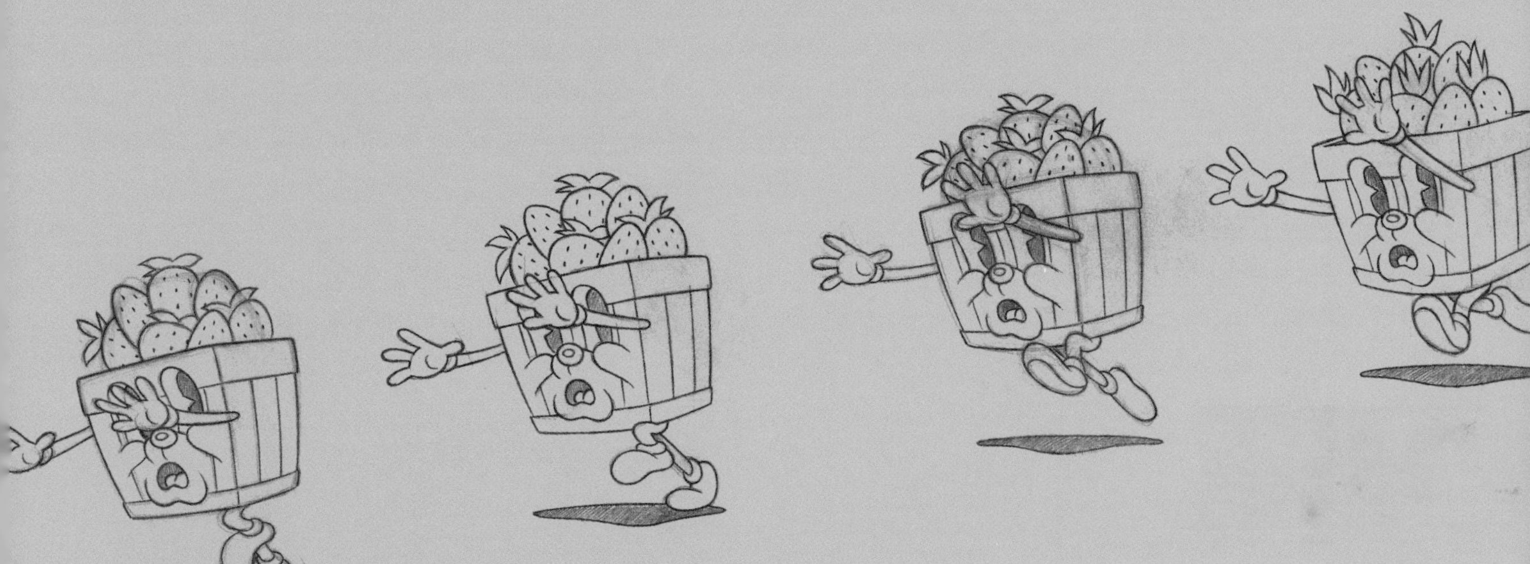

I0824249

CUPHEAD

-in-

"THE DELICIOUS LAST COURSE"

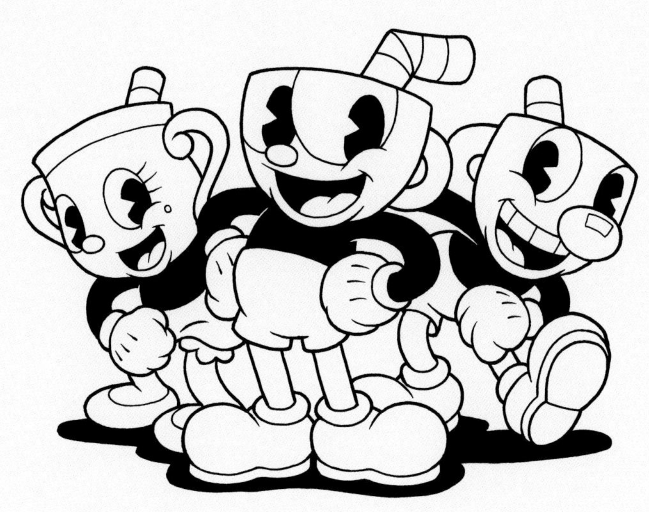

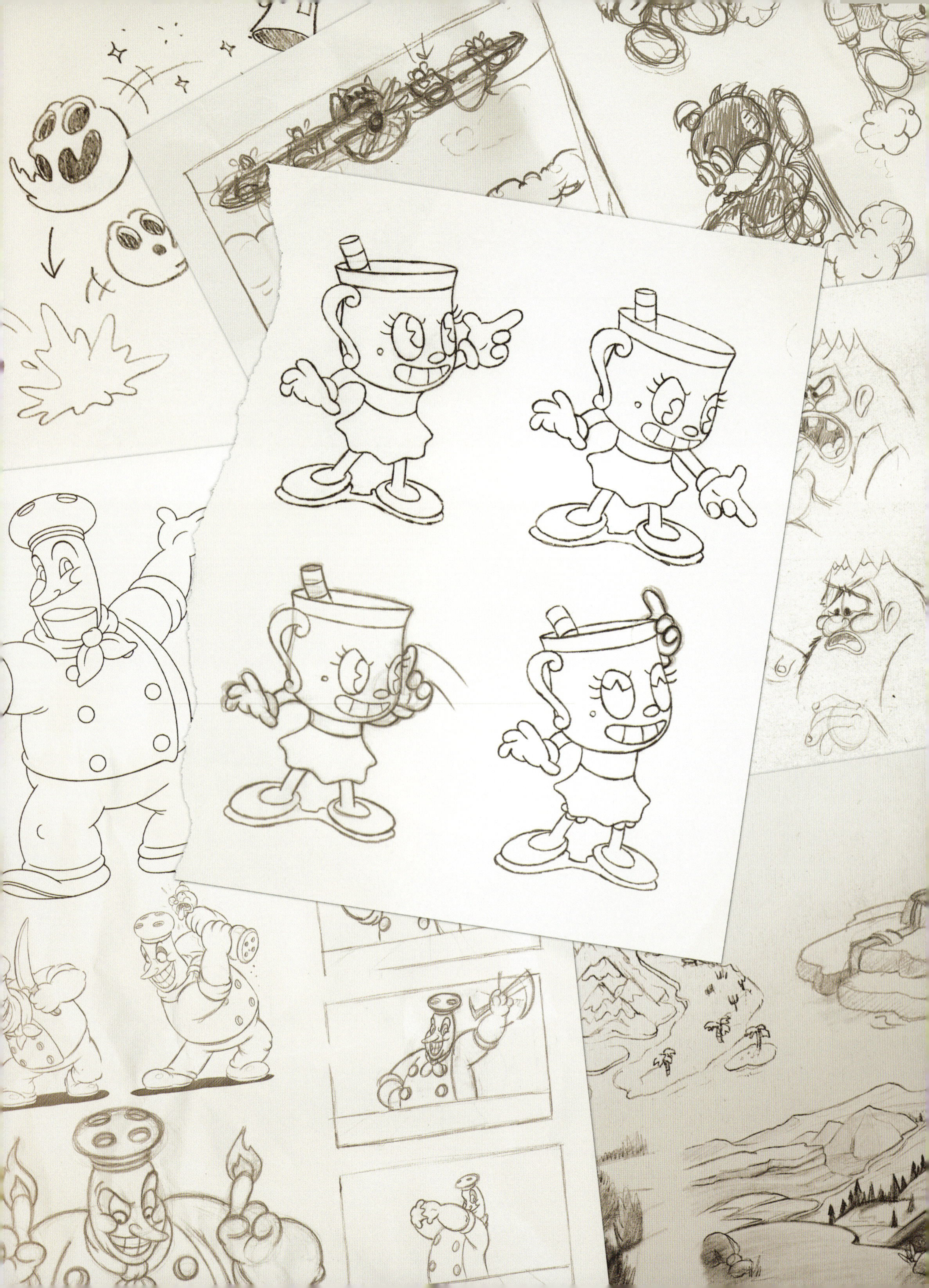

THE ART OF CUPHEAD
-in- "THE DELICIOUS LAST COURSE"

Writers
ELI CYMET AND TYLER MOLDENHAUER
WITH INSIGHTS FROM CHAD AND JARED MOLDENHAUER

Art Direction and Cover Design
IAN CLARKE, CHAD MOLDENHAUER,
AND RYAN MOLDENHAUER

Process and Model Photography
CAITLIN RUSSELL, ALI MORBI,
AND SCREEN NOVELTIES

Cover Illustration
LANCE INKWELL AND JOSEPH COLEMAN

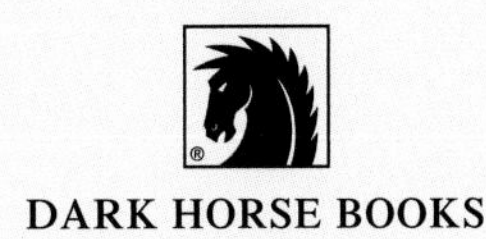

DARK HORSE BOOKS

Publisher
MIKE RICHARDSON

Editor
RACHEL ROBERTS

Assistant Editor
ANASTACIA FERRY

Designer
ETHAN KIMBERLING

Digital Art Technician
BETSY HOWITT

Special editorial thanks to
IAN CLARKE AND ELI CYMET AT STUDIOMDHR AND BERIT GINSBERG, CHRISTINA NIX LYNCH, AND BETH NOCK AT KING FEATURES.

THE ART OF CUPHEAD: DELICIOUS LAST COURSE

Published by Dark Horse Books
A division of Dark Horse Comics LLC
10956 SE Main Street, Milwaukie, OR 97222
DarkHorse.com

Represented in the EU by Authorised Rep Compliance Ltd.
Ground Floor, 71 Lower Baggot Street, Dublin, D02 P593, Ireland
ARCCompliance.com

First Edition: October 2024
Digital ISBN: 978-1-50674-807-8
Standard Edition ISBN: 978-1-50674-737-8
Deluxe Edition ISBN: 978-1-50674-738-5

2 4 6 8 10 9 7 5 3
Printed in China

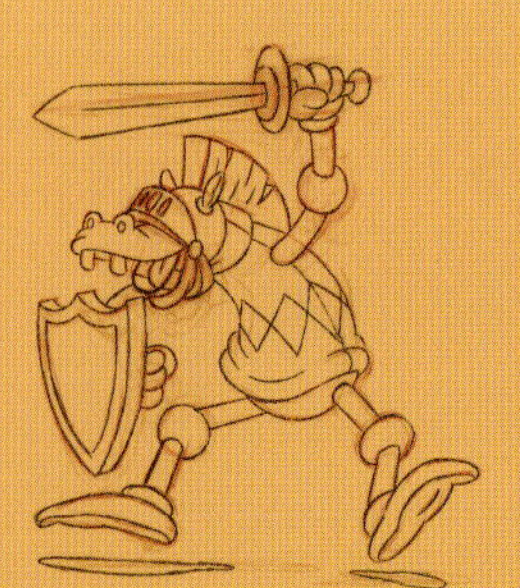
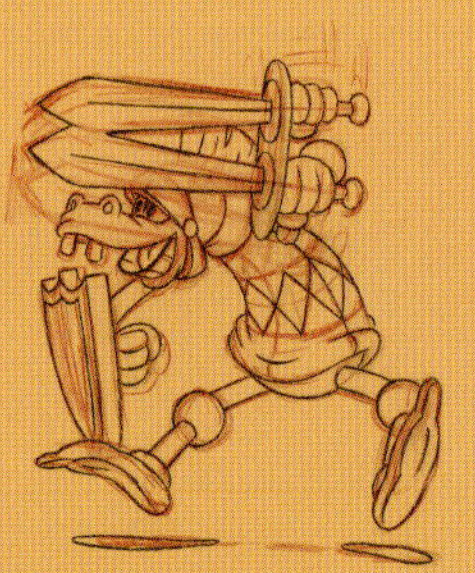
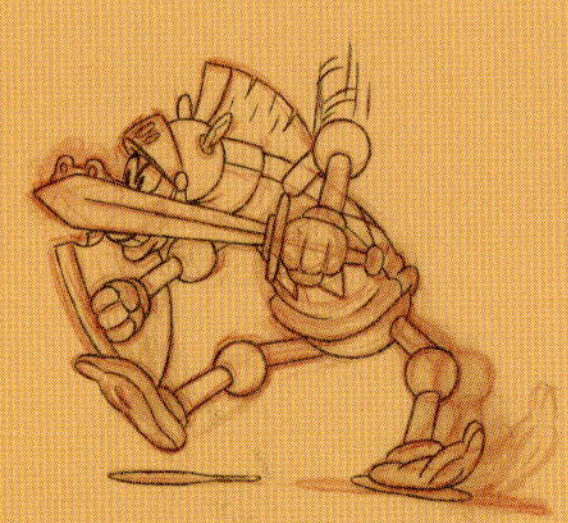
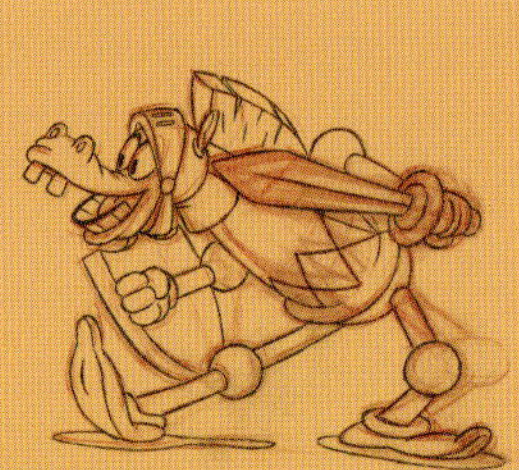
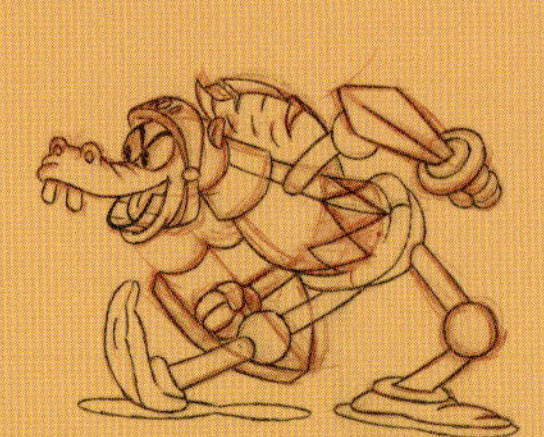

TABLE *of* CONTENTS

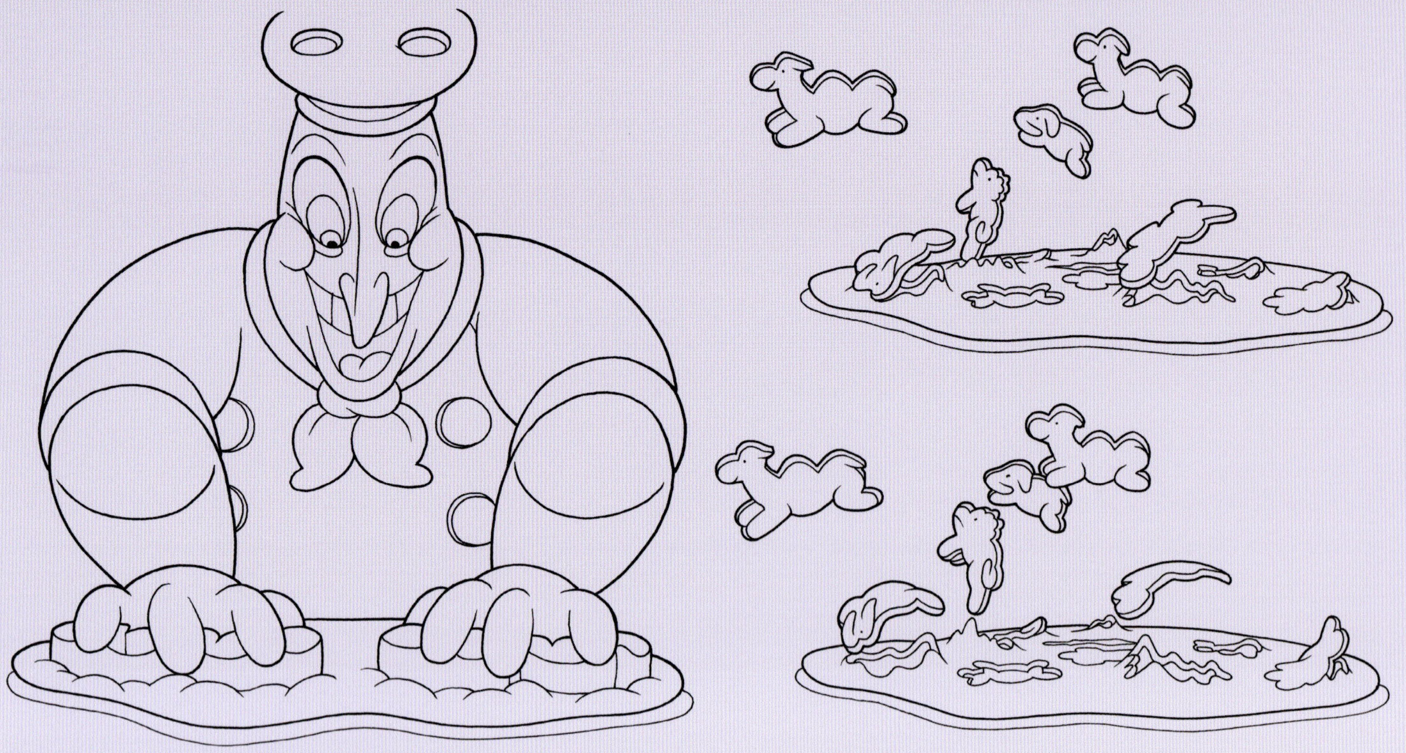

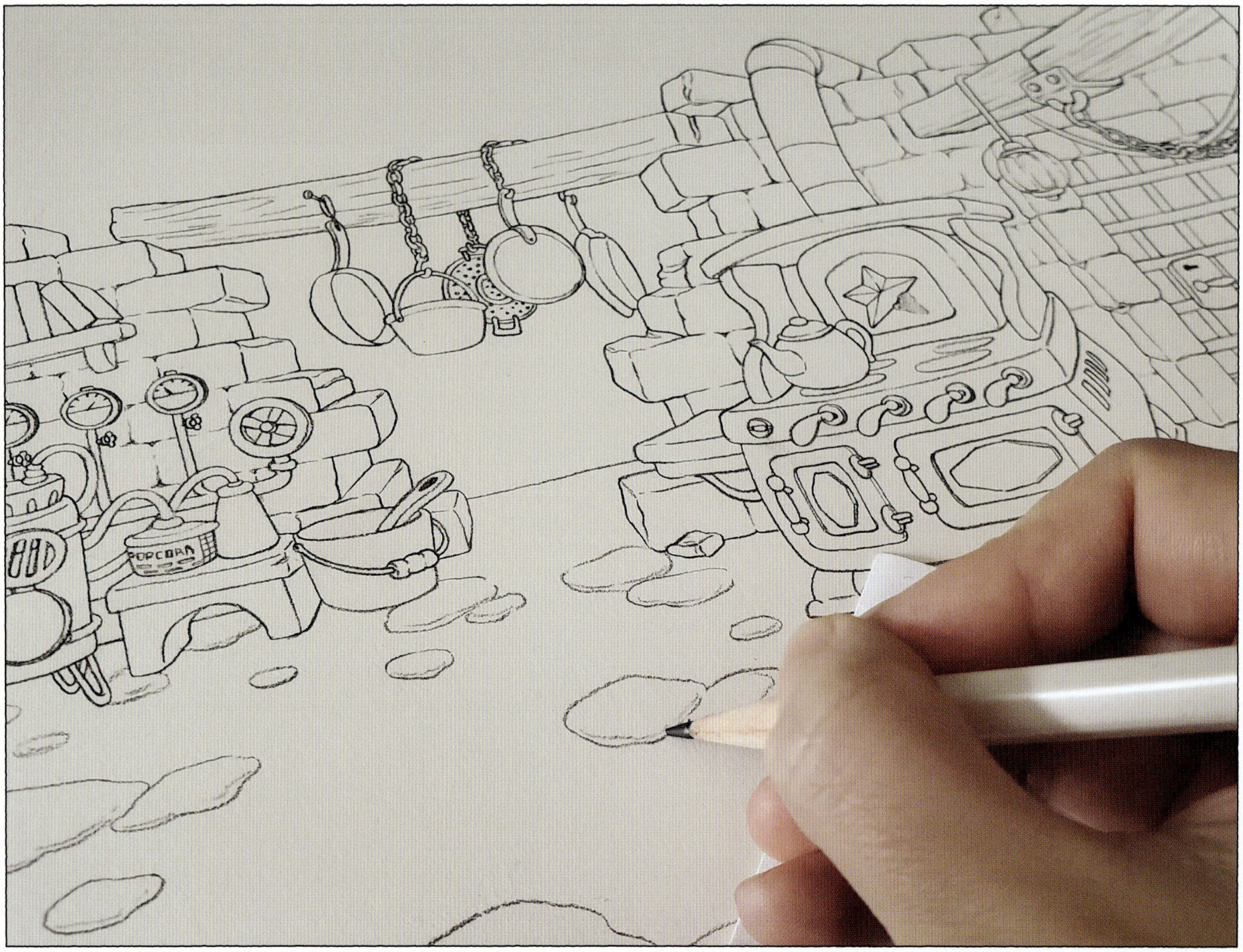

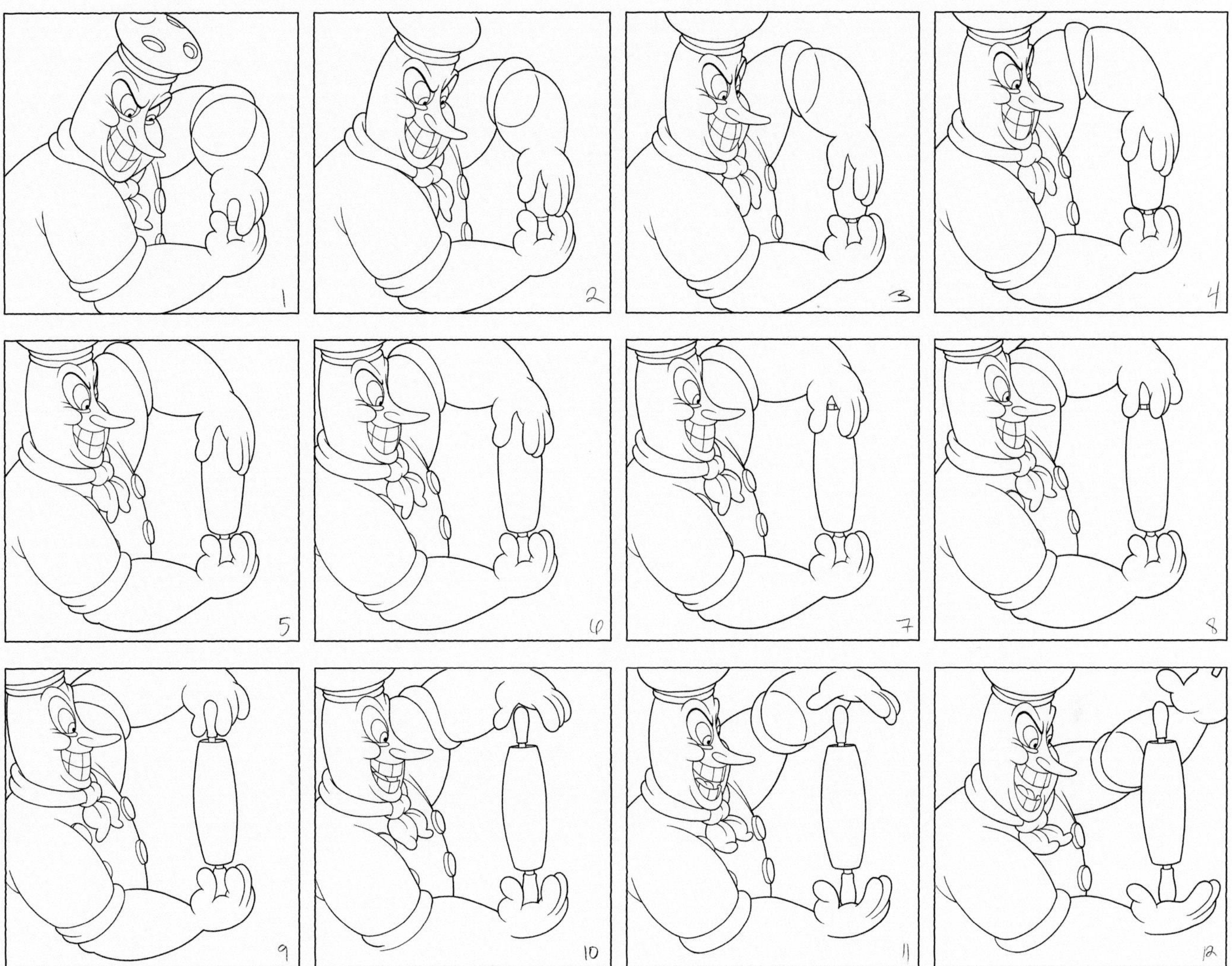

Introduction

IT'S OFTEN SAID THAT "you can't go home again." That it's impossible to return to something once-familiar and expect it to be the same as it was. But when *Cuphead* released in 2017 and found an audience with such an amazing community, we were given the chance to do the impossible—to return once more to the fantastical cartoon shores of the Inkwell Isles.

Like any developer making their first game, we released *Cuphead* with a laundry list of ideas we wish we could have explored. But thankfully, the way the audience embraced our little animated adventure put us in the position to revisit the world and characters we loved so much. And good thing, too, as there was one character's story in particular we had been itching to tell throughout the time spent making the original game. A certain ghostly gal who could be found floating around the Mausoleums of the Inkwell Isles...The Legendary Chalice. Once created, we began to see her as part of a trio of main characters, but the realities of indie development forced us to give her a smaller role than we would have liked.

As we bounced around ideas for what a Chalice-focused return to the world of *Cuphead* might look like, a high level idea came into focus. A surprise summons to a far away isle off the coast. Diverse geography to allow for a wider array of boss themes. A quest to free the Legendary Chalice from the mysterious Astral Plane. And at the center of it all, a brand new friend (turned foe)...Chef Saltbaker. And so, like Cuphead and Mugman, we set sail for a brand-new adventure as a team. In true Studio MDHR fashion, however, going home again meant doing some renovations.

We often say that our aspiration with the original *Cuphead* experience was to design boss battles that would have felt suitable to be the last boss of any other game. With *The Delicious Last Course*, we pushed to make every boss feel like they could be on par with the final fight of the original *Cuphead*. This meant upping the ante in every discipline, from painting to animation to design. In the end, there were some single boss phases in this expansion that exceeded the frame count of *entire bosses* from the original game.

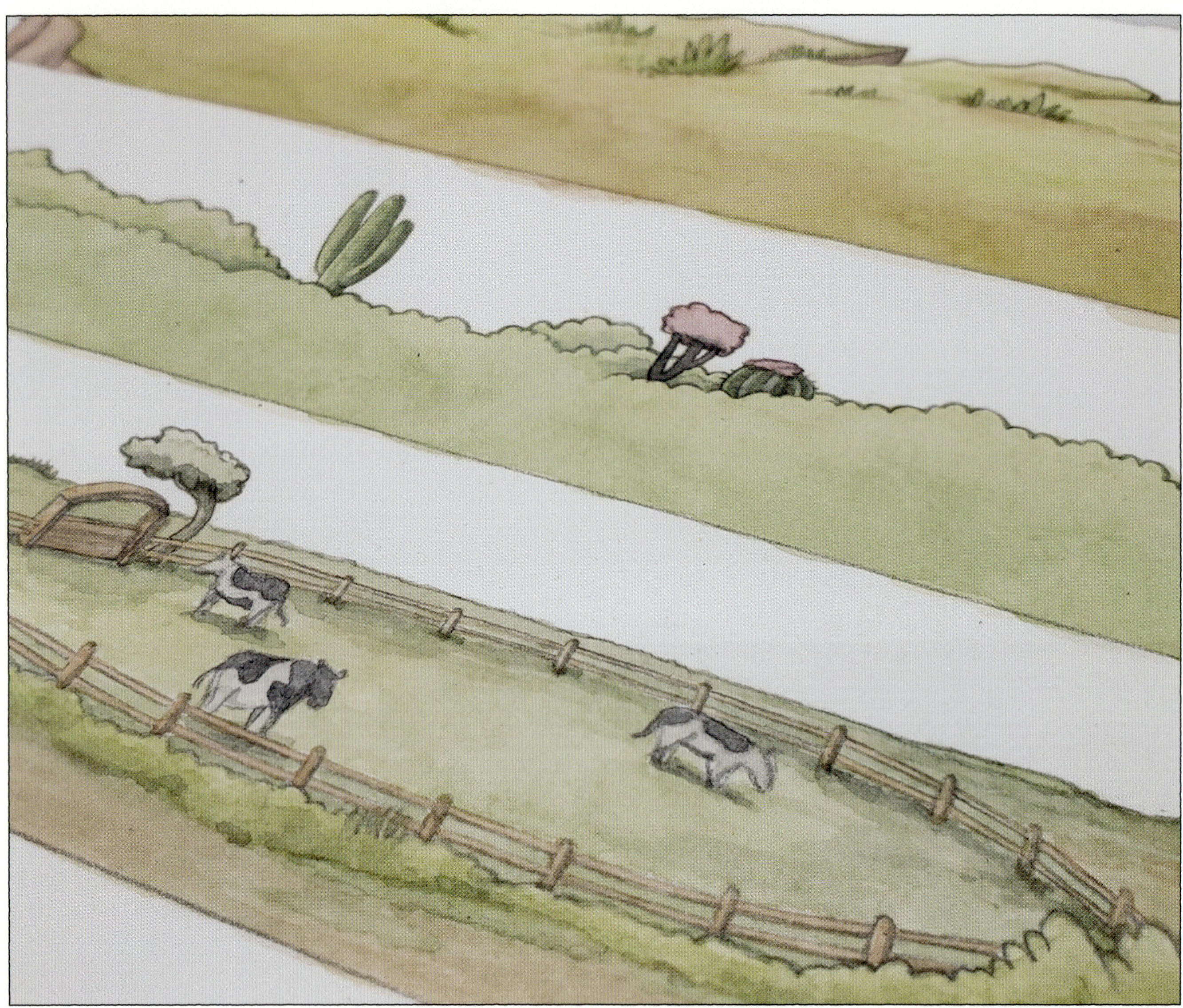

More than just *more*, though, we challenged ourselves to improve our craft as an entire studio. We expanded *Cuphead*'s aural atmosphere beyond the high-tempo jazz of the original to include tracks reminiscent of animated feature films, replete with a 120-person orchestral accompaniment. We worked to achieve greater levels of detail in our backgrounds by using experimental painting techniques and implementing our first fully animated painted background. Our animators pushed themselves further, creating fluid, screen-filling animations that were more complex, layered and detailed than anything in the original game. And as for the bosses themselves, we were laser-focused on designing frenetic and screen twisting gameplay scenarios beyond anything we had attempted before.

In hindsight, it's fair to say that we may have got lost in the joys of taking this trip back to the Inkwell Isles, as our development timeline stretched beyond anything we had initially forecast. And yet, even through pushed release dates and the shifting realities brought on by a global pandemic, there was one constant. You. That same amazing community of pals who was there for us when *Cuphead* first launched, remaining steadfast in your support and excitement. All our amazing team members are deservedly mentioned as the credits roll on this latest adventure, but if you've ever played through *Cuphead* or drawn some fan art or sent a supportive word or thought our way, we wouldn't be here without you and you ought to consider your name there right there too.

In the end, it may well be true that you can't go home again. At least not in exactly the same way or as exactly the same person as you were before. But perhaps that makes the trip back all the better. And one thing is for certain: whether you can go home or not, you can always come visit us on the Inkwell Isles.

Sincerely,
Chad and Jared Moldenhauer

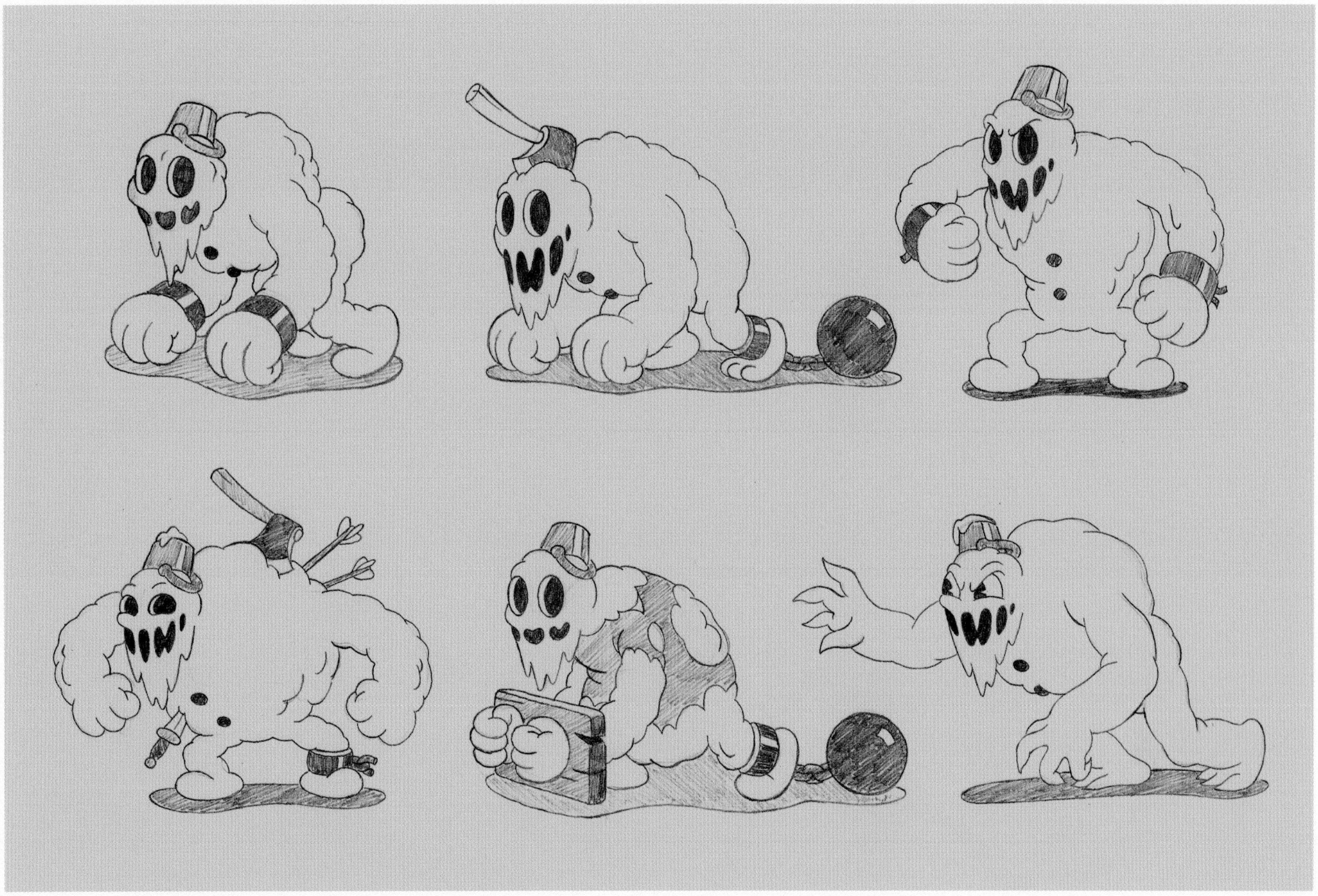

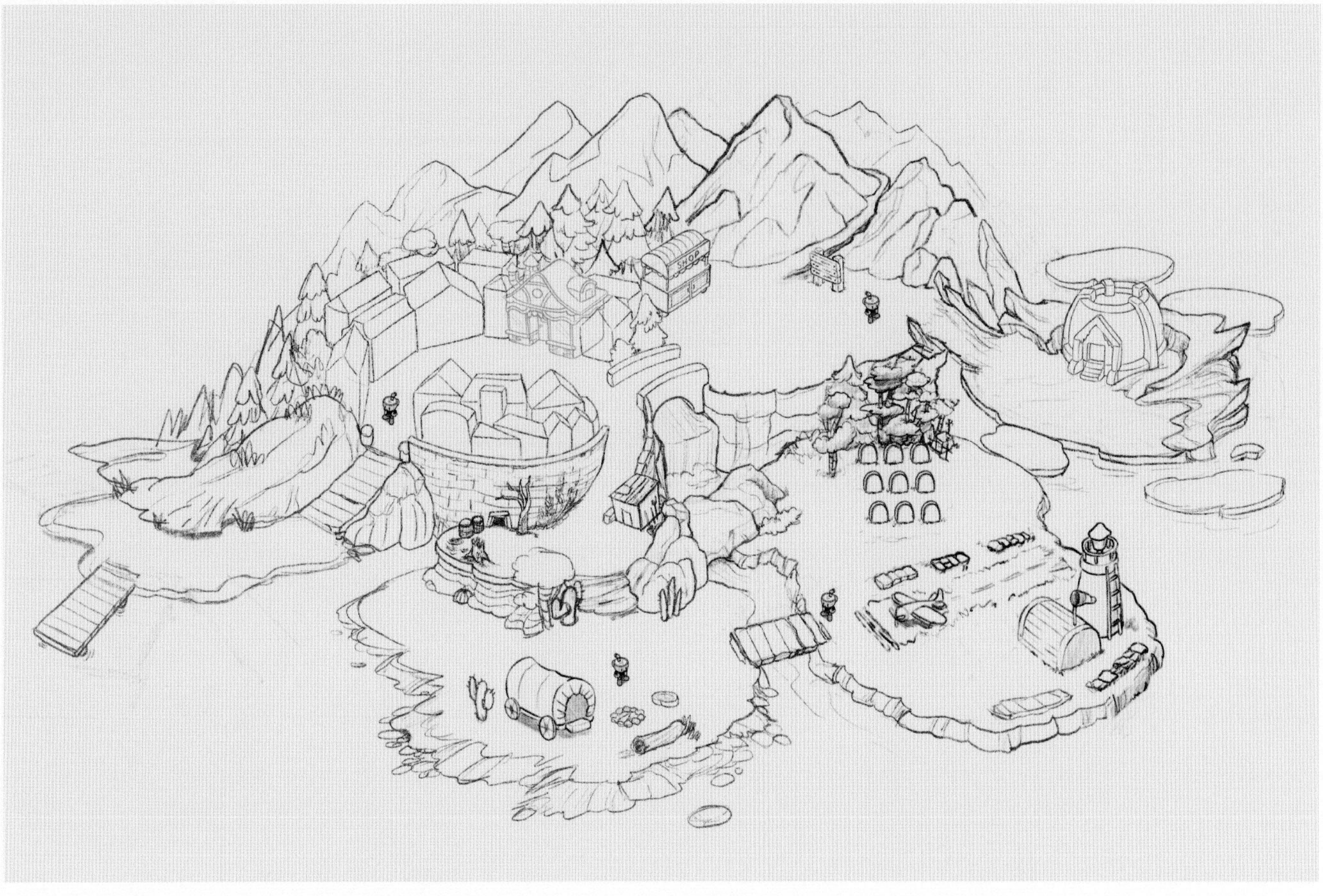

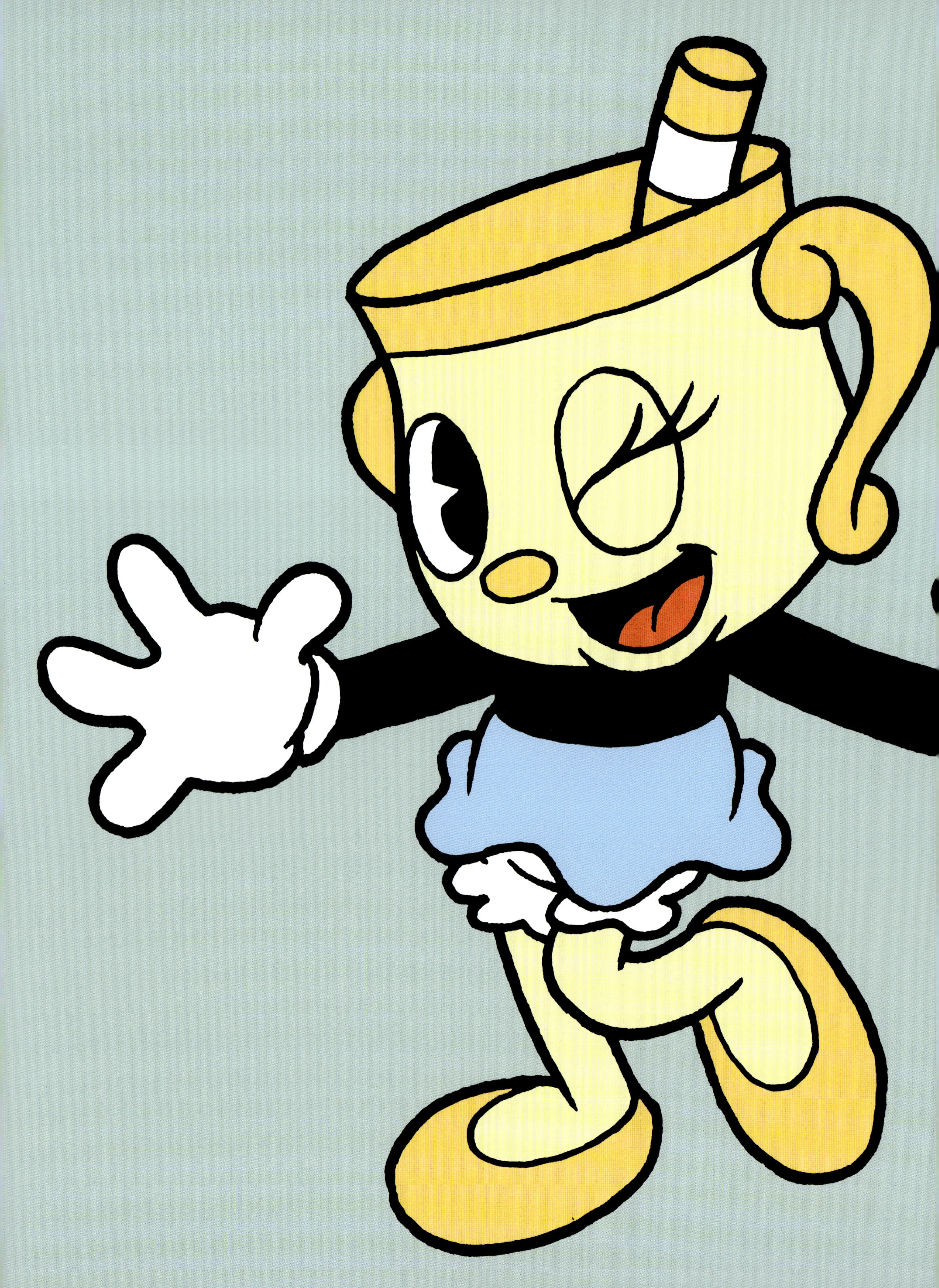

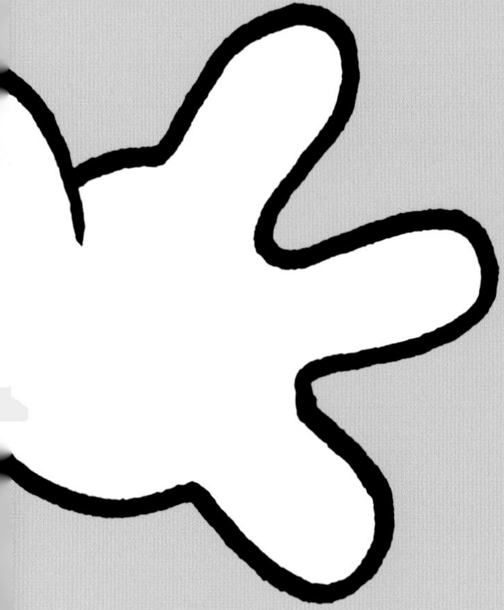

Chapter I:
Ms. Chalice

MORE THAN JUST AN OPPORTUNITY to revisit the Inkwell Isles and explore exciting new boss designs, *The Delicious Last Course* was a chance to flesh out the story of a character for whom we always had bigger aspirations: The Legendary Chalice. Many *Cuphead* fans know her as the helpful ghostly gal that you meet across the game's Mausoleum stages, who bestows Cuphead and Mugman with all-powerful Super Arts. However, the truth is that we had long dreamt of including her as Cuphead's third playable character—even going as far as to plan the idea very early in the original game's development. However, as with so many first-time developers facing the reality of time and cost constraints, we ultimately had to make the difficult decision to put her development aside.

So, when we made the exciting decision to take another trip to the all-cartoon wonderland we loved so much, perhaps nothing excited us more than the knowledge that Chalice would be getting her day in the sun (and her feet on the ground). Inspired by everything from cartoon legends like Betty Boop and Minnie Mouse to real life icons like Amelia Earhart, Ms. Chalice is no damsel in distress, but rather an intrepid, sparky heroine ready for a grand adventure of her very own.

MS. CHALICE

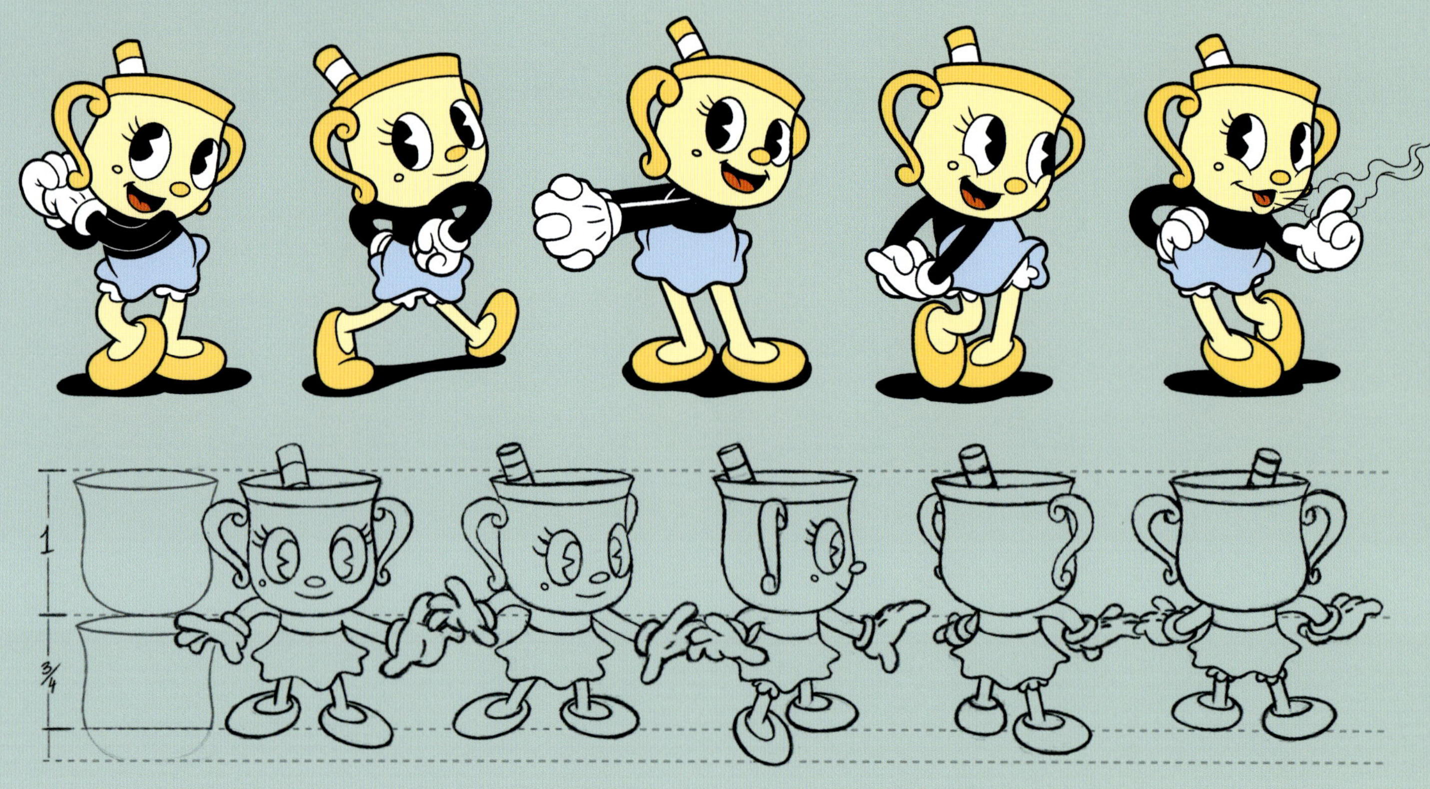

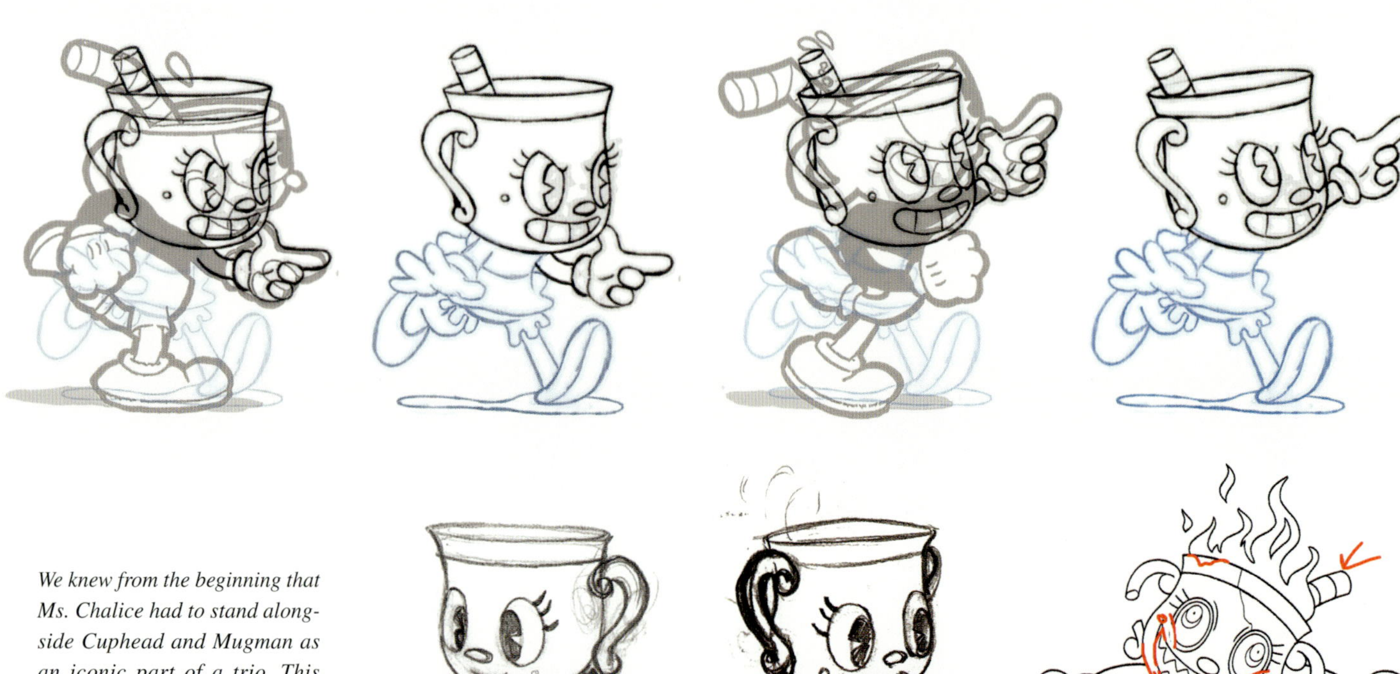

We knew from the beginning that Ms. Chalice had to stand alongside Cuphead and Mugman as an iconic part of a trio. This meant meticulous iteration on her character expressions, including the existence of an "evil" form—Ms. Malice!

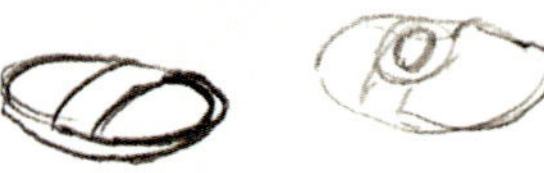

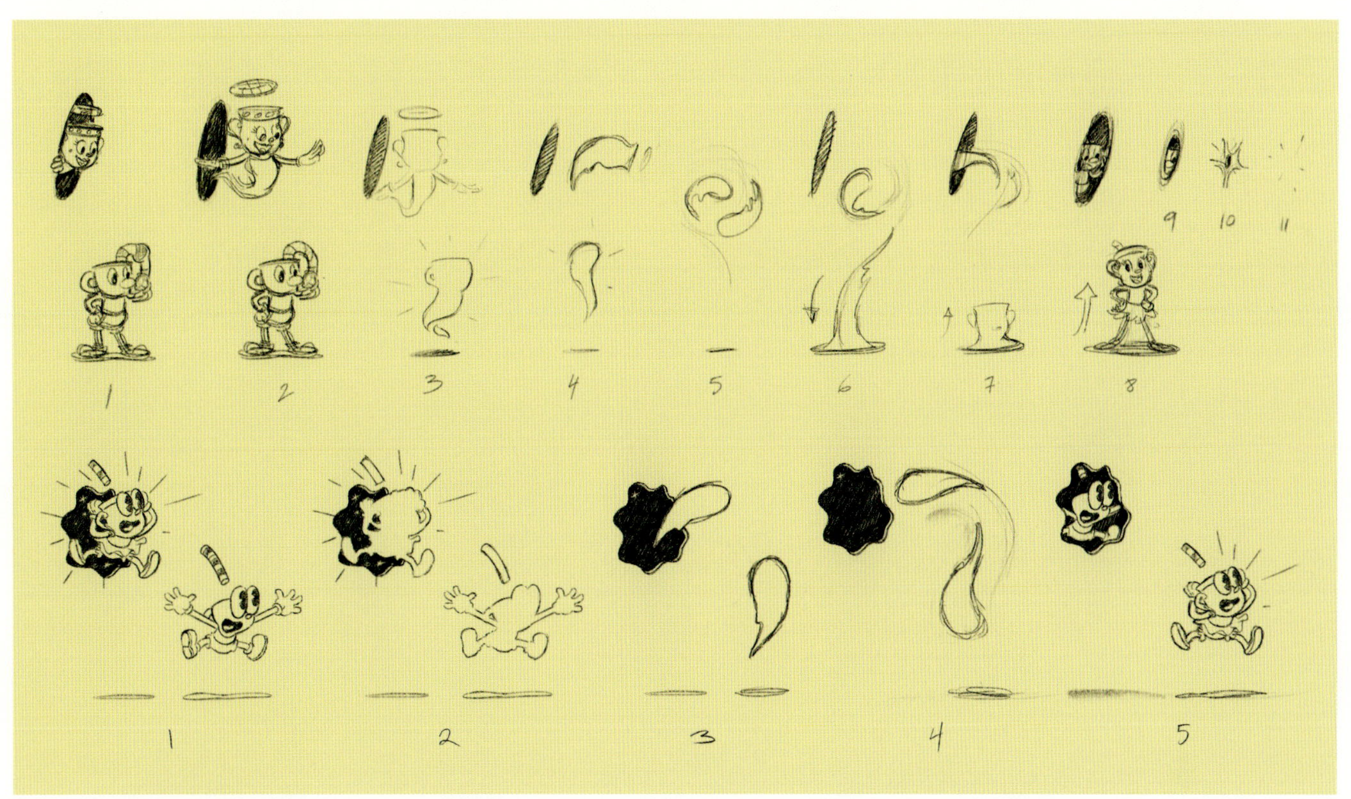

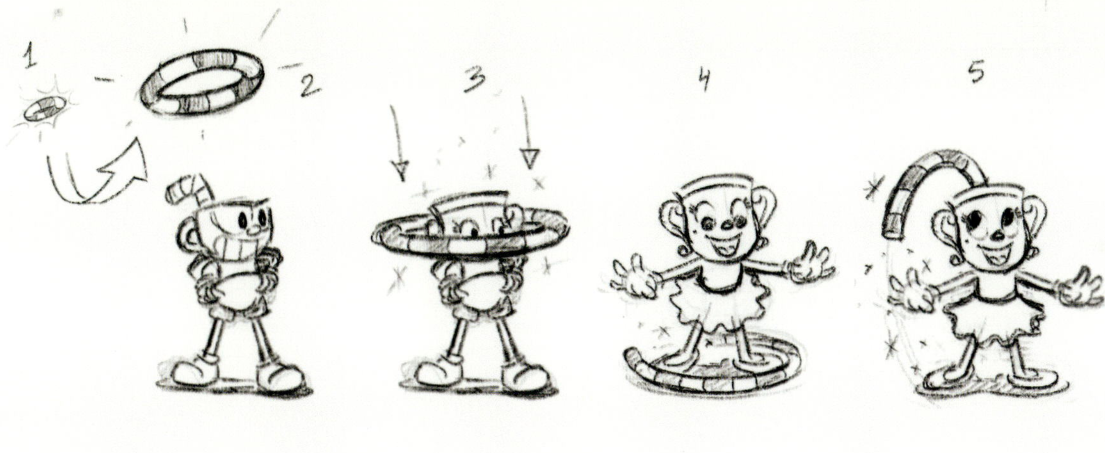

Unlike Cuphead and Mugman, Ms. Chalice only takes corporeal form within a level. These character intro concepts from Animation Supervisor Hanna Abi-Hanna illustrate the challenge of capturing Chalice's emergence from the Astral Plane.

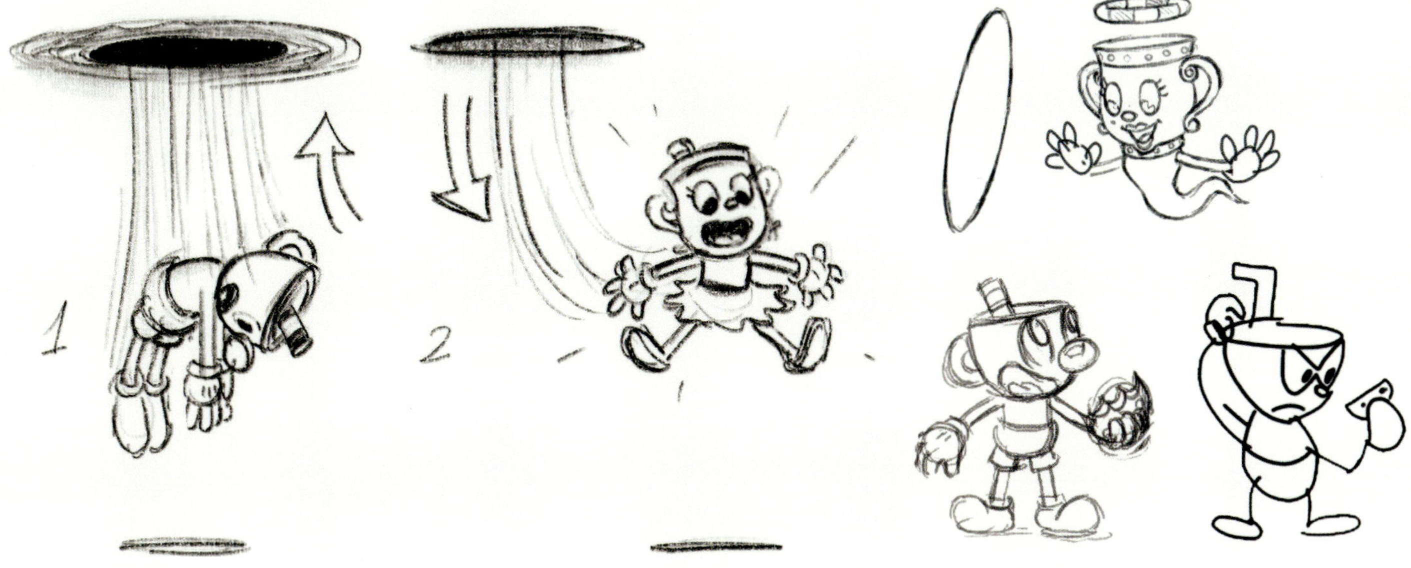

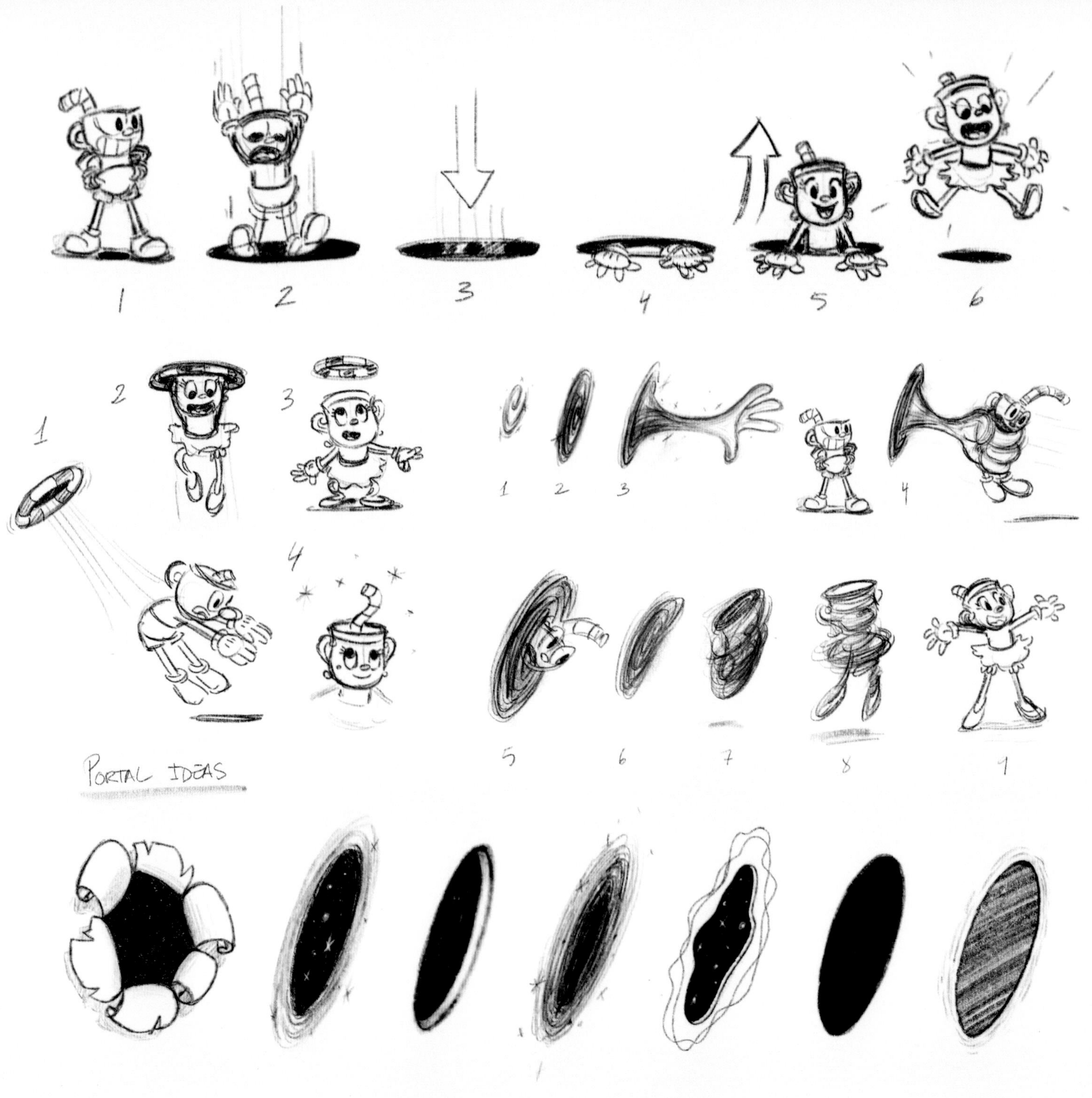

From attacks to character introductions to super moves, every one of Ms. Chalice's in-game actions is uniquely animated to suit her character and personality. In total, her character alone represents approximately 1,200 new frames of animation. Compounding the challenge of animating a brand-new playable character from scratch was the central narrative conceit we built around Ms. Chalice—the Astral Plane.

Having existed previously only as the spectral Legendary Chalice, our story discussions eventually led us to one clear conclusion: *The Delicious Last Course* would need to explain how Ms. Chalice came to life. This meant bending one of our core storytelling principles at Studio MDHR—giving out specific information about a character's origins. In keeping with the 1930s style of cartoon storytelling, we like to leave wide open narrative space for our players to fill in the blanks with their imagination.

Here, however, we needed to weave the mystical Astral Plane into the fabric of *The Delicious Last Course* through the story of Cuphead and Mugman's journey. Pictured above are concepts for the types of portals Ms. Chalice might emerge from, including one unused idea in which the Astral Plane breaks the fourth wall by puncturing the imaginary paper on which the character is drawn.

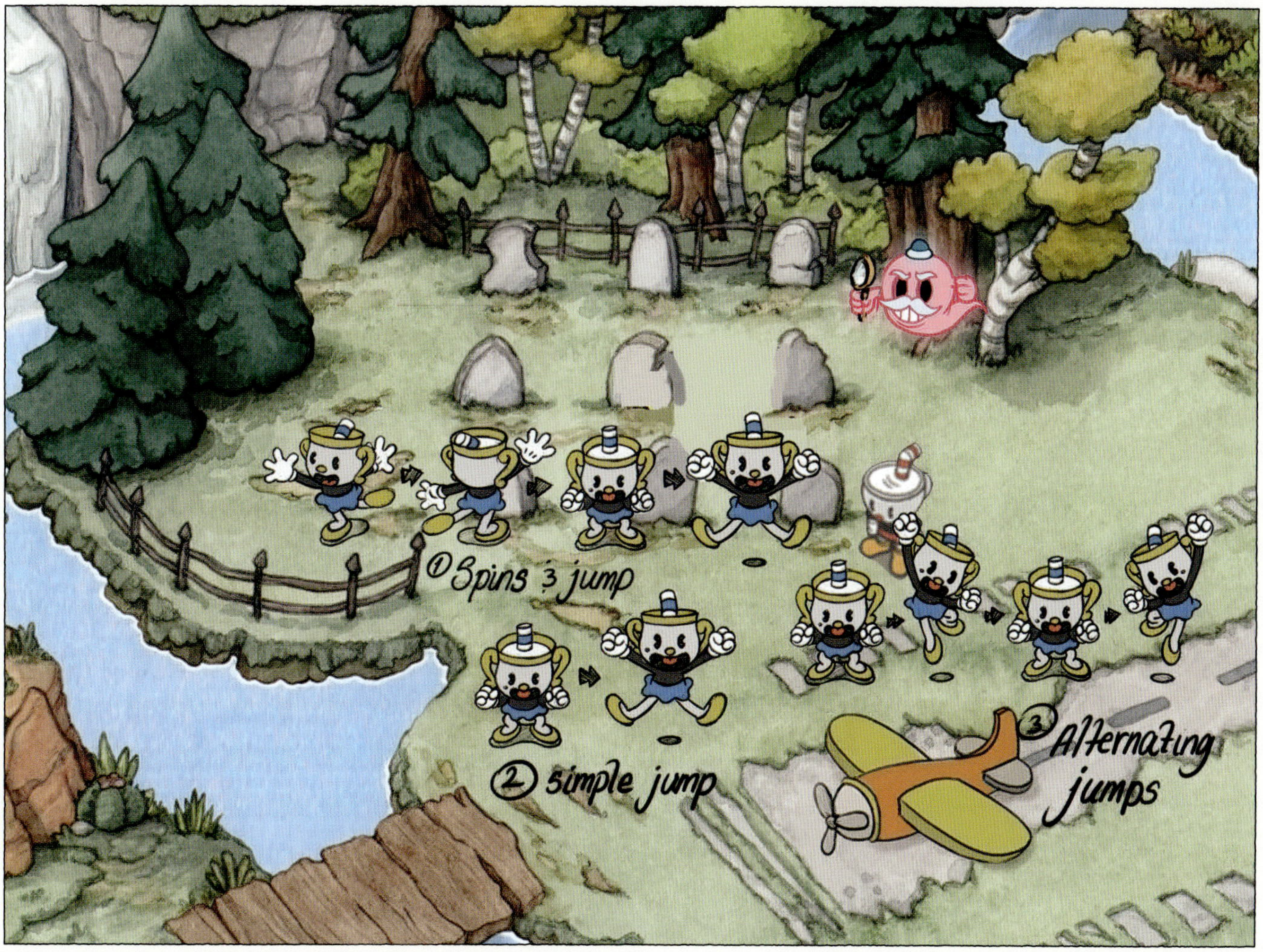

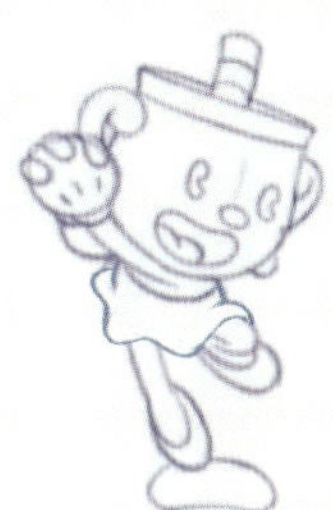
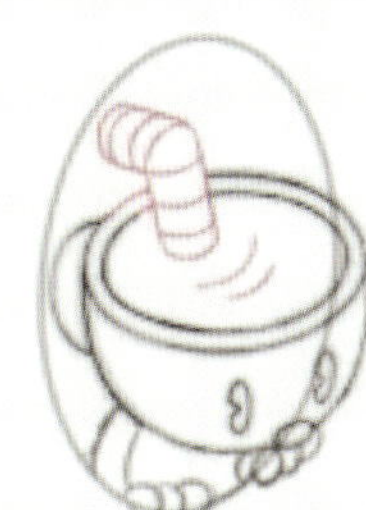
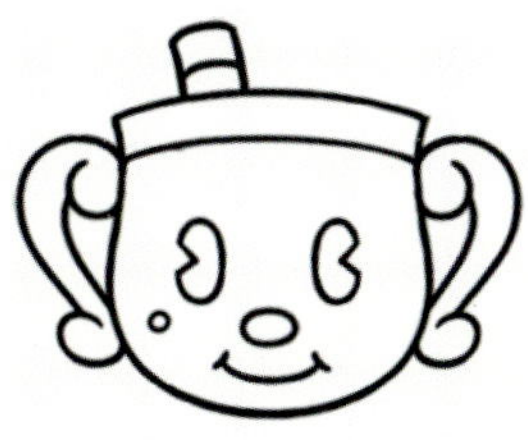
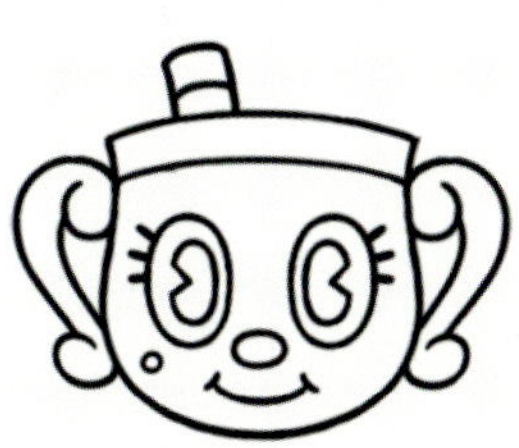

Before returning to the Astral Plane, we knew we wanted Ms. Chalice to celebrate a player's hard-earned victory. This required Animator Joseph Coleman to come up with concepts for an iconic, simplified "map sprite," pictured above.

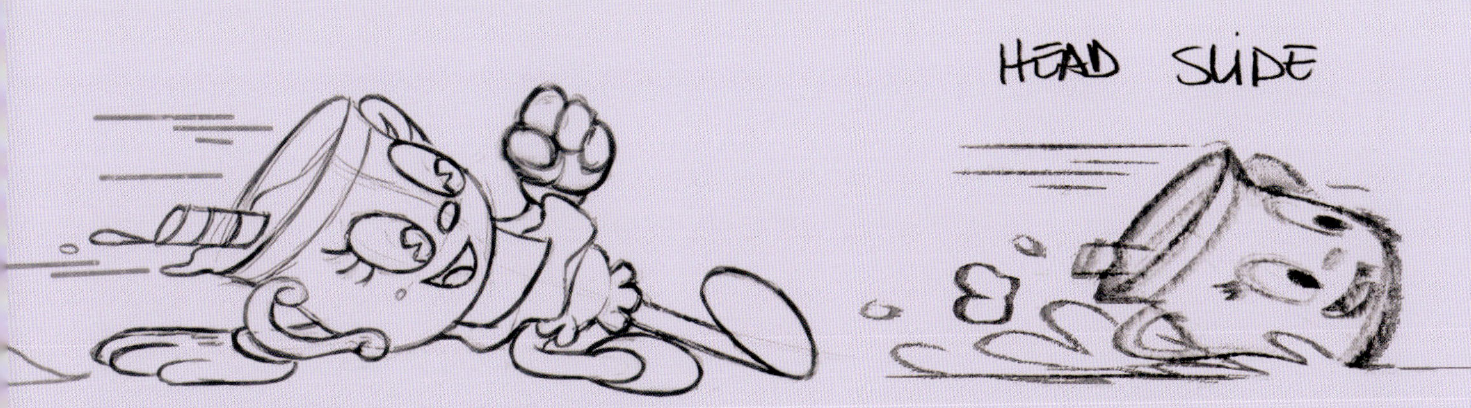

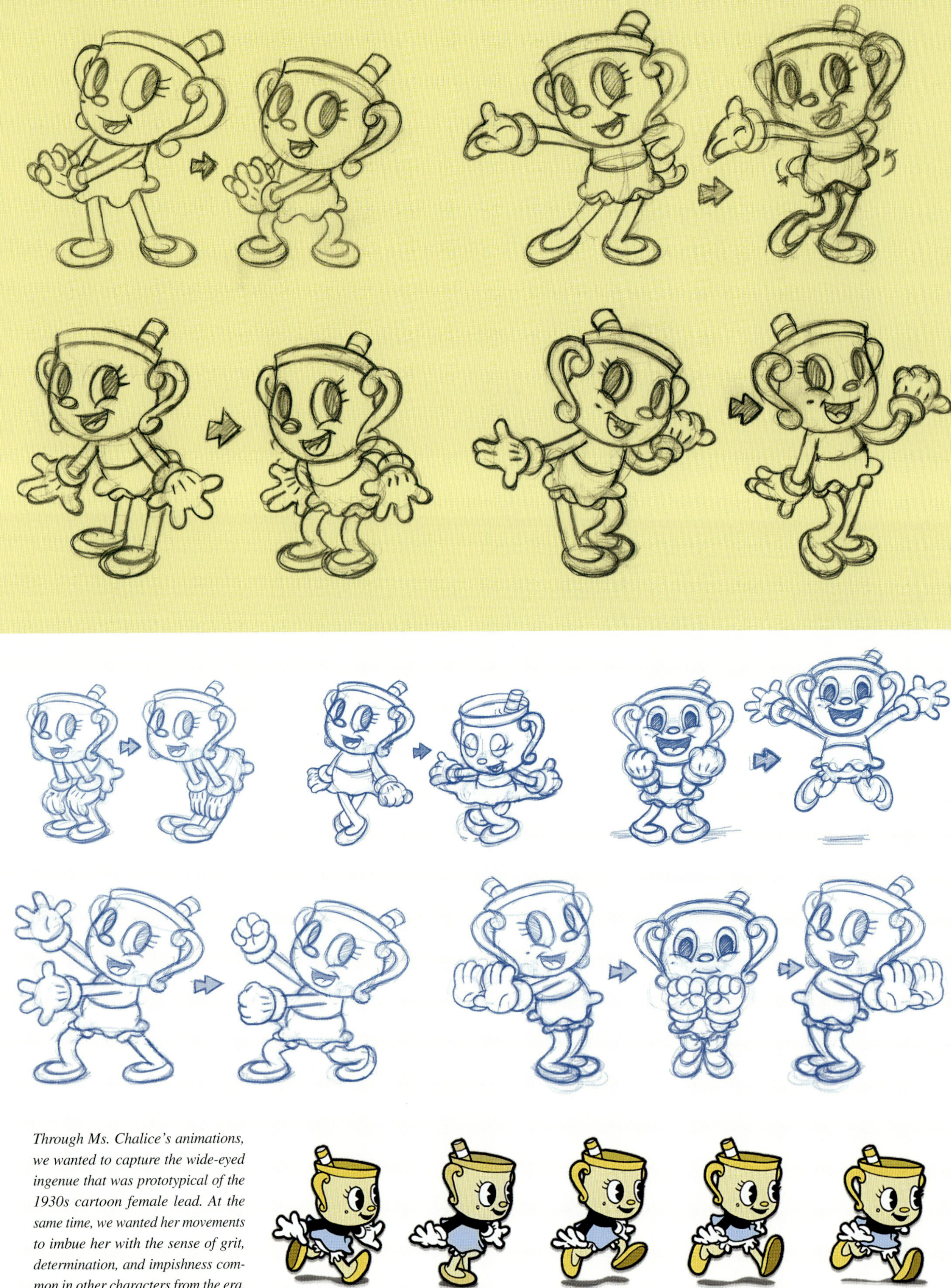

Through Ms. Chalice's animations, we wanted to capture the wide-eyed ingenue that was prototypical of the 1930s cartoon female lead. At the same time, we wanted her movements to imbue her with the sense of grit, determination, and impishness common in other characters from the era.

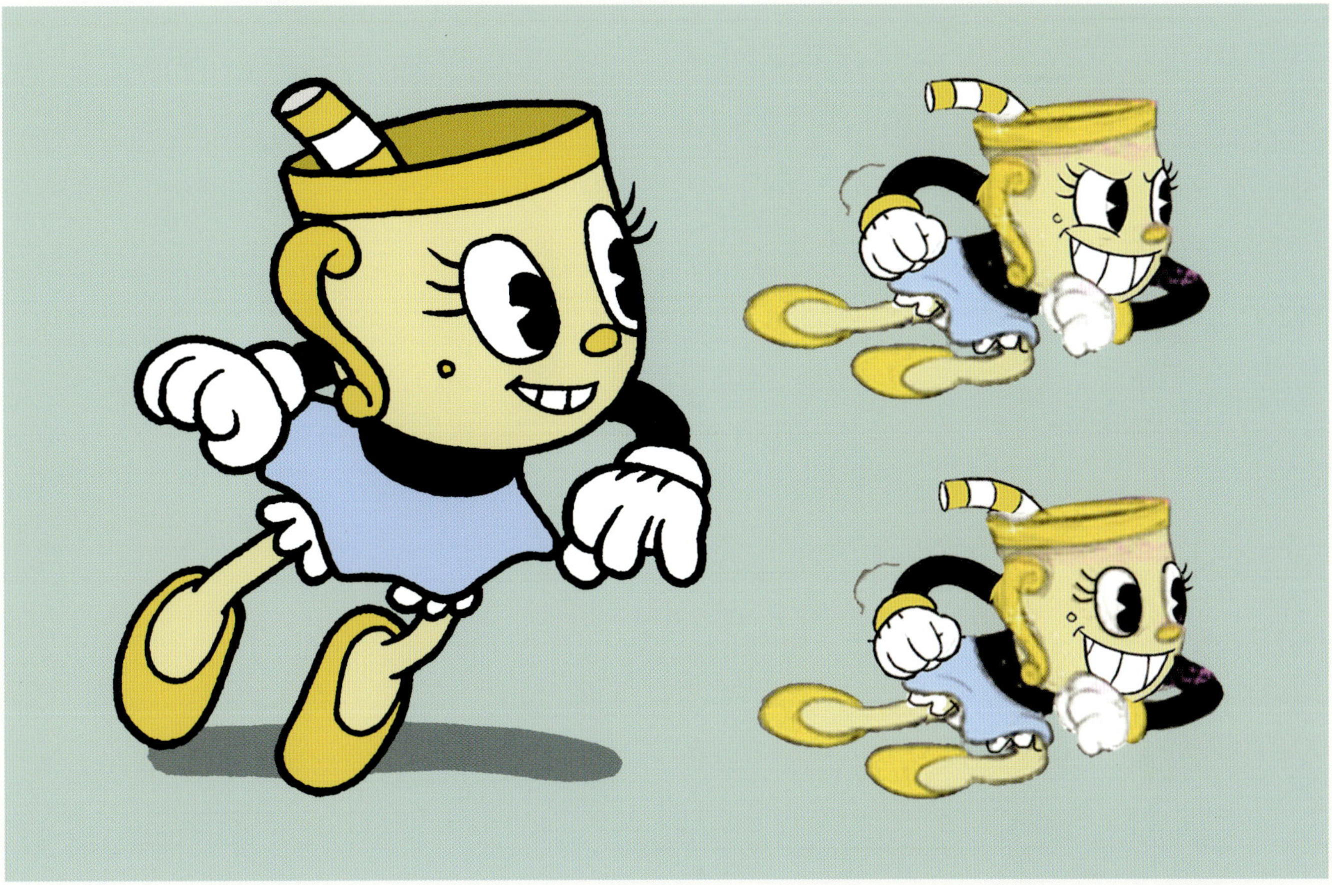

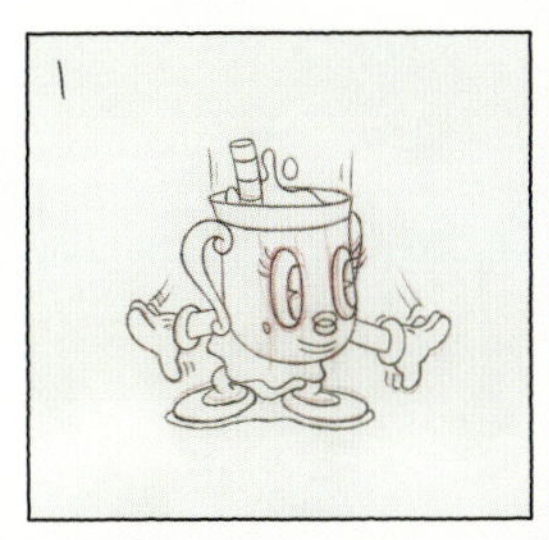
1
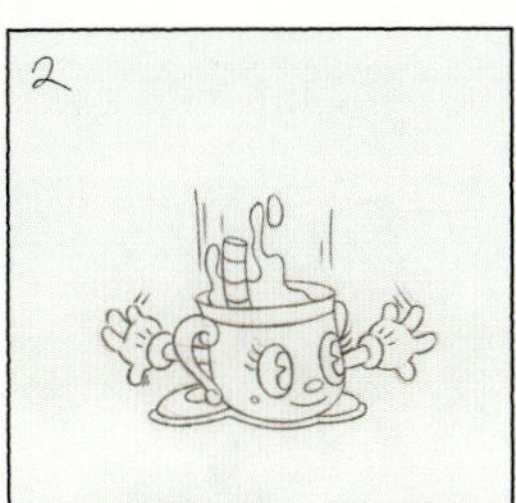
2
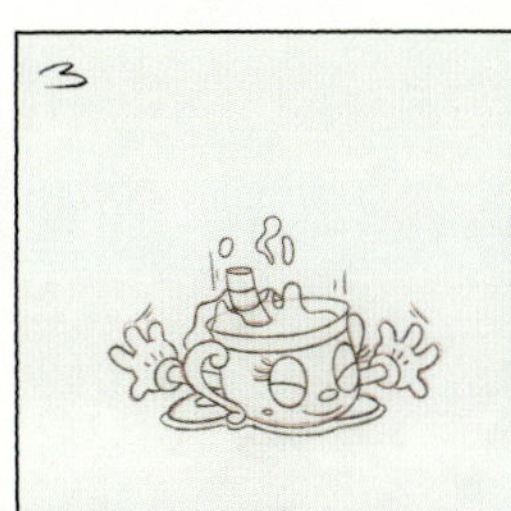
3
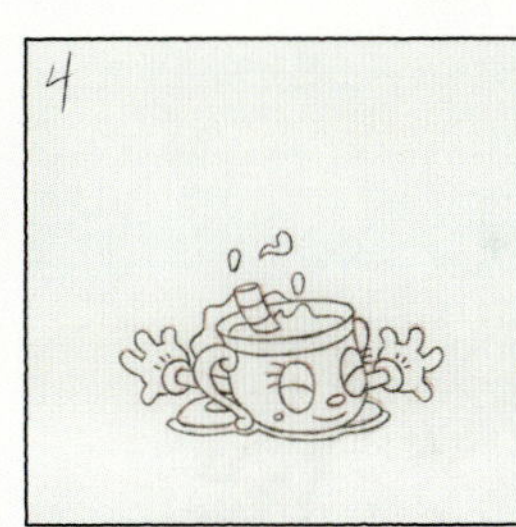
4
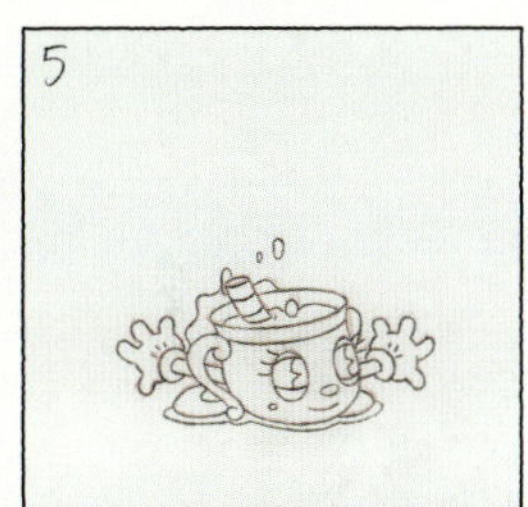
5
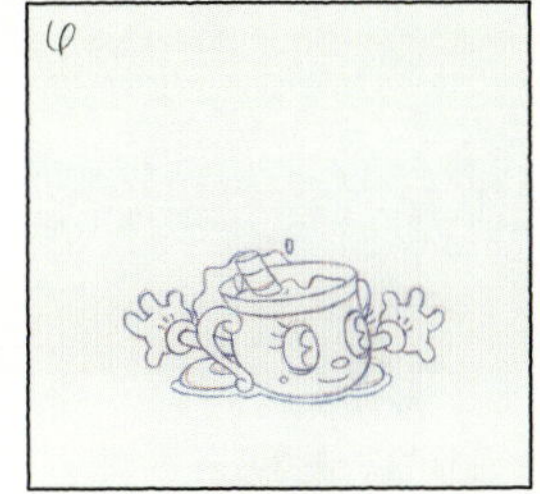
6
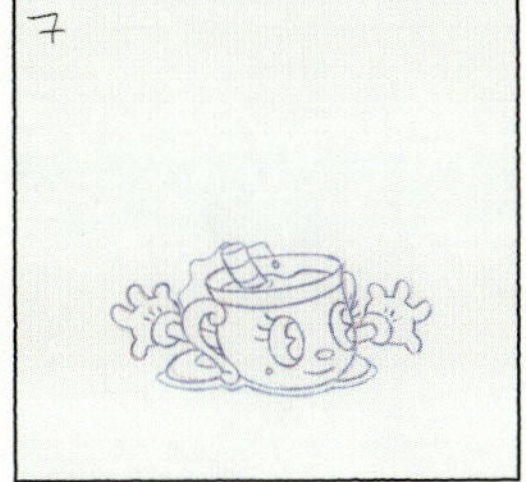
7
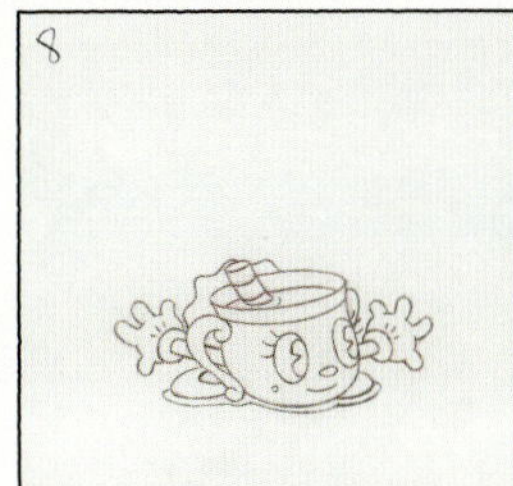
8
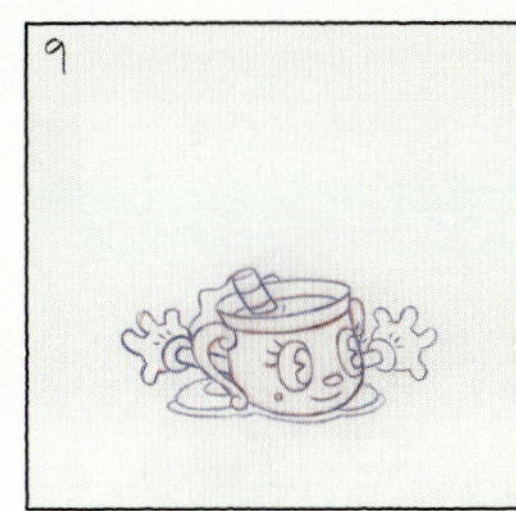
9
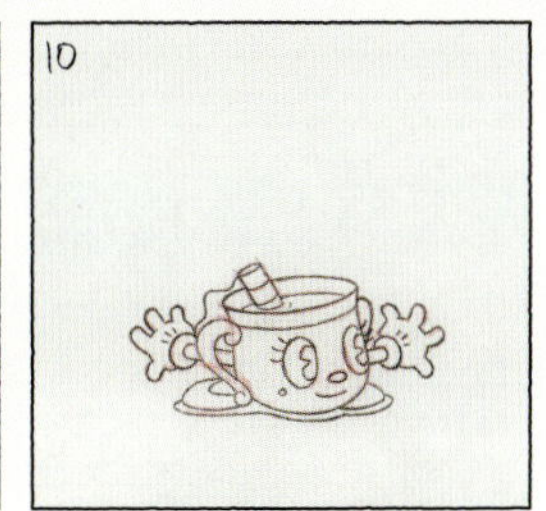
10
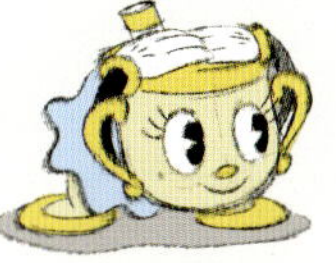
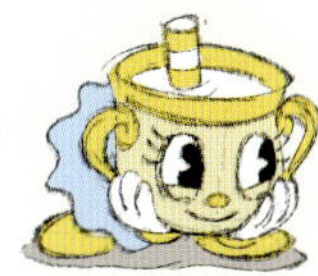
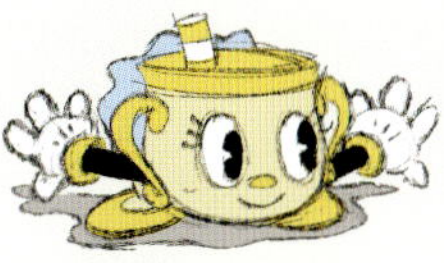
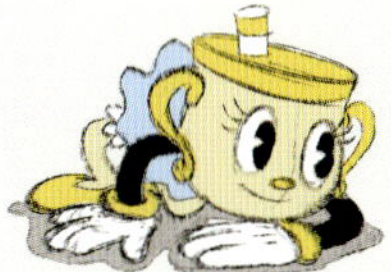
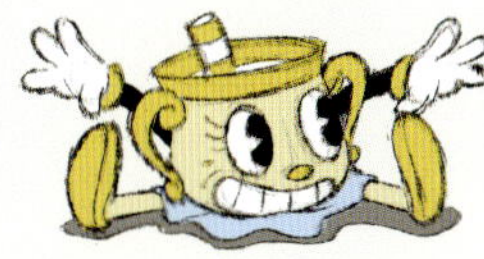
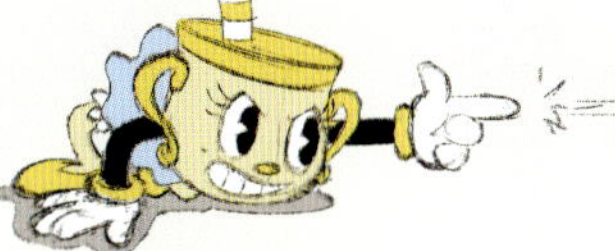
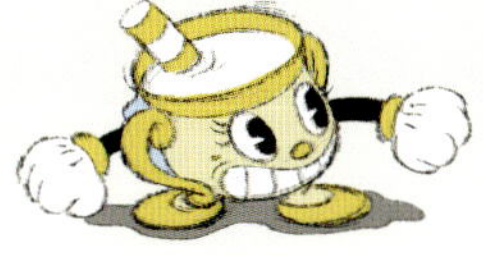
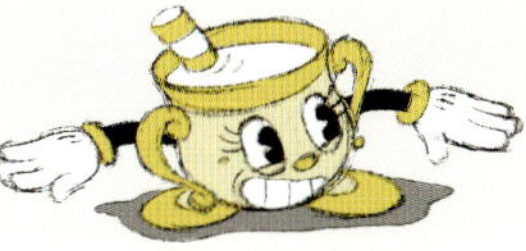
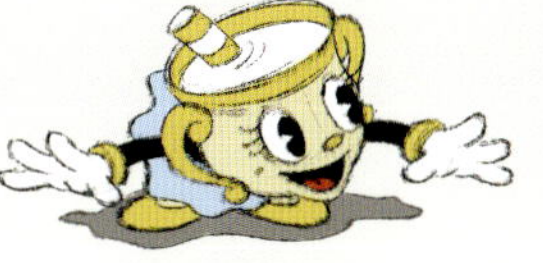
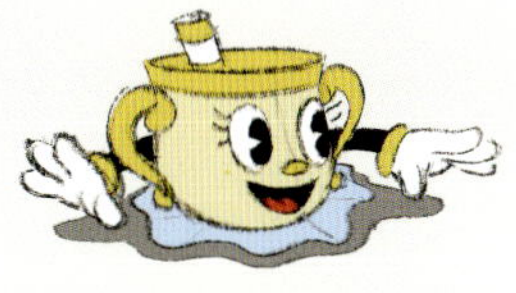
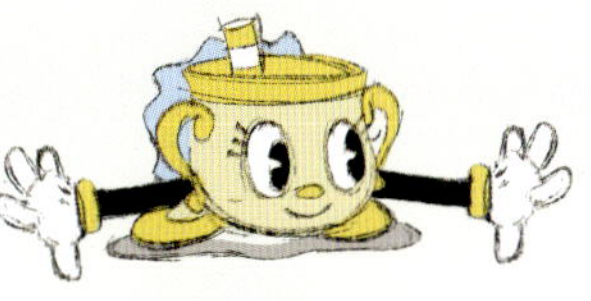

TH— THANK YOUUUU!

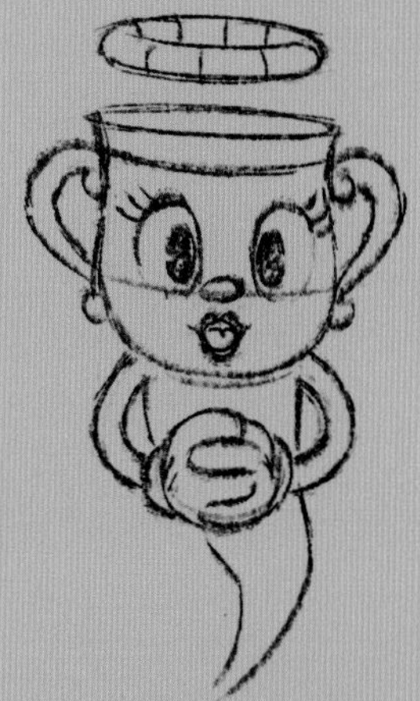

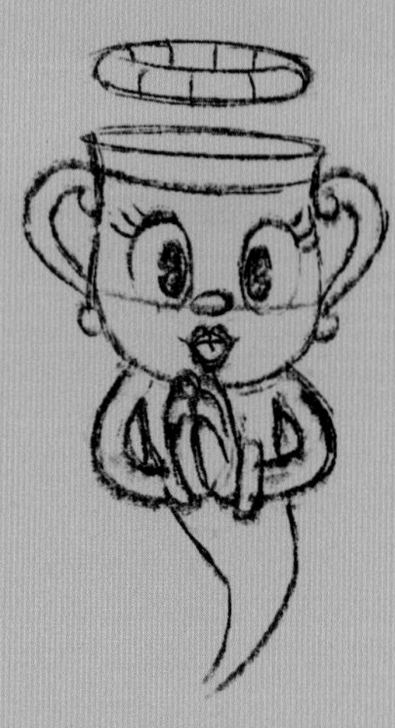

As with Cuphead and Mugman, Ms. Chalice needed her very own "death ghost"—the sprite which players see after your character has lost their last hit point. In a multiplayer game, players can bounce off this death ghost with a parry move to bring their friend back to life, resulting in one of the only spoken lines by our main trio. Illustrated here is the complexity of blocking out even the simplest of spoken lines in hand animation. Fun fact: the spoken "thank you" heard by Ms. Chalice in-game is voiced by none other than Doutzen Moldenhauer, daughter of Art Director Chad Moldenhauer and Studio Director Maja Moldenhauer.

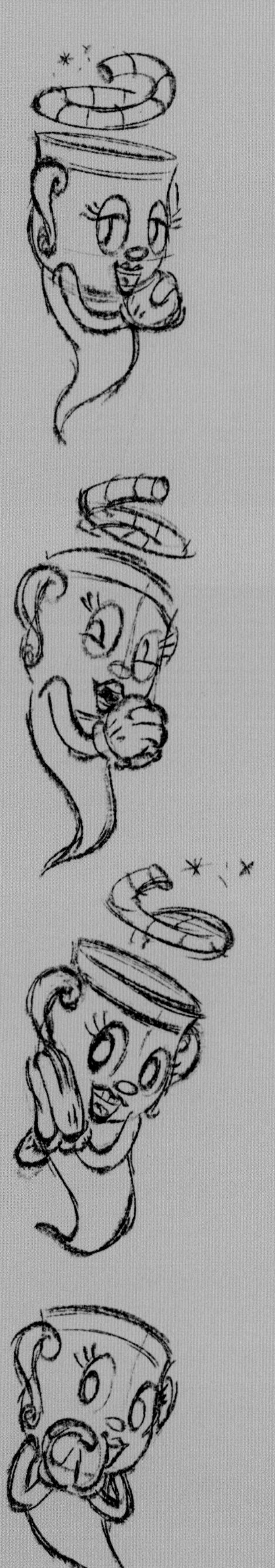

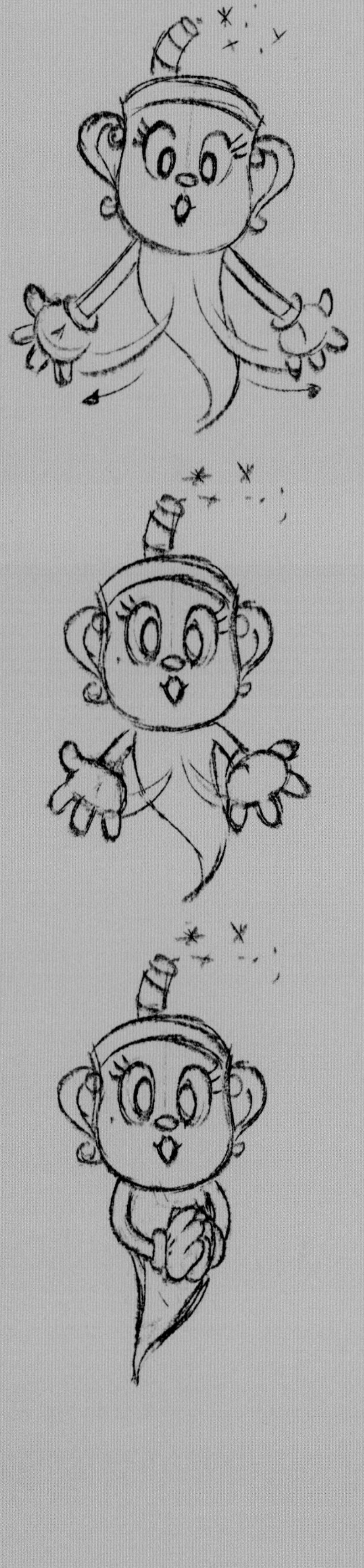

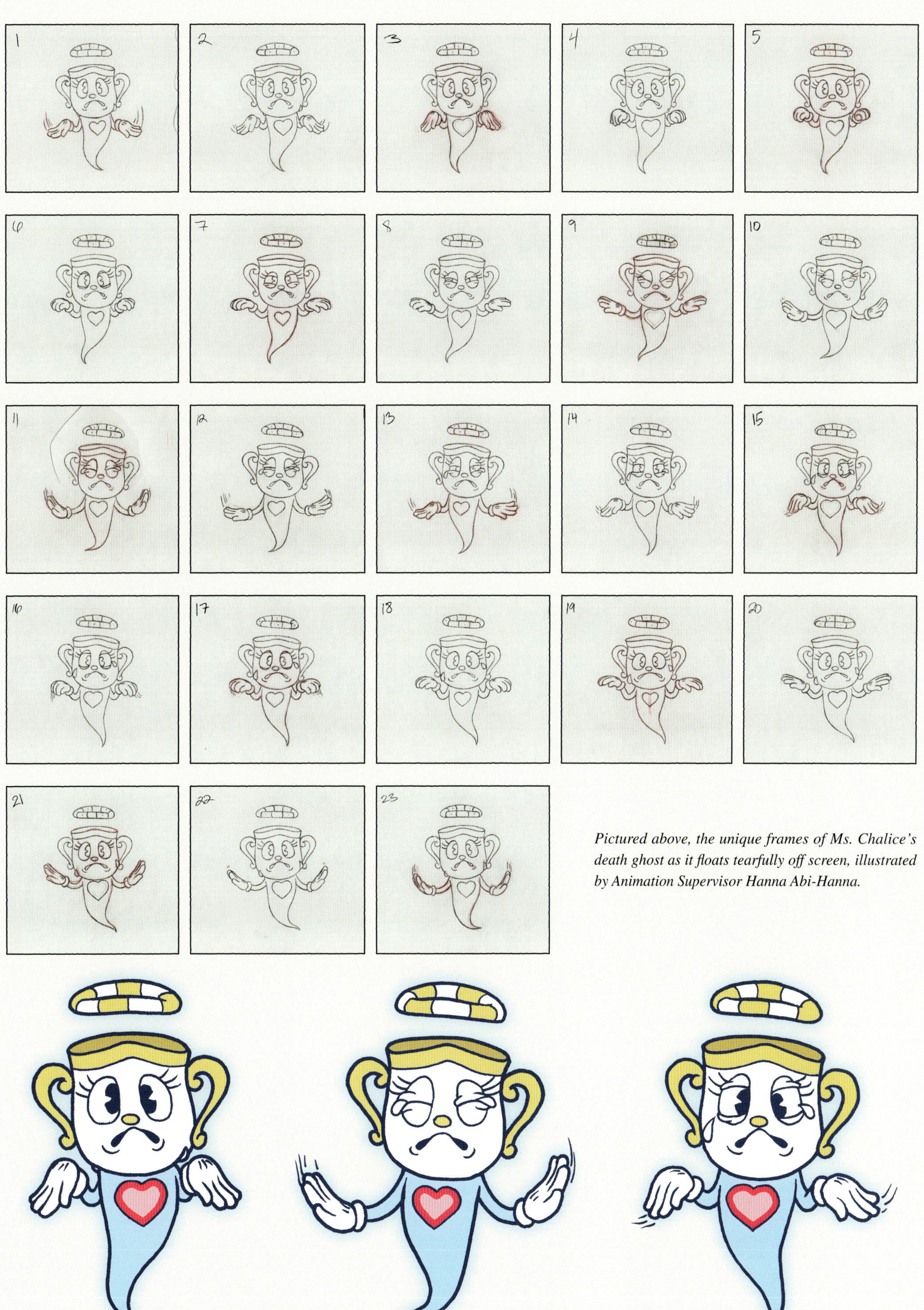

Pictured above, the unique frames of Ms. Chalice's death ghost as it floats tearfully off screen, illustrated by Animation Supervisor Hanna Abi-Hanna.

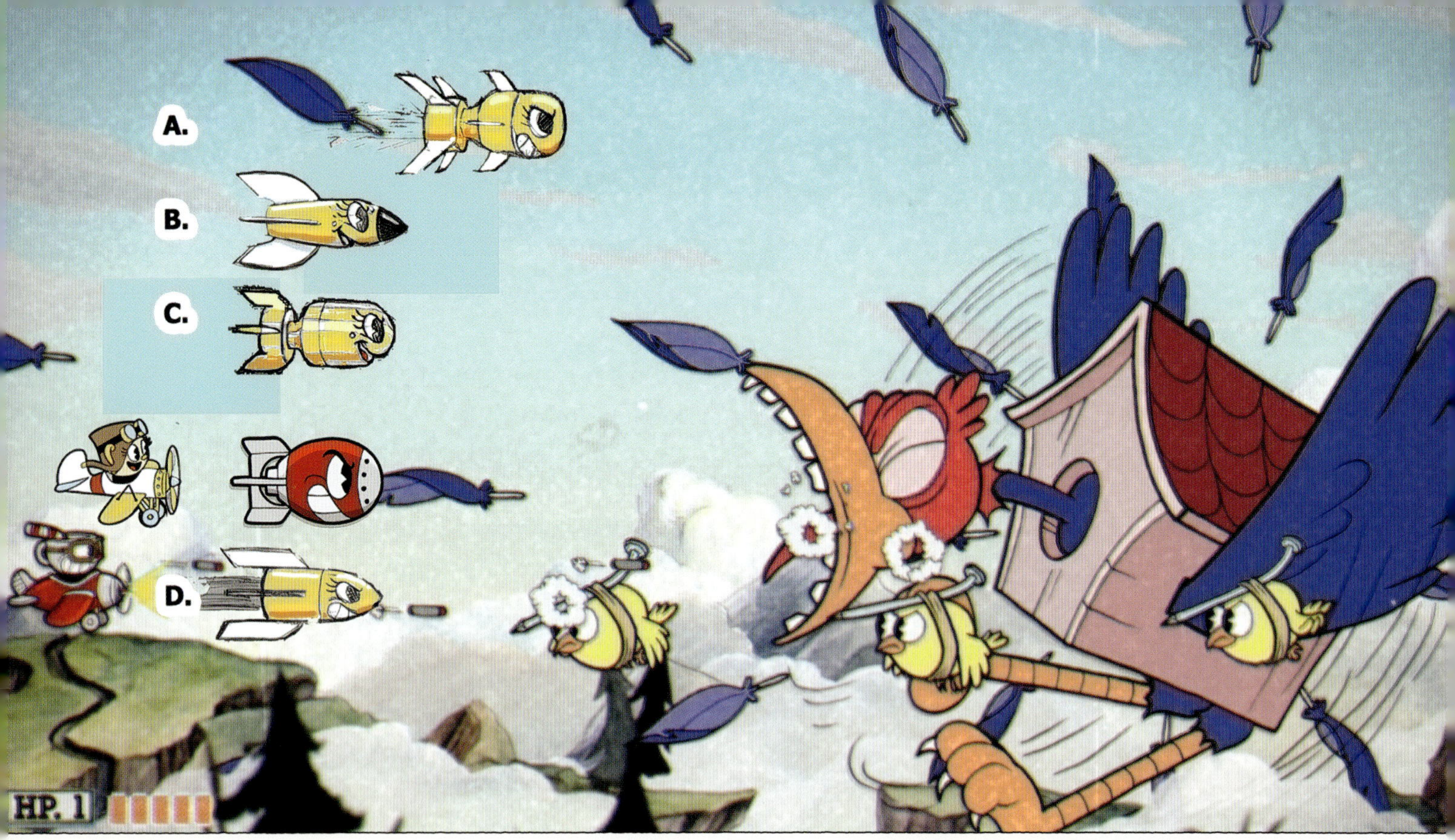

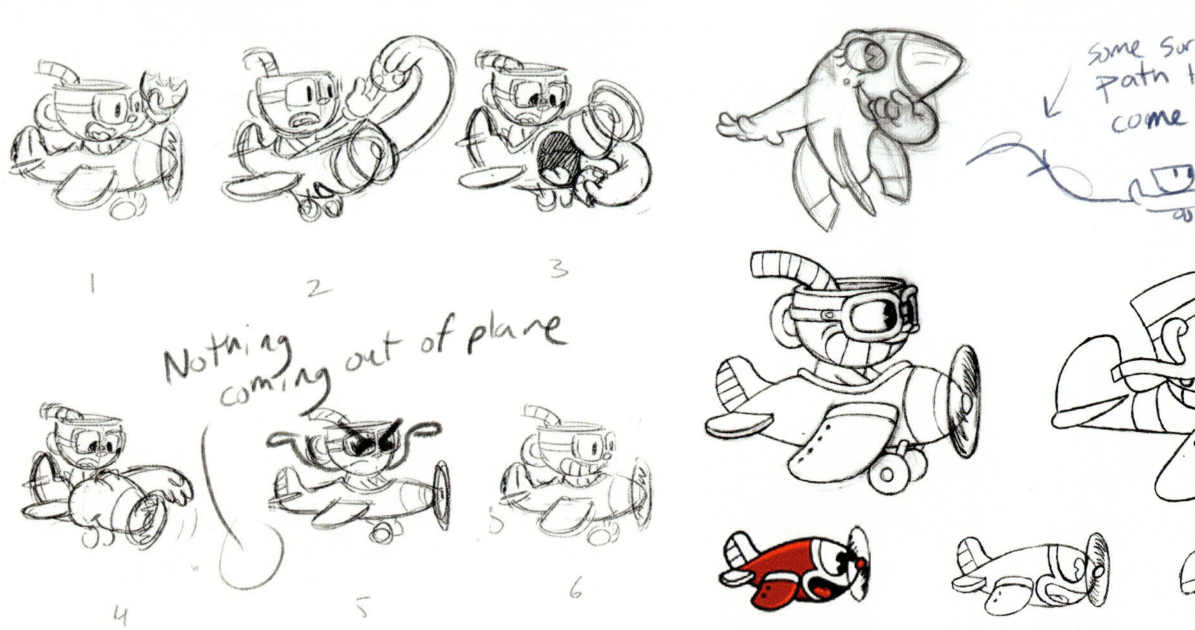

As a team, we had a lot of fun creating bespoke designs for all of Ms. Chalice's many character actions, but perhaps nowhere did we have more fun than with the "plane form" seen in the game's airborne shoot-'em-up stages. After much experimentation, we ended up settling on a design for Ms. Chalice inspired by aviation pioneer Amelia Earhart, the first female pilot to fly solo across the Atlantic Ocean. From the little strap of her cap flapping in the wind to her handle-ear sticking out the side, Animation Supervisor Hanna Abi-Hanna's chosen design was one of those fantastic "know it when you see it" moments in game development where we all felt like we had landed on something special.

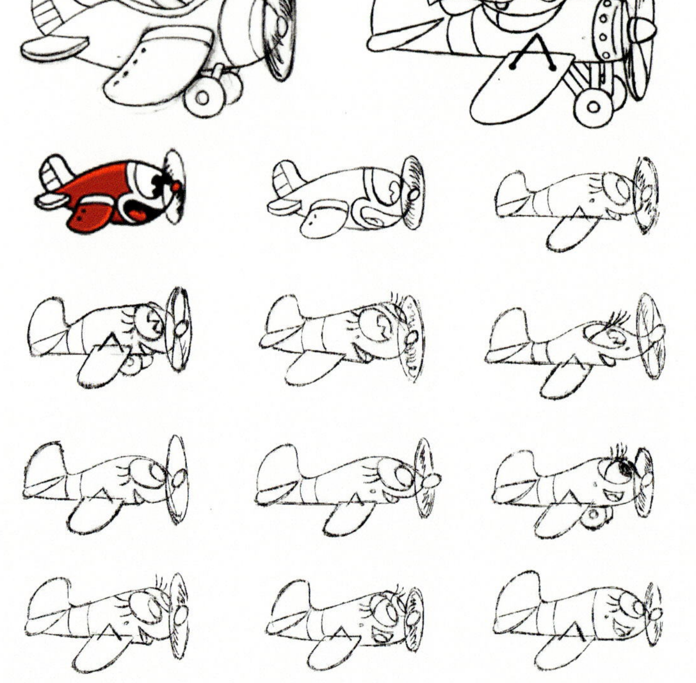

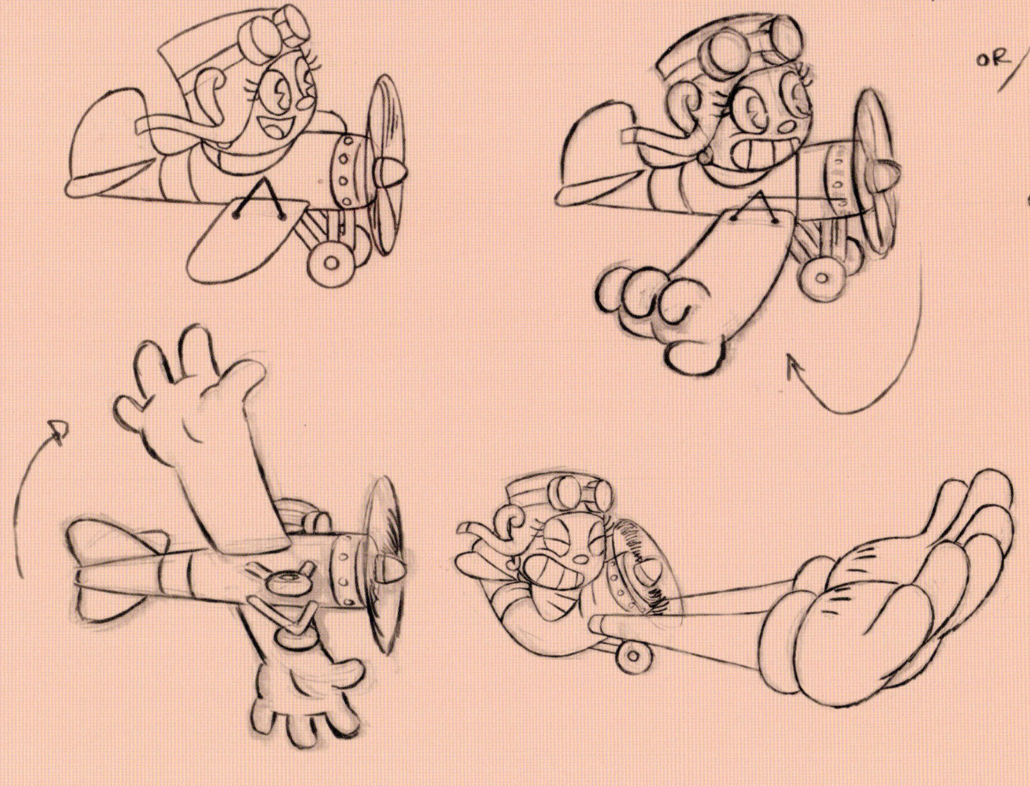

Left, key frame concept of Ms. Chalice's plane EX animation by Animator Hanna Abi-Hanna. Below, a variety of concepts trying to capture of the personality of Ms. Chalice in her unique, more streamlined bomb super anthropomorphization.

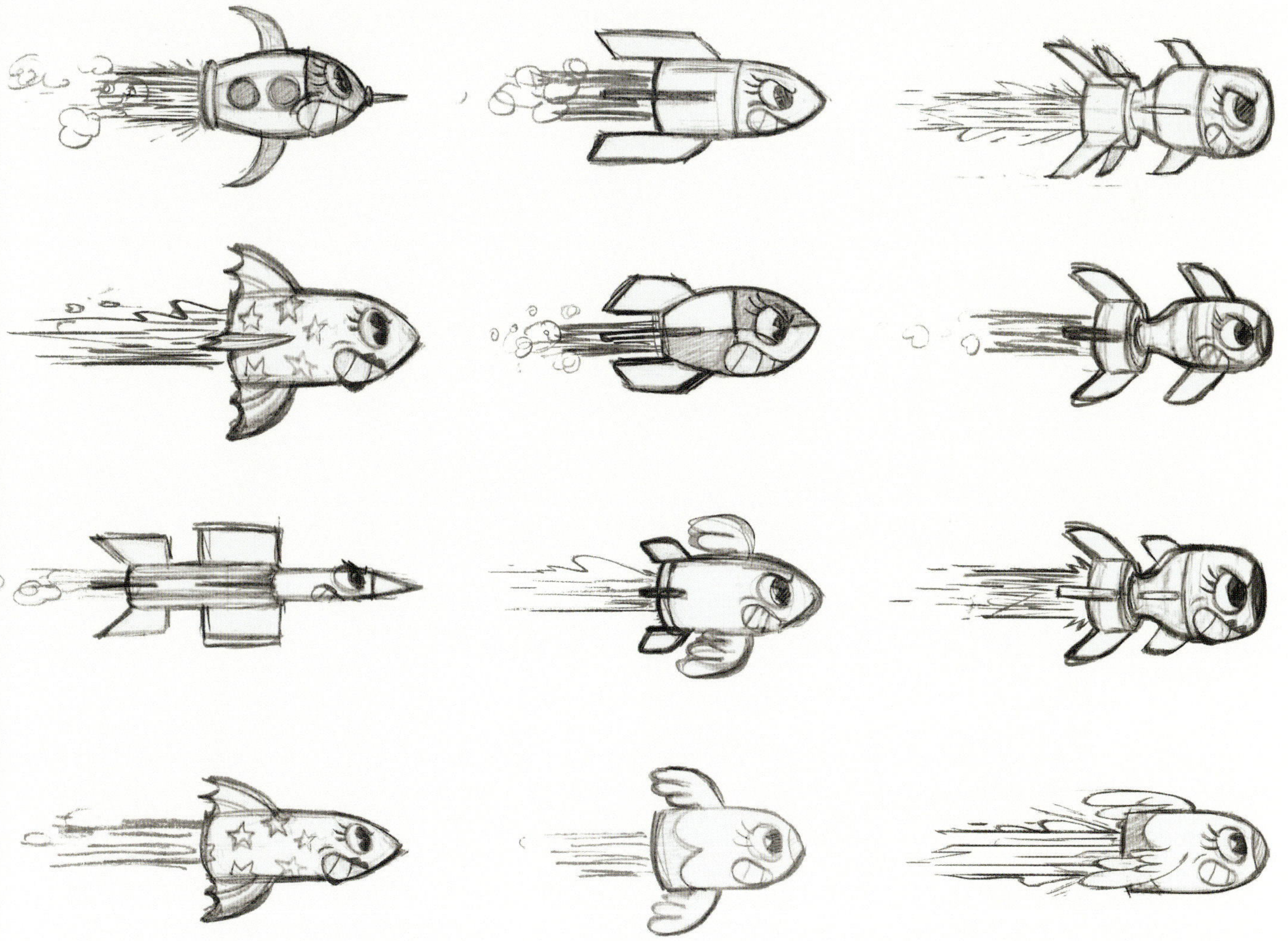

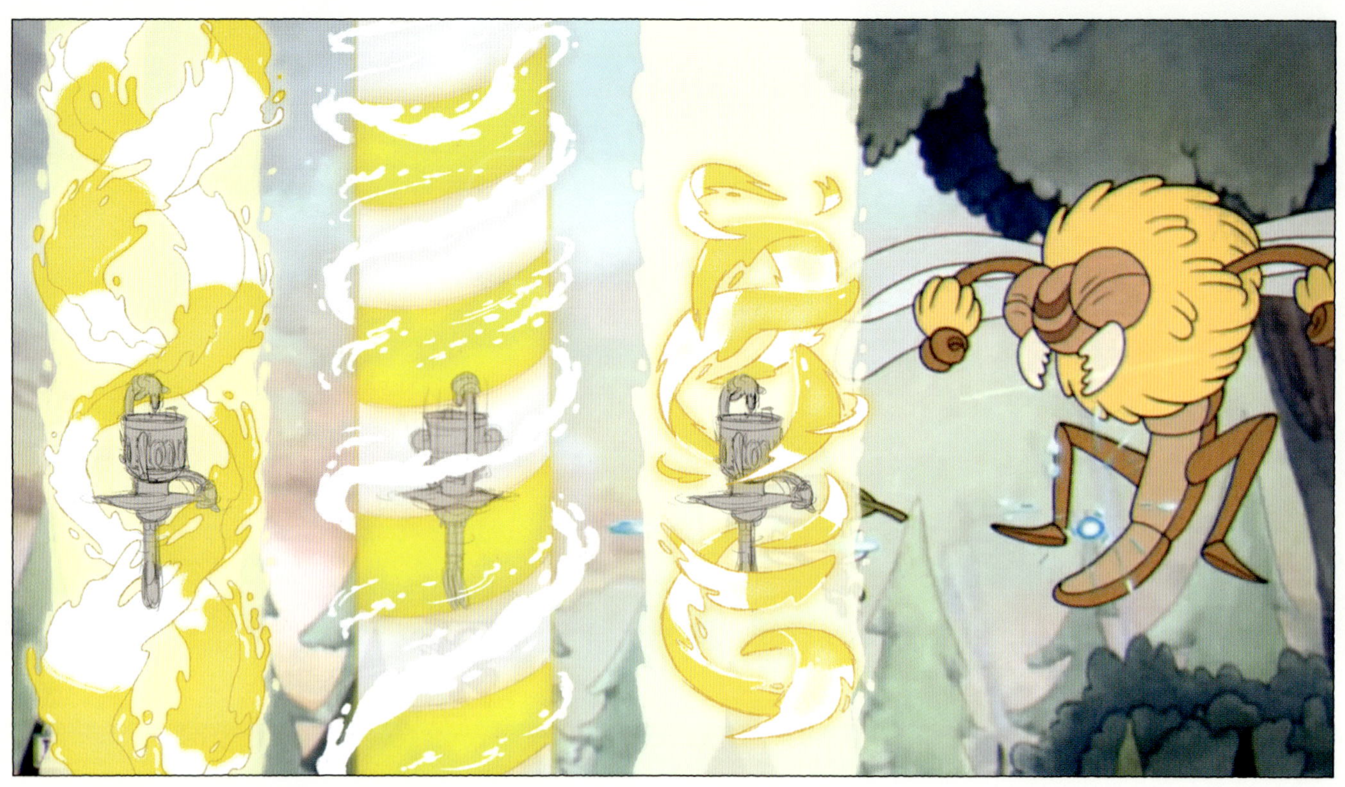

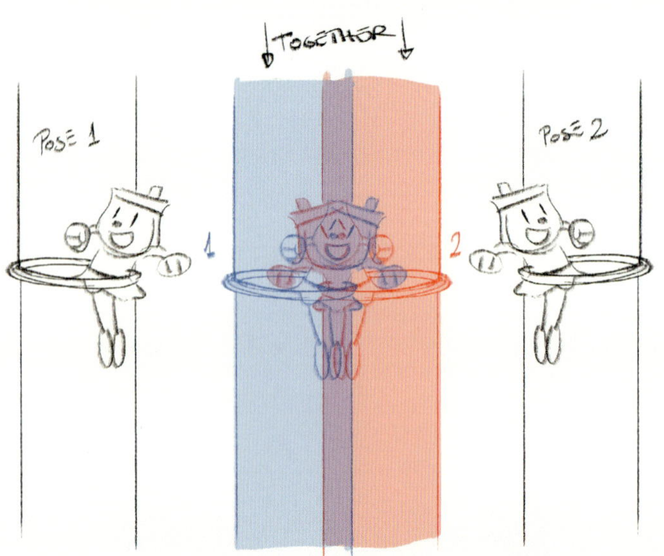

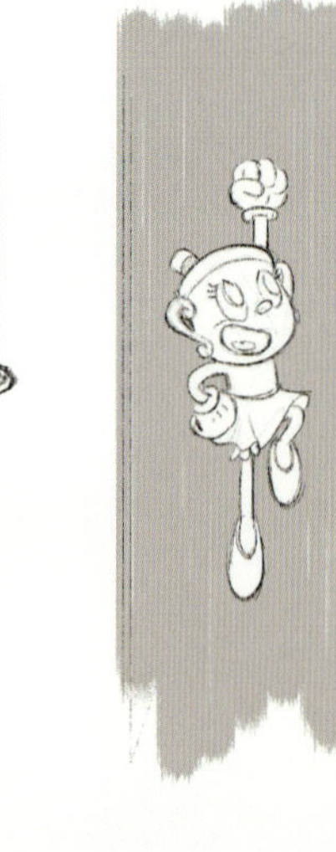

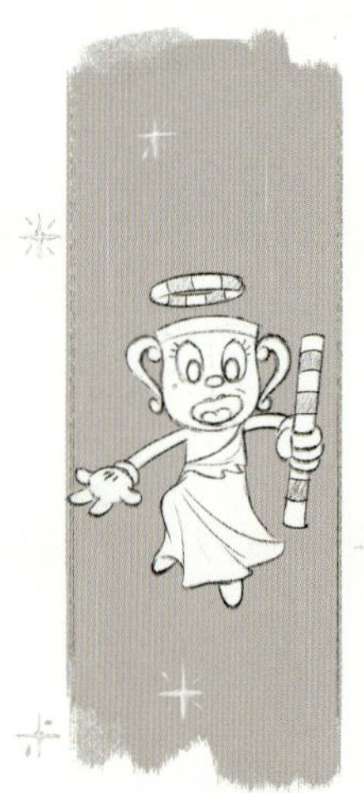

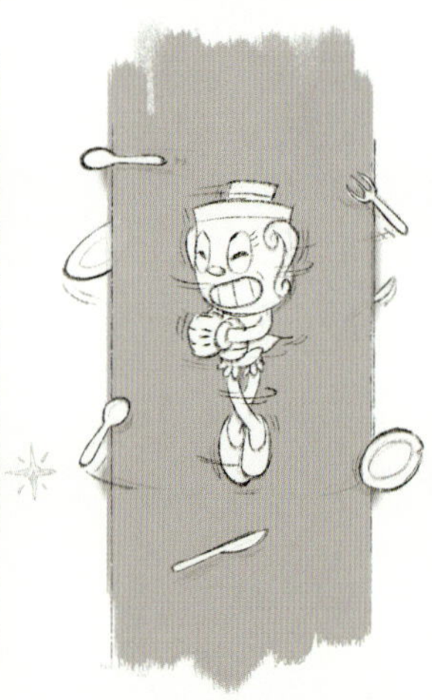

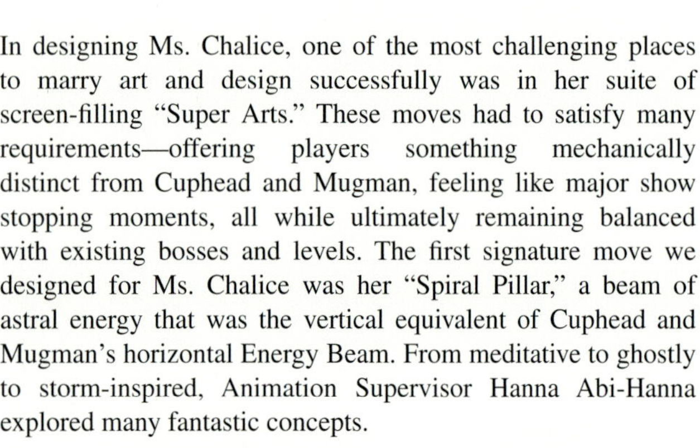

In designing Ms. Chalice, one of the most challenging places to marry art and design successfully was in her suite of screen-filling "Super Arts." These moves had to satisfy many requirements—offering players something mechanically distinct from Cuphead and Mugman, feeling like major show stopping moments, all while ultimately remaining balanced with existing bosses and levels. The first signature move we designed for Ms. Chalice was her "Spiral Pillar," a beam of astral energy that was the vertical equivalent of Cuphead and Mugman's horizontal Energy Beam. From meditative to ghostly to storm-inspired, Animation Supervisor Hanna Abi-Hanna explored many fantastic concepts.

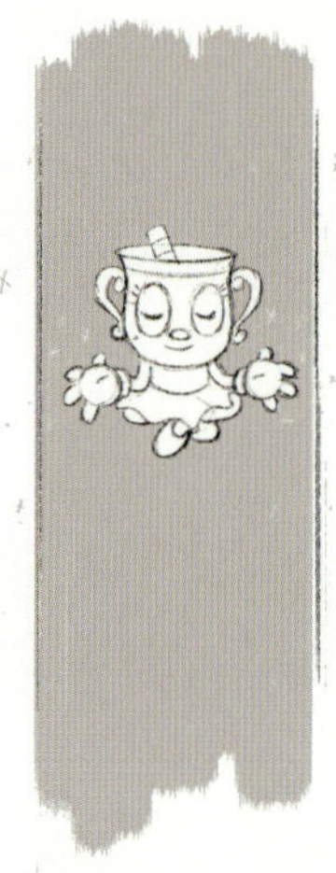

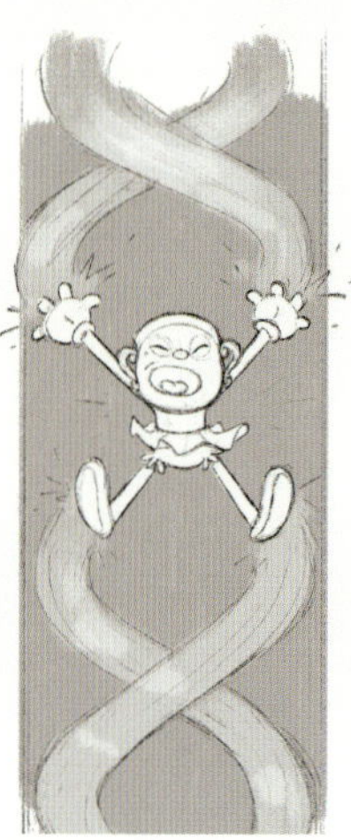

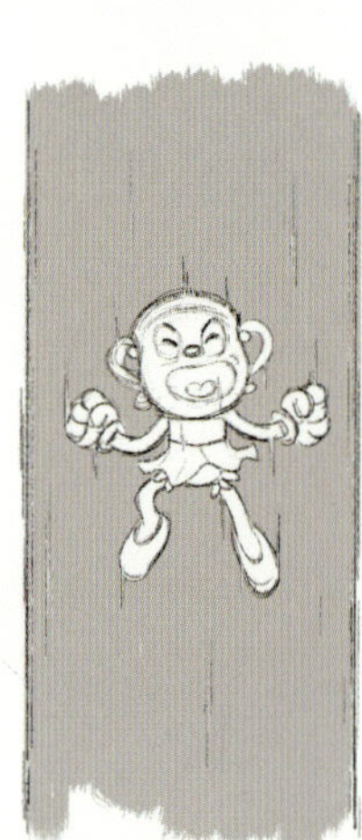

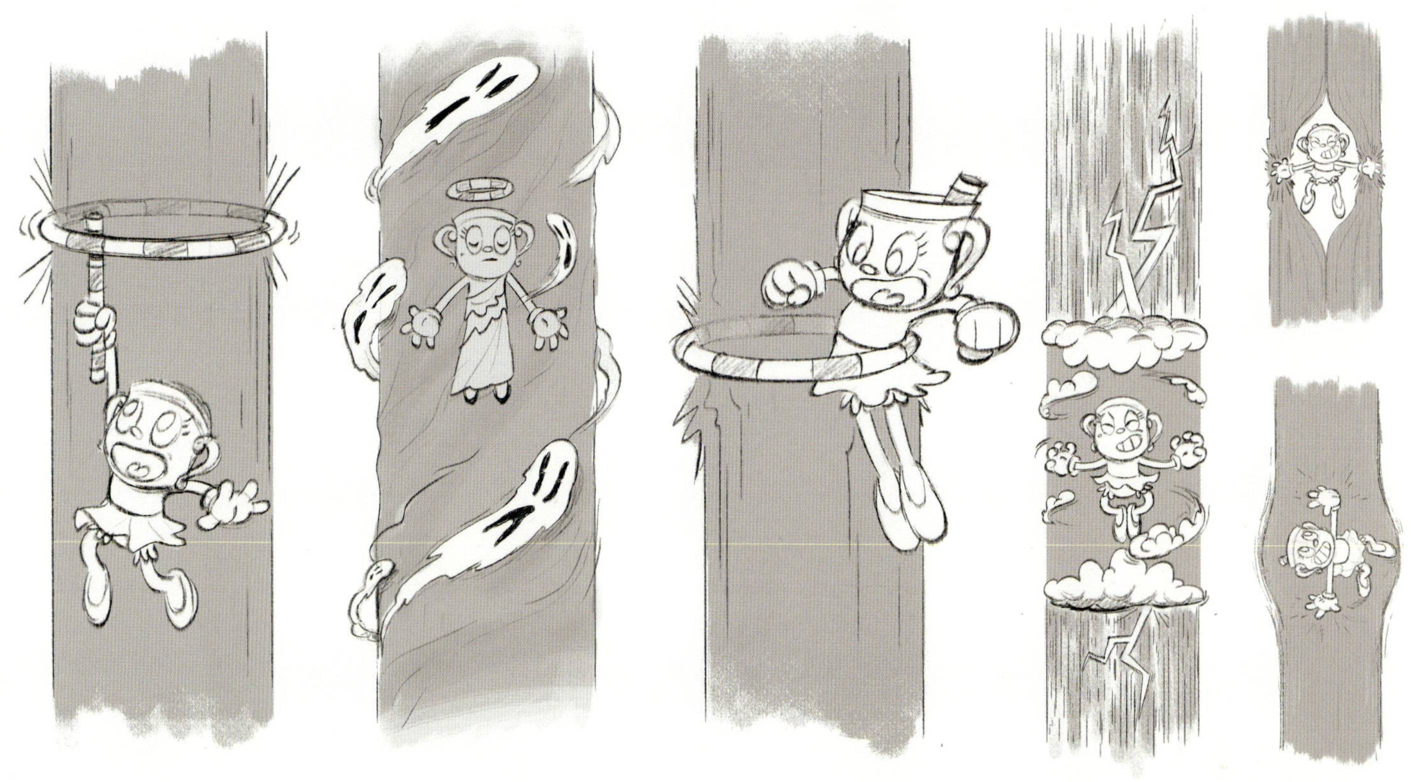

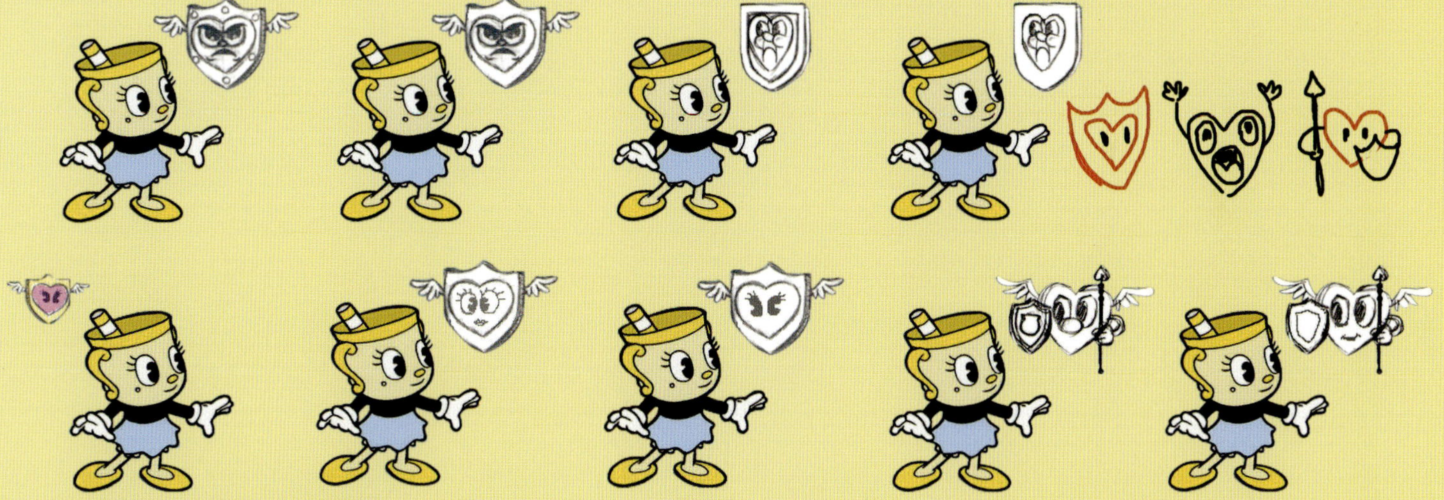

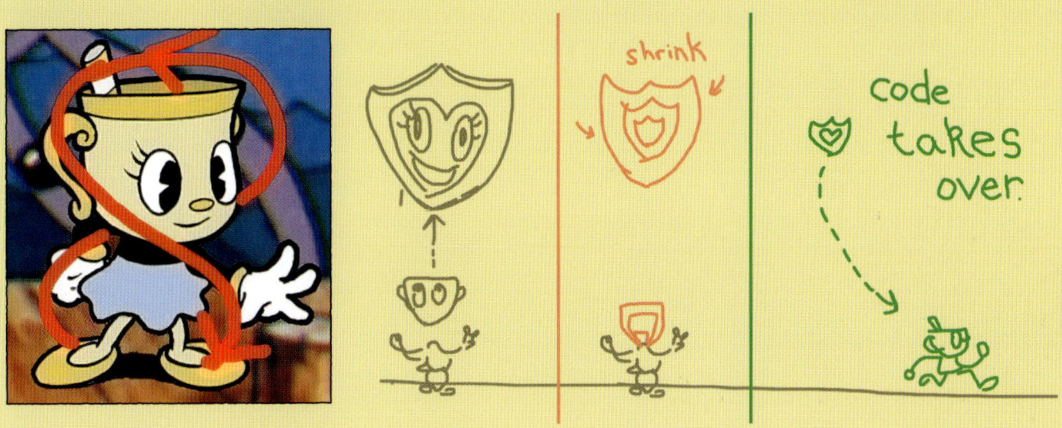

Various elements in Cuphead require movement animation driven by programming to facilitate a more reactive sense of movement. Shown above and left, Ms. Chalice's floating shield super required a combination of hand animation and slick mathematical integration.

When creating something, it's often necessary to see a massive amount of what you don't quite want in order to know for certain what you do want. In developing *The Delicious Last Course*, there is arguably no place that this rang truer than in the development of the art and design for Ms. Chalice's final Super Art, the Ghostly Barrage.

What ended up as the third bombastic, screen-filling attack started its life as an entirely different design…but that's a story for the next page of this book. Ultimately, our "lightbulb" moment with the Ghostly Barrage came when took a look at the past—literally and metaphorically speaking! Finding ourselves creatively blocked, we ended up fascinated by the statues littered throughout *Cuphead*'s "Rugged Ridge" platforming stage, which harkened to an imagined past of the Inkwell Isles filled with cutlery heroes long gone. Studying these statues unlocked the idea of having Ms. Chalice tap into her ancient lineage, and call forth a volley of spectral warriors to do battle with her. Sometimes in game development, the best way to figure out where you need to go is to remind yourself of where you—and your characters—have already been.

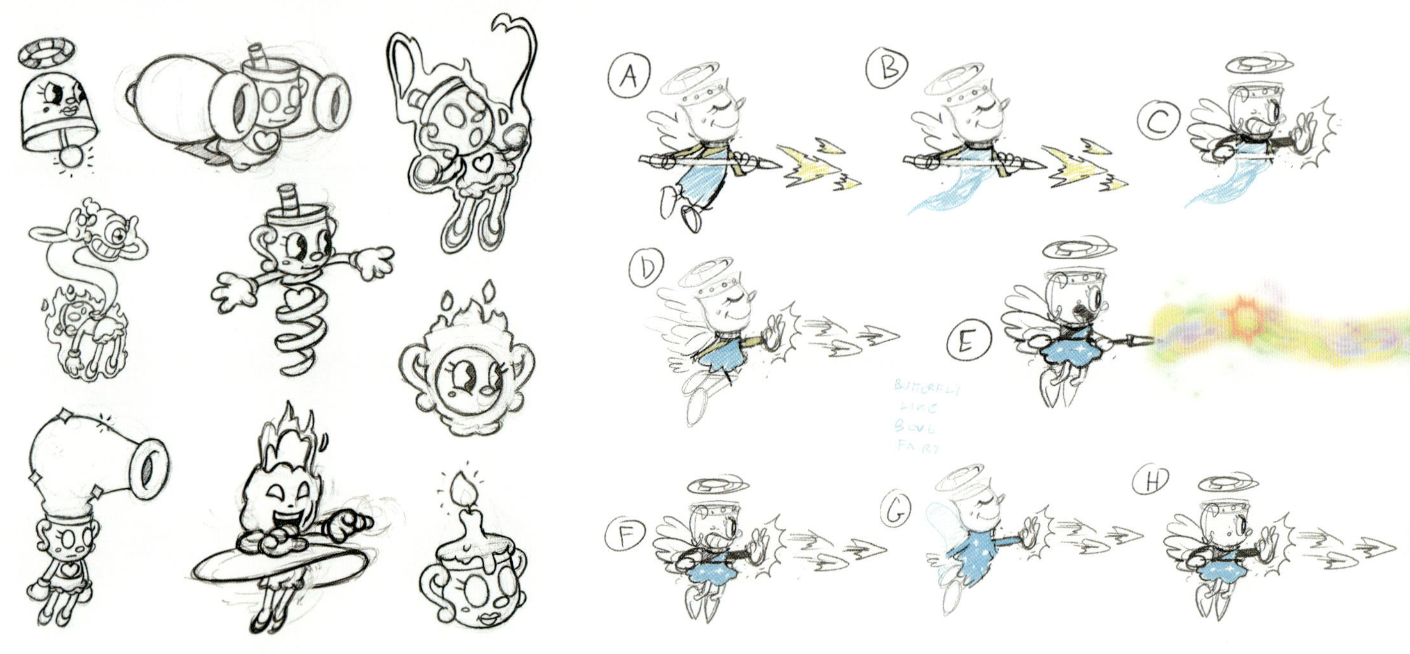

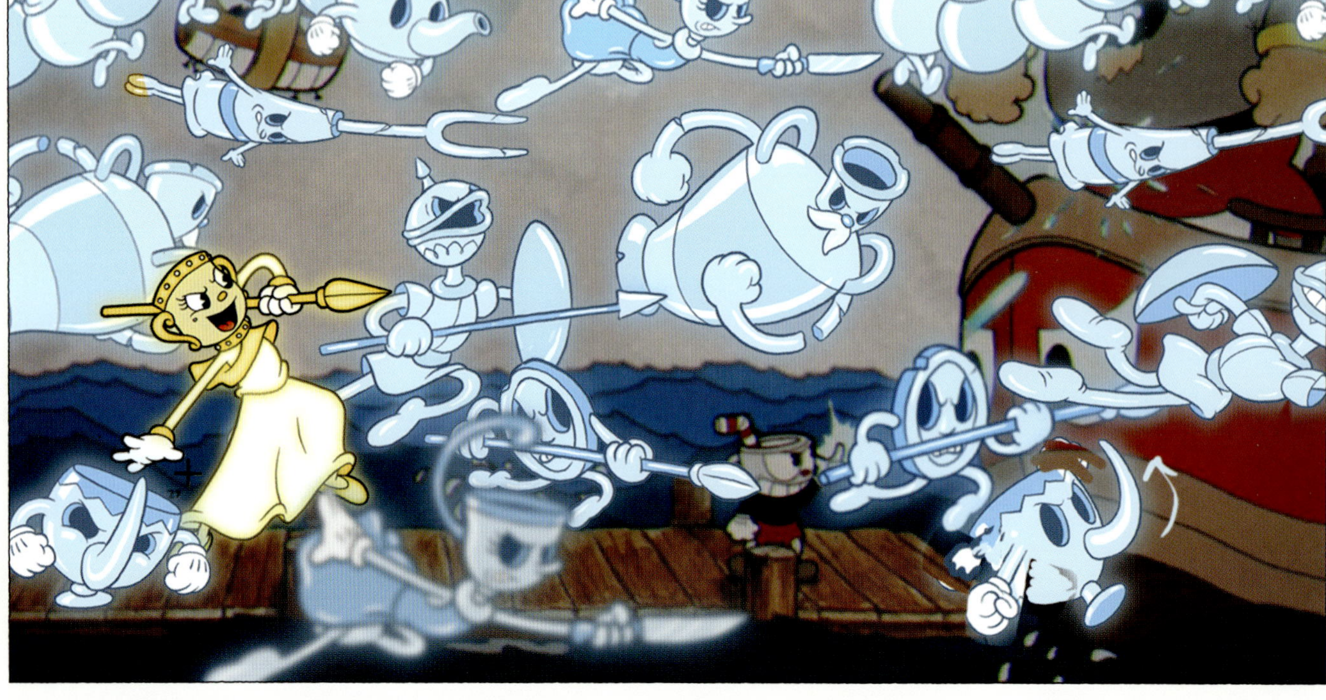

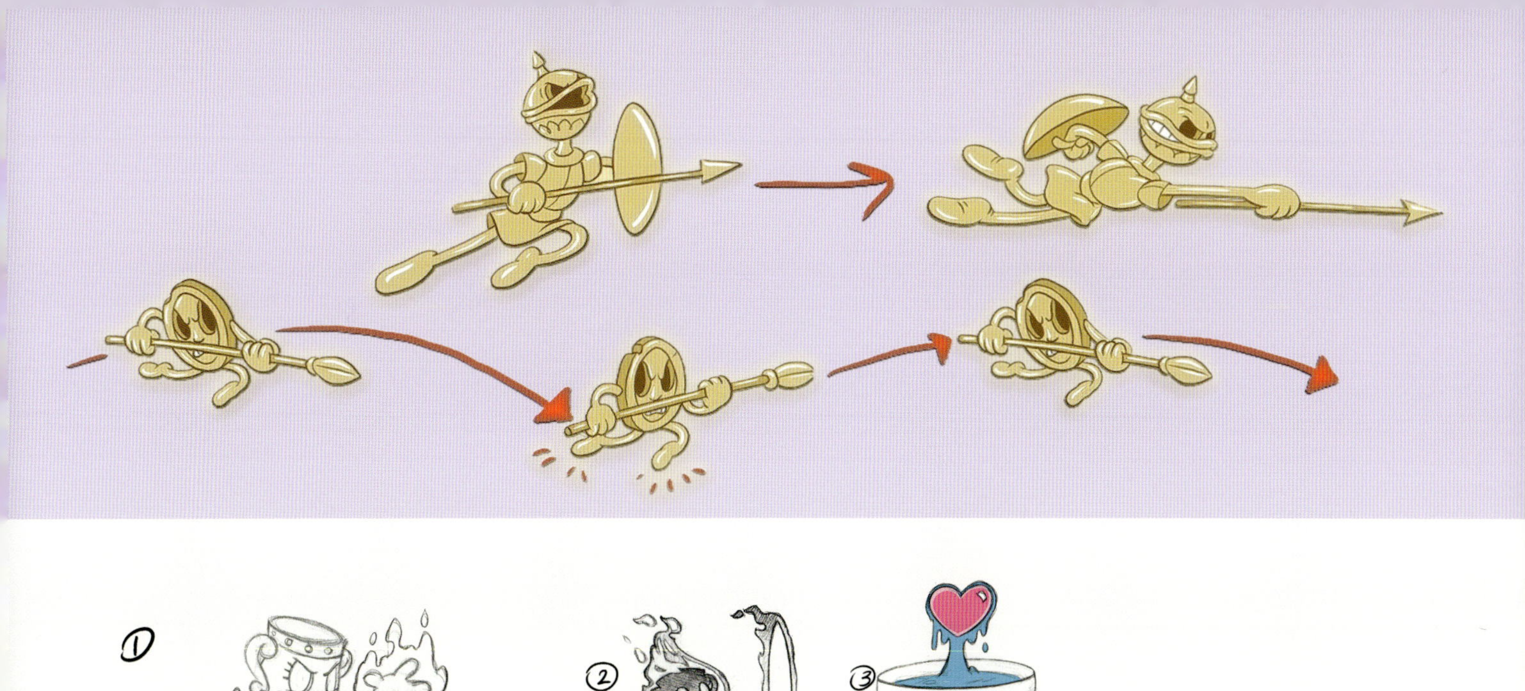

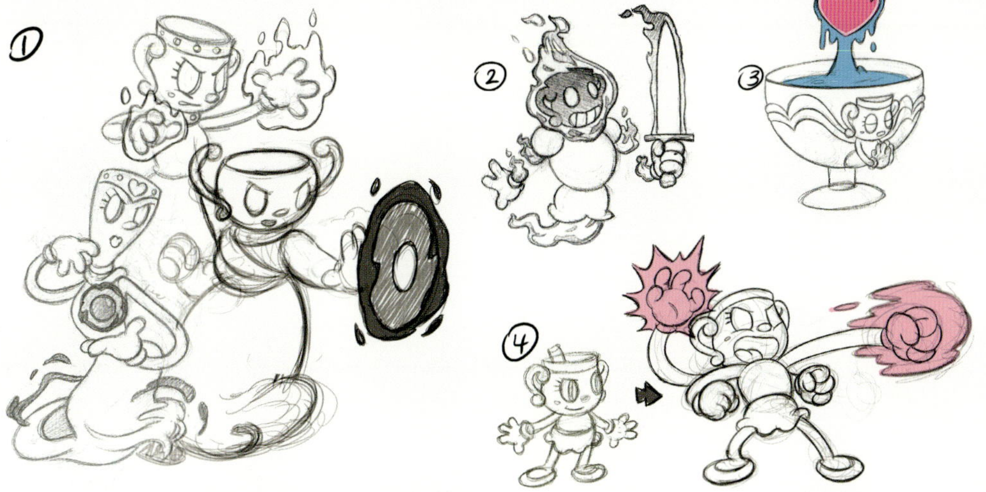

Left, Animator Joseph Coleman explored a host different options for the attack which ultimately became the Ghostly Barrage. At one point, we considered a version of this super involving a team-up with Chalice's spectral ancestors.

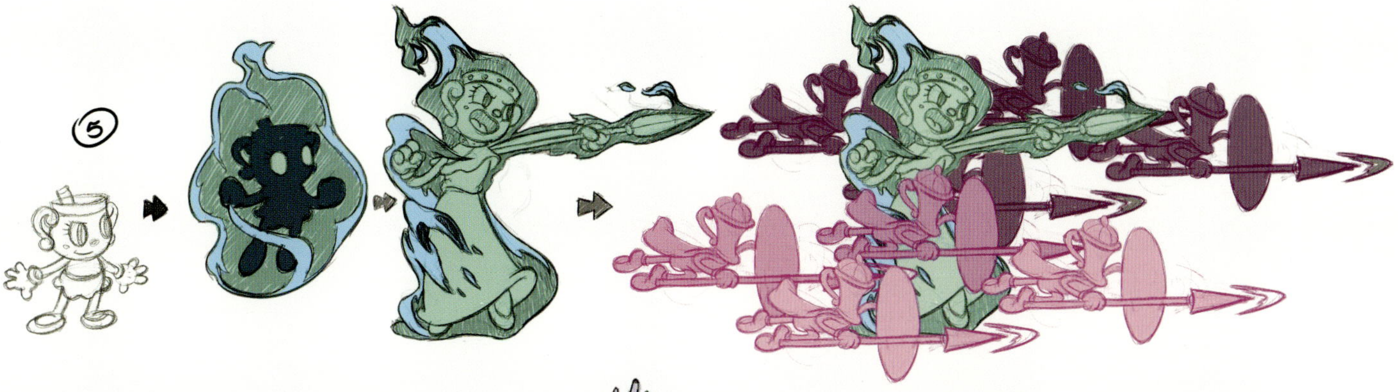

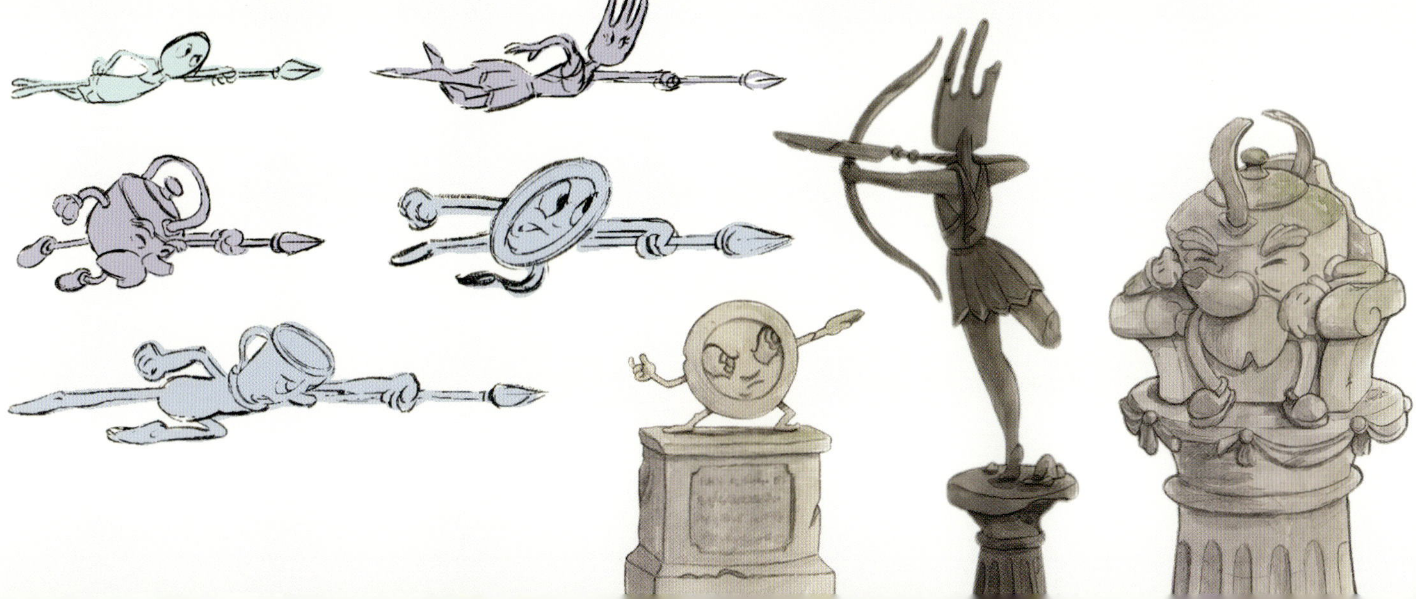

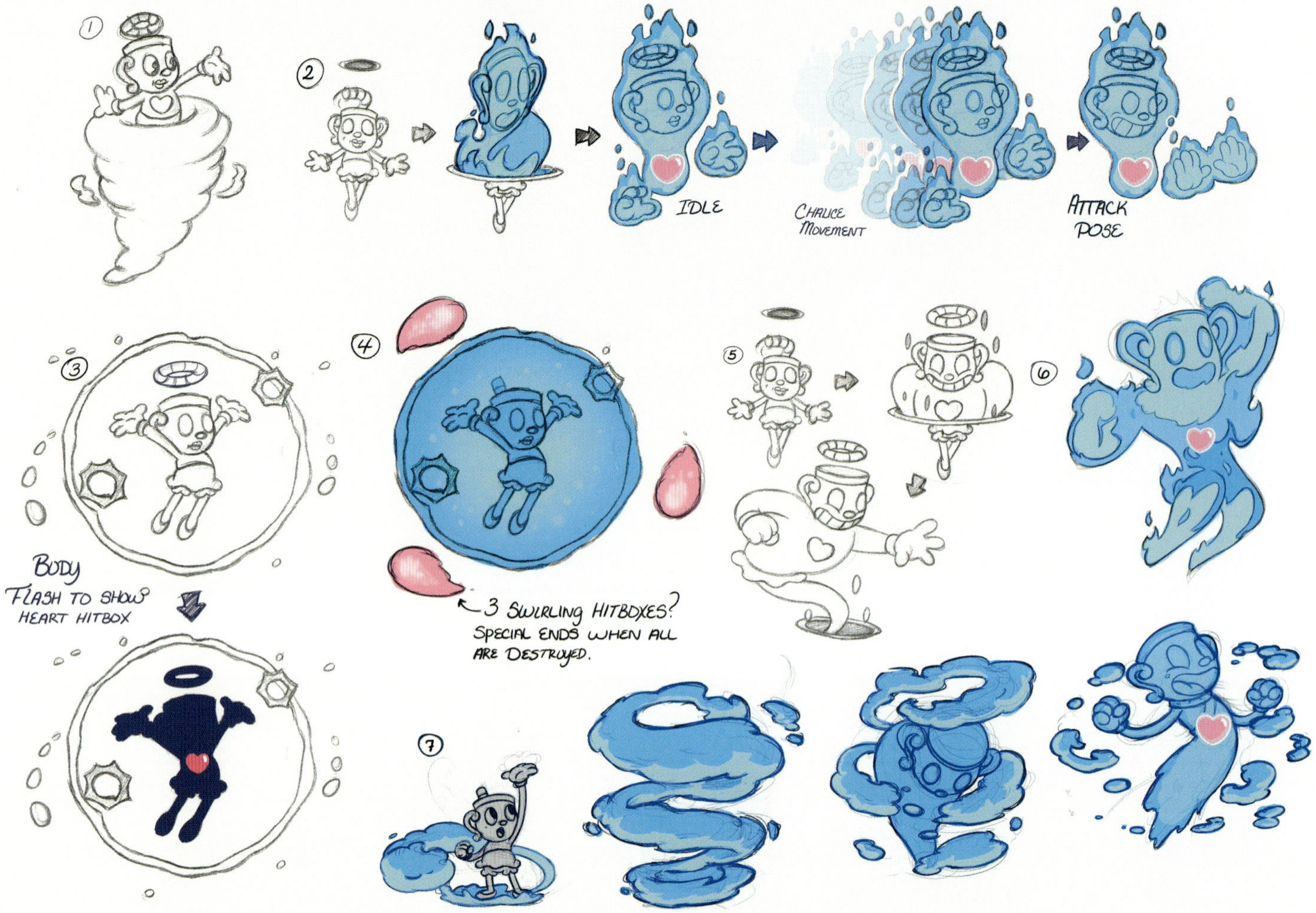

1

2

IDLE

CHALICE
MOVEMENT

ATTACK
POSE

3

4

5

6

BODY
FLASH TO SHOW
HEART HITBOX

← 3 SWIRLING HITBOXES?
SPECIAL ENDS WHEN ALL
ARE DESTROYED.

7

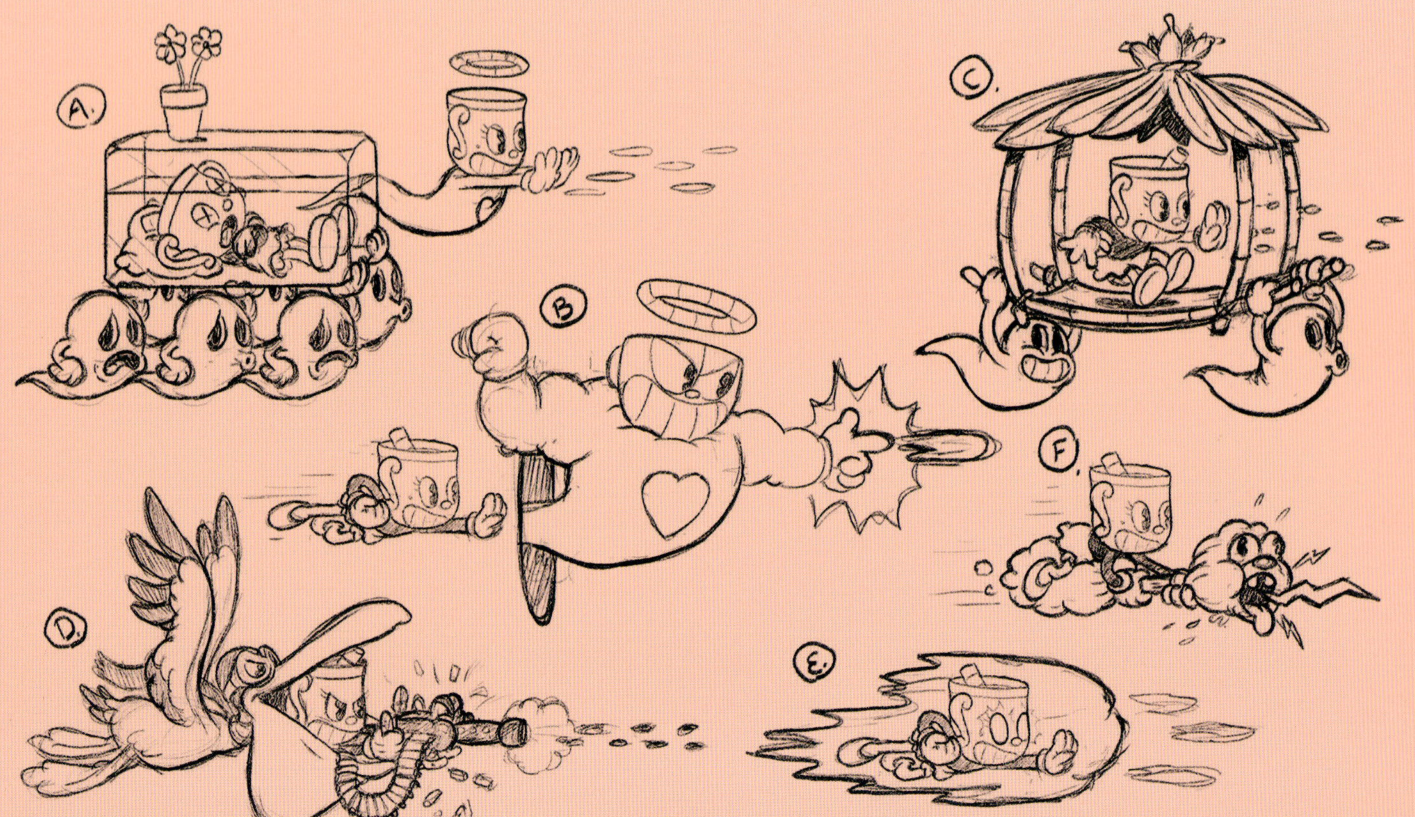

A.

B

C.

F.

D.

E.

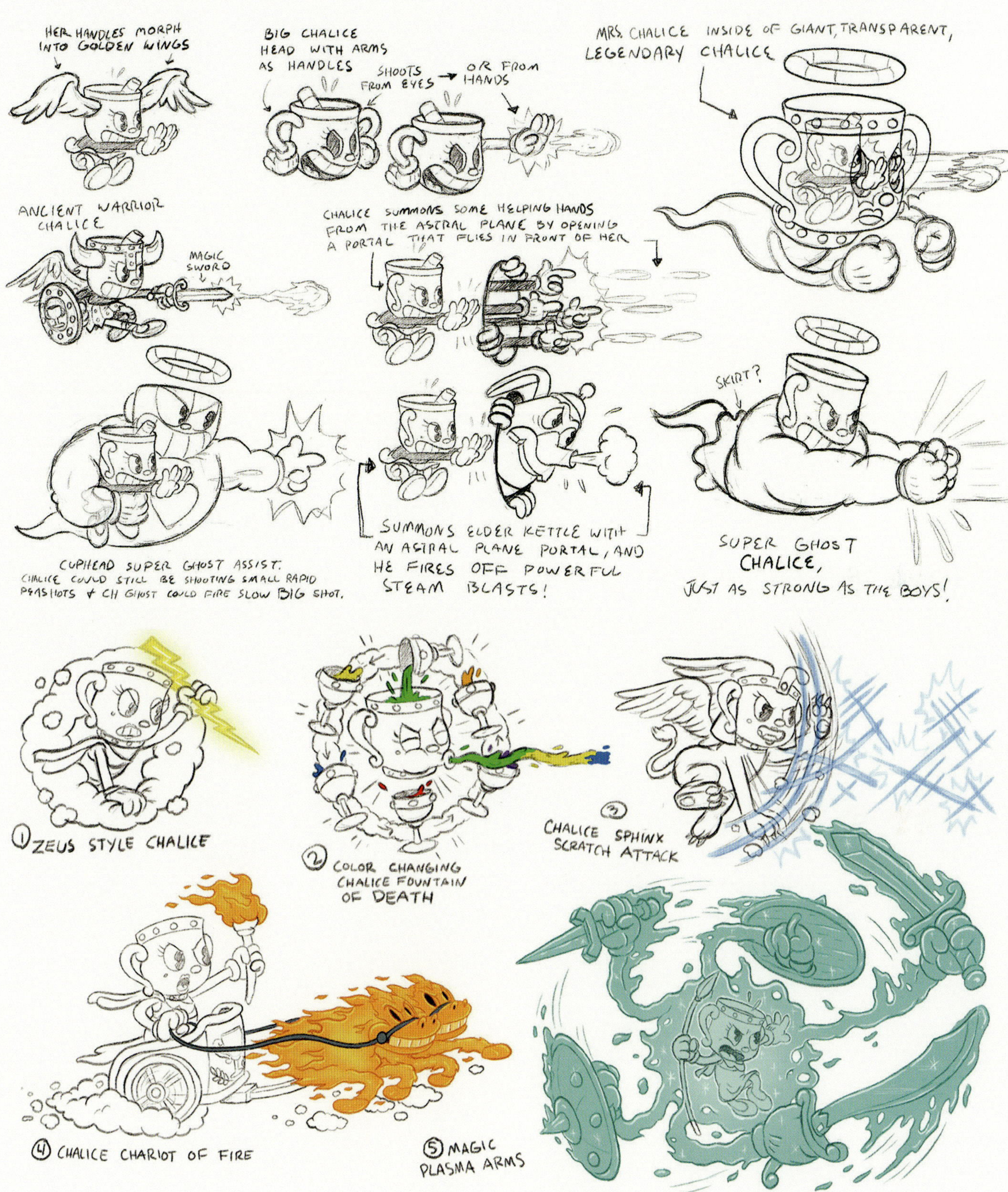

There is perhaps a different universe in which Ms. Chalice's Ghostly Barrage ended up as something altogether different. For much of the game's early development, we had conceptualized Ms. Chalice's third Super Art as one in which the player controlled a ghostly abstraction of Ms. Chalice as she moved around the screen firing projectiles at enemies. Affectionately referred to as the "Shmup Super" in reference to the game's shoot-'em-up plane mode, it was ultimately decided that the attack as designed bore too many similarities to those levels. Before shifting gears to a different design, however, our artists explored a dizzying array of concepts—just some of which you can see pictured here, from Animator Joseph Coleman and Lead Concept Artist Lance "Inkwell" Miller.

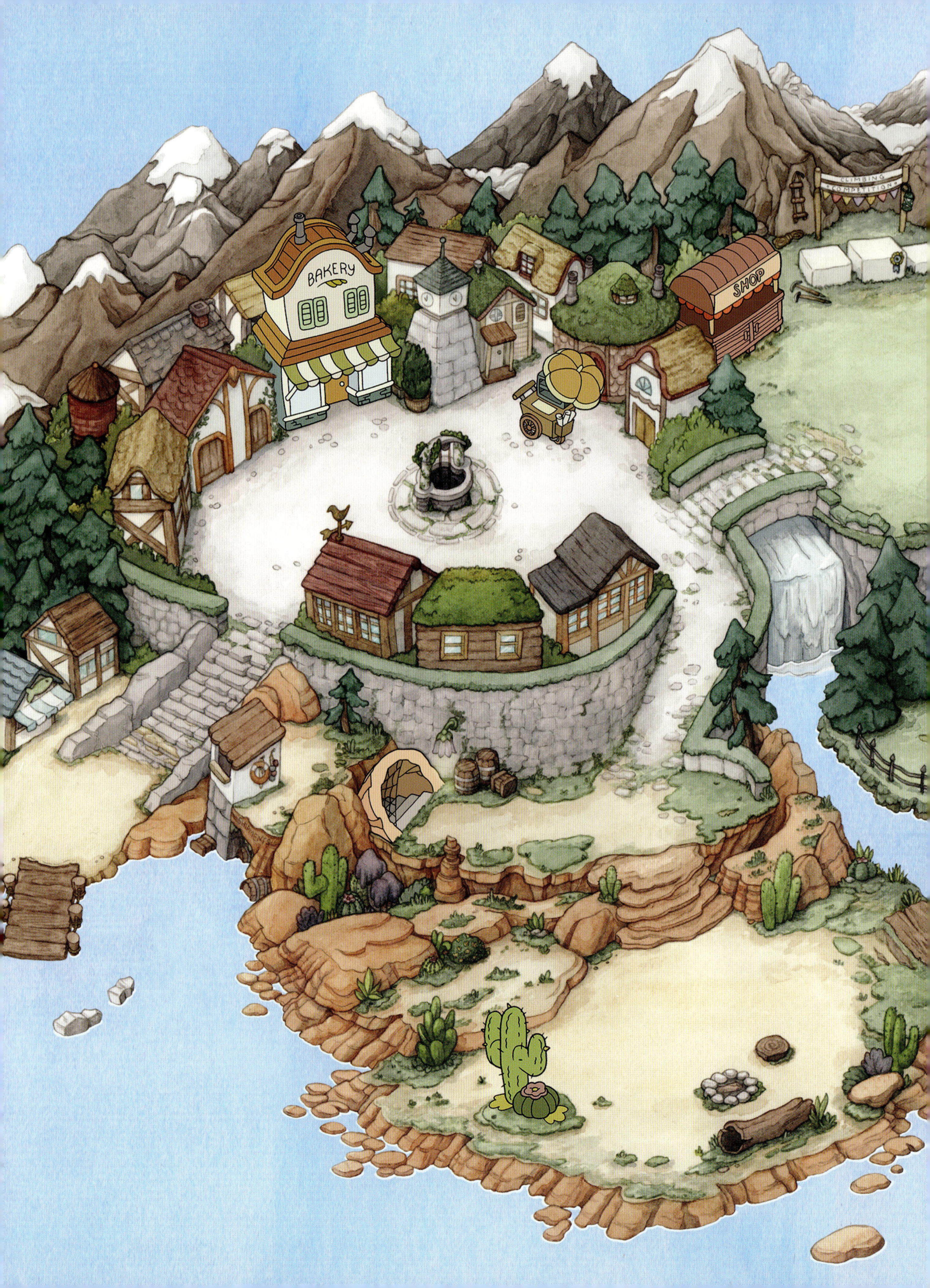

BAKERY
SHOP
CLIMBING
COMPETITION

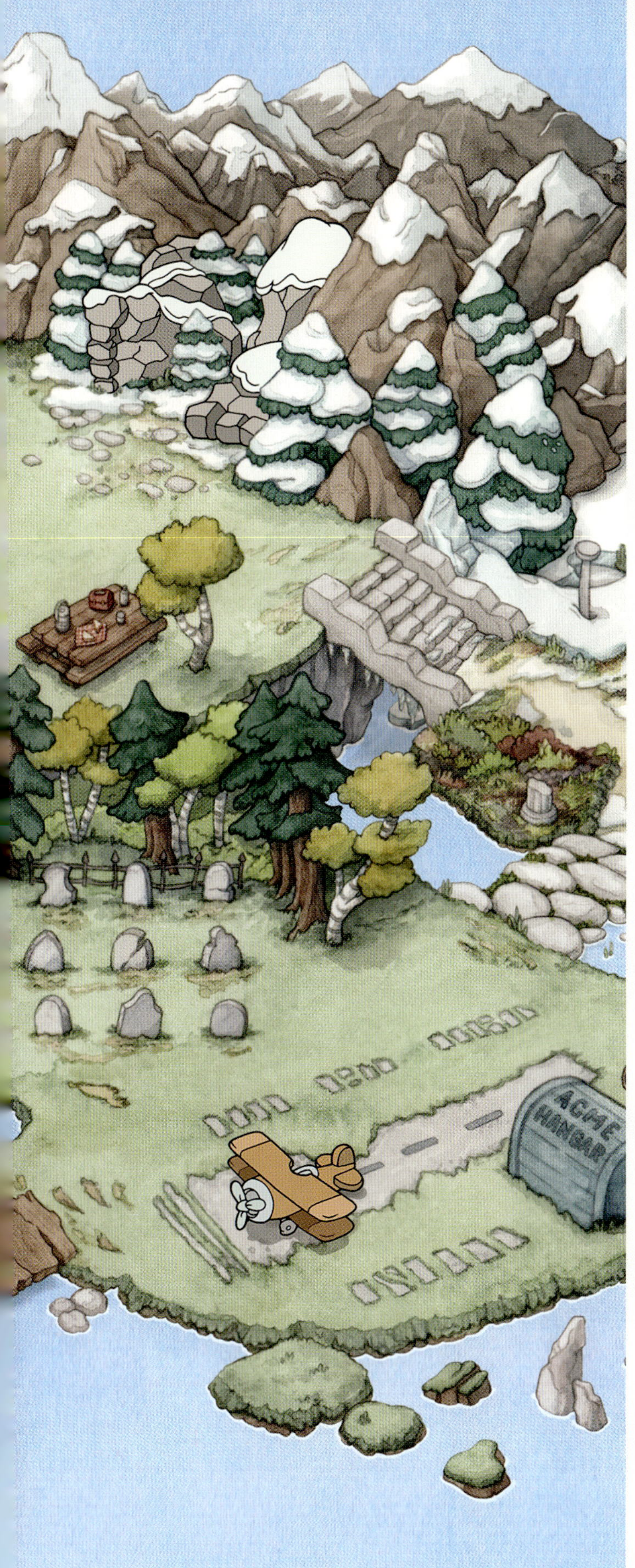

Chapter II:
DLC Island

FROM VERY EARLY ON in the development of *The Delicious Last Course*, we knew that the call to adventure for our intrepid cups would mean a trip to an entirely new Inkwell Isle. The thought of expanding the size of the "known world" of *Cuphead* was both exciting and daunting, and required a lot of careful iteration over the course of development.

Where the original game's world map was a progression through themed zones that saw players travelling from a placid forest to a thrilling carnival, through a bustling metropolis, and eventually to the gates of Inkwell Hell itself, this new adventure called for something different entirely. Our artistic and design goal for *The Delicious Last Course* was to find a home for boss patterns, thirties cartoon homages, and character concepts that never made it into the core *Cuphead* experience. This meant acknowledging from the beginning that any new island would have to be a more eclectic mixture of locales, all coexisting in the same space. Thankfully, the Inkwell Isles are an all-cartoon wonderland where anything is possible…even having a moonshine-running gang of insects live next door to a bovine cowgirl outlaw.

Concepts

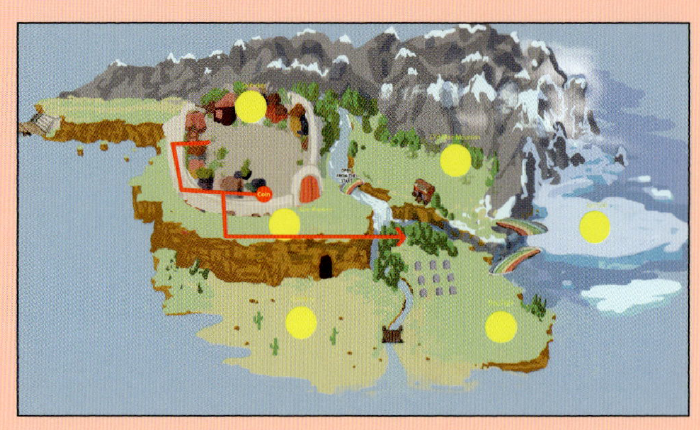

BRINGING THE WORLD MAP in *Cuphead* to life is as much a design exercise as it is an artistic one–arguably more so the former. In addition to considering how we're going to thematically transport players to a cartoon world, we also need to carefully sculpt the player's walking path in a way that guides them to key points of interest. It's a delicate balance of restricting access to certain areas while still offering space for players to explore. The first step often involves creating the kind of rudimentary visual pictured right, on which we outline boss nodes, progression "gates," and hidden walking paths.

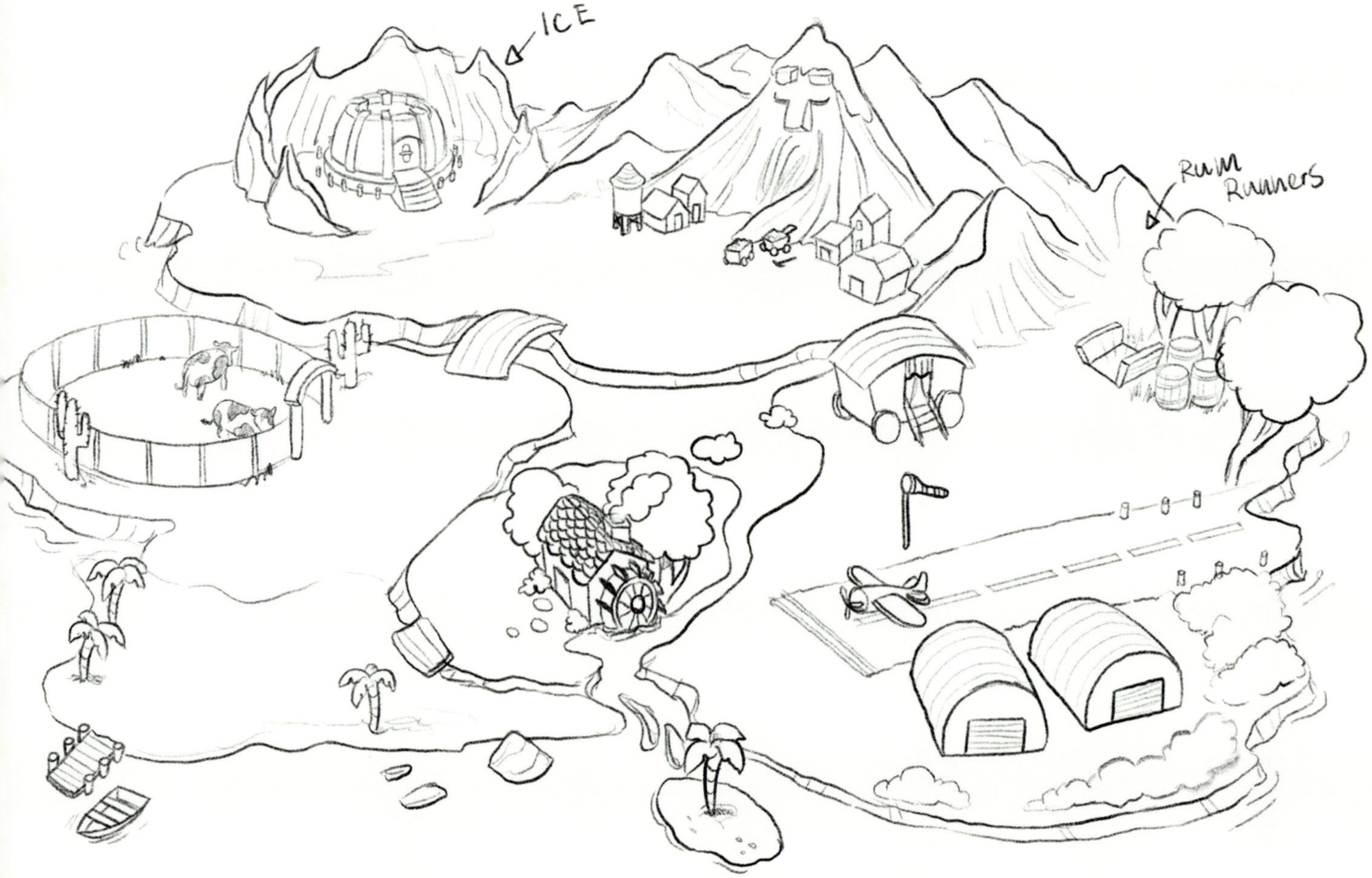

Before sketching out early conceptual layouts, Background Painter Caitlin Russell (above) often starts with heavily simplified "color stories" (right) that inform the biomes we're hoping to see.

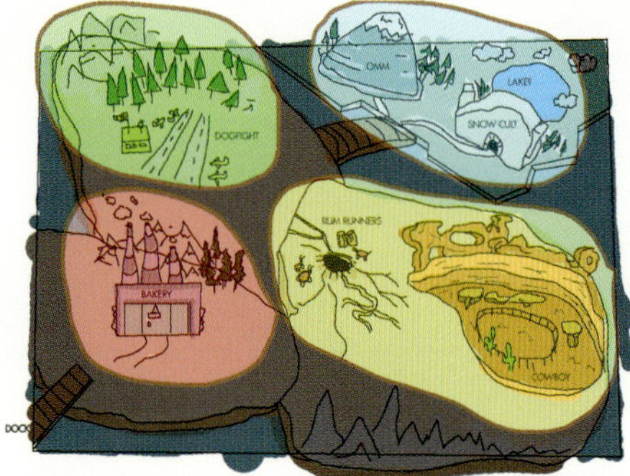

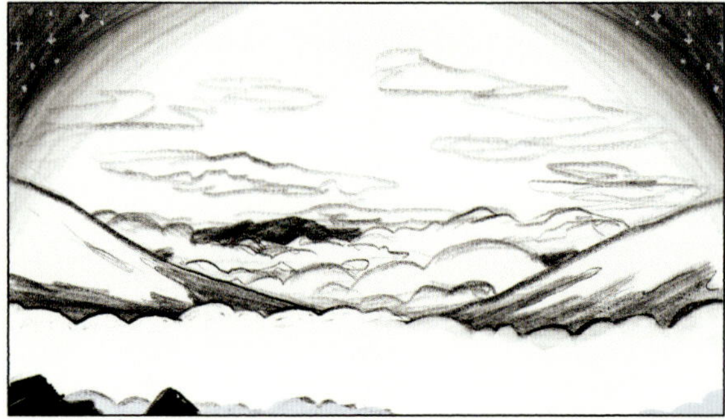

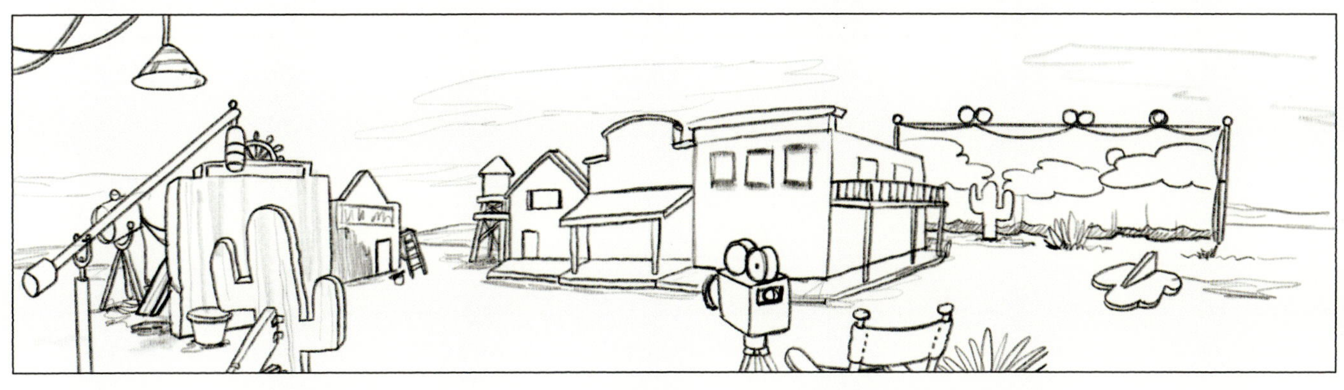
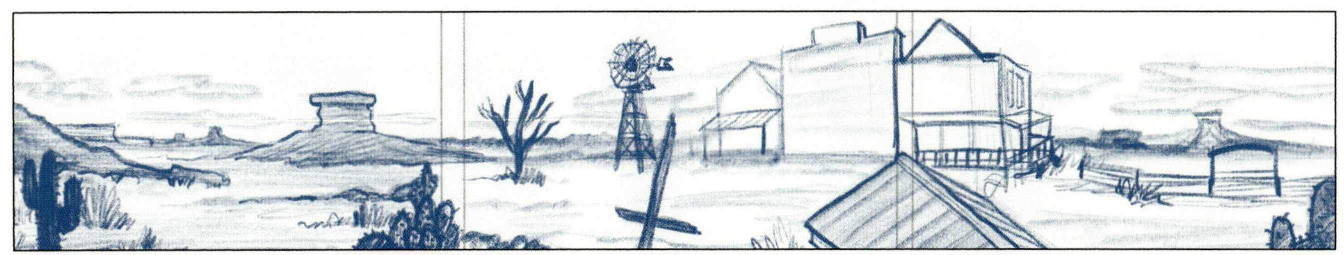
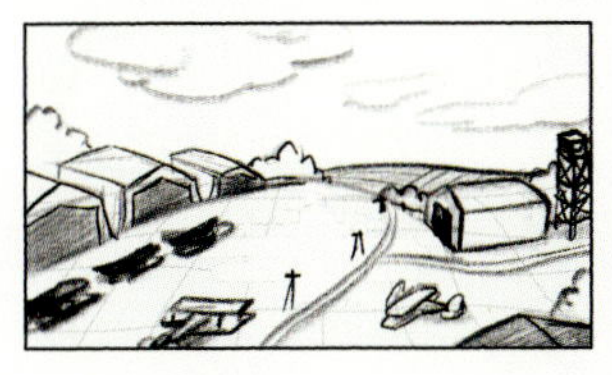
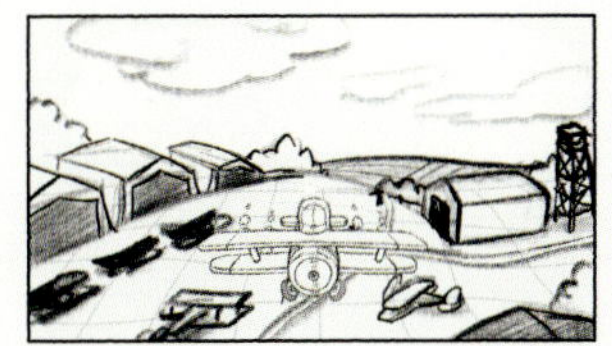
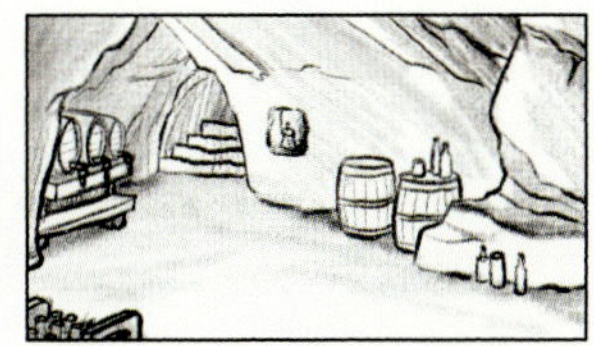
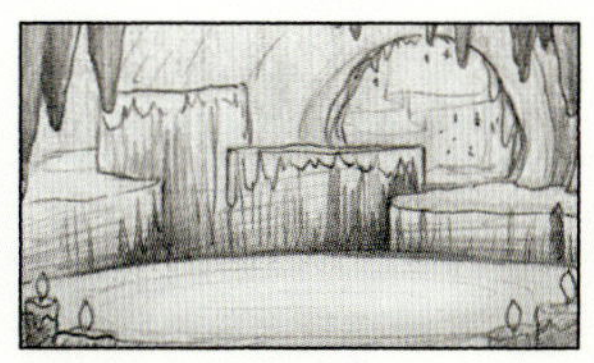
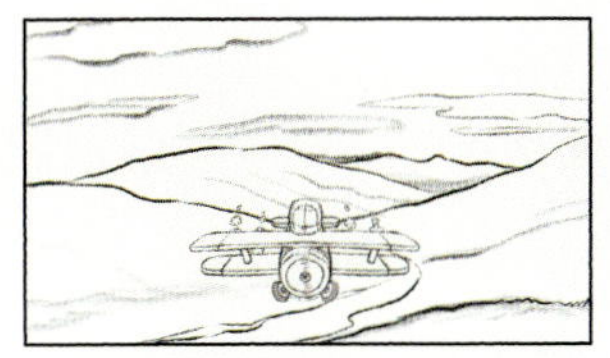
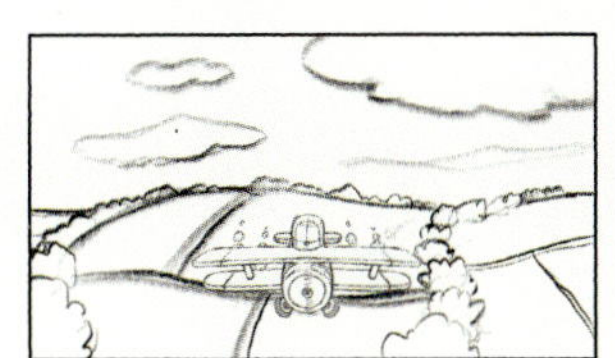
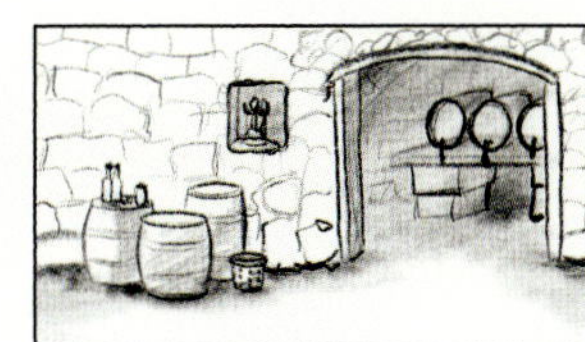
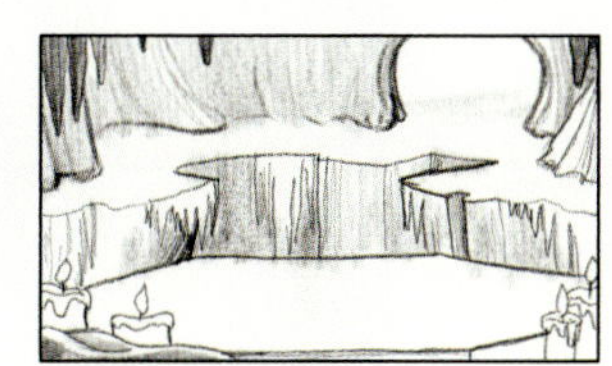
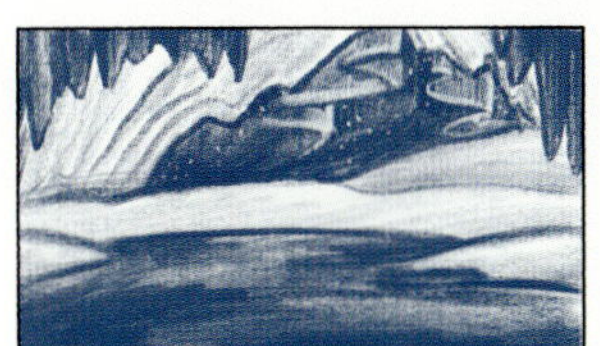
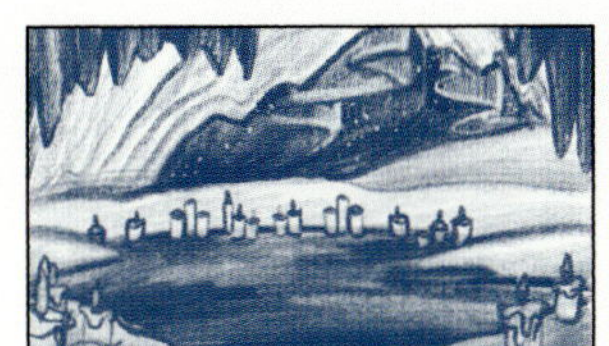
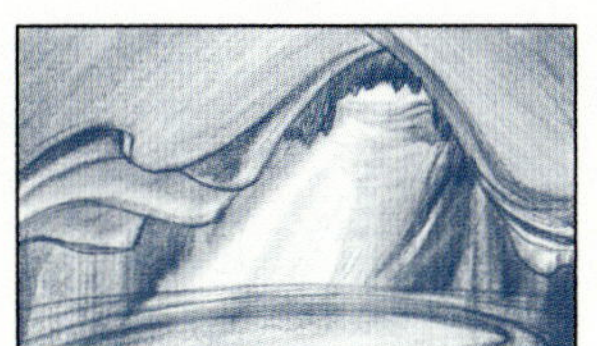
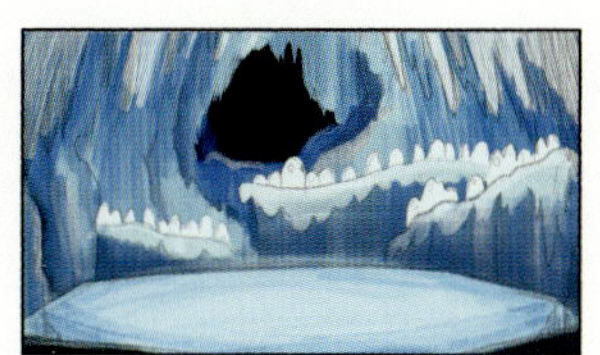
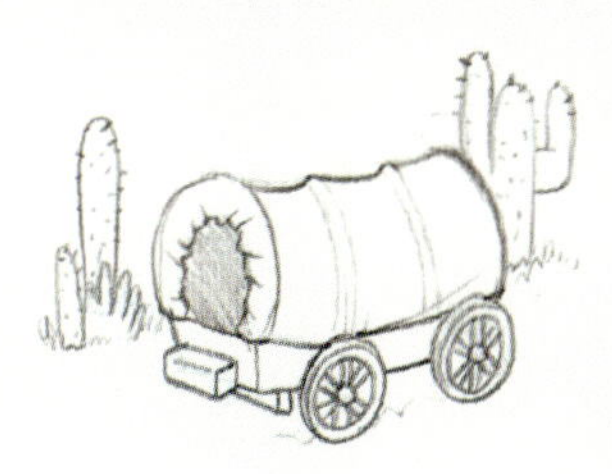
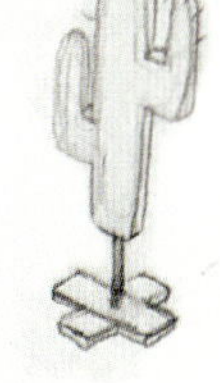
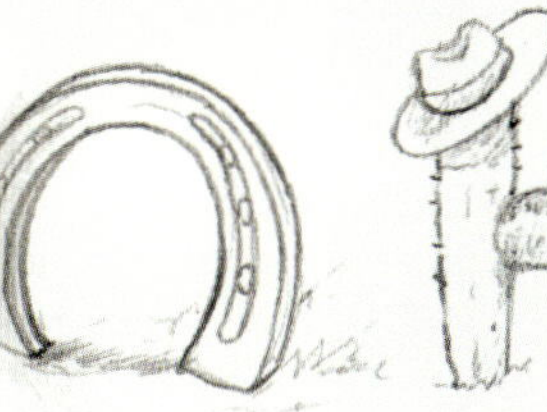
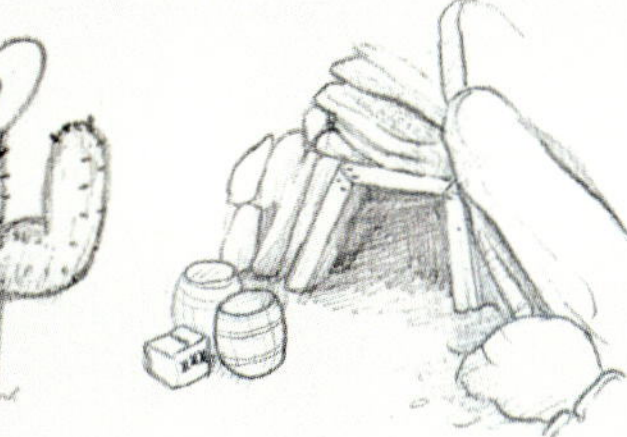
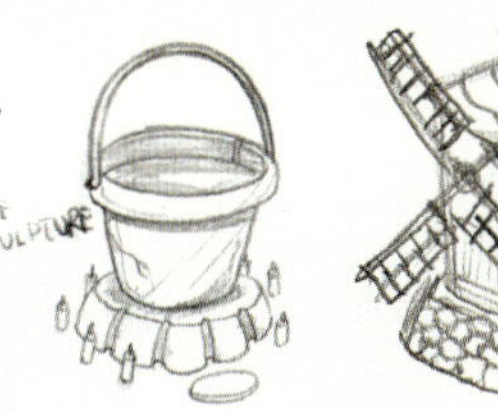
ICE SCULPTURE
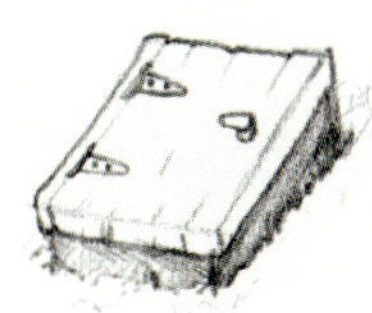
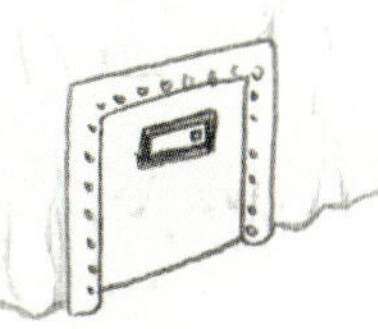
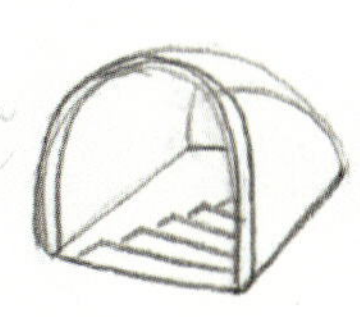
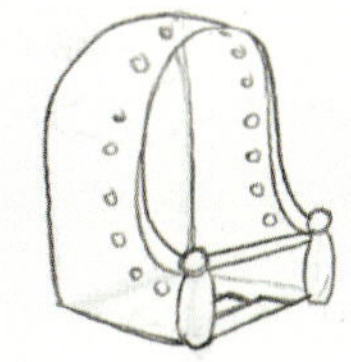
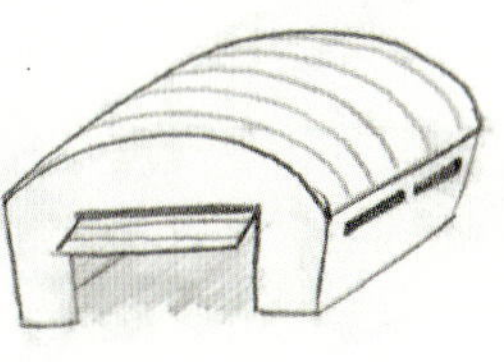
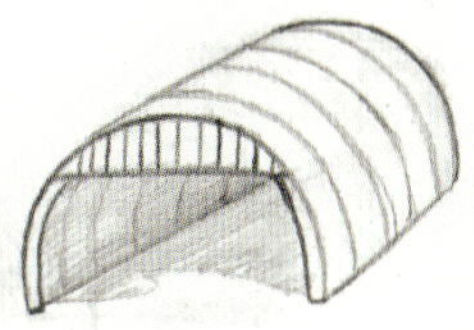

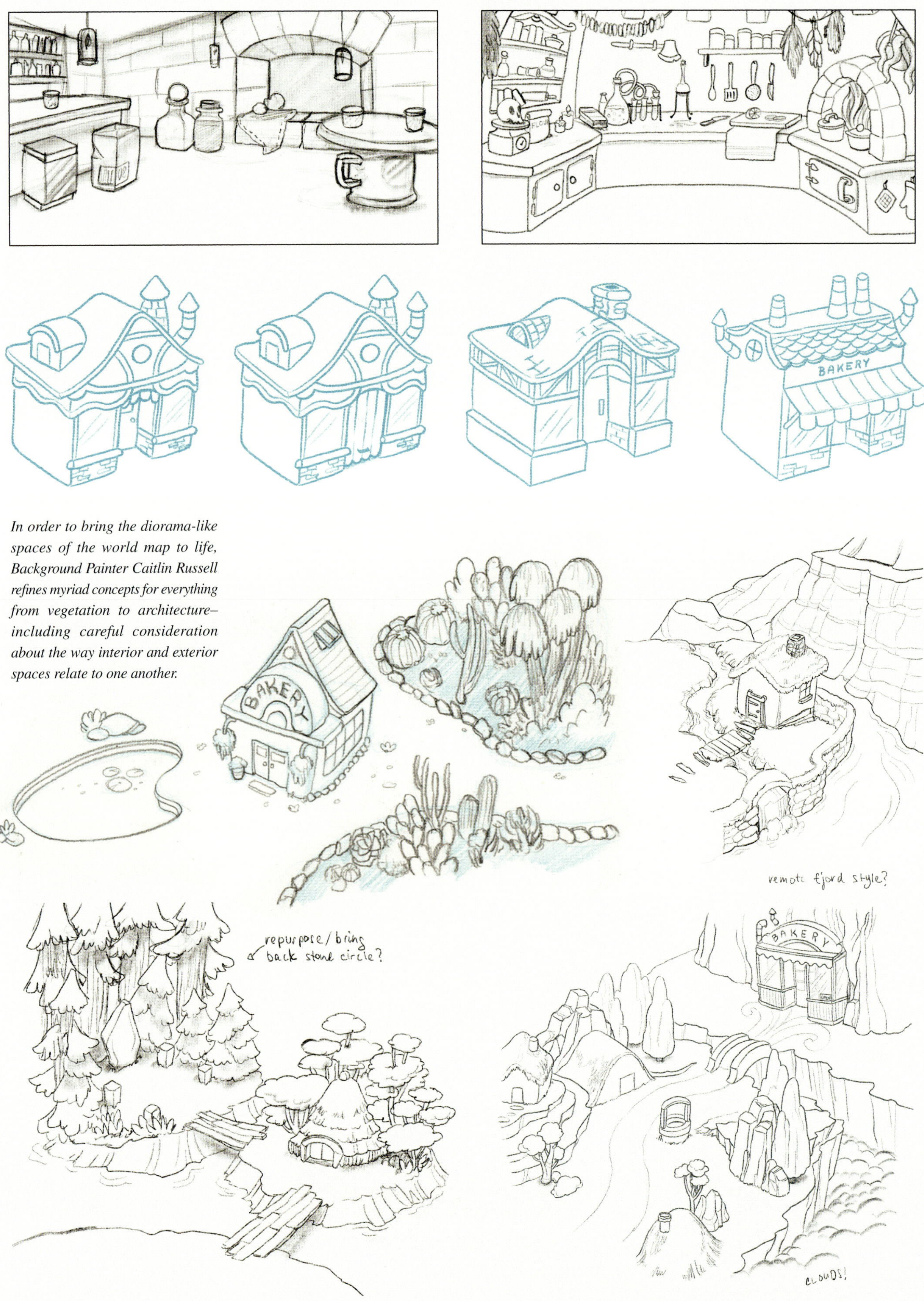

In order to bring the diorama-like spaces of the world map to life, Background Painter Caitlin Russell refines myriad concepts for everything from vegetation to architecture–including careful consideration about the way interior and exterior spaces relate to one another.

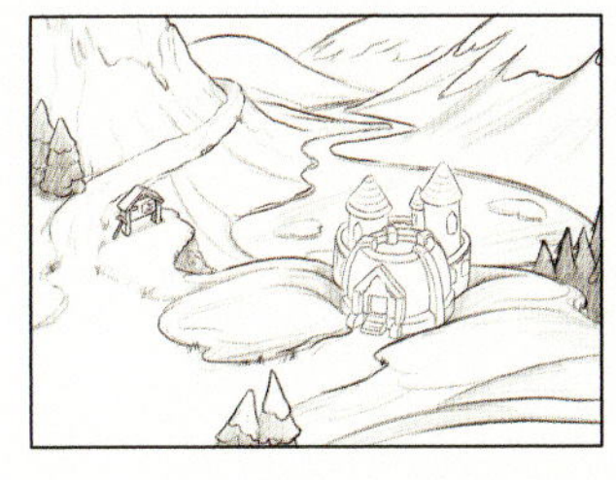
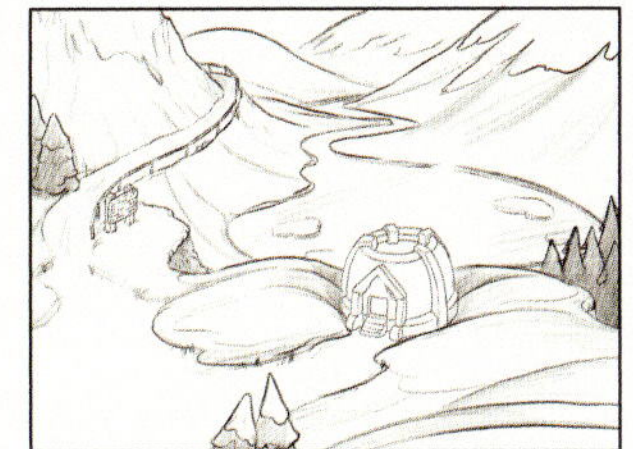
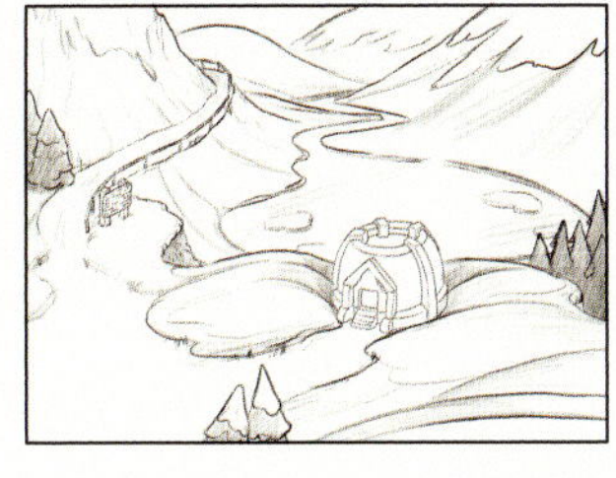
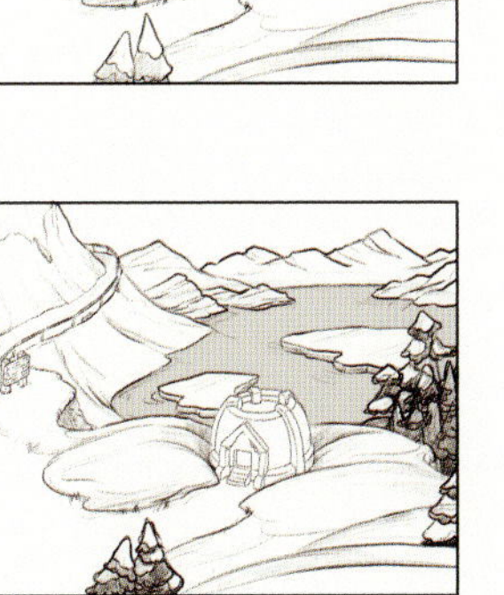
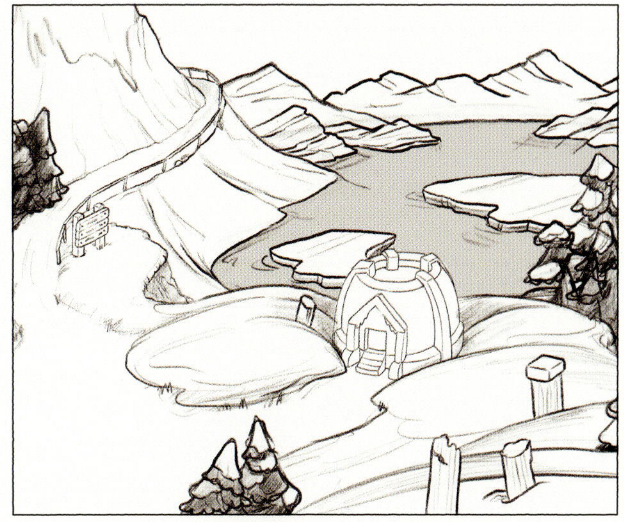
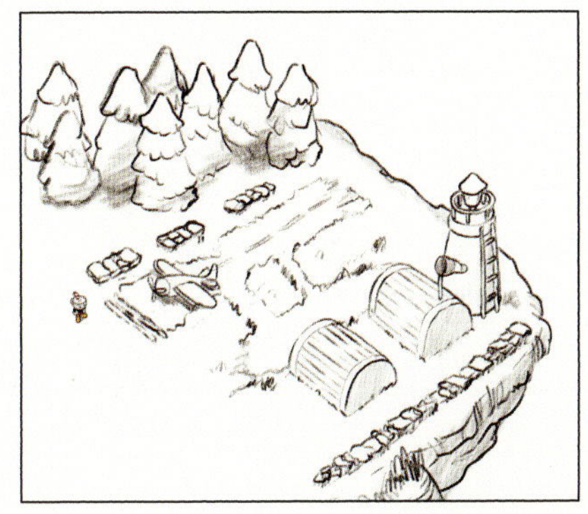
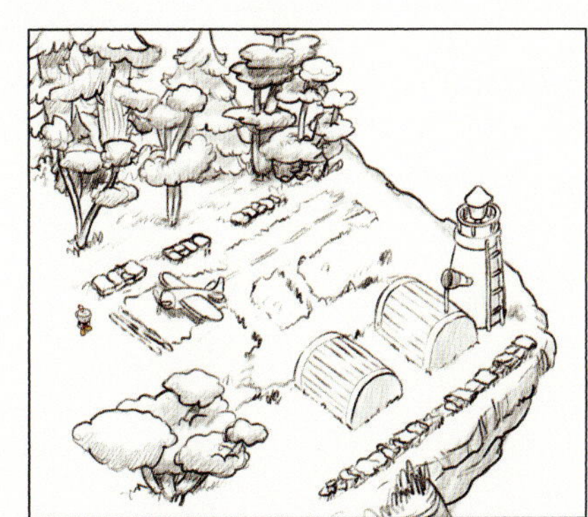
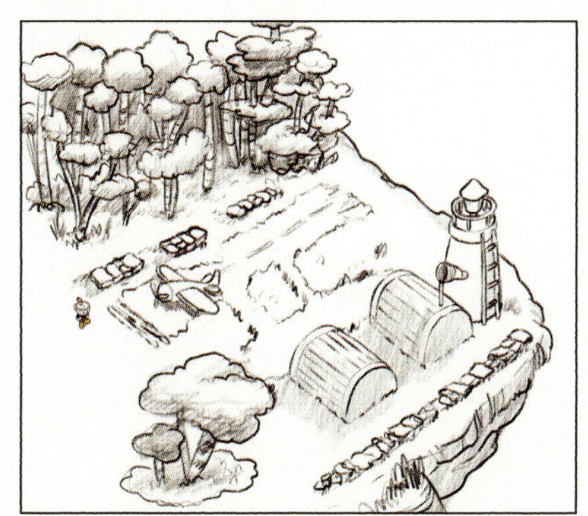
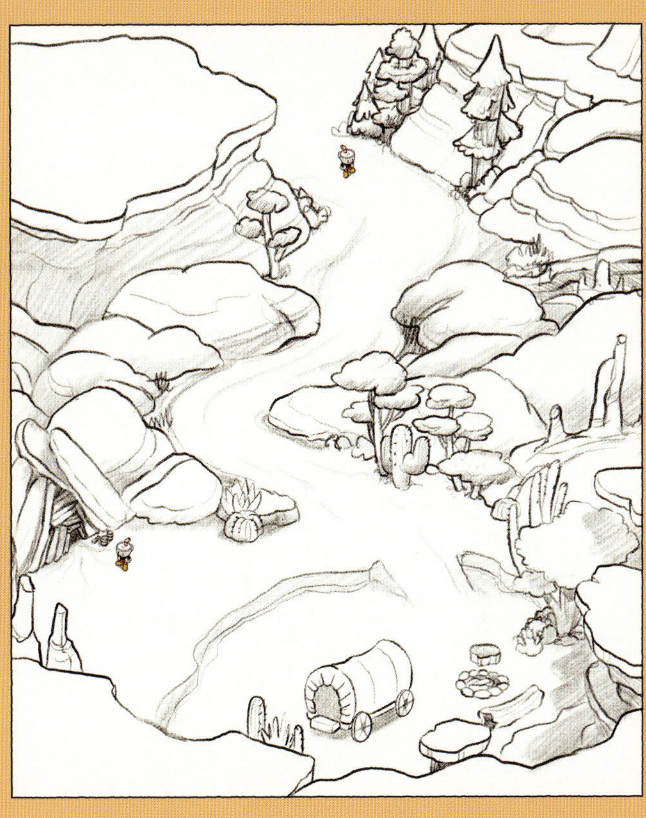
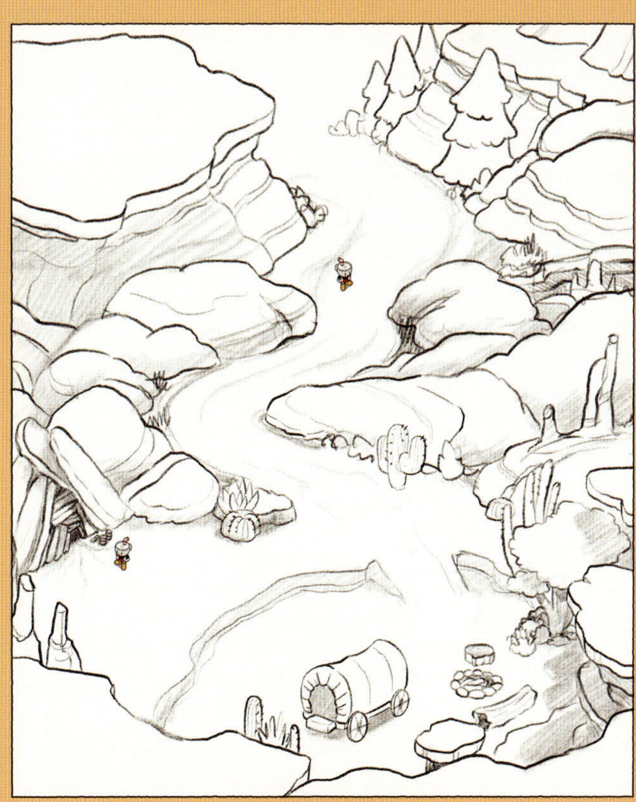

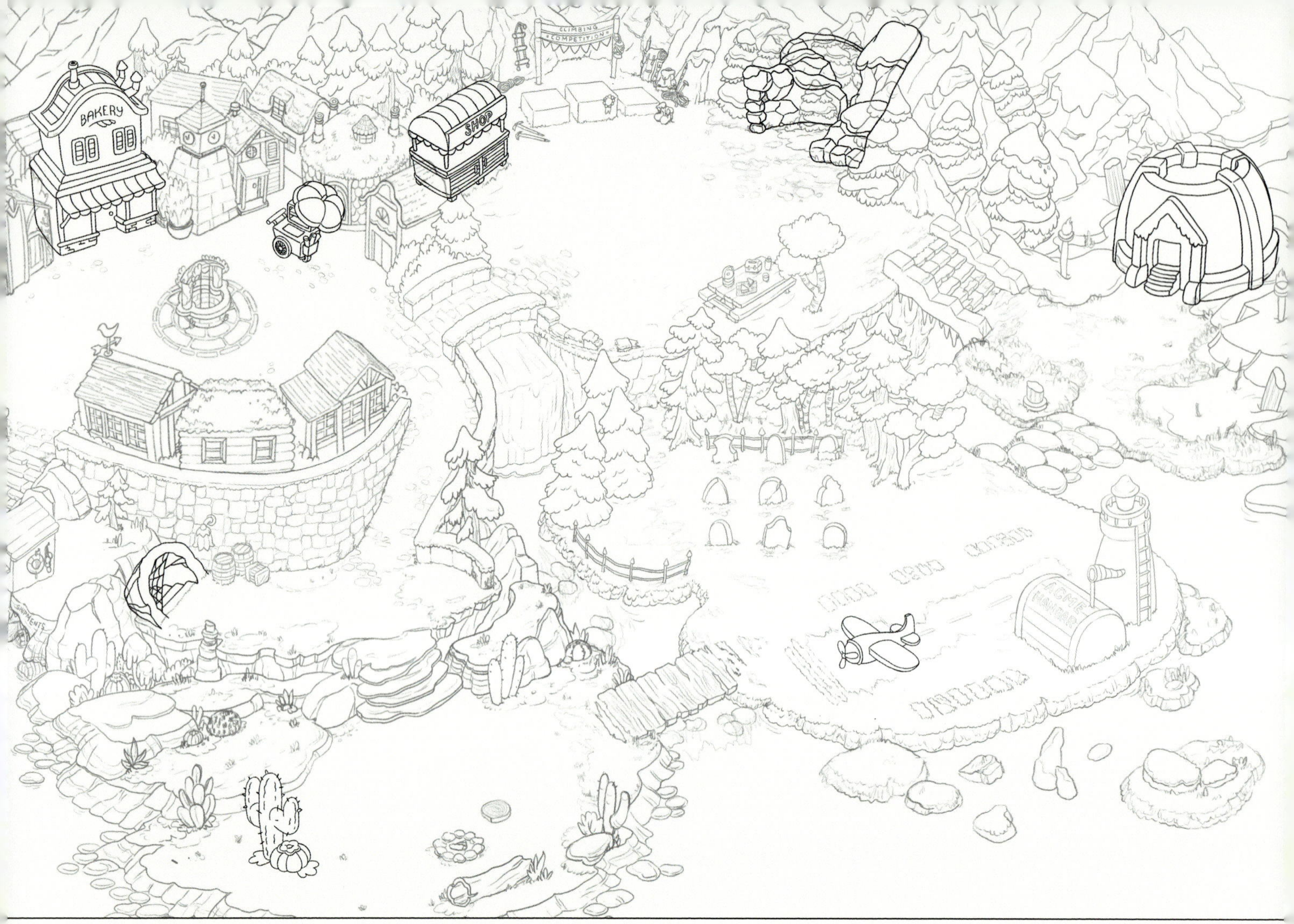

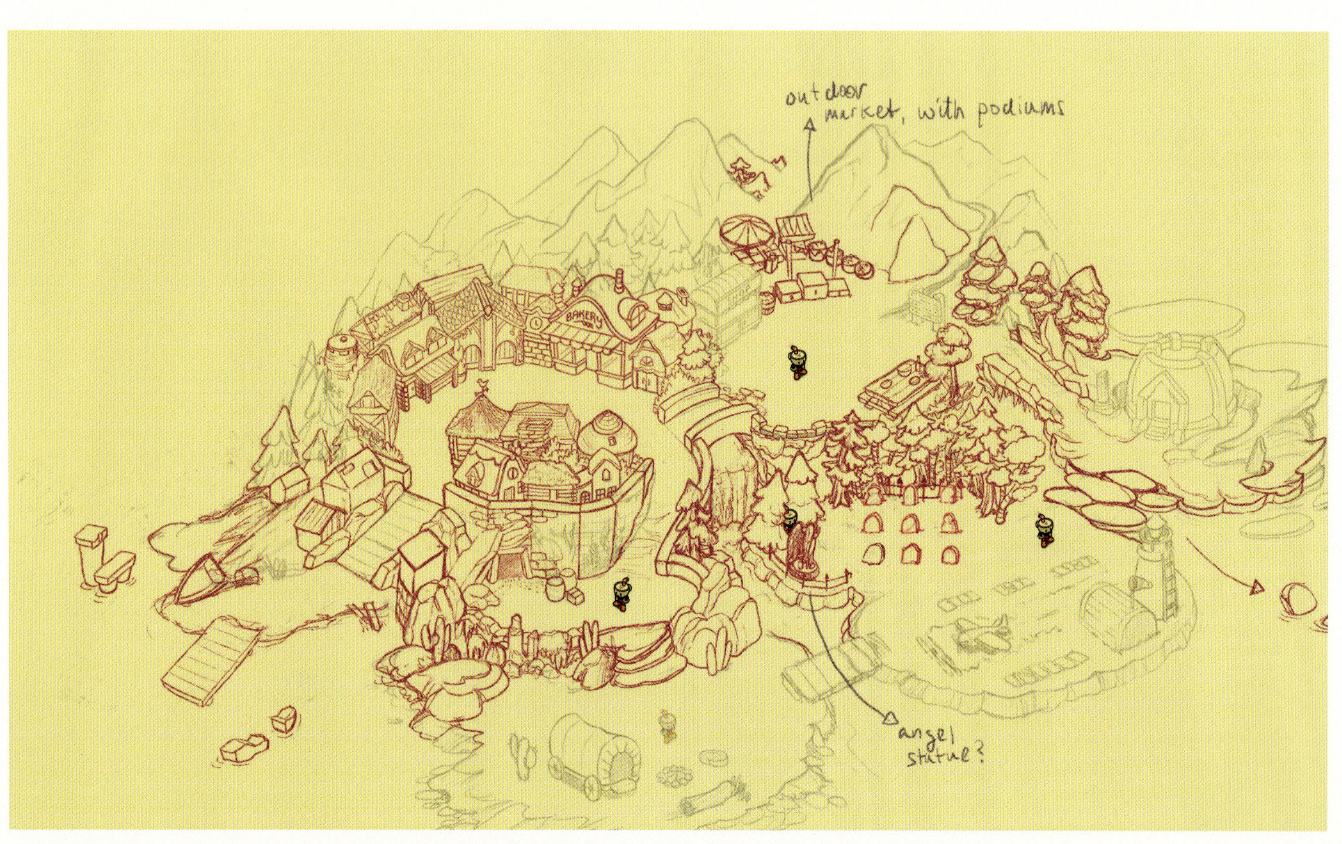
outdoor market, with podiums
BAKERY
angel statue?

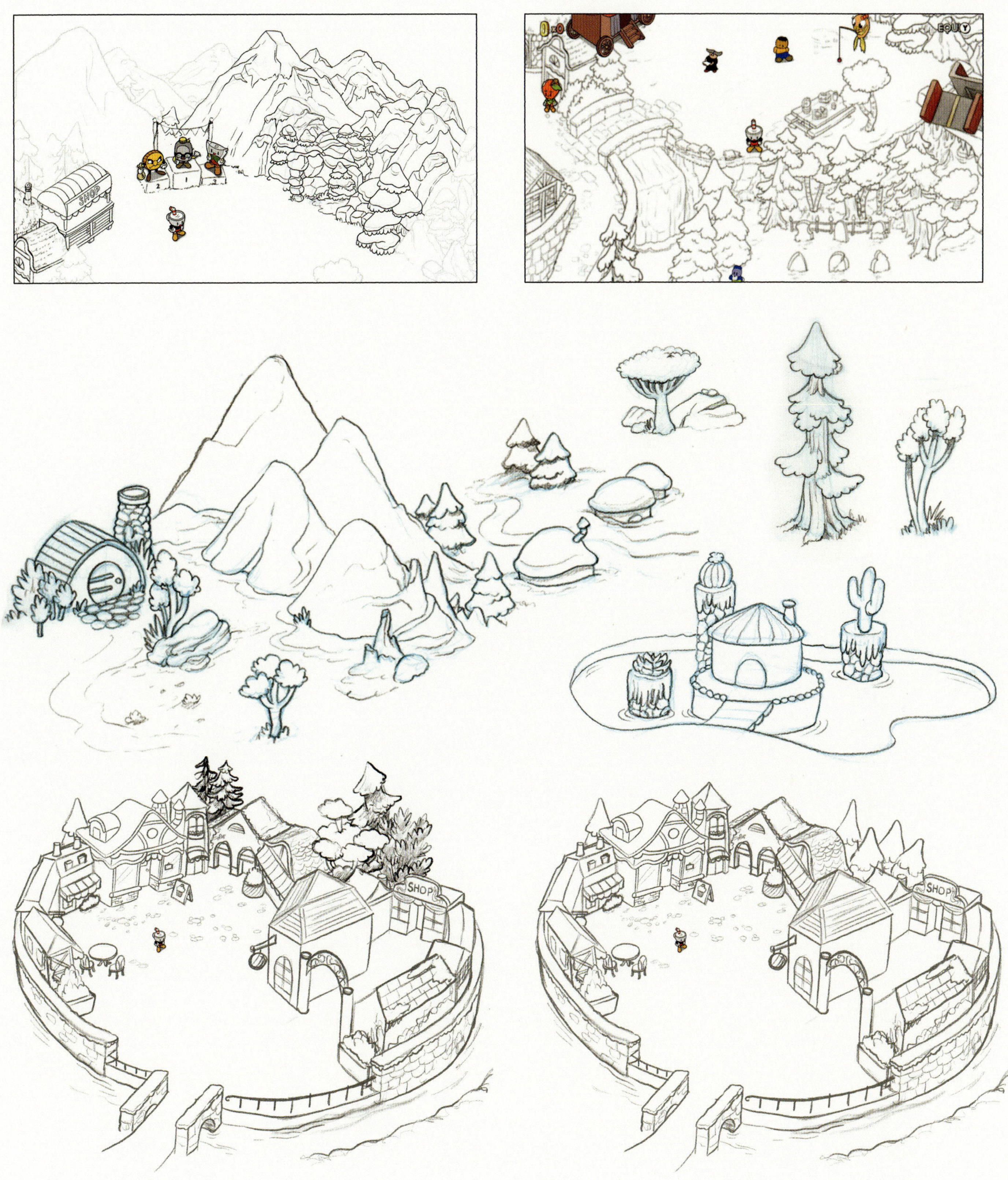

A major goal for the new island in *The Delicious Last Course* was to populate it with more things for the player to interact with–secrets to find, characters to talk to, and even hidden puzzles to solve. This took careful coordination between our art and design teams to fill the map with a higher density of meticulous detail and more non-playable characters while still offering players the space to move unencumbered. Pictured on page left, you'll see DLC Island's key points of interactivity, each of which was illustrated separately and drawn over multiple times to create a visual "boil" that wobbles the hand-drawn lines in order to draw the eye as players explored the map.

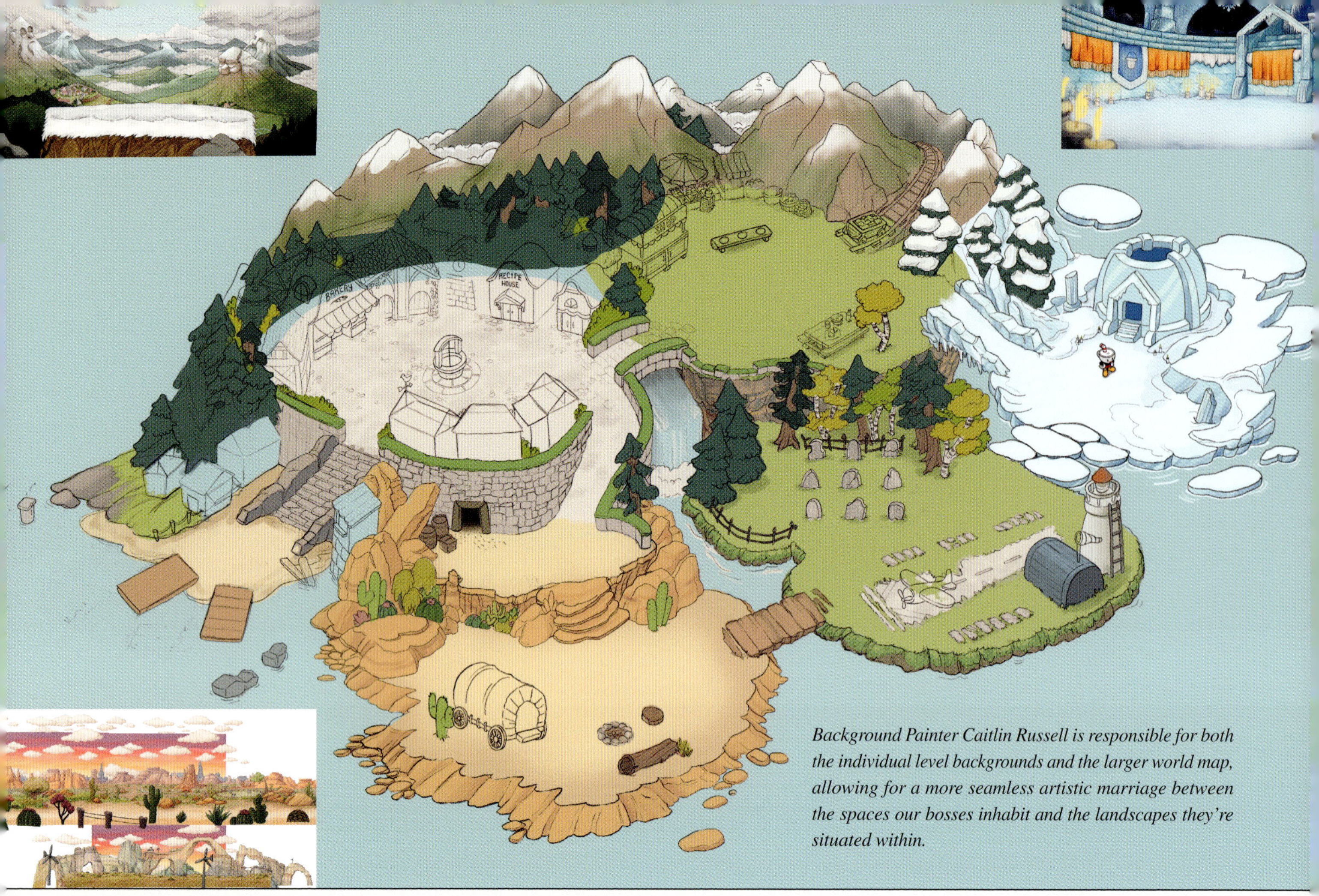

Background Painter Caitlin Russell is responsible for both the individual level backgrounds and the larger world map, allowing for a more seamless artistic marriage between the spaces our bosses inhabit and the landscapes they're situated within.

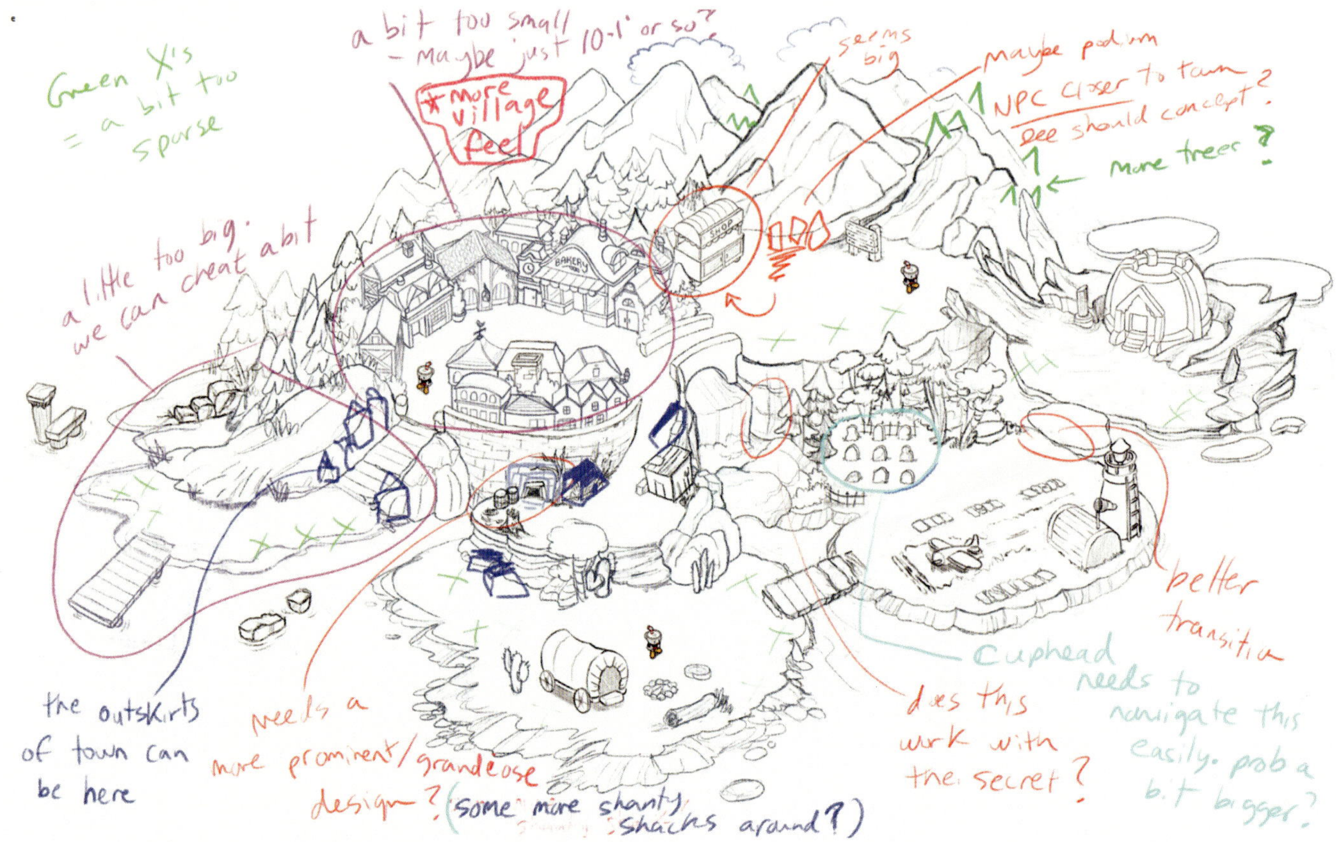

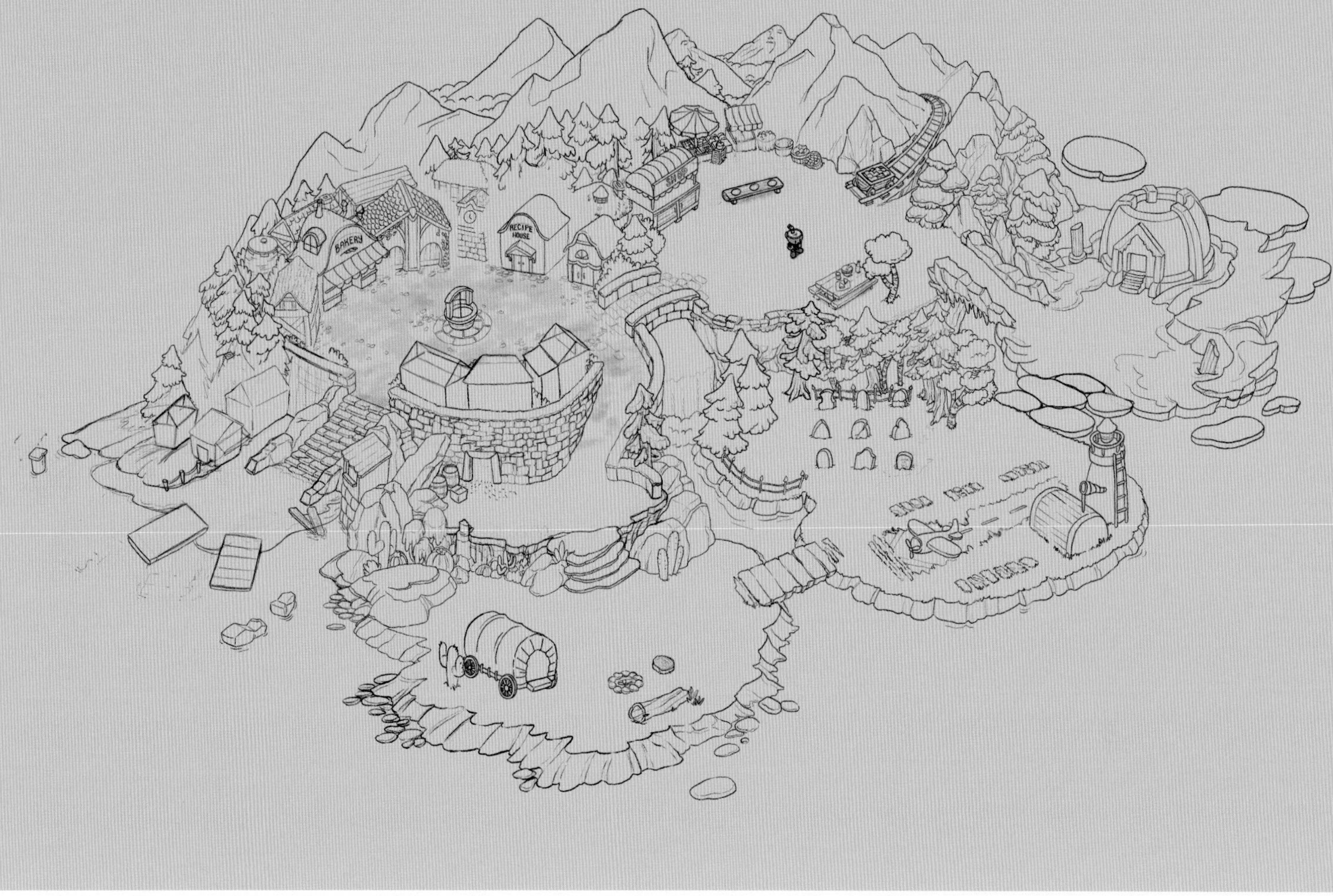

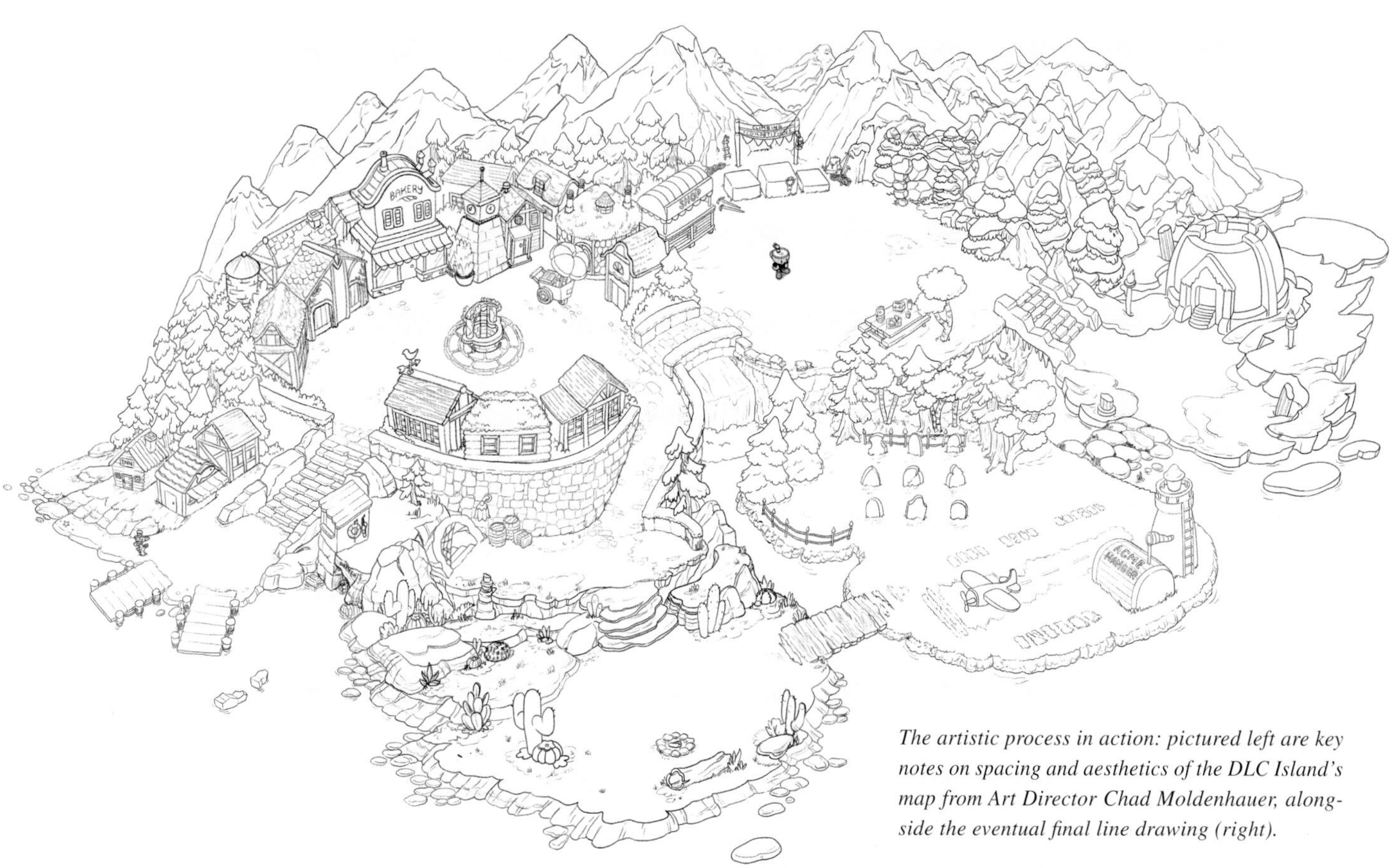

The artistic process in action: pictured left are key notes on spacing and aesthetics of the DLC Island's map from Art Director Chad Moldenhauer, alongside the eventual final line drawing (right).

Process

AS WITH ALL OUR WORLD MAP backgrounds, the DLC Island was painted by hand on 140lb stock hot press watercolor paper. The smooth surface of hot press is important to get the same feel of 1930s backgrounds. Normal cold press watercolor paper is textured, and the texture creates unwanted shadows and noise when scanned digitally. Pictured below are various shots of the world map in different states of completion, from pencil-drawn "linear" to final painting.

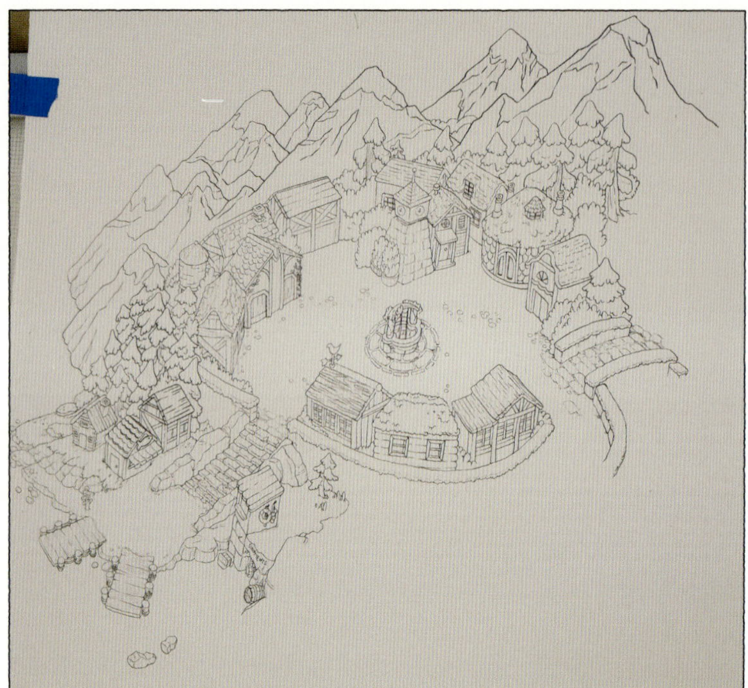

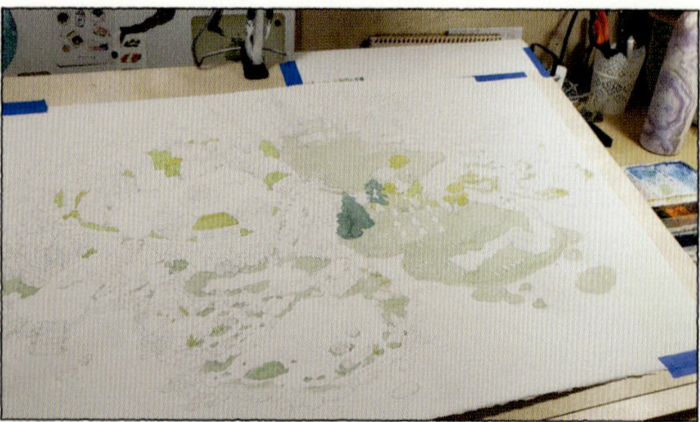

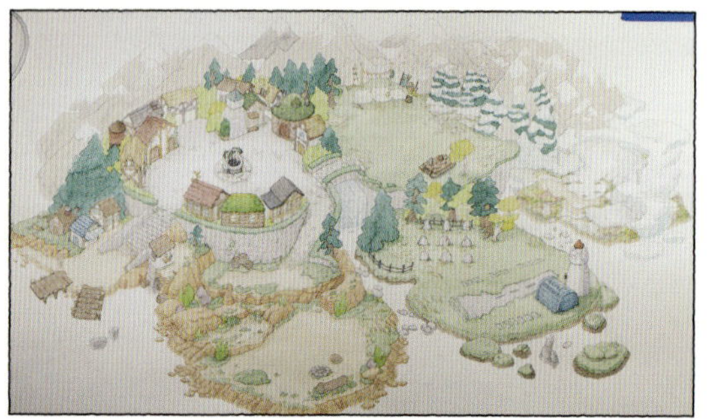

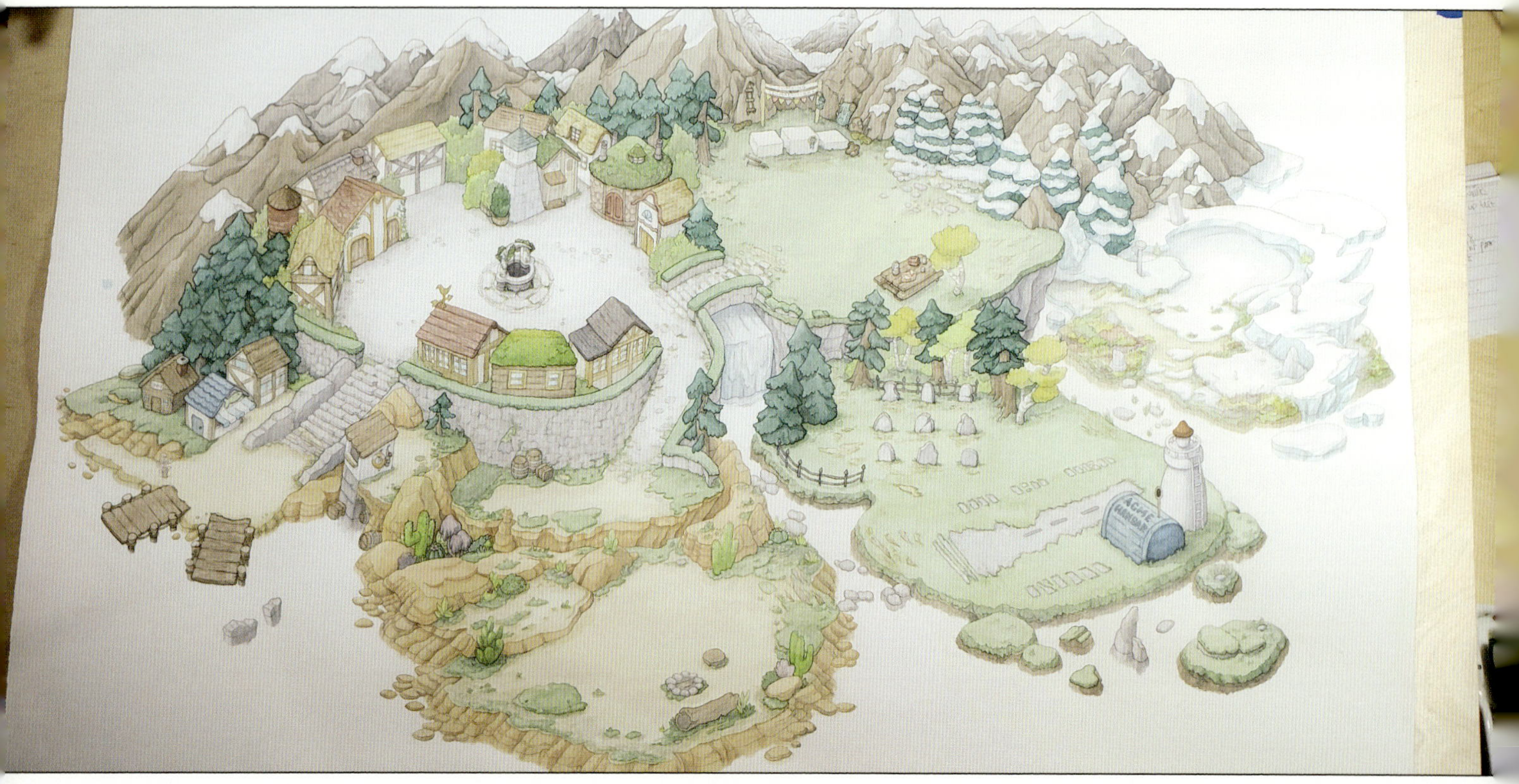

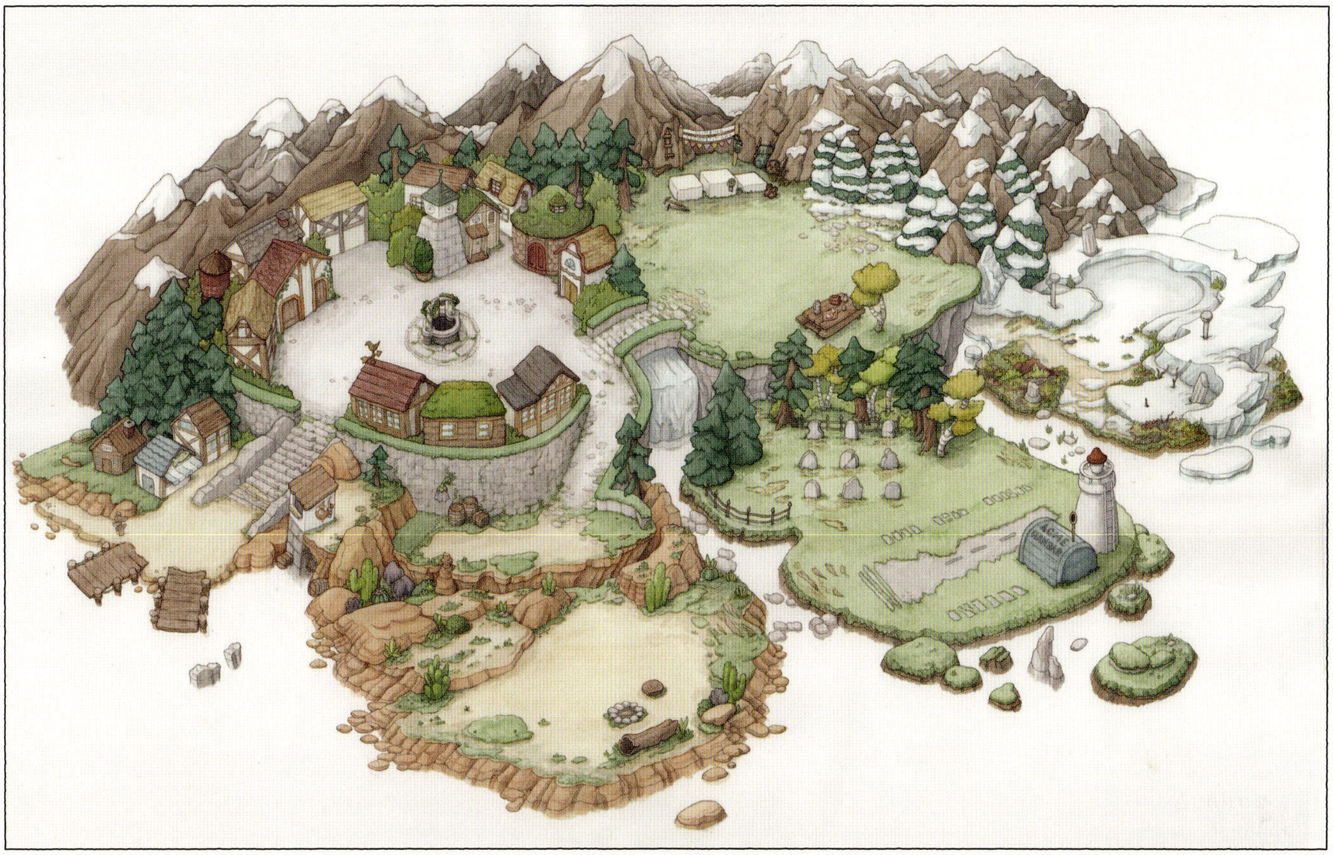

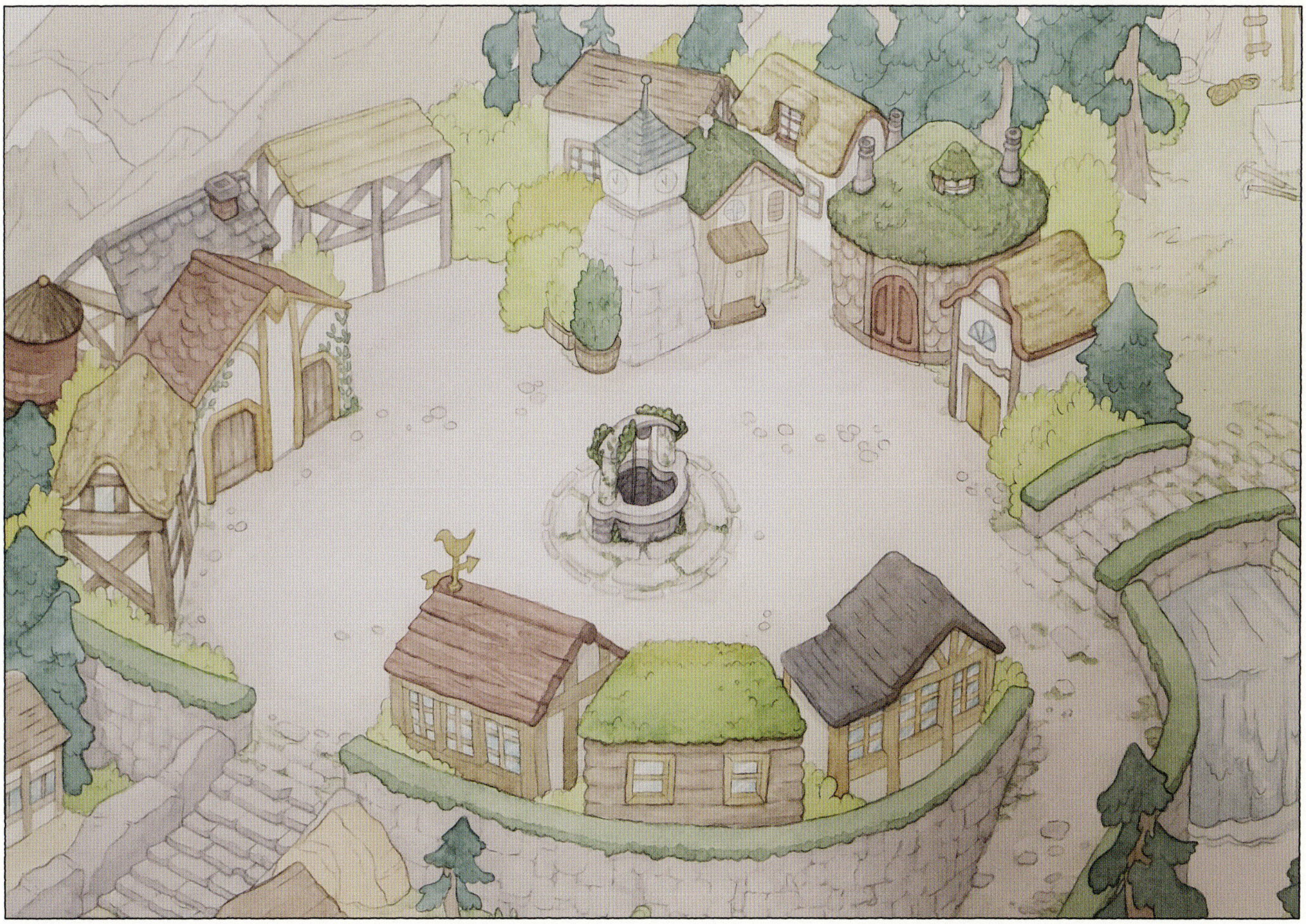

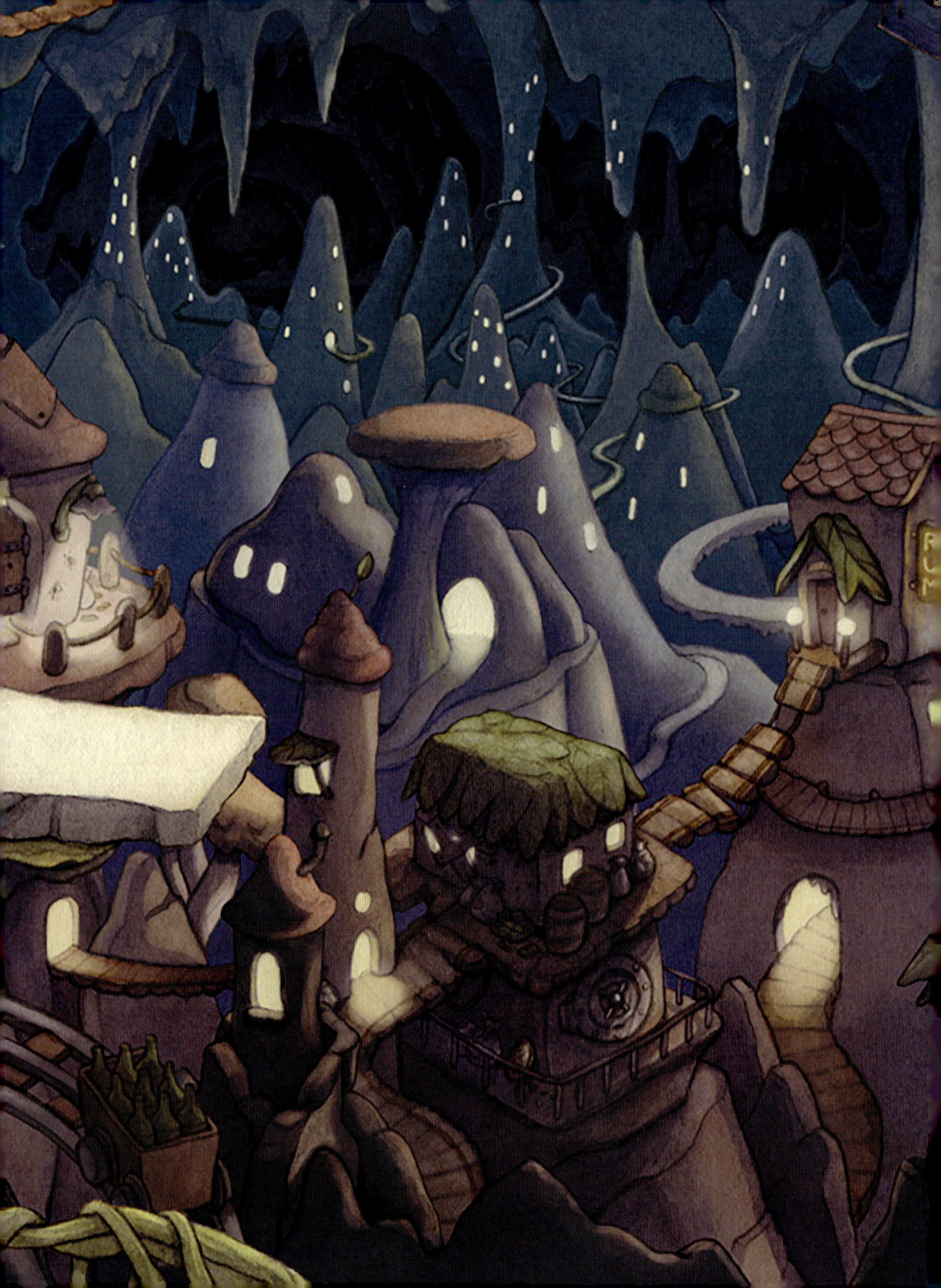

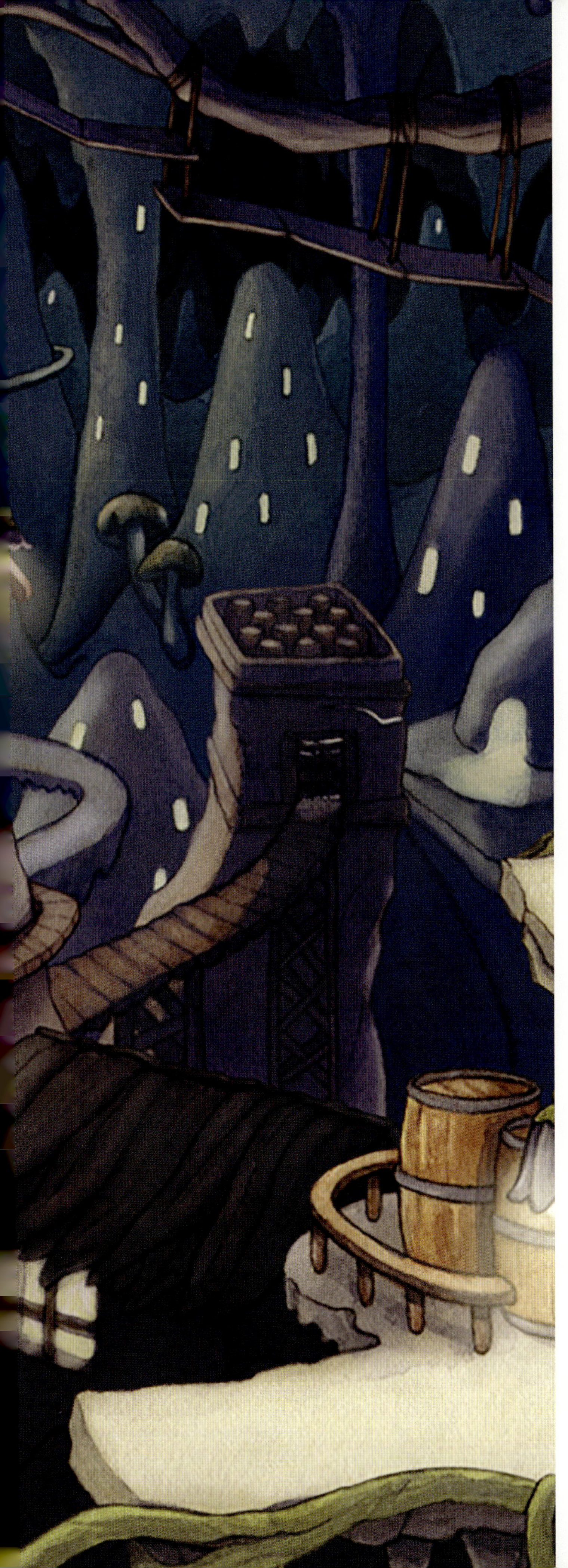

Chapter III:
Bootlegger Boogie

DEEP BENEATH THE PASTORAL COUNTRYSIDE of the Inkwell Isles lies a bustling, interconnected network of shipping and receiving lines operated by the ever-present insects that inhabit subterranean cities. Previously, we established our busy bee tower in the original *Cuphead* with Rumor Honeybottoms and her endless cubicles of worker drones toiling away. It felt like a natural next step in cartoon world-building to expand our insectoid universe by delving deep into the seedy underbelly of urban exports. Setting this boss battle in the middle of a shakedown between a syndicate of smugglers and a cluster of crazy coppers seemed like the perfect chance to flesh out the fiction of our felons.

The fact that our take on early thirties prohibition criminal "business" is set quite literally underground is both on-the-nose and reverential—with classic Fleischer cartoons like the 1930 *Wise Flies* and 1936's *The Cobweb Hotel*, there is no shortage of rubber hose inspiration from the era. Beyond the creepy crawly cartoons, the motley band of snide fly wise guys gave us the opportunity to pay homage to some of our favorite silent film comedians from the era, with our own Charlie Left Legs and Hardtop Harold named after Charlie Chaplin and Harold Lloyd. Can Cuphead and pals survive this dust up in the middle of a bust-up?

Moonshine Mob in "BOOTLEGGER BOOGIE"

THE MOONSHINE MOB FIGHT, known internally as the "Rum Runners" for the majority of development, was originally conceptualized as a battle where the player would find themselves caught in the middle between two warring factions. To sell this story, the gameplay design consisted of many small threats that would pour in from all sides of the arena, rather than focus the action on one large adversary. With the eventual cops vs. mobsters concept locked, we went about finding our micro mafia.

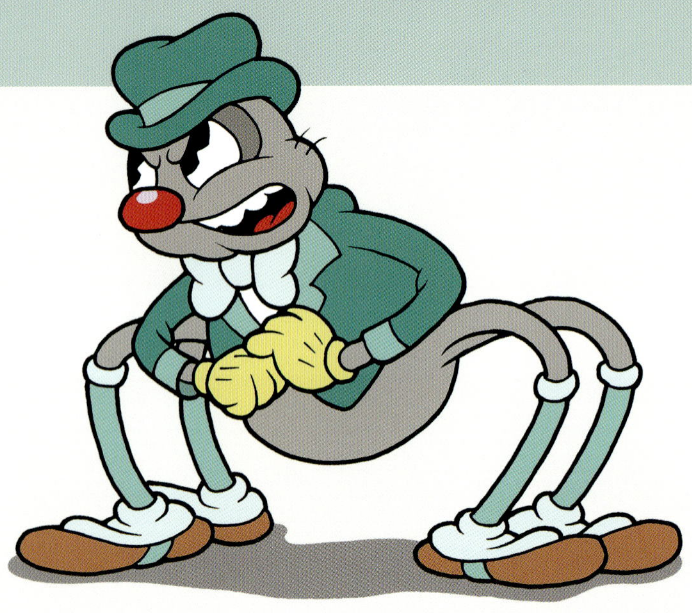

Charlie Left Legs

THE MUSCLE OF THIS OPERATION, Charlie Left Legs acts as the linchpin for Phase 1 of the fight, calling in all matter of goons and grubs to take out our heroes. Charlie's initial design was based off of a much more gentlemanly spider concept that eagle-eyed fans may remember from early development images released back when we had barely started working on the original game. We dressed that spider down a bit and gave him a surly attitude and he fit perfectly as the initial buster in this feud against the fuzz.

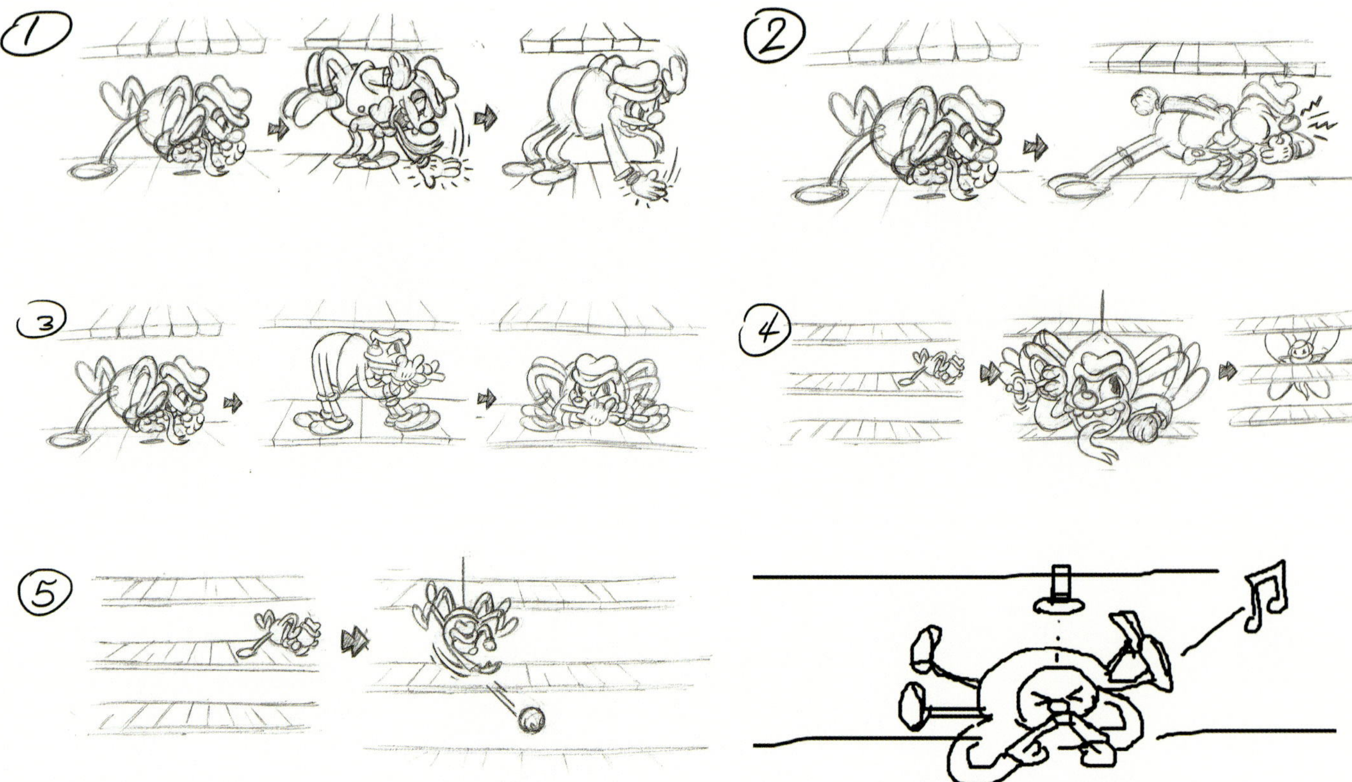

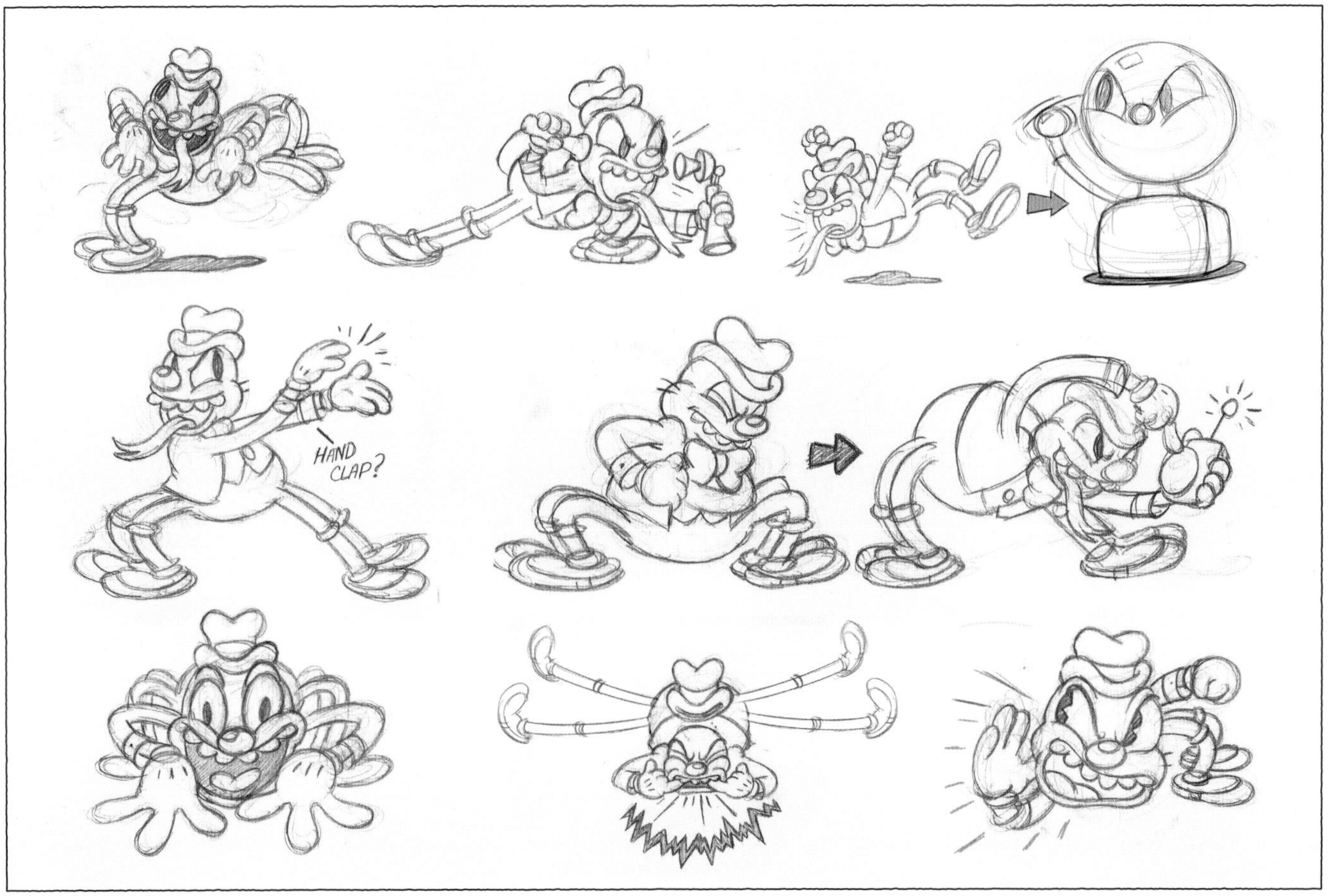

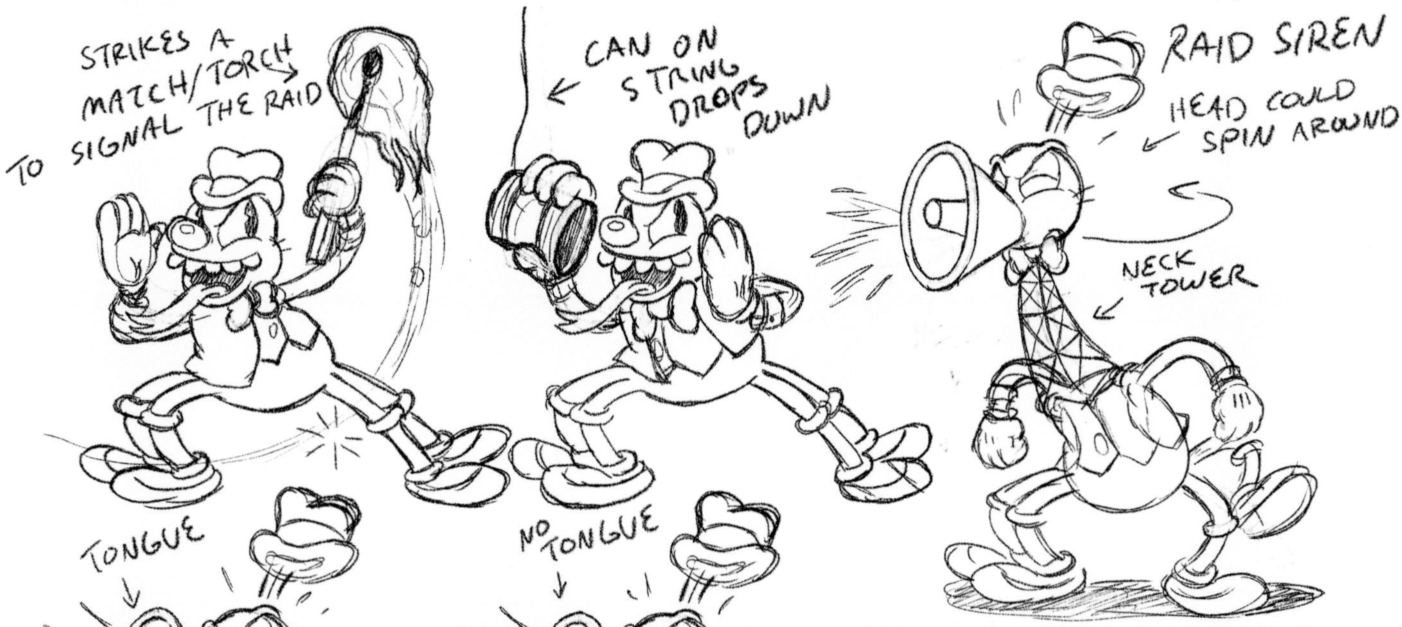

We wanted unique animations for each different enemy type summoned. Above, Animator Joseph Coleman explores different ways for Charlie to call the gang into the fray.

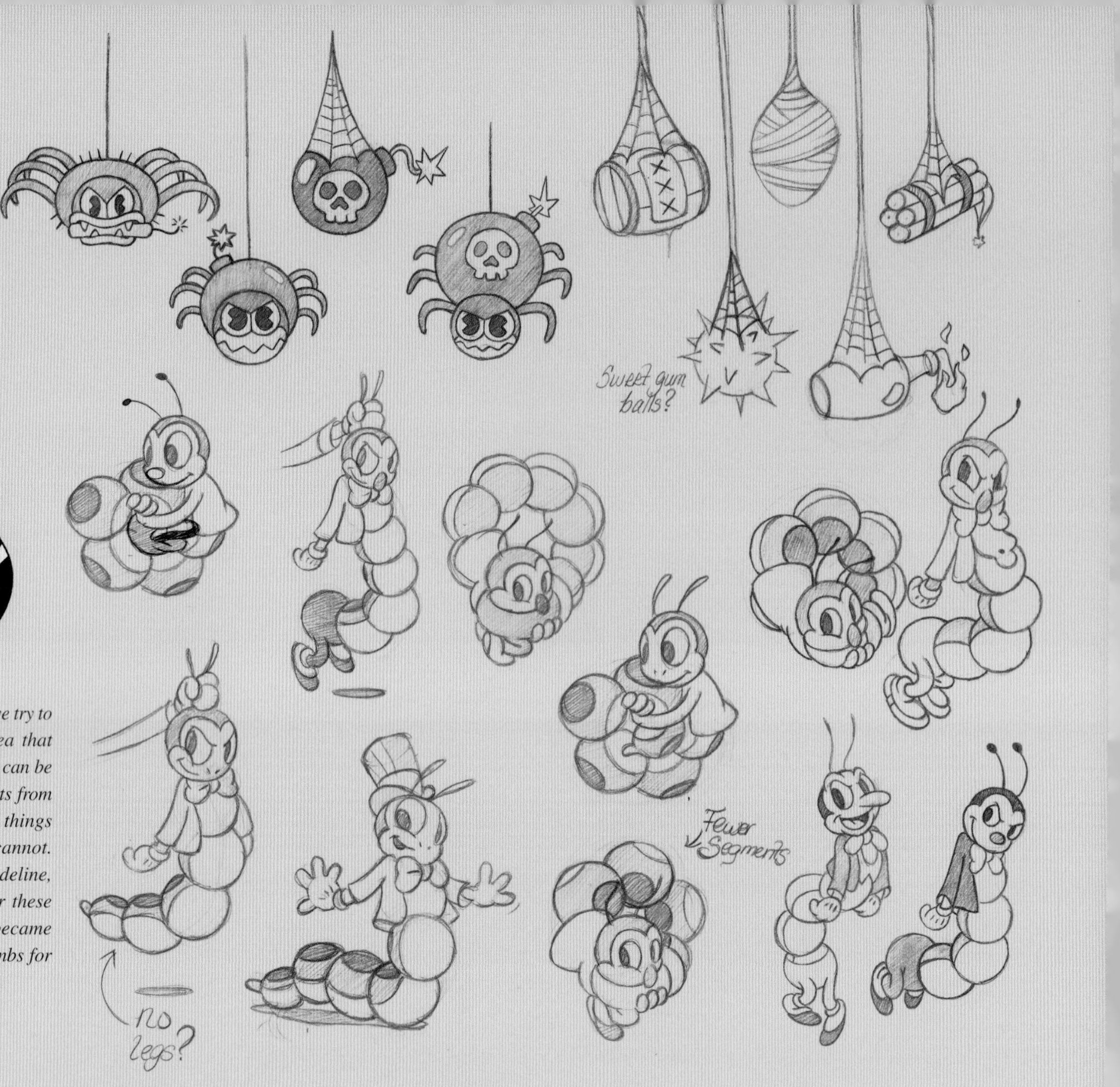

A rule of thumb we try to follow is the idea that things with faces can be destroyed by shots from the player, and things without faces cannot. True to this guideline, bug concepts for these mine hazards became more classic bombs for the final design.

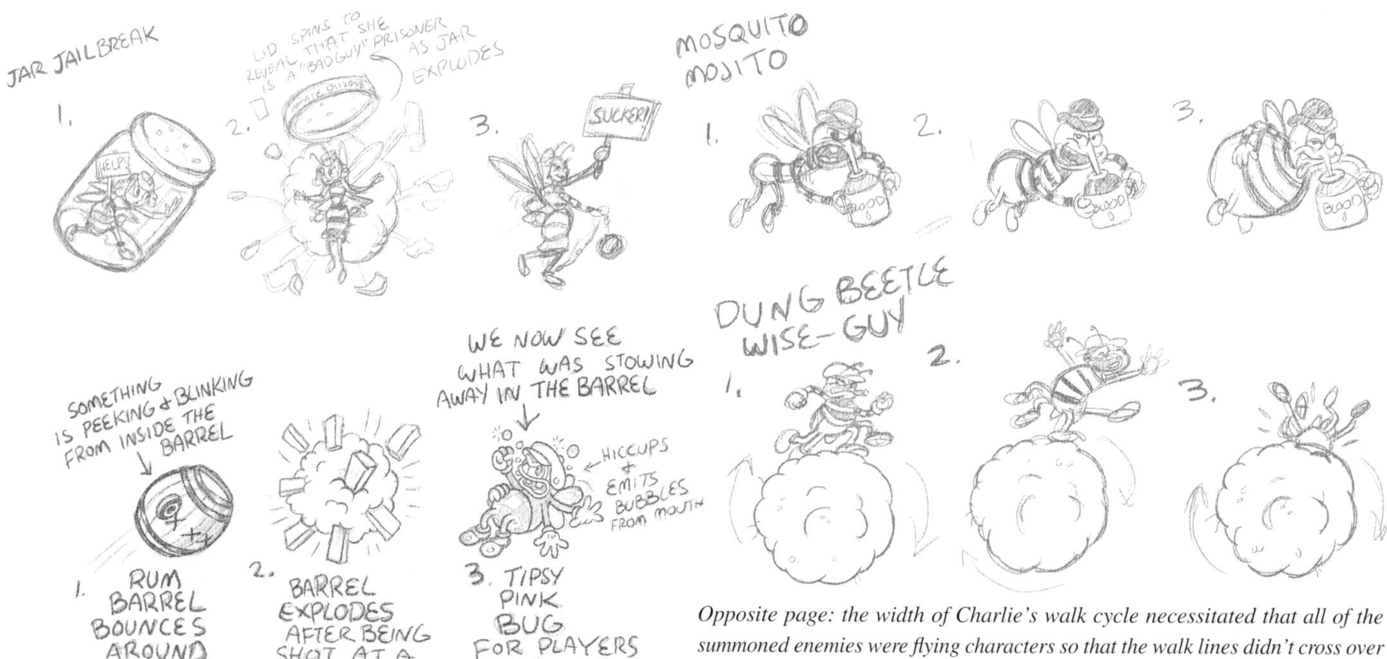

Opposite page: the width of Charlie's walk cycle necessitated that all of the summoned enemies were flying characters so that the walk lines didn't cross over each other in an awkward way that might break the seamless cartoon presentation.

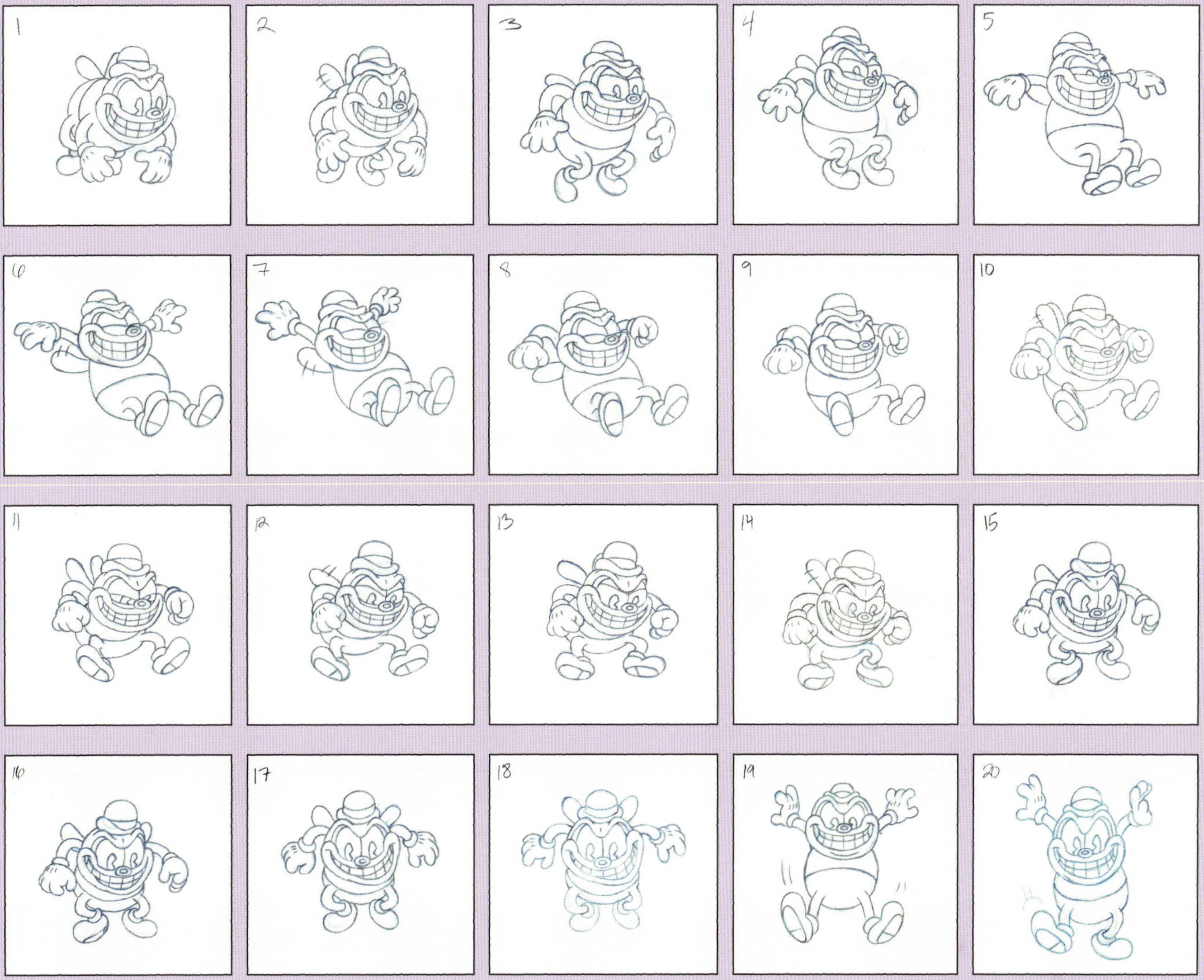

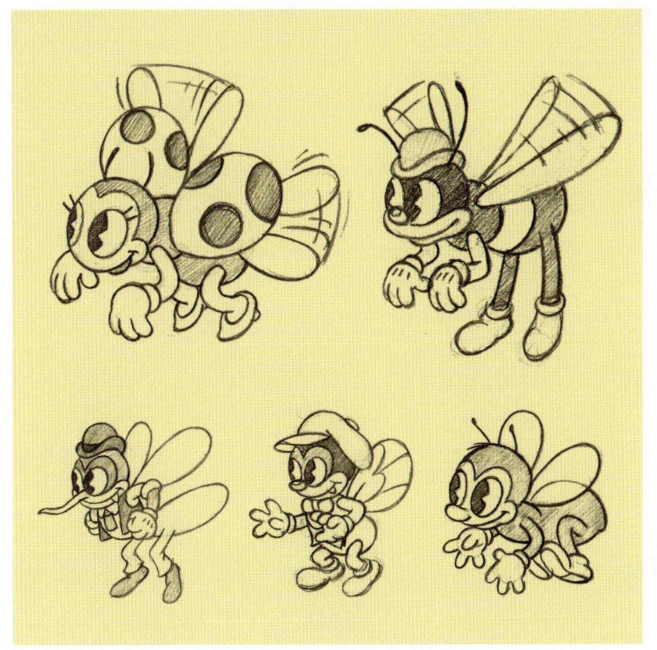

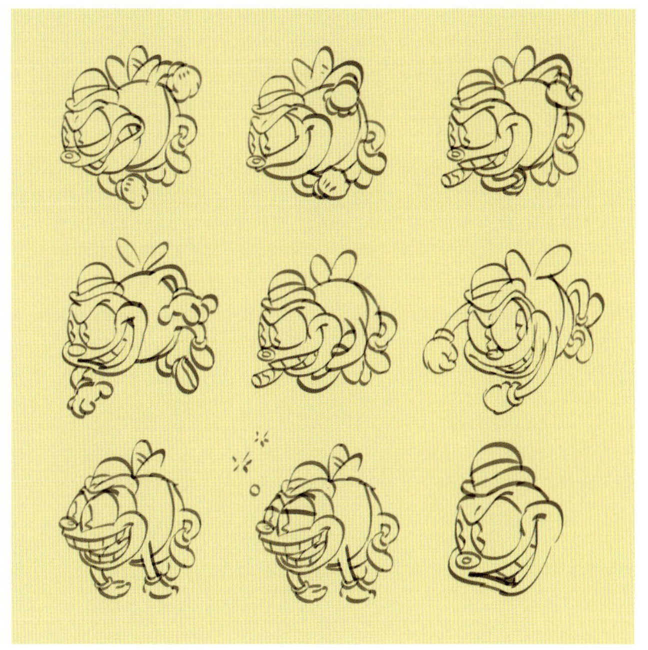

Madcap Maddie

BASED ON A CUT KING DICE MINIBOSS fight from the original *Cuphead*, the original visual idea for Maddie was to have her descend from the top of the screen on a diamond. Upon landing, a spotlight would shine on the jewel, cascading different colored lasers around the screen. Inspired by composer Kris Maddigan's scat-filled music for this stage, we eventually moved to a more speakeasy-style tune, complete with swirling music notes and flappers dancing and kicking as a nod to Disney's 1937 *Silly Symphony–Woodland Cafe*.

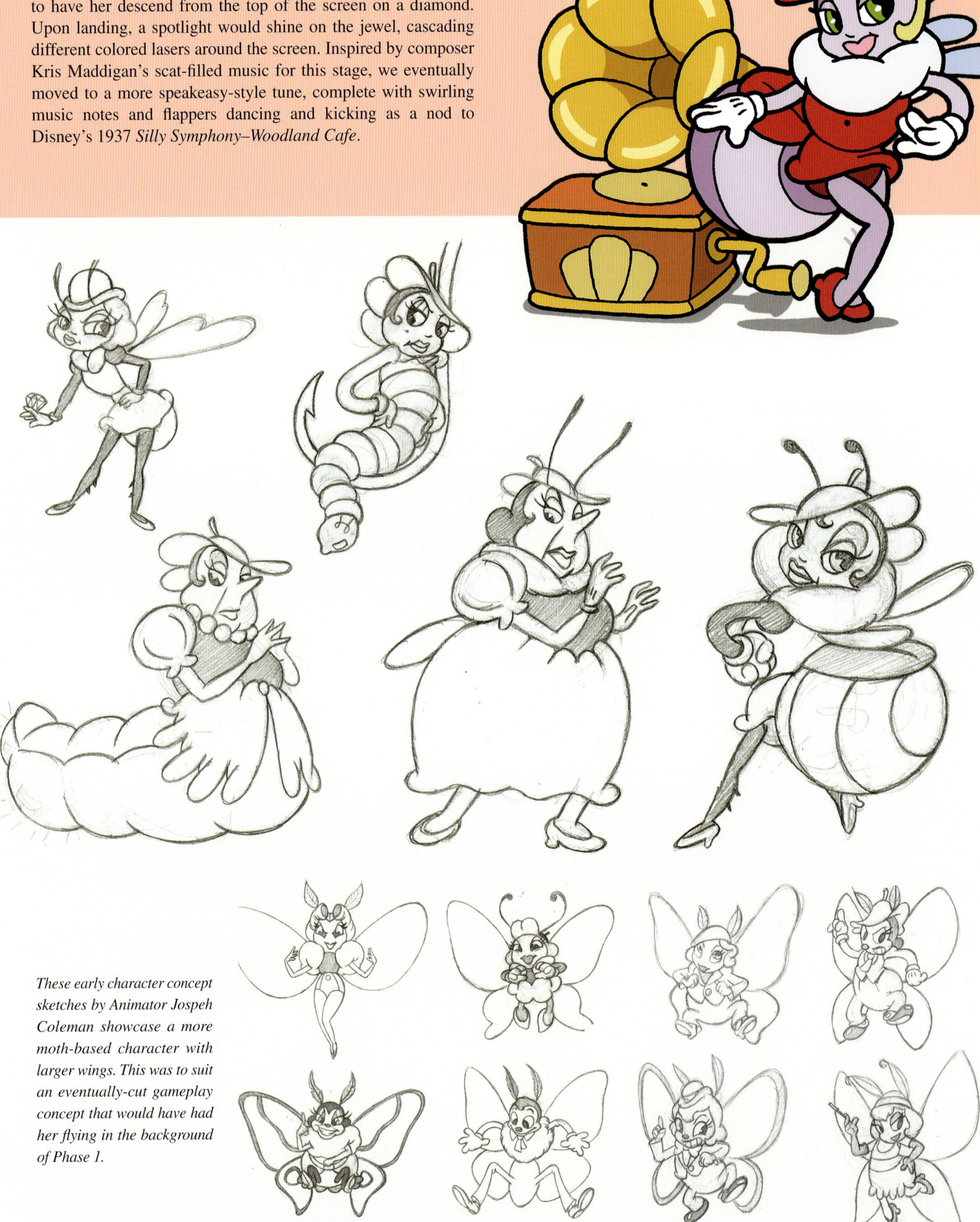

These early character concept sketches by Animator Jospeh Coleman showcase a more moth-based character with larger wings. This was to suit an eventually-cut gameplay concept that would have had her flying in the background of Phase 1.

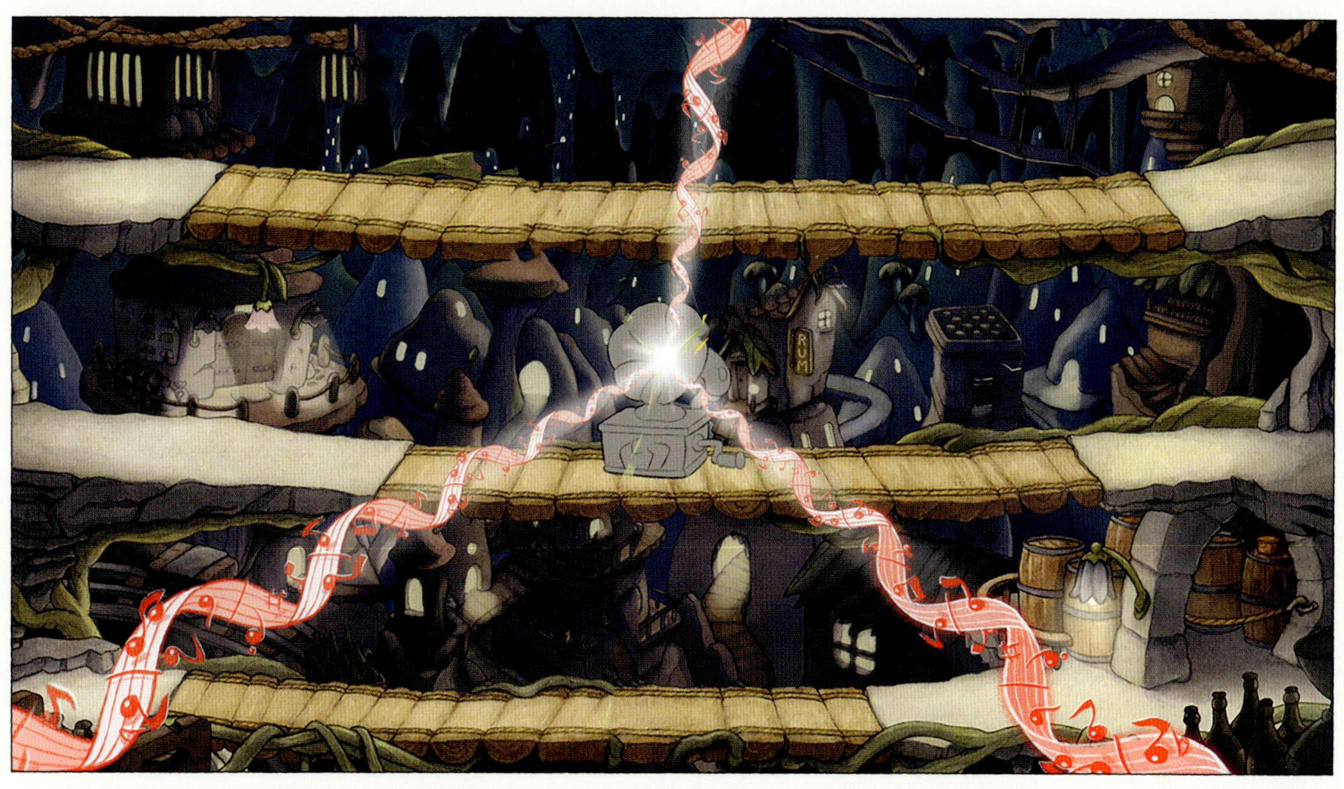

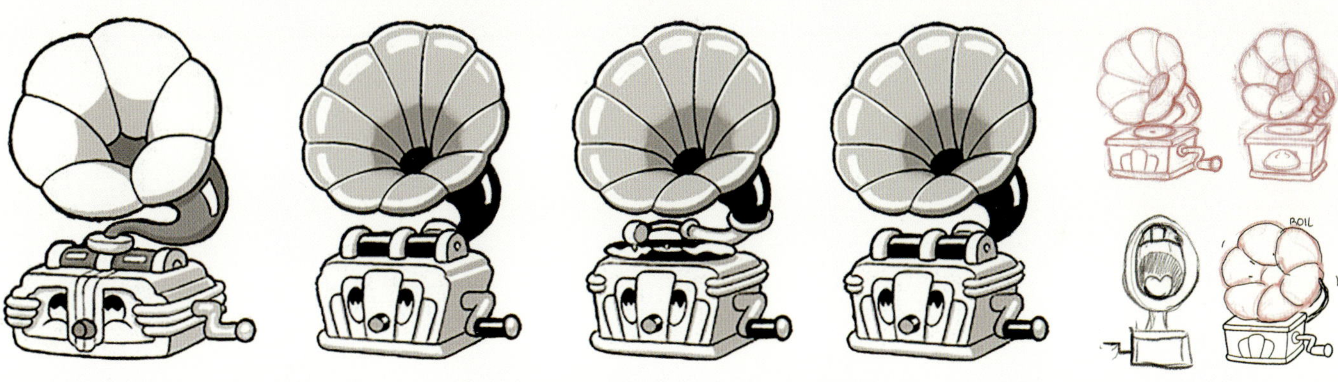

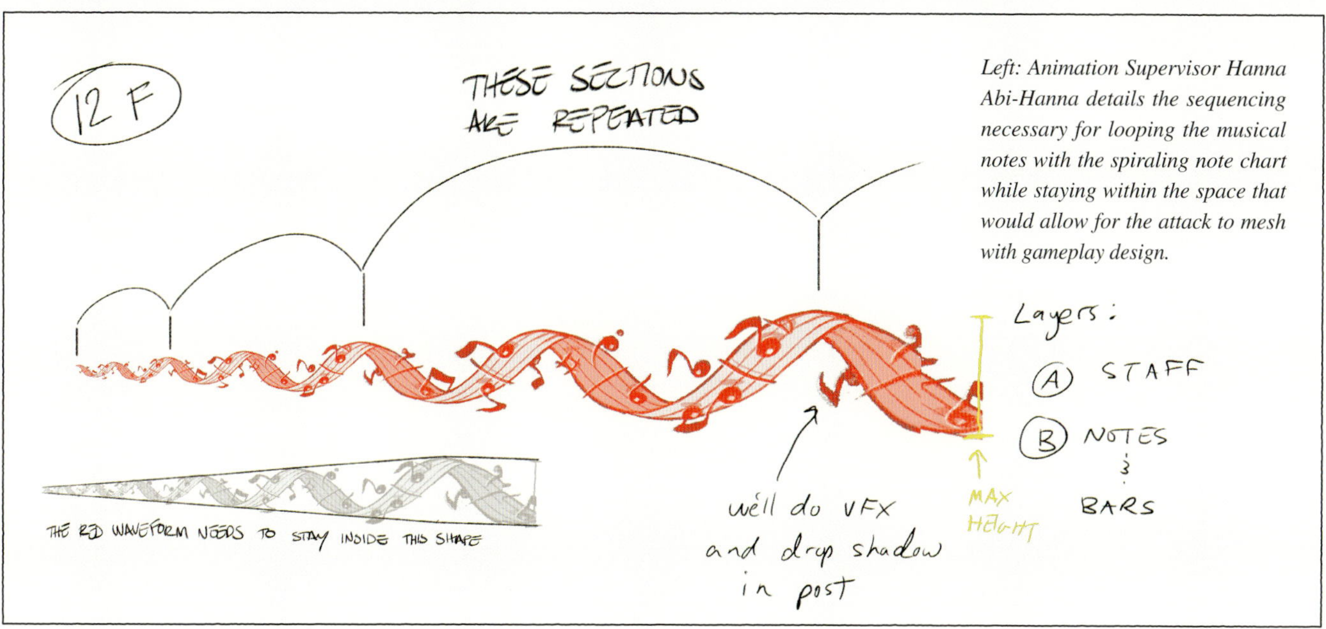

Left: Animation Supervisor Hanna Abi-Hanna details the sequencing necessary for looping the musical notes with the spiraling note chart while staying within the space that would allow for the attack to mesh with gameplay design.

Sidney the Snout

EARLY DESIGN OF THE third phase for Bootlegger Boogie only had an anteater's snout poking in from the top of the screen, with the actual full character remaining mostly unseen. But something felt missing in a fight which was already so full of smaller creatures. So, taking cues from the legendary robo-skeleton boss from the 1993 Konami game *Contra III*, we decided to have Sidney crash into the play space one hand at a time, destroying the scenery on his way. As the natural adversary of our ant cops, we saw his sticky "snout grabs" as the suitable crescendo to this dust up.

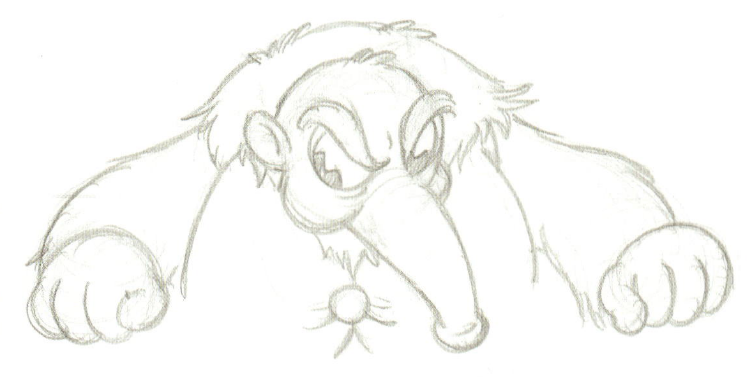

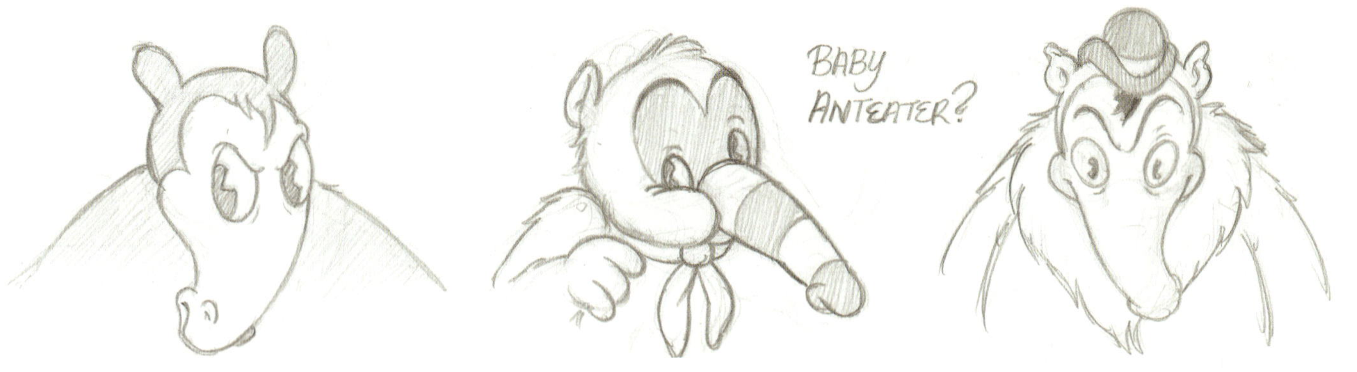

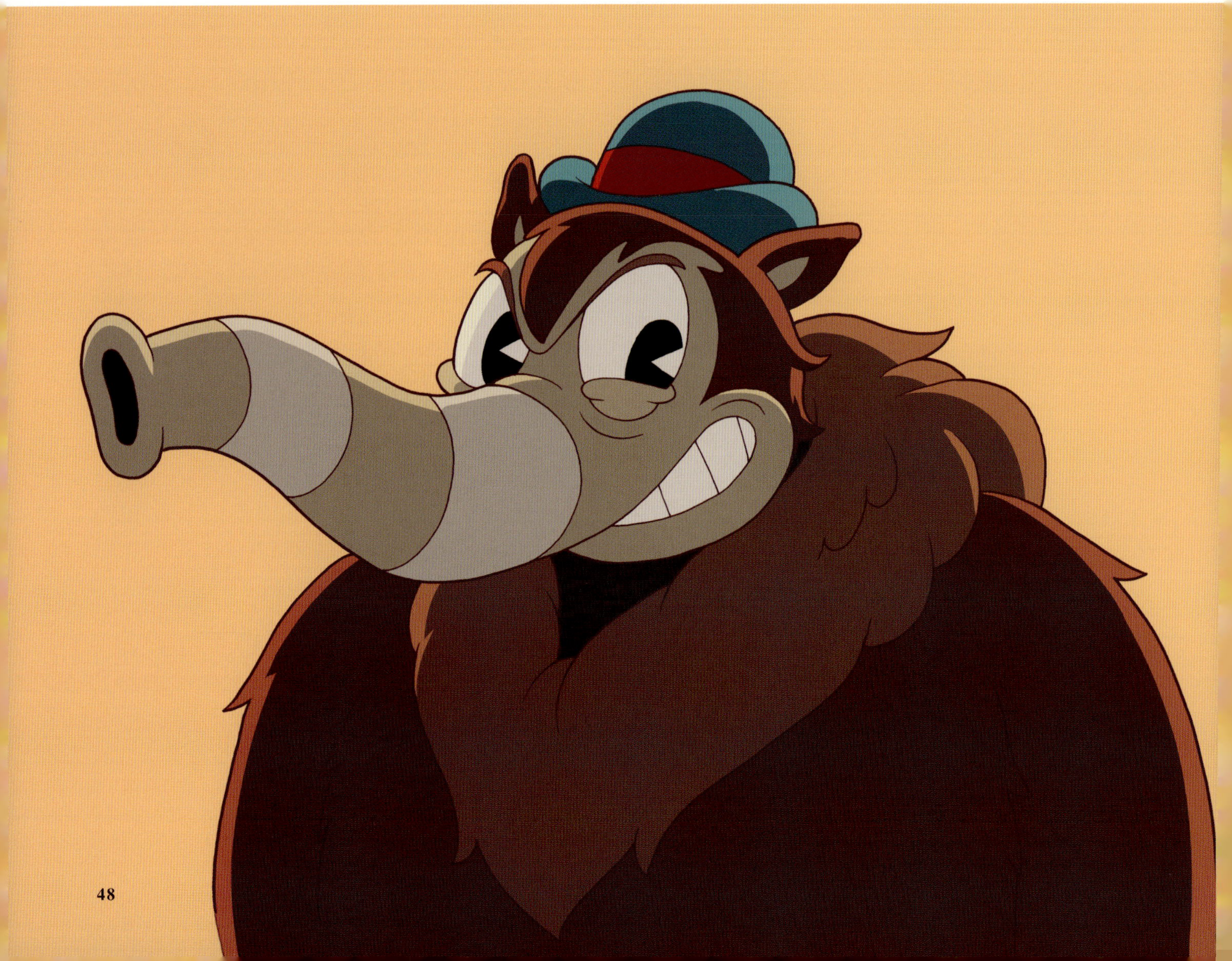

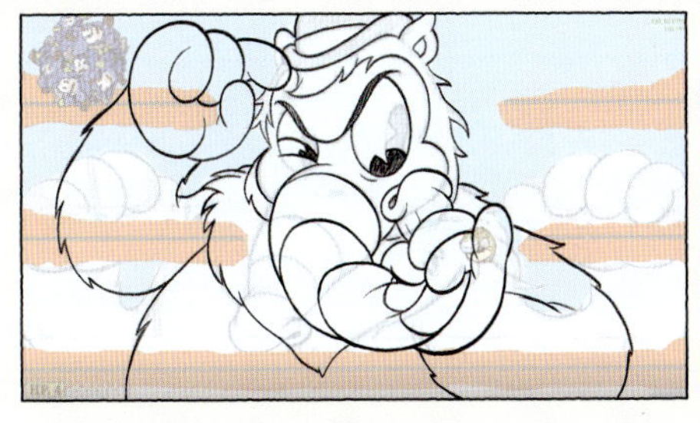
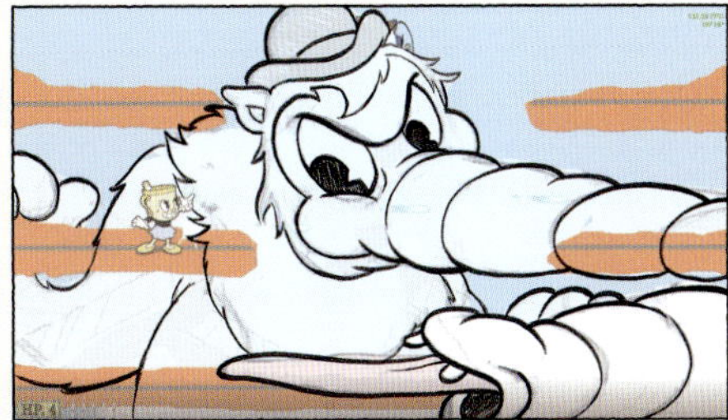
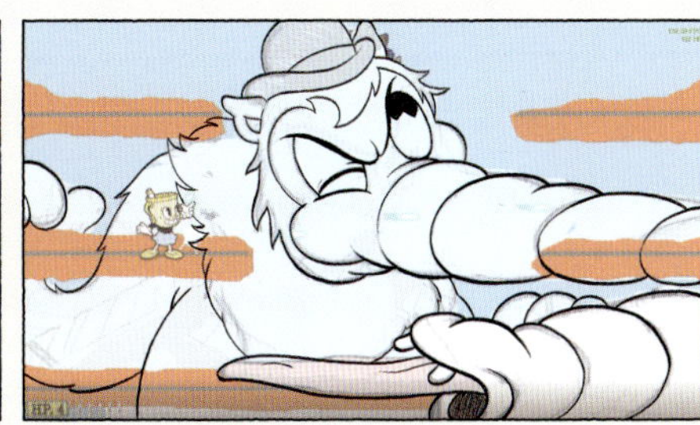
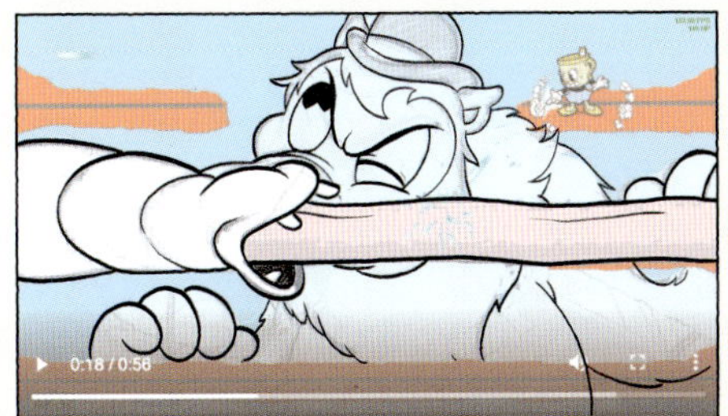
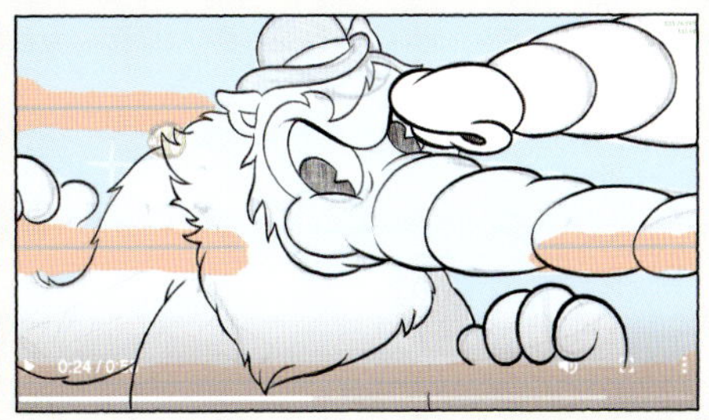

Initial animation blocking and spacing by Concept Artist Lance Inkwell for Animator Jamie Oliff. Using drawings directly over screen captures from the in-engine fight prototypes helps us to ensure final art matches gameplay design.

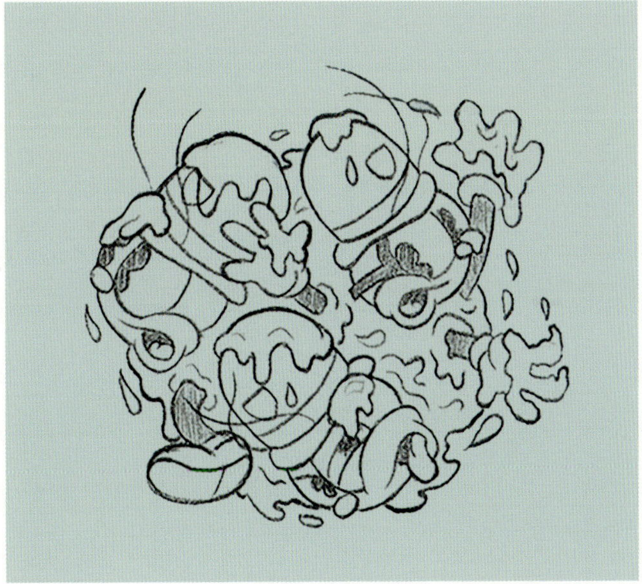
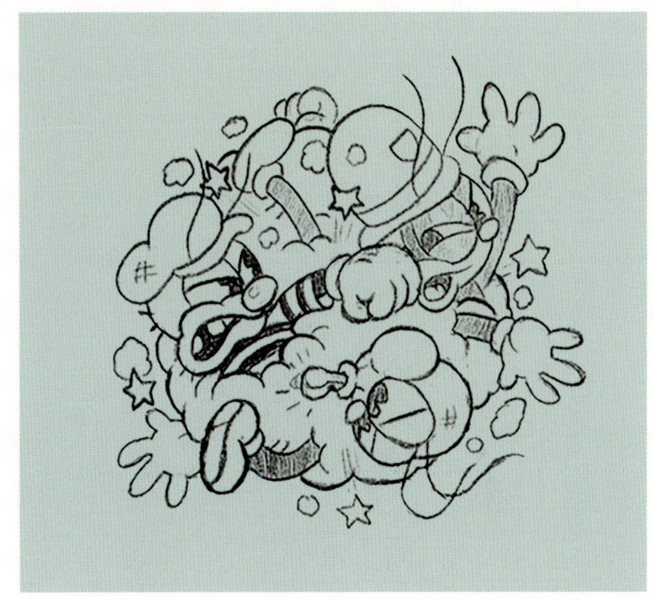

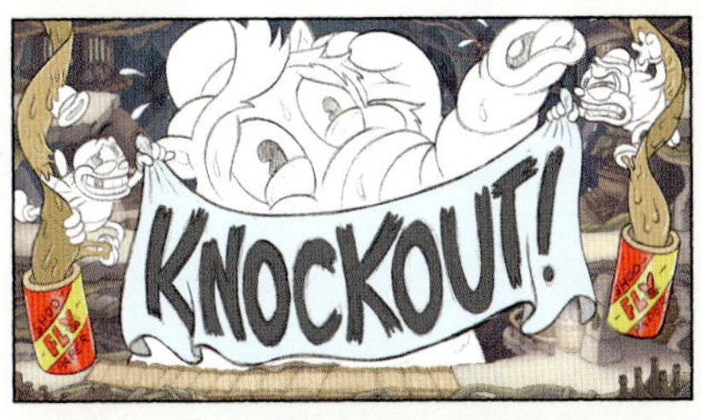

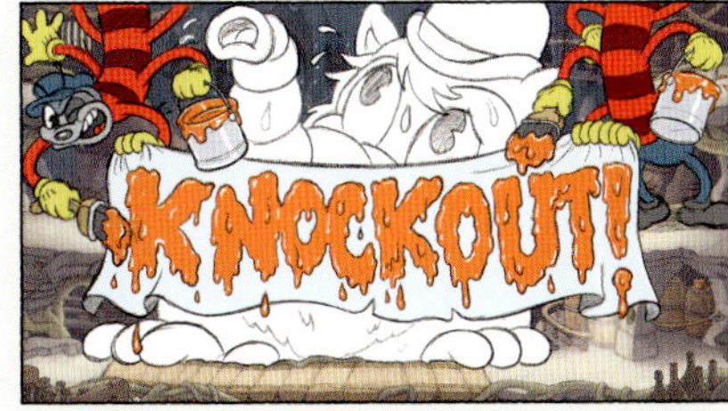

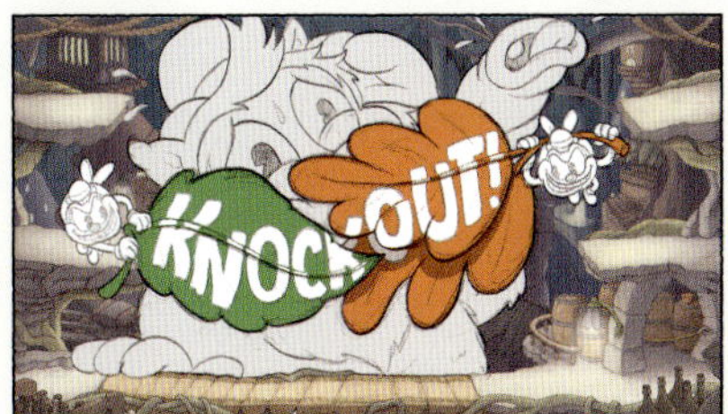
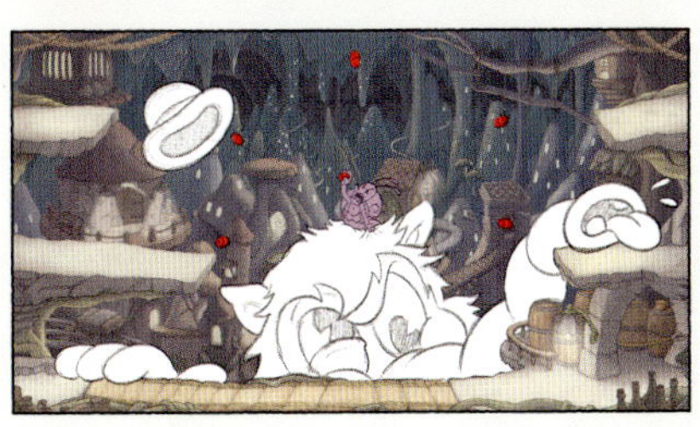
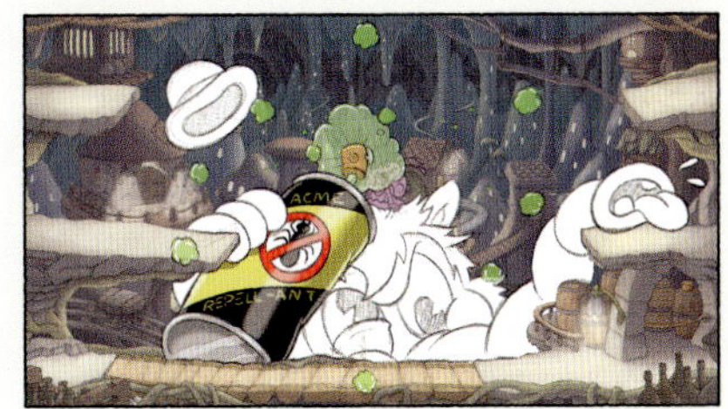
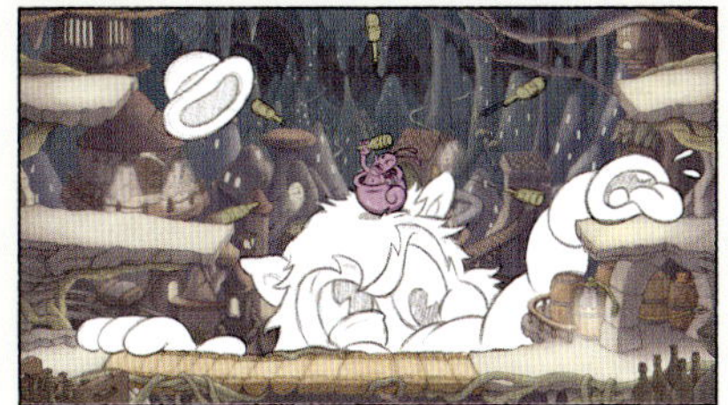

Above, Concept Artist Lance Inkwell's different takes on the fake knockout sign and subsequent transition into the final phase. Coordinating Sidney's death and Harold's reveal with a fake knockout sign proved challenging with respect to screen spacing and gameplay timing.

Hardtop Harold

AS OUR FINAL SURPRISE to players, we had always planned to do a gameplay trick similar to Goopy LeGrande's "tombstone fake out" from the original game–only much more elaborate this time around. Even with lots of clues, from his flyaway during the battle's intro animation, to his reveal under Sydney's hat, to the clearly customized Knockout sign, we still think we managed to catch a few players unaware with this micro mob boss's reveal. Following the cartoon trope of the smallest character being the biggest baddie, Hardtop Harold's commanding megaphone is also a nod to Cait Sith from *Final Fantasy VII* (1997).

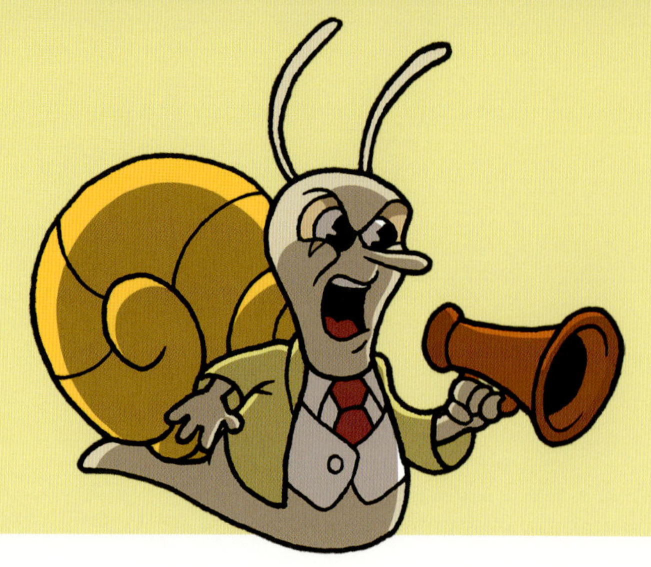

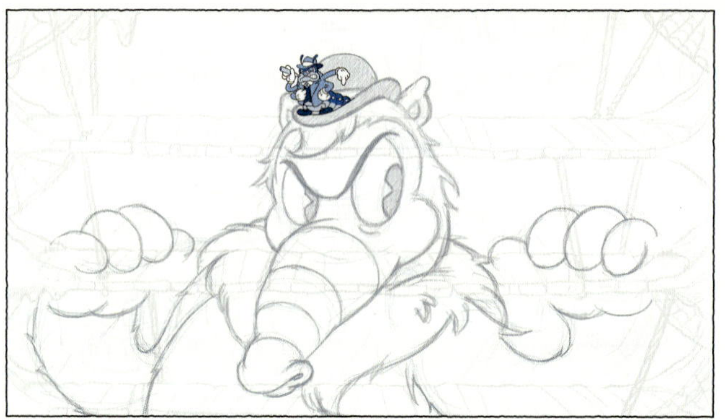

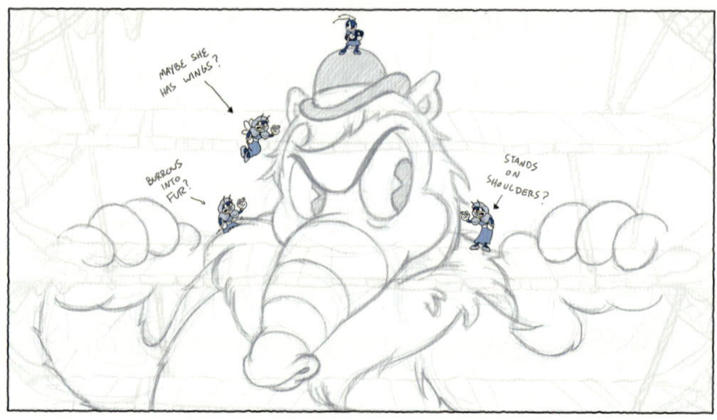

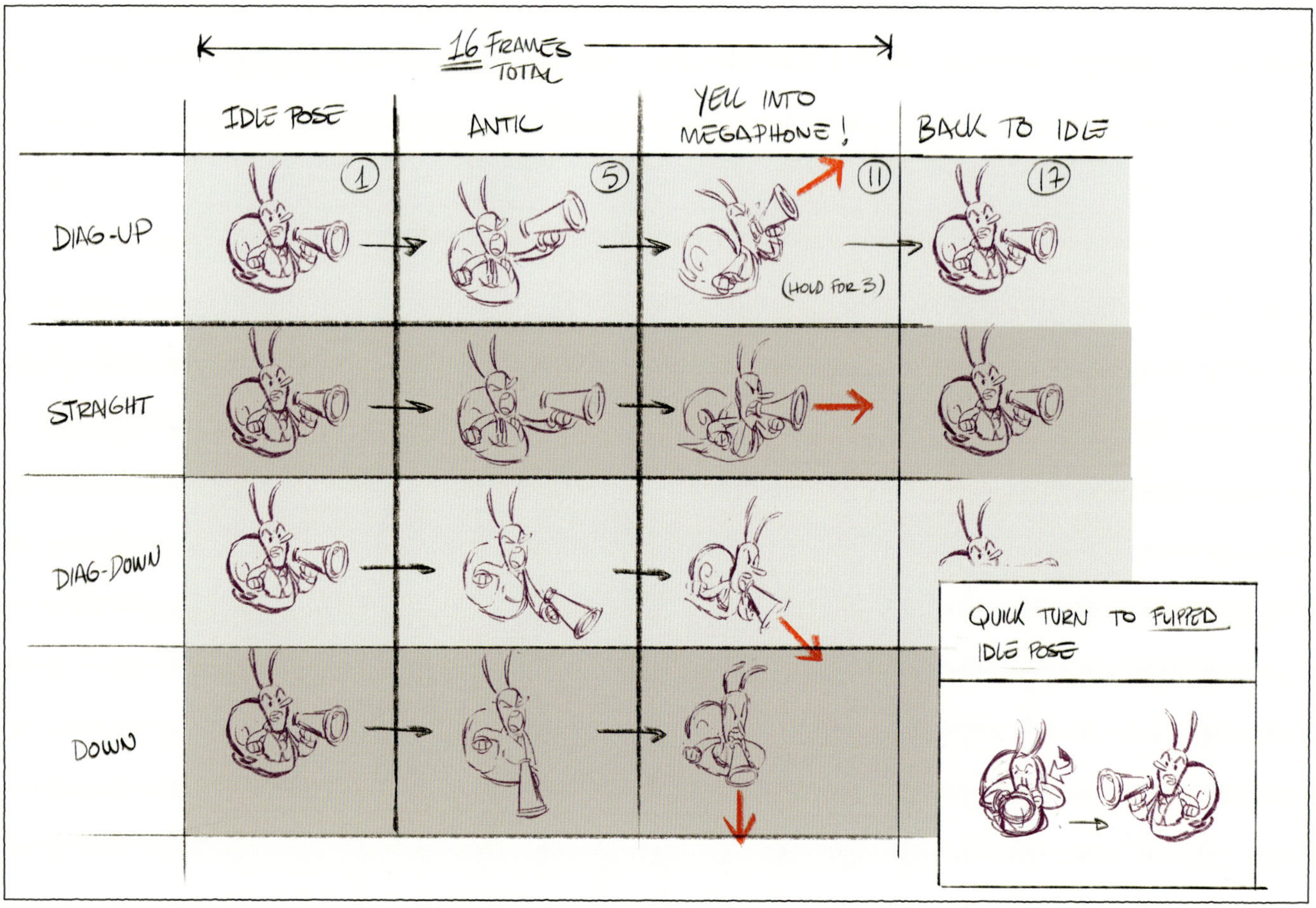

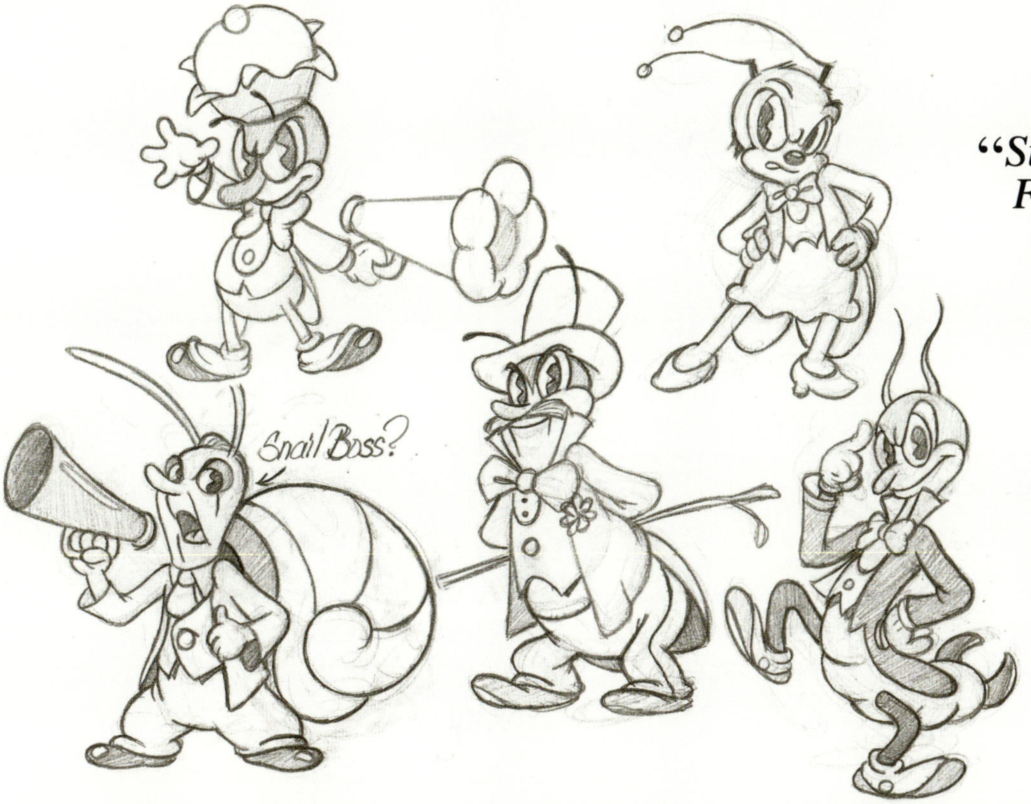

"Surprise! Forgetting about da boss ain't wise."

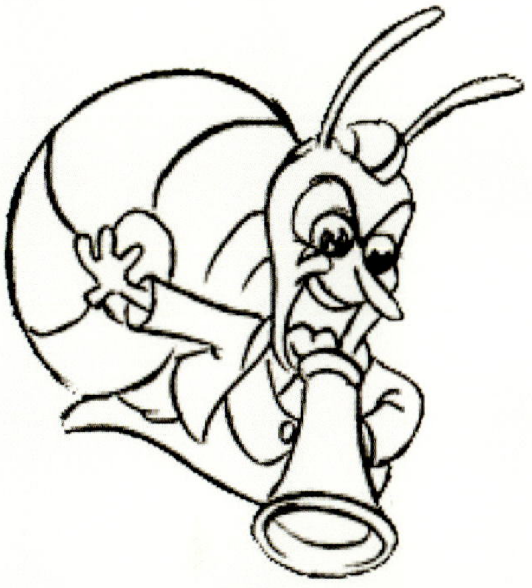

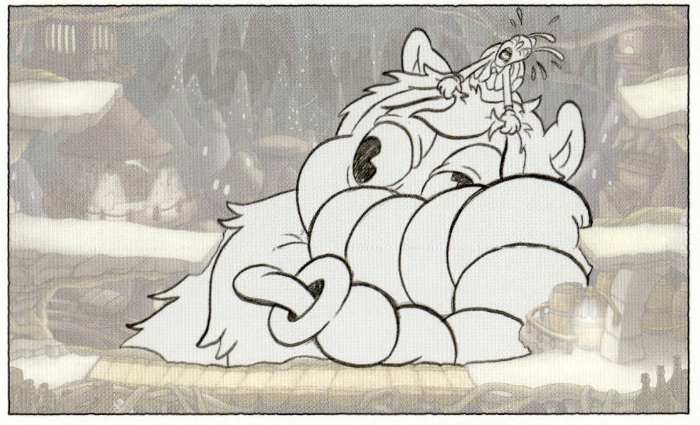

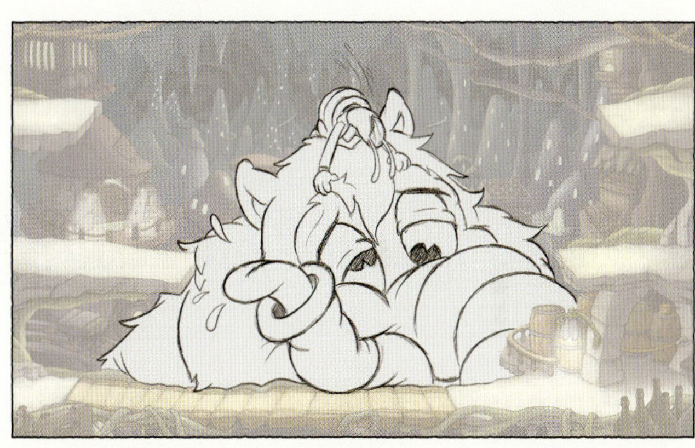

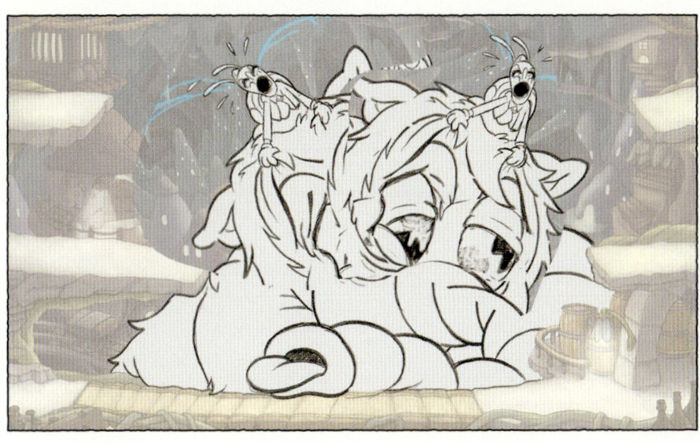

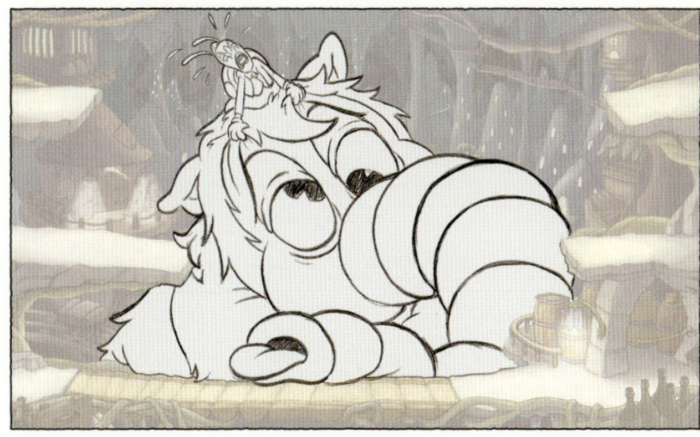

Above top, Animator Joseph Coleman's initial concept exploration of the final mob boss. Note the near-final design of Harold with a pompadour haircut, which made it all the way through animation and inking before we decided to shave him bald for his final design. Above, for Harold's final actual death, we tried to sell the idea that–as the quintessential mob boss to the end–he'd blame his underlings for his defeat. As such, his death animation showcases him taking out his frustrations on the defeated anteater.

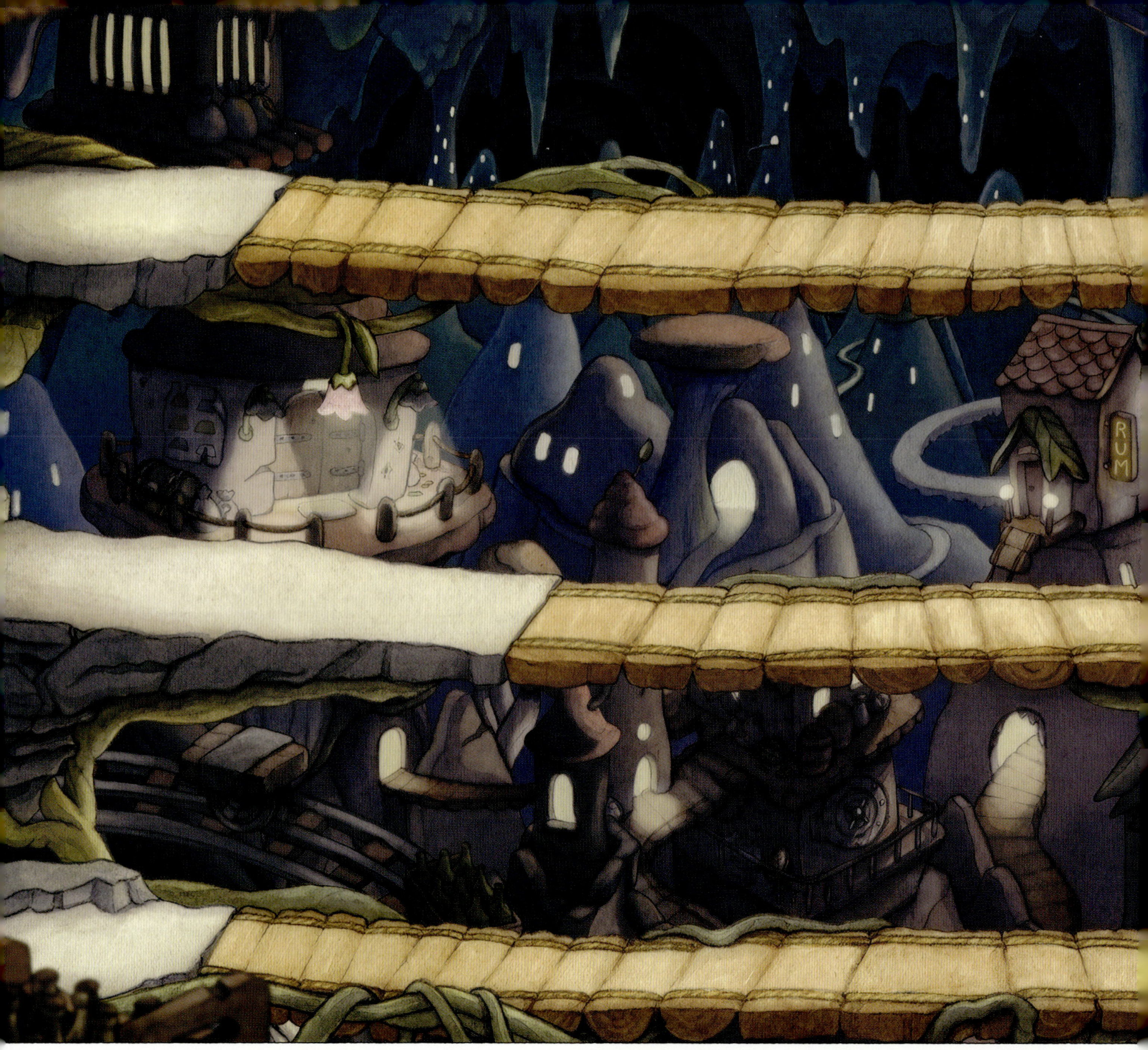

Moonshine Mob Background

WITH GAMEPLAY DESIGN that required a three-tiered layout to facilitate the swarms of enemies, Background Painter Caitlin Russell explored interiors that could convey a criminal syndicate's hideout getting raided by cops. Eventually, we decided to open up the above vista, endeavoring to create a bustling bug city with a criminal element operating within. With visual notes from the Fleischer classic *Mr. Bug Goes To Town* (1941) and thematic inspirations from Jim Henson's *Fraggle Rock* (1983) and *The Hobbit*'s (1937) goblin-town, we wanted to give the city a quickly-constructed but lived-in feel.

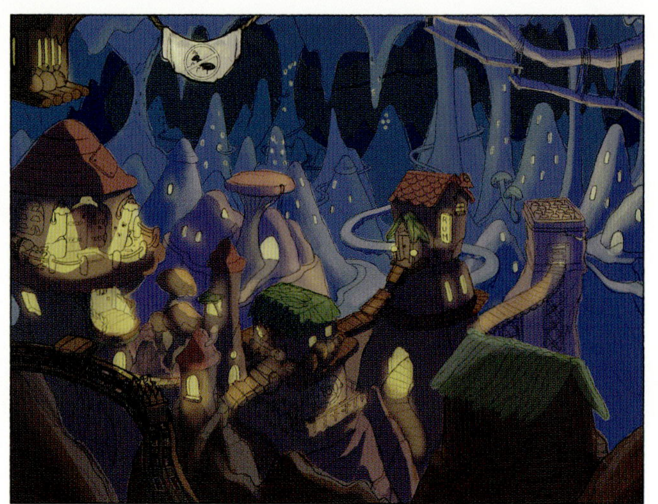

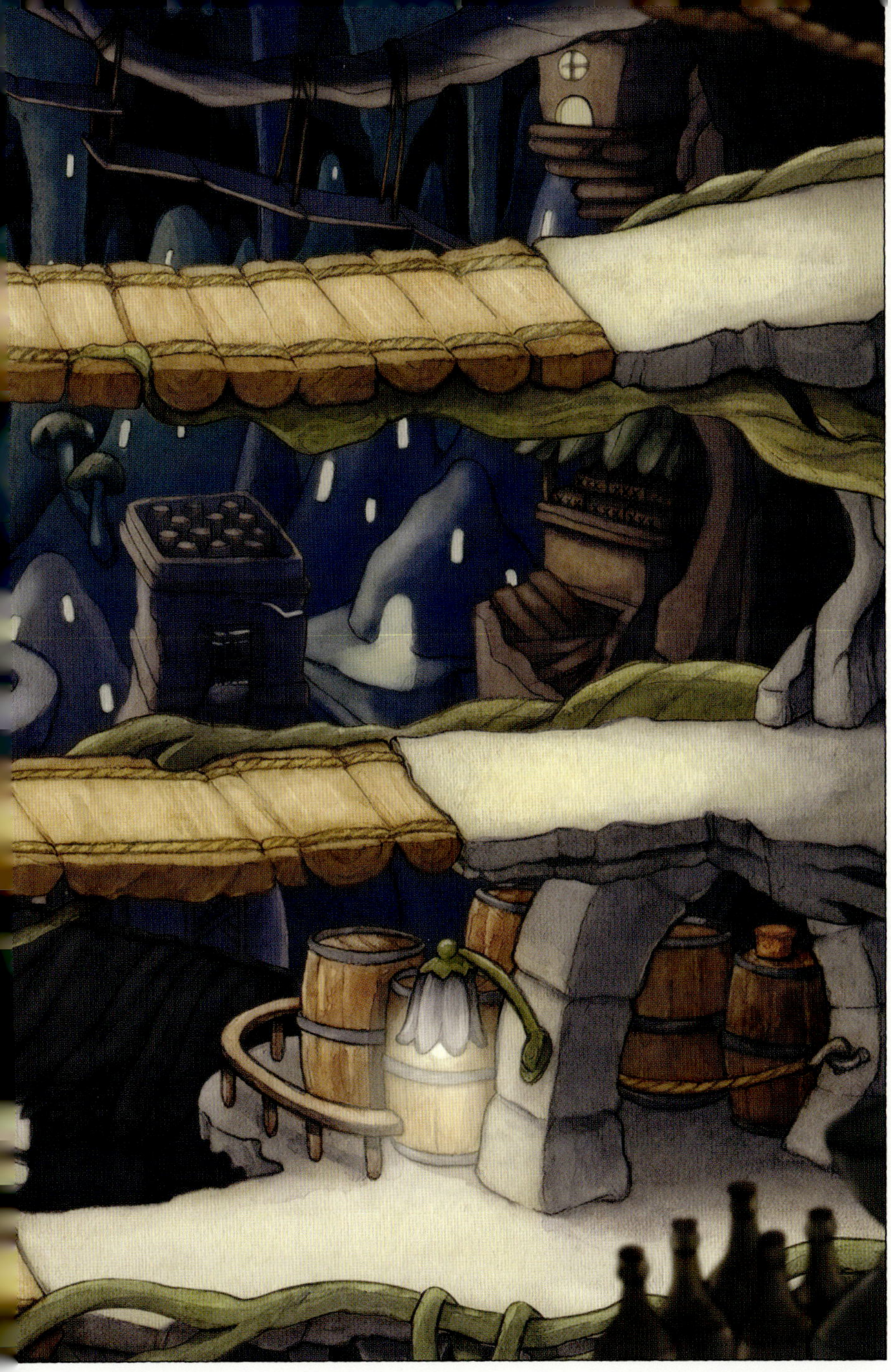

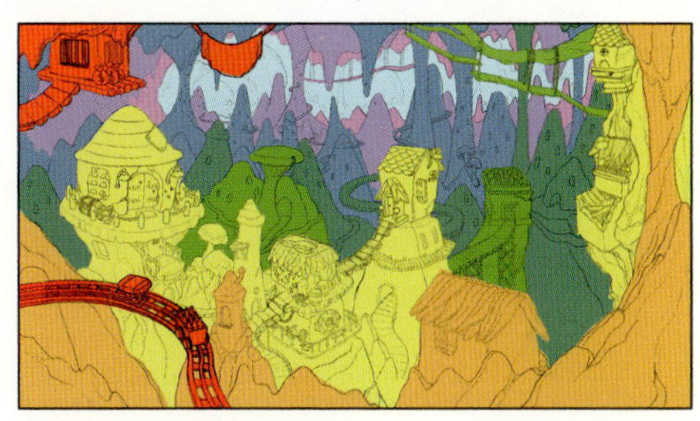

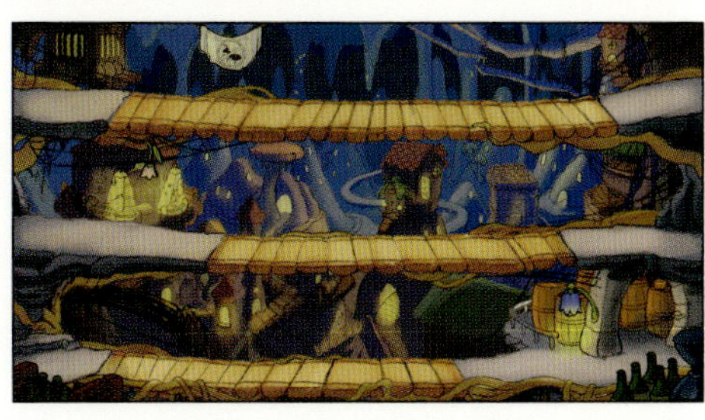

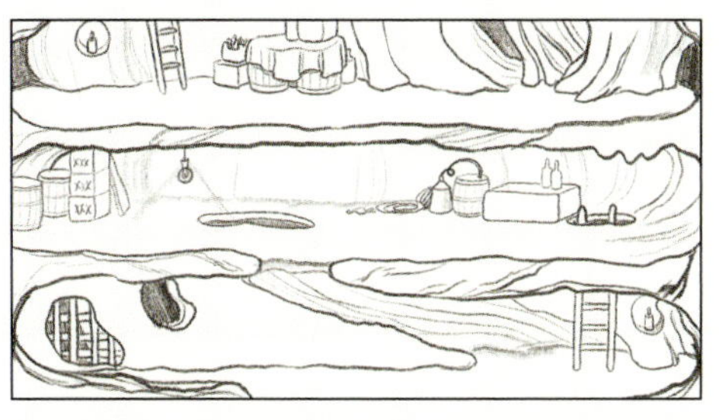

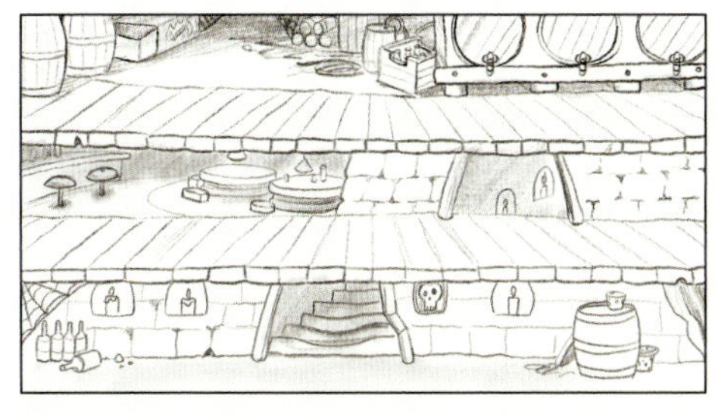

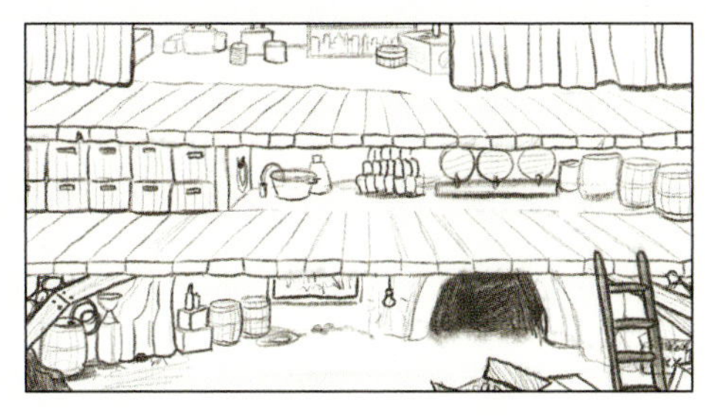

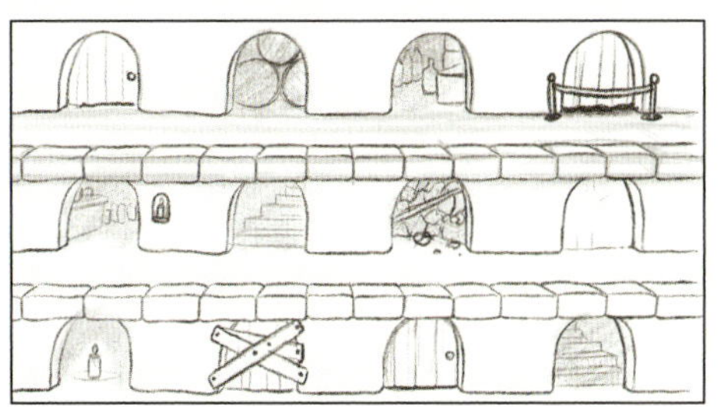

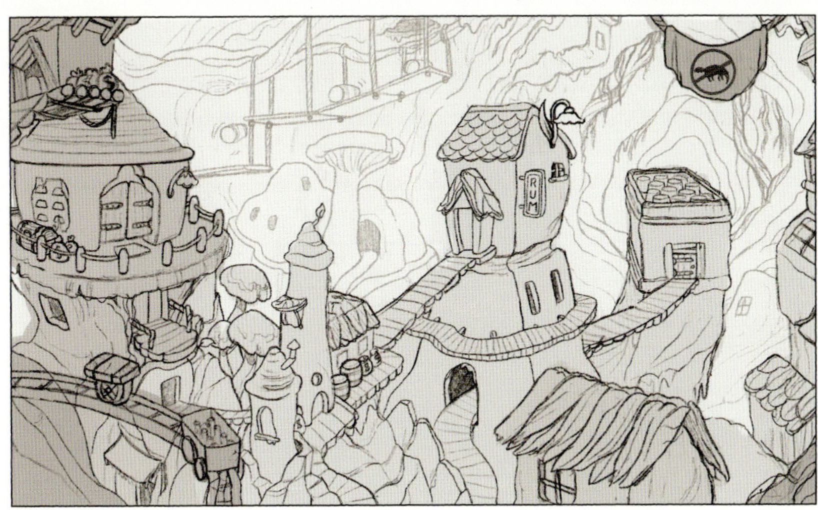
RUM

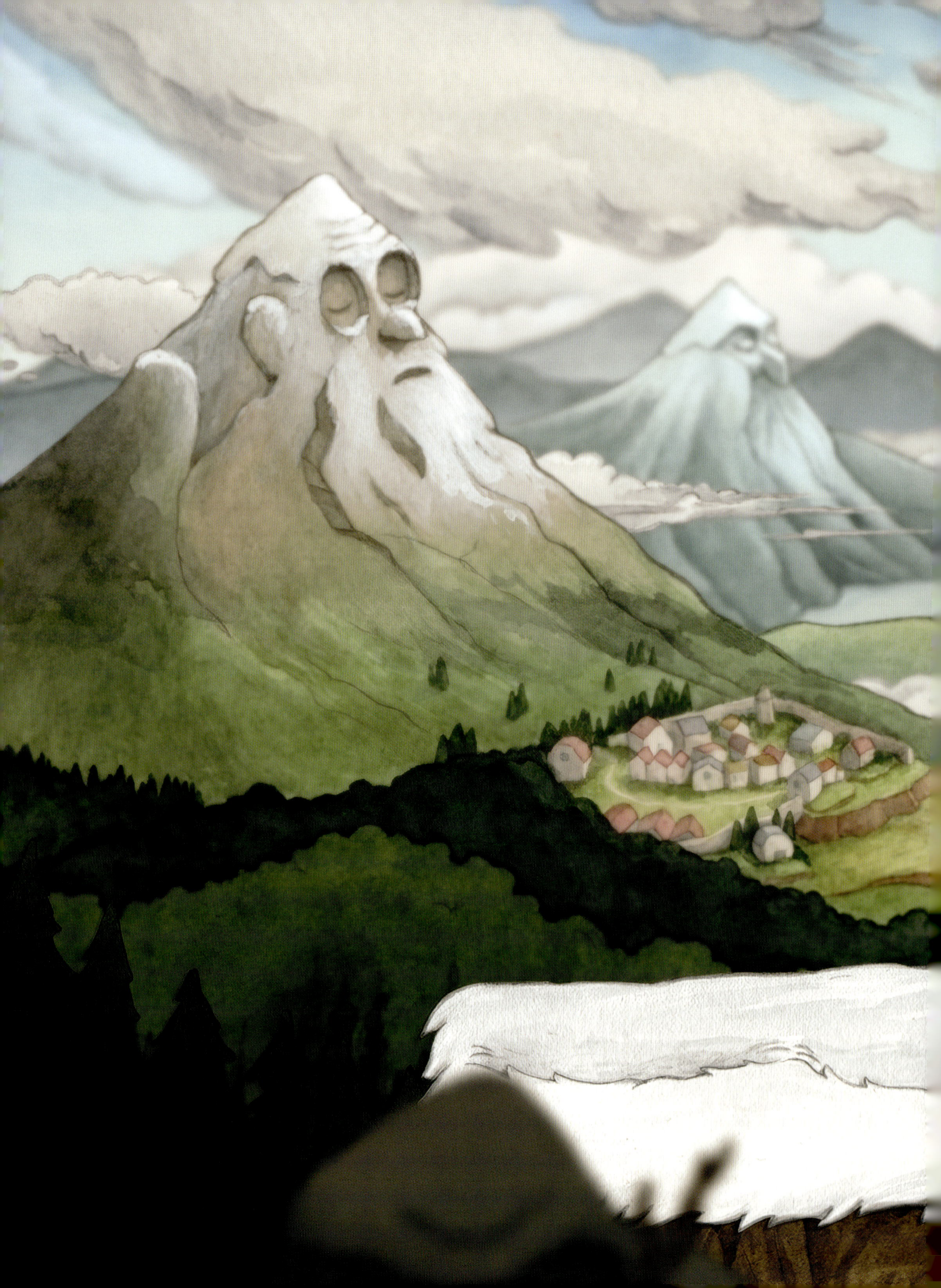

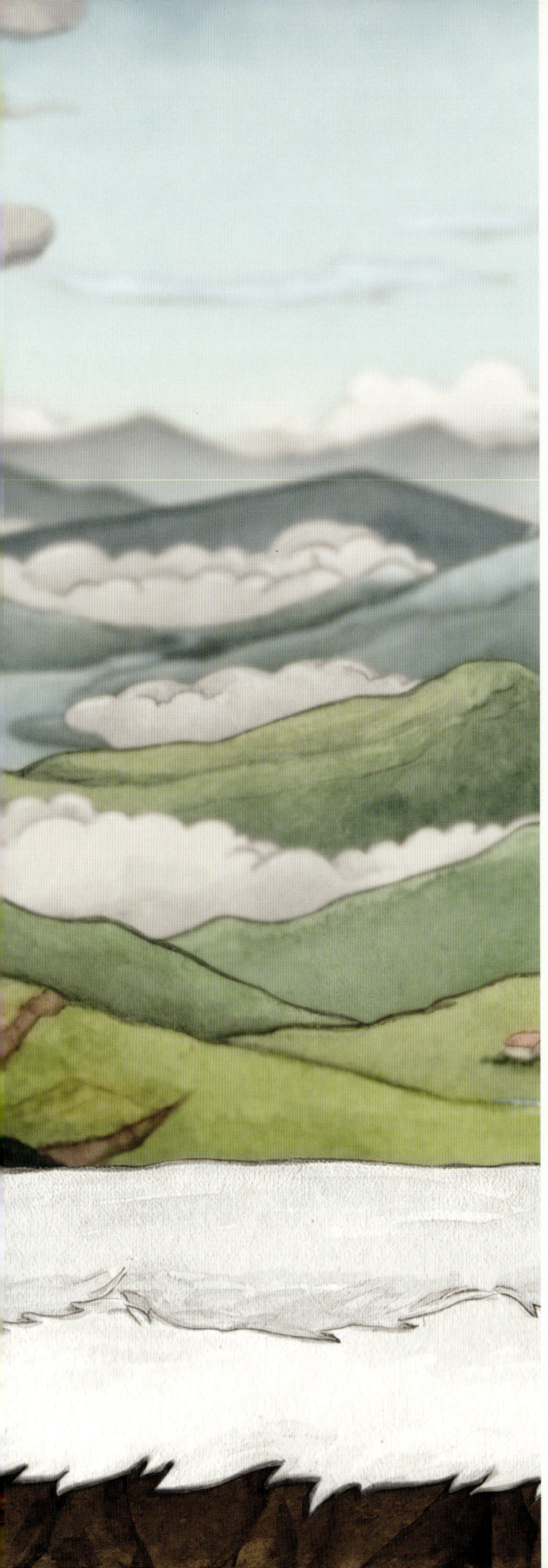

Chapter IV:
Gnome Way Out

THERE'S NOTHING QUITE LIKE taking in the mountain air. Escaping the doldrums of daily life, getting away from the hustle and bustle of the big city, and taking in the world from up in the clouds. That is, unless you live on the Inkwell Isles, where some of those mountains are alive and none too pleased to find you standing on their face.

As one of the major archetypes from classic films and shorts of the 1930s and '40s that was initially planned for inclusion in the original Cuphead, the "cartoon giant" was a character we knew we wanted to bring to life from very early in the production of *The Delicious Last Course*. We've always played with scale in our game–pitting Cuphead and pals against a variety of impossible, screen-filling enemies. But with a literal giant, this took on a whole other dimension, challenging our artists and designers to consider how we could convey the idea of battling a creature this humongous. After much experimentation, art concepts, and testing, the result was a standoff with a conceit not seen anywhere else in all of *Cuphead*: a fight that starts on the outside of a foe, and ends up in their stomach.

Glumstone the Giant
in
"GNOME WAY OUT"

ORNERY BUT PLAYFUL, our very own Glumstone the Giant pays homage to one of cartooning's absolute classics: Disney's *Brave Little Tailor* (1938). The short, which sees Mickey Mouse nearly dumped into a giant's mouth as he snacks on a cart full of pumpkins as if they were tiny grapes, had our brains swirling with ways we could design and animate a *Cuphead* battle that progressed naturally into a giant's insides.

A real breakthrough came when we settled on the idea to use the character's bushy beard as a stand-in for the snowcaps atop a mountain peak, allowing us to play with a story progression that begins by disturbing Glumstone from his nap. A fun fact, pictured below: the pose for our "Geese Crossing" sign is modelled after the iconic attack pose of the *Fatal Fury* character Geese Howard.

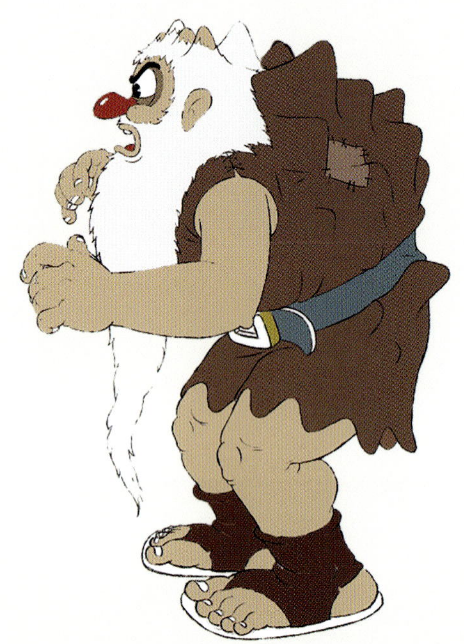

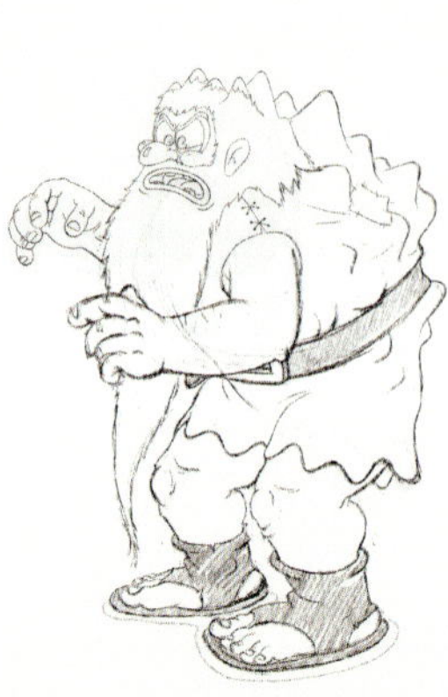

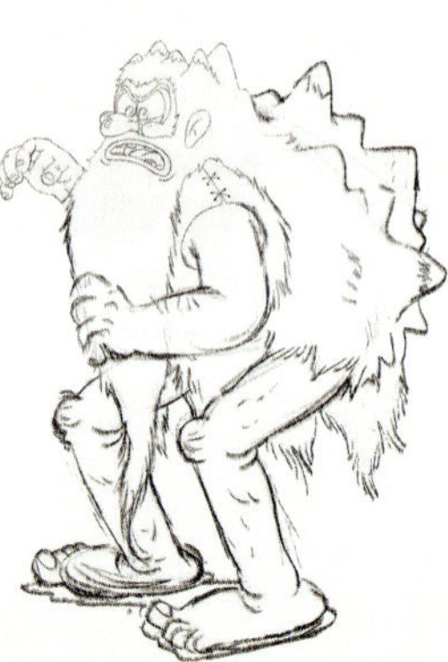

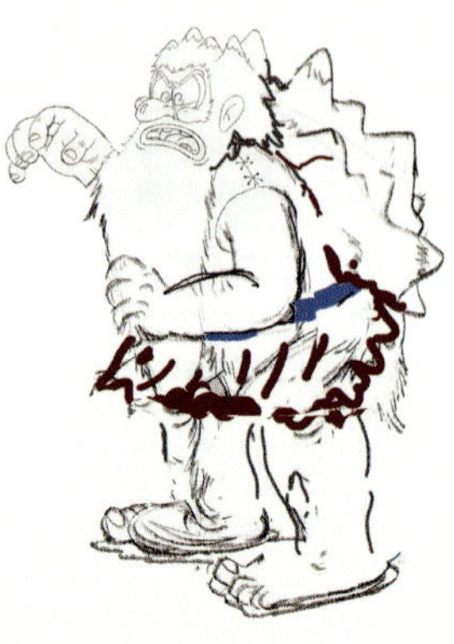

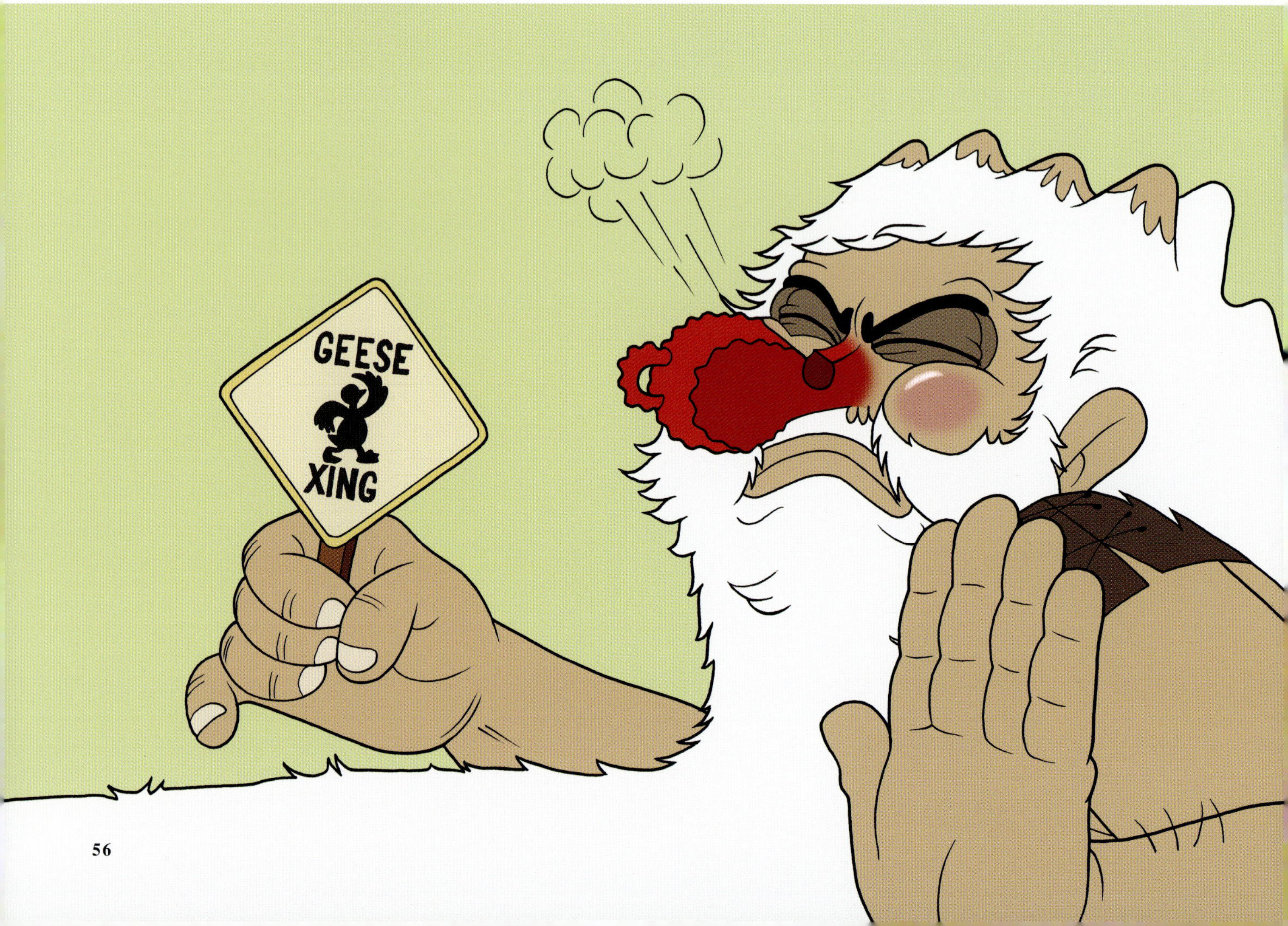

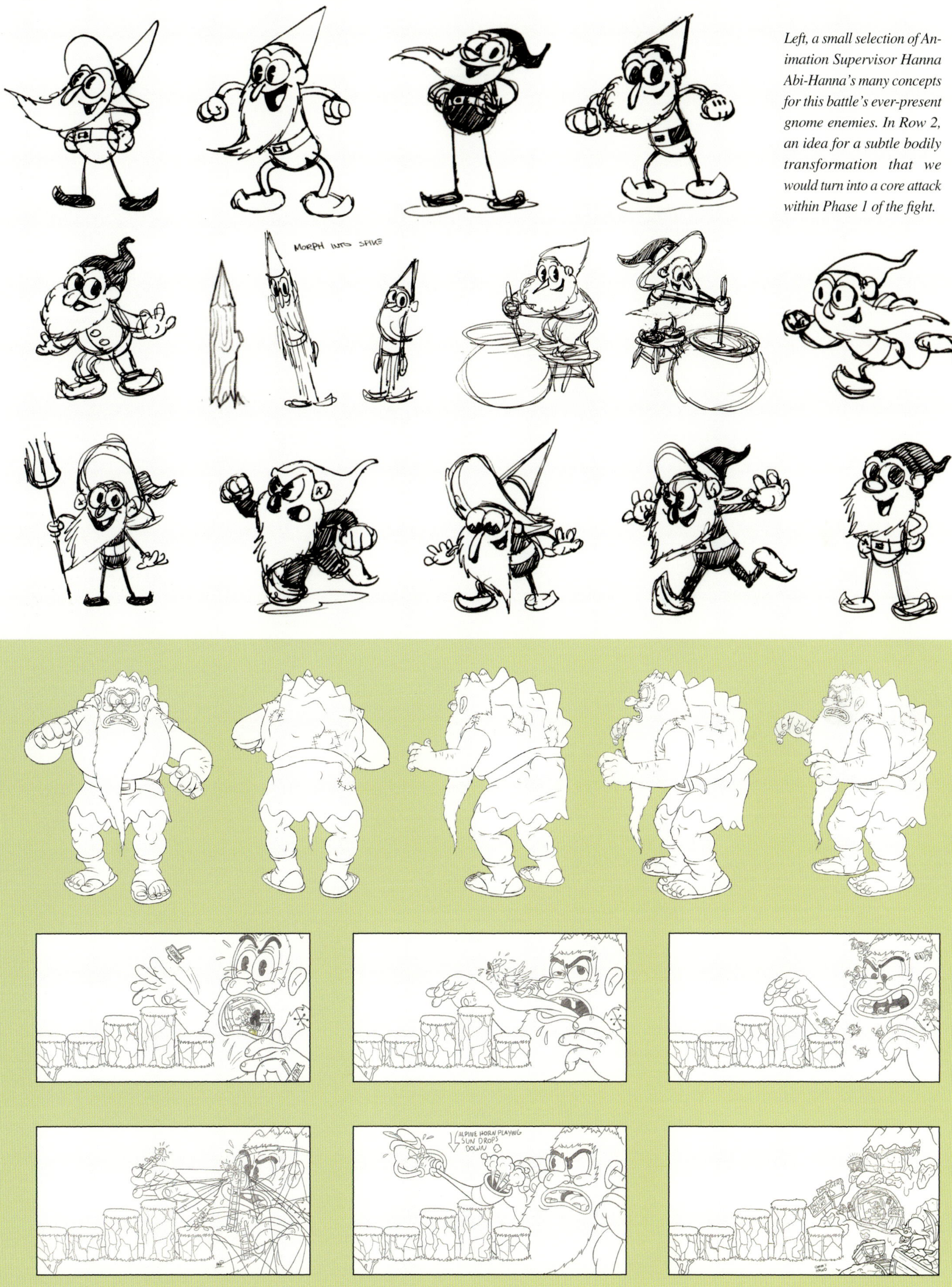

Left, a small selection of Animation Supervisor Hanna Abi-Hanna's many concepts for this battle's ever-present gnome enemies. In Row 2, an idea for a subtle bodily transformation that we would turn into a core attack within Phase 1 of the fight.

During the design process for Glumstone's battle, we bandied around the notion of including a fun-but-gimmicky secret moment where players could catch Glumstone sleeping by rushing up to him quickly during the opening sequence. While this idea was ultimately scrapped, it did lead us down the rabbit hole to thoughts of attack sequences based on a giant's morning routine, complete with bad breath and all. Evidenced below in concepts from Animation Supervisor Hanna Abi-Hanna, a real challenge with this

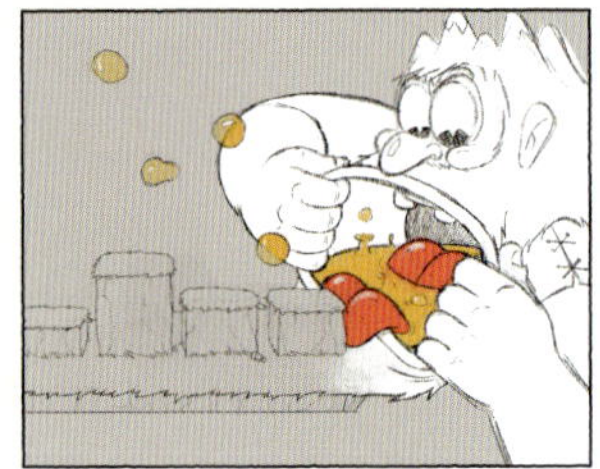

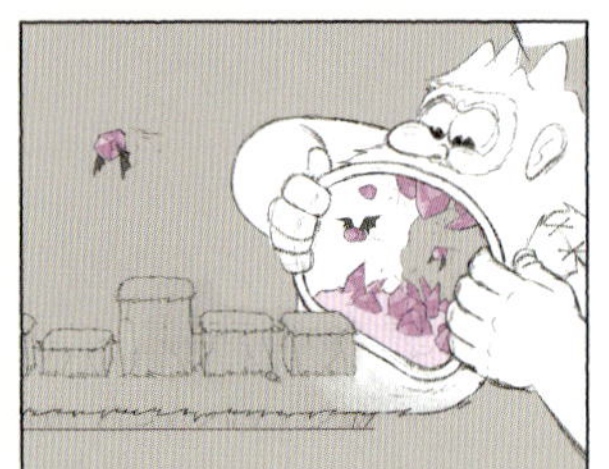

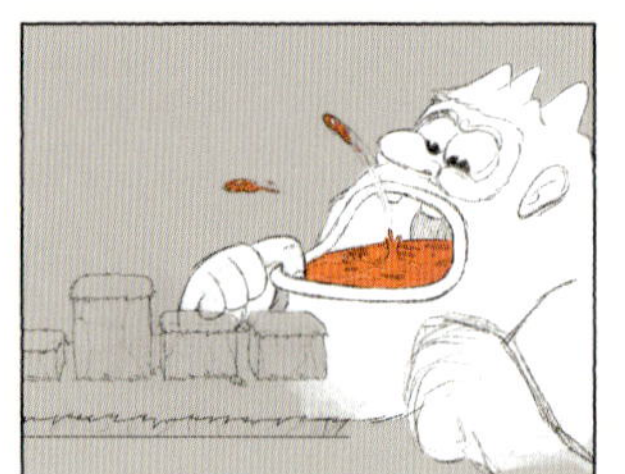

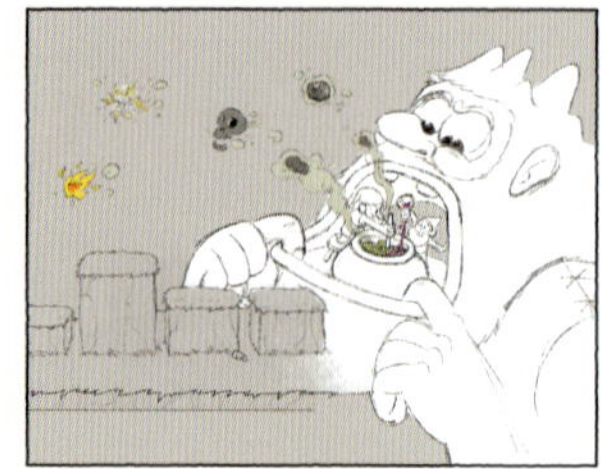

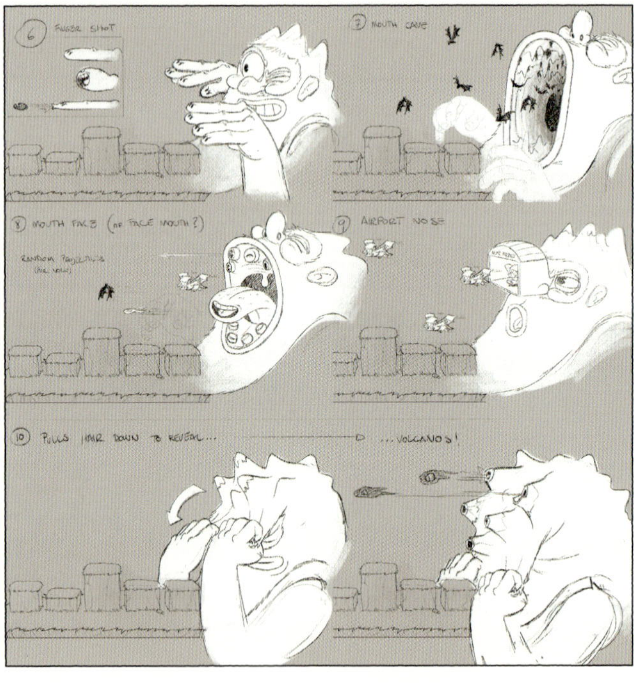

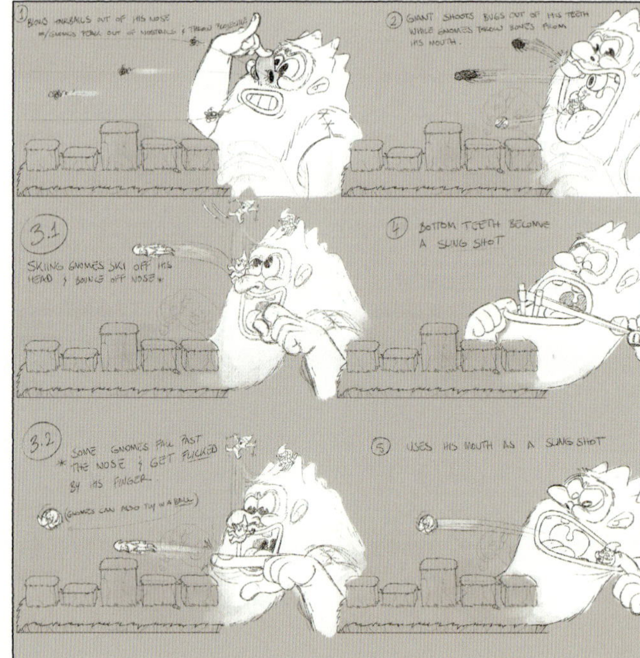

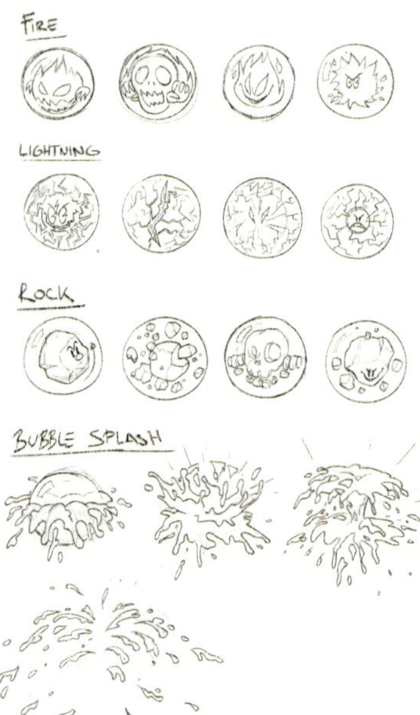

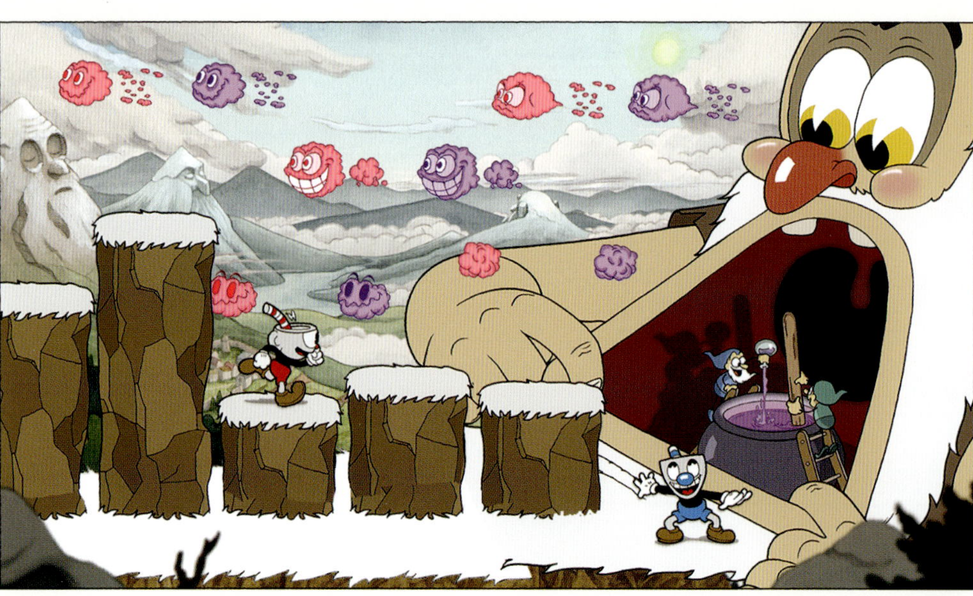

fight's opening phase involved coming up with clever ways to use the stage's layout (a horizontal platform with a massive obstacle on the right) to convey the wide range of wacky cartoon transformations that have become such hallmarks of the *Cuphead* universe.

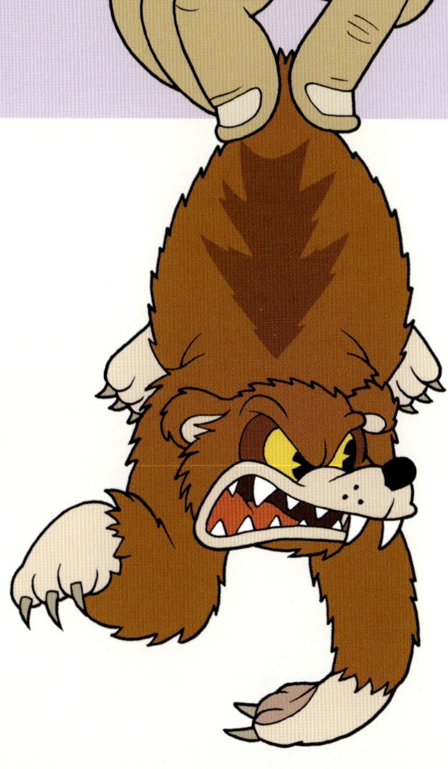

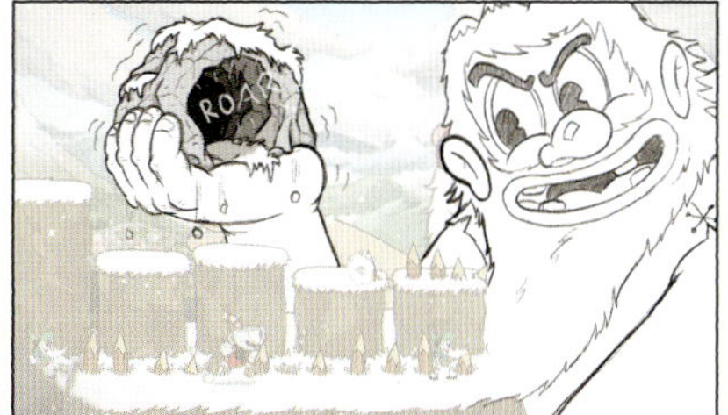

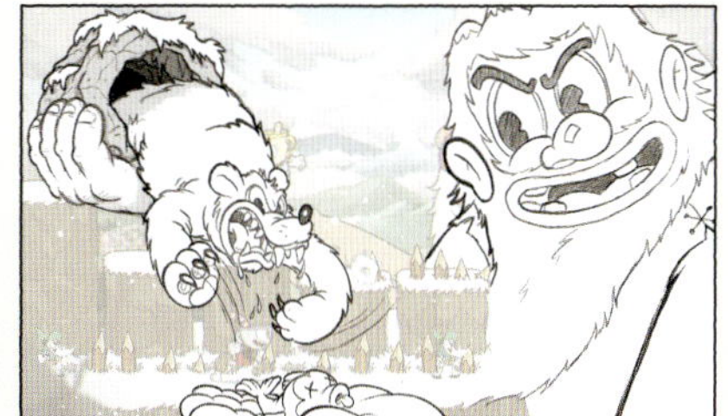

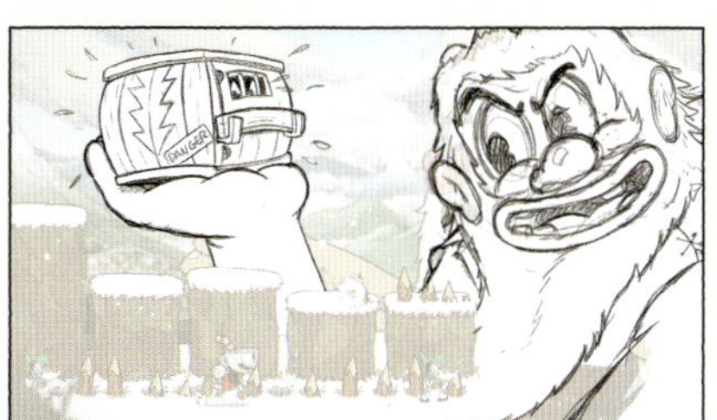

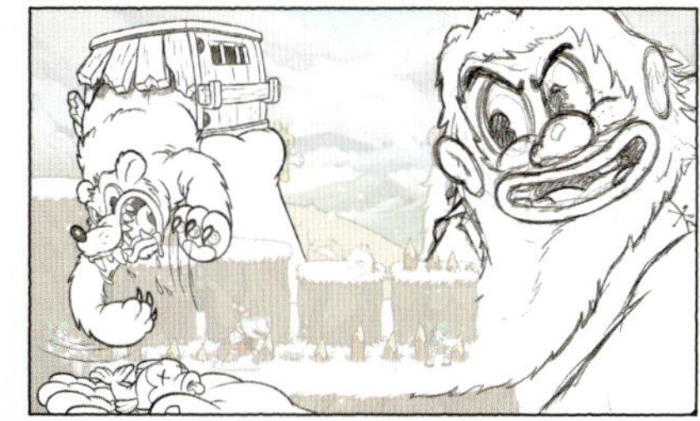

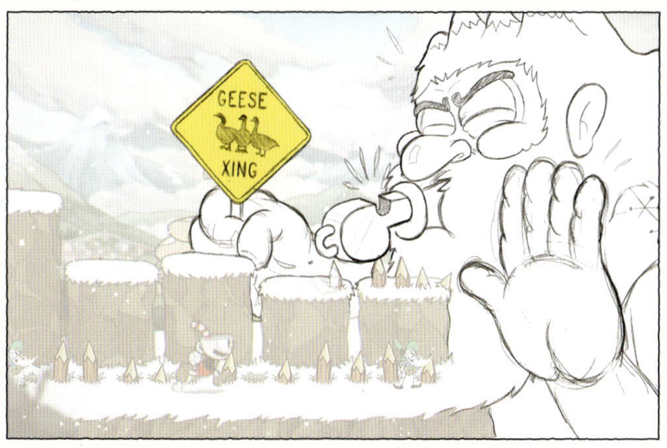

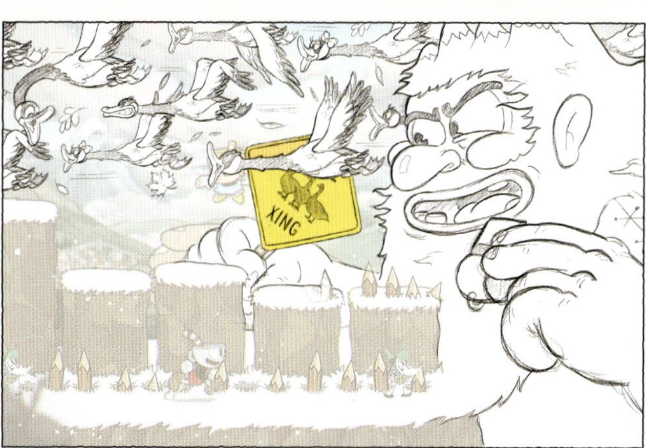

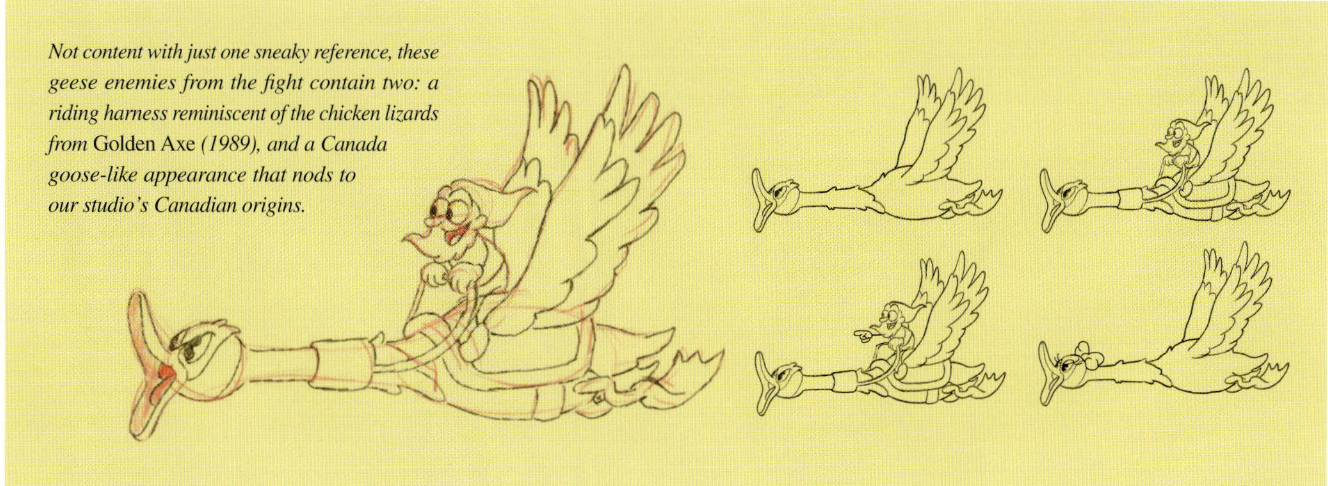

Not content with just one sneaky reference, these geese enemies from the fight contain two: a riding harness reminiscent of the chicken lizards from Golden Axe *(1989), and a Canada goose-like appearance that nods to our studio's Canadian origins.*

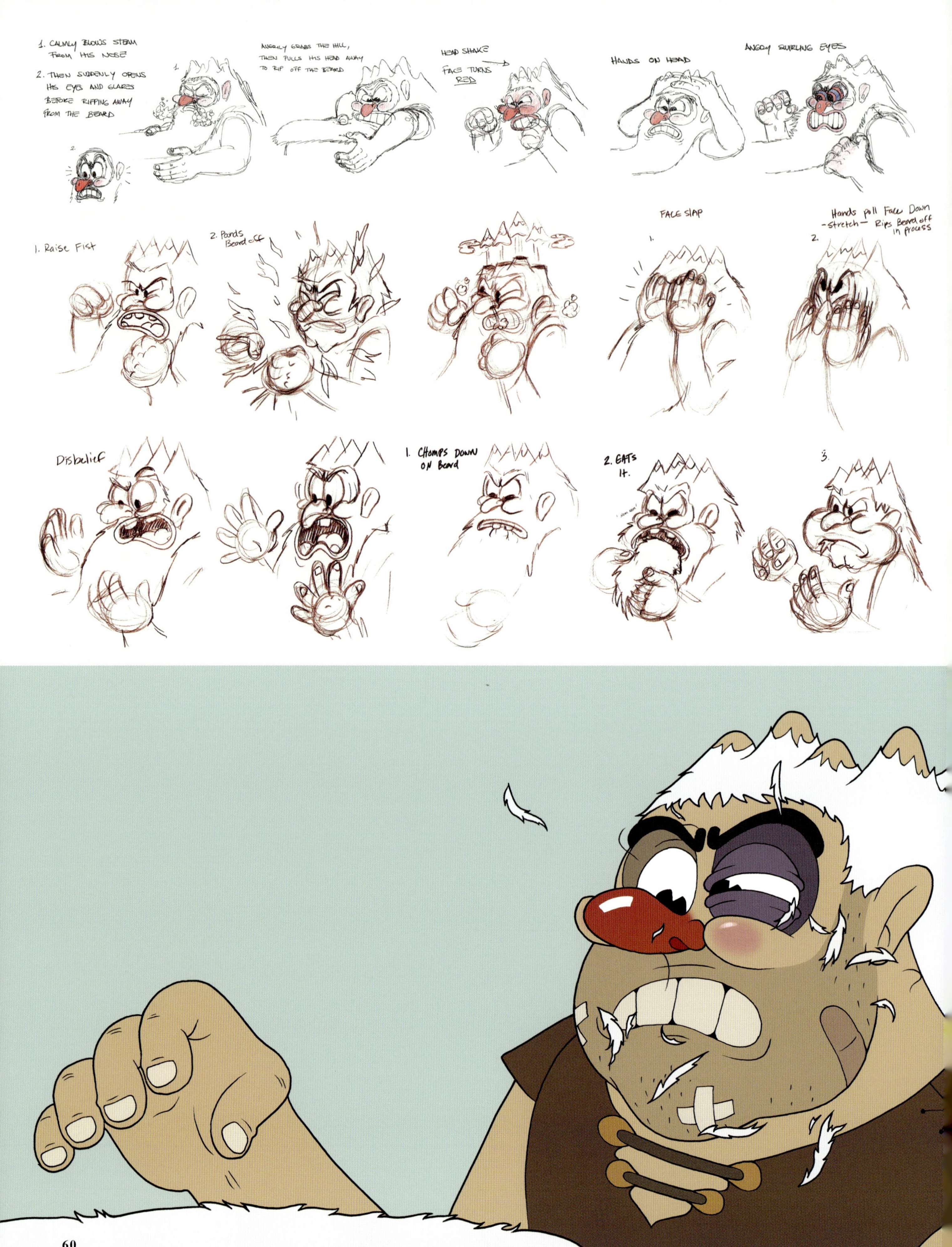
1. CALMLY BLOWS STEAM FROM HIS NOSE
2. THEN SUDDENLY OPENS HIS EYES AND GLARES BEFORE RIPPING AWAY FROM THE BEARD
ANGRILY GRABS THE HILL, THEN PULLS HIS HEAD AWAY TO RIP OFF THE BEARD
HEAD SHAKE
FACE TURNS RED
HANDS ON HEAD
ANGRY SWIRLING EYES
1. Raise Fist
2. Pounds Beard off
FACE SLAP
Hands pull Face Down -stretch- Rips Beard off in process
Disbelief
1. CHOMPS DOWN ON Beard
2. EATS it.

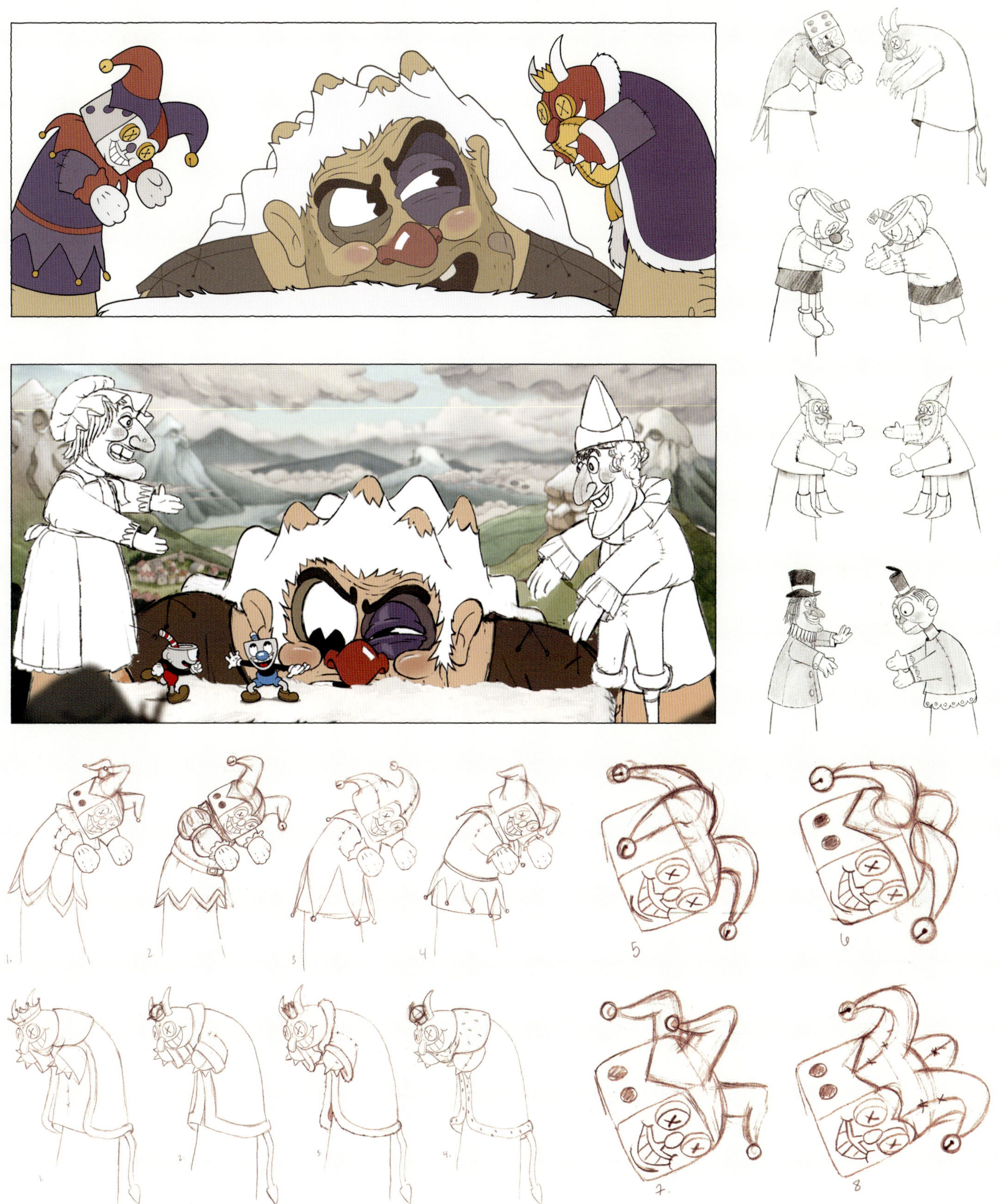

In the spirit of ratcheting up the action with each new stage of a boss, we sought to involve Glumstone's hands in Phase 2 of his battle. And what better way to involve a giant's hands than…a giant puppet show! We initially explored puppet concepts rooted in the classic "Punch and Judy" characters that originated as far back as sixteenth-century Italian puppet theatre, but wound up feeling like hand-stitched puppets were more in line with the modest garb worn by Glumstone himself. Better still, the "medieval" imagery of giants opened up the door for us to explore the way theatre of that period was often used to satirically mock the upper crust–or in our case, our very own *King* Dice and throne-sitting Devil.

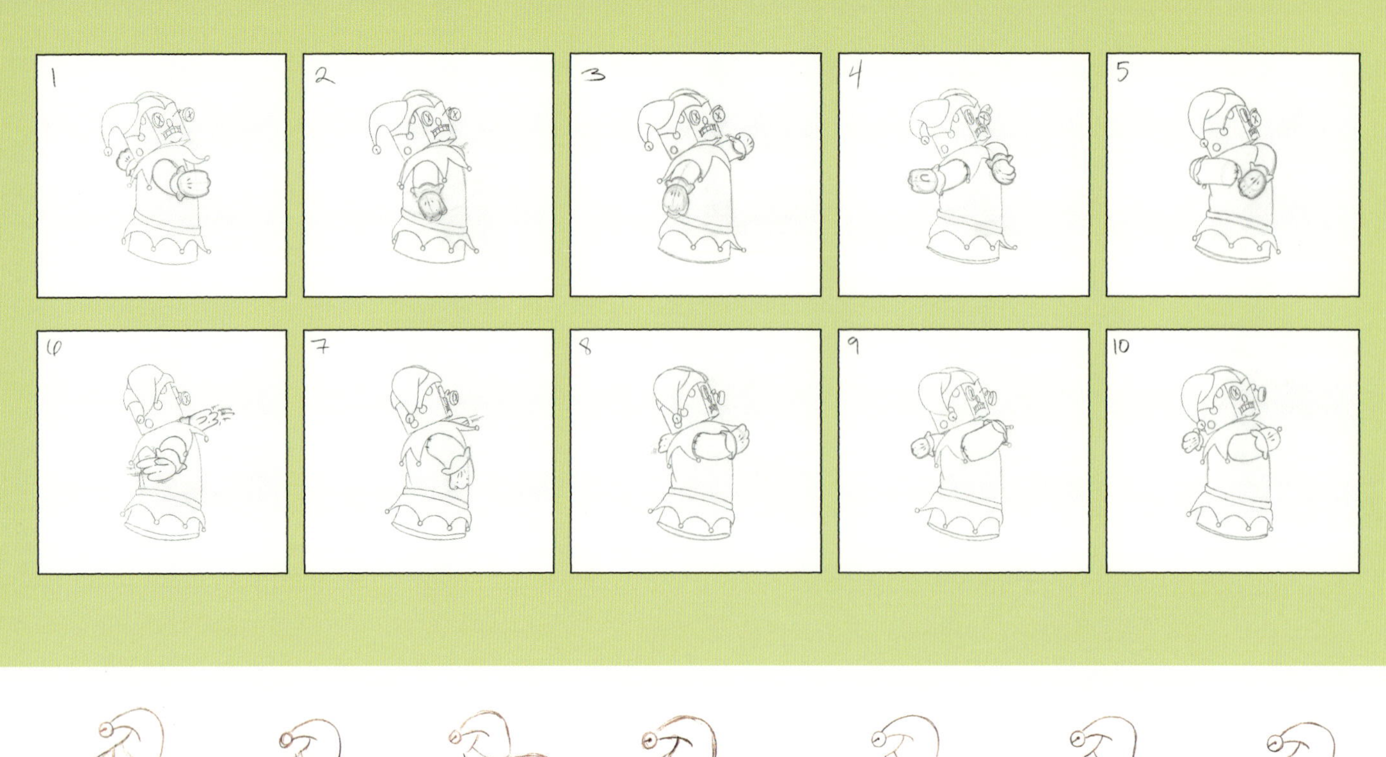

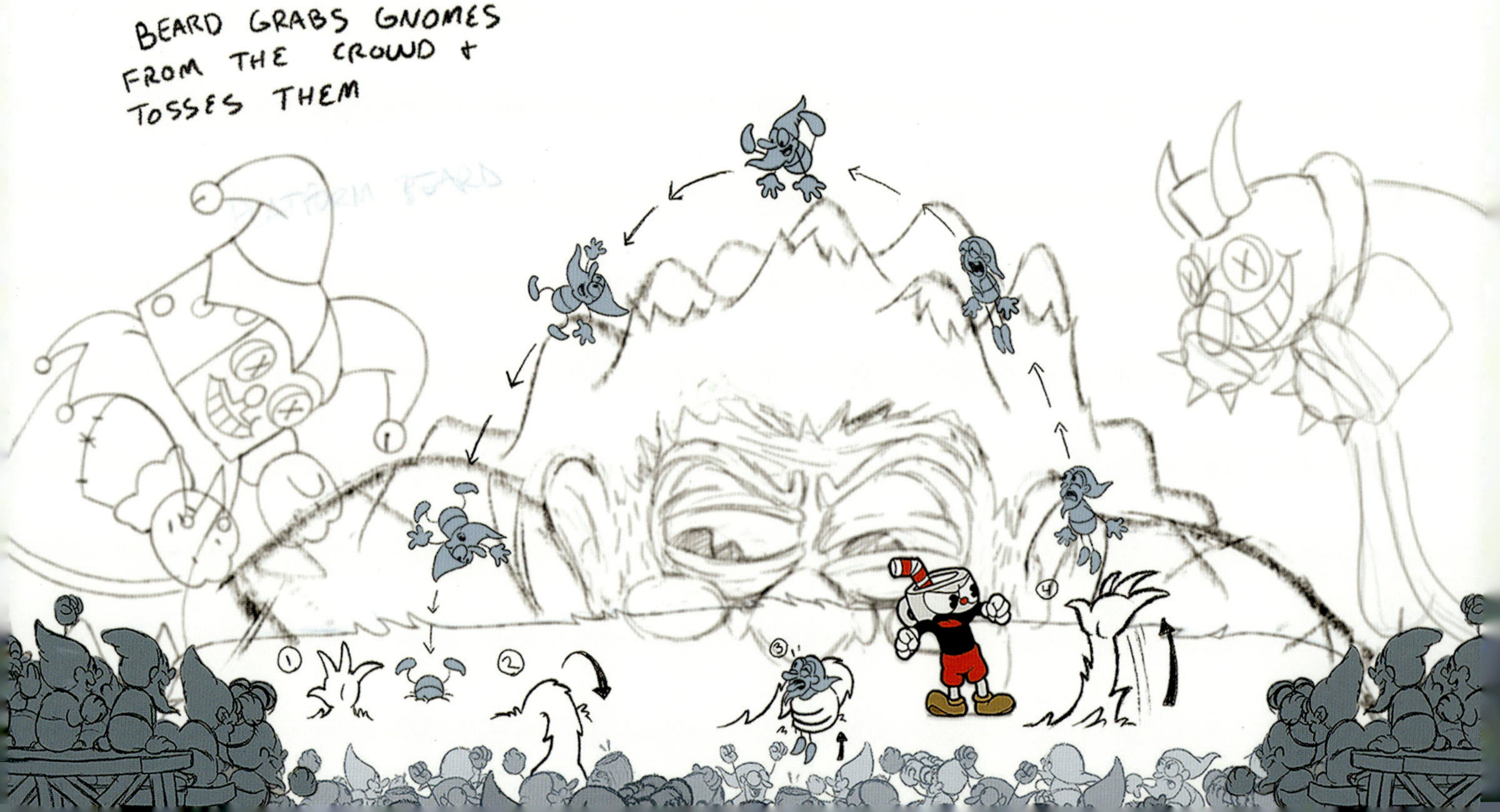

BEARD GRABS GNOMES FROM THE CROWD + TOSSES THEM

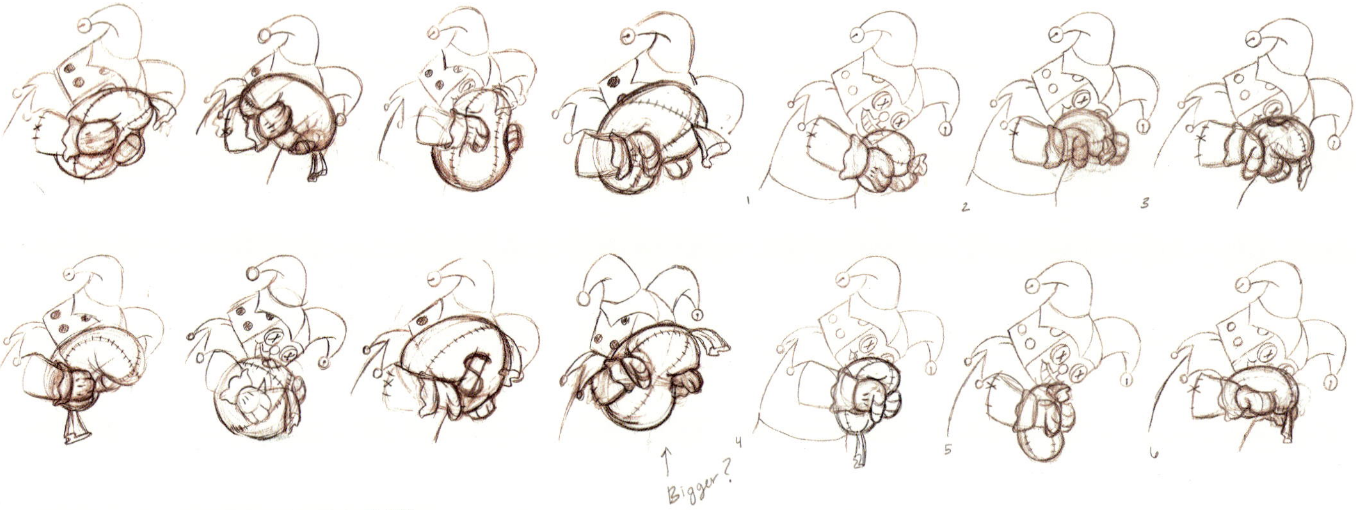

↑ Bigger?

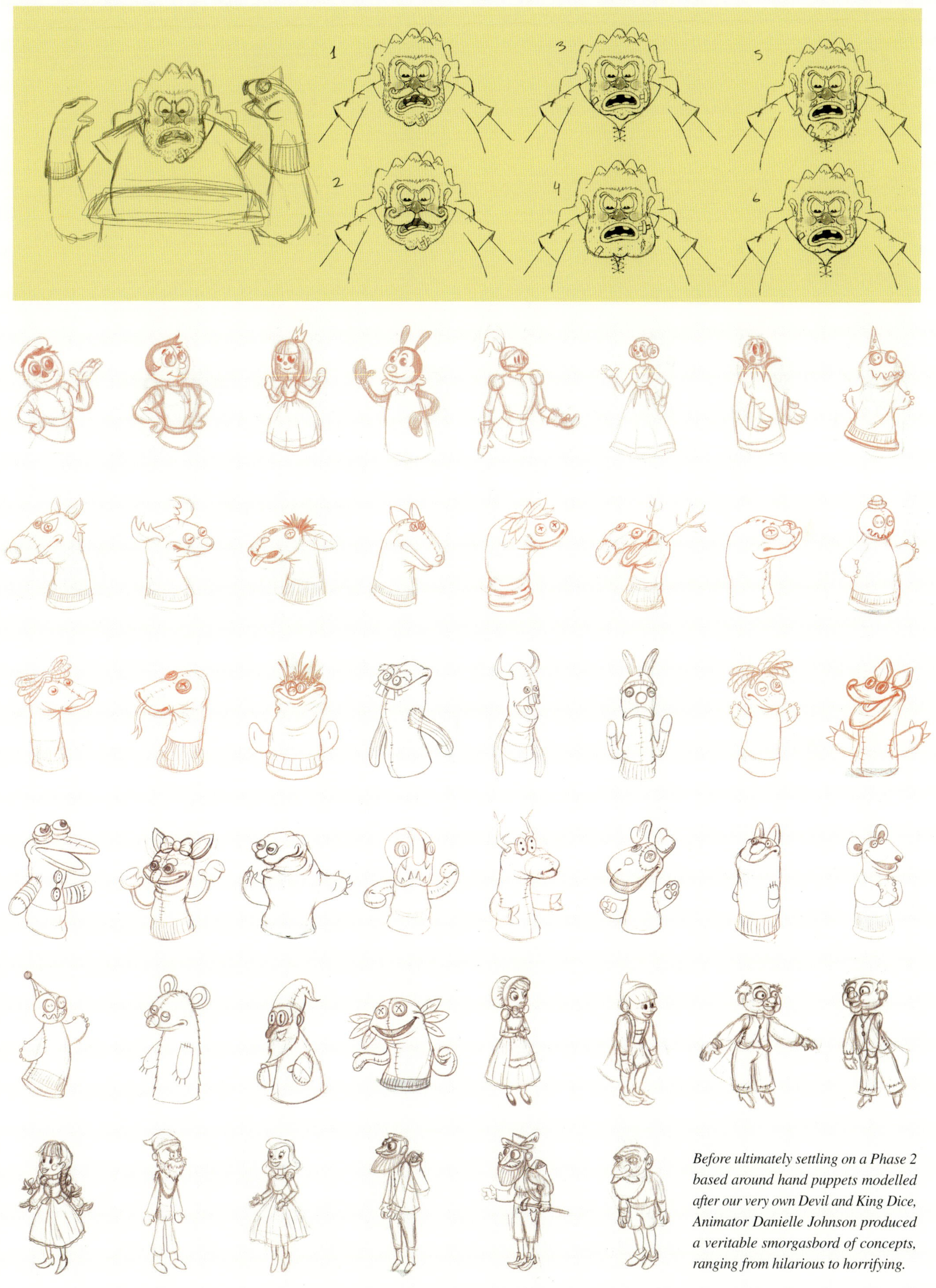

Before ultimately settling on a Phase 2 based around hand puppets modelled after our very own Devil and King Dice, Animator Danielle Johnson produced a veritable smorgasbord of concepts, ranging from hilarious to horrifying.

Planning and executing a big phase transition, like the one into the Glumstone's stomach, requires a delicate dance between art, design, and programming. Great pains went into finding a visually compelling way for the giant to eat Cuphead and pals while not removing control from our players–something we're very mindful in a game filled with as much frenetic action as ours.

See below for an ultimately unused concept from Illustrator Lance Inkwell in which Glumstone would have picked up the stage and dumped its contents (you included) down the hatch!

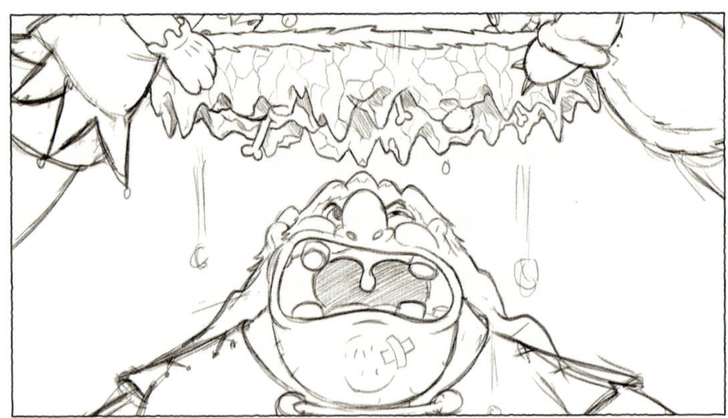

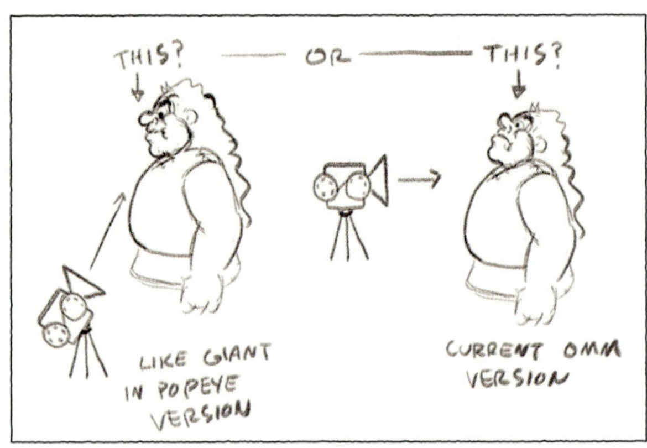

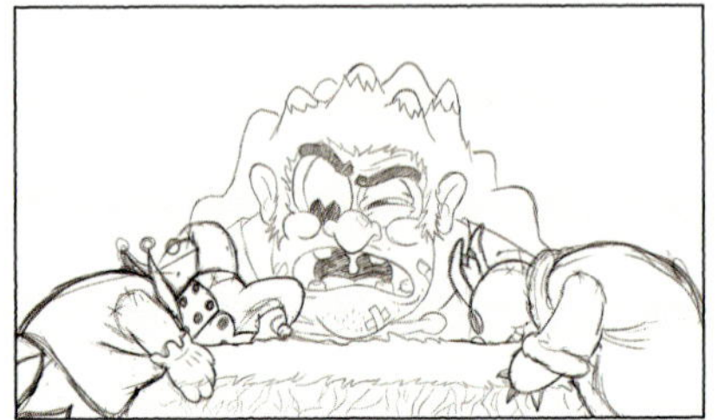

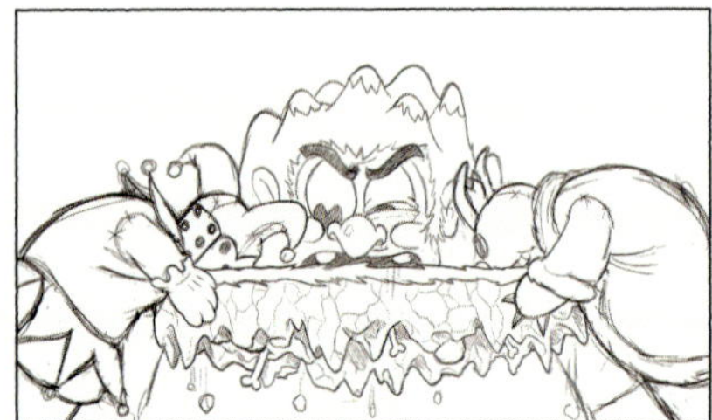

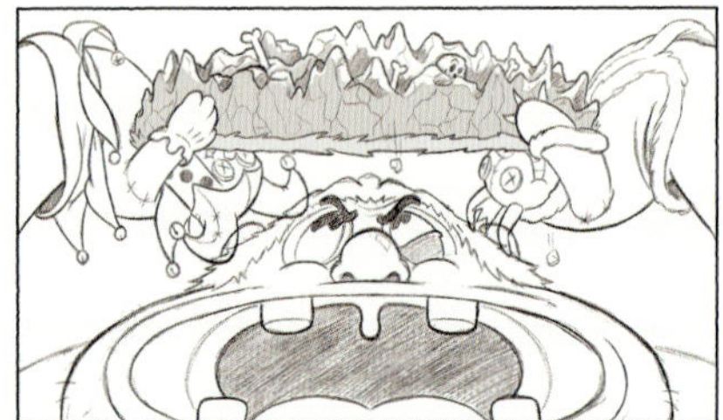

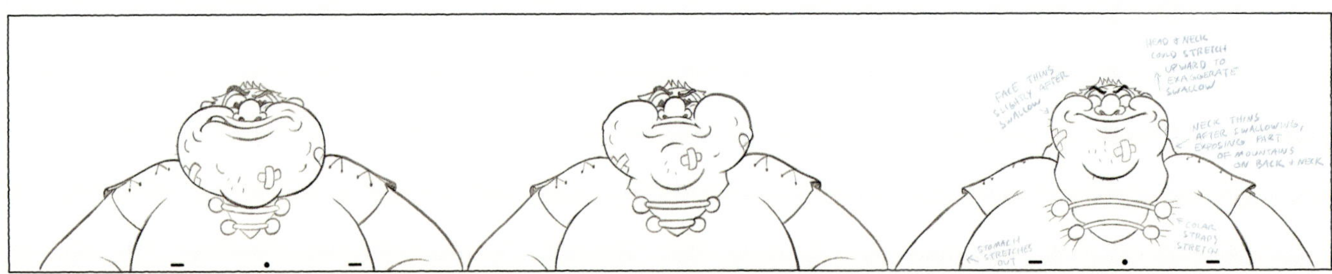

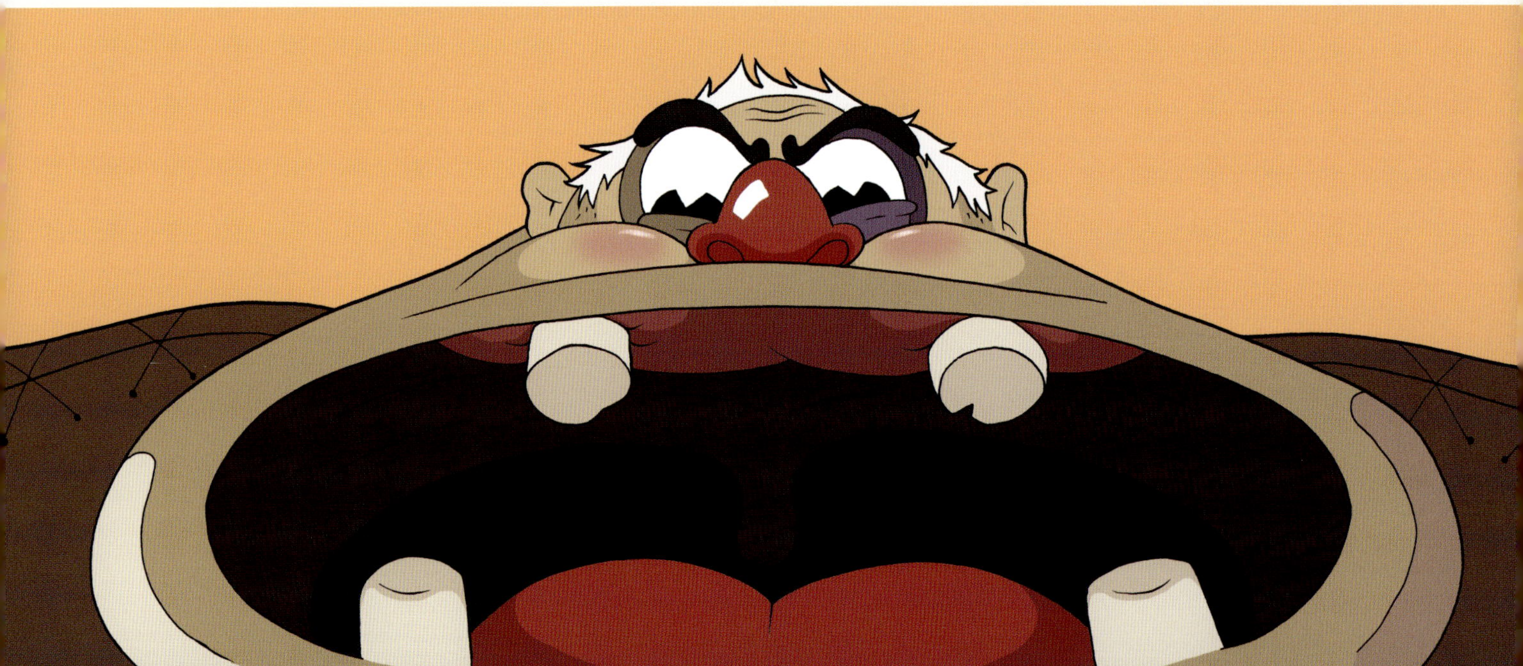

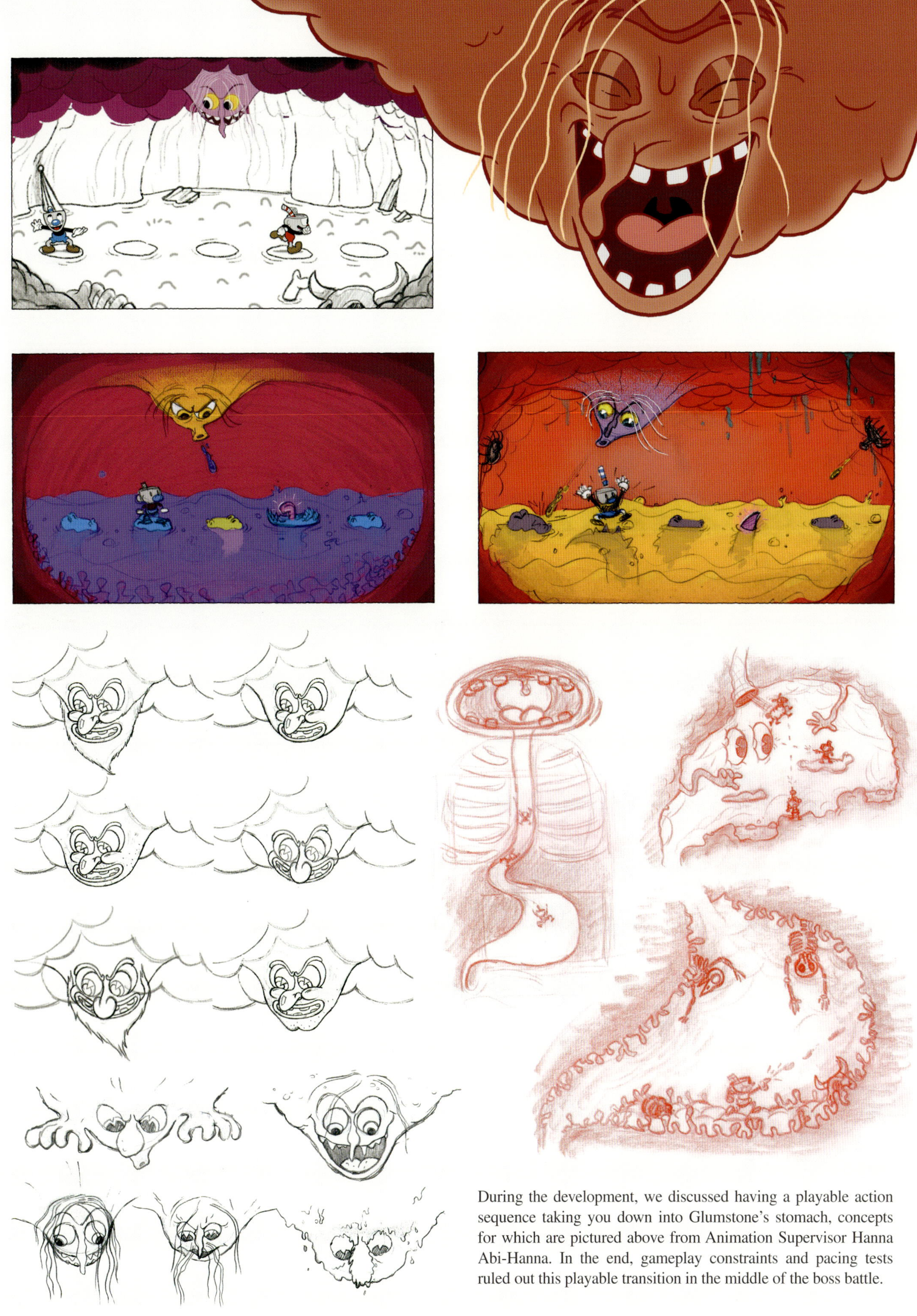

During the development, we discussed having a playable action sequence taking you down into Glumstone's stomach, concepts for which are pictured above from Animation Supervisor Hanna Abi-Hanna. In the end, gameplay constraints and pacing tests ruled out this playable transition in the middle of the boss battle.

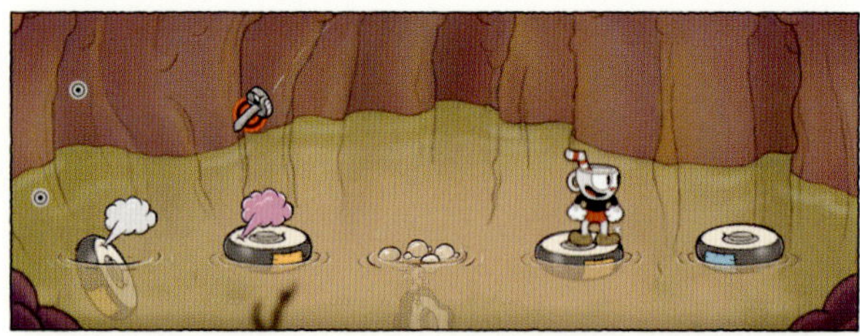

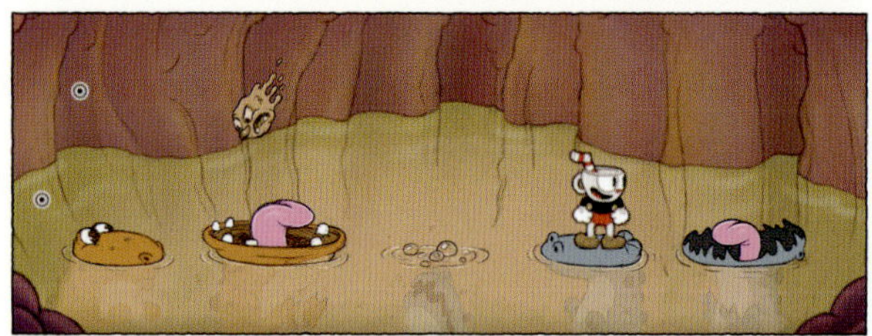

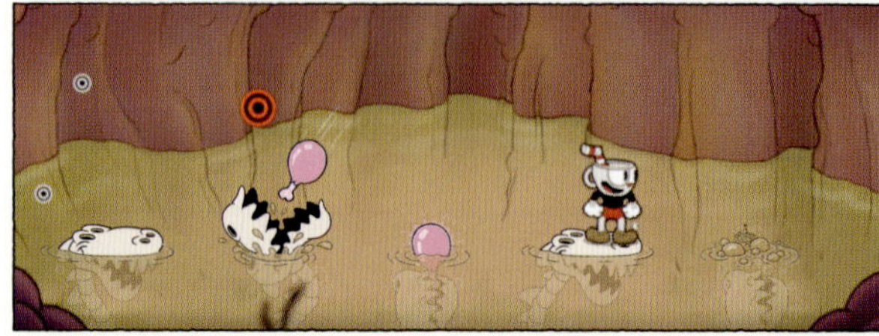

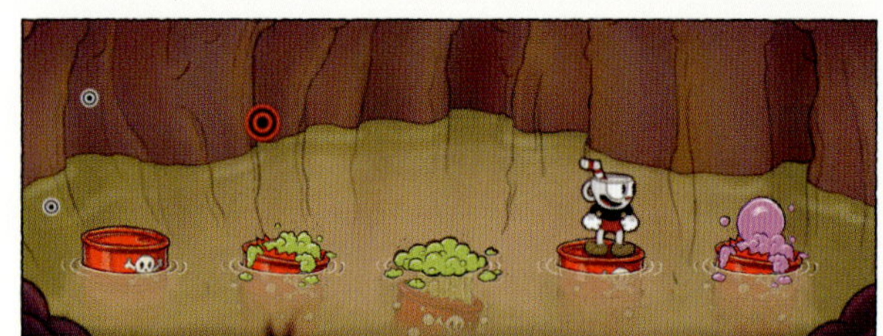

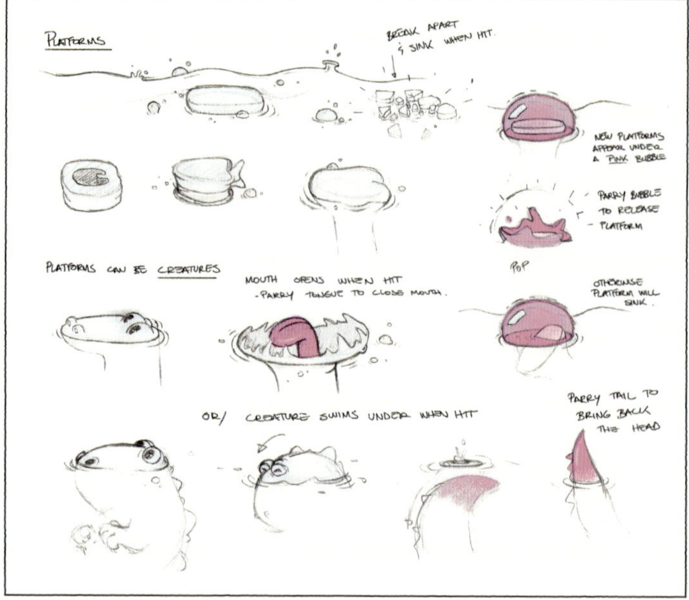

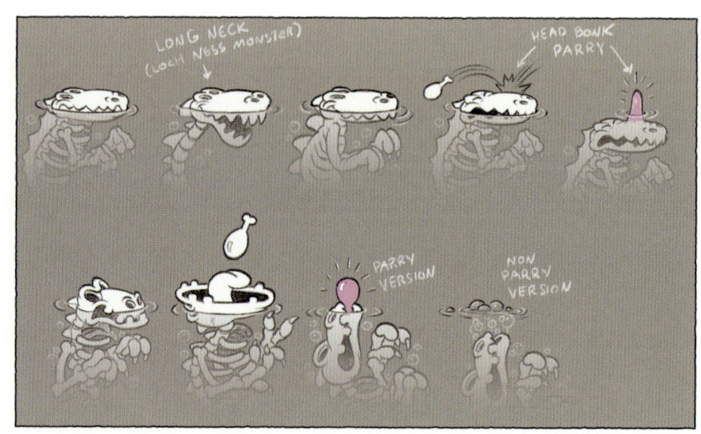

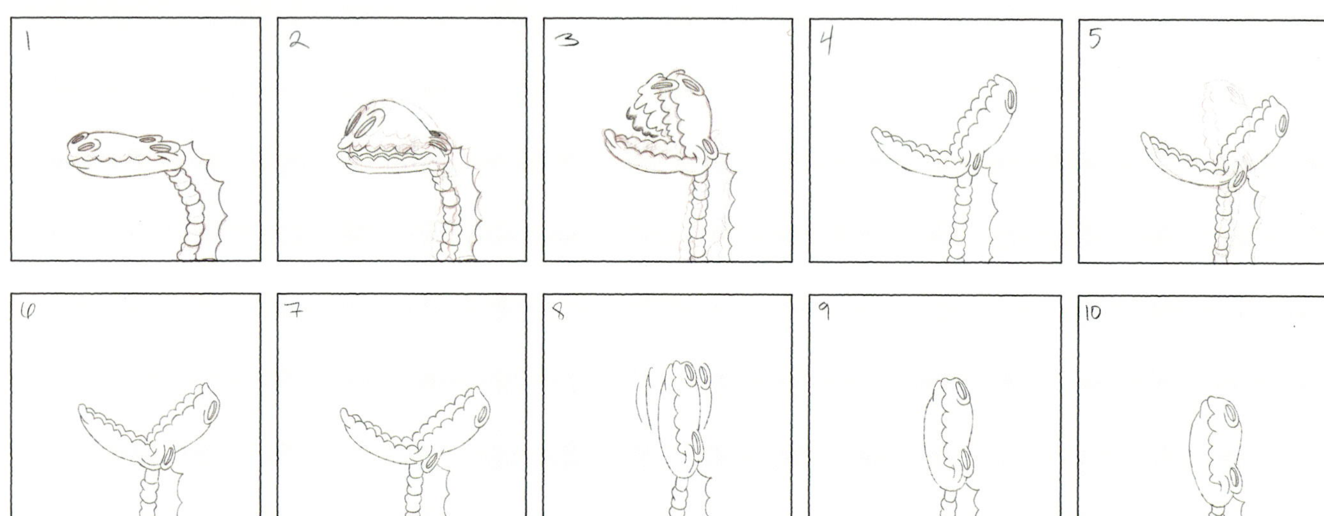

At the heart of thirties and forties toons is a quality we like to call "nightmare cute"–that razor's edge between adorable and eerie. Keeping on this theme, we springboarded from concepts (seen above) by Animation Supervisor Hanna Abi-Hanna to refine a design for platforms made from "bone salamanders"–nightmare cute creatures that might be the remains of something Glumstone ate, but are nonetheless content to power their giant keeper's digestion.

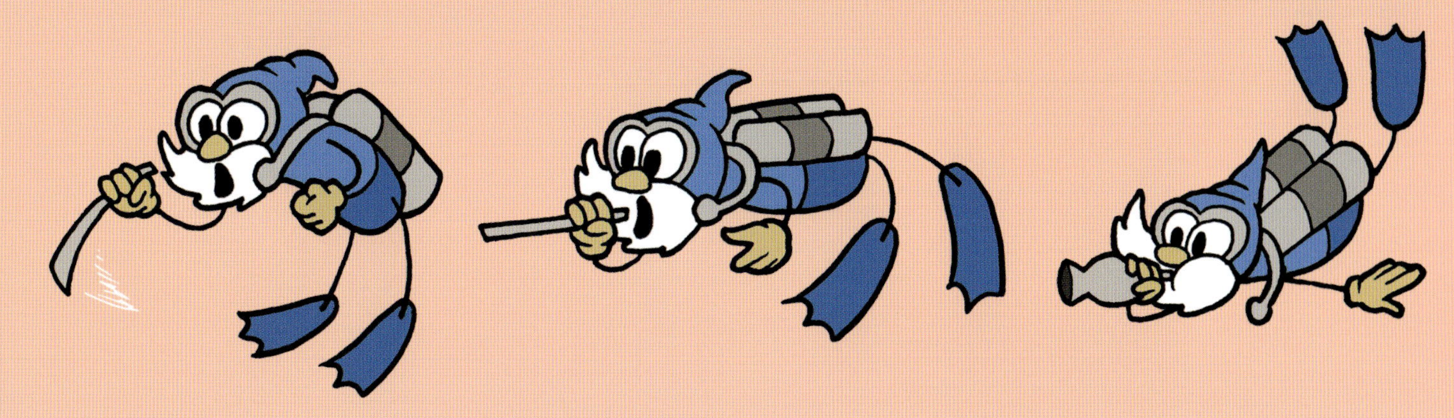

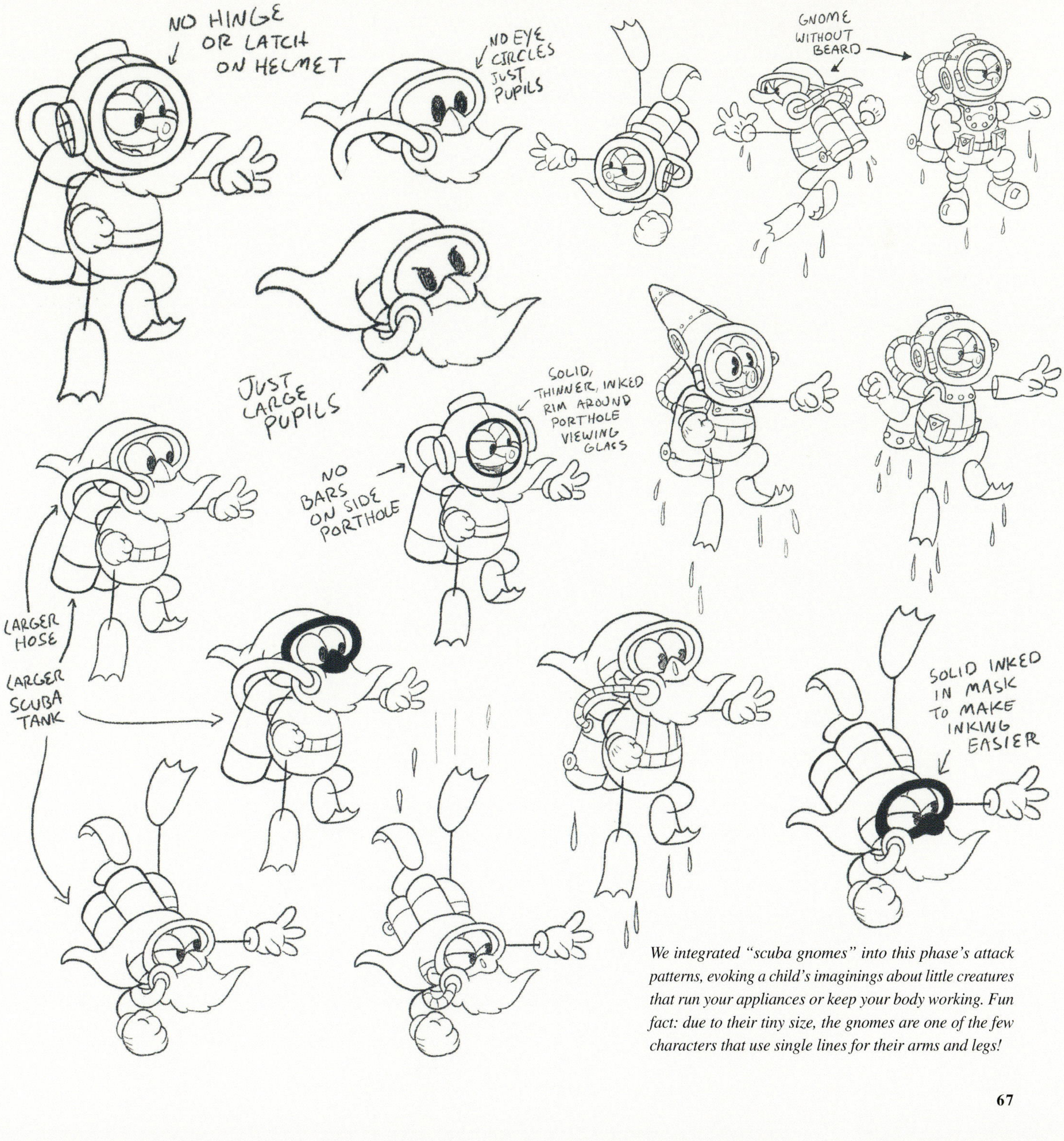

We integrated "scuba gnomes" into this phase's attack patterns, evoking a child's imaginings about little creatures that run your appliances or keep your body working. Fun fact: due to their tiny size, the gnomes are one of the few characters that use single lines for their arms and legs!

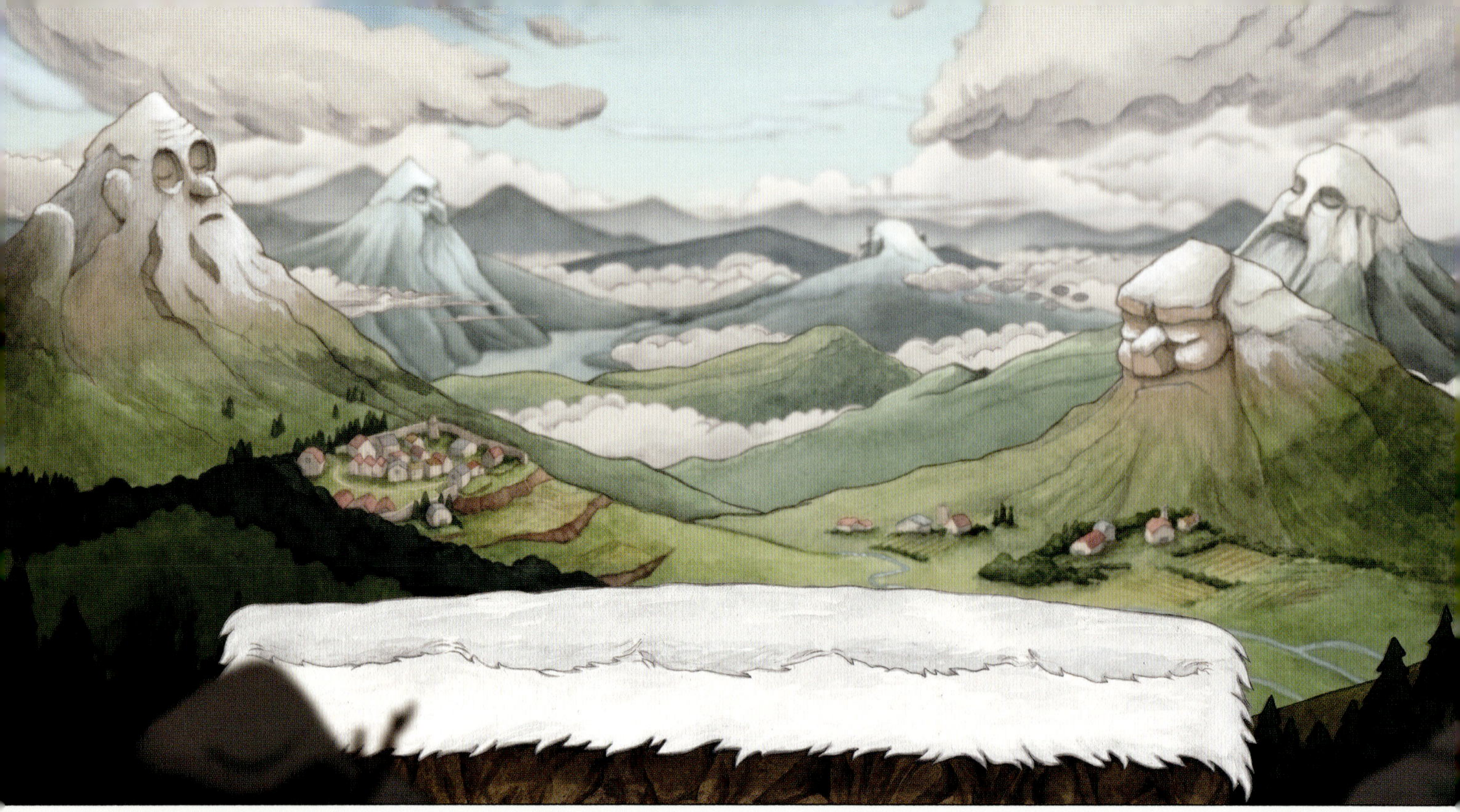

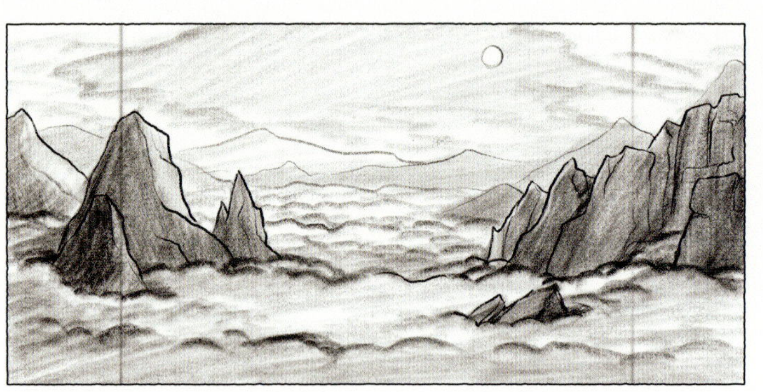

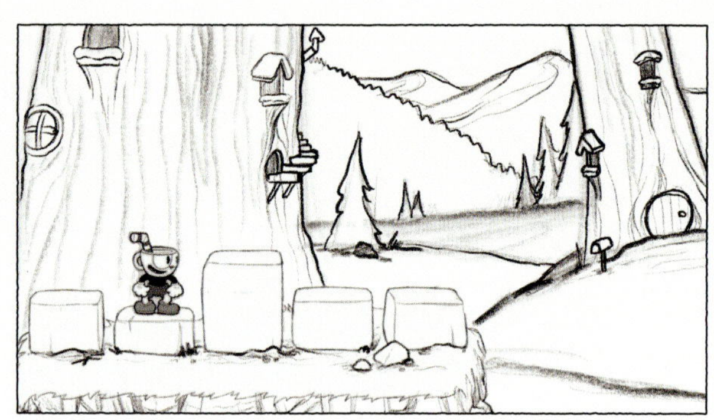

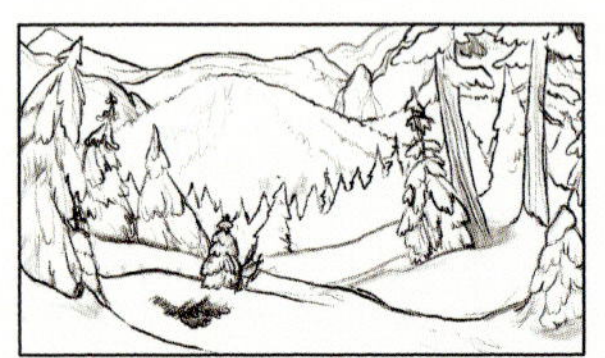

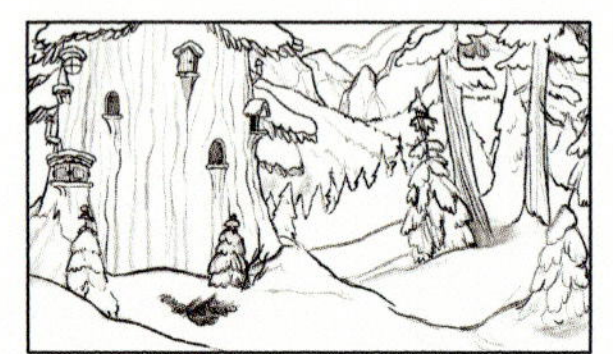

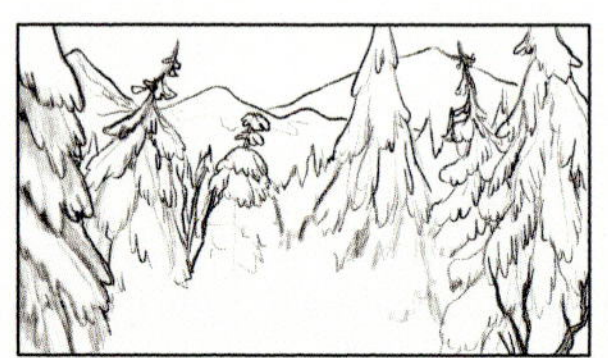

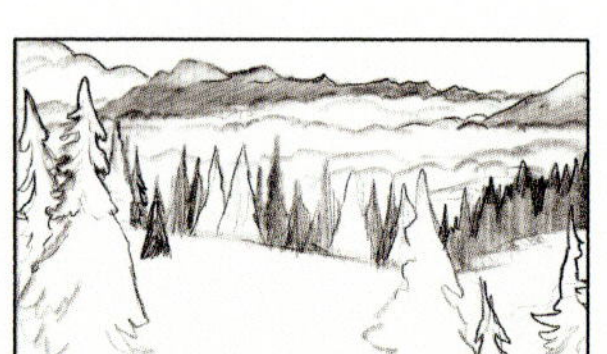

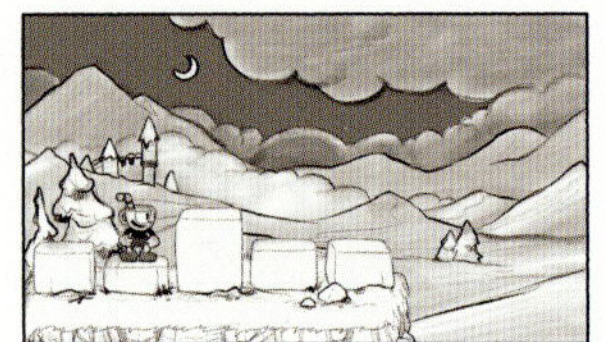

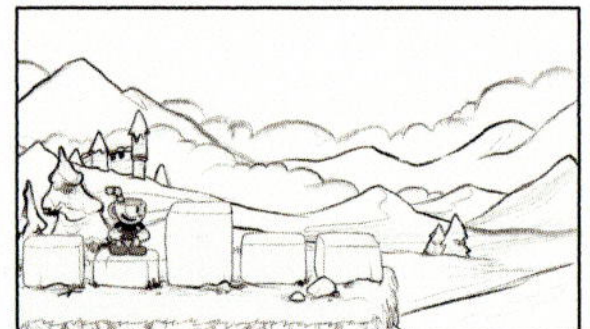

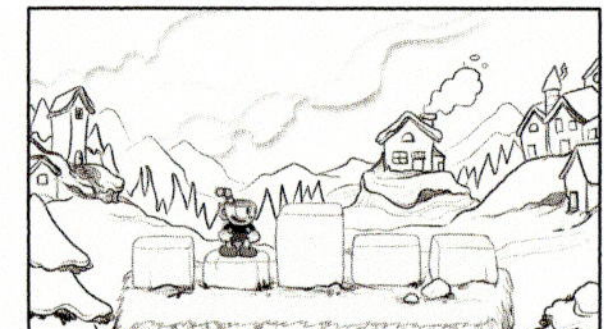

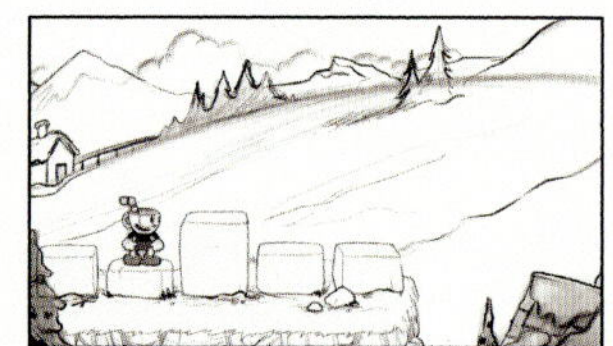

Gnome Way Out Background

ONE OF THE KEY CHALLENGES faced by Background Painter Caitlin Russell as she brought the scenery for Gnome Way Out to life was the process of capturing the size of Glumstone himself. As seen in early concept experiments above, ideas ran the gamut from a gnome-filled forest to a bucolic hilly field. The key ended up being threading the needle between too low lying an environment, and one so high it felt divorced from the landscape Glumstone was a part of.

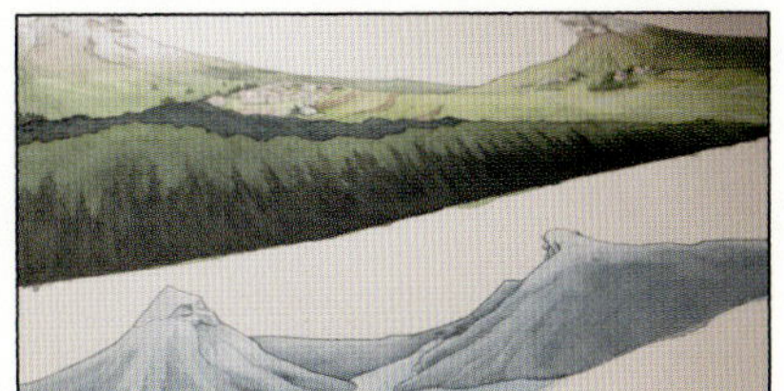

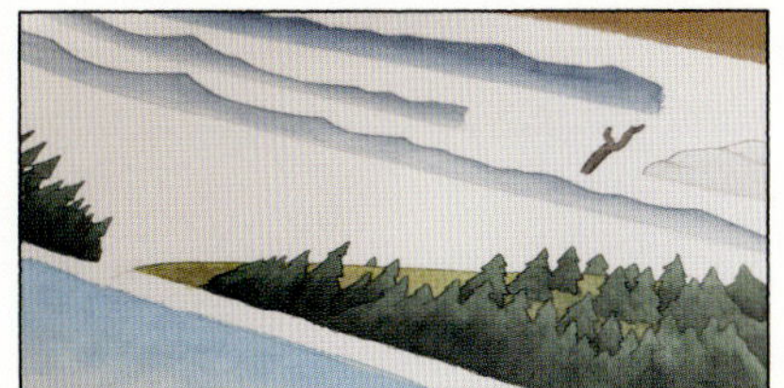

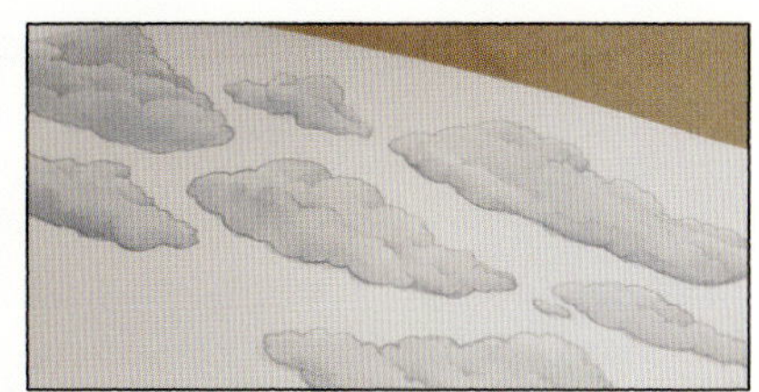

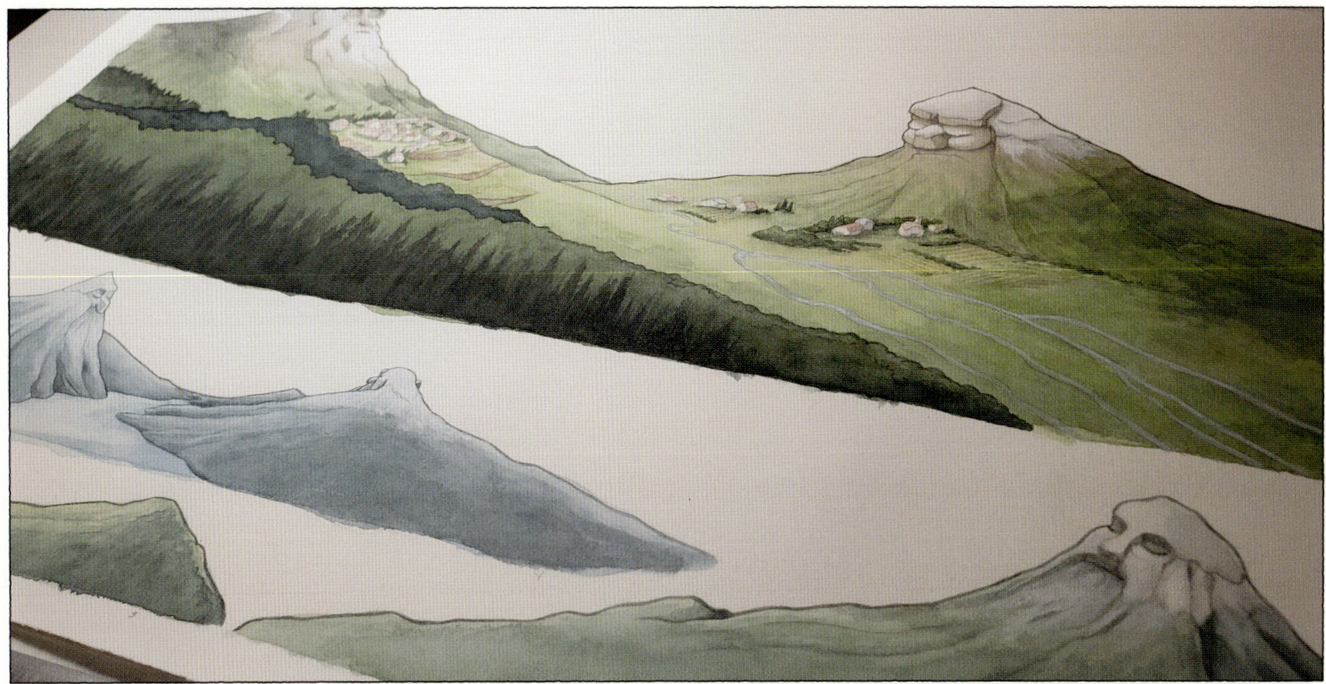

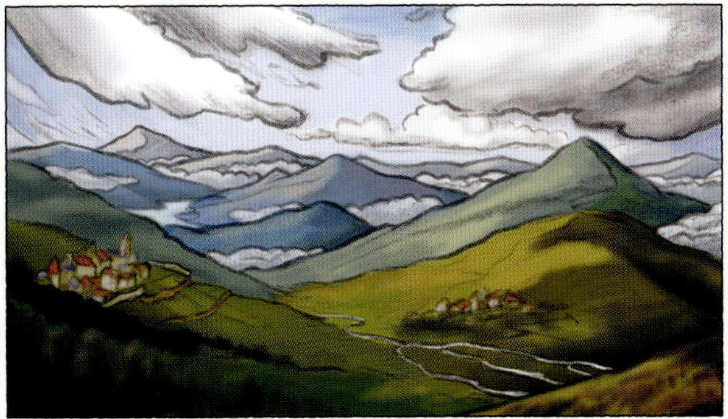

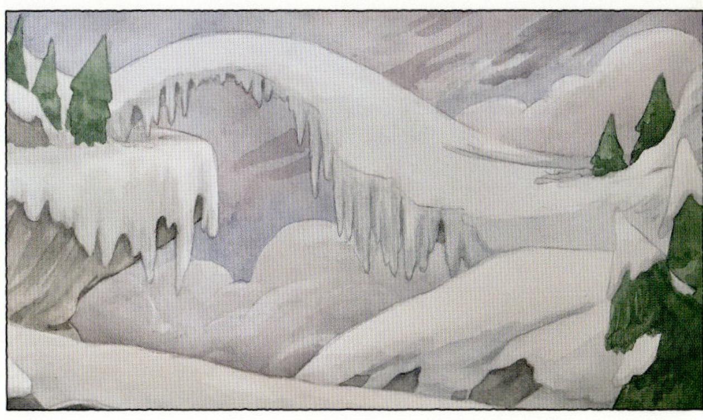

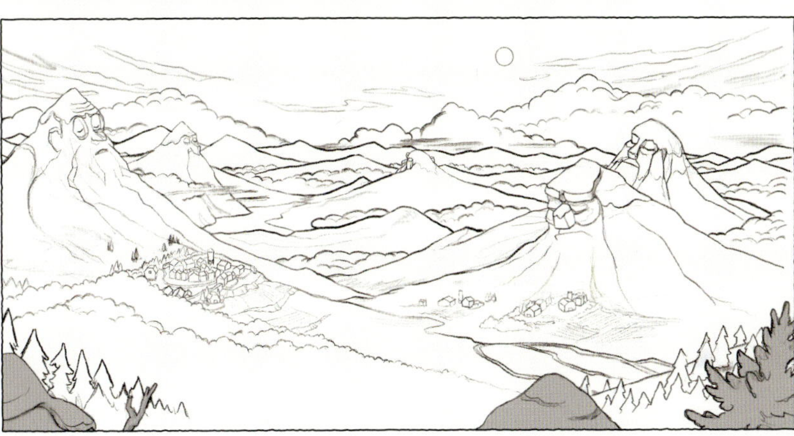

Left: this linear from Background Painter Caitlin Russell reveals the key breakthrough that solved this concept–the inclusion of an implied race of mountain giants that gave a sense of mystery and grandeur to the stage.

In animation, a "boil" is the effect created when multiple drawings of the same line are created and played back in sequence to create a visible wobble, giving the subject "life" while stationary. To create the eerie, off-putting undulation of Glumstone's stomach, Background Painter Caitlin Russell attempted our first and only "painted boil," creating three instances of all watercolor elements which warbled and rippled when layered atop one another. A whopping total of twenty-four individual paintings were layered at the top to create an unsettling undulation effect that animates as the boss's head moves! Meanwhile, the particular green coloring of the hazardous stomach acid was inspired by the iconic "Dead Pool" from *Mortal Kombat 2* (1993).

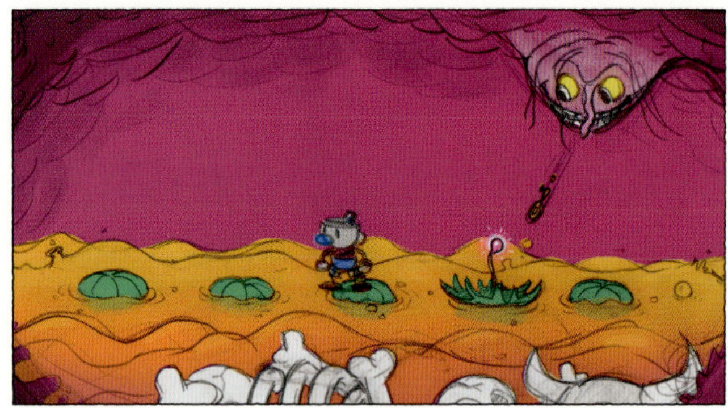

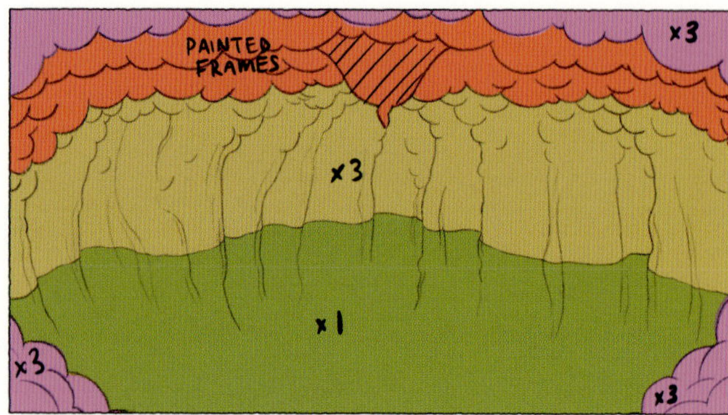

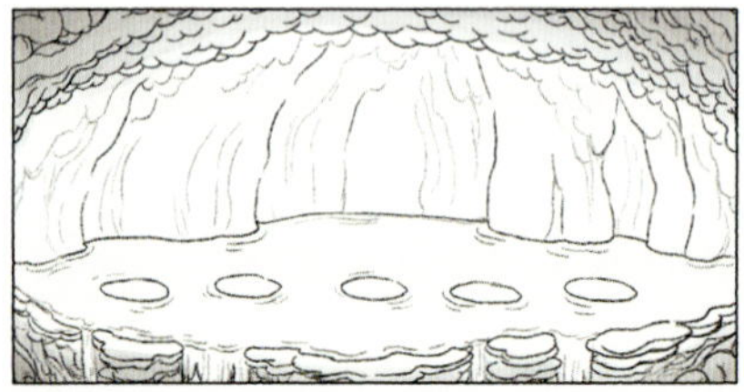

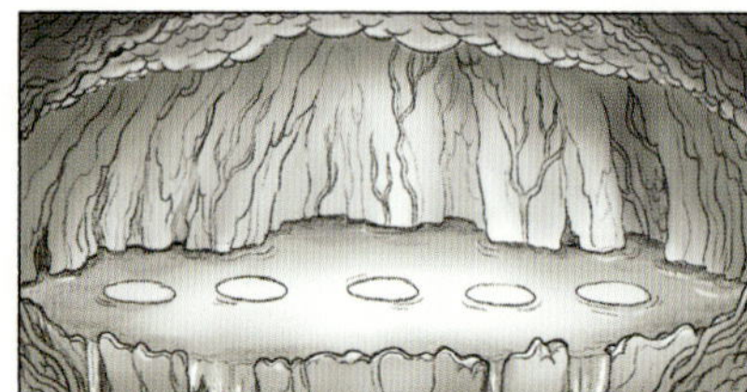

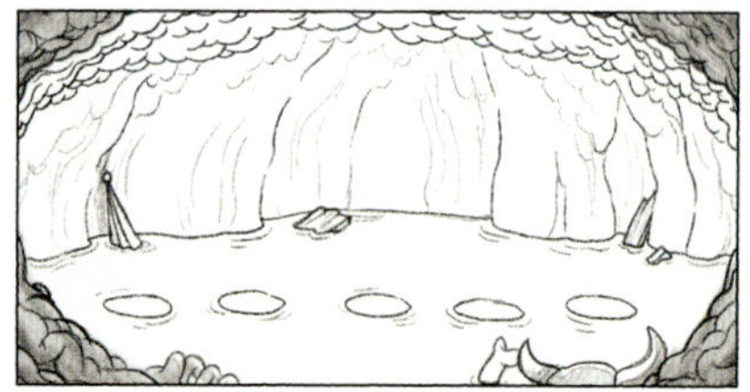

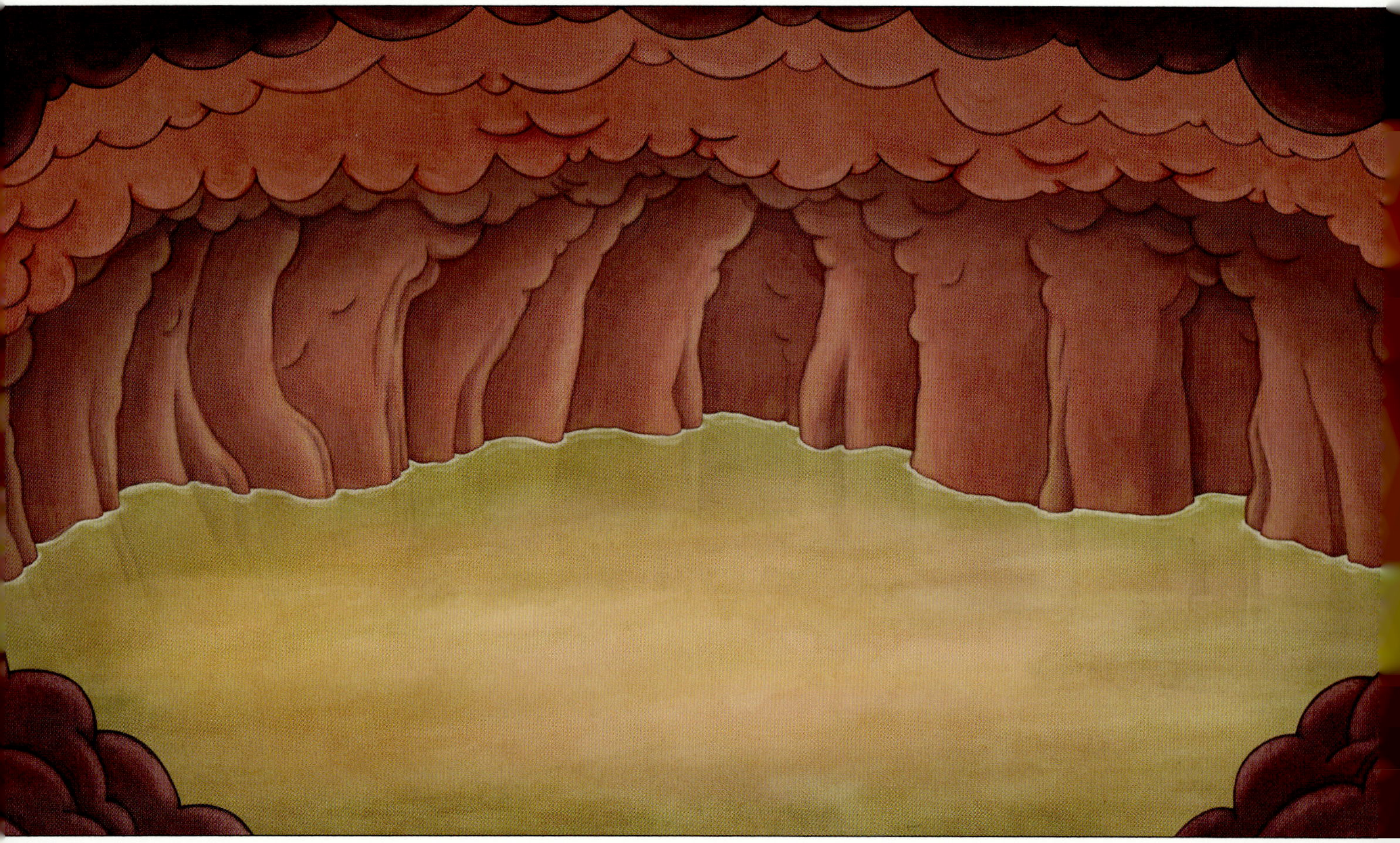

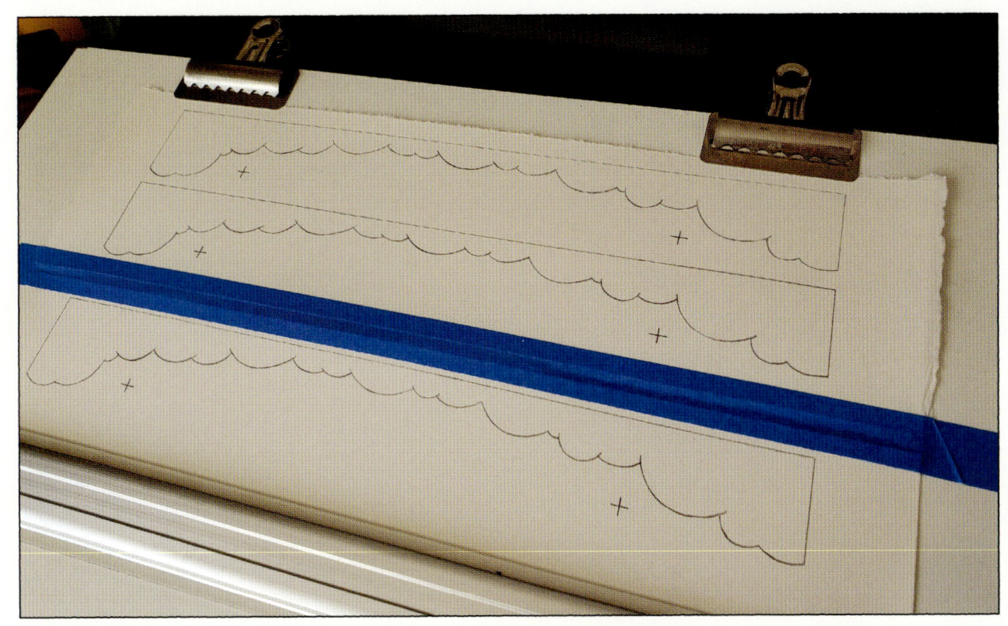

While seemingly identical at a glance, each hand-painted element of Glumstone's background had slight variance in color and gradient that contributed to the final "rippling" effect.

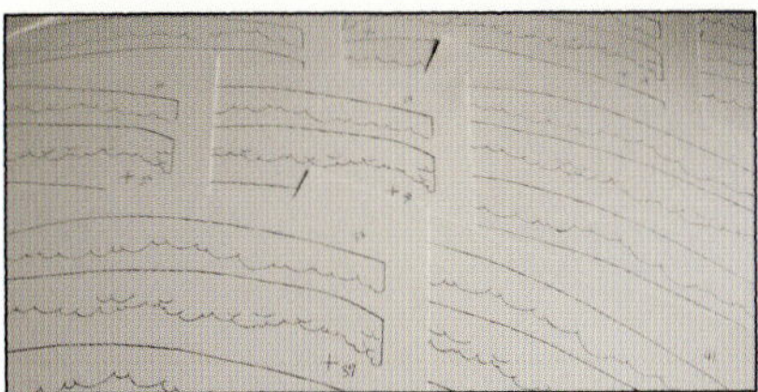

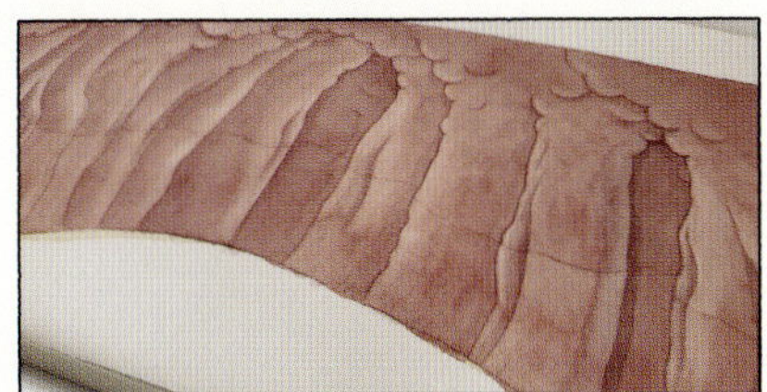

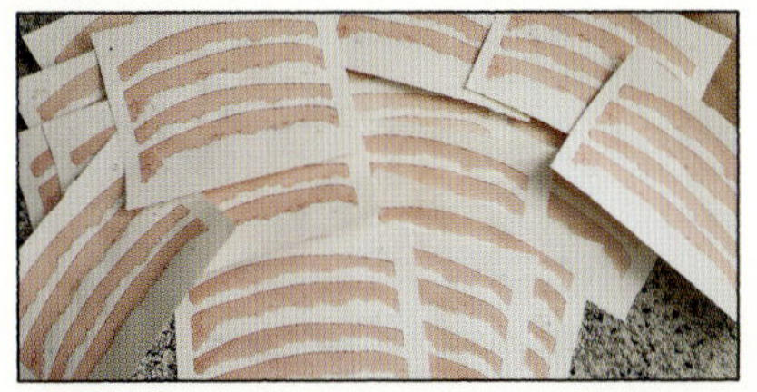

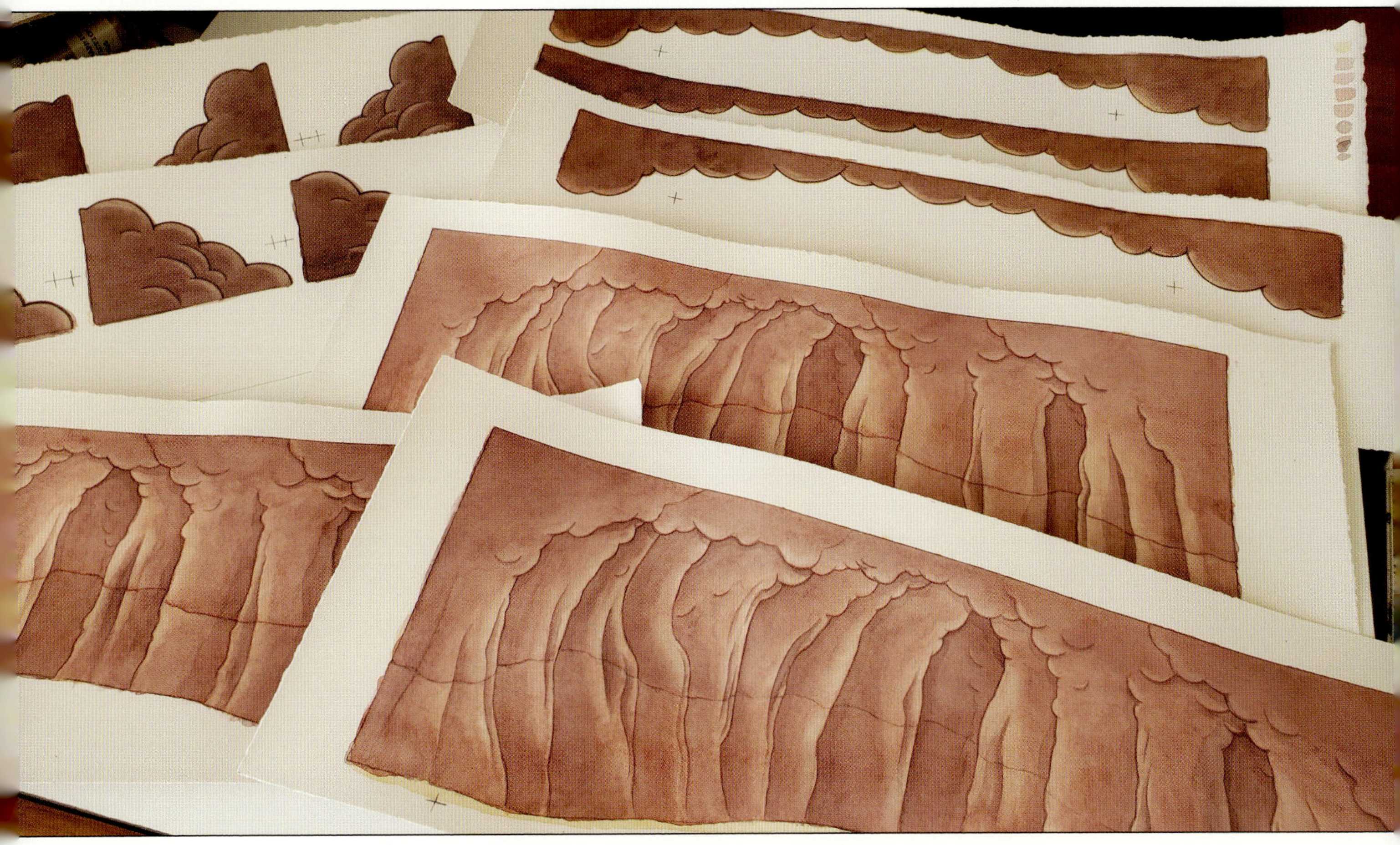

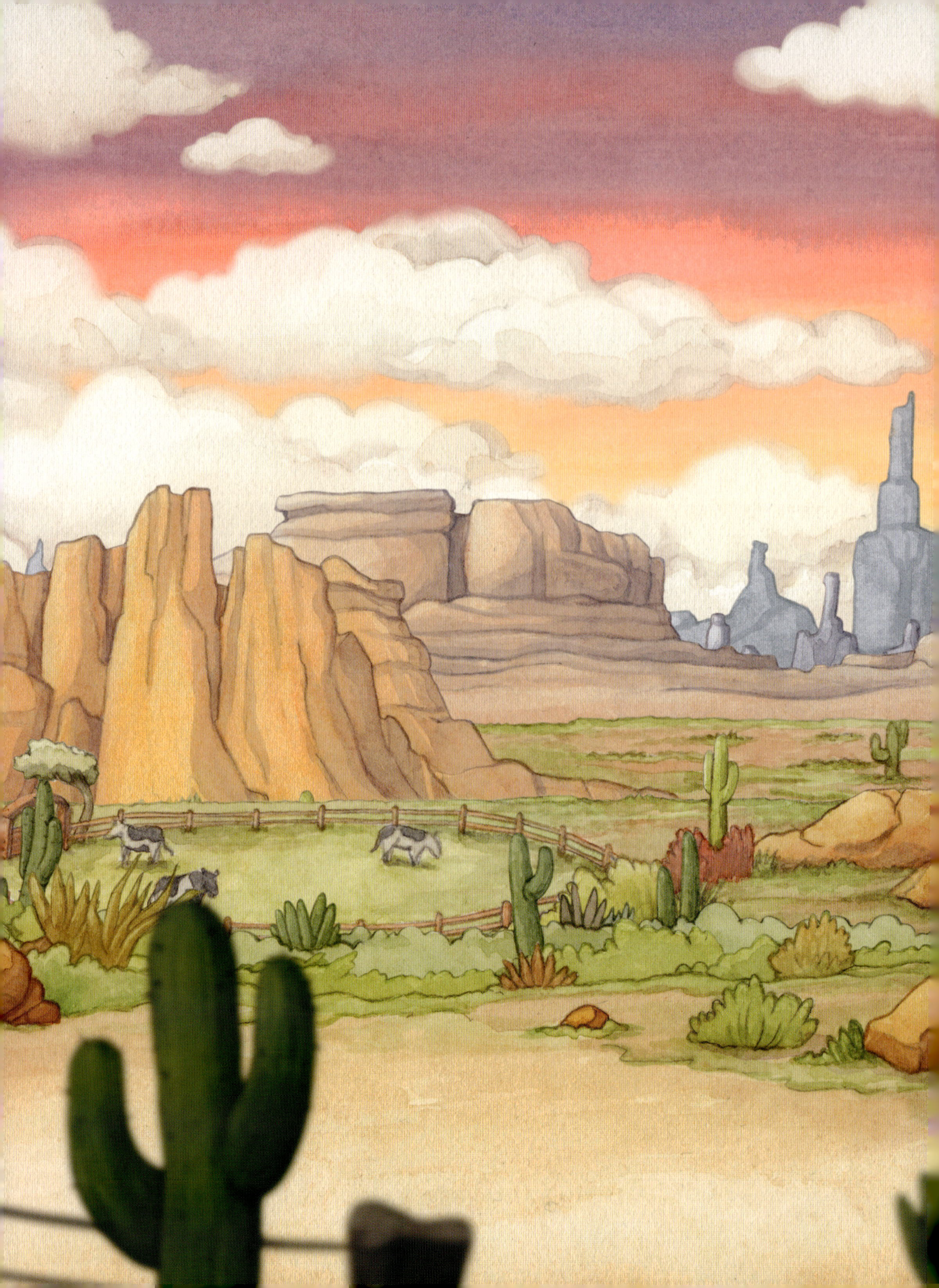

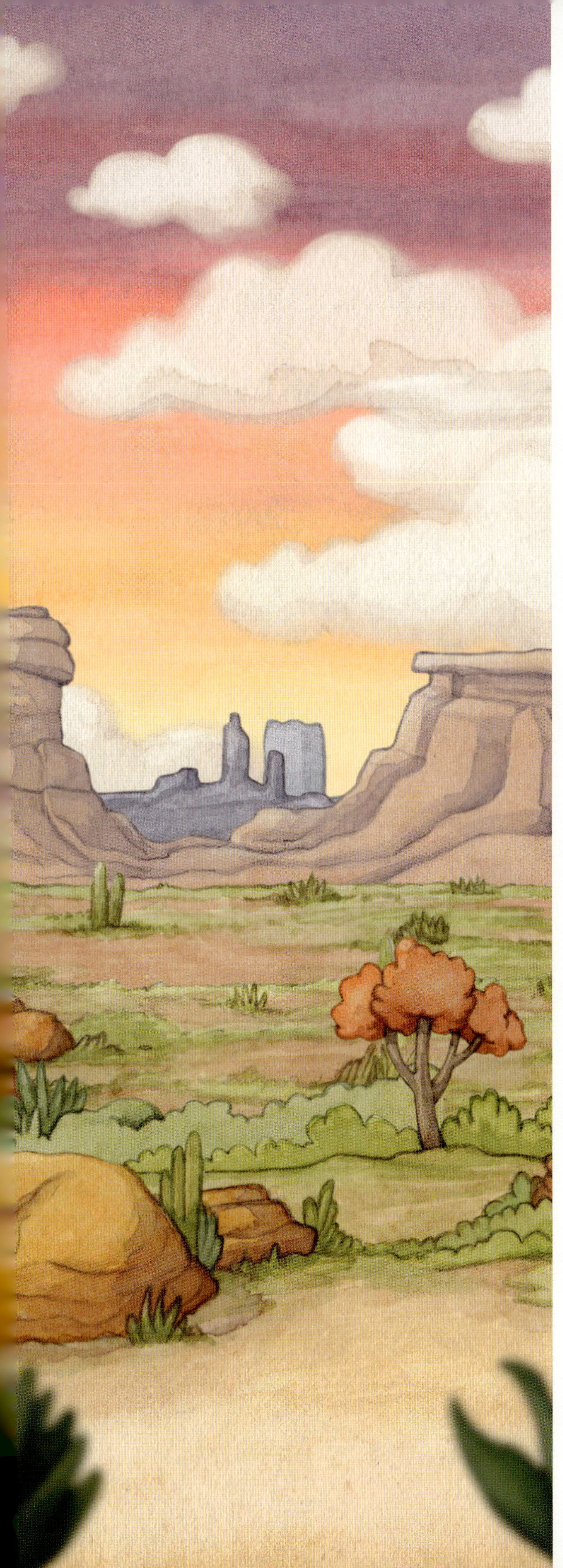

Chapter V:

High-Noon Hoopla

BEFORE *THE DELICIOUS LAST COURSE* centered around Chef Saltbaker and a quest for Ms. Chalice's life, the game was originally going to be about an island filled with outlaws, with each boss fight a way to slot in every remaining rubber-hose character theme we couldn't fit into the original game. Of those outlaws, we wanted to touch on the oft-tread 1930s cartoon barnyard scene, with our very own cowboy. Well, a cow, girl, cowgirl to be exact. The most rootin,' tootin,' six-shootin,' bank robbin' outlaw out to fend off any no-good varmints tryin' to steal her desert limes!

Esther Winchester's boss fight ended up coming together quite late in *DLC*'s development, going through a number of different iterations that had her doing everything from rumbling in a screen filling bar fight with a bunch of pigs to riding a giant cactus spouting pink flowers players had to parry back at her. Eventually the race through the desert came together, with our beefy buckaroo lassoing giant cacti and quick drawing whisky jugs full of snake oil, culminating in an evolution only possible in the weird world of *Cuphead*.

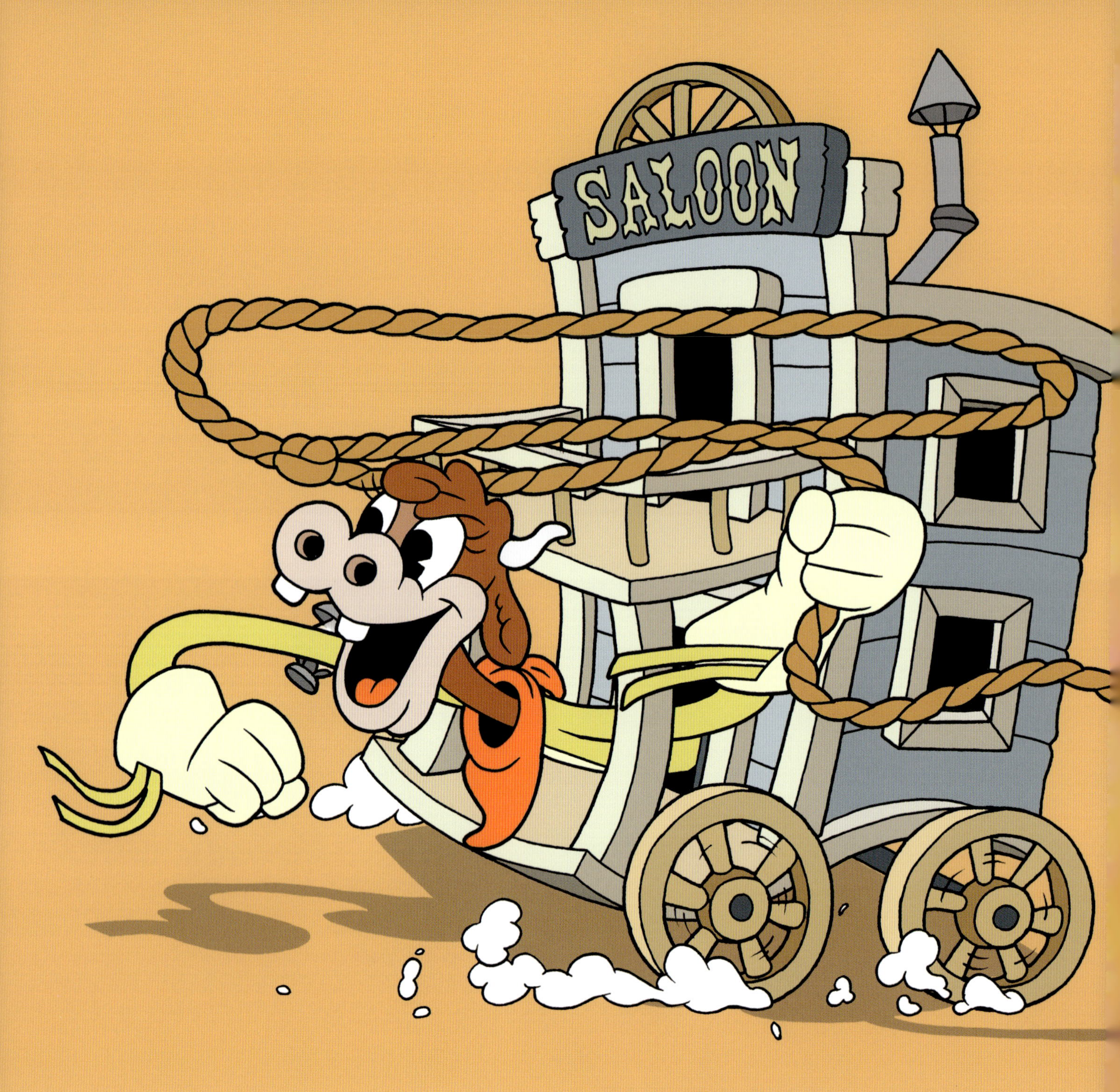

Esther Winchester in "HIGH-NOON HOOPLA"

As the final shoot 'em up battle created for *Cuphead*, we wanted to incorporate every possible Western-themed gag we could think of, sequenced through a visually-told storyline with a crescendo that was as much a surprise as it was a punchline. The original pitch was to have Esther and her supporting posse of outlaw pigs, careening through the desert in a ramshackle connected caravan, with each phase having her follow you from cart to cart, each with a different theme; a saloon, a stage show, a horse chase, etc. Multiple iterations of this concept were tried and eventually discarded, as their complexity and readability proved difficult to balance.

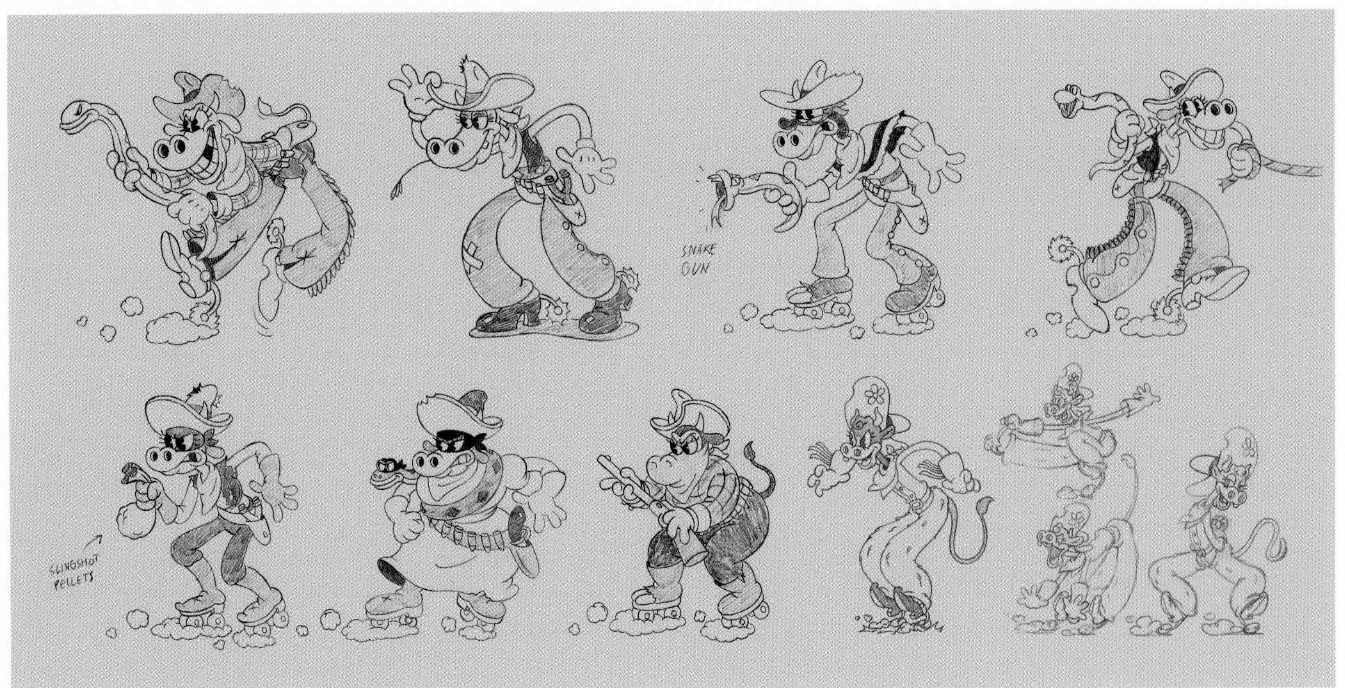

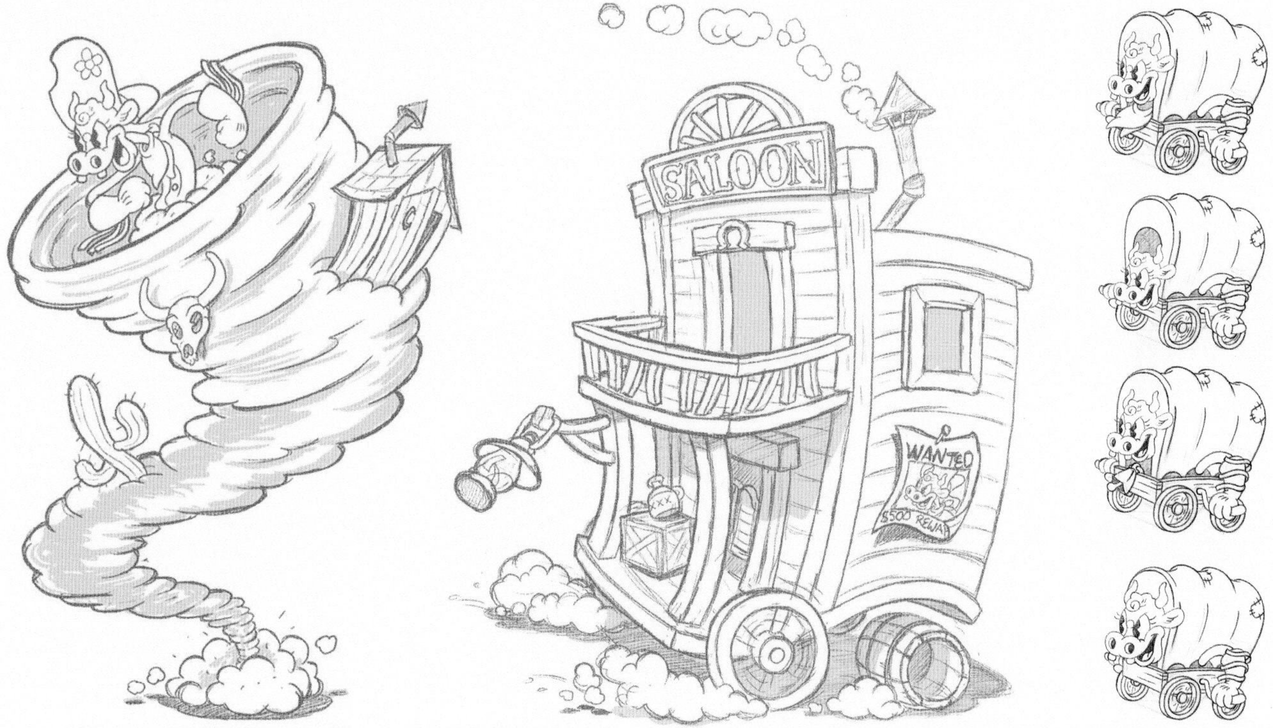

Going back to the drawing board, we decided to focus directly on Winchester herself for the visual theme and a simple gameplay concept: up and down. As each phase showcased Esther fervently fighting back as she is further flattened into foodstuffs, the interactive attacks would explore bifurcating the top and bottom halves of the screen with cartoon puns.

Early refinements of Esther's core character design were shaped by Animators Jake Clark and Joseph Coleman, with Concept Artist Lance Inkwell exploring different possibilities of her phase 1 core structure. While we eventually settled back on the rickety travelling saloon concept from the initial caravan pitch, early investigations into other possibilities encompassed everything from a shrinking and growing desert twister to a cart contraption that would elevate and descend on classic cartoon seesaw legs. The final saloon wagon proved to be an unanticipated animation challenge, though, with each frame of its basic idle requiring seventeen different layers to allow for the cowgirl to weave seamlessly in and out of it.

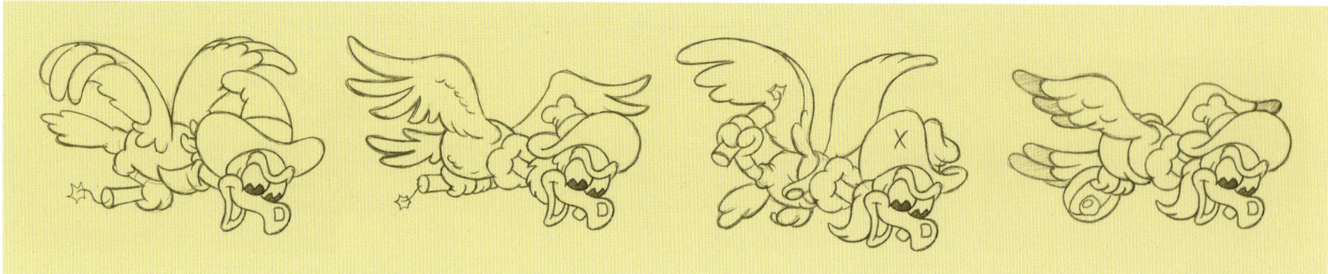

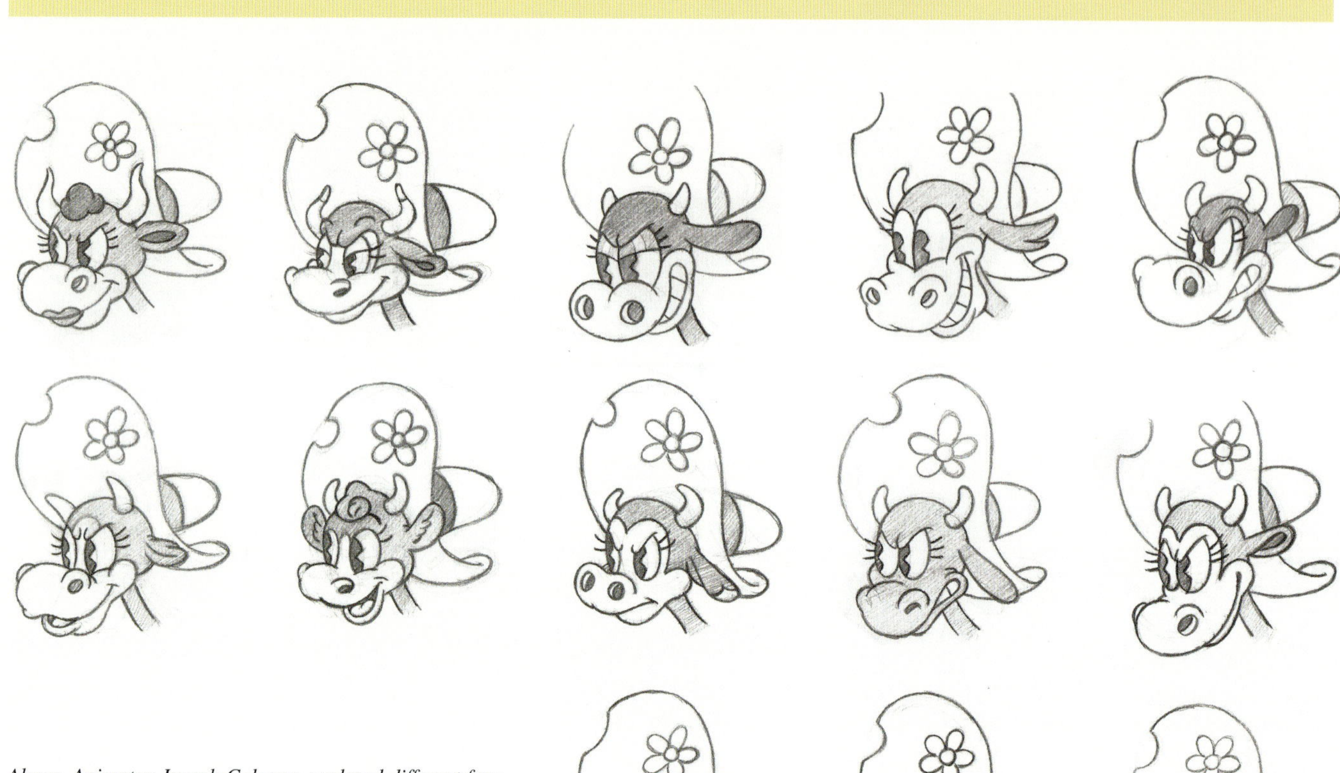

Above, Animator Joseph Coleman explored different face shapes for Esther to refine her tomboy personality to the perfect amount of mischief and charm. Below, Animator Patt Jewanarom illustrates the how the individual pieces of the saloon break down, seamlessly transitioning into phase 2.

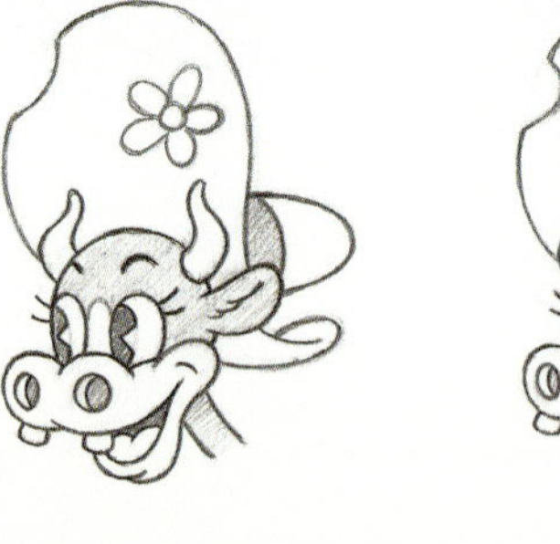

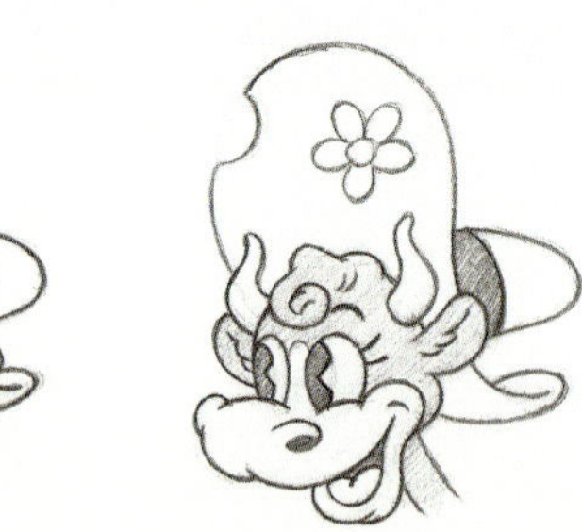

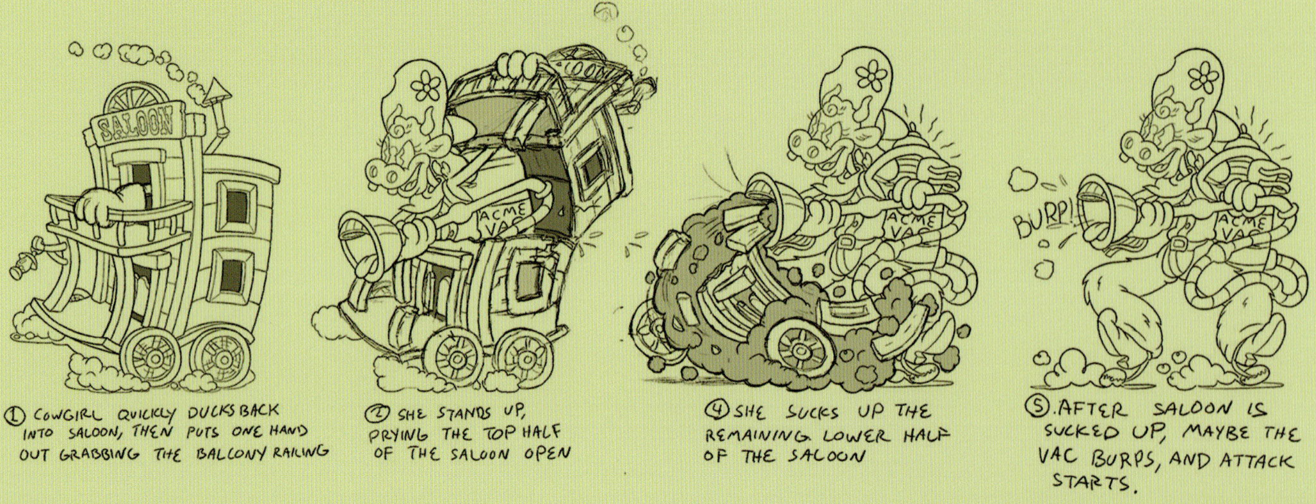

The gameplay concept for phase 2 was to be the inverse of the tried and true "bullet hell" patterns previously seen with Wally Warbles and Dr. Kahl, with the added complexity of the vacuum's pulling effect on the player. Seen below, we investigated a number of different possible "vacuums," eventually settling on wacky wide-mouthed contraption inspired by a similar device held by the protagonist from 1991's Data East arcade game, *Tumblepop*.

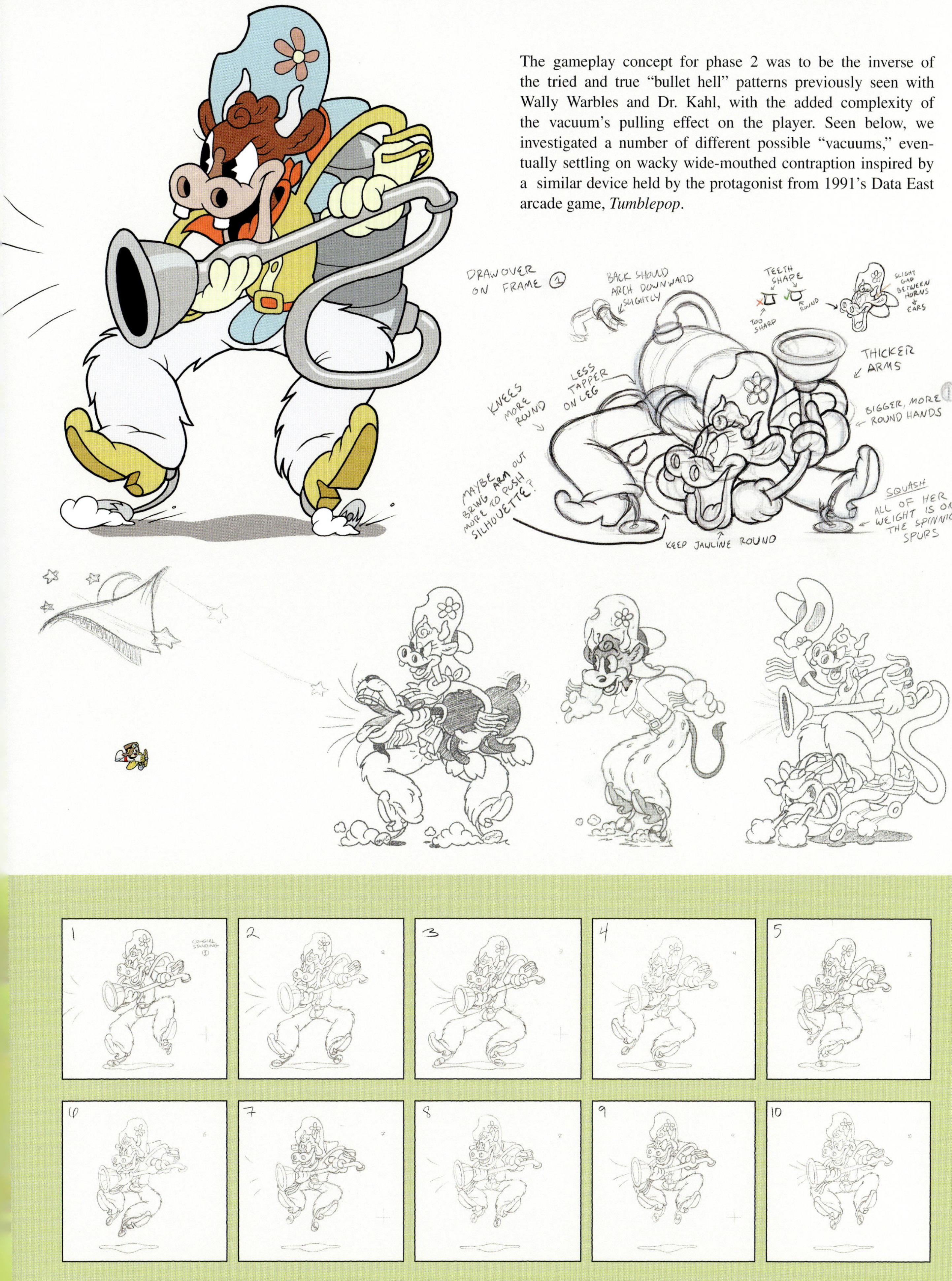

As the fight progresses and Esther's contraptions continue to foible her, we tried to toe the nineteen thirties' line of "horror-cute" while progressing her through the various stages of commercial meat production. To undercut the extreme nature of what's actually happening, Animator Jared Beckstrand has Esther react to the metamorphosis into meat the same way someone might react having just received a bad haircut. At bottom, Concept Artist Lance Inkwell details the how the vacuum pack transforms into a pressure cooker to initiate the transformation.

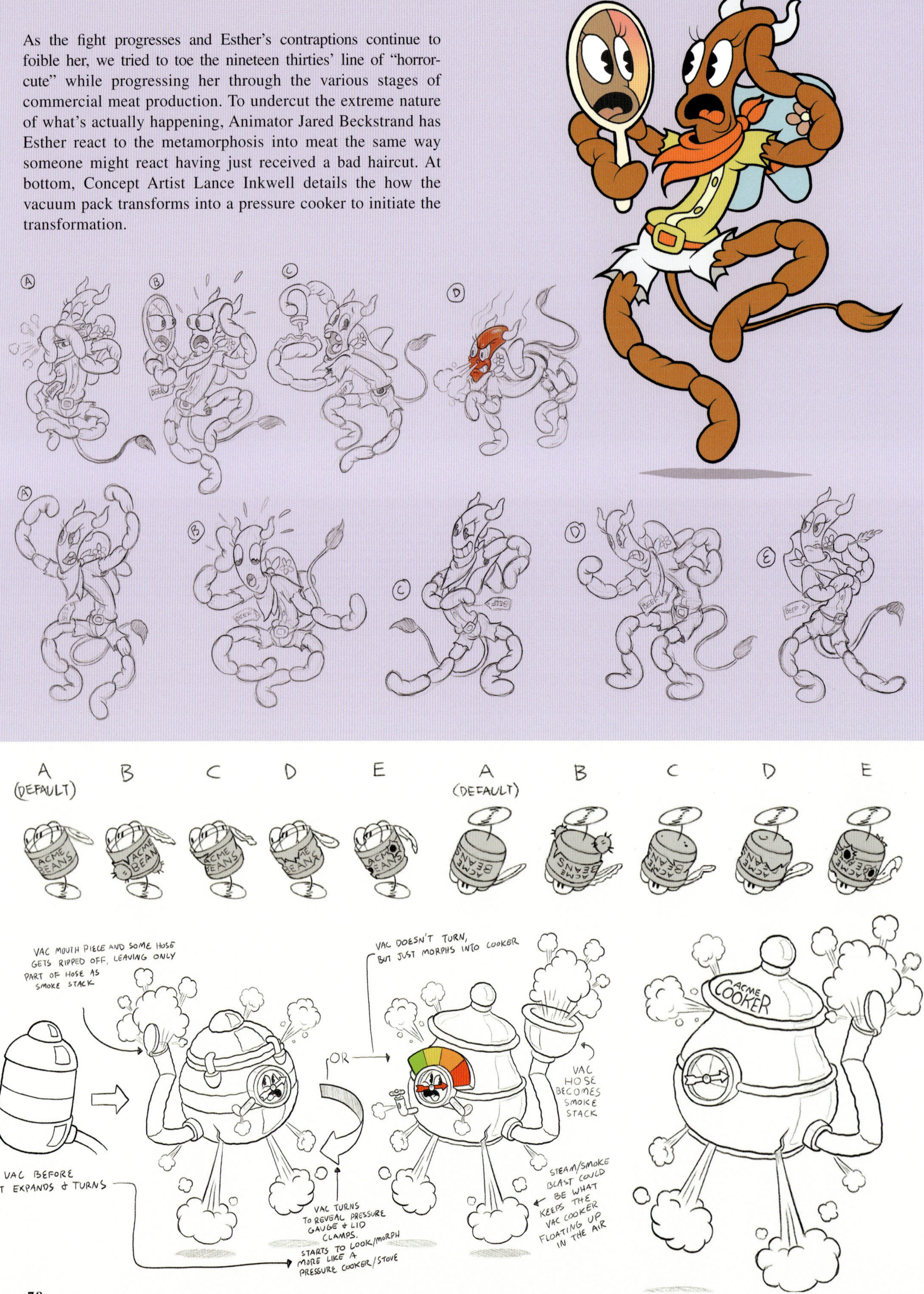

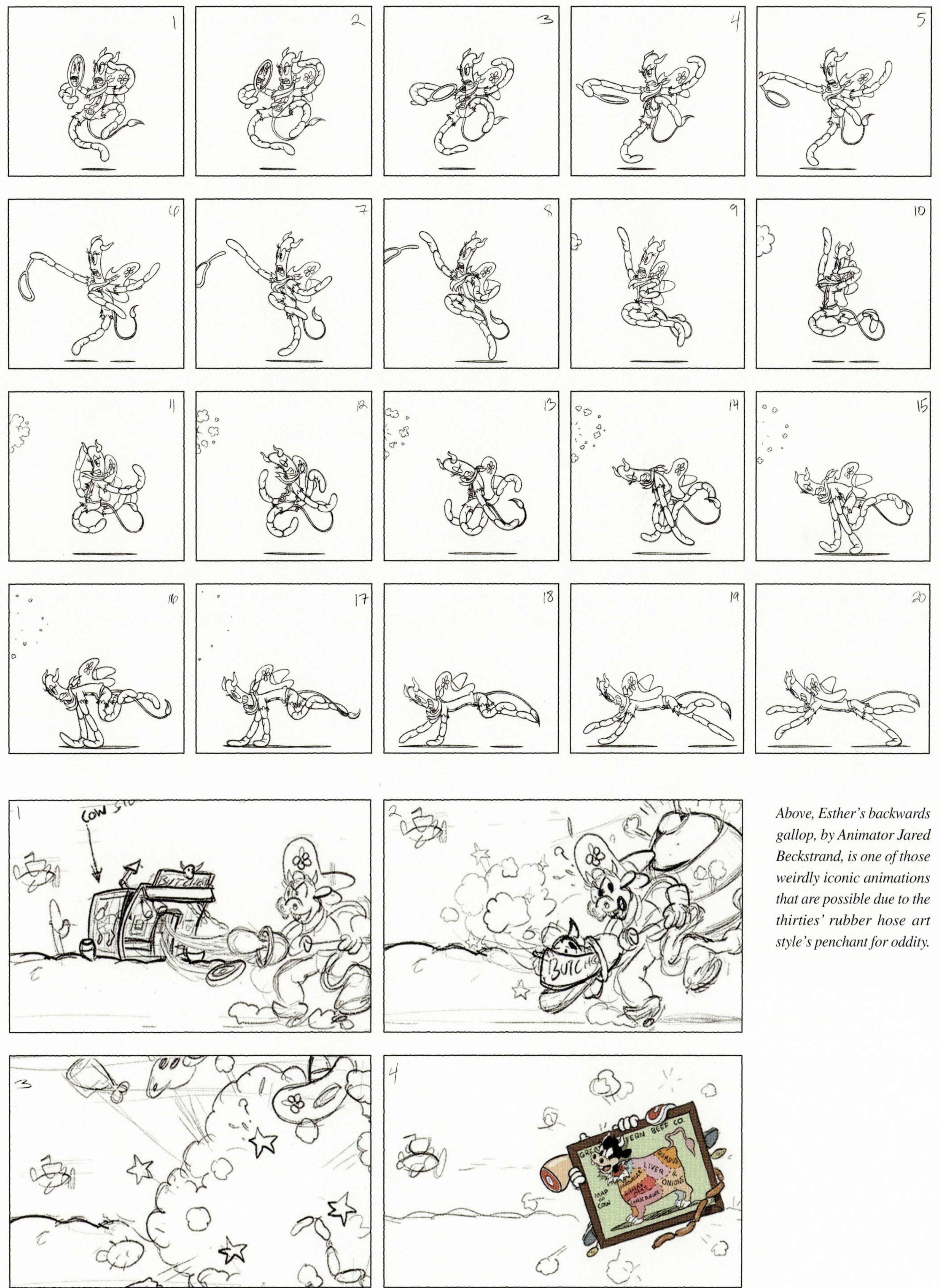

Above, Esther's backwards gallop, by Animator Jared Beckstrand, is one of those weirdly iconic animations that are possible due to the thirties' rubber hose art style's penchant for oddity.

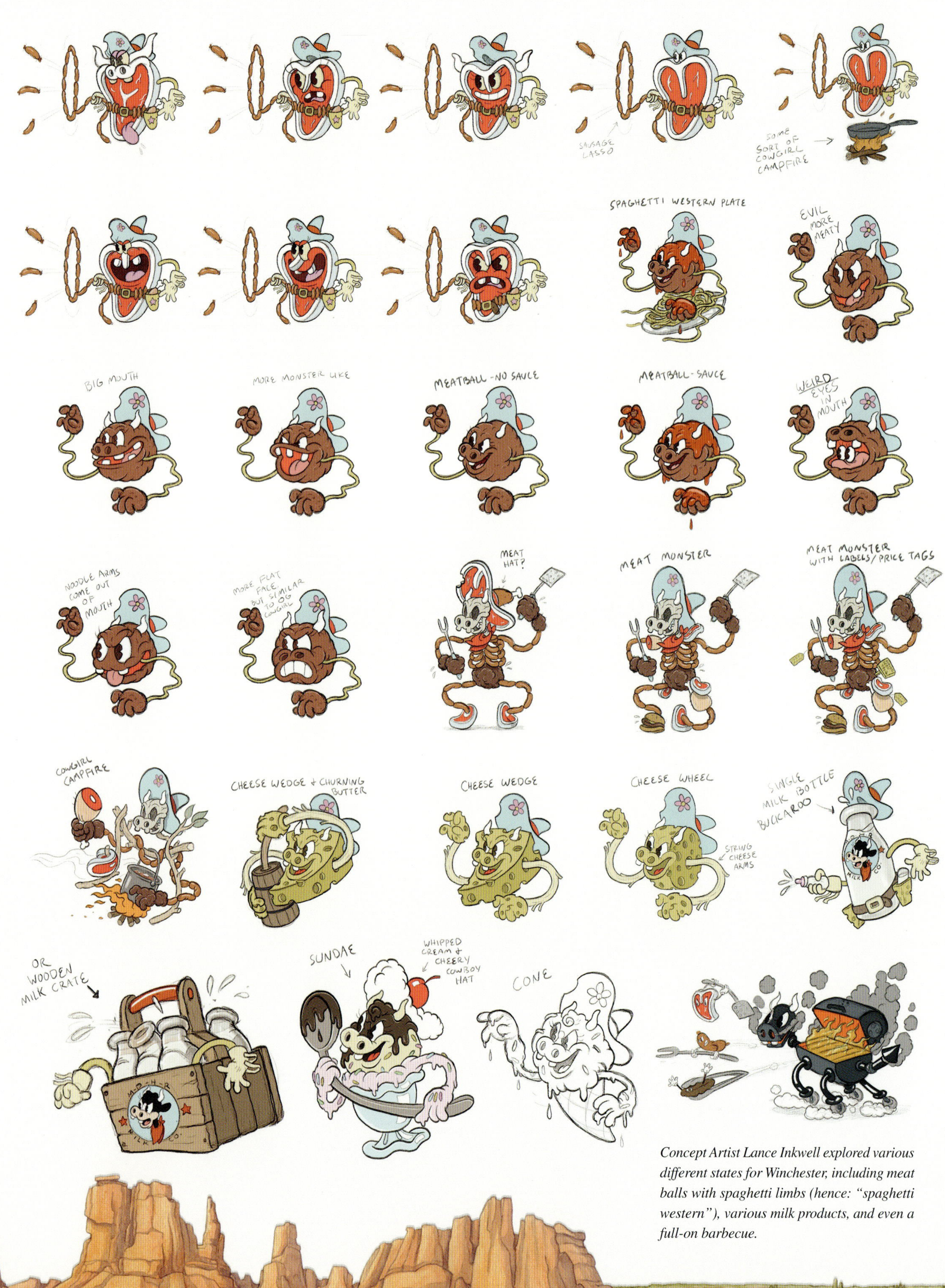

Concept Artist Lance Inkwell explored various different states for Winchester, including meat balls with spaghetti limbs (hence: "spaghetti western"), various milk products, and even a full-on barbecue.

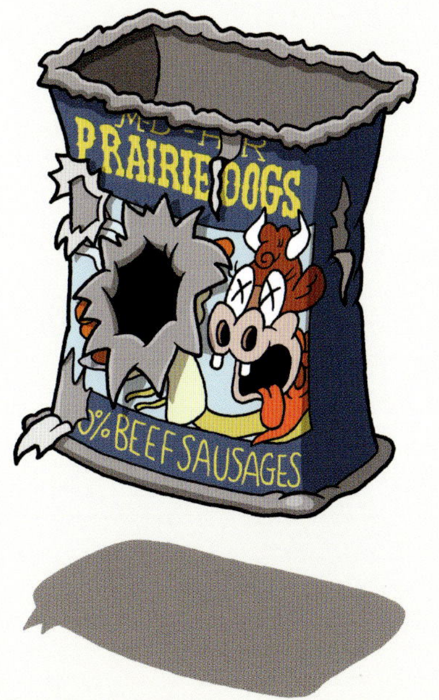

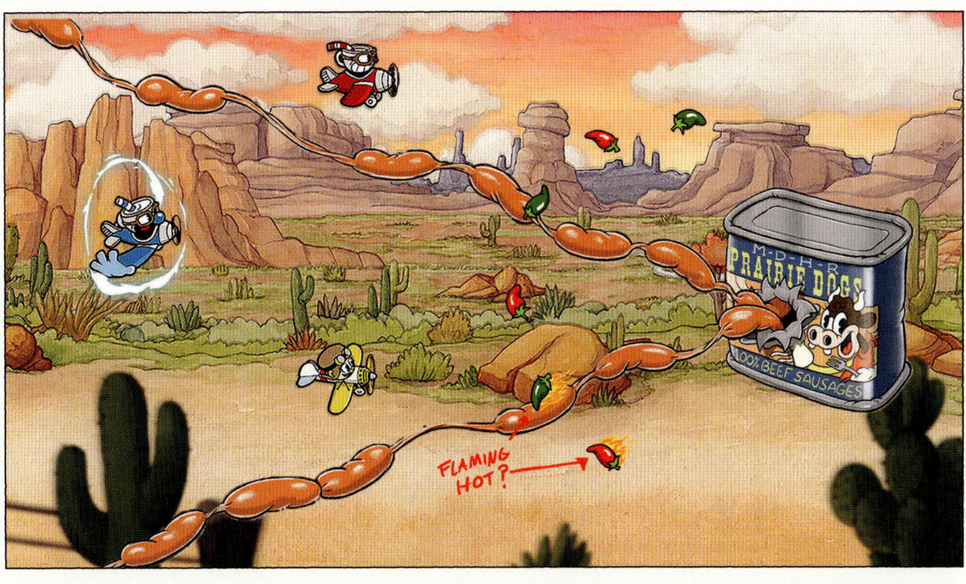

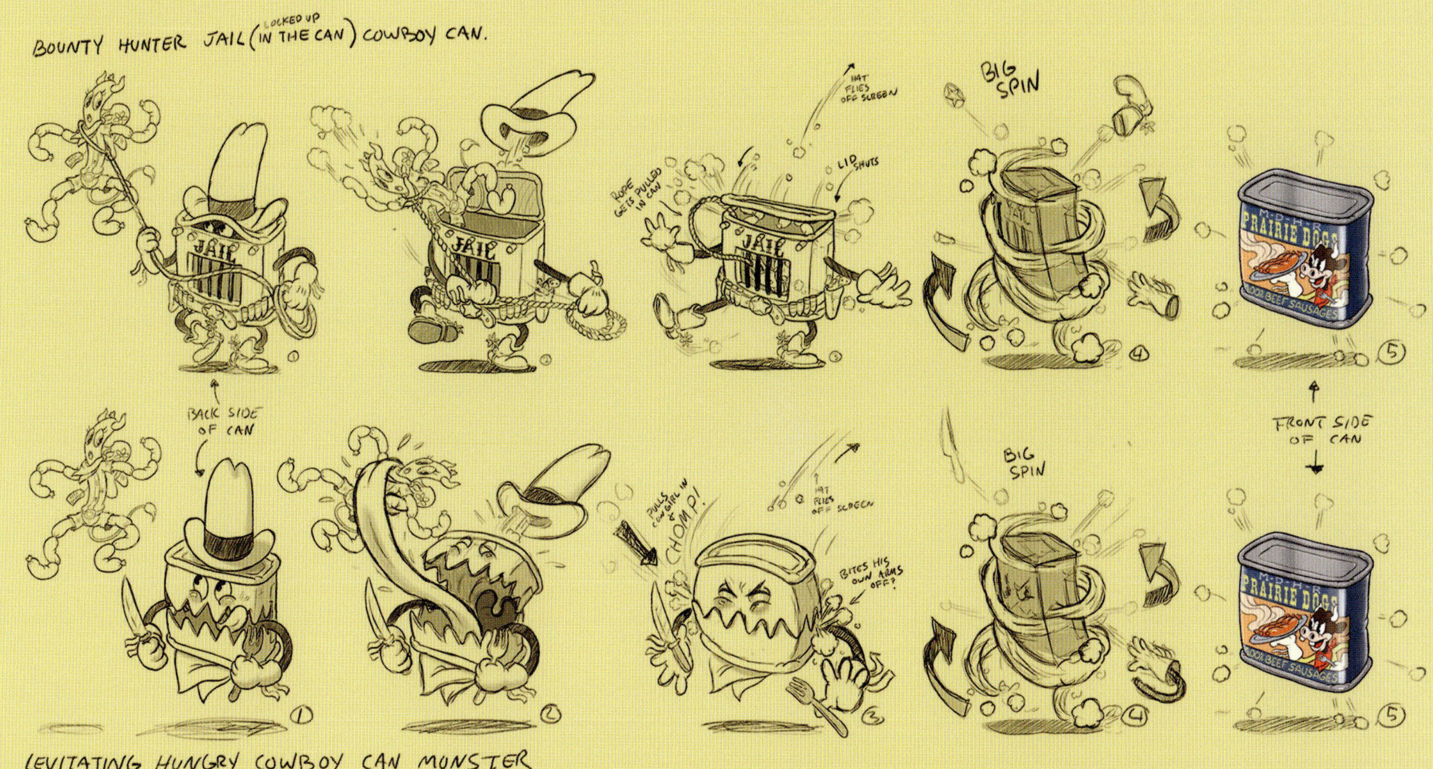

Esther's journey through commercial meat processing was originally conceptualized to be three brief phases (T-bone, meatball, sausage), but due to time constraints in the fight, the metamorphosis was eventually reduced to just two: sausages and canning. Keeping Esther's character and likeness through the various stages proved challenging, as we didn't want the designs to just look like we crudely drew her face on different meats. So, for phase 4, Concept Artist Lance Miller proposed Esther as the mascot character for the can of her own sausages. The product's "Prairie Dogs" name is a pun on the rodents that litter the countryside of Directors Chad and Jared Moldenhauer's home province of Saskatchewan.

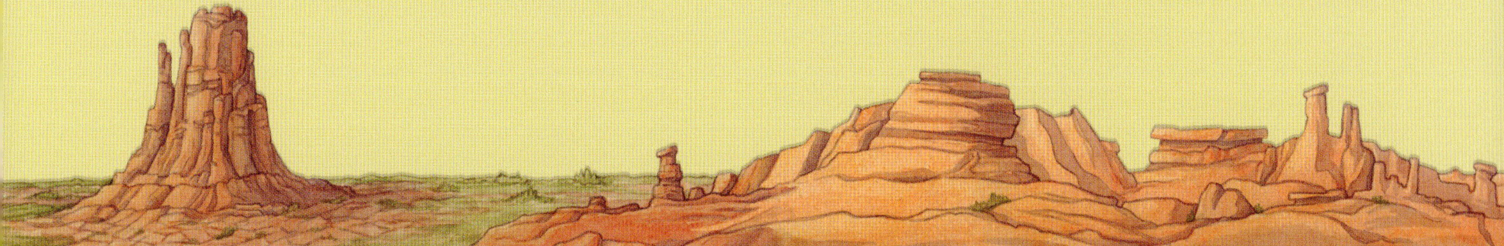

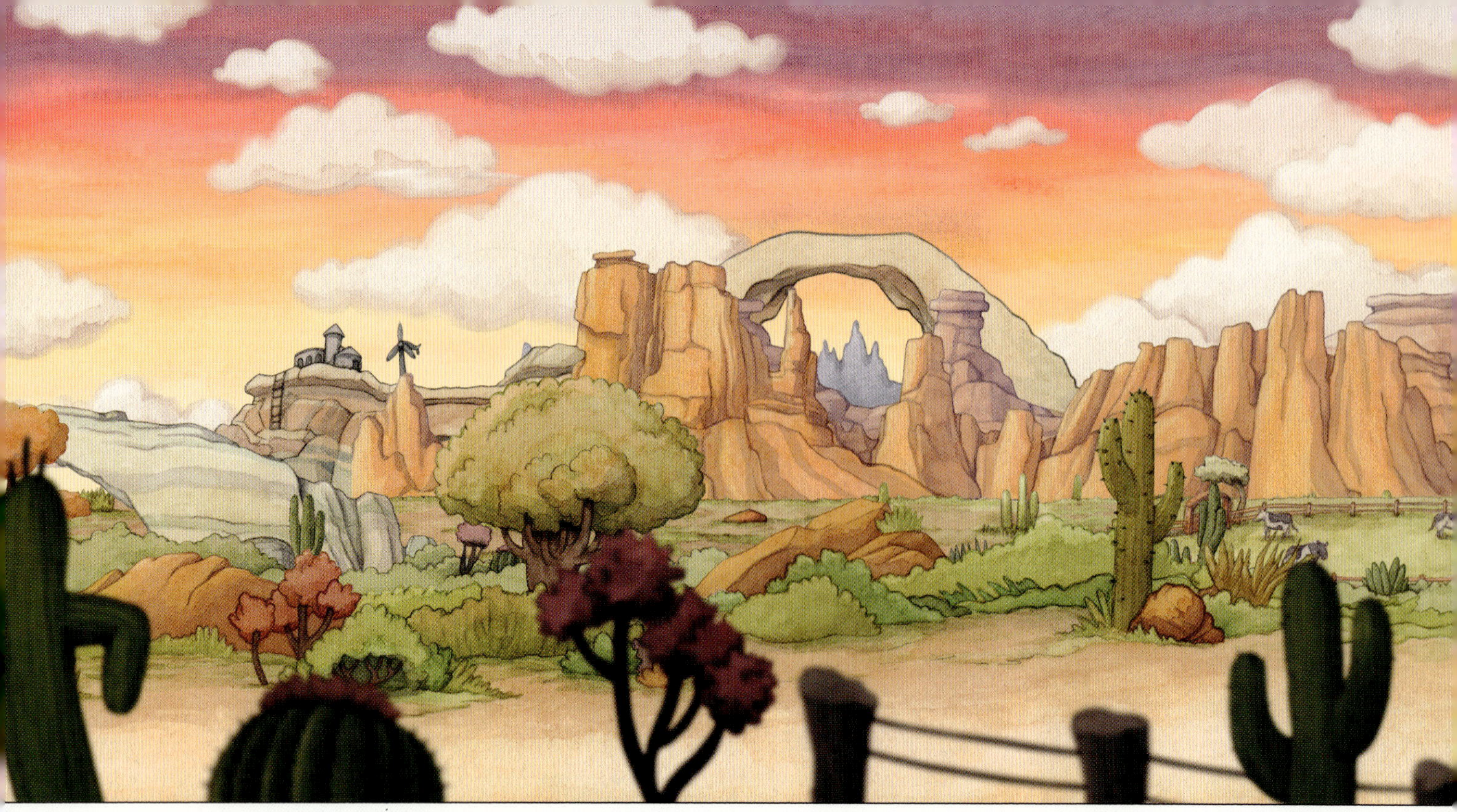

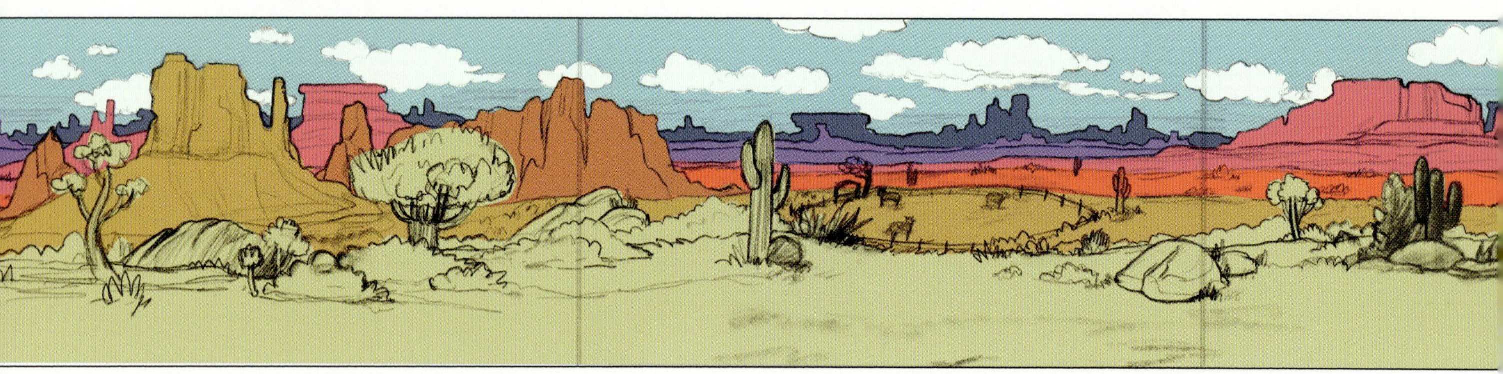

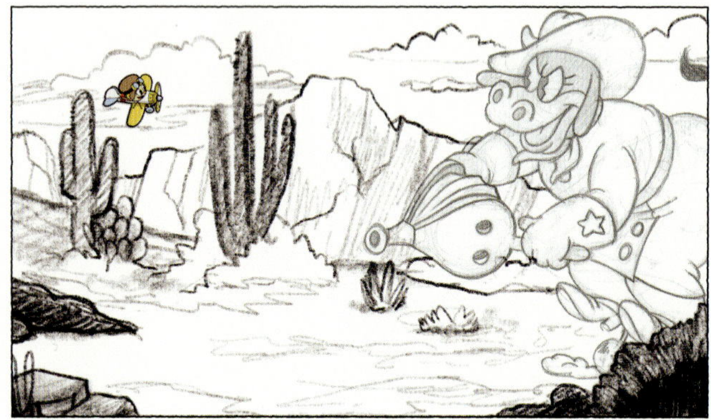

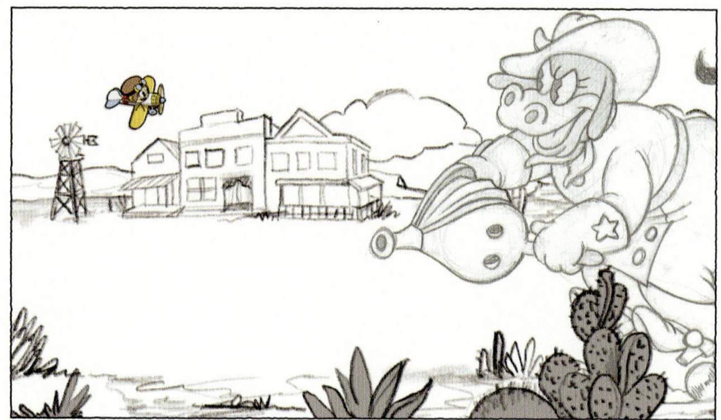

High-Noon Hoopla Background

TO GIVE THE ILLUSION OF travelling through a vast desert, Winchester's enormous background, by Background Painter Caitlin Russell, encompasses dozens of unique objects that are procedurally spawned on various layers of parallax based on different timing triggers during the fight. We included a number of subtle nods and references to classic video game deserts, from *Super Mario Bros. 2* and *Samurai Shodown*, to Cosmo Canyon from *Final Fantasy VII*. As the sun slowly sets on the rocky formations, you might even spot a Cactuar if you look close enough.

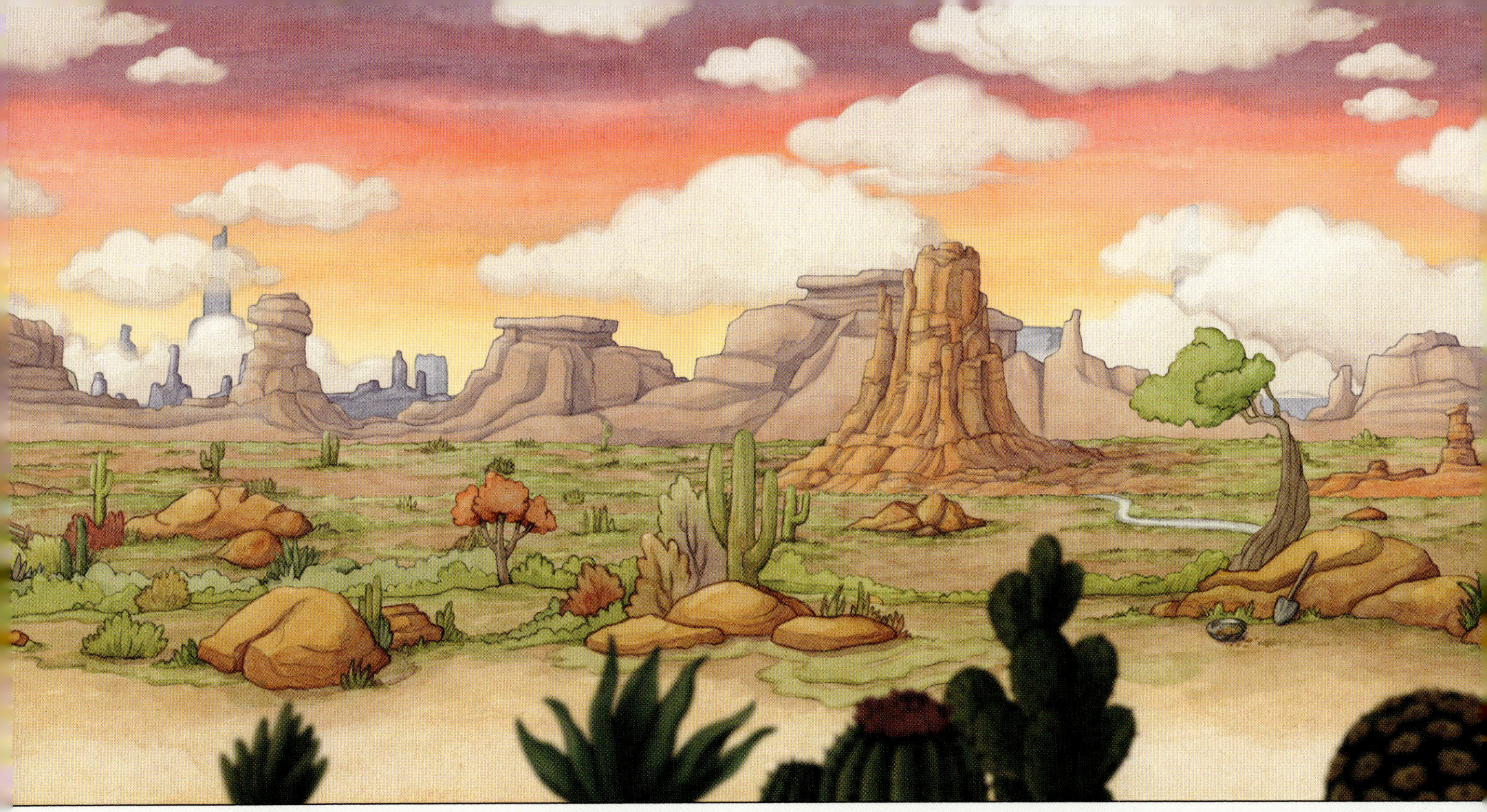

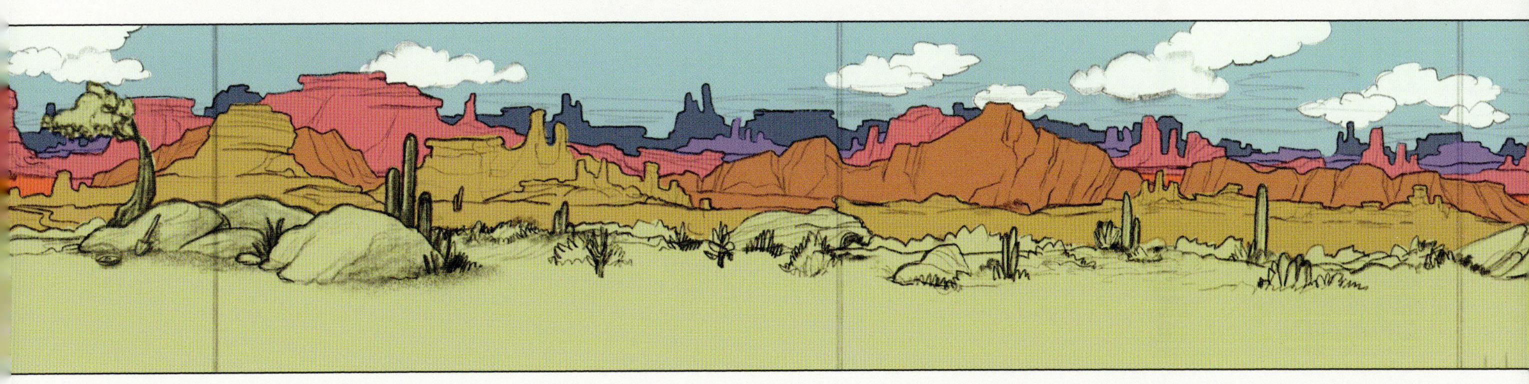

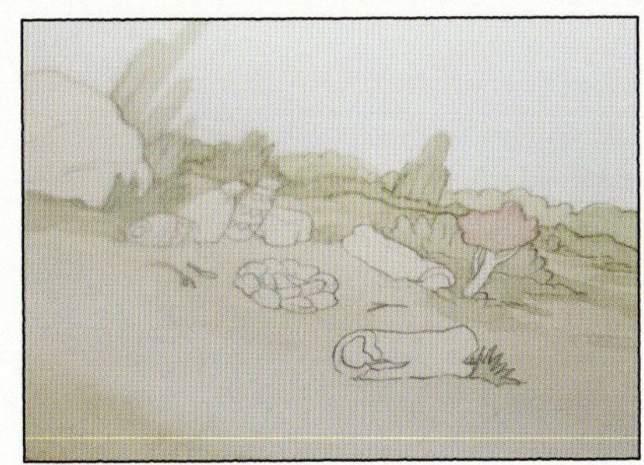

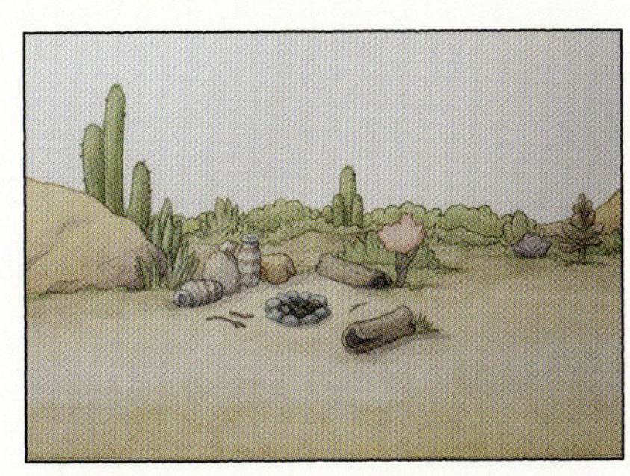

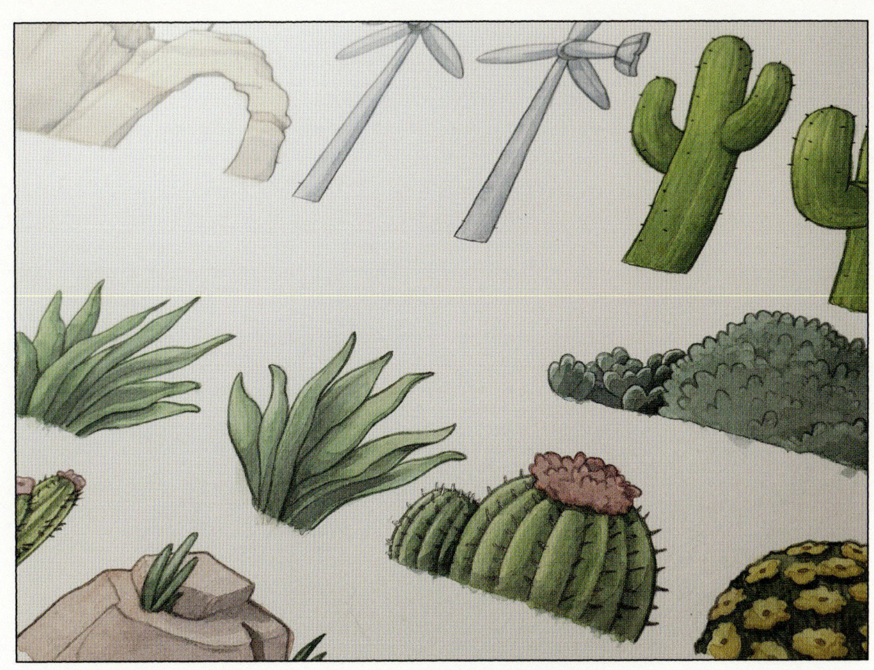

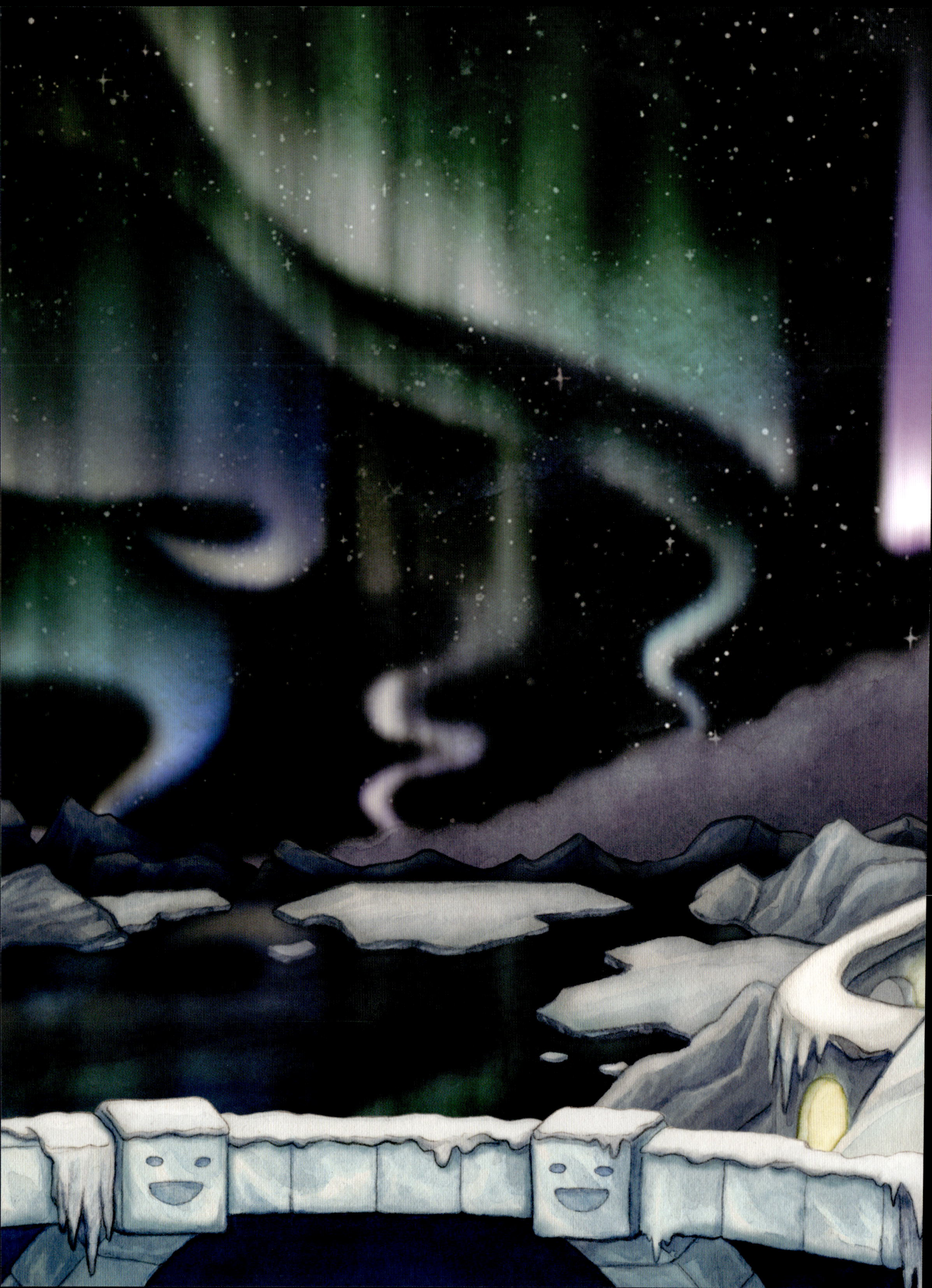

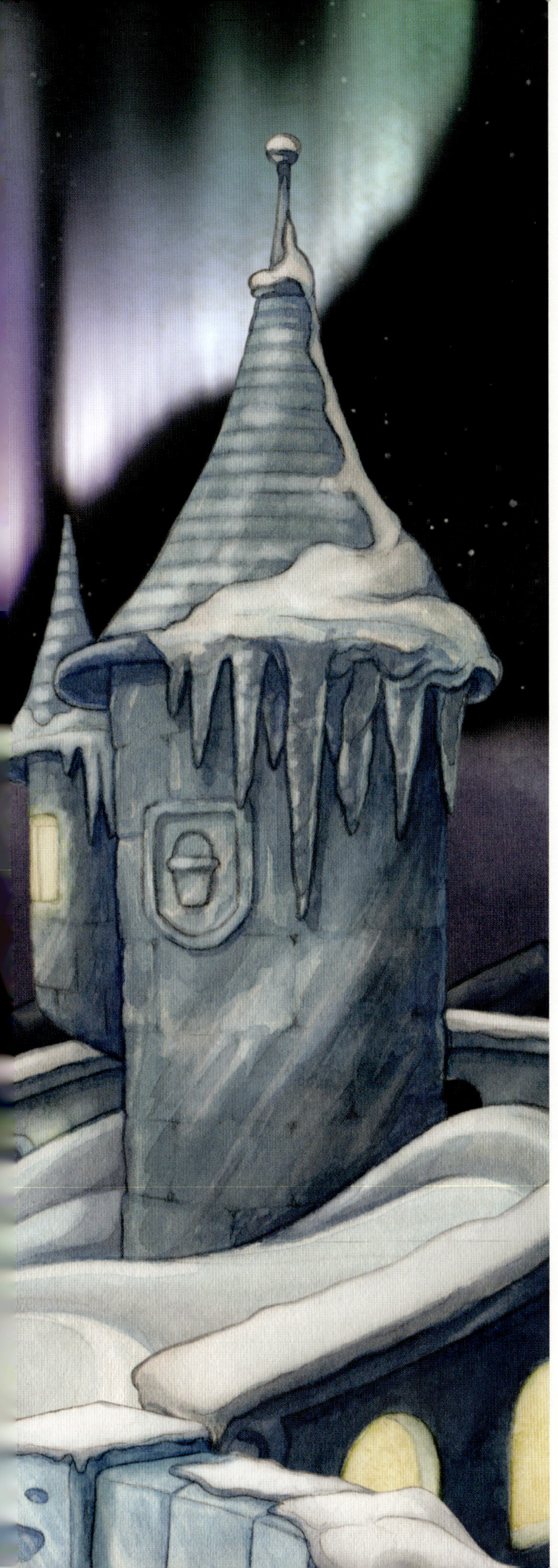

Chapter VI:
Snow Cult Scuffle

SITUATED JUST OFF THE COAST, nestled in the shade of the mountains, lives the coldest congregation in all the lands. Led by the garrulous and mystical wizard Mortimer Freeze, this frigid flock of frosty followers worships at the altar of the mysterious bucket, protecting their secrets from all outsiders in a candlelit coliseum.

While looking for unused environment types and visual themes to explore in the DLC, we realized that we hadn't done an ice level of any kind in the base game. And while Fleischer's *Bimbo's Initiation* (1931) had been oft-touted as our "magnetic north" for both the tone and art style of the original *Cuphead* game, we hadn't ever touched on the actual cult-like themes portrayed in the seminal cartoon. So it was that Snow Cult Scuffle became the melting pot (freezing pot?) of both ideas, all through the lends of arcane magics previously unseen in the Cuphead universe. Apart from Djimmi's wish-based magic and Hilda Berg's zodiac bewitchment, Mortimer Freeze's occult tarot mysticism seemed a perfect fit to ensnare the minds of his icy ideologues, all while giving us ample opportunity to create interesting attacks and outrageous animations!

Mortimer Freeze in "SNOW CULT SCUFFLE"

WHILE THE INKWELL ISLES are rife with all manner of characters who can magically shift through various bodily transformations, we hadn't explored the idea of a true spell-slinging sorcerer until we needed to find an iconic leader for this frosty faction. With visual inspiration from the eponymous Jack Frost of Fleischer's 1934 classic and some personality touches from the King of Neptune in Ub Iwerks' *Willie Whopper in Davy Jones' Locker* (1933), Mortimer Freeze's jovial mischief is emblematic of the tone of many iconic rubber hose characters.

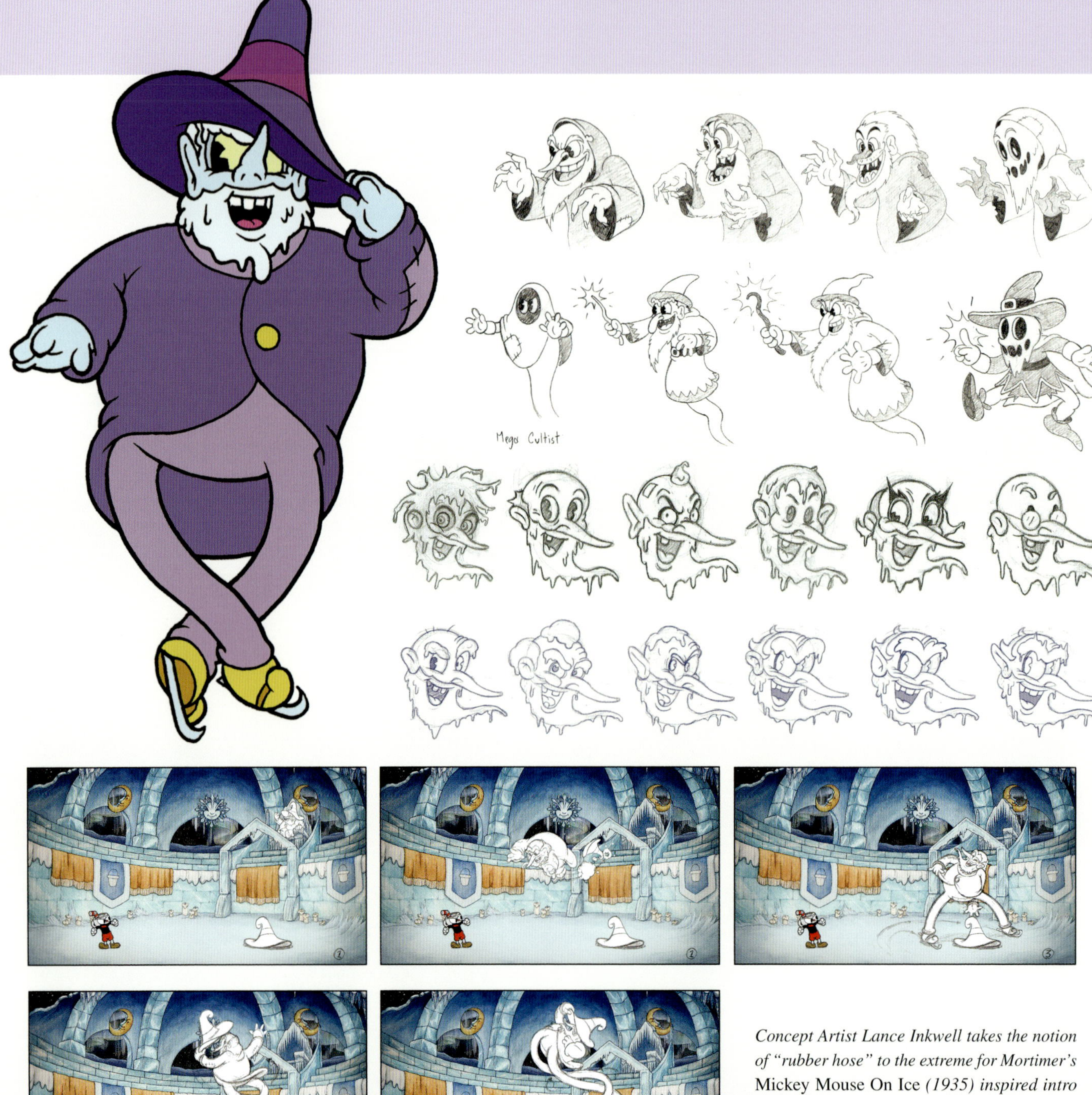

Concept Artist Lance Inkwell takes the notion of "rubber hose" to the extreme for Mortimer's Mickey Mouse On Ice *(1935) inspired intro animation.*

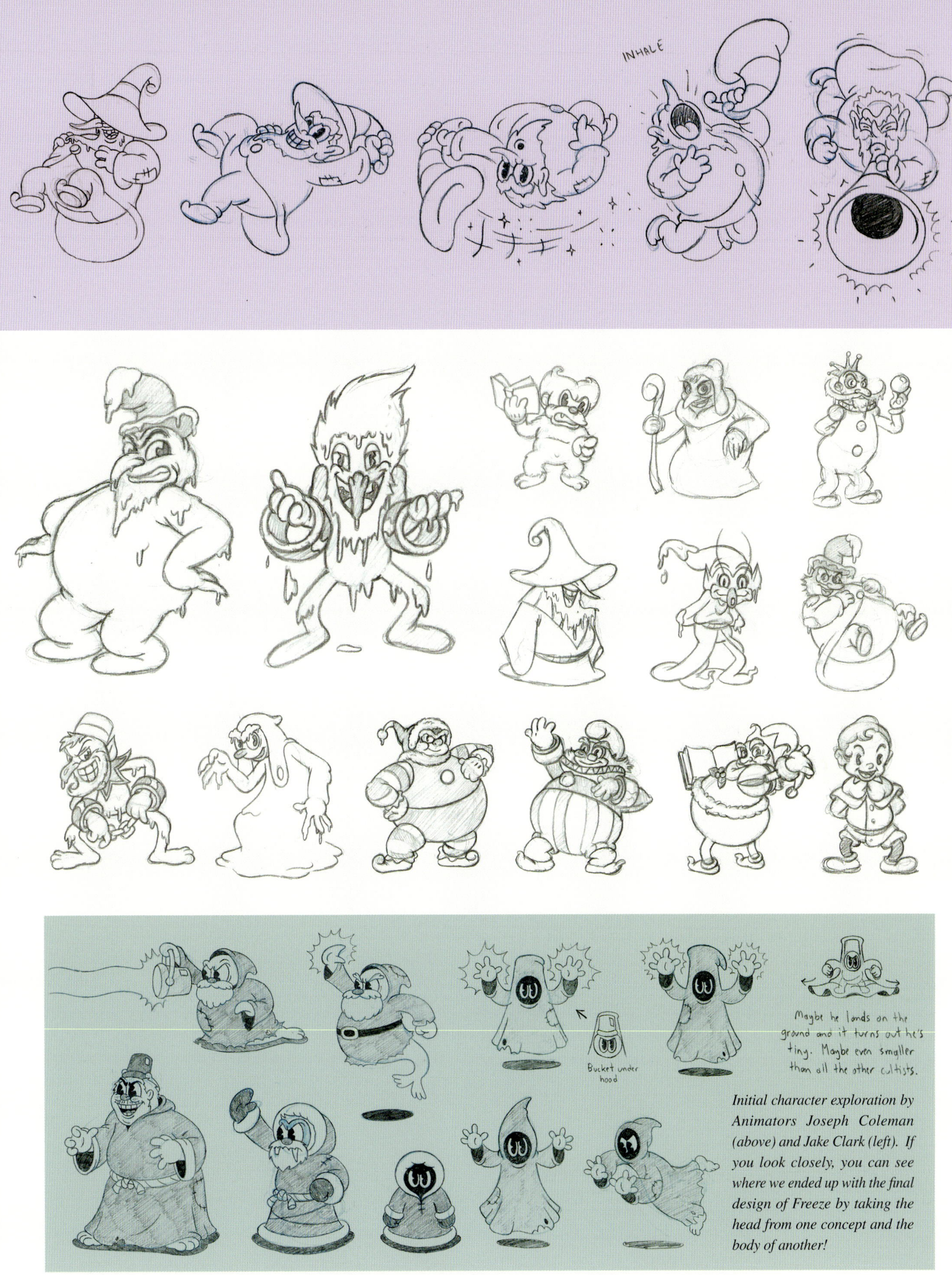

Initial character exploration by Animators Joseph Coleman (above) and Jake Clark (left). If you look closely, you can see where we ended up with the final design of Freeze by taking the head from one concept and the body of another!

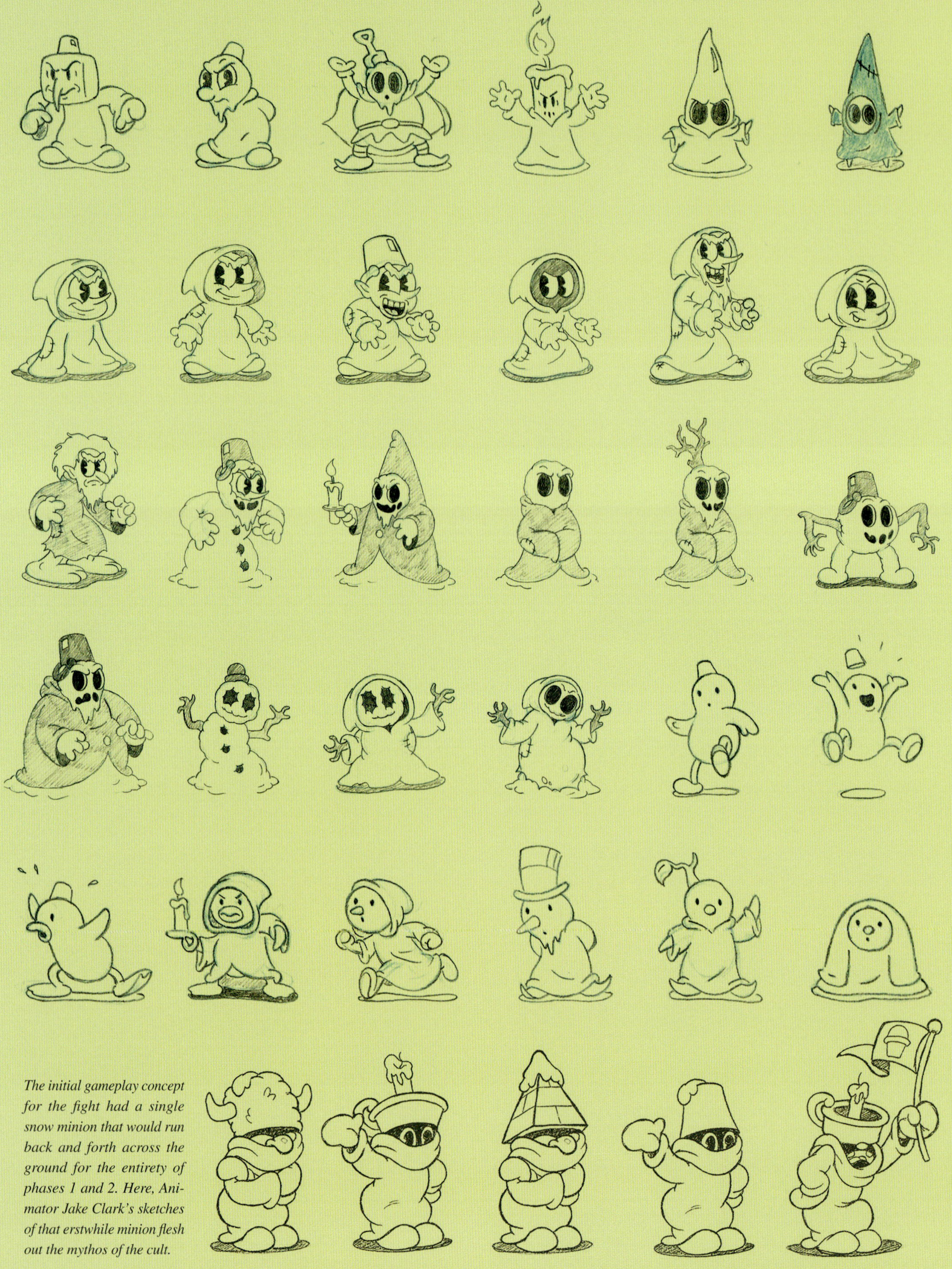

The initial gameplay concept for the fight had a single snow minion that would run back and forth across the ground for the entirety of phases 1 and 2. Here, Animator Jake Clark's sketches of that erstwhile minion flesh out the mythos of the cult.

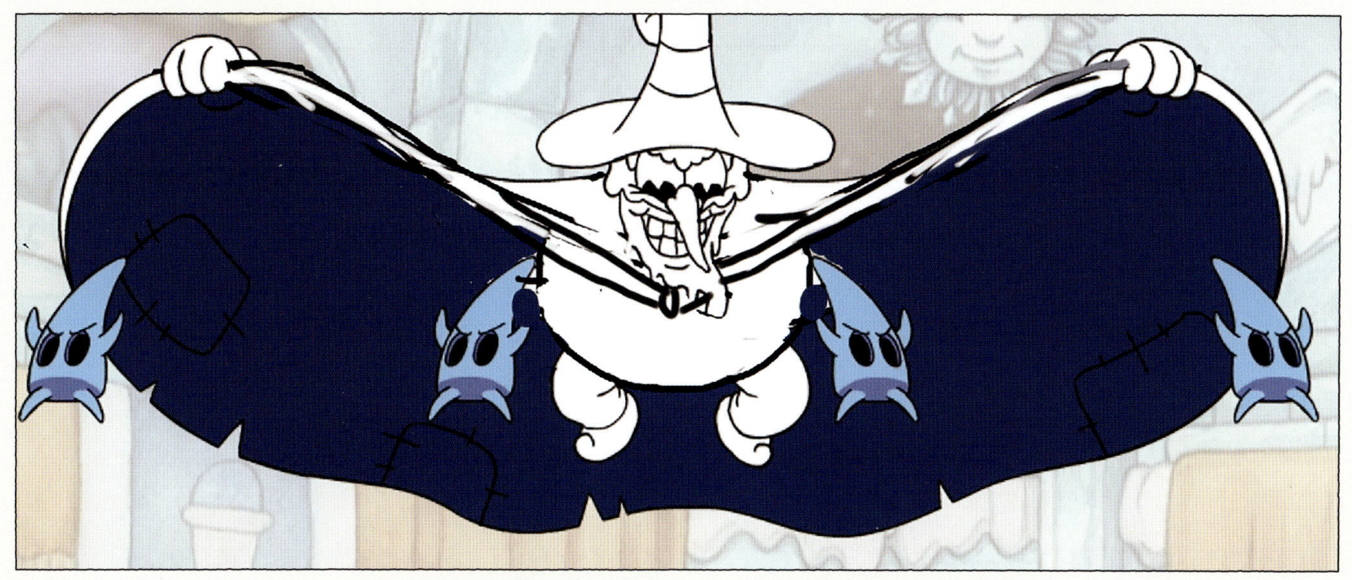

That single minion concept seen opposite was repurposed into a four-piece of familiars that Mortimer could summon to dispense hazards during the fight. Clark's concepts, above, propose various methods of launching the frigid followers.

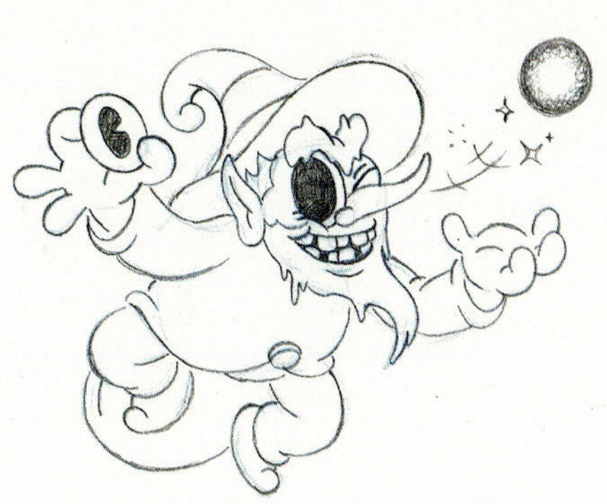

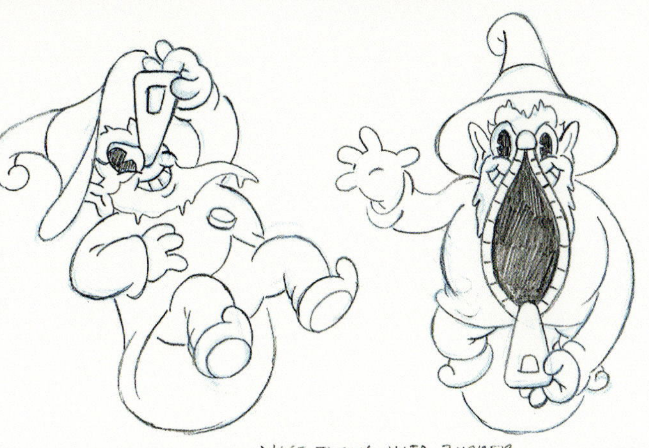

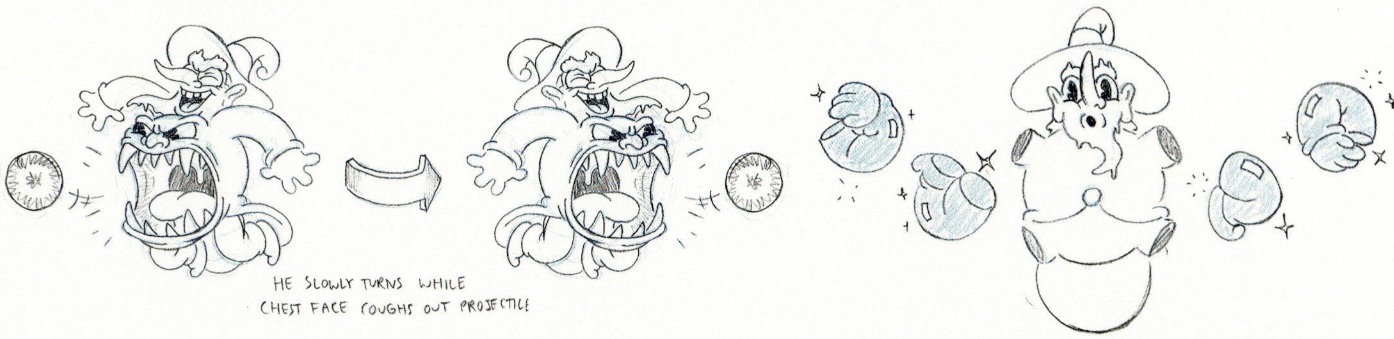

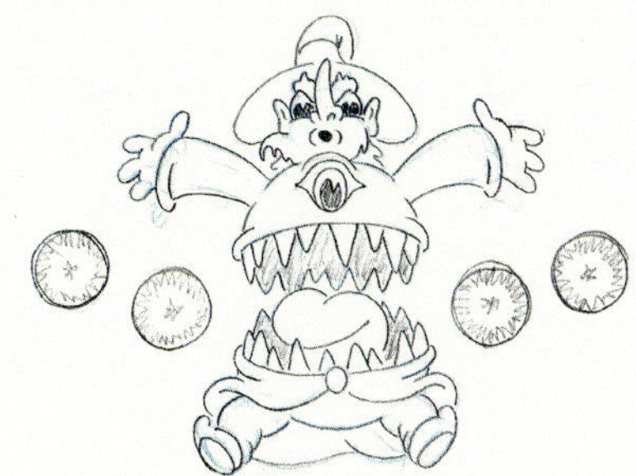

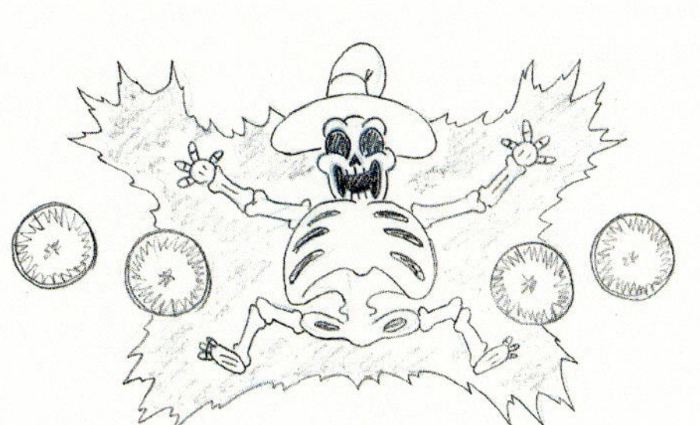

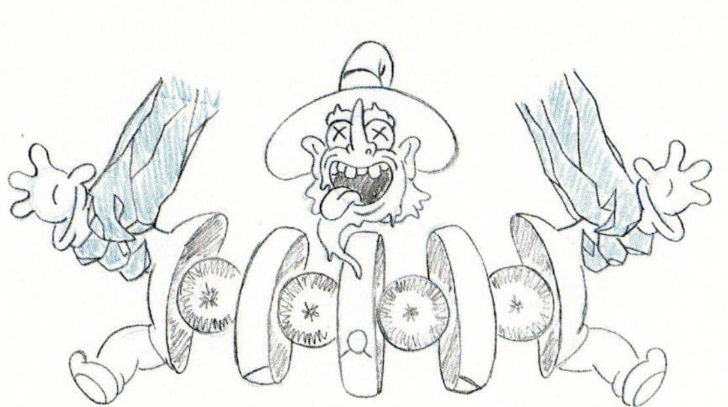

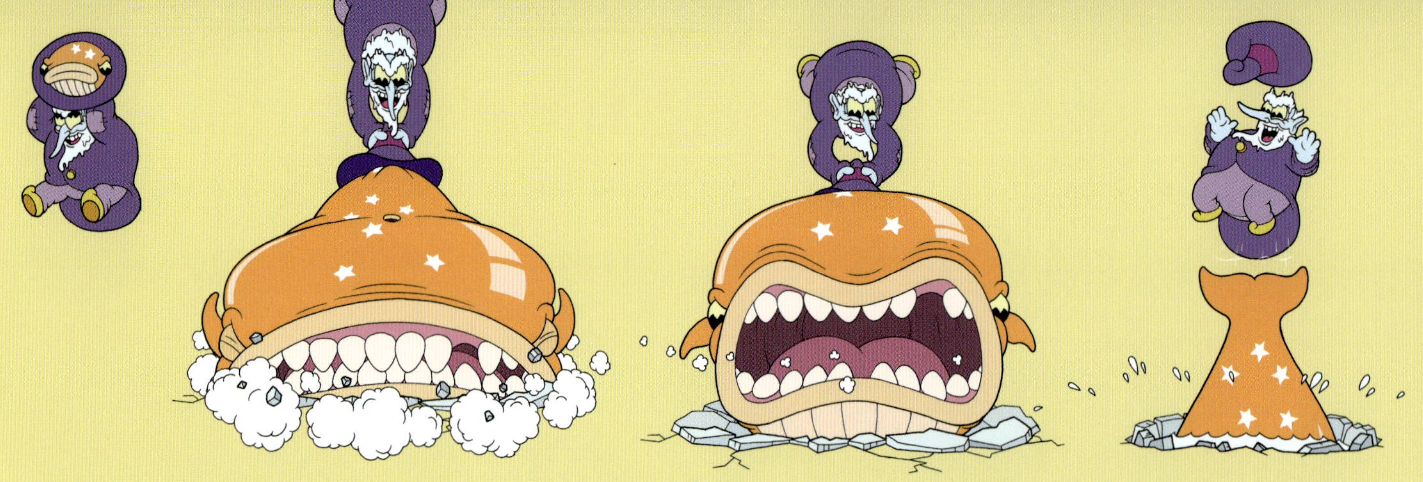

When building the lore of the Inkwell Isles, we try to tie common facets together with visual themes in order to give a logical structure to the way a cartoon world might work. We had already established mystical properties to the zodiac symbols of Hilda Berg's transformations, and wanted to build on that with Mortimer's take on the magician's trick of "pulling a rabbit out of a hat"–his whale slam. The whale's astrological star pattern is both a literal reference to Cetus, the whale constellation, and a nod to *Ecco the Dolphin's* (1994) Delphinus constellation markings, while his missing tooth is an homage to the grandest cartoon whale of all time, Monstro from Disney's *Pinocchio* (1940).

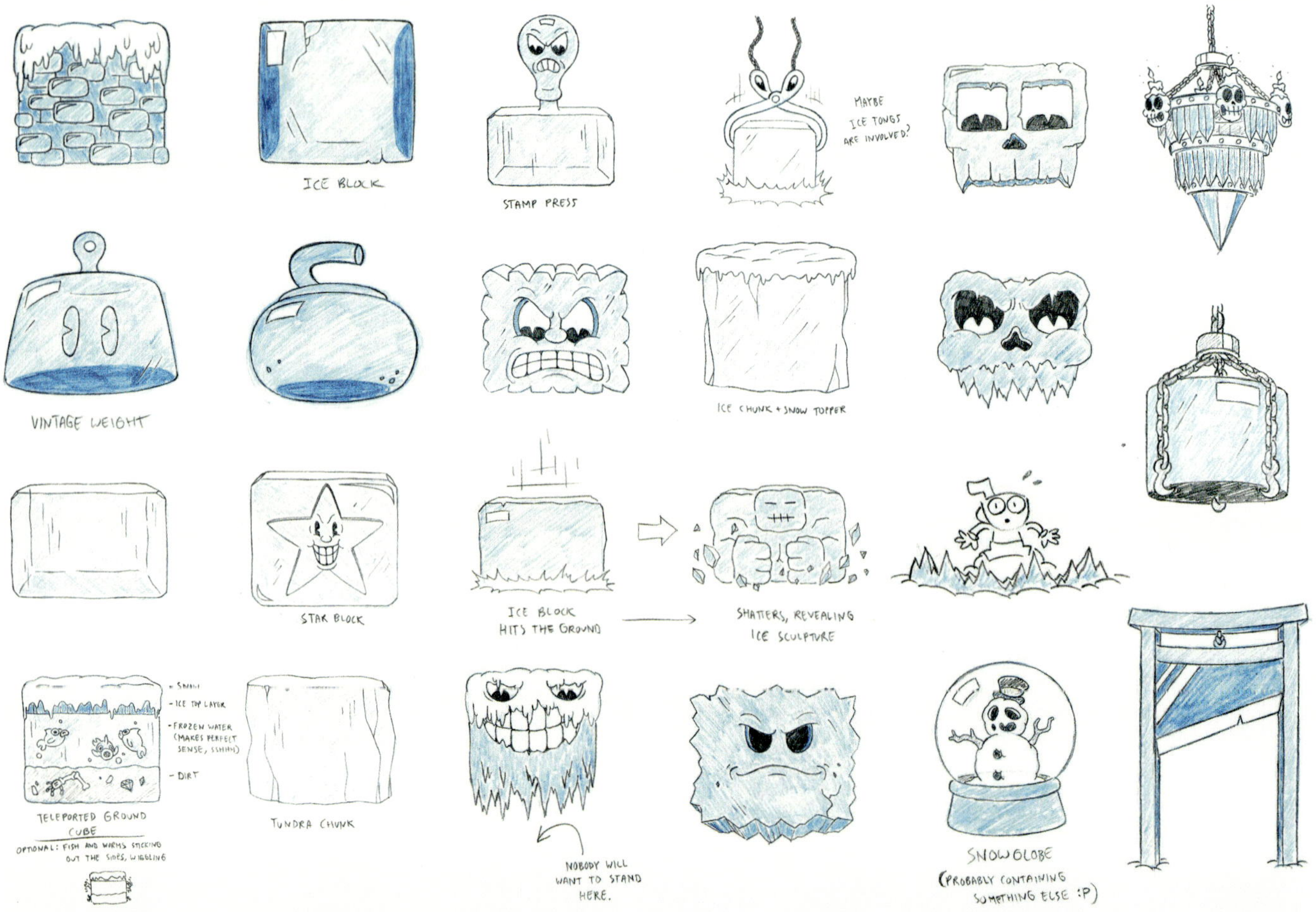

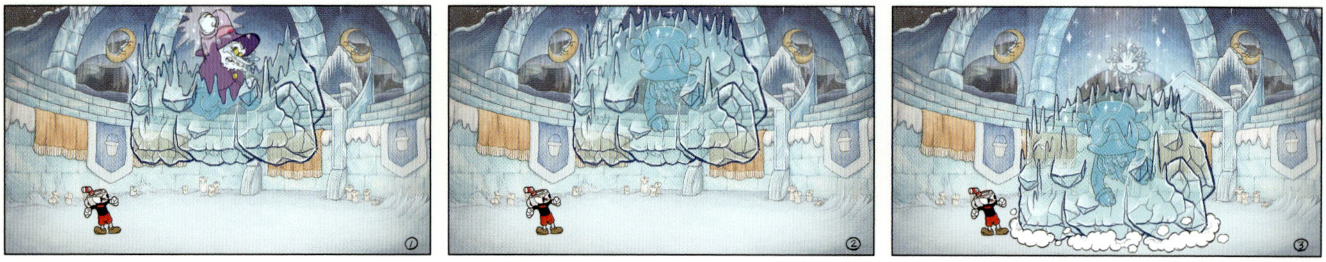

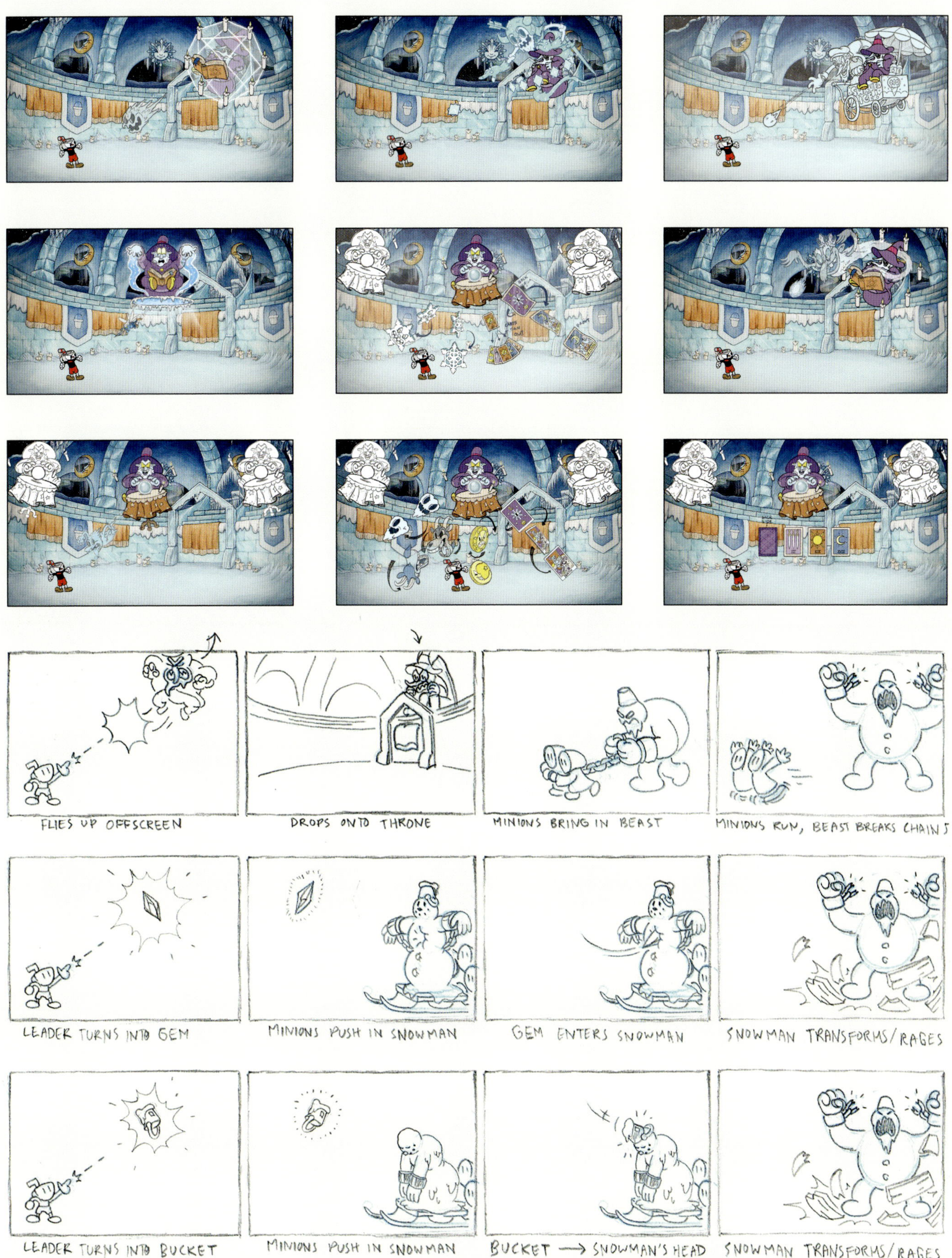

Top, Lance Inkwell's concepts for ways Mortimer could shoot basic projectiles that would demonstrate suitable grandeur for a wizard cult leader. Above, Animator Jake Clark proposes various ways to summon the beast, who we named Jupiter.

Jupiter

OUR OWN TAKE ON THE abominable snowman archetype, Jupiter's place in the DLC shifted over the course of development. Initially envisioned as a singular monster, Jupiter eventually took on a grander role as a sort of legendary "living armor" in the ever-expanding lore of the cult's devotion to the bucket. What started as a goofy nod to Toaplan's *Snow Bros.* (1990), the orange bucket on his head ended up becoming a focal point for the cult's iconography and a gag we could keep calling back to throughout the fight.

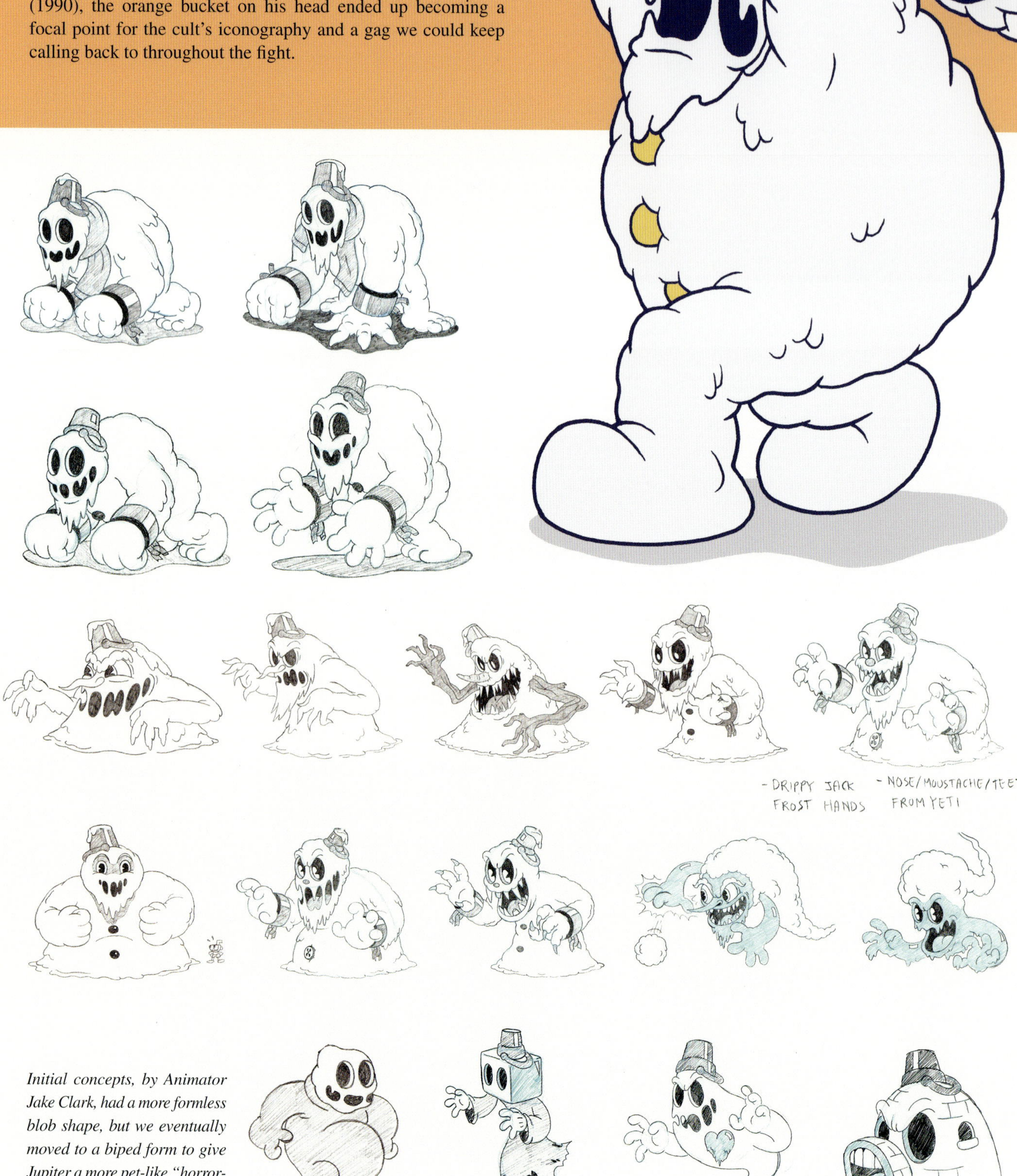

Initial concepts, by Animator Jake Clark, had a more formless blob shape, but we eventually moved to a biped form to give Jupiter a more pet-like "horror-cute" charm.

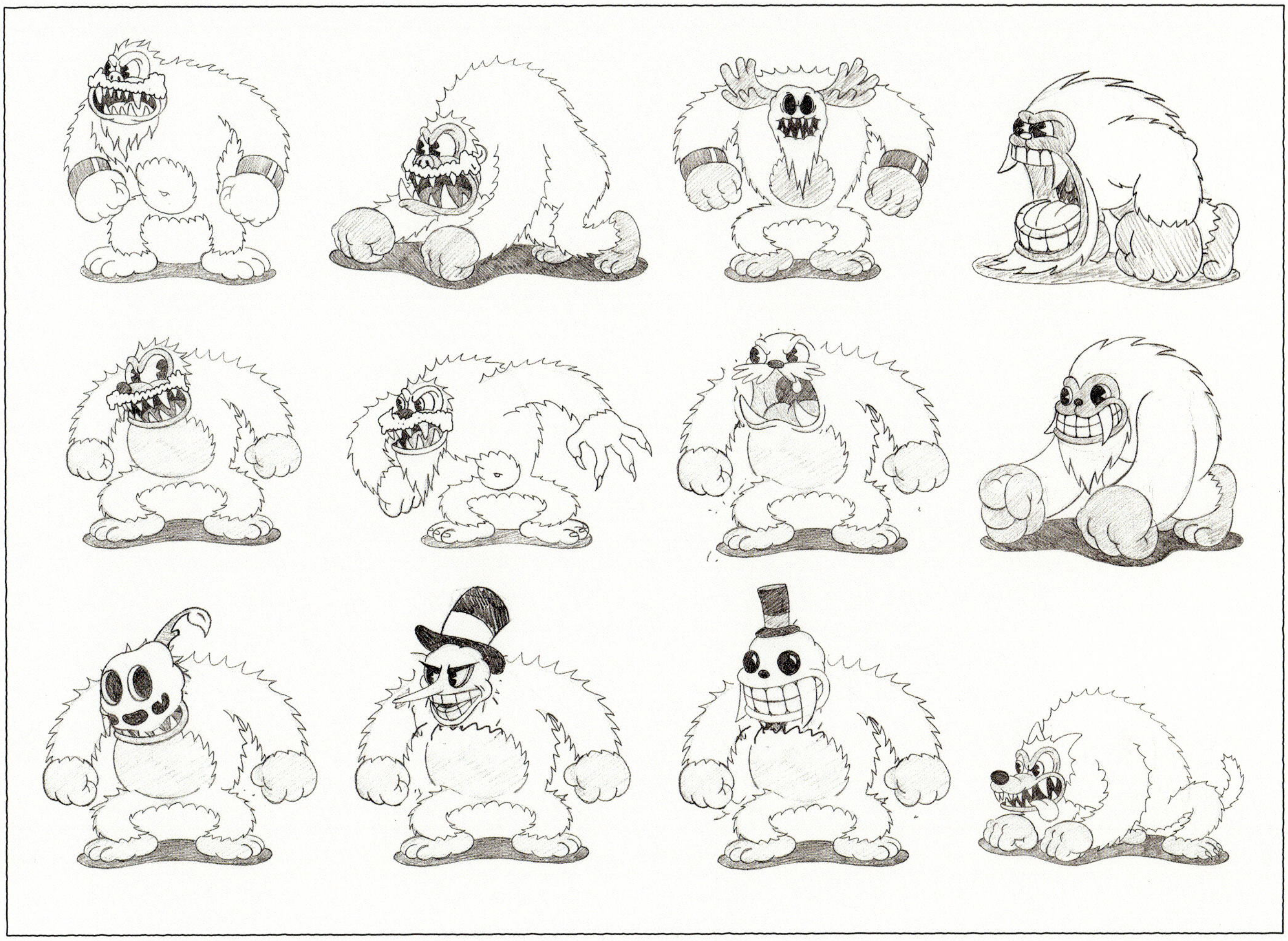

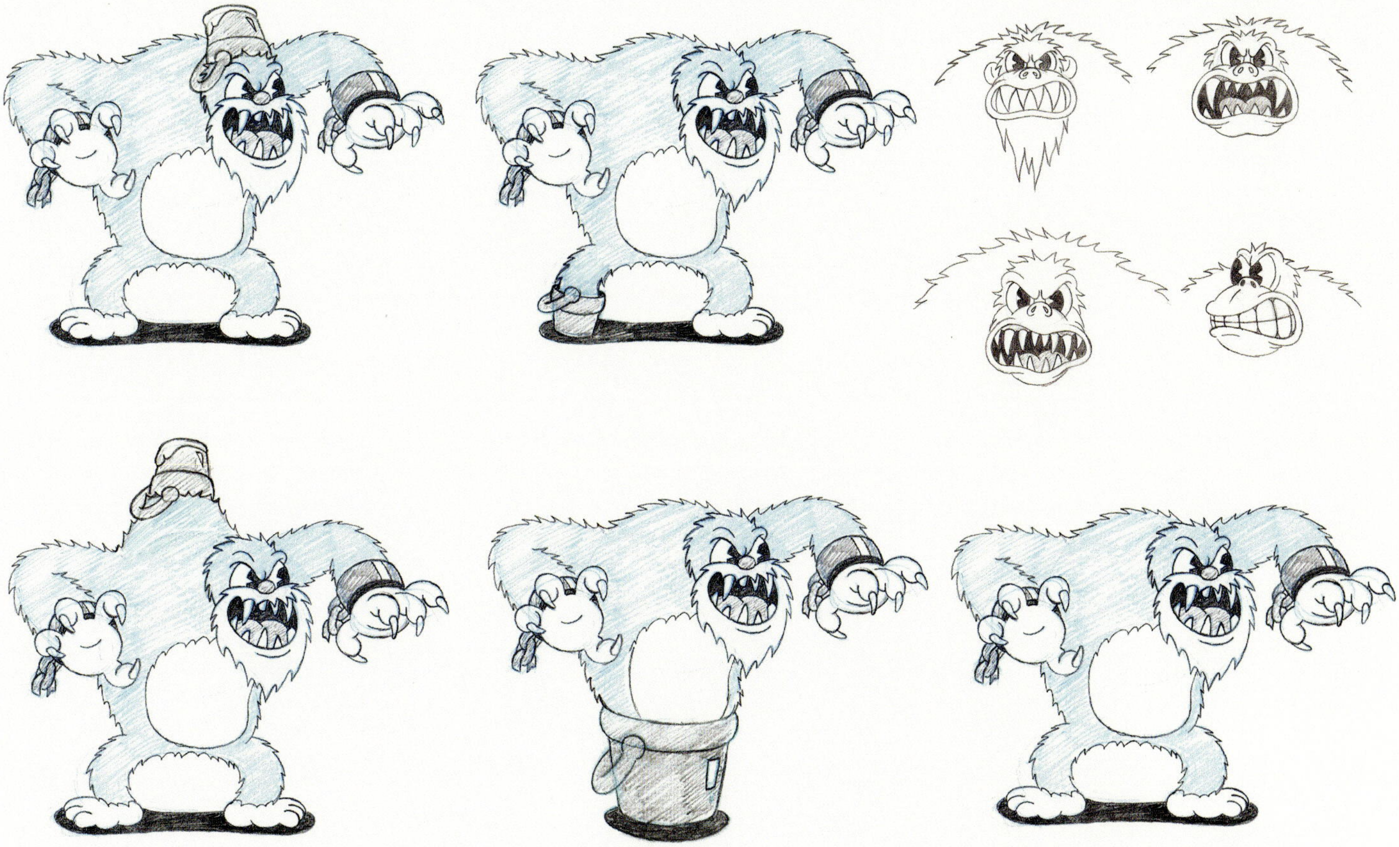

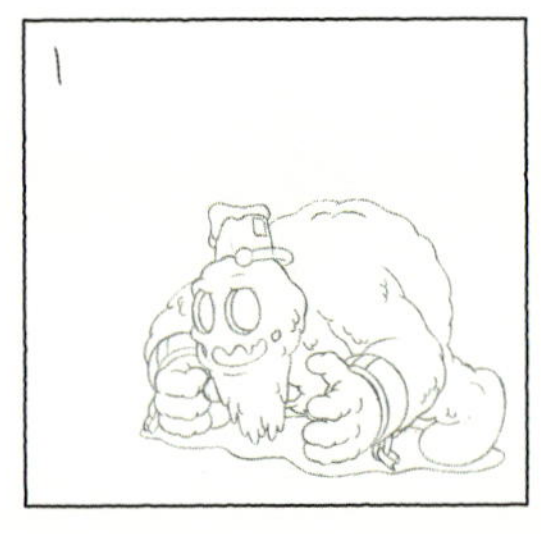

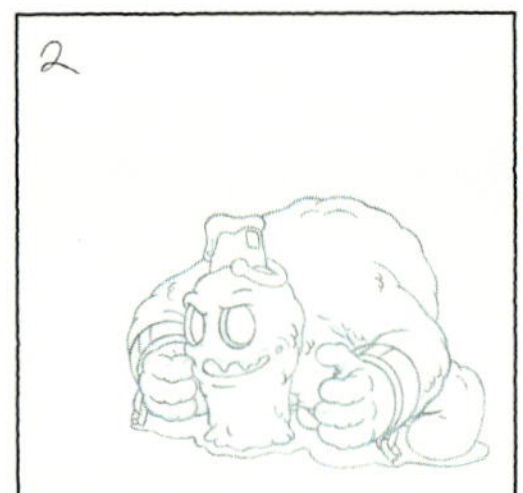

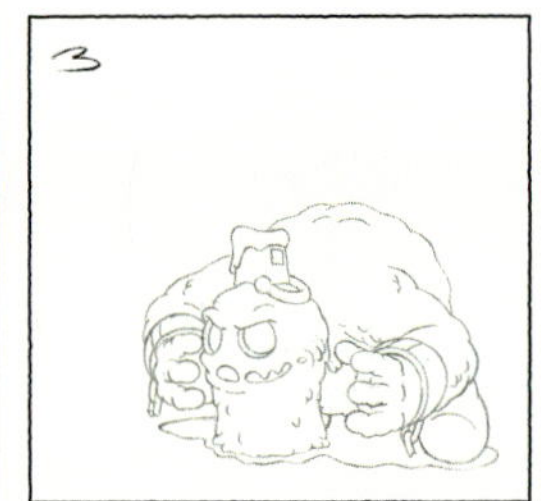

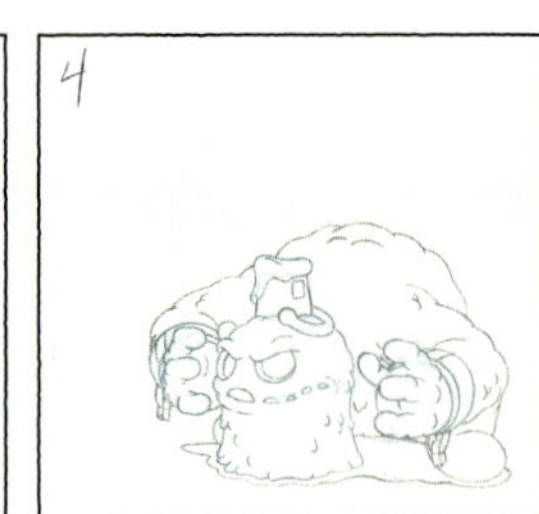

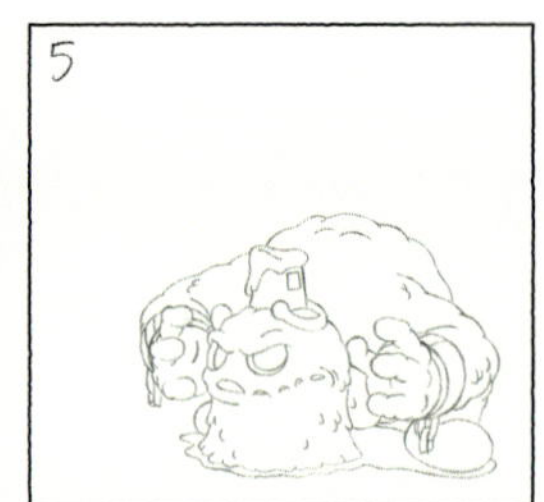

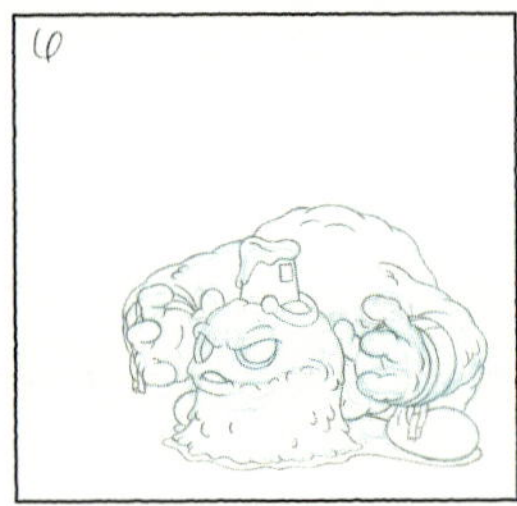

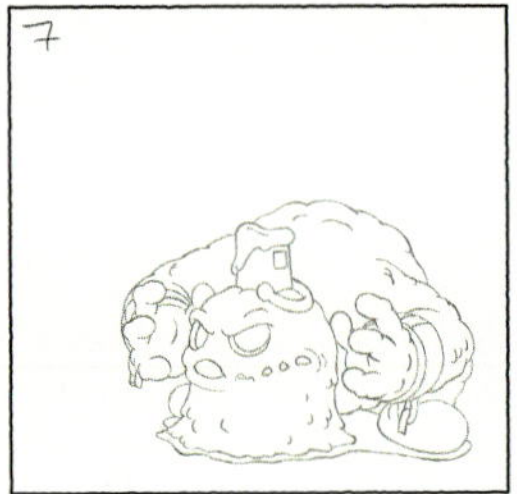

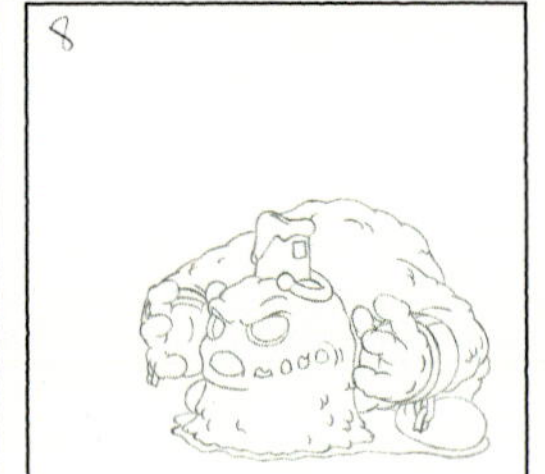

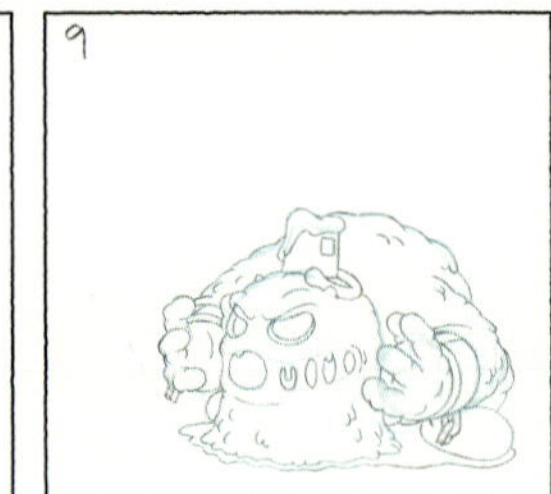

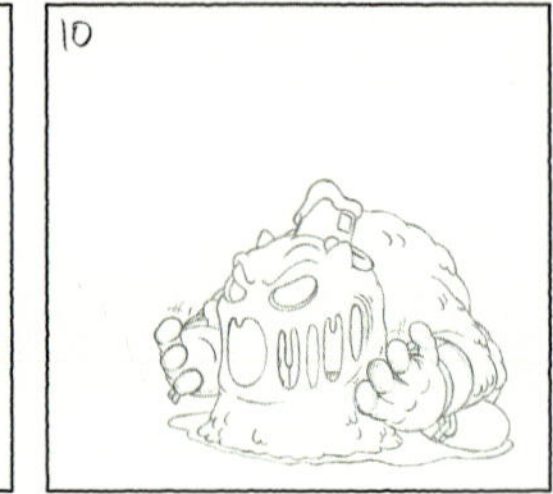

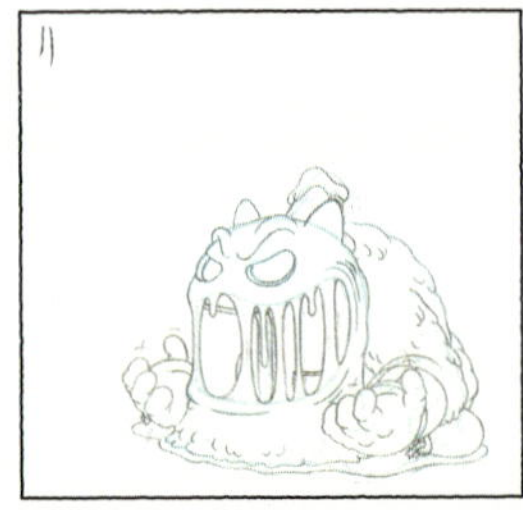

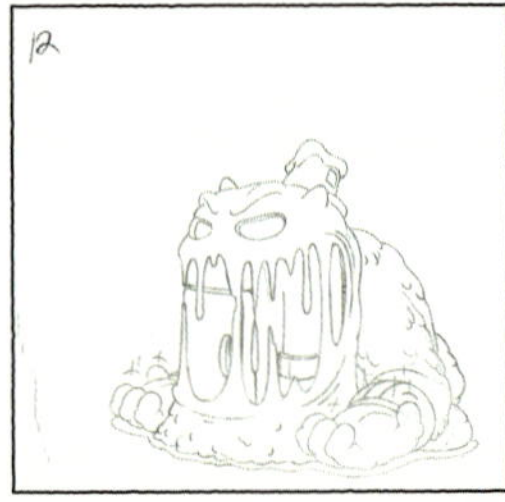

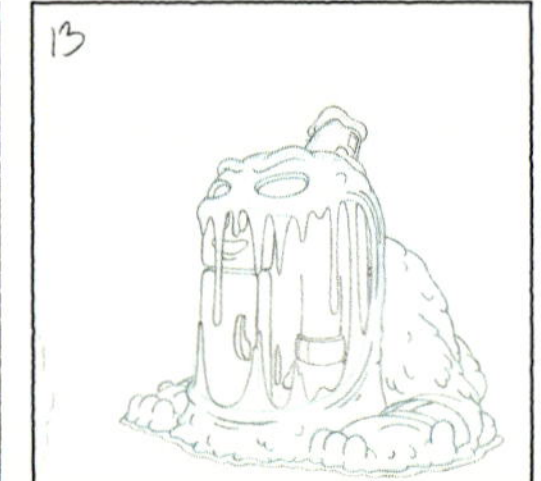

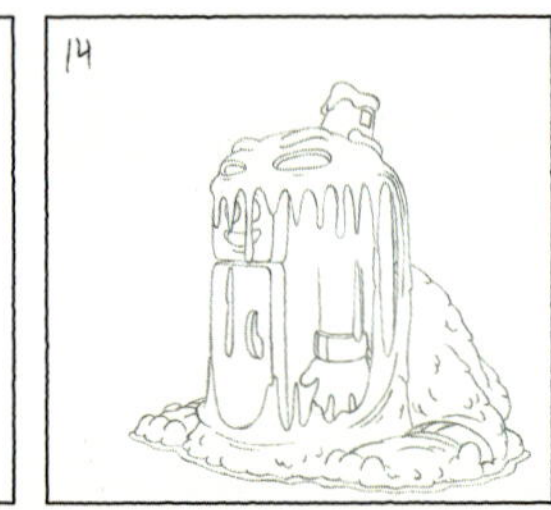

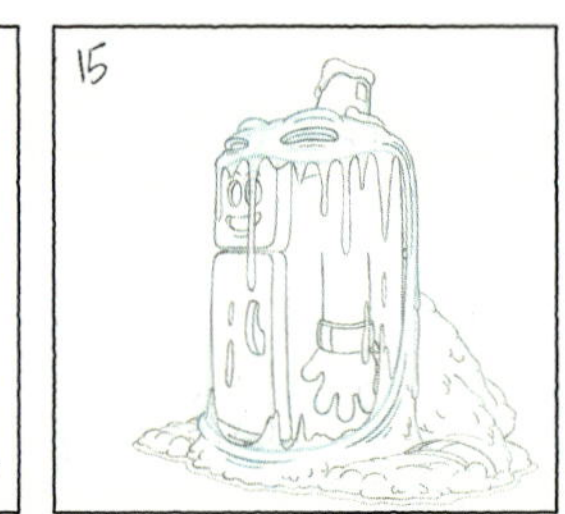

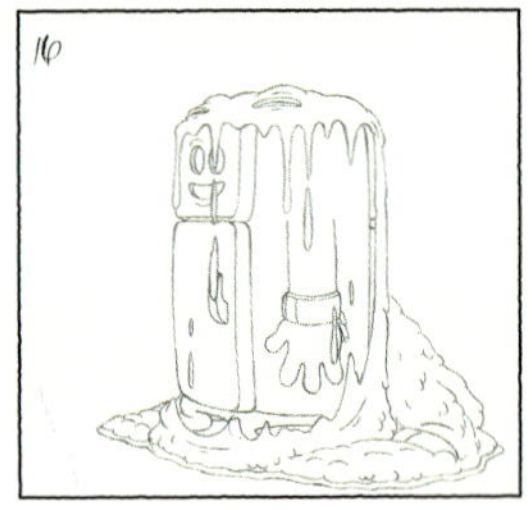

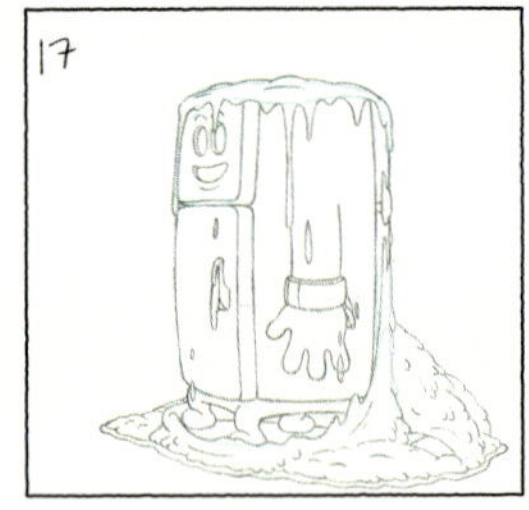

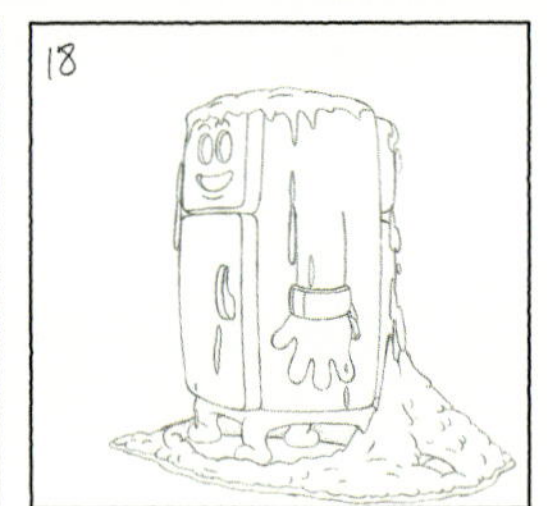

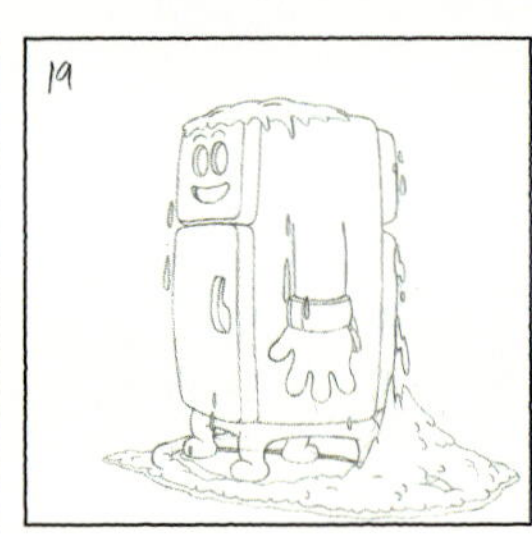

One of our more elaborate morphs, Jupiter's fridge transformation took extensive planning by Animator Jake Clark to balance visual richness with gameplay restrictions.

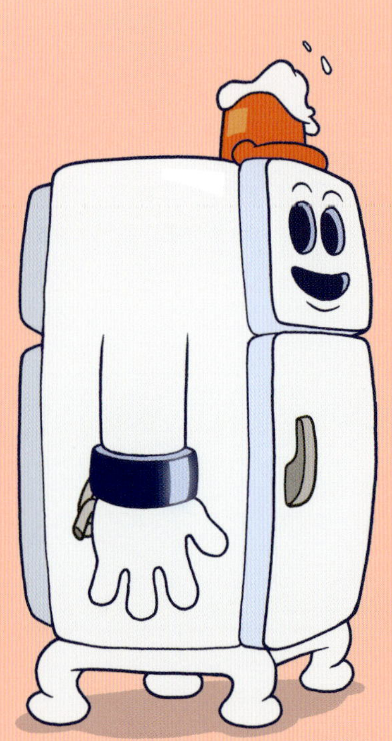

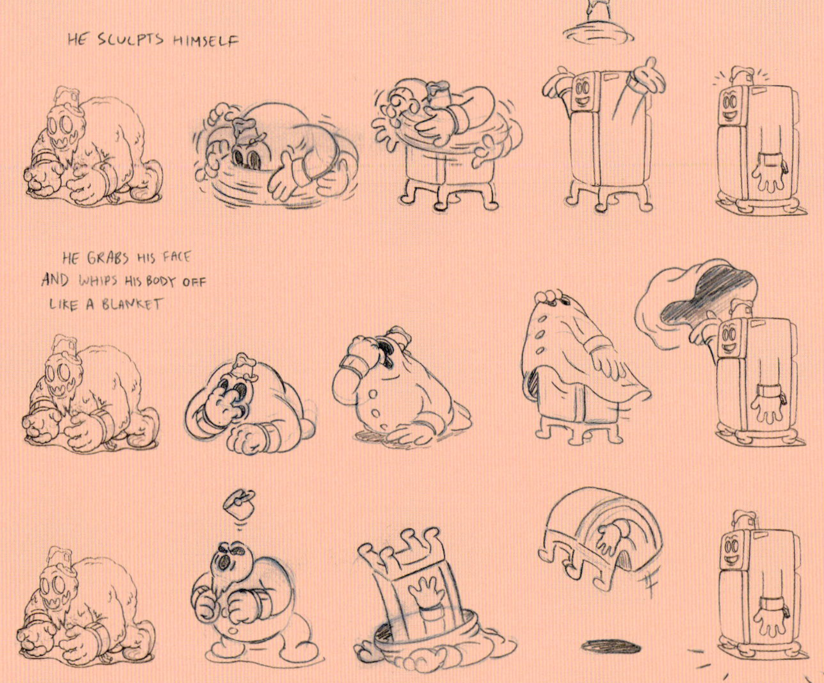

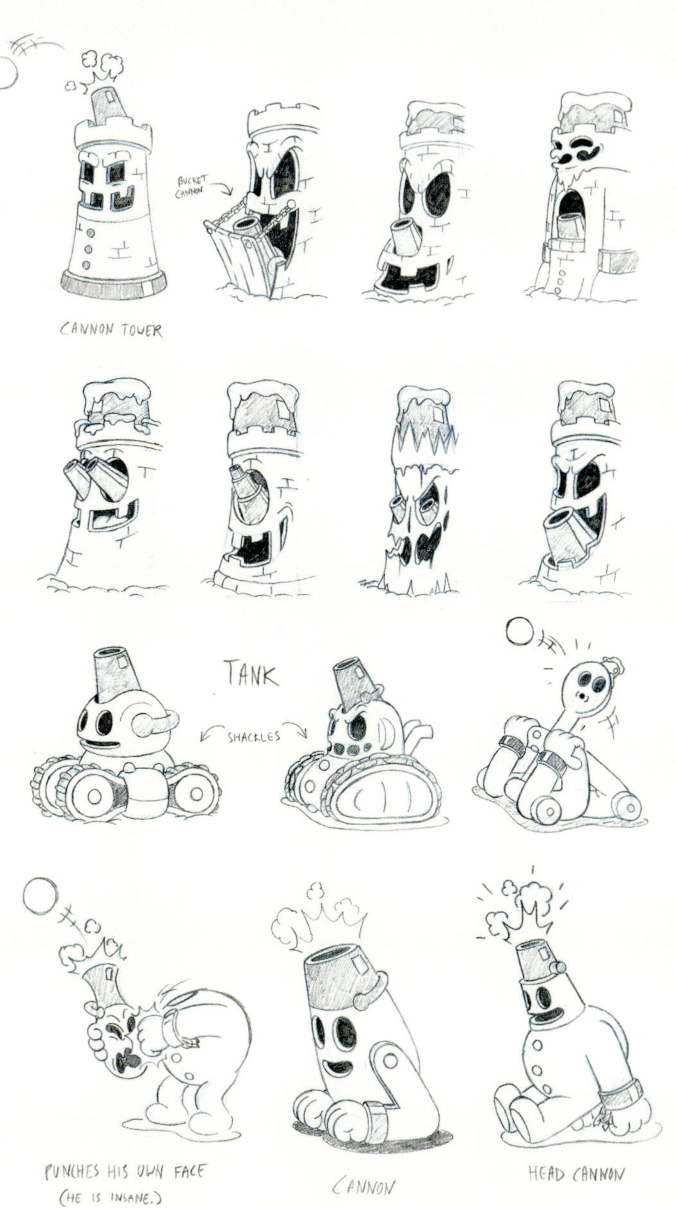
BUCKET CANNON
CANNON TOWER
TANK
SHACKLES
PUNCHES HIS OWN FACE
(HE IS INSANE.)
CANNON
HEAD CANNON

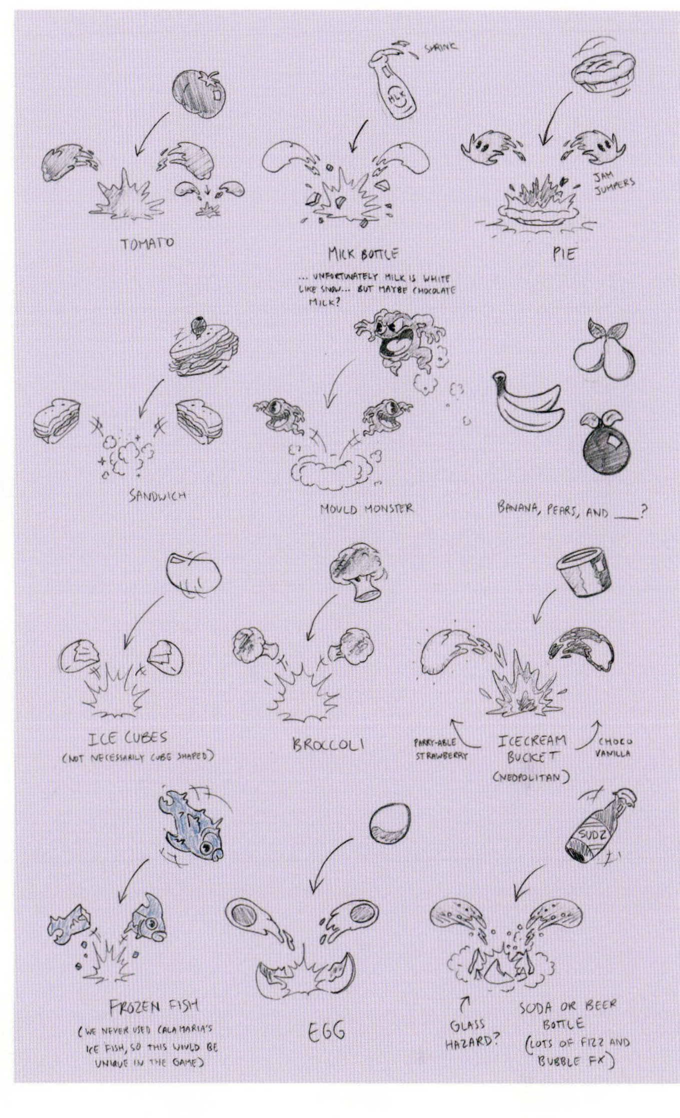
TOMATO
MILK BOTTLE
... UNFORTUNATELY MILK IS WHITE LIKE SNOW... BUT MAYBE CHOCOLATE MILK?
PIE
JAM JUMPERS
SANDWICH
MOULD MONSTER
BANANA, PEARS, AND ___?
ICE CUBES
(NOT NECESSARILY CUBE SHAPED)
BROCCOLI
PARRY-ABLE STRAWBERRY
ICECREAM BUCKET
(NEOPOLITAN)
CHOCO VANILLA
SUDZ
FROZEN FISH
(WE NEVER USED CALA MARIA'S ICE FISH, SO THIS WOULD BE UNIQUE IN THE GAME)
EGG
GLASS HAZARD?
SODA OR BEER BOTTLE
(LOTS OF FIZZ AND BUBBLE FX)

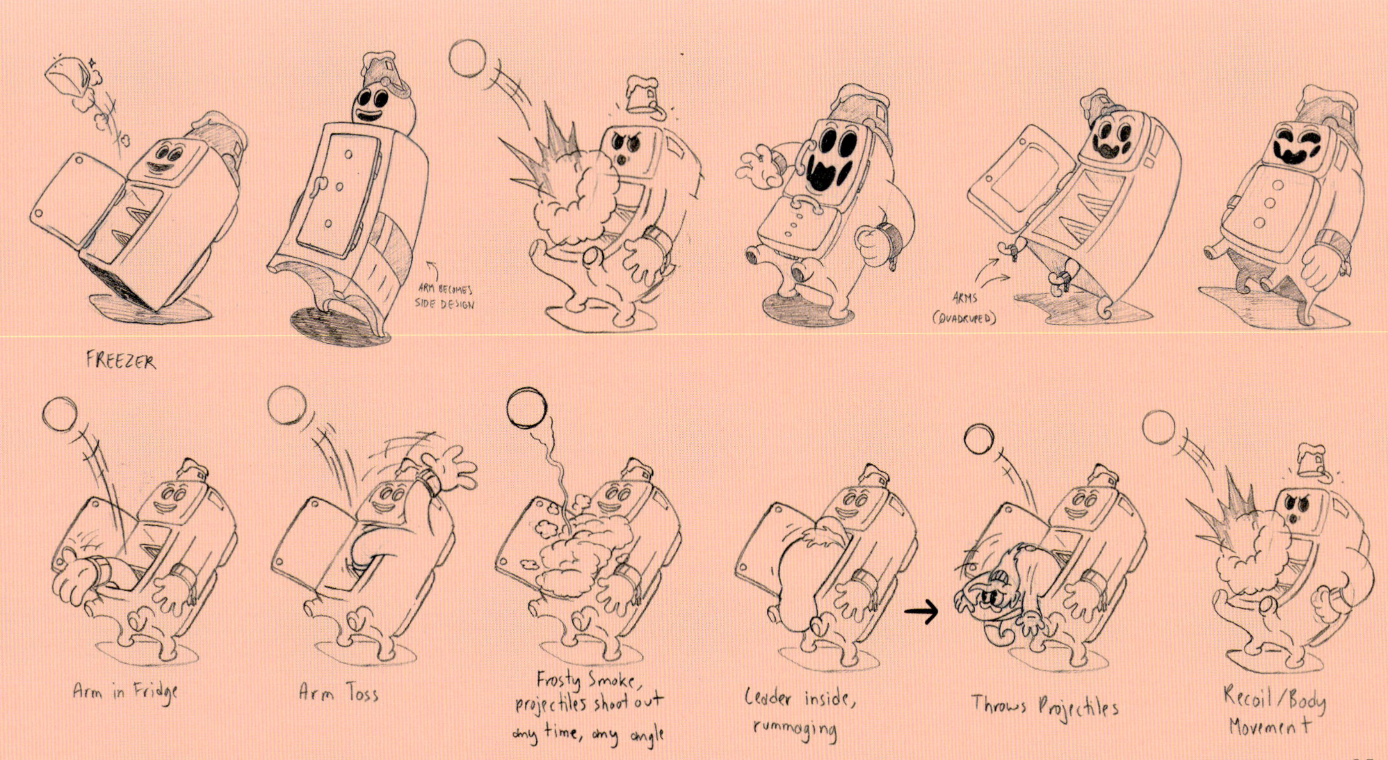
ARM BECOMES SIDE DESIGN
ARMS
(QUADRUPED)
FREEZER
Arm in Fridge
Arm Toss
Frosty Smoke, projectiles shoot out any time, any angle
Leader inside, rummaging
Throws Projectiles
Recoil / Body Movement

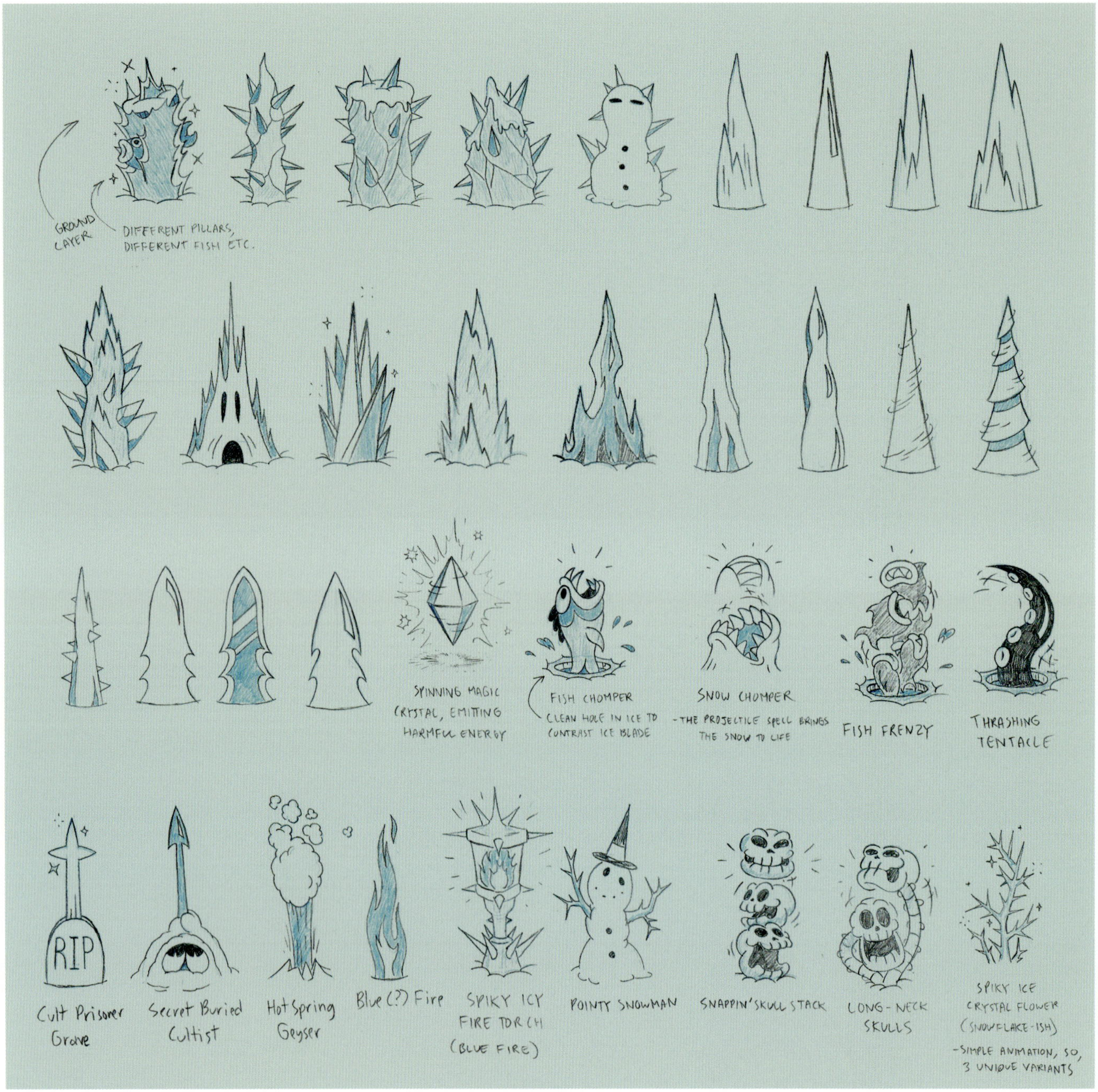

GROUND LAYER

DIFFERENT PILLARS, DIFFERENT FISH ETC.

SPINNING MAGIC CRYSTAL, EMITTING HARMFUL ENERGY

FISH CHOMPER

CLEAN HOLE IN ICE TO CONTRAST ICE BLADE

SNOW CHOMPER

-THE PROJECTILE SPELL BRINGS THE SNOW TO LIFE

FISH FRENZY

THRASHING TENTACLE

Cult Prisoner Grave

Secret Buried Cultist

Hot Spring Geyser

Blue (?) Fire

SPIKY ICY FIRE TORCH (BLUE FIRE)

POINTY SNOWMAN

SNAPPIN' SKULL STACK

LONG-NECK SKULLS

SPIKY ICE CRYSTAL FLOWER (SNOWFLAKE-ISH)

-SIMPLE ANIMATION, SO, 3 UNIQUE VARIANTS

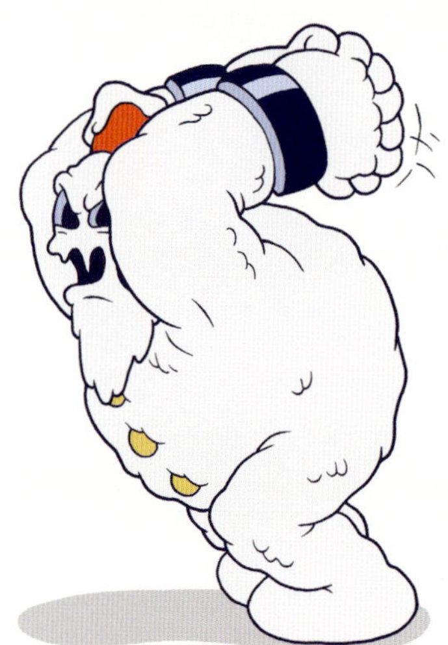

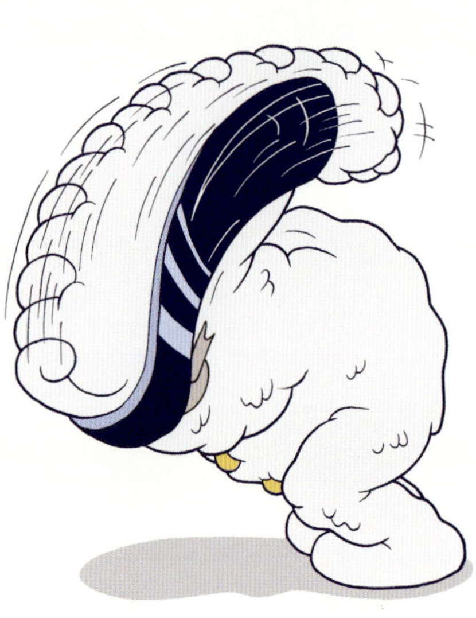

"Iced already? Where puny cups go?"

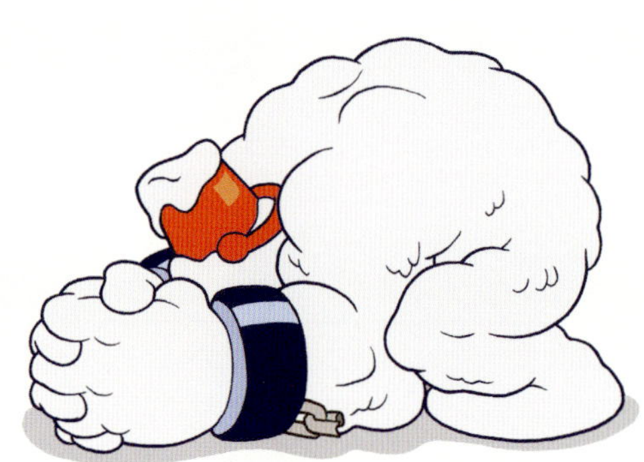

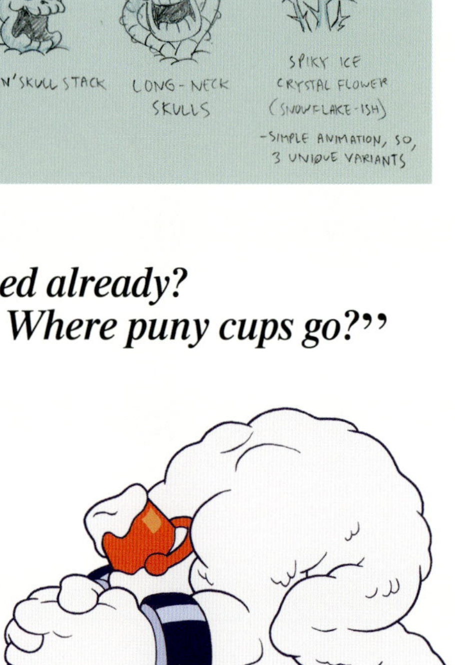

Bursting from the chest of Jupiter, Mortimer Freeze's final magic trick is a total body transformation! Awaiting you in the sky is a side-switching snowflake standoff on some perilous platforms. We're always looking for finales that can showcase the faces of our foes as large as possible, as their comical expressions really sell their personality. Mortimer's snowflake form gave us an opportunity to flex our imaginations. With Glumstone the Giant already filling our large-bearded-man quota, we moved from just a large representation of Mortimer's face to a snowflake shell design inspired by classic face-flipping bosses of eras gone by, including Toaplan's *Snow Bros. 2* (1994) and Sega's *Ghostbusters* (1990).

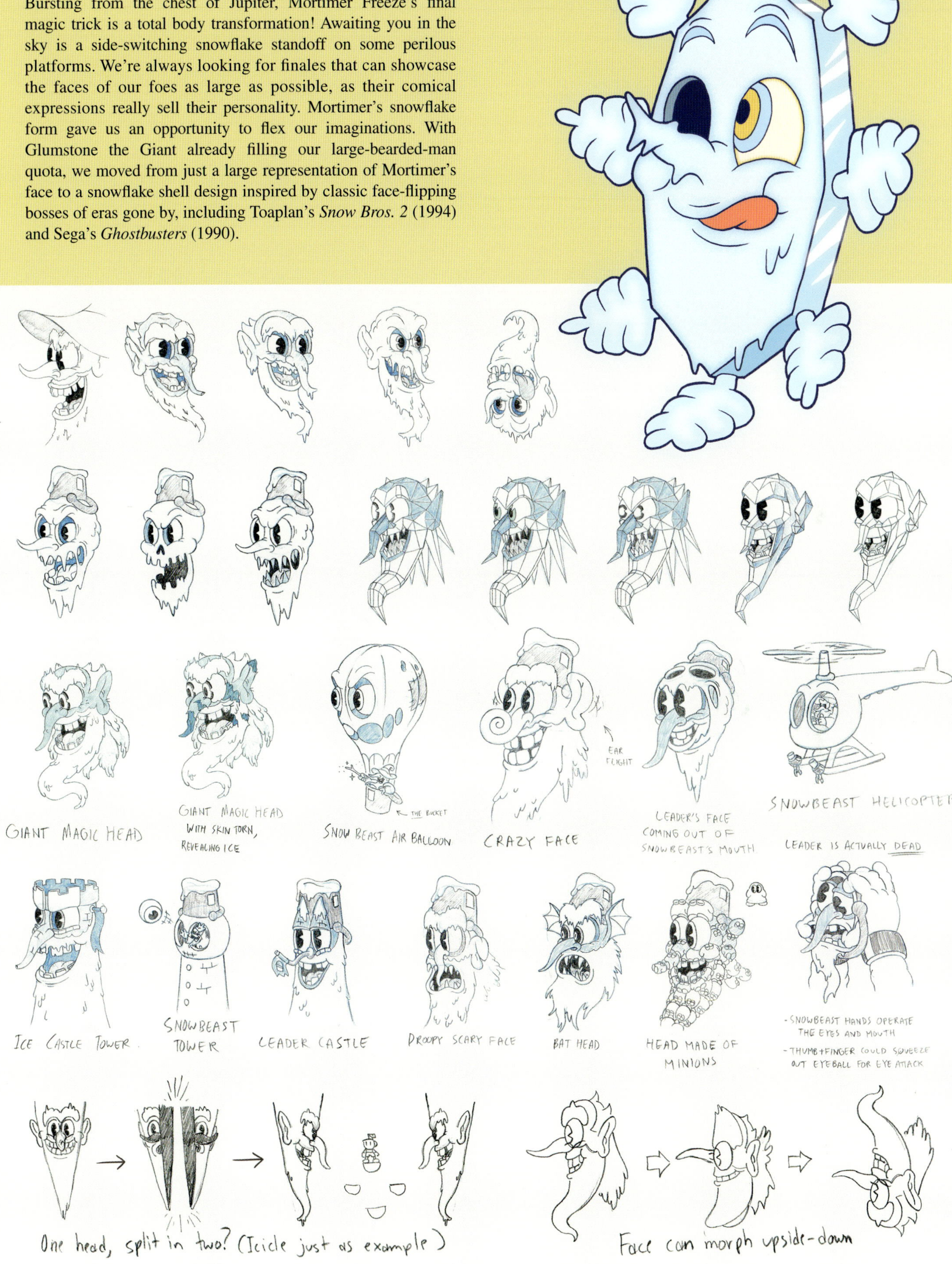

While going through the visual design process for Mortimer's snowflake, we often had to strike a balance between what the real properties of a snowflake were and what we thought would look and operate best for our design. For instance, real snowflakes have six points, but we broke that rule and went with eight points because it placed the points along the sides in a more "arm-like" position that would work with various animations. Additionally, we had to keep shrinking Mortimer's snowflake nose, as it was jutting out into the space the players would be moving within, and we didn't want it interfering with the platforms.

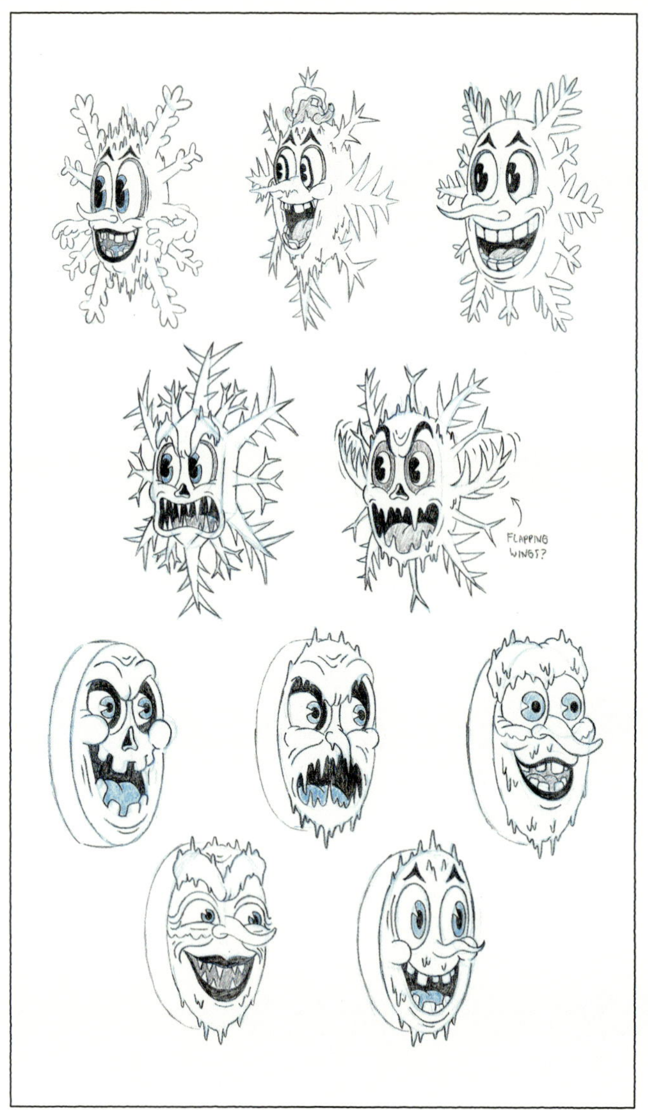

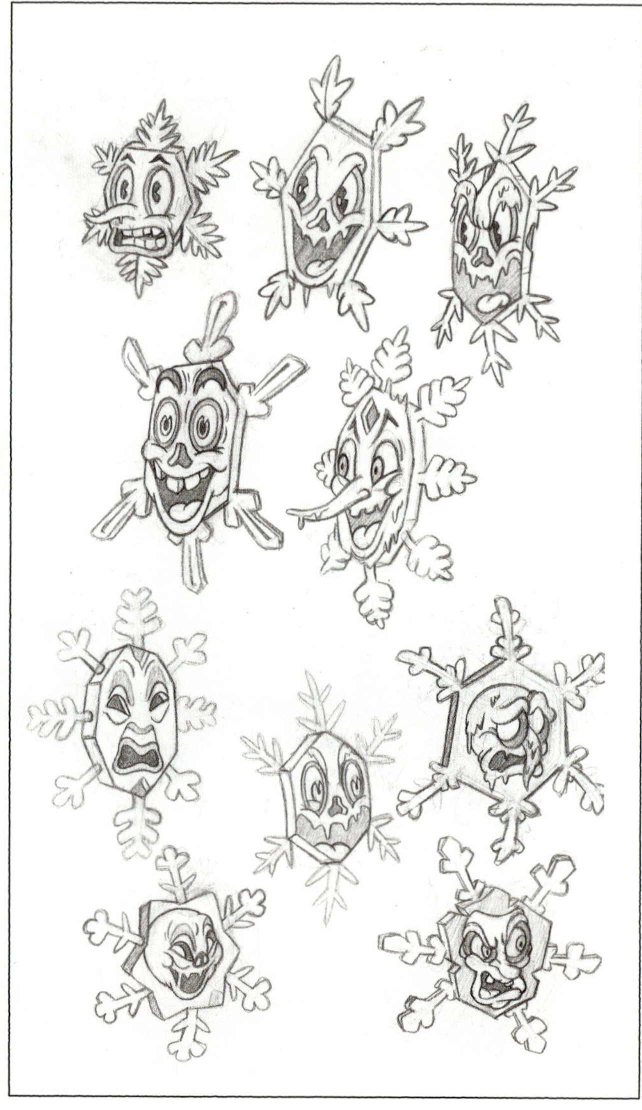

In true Studio MDHR fashion, we were not content with a simple side-switching animation. Instead, we created three bespoke side switching animations for each of the possible ways Mortimer could move and rotate during the fight.

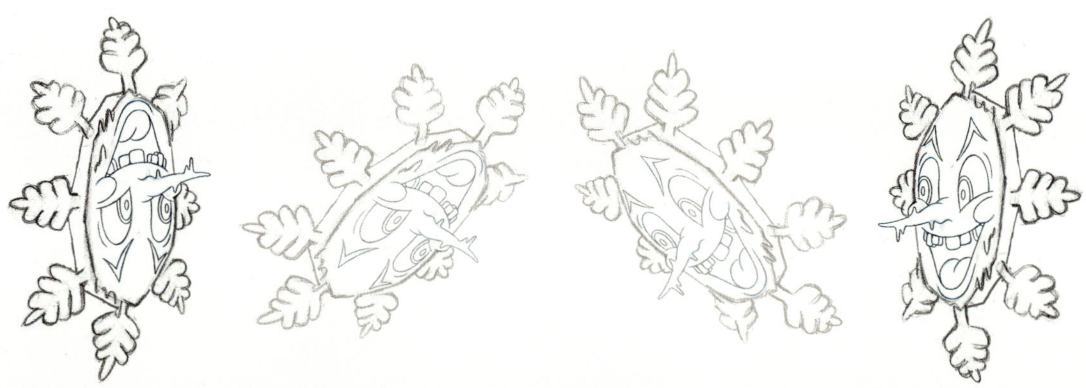

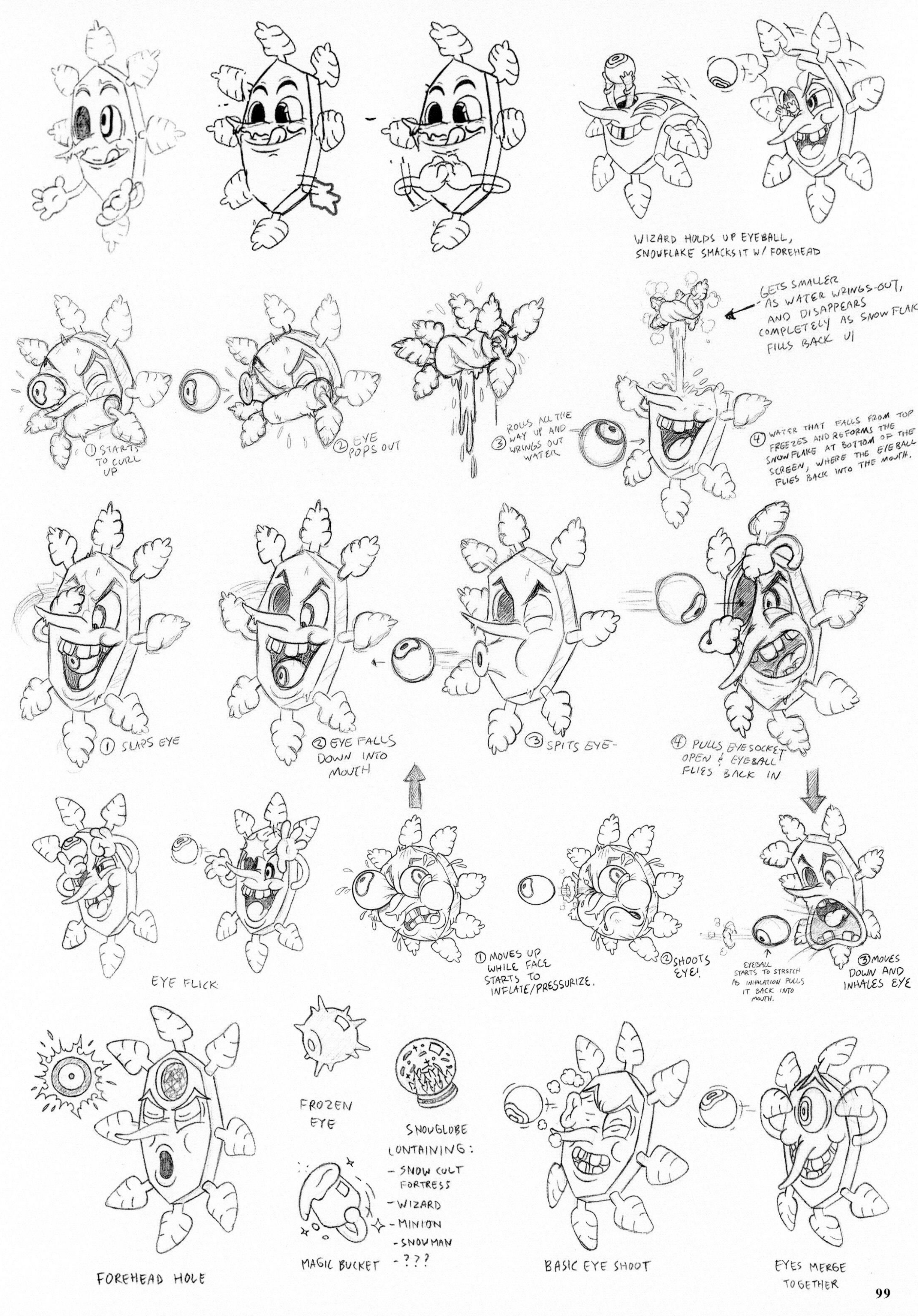
WIZARD HOLDS UP EYEBALL,
SNOWFLAKE SMACKS IT W/ FOREHEAD
GETS SMALLER AS WATER WRINGS-OUT, AND DISAPPEARS COMPLETELY AS SNOW FLAKE FILLS BACK UP
① STARTS TO CURL UP
② EYE POPS OUT
③ ROLLS ALL THE WAY UP AND WRINGS OUT WATER
④ WATER THAT FALLS FROM TOP FREEZES AND REFORMS THE SNOWFLAKE AT BOTTOM OF THE SCREEN, WHERE THE EYEBALL FLIES BACK INTO THE MOUTH.
① SLAPS EYE
② EYE FALLS DOWN INTO MOUTH
③ SPITS EYE-
④ PULLS EYE SOCKET OPEN & EYEBALL FLIES BACK IN
EYE FLICK
① MOVES UP WHILE FACE STARTS TO INFLATE/PRESSURIZE.
② SHOOTS EYE!
EYEBALL STARTS TO STRETCH AS INHALATION PULLS IT BACK INTO MOUTH.
③ MOVES DOWN AND INHALES EYE
FOREHEAD HOLE
FROZEN EYE
SNOWGLOBE CONTAINING:
- SNOW CULT FORTRESS
- WIZARD
- MINION
- SNOWMAN
- ???
MAGIC BUCKET
BASIC EYE SHOOT
EYES MERGE TOGETHER

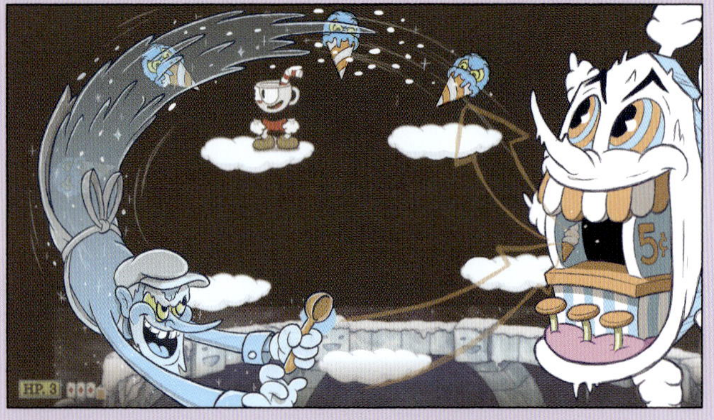

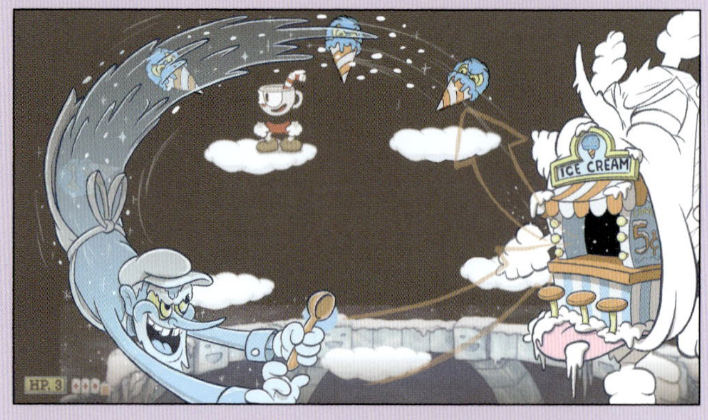

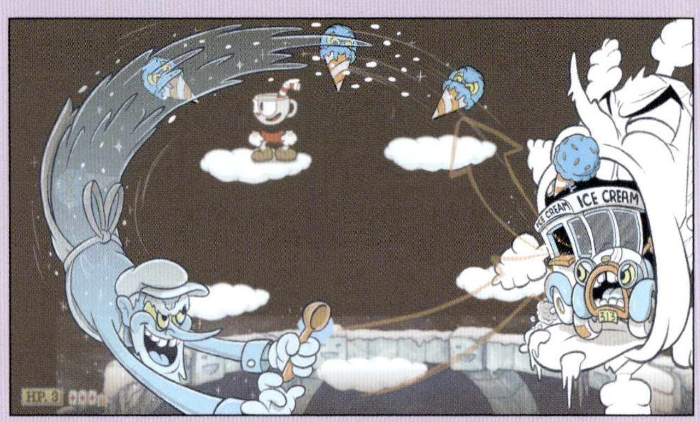

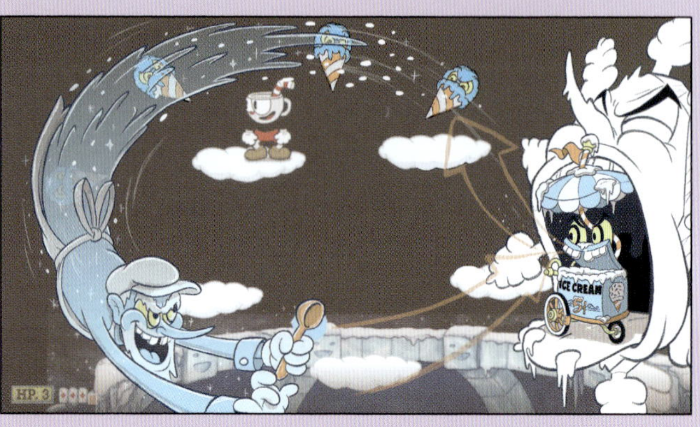

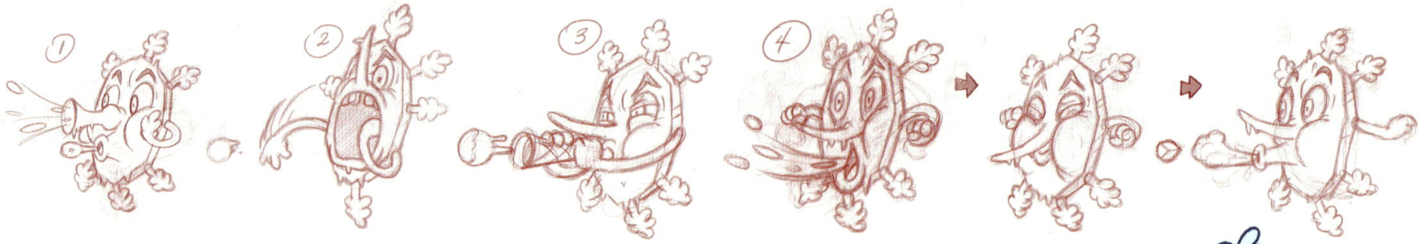

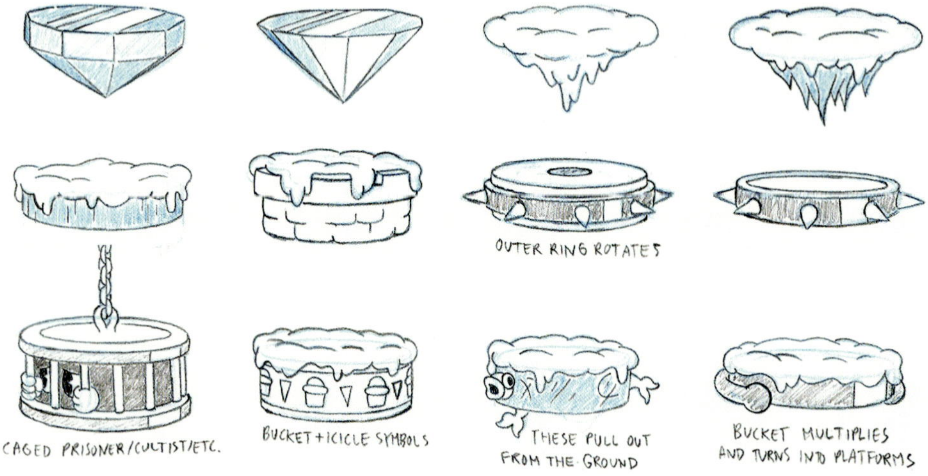

1 2 3 4

OUTER RING ROTATES

CAGED PRISONER/CULTIST/ETC.

BUCKET + ICICLE SYMBOLS

THESE PULL OUT FROM THE GROUND

BUCKET MULTIPLIES AND TURNS INTO PLATFORMS

We never miss an opportunity to do something elaborate, so the summoning of the ice cream cones required a full character transformation into an old-timey ice cream stand (with an awning top made of teeth, of course), as Mortimer's frosty spirit leaves his mouth and spirals around the stage.

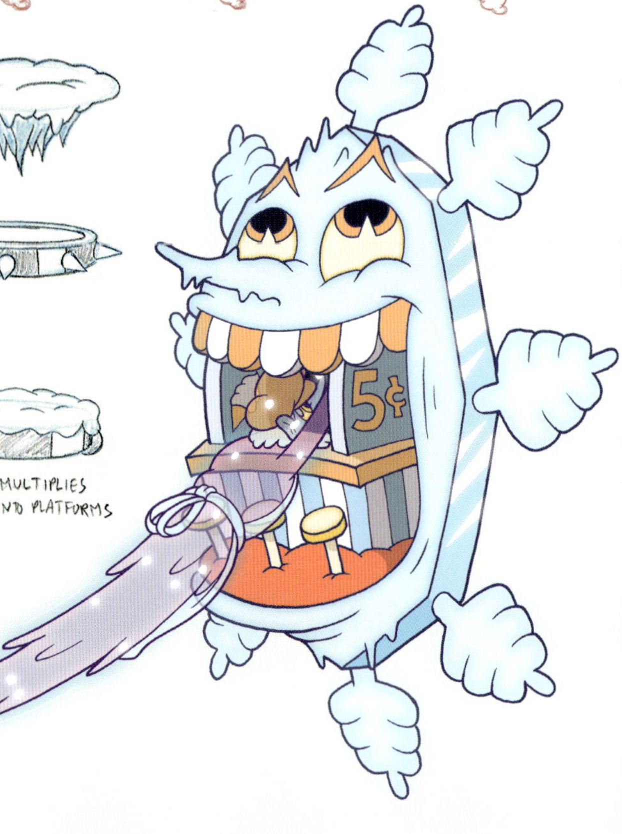

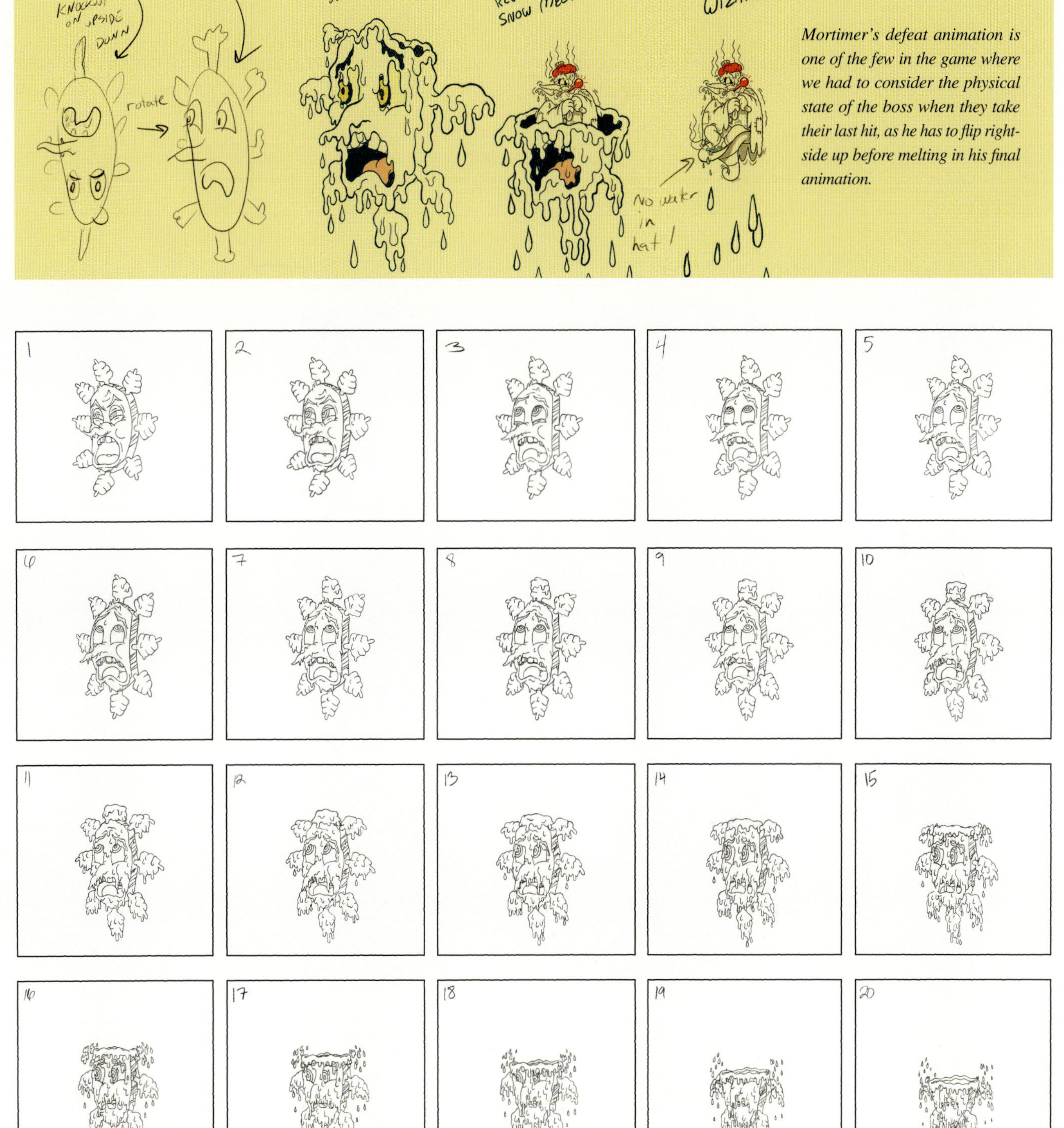

Mortimer's defeat animation is one of the few in the game where we had to consider the physical state of the boss when they take their last hit, as he has to flip right-side up before melting in his final animation.

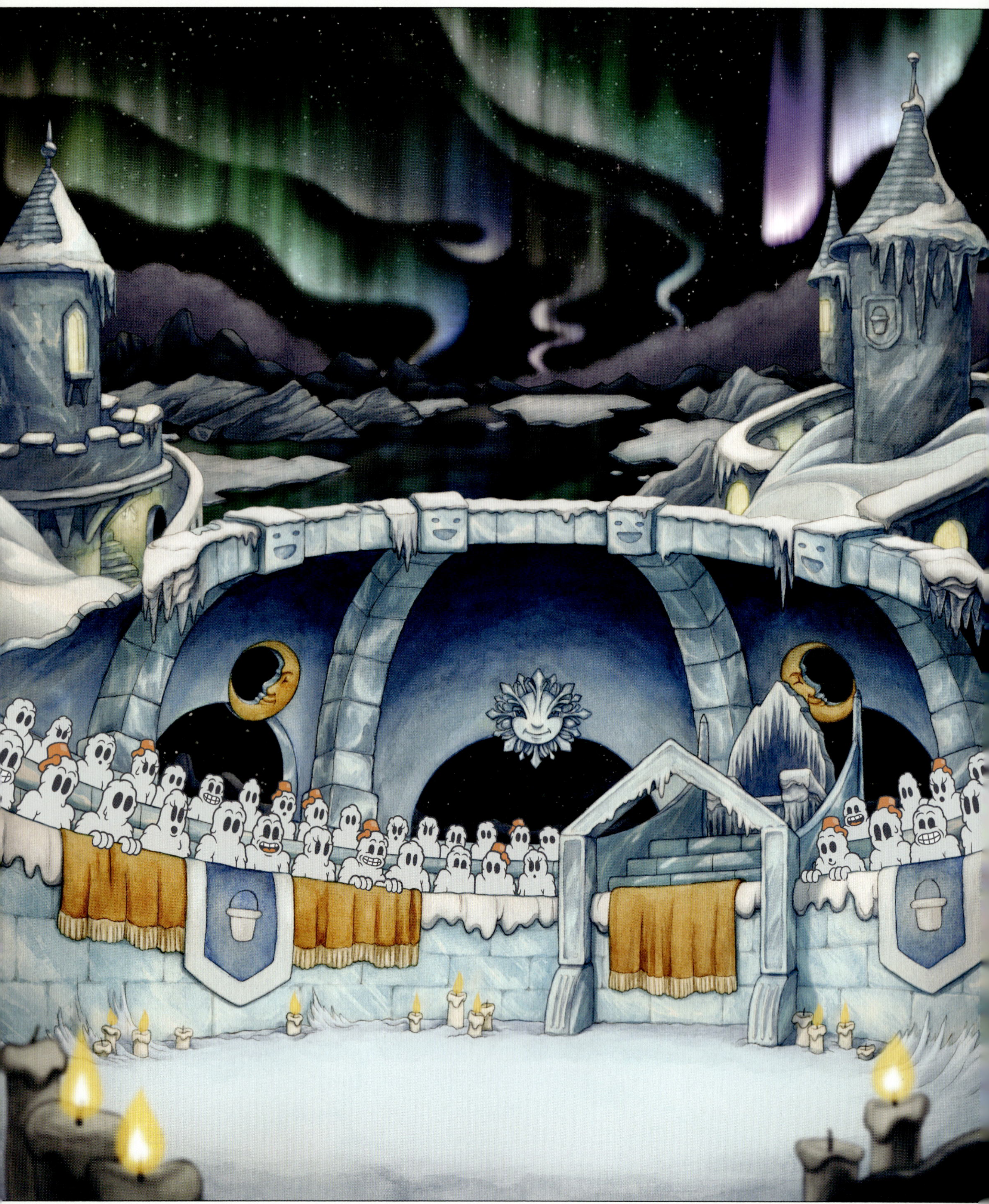

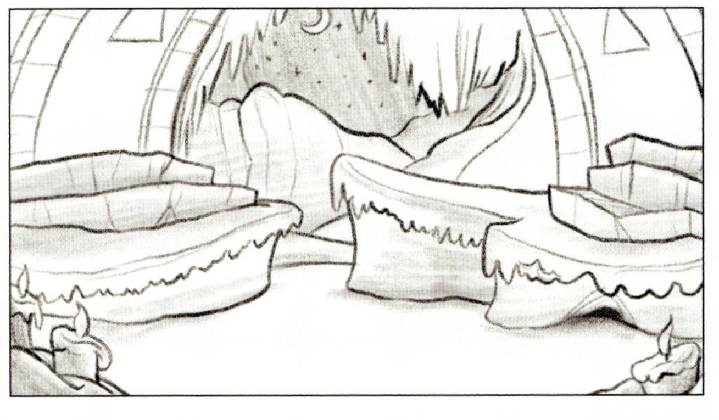

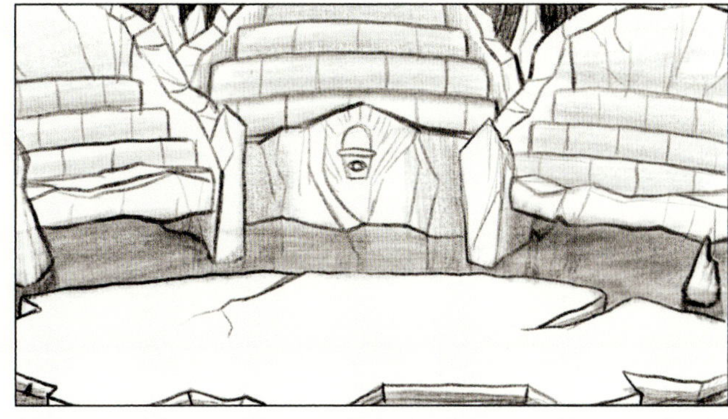

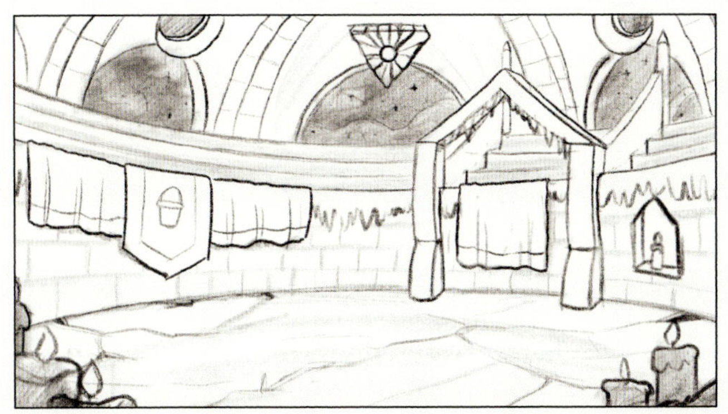

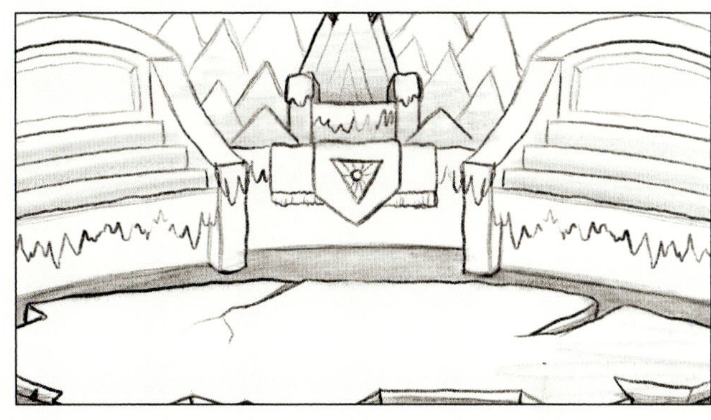

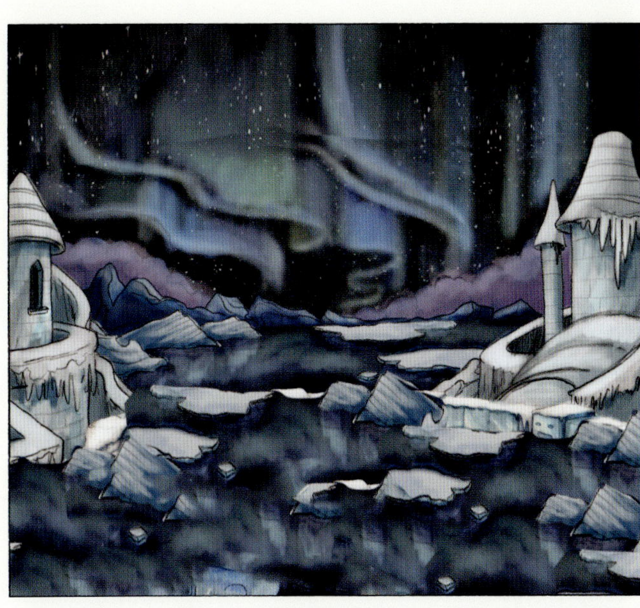

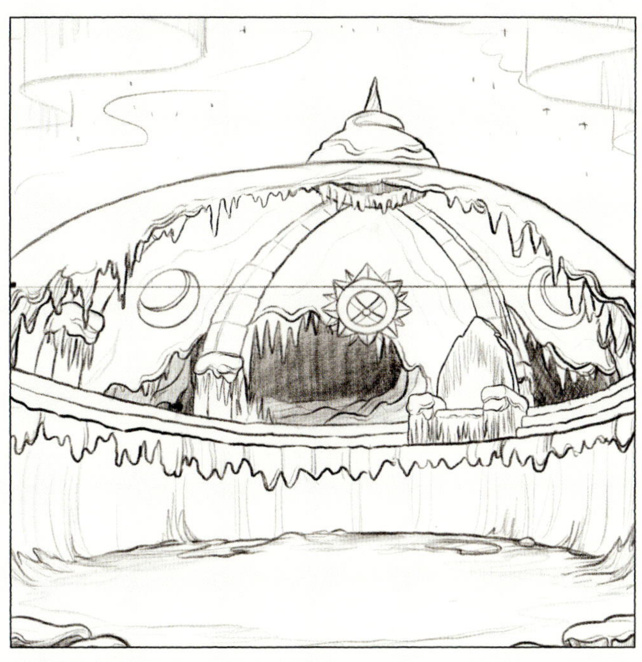

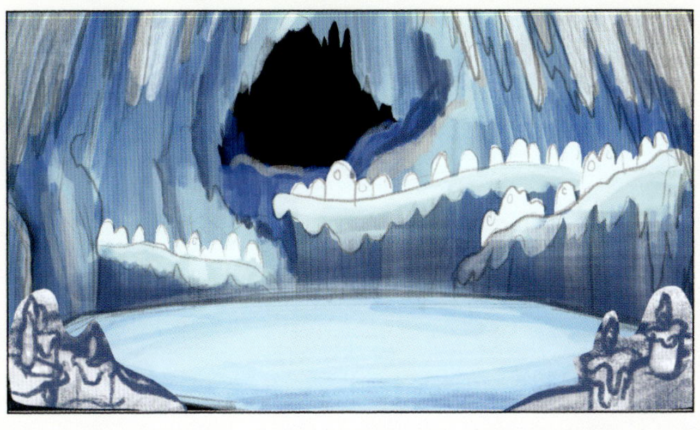

Snow Cult Scuffle Background

FROM THE COLISEUM FULL OF religious iconography to the Northern Lights glimmering above, to the amassed congregation watching the proceedings, the background to Snow Cult Scuffle took significant coordination between the various art disciplines. Animator Jake Clark brought the snowy patrons to life, while FX Artist and Animator Danielle Johnson created the ethereal glimmering of the aurora borealis, all above a stage painted by Caitlin Russell.

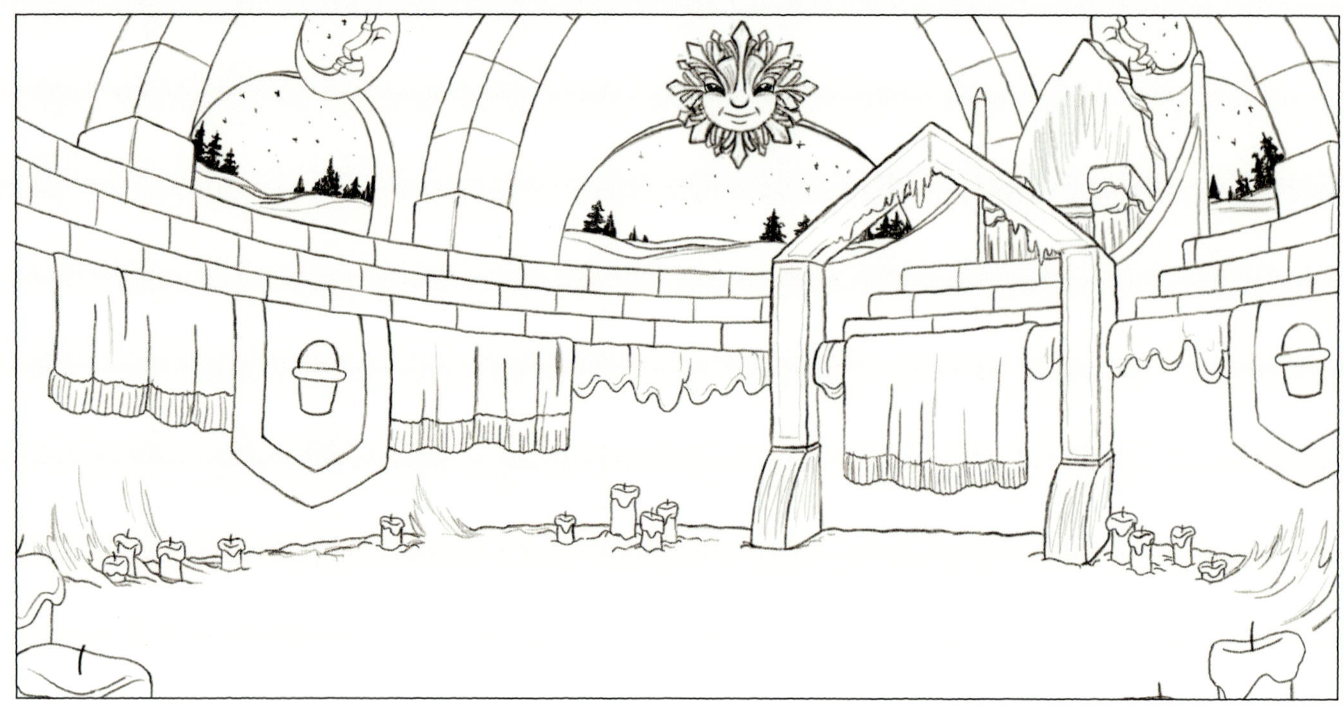

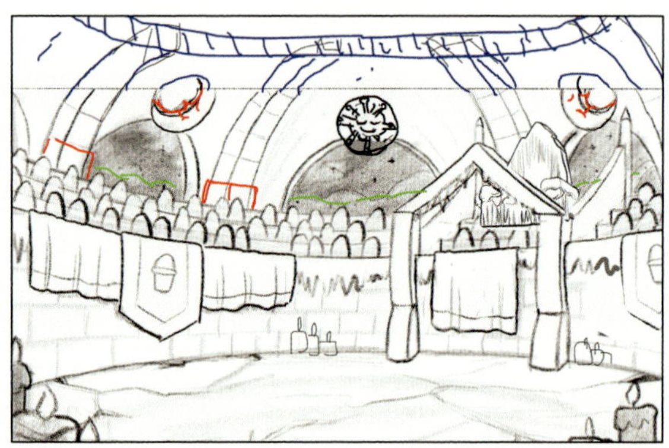

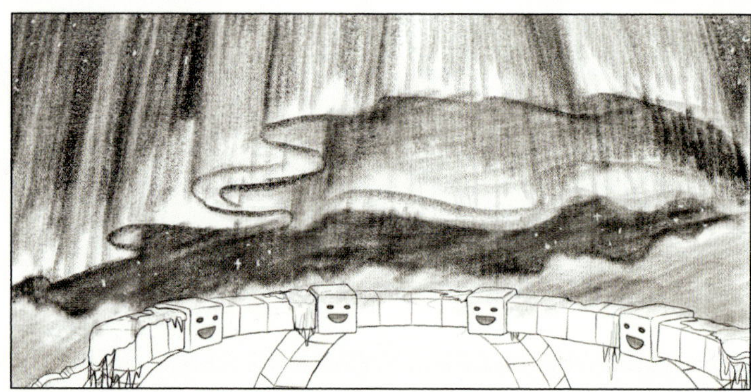

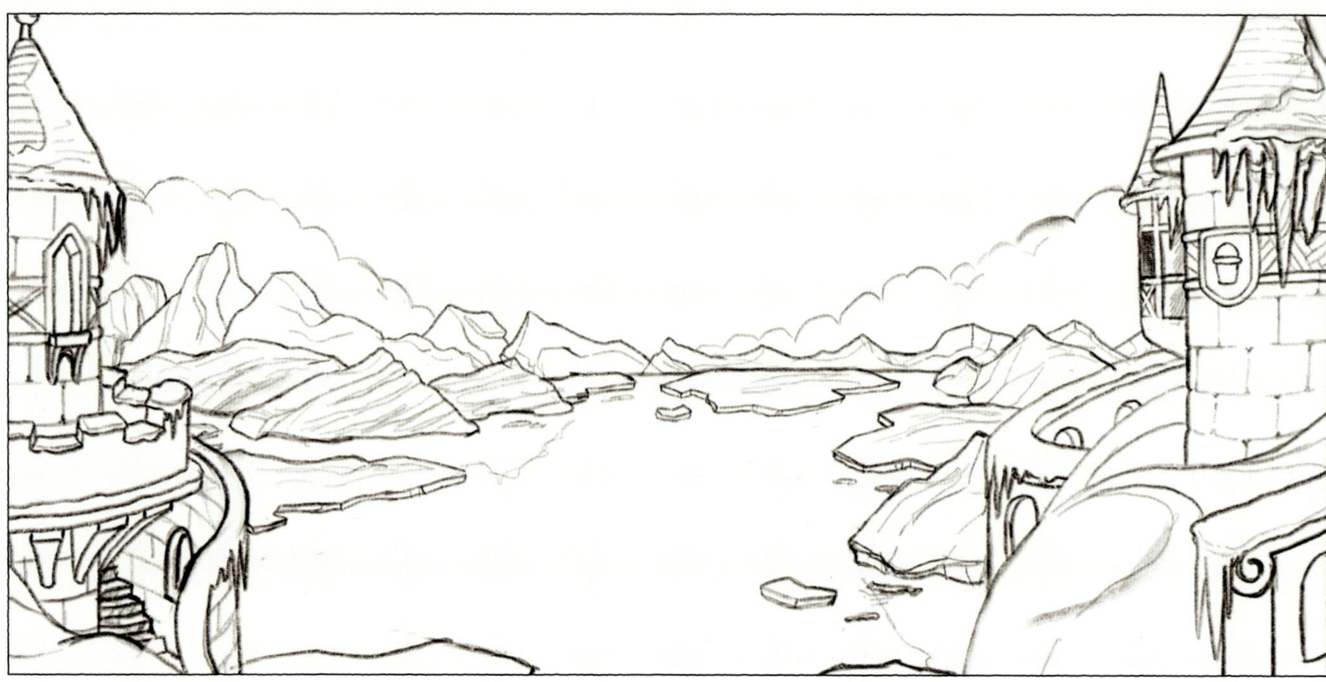

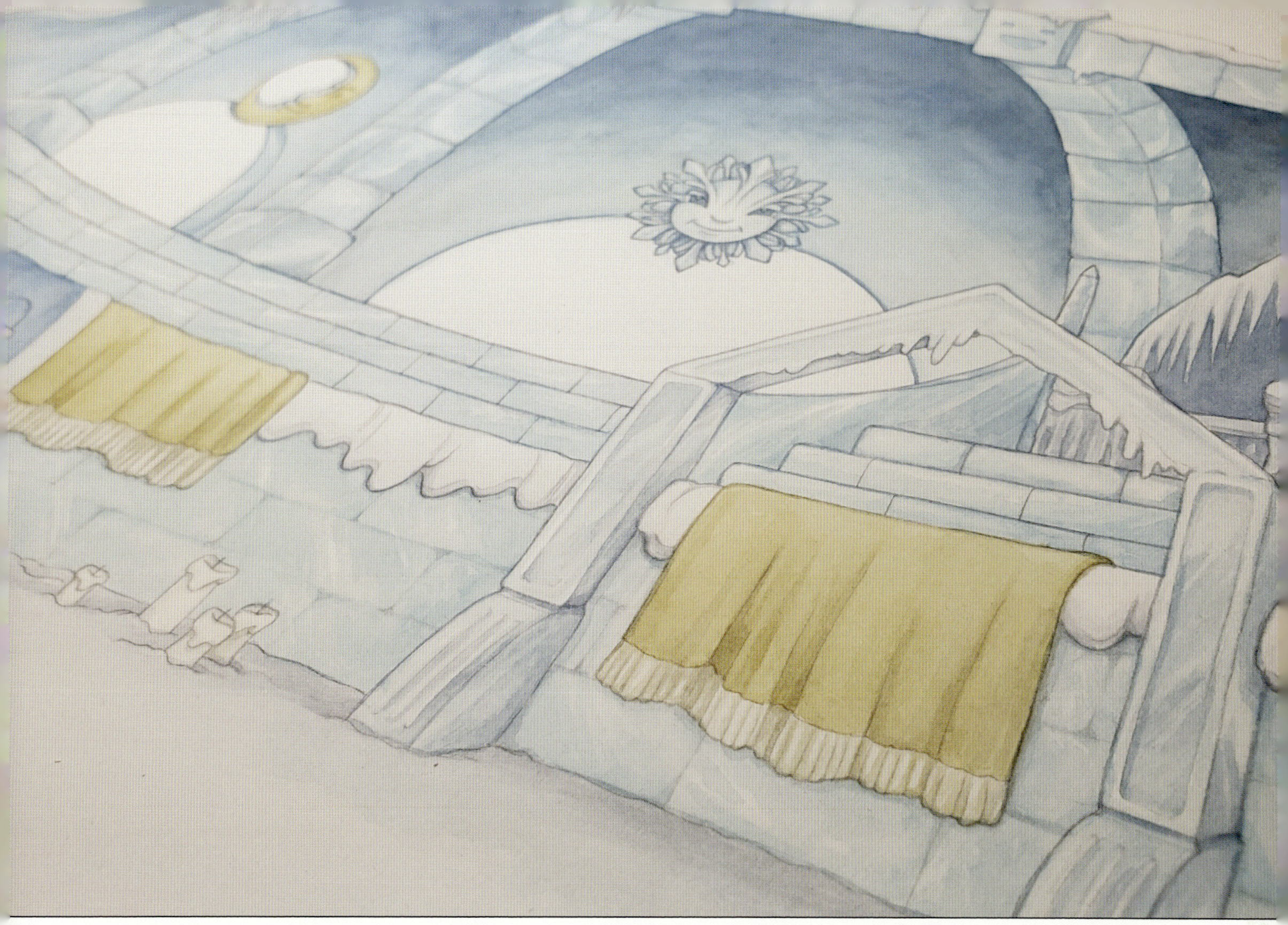

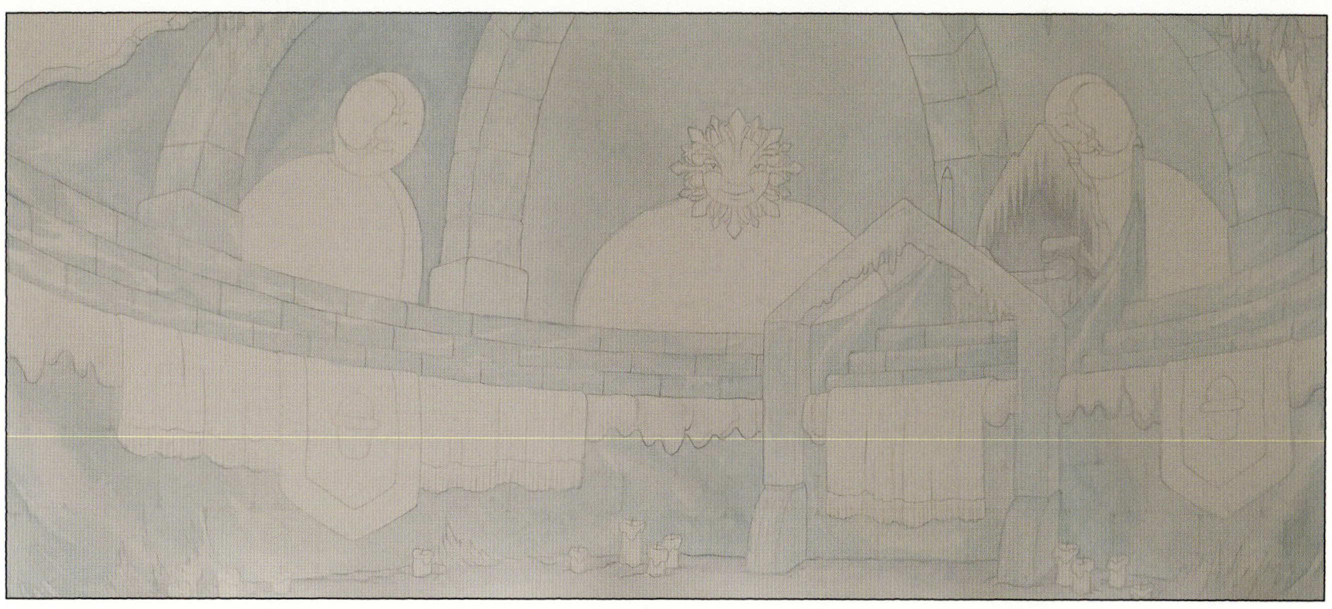

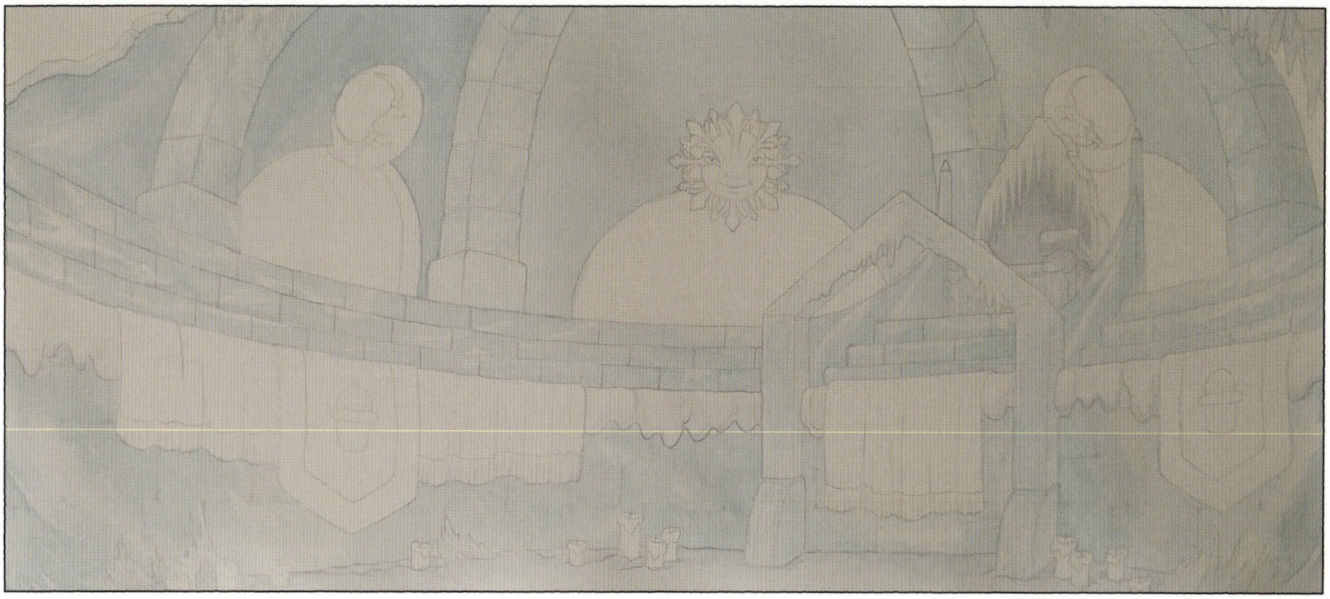

Since the gameplay design of the Snow Cult went through a number of iterations, the transition between the congregation's coliseum (completed early in development) to the skies above the lake for phase three (developed later), forced us to break a few perspective rules and apply a few tricks to make things work visually. During the ascent, the mountains seen through the windows in phase one are subtly swapped for the lake and new mountain range, allowing us to have both a low horizon line for the ground level fight and scenic view while up above.

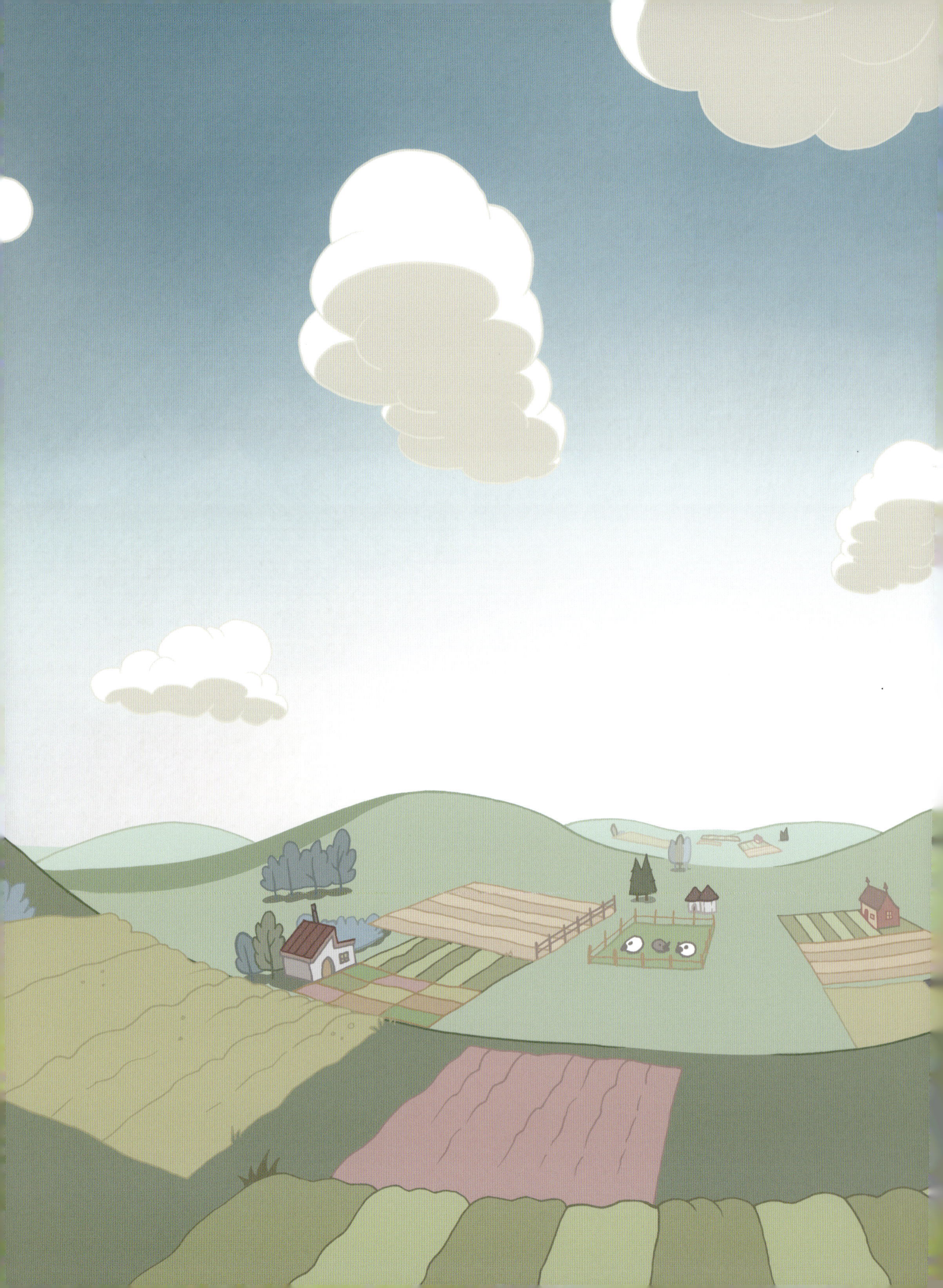

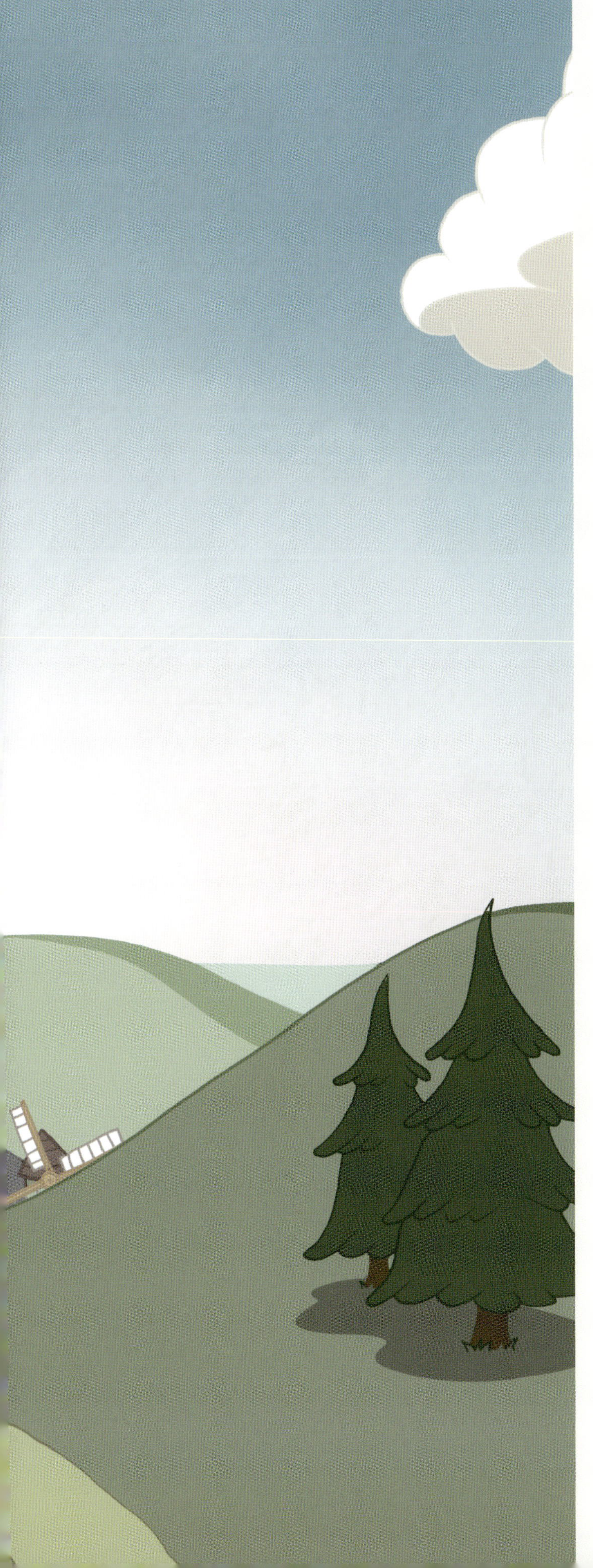

Chapter VII:
Doggone Dogfight

AT (UN)EASE, SOLDIER! Your mission, should you be able to survive it, is to go toe to paw with the meanest military mutts around in a spectacular scuffle in the skies. For your airborne amusement, we present The Howling Aces in… Doggone Dogfight! As a home to many of the ideas we couldn't fit into the original *Cuphead* experience, "DLC Island" was the perfect place to situate this battle against one of the classic archetypes of vintage cartoons: the aviator.

When we began exploring a boss fight in the skies, we very quickly coalesced around the idea of a military-adjacent theme so often seen in shorts of the era. And what better way to represent a *dogfight* than with a literal pack of hounds looking to blast you out of the skies. If the player's goal was to put these pesky pups in their place, however, ours was something altogether more ambitious: to craft a *Cuphead* battle in which the player was travelling *into* the screen. The result was a complex series of experiments with physical models of everything from spinning globes to moving movator fields of grass, before arriving at the decision to create something truly one-of-a-kind in the world of the Inkwell Isles: our only fully hand-animated boss background ever.

The Howling Aces in "DOGGONE DOGFIGHT"

WE KNEW FROM THE OUTSET of this battle's design that we wanted to give it the distinct feeling of participating in an airborne dogfight without conflating the experience with the game's other plane-based "shoot-'em-up" levels. Taking inspiration from the lightly controllable platform in our original game's battle against The Phantom Express, and 1992's *Sonic the Hedgehog 2*–in which the titular hero rode a plane while his pal Tails piloted–we landed on the notion of staging the first phase of this fight atop a biplane you control with your movement.

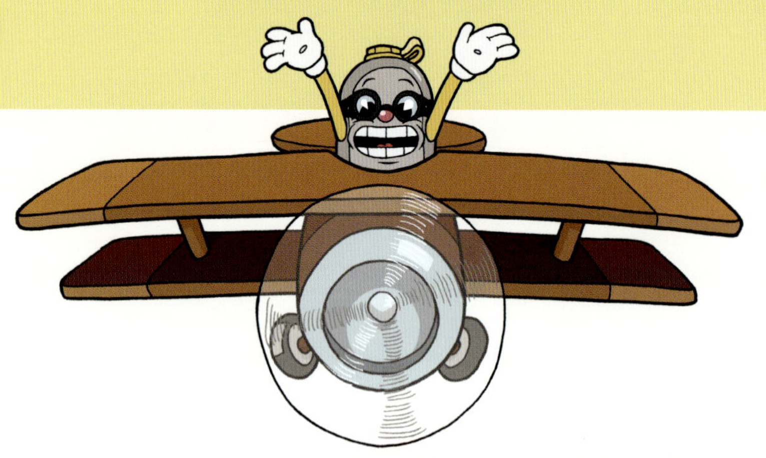

Canteen Hughes

PLAYING THE ROLE OF Cuphead's co-pilot in his fight against The Howling Aces is none other than the Inkwell Isles' mentor in all things aviation, Canteen Hughes. Inspired by plane magnate Howard Hughes, eagle-eyed fans will recognize Canteen as the character who leads the early-game tutorial for the plane-based shoot-'em-up levels.

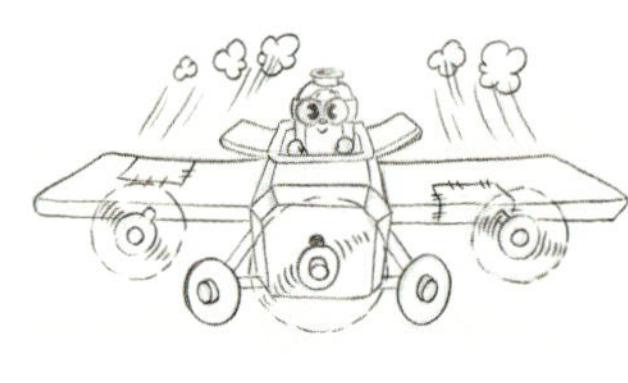
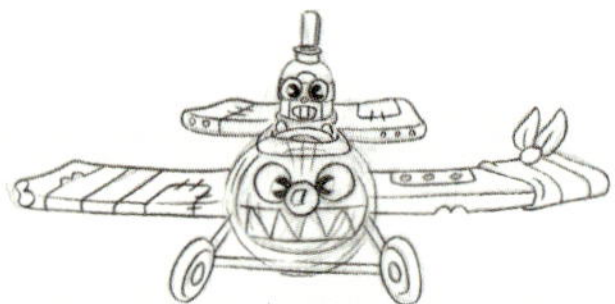
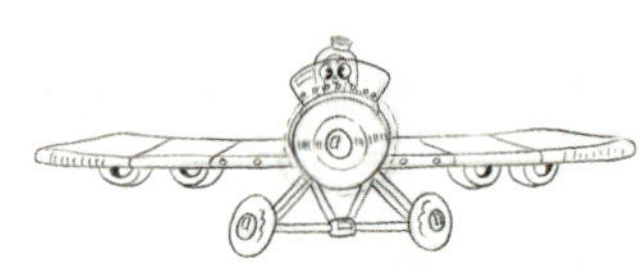
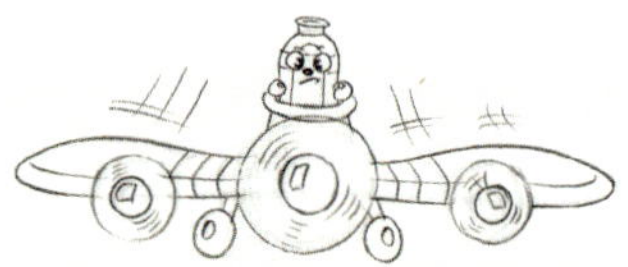
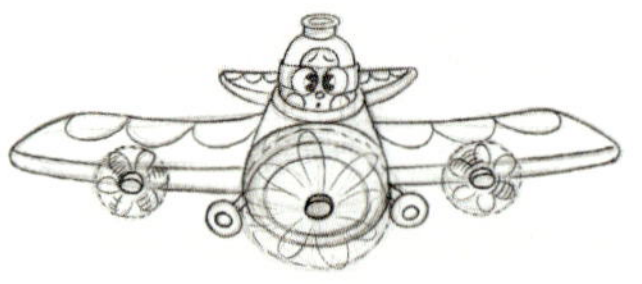
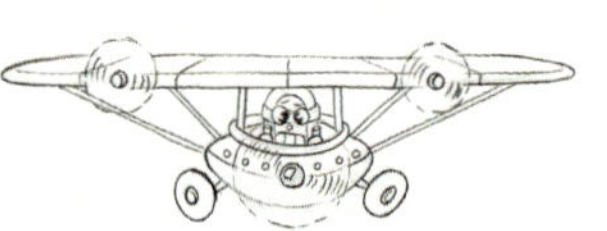
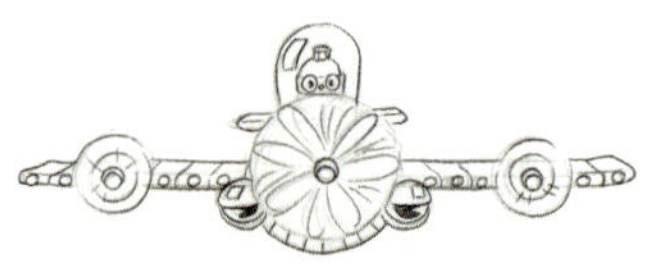
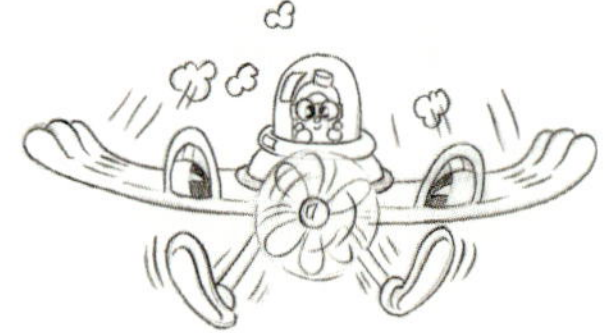
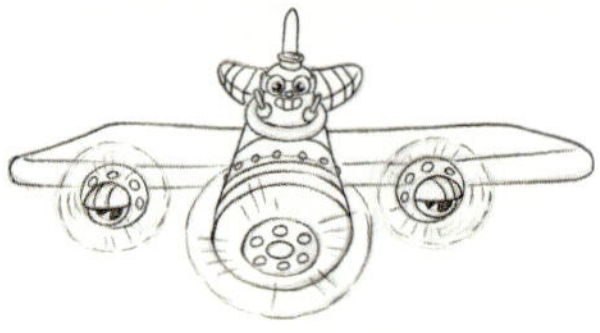
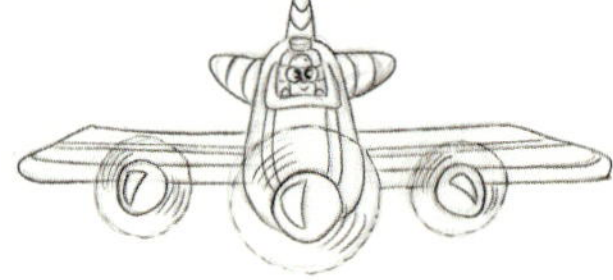
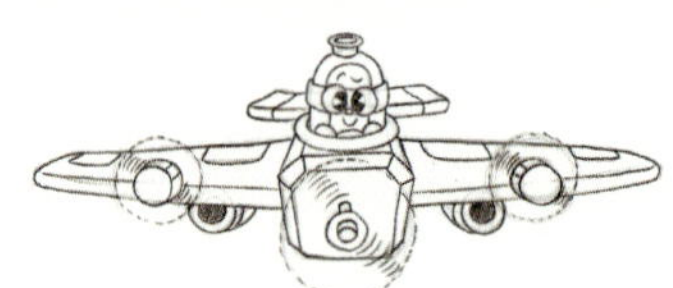
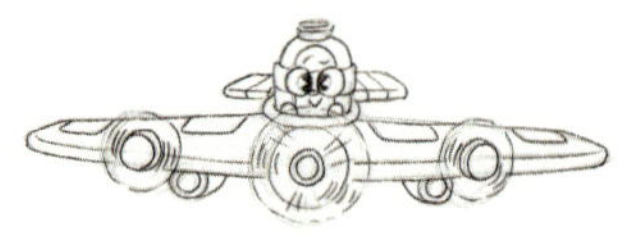
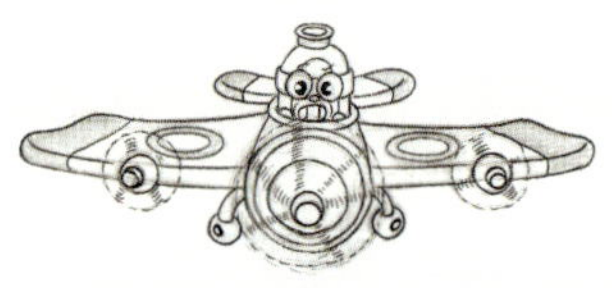
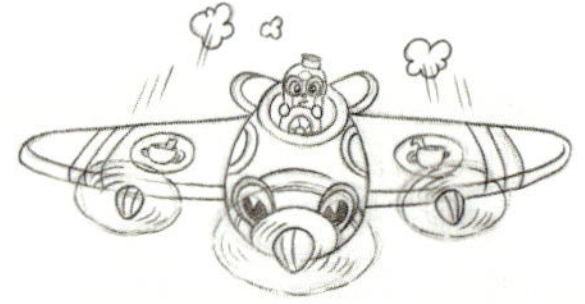
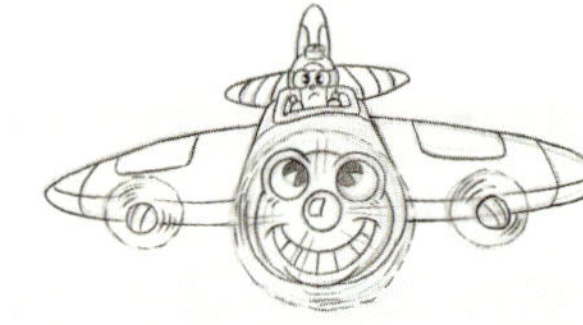
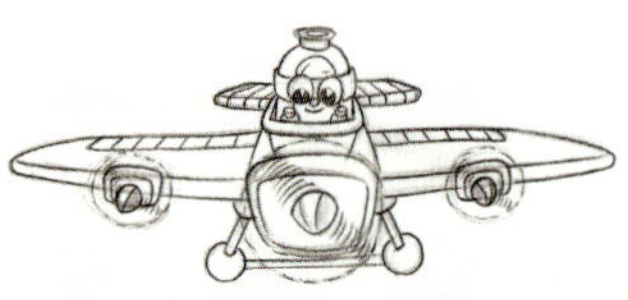
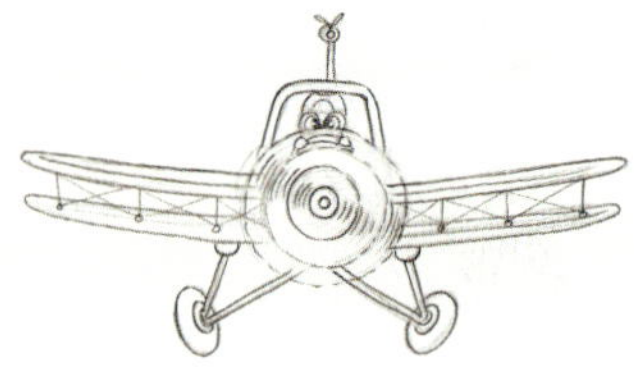
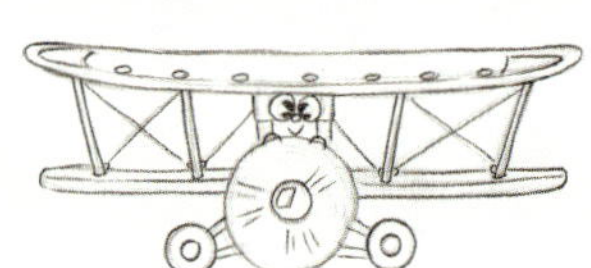
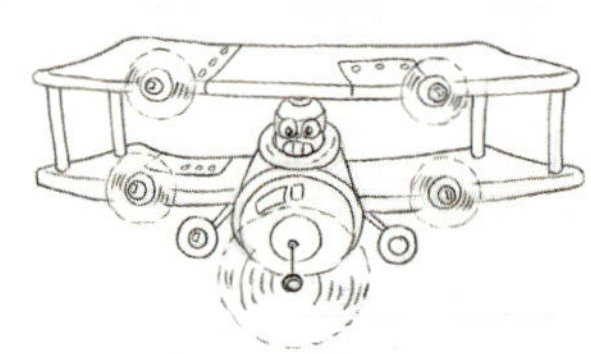
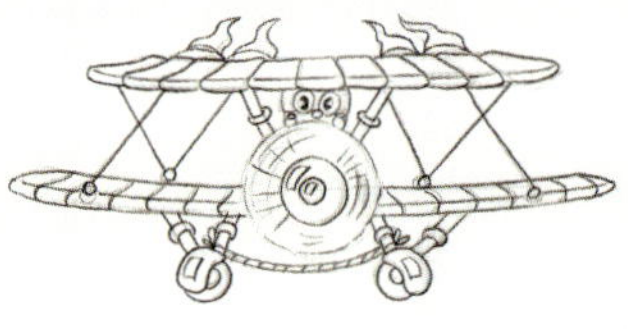

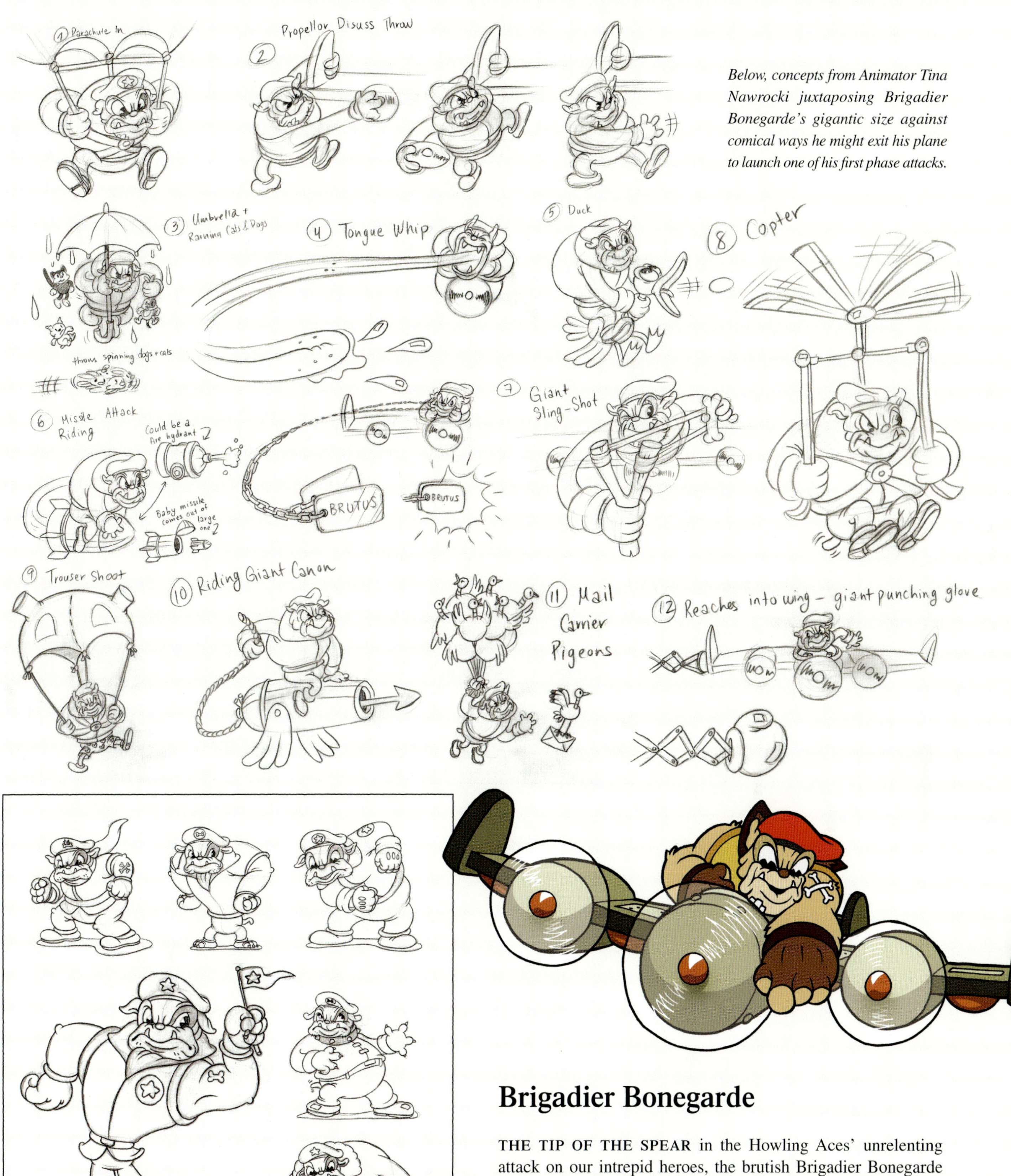

Below, concepts from Animator Tina Nawrocki juxtaposing Brigadier Bonegarde's gigantic size against comical ways he might exit his plane to launch one of his first phase attacks.

Brigadier Bonegarde

THE TIP OF THE SPEAR in the Howling Aces' unrelenting attack on our intrepid heroes, the brutish Brigadier Bonegarde is emblematic of the swirl of cartoon and video game inspiration that often leads us to our character designs. With a beret, tattoos, and final outfit coloring that are reminiscent of military man Rolento from Capcom's *Final Fight* (1989), Bonegarde also contains visual notes of *Tom and Jerry* mainstay Spike the Bulldog. Seen left, in Animator Tina Nawrocki's concept work: ideas for the Howling Aces' uniform iconography, which we sought to keep consistent to sell their status as a unit.

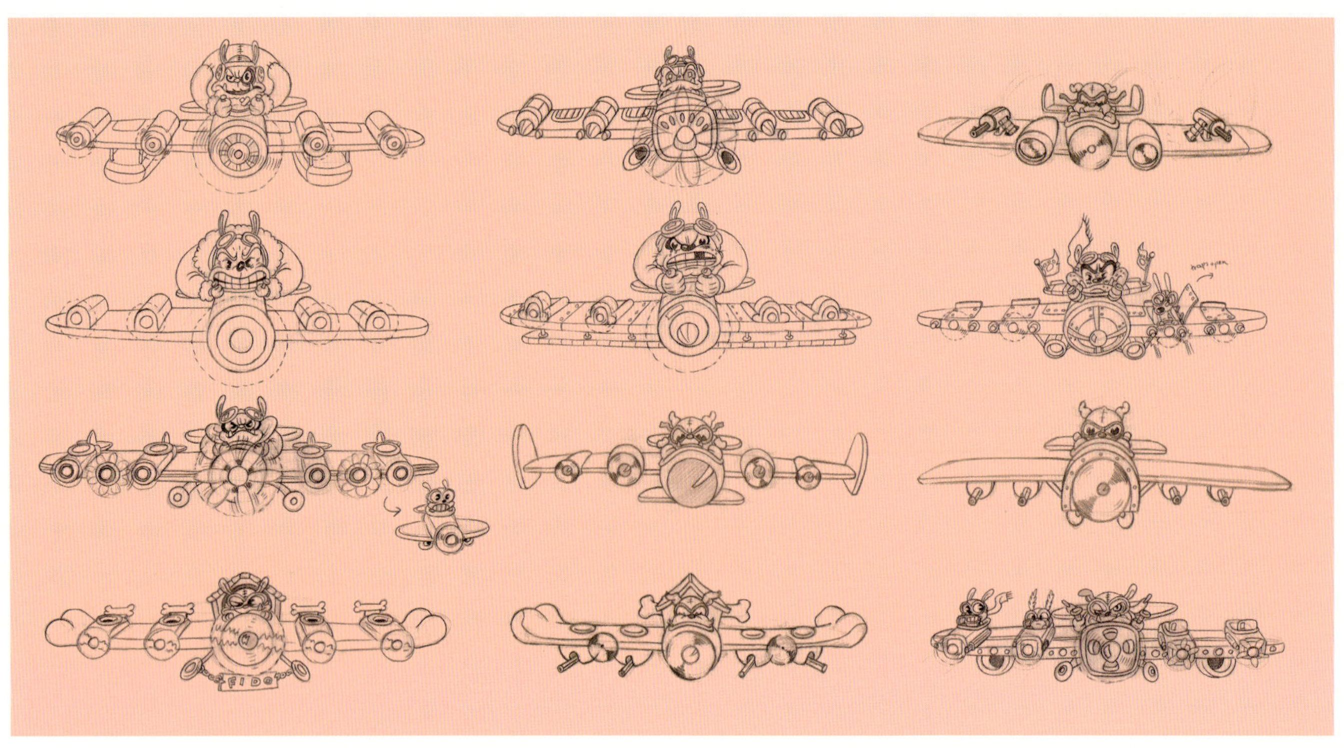

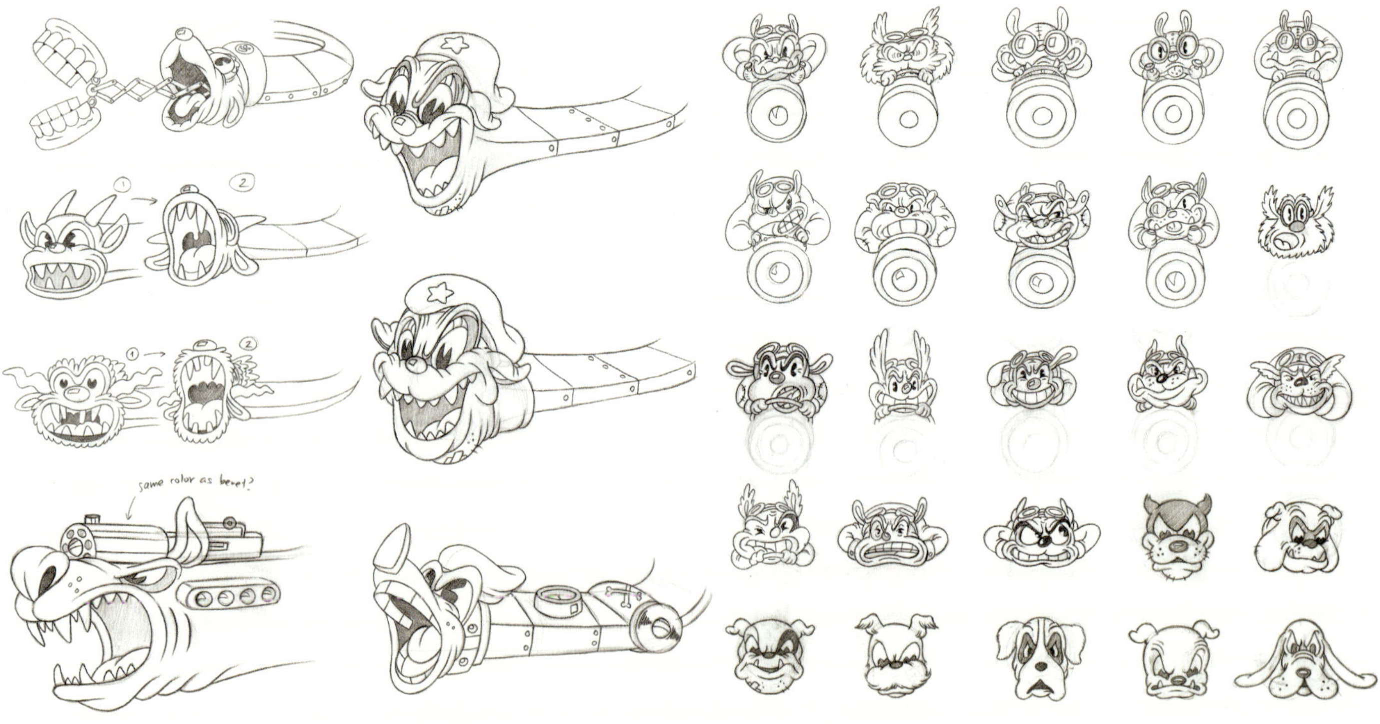

An early version of Bonegarde's "cat and yarn ball" attack had him spitting dog food can bullets out of his own mouth, each laden with references like the one pictured right to iconic Animator Ward Kimball.

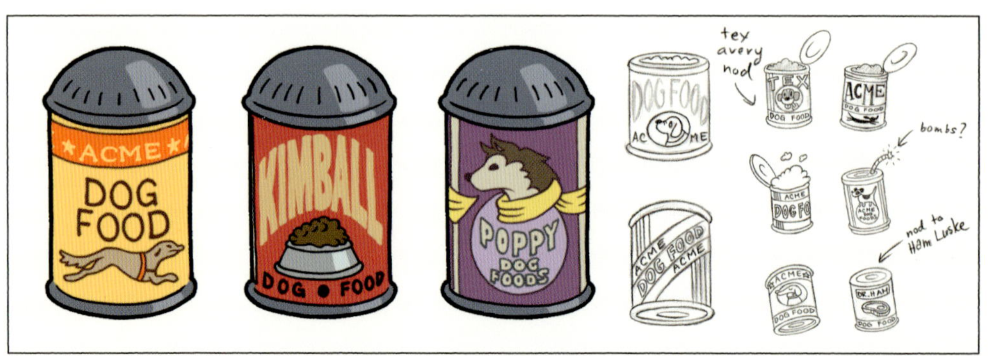

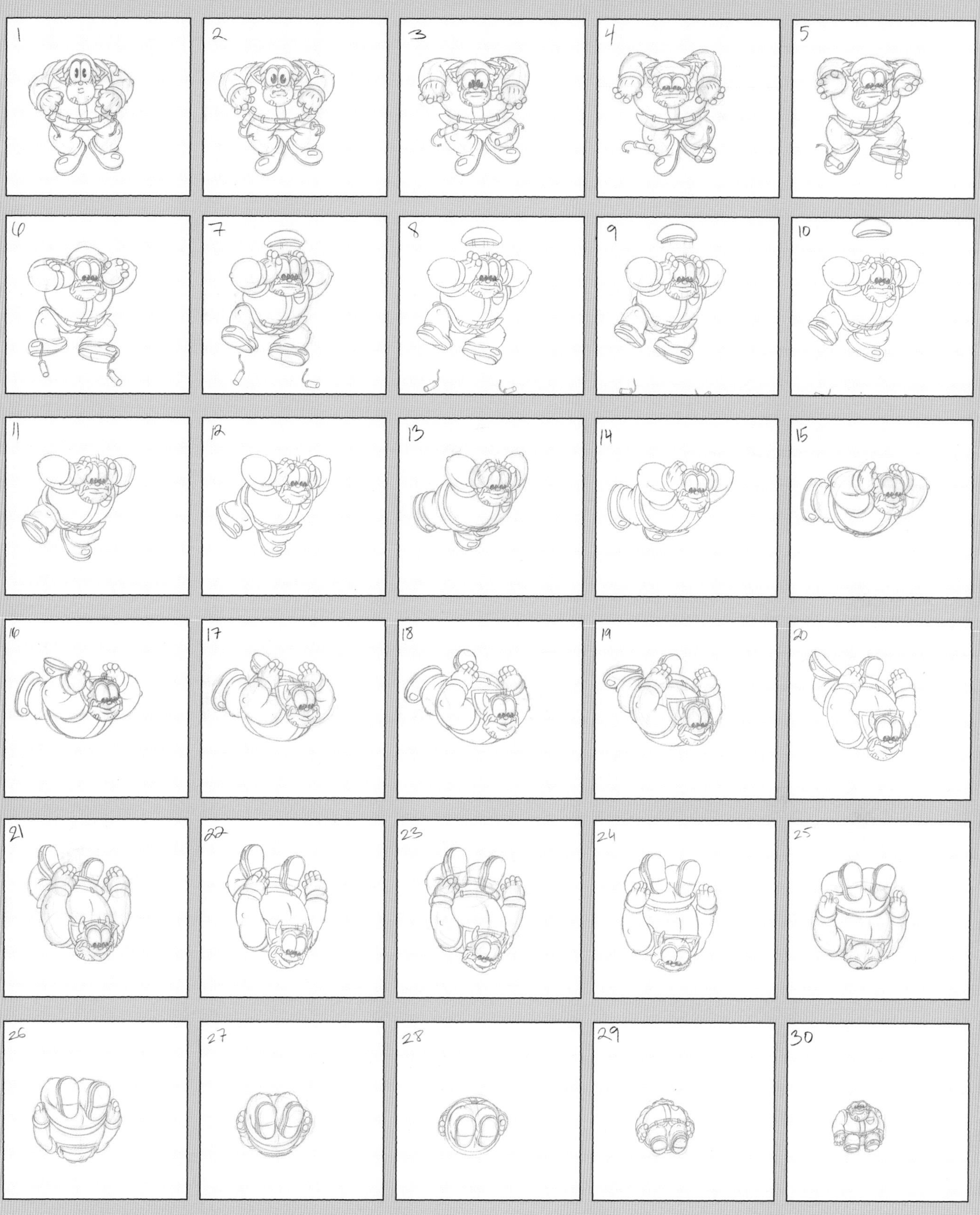

Among many other sequences of this battle, this character defeat animation from Animator Tina Nawrocki (pictured in a frame breakdown above) was one which had to be meticulously planned against the reality of a constantly-moving background. Bonegarde's expression here is inspired by a similar moment in the obscure 1934 Disney short *Two Gun Mickey*.

Yankee Yippers

FULL OF GRIT AND DETERMINATION, but not much in the way of strategic prowess, it's Yip, Yap, Yelp, and Arf…the Yankee Yippers! This little litter represents Phase 2 of Doggone Dogfight, and was loosely inspired by enemy attack patterns from the 8-bit action platformer *Rockin' Kats* (1991) by developer Atlus. Encircling your plane and launching a verbal volley of literal letters your way, the "B-O-W W-O-W" projectiles this quartet fires call out to the many physicalized onomatopoeia of cartoons past, while making more direct reference to canine enemies from Sega's 1986 classic *Alex Kidd in Miracle World*.

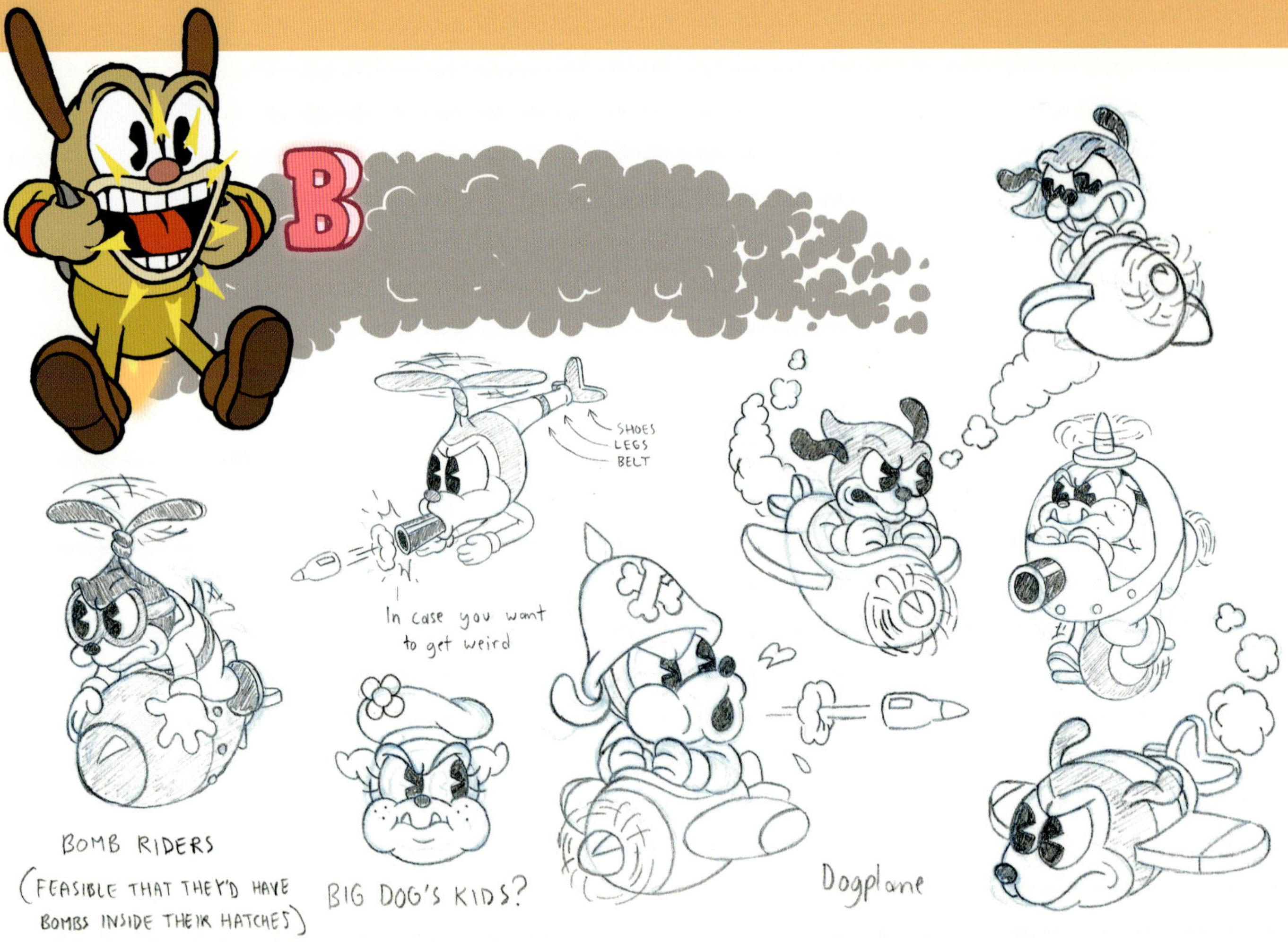

SHOES
LEGS
BELT

In case you want to get weird

BOMB RIDERS
(FEASIBLE THAT THEY'D HAVE BOMBS INSIDE THEIR HATCHES)

BIG DOG'S KIDS?

Dogplane

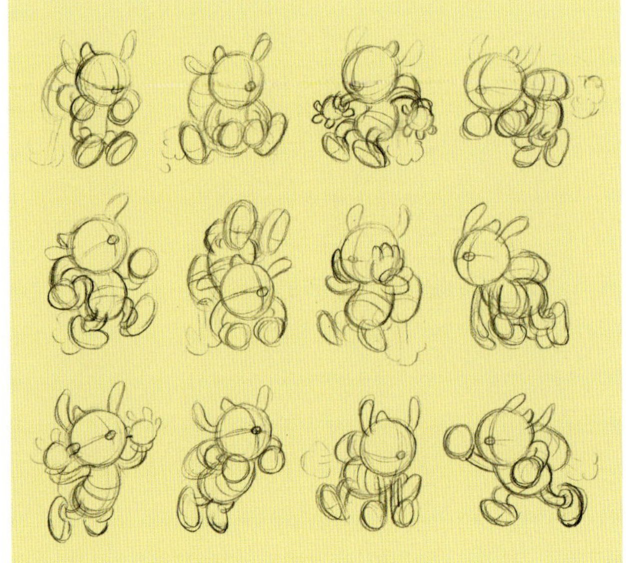

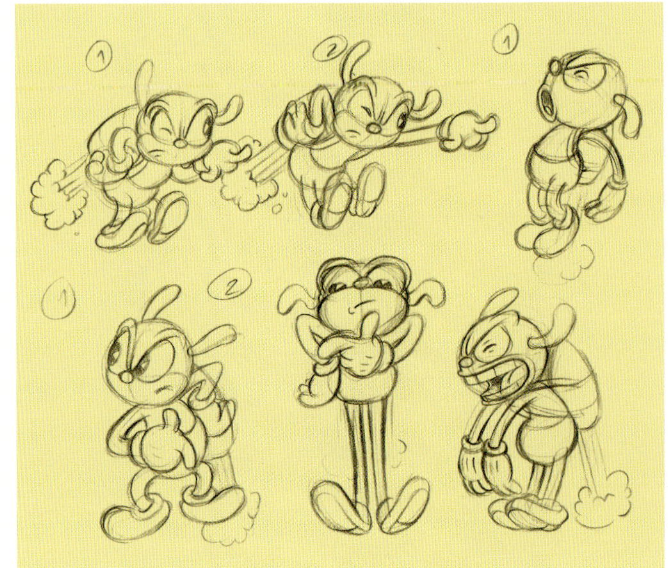

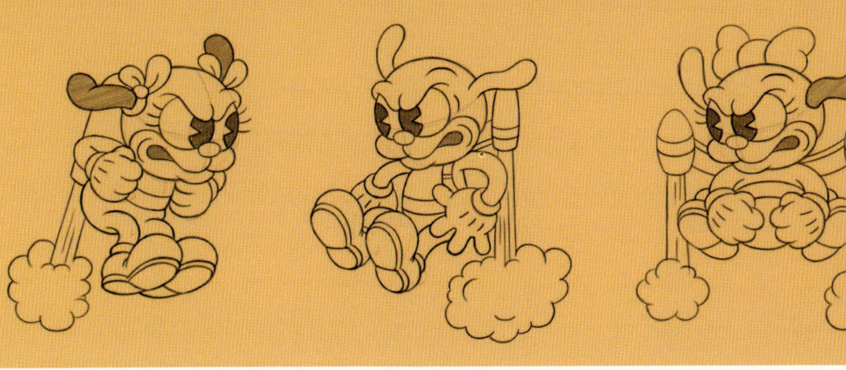

Below, a slew of concepts from Animator Tina Nawrocki exploring various vehicles the Yippers could pilot. We ultimately settled on rocket packs, which seemed appropriately retro-futuristic for our cartoon army.

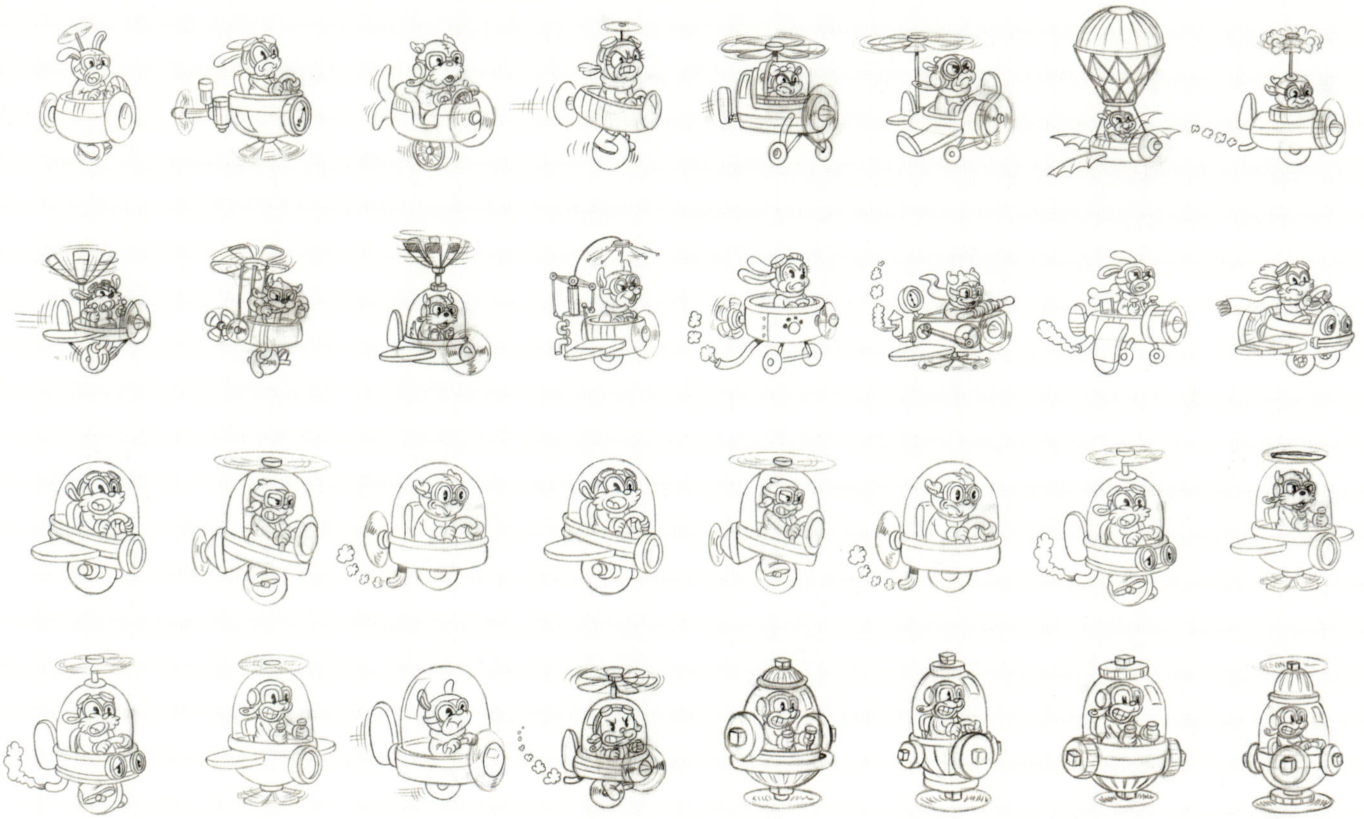

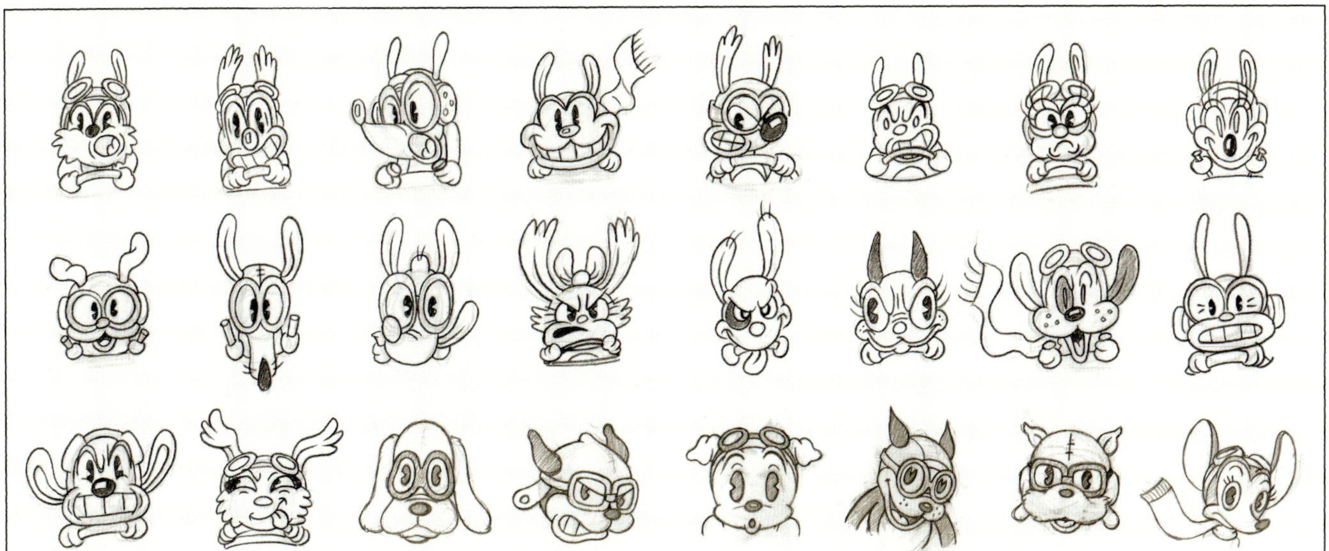

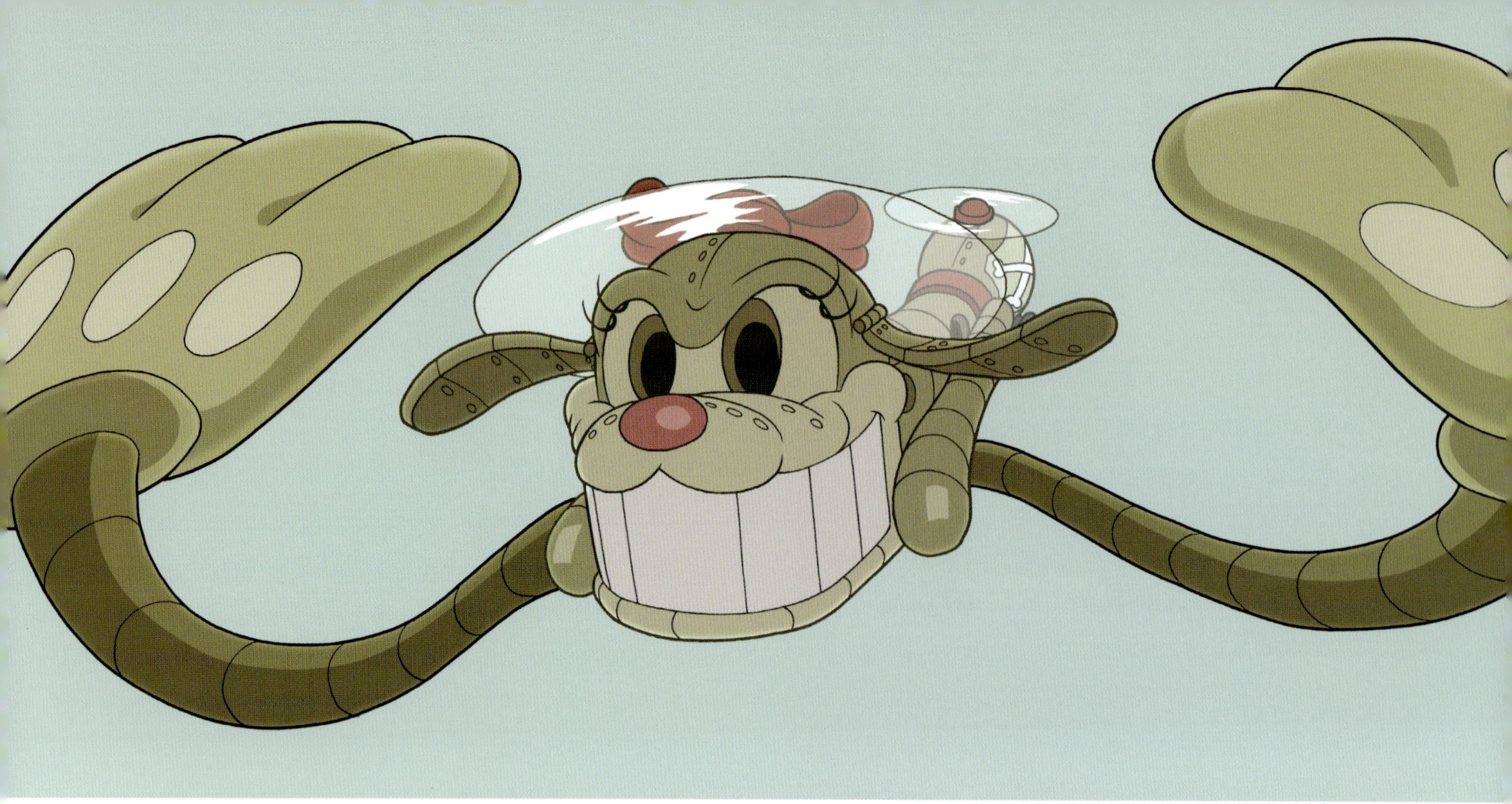

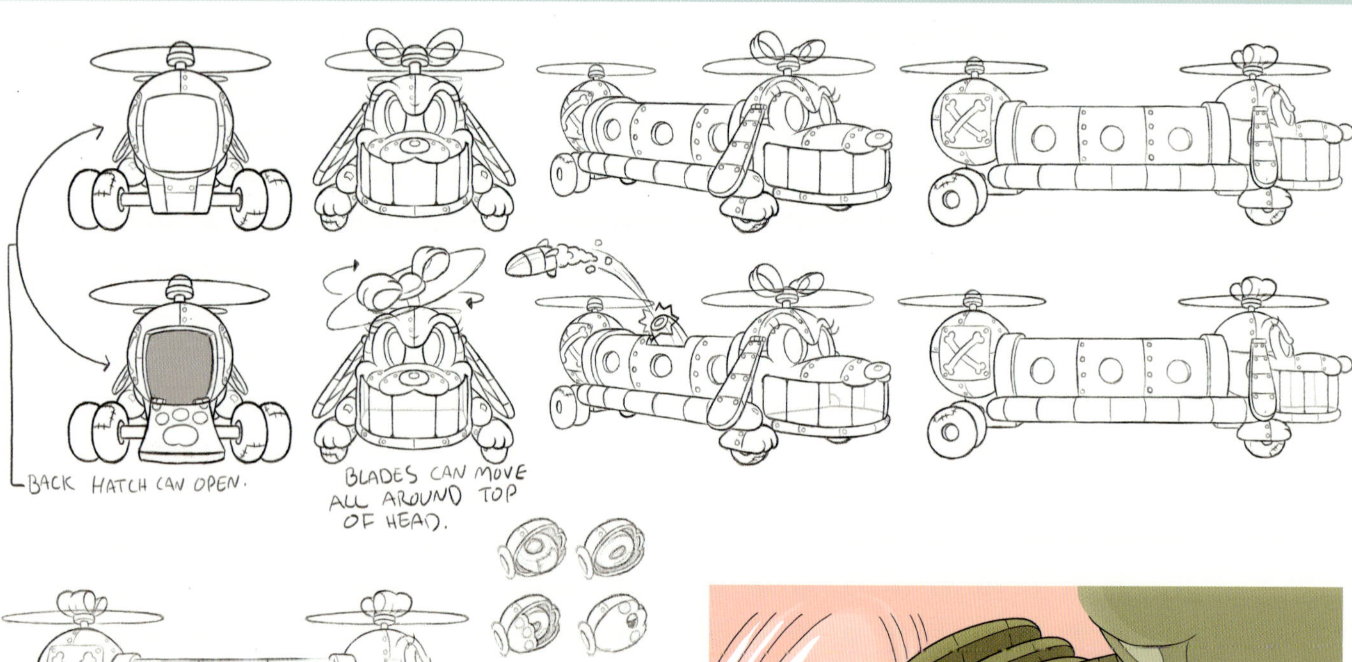

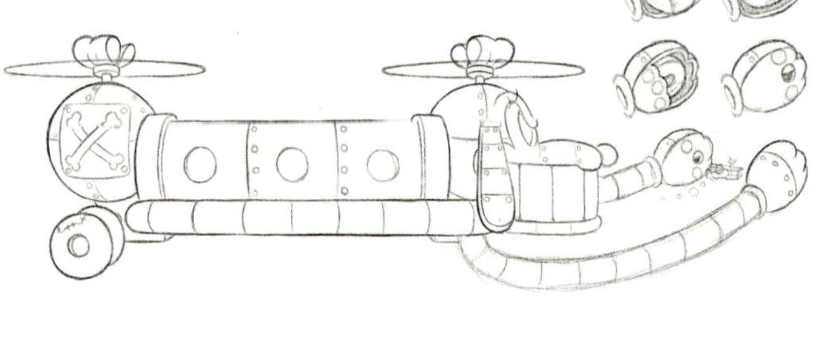

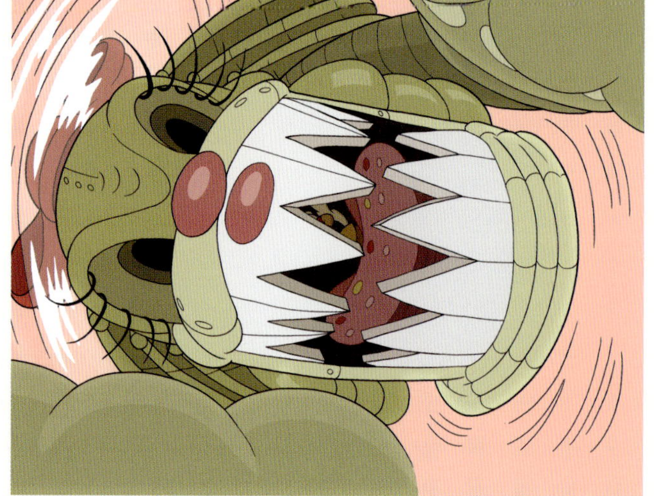

In a boss battle littered with challenges both technical and artistic, squadron leader Sergeant O'Fera's Dachshund Destroyer was one of the biggest of them all–quite literally. Knowing that the design ambitions for this final phase of the fight involved rotating the screen and play area, we had to work with principal Concept Artist Lance Inkwell to refine a concept that felt both alive and mechanical, both imposing and comical. In the end, the classic form factor of the much-loved "Weiner Dog" combined with a tandem rotor aircraft cut the perfect doglike silhouette we wanted.

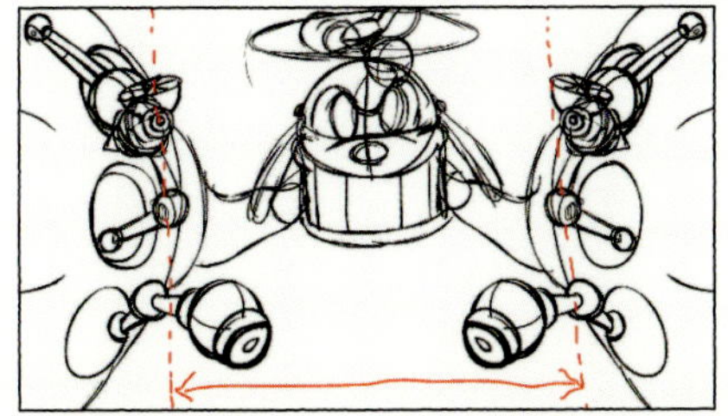
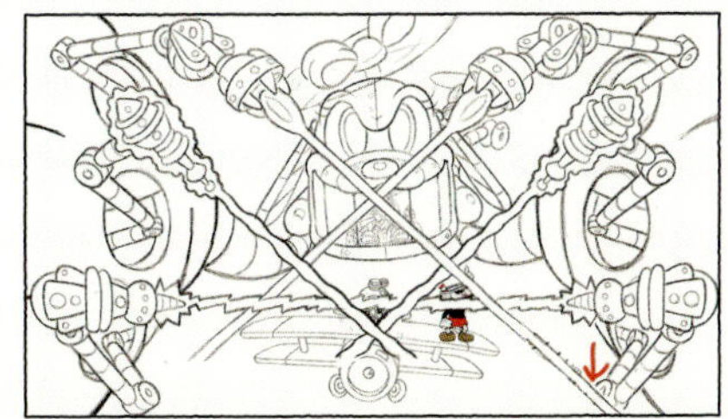
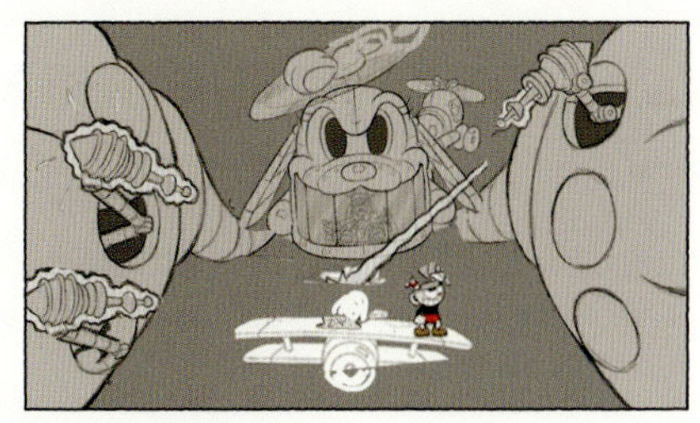
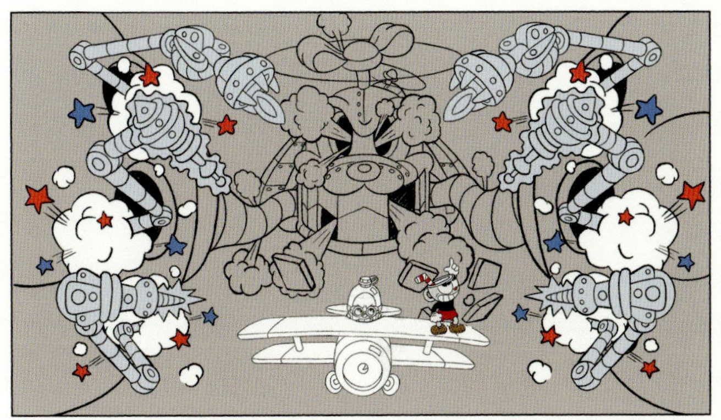
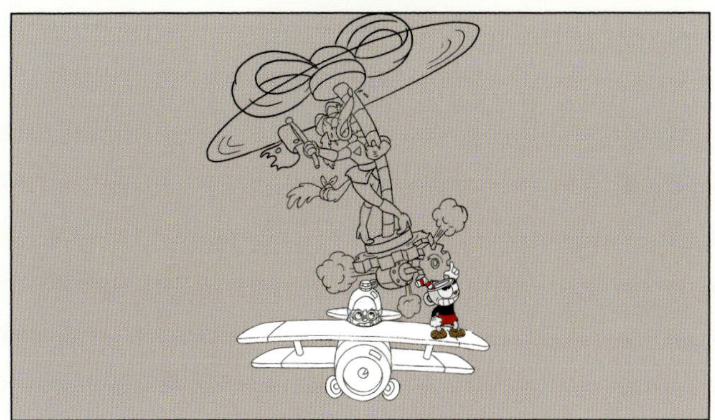
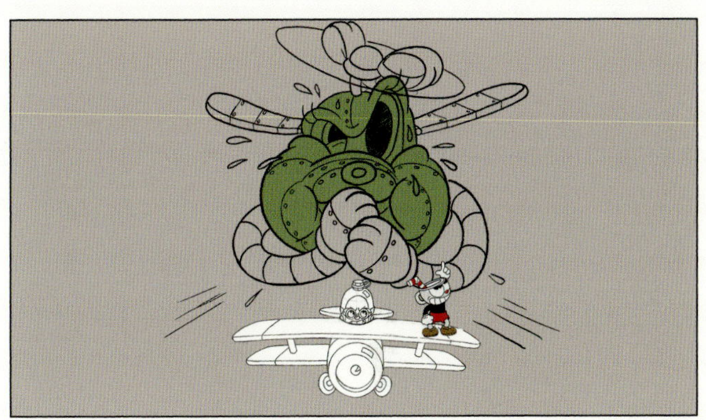
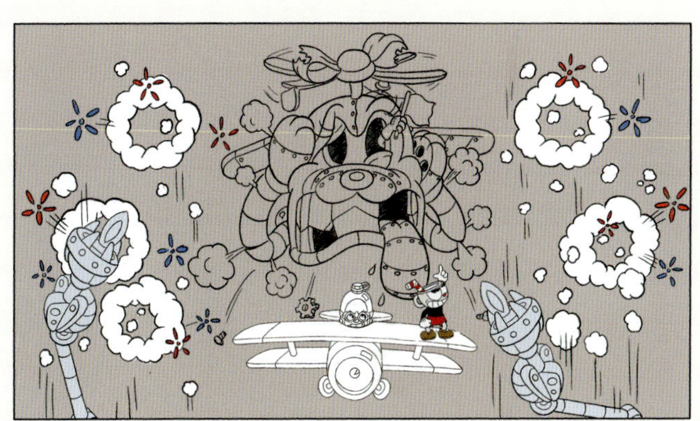

Below, alternate (and significantly more menacing!) options for ways to personify Sergeant O'Fera's aircraft from Animator Tina Nawrocki. There's something quite eerie about arms-turned-faces-turned-cannons.

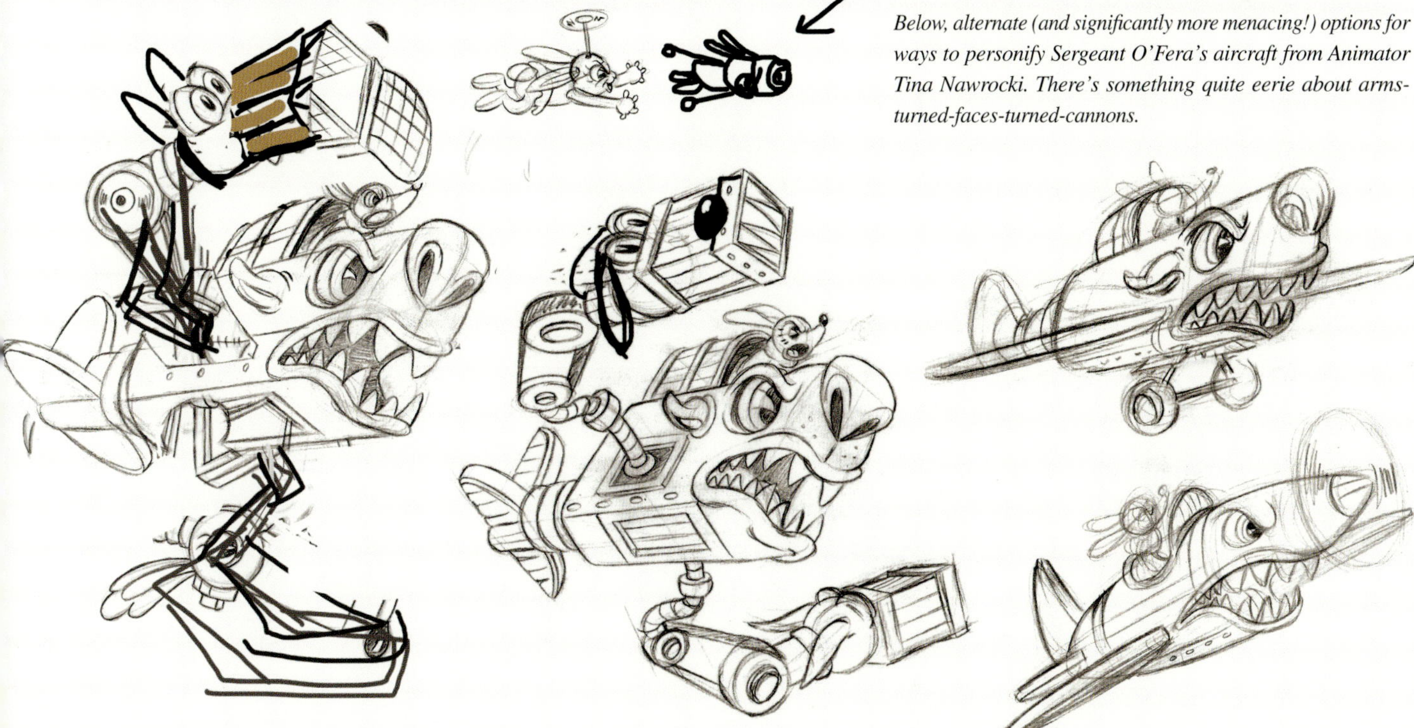

Sergeant O'Fera

WITH A NAME THAT IS LATIN for "wild animal," but a sense of authority and composure that is anything but, Sergeant O'Fera is the alpha authority of the Howling Aces. Heavily inspired both in form and animation by the *Street Fighter* series' Cammy, this ruthless pack leader's facial features are modelled after the Saluki dog (or "Afghan"), whose ears provided the perfect corollary to long hair. Pictured below: Sergeant O'Fera's long snout offered just the right complement to her defeated "death animation", accentuating the sense of dismay at her dishonorable discharge from the fray.

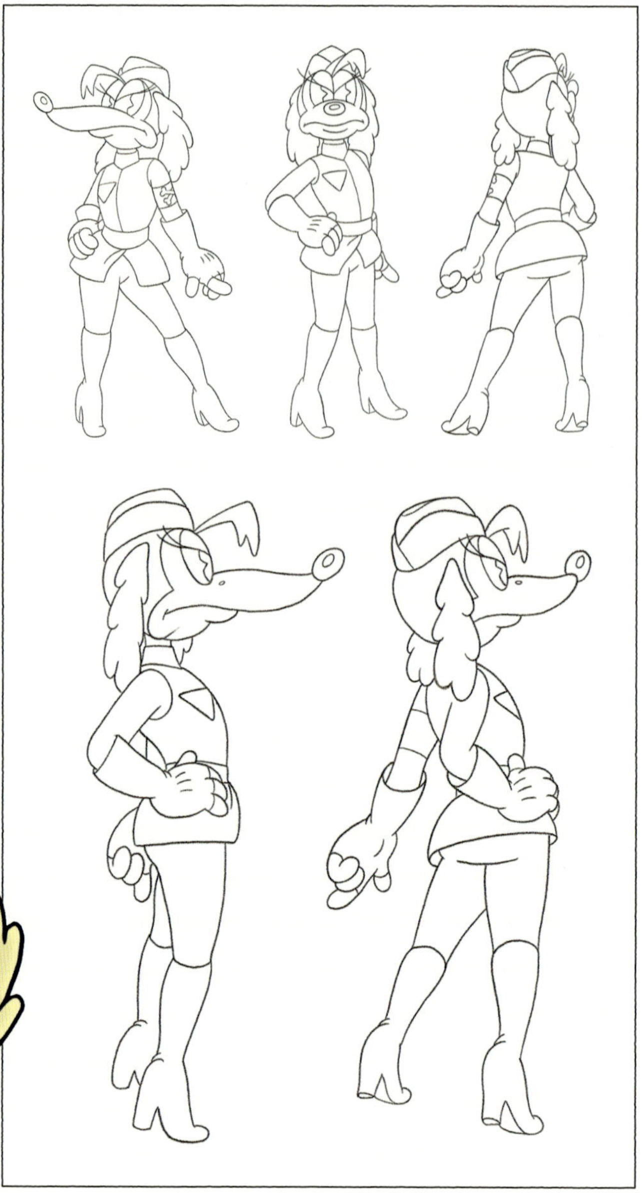

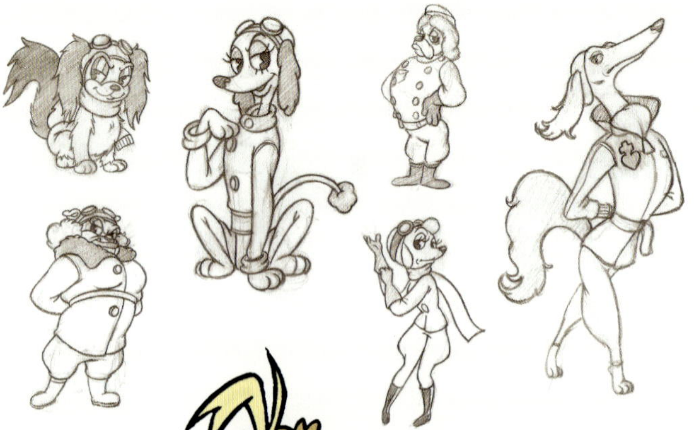

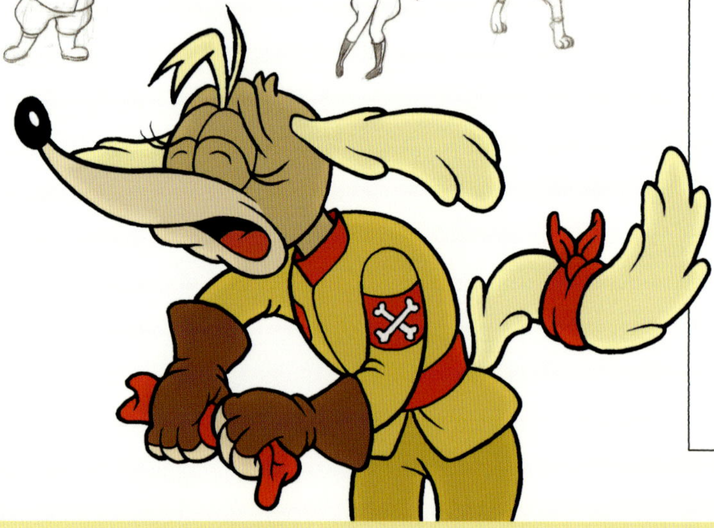

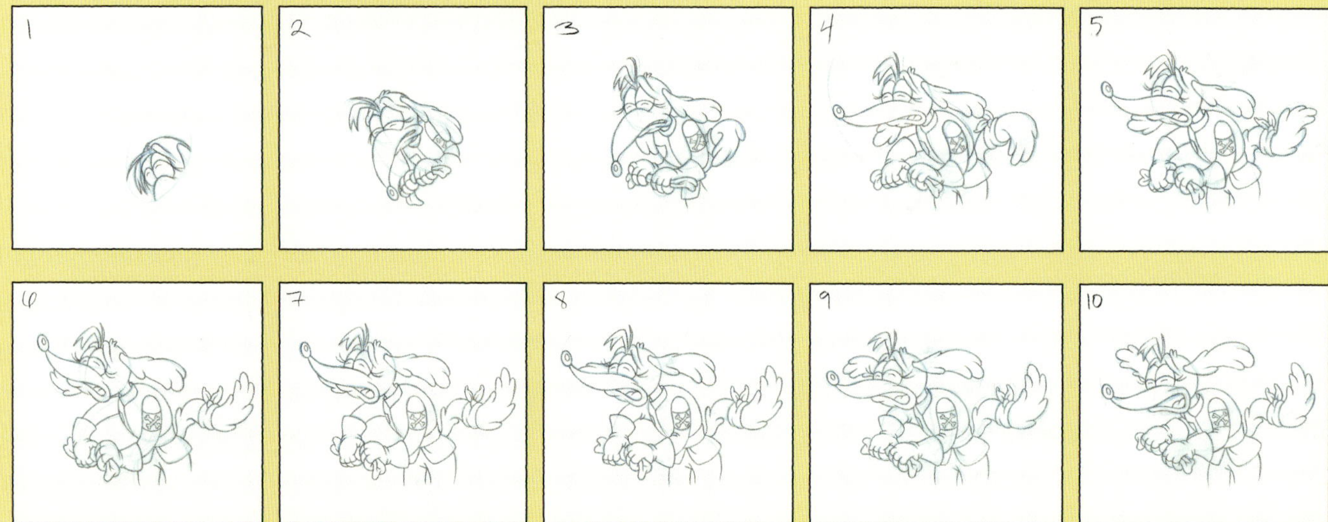

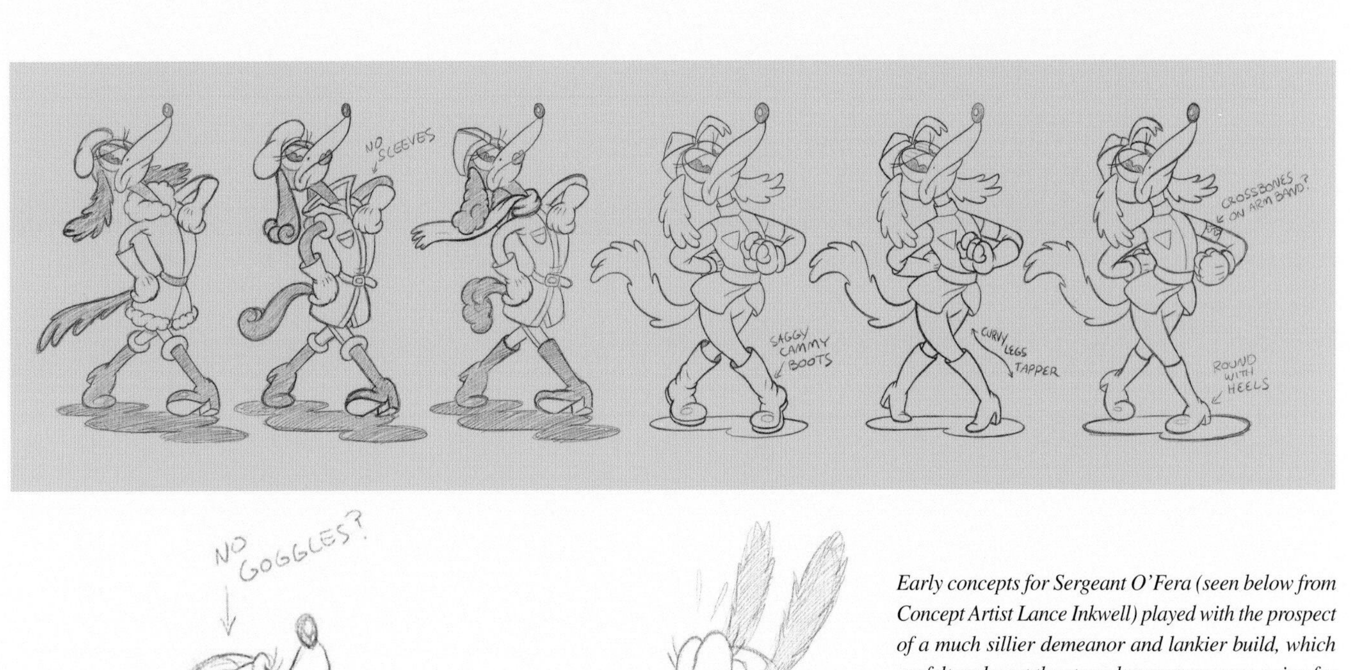

Early concepts for Sergeant O'Fera (seen below from Concept Artist Lance Inkwell) played with the prospect of a much sillier demeanor and lankier build, which we felt undercut the stern decorum we were going for with the leader of the Aces.

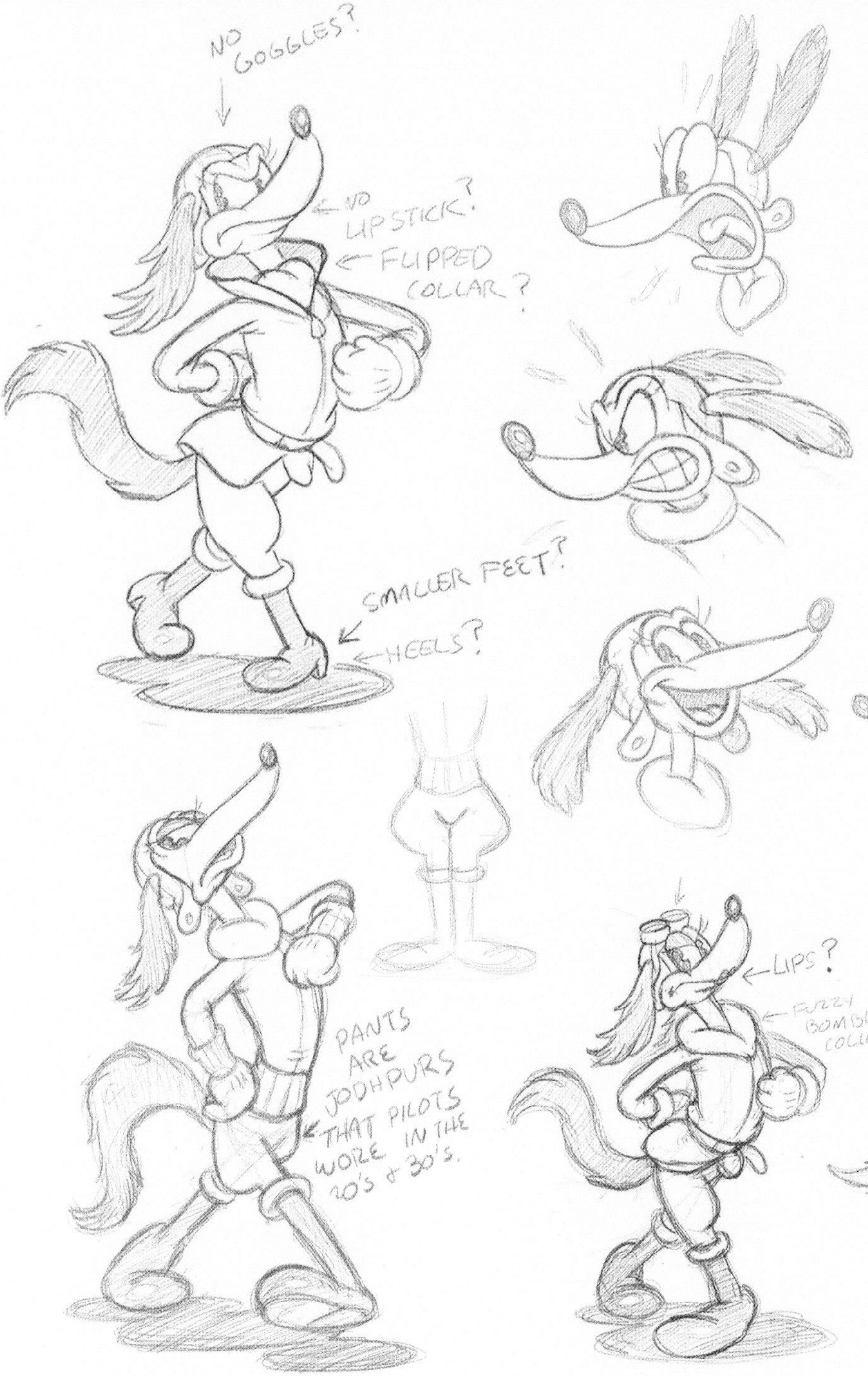

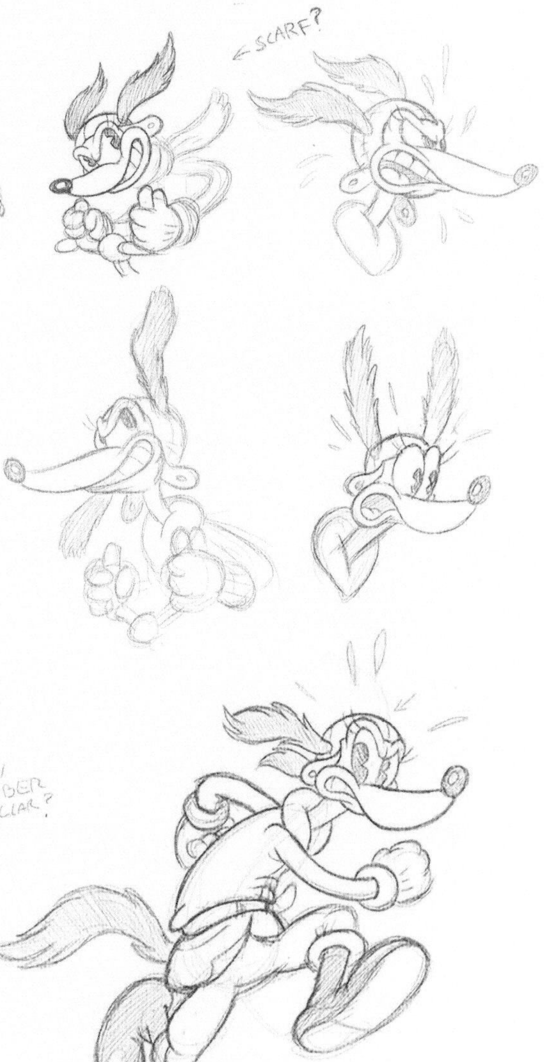

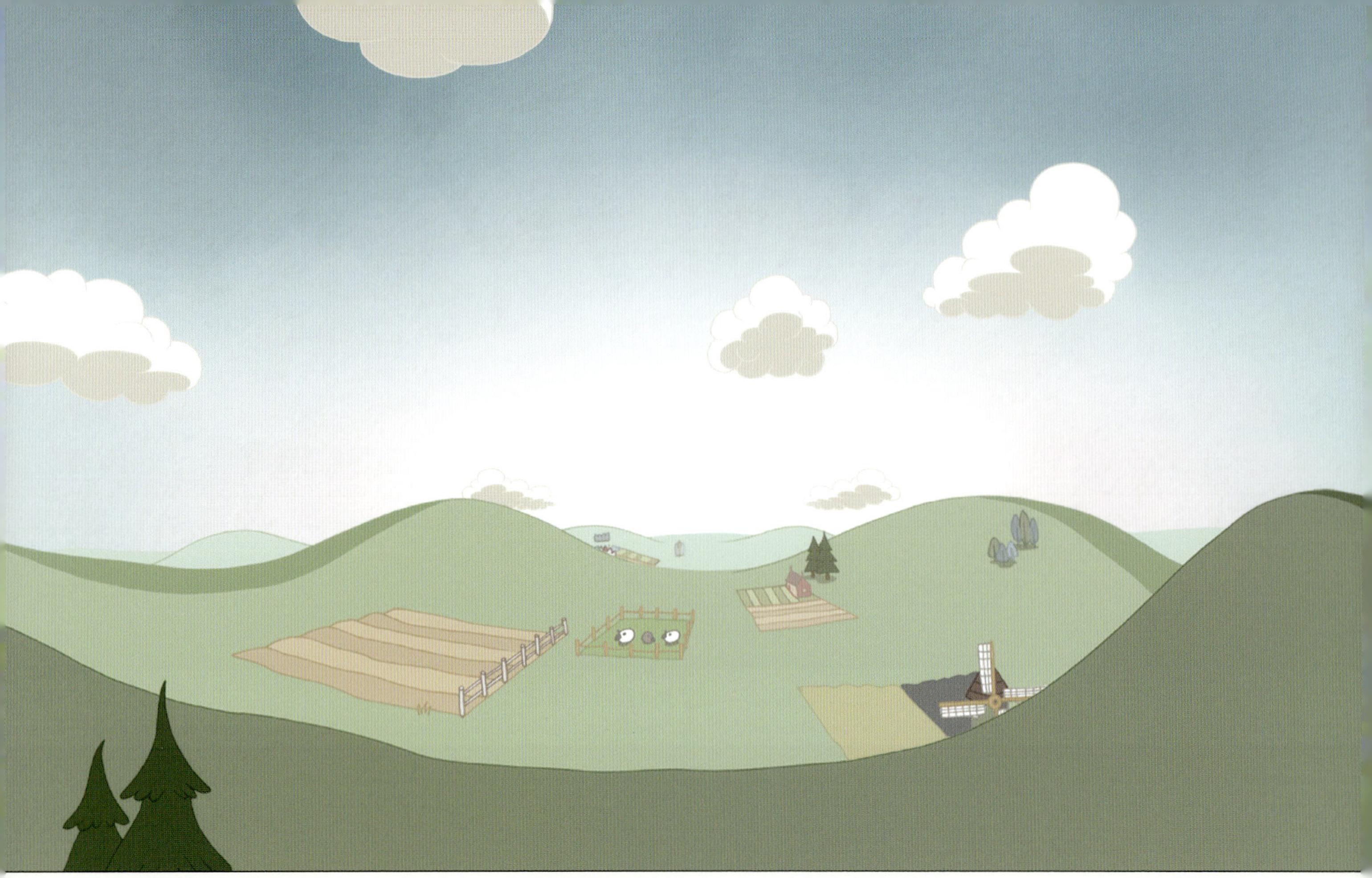

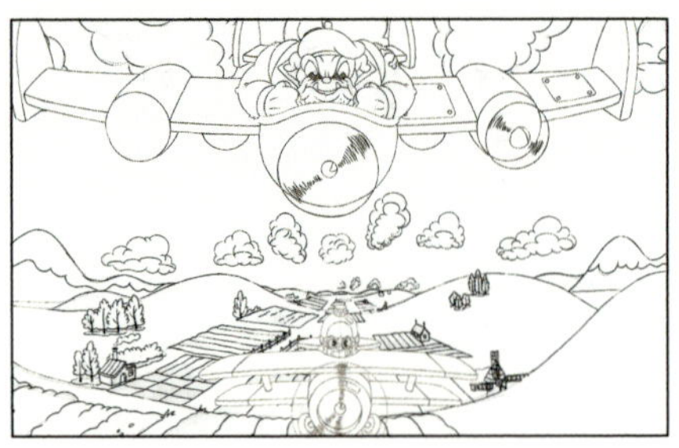

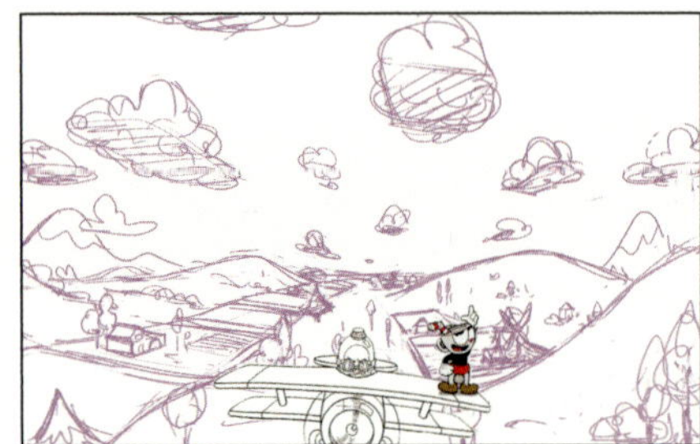

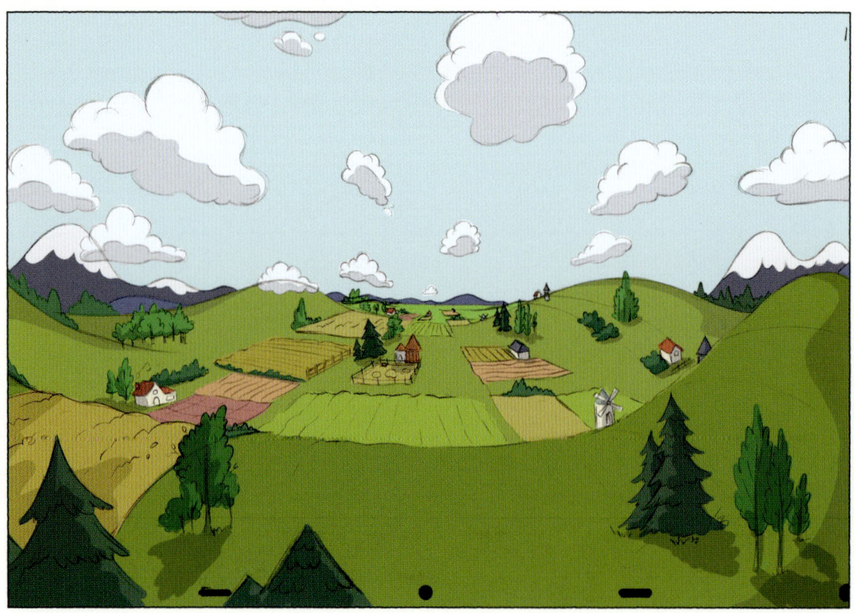

Doggone Dogfight Background

IT'S NO EXAGGERATION TO SAY that the background for Doggone Dogfight represents one of our single-most complex pieces of animation in *The Delicious Last Course*. A deeply technical exercise in precision, the constantly-rolling hills unfurling beneath the player went through countless rounds of experimentation and revision as we pushed to find the correct perspective and vanishing point to convey the feeling of zooming quickly (but not nauseatingly quickly!) away from a rolling horizon. Every discipline at the studio was critical in bringing this piece to life, with our engineers going as far as to rewrite our animation sequencer specifically for this background so that no individual elements were out of sync.

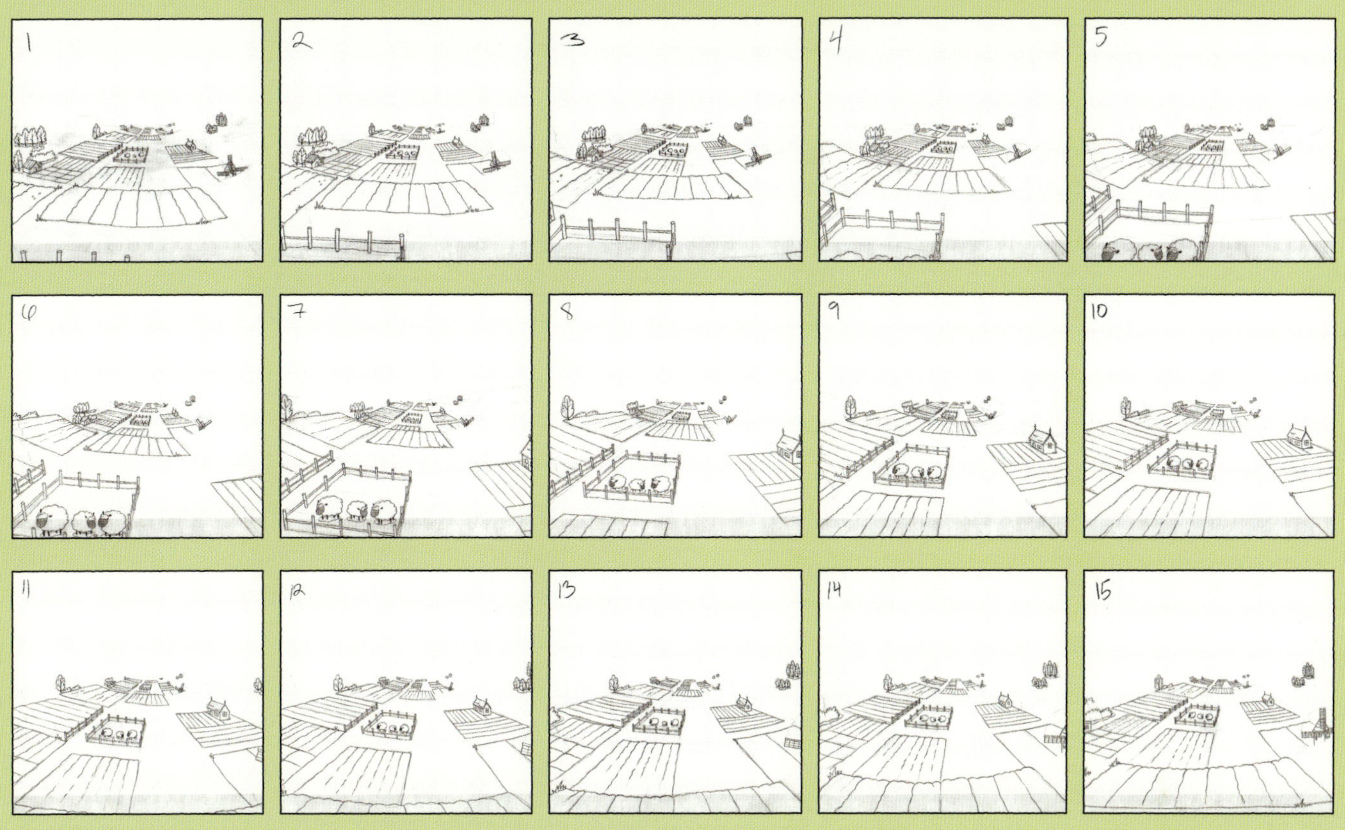

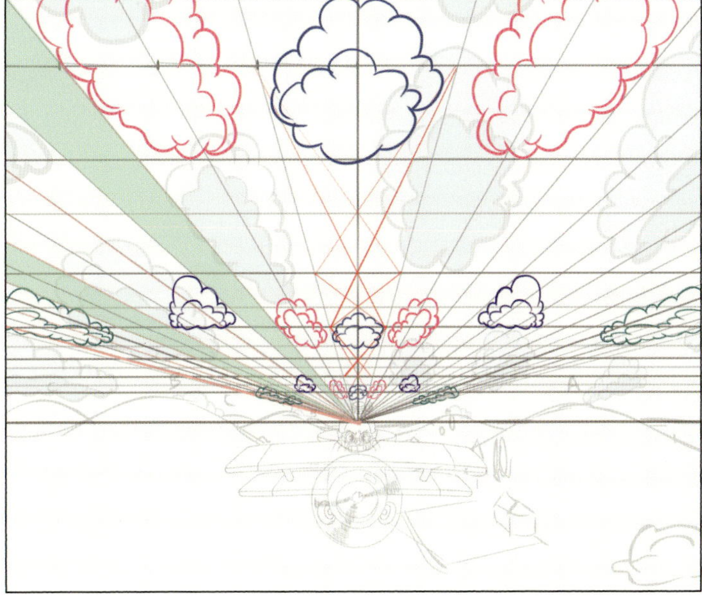

From hand-placed cloud patterns to carefully mapped-out trees, houses, and fields, the landscape below the battle is filled with details that are sequenced procedurally to prevent visible looping.

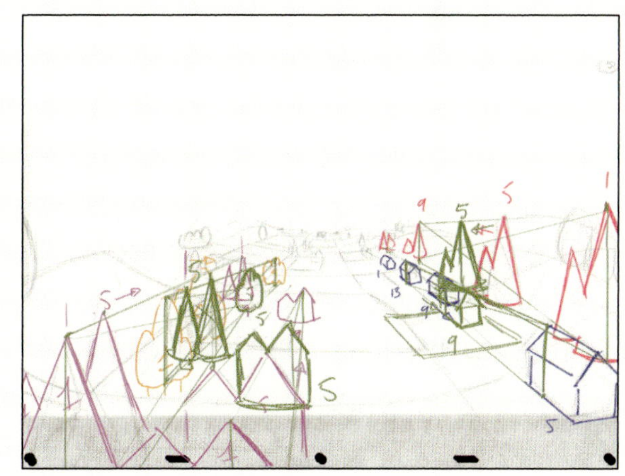

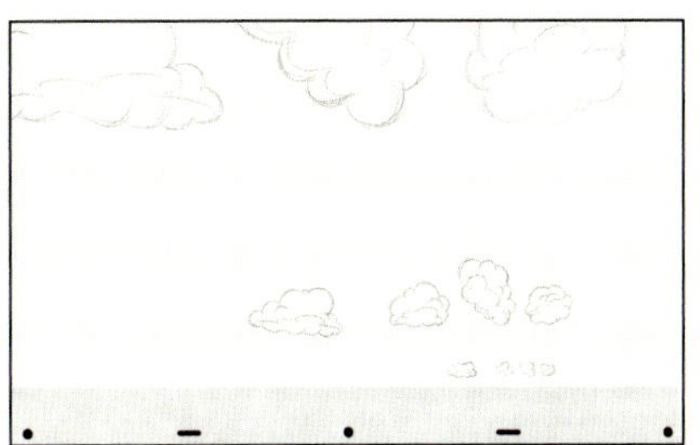

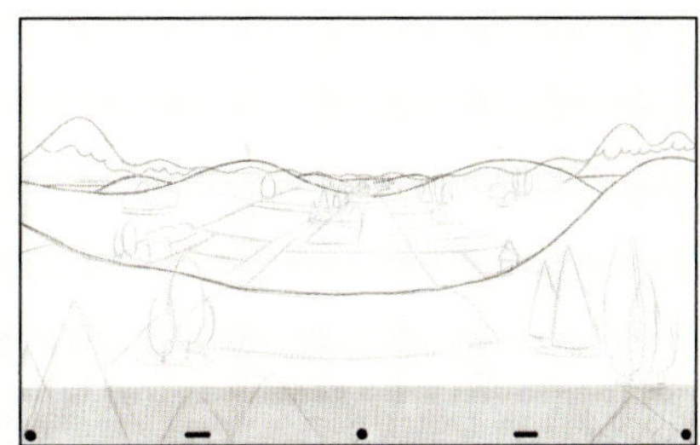

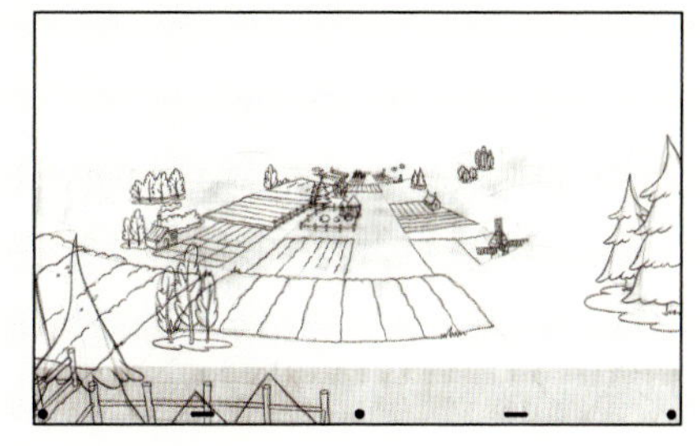

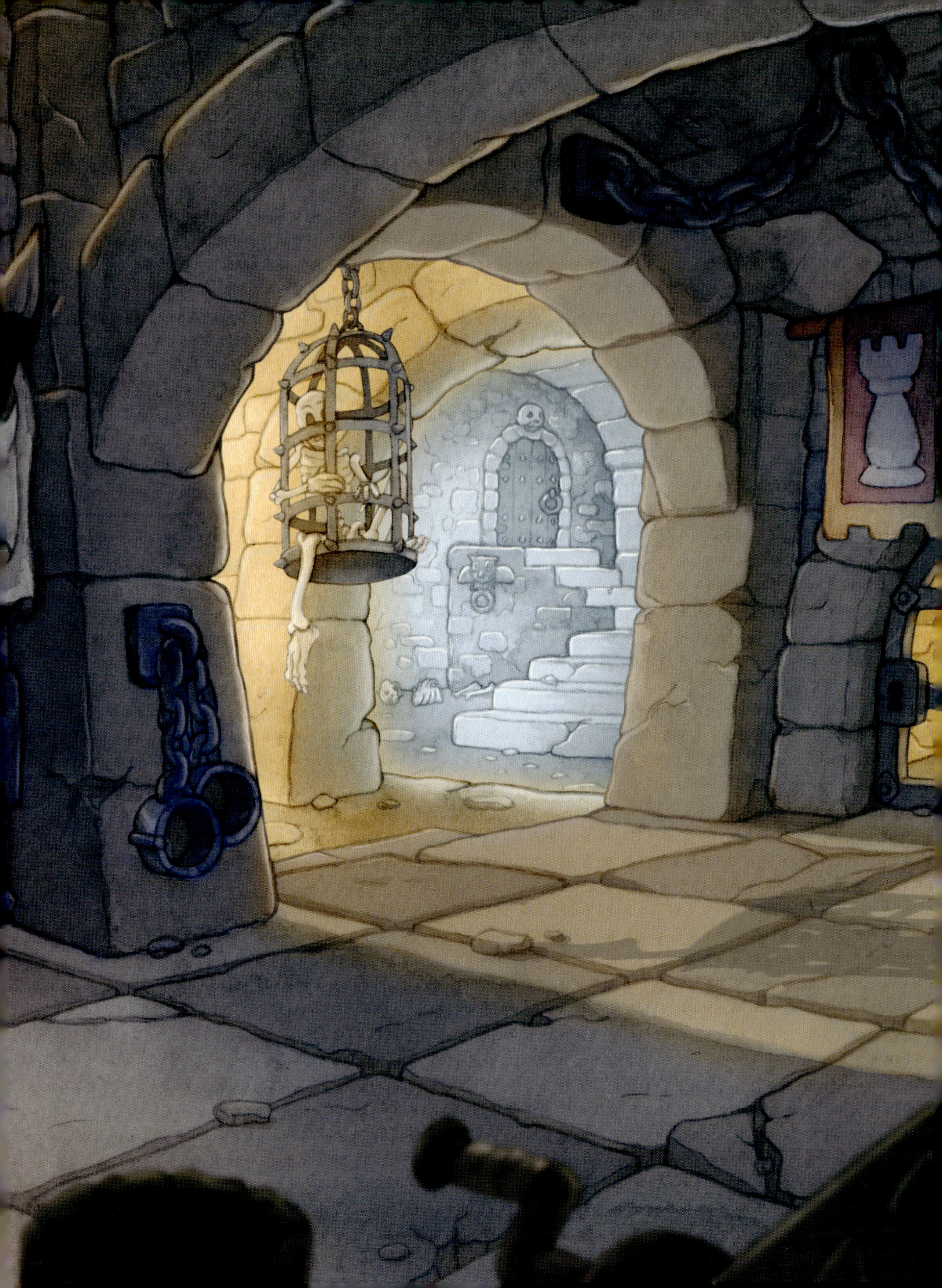

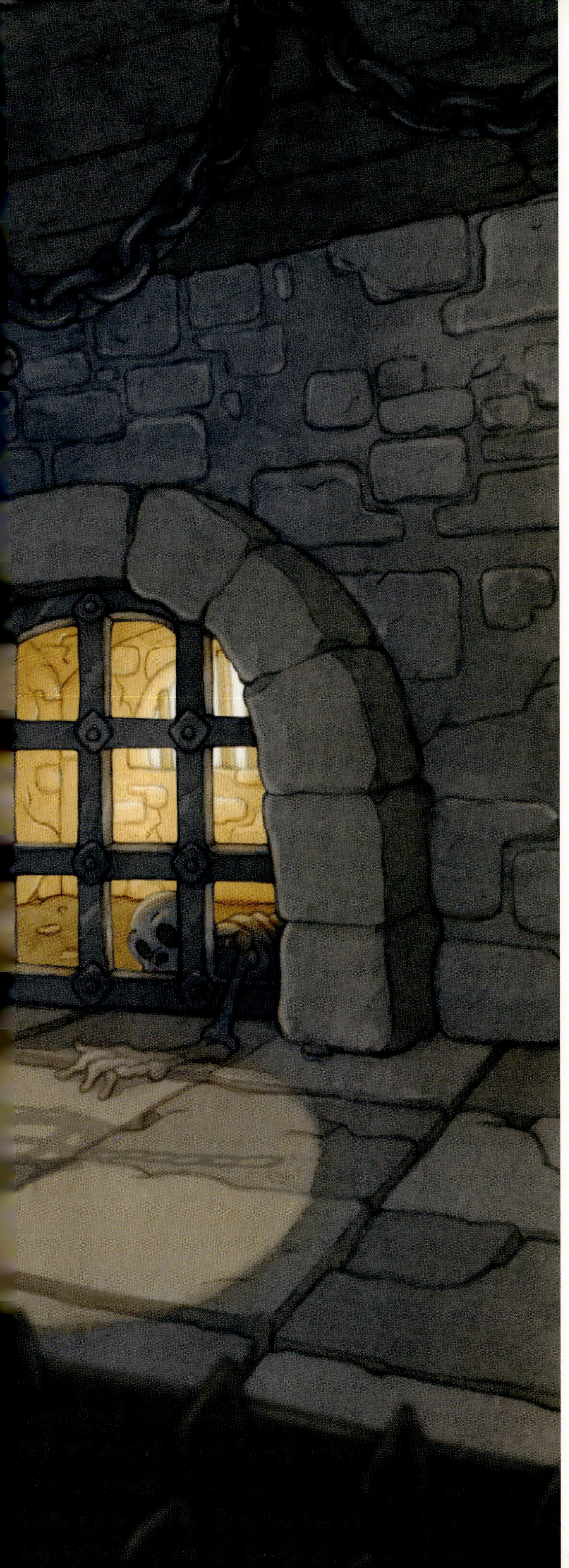

Chapter VIII:
The King's Leap

ONE OF THE BIG LESSONS you learn making video games is that no concept ever really goes to waste. Any developer can attest: while the road to release is littered with ambitious ideas that never see the light of day, those unfinished prototypes, half-completed stages, or partial designs often get a new lease on life when the time is right. Case in point for us: The King's Leap parry bosses.

These chess-themed challenges are the player's way of earning coins in *The Delicious Last Course*, and rose from the ashes of the "Airship" stages that we originally concocted for the base *Cuphead* game (see the "Lost Levels" chapter of this book for more on that). As design took shape on our DLC expansion, it became apparent that we weren't going to include any classic "run and gun" platforming stages, and would therefore need a suitable way for people to earn the currency necessary to buy charms and weapons at Porkrind's store (after all, Porkrind doesn't offer to run a tab!). We knew as well that whatever solution we came up with needed to be mobile, so it could touch down wherever the player might be located on the map. After much hemming and hawing and countless concepts, an idea sprung up in our heads: a floating castle occupied by a haughty king looking for a challenger noble enough to overcome his gaming gauntlet.

King of Games in "THE KING'S LEAP"

PUTTING THE "POMP" IN "POMPOUS," the figurehead of The King's Leap is naturally none other than the head regent himself. While never made explicitly clear, we always envisioned an implied rivalry between the King of Games and classic *Cuphead* villain King Dice–a stately and distinguished host of skill-based challenges flying literally and metaphorically above the moral turpitude of more flashy, tempting games of luck and chance. At the same time, however, we found that there was something humorous and era-appropriate about a delusional royal giving you a few measly coins while claiming to shower you with riches, like an out-of-touch grandparent giving you a shiny nickel for your birthday.

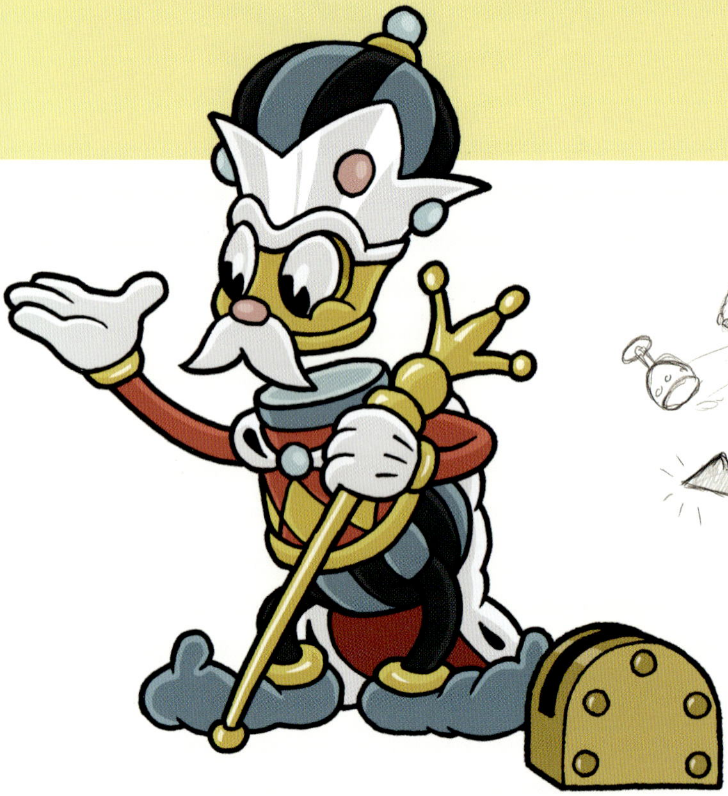

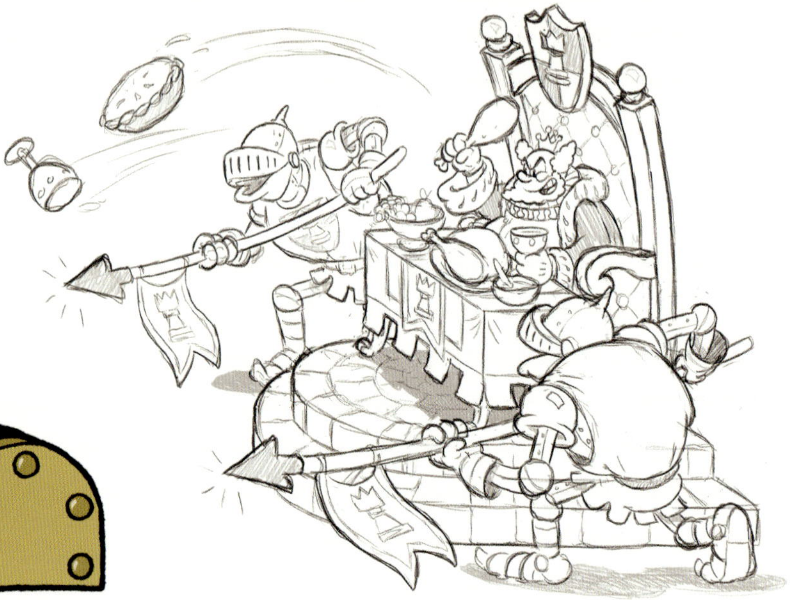

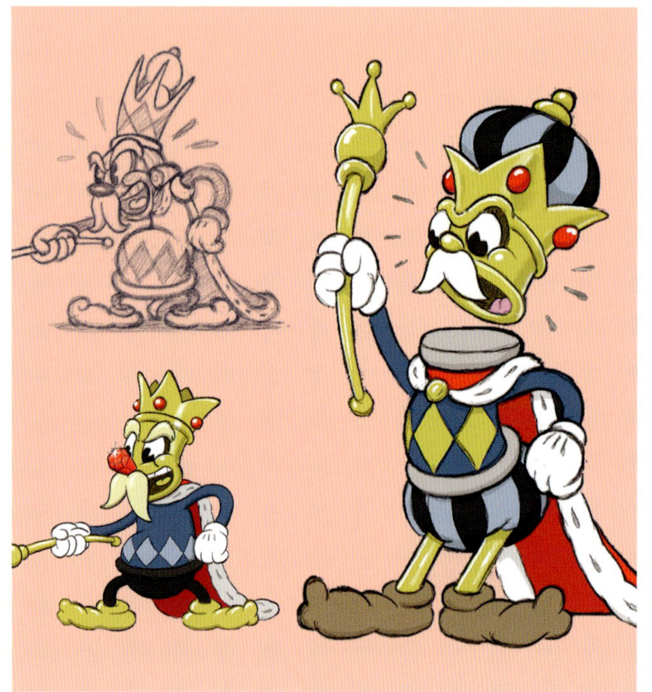

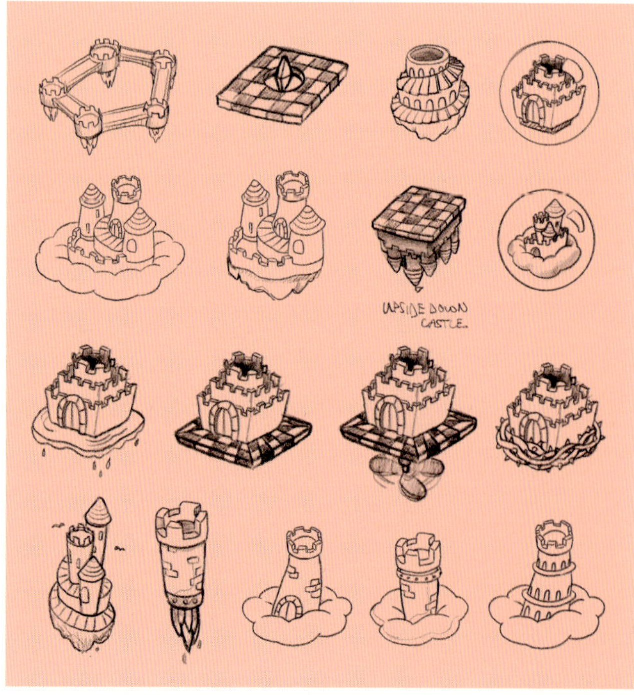

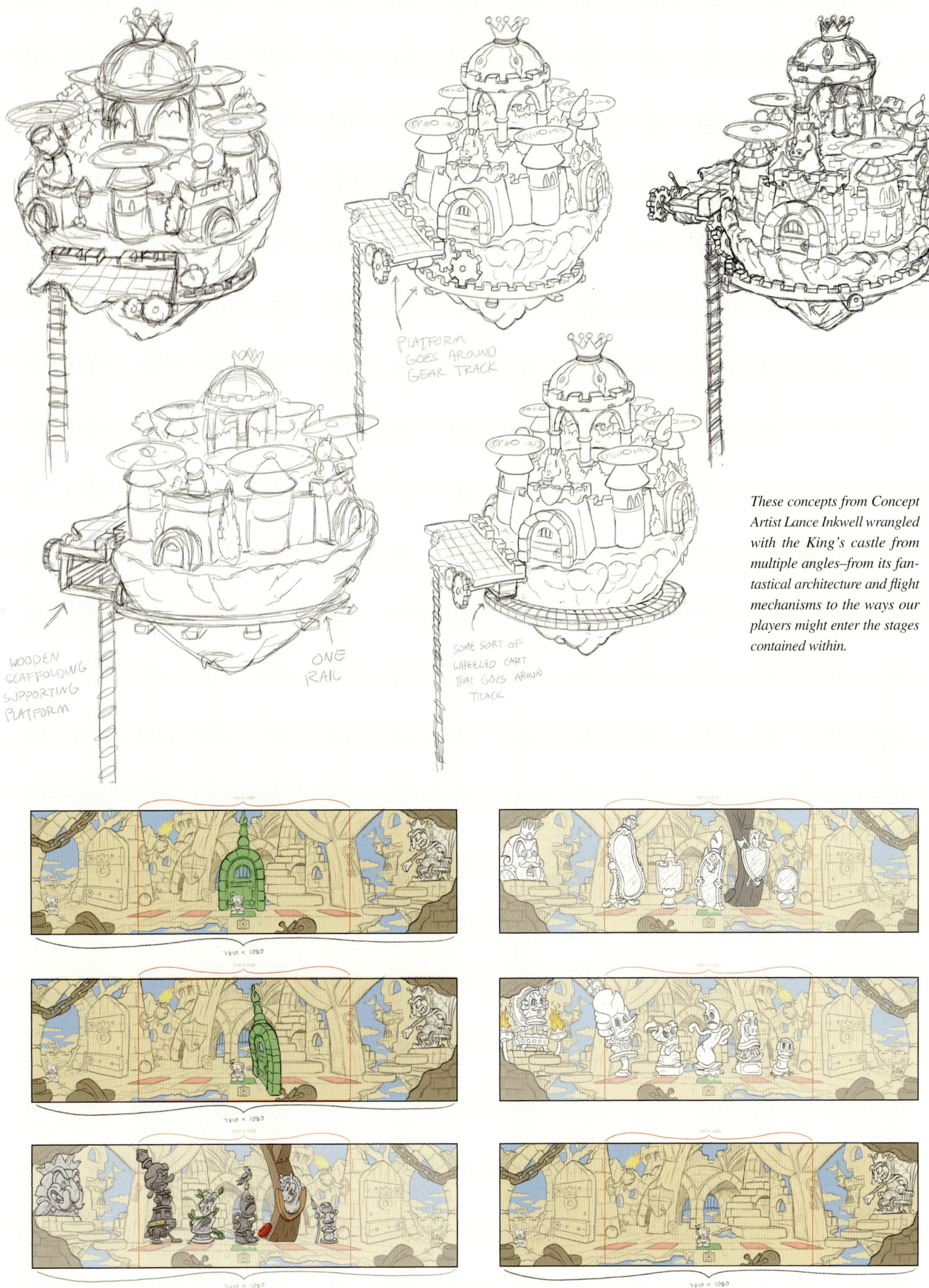

These concepts from Concept Artist Lance Inkwell wrangled with the King's castle from multiple angles–from its fantastical architecture and flight mechanisms to the ways our players might enter the stages contained within.

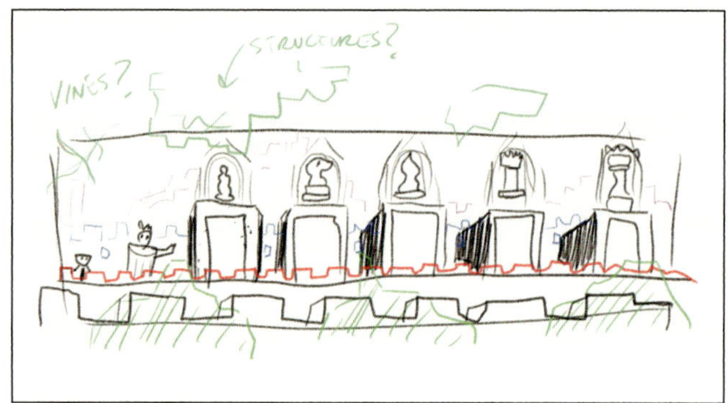

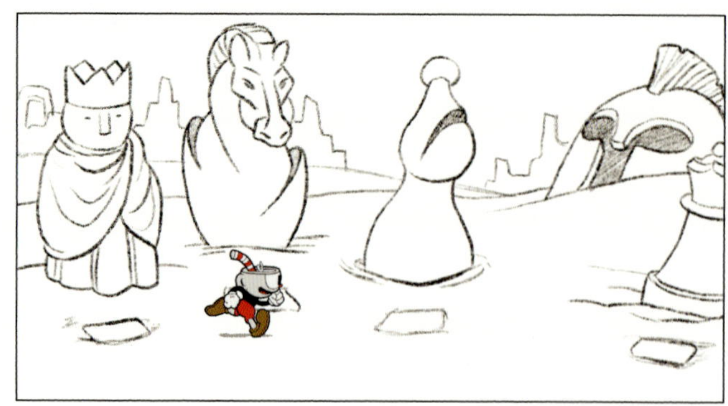

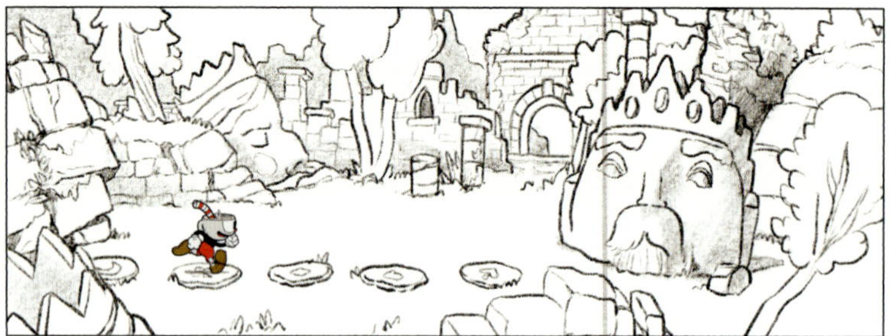

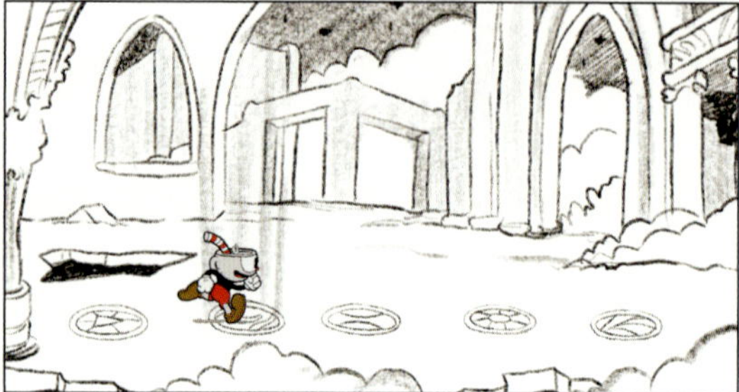

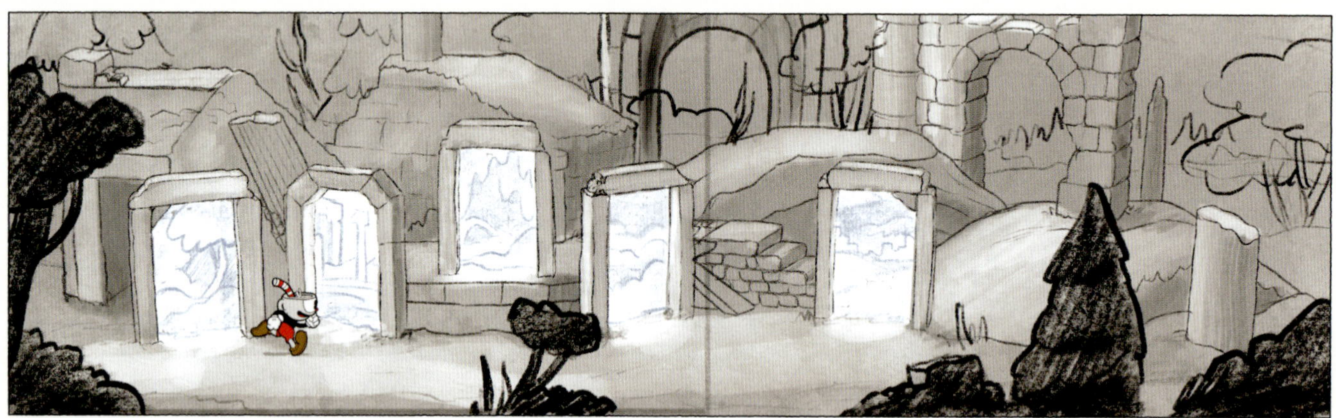

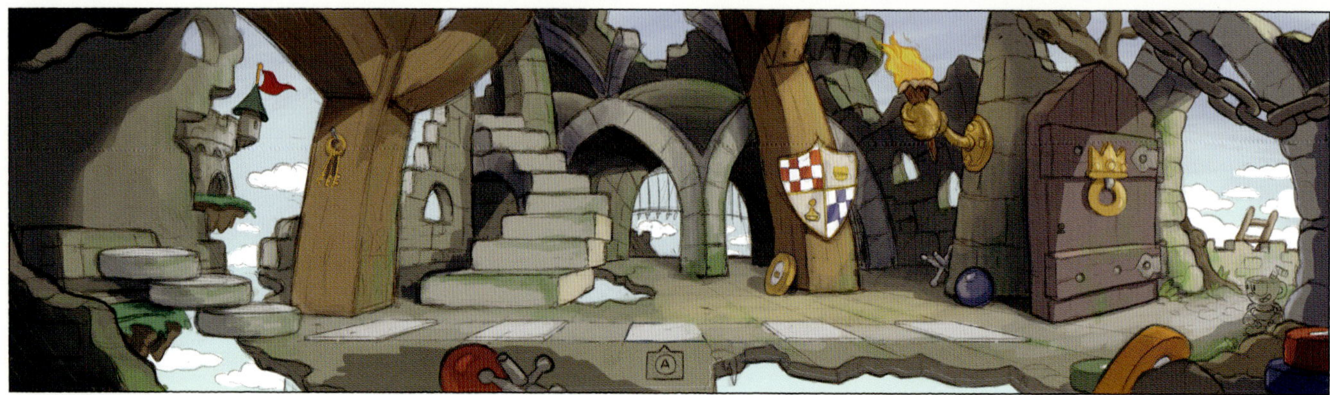

Before making the *leap* and working with our partners at Screen Novelties in Los Angeles to construct a physical stop motion set for the King's castle, we worked on an array of more traditional background ideas with Painter Caitlin Russell and Layout Artist Lance Inkwell.. Inspired by the labyrinthian geometry of Dutch graphic artist M.C. Escher, ideas ranged from a liminal desert containing chess piece statues to mysterious stone doors filled with portals to other worlds. It's to Russell's credit that each idea felt truly magical, but we ultimately decided that the painted medium as a whole fell short of conveying a physical space where a royal court of chess pieces might actually live.

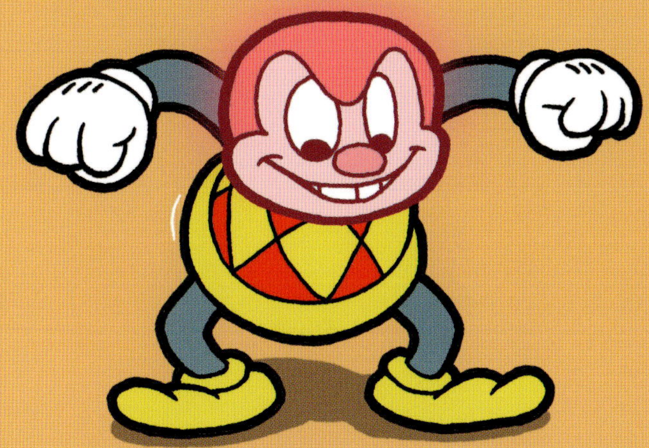

Pawn

ATTACKING DIAGONALLY but moving straight, it's an army of pawns–to be precise, eight! Paying homage to an attack pattern from Konami's 1992 run and gun *Contra III: The Alien Wars*, the first parry challenge in The King's Leap is a contest against chess's most iconic little fighters. In early concepts, we envisioned this stage as a battle on a physical board, with the players on one side and a group of attacking pawns on the other. After putting the more complex patterns we implemented through their paces, however, things didn't feel quite right, so we simplified both the design and visuals to use this first stage as a way to ease players into the parry challenges.

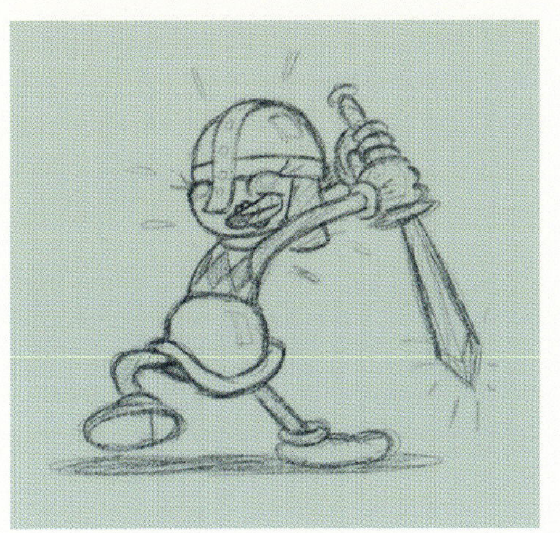

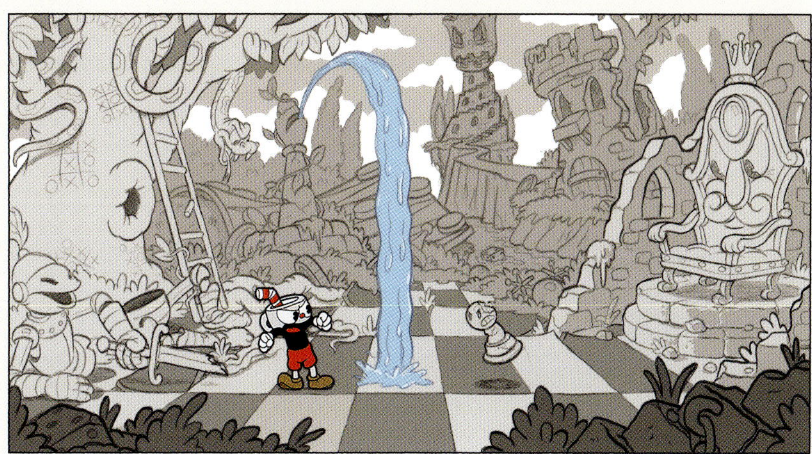

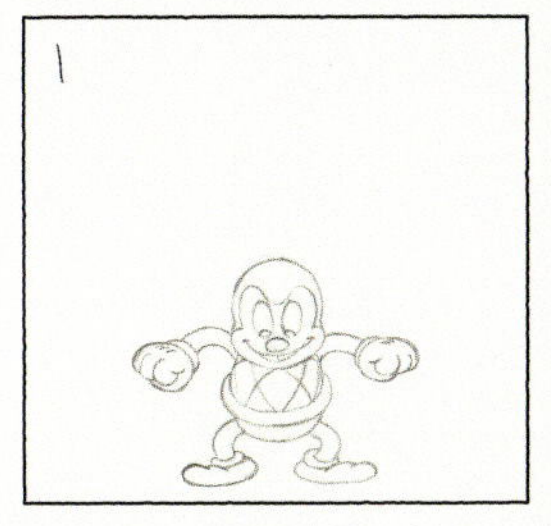

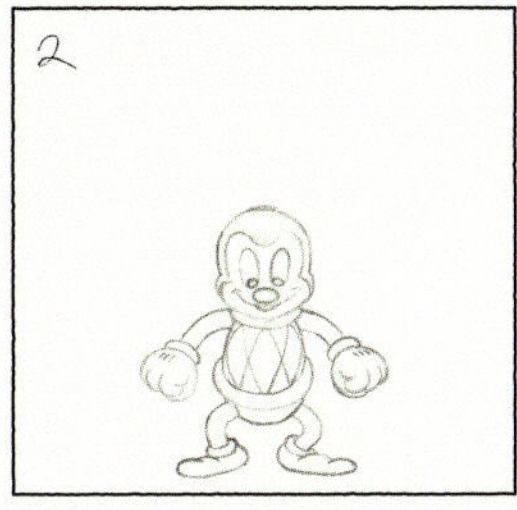

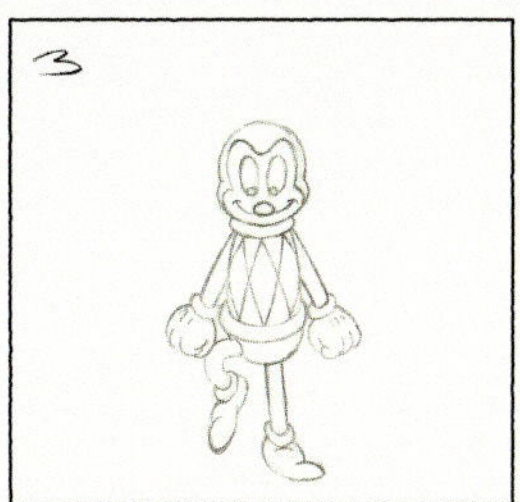

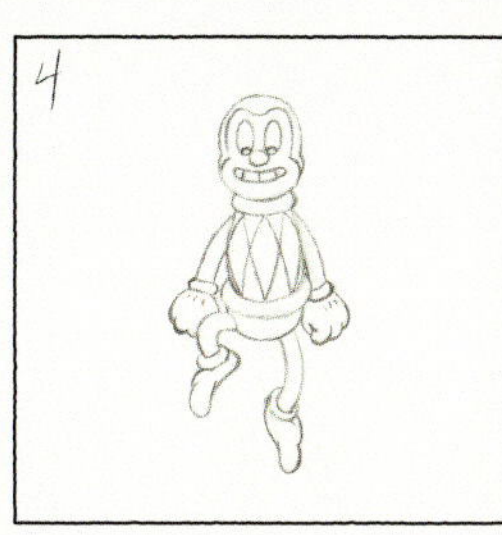

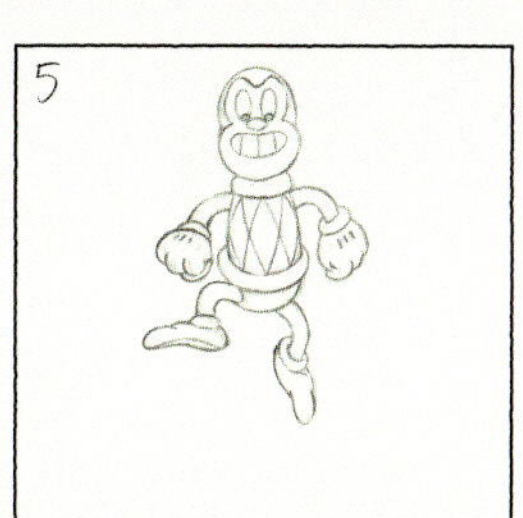

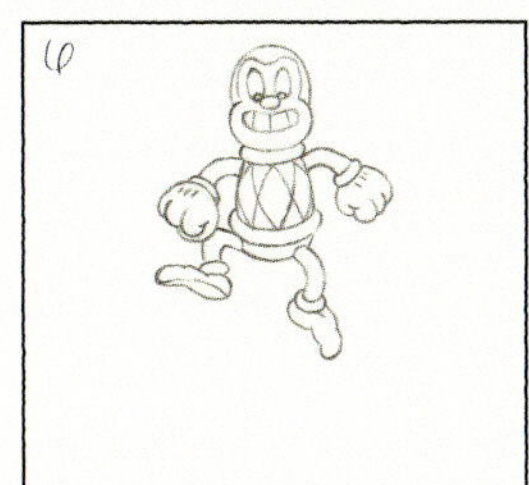

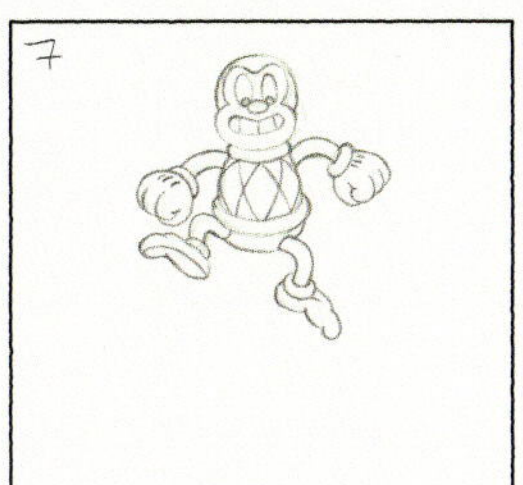

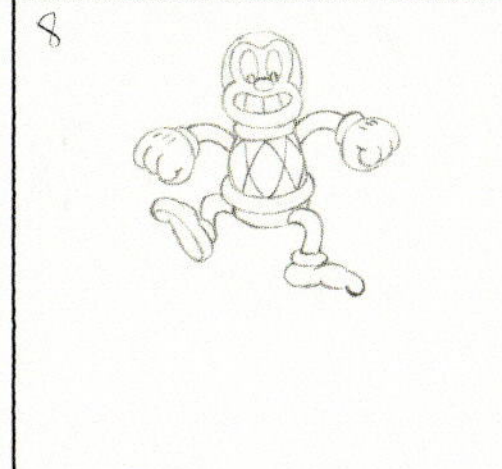

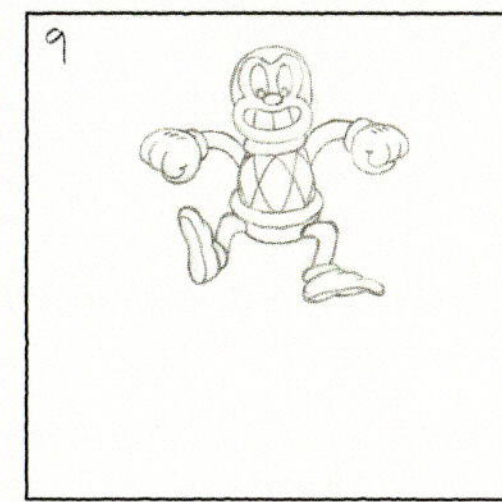

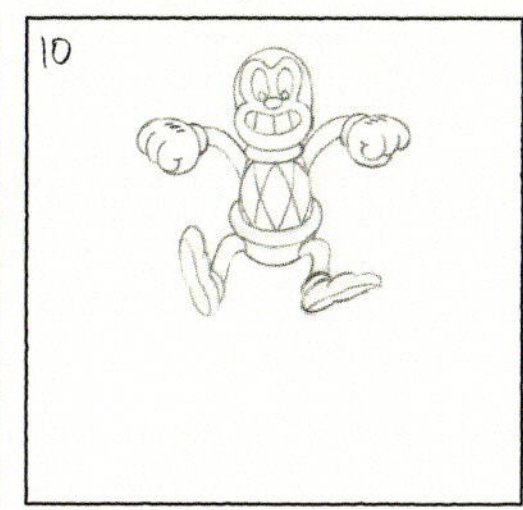

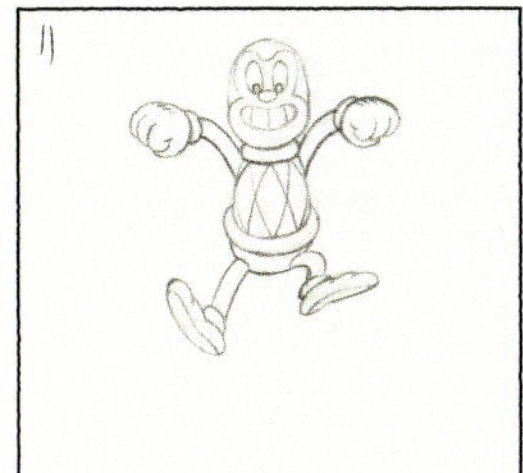

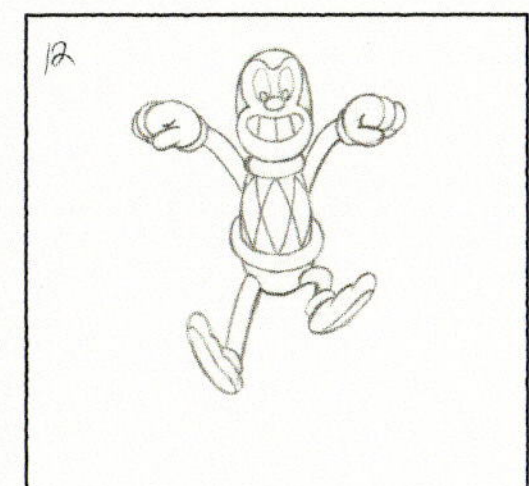

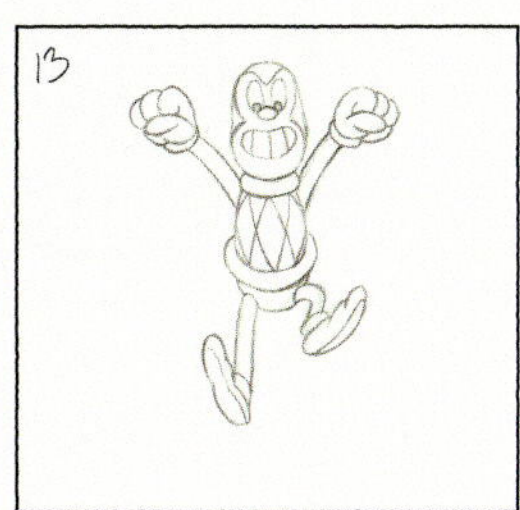

Above, animation frames of the pawns from Rapeepat Jewanarom in its "leap down" animation. Great care was taken with each King of Games battle to represent the true shape of each chess piece in its suite of animations.

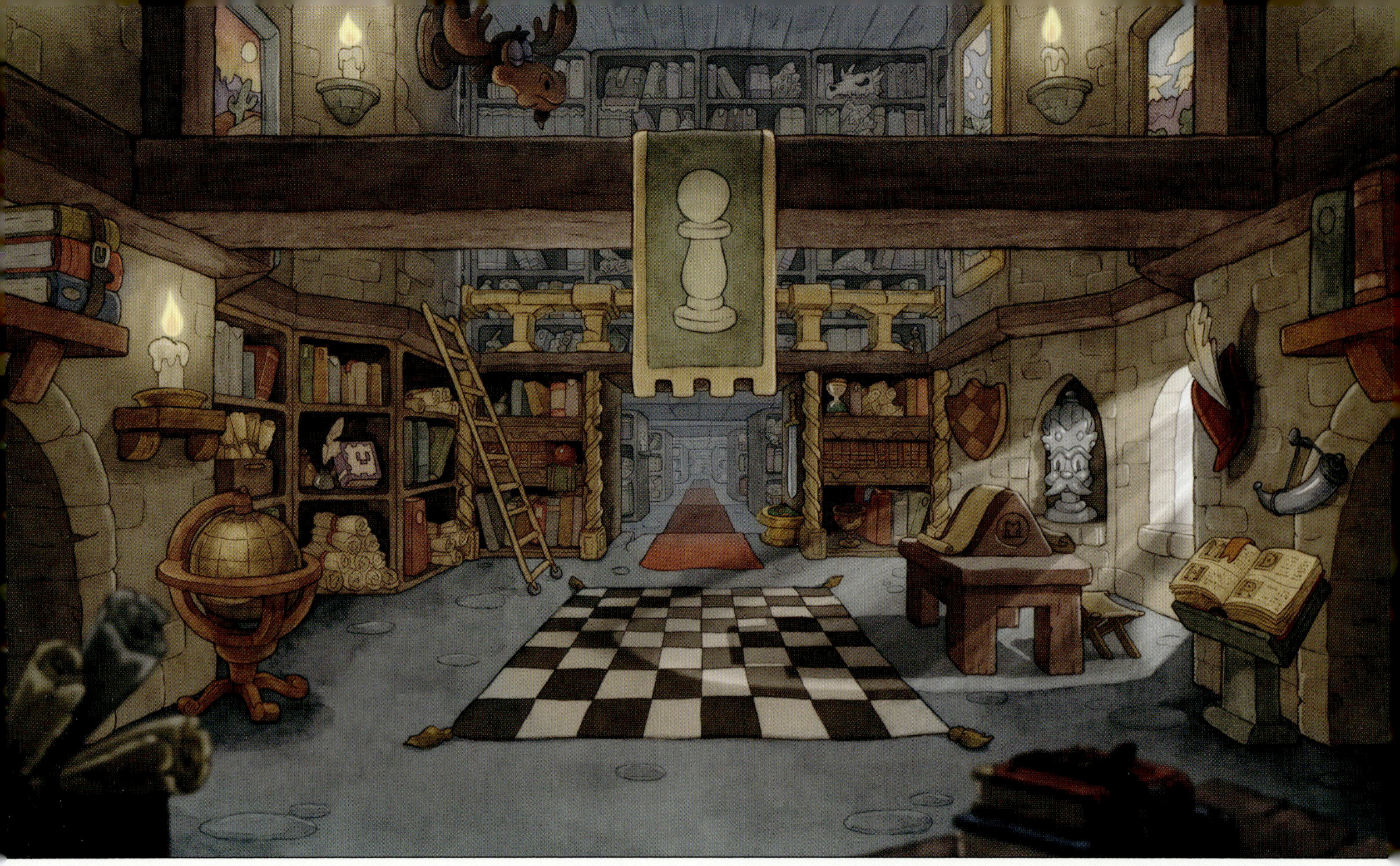

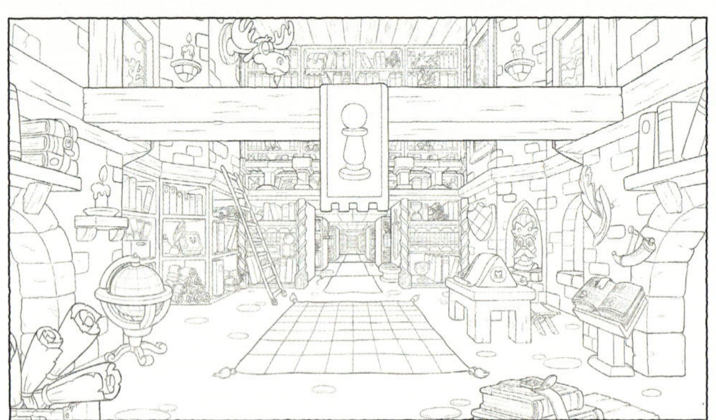

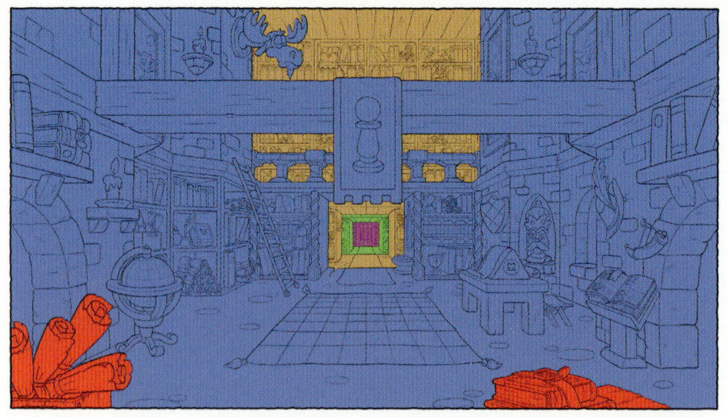

Pawn Background

ANYONE WHO PLAYS CHESS can attest that at the heart of the experience is the constant willingness to learn. We knew that a series of boss fights that stripped away all of your classic *Cuphead* tools except for the parry would similarly be a learning experience for players, so it felt only natural for the first battle in this gauntlet to take place in a library. Perhaps surprisingly, this may be the background with more references-per-inch than any other in the Inkwell Isles. We won't spoil them all, but here's a fun one we enjoy: the paintings up in the library rafters depict other levels from the DLC Isle, and pay homage to *Super Mario 64*'s painting-based level travel!

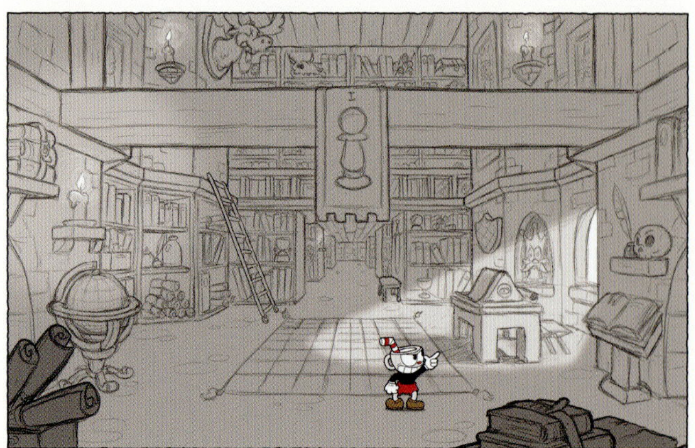

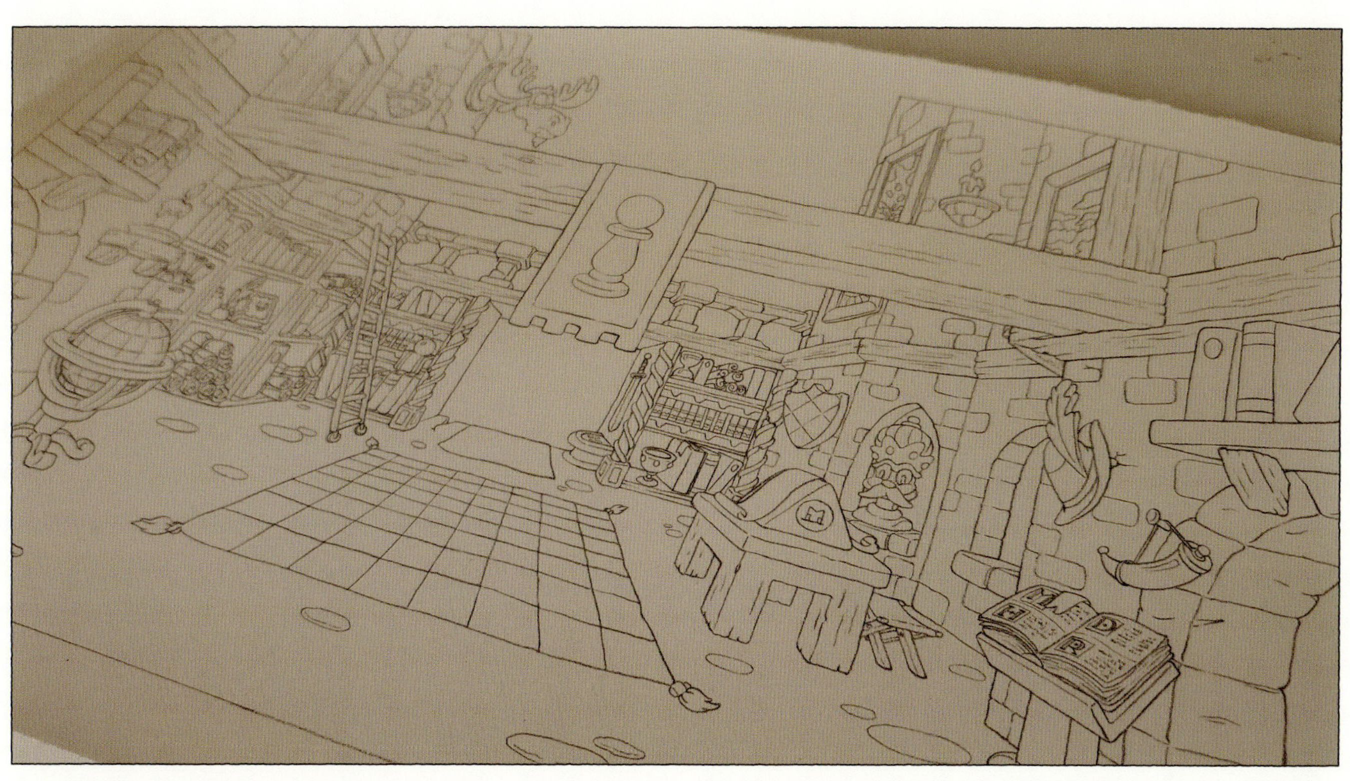

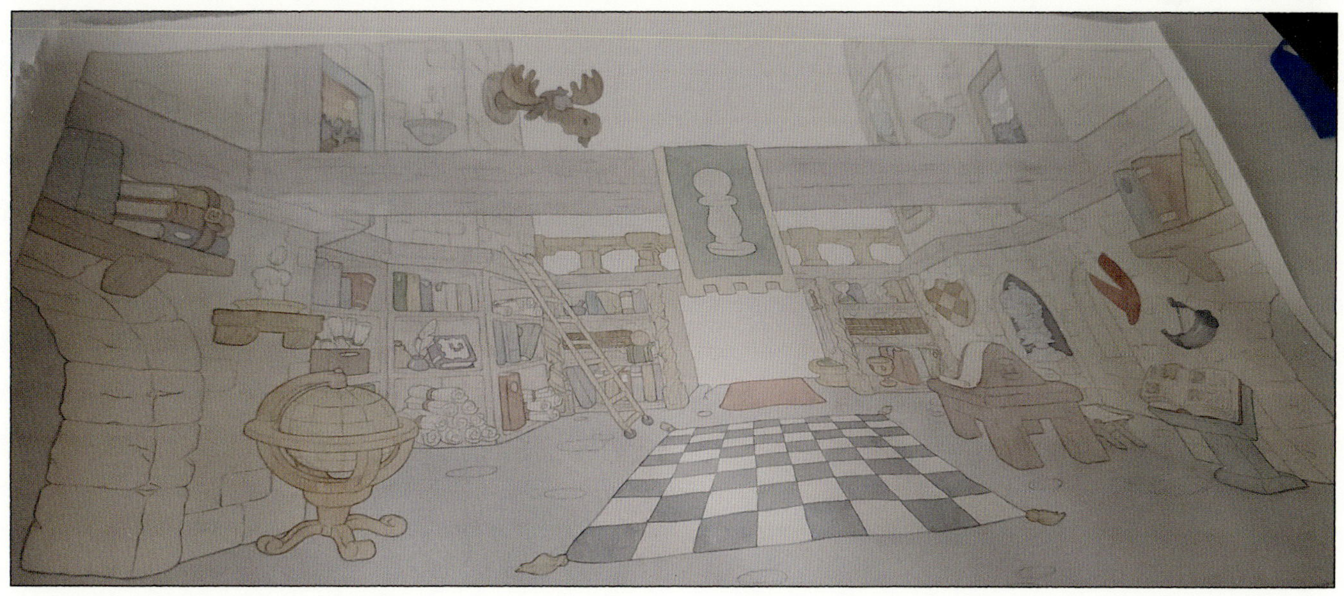

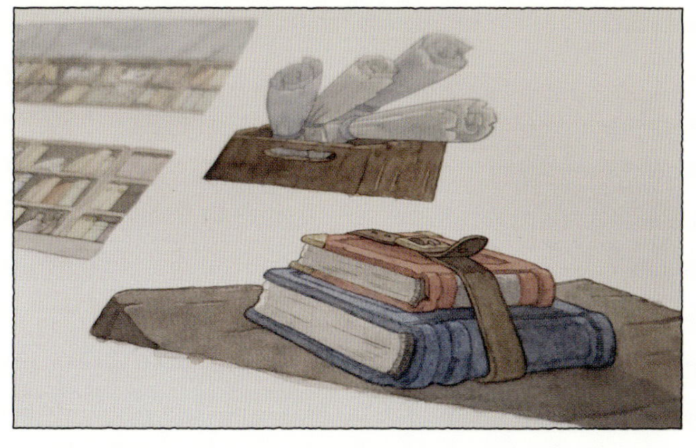

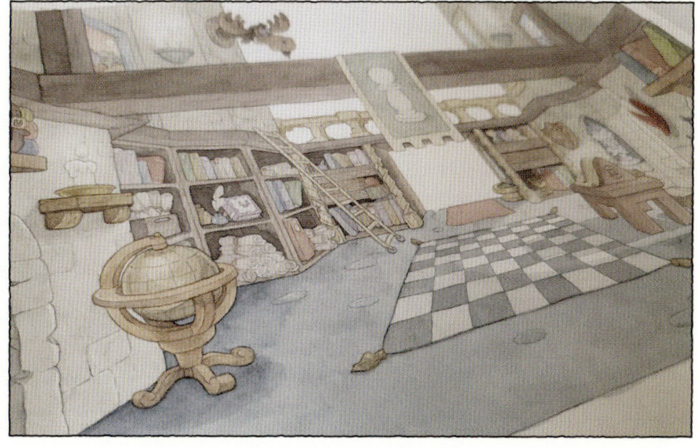

Knight

SOMETIMES IN THE CREATIVE PROCESS, things just… come together. For example, a knight boss in a chess-themed battle arena required very little creative ideation to settle on a lanky cartoon horse—especially given the thirties cartoon tendency to anthropomorphize animals. While taking some inspiration for his mannerisms from Disney's iconic Goofy, our knight is still one serious combatant. The fight itself pays homage to Nintendo's 1987's boxing brawler *Punch-Out!!*, where it's critical to analyze your opponent's movements, and pick between a series of simple responses performed with precision. En garde, cups!!

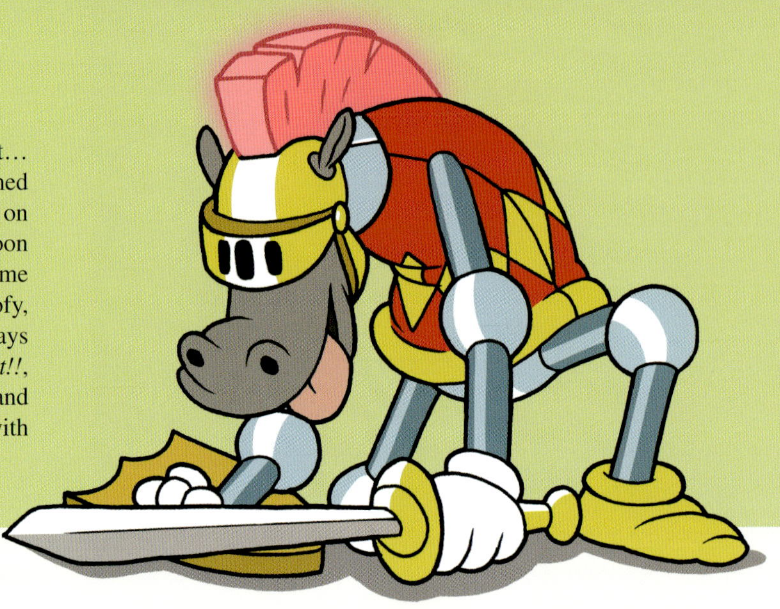

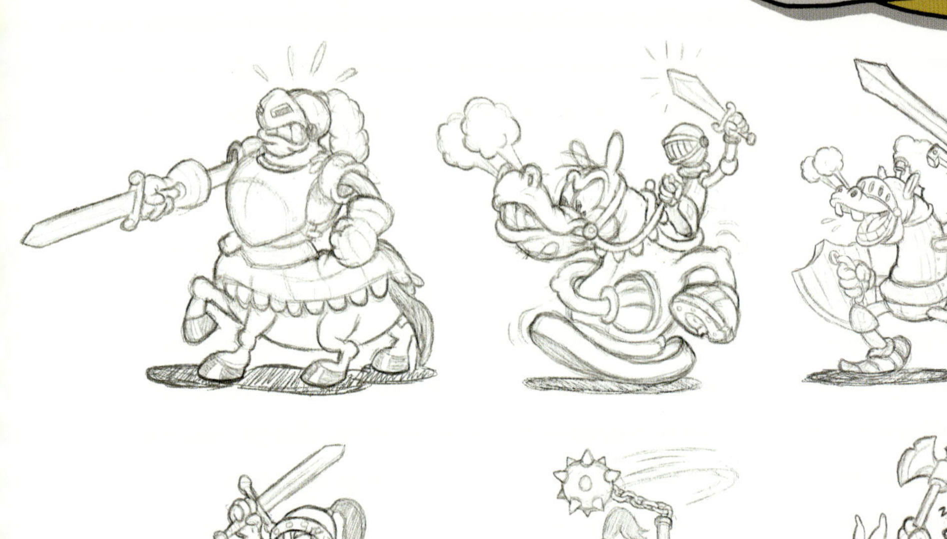

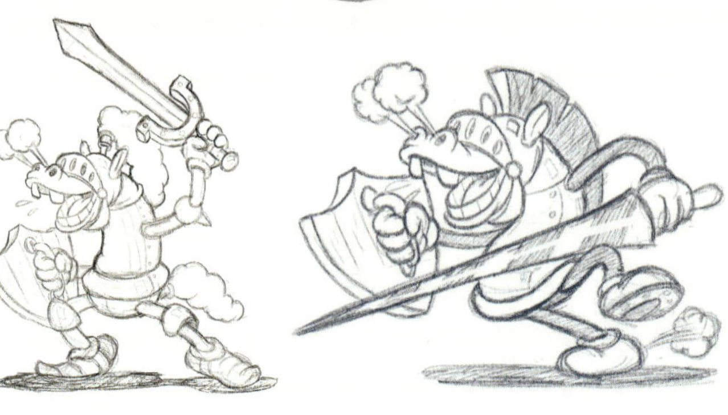

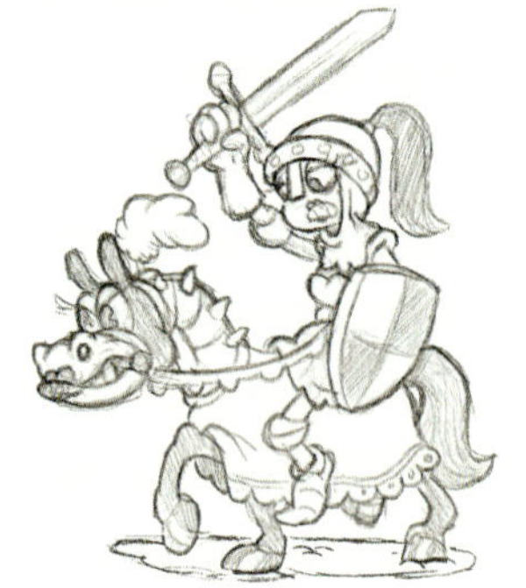

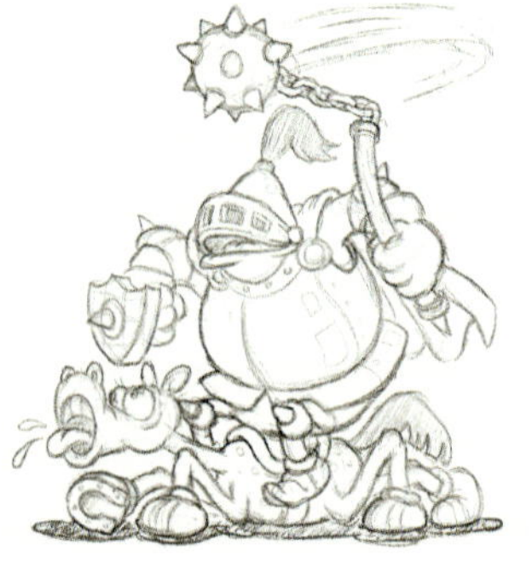

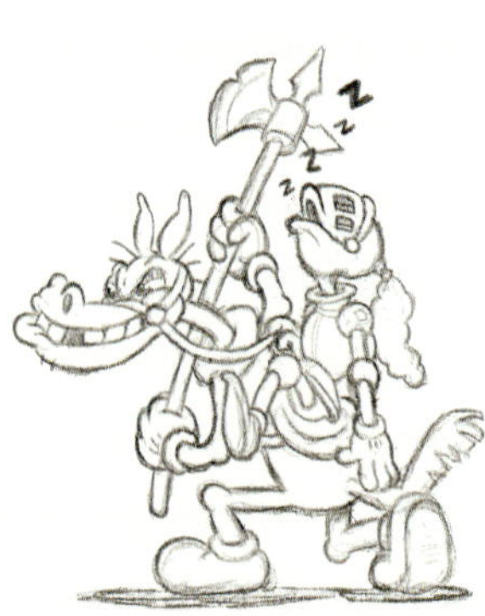

Conceptual exploration from Artist Lance Inkwell, pictured right, shows a brief dalliance with the idea of our knight having a rider. Like our knight at the thought of having a person on his back, this is a line of exploration we quickly bucked.

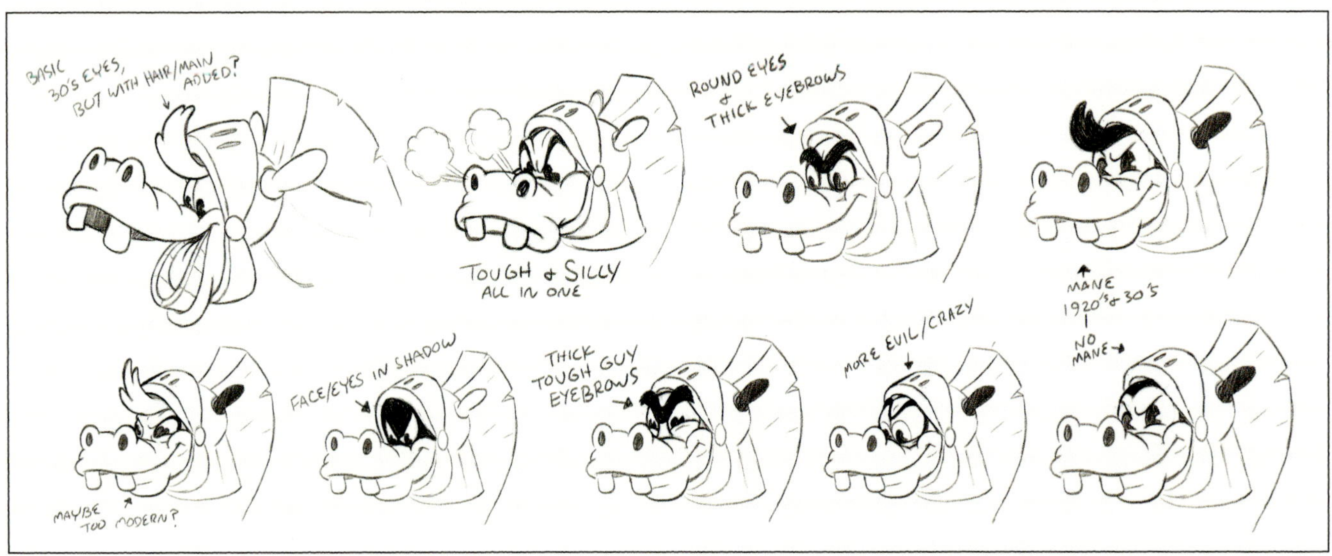

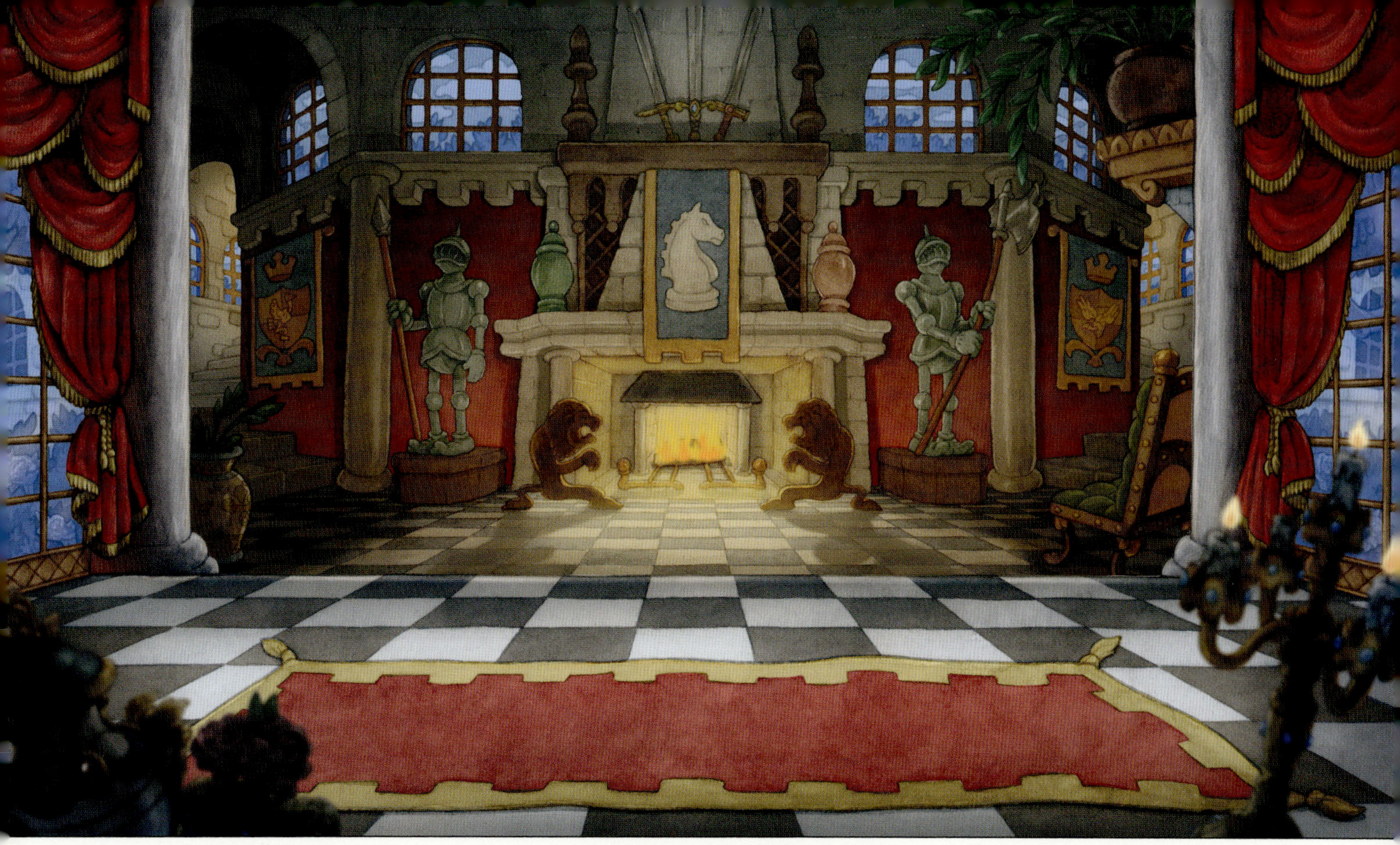

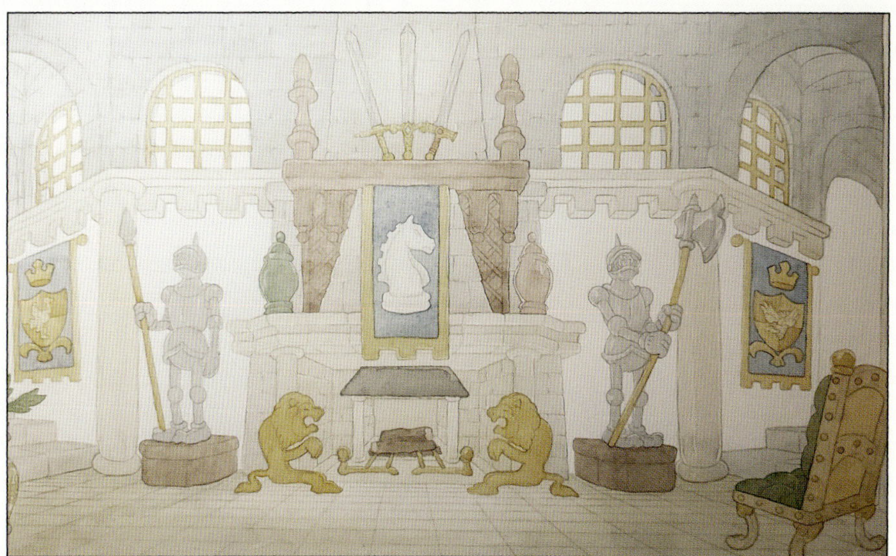

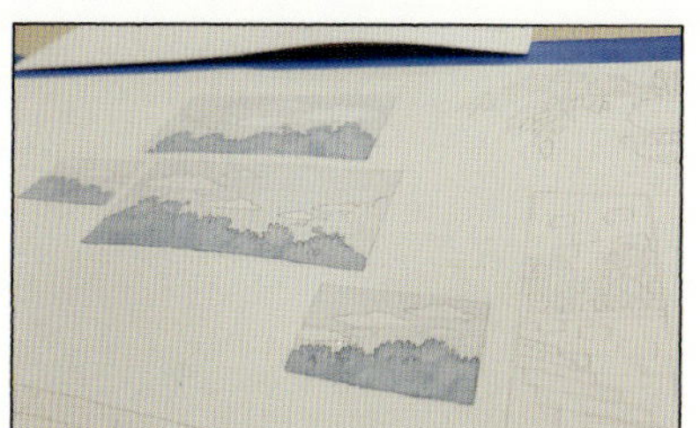

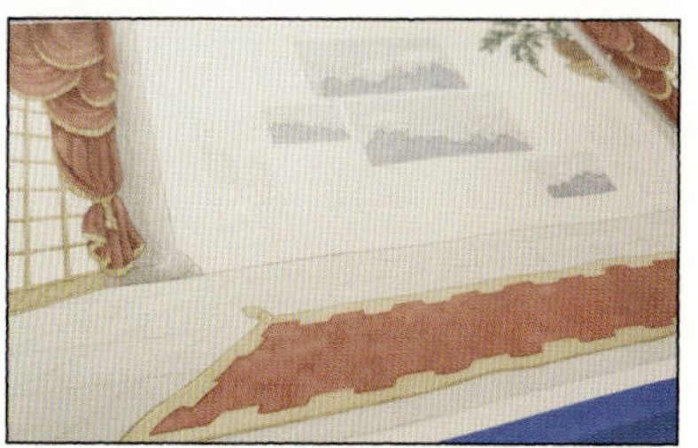

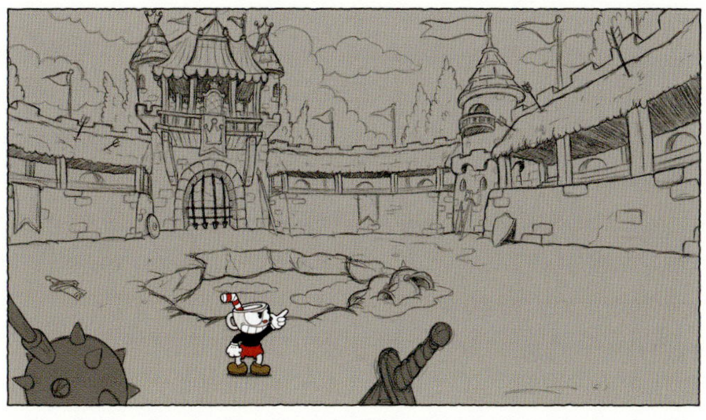

Knight Background

WITH DRAPERY AND floor-to-ceiling windows inspired by the background of character Charlotte Colde's stage from SNK's 1994 arcade fighter *Samurai Showdown II*, our Knight's regal foyer is the perfect place for showdown at sword-point. Key recurring details like the chess piece banner and checkered flooring help to achieve the light sense of "world building" we like in *Cuphead*, in which artistic flourishes create a sort of internal logic for the rituals and customs our characters might adhere to.

Bishop

IN AN IRONIC TWIST for a character inspired by a man of the cloth, our bishop battle in the King of Games gauntlet contains heavily reworked mechanics from a much more malevolent idea cut from the original *Cuphead*–a secret "death reaper" character who would have emerged if players lingered for too long within our boss fights! As design for this stage progressed, it became apparent that there was a risk of players simply standing around and waiting for the enemy to come to them. Thus was born the idea of required you to snuff out a series of candles in order to make your pious rival reappear!

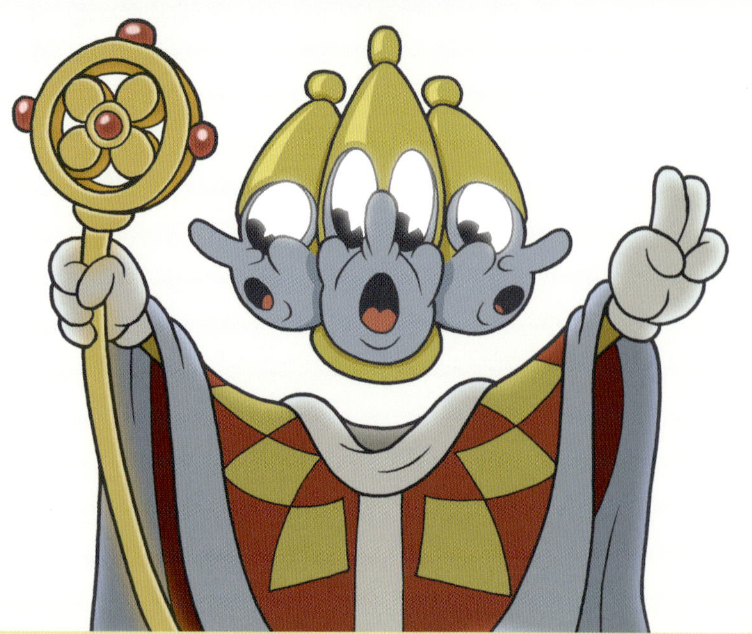

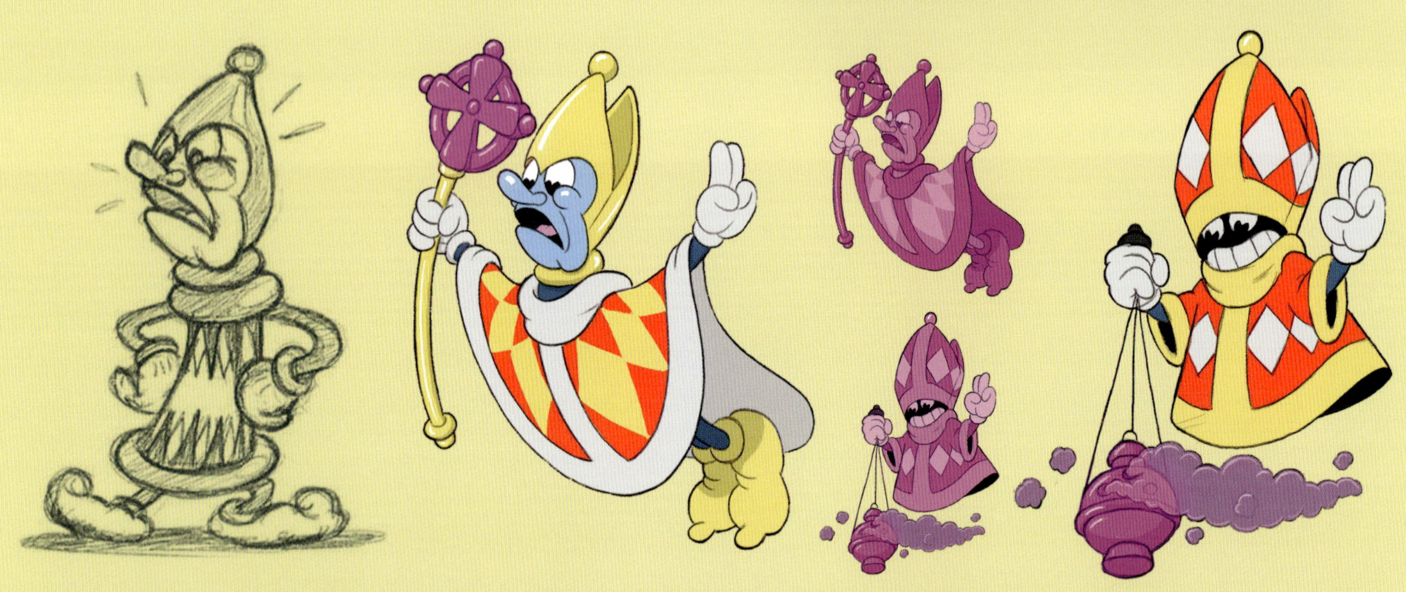

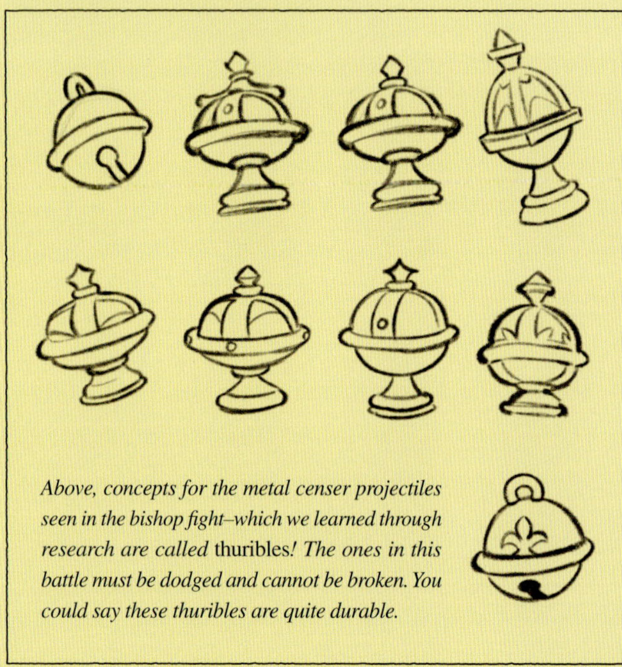

Above, concepts for the metal censer projectiles seen in the bishop fight–which we learned through research are called thuribles! *The ones in this battle must be dodged and cannot be broken. You could say these thuribles are quite durable.*

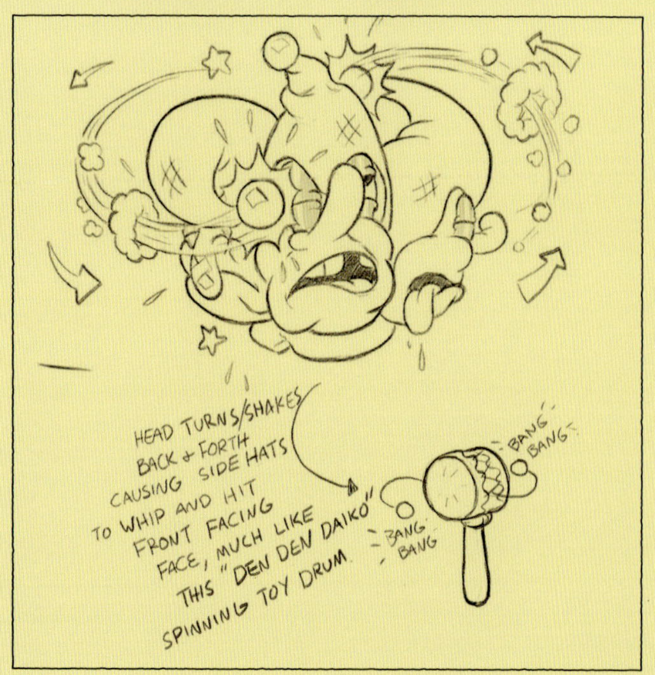

Bishop Background

A KEEN STUDY WILL NOTICE that the background of our bishop battle (say that ten times fast!) contains an abundance of X-shaped iconography–a nod to the diagonal movement pattern of the chess piece on which this character is based. Meanwhile, thuribles carved into the foreground pillars are deliberately reminiscent of the bell projectiles thrown by the titular character in developer Taito's 1992 platformer *Little Samson*. The whole scene is tied together with stained glass art designed both to add an air of reverence and spirituality, and to link the architecture here to that in our Inkwell Isle Mausoleums.

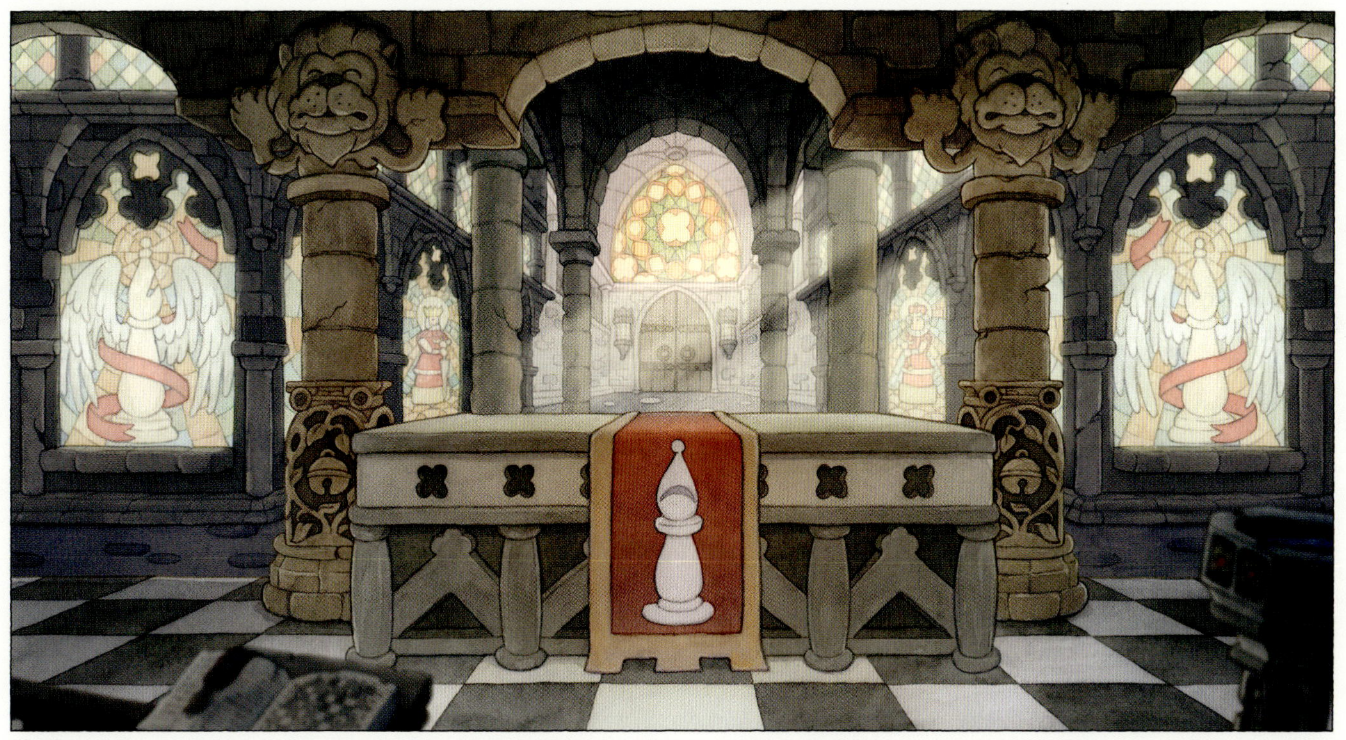

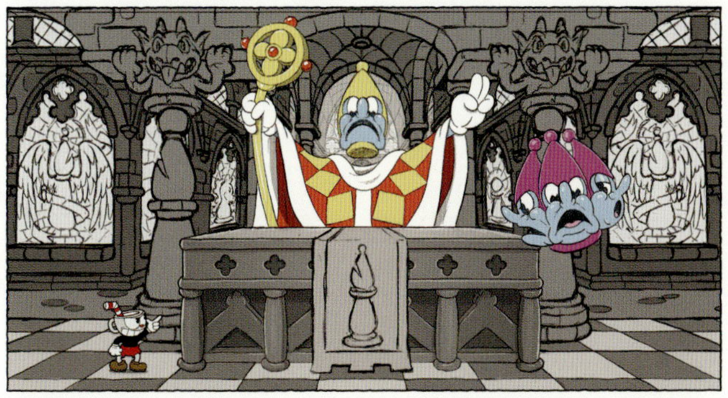

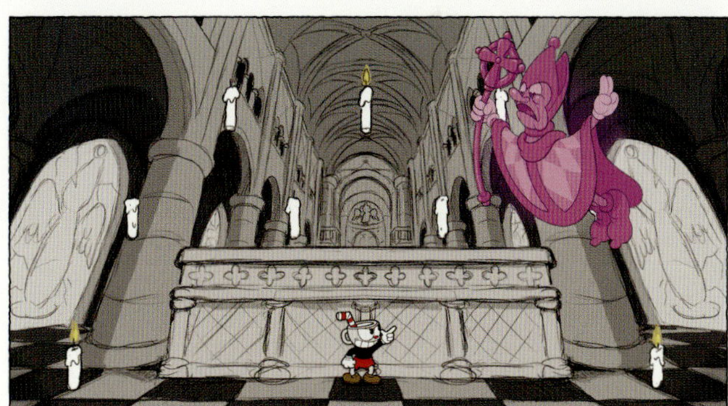

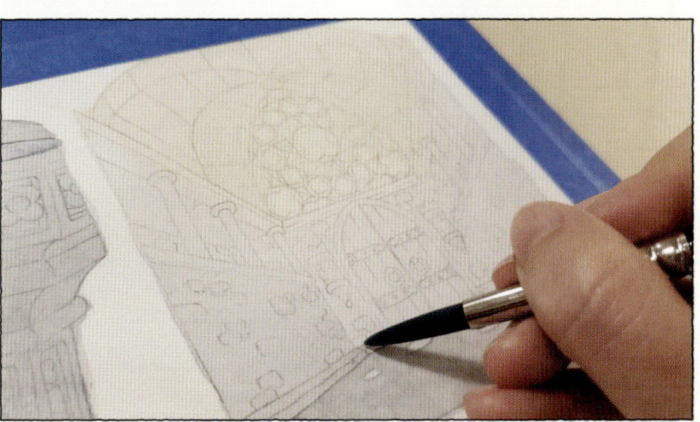

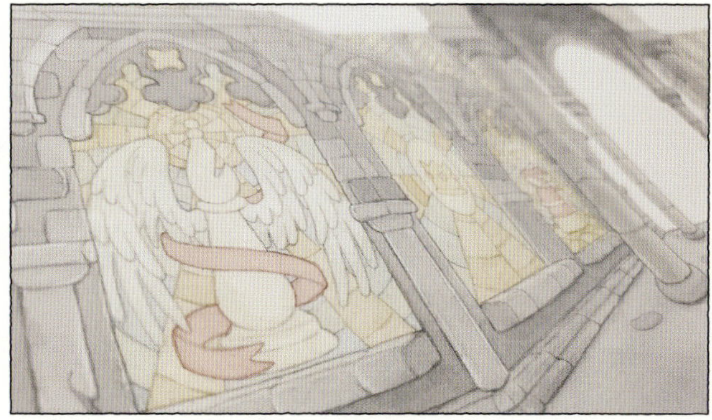

Rook

ONE TOUGH CASTLE TO CRACK, our Rook mini-boss was a hard-fought concept that we initially envisioned as a much more literal representation of a classic parapet. Knowing this would be a stationary enemy, the breakthrough in visual design happened when we arrived at concepts of a character who used his stone base as a seat—leading us down the path of rook as executioner, toiling away on his tools in the King's dungeon. If you can guess the inspiration for the floating head emerging from his axe, let's just say we'll let you eat cake.

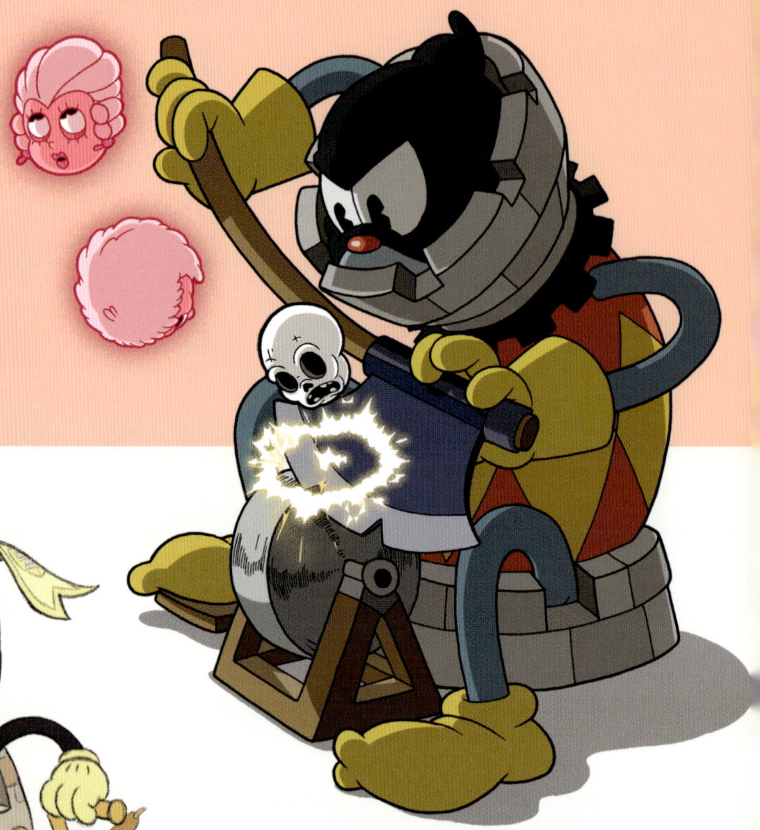

Another fun fact about the projectiles in this battle: their expression changes based on whether they are emerging from the grindstone (spooky!) or bouncing toward the rook (happy for revenge!)

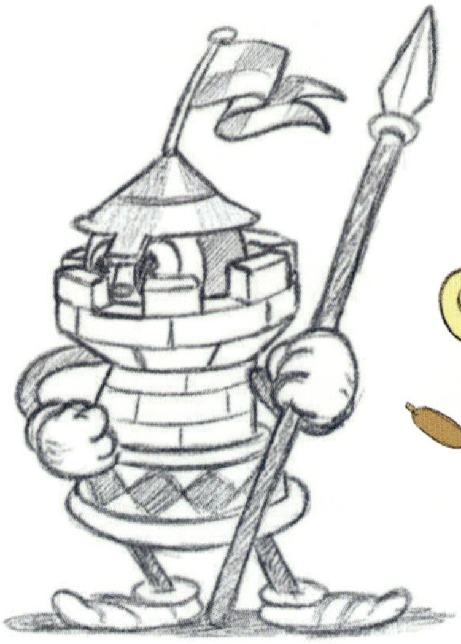

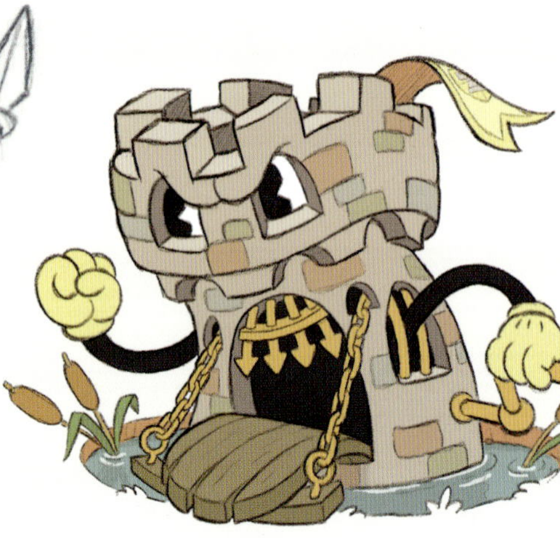

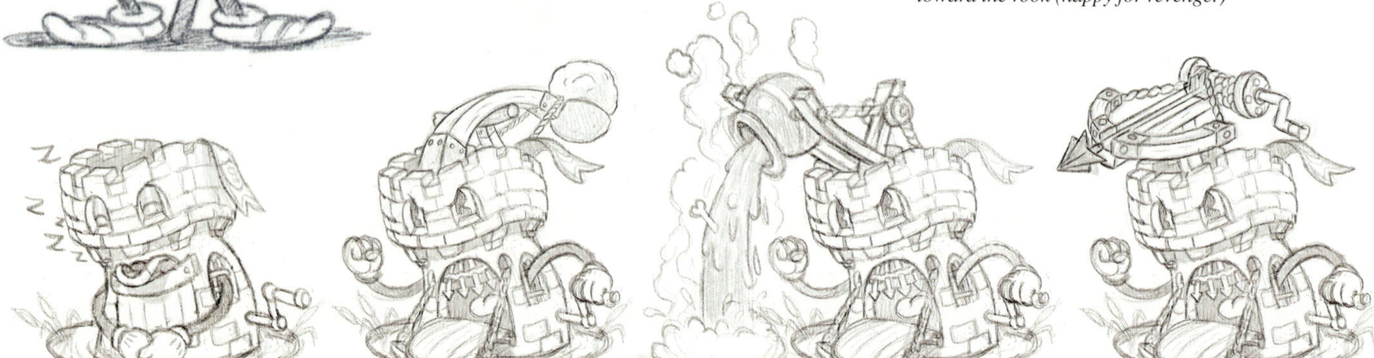

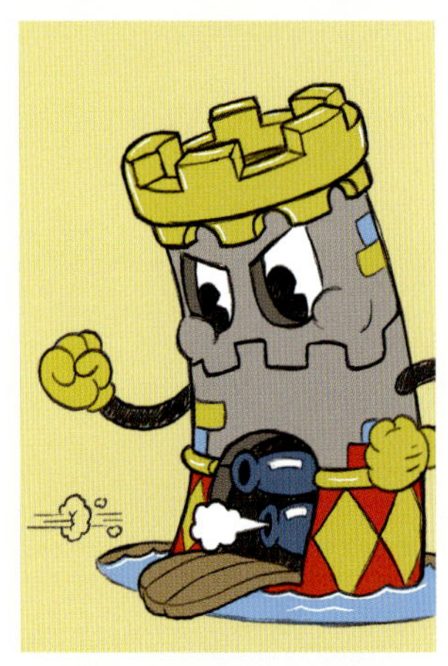

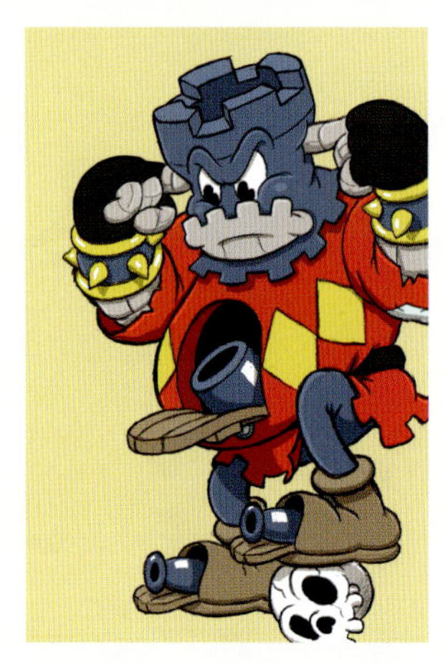

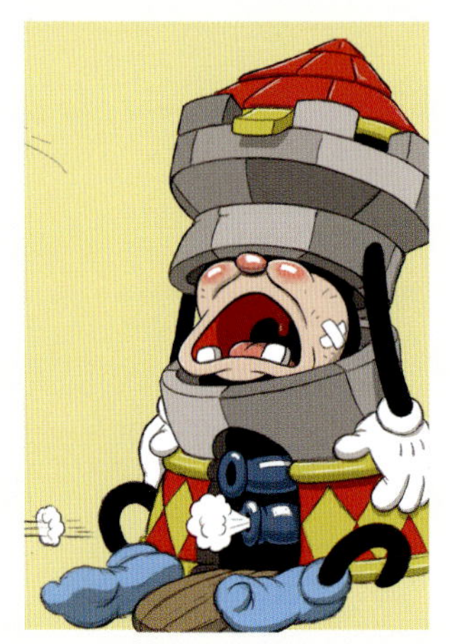

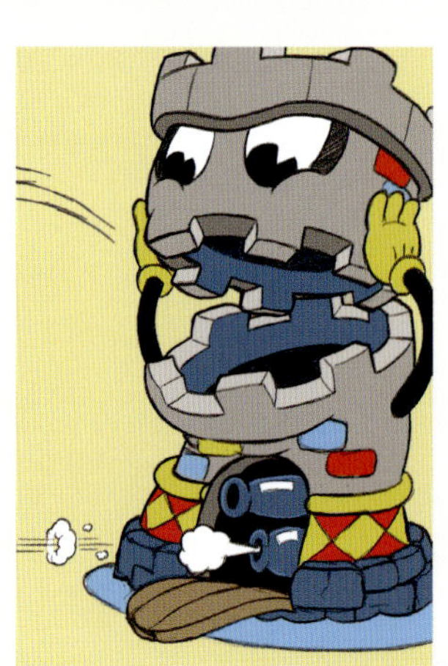

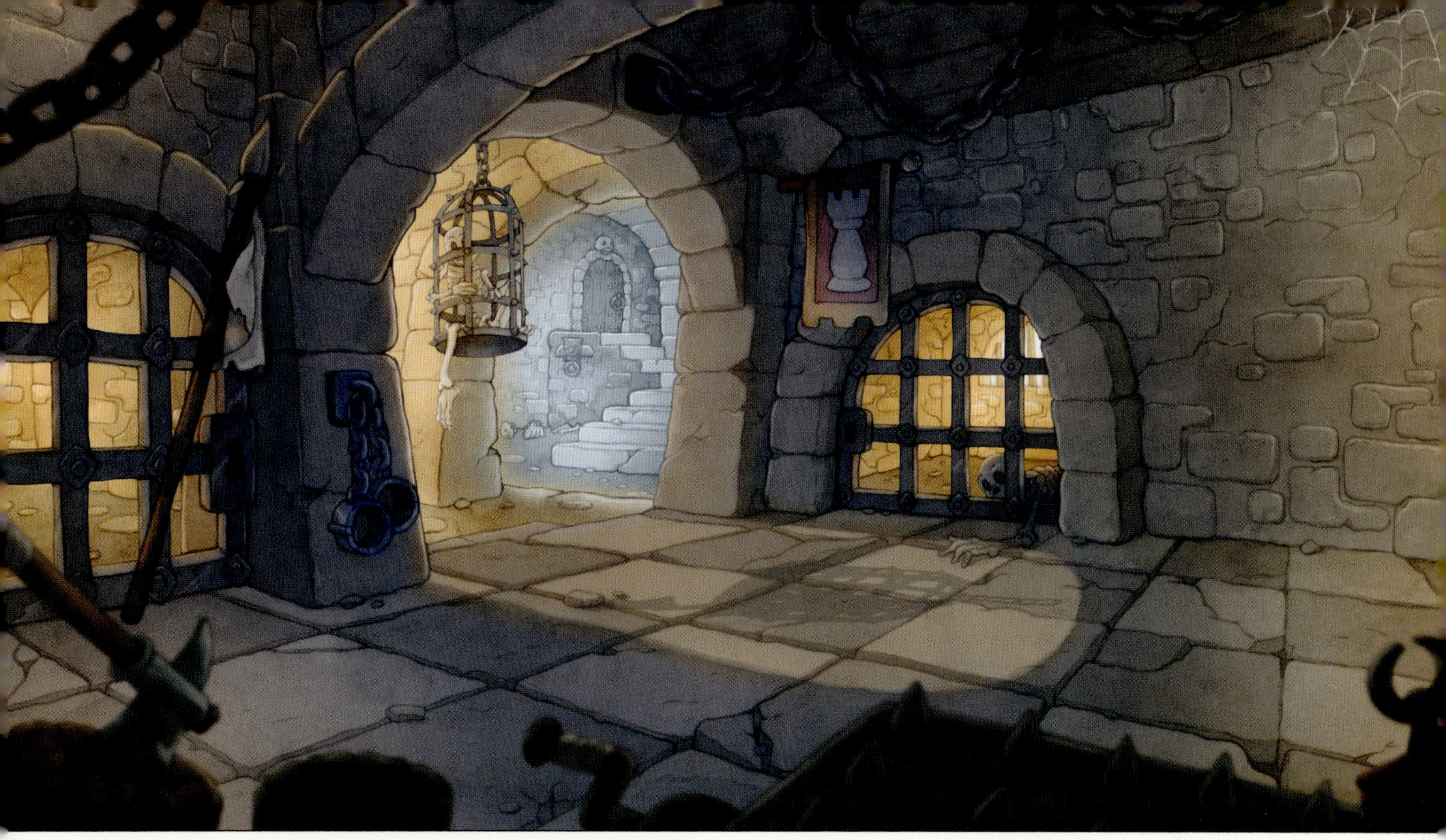

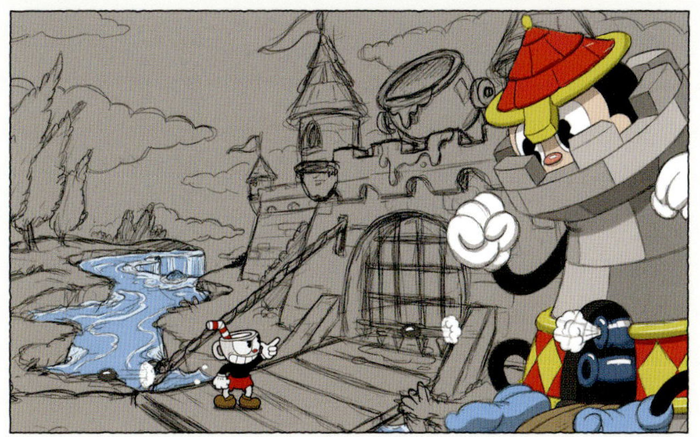

Rook Background

THE DUNGEON SETTING FOR the Rook's stage required us to get playful with the motifs we were looking to carry across the King of Games fights. Here, we opted to represent the chess board pattern on cracked stone flooring rather than with black and white tiles to better suit the diegesis of the scene. Little-known fact: the brick pattern on the wall is a nod to iD Software's 1991 shooter threequel *Catacombs 3D*–notably, the first game to give *Cuphead* Design Director Jared Moldenhauer motion sickness!

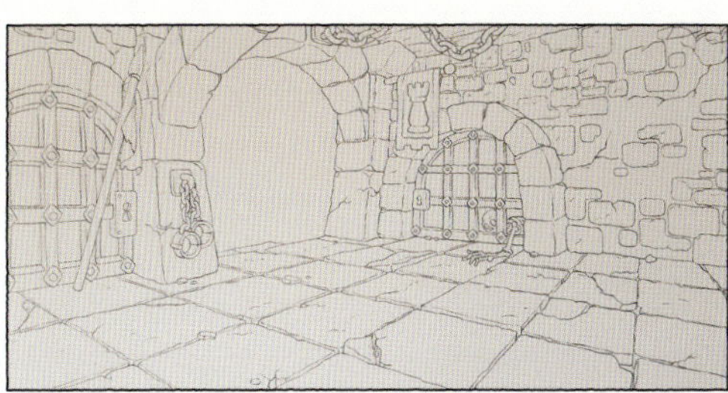

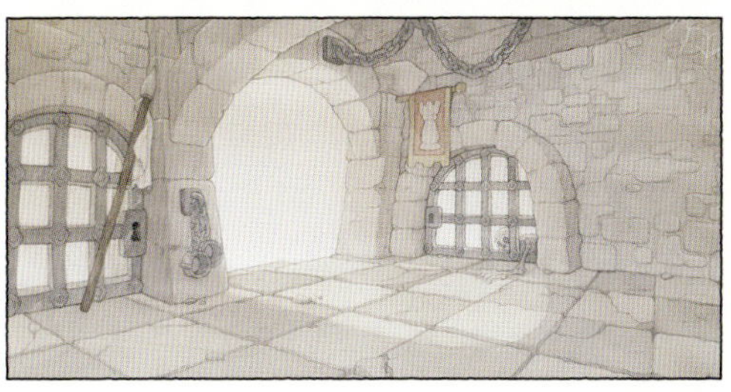

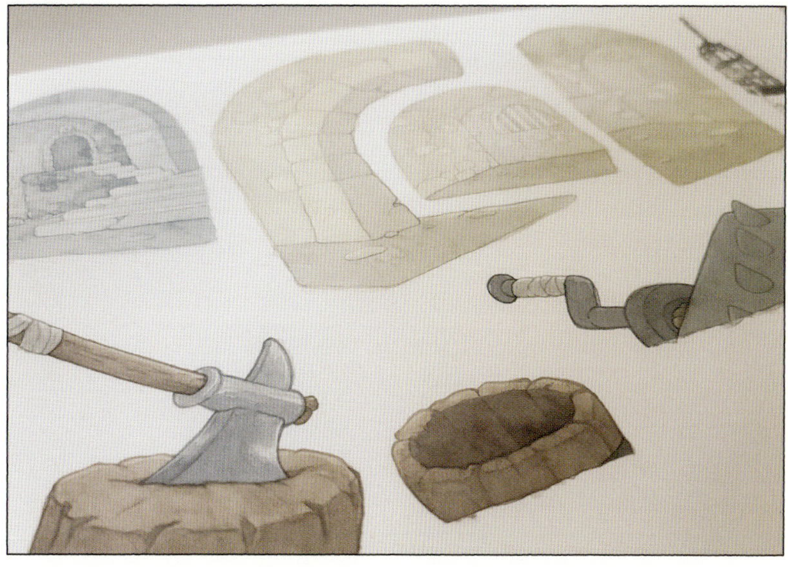

Queen

THE EVER-IRATE HEAD OF STATE, our Queen rounds out this parry gauntlet as the final boss in order to signal to players what all chess enthusiasts know to be true: that it is she, and not the king, who is the most versatile combatant on the board. To mirror this versatility, we pushed to find interesting ways to interact with the boss indirectly, experimenting at first with three cannons placed in different zones on the screen. We ultimately felt flattening them out into one row made for a more legible design experience, and thus was born the idea of working with a gaggle of *Robin Hood* (1973)-inspired rodents against this rude royal!

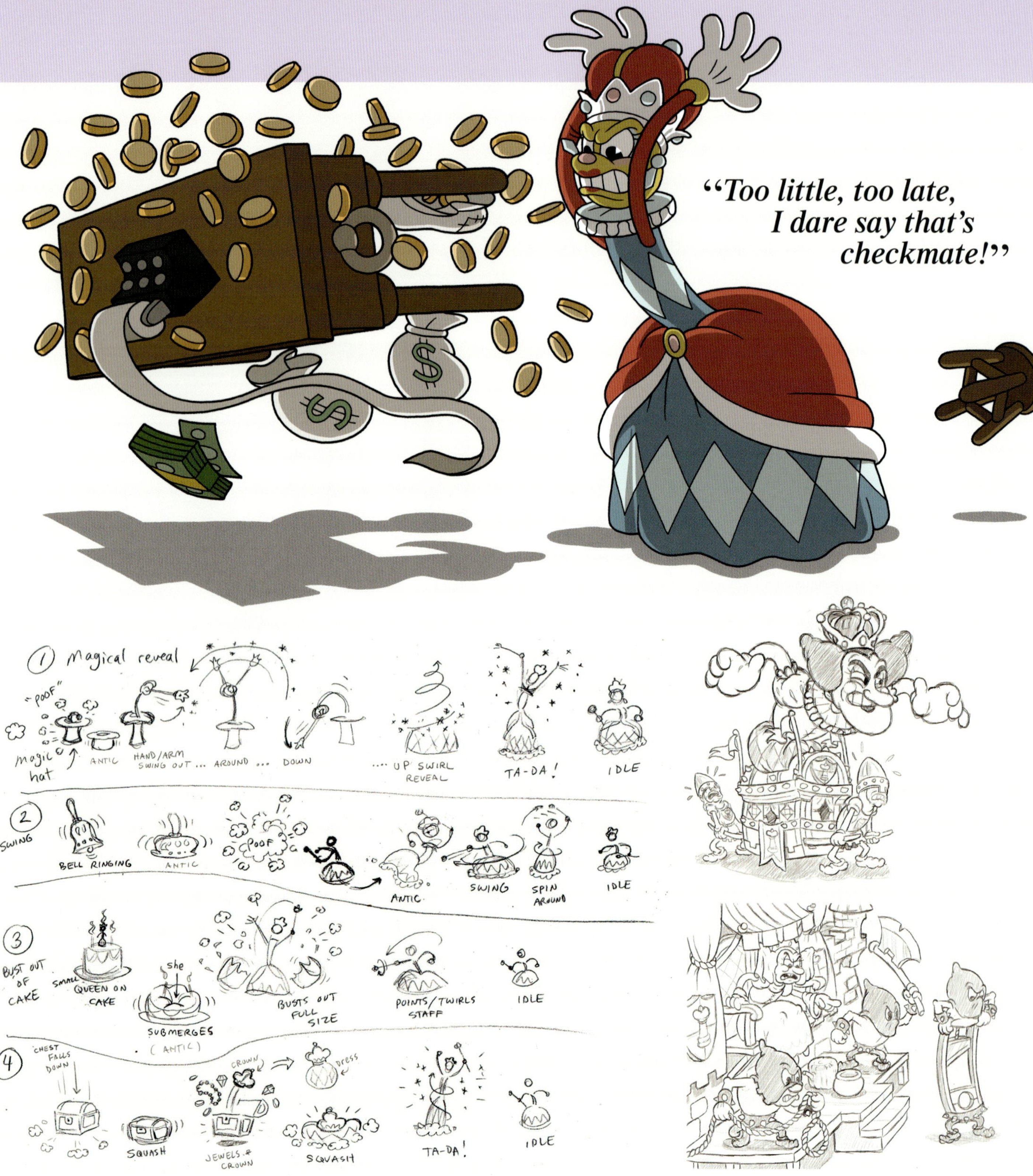

"Too little, too late, I dare say that's checkmate!"

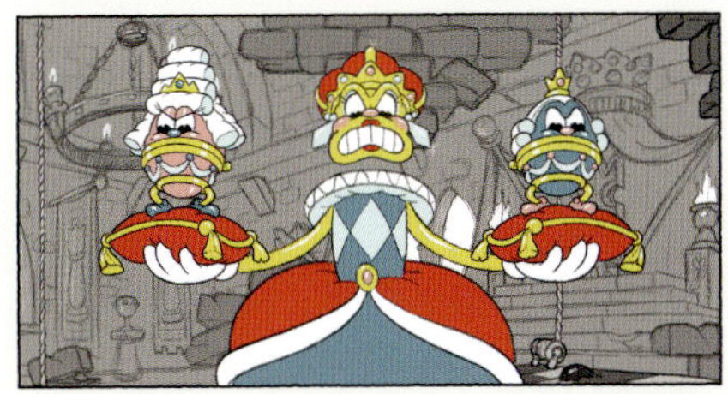

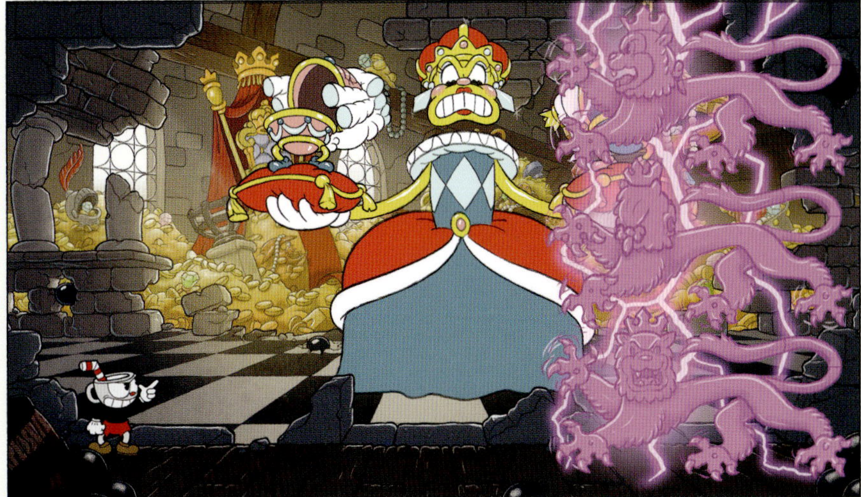

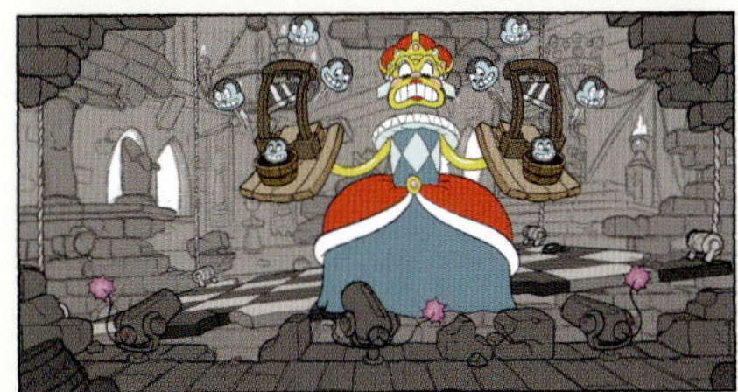

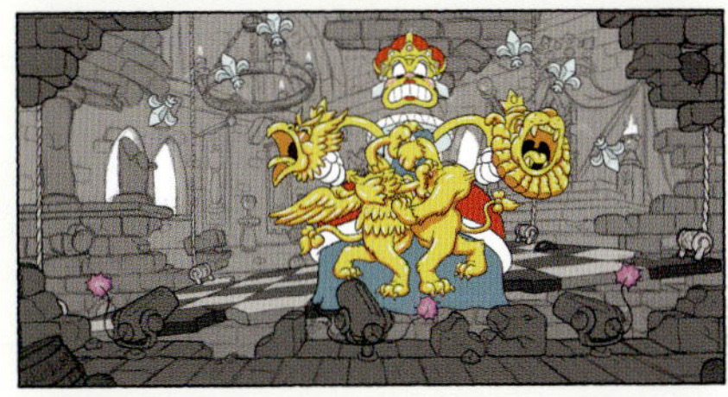

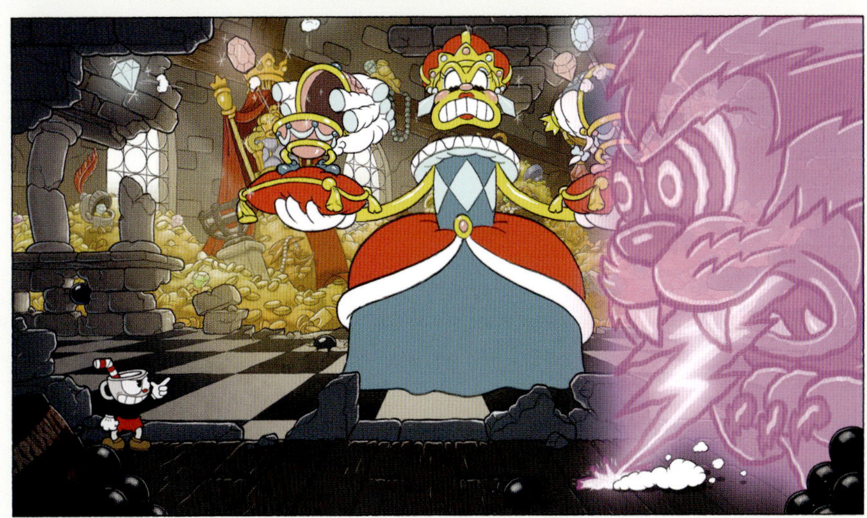

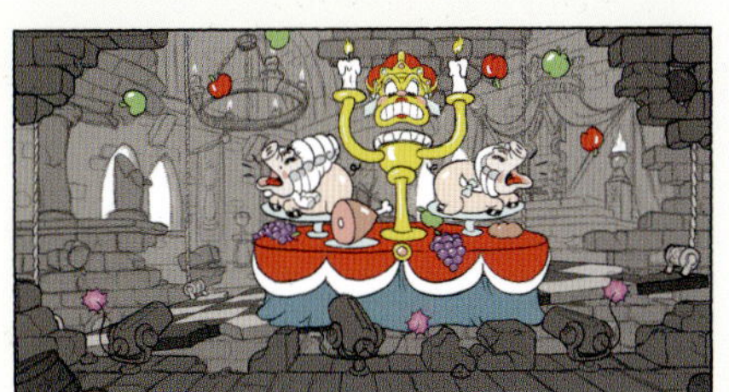

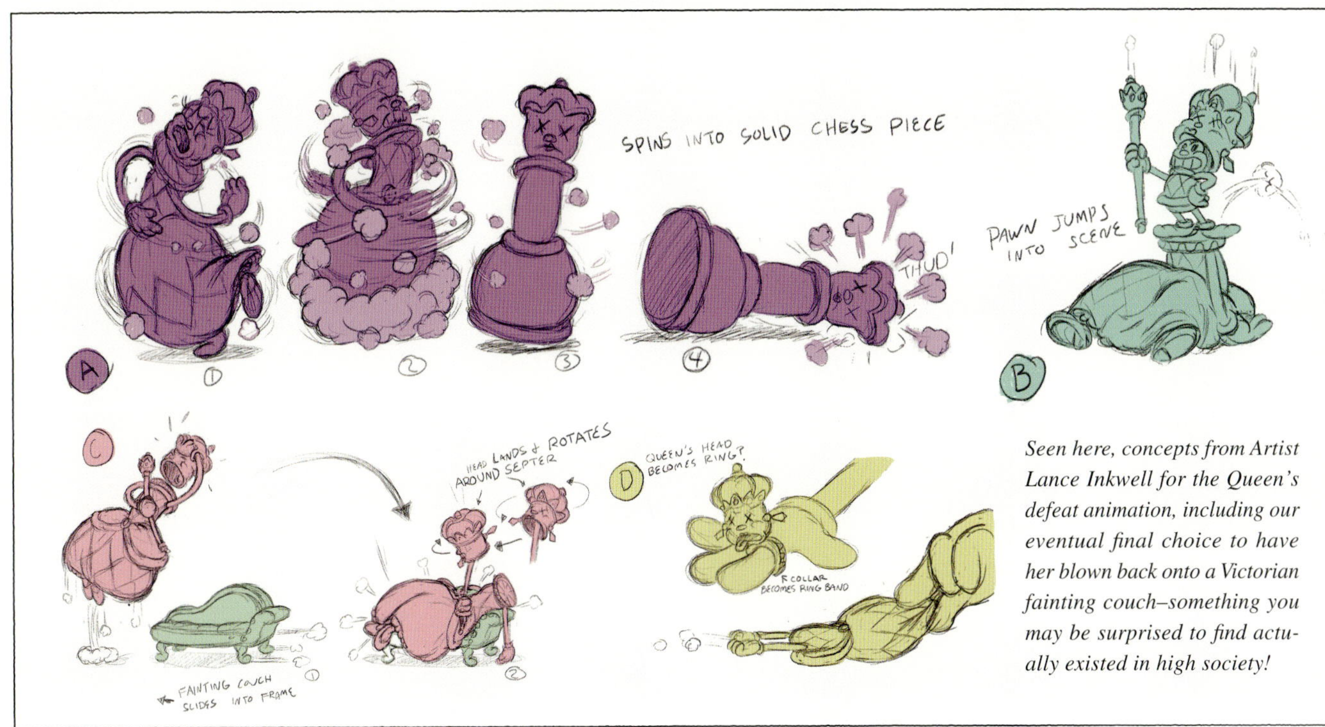

Seen here, concepts from Artist Lance Inkwell for the Queen's defeat animation, including our eventual final choice to have her blown back onto a Victorian fainting couch–something you may be surprised to find actually existed in high society!

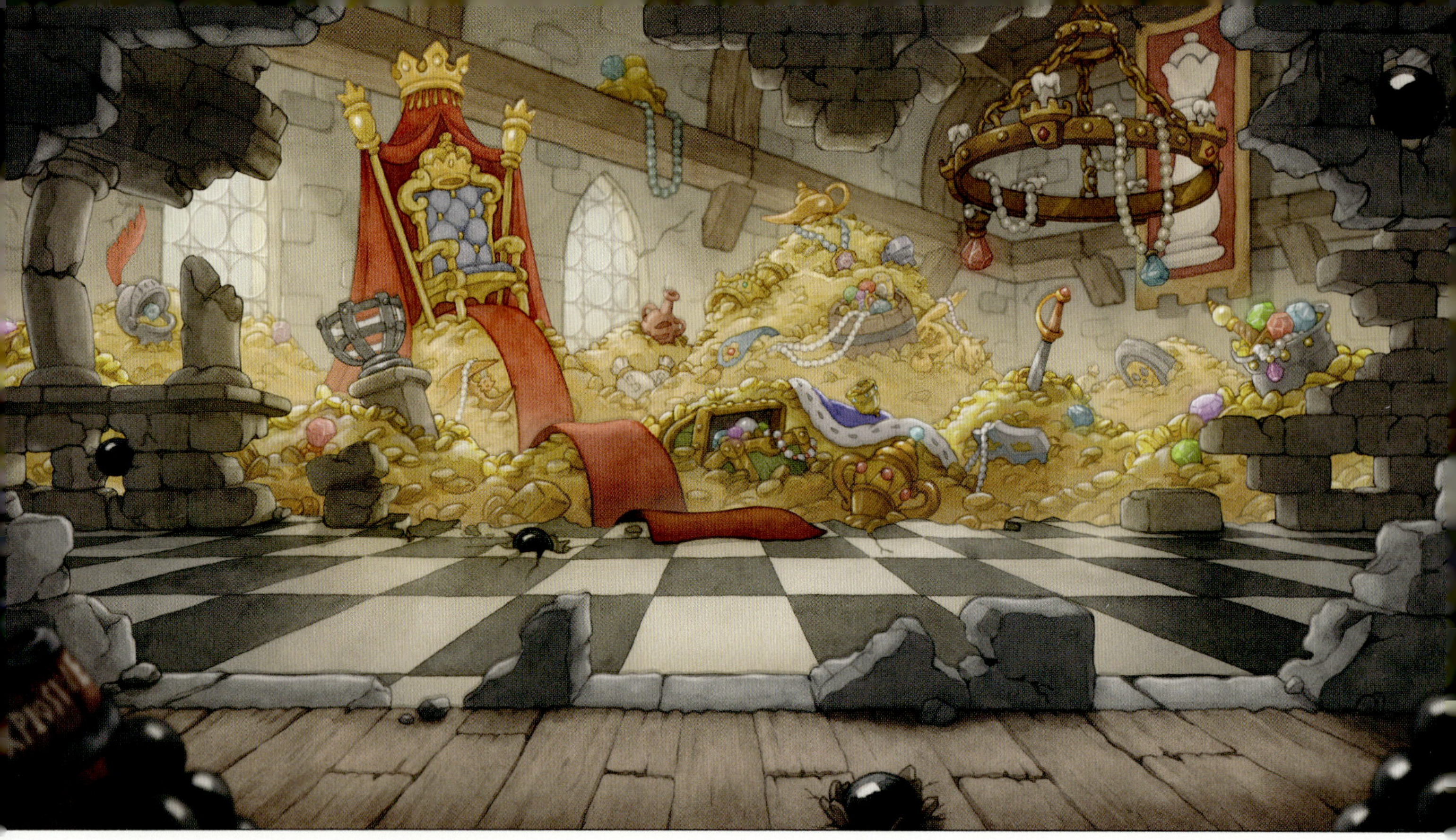

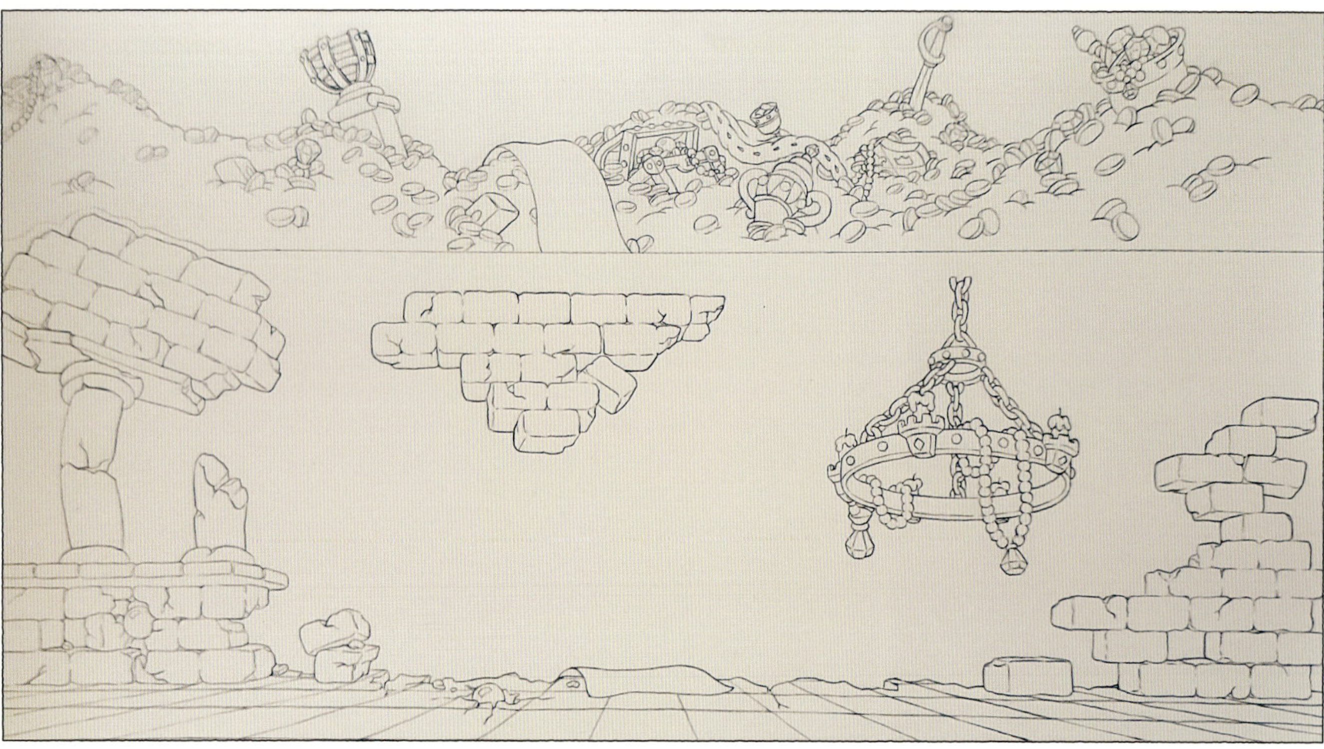

Queen Background

ONE OF THE KEY DIFFICULTIES with the Queen's background was conveying the right sense of depth, something we ultimately chase in any *Cuphead* boss battle. Tests on a standard throne room didn't yield the results we wanted, so we moved to flesh out the story of the battle more with the idea of the Queen's gold stores under assault, cannon-blasted walls and all. Speaking of the royal riches, it's no accident if those glittering piles of coins and gems evoke images of Disney's 1987 hit *DuckTales*–don't you just want to take a dive?

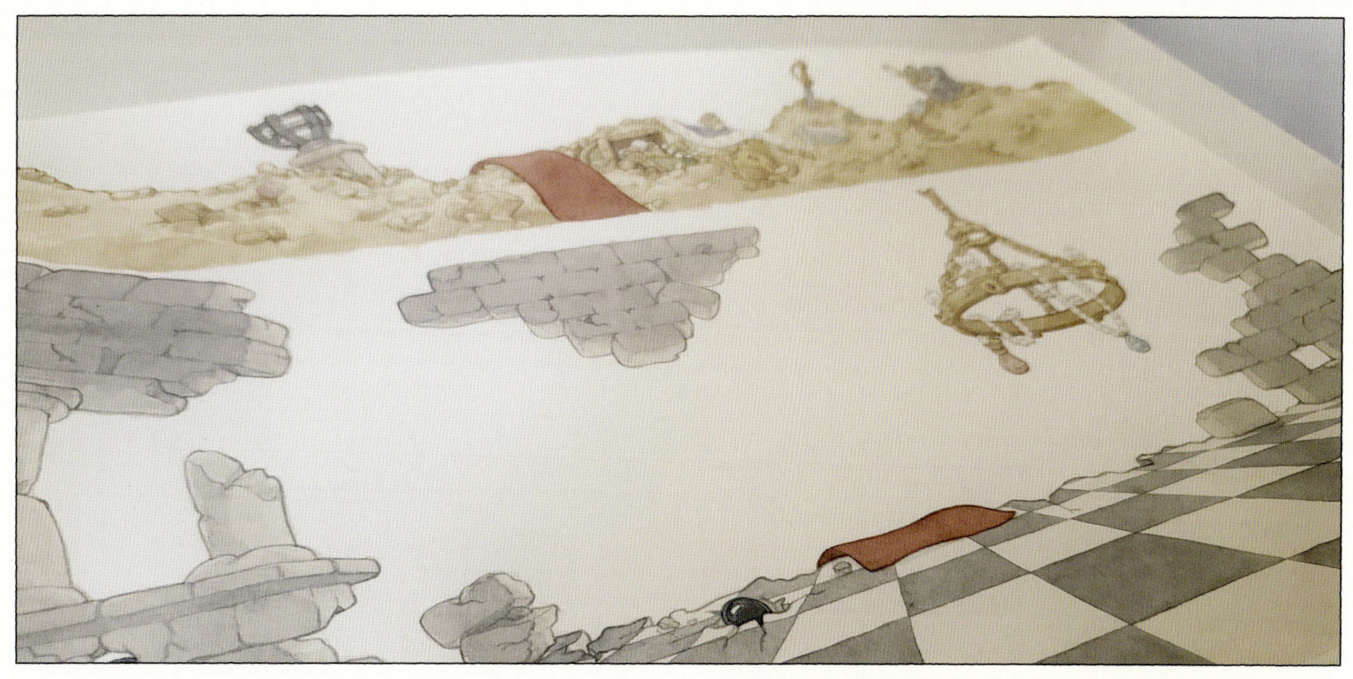

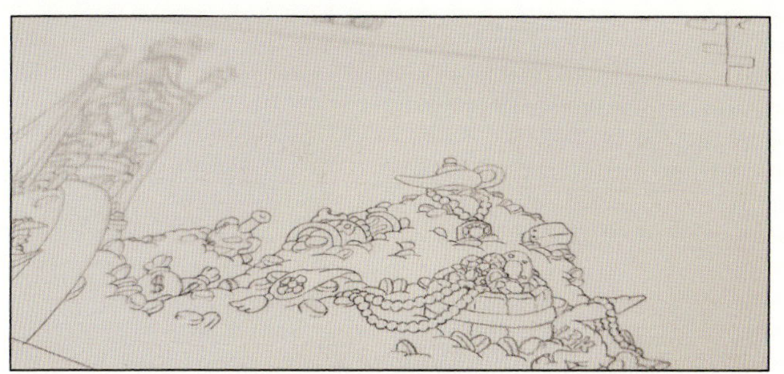

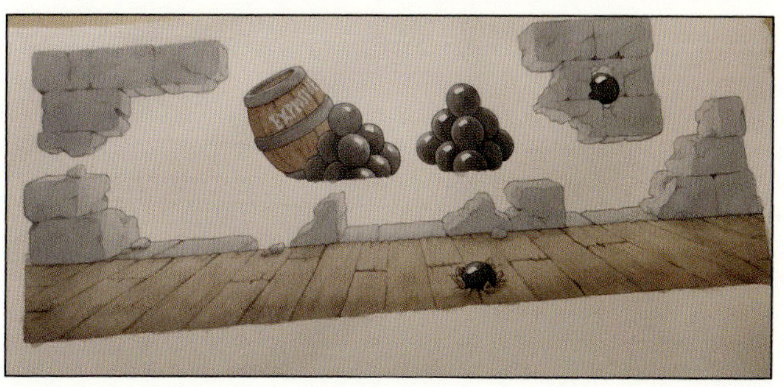

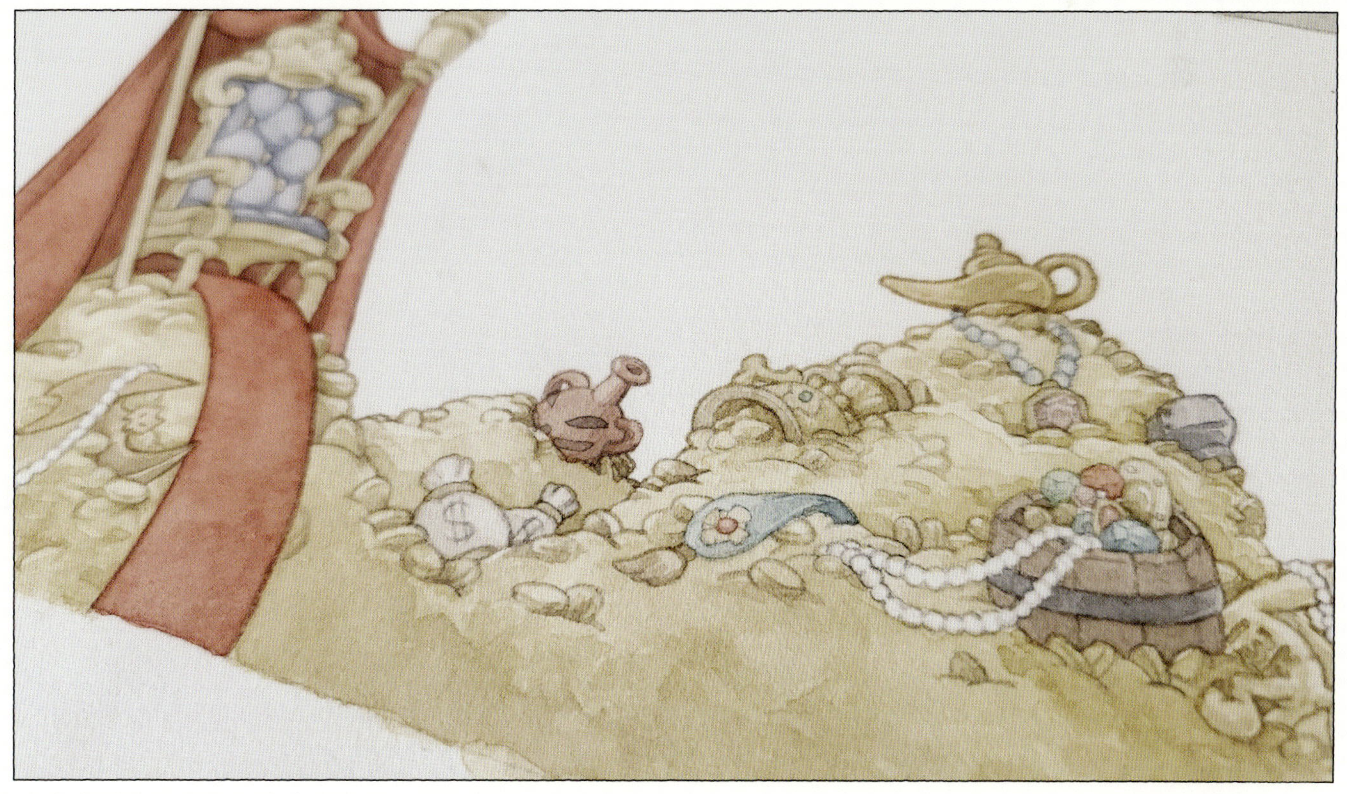

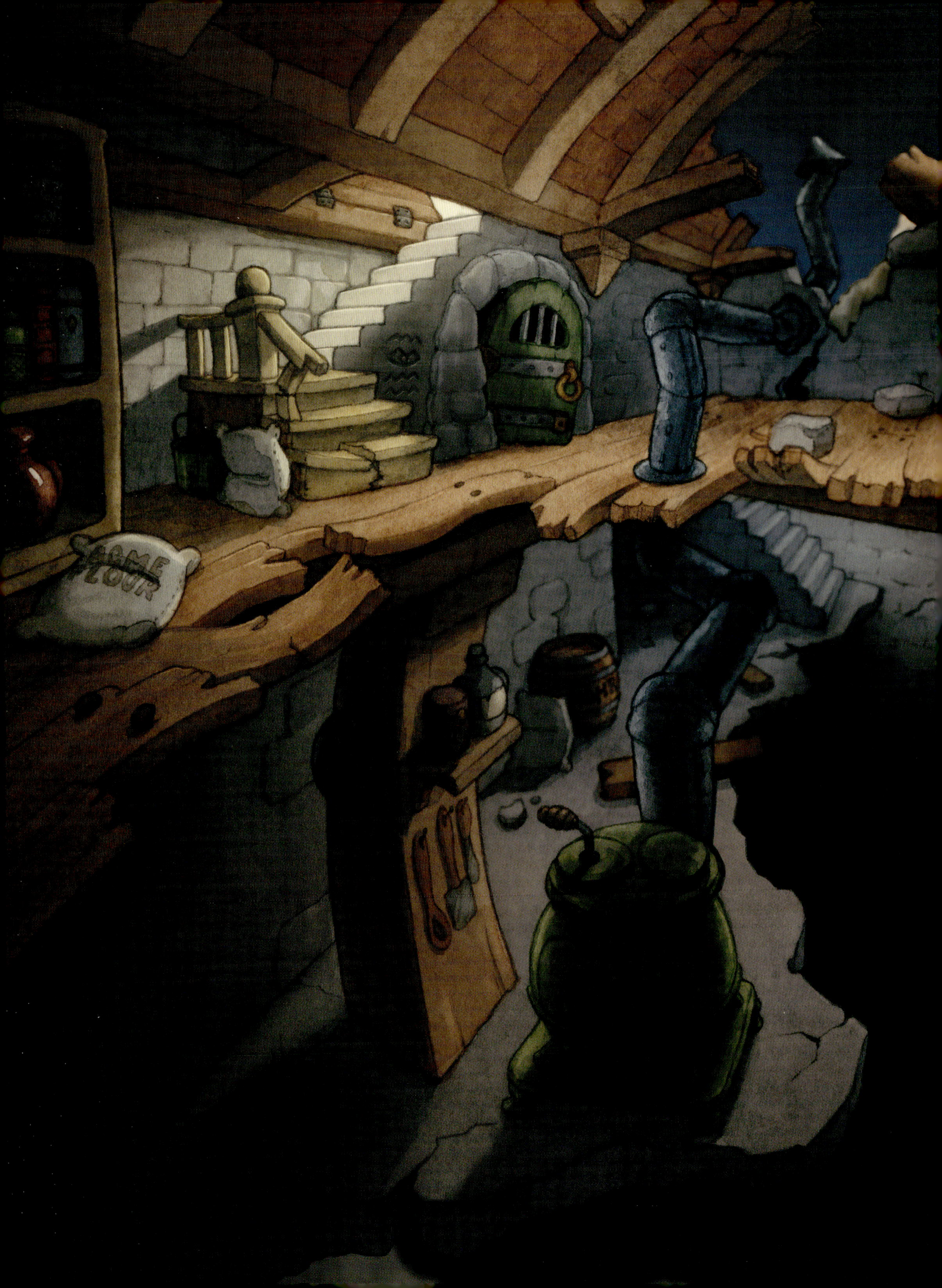
FLOUR

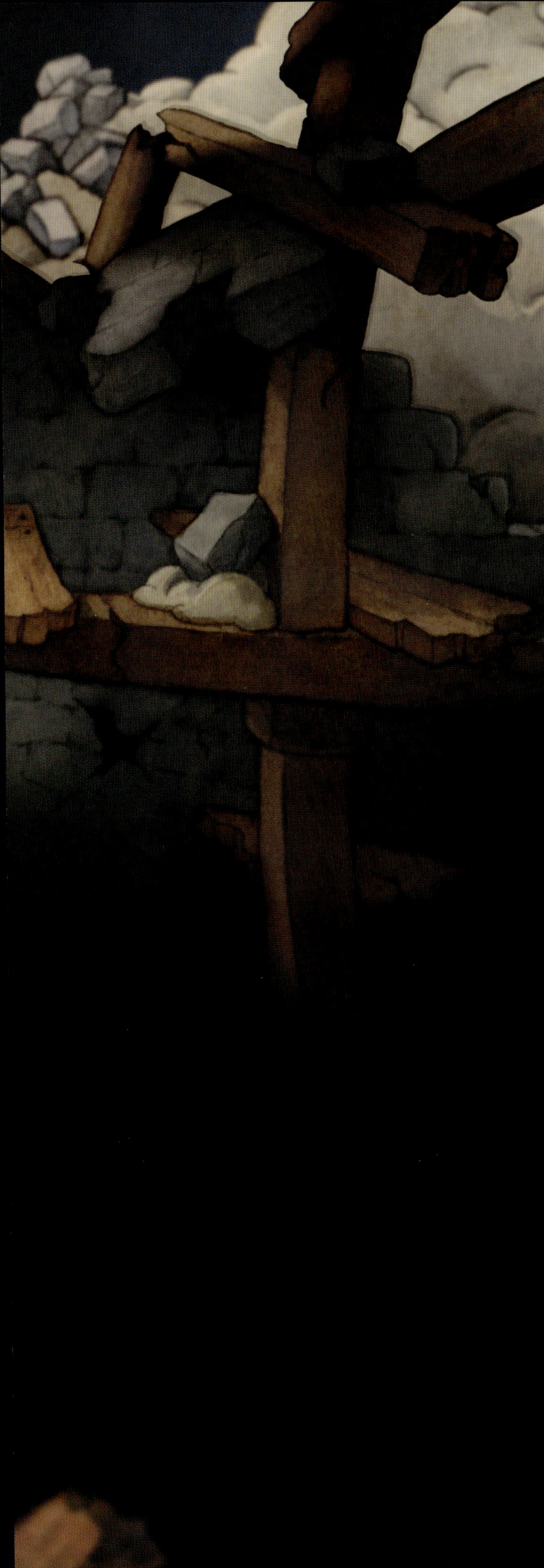

Chapter IX:
A Dish To Die For

IT'S NOT WELL KNOWN WHAT DROVE the otherwise magnanimous Chef Saltbaker down such a dark path as to lure our heroes into a devious trap. Was it simply a lust for power, or was it the mysterious pull of the ethereal astral plane? Either way, the duality of Chef Saltbaker's personality was planned from the very start of *The Delicious Last Course*'s story development. Originally, we had concepts for a pair of wacky wizards, one good and one evil, who would in turn guide the player and lead them astray on their quest to make Ms. Chalice real again. As we looked to make our antagonists more novel, however, we decided that the oft-seen jolly chef trope from 1930s cartoons could fill the role of both wizards: a wondrous baker whose fantastical culinary concoctions had the ability to grant magical powers *and* a duplicitous schemer, driven mad by the thirst for greater control of the cosmos!

While the player initially meets a warm-hearted Chef Saltbaker in a scene purposely meant to evoke the nurturing hearth of Elder Kettle's abode, we placed some sneaky puns in Saltbaker's initial dialogue lines to hint at the dastardly plan he had in store for the trio. Upon returning with the Wondertart's ingredients, this final battle—the grandest production endeavor in our company's history—is all that stands between our heroes and a dire fate for their captured friend!

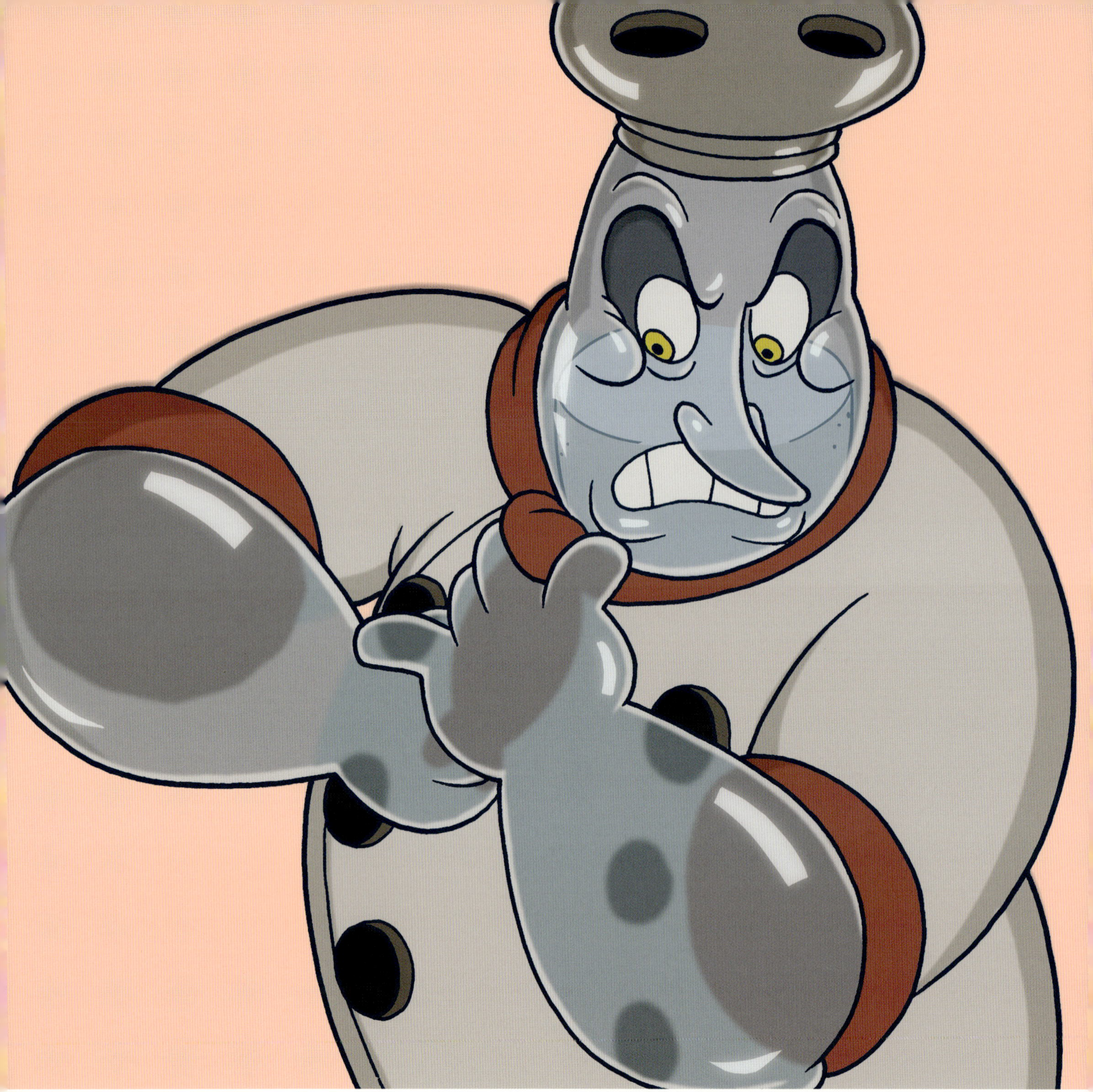

Chef Saltbaker
in
"A DISH TO DIE FOR"

FOR CHEF SALTBAKER, we wanted an iconic and timeless visual design that could join the roster of our other main characters as both a friend and foe. When deciding on the chef's archetype, we explored a variety of different animals, foods, and abstractions in search of his archetypal form. Once we landed on an anthropomorphized salt shaker, we knew we had our celebrated chef. Adjacent to our other "utensil universe" characters like Cuphead and Silverworth, Chef Saltbaker's frosted-glass salt shaker form matched perfectly, and his bulbous tin top perfectly represented the classic chef's

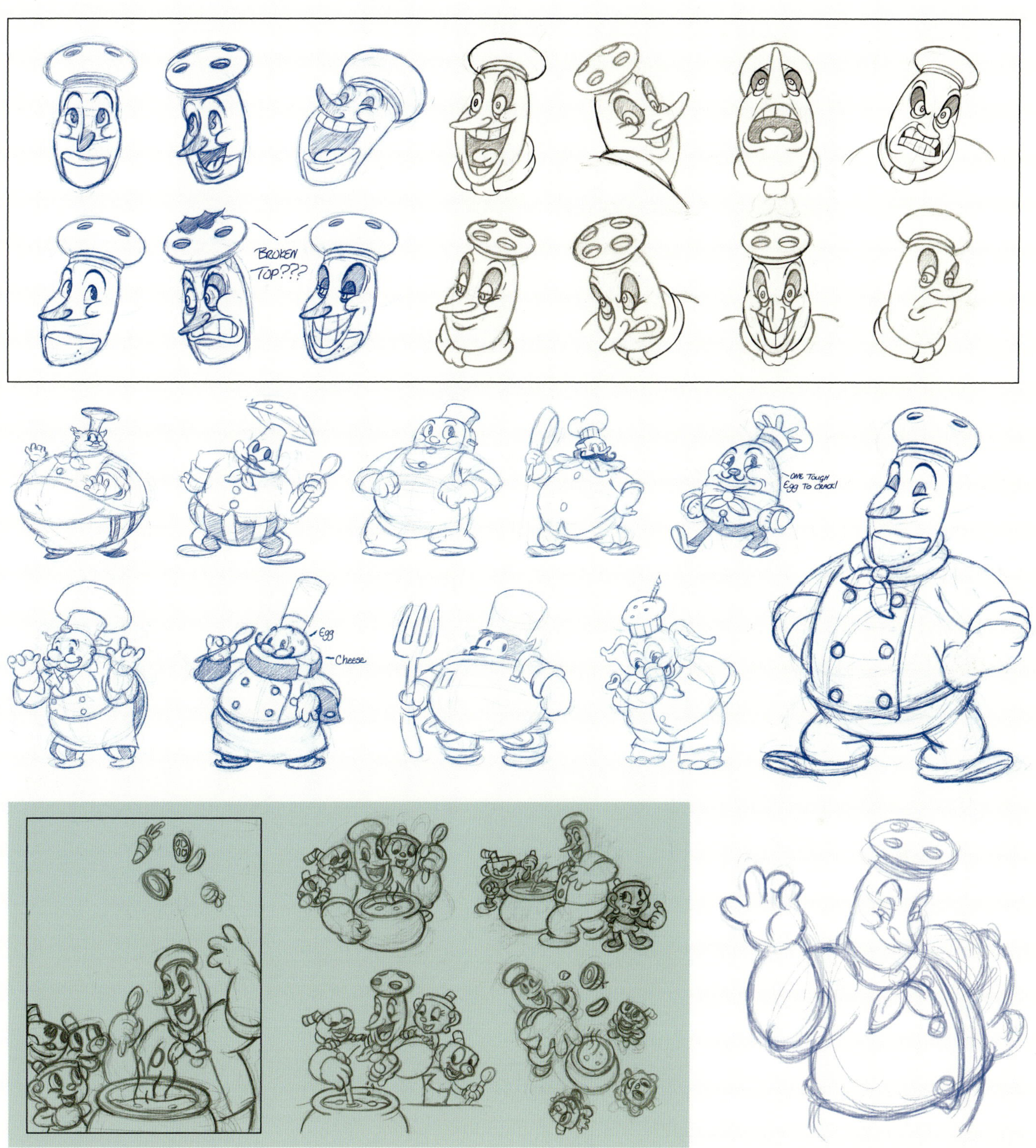

toque blanche. For his uniform, we added notes from traditional French and British culinary garb to denote an artist's experience and rank, while Saltbaker's jovial personality and overall body language were inspired by both the king in the 1933 Silly Symphony *Old King Cole* and the garrulous bakers in *Pastry Town Wedding* (1934).

While many players find the battle with Chef Saltbaker to be the ultimate *Cuphead* challenge, the production and animation of the DLC's last boss was also the ultimate challenge for us at the studio. Containing more frames of animation than any other boss we'd ever built, this corrupt culinarian's frosted glass design provided an additional complication. Every frame of Saltbaker's animation required three total art treatments to complete: the initial body animation, the animation of all of the internal salt and parts seen through the transparencies, and finally, the layered frosting effects and glares on the surface of the glass. Altogether, bringing Chef Saltbaker to life required thousands of hours of craftsmanship by a dozen artists.

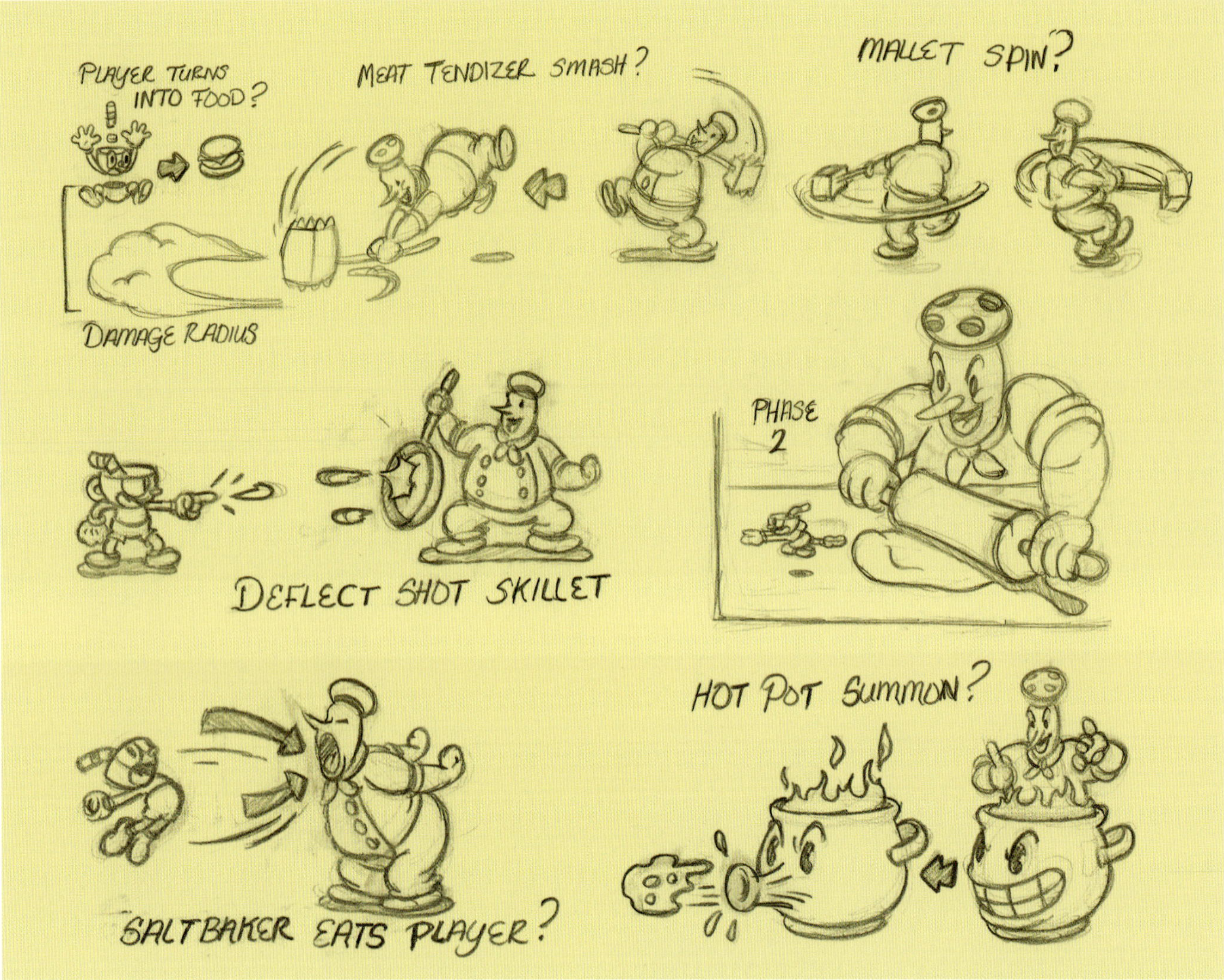

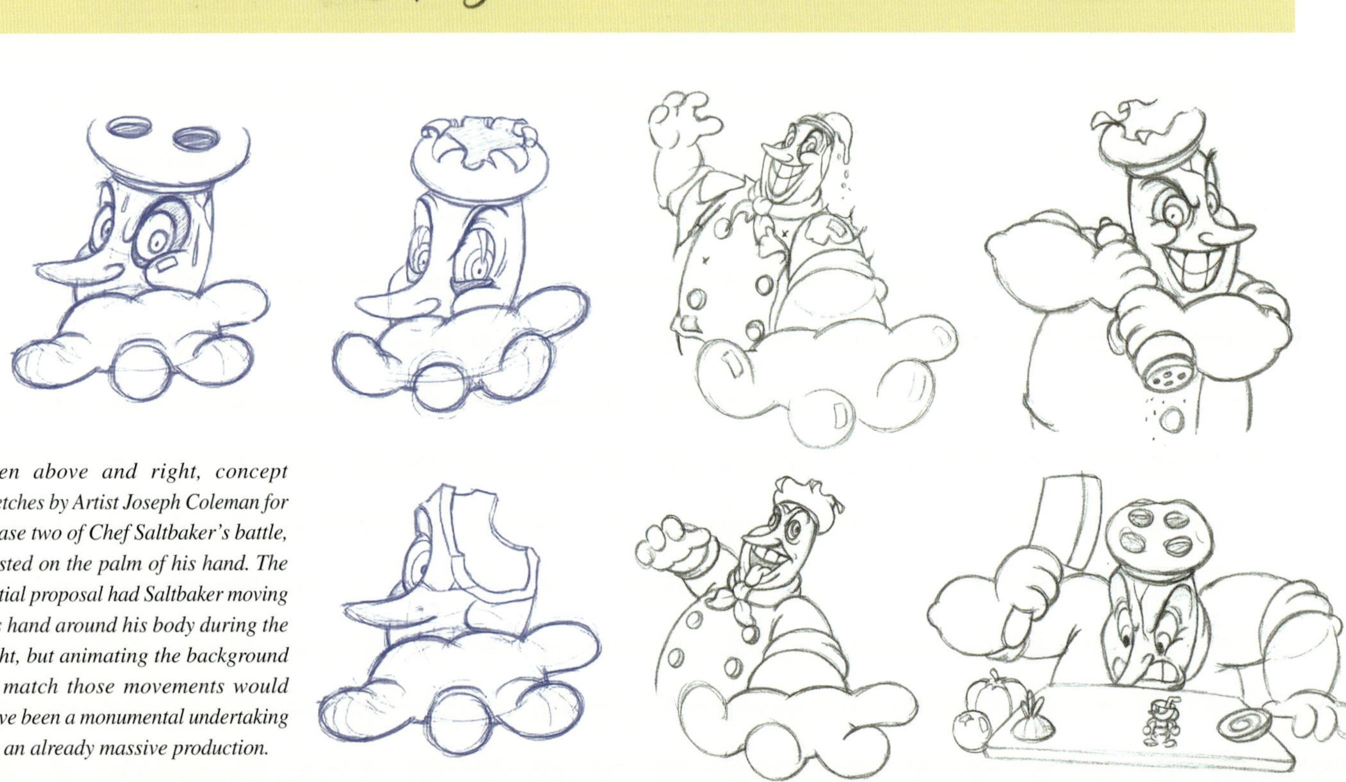

Seen above and right, concept sketches by Artist Joseph Coleman for phase two of Chef Saltbaker's battle, hosted on the palm of his hand. The initial proposal had Saltbaker moving his hand around his body during the fight, but animating the background to match those movements would have been a monumental undertaking on an already massive production.

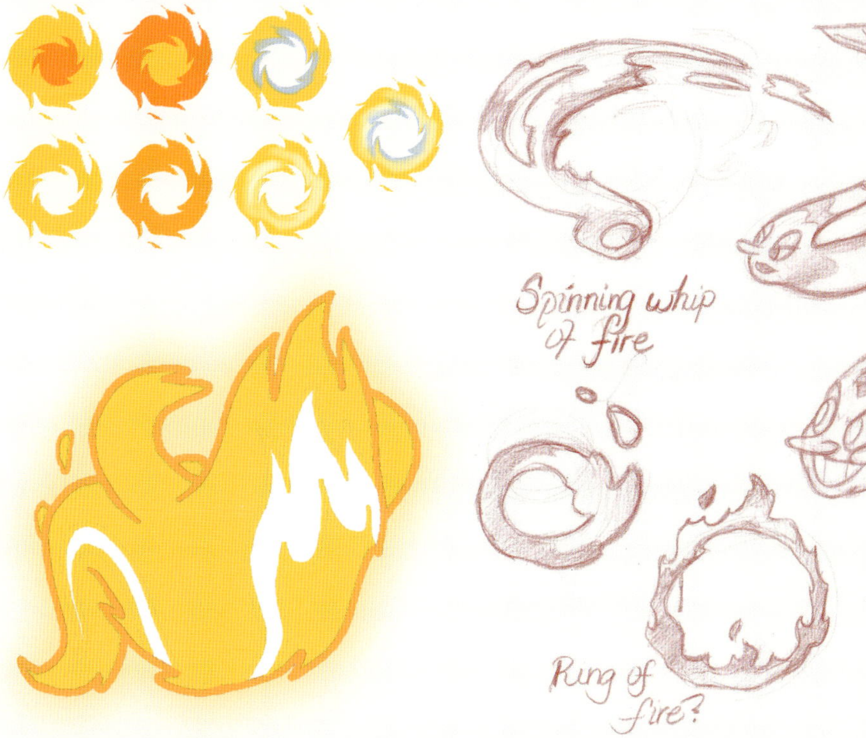

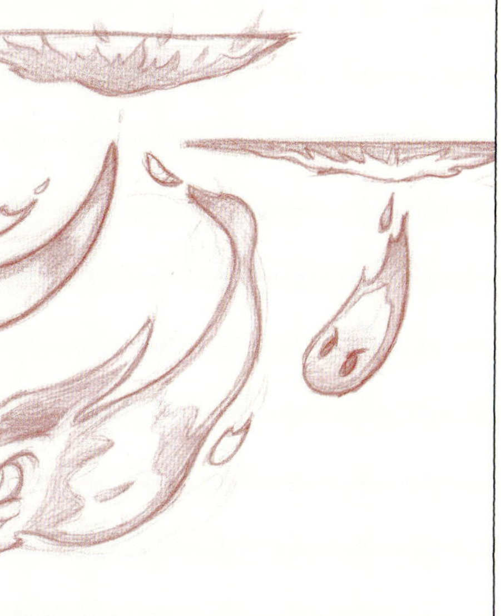

With a final design inspired by the mischievous fire beings in the Disney short Mickey's Fire Brigade *(1935), our swooping, jumping, dancing flame sprites originally donned Saltbaker's grinning guise before being simplified for gameplay reasons.*

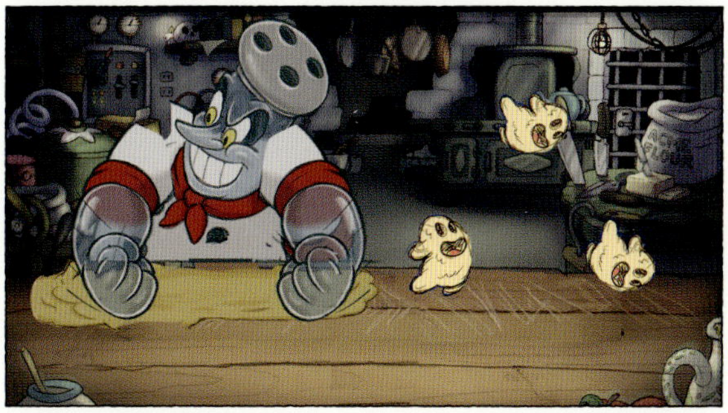

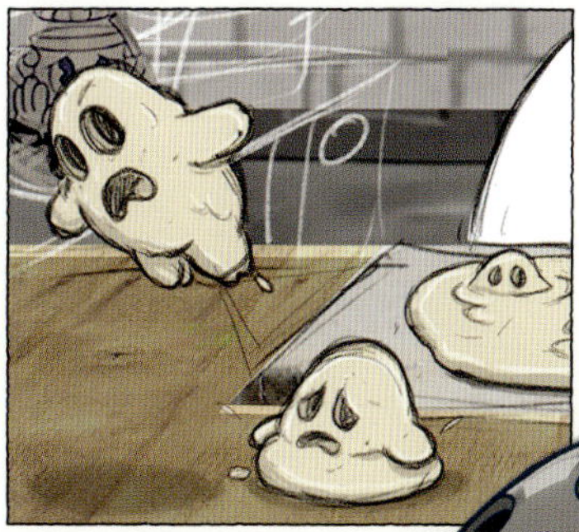

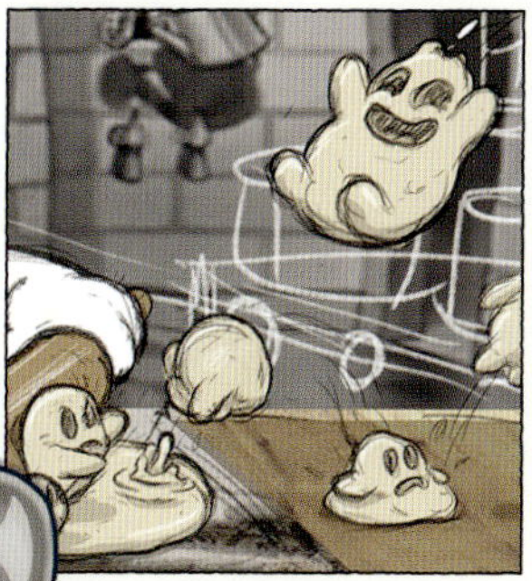

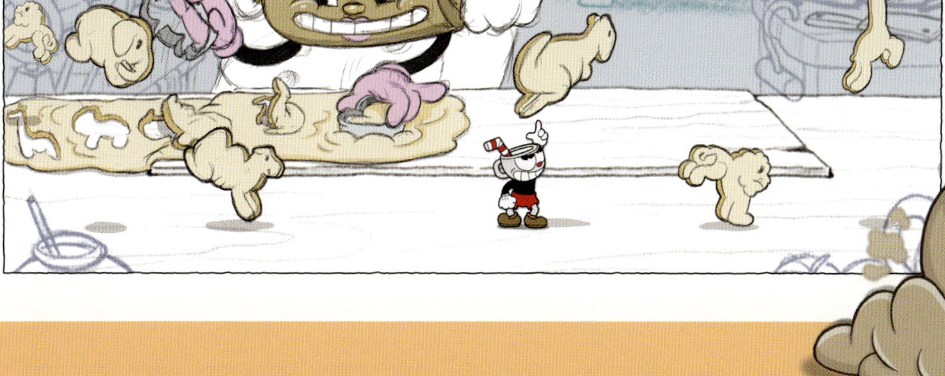

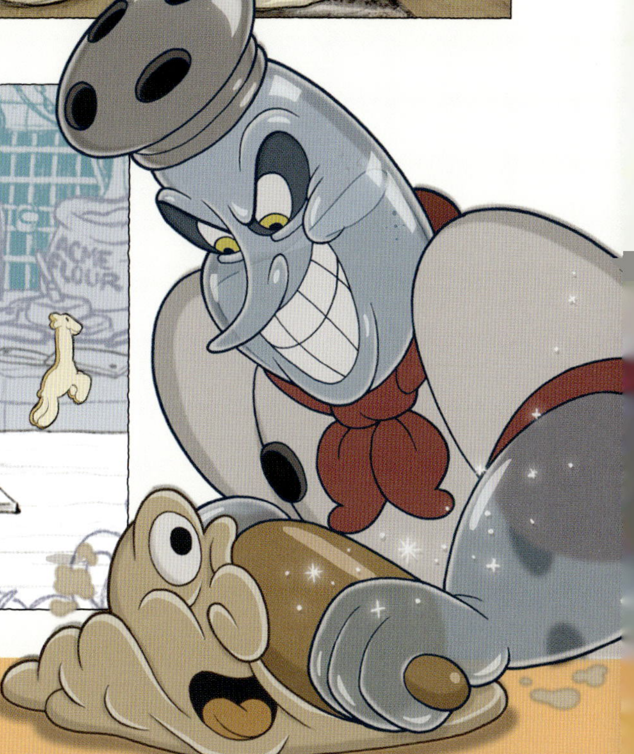

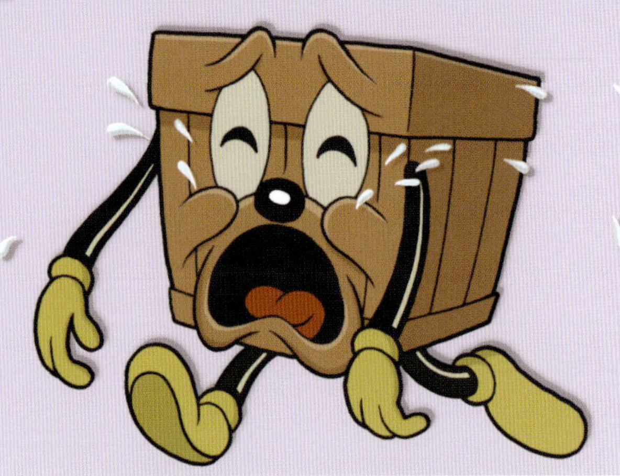

We had three goals when it came to Saltbaker's dastardly dicing of the Wondertart ingredients: firstly, we wanted to have a visual representation that tied to the quest for ingredients during the DLC's campaign. Second, we wanted to show the process of prepping all of the ingredients through the progression of the fight, ramping up the desperation of the battle. And finally, we wanted to portray how sinister the chef had become in his quest for astral power, so seeing the friendly foodstuffs get fricasseed really sold his turn to the dark side.

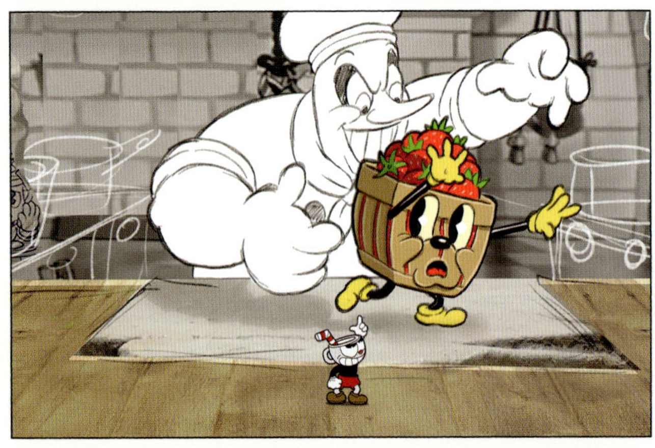

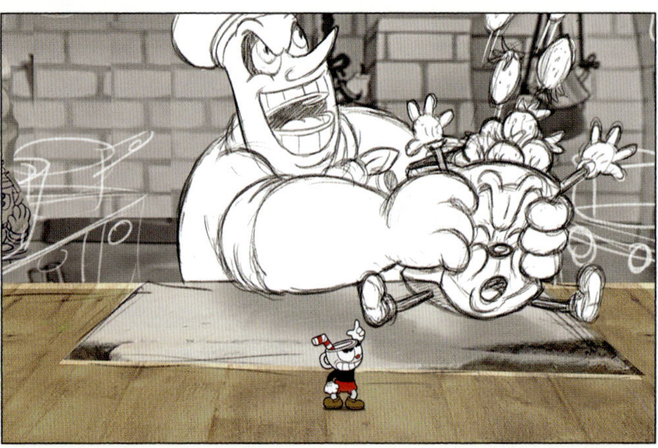

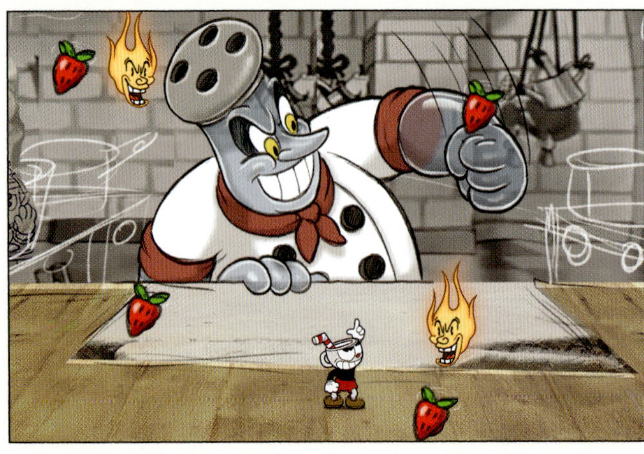

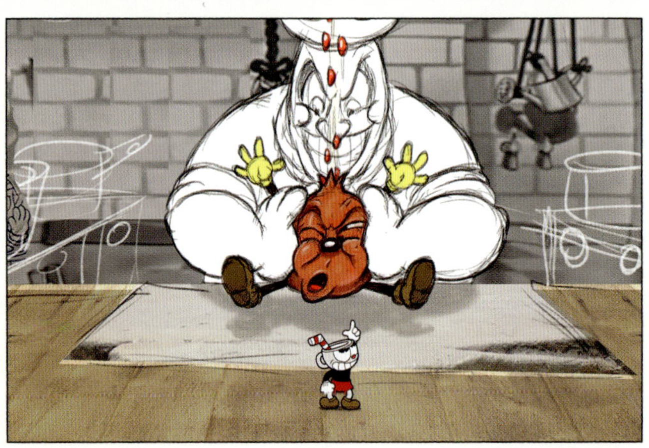

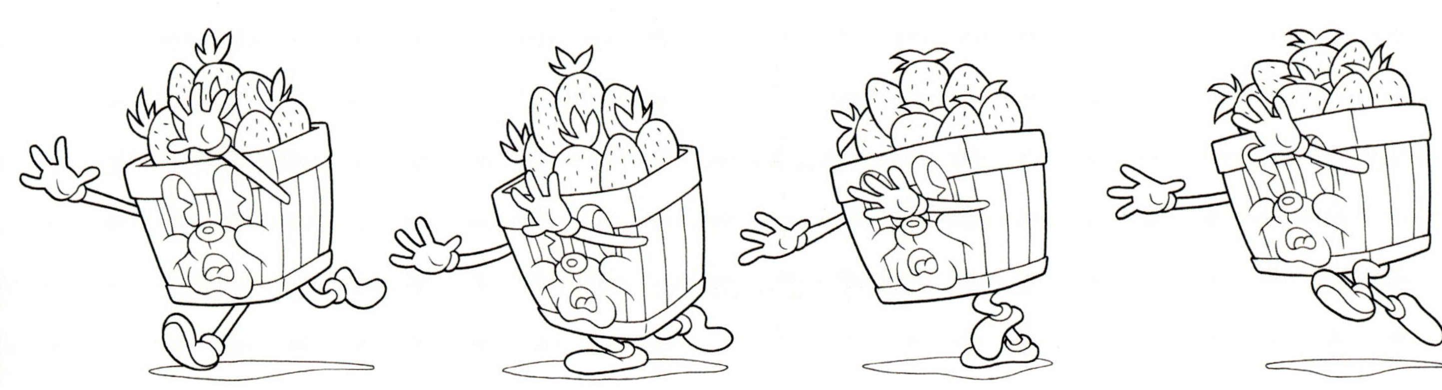

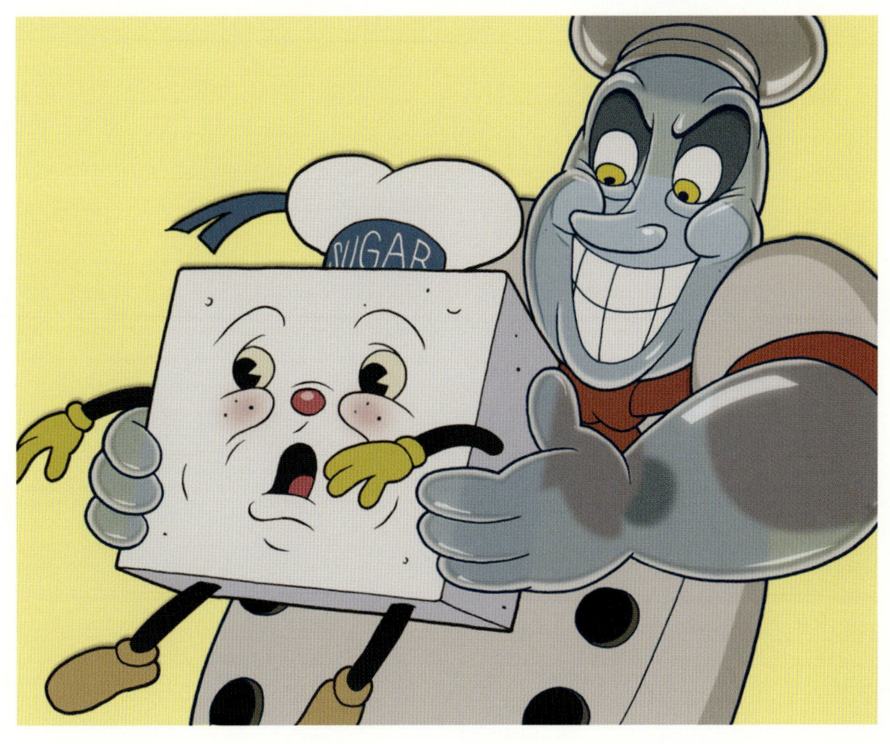
SUGAR

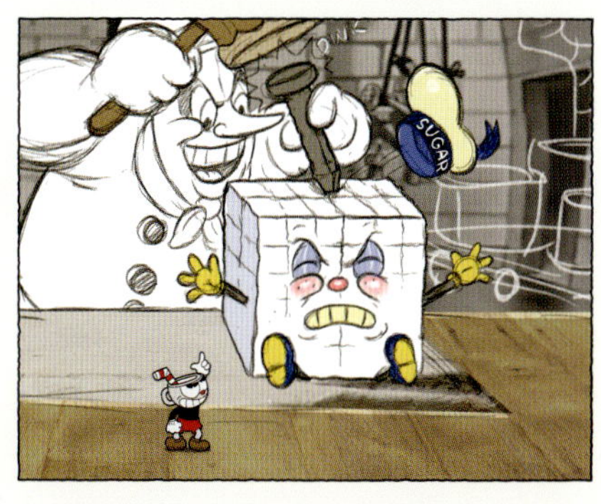
SUGAR

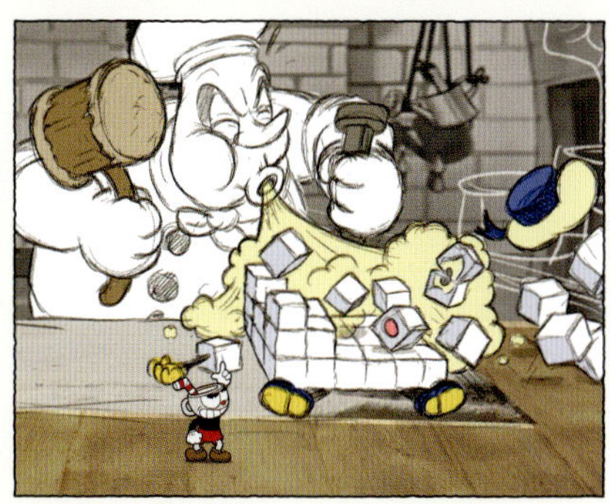

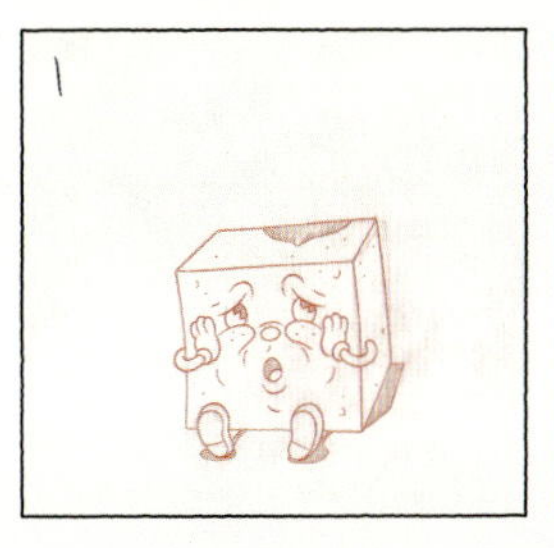
1

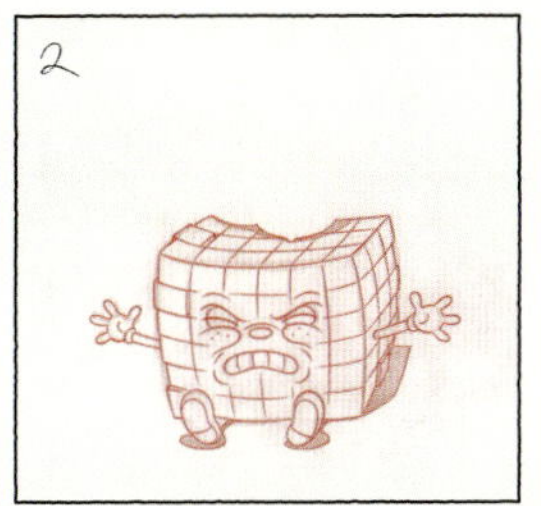
2

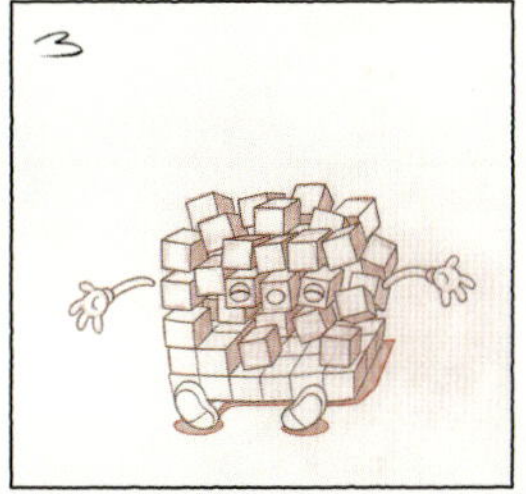
3

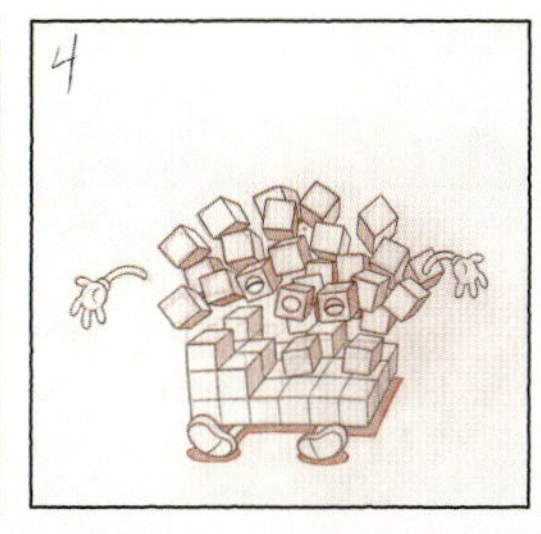
4

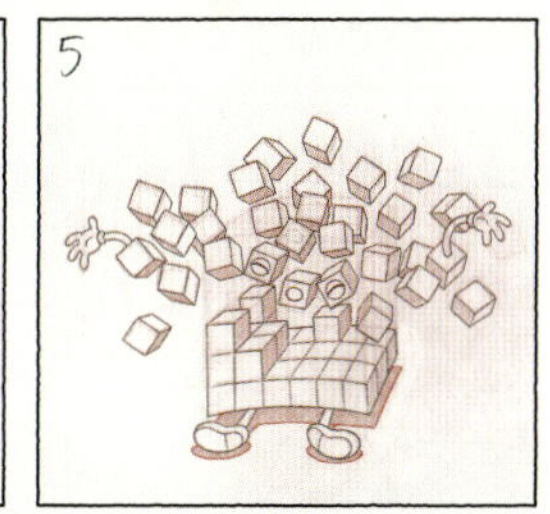
5

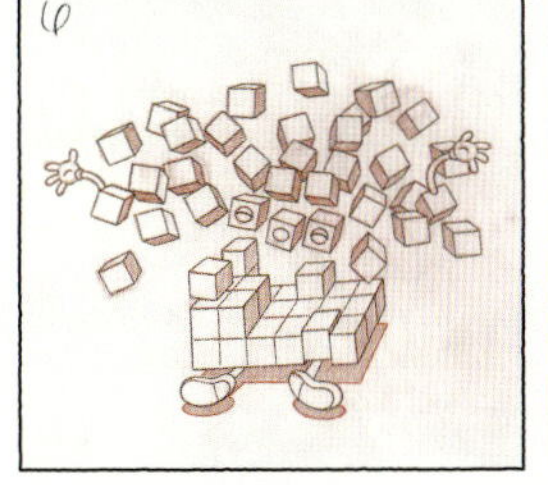
6

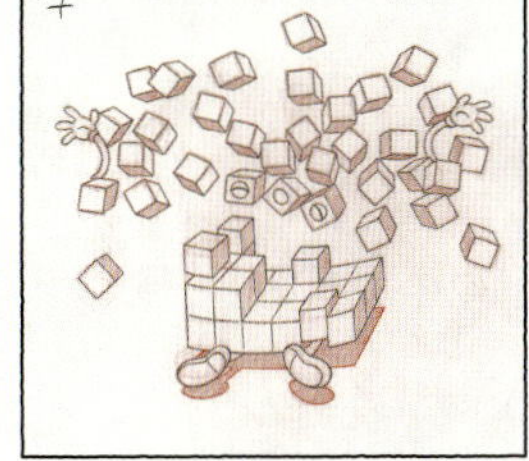
7

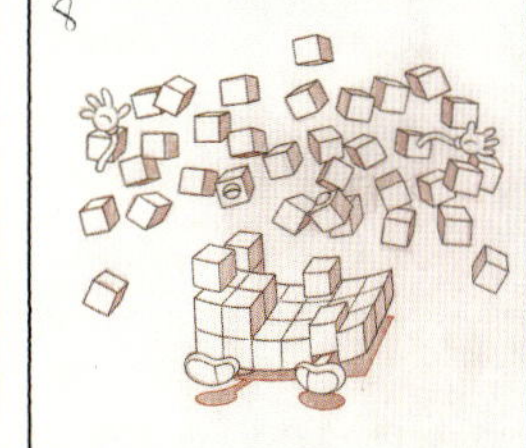
8

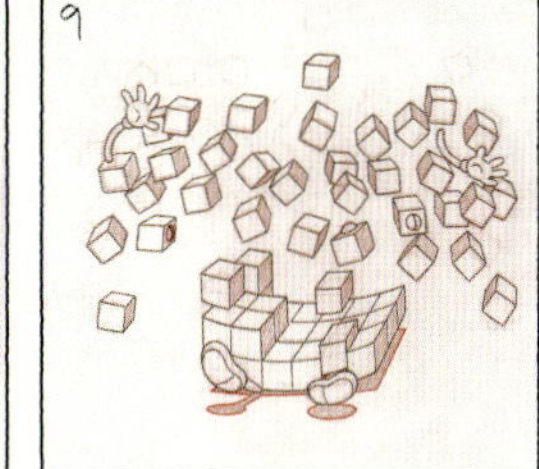
9

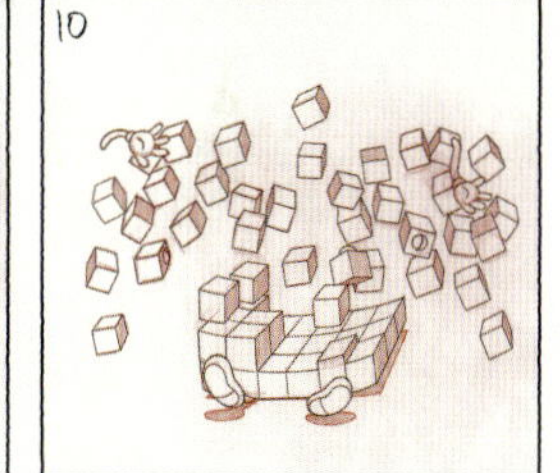
10

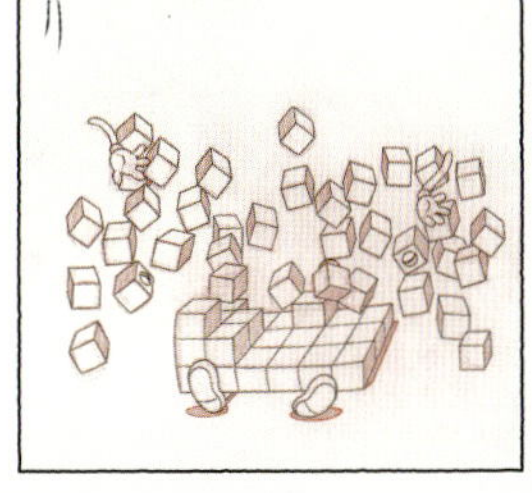
11

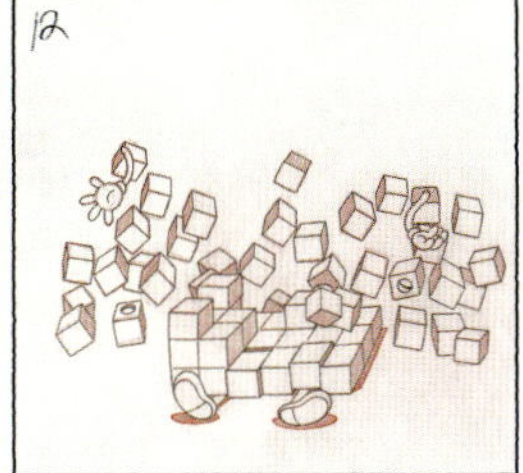
12

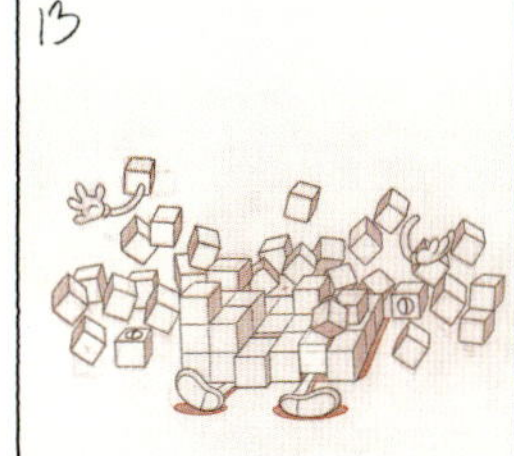
13

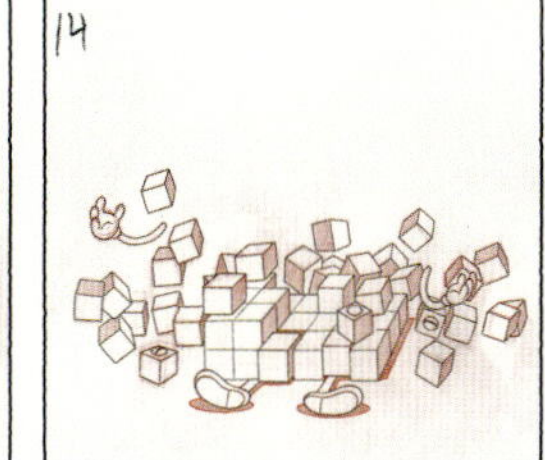
14

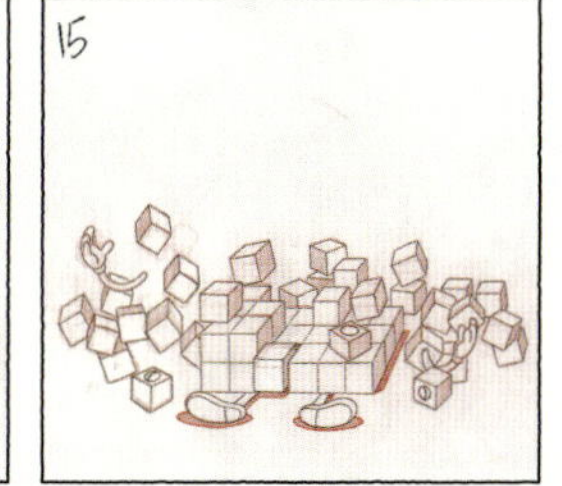
15

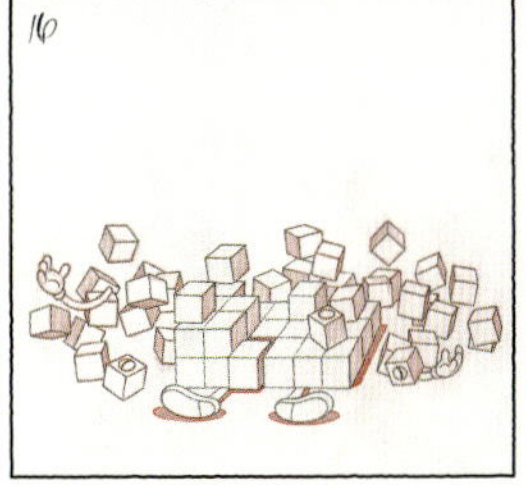
16

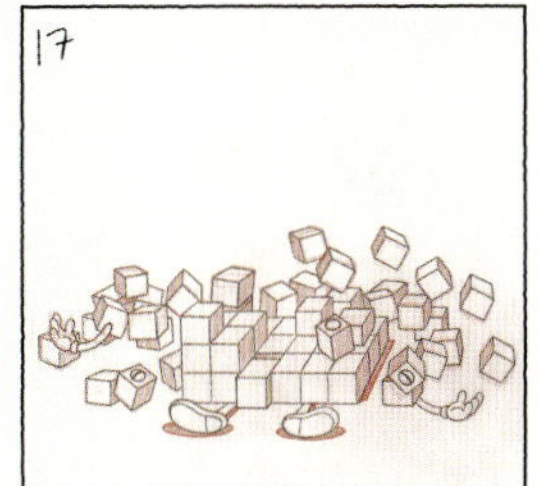
17

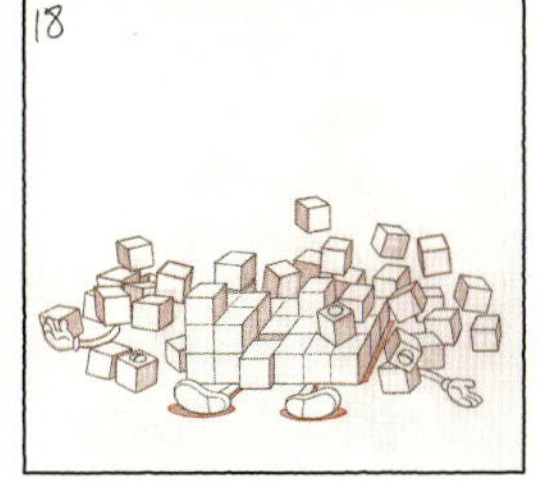
18

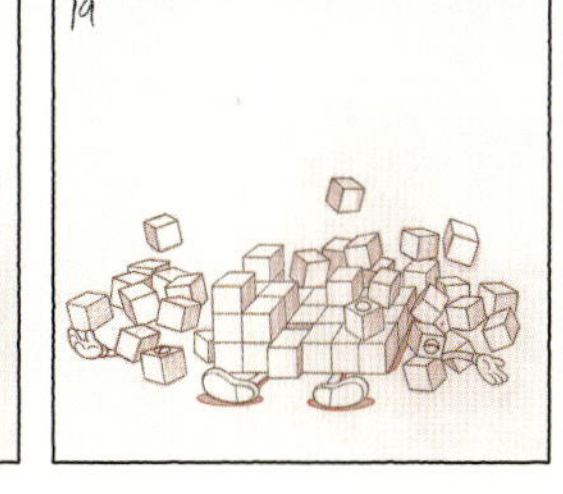
19

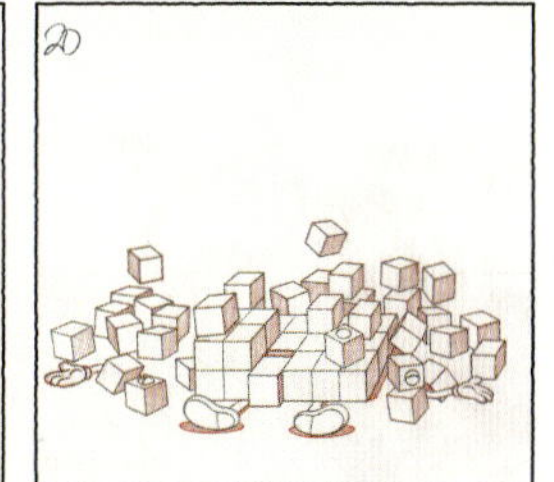
20

Setting Saltbaker's body behind the main play space for phase one allowed us to create extended and intricate animations not seen in any other boss fight in the game. The complexity of these animations, often involving multiple intersecting characters, required extensive planning and spacing to match the appropriate area and gameplay timing cues. Below, a series of breakdown images progressing from Illustrator Lance Inkwell's concepts to Animator Jared Beckstrand's final layout.

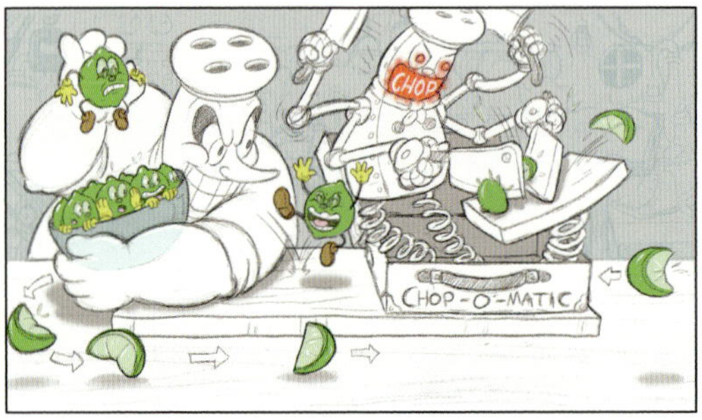

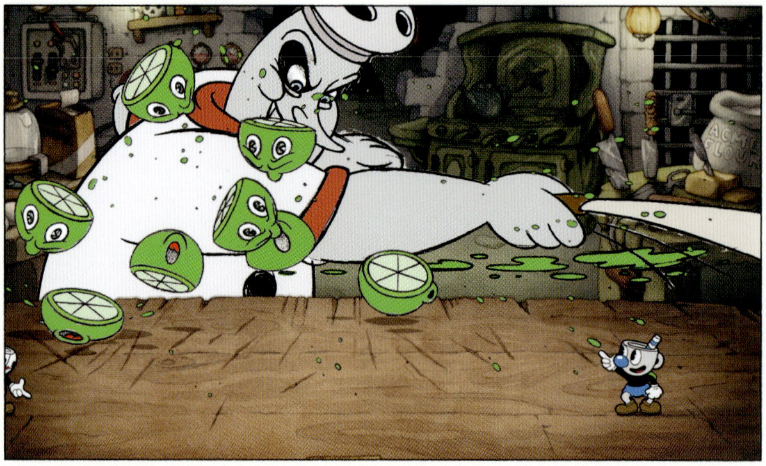

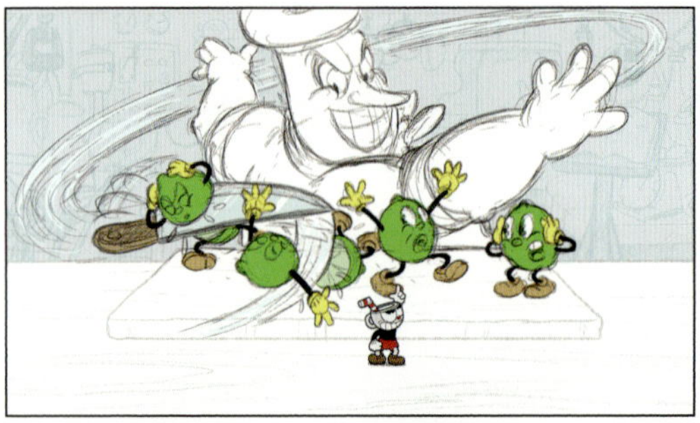

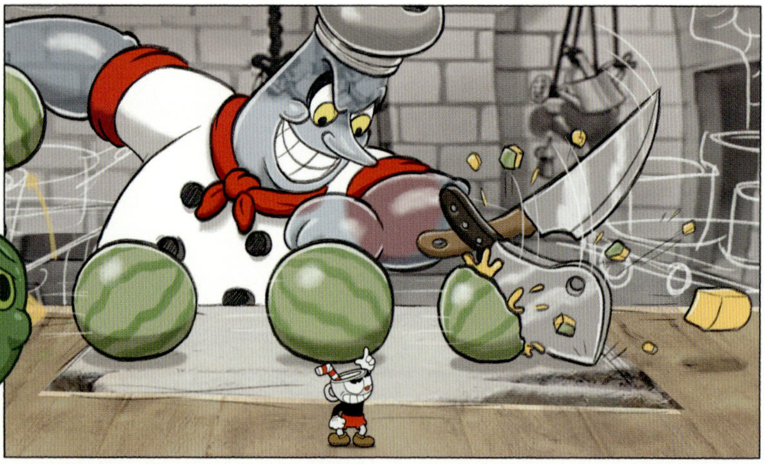

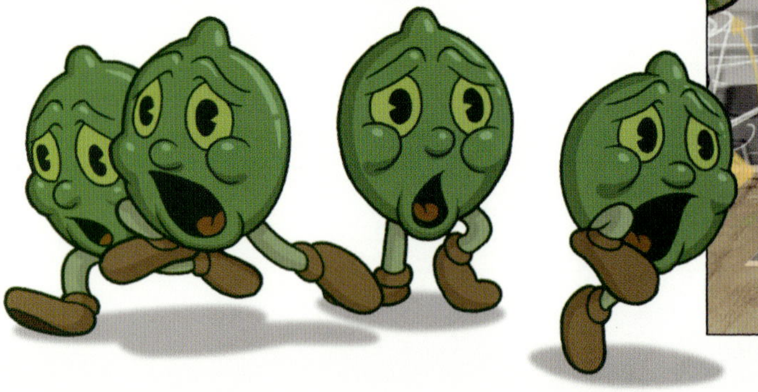

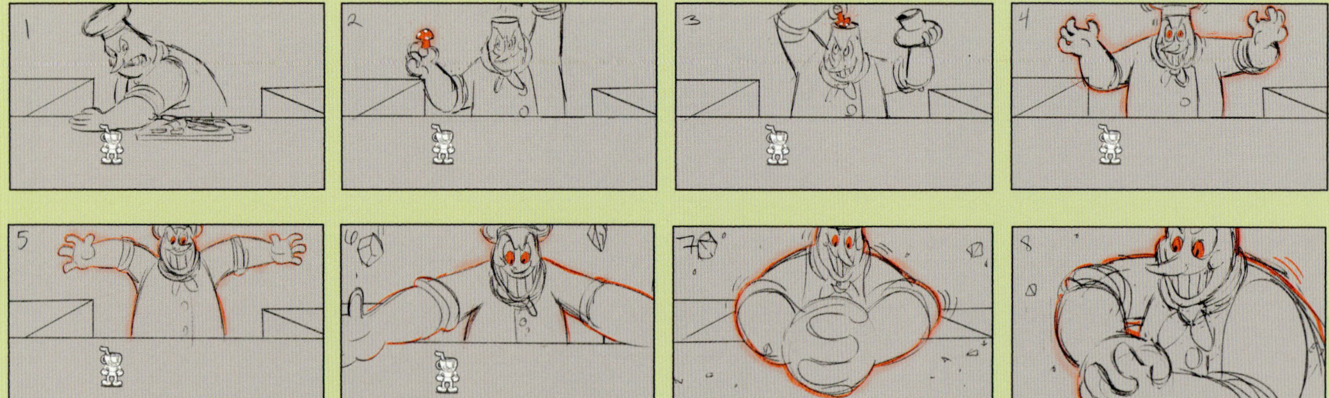

Above, an initial animatic of Saltbaker's transition from phase one to phase two by Supervising Animator Hanna Abi-Hanna. There's a single frame during this transition where Saltbaker's hands cover the entire screen, allowing us to sneakily swap out the background for the second phase.

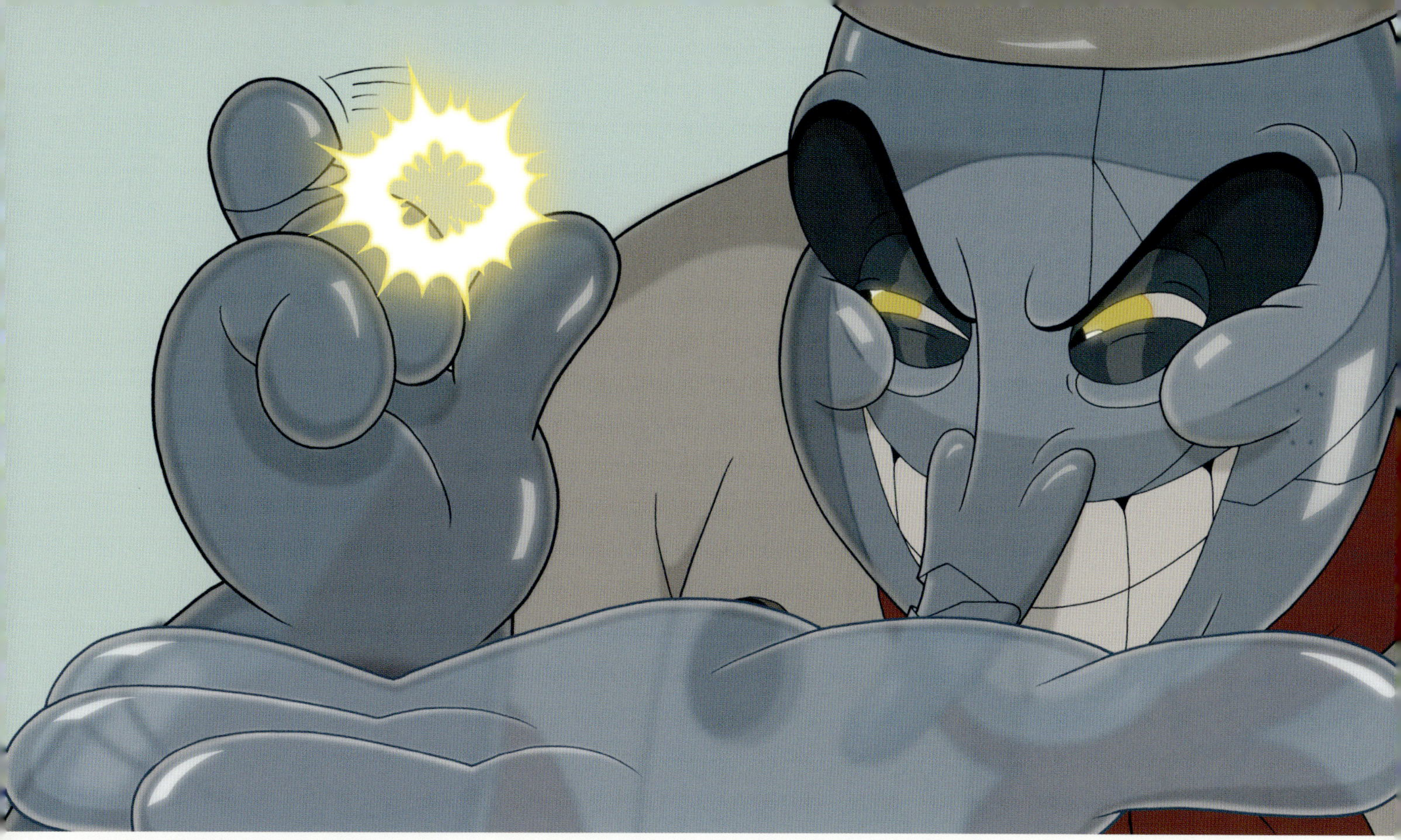

After ingesting a mysterious magical mushroom and growing super-sized (our nod to a legendary turtle stomping plumber), Chef Saltbaker finally has the heroes in the palm of his hand, even if the cracks are beginning to show in his façade. Like the Devil that came before him, this penultimate scene allowed phase two Animator Rapeepat "Patt" Jewanarom to portray Saltbaker's personality as bombastically as possible, all while keeping the fight as fast and frenetic as befitting a last boss!

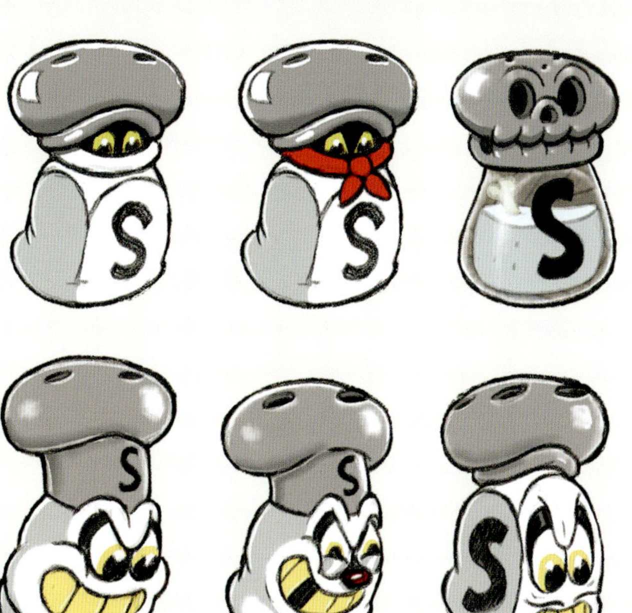

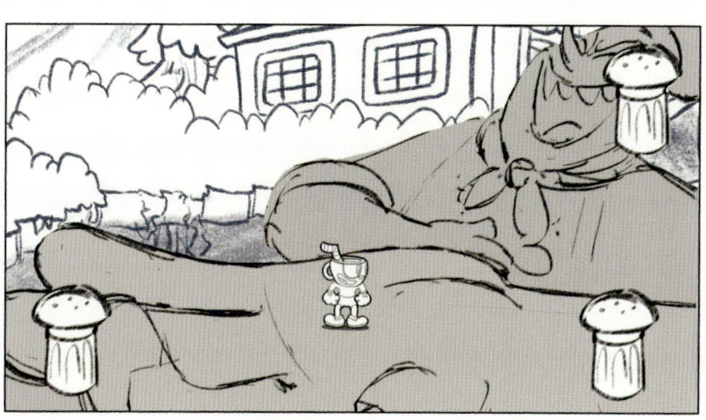

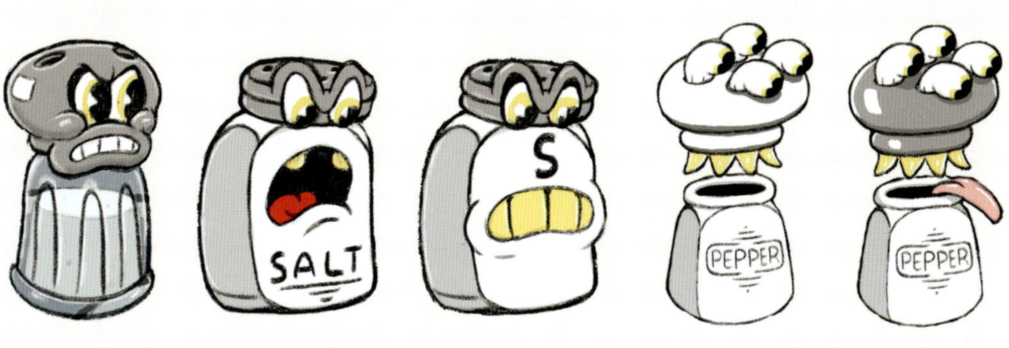

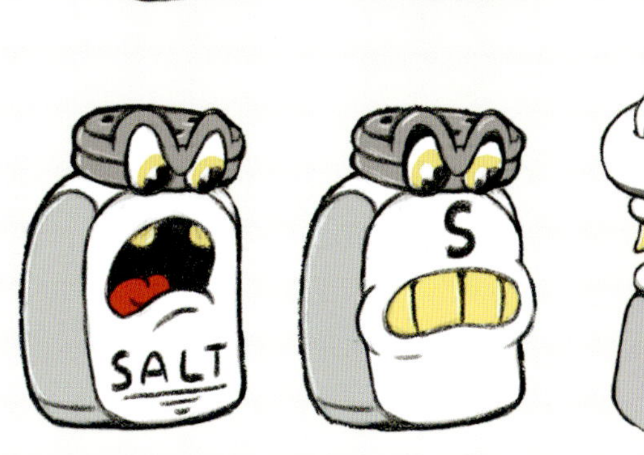

Initial concepts for Saltbaker's minions had them as a quartet of mini salt shakers. Concept Artist Lance Inkwell's idea of making them sneezing pepper shakers proved too clever to resist.

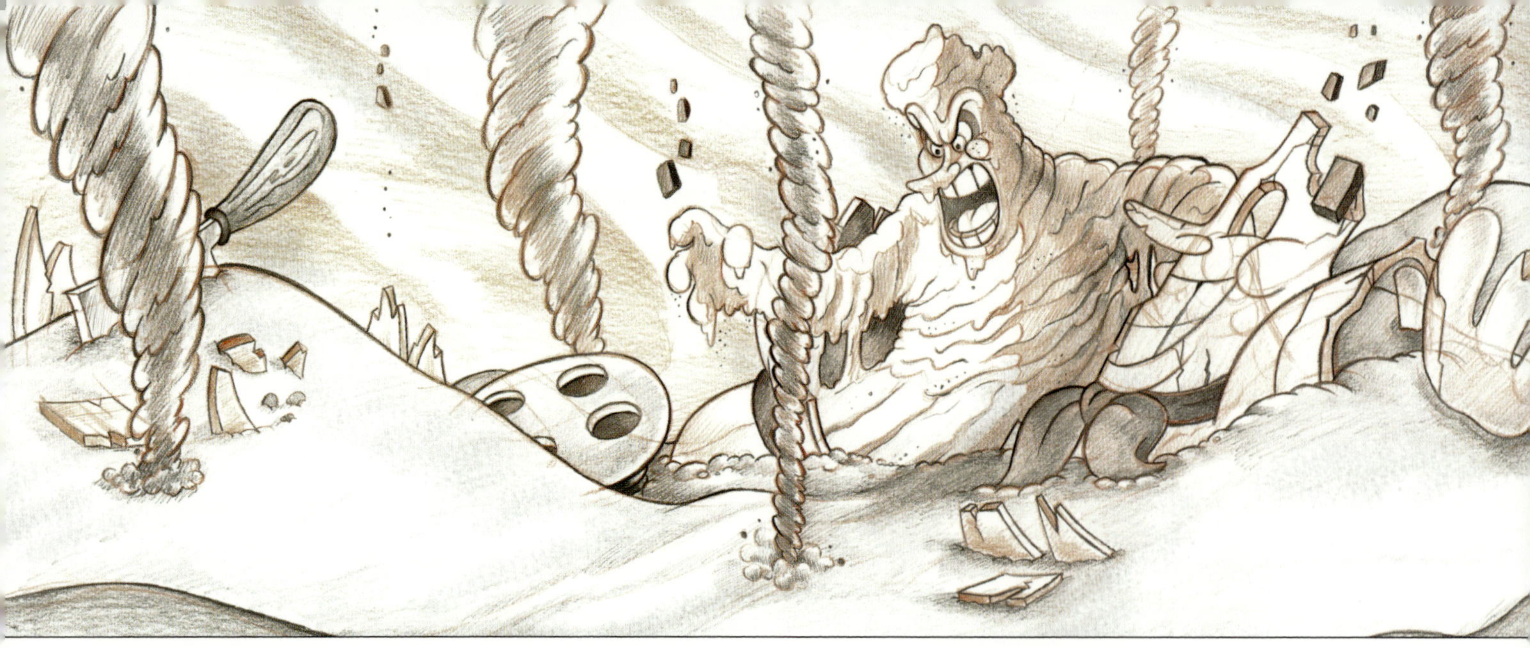

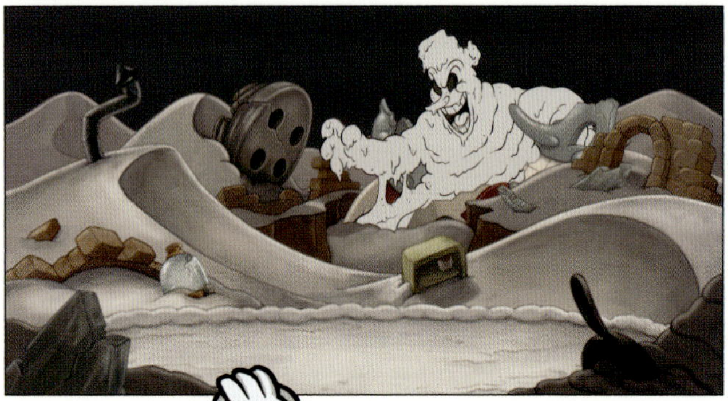

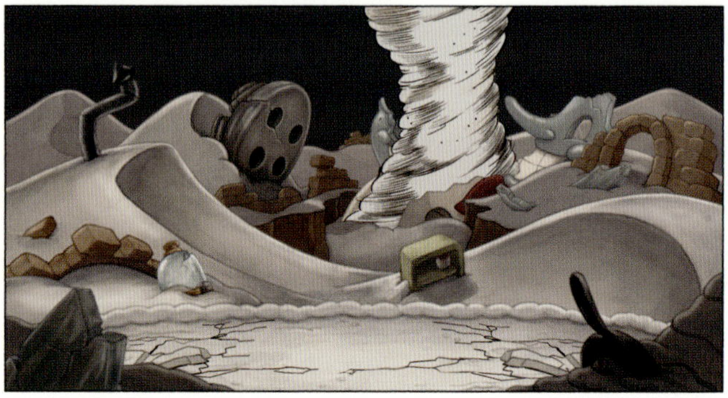

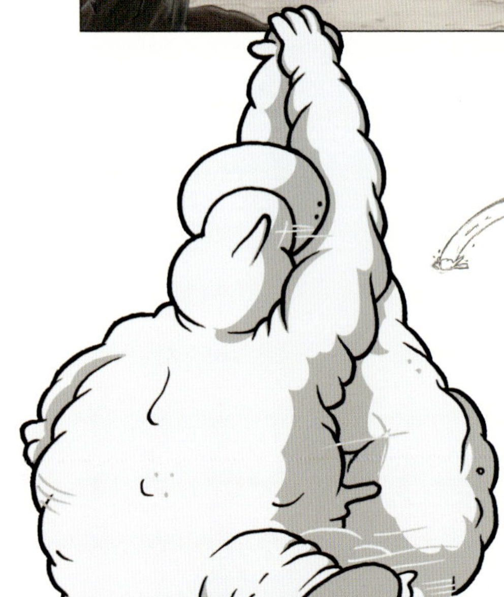

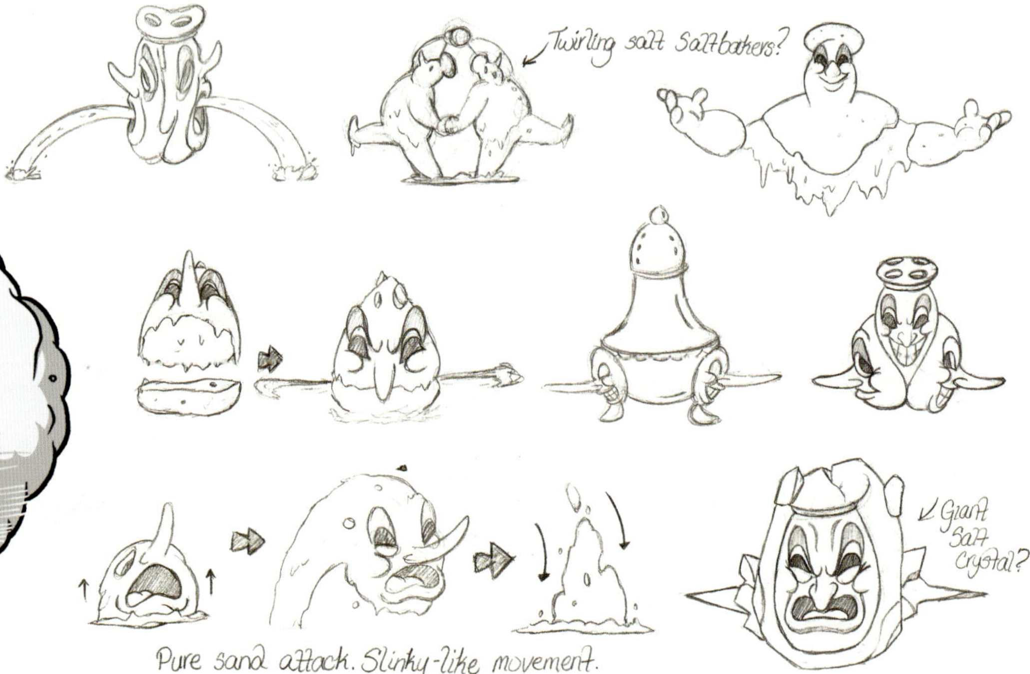

Twirling salt Saltbakers?

Giant Salt Crystal?

Pure sand attack. Slinky-like movement.

Saltbaker's spinning salt "dancers" came at the tail end of a lot of conceptual iteration. The original gameplay design for this attack was to have a bouncing foe with hazards poking out of its sides that the player would have to duck. This led to a lot of off-putting concepts, seen above, that never quite fit with the elegance and absurdity of 30s cartoons. Ultimately, Animator Joseph Coleman proposed a dancing duo, and thus we found the perfect twirling test to transition to the finale.

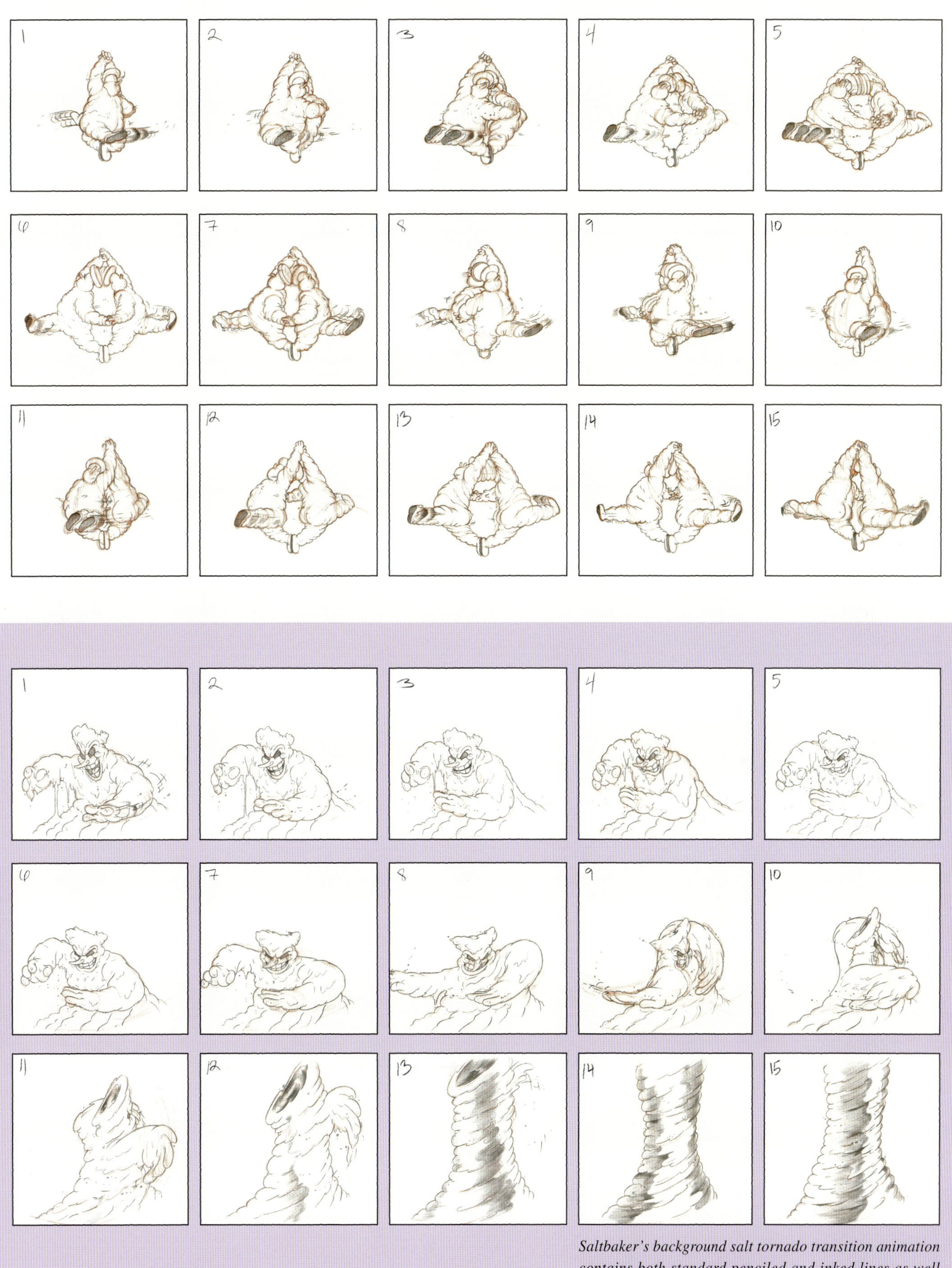

Saltbaker's background salt tornado transition animation contains both standard penciled and inked lines as well as charcoal accents by Animator Simone Cirillo used to convey the chaotic motion of the spiral.

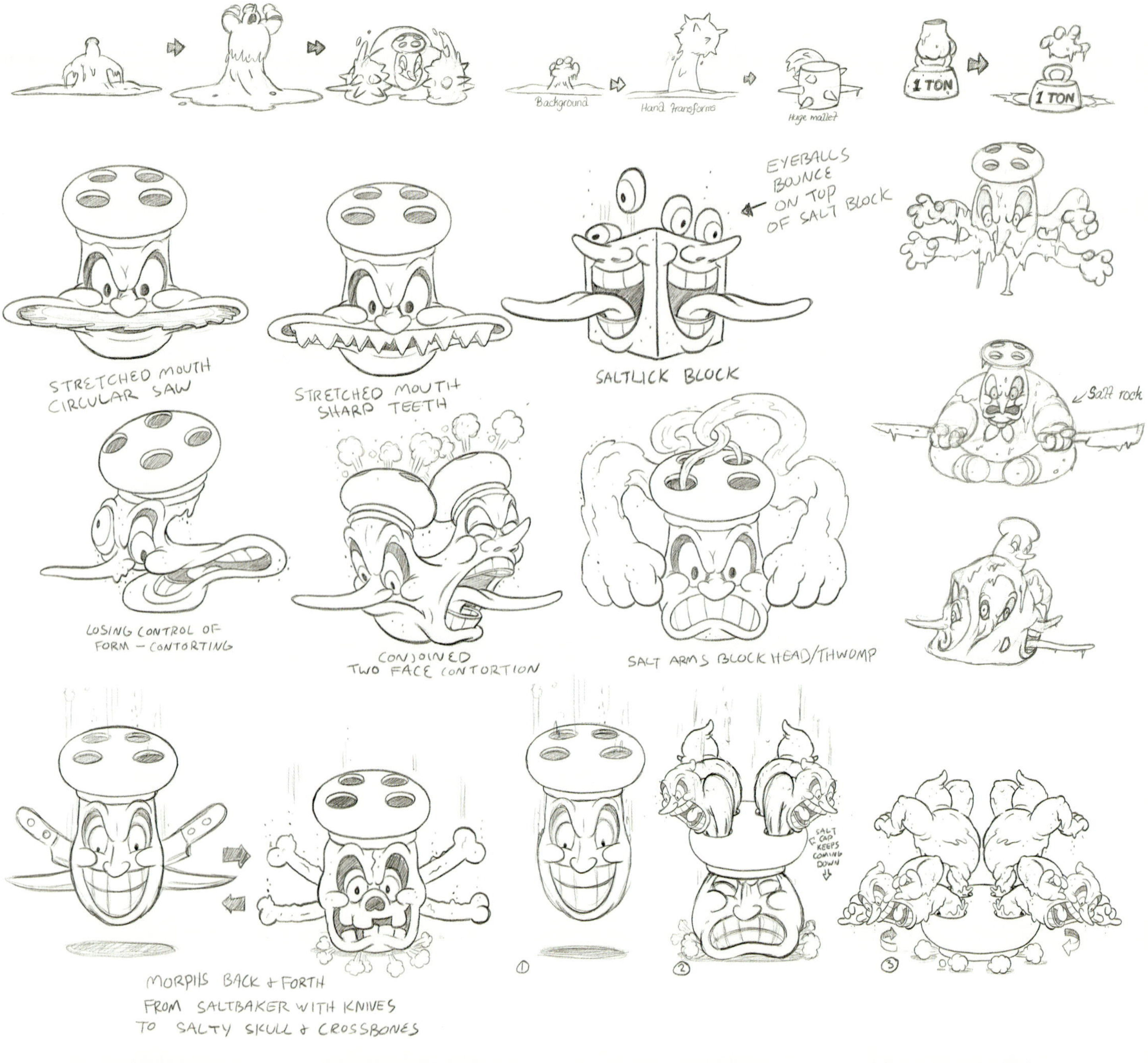

Background

Hand transforms

Huge mallet

1 TON

1 TON

EYEBALLS BOUNCE ON TOP OF SALT BLOCK

STRETCHED MOUTH CIRCULAR SAW

STRETCHED MOUTH SHARP TEETH

SALTLICK BLOCK

Salt rock

LOSING CONTROL OF FORM – CONTORTING

CONJOINED TWO FACE CONTORTION

SALT ARMS BLOCK HEAD/THWOMP

SALT CAP KEEPS COMING DOWN

① ② ③

MORPHS BACK & FORTH
FROM SALTBAKER WITH KNIVES
TO SALTY SKULL & CROSSBONES

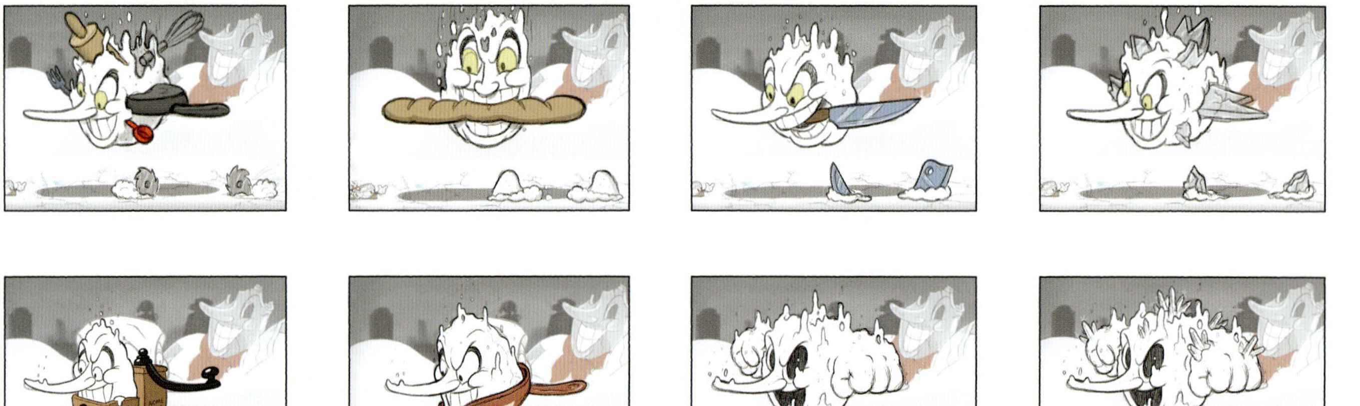

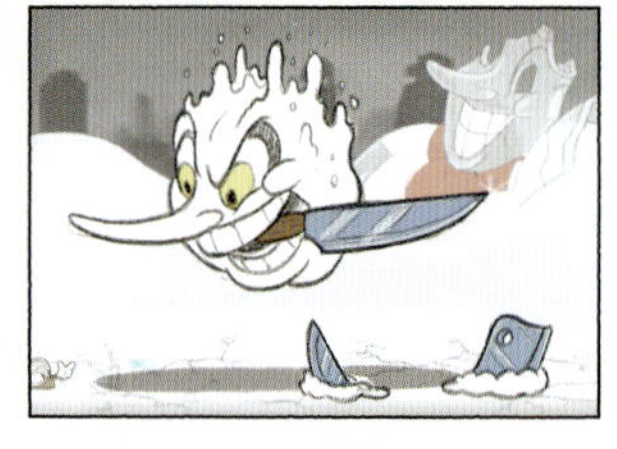

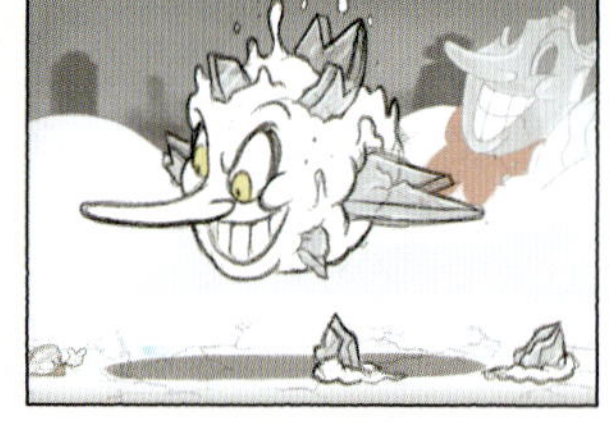

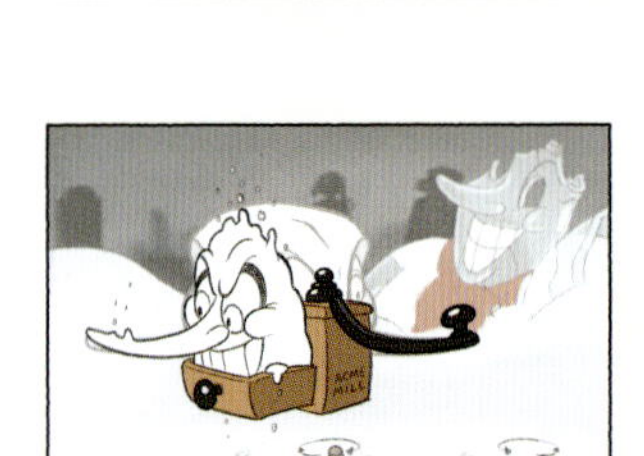

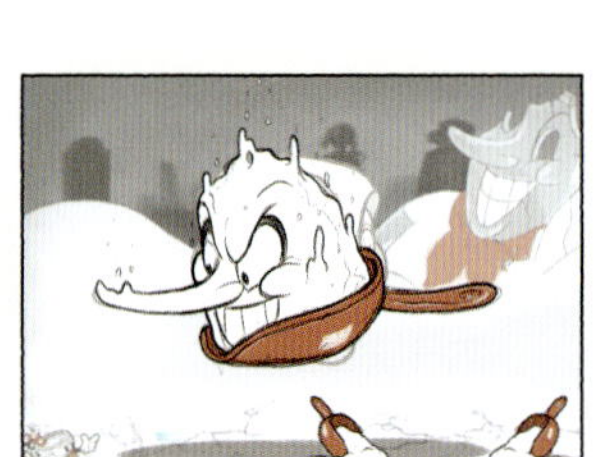

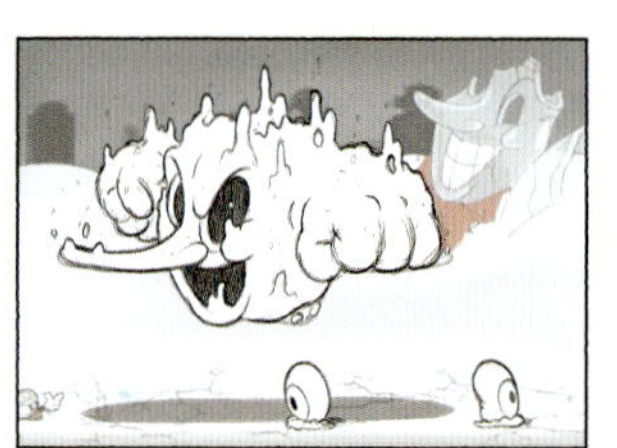

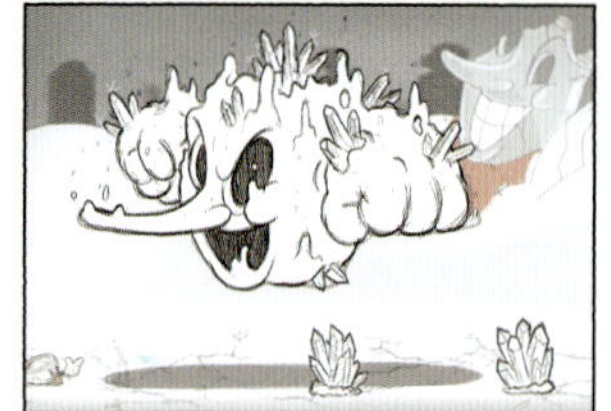

As the salt-covered ground cracks and opens up and the radiating skies fill with towering tornadoes of salinity, the sneering dark heart of Saltbaker's twisted intentions reveals itself…it's up to our heroes now to put the final kibosh on the chef's diabolical plan! Like many classic 8- and 16-bit games we played in our youth, facing off against the true physical heart of your ultimate enemy often accompanied many final bosses and we wanted to pay homage to that in our own twisted way.

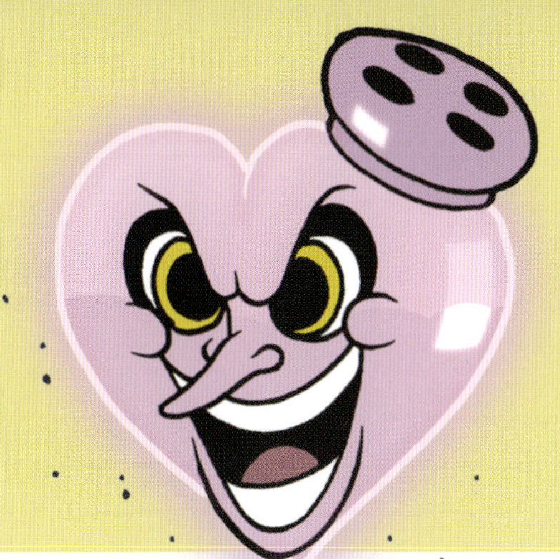

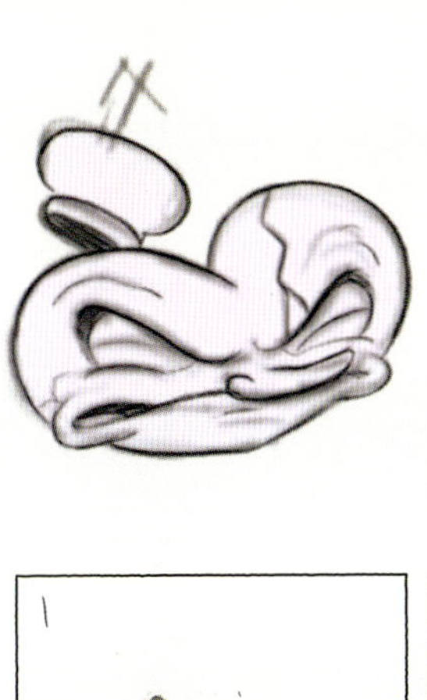
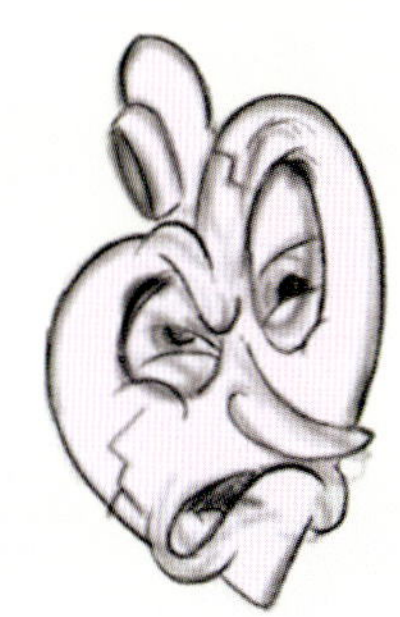
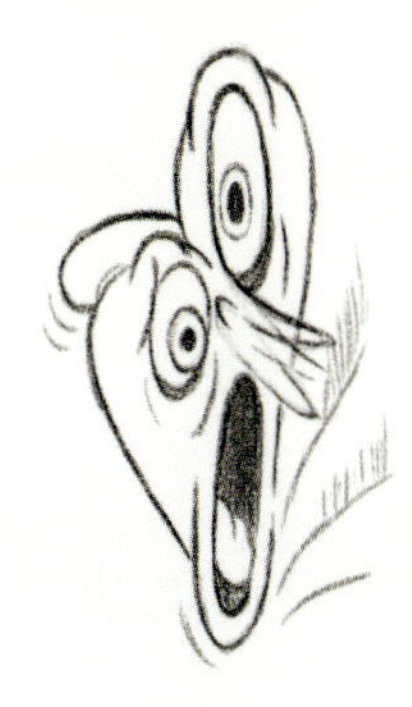
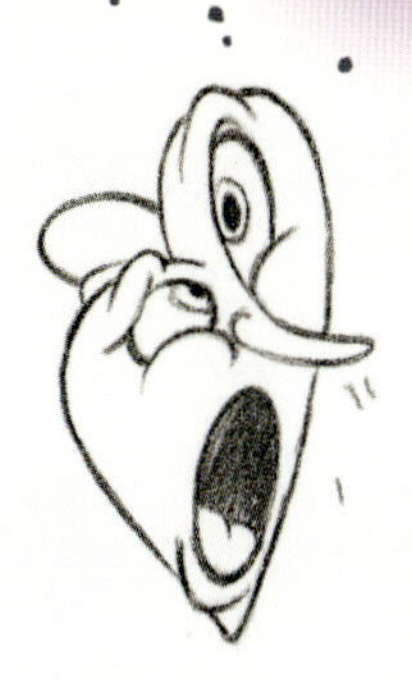
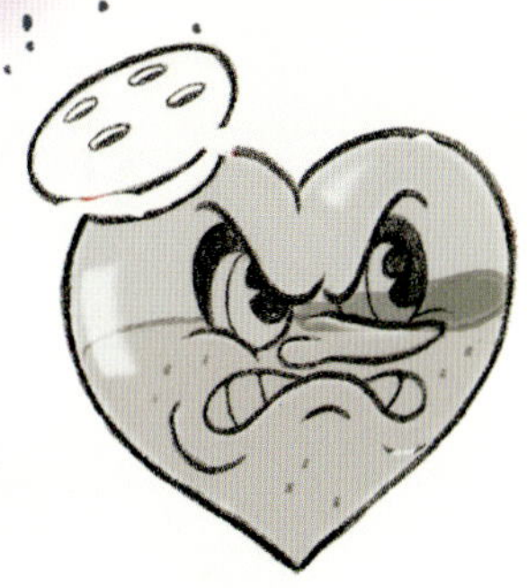

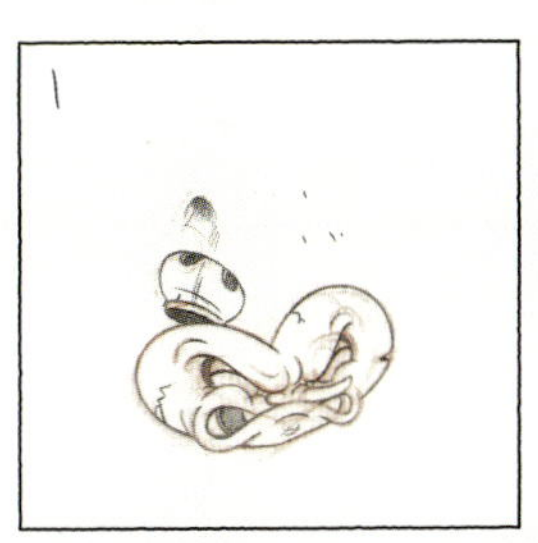

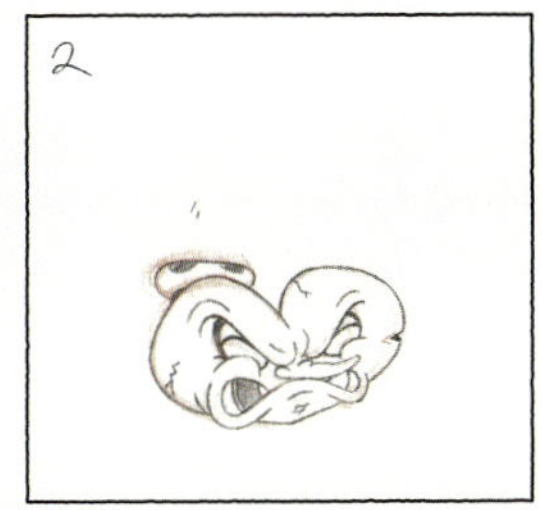

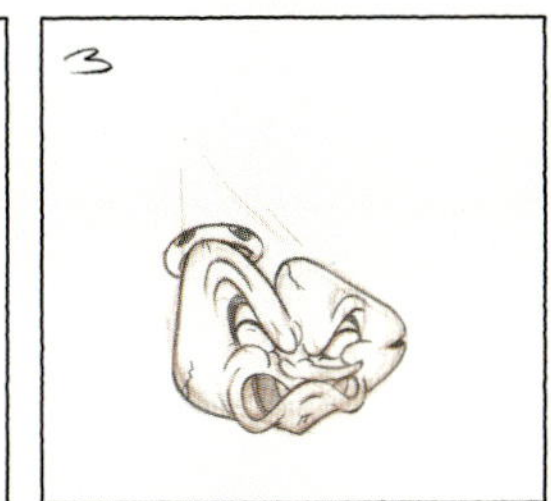

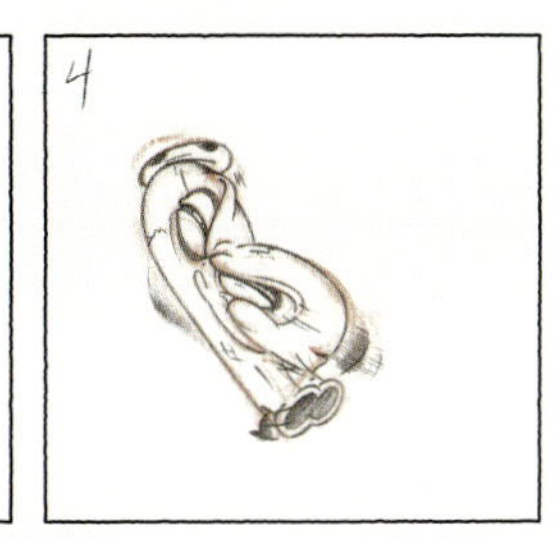

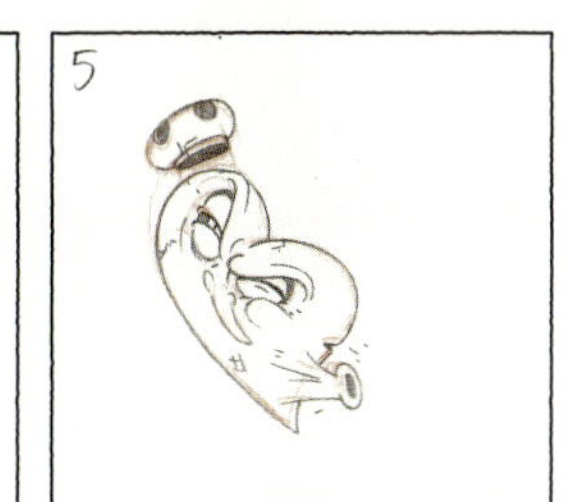

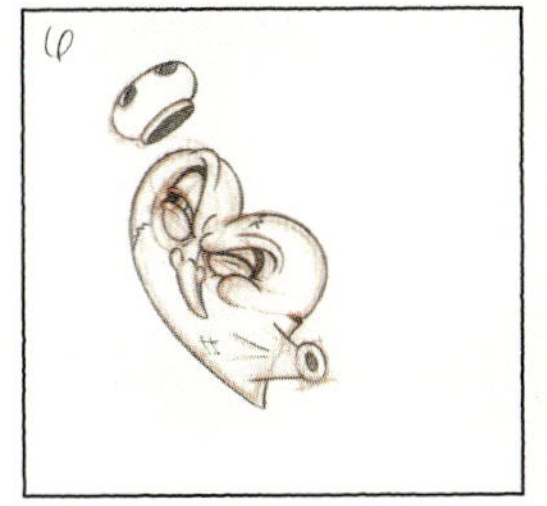

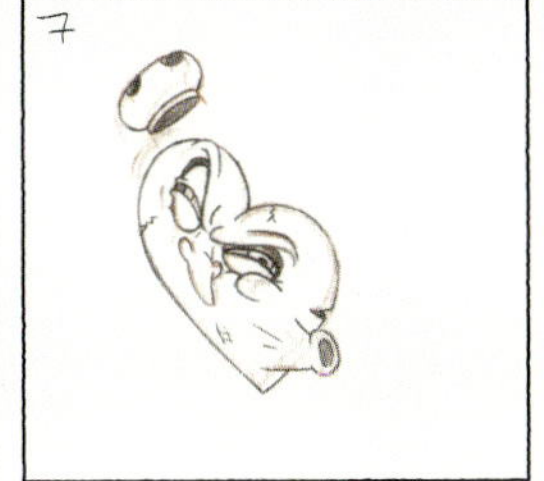

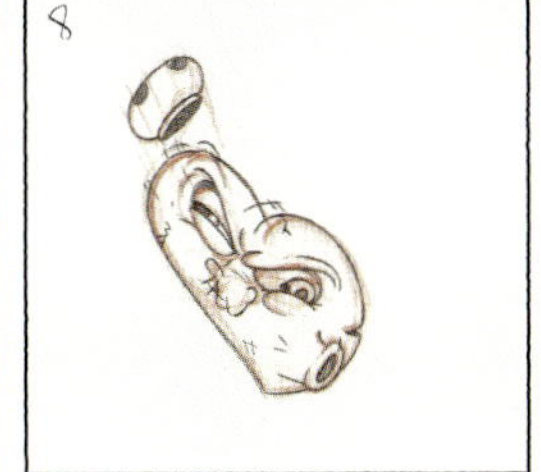

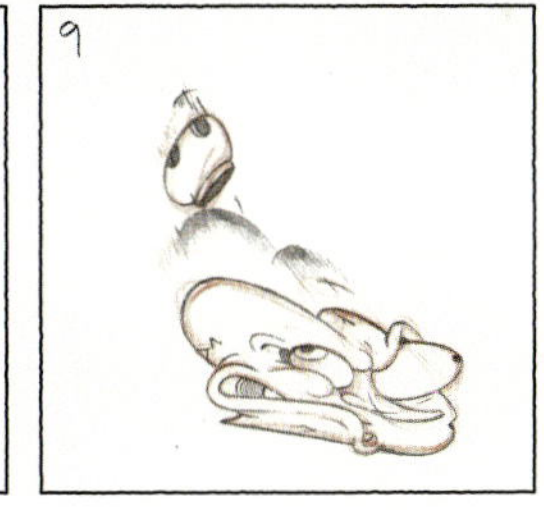

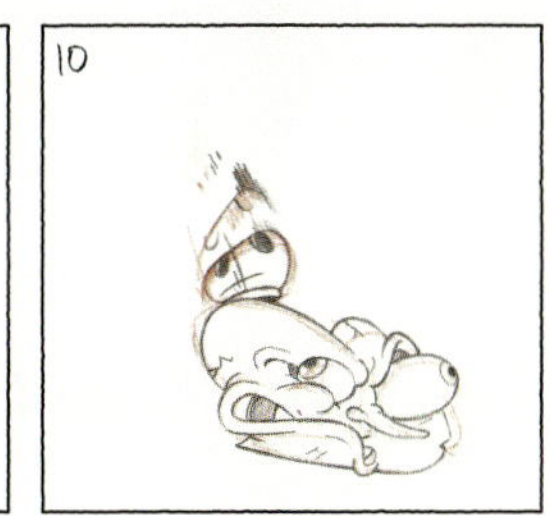

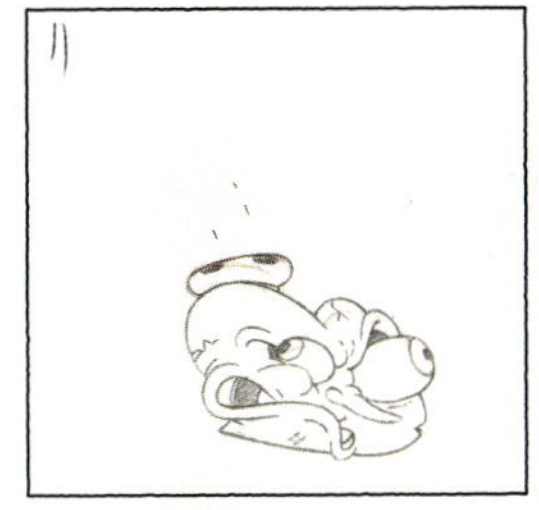

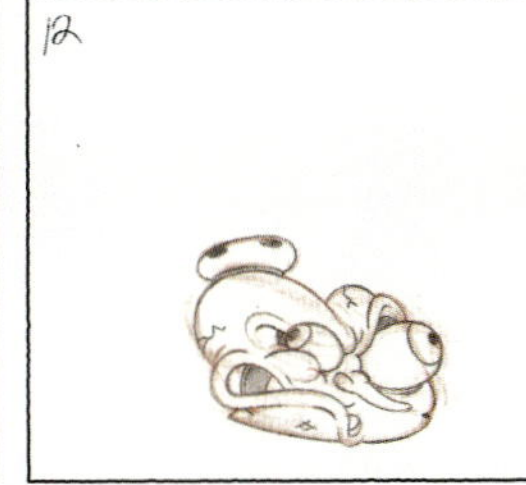

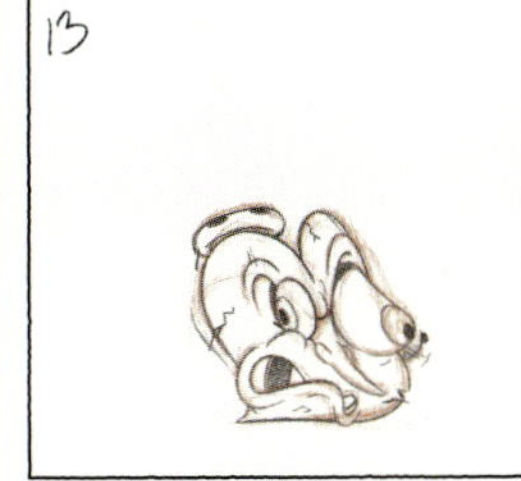

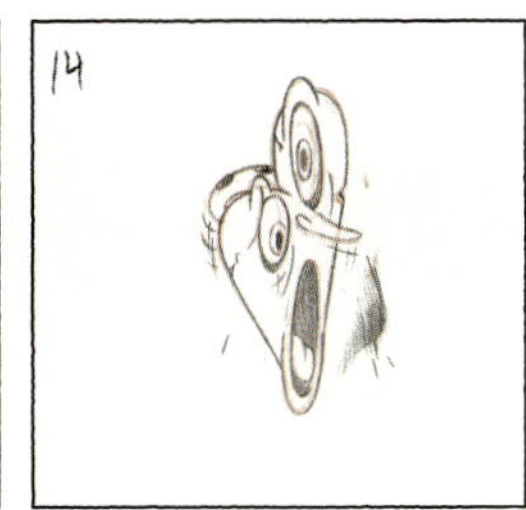

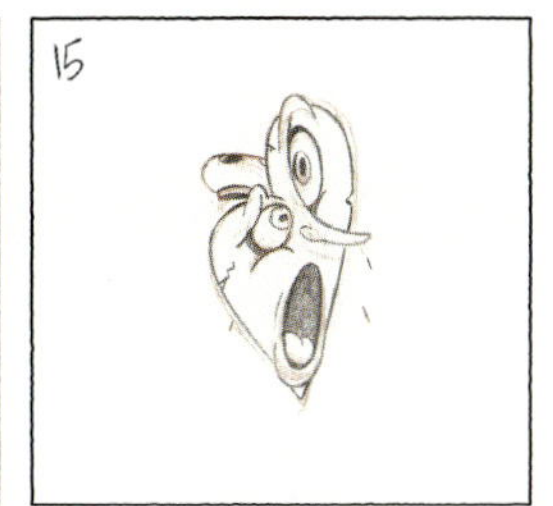

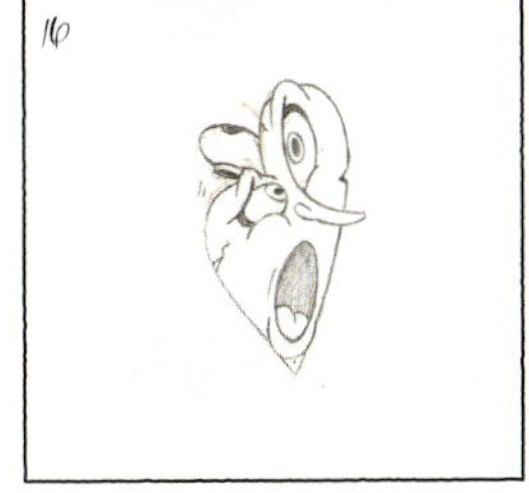

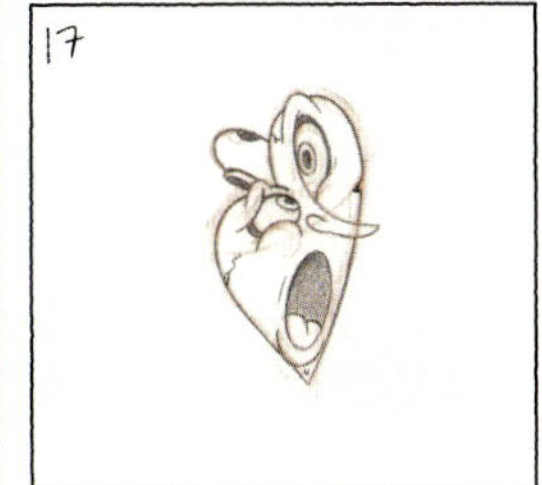

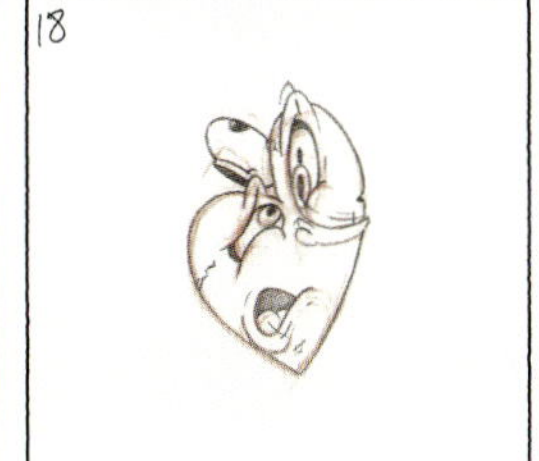

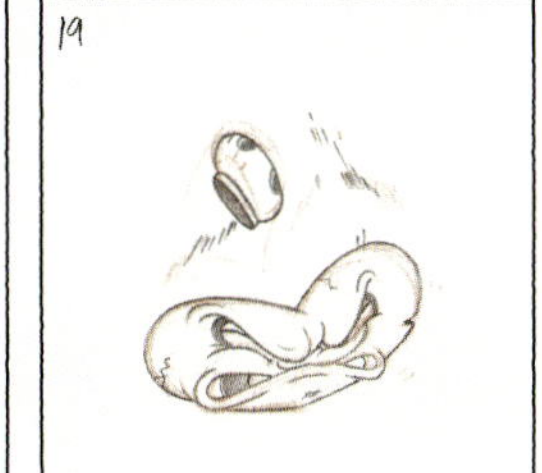

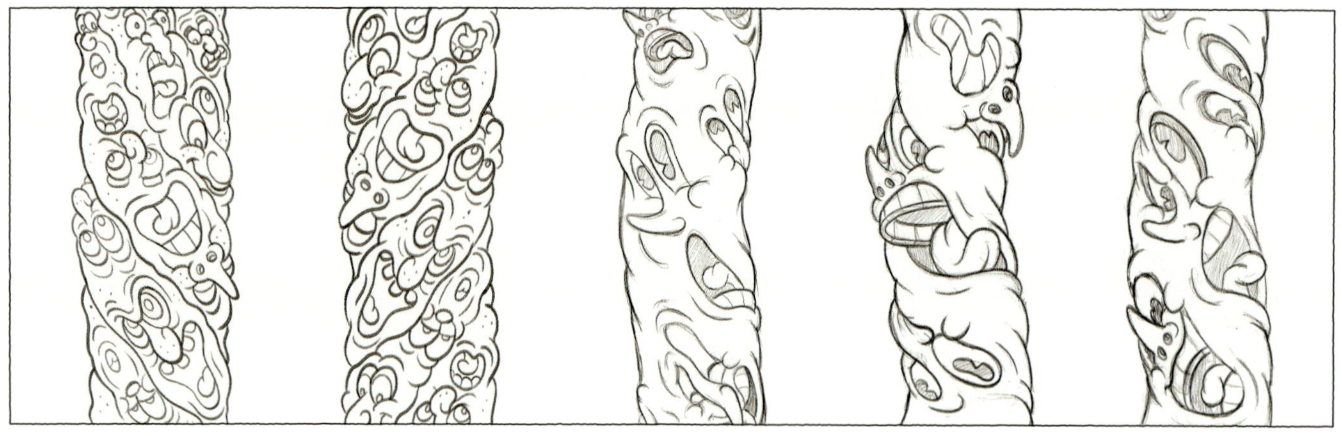

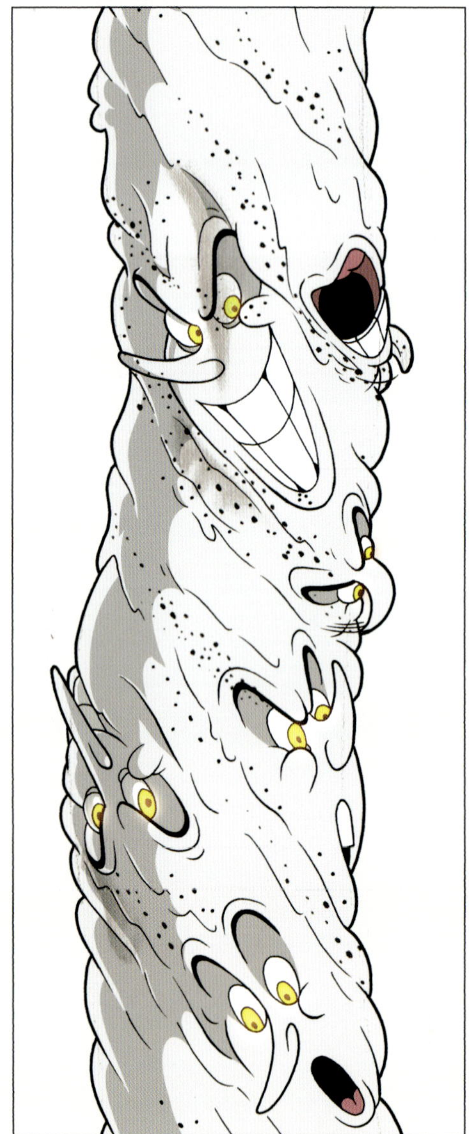

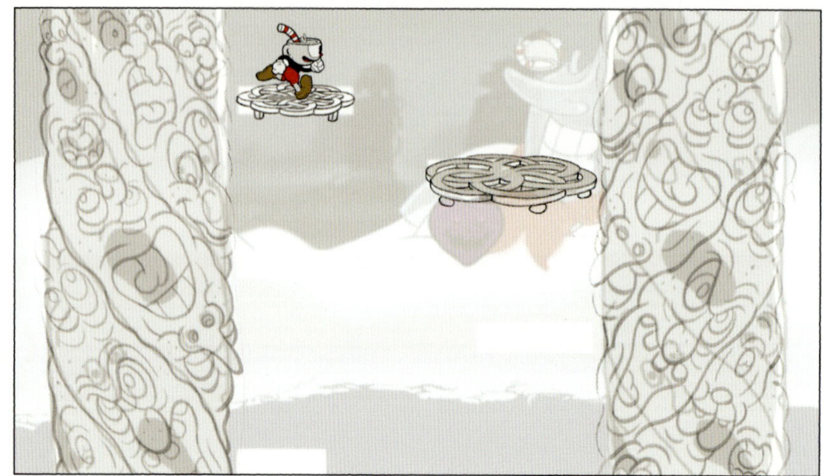

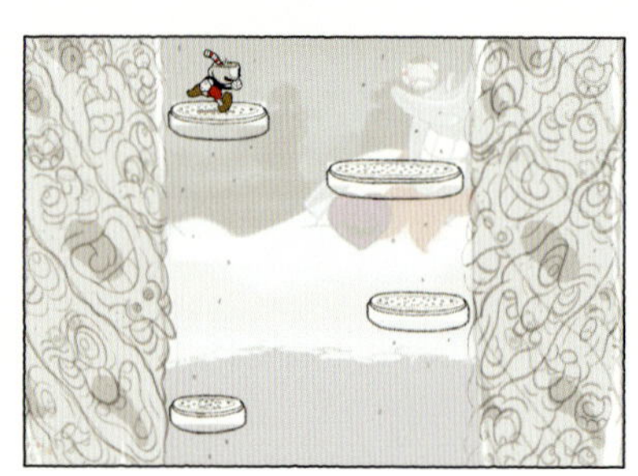

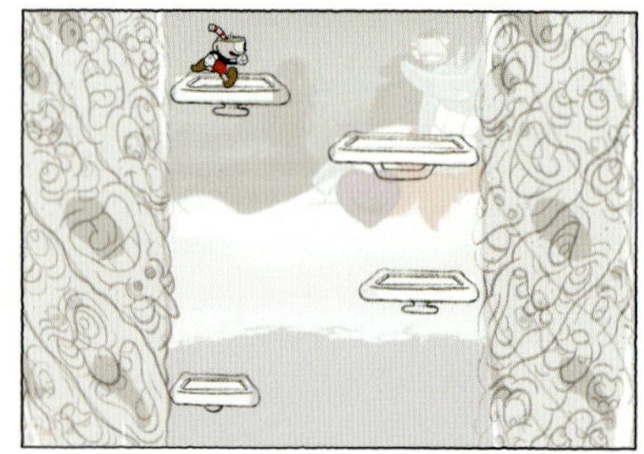

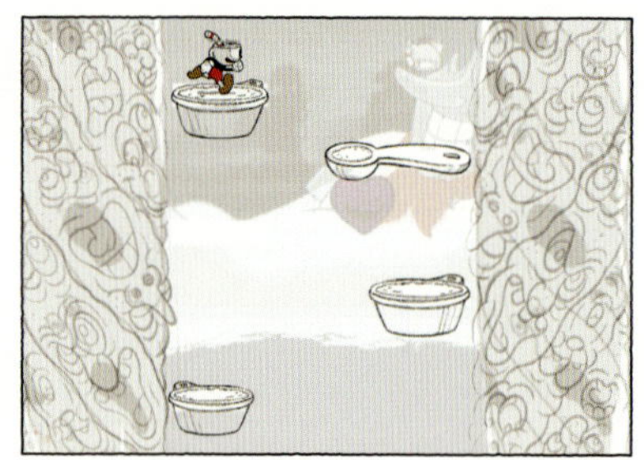

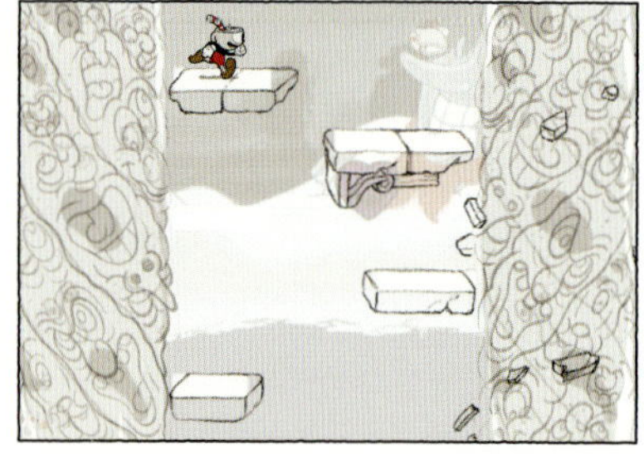

Very early in the gameplay prototypes for Saltbaker's final phase, we conceptualized a giant wall of salt with multiple twisted versions of the chef's visage forming on the surface of it to attack the player. While that concept was eventually scrapped, we liked the idea of Saltbaker's internal contents being the manifestation of his very being, all fighting back with every *grain* against his inevitable defeat.

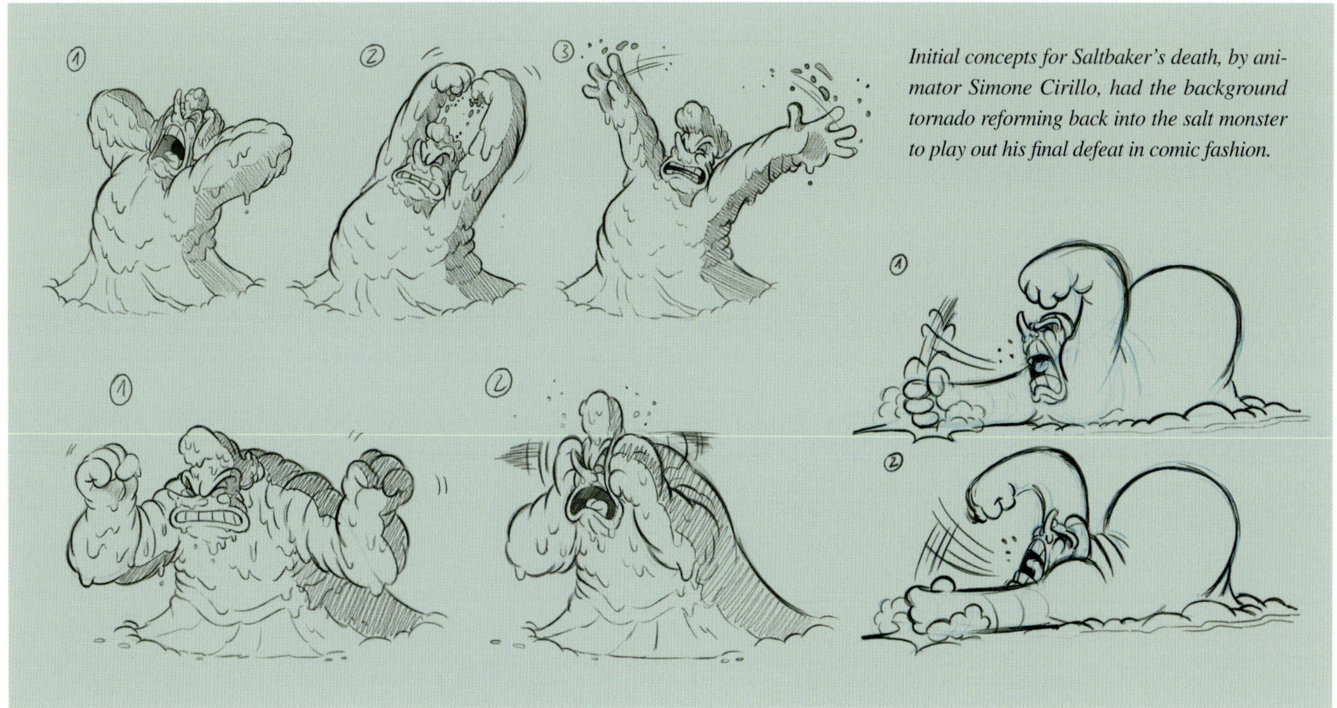

Initial concepts for Saltbaker's death, by animator Simone Cirillo, had the background tornado reforming back into the salt monster to play out his final defeat in comic fashion.

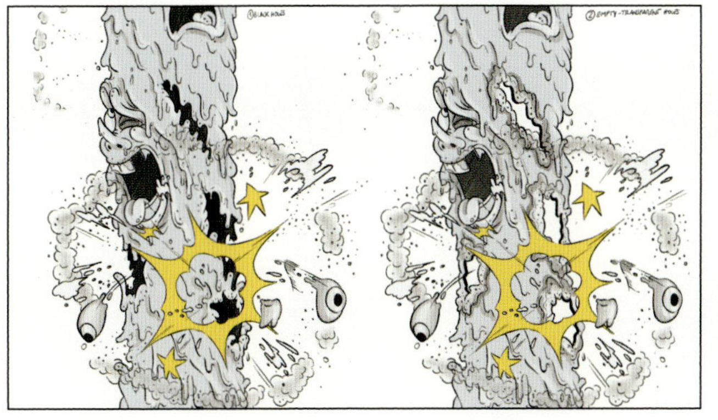

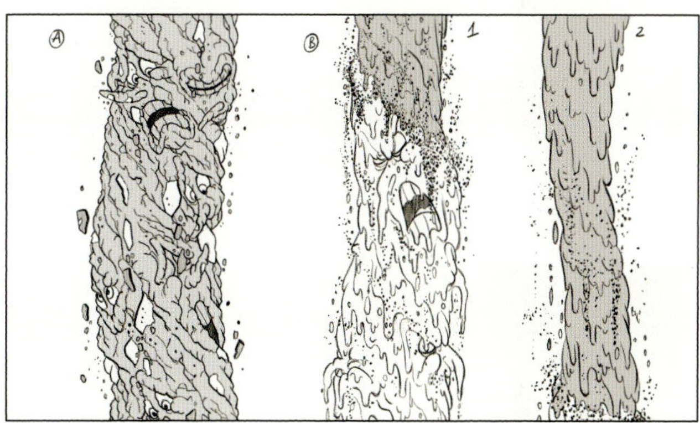

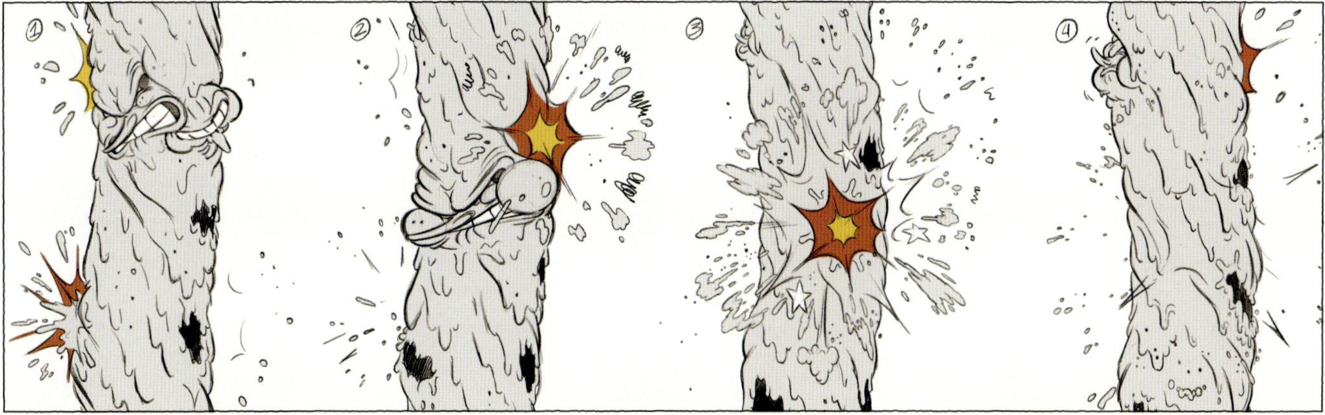

Initial prototypes for the salt pillars had them close together for the entire phase while the player fought against Saltbaker's bouncing heart and jumped up pillar-attached platforms descending into the pit. To give the fight a more desperate feel, we eventually decided to start with the pillars far apart and continuously close the walls in to narrow the maneuverable space and enhance the feeling of the walls closing in.

A Dish to Die For Background

DEEP BELOW CHEF SALTBAKER'S COZY and inviting bake shop lies a secret testing laboratory replete with mysterious eldritch contraptions and sinister instruments of dissection. From the grey stone crumbling walls of the witch's dungeon in *Snow White* (1937) to the twisted tubing and glossy beakers of *The Mad Doctor*'s (1933) torturous science lab, we took inspiration from a variety of villainous lairs of the era. A maniacally gouged butcher's table capped the whole scene off as a fitting setting for this fight. After all, our intrepid cups are on the chopping block!

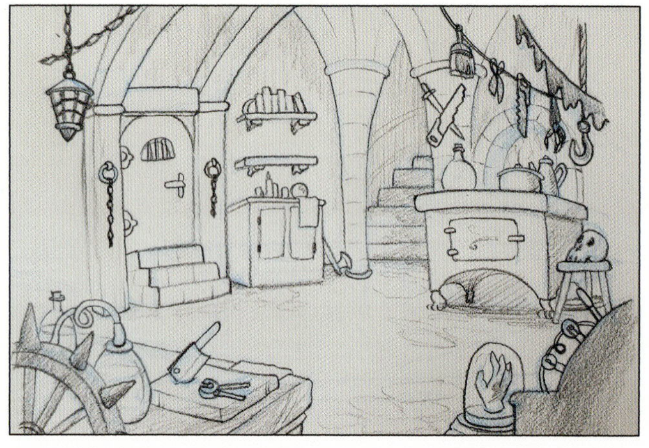

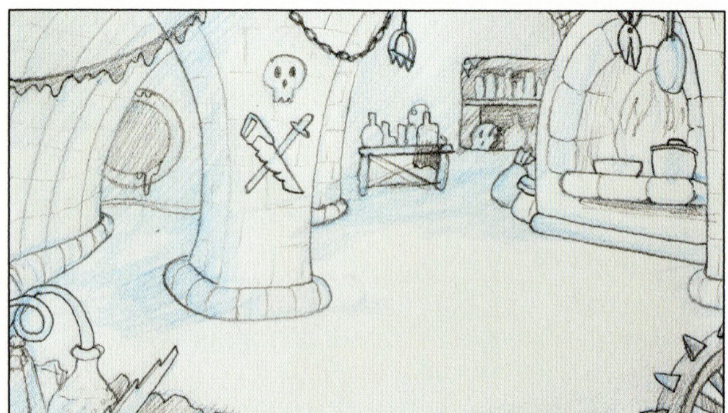

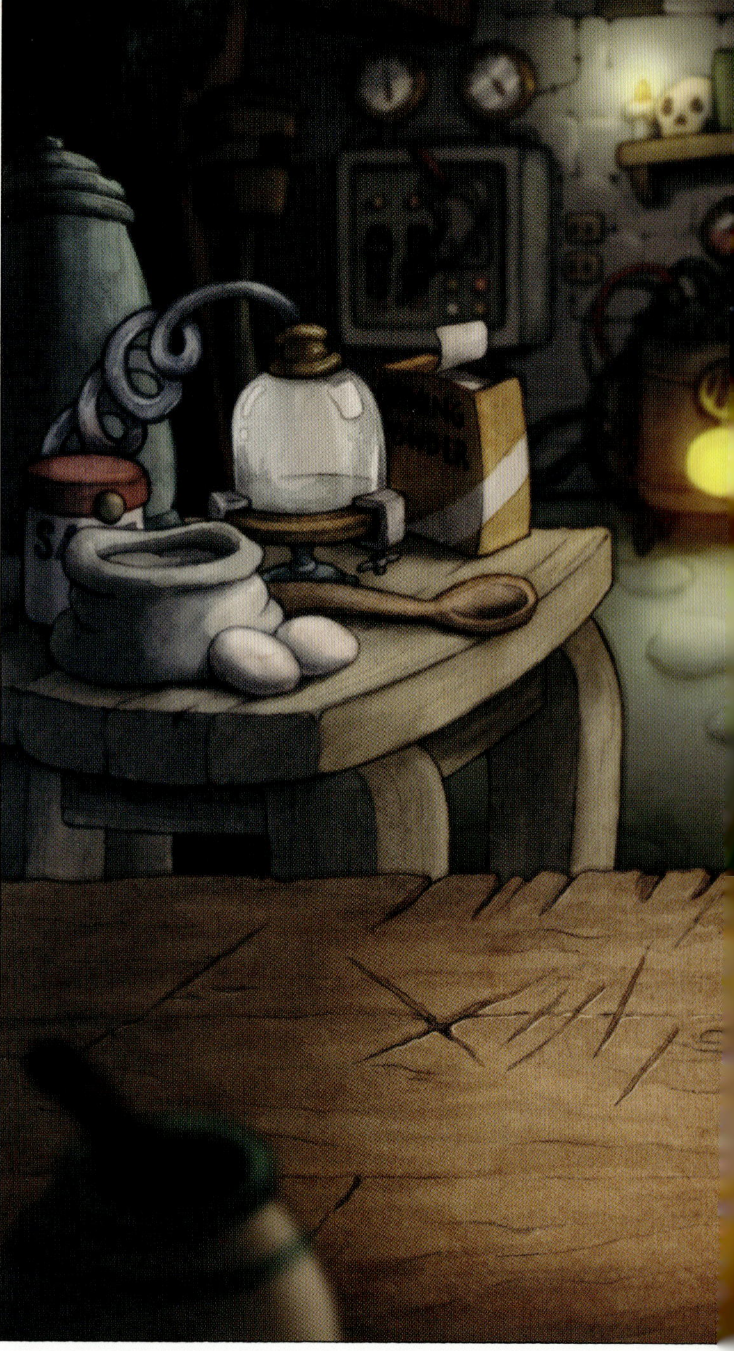

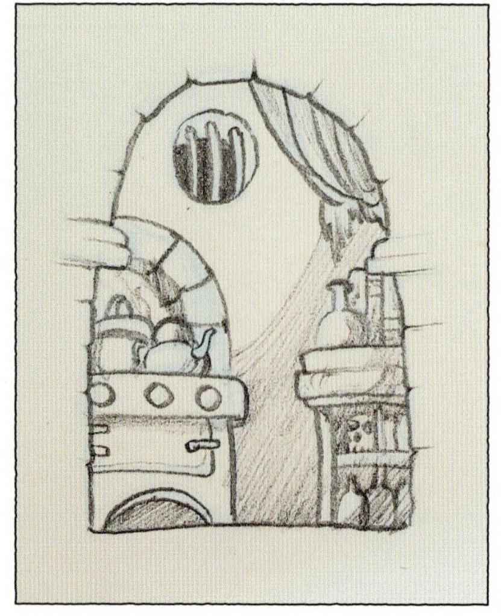

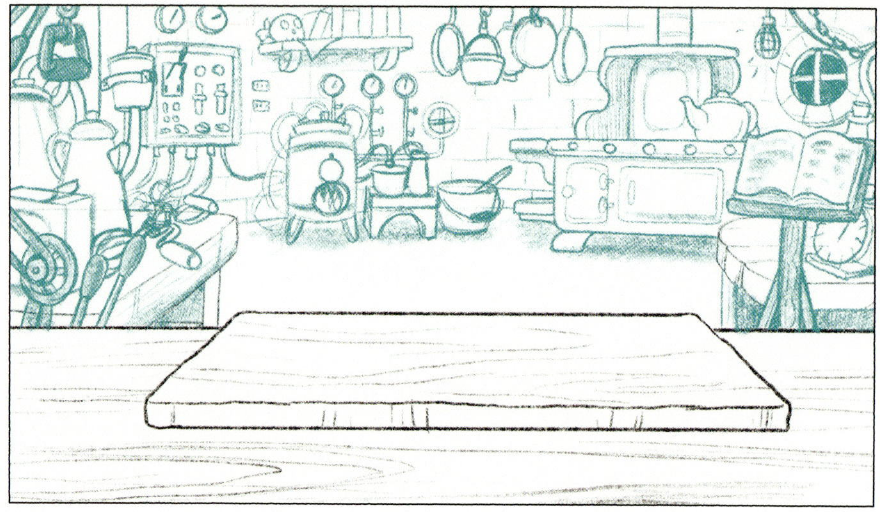

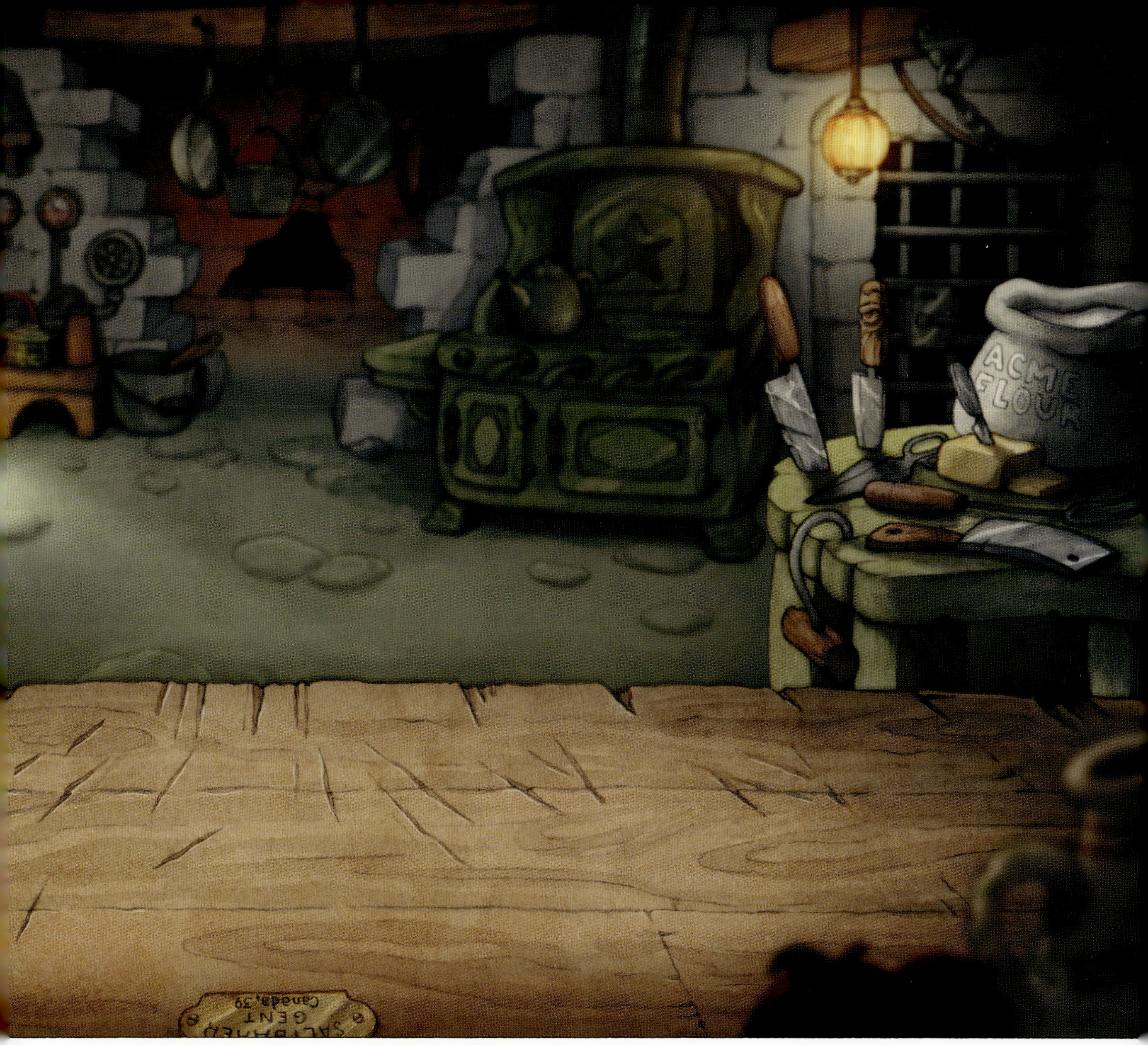

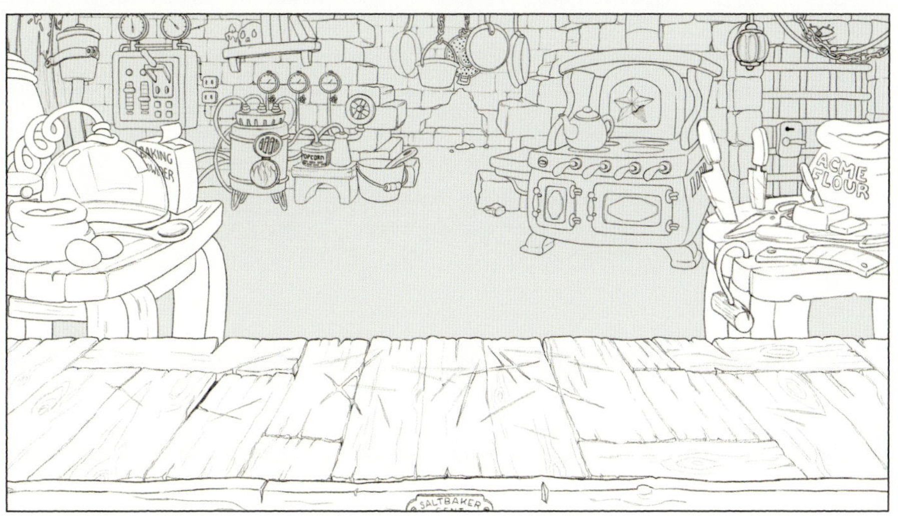
ACME FLOUR
SALTBAKER

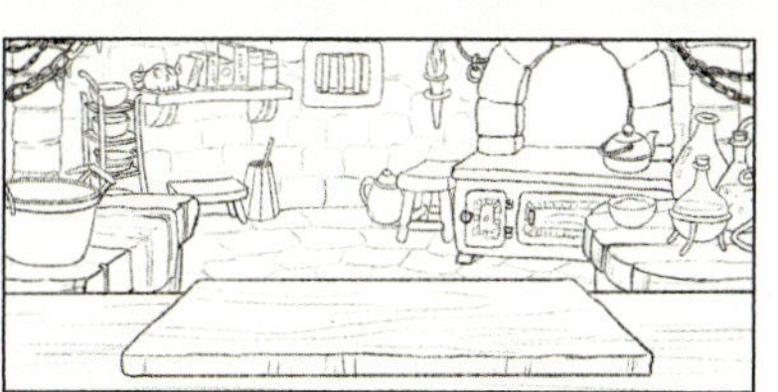

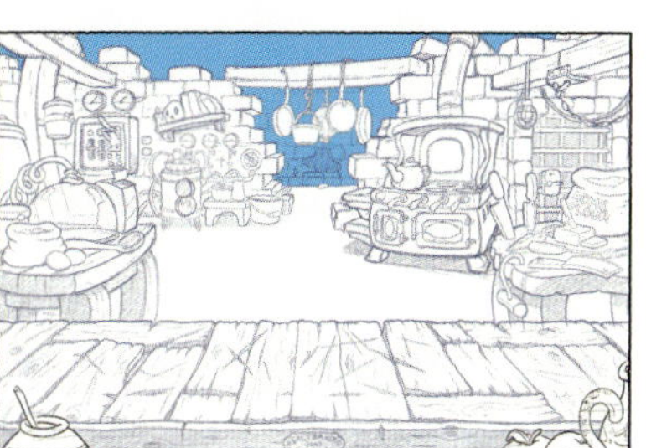

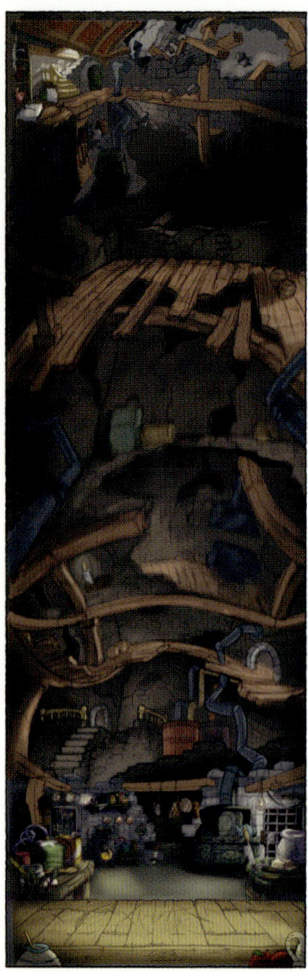

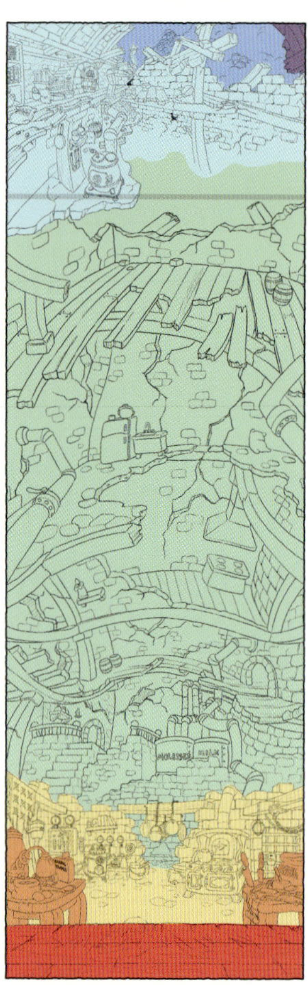

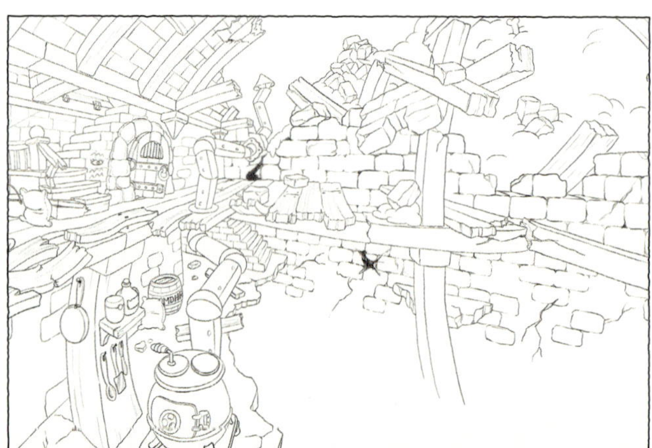

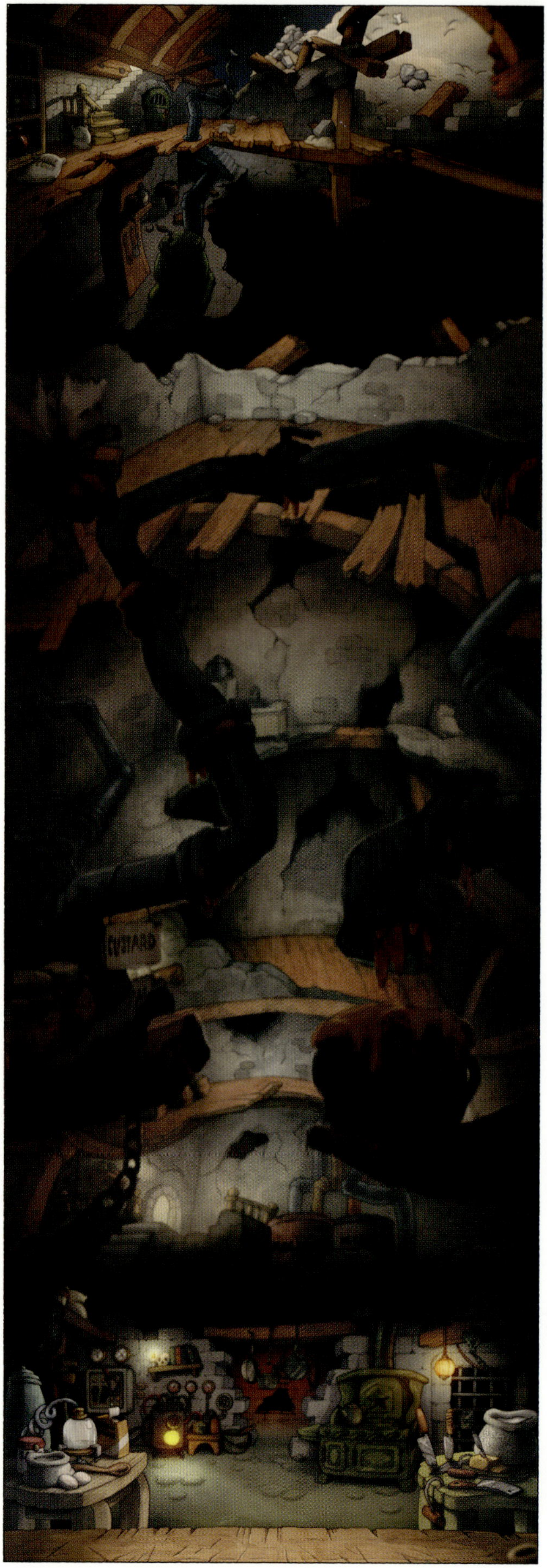

For Chef Saltbaker's expansion into his colossal giant form in phase two, we had to construct a way for the background of phase one to seamlessly transition through the various levels of his secret underground bakery and bust out of the ceiling. Almost a dozen different layers of painted parallax depicting busted pipes, broken floor boards, and mysterious culinary contraptions are seen for barely a second as the camera whip-pans to follow Saltbaker's rapid growth. For the design of the background, Concept Artist Lance Inkwell and Background Painter Caitlin Russell collaborated on defining the layout of the floors, and then Russell separated them into their specific layers and painted each independently.

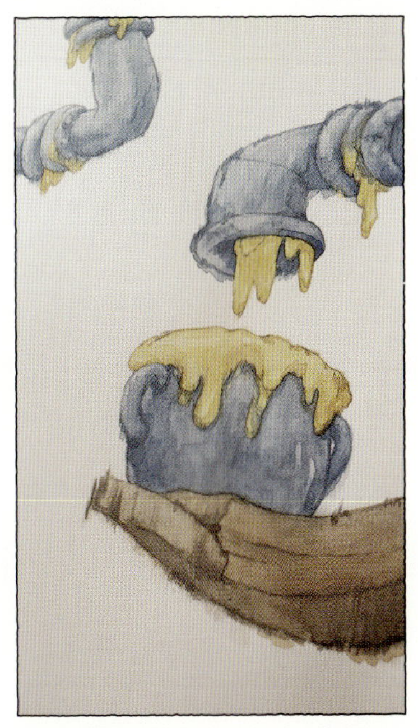
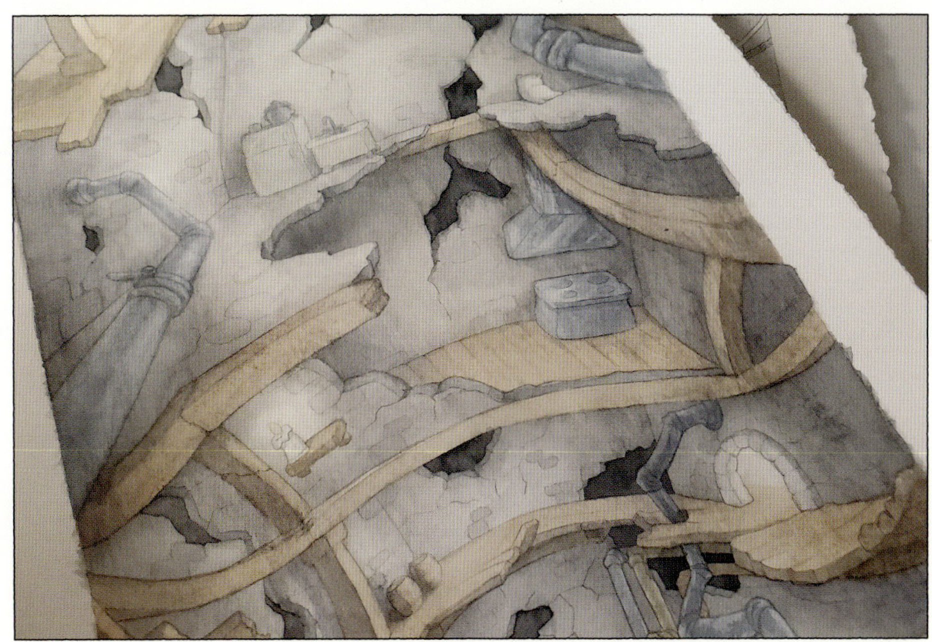
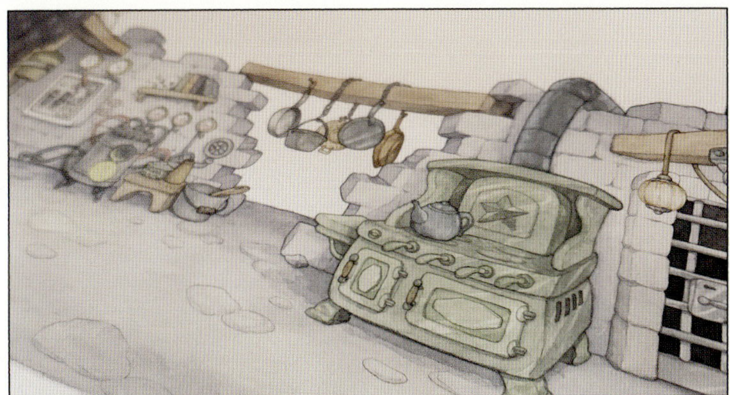
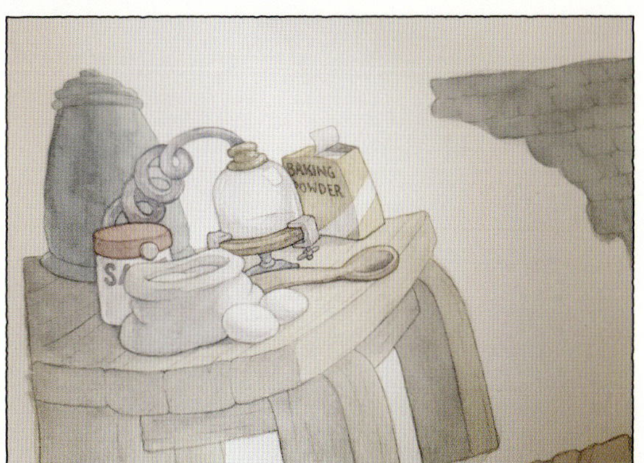
BAKING
POWDER
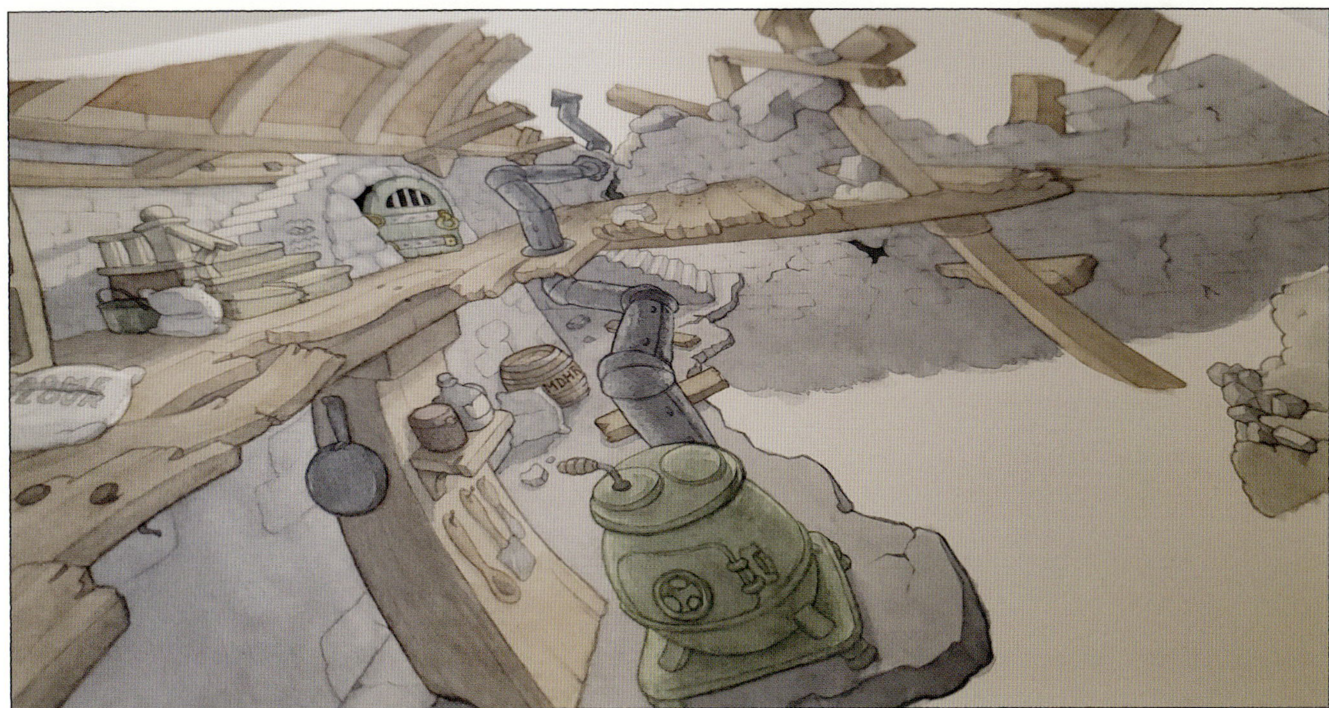

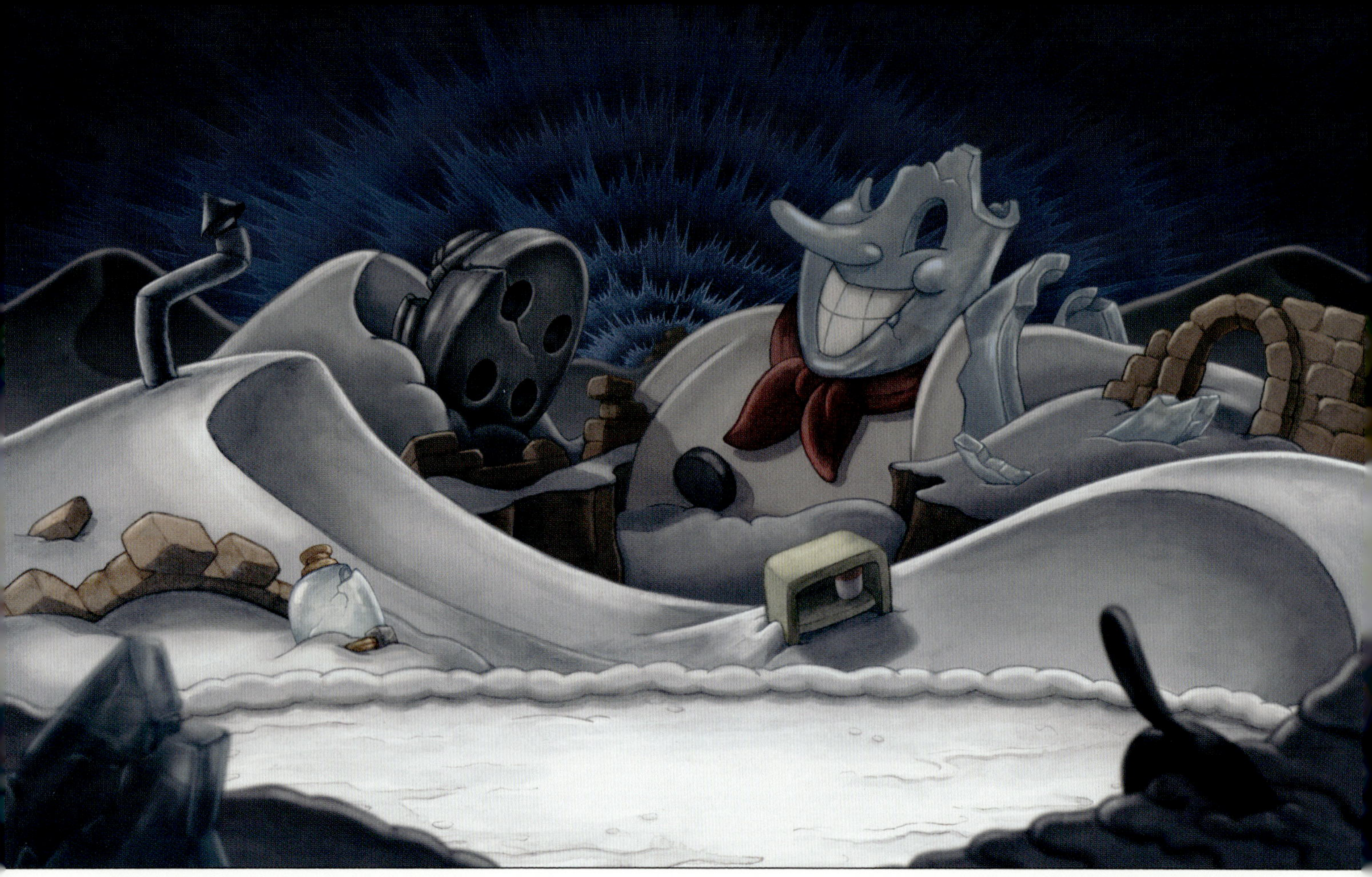

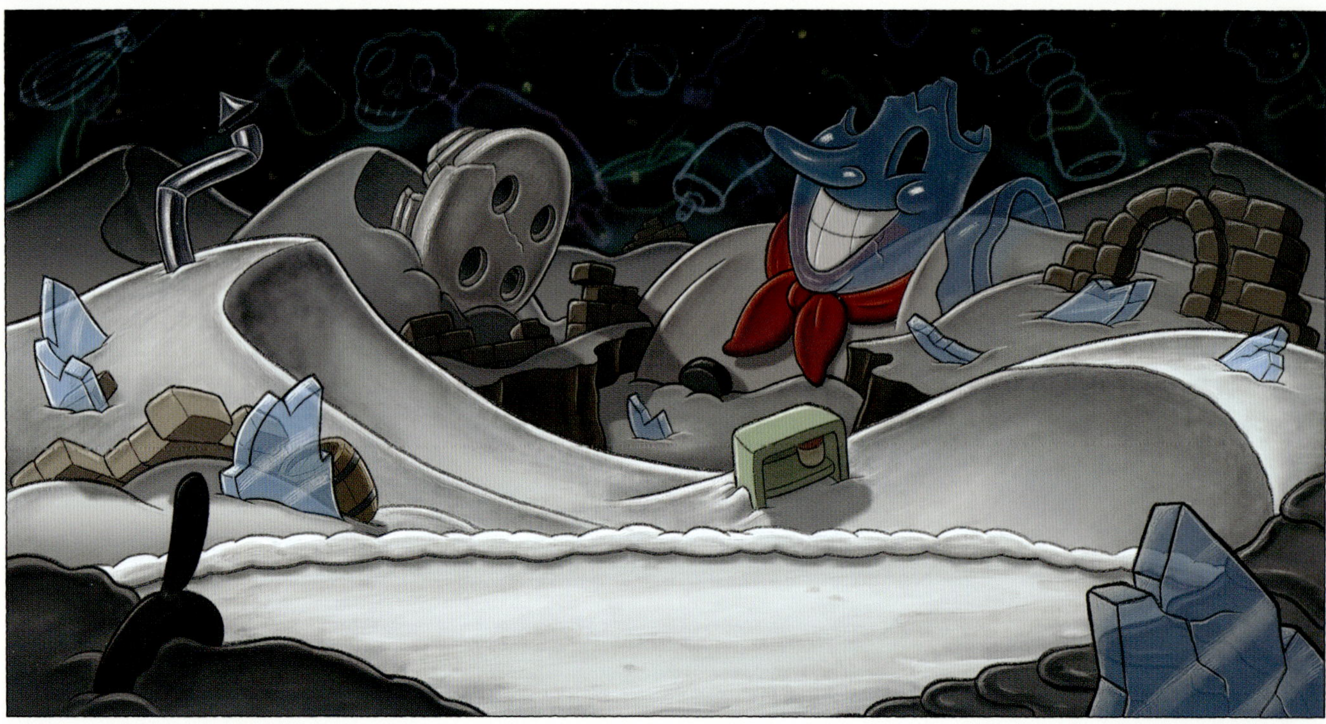

For the absolute finale of *The Delicious Last Course*, we wanted the player to feel like they were fighting against impossible odds in a truly apocalyptic scenario. This nightmarish desert lives in a liminal void filled with the Salvador Dalí-inspired shattered glass remnants of Saltbaker's monstrous façade, while a windswept wasteland of salt stretches as far as the eye can see. The concluding struggle against the chef's displaced and exploded form, with your friend's stolen soul cheering you on, suggests a battle at the very end of the world.

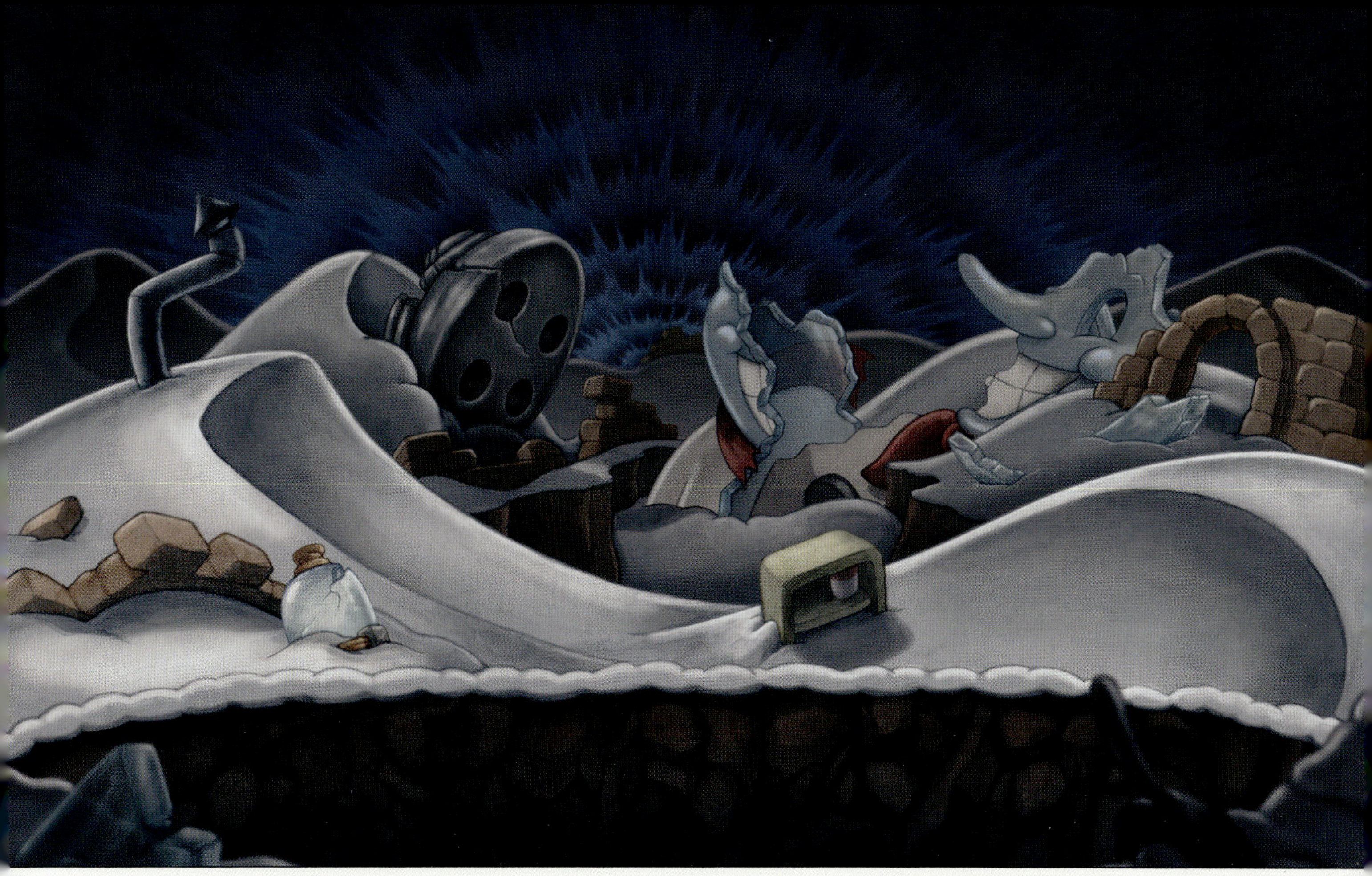

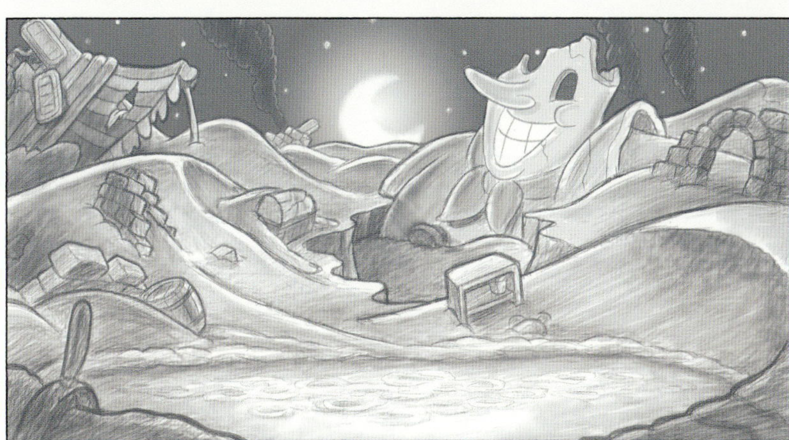

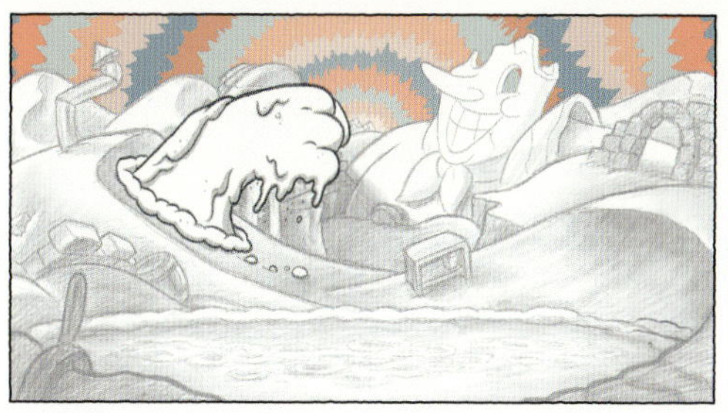

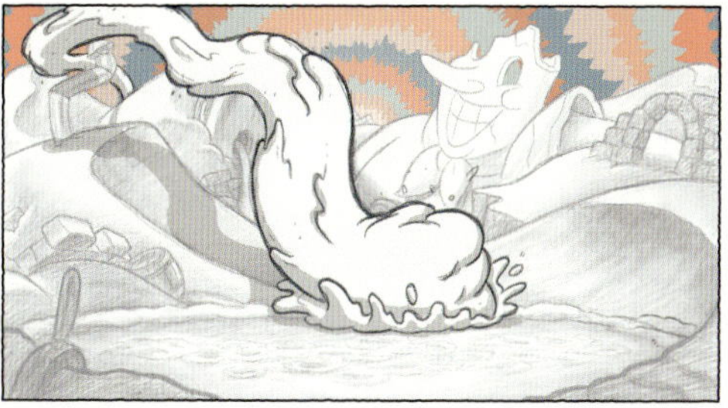

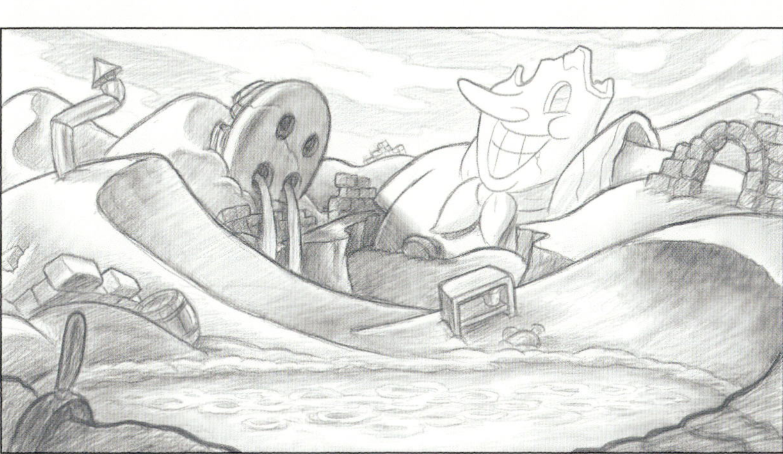

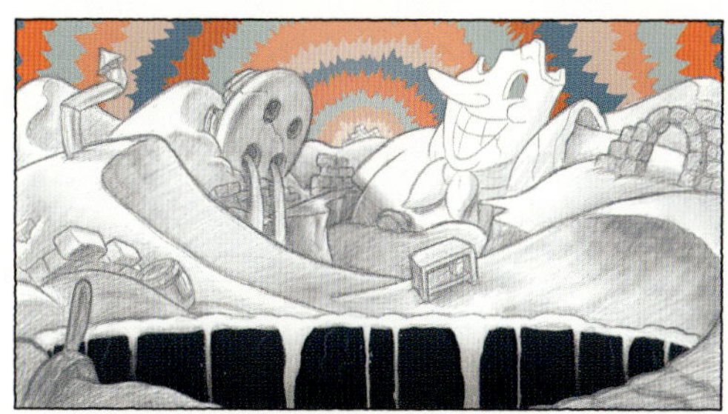

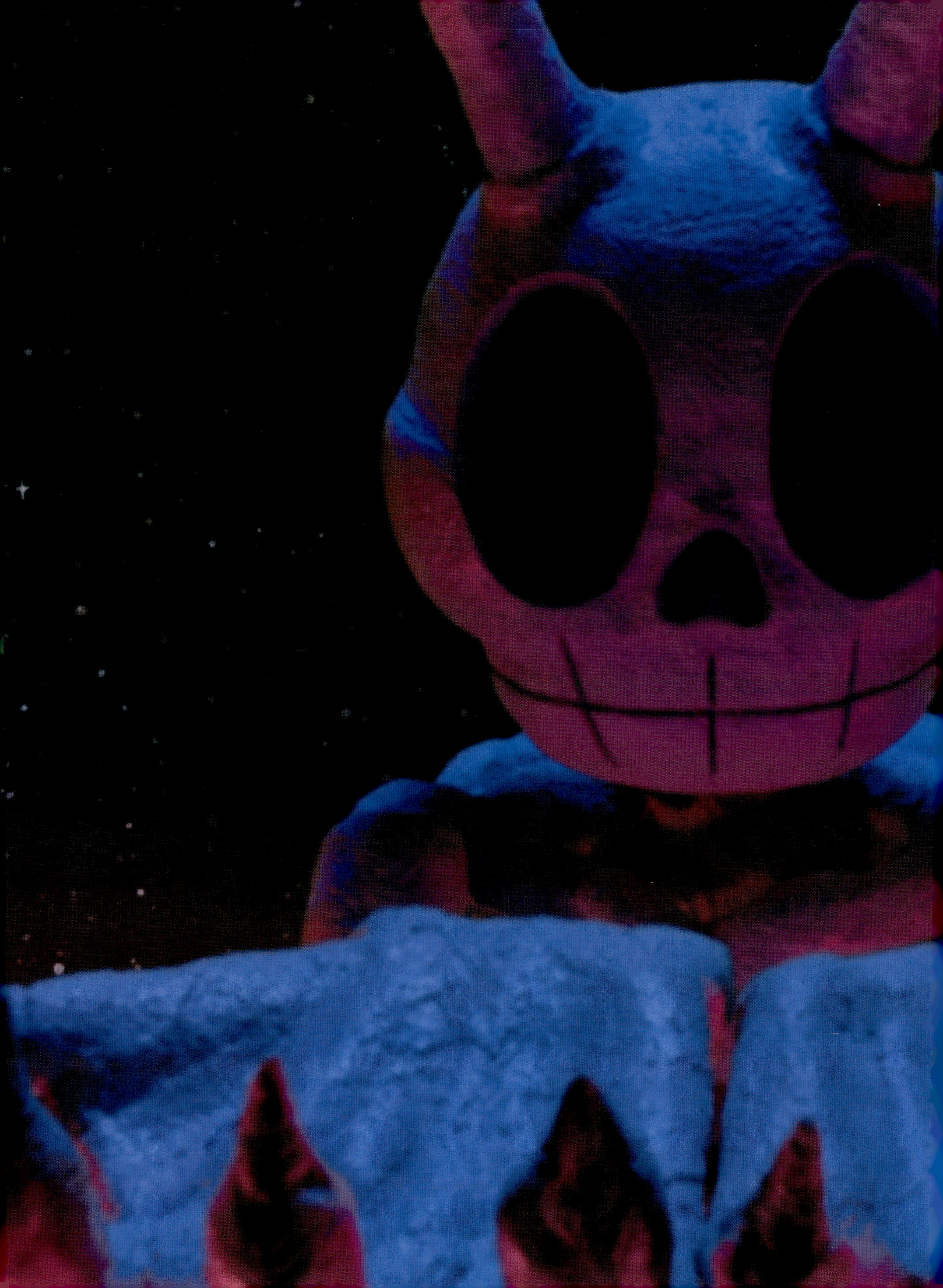

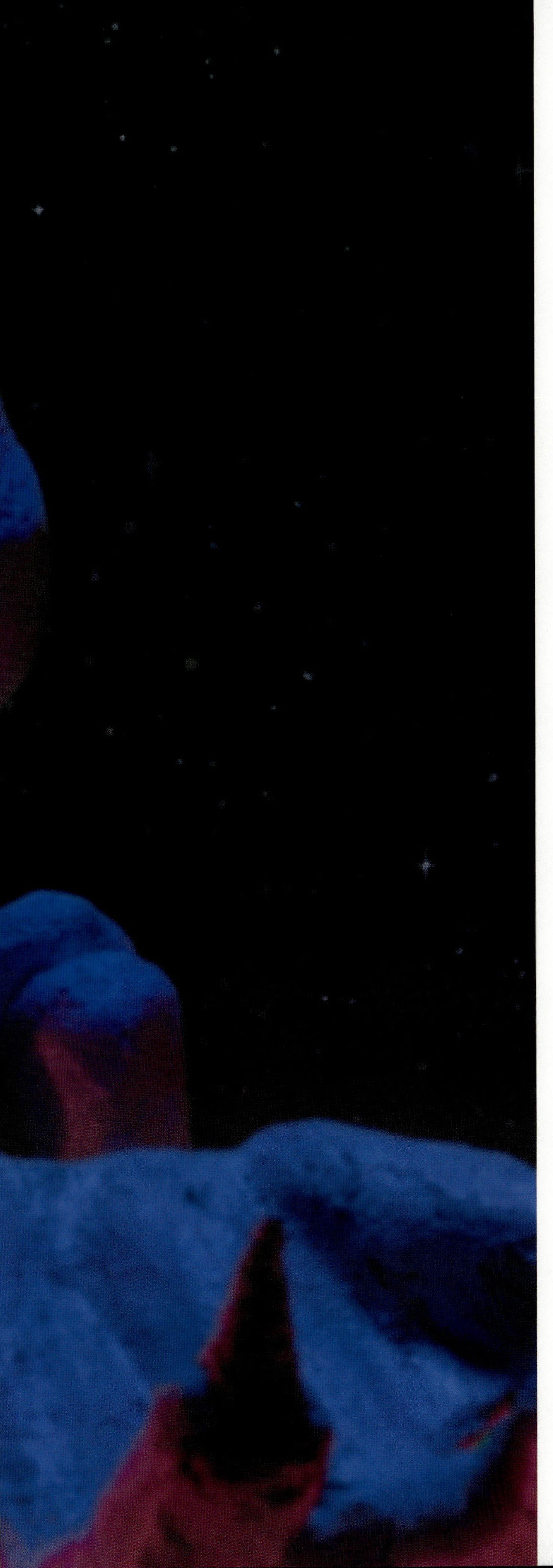

Chapter X:
One Hell Of A Dream

DEEP IN THE GRAVEYARD of this far off Inkwell Isle lies a mysterious concentration of astral energy. By harnessing the power of an ancient cursed relic, our heroes are thrust into a nightmarish encounter within the recesses of their own minds! Is this battle a hint at the origins of Cuphead's greatest foe, or just a dreaming manifestation of the unknowable astral plane? One thing's for sure, the devil's in the details…and we loaded up this fight with as many as we could in order to create an atmosphere unlike anything else in the game. From the blurred fade-out of the cups falling asleep in the cemetery, to the broken hourglass character on the loading screen, to the ethereal announcer and the endlessly looping haunting dirge, we strove to make this nightmare feel as detached as possible from anything in the main quest.

Visually, this battle was inspired by popular iconography representing the conscience—an angel on one shoulder urging you to do good, and a demon on the other tempting evil. There are countless influential examples of this classic trope across cartoons of the era, but we were taken with one in particular: the representation of the angel and demon from Disney's 1942 comedy short *Donald's Decision*. Funded by the National Film Board of Canada, this short was used as wartime propaganda to convince Canadian citizens to buy bonds during the Second World War! In true Studio MDHR fashion, we often like to stray from the beaten path to find reference points that are off-kilter and esoteric.

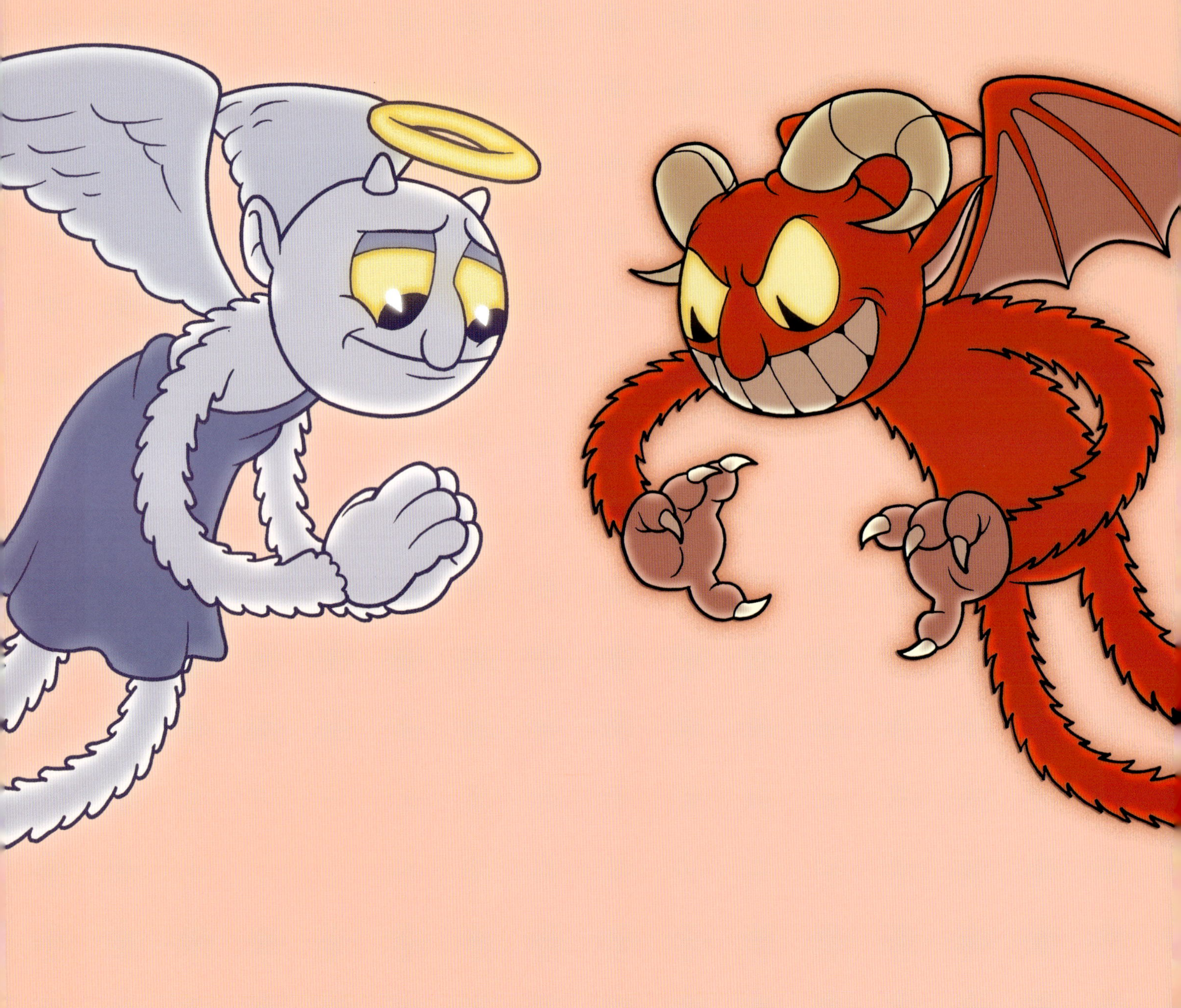

The Angel and The Devil in "ONE HELL OF A DREAM"

CONCEPTUALLY, THE SEED OF this battle came from Design Director Jared Moldenhauer's love of classic game developer Treasure's mode-switching combat design. From the color-swapping "shmup" action of their arcade classic *Ikaruga* (2001), to their direction-switching Sega Saturn platformer *Silhouette Mirage* (1997), our nightmare fight was heavily inspired by this mind-bending process of maneuvering safely within a color-coded storm of hazards.

Initially, this fight was designed as the second phase of the climactic final battle against The Devil in the original campaign,

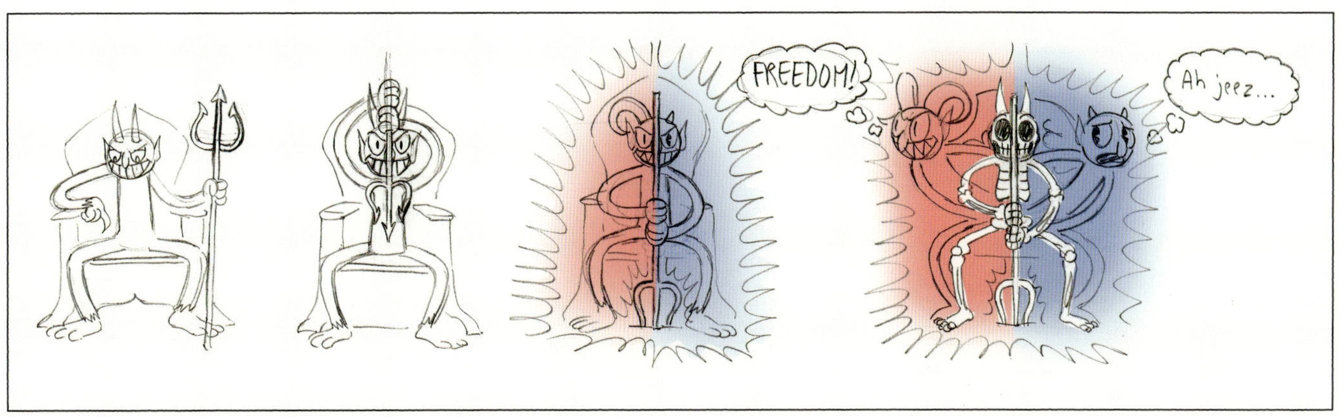

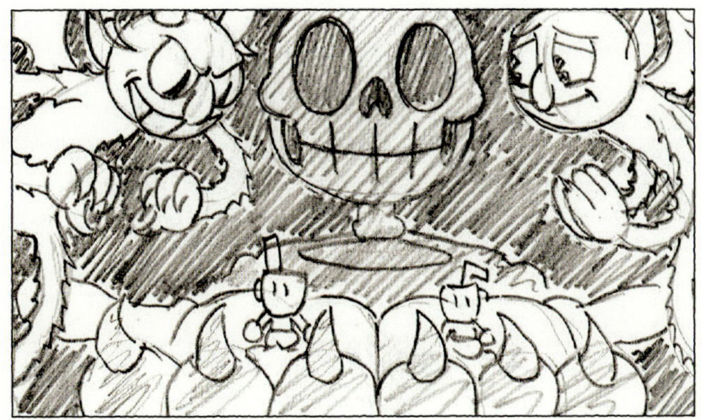

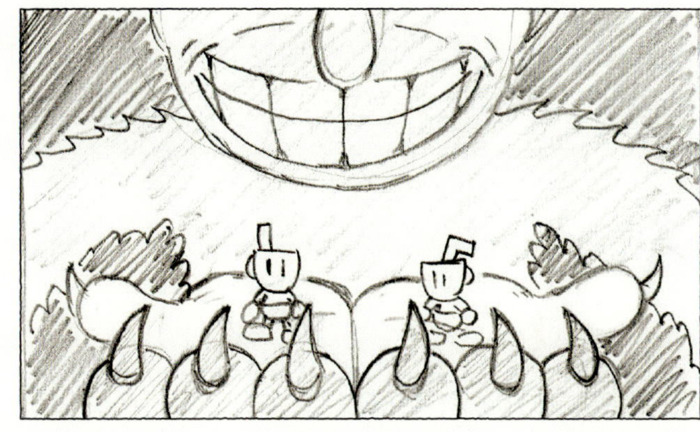

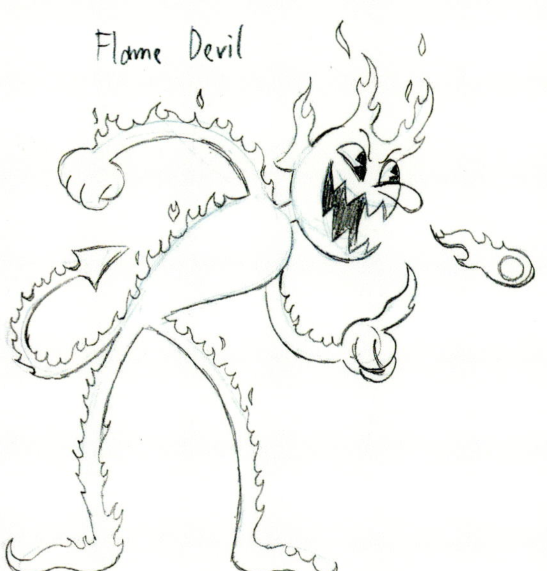

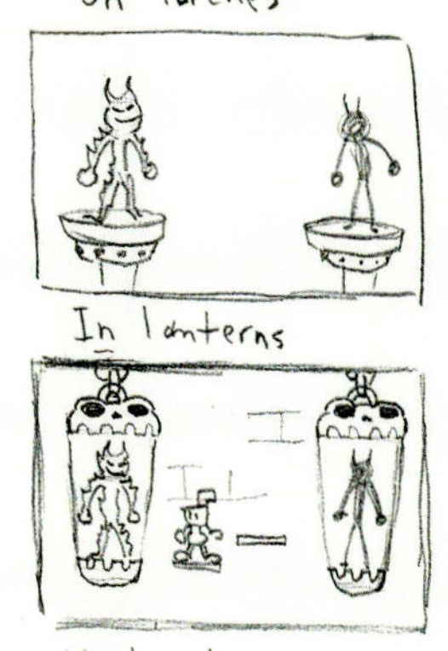

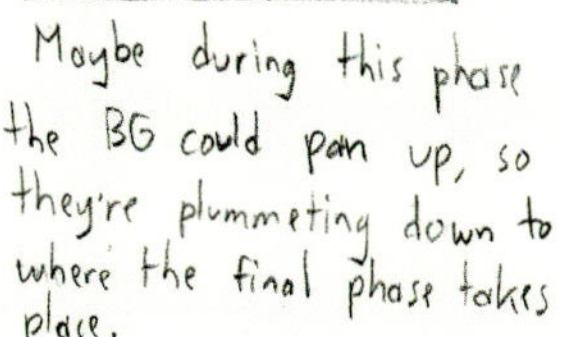

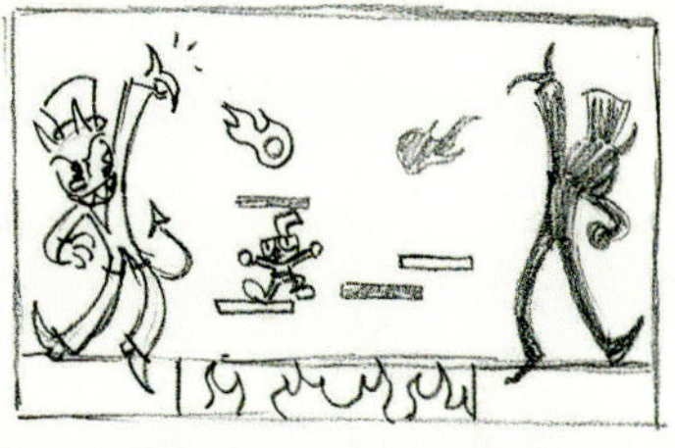

but we decided to cut it both for pacing reasons and because the complexity of the direction-swapping mechanic was too difficult to teach the player in the middle of an otherwise epic fight. With the DLC, we were able to break the fight out into its own unique set piece and let the gameplay mechanics gel better with players over the course of a self-contained experience.

From a development perspective, this fight was by far the most complicated to produce in the history of our studio. To allow the angel and demon to seamlessly morph into each other at any point of their animations without having to wait for the transitions to finish before executing their next action, Animator Jake Clark drew three morphing animation frames for every third standard attack or idle animation frame. From there, our programmers wrote custom sequencing code to check the state of the player, queue up the demon-angel morphs, and progress through them without interrupting any of the bosses' attack timings. A monumental task, but very much emblematic of the type of challenge we pushed for in the *Delicious Last Course*'s creation.

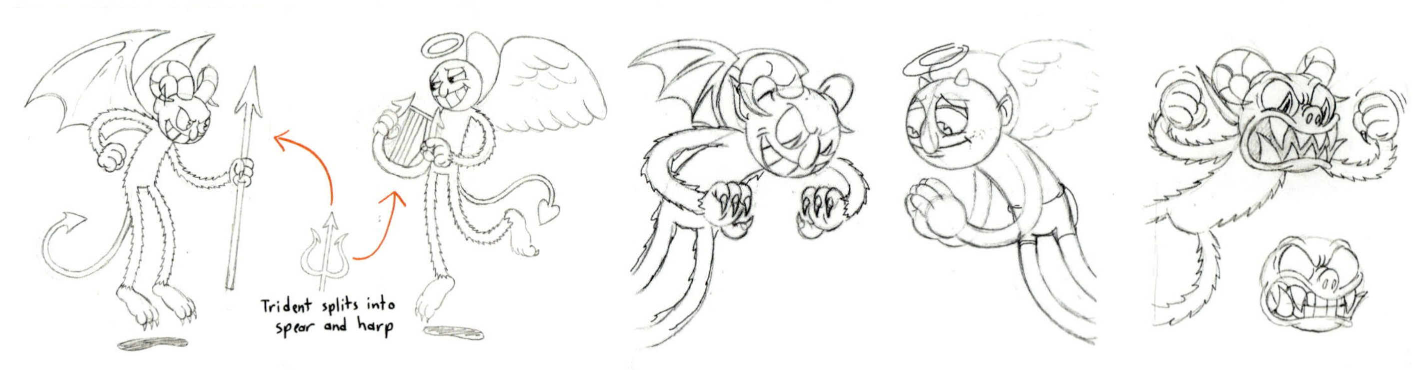
Trident splits into
spear and harp

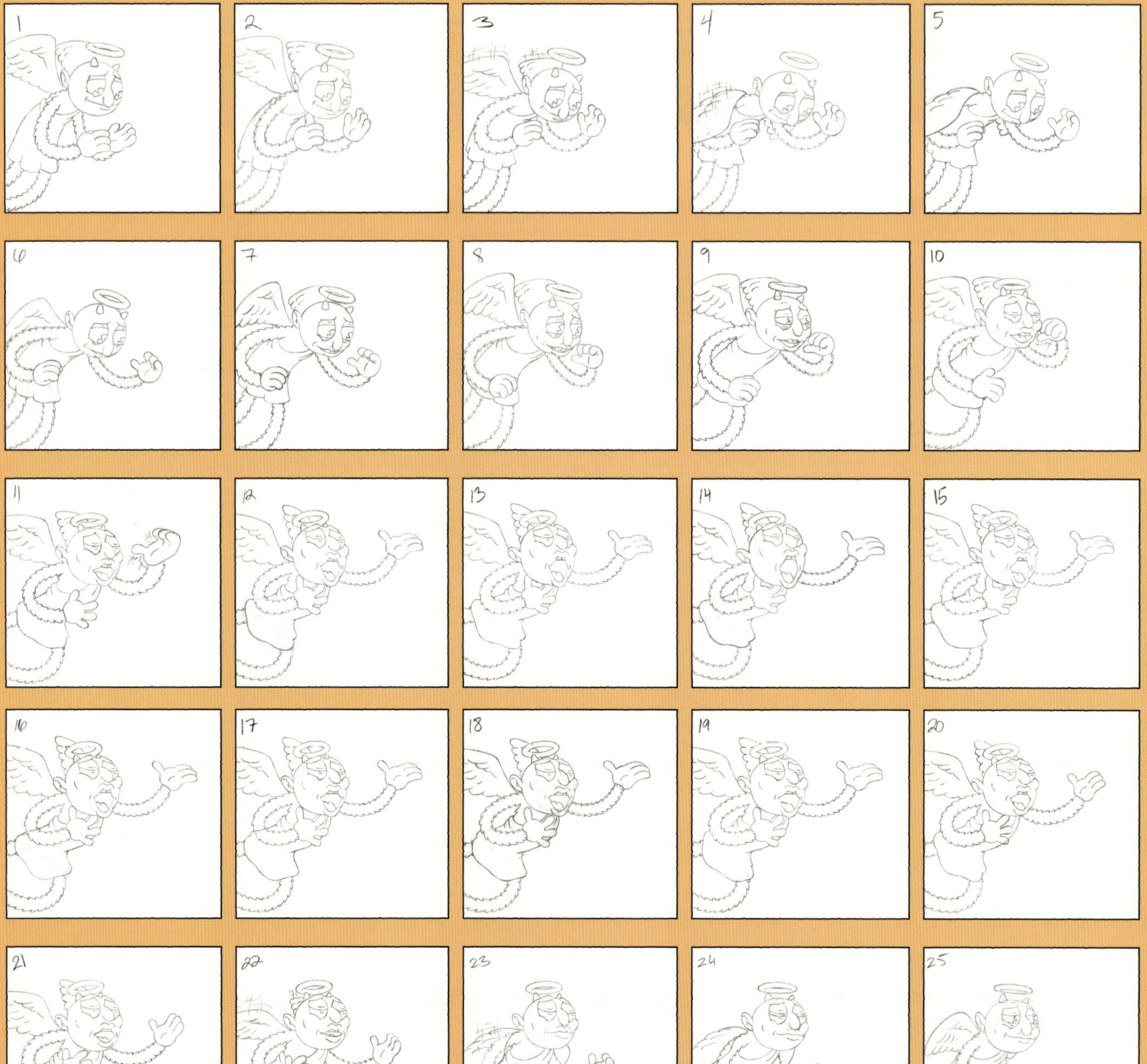

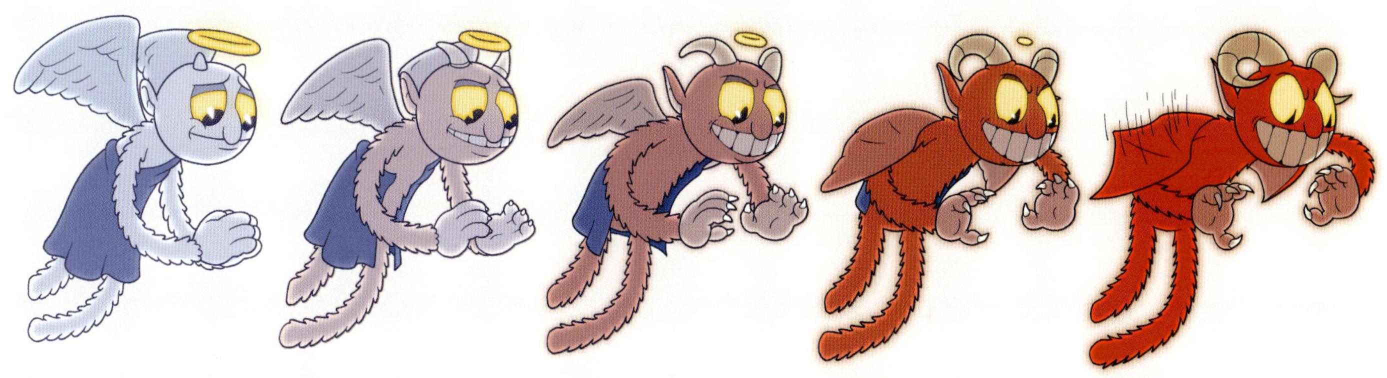

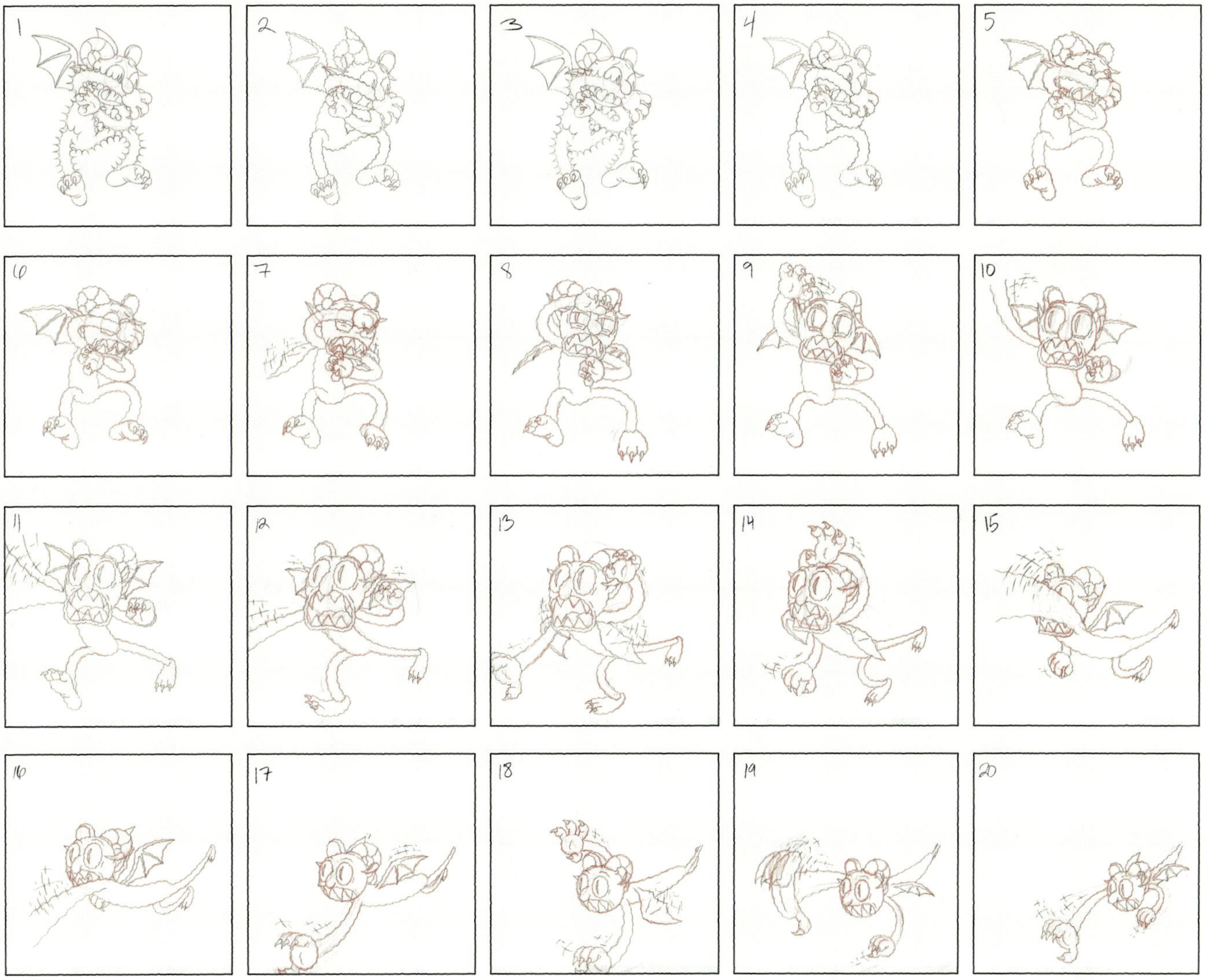

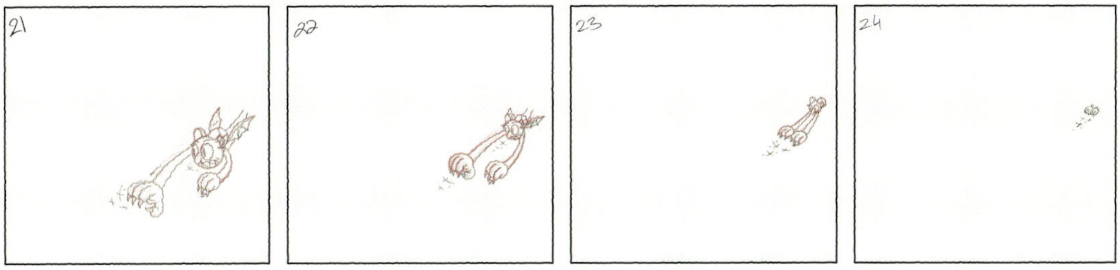

It's no coincidence that the demon and angel are presented in the same colors as Cuphead and Mugman—the red represents mischief and the blue peace, just like our heroes!

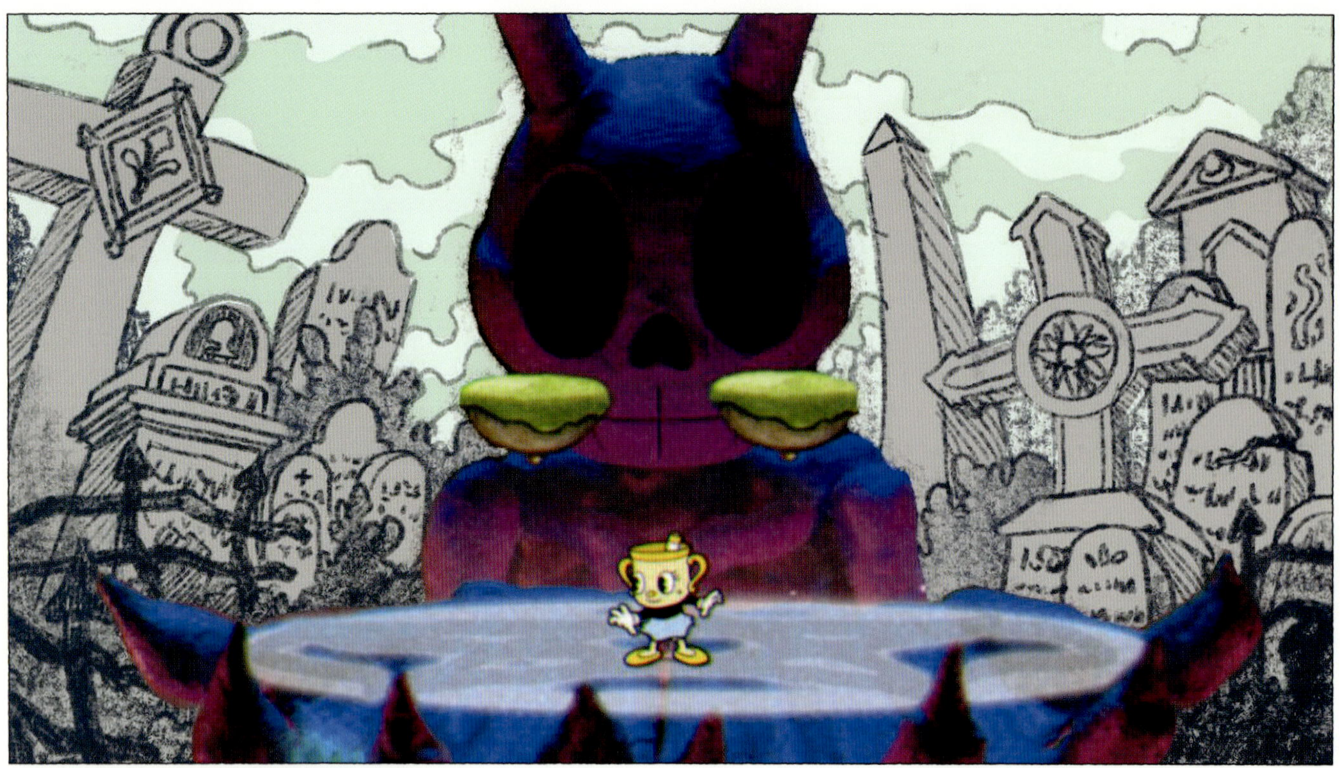

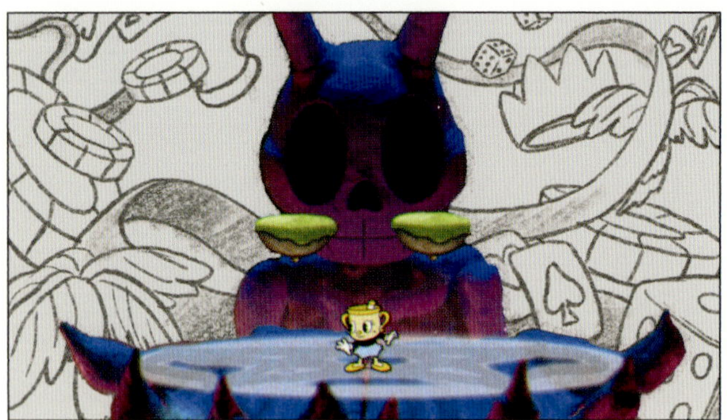

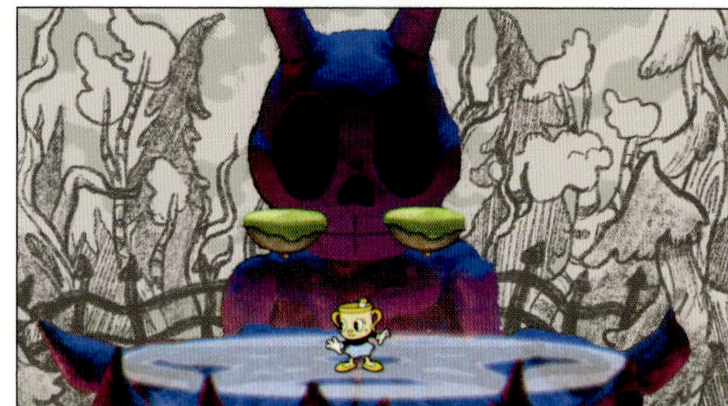

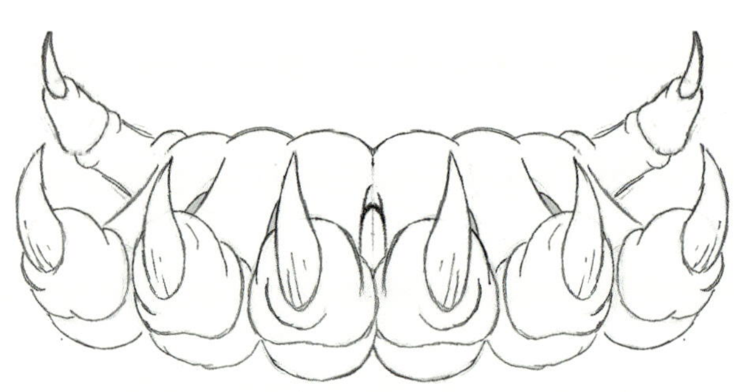

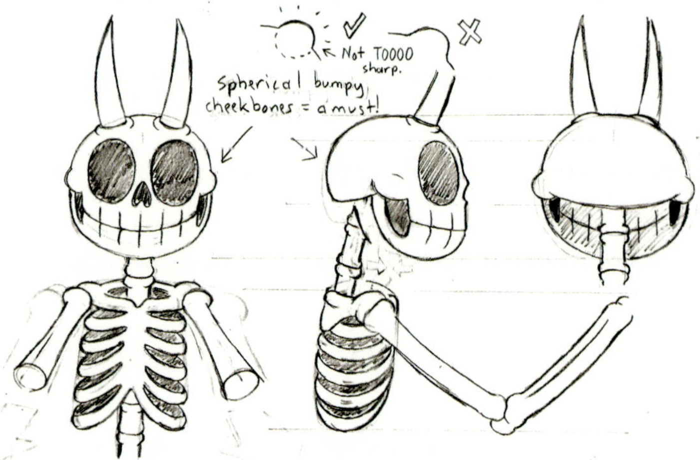

One Hell Of A Dream Background

WE'D BE HARD PRESSED to imagine anything more nightmarish for our intrepid cups than literally being the in palms of the Devil's hands! Inspired by the giant skeleton in the player select screen of Sega's 1989 arcade game *Golden Axe*, we needed to add some swirling otherworldly magic to the skeleton's hands to create a suitably flat play space for this otherwise unconventional battle. While the original stage design had two floating platforms, we eventually simplified the stage to contain a singular floating cloud with an ever-present bolt of lightning color-coded to neither the demon nor angel's morphing hazards.

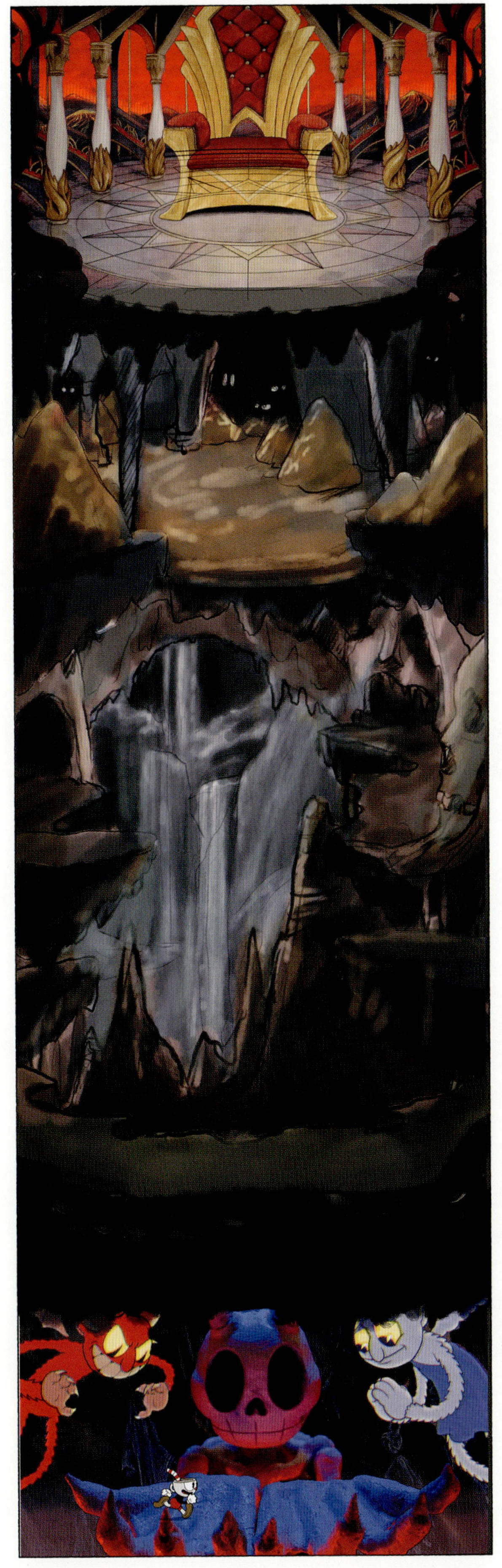

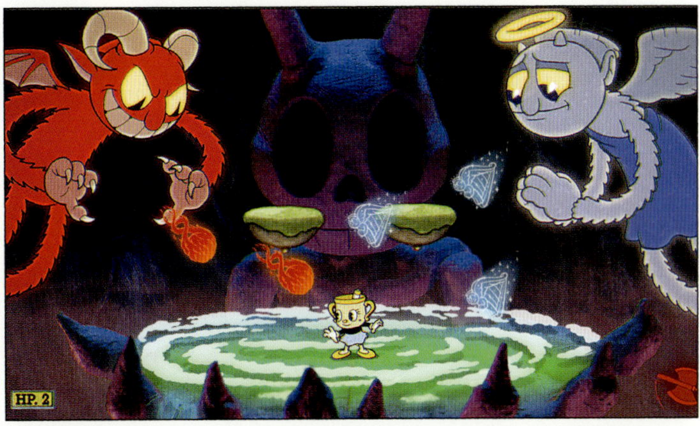
HP. 2

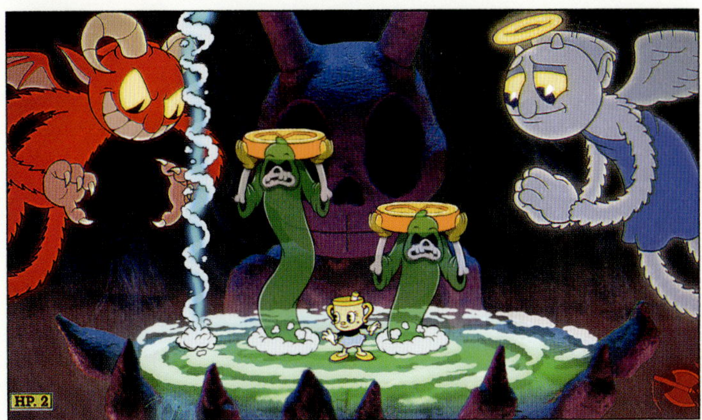
HP. 2

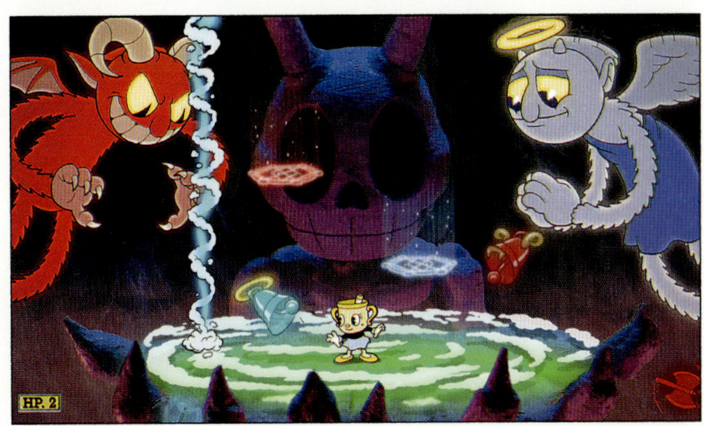
HP. 2

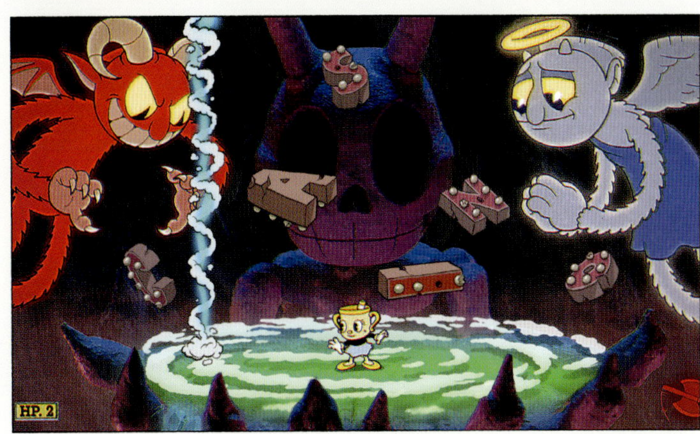
HP. 2

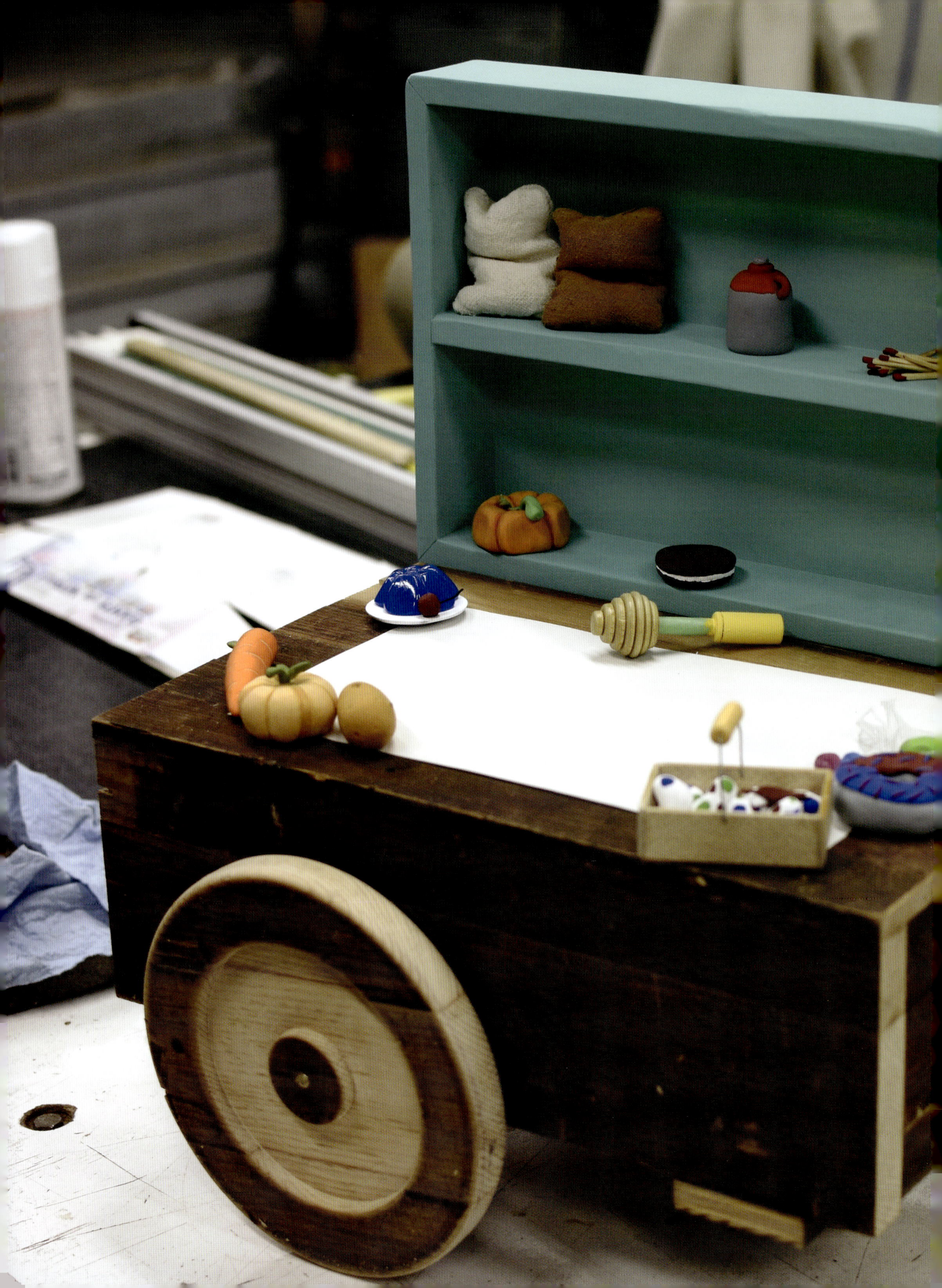

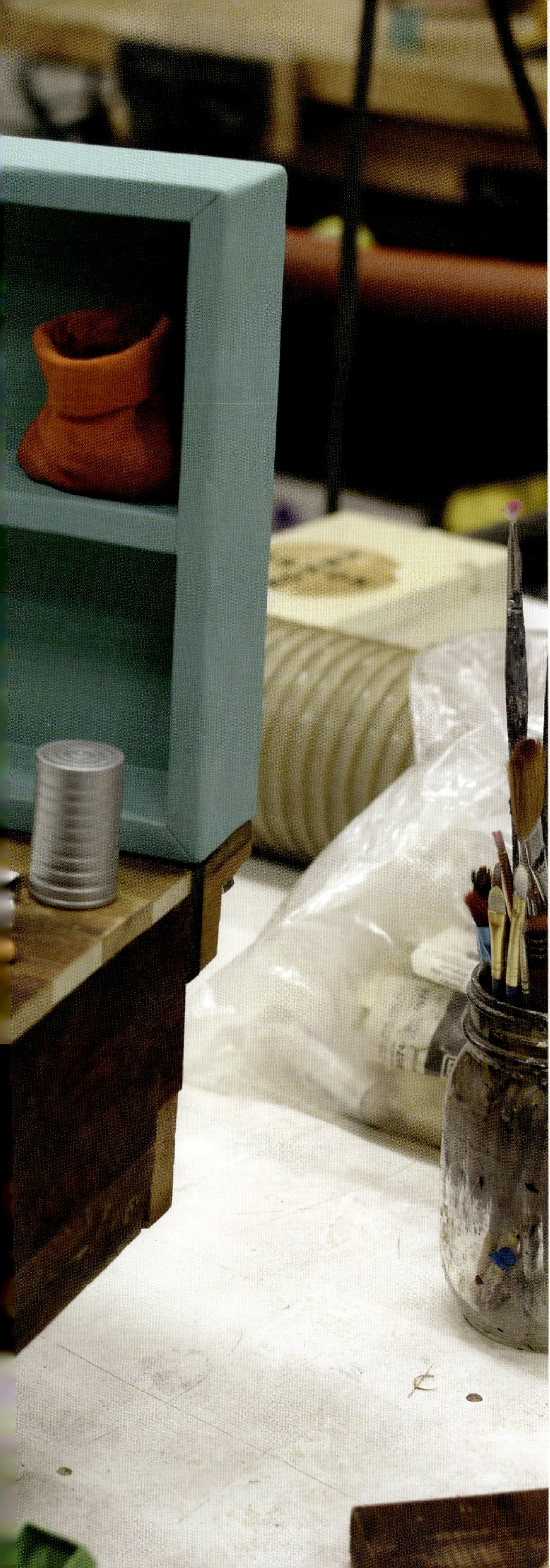

Chapter XI: Model Making and Physical Sets

THE ERA OF CARTOONING to which *Cuphead* owes its existence was defined by creativity and experimentation. In order to get the most out of the constraints within which they were working, individual artists and studios alike would push the limits of the medium by employing outside-the-box techniques for everything from animation to coloring to painting. One of the places where this is most evident was in the use of physical models as background elements for complex shots.

Perhaps the most famous example of this technique can be found in Fleischer Studios' *Popeye the Sailor Meets Sinbad the Sailor* (1936). Around eight and a half minutes into the short, as Popeye steels himself to enter the Isle of Sinbad, the scene transitions from a traditional painted background to a physically modelled cave interior, replete with jewel tone lighting and rich shadows. The technique lends the scene a sense of exaggerated realism—as if the titular sailor man is leaping off the screen and into the world around you. Inspired by this iconic moment and many like it from the era, we integrated several prominent physical model backgrounds into the original *Cuphead*, and upped the ante for *The Delicious Last Course* with even more of them. Here is a small peek behind the curtain at how those set pieces came together!

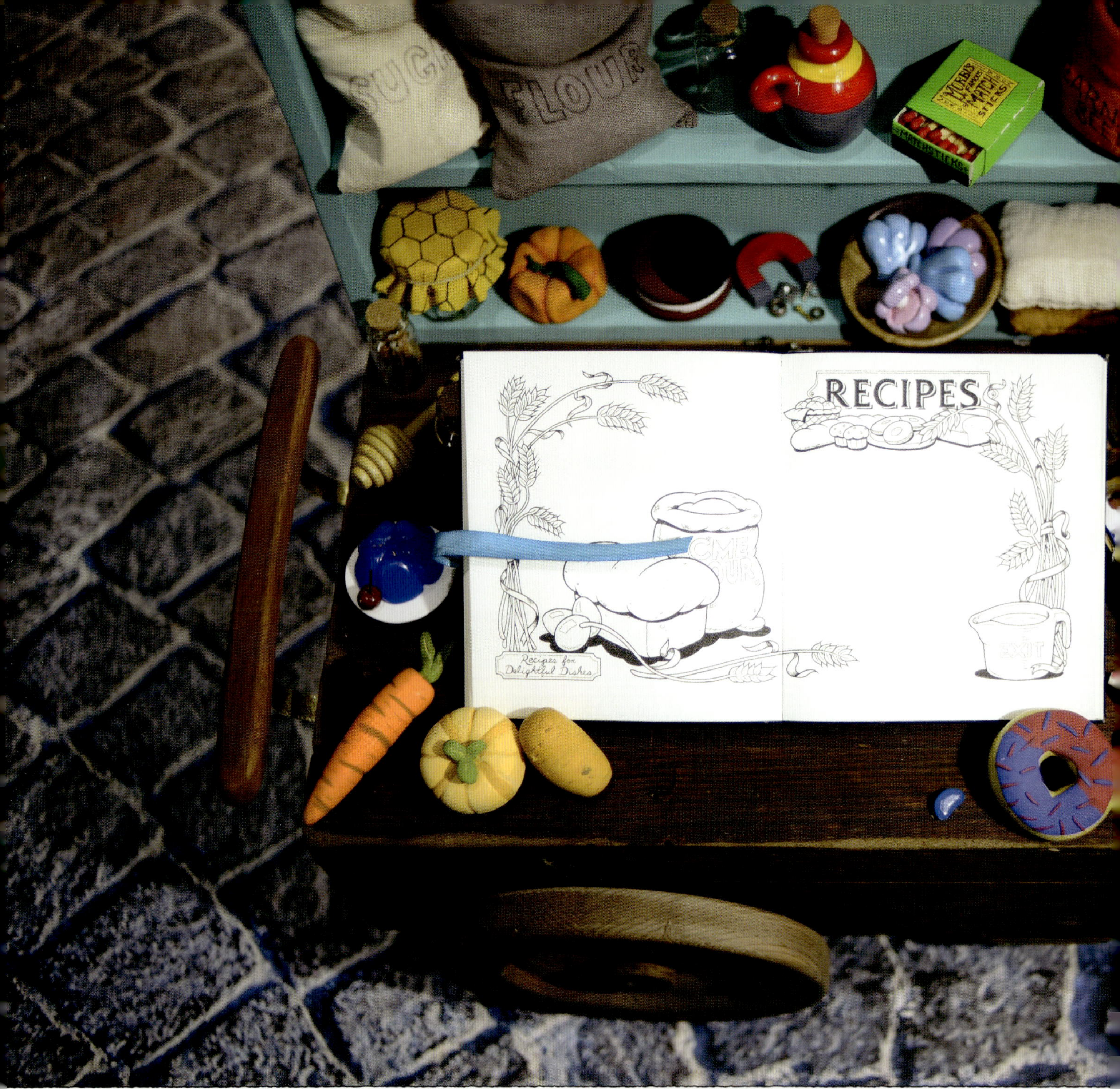

Ms. Chalice Tutorial Fabrication

IN THE WORLD OF *CUPHEAD*, all the player tutorials happen on some form of paper—from the introductory tutorial on drawing paper to the game's airplane control tutorial on blueprint paper. With *The Delicious Last Course* focusing on a quest to recover magical ingredients, it only made sense that the tutorial for Ms. Chalice's character controls be hosted within a recipe book (for what is a recipe book if not a tutorial for your meal?). Once we landed on this idea, it felt like the perfect excuse to bring in model fabricator and longtime collaborator Ali Morbi to construct a physical food cart, complete with handcrafted miniatures referencing almost all of the baddies from across the Inkwell Isles. Some standout favorites include wonderful abstractions like a plate of blue jelly representing Goopy LeGrande, a sprinkle donut whose colors match Beppi the Clown, and a pack of matches that call out to infamous dragon Grimm Matchstick. Fun fact: the matches are from imaginary brand "Morbi's Famous Matches," as a nod to the maquette maestro himself.

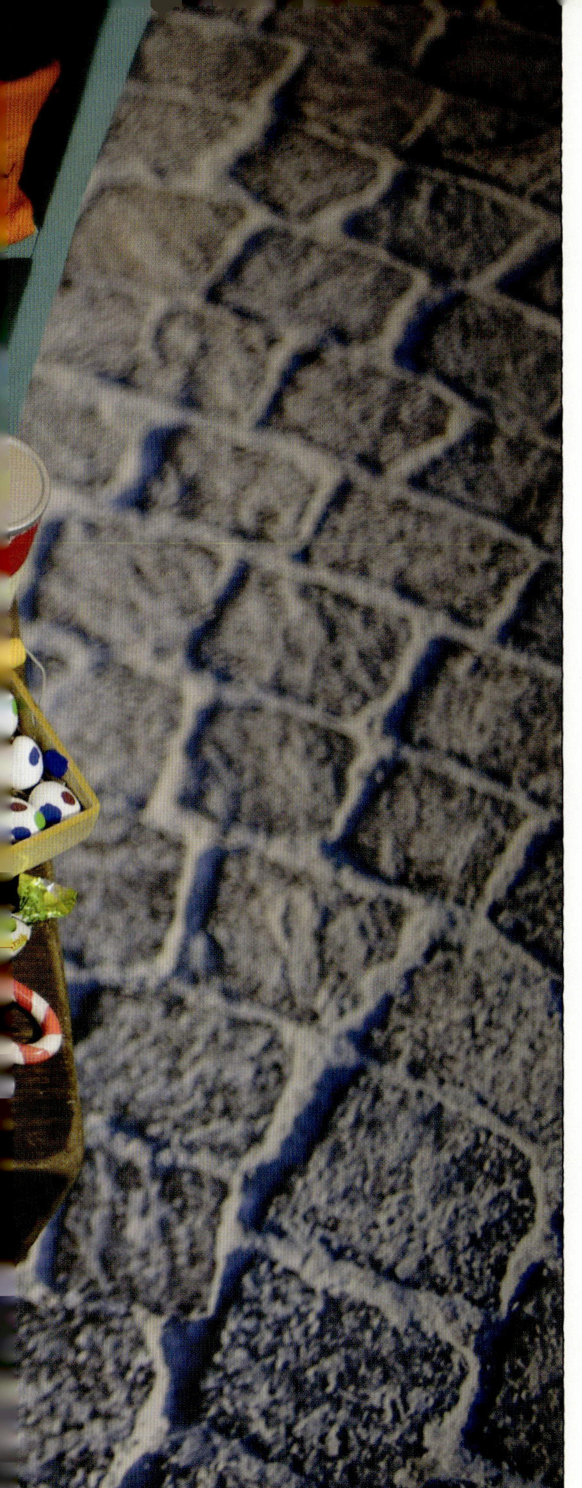

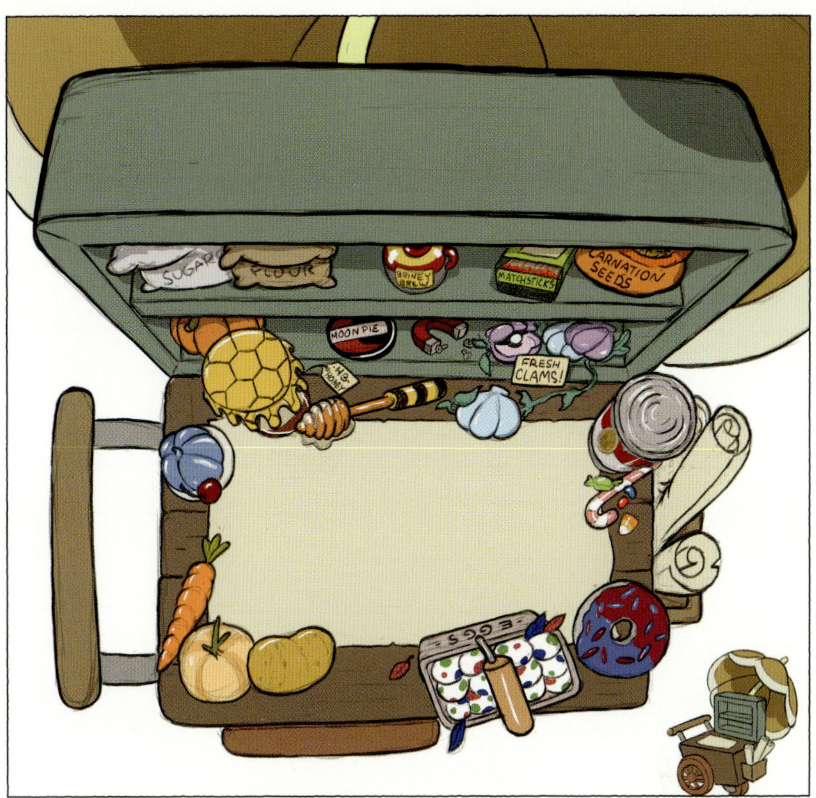

SUGAR
FLOUR
BRINEY BREW
MATCHSTICKS
CARNATION SEEDS
MOON PIE
FRESH CLAMS!
EGGS

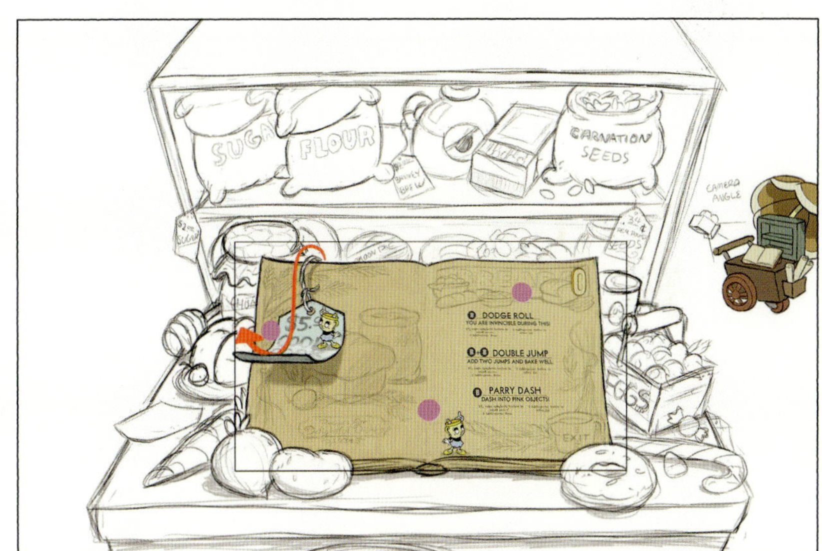

SUGA
FLOUR
BRINEY BREW
CARNATION SEEDS
CAMERA ANGLE
DODGE ROLL
YOU ARE INVINCIBLE DURING THIS!
DOUBLE JUMP
ADD TWO JUMPS AND BAKE WELL
PARRY DASH
DASH INTO PINK OBJECTS
EGGS
EXIT

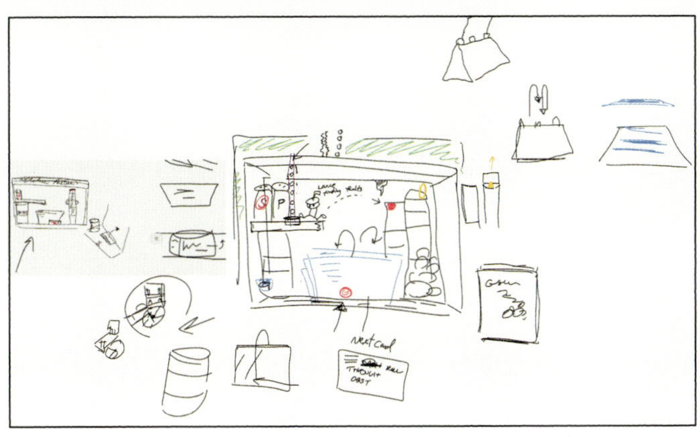

next card

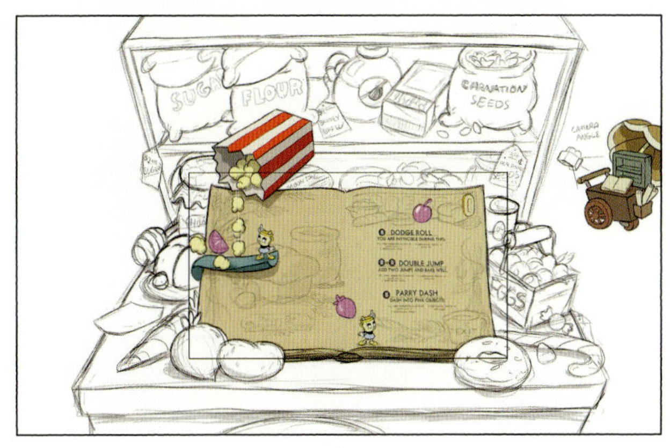

SUGA
FLOUR
CARNATION SEEDS
CAMERA ANGLE
DODGE ROLL
DOUBLE JUMP
PARRY DASH
EGGS

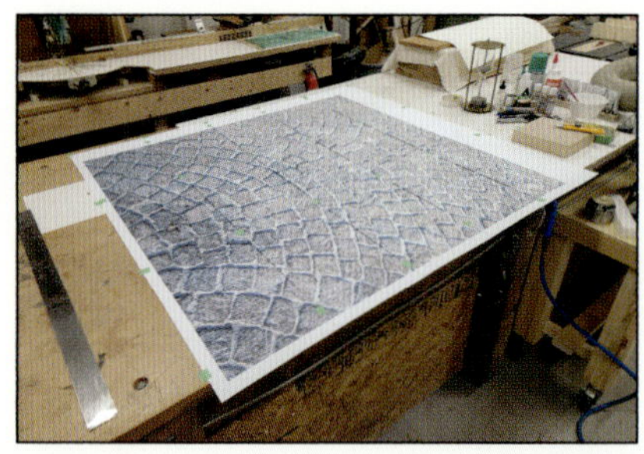

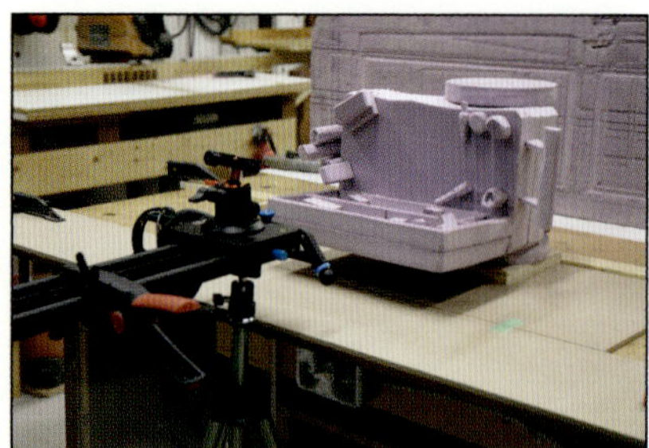

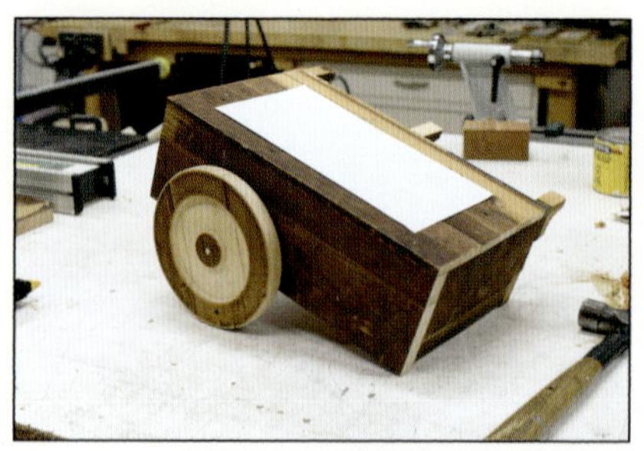

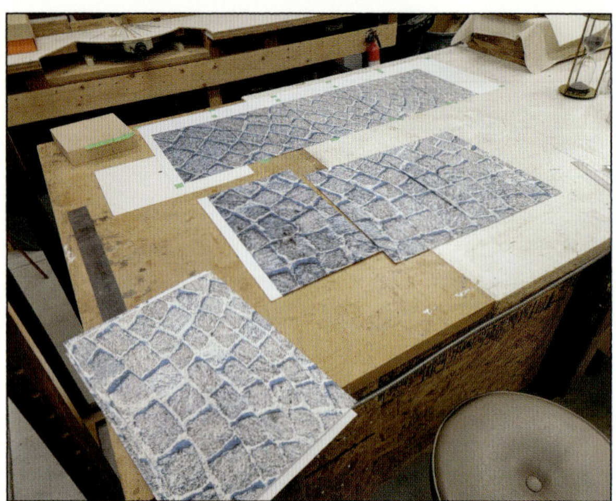

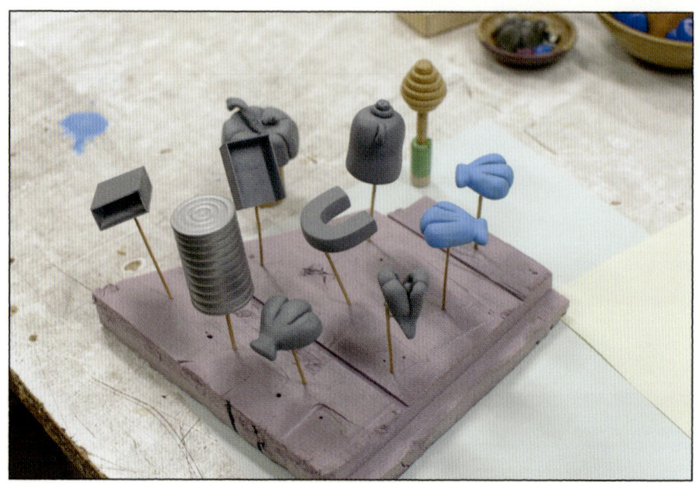

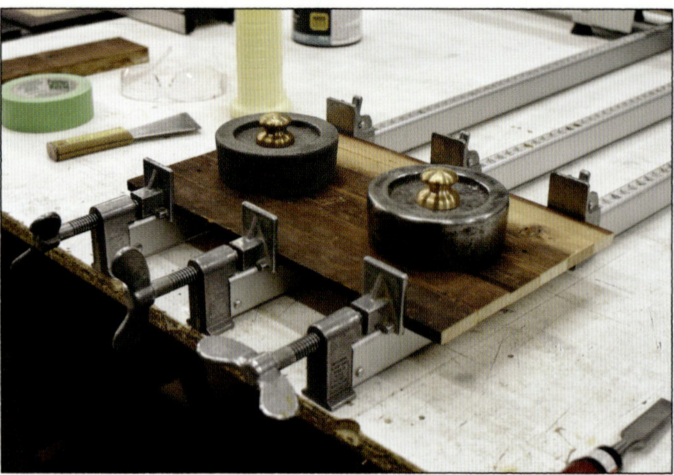

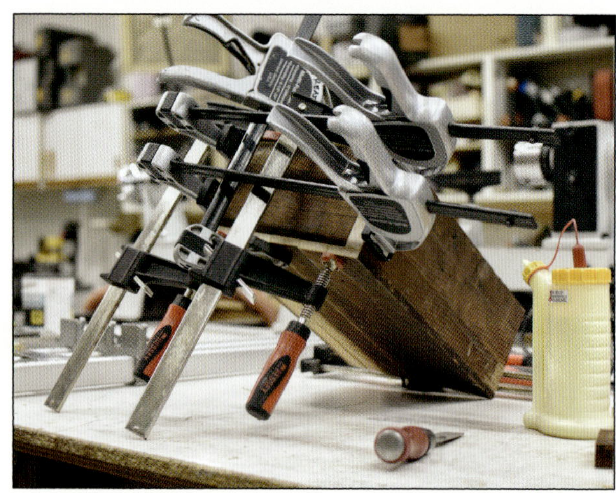

A rare look inside Model Fabricator Ali Morbi's workshop where the Ms. Chalice tutorial cart was assembled. The massive black apparatus you see, pictured page right, is a camera rig used to execute the zoom shot players see when opening the tutorial.

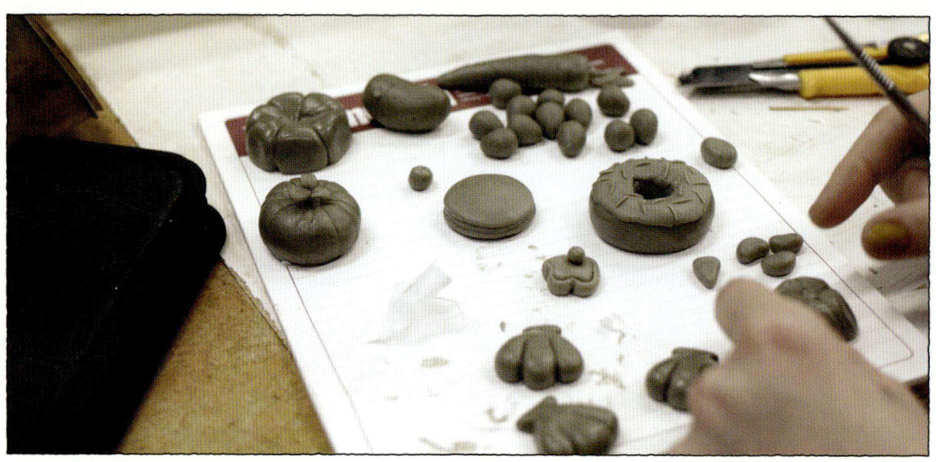

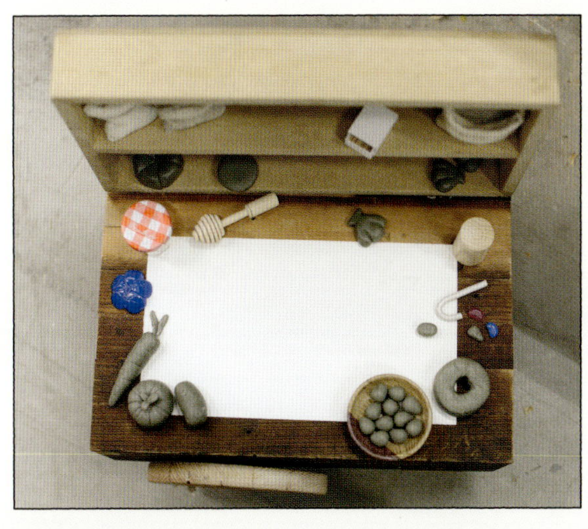

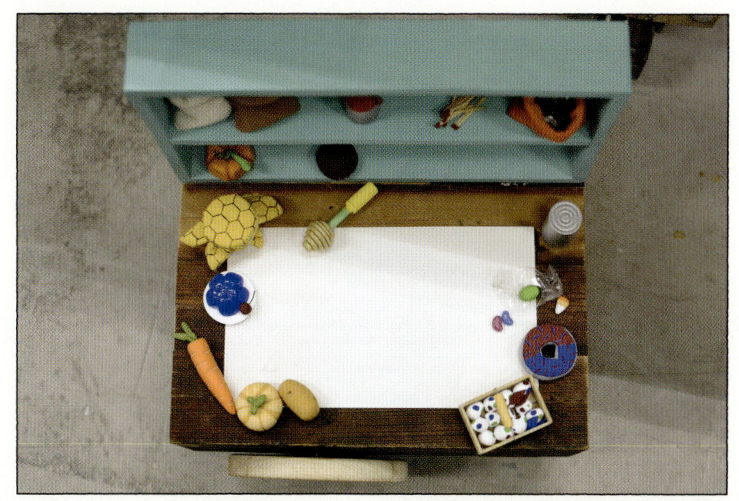

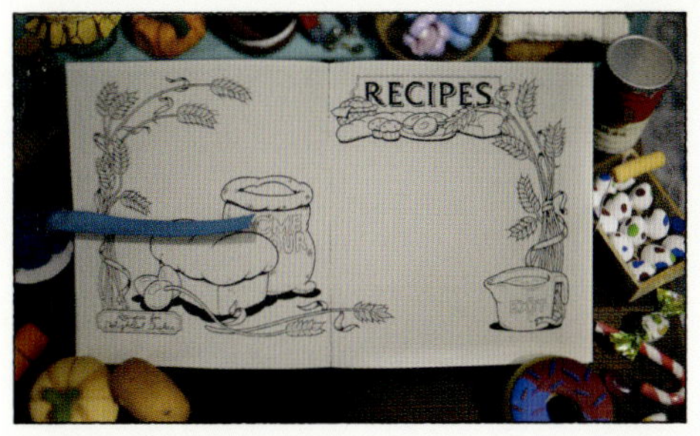
RECIPES

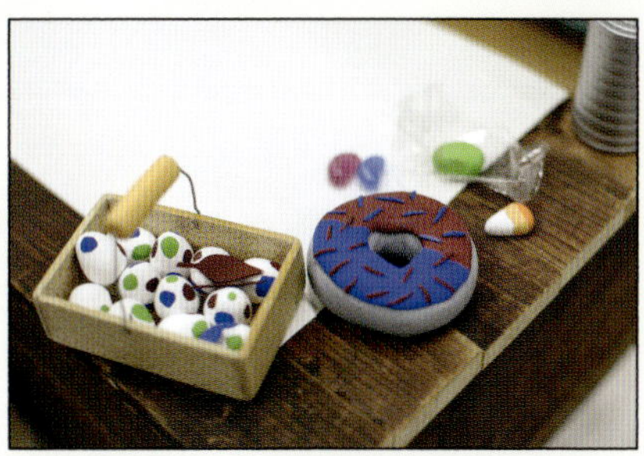

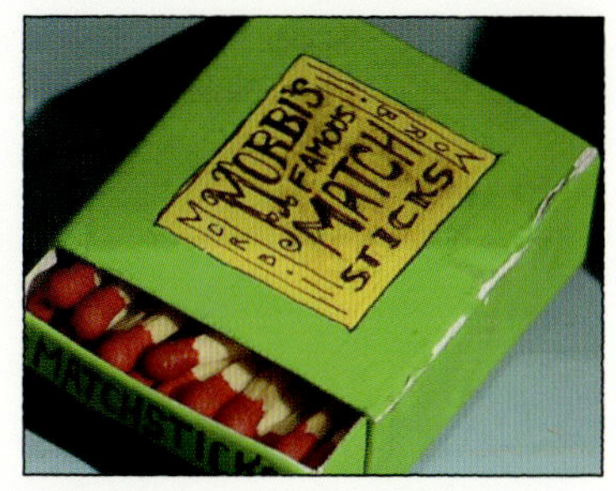
MORBI'S
FAMOUS
MATCH
STICKS

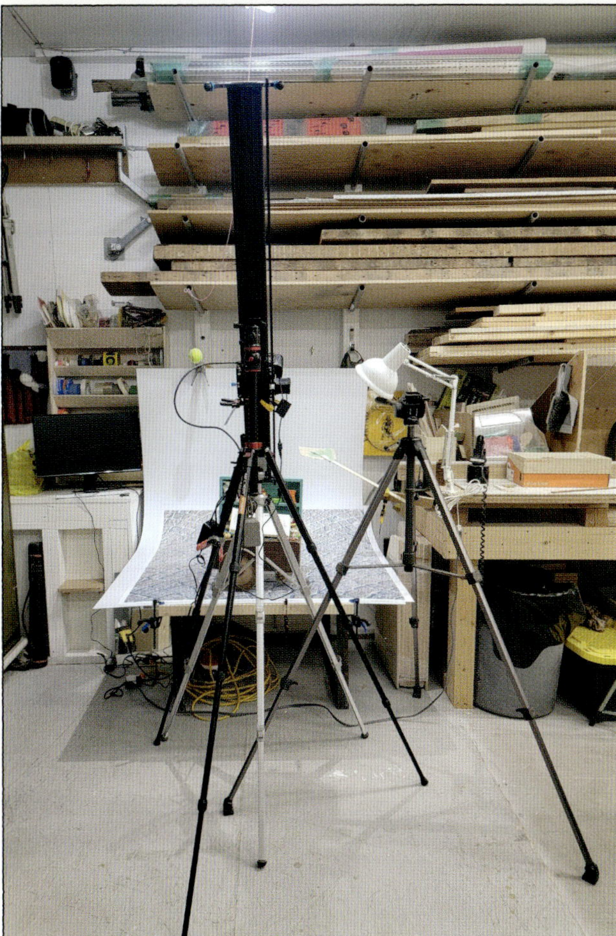

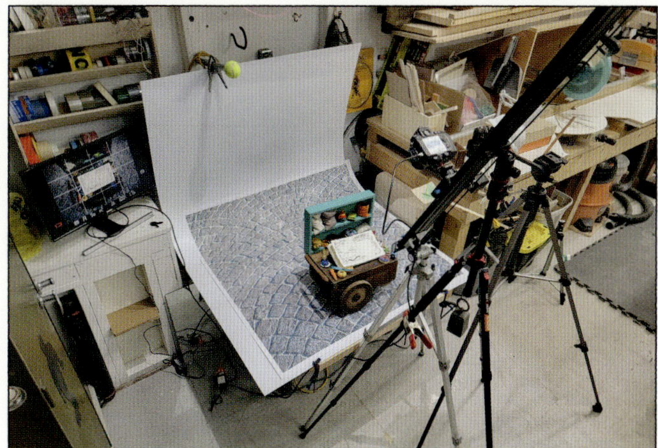

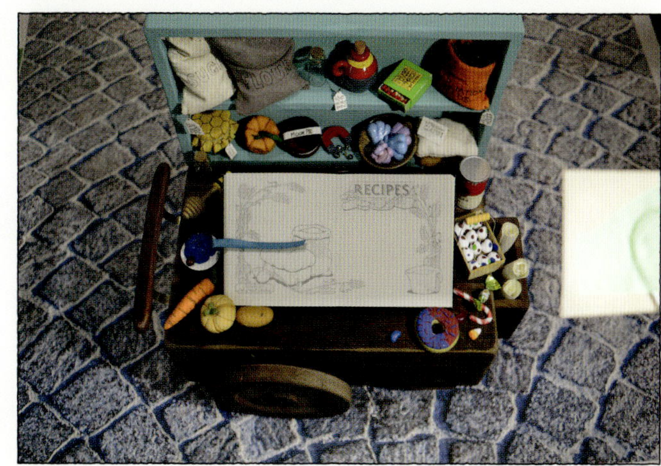
RECIPES

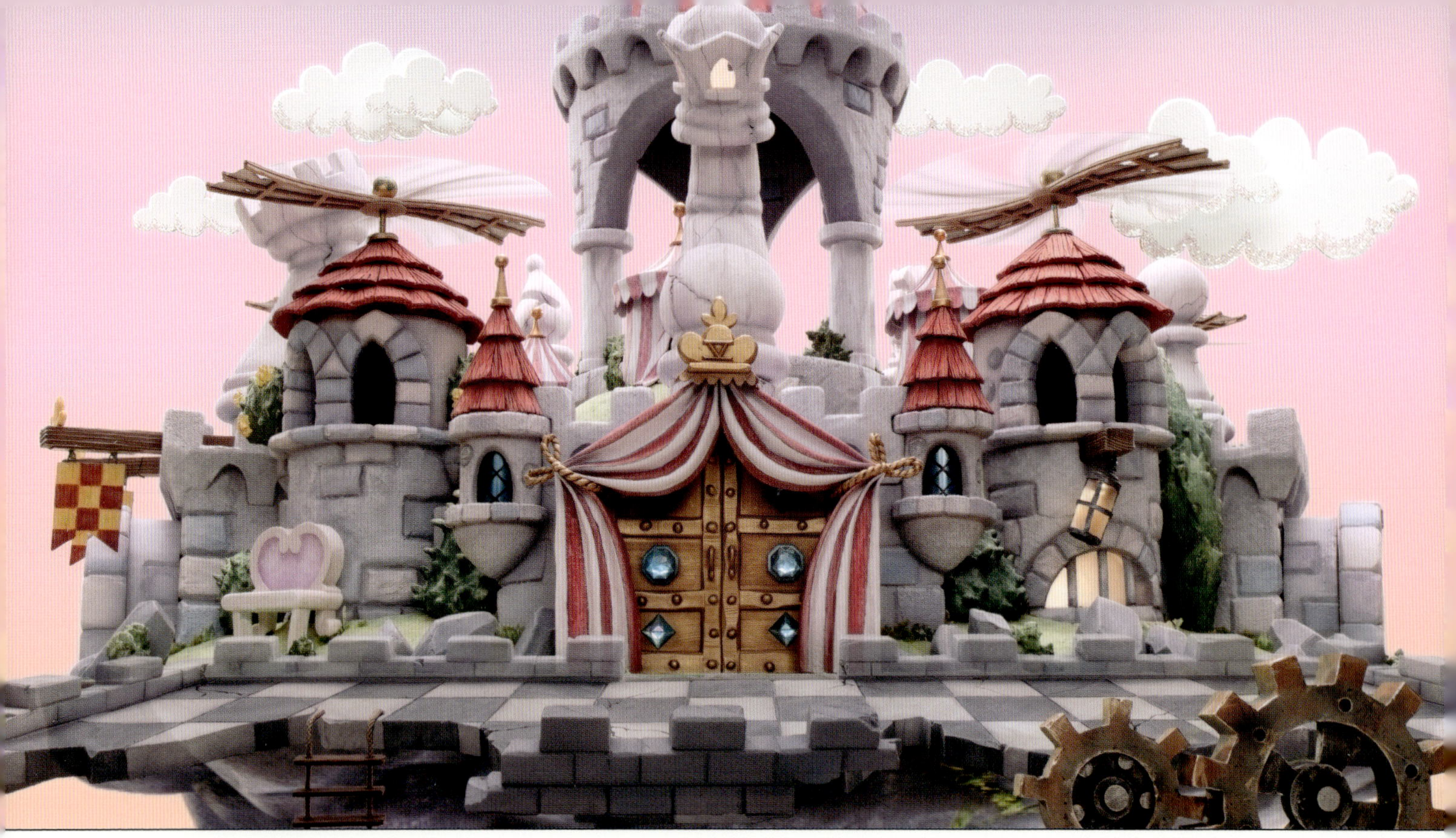

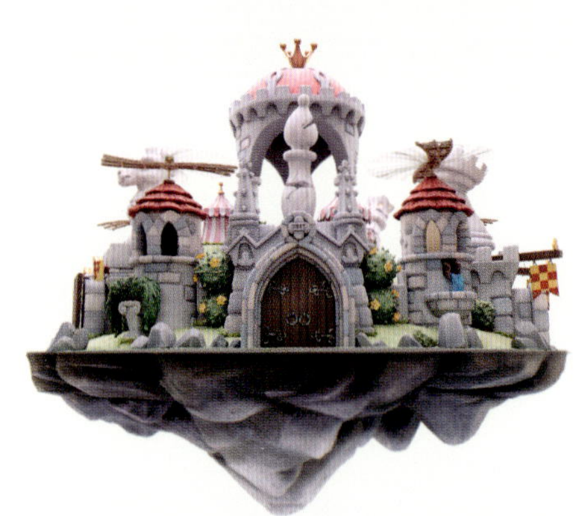

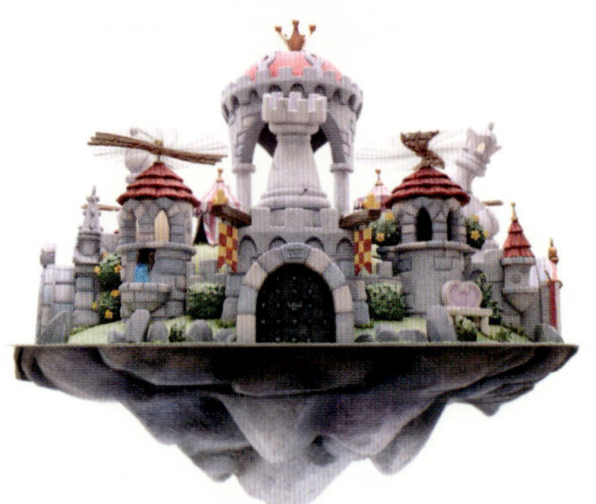

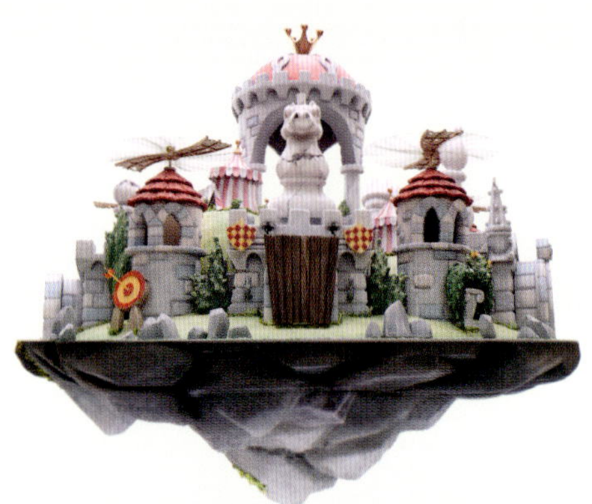

King's Leap Set Fabrication

FAR AND AWAY THE most complex piece of filmed model work ever included in the world of *Cuphead*, the portal for the King's Leap stages is in many ways the *pièce de résistance* of *The Delicious Last Course*. Created over several months by the talented team of fabricators and artists at Screen Novelties in Los Angeles, and then filmed from all angles in stop motion, the King's castle represents the most interactive physical model we've ever included in the game. The seemingly mechanized castle moves in response to the actions of our animated characters—the King of Games pulling a lever to rotate the platform and the various doors opening to new boss battles, for example. Aesthetically, the final design was inspired by the prescient inventions and schematics of famed artist Leonard DaVinci, complete with propellers and interlocking gears. Look closely as you play, and you'll even notice the chess piece parapets rotate with the castle to face the most eye-catching direction as it spins!

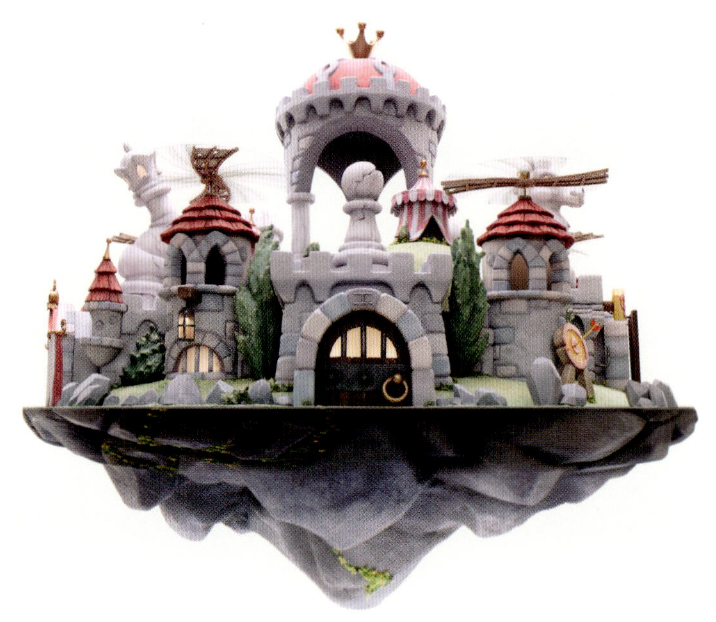

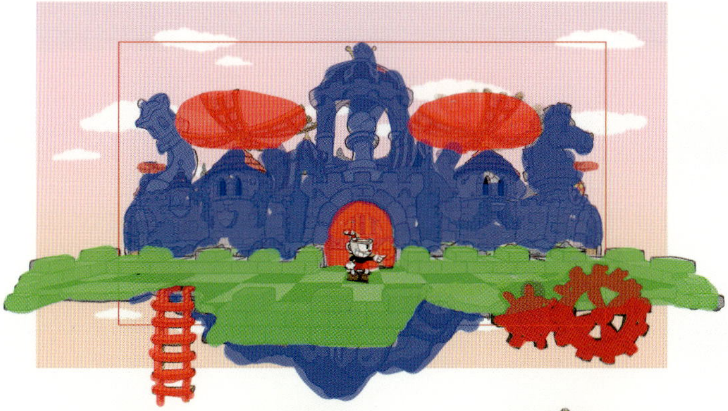

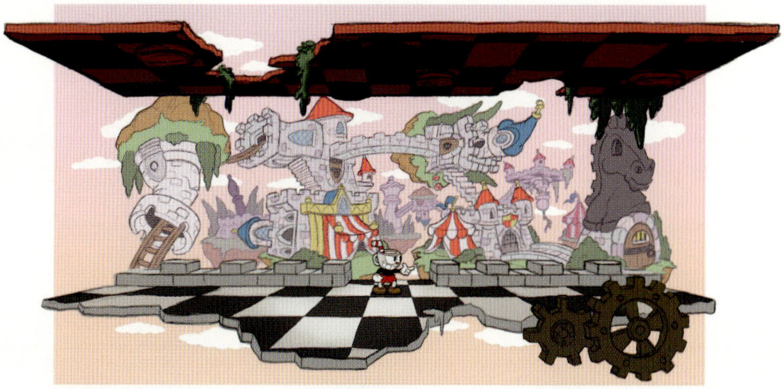

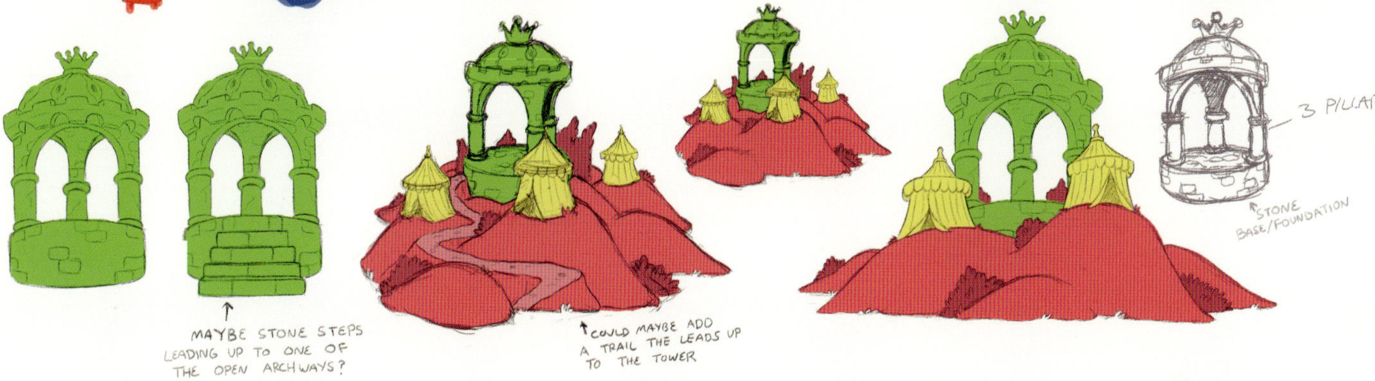

MAYBE STONE STEPS LEADING UP TO ONE OF THE OPEN ARCHWAYS?

COULD MAYBE ADD A TRAIL THE LEADS UP TO THE TOWER

3 PILLARS

STONE BASE/FOUNDATION

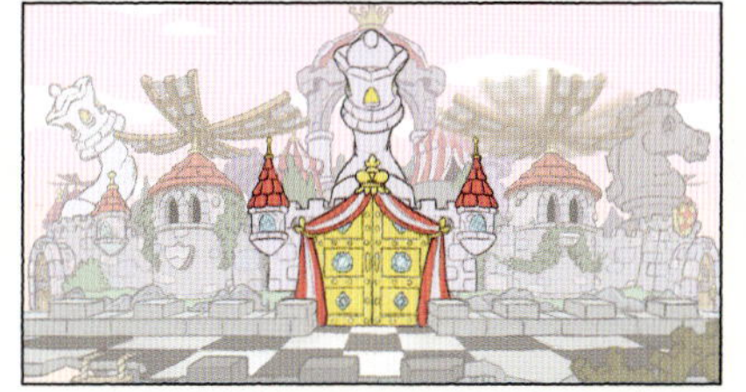

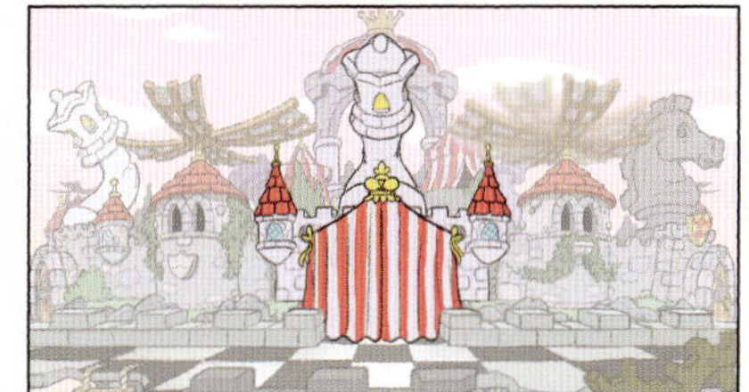

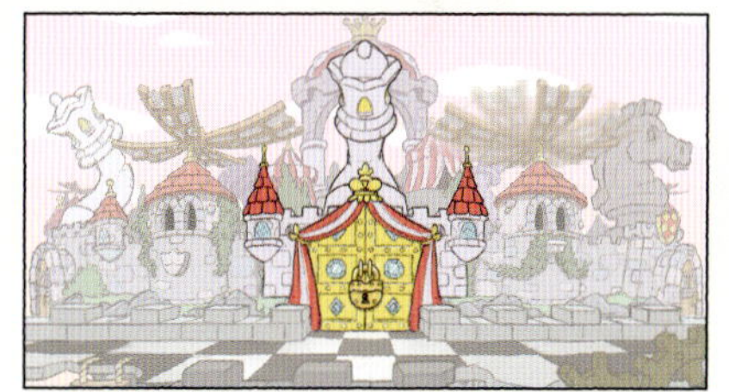

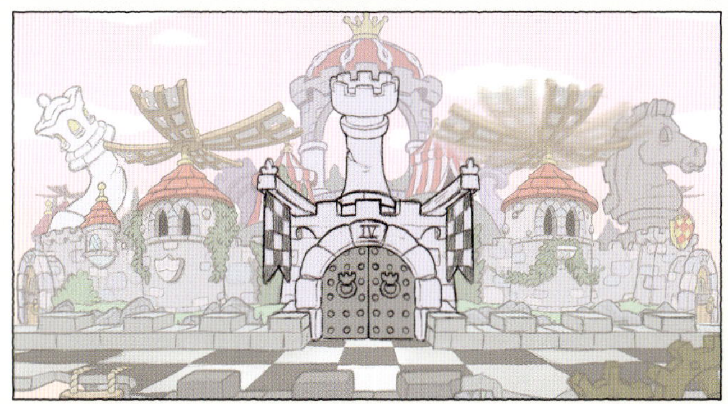

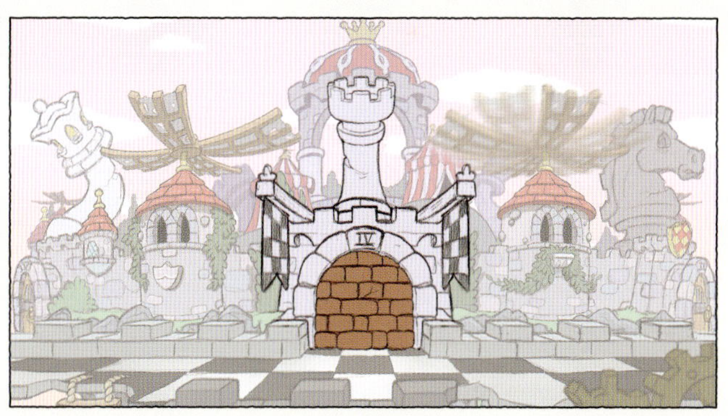

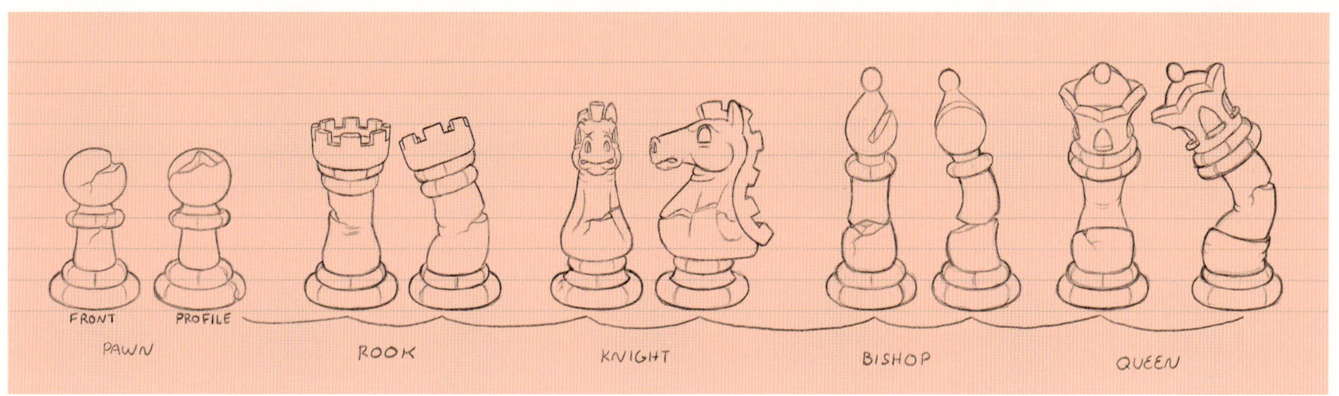

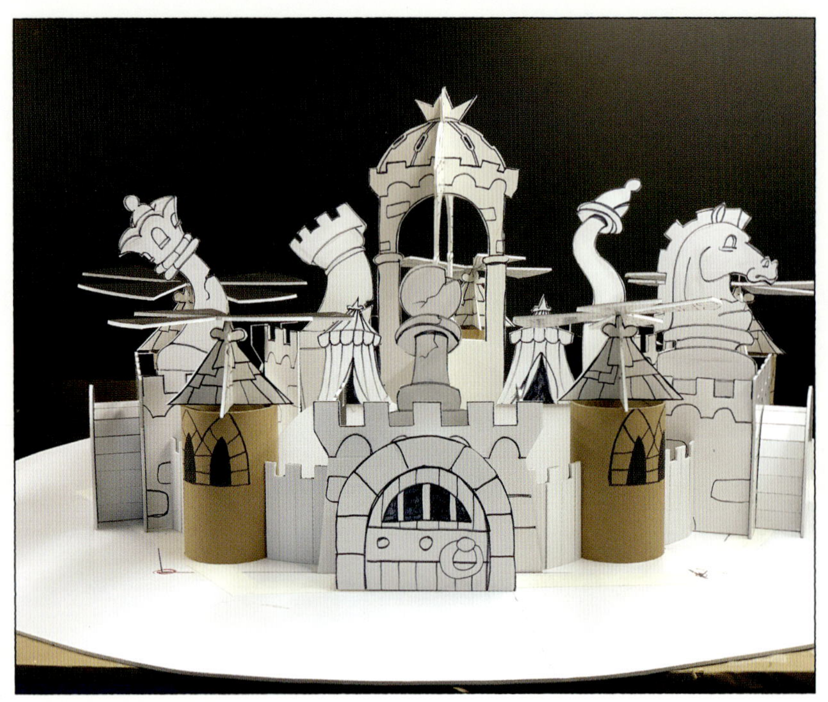

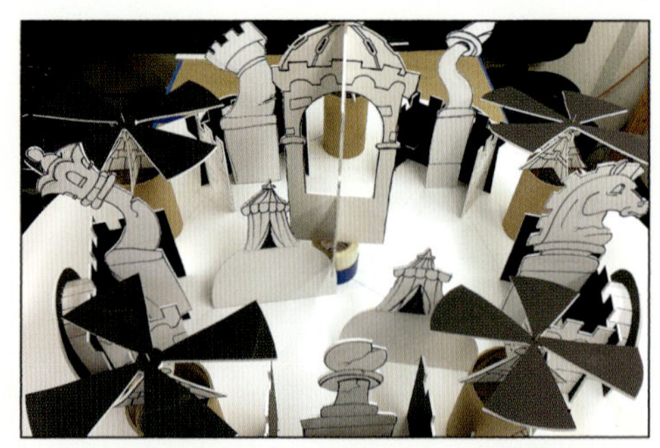

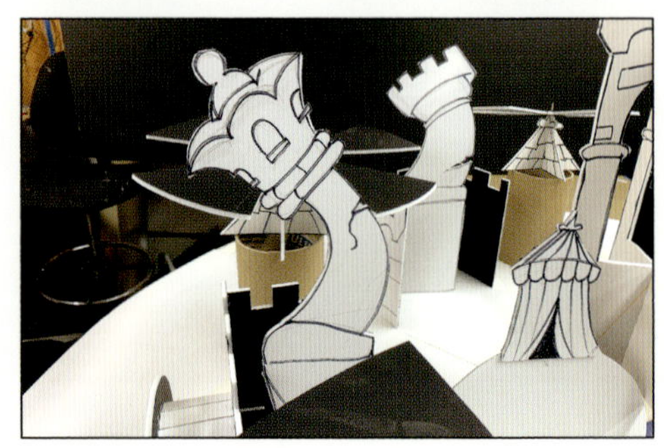

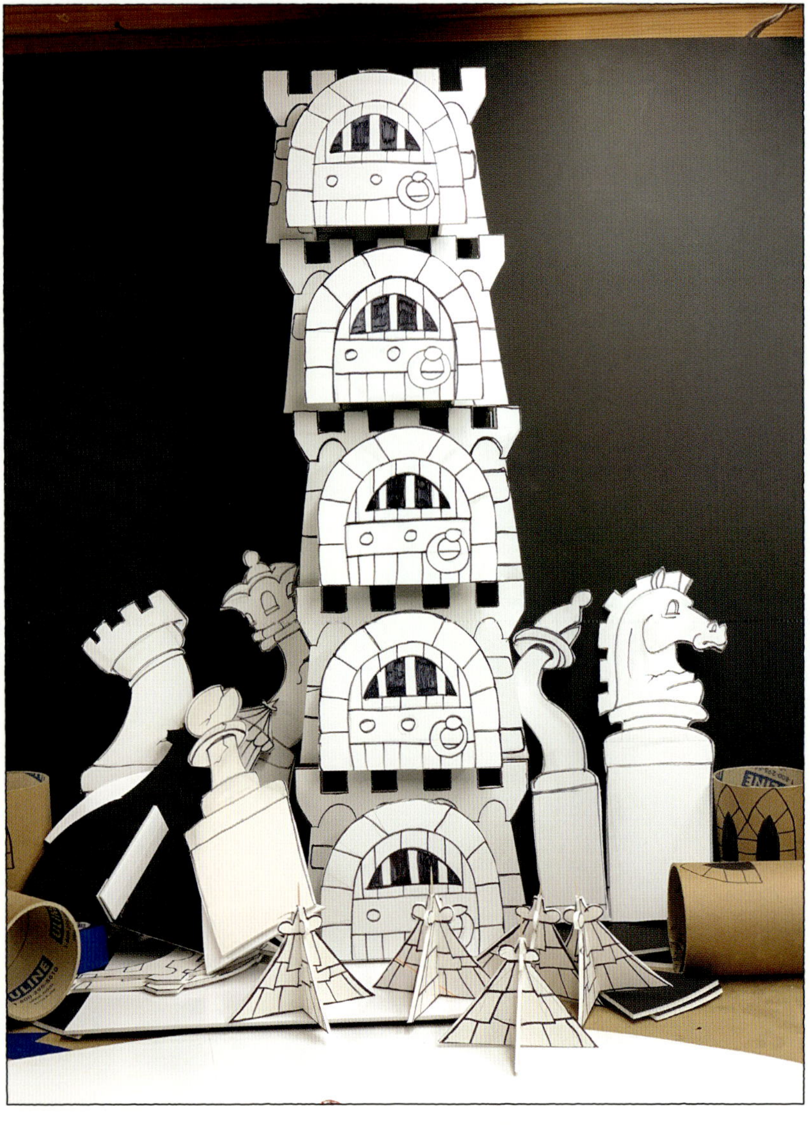

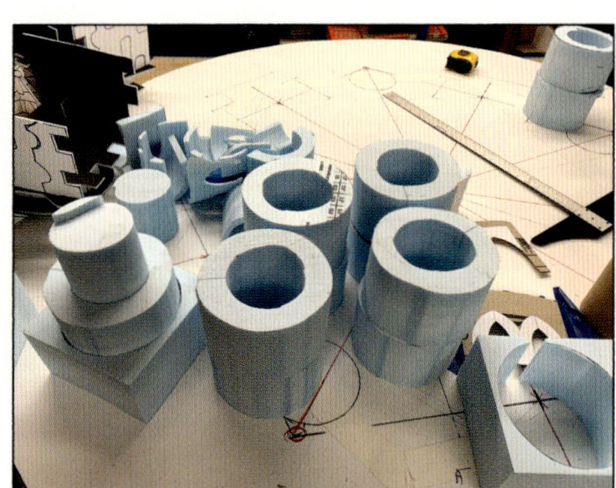

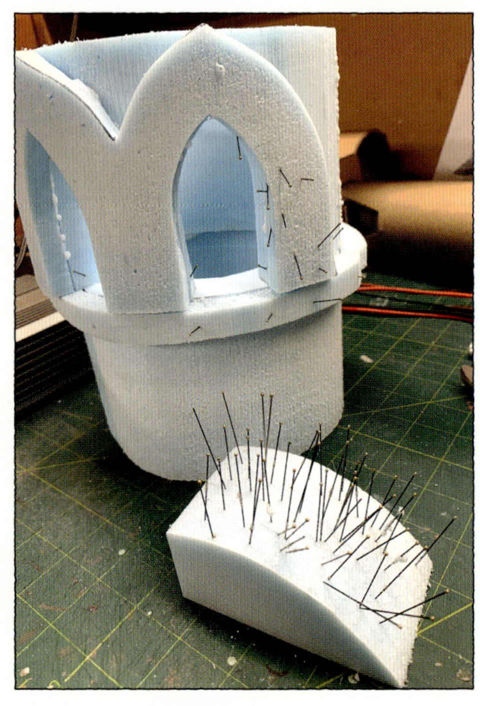

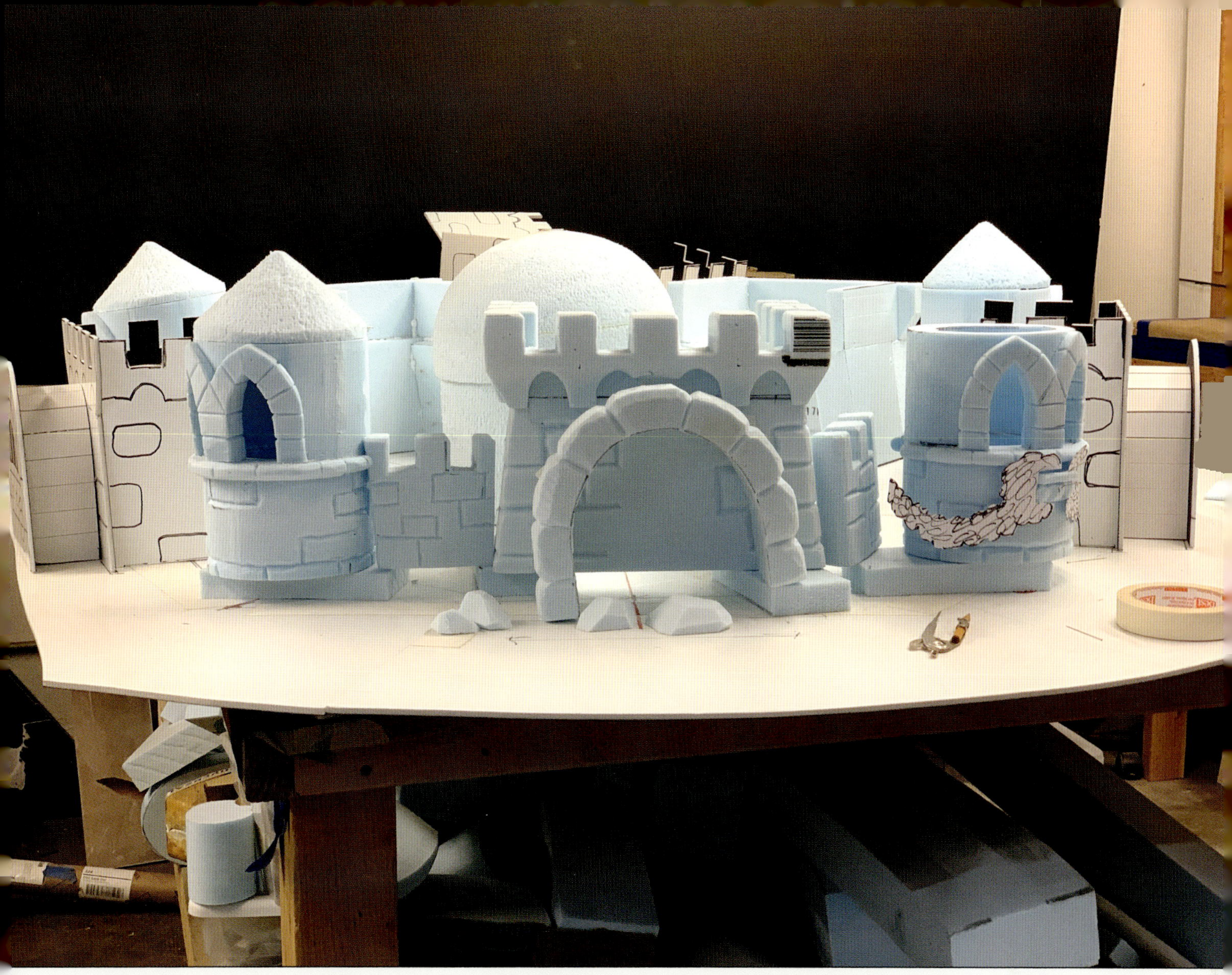

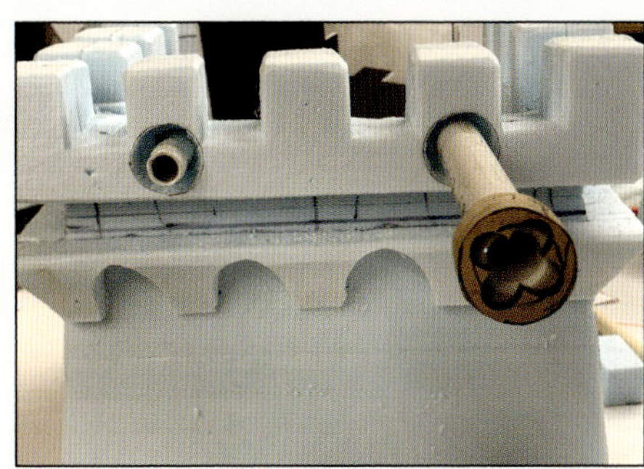

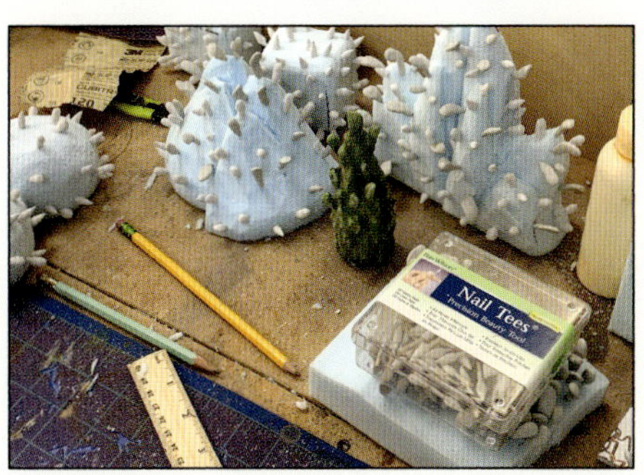

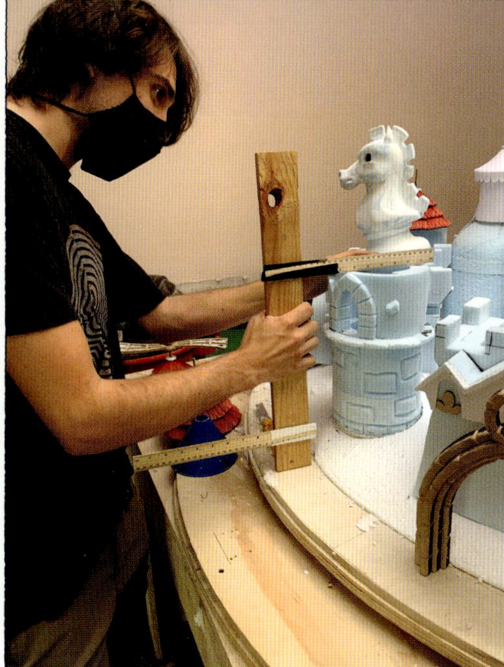

Every second counts on a project like the King's Leap, so the team at Screen Novelties begins their work by capturing the look and feel of the set with materials like paper and cardboard to quickly validate assumptions.

Once the design and direction of the model is locked, fabrication and filming begins in earnest. With so many individual moving elements, it is often necessary to film small pieces of the larger whole in isolation—as seen below, left, with the filming of just a single door. All told, the final King's Leap set represents 170 frames of animation for the core castle rotation, with many hundreds more layered atop for odds and ends like spinning towers, rotating propellers, and turning gears. Meticulousness is the name of the game throughout this process, as seen below on page right, with each unique component of the castle often having its own touch-up and care instructions!

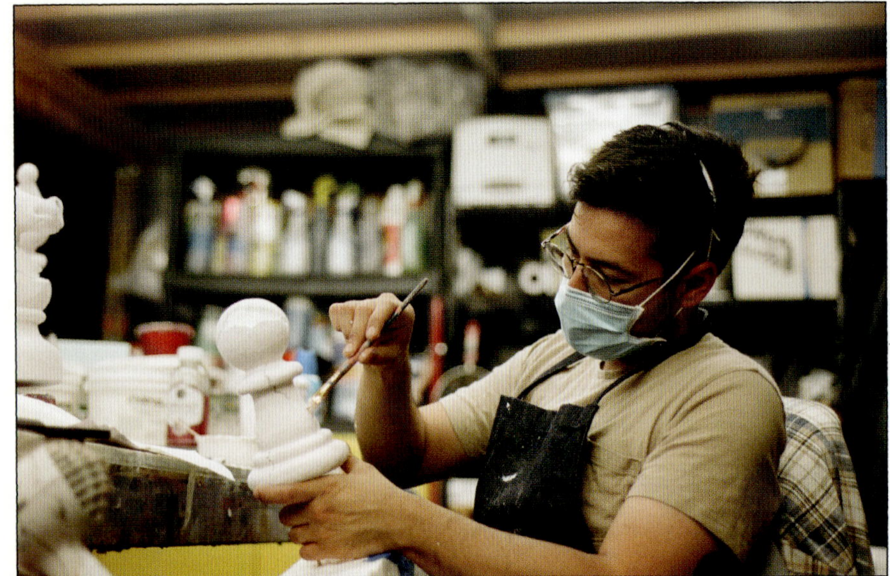

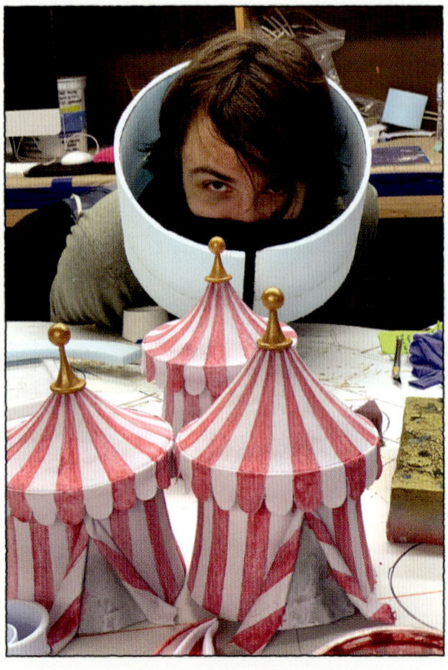

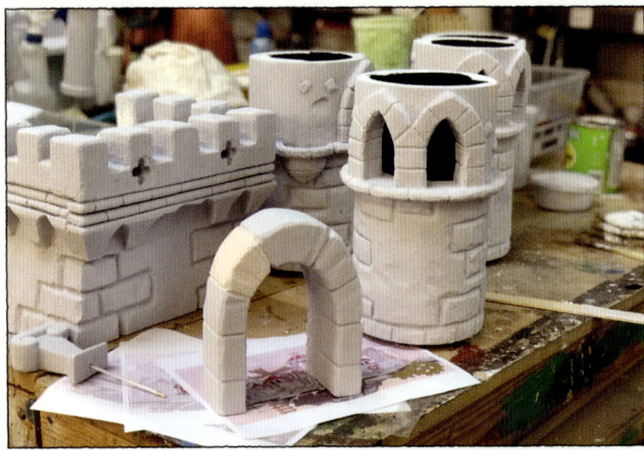

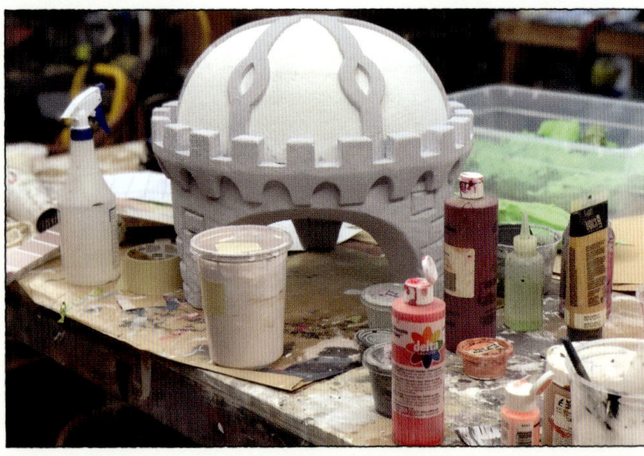

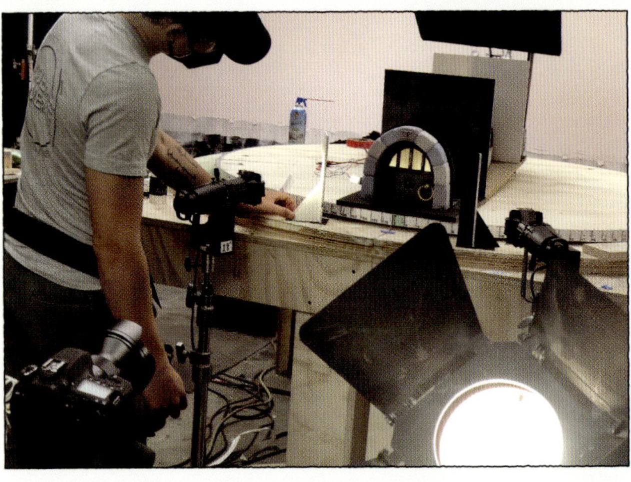

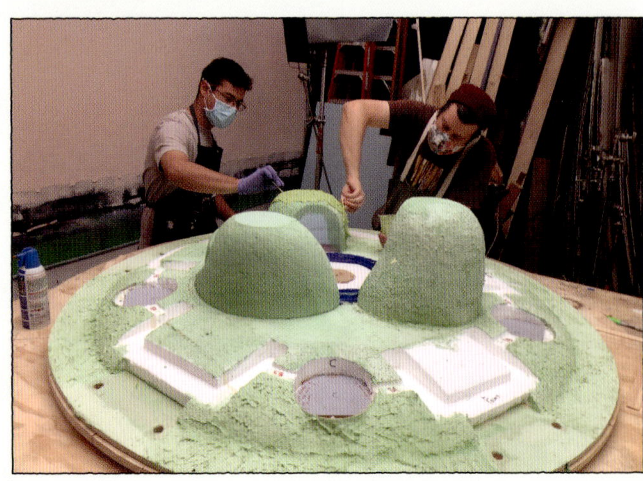

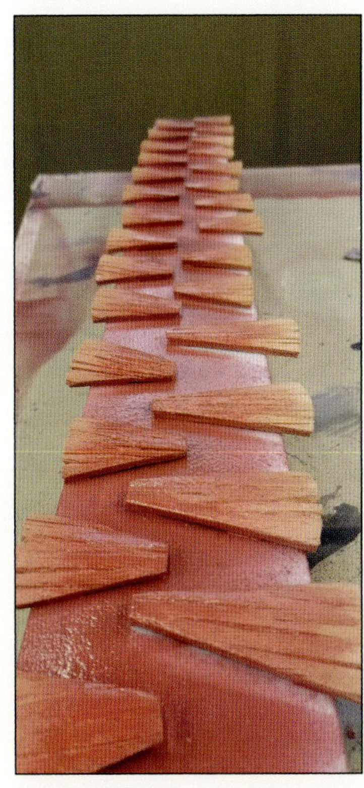

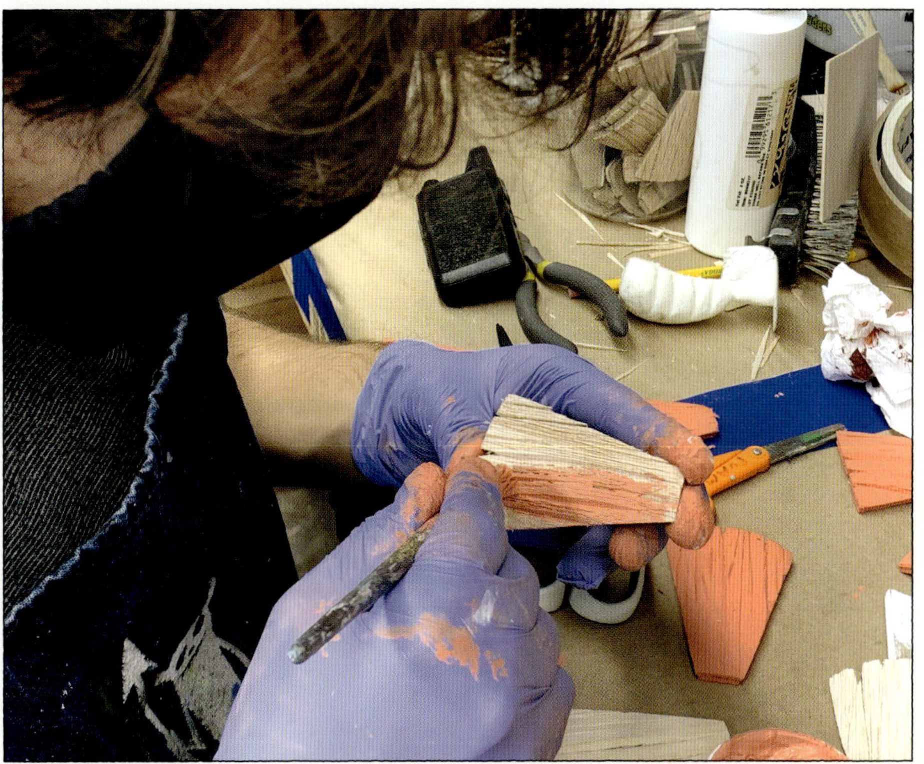

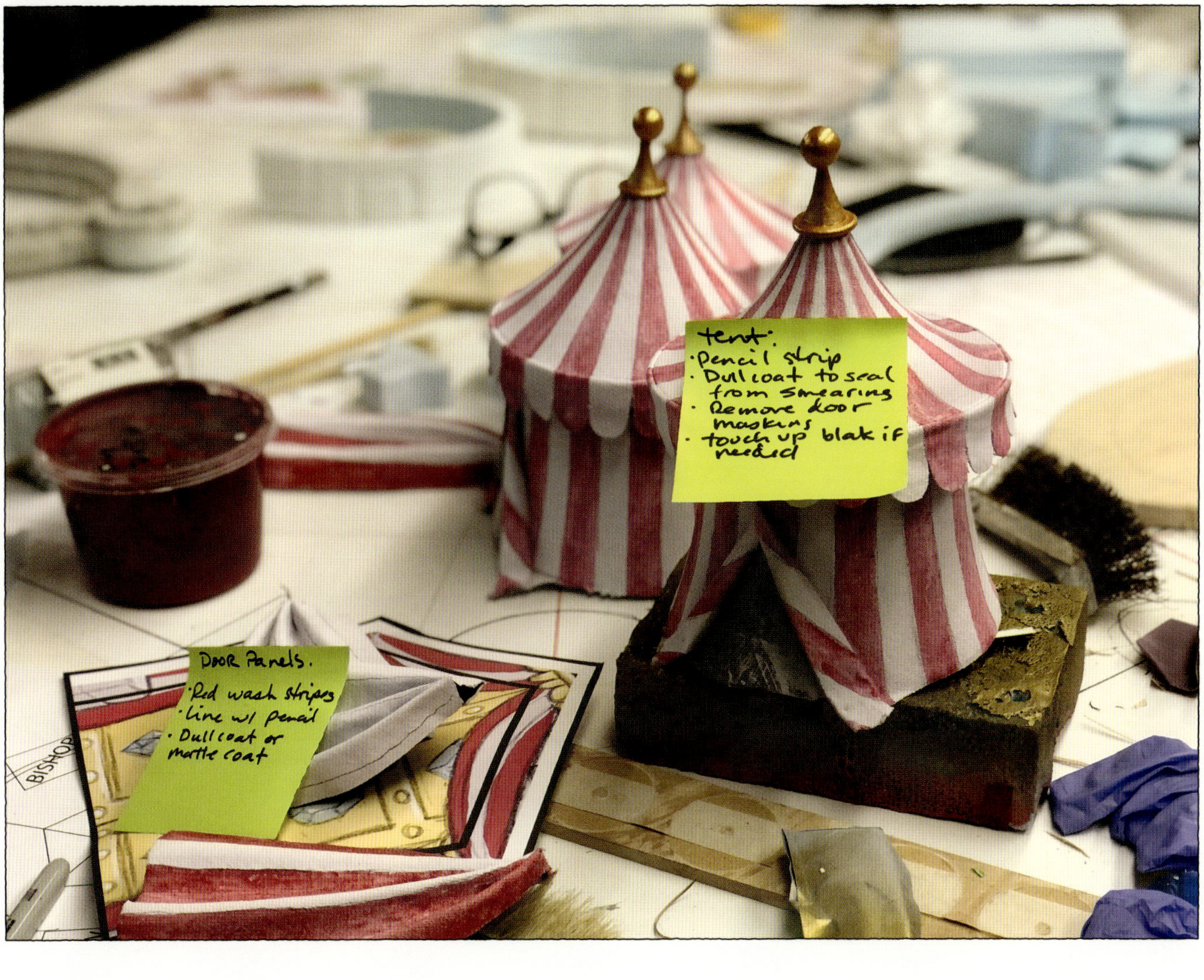

tent:
·Pencil strip
·Dullcoat to seal from smearing
·Remove door masking
·touch up blak if needed
Door Panels.
·Red wash stripes
·Line w/ pencil
·Dullcoat or matte coat
BISHOP

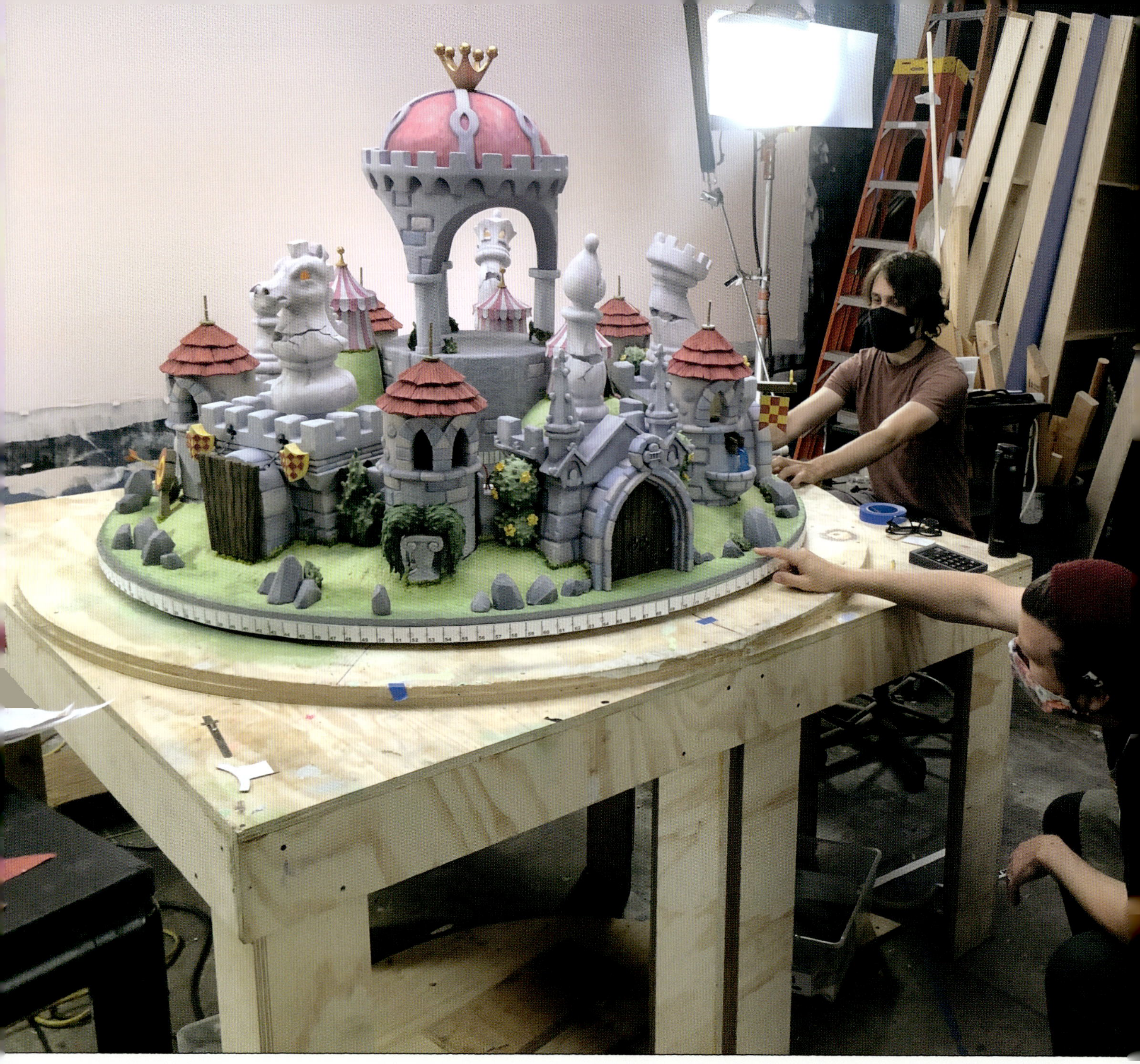

Arguably the "secret sauce" of the King's Leap set is the castle garden atop which it is built, which functions as its method of rotation. Think of the base of the model like a "lazy susan" rotating table tray, which can move the castle seamlessly around in a circle. This allowed Screen Novelties to film and light the castle from all angles and set up new shots more efficiently. Seen to the right, more delightful details from the team's amazing fabrication process, including the clever hiding of wiring connected to the lights inside of the chess piece statues atop the castle.

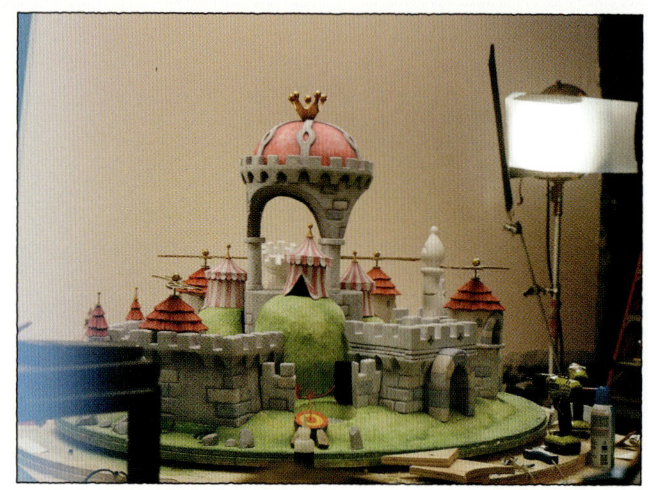

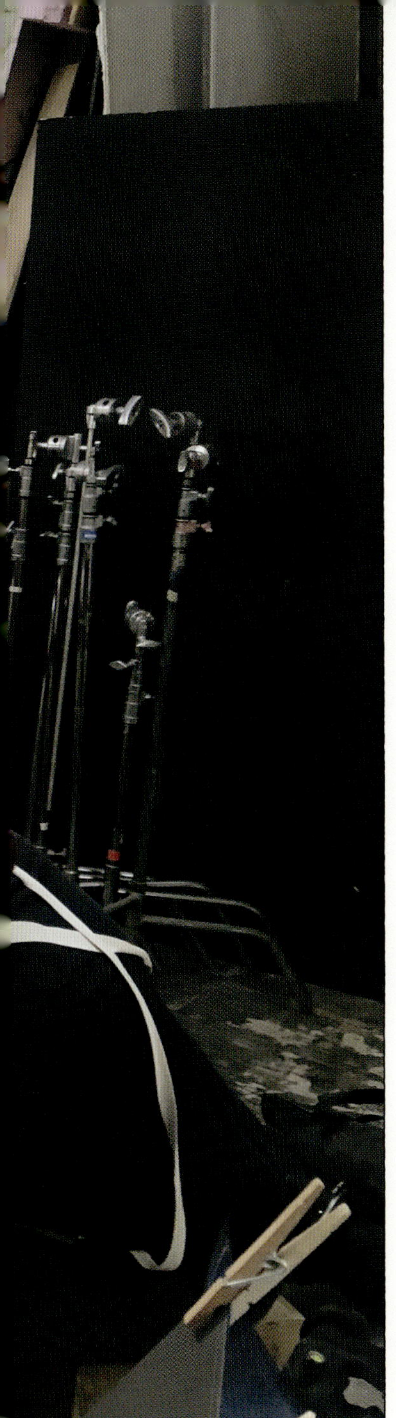

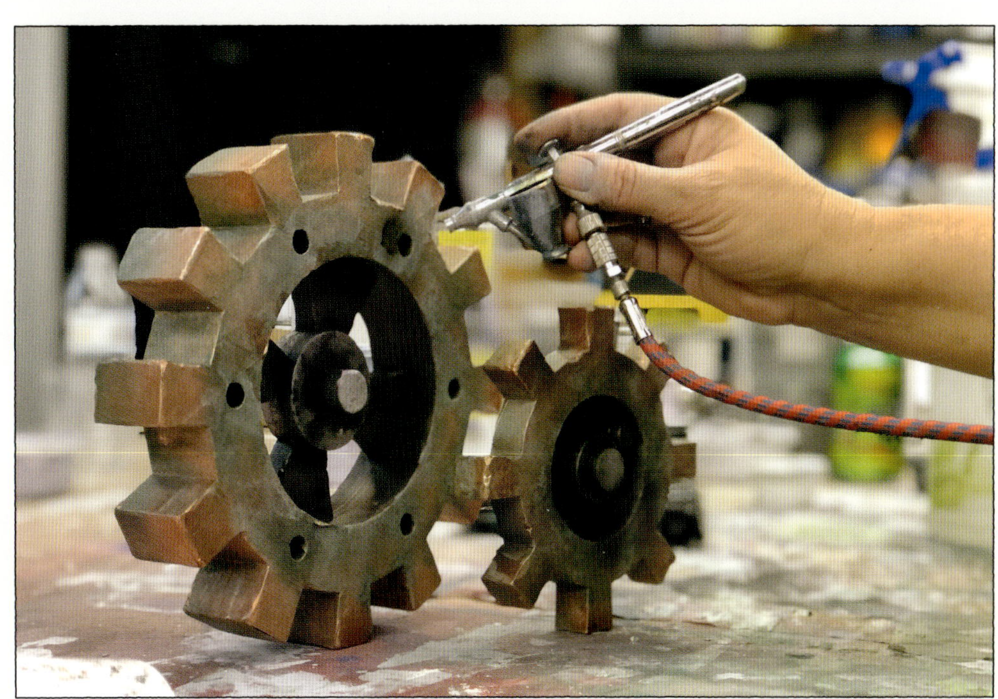

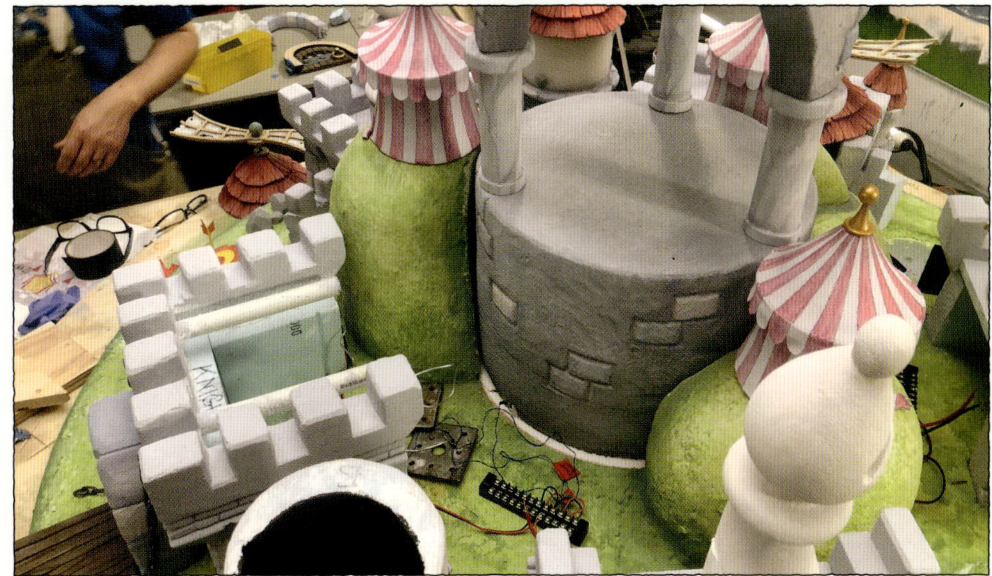

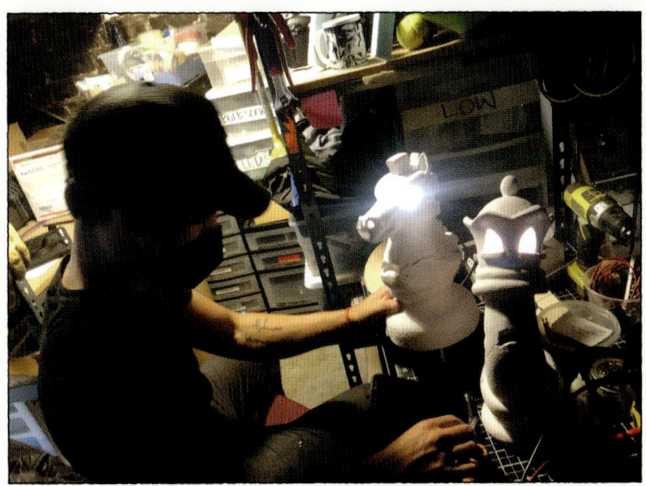

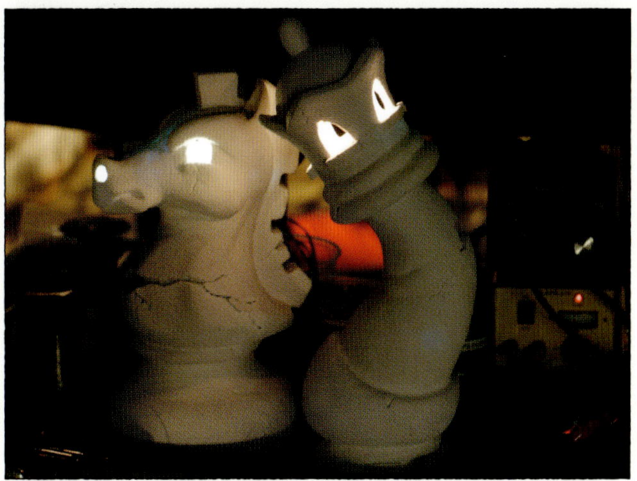

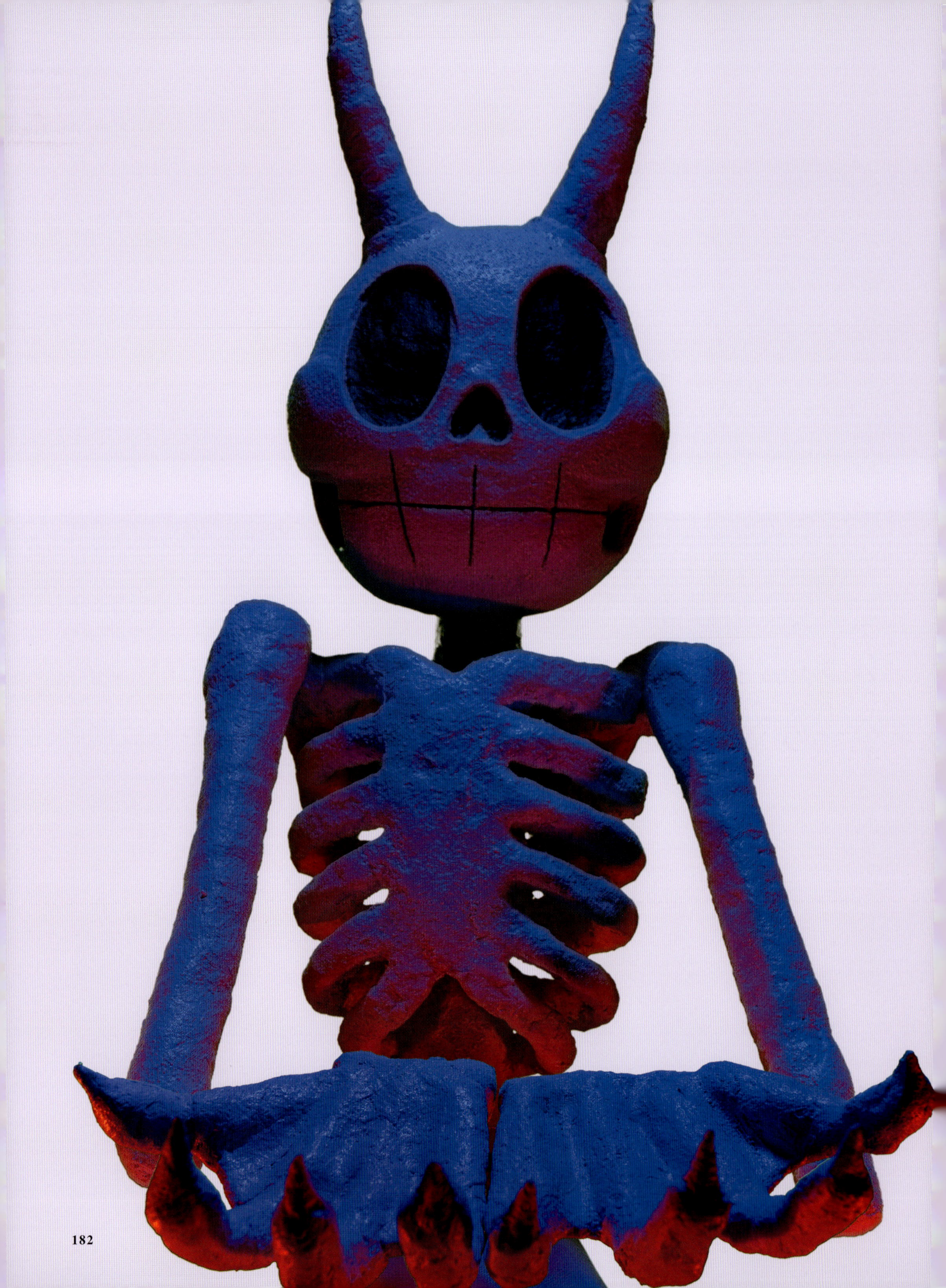

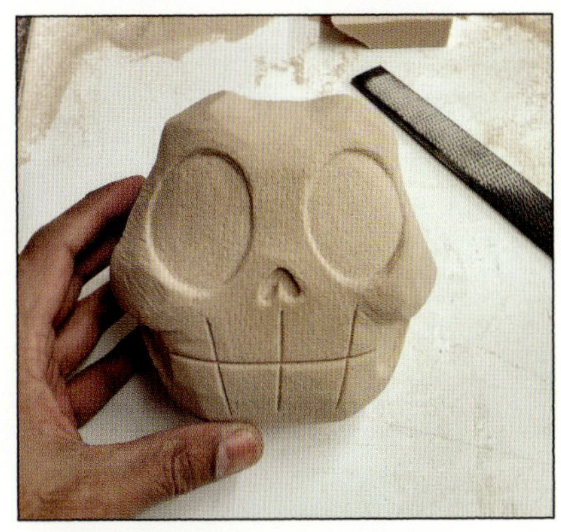
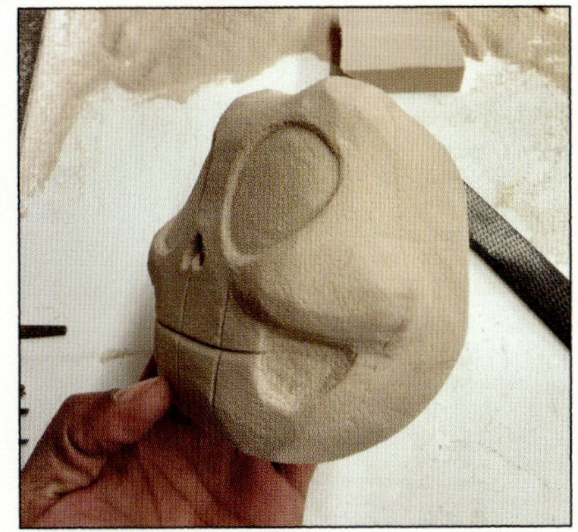
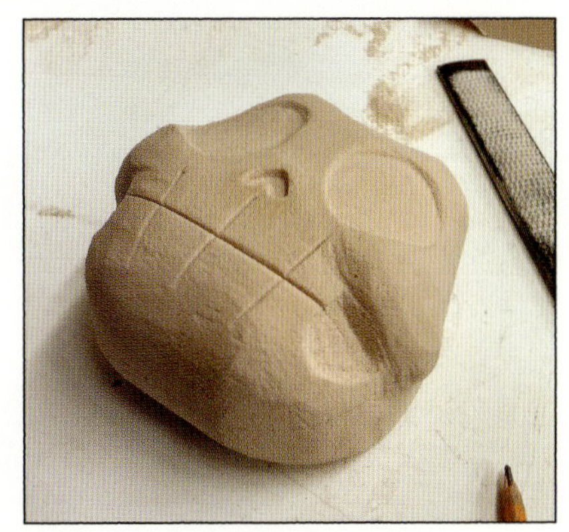
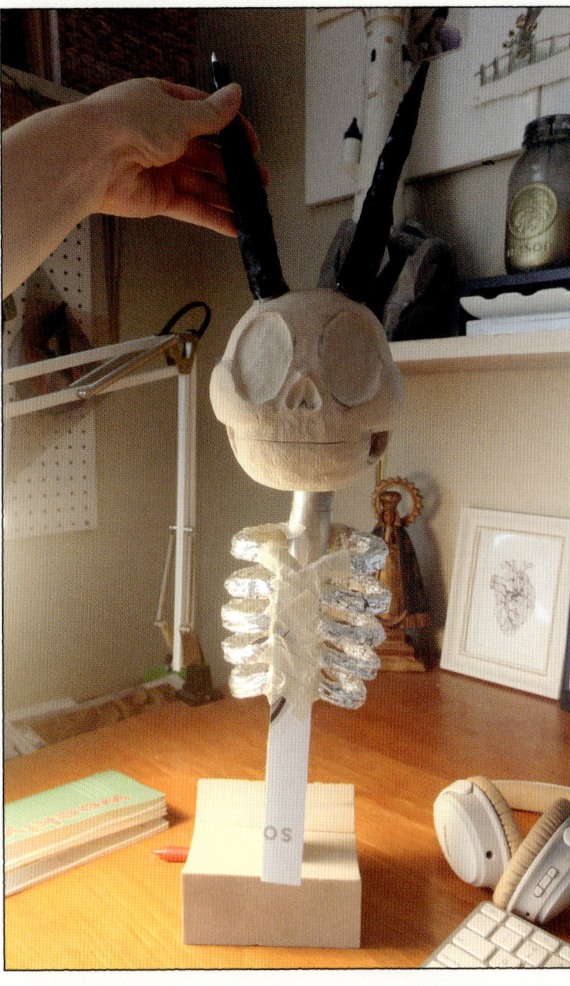
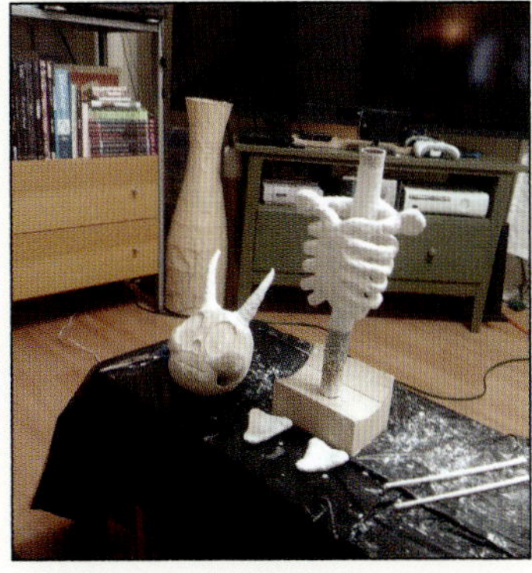
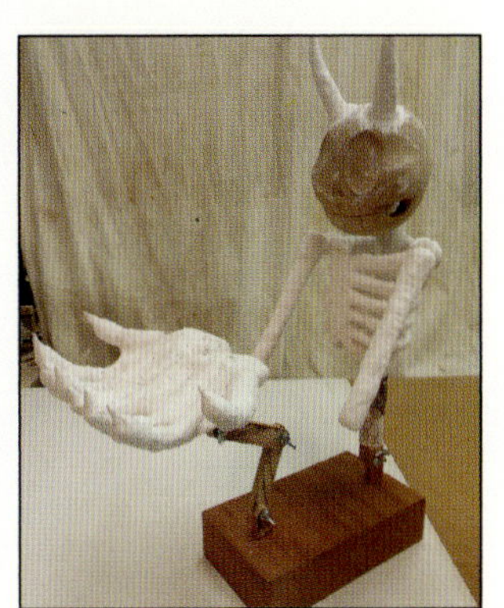
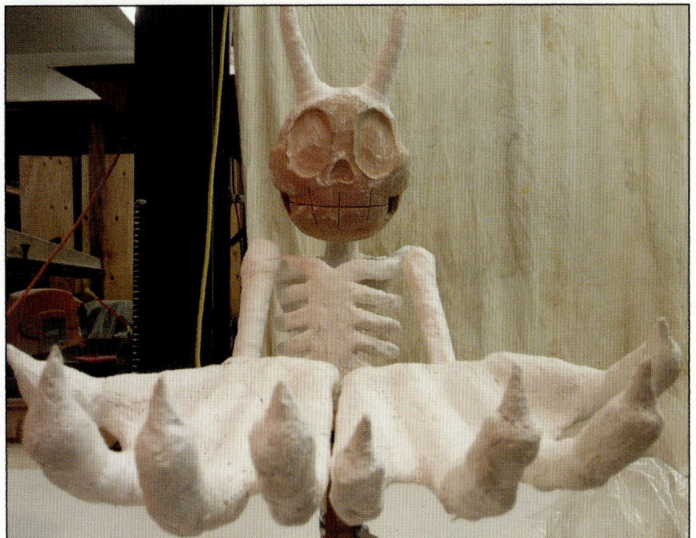

One Hell of a Dream Set Fabrication

THE FINAL PHYSICAL MODEL included in *The Delicious Last Course* is one that not all players will even see! Originally created for an eventually-cut second phase of the climactic battle against The Devil, this imposing skeleton serves as both the background and the platform for *The Delicious Last Course*'s hidden boss battle against a nightmarish manifestation of Ol' Scratch. Fabricated and filmed by Ali Morbi, this set piece contains deceptively detached limbs, with the body-and-arm combination being anchored to one hinge of the model's wooden base, and the hands being fixed to another (seen above). This separation allowed for Ali to better coordinate the movement of each body part to create the illusion of The Devil reaching out of the screen and at the player. Conceptually, this set piece owes a great debt to stop motion pioneer Ray Harryhausen, whose Dynamation technique captured some of the most iconic monster and skeleton sequences in cinema history.

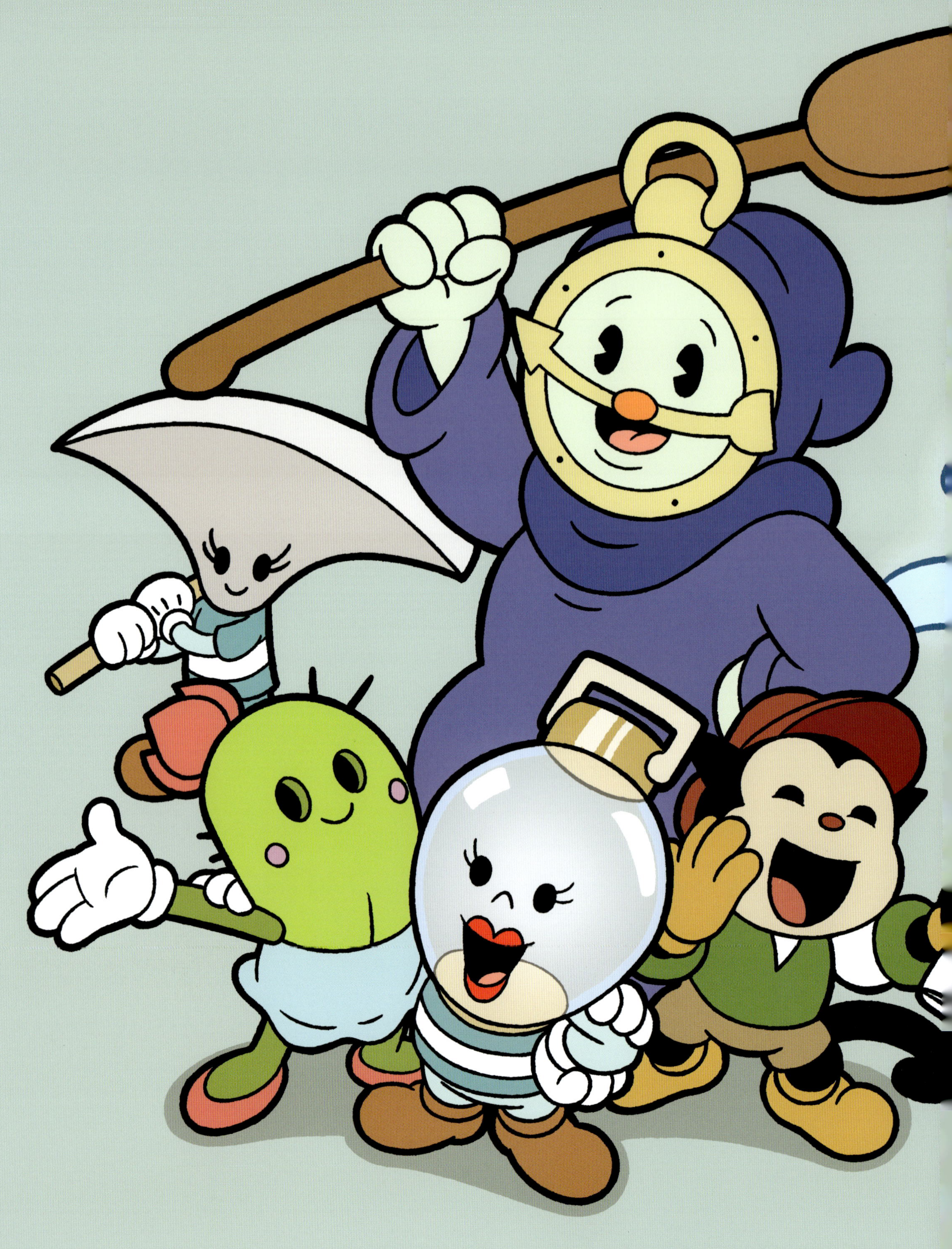

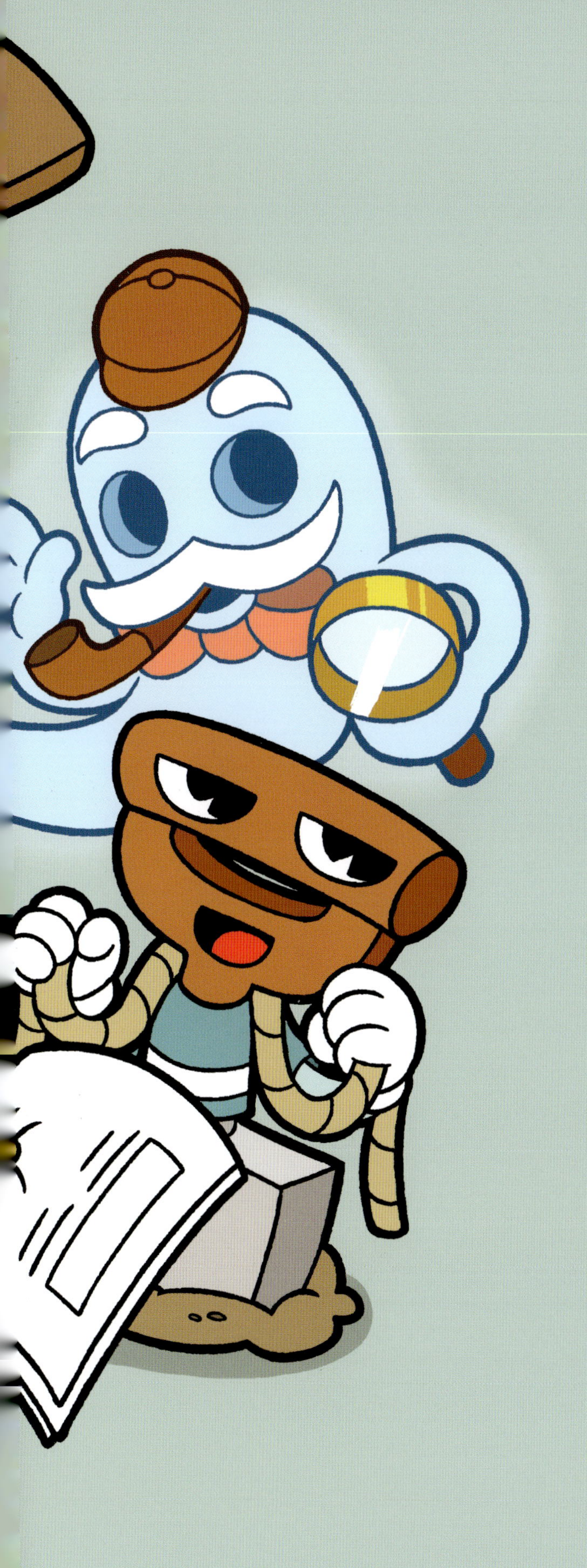

Chapter XII: NPCs

THE SPRAWLING, ECLECTIC Inkwell Isle we envisioned for the DLC required an equally eclectic band of merry characters to inhabit it. While foreign to Cuphead and Mugman, this region needed to be home to a populace with a history and culture all its own in order truly make it feel lived in. With initial inspiration taken from the various biomes our boss fights inhabited, we continued our tradition of making our non-playable characters both flavorful and functional. Their purpose often dictated their personality, and where the original game's cast tended to have a singular tone and tenor to their speech, we strove to give this new cast more of a distinct linguistic cadence.

Of special note: for the first time, our NPCs were key to deciphering a puzzle that involved multiple in-game mechanics–from the shop to the dialogue of the climbing competitors to gravestone interactions. The nature of the puzzle clues and position of the pertinent NPCs changed a number of times as we refined the population of the island down to allow for the smoothest possible progression. Like in life, as the land changed, so did the people within it.

The Boatman

THE BOATMAN STARTED FROM a central mechanical problem–how could our intrepid heroes get whisked away to a brand-new island of dangers? We needed a character who could logically appear on any of the original three Inkwell Isles after a completed Mausoleum to impart a message of a foreboding challenge ahead. With a gloomy silhouette inspired by Charon, Greek mythology's ferryman of the dead, our Boatman is nonetheless a lighter take on that nautical navigator.

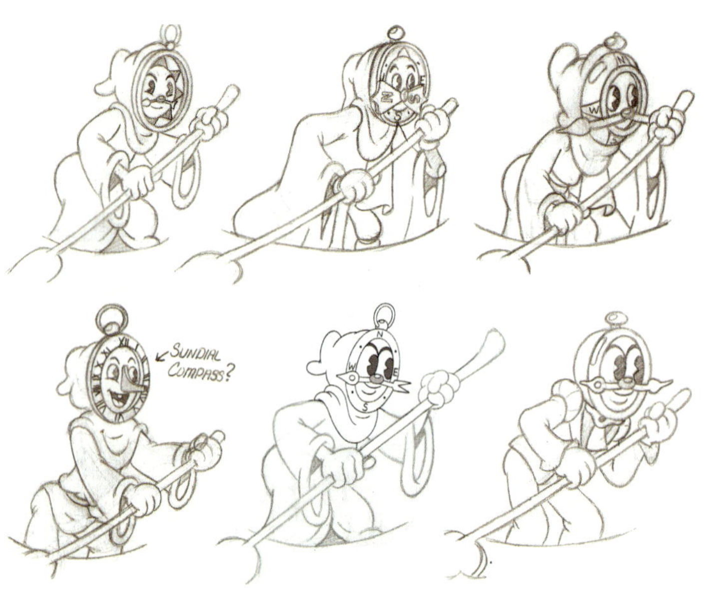

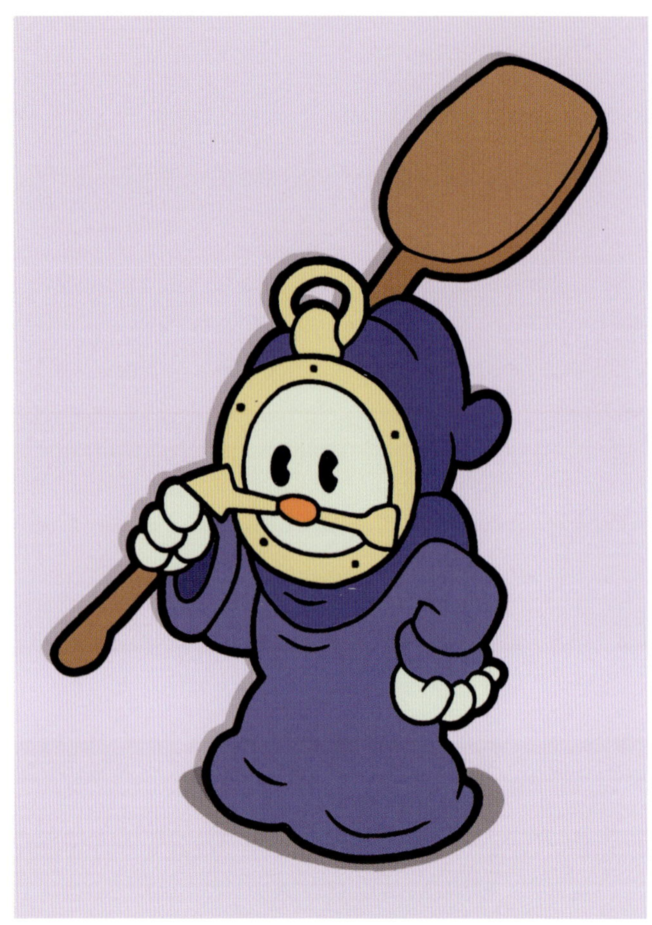

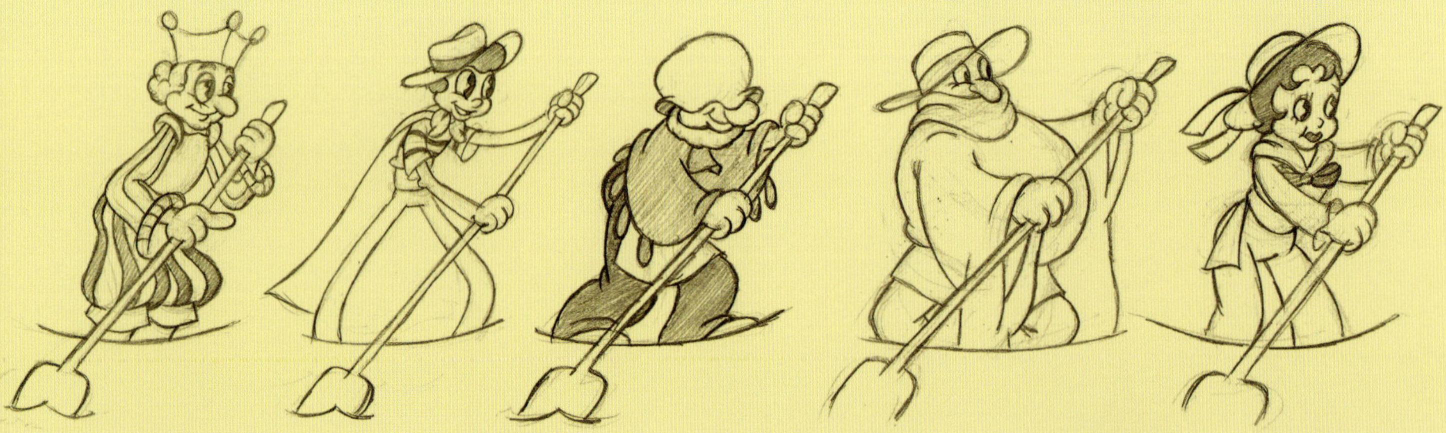

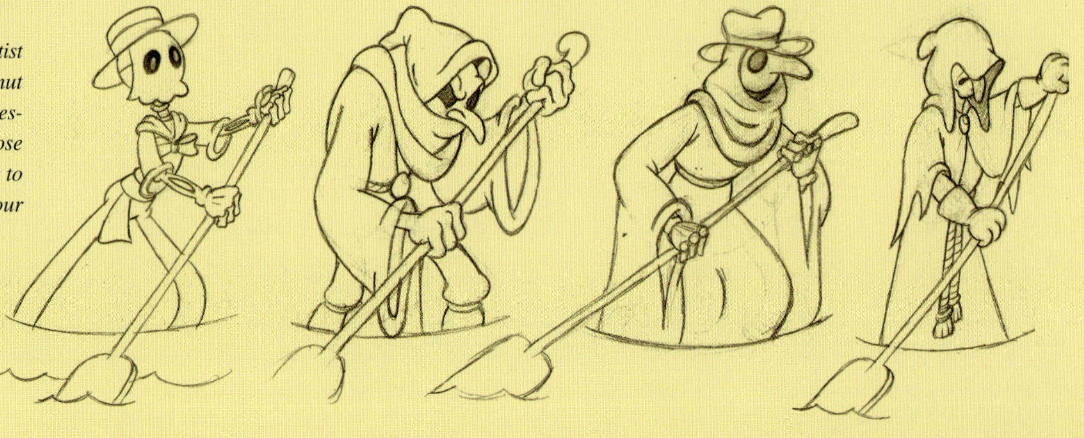

These concept sketches from Artist Joseph Coleman ran the gamut from exceptionally grim to expressively jovial. In the end, we chose an anthropomorphic compass to imply a light connection to our porcelain pals.

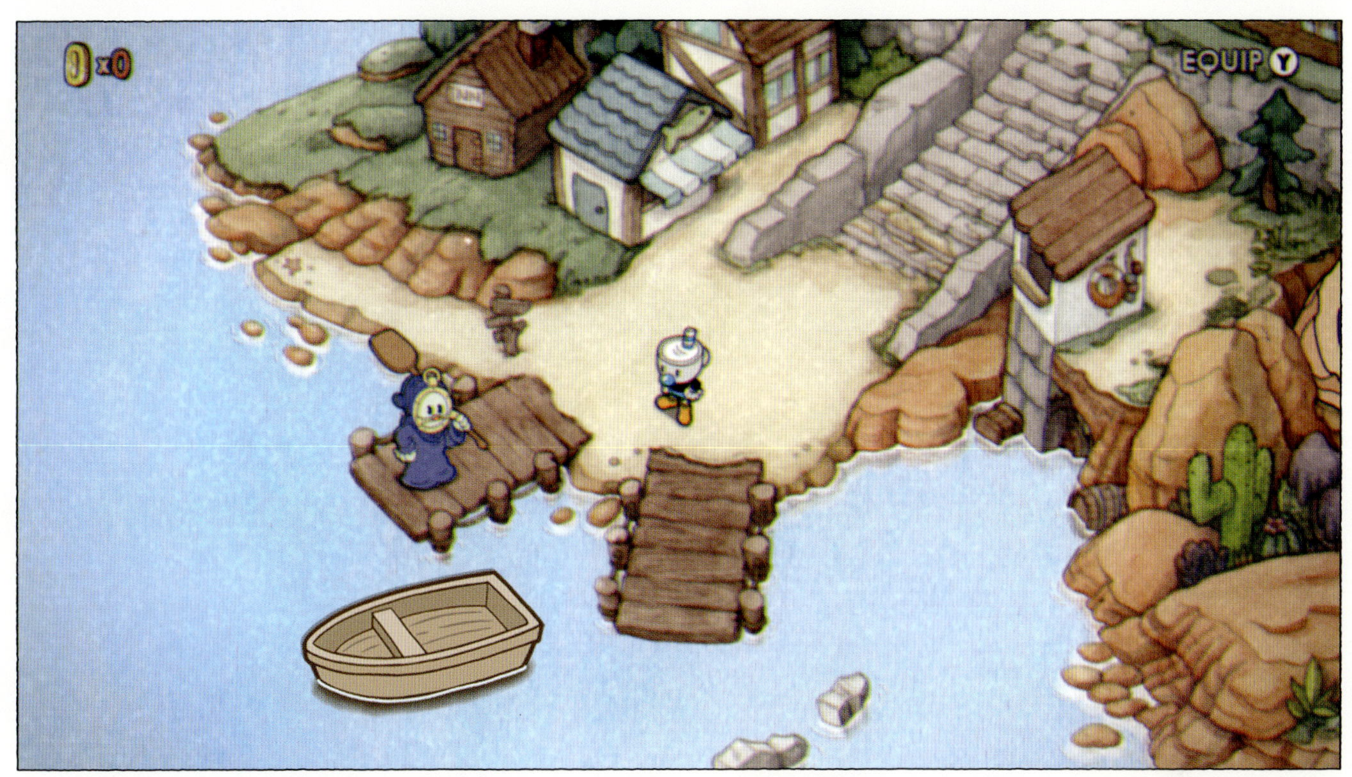
EQUIP

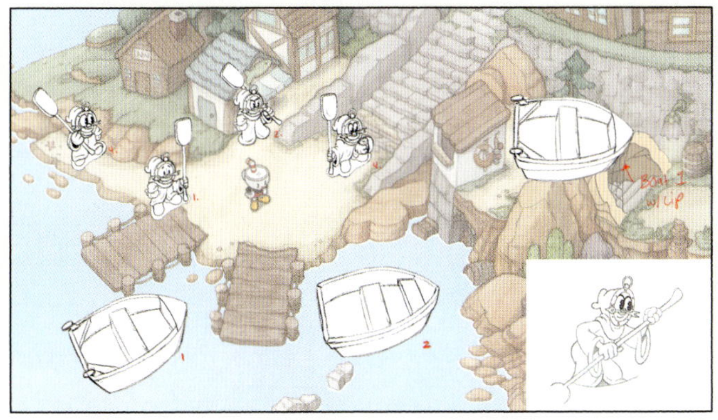

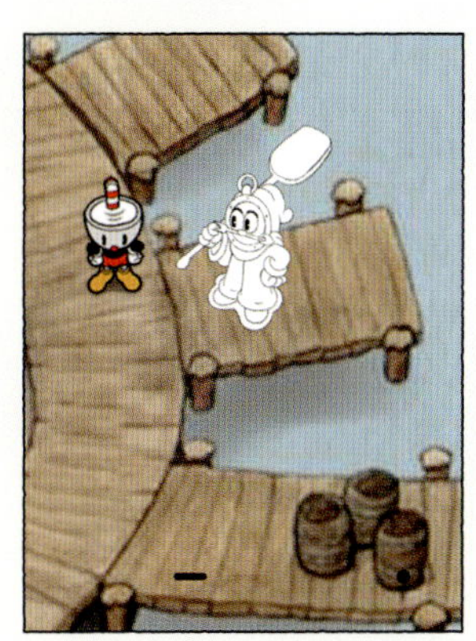

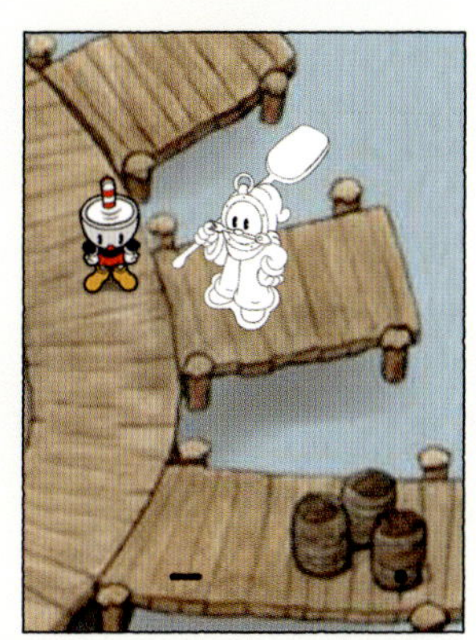

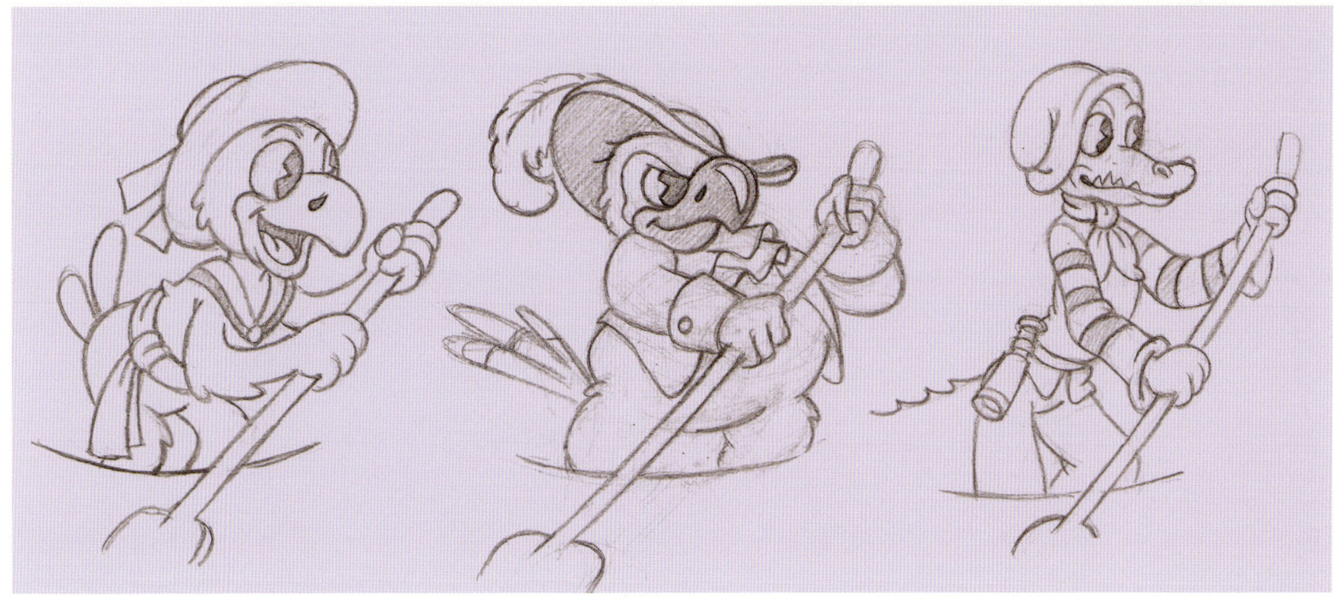

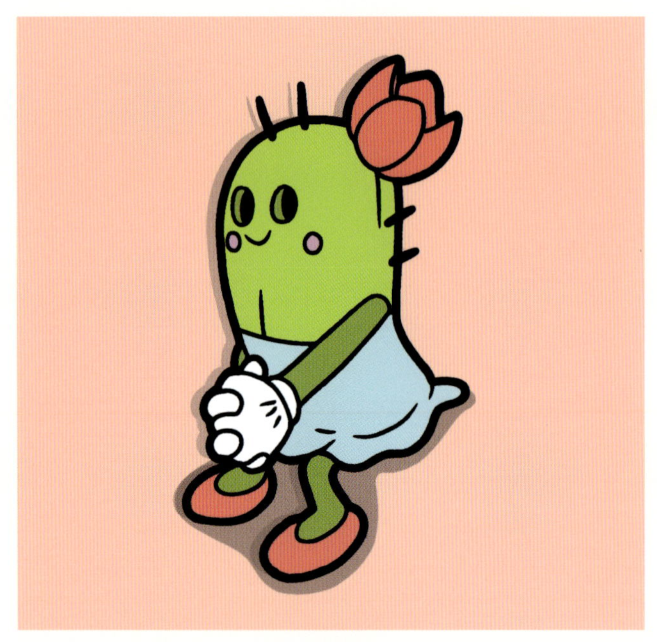

Senita

WE KNEW THAT WE'D HAVE PLAYERS that would want to defeat every boss in the original game and DLC with the newly playable Ms. Chalice, so we pushed to include an NPC that could assist in tracking that progress in a diegetic way. Known through prototype development as "Chalice Fan," Senita eventually became the ghost-story-loving cactus continuously pushing the player to help her finish her epic anthology of campfire tales.

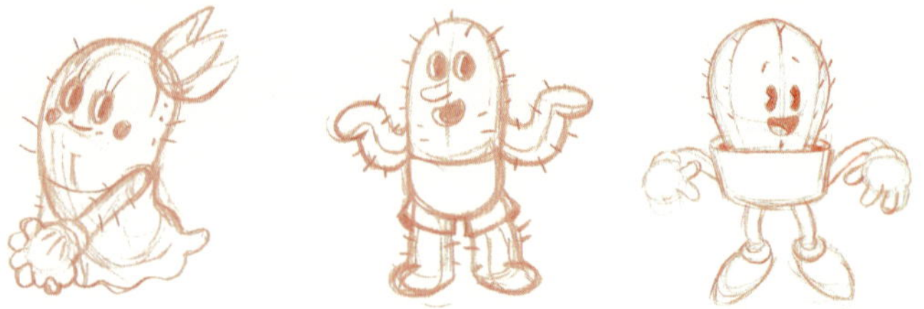

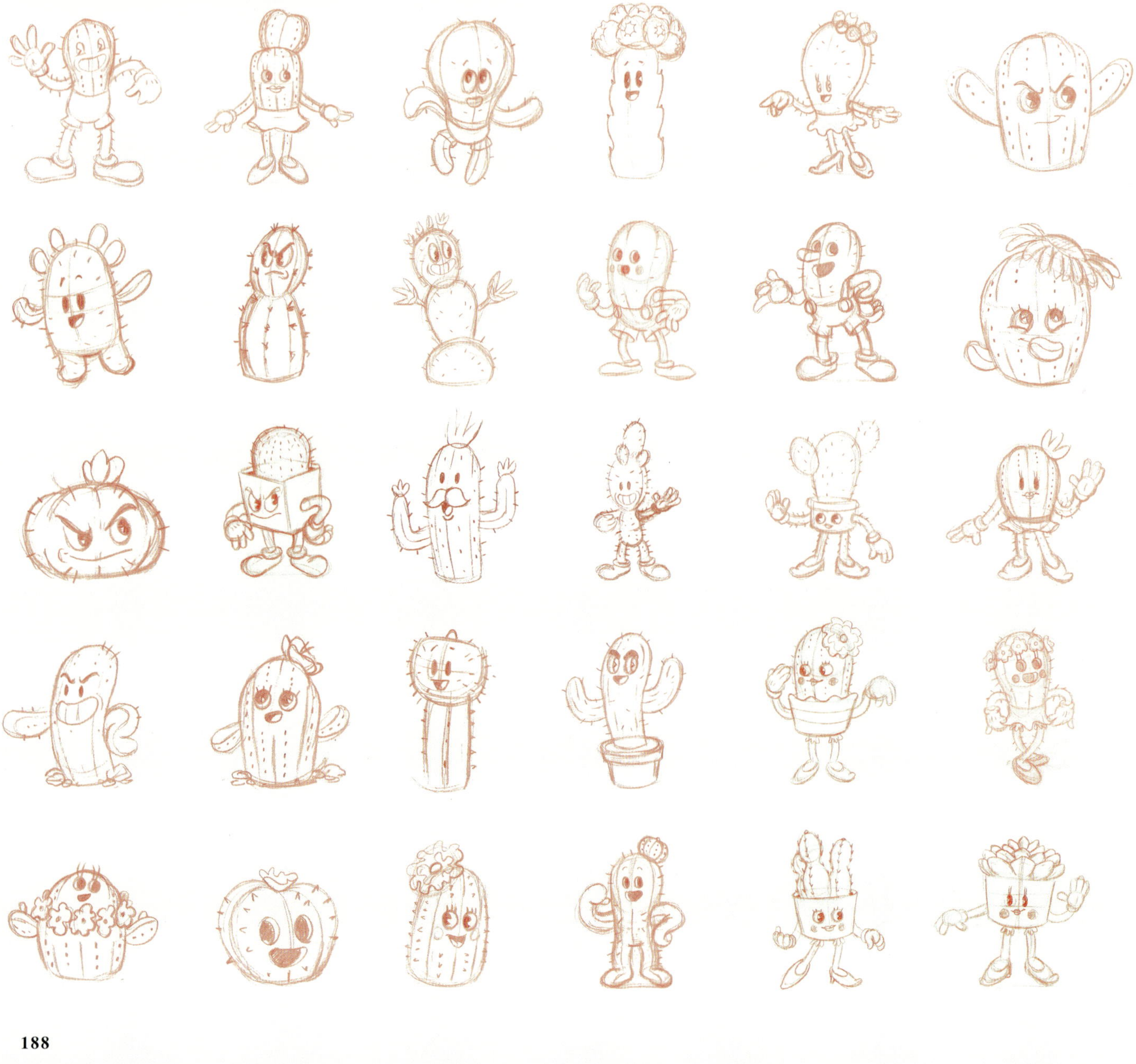

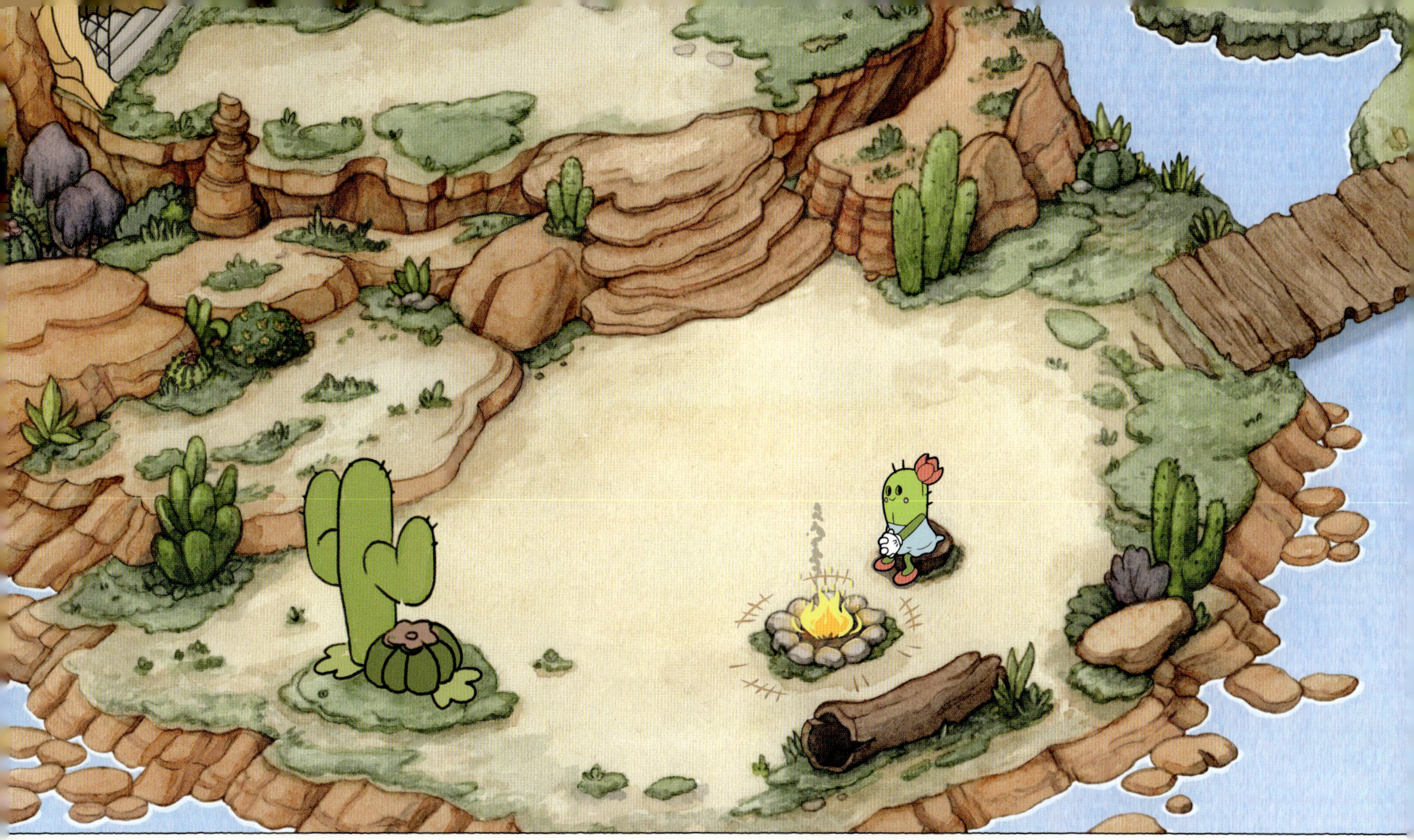

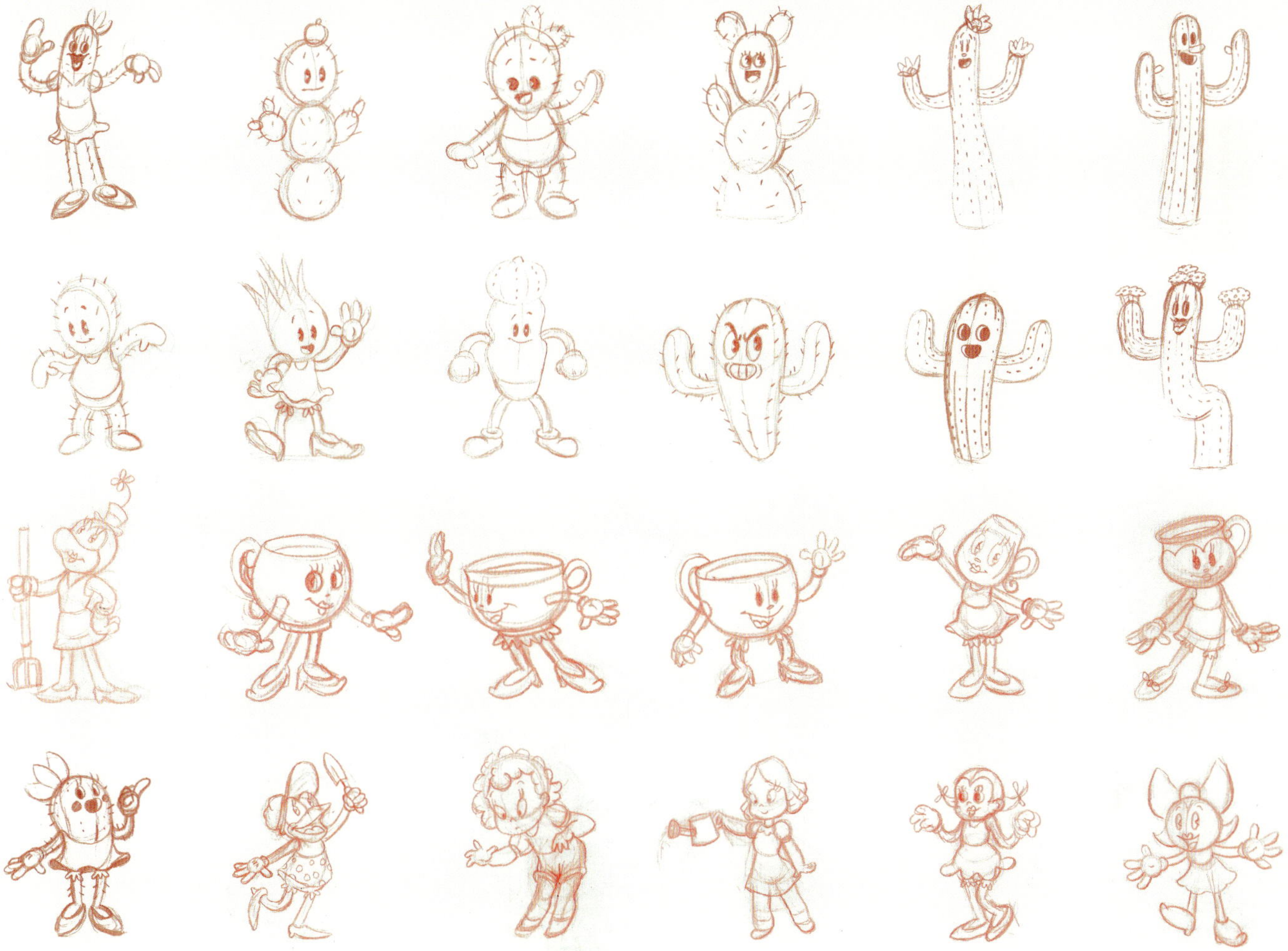

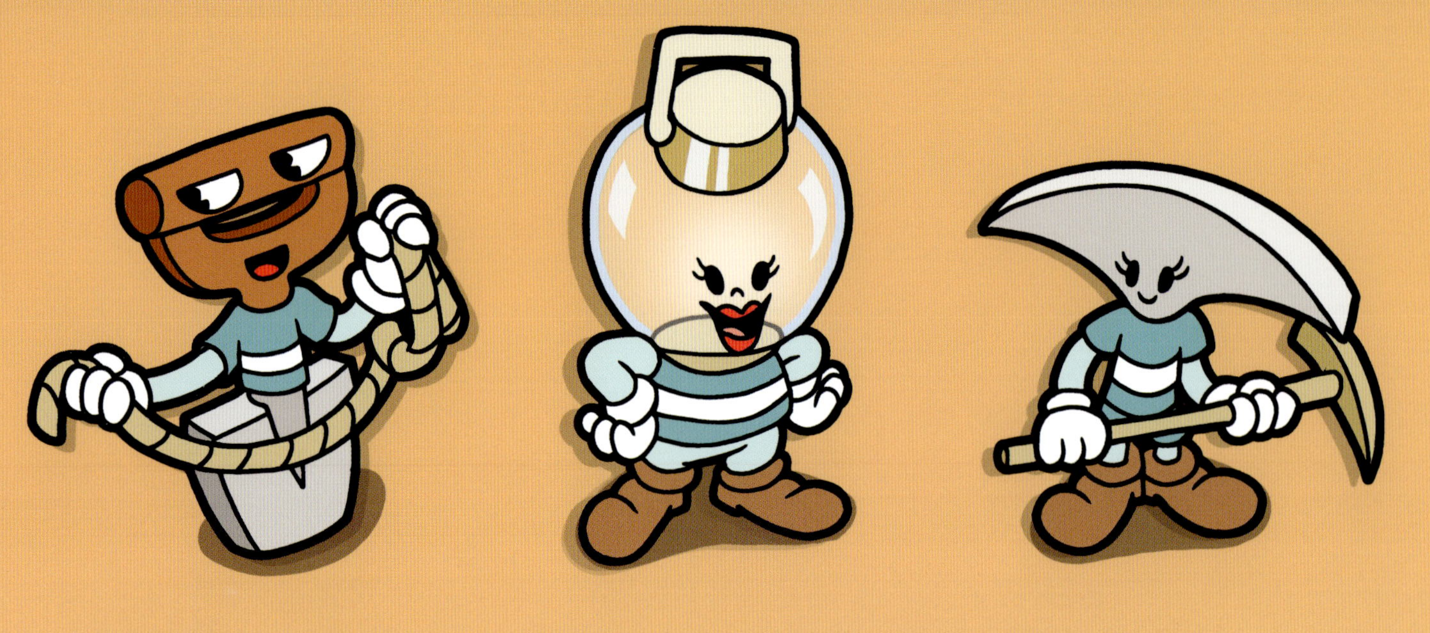

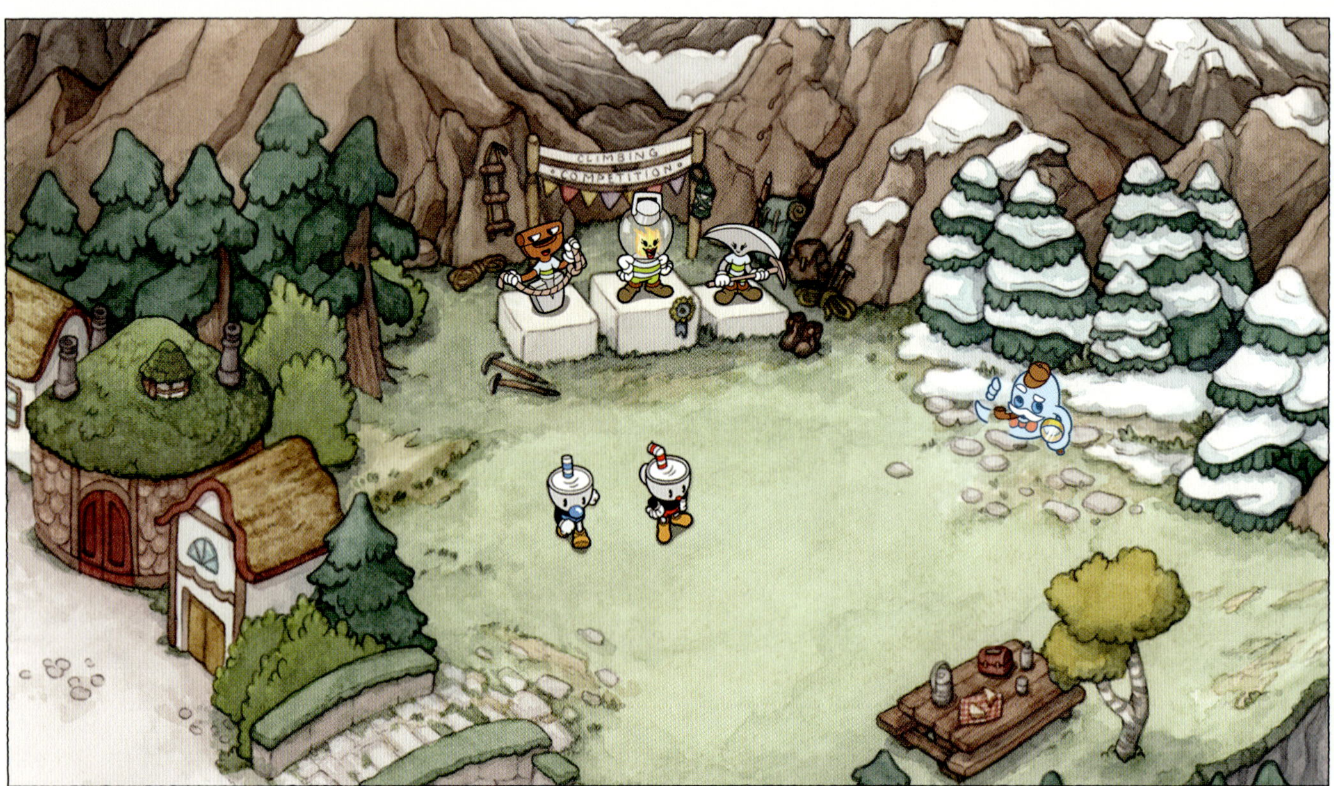

Digby, Lumin, and Prynne

JUST OUTSIDE OF the Inkwell Isle IV's cozy little town square, a small band of ambitious athletes compete for climbing aplomb, all the while being unknowing instruments in the astral plane's mysterious influence on the land. The trifecta of inadvertent clue-givers didn't start out as alpiners; in development we explored a variety of competitions, from a Saltbaker-inspired baking contest to a simple foot race around the island. While sketching out the final iteration of the DLC island map, Background Painter Caitlin Russell, an avid climber herself, suggested that a climbing contest would fit perfectly within Glumstone's mountain range along the Northern Coast–and thus we had our inspiration!

Originally, the puzzle called for five unique NPCs, with an additional challenger who came in last place sulking at the picnic table and a judge residing nearby with more hints. Eventually, we simplified the dialogue down to the bare minimum to reduce the number of distractions that could lead players astray.

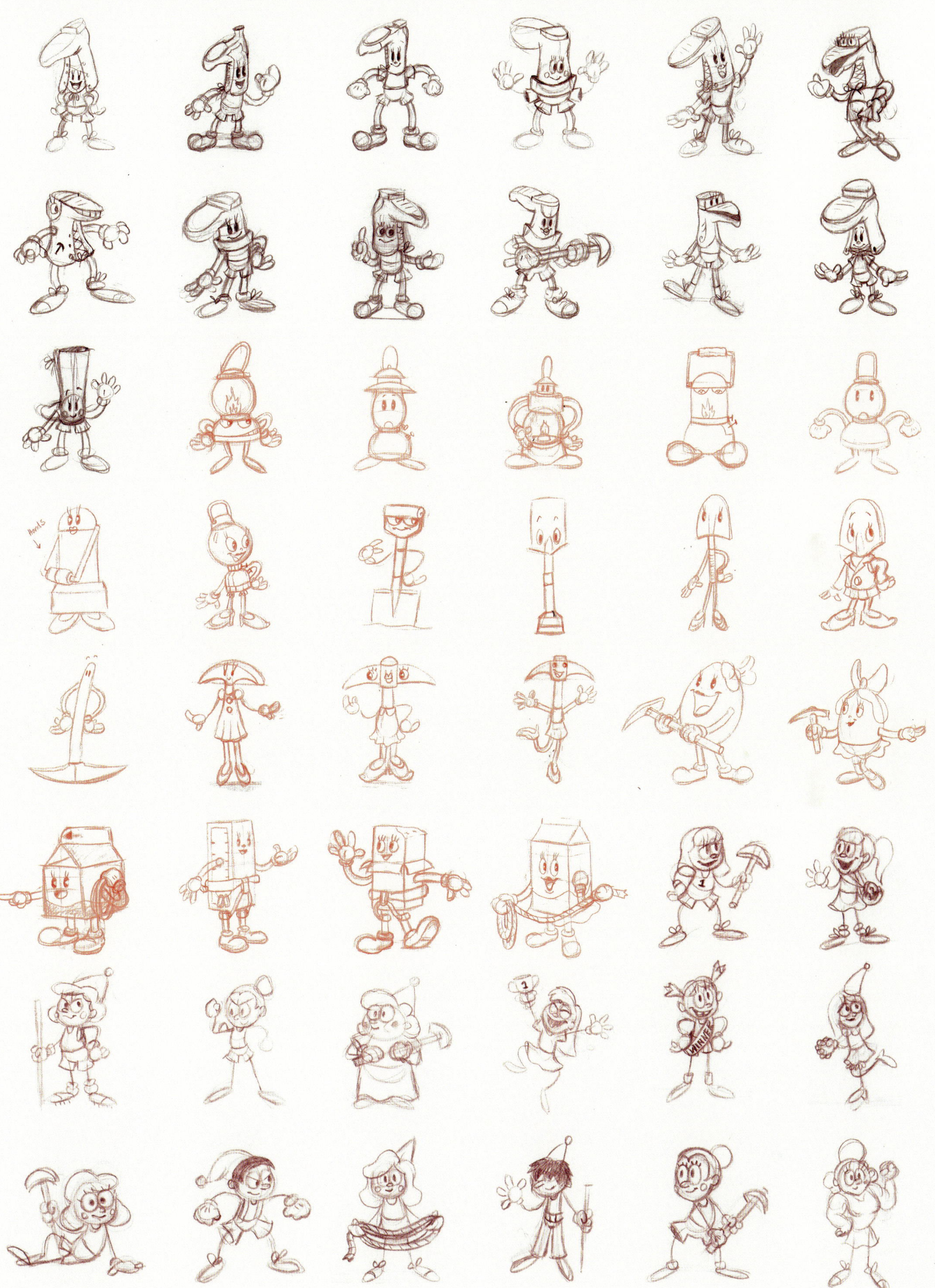

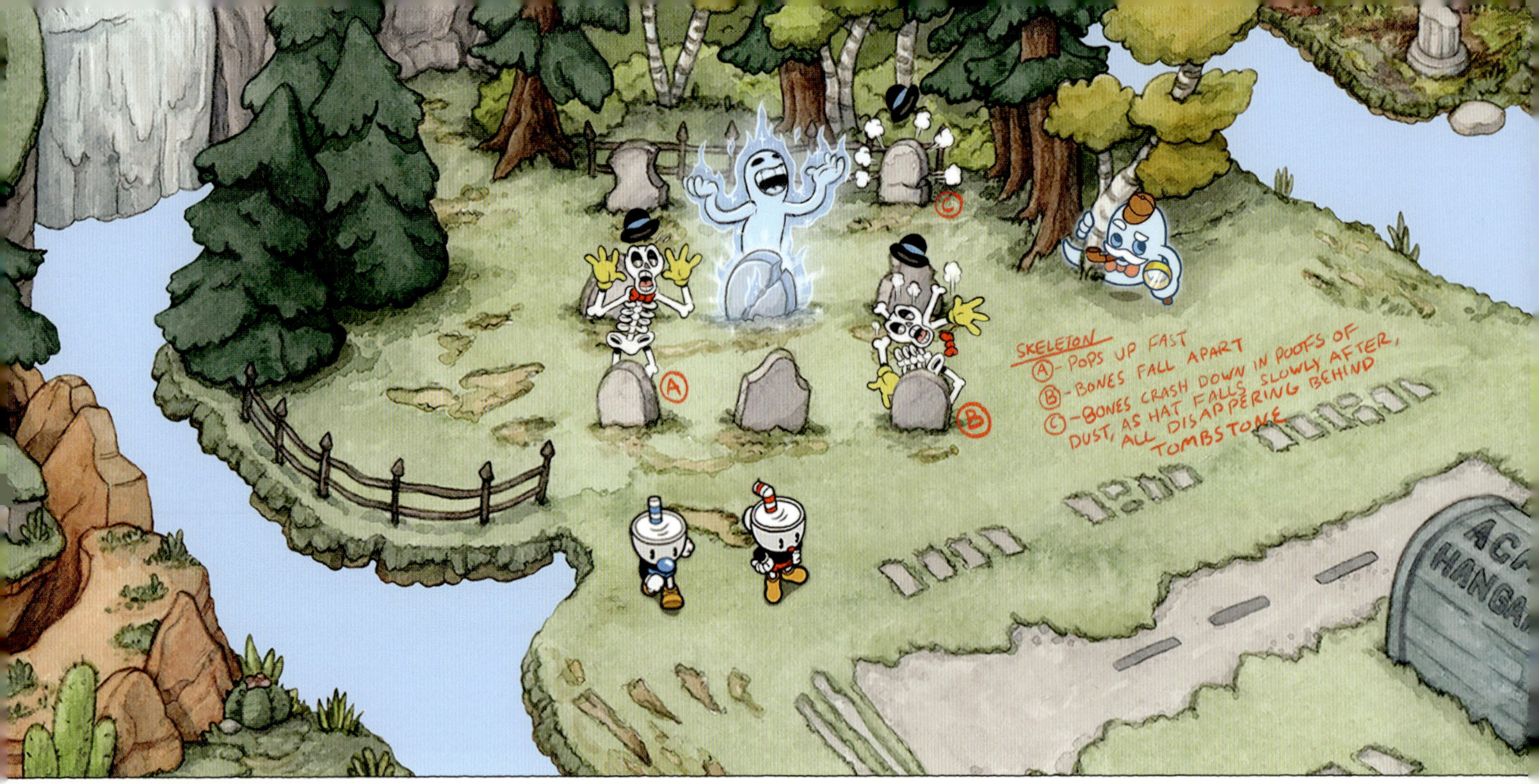

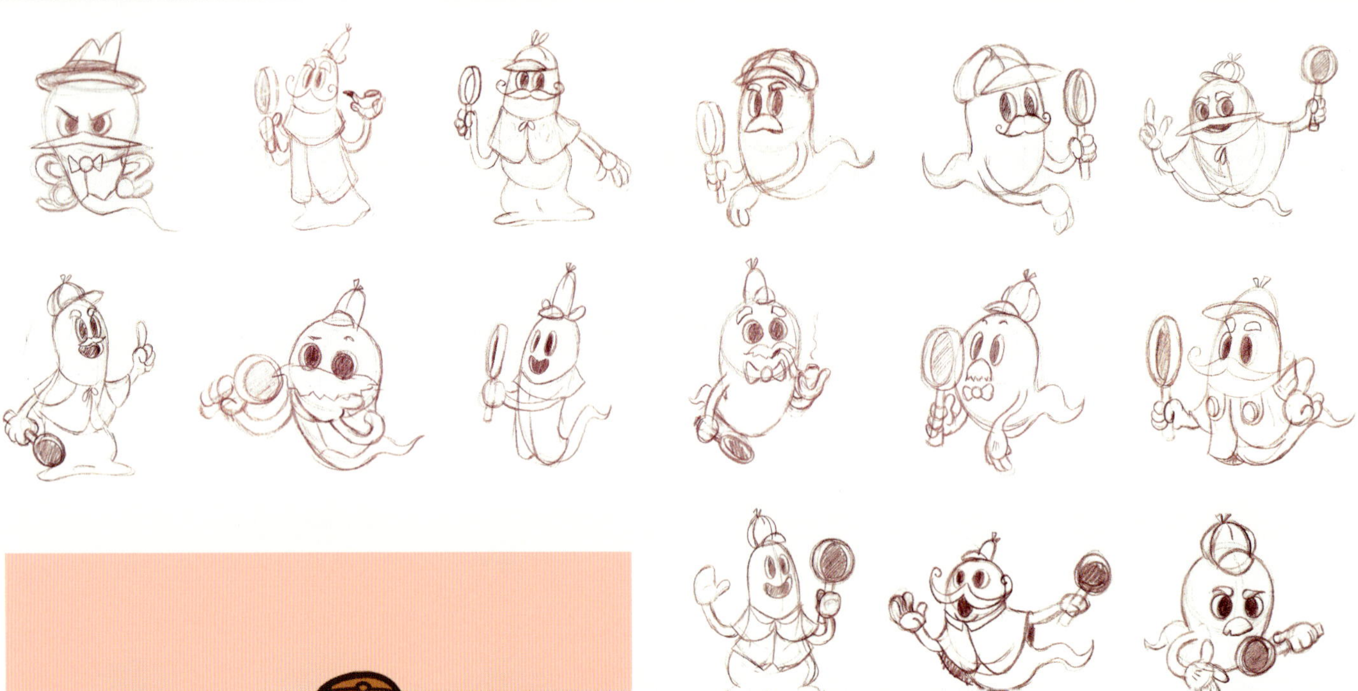

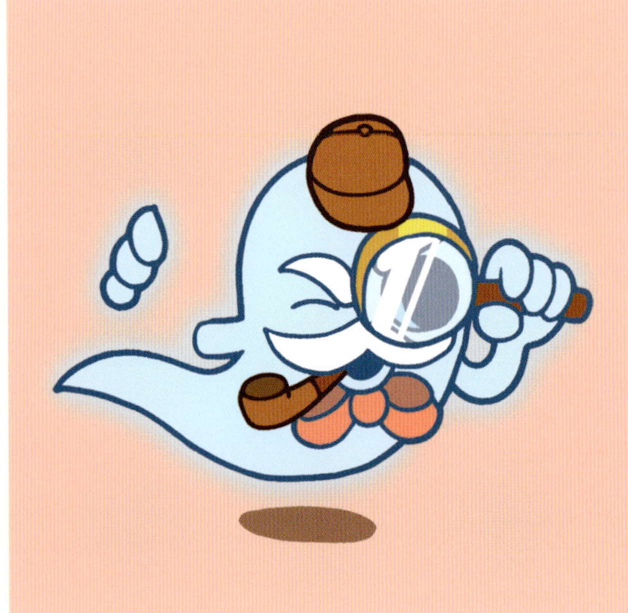

Inspector Graves

LINGERING AROUND A GRAVEYARD, as ghosts are wont to do, our fastidious phantom detective is perpetually dumbfounded by the case of the errant astral energy! Inspired by Agatha Christie's storied sleuth Hercule Poirot, Inspector Graves acts as the primary instigator for the secret quest to obtain the legendary Paladin Charm. While we didn't specifically start with an investigative NPC, Animator Danielle Johnson's many visual explorations of the character convinced us that the character leading you on your quest should also be one who was searching for the answer themselves.

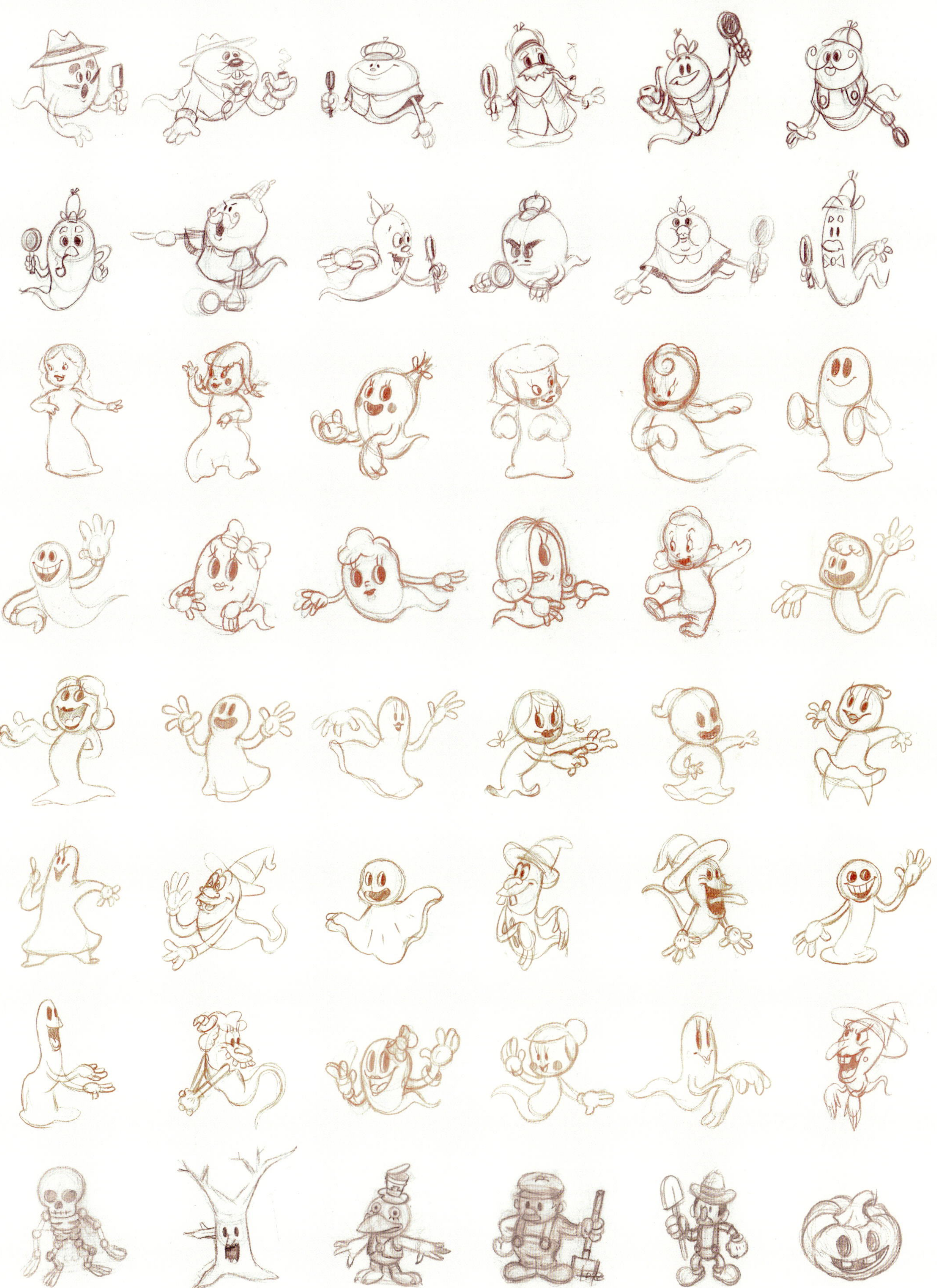

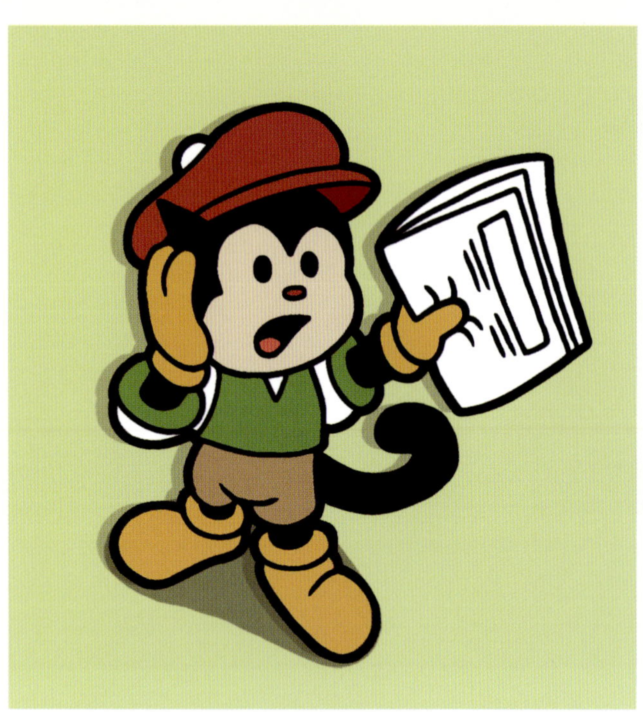

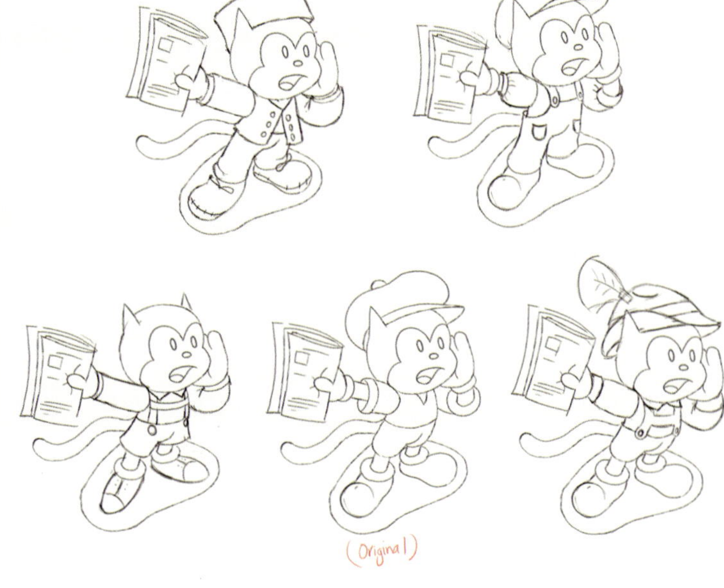

Buckley

UPON SETTING OUT ON your brand-new quest on DLC Isle, your initial encounter is most likely to be a sass-mouthed newsie who'll give a tough but fair analysis of whether you're cut out for the challenges ahead. Since we knew that there would be some first-time players who would gain access to the DLC near the outset of their journey through the Inkwell Isles, we needed a character who would warn them of the high-level battles ahead and maybe recommend they come back later.

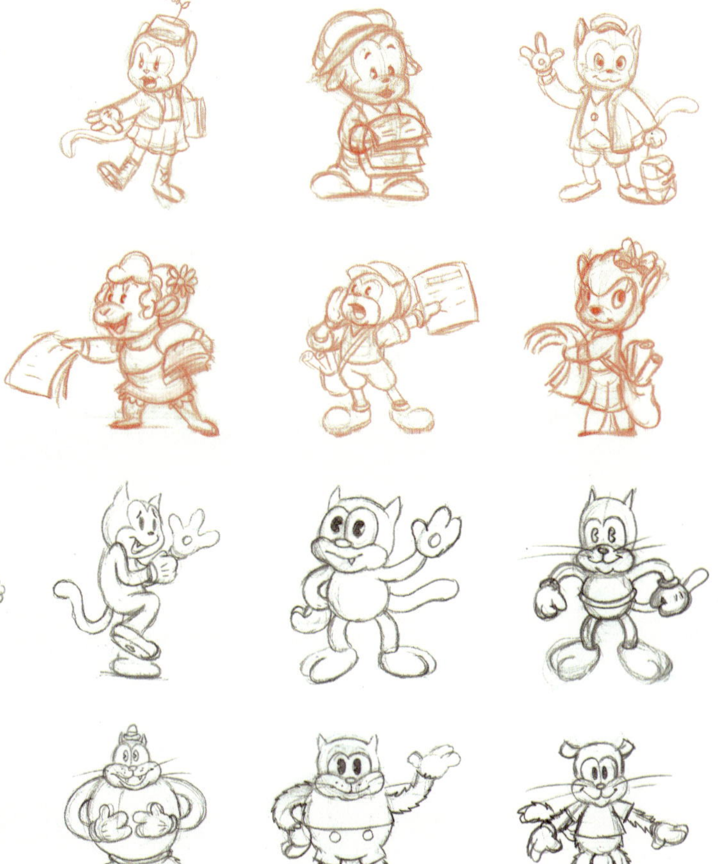

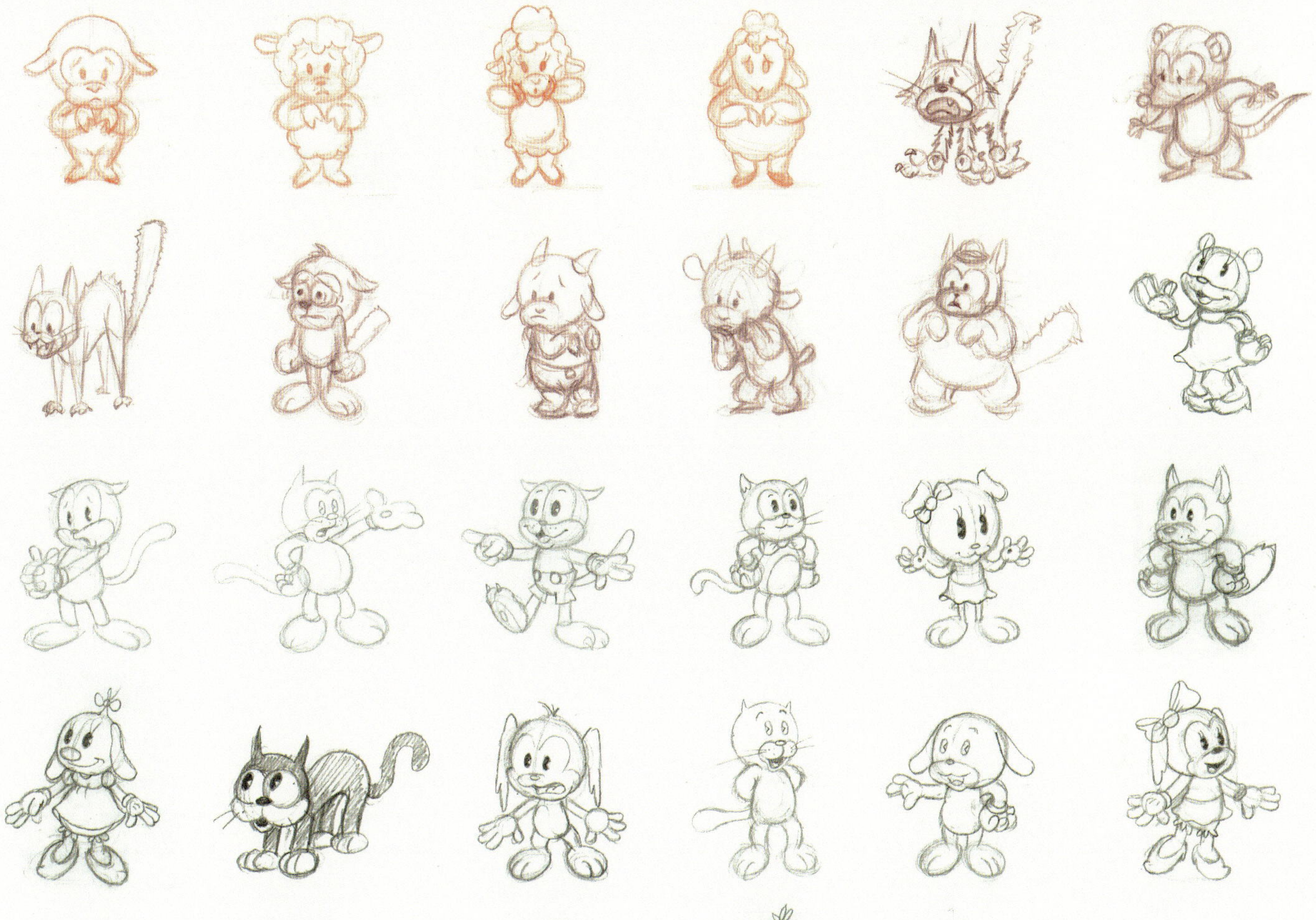

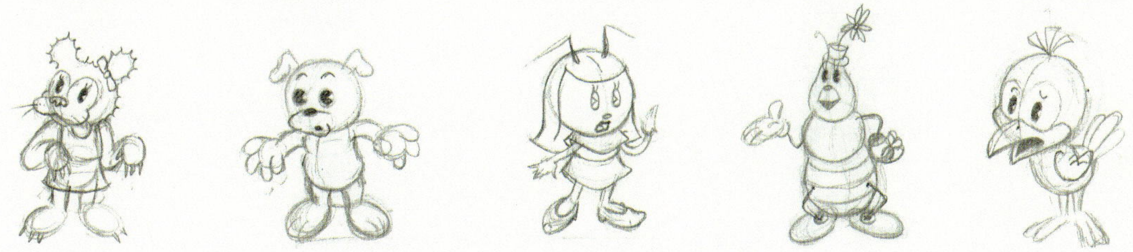

Early in development, Buckley was known as "Scaredy Cat," a timid little creature who was fearful of the fearsome foes found across DLC Isle, and would warn you to stay away.

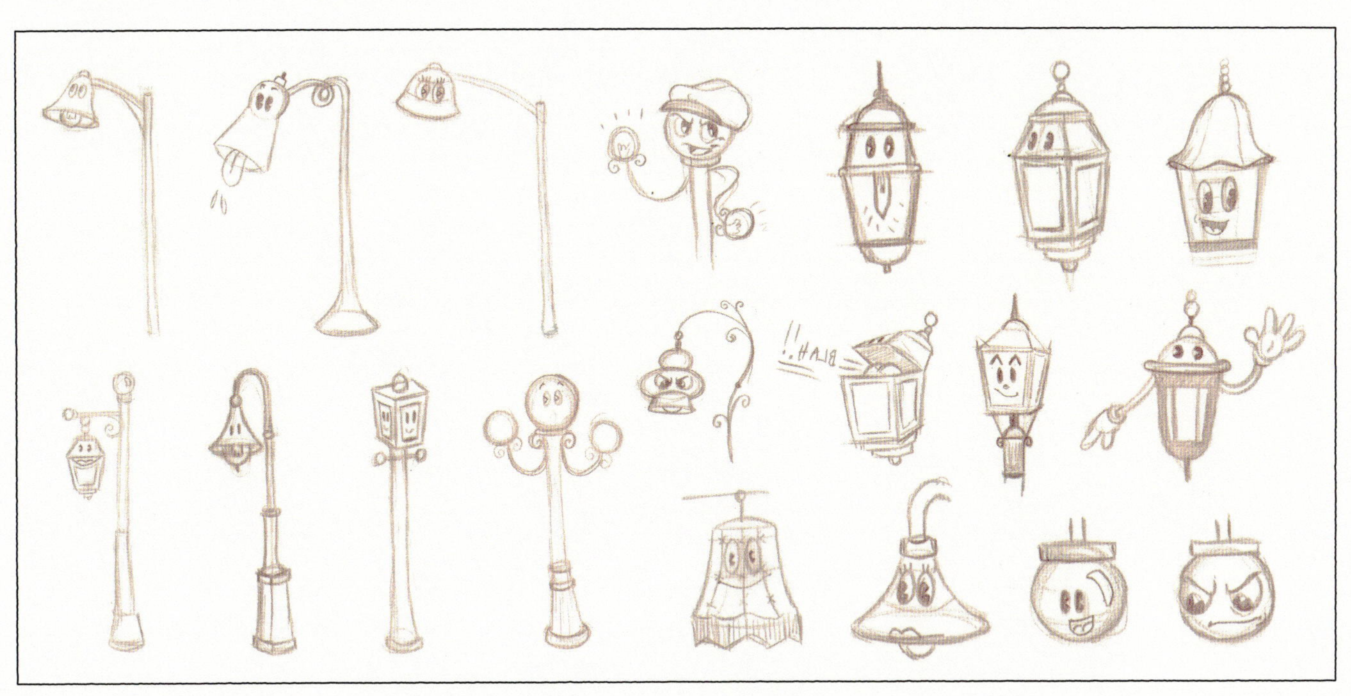

Unused NPC Designs

FROM BAKING COMPETITION ENTRANTS to climbing judges to friendly birds and other townspeople, there's an unfortunate number of characters that inevitably get cut during development, simply due to the shifting priorities of quest lines and features. While we love each and every one of our characters, sometimes we have to make the difficult decision to let them go. At least here they get some time to shine!

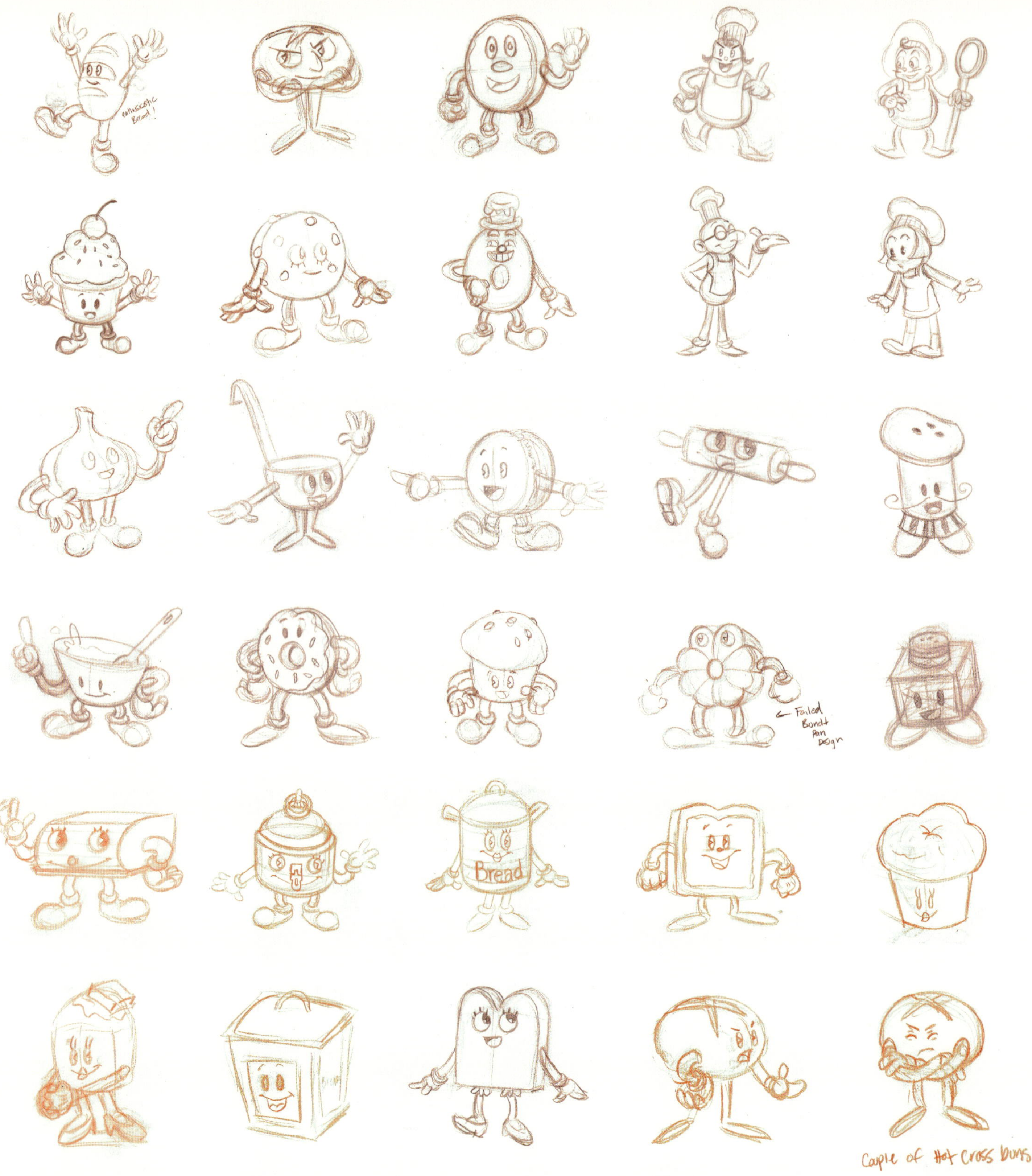

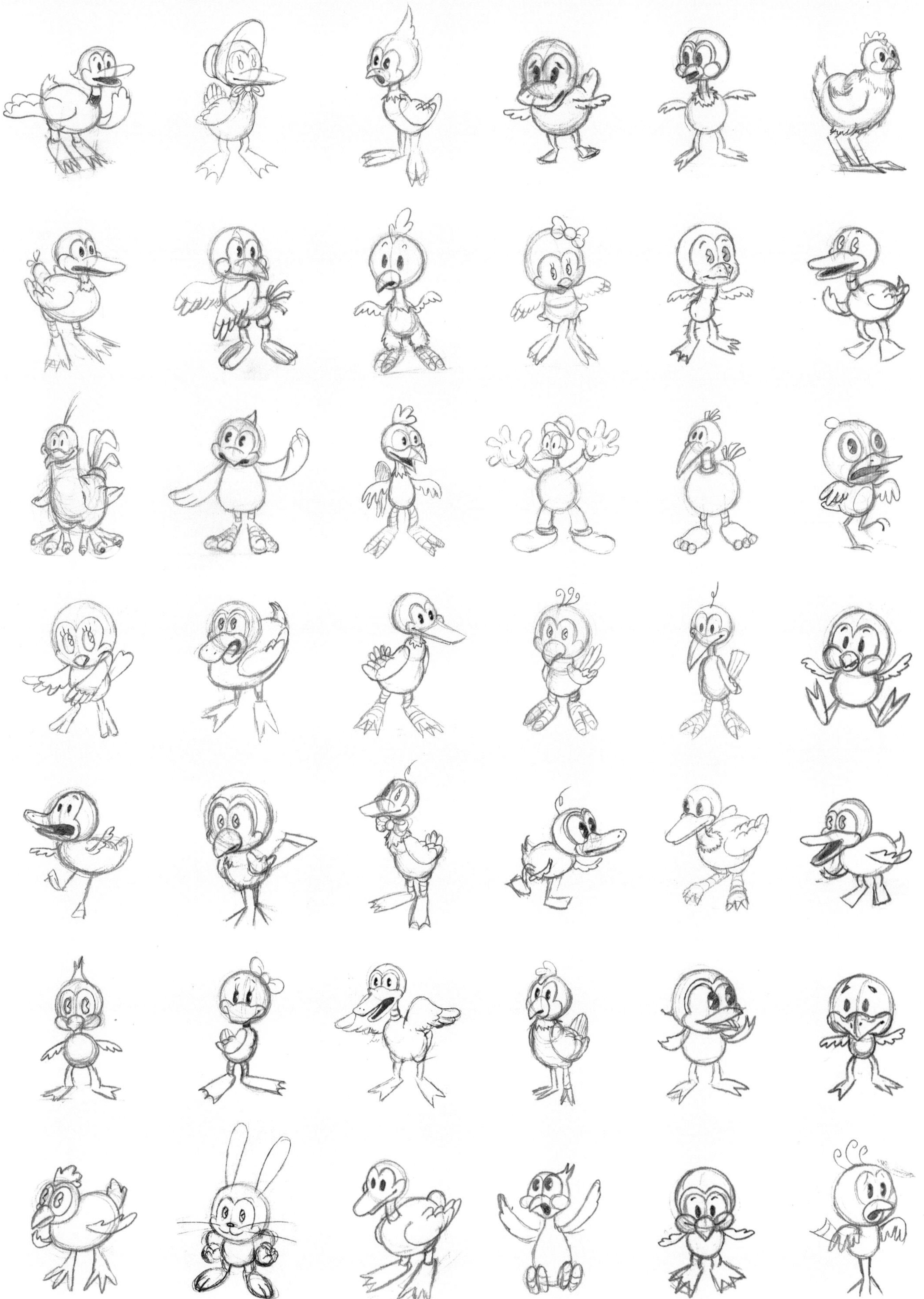

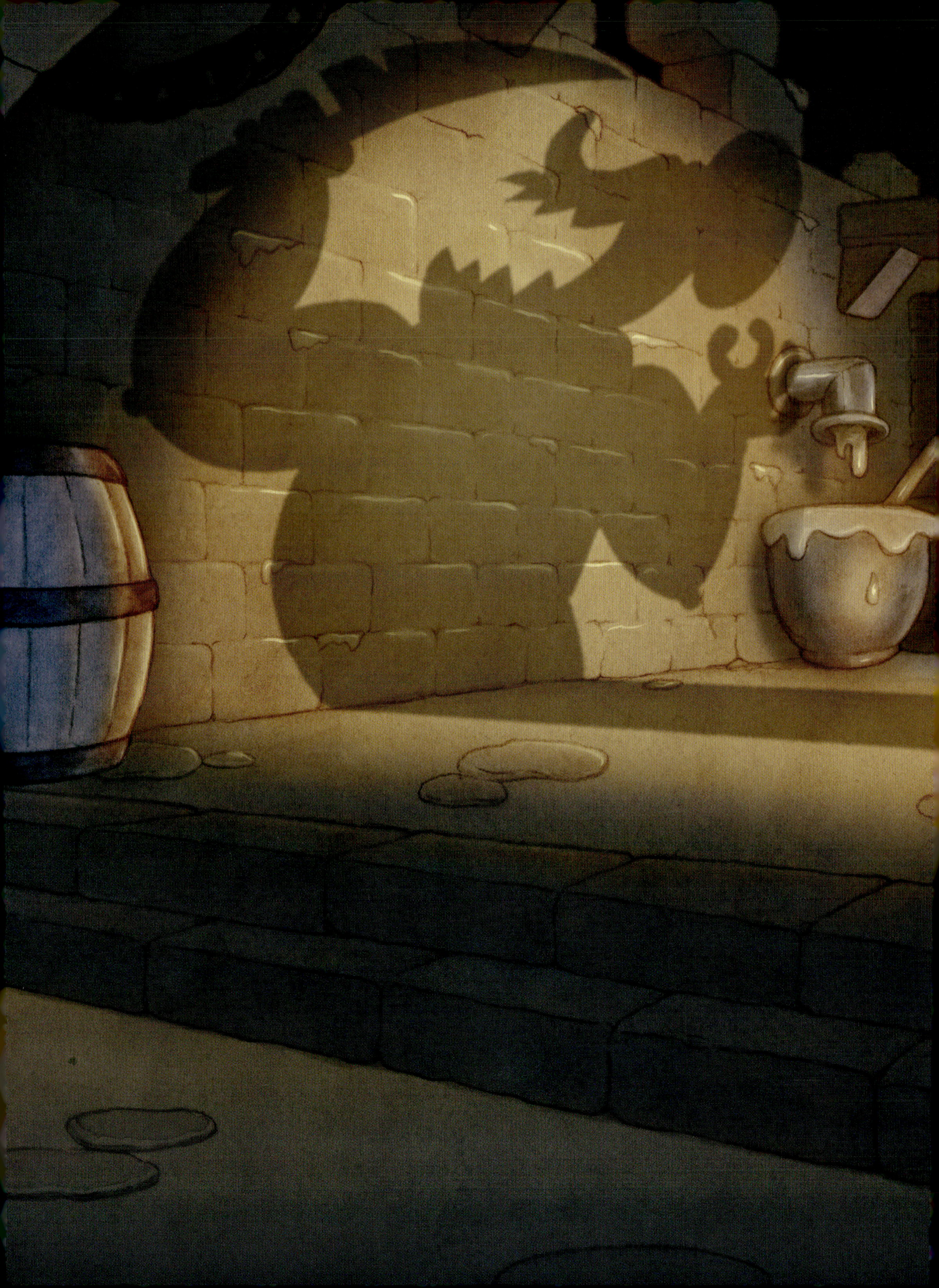

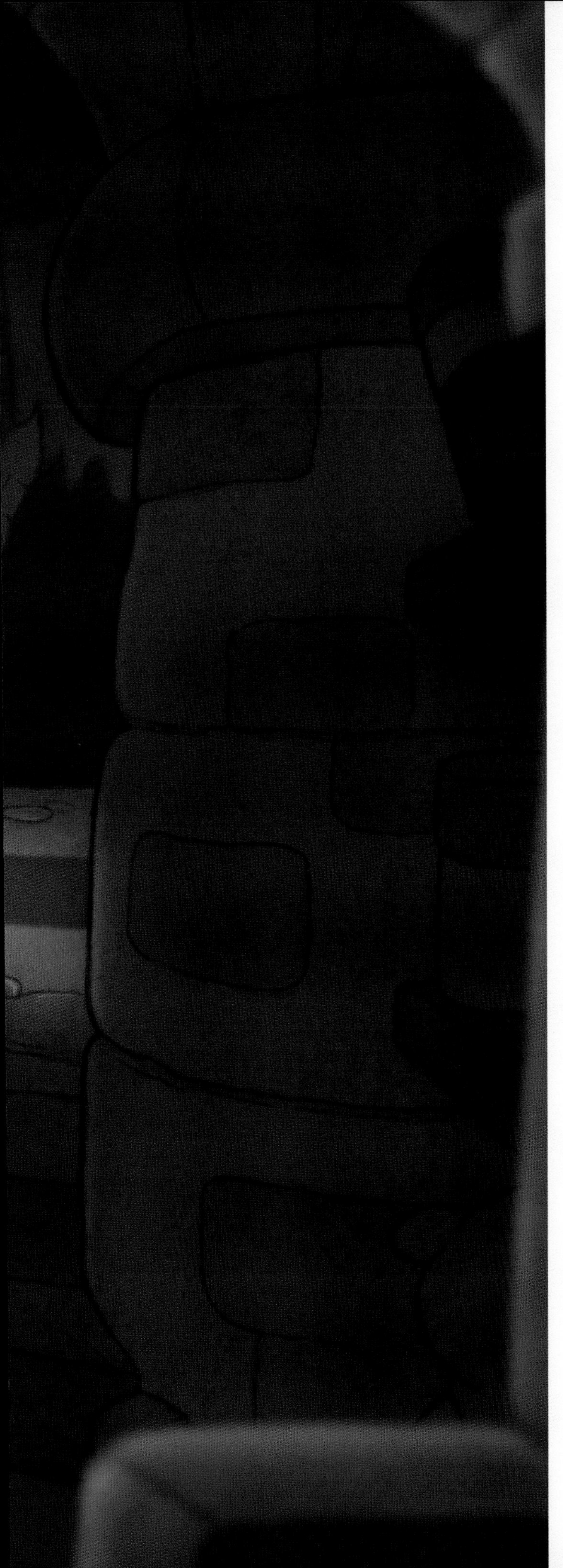

Chapter XIII: Cutscenes

CUPHEAD'S VISUAL IDENTITY is rooted in the cartoon shorts of the 1930s, and nowhere is that more evident than in the game's story-driven cutscenes. While gameplay has always come first, we always revel in the opportunity to stretch our cinematic legs by showcasing narrative interstitials in all their hand-drawn glory.

Like most other aspects of *The Delicious Last Course*, we wanted to push our cutscenes beyond the standard set created for the base game. By using more dynamic camera angles, more expressive character motions, and more interesting shot composition, the DLC cutscenes hew more closely to the sophistication of our 1930s inspirations. While we maintained a commitment to the brevity of dialogue found in those rubber hose cartoons, the DLC's somewhat more complex story (full of twists and turns and double crosses!) required a greater number of individual shots and character interactions. But wherever possible we still tried to opt for visual storytelling, whether in the background set dressing details or character facial expressions, playing to the original strength of the medium.

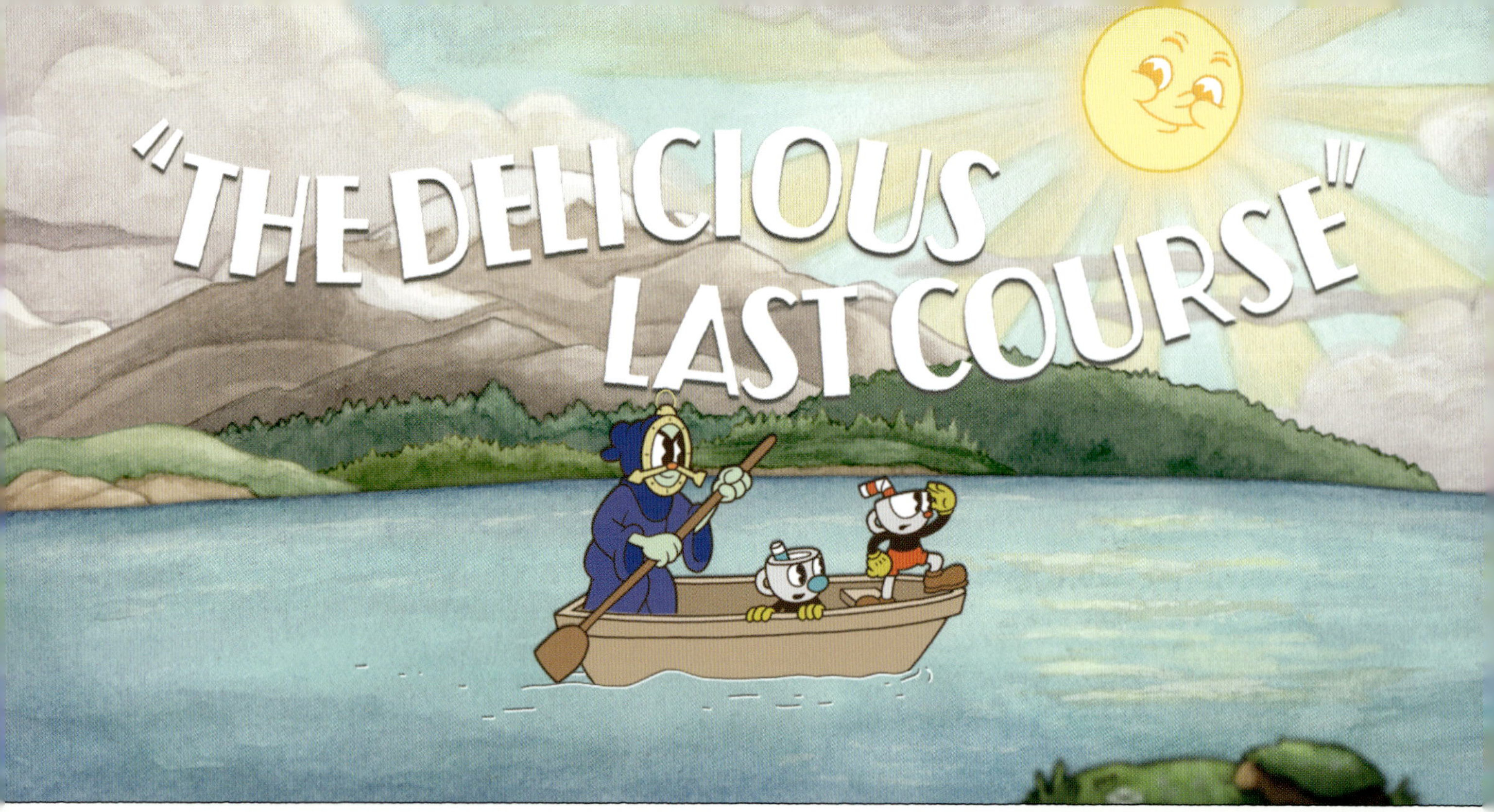

"THE DELICIOUS LAST COURSE"

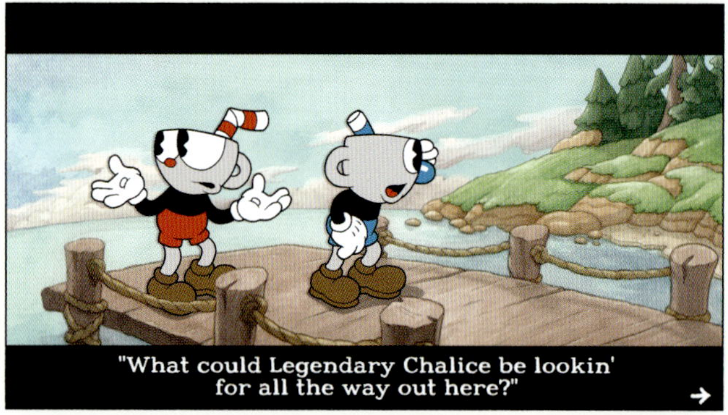

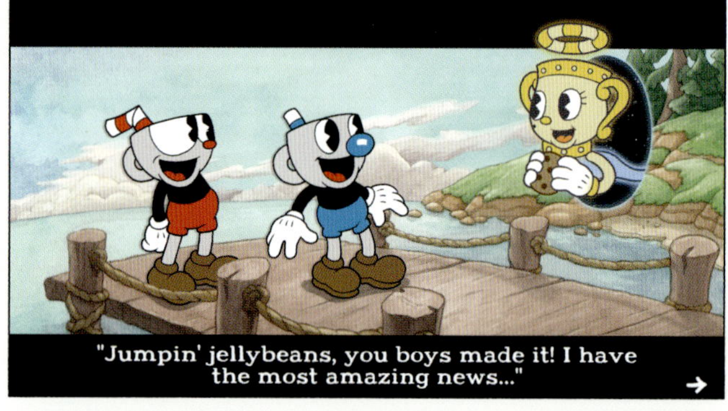

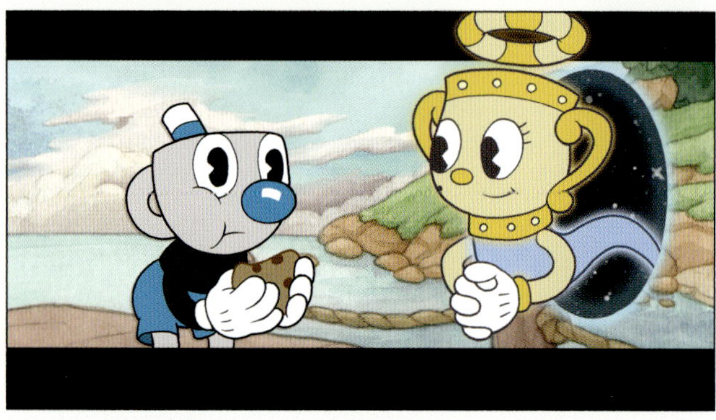

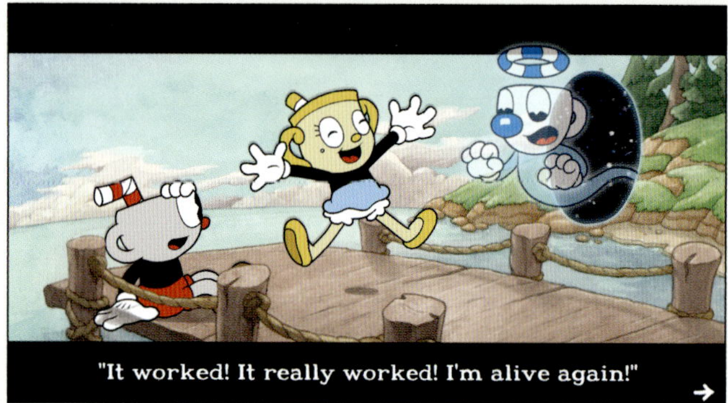

Opening Cutscene

AS THE *DELICIOUS LAST COURSE*'s adventure was an extension of the original *Cuphead*'s mission, we opted not to do another physical storybook introduction so as to maintain the consistency of the in-world storytelling. Upon arriving on this unknown isle, we wanted to get right into the core of the DLC's *raison d'être*, so we decided to demonstrate the magical cookie's soul-swapping powers right from the first shot, with little introduction or fanfare. Much like the 1930s cartoon shorts that inspired us, this approach helps to maintain an air of breezy adventure.

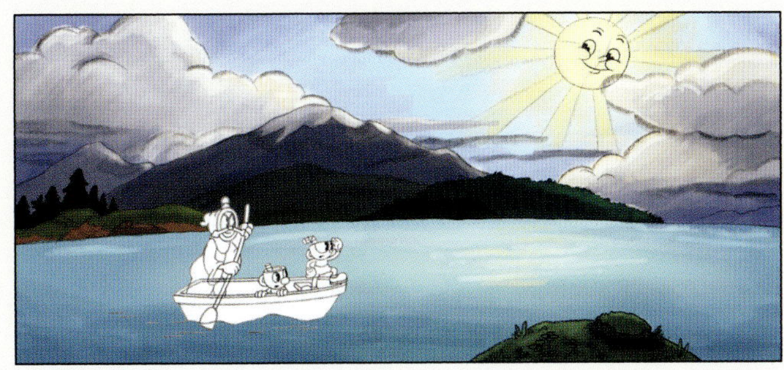
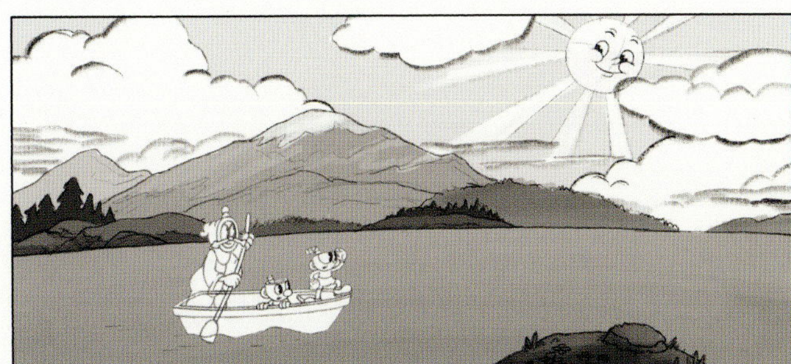
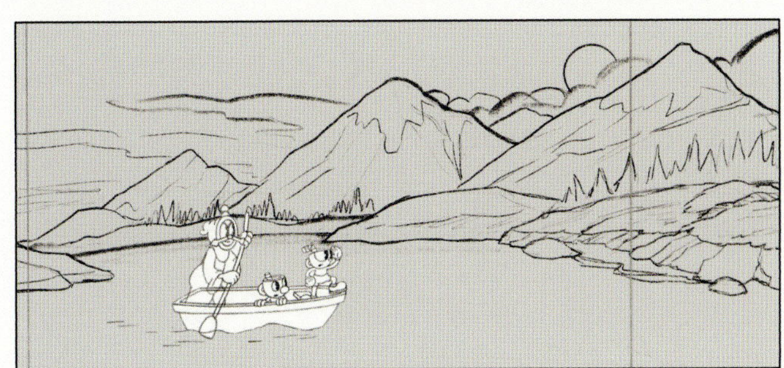
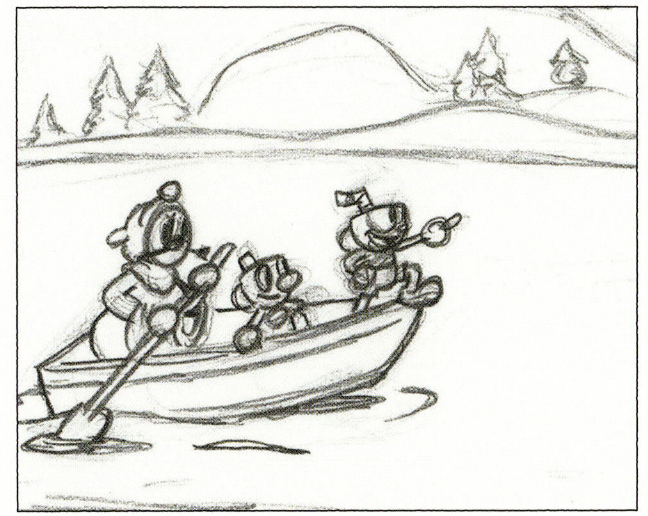
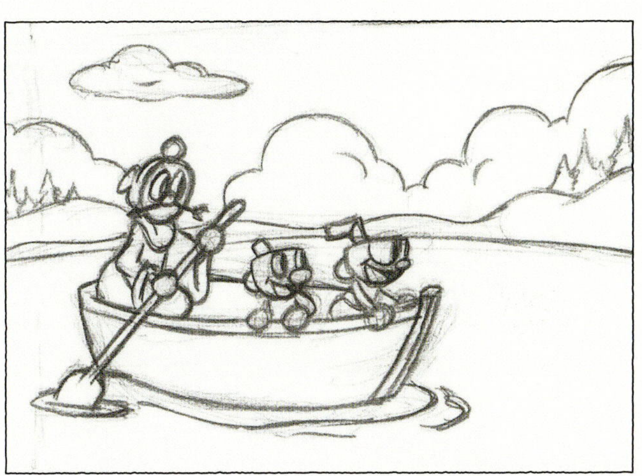
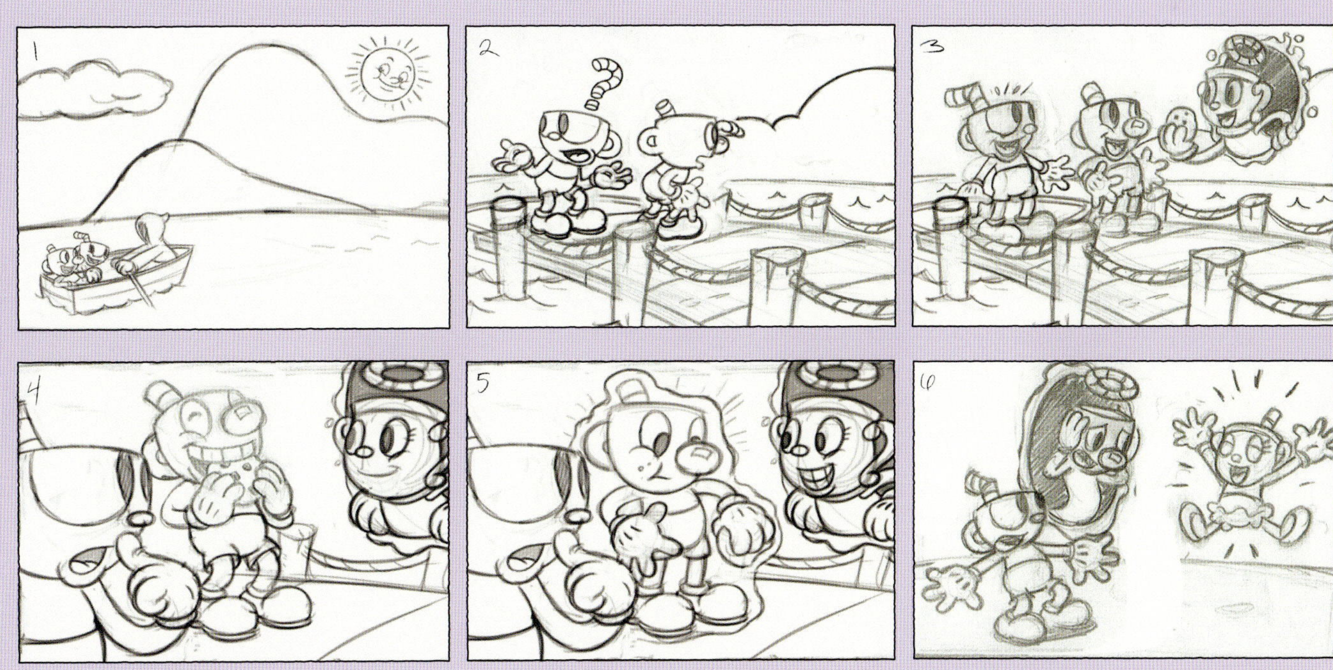
1
2
3
4
5
6

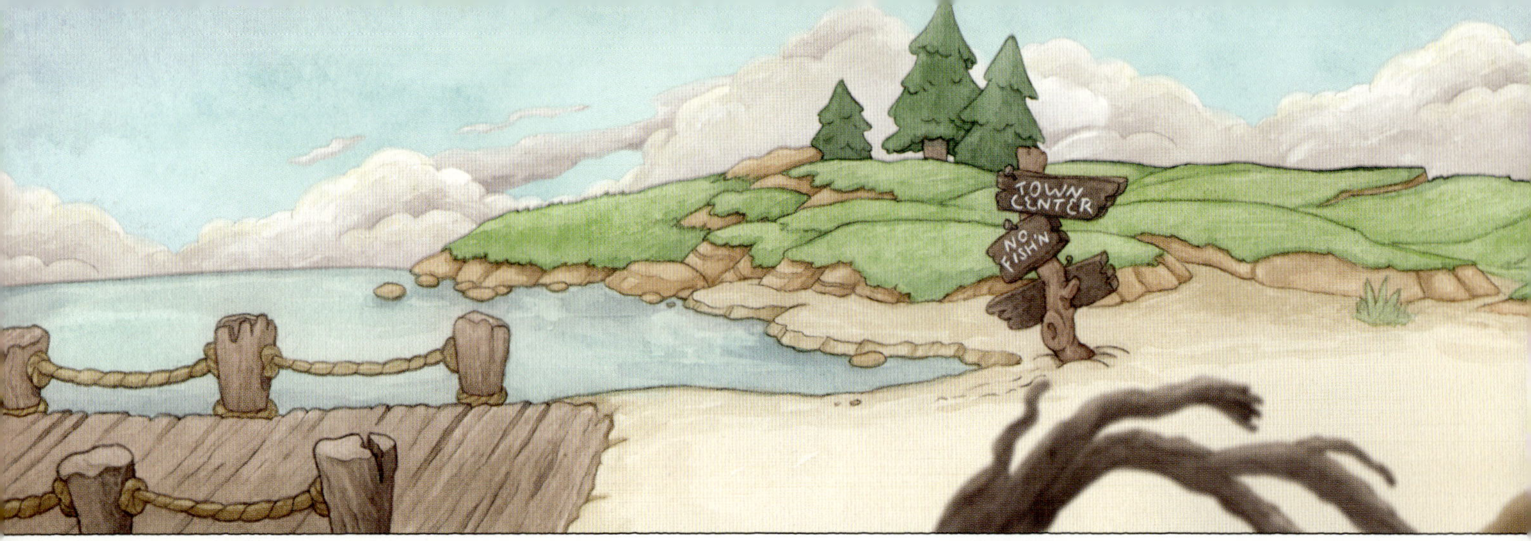

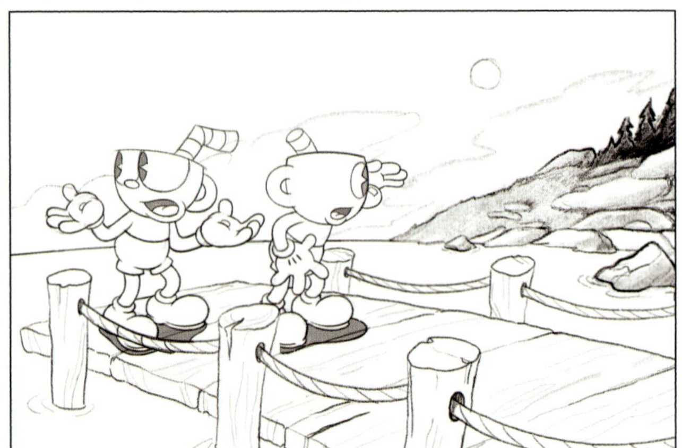

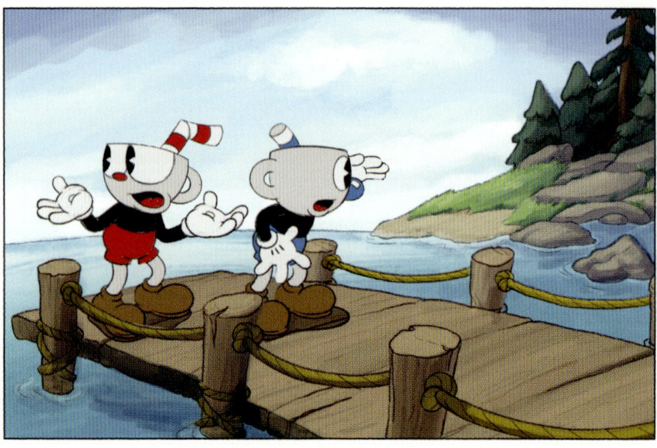

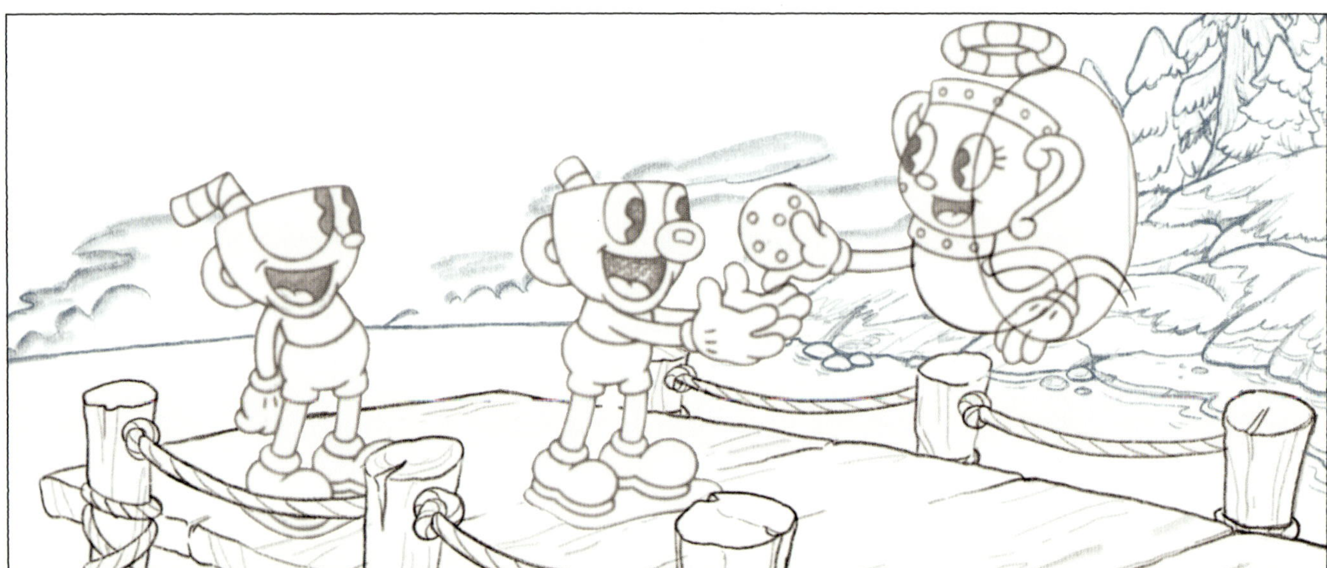

All of the original cutscenes for the base game used static shots to portray characters moving the plot along, but to keep the pace up for the DLC's opening sequence, we needed to show our trio of heroes talking while traversing the space from the docks to the bakery. This sequence required some artistic trickery, as we couldn't know exactly how long a player would spend on each line of dialogue as the background scrolled past the screen. To make the shot seamless, we connected the docks painting to a sequence of beach layers that could loop for an indeterminate amount of time, then queued up the town art to conclude the shot once the players advanced the last line of text.

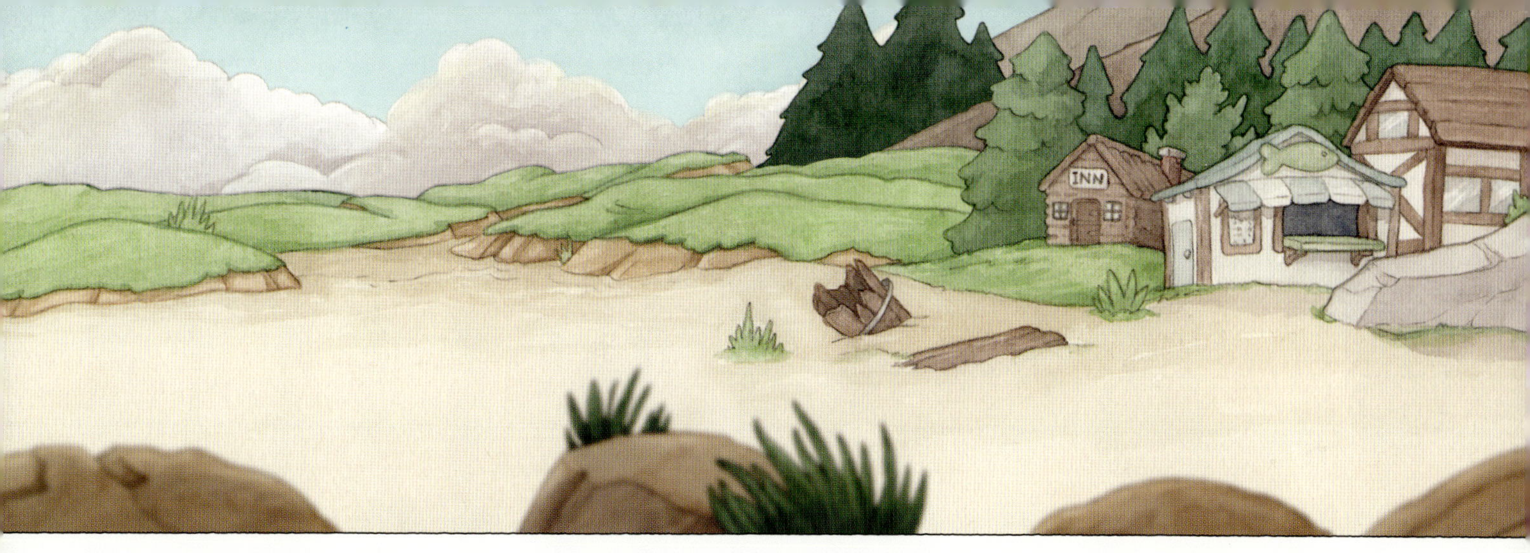
INN

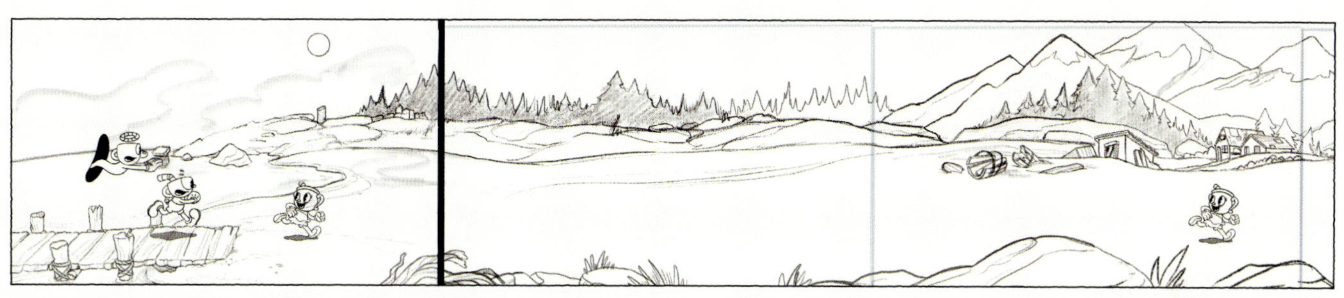

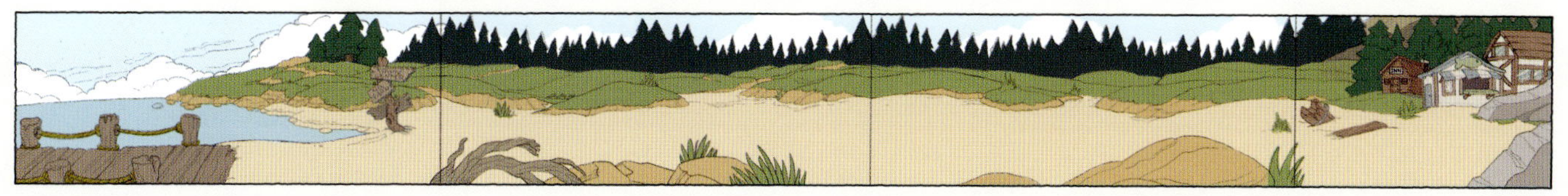

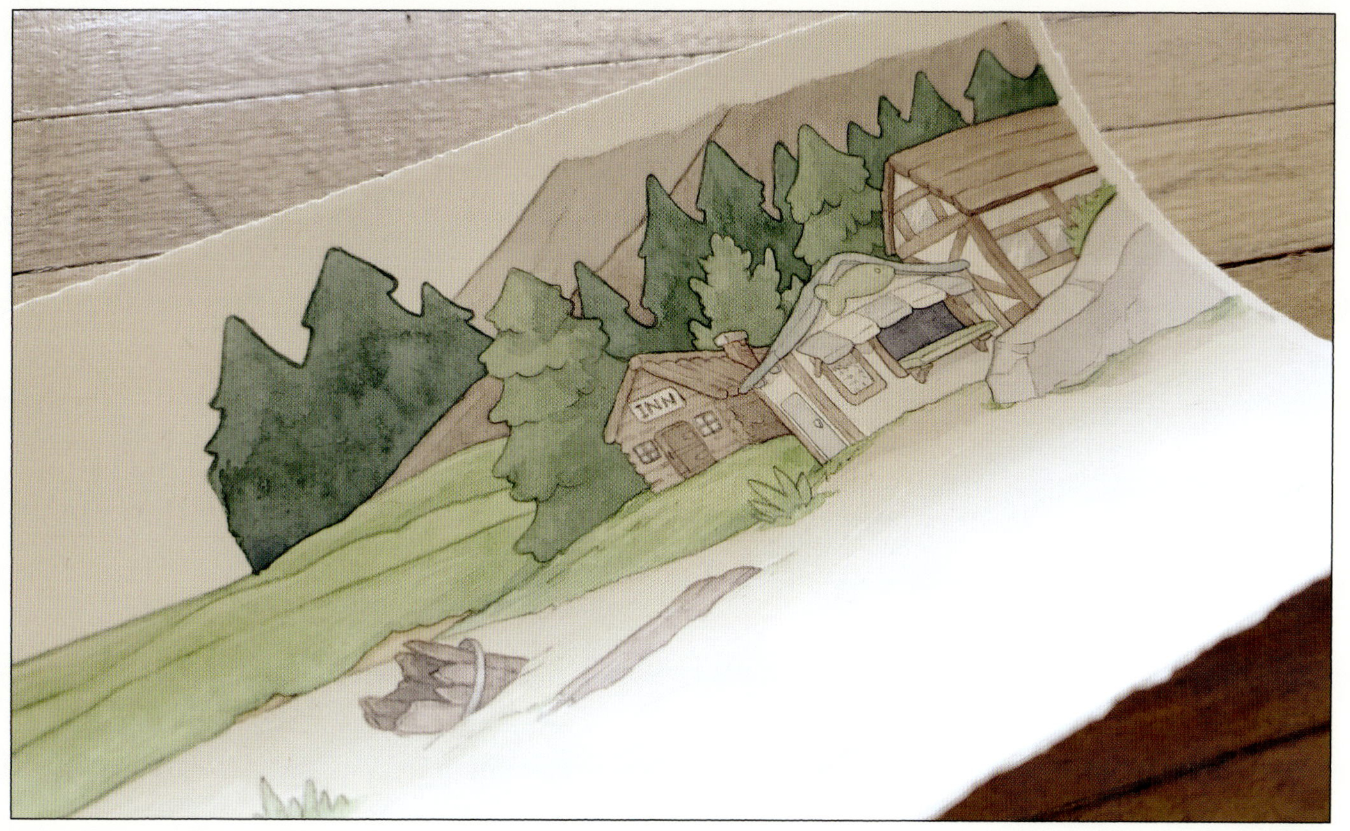
INN

For the development of all of our cutscenes, we go through a number of iterations involving multiple disciplines. We start with a basic plot outline and then budget and block out the number and style of shots it would take to convey that story in the most concise way possible. From there, the writers flesh out dialogue and character interactions, allowing the storyboard artist to draw basic staging and key frames to match that dialogue. We iterate on both shot composition and dialogue for flow and clarity, continuing to edit both down until we have our final shots. These shot templates are then used by the background artists and animators to complete the final assets for the game.

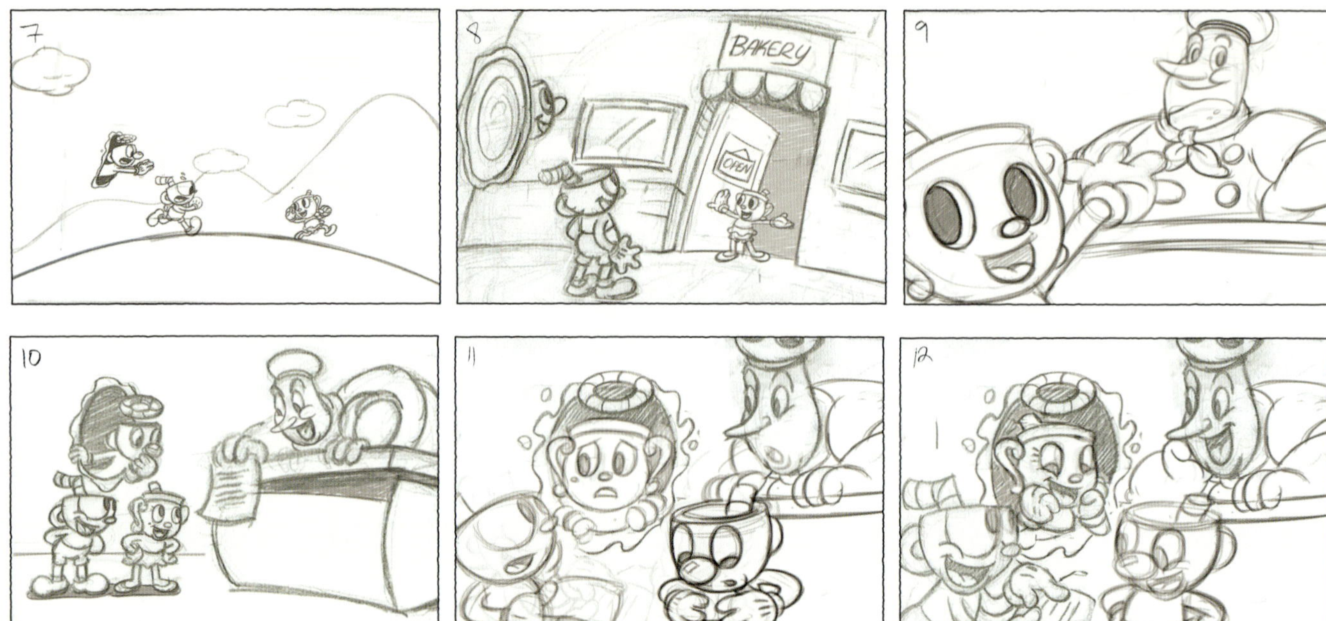

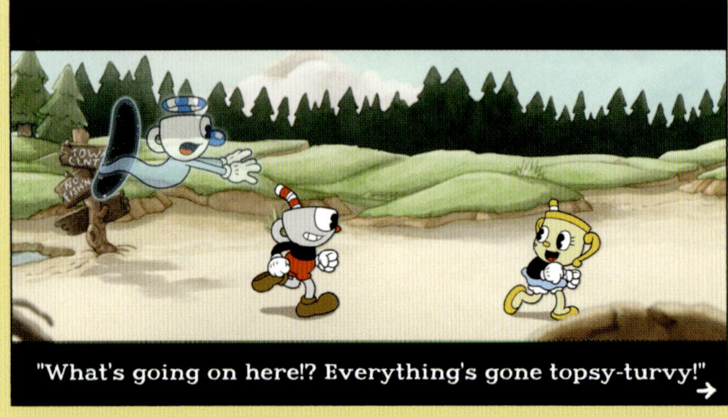

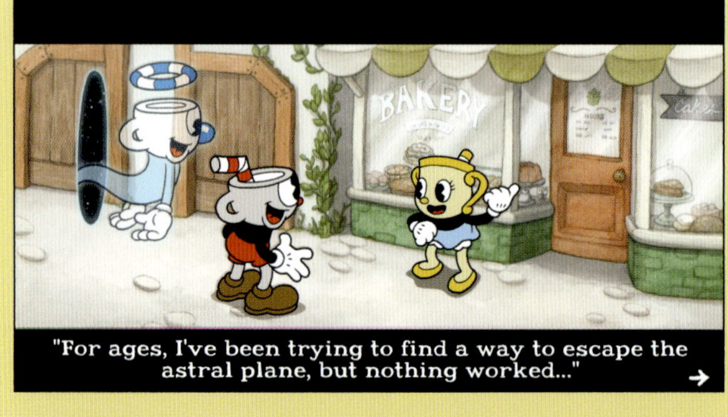

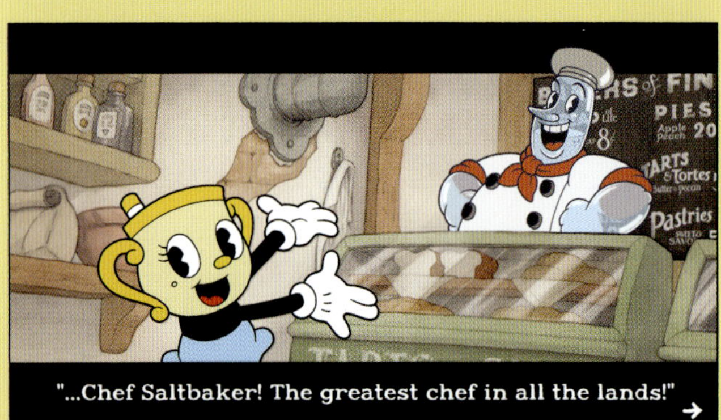

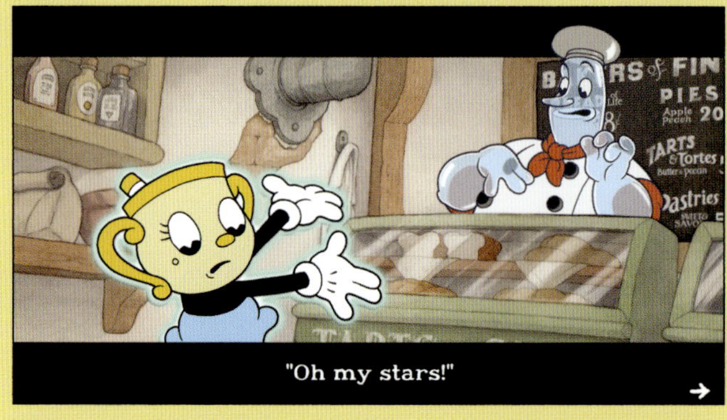

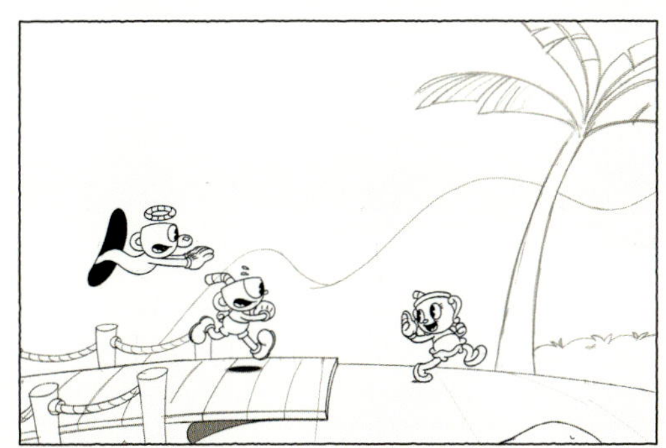

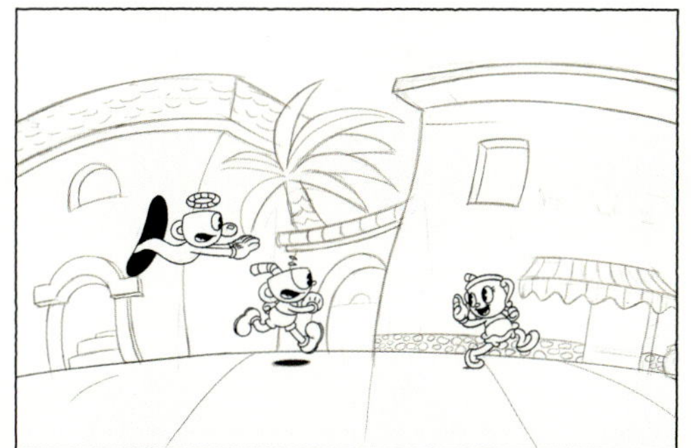

Pictured left, pencil iterations by Cutscene Animator Joseph Coleman. Note the palm trees in the town, a vestigial artifact from a time when the DLC town was depicted as a resort.

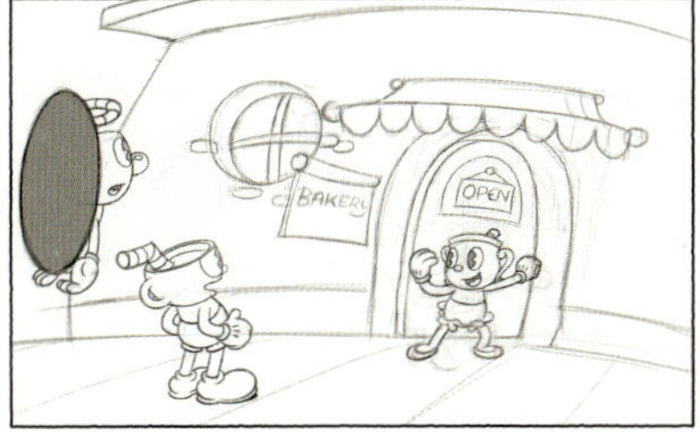

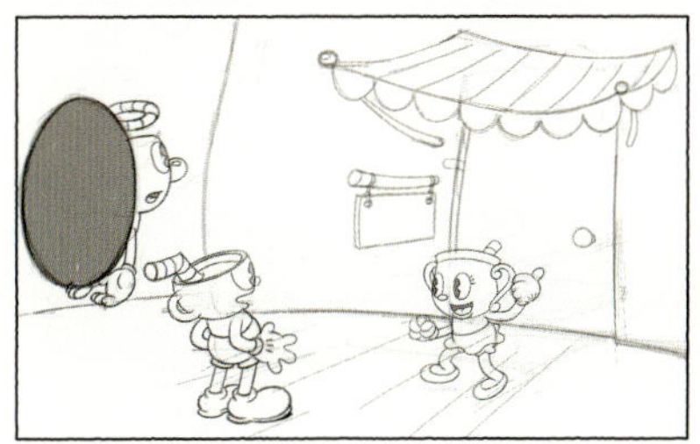

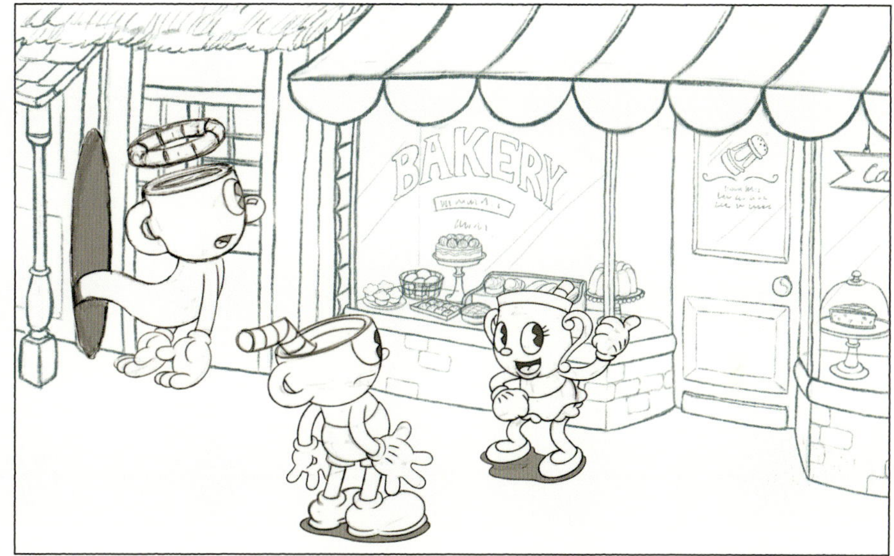

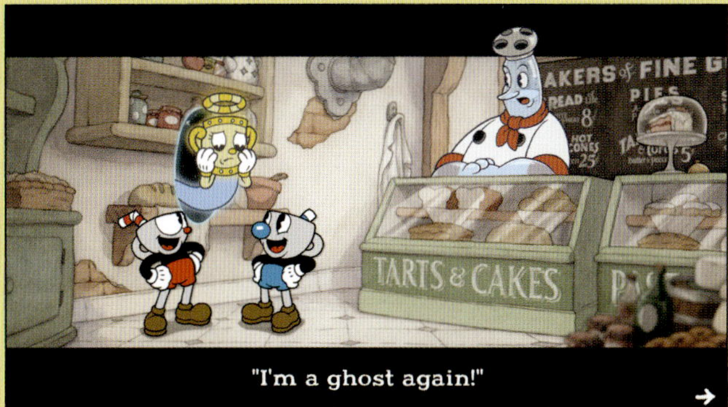

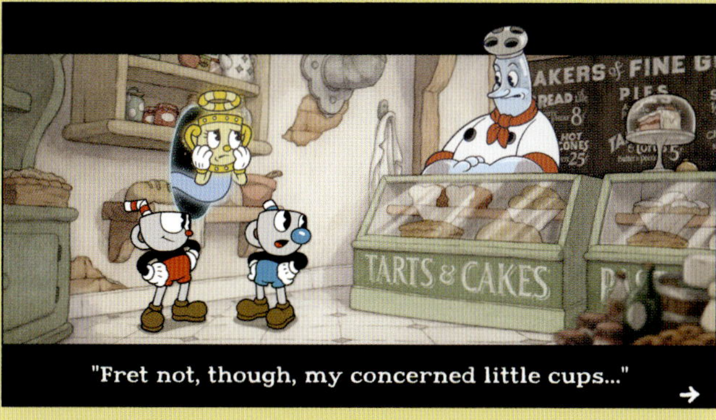

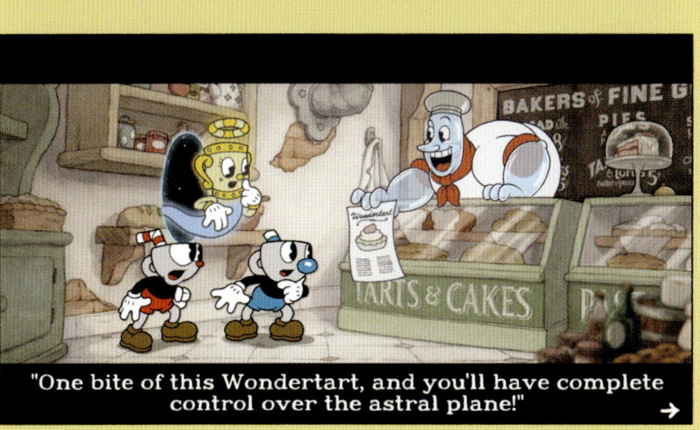

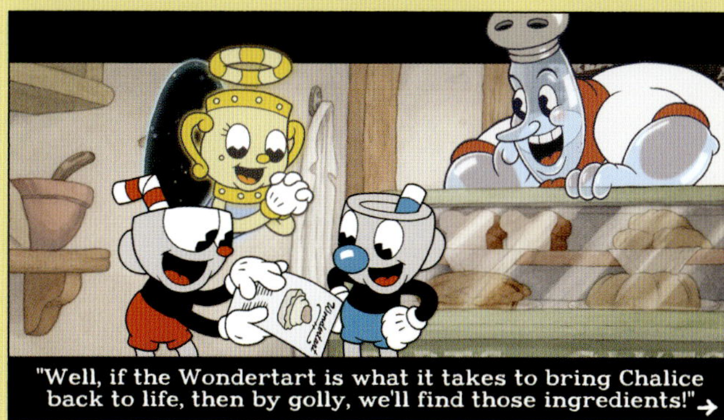

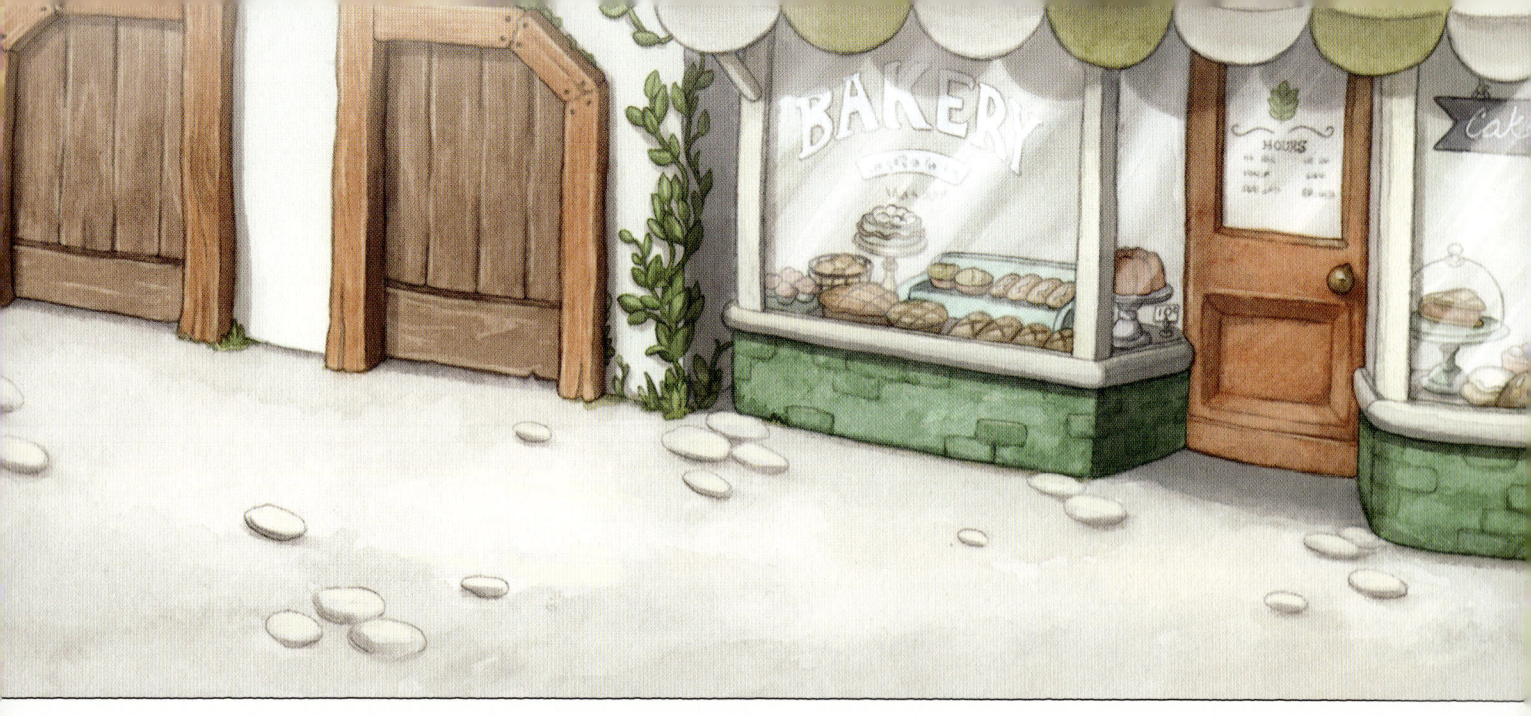
BAKERY
HOURS

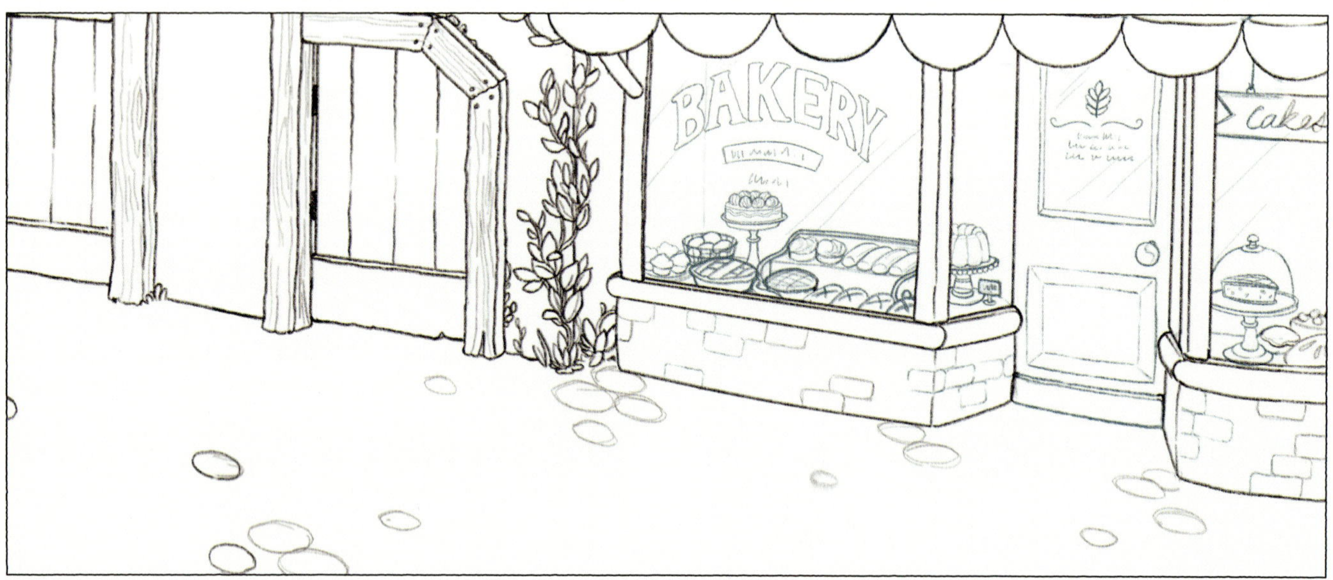
BAKERY

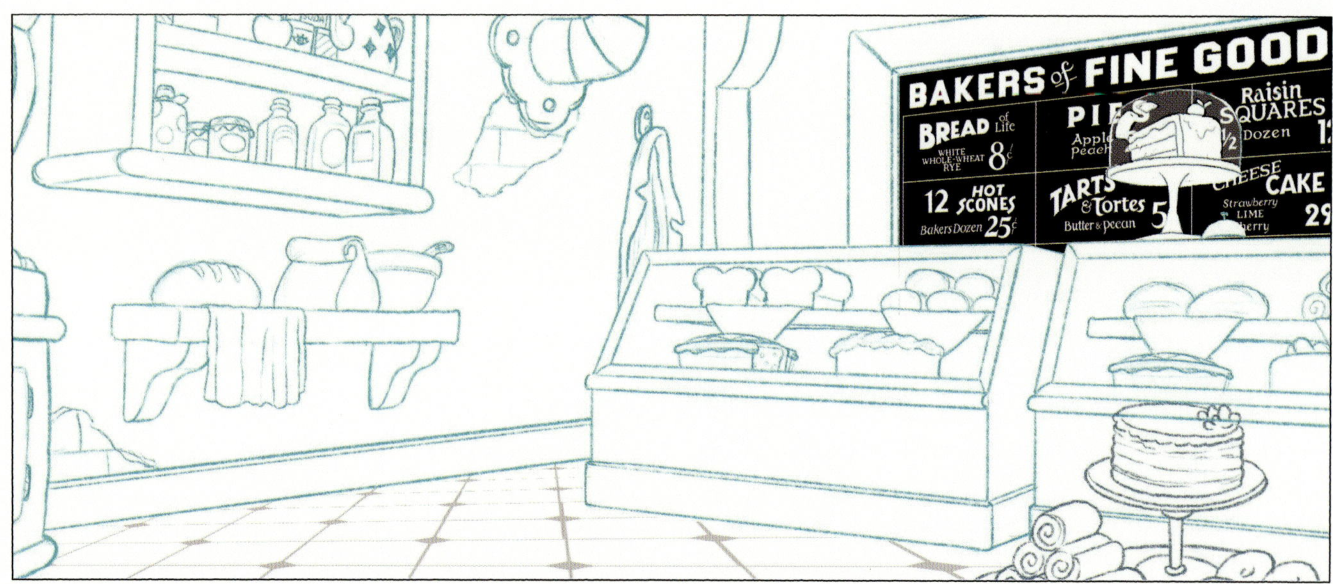
BAKERS of FINE GOOD
BREAD of Life
WHITE
WHOLE-WHEAT
RYE
8¢
Apple
Peach
Raisin
SQUARES
Dozen
12 HOT SCONES
Bakers Dozen 25¢
TARTS
& Tortes
Butter & Pecan
CAKE
Strawberry
LIME

BAKERS of FINE GOODS

BREAD of Life
WHITE
WHOLE-WHEAT
RYE
8¢

PIES
Apple
Peach
20¢

Raisin
SQUARES
½ Dozen
12¢

12 HOT SCONES
Bakers Dozen 25¢

TARTS & Tortes
Butter & Pecan
5¢

CHEESE CAKE
Strawberry
LIME
Cherry
29¢

SHORTCAKE
Fresh
Cream
10¢

Pastries
SWEET & SAVORY
5¢

FRUITcake
18¢ Each

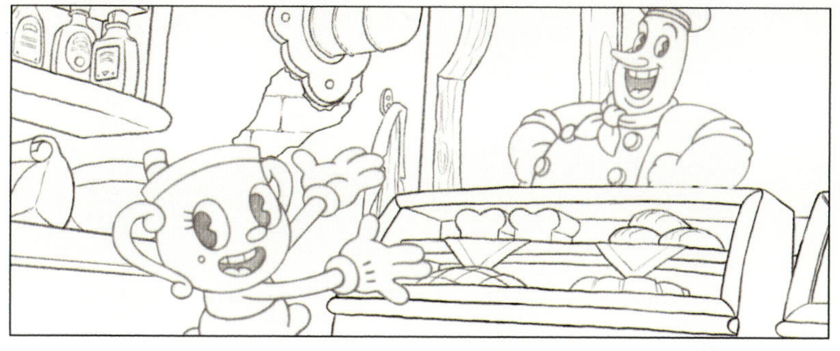

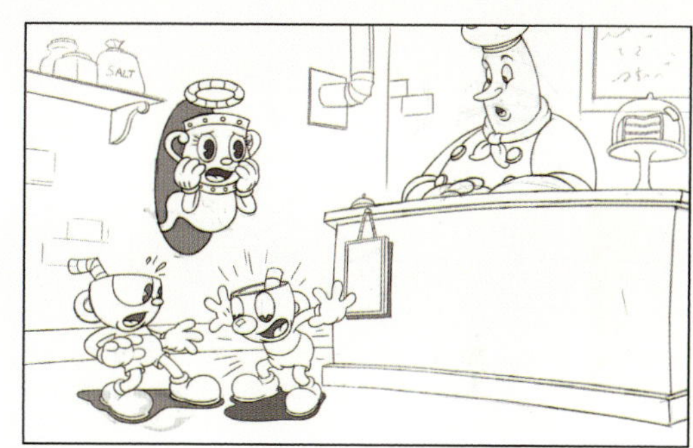

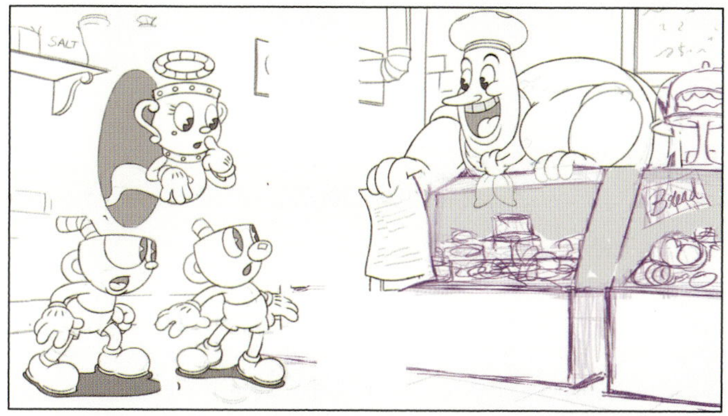

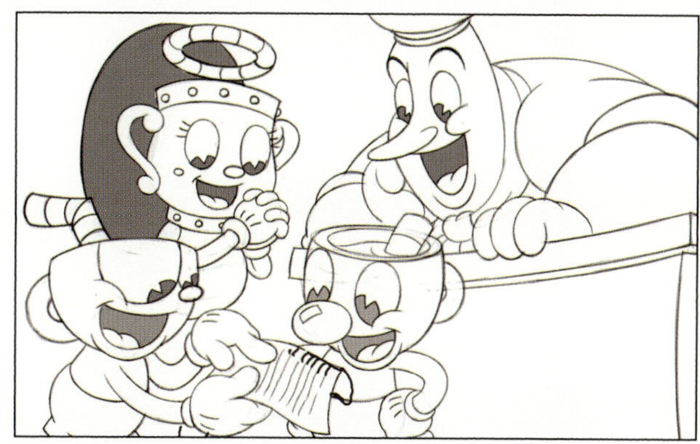

The interior of Chef Saltbaker's bakery ultimately became a key location in the story, bookending the adventure as the home-away-from-home for our heroes as well as the venue for the climactic double cross. On the player's initial visit, we wanted the bake shop to feel as warm and welcoming as Elder Kettle's cottage. For the specific baked goods depicted, we researched popular items of the 1930s and, commissioned Lettering Artist Warren Clark to hand draw a custom sign for the back of Saltbaker's business. Fun fact that few have spotted: the advertised "Bakers Dozen" is one short of the customary 13, hinting at Saltbaker's greediness in plain sight.

Chef Saltbaker Fight Cutscene

FOR THE REVEAL OF Chef Saltbaker's turn to the dark side, we needed a big bombastic display of his altered visual design that would parallel Cuphead and Mugman's final confrontation with the Devil. So, like that original penultimate cutscene in Inkwell Hell, this preamble to the final showdown with the crooked cook is delivered from the hero's first-person perspective, as if Saltbaker is talking directly to you.

We went through a number of iterations for the scene, with different angles and expressions culminating in the reveal of your captured friend. On the opposite page, you can see how the initial staging sketches from Assistant Art Director Ryan Moldenhauer eventually developed into the final shots by Cutscene Animator Joseph Coleman.

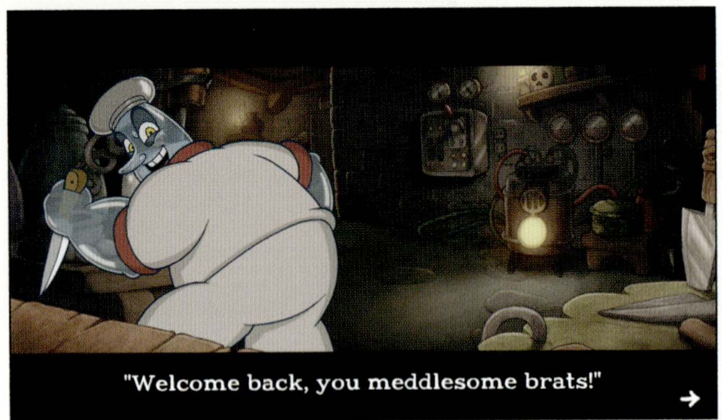

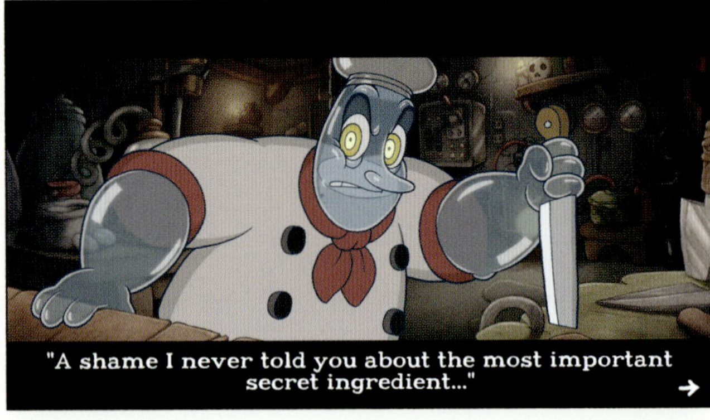

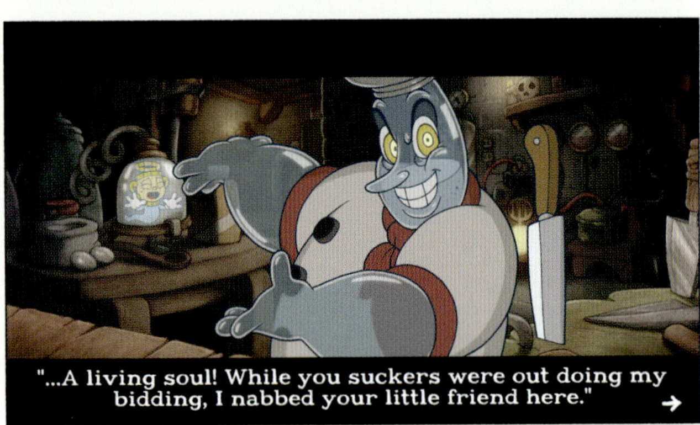

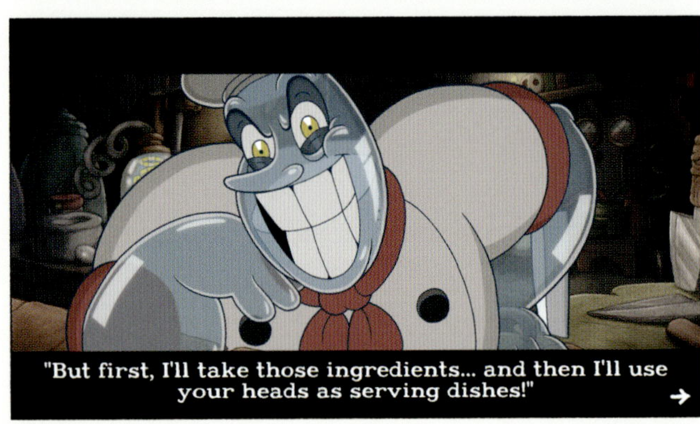

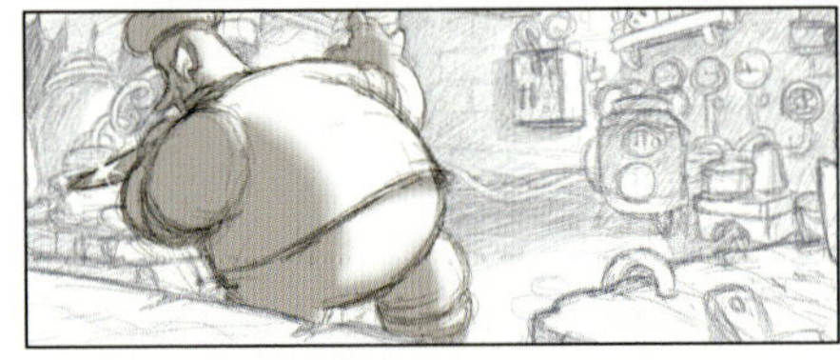

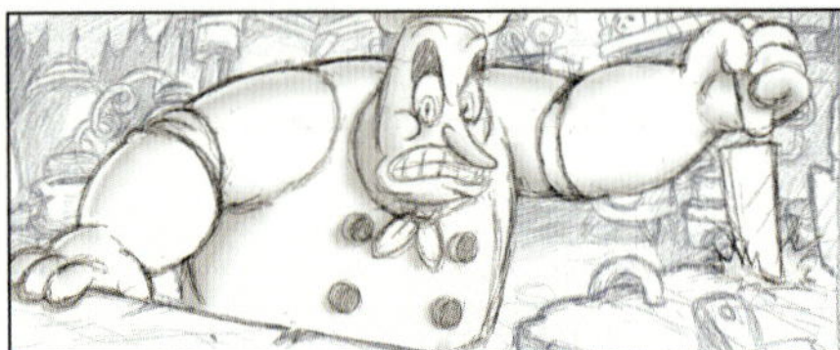

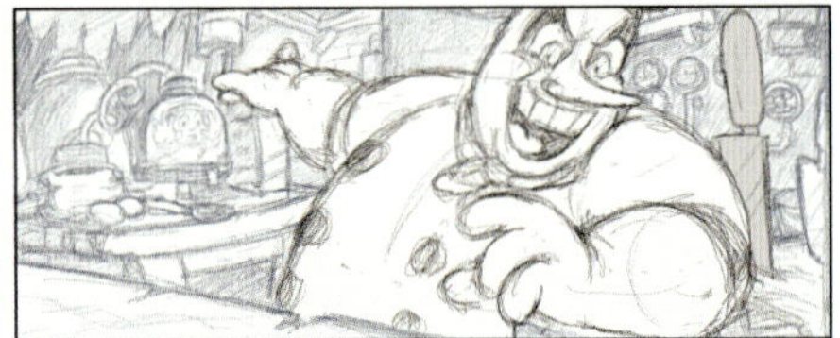

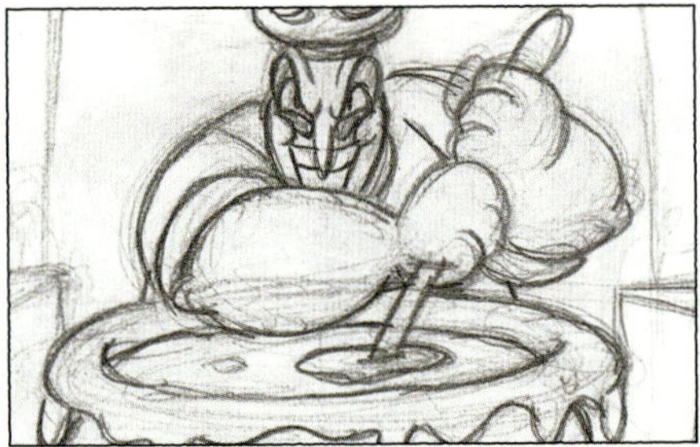

Saltbaker: *I didn't think you would make it back so quickly . . .*

Alas, there's no point in maintaining the ruse any longer.

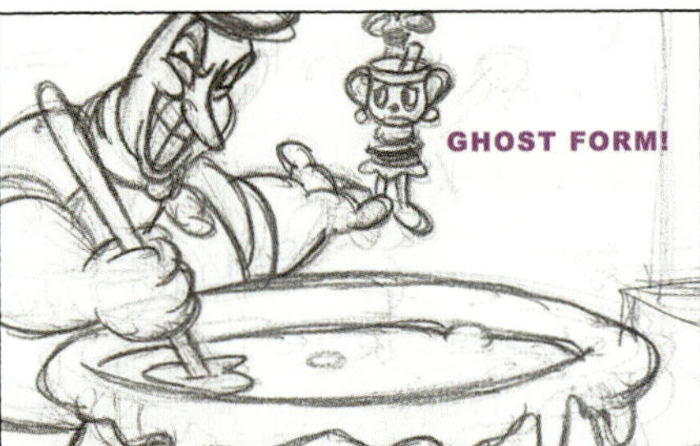

Saltbaker: *Foolish Children! Those ingredients are not enough to bake a cake of this power. A recipe of this magnitude requires a living soul as the final ingredient . . . and your friend will do just perfect!*

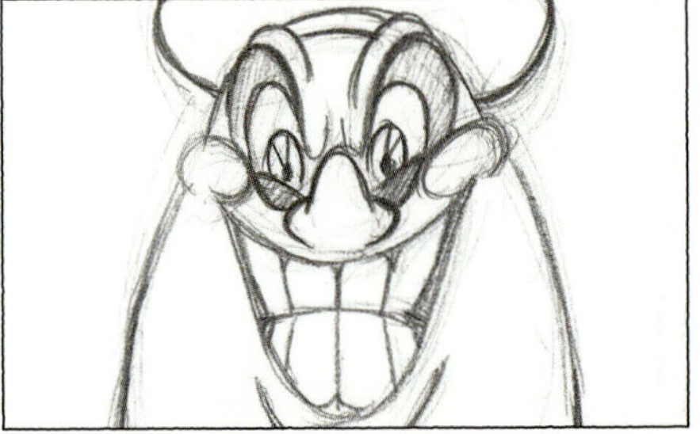

Saltbaker: *Once baked to perfection, one bite of this masterpiece will make me stronger than the Devil himself!*

After I crush you, I'm going to add you to the recipe, too!

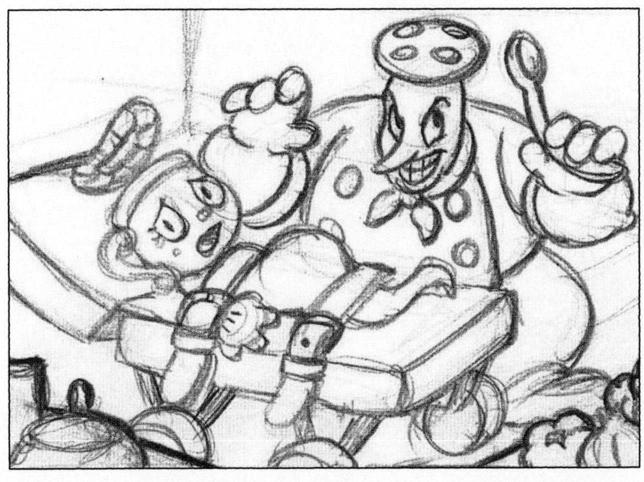

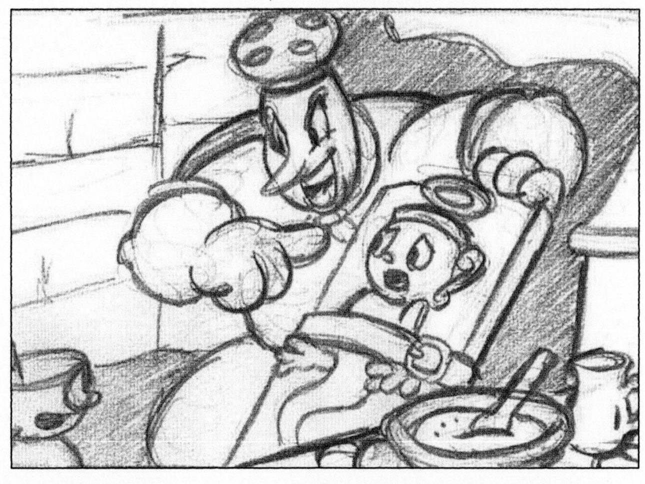

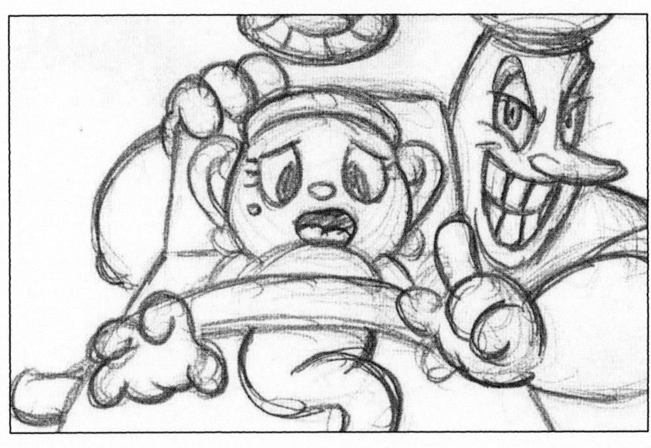

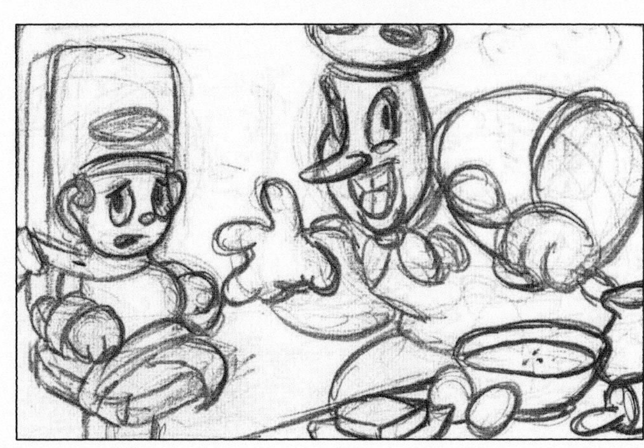

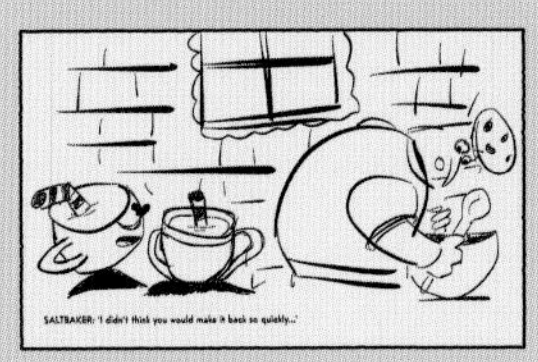

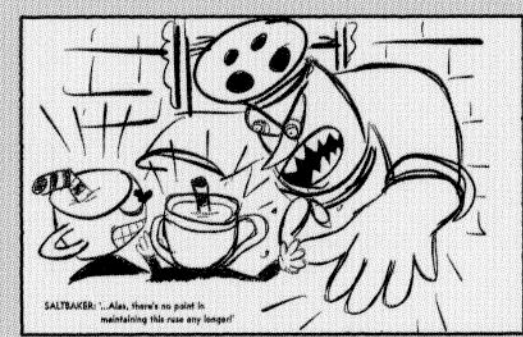

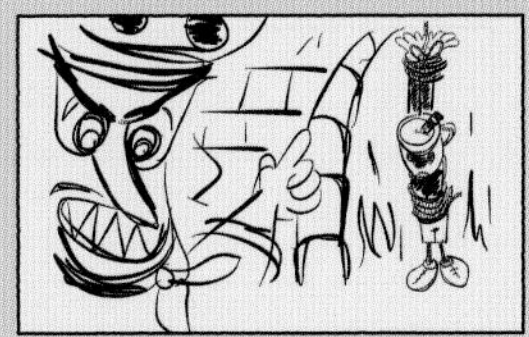

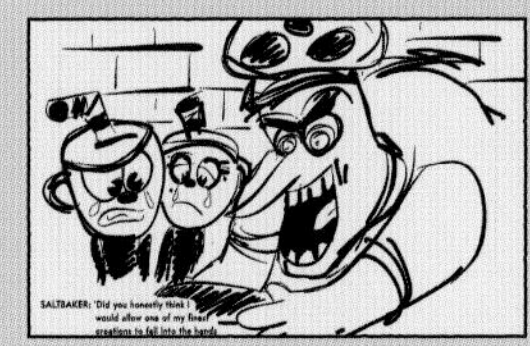

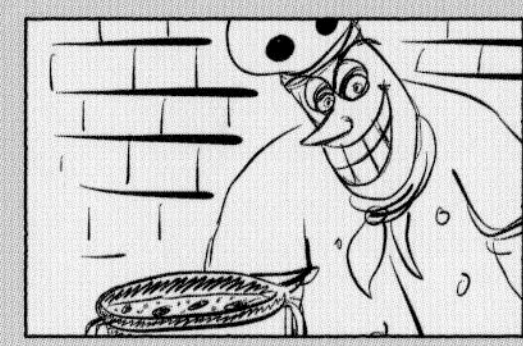

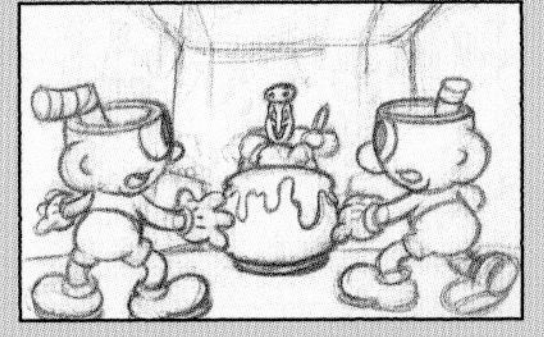

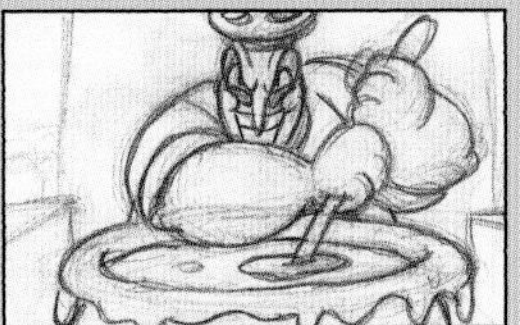

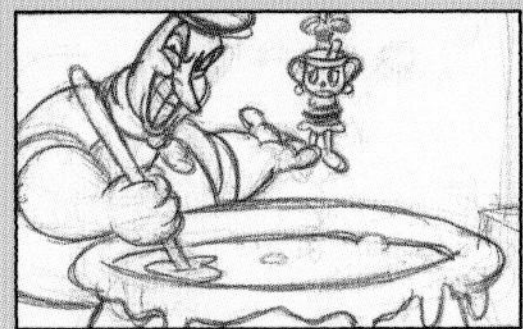

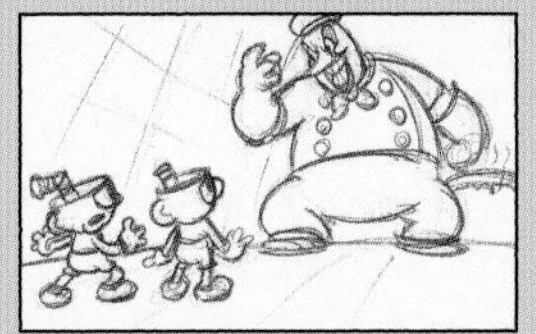

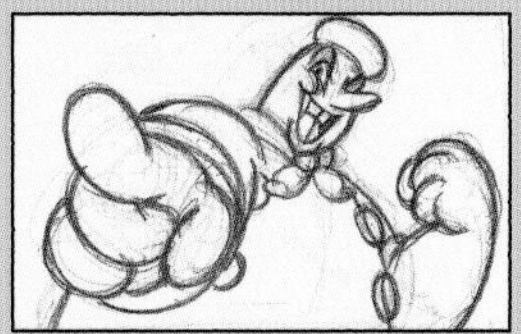

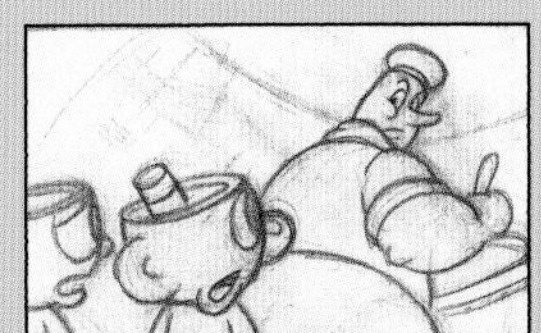

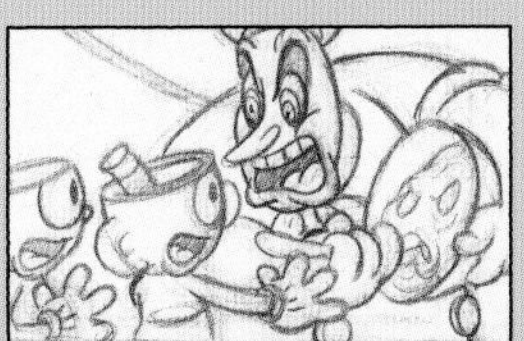

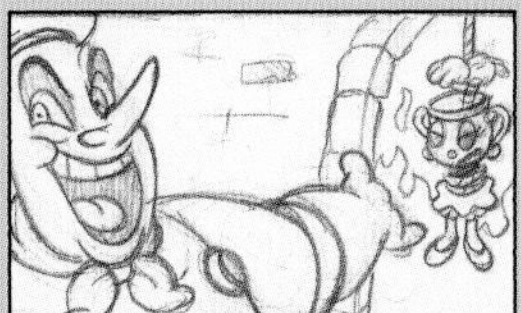

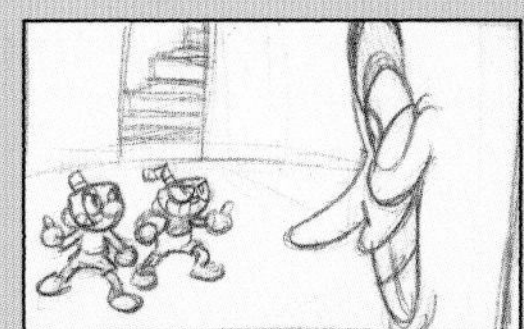

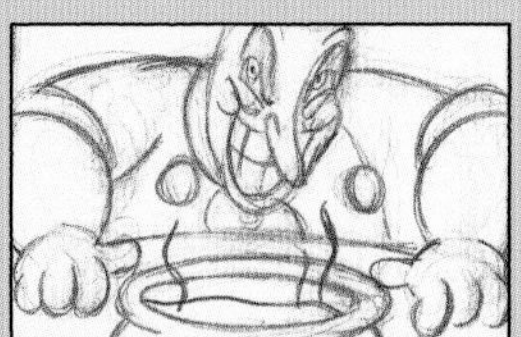

Saltbaker: *I didn't think you would make it back so quickly . . .*

Saltbaker: *Alas, there's no point in maintaining the ruse any longer.*

Saltbaker: *Foolish Children! Those ingredients are not enough to bake a cake of this power. A recipe of this magnitude requires a living soul as the final ingredient . . . and your friend will do just perfect!*

Saltbaker: *Once baked to perfection, one bite of this masterpiece will make me stronger than the Devil himself!*

Saltbaker: *After I crush you, I'm going to add you to the recipe, too!*

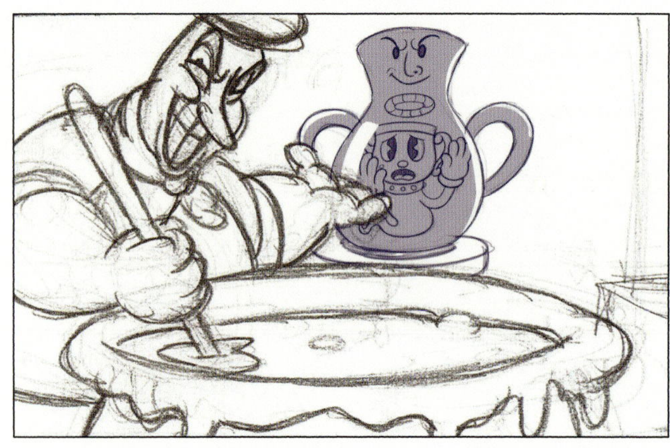
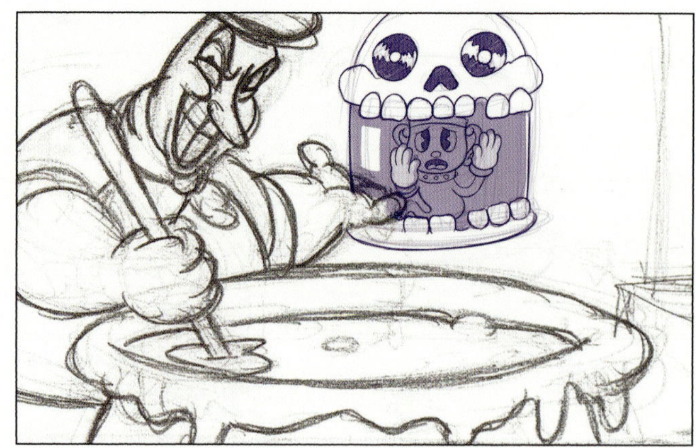
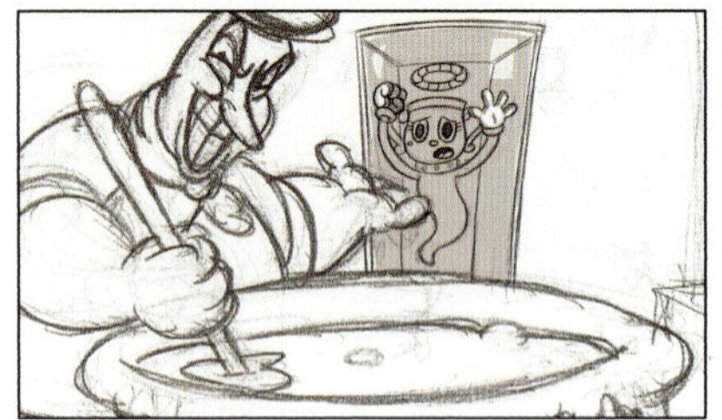
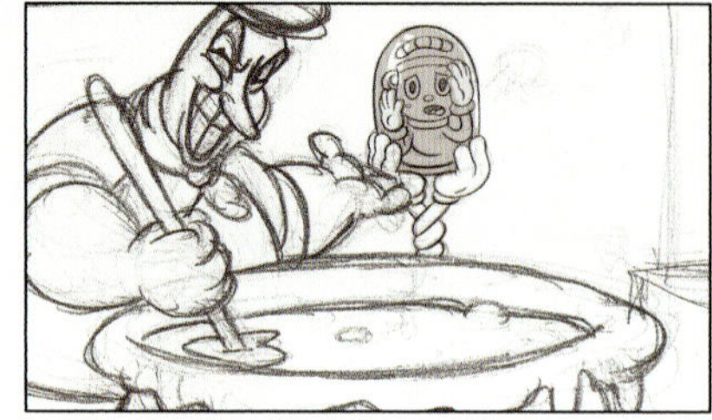
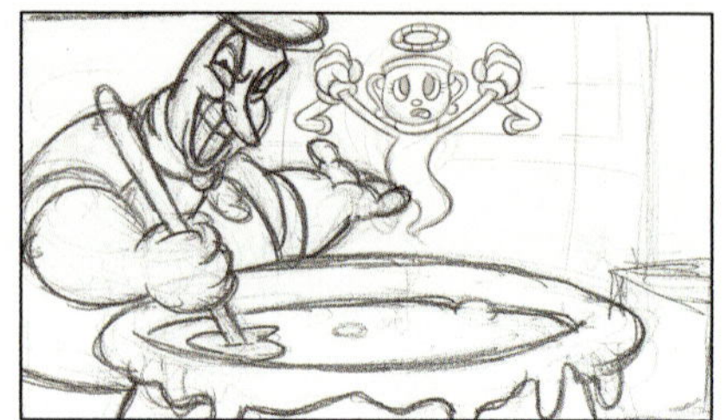
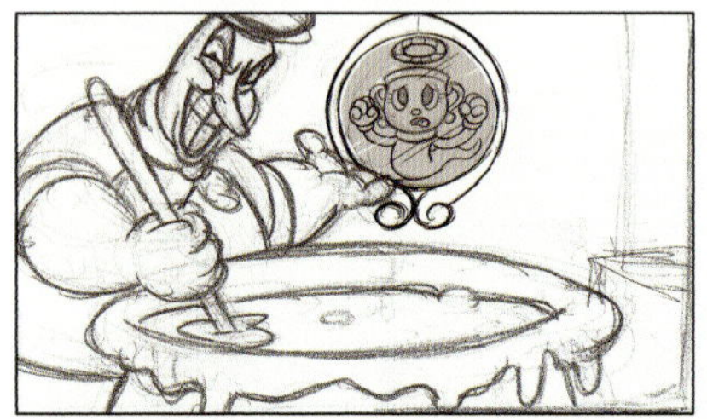
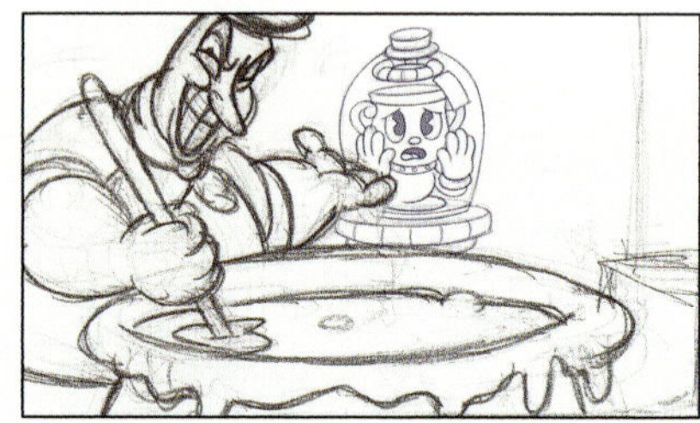
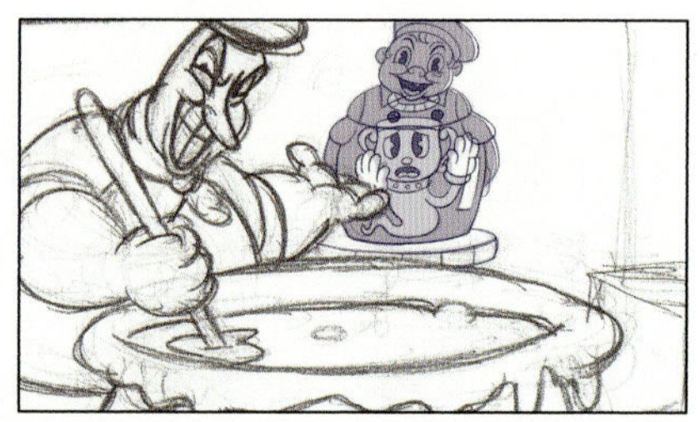
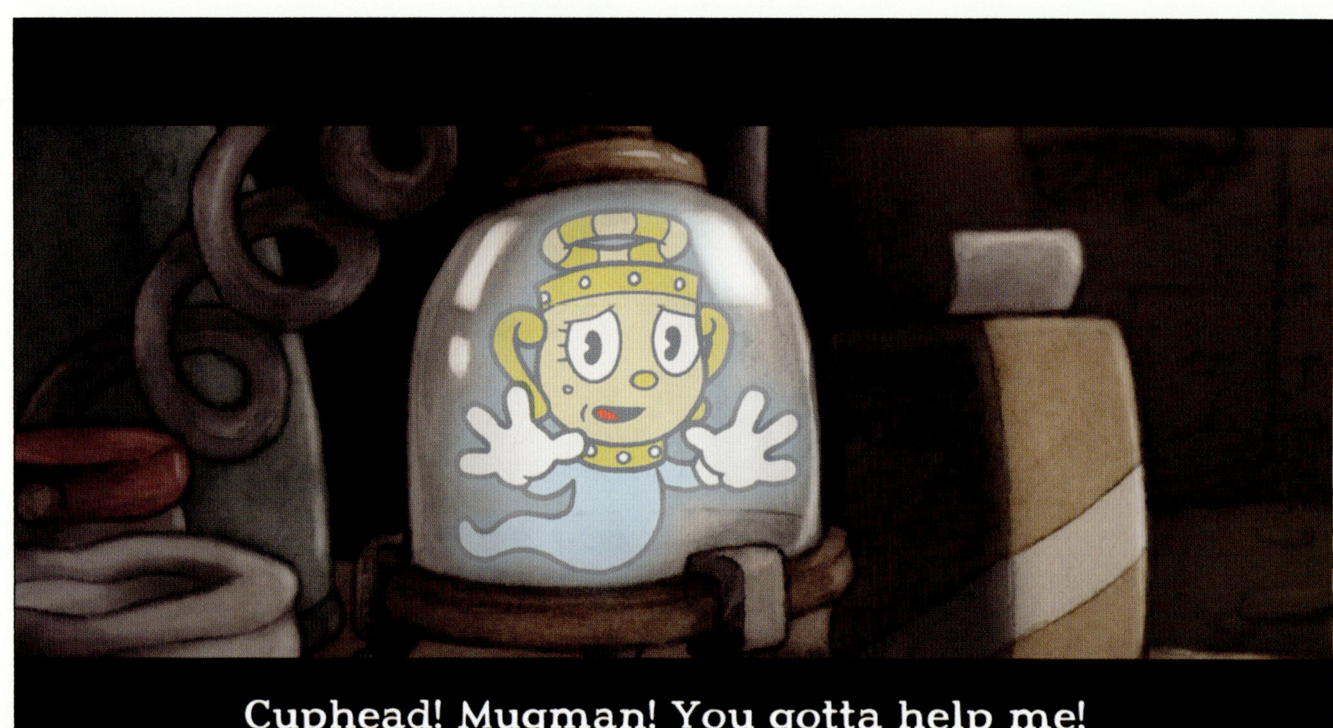
Cuphead! Mugman! You gotta help me!

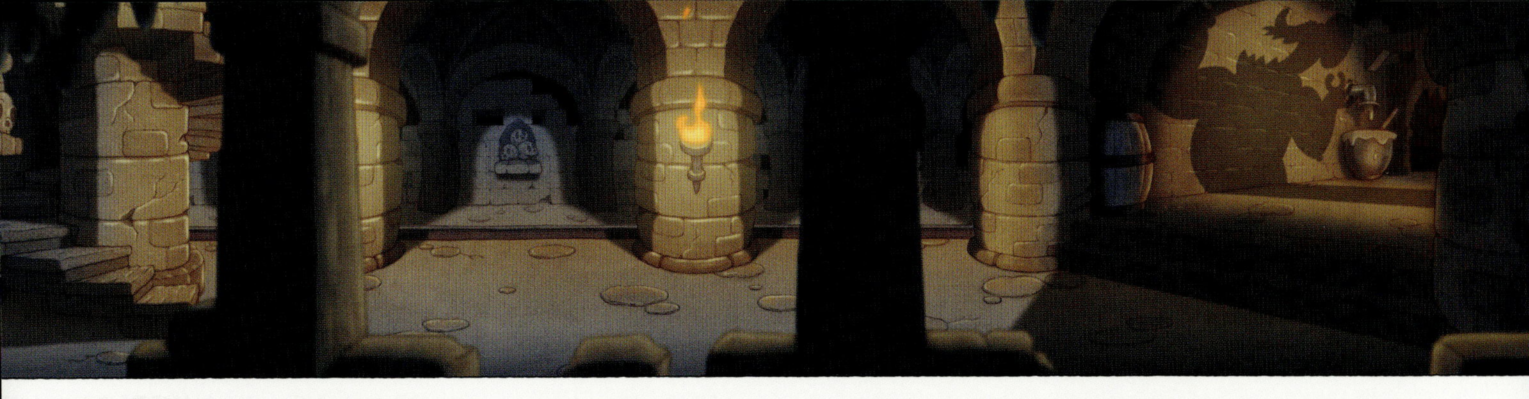

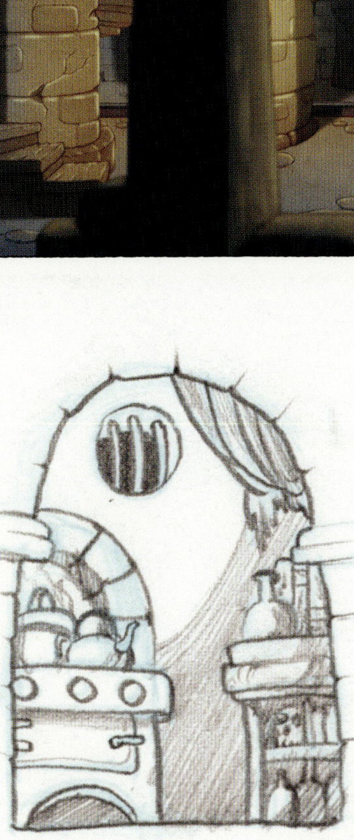

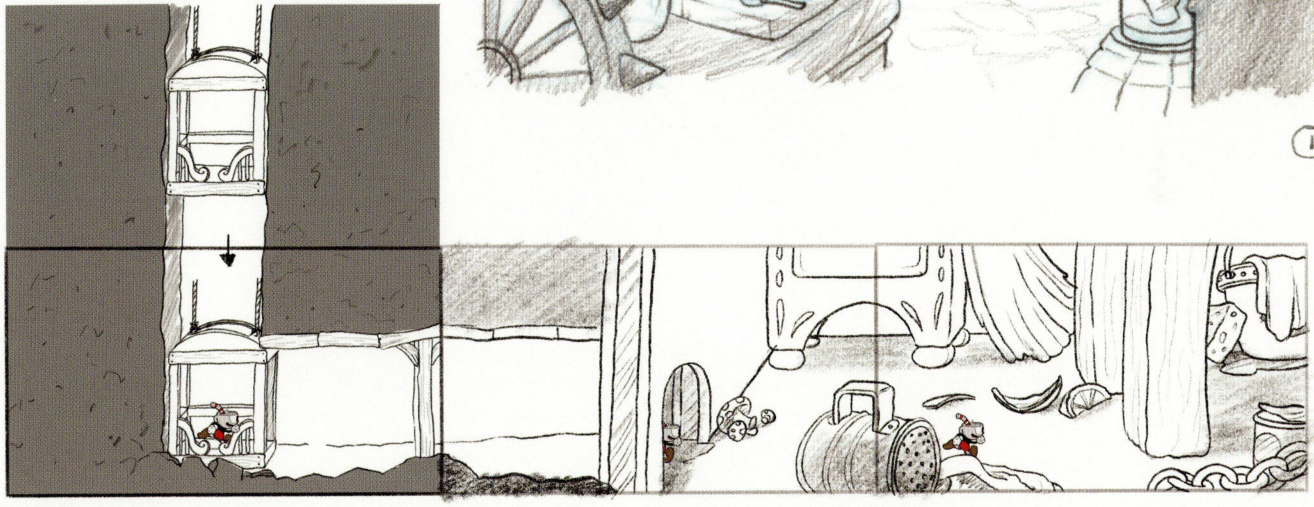

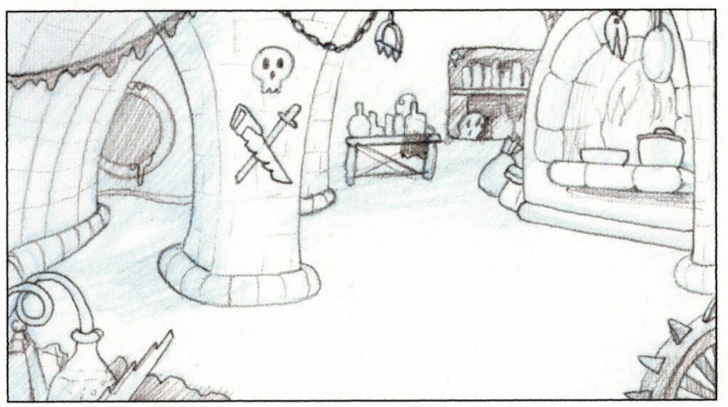

Background Design

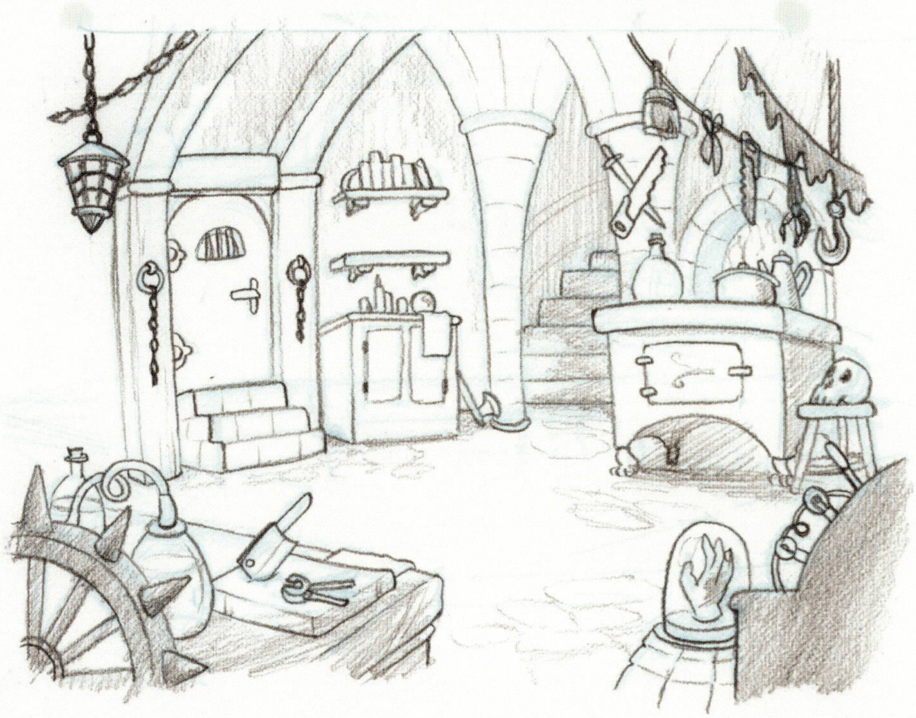

FROM CHEF SALTBAKER'S warm and welcoming bakery down to the ominous secret laboratory where he toils away on dastardly desserts, we wanted to build anticipation for the upcoming surprise. An homage to the pre-Dracula hall of torches in Konami's *Super Castlevania IV* (1991), our original plan for the liminal space involved a creaky elevator descent that was cut for pacing reasons. As a little secret, after defeating Chef Saltbaker, if a player wants to experience the spooky approach again, they can hold L & R on the controller outside Chef Saltbaker's Bakery before entering the fight!

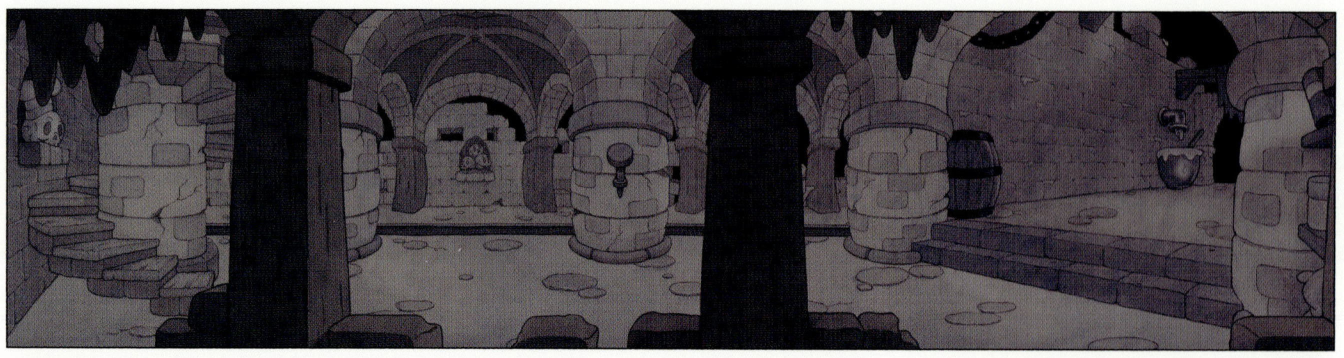

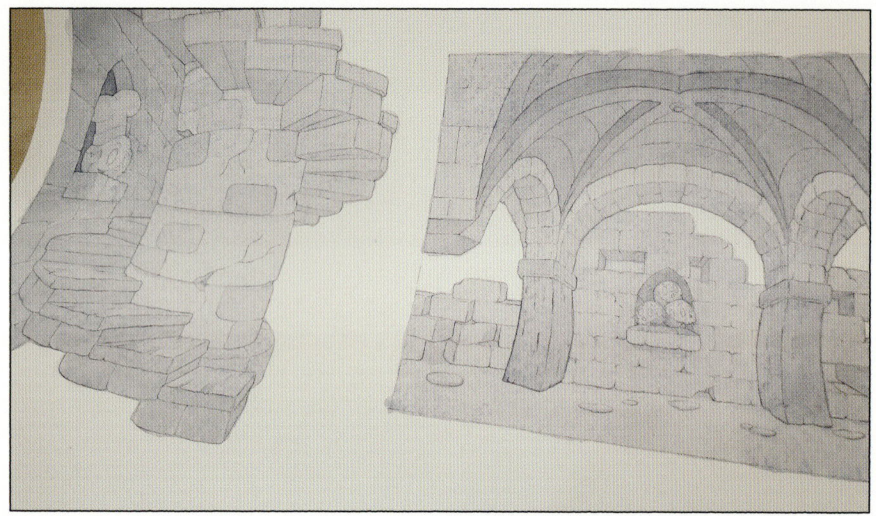

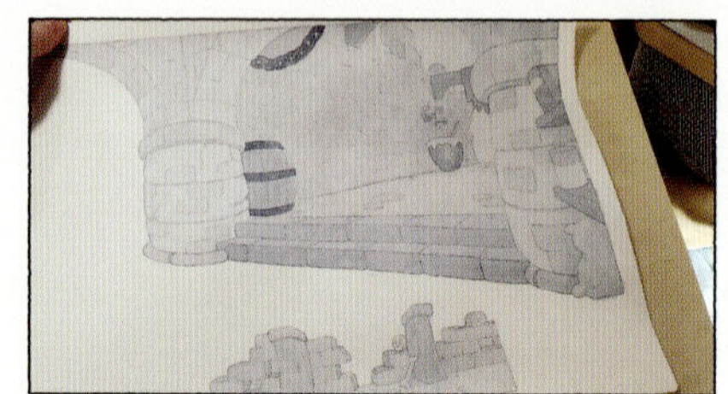

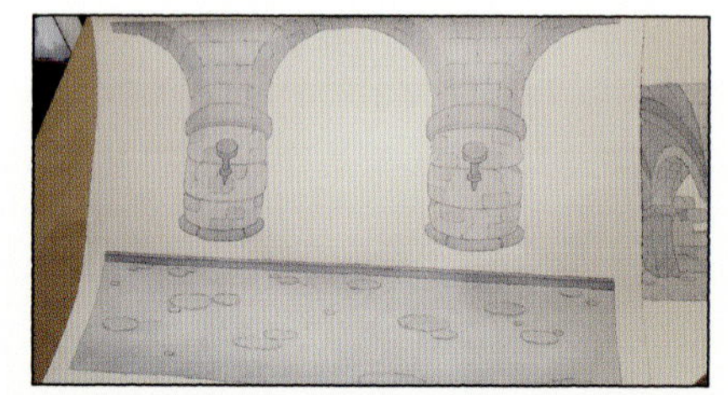

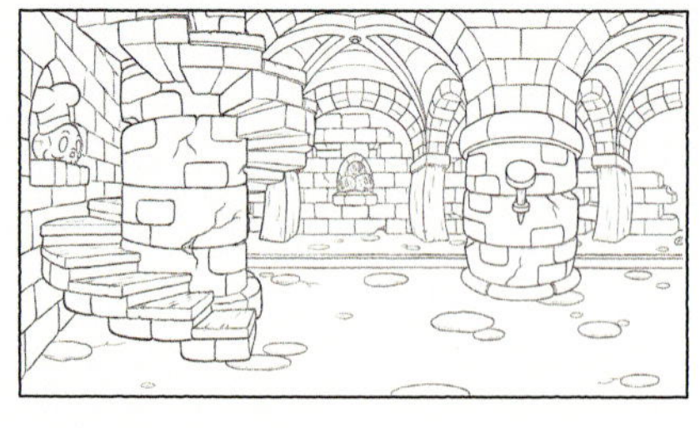

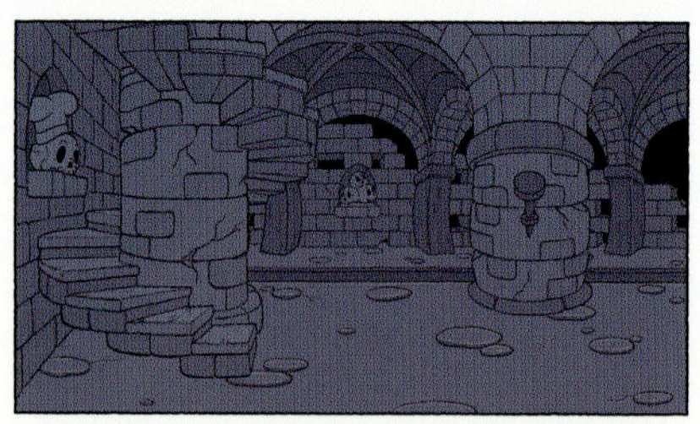

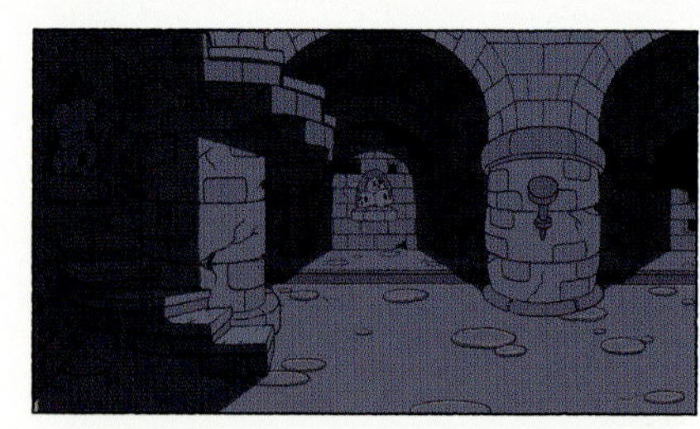

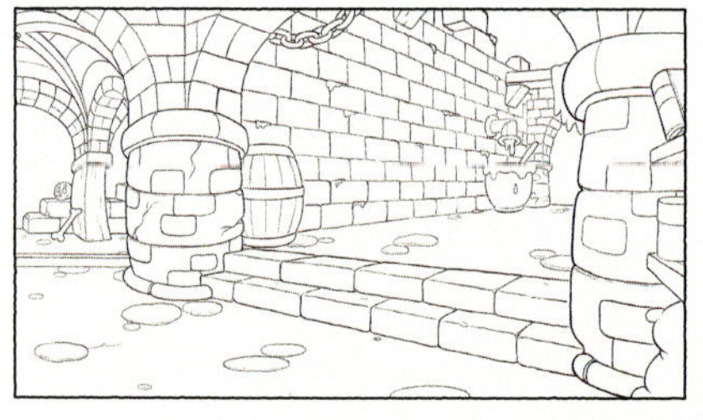

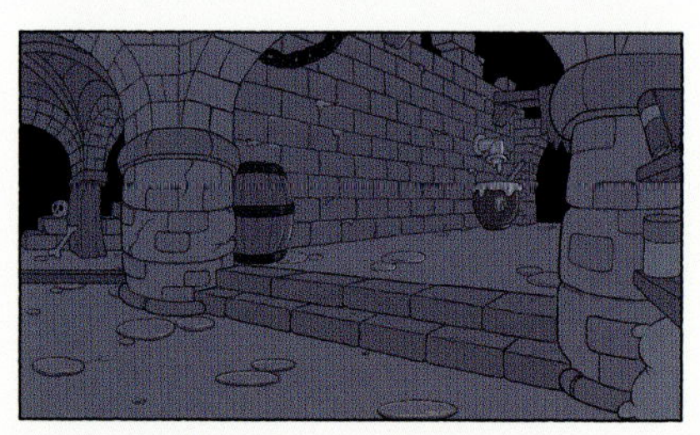

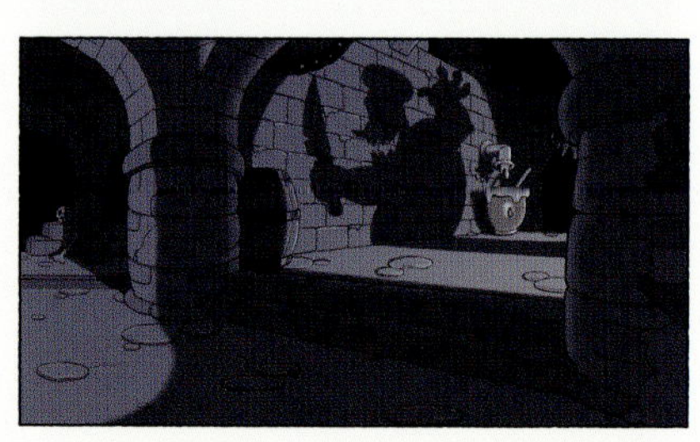

Seen right, Concept Artist Lance Inkwell color codes the different elements that make up his sequenced background design so that Background Painter Caitlin Russell can paint them independently.

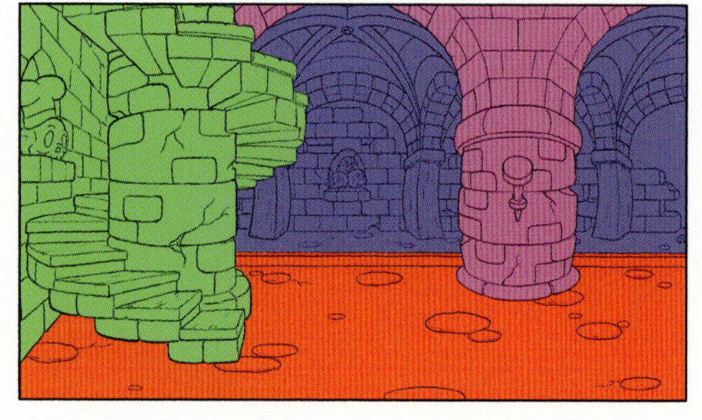

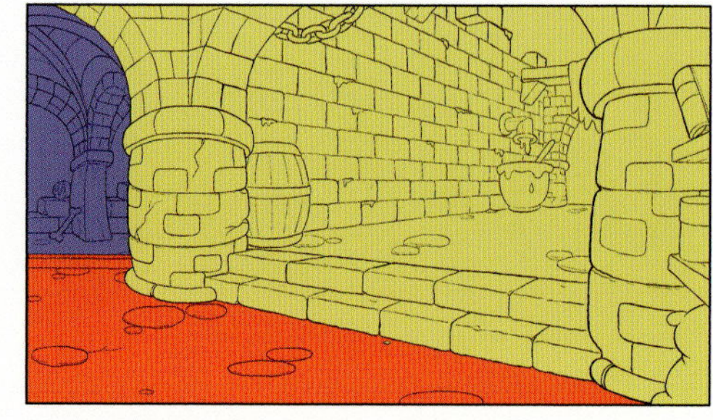

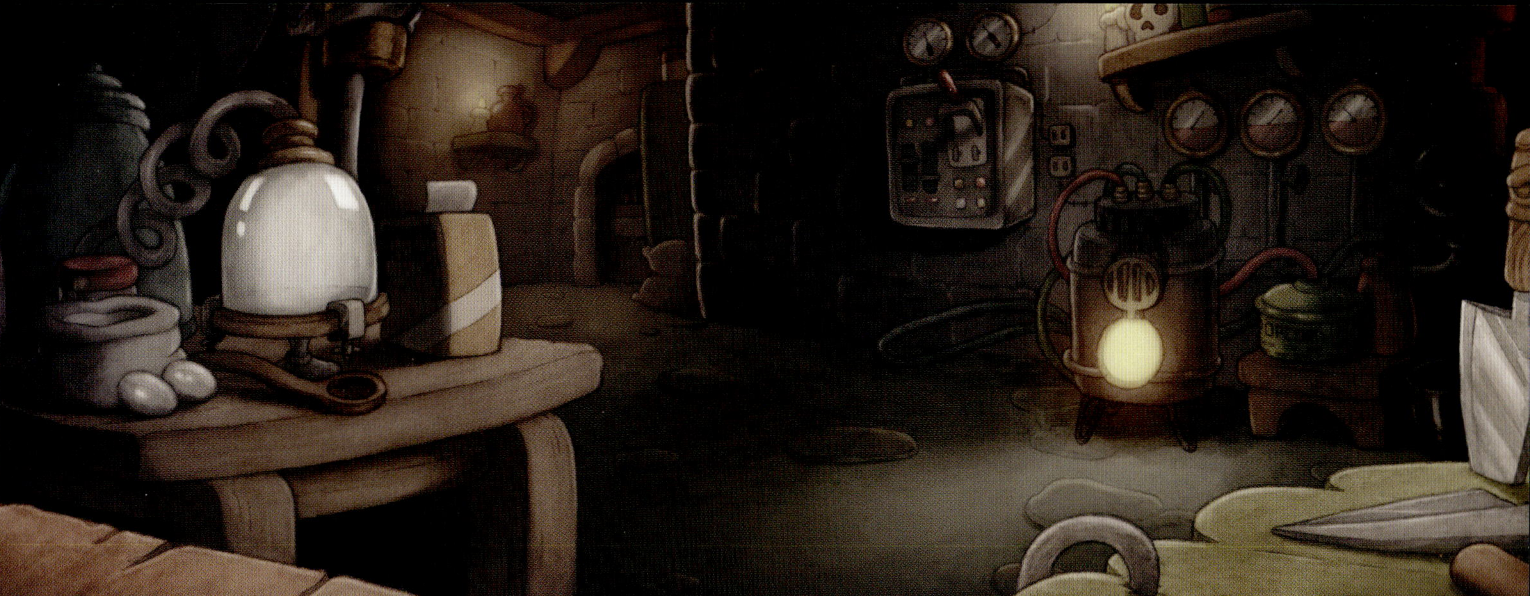

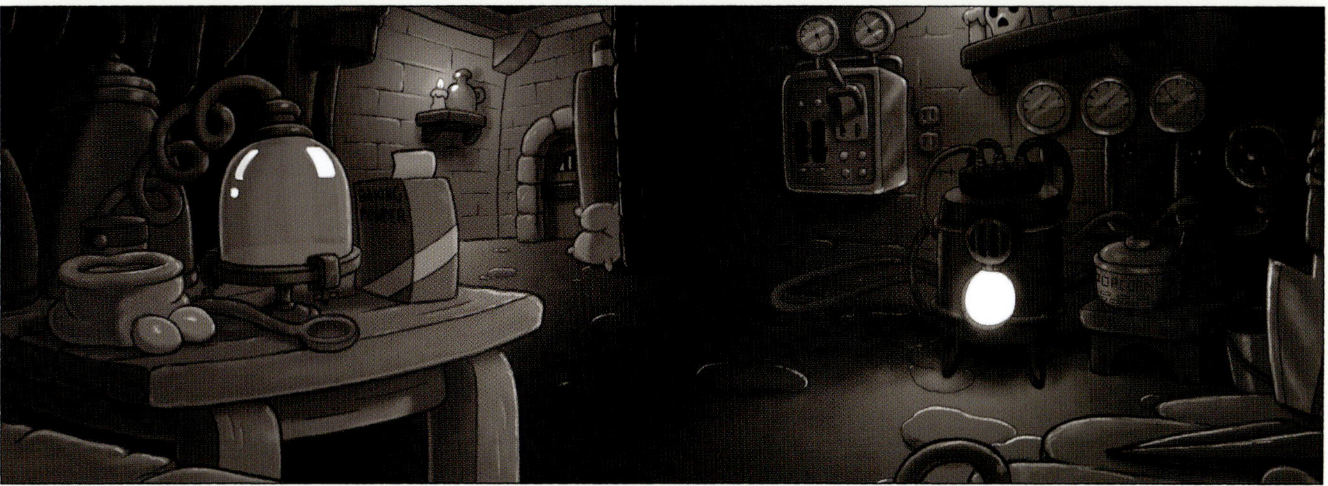

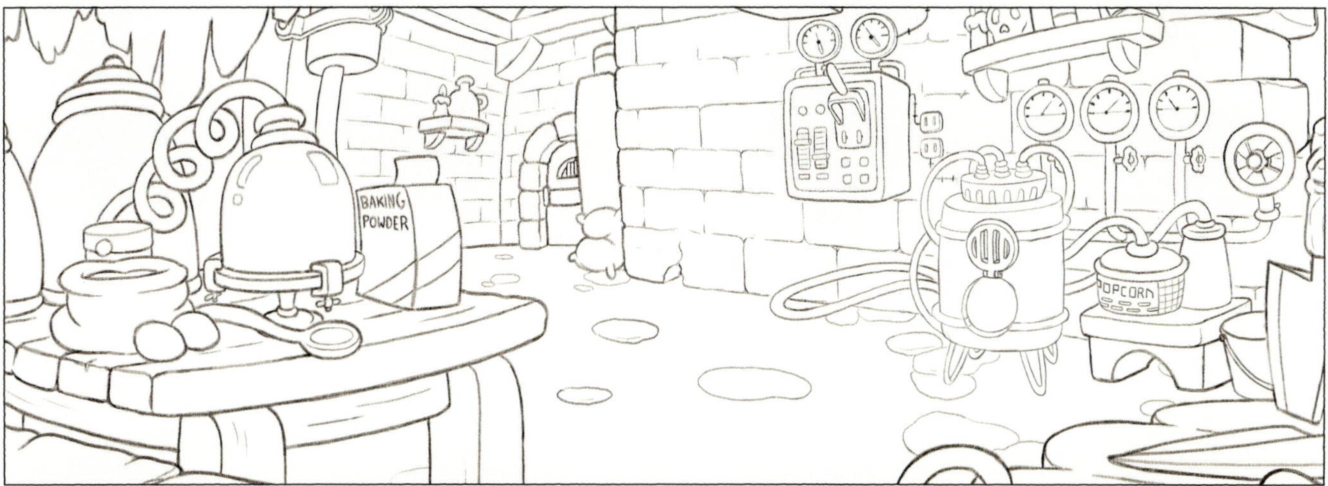

While the overall story for the *Delicious Last Course* was solidified relatively early in production, the actual animation and painting of our cutscenes tends to happen near the tail end of development. We originally designed Chef Saltbaker's laboratory to create a visually dynamic fight scene from the gameplay perspective. For the background of this cutscene, which flows directly into the final fight, we needed to match the previously-created stage's set dressing and frame the camera in a way that would allow Saltbaker's body to obscure the captured character while presenting him as intimidatingly as possible.

Ending Cutscene

AFTER LAYING WASTE TO Saltbaker in his salted wasteland, our heroes have nary a moment to celebrate their hard-won victory or lament the loss of Chalice's dream to be real again before needing to scramble out of the crumbling bakery. Like the rubber hose shorts that *Cuphead* is inspired by, we kept our fable light on dialogue, brisk in pacing, and heavy on visual storytelling, even in resolution. One interesting production note: we had to animate the first scene of the ending three different ways for the three possible characters that could have been kidnapped.

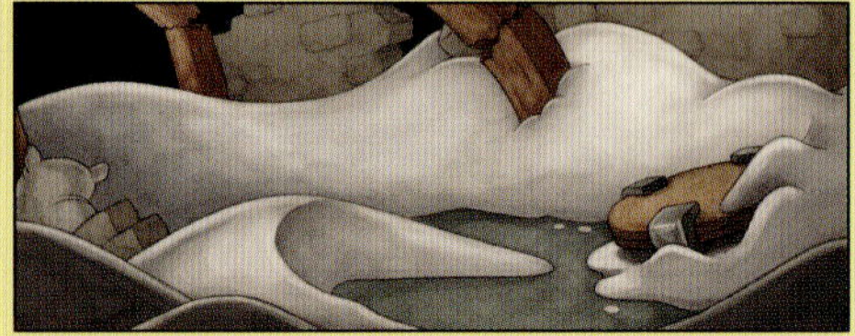

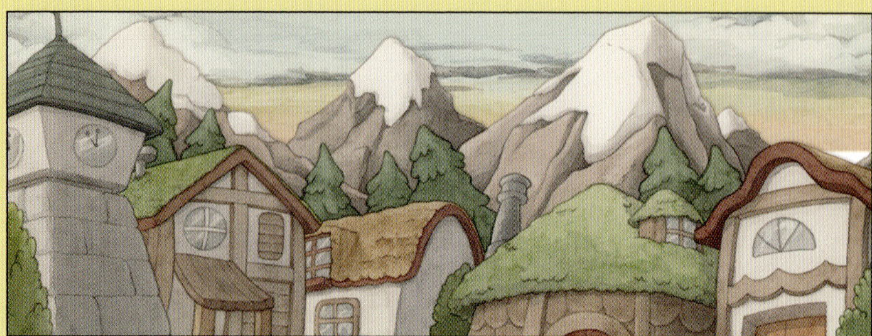

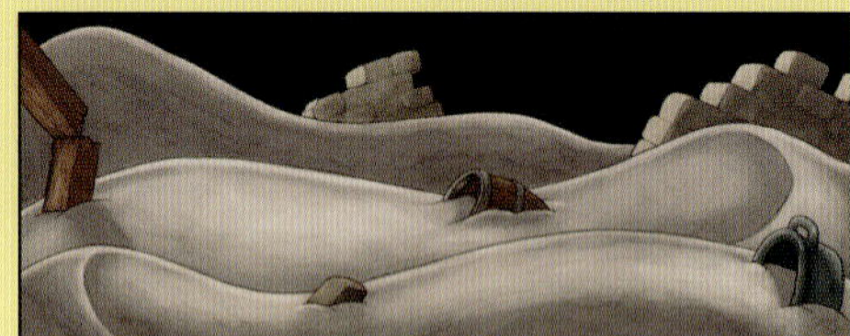

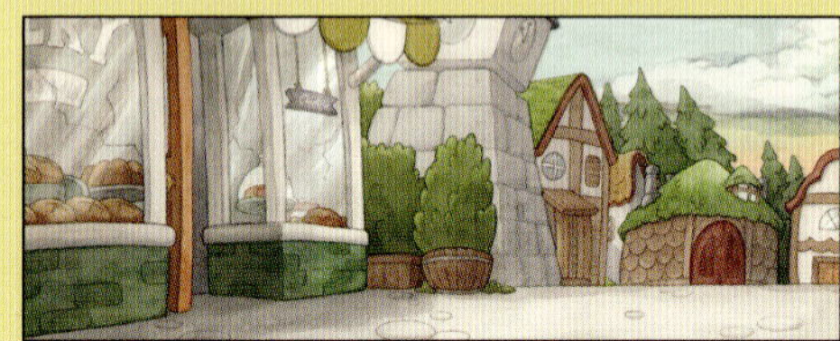

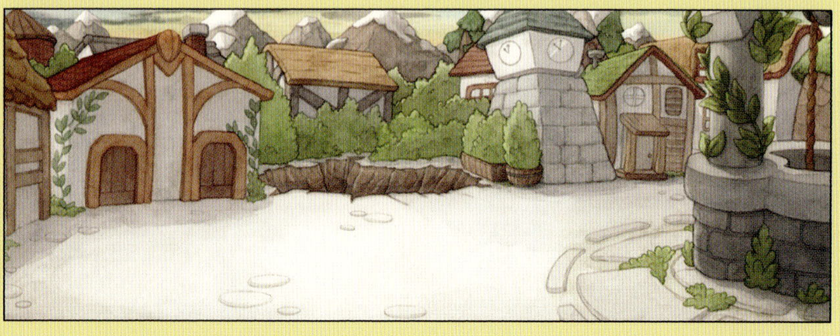

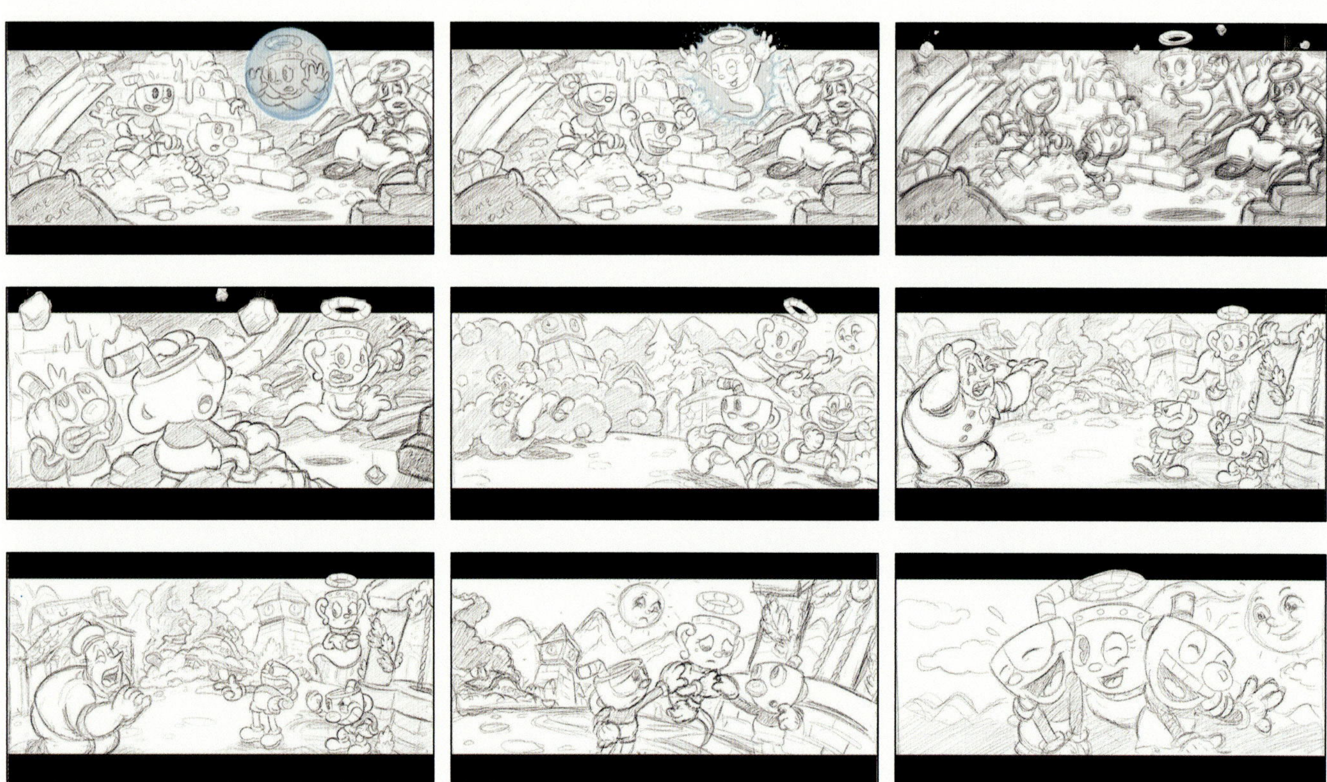

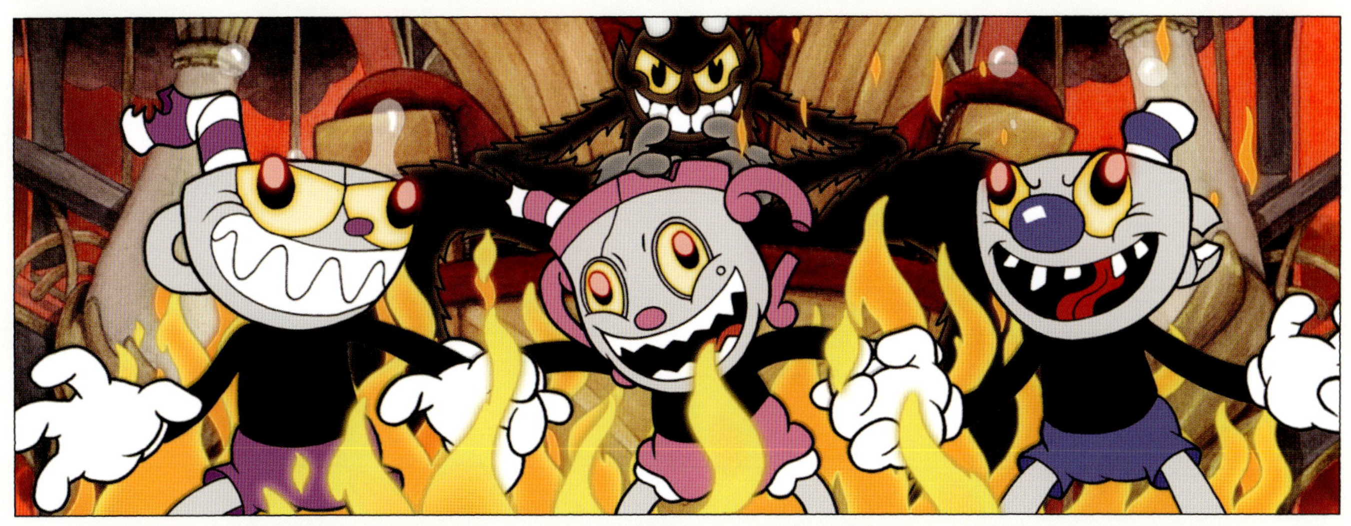

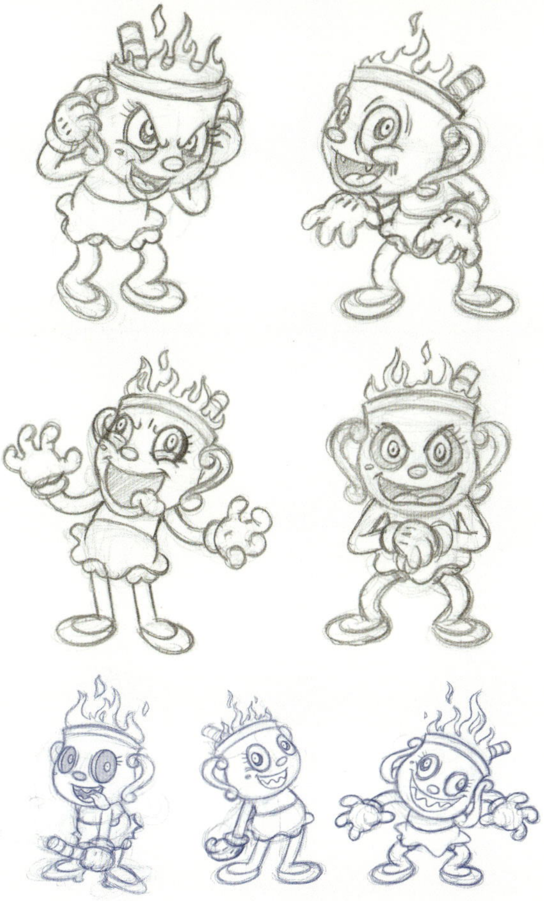

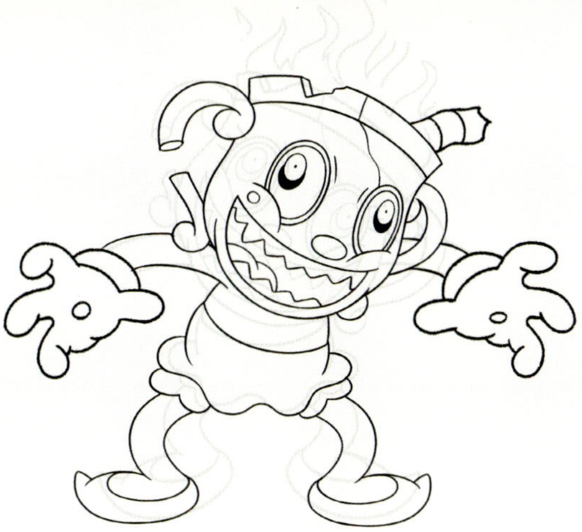

Ms. Malice's original concept sketches by Artist Joseph Coleman trended towards a more "cuddly" style, similar to how Evil Cuphead and Vile Mugman have been depicted in media since the original game's release.

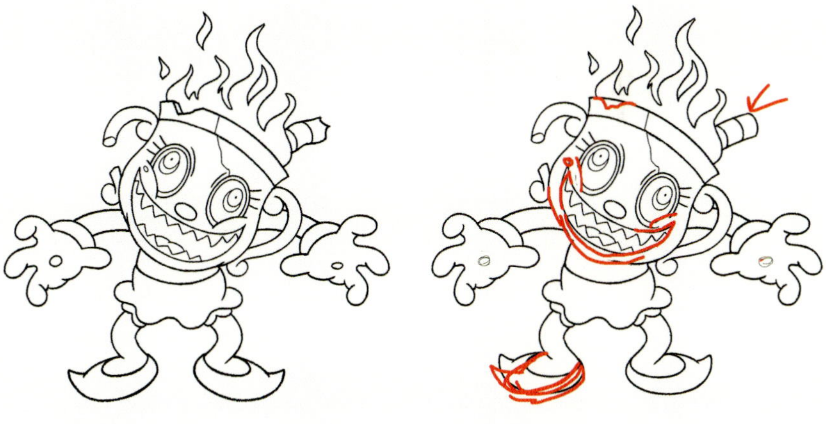

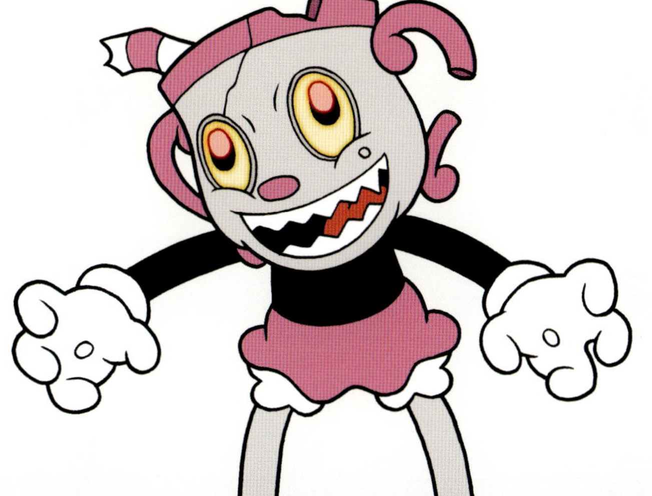

Bad Ending

WHILE A LITTLE NONSENSICAL from a lore perspective, we nonetheless thought it would be fun to have an evil version of Ms. Chalice, dubbed Ms. Malice, join Evil Cuphead and Vile Mugman in the bad ending of the original game–obtained by agreeing to side with the Devil. To match with her dastardly doppelganger pals, Ms. Malice's pink highlights coincided nicely with the purple-toned schema of the hell-bound schemers.

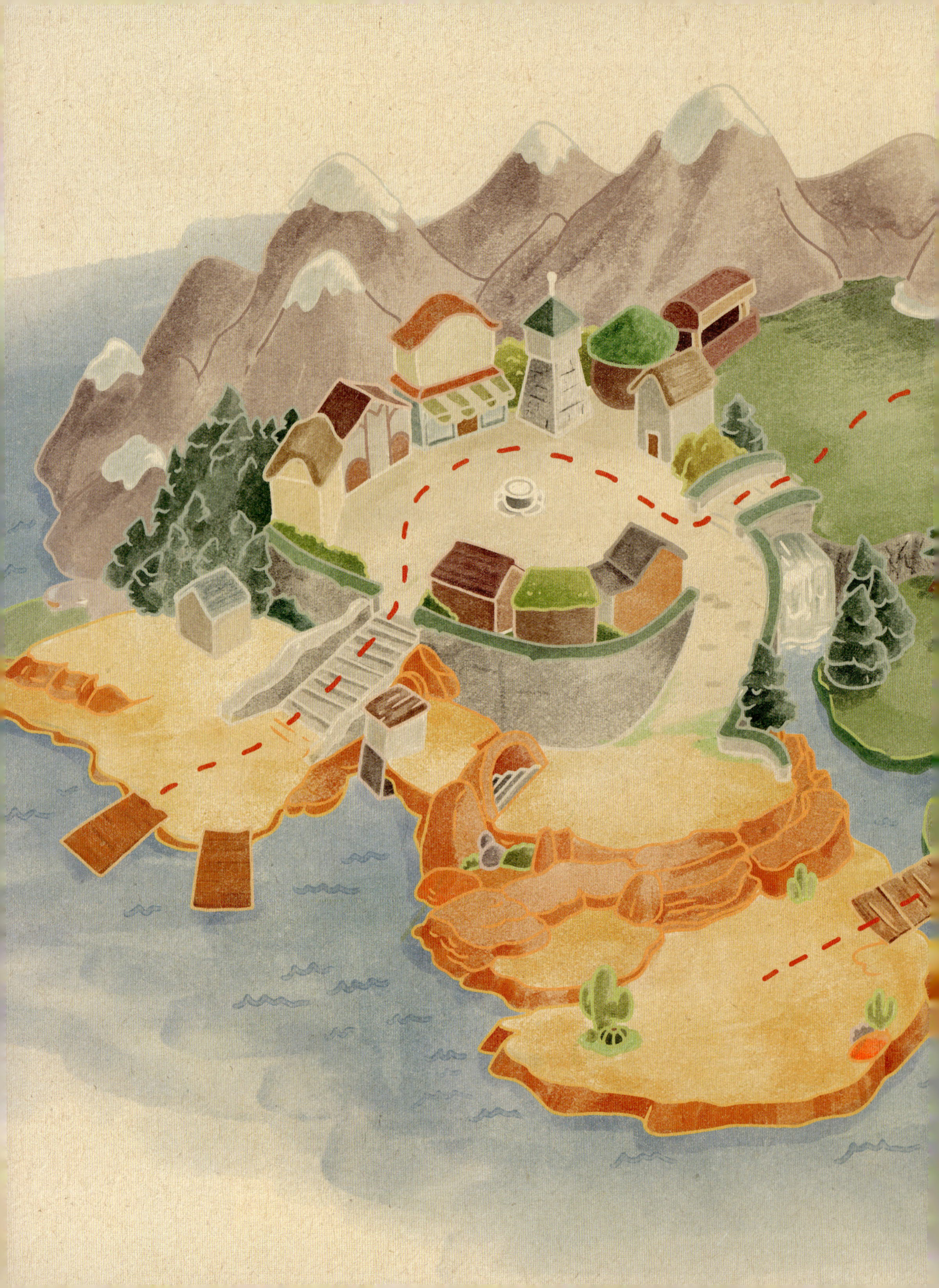

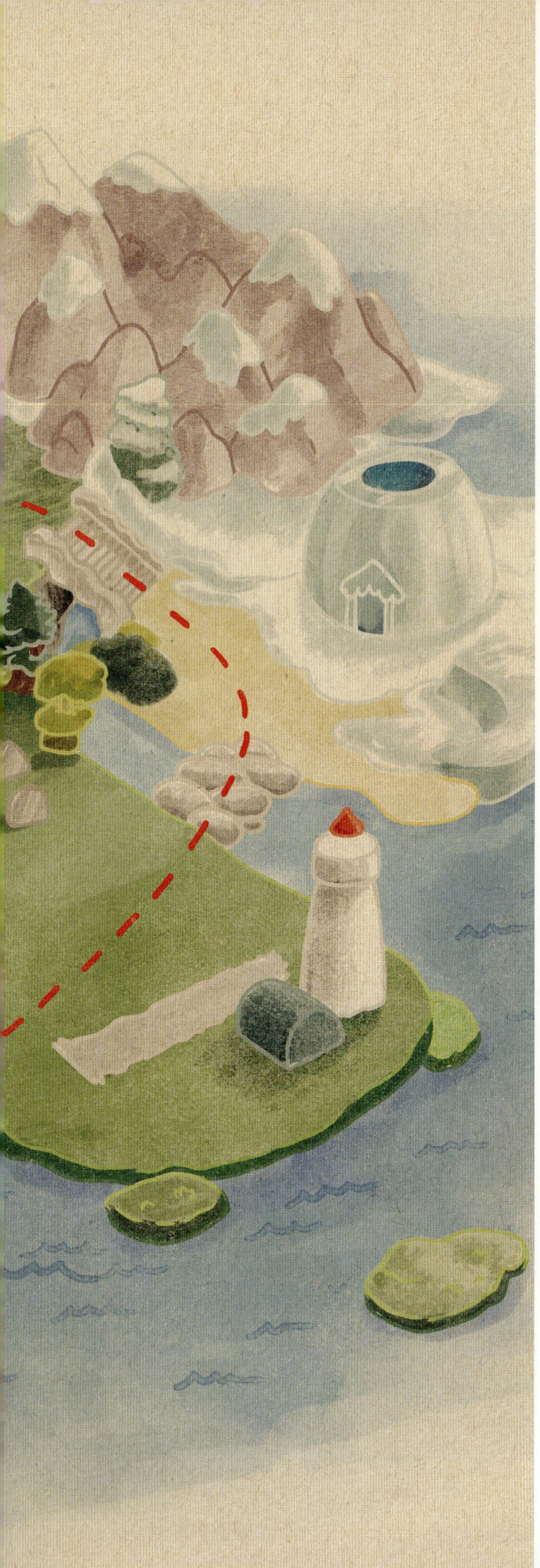

Chapter XIV:
Delicious Details

THERE IS A PHILOSOPHY ABOUT little details that really resonates with us here at the studio. The perhaps-apocryphal story goes that, when he was a young boy, eventual Apple Computer founder Steve Jobs was helping his father build a fence in their backyard. When told by his dad to take as much care with the back of the fence as with the front, Jobs pushed back, insisting that it made no difference; nobody passing by would know. "But," his father replied, "you will know."

This principle–of devoting meticulous attention to small design elements that not everyone will notice–is central to the way we build things at Studio MDHR. One of our core beliefs is that these understated flourishes, from typeface to lettering to iconography, all matter. They are part of that ephemeral sort of artistry, whose absence is often felt more than its presence. Individually they may not make or break the aesthetic of our games, but taken together, these delicious details help as much as bombastic music or complex animation to immerse players in a faraway cartoon wonderland.

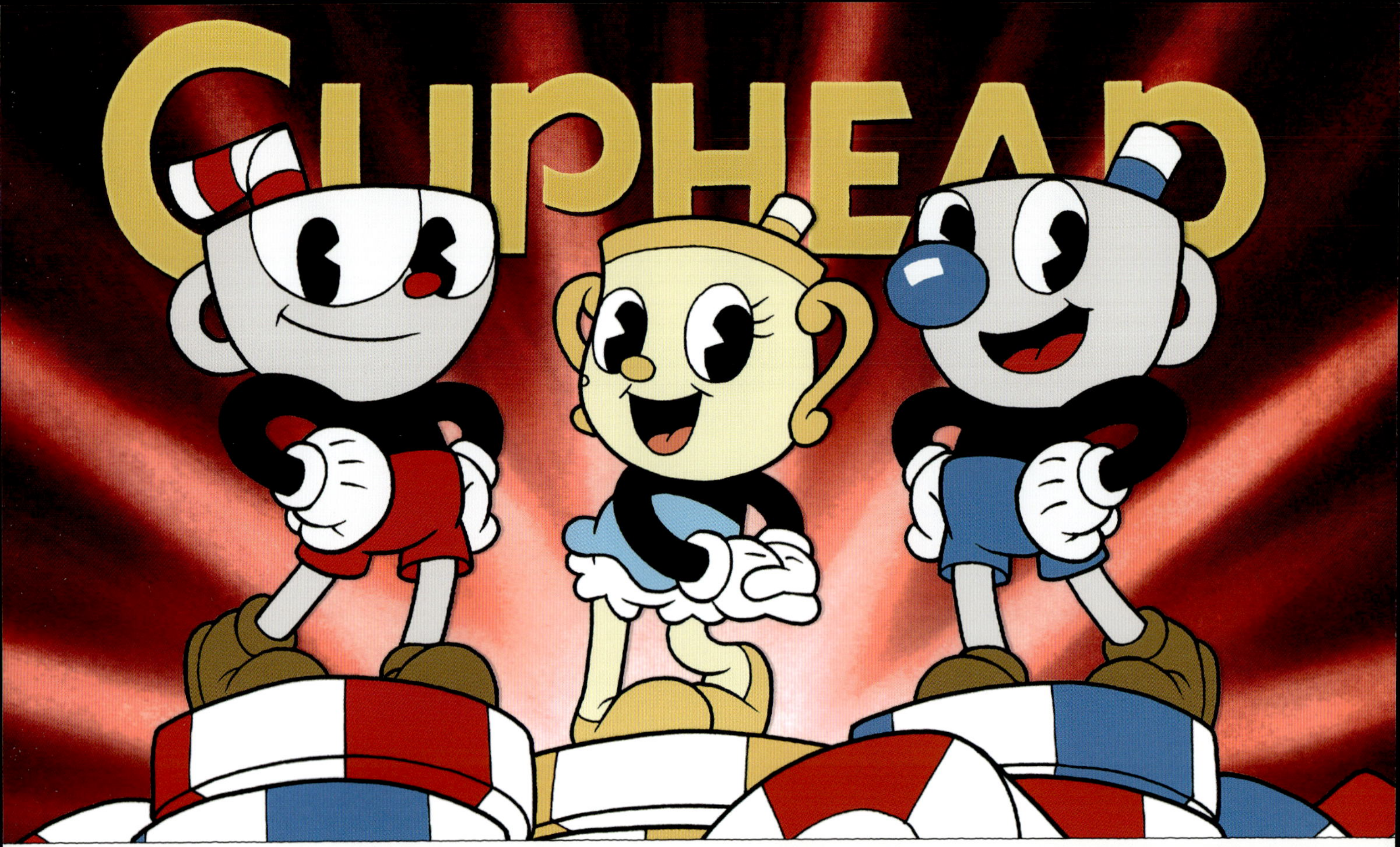

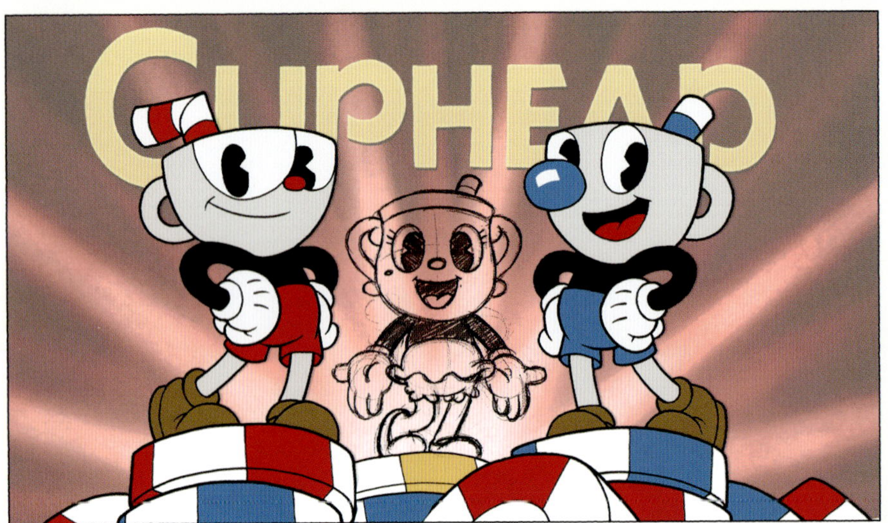

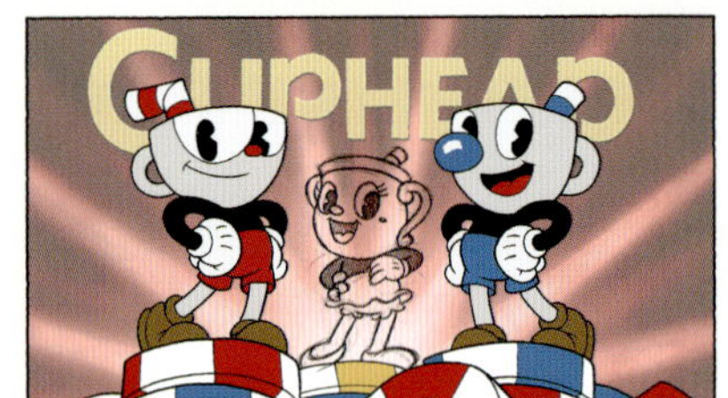

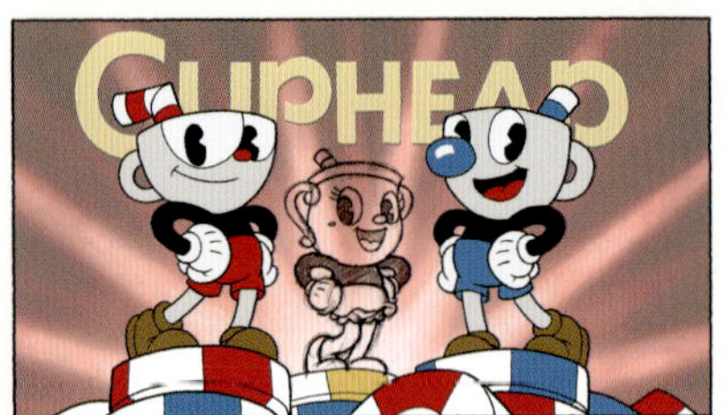

Title Screen

WITH *THE DELICOUS LAST COURSE* focusing on the story of brand-new character Ms. Chalice, we knew from quite early on in development that we wanted her presence to be felt front and center–literally. To that end, we undertook a redesign of the game's opening title screen which added our plucky new porcelain pal to her very own color-coded casino chip, dancing alongside Cuphead and Mugman. Of course, the new trio needed something to dance *to*, and Composer Kristofer Maddigan rose to the occasion with the creation of an eponymous overture summarizing the adventure ahead.

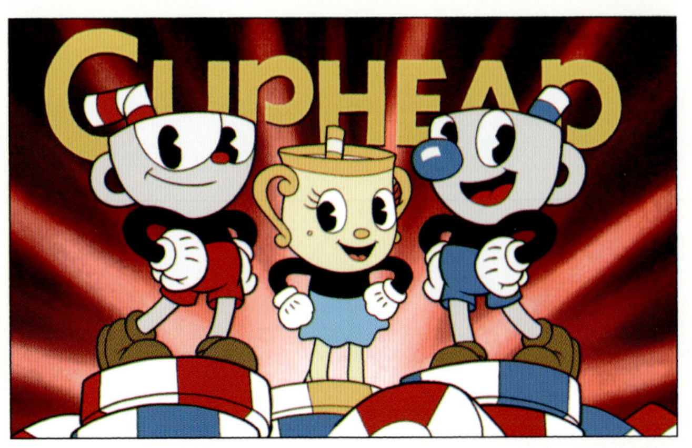

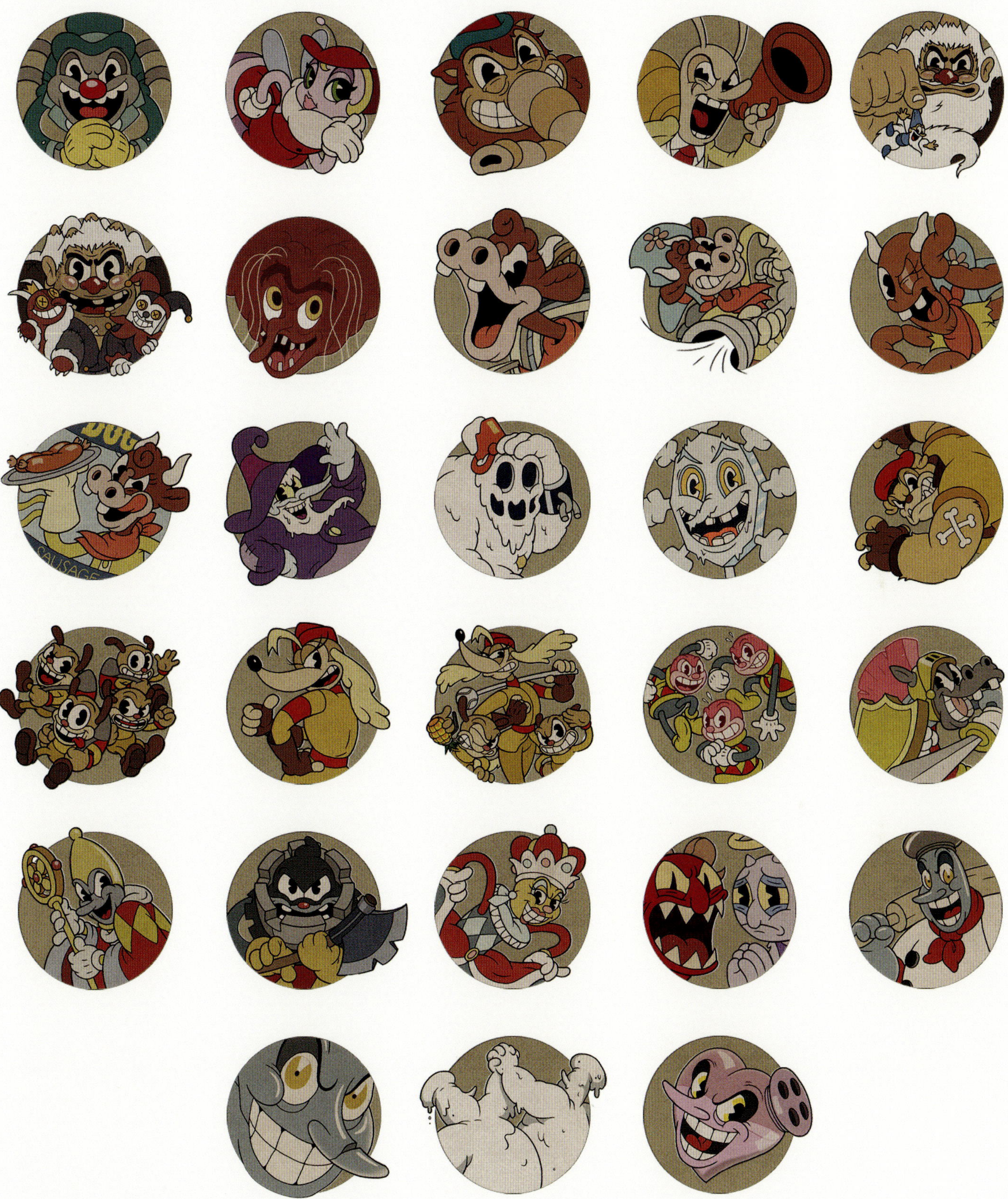

Death Cards

EACH DEFEAT AT THE HANDS OF one of the Inkwell Isles' fearsome foes comes complete with a "Death Card" that adds a dose of posthumous pain by informing players just how close they got to the end of the battle. On our part, a great deal of effort went into ensuring that each phase of the boss came complete with a character pose that exuded personality–alongside some deliberately dreadful puns rooted in references and vocabulary of the era. For the DLC, we upped the ante by experimenting with poses that extended beyond the borders of the frame!

Ticket to DLC Isle

EASE OF ACCESS dictated that we offered players a chance to purchase *The Delicious Last Course* from within *Cuphead*, but we were determined to find a way to do so that felt like it fit within the world of the Inkwell Isles. The result is a screen we internally called the "DLC Passport." Designed by Brand Design Director Ian Clarke with miniature map art by Background Painter Caitlin Russell, this screen's aesthetic is rooted in travel brochures and boat tickets of the 1930s and 40s. Once the DLC is installed, the accoutrements spilling out of the wallet tuck inside to signal that players are ready for their trip!

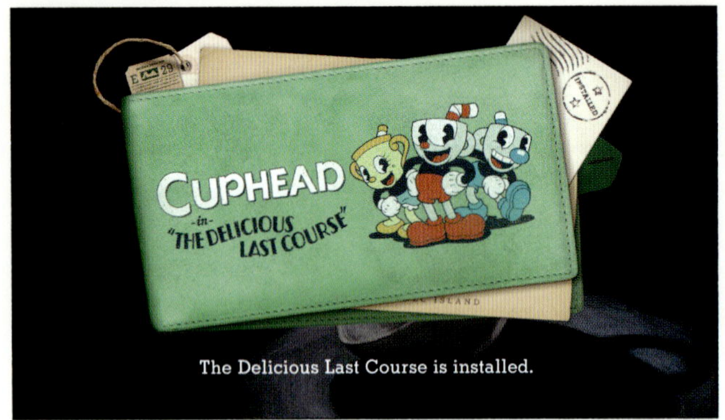

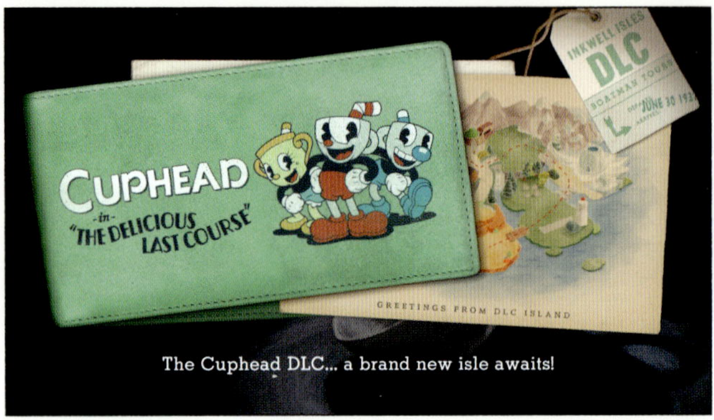

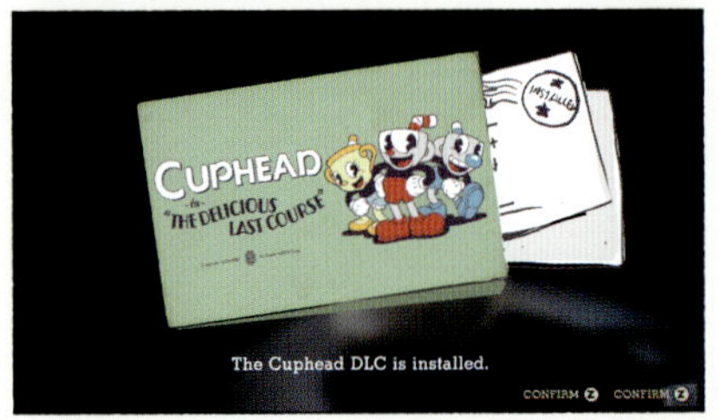

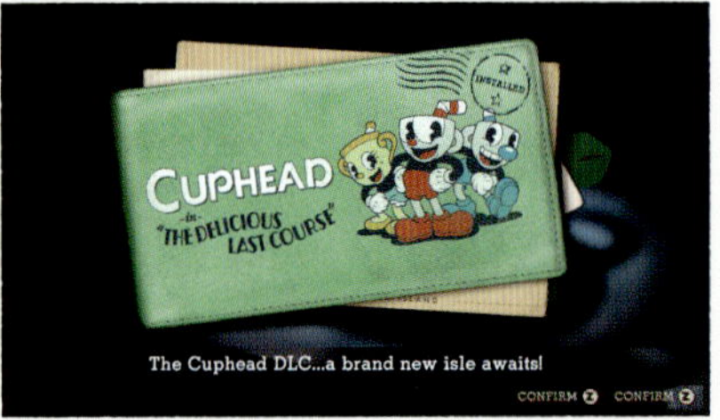

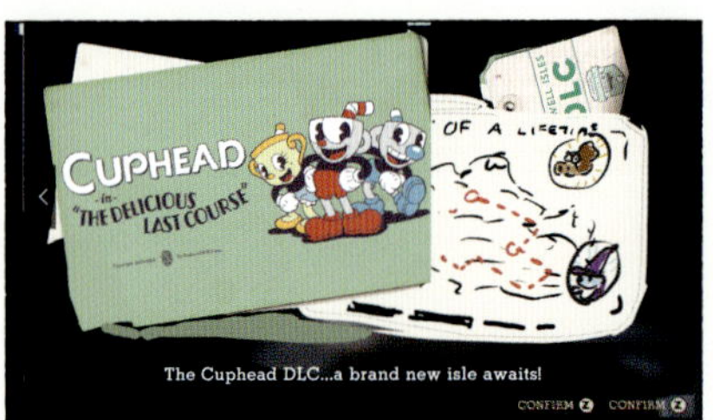

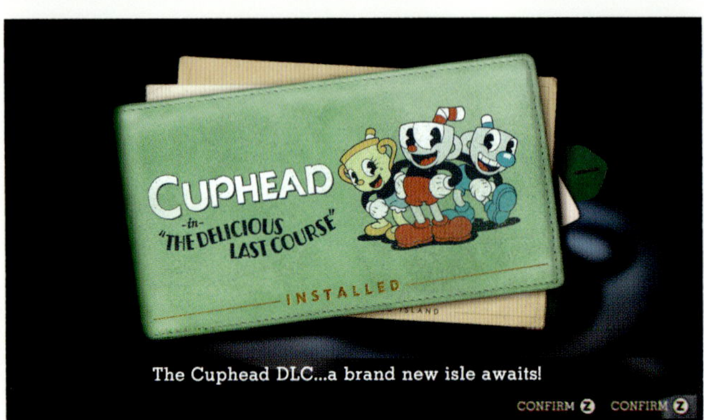

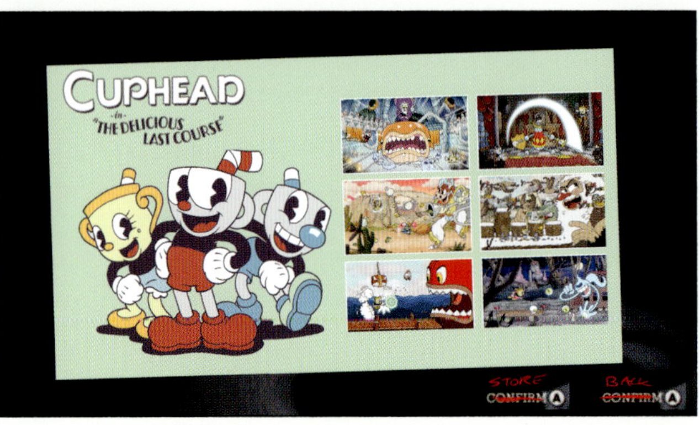

Pictured right, concepts from Ian Clarke for hang tags and in-world tourism iconography to complement the passport. Early ideation envisioned a boat tour offered by none other than the compass-headed Boatman character himself.

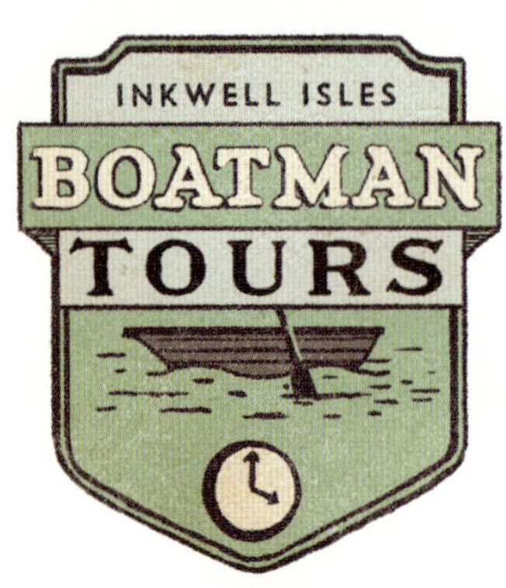

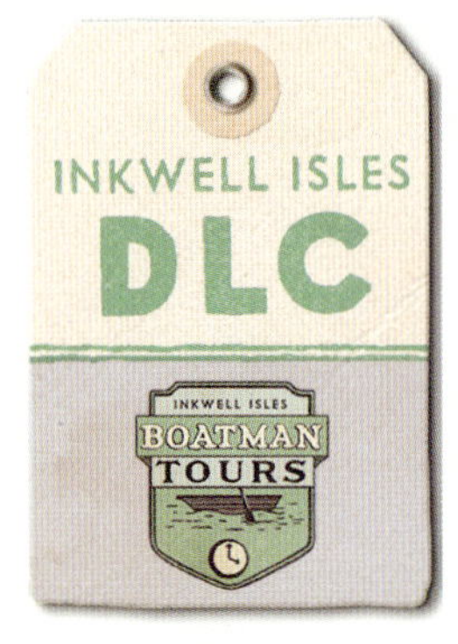

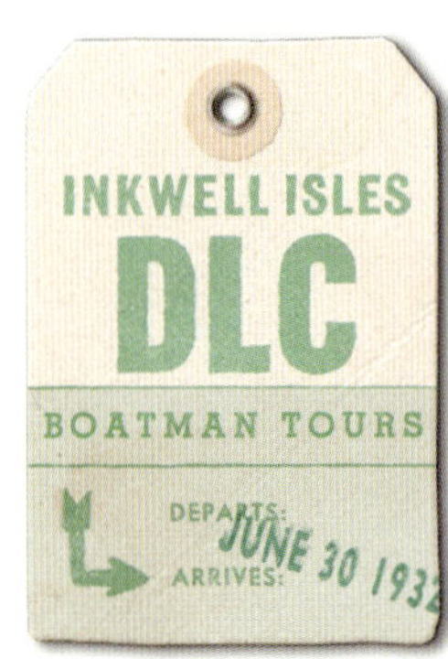

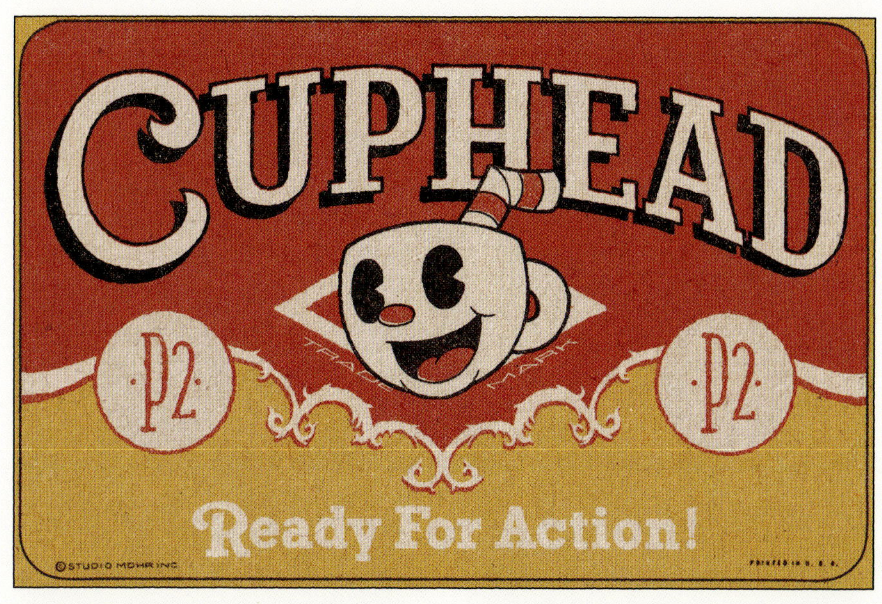

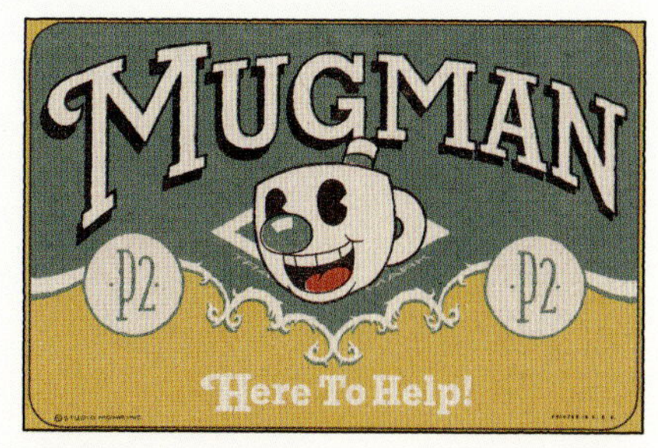

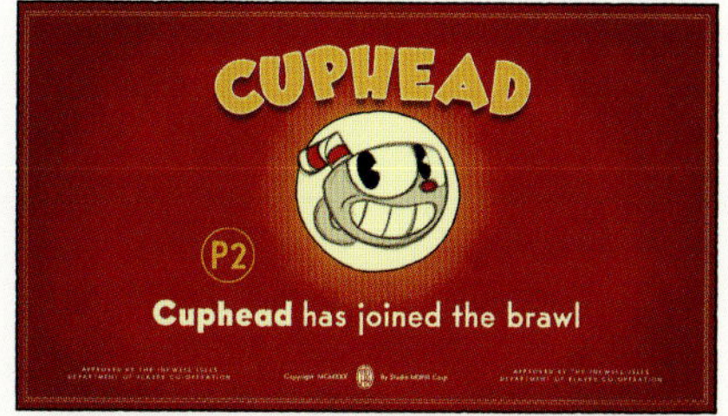

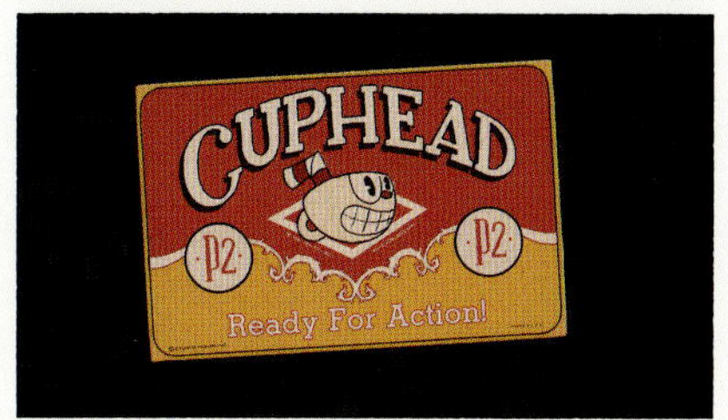

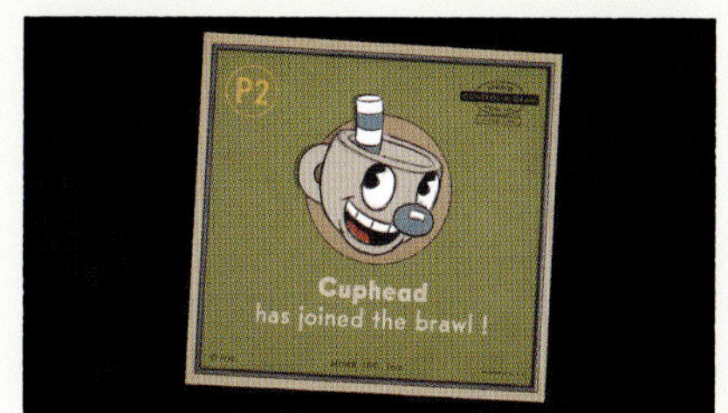

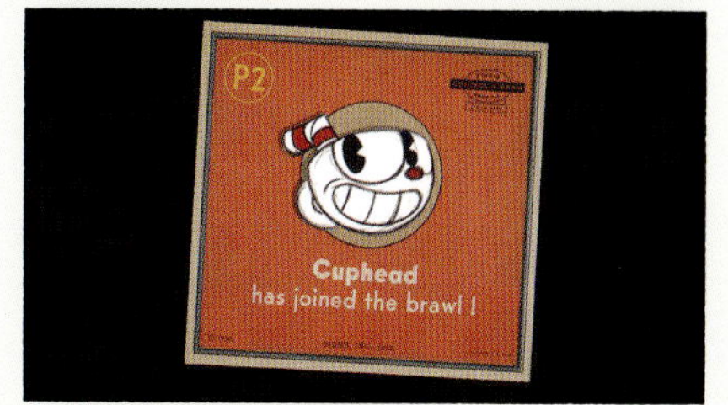

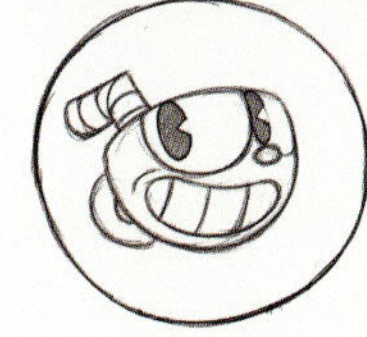
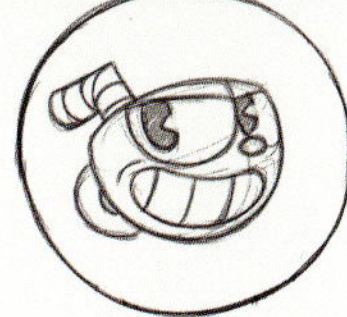
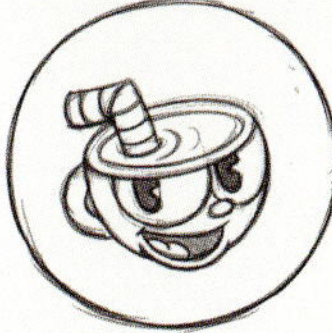
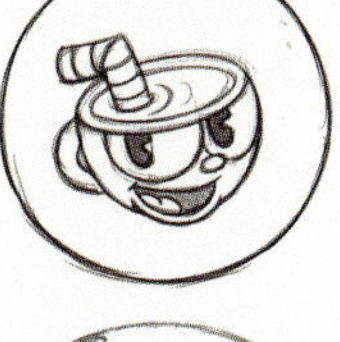
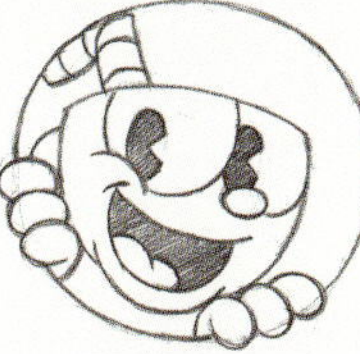
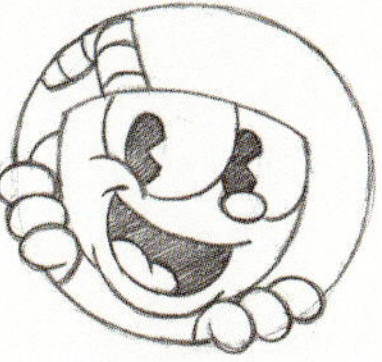
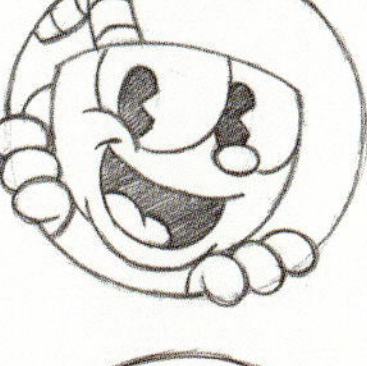
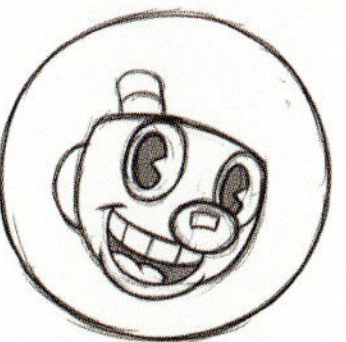

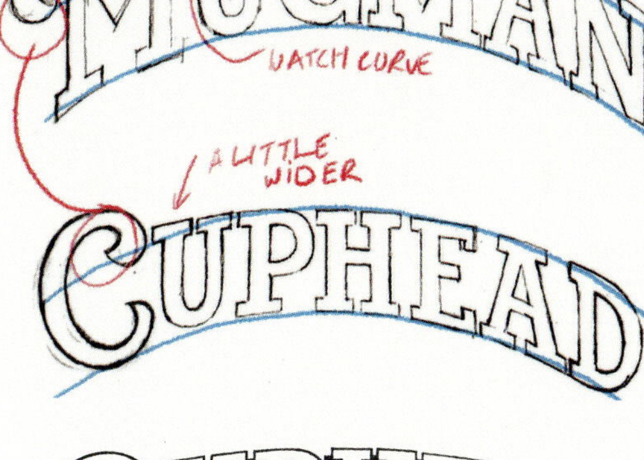

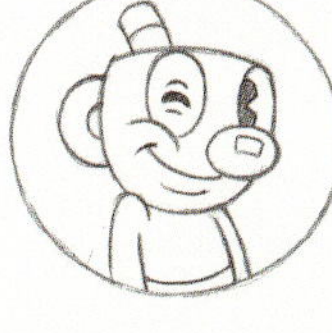
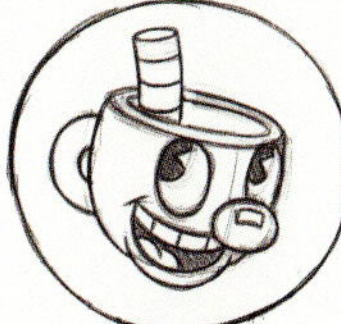
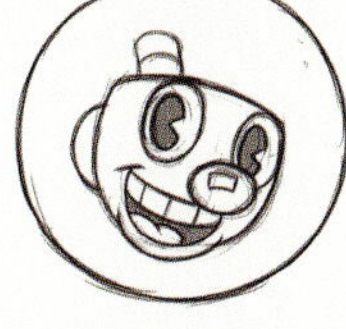

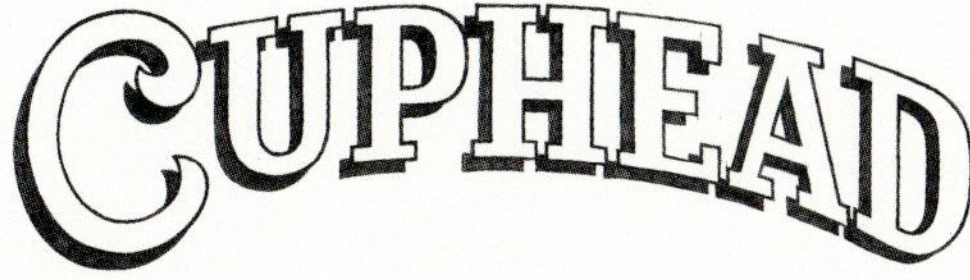

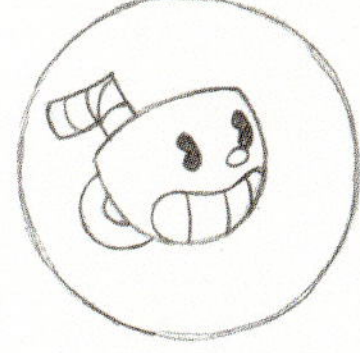
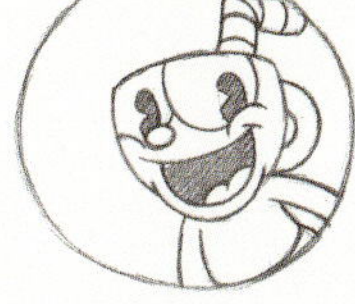
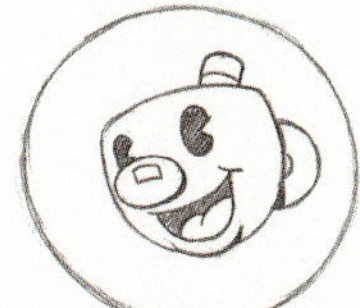
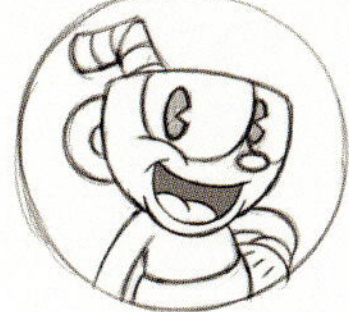
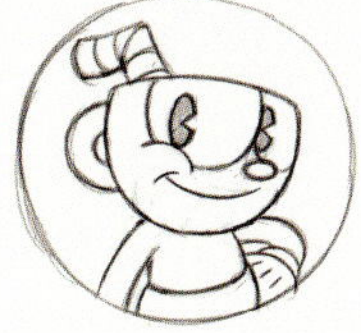
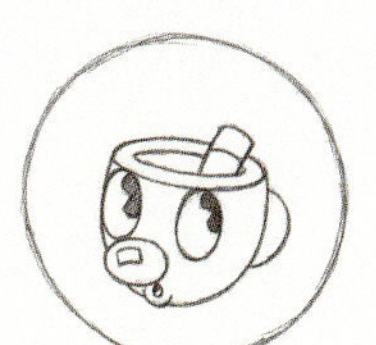

Player Join Screen

THE RELEASE OF *The Delicious Last Course* gave us the chance to spruce up a few areas of the original game with which we were less than satisfied. This included the screen players see when a friend joins for a multiplayer session, which we re-envisioned as physical packaging labels from imagined confectionery packages of the era. The final designs, pictured at the top of the page, use whimsical wordmarks from master Letter Artist Warren Clark and simplified character faces from Artist Joseph Coleman to evoke the idea of mascots adorning a commercial product.

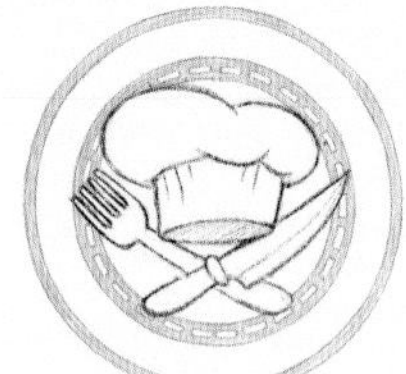

COMPLIMENTS TO THE CHEF
(COMPLETE YOUR QUEST ON INKWELL ISLE IV)

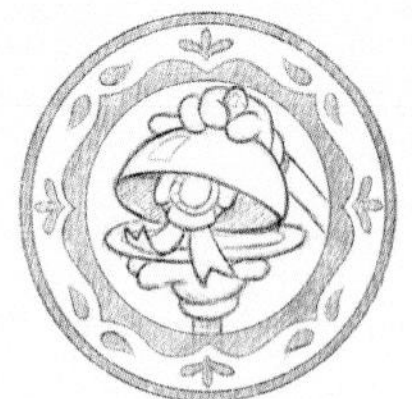

COOKED TO PERFECTION
(GET S-RANK ON A STAGE OF INKWELL ISLE IV)

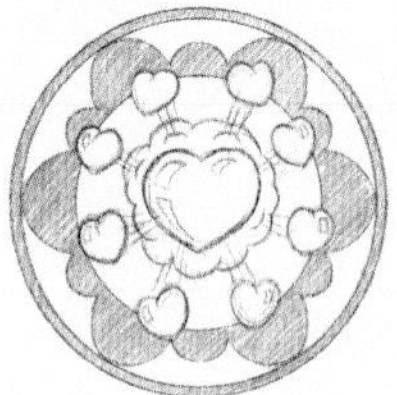

HEARTY
(HAVE 9HP AT ONE TIME)

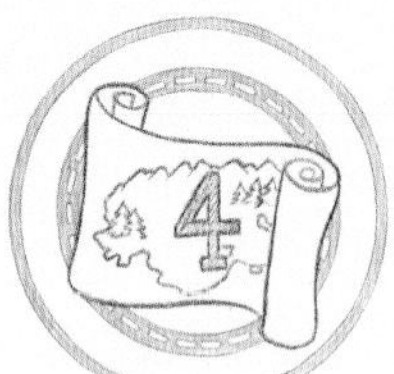

A VACATION IN THE WILDS
(DEFEAT EVERY BOSS IN INKWELL ISLE IV)

RANGER
(OBTAIN A-RANK OR HIGHER ON ALL BOSSES IN INKWELL ISLE IV)

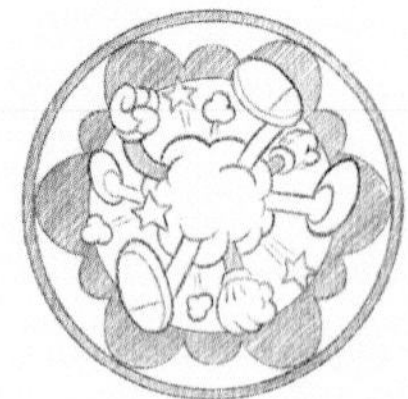

ALIVE + KICKING
(DEFEAT A BOSS WITH MC)

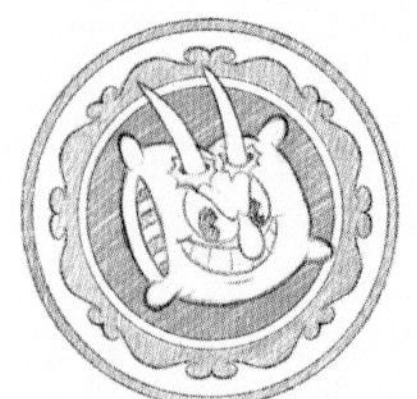

WHAT A HORRIBLE NIGHT TO HAVE A CURSE
(SURVIVE THE NIGHTMARE)

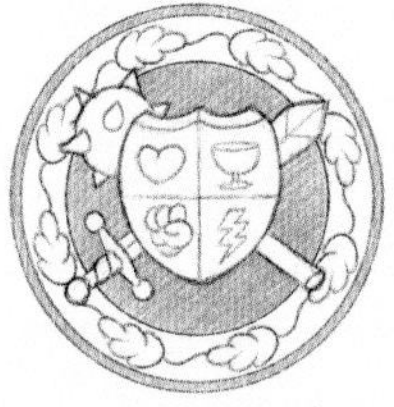

PALADIN
(OBTAIN GREAT POWER)

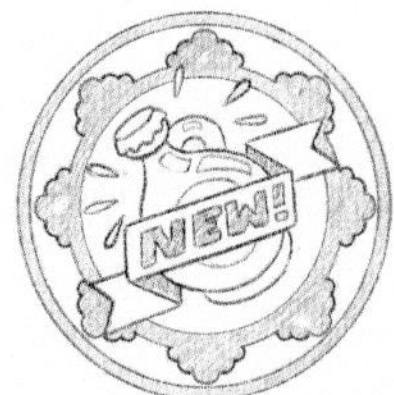

THE LATEST SENSATION
(DEFEAT A BOSS WITH ONE OF PORKRIND'S NEW WEAPONS)

ALMIGHTY GRAIL
(DEFEAT ALL BOSSES WITH MC)

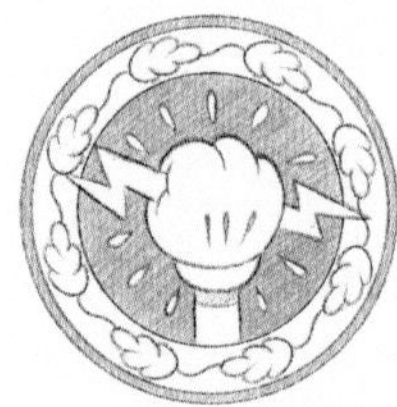

THE GOLDEN TOUCH
(DEFEAT A BOSS WITH ONE OF MC'S SUPER ARTS)

CHECKMATE
(DEFEAT ALL OF THE KING OF GAMES CHAMPIONS)

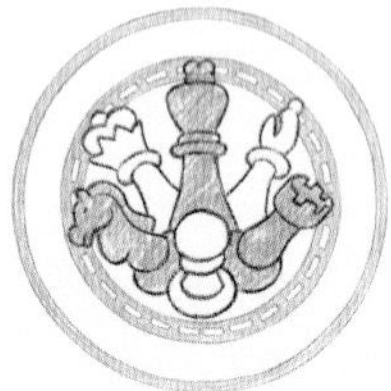

ENDURE

THE HIGH HAT
(DEFEAT A BOSS ON INKWELL ISLE IV WITHOUT KILLING ANY OF THE ENEMIES)

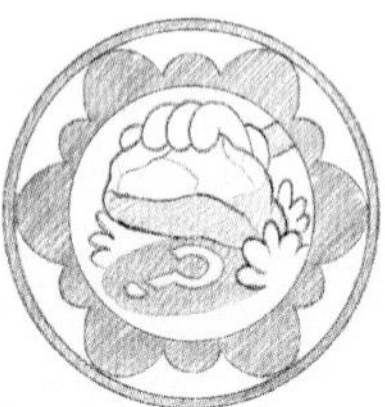

NO STONE UNTURNED
(DEFEAT ALL SECRET BOSS PHASES)

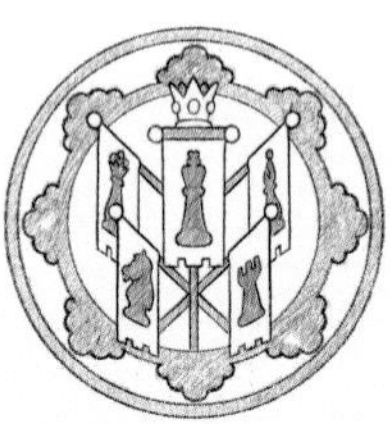

ENDURE

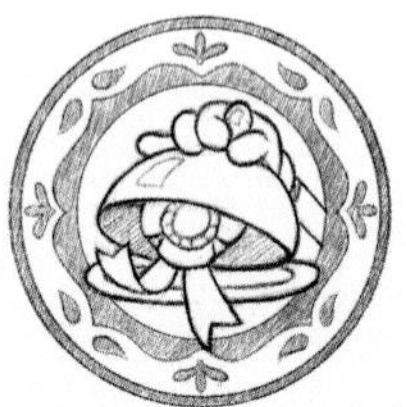

COOKED TO PERFECTION
(GET S-RANK ON A STAGE OF INKWELL ISLE IV)

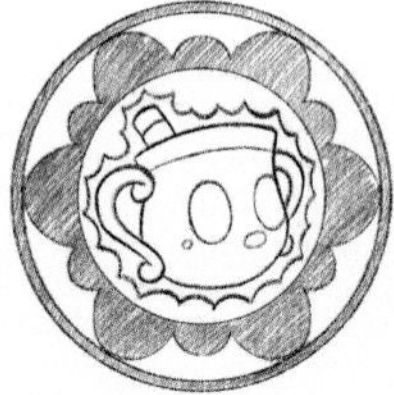

ALIVE + KICKING
(DEFEAT A BOSS WITH MC)

NOTHING LEFT ON YOUR PLATE
(COMPLETE INKWELL ISLE IV ON EXPERT)

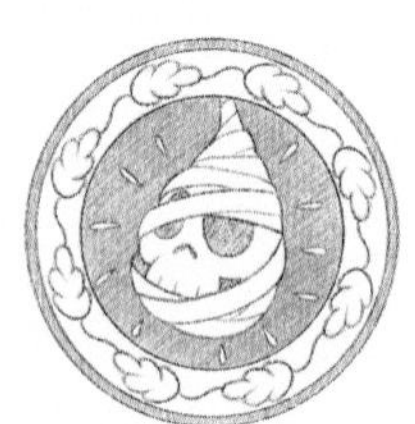

BLOWN TO ITSY-BITSIES
(DEFEAT THE SPIDER IN BOOTLEGGER BOGGIE WITH ONE OF HIS OWN MINES)

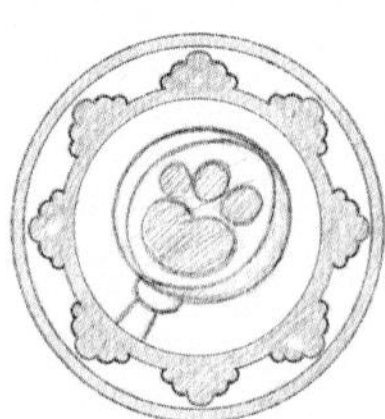

SNIFF IT OUT
(FIND THE DOGFIGHT SECRET)

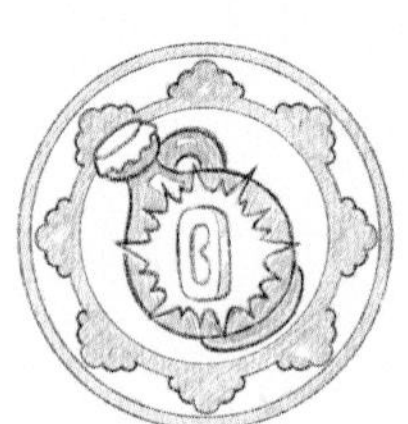

THE LATEST SENSATION
(DEFEAT A BOSS WITH ONE OF PORKRIND'S NEW WEAPONS)

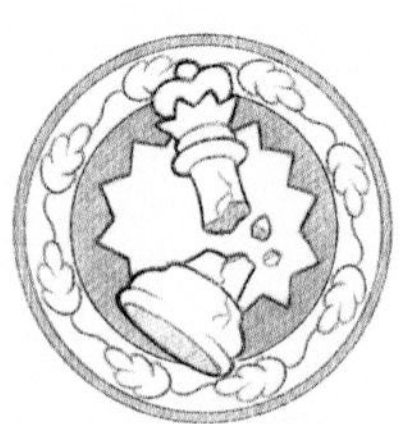

CHECKMATE
(DEFEAT ALL OF THE KING OF GAMES CHAMPIONS)

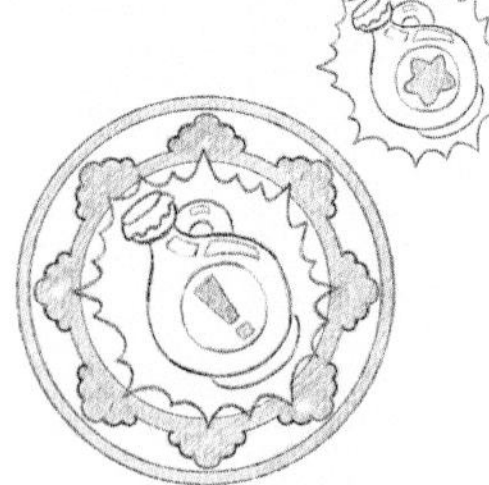

THE LATEST SENSATION
(DEFEAT A BOSS WITH ONE OF PORKRIND'S NEW WEAPONS)

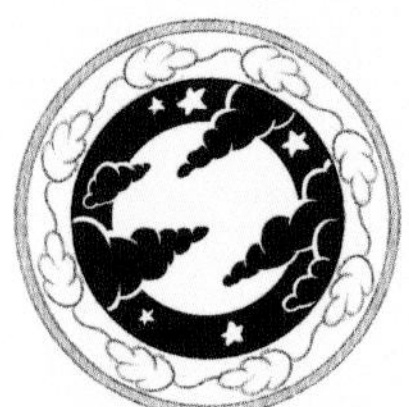

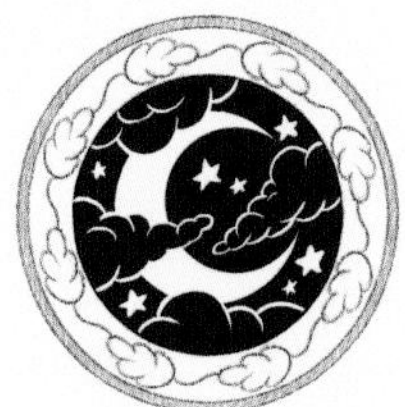

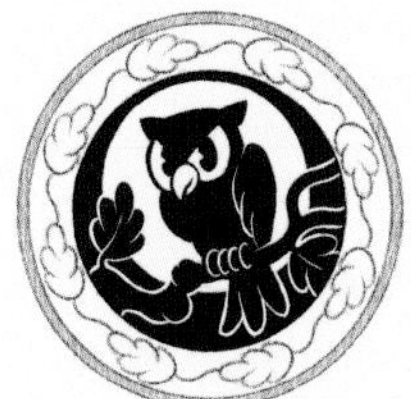

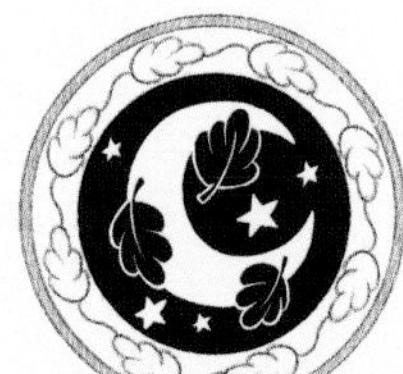

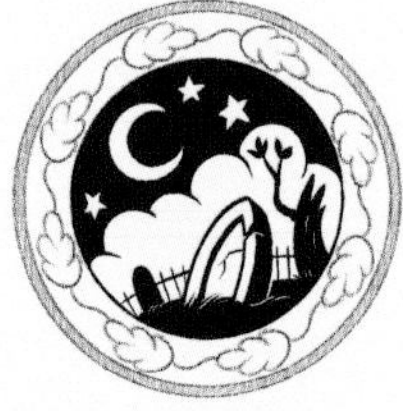

WHAT A HORRIBLE NIGHT TO HAVE A CURSE
(SURVIVE THE NIGHTMARE)

Achievements

ONE OF OUR MANTRAS during the development of *The Delicious Last Course* was "depth over breadth," with an internal focus on meticulous craftsmanship and increased detail rather than doing more for the sake of more. This philosophy extended even to our in-game achievements, the badges players earn by completing key milestones during the adventure. Illustrated by Artist Lance Inkwell, these icons contain unique framing to allow players to differentiate them from base game achievements when looking at a list. Above, keen eyes will spot several achievements that never made it into the final game!

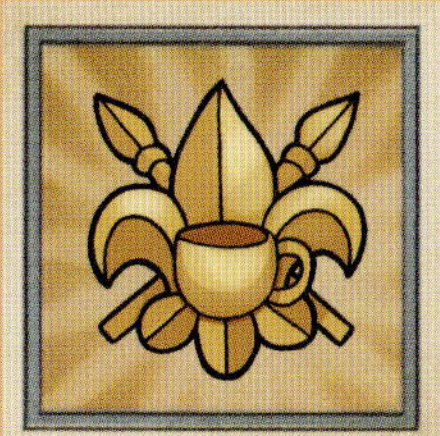
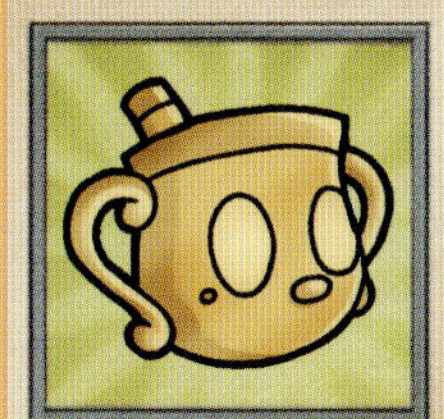
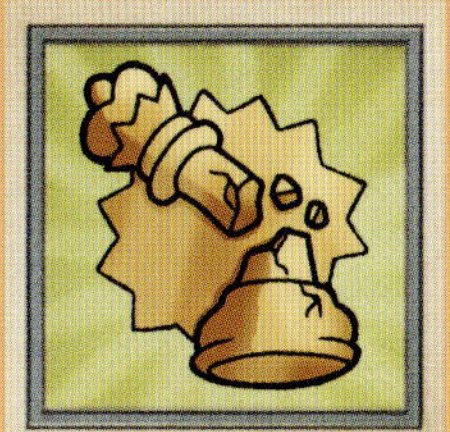
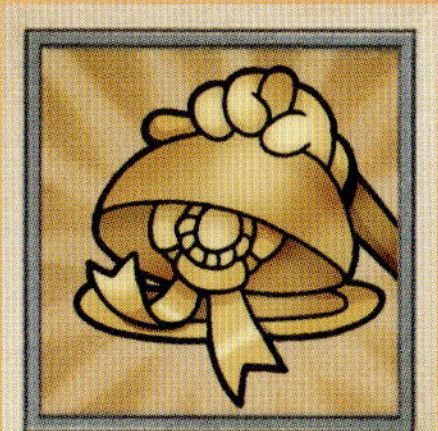
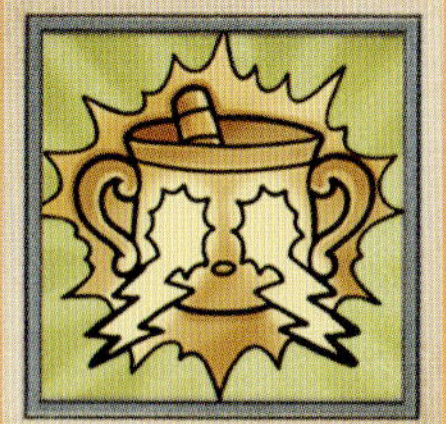

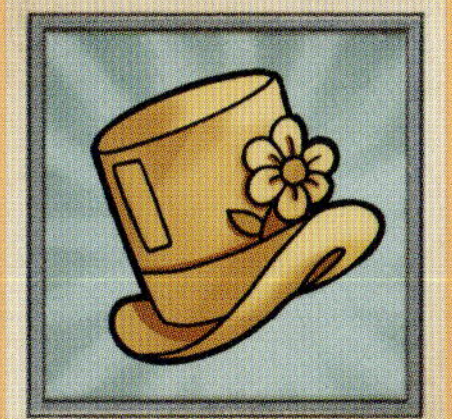
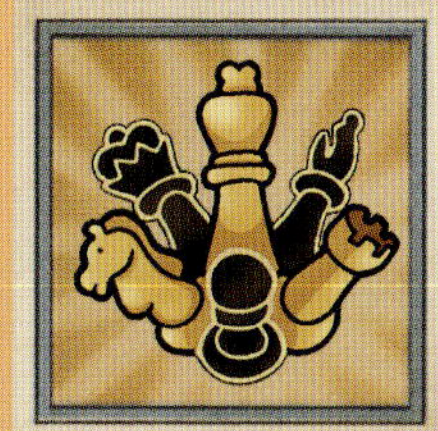
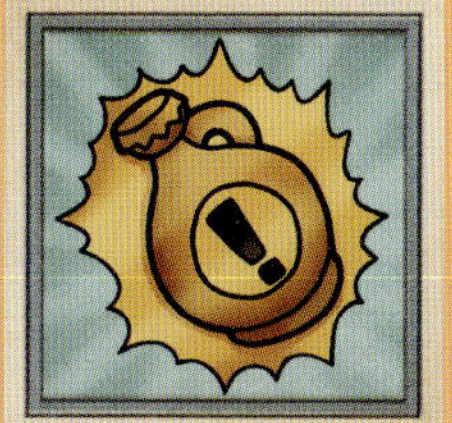
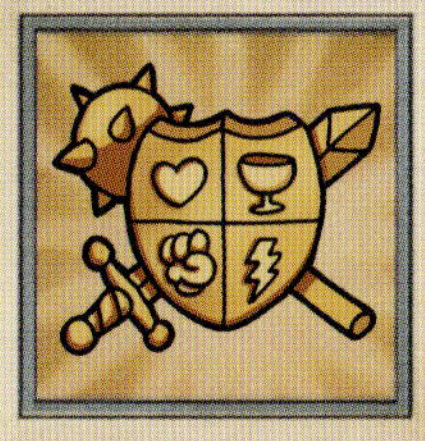
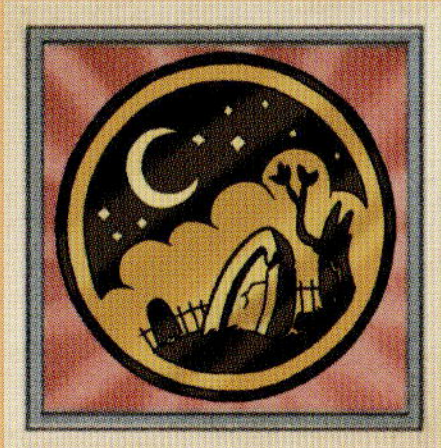

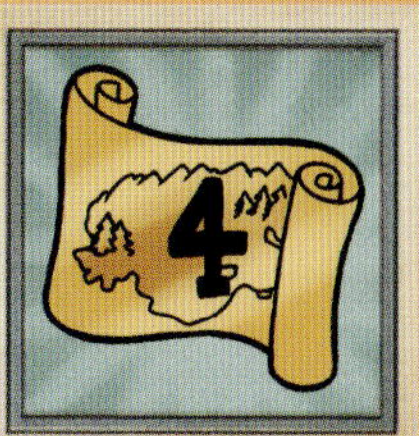
4
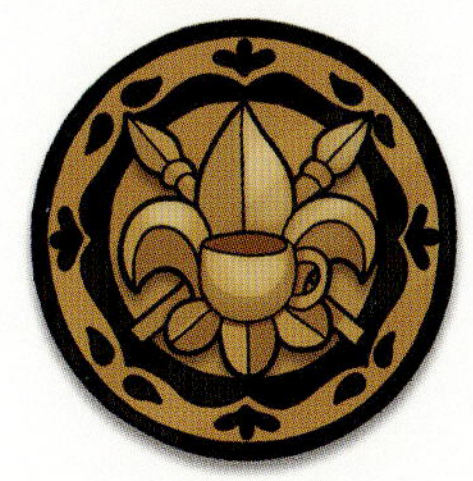
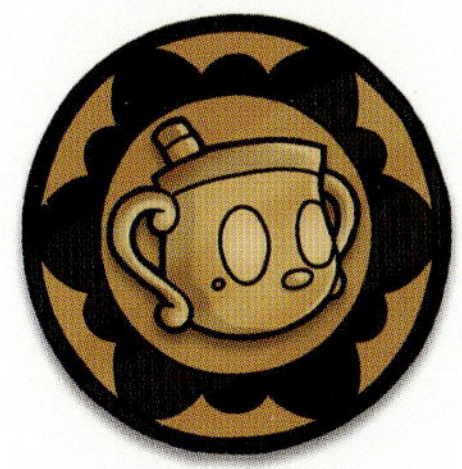
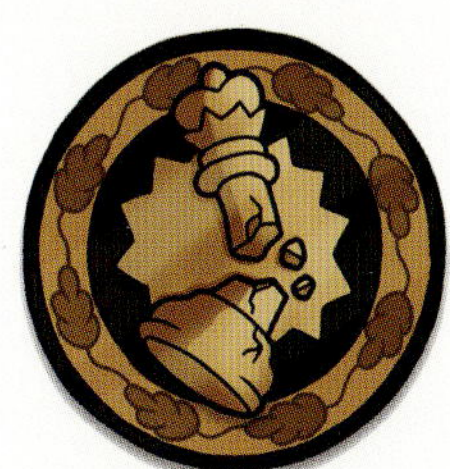
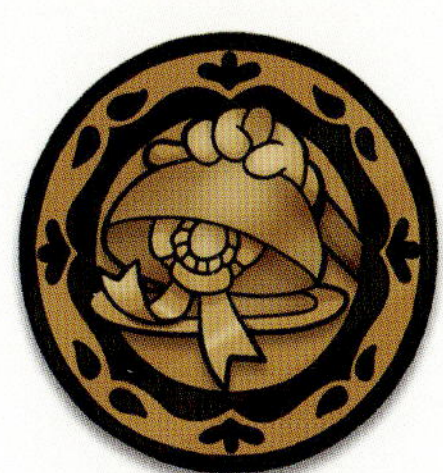
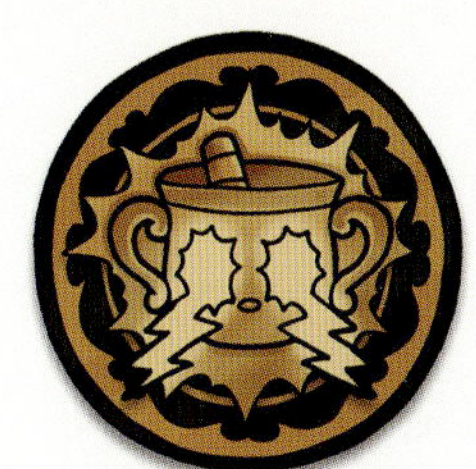
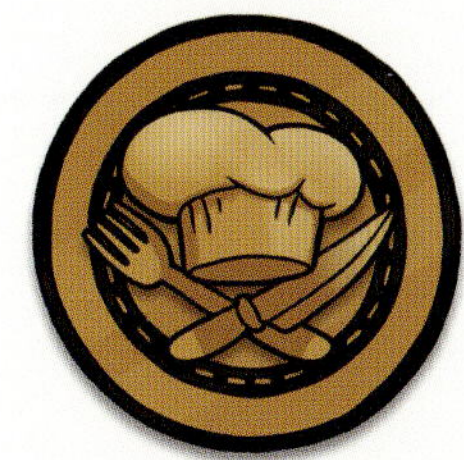
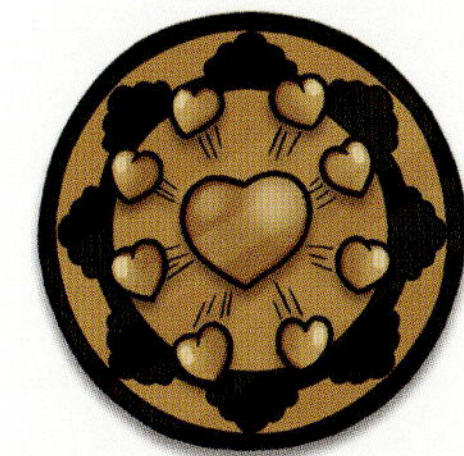

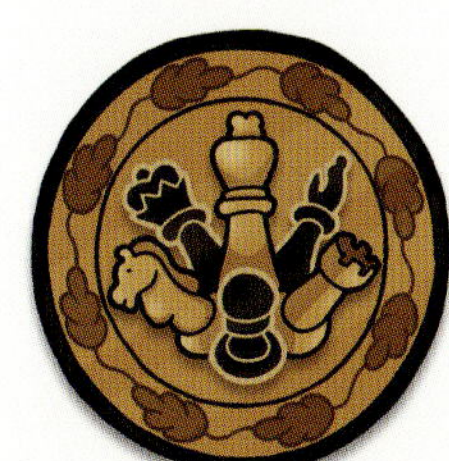
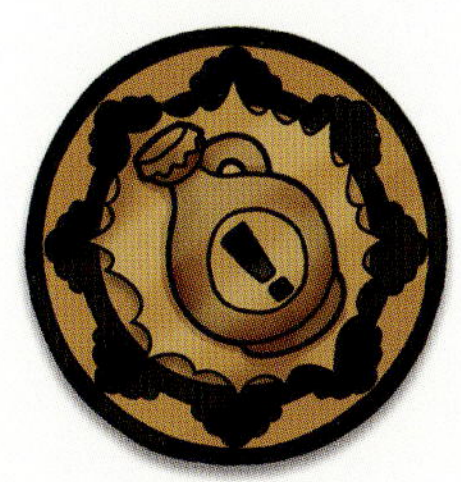
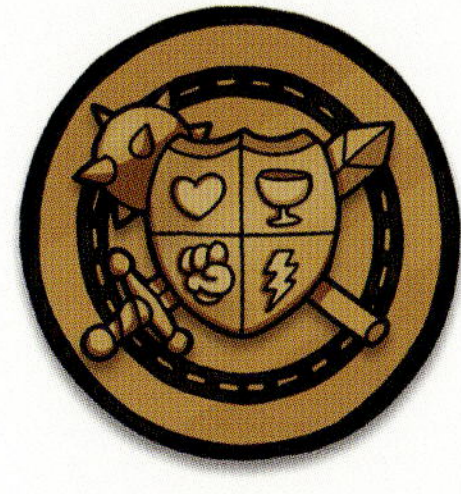
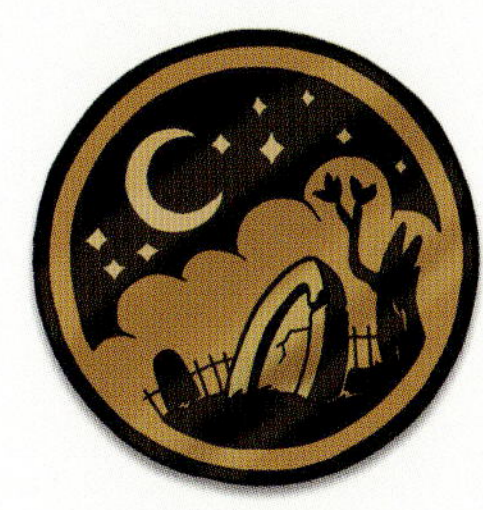
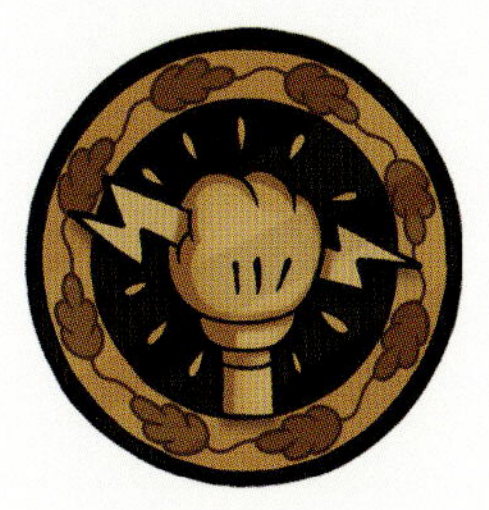
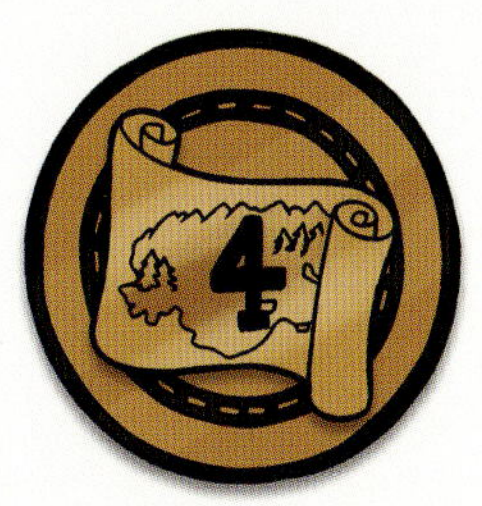
4

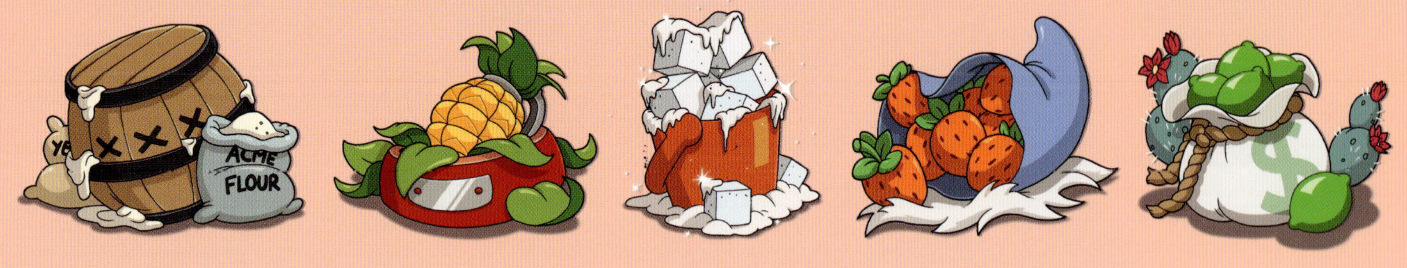

Ingredients

THE DELICIOUS LAST COURSE tasks our intrepid trio with collecting a laundry list of magical ingredients necessary to bake a magical tart that will bring Ms. Chalice to life. Initially, we imagined each ingredient as an anthropomorphized rubber hose character (see some pictured page right), but ultimately felt it would be a more morbid surprise when players later saw the living ingredients for the first time when they are chopped and julienned by the maniacal Chef Saltbaker!

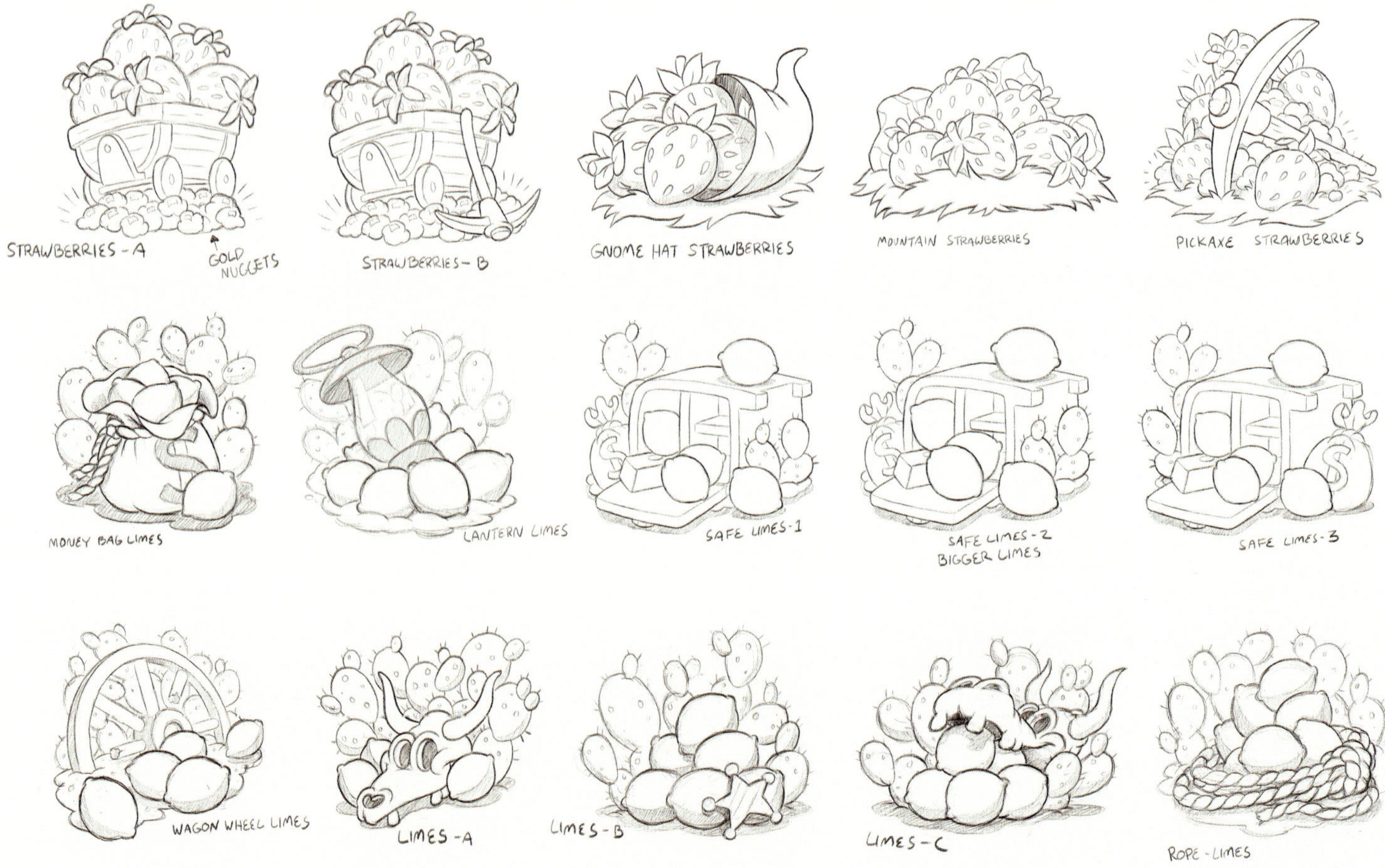

Pictured to the right, unused concepts for the collectible ingredients from Artist Lance Inkwell. Final ingredients were brought to life with buoyancy from Animator Simone Cirillo.

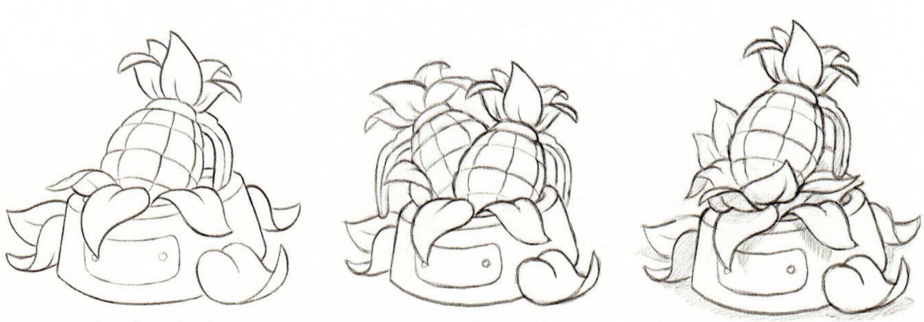

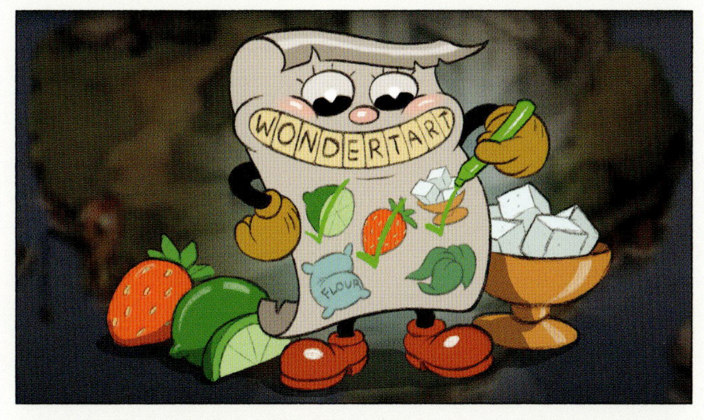
WONDERTART
FLOUR
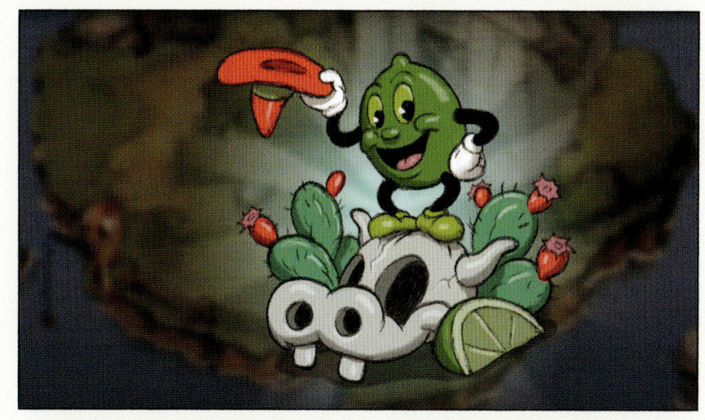
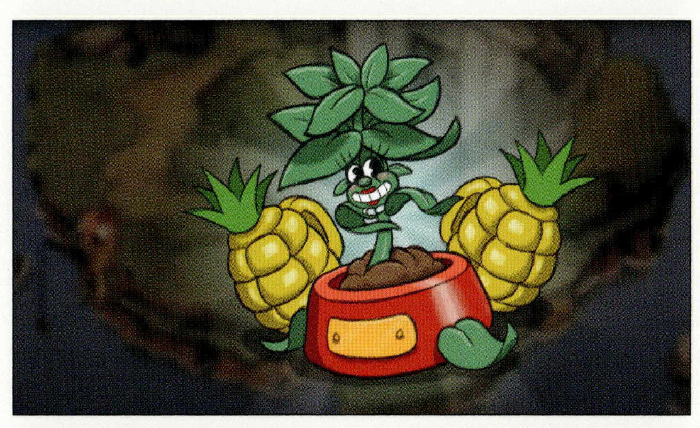
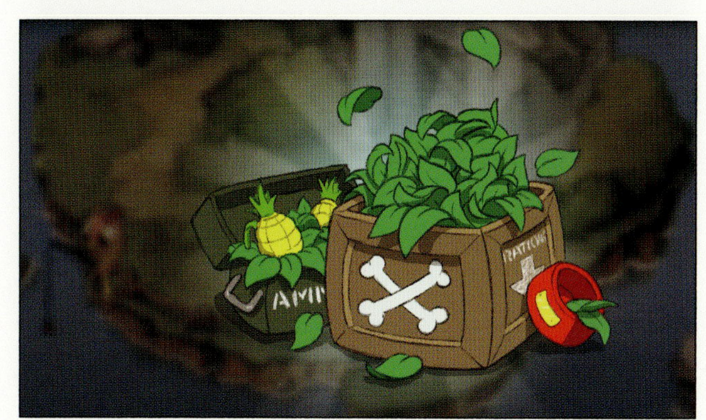
AMM
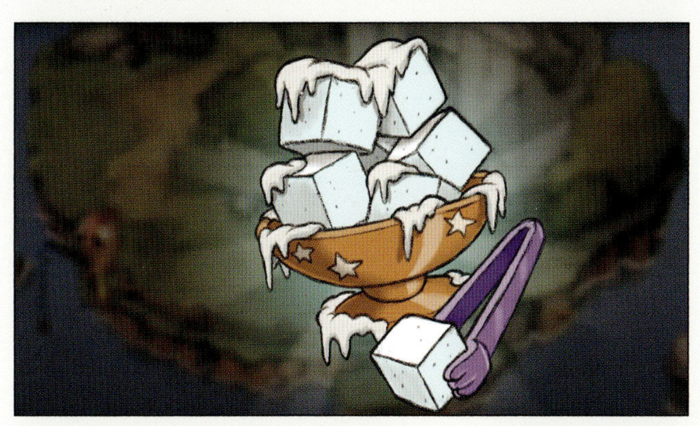
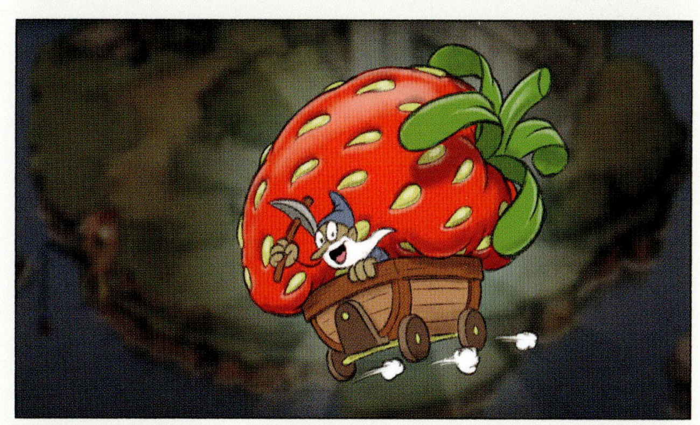
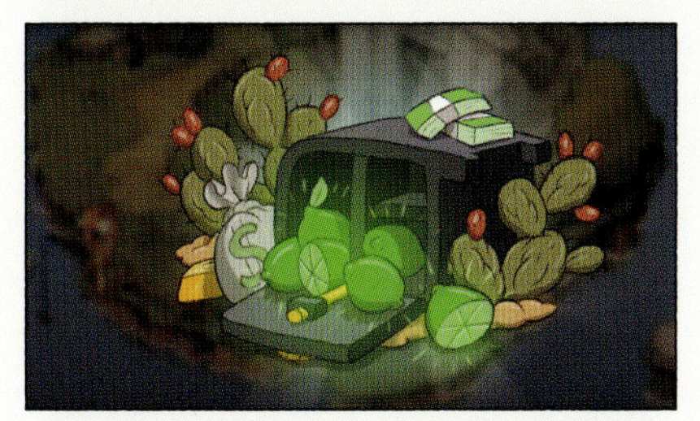
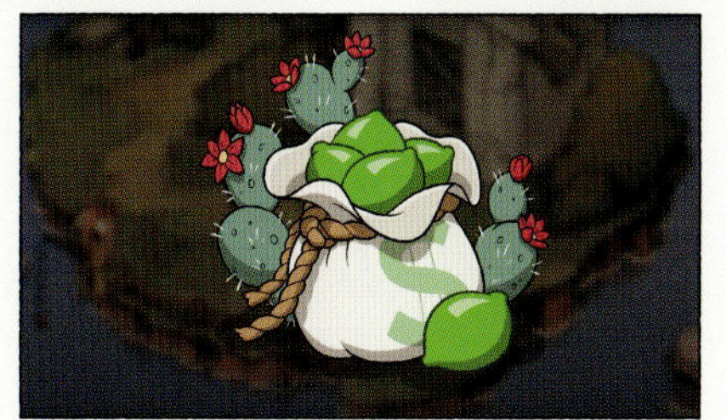
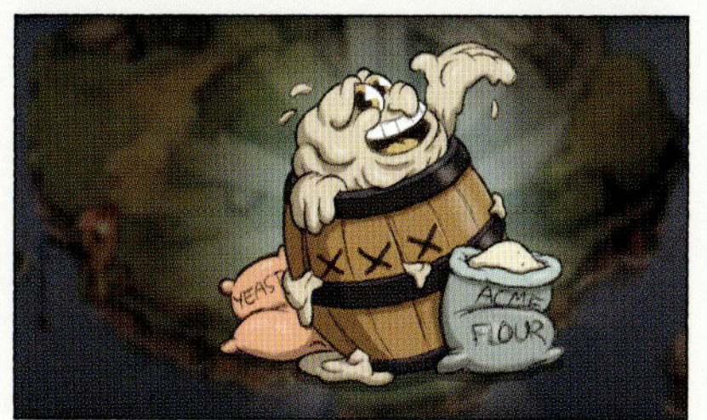
YEAST
ACME
FLOUR
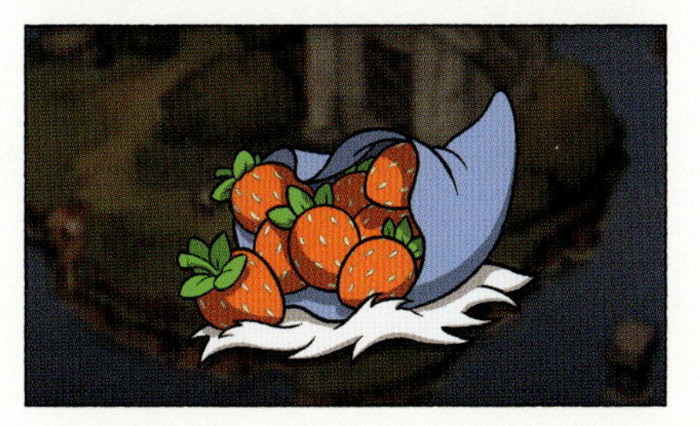
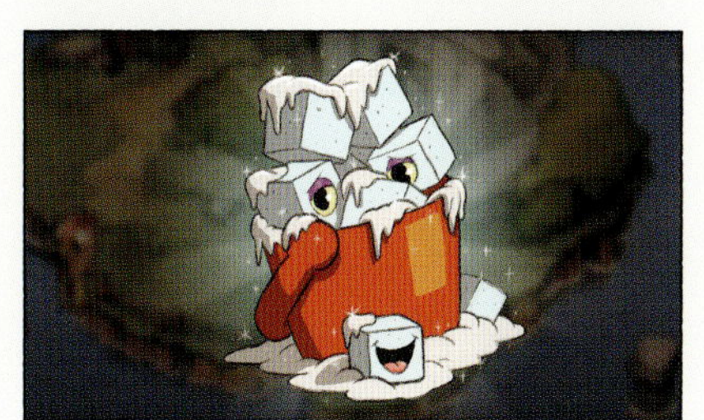
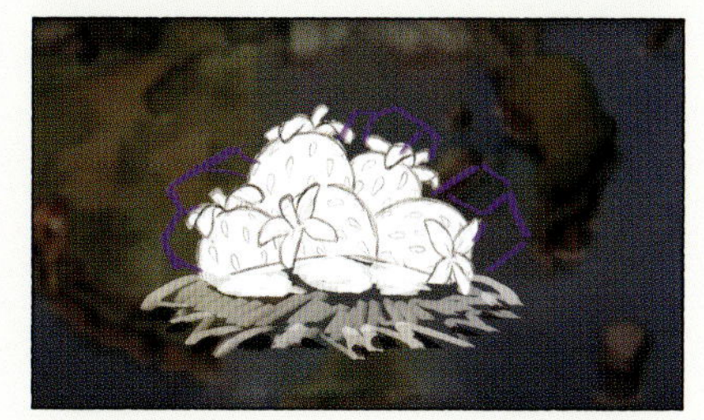

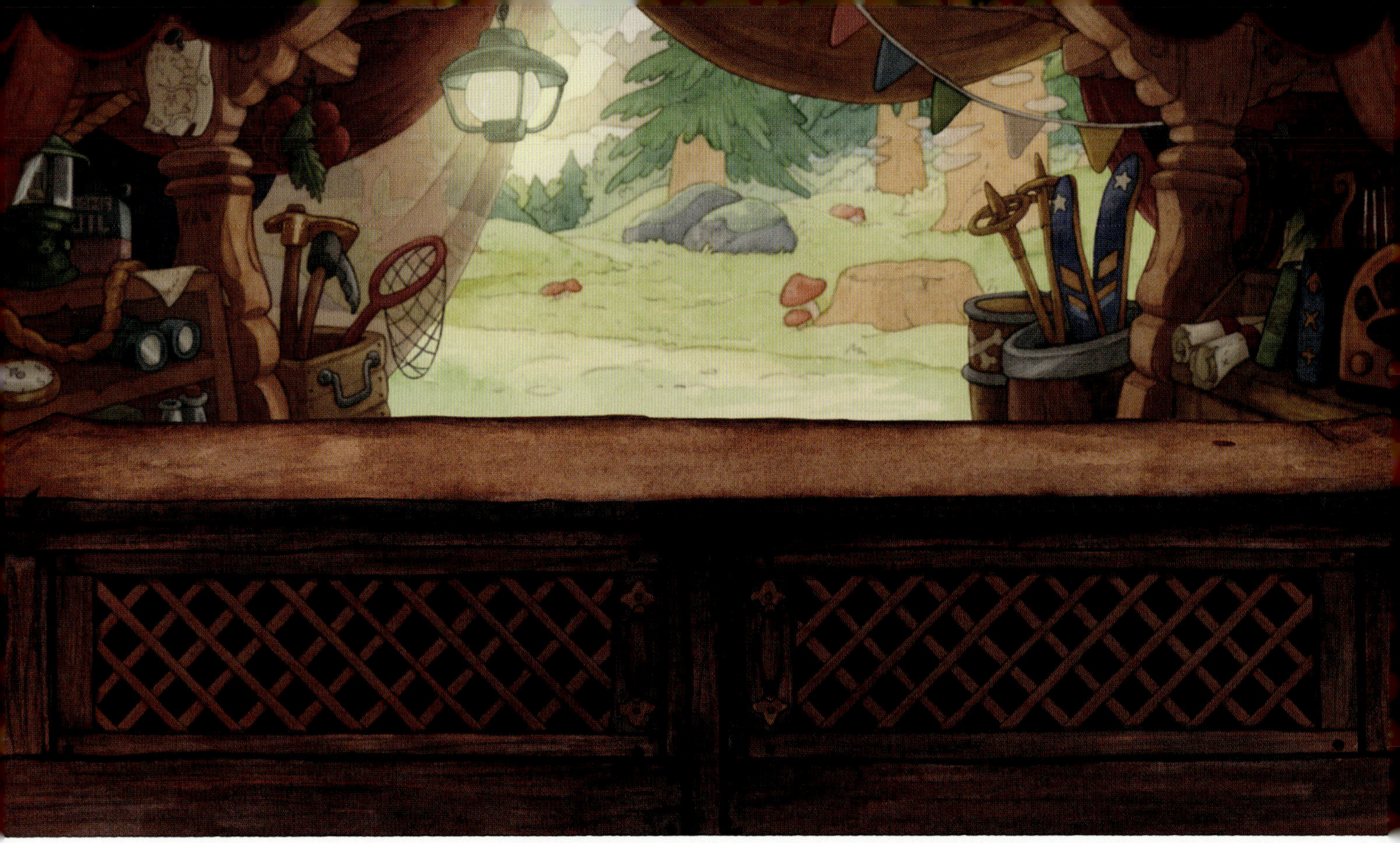

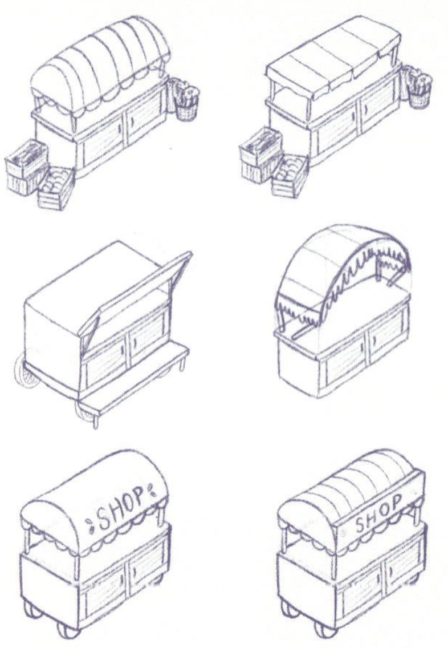

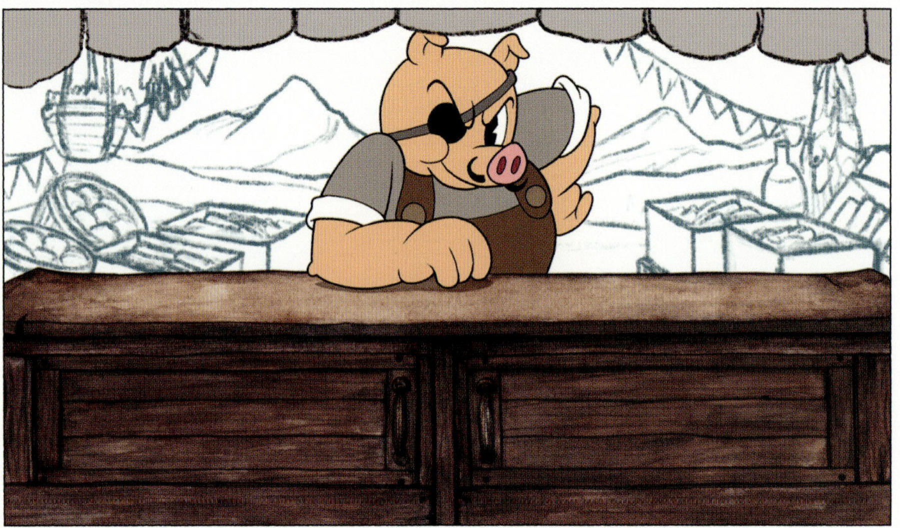

Porkrind's Shop

AN EPIC NEW QUEST on a brand new, unexplored Inkwell Isle can only mean one thing…a chance for surly porcine shopkeep Porkrind to hawk new wares! For the DLC, we took on the task of imagining how Porkrind might mount a more *plein air* version of his iconic travelling shoppe from the original game. As with all of our backgrounds, this one is packed with more references than you can shake a ski pole at, including the map pinned up in the top left corner–which pays homage to Sega's 1988 side-scroller *Lord of the Sword*.

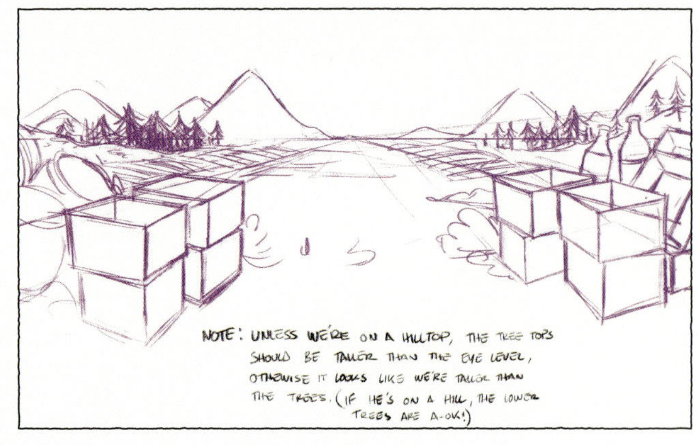

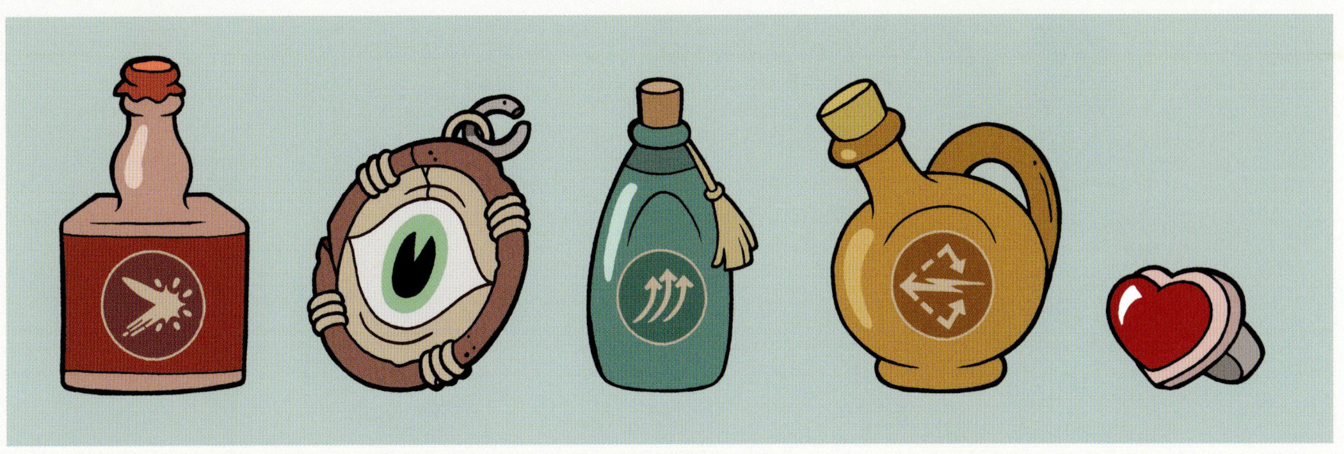

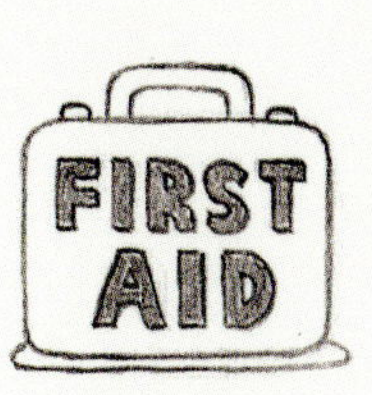

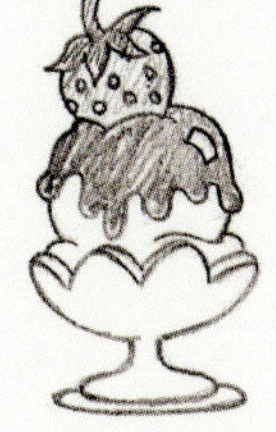

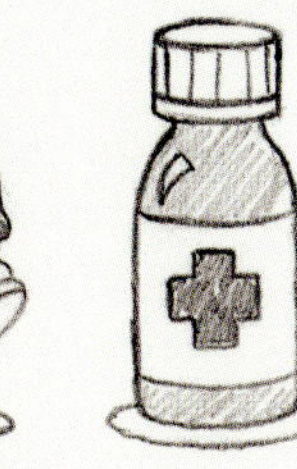

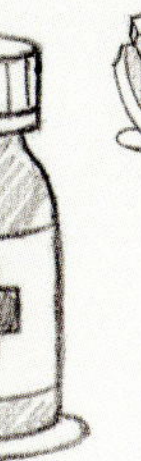

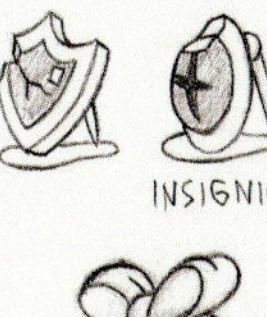

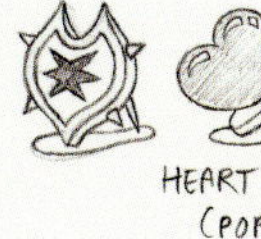

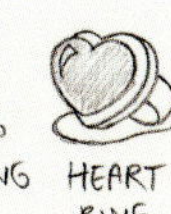

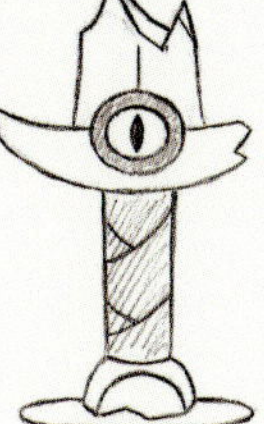

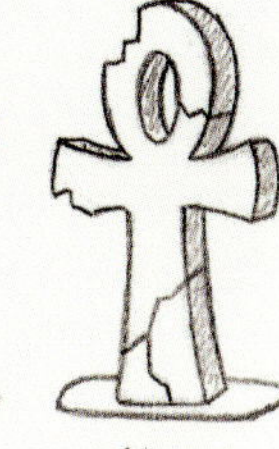

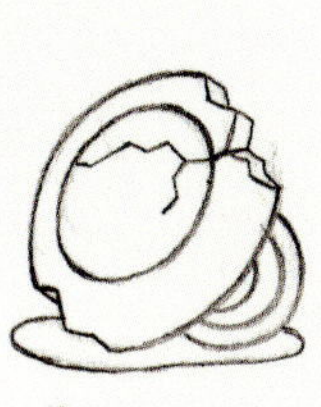

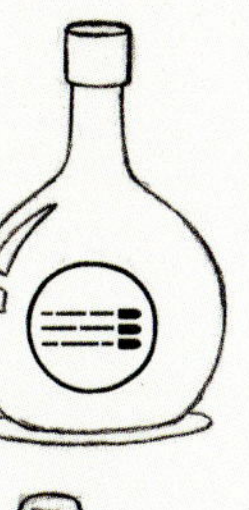
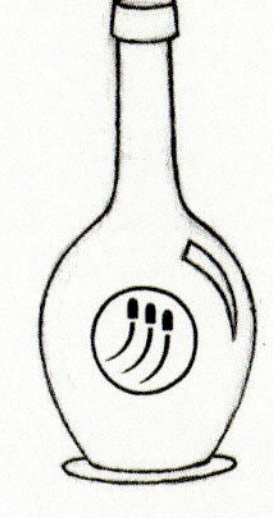
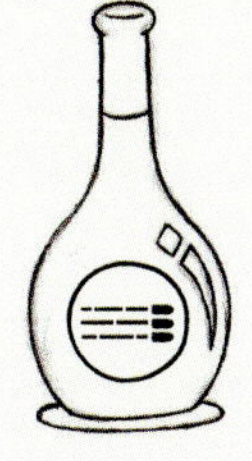
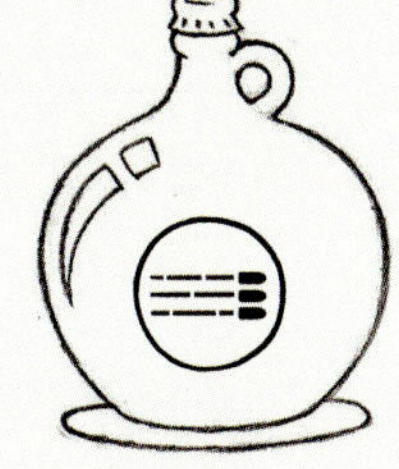
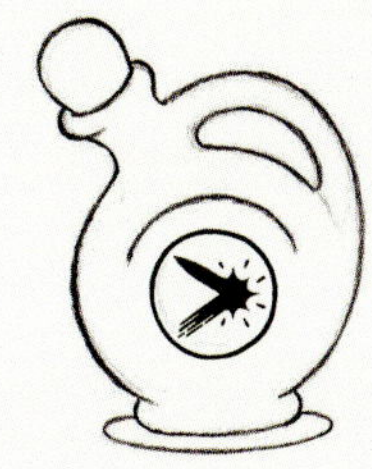
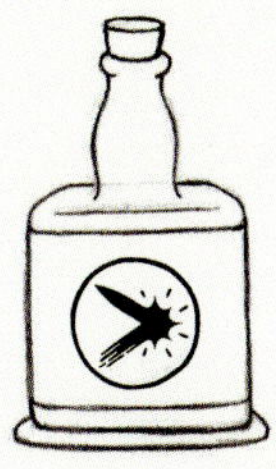
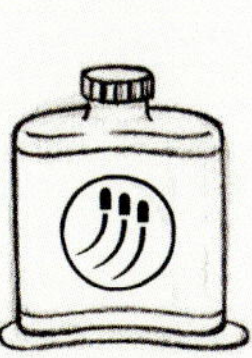

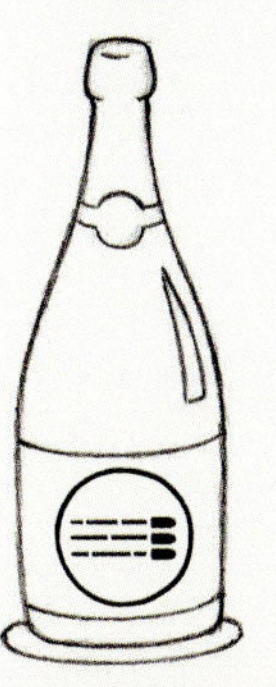
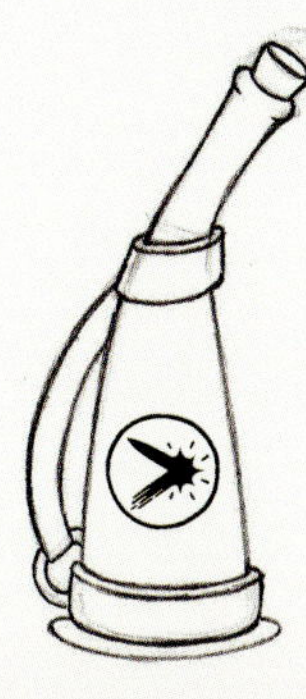
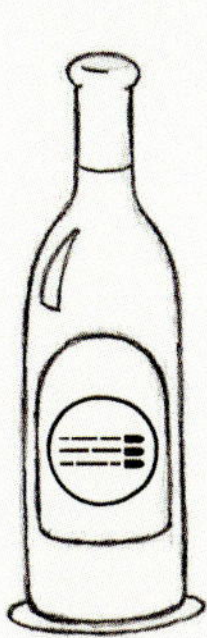
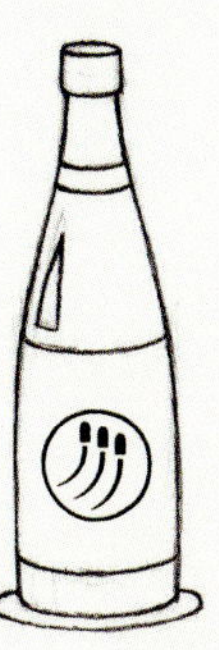
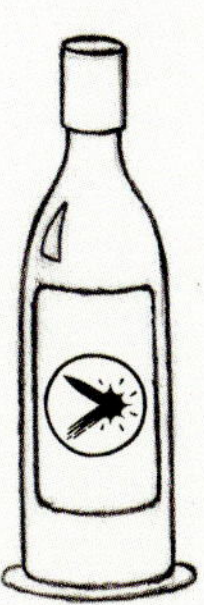
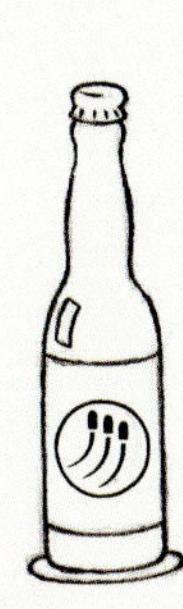
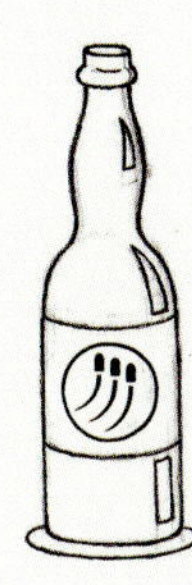
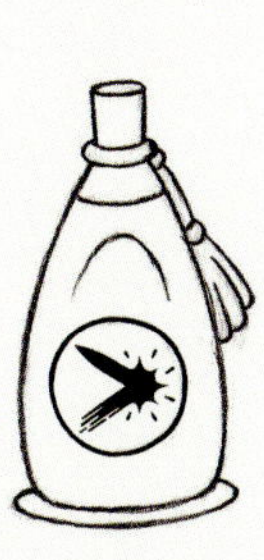

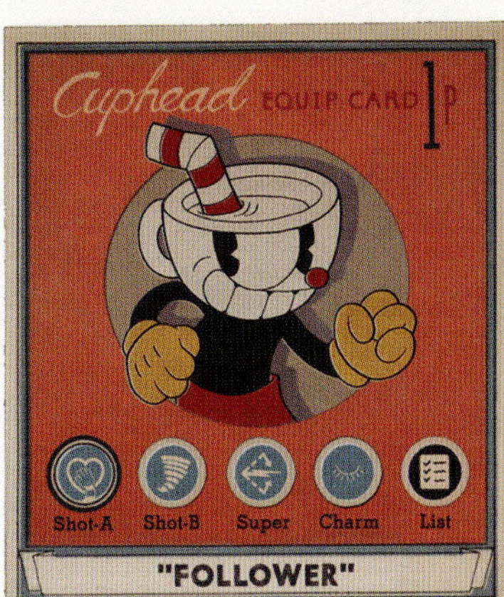

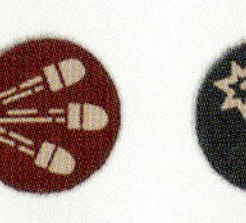
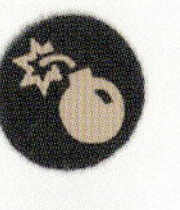
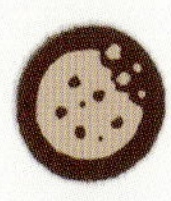
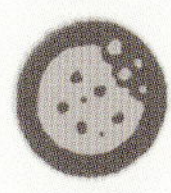

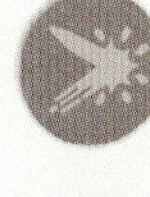
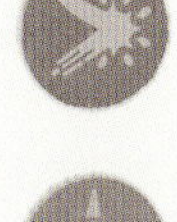
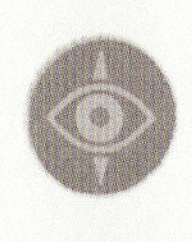
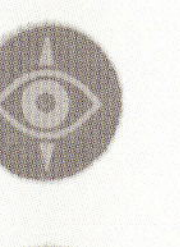

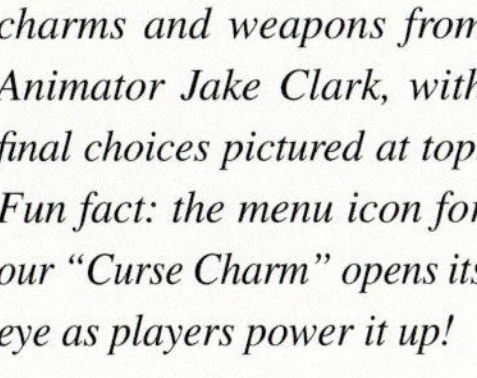

Concepts for this new Isle's charms and weapons from Animator Jake Clark, with final choices pictured at top. Fun fact: the menu icon for our "Curse Charm" opens its eye as players power it up!

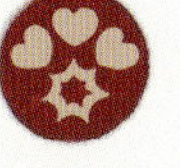
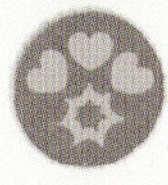
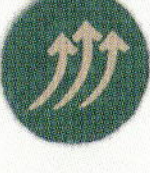

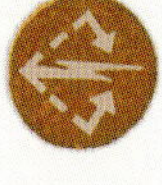
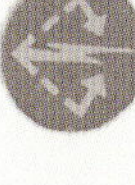

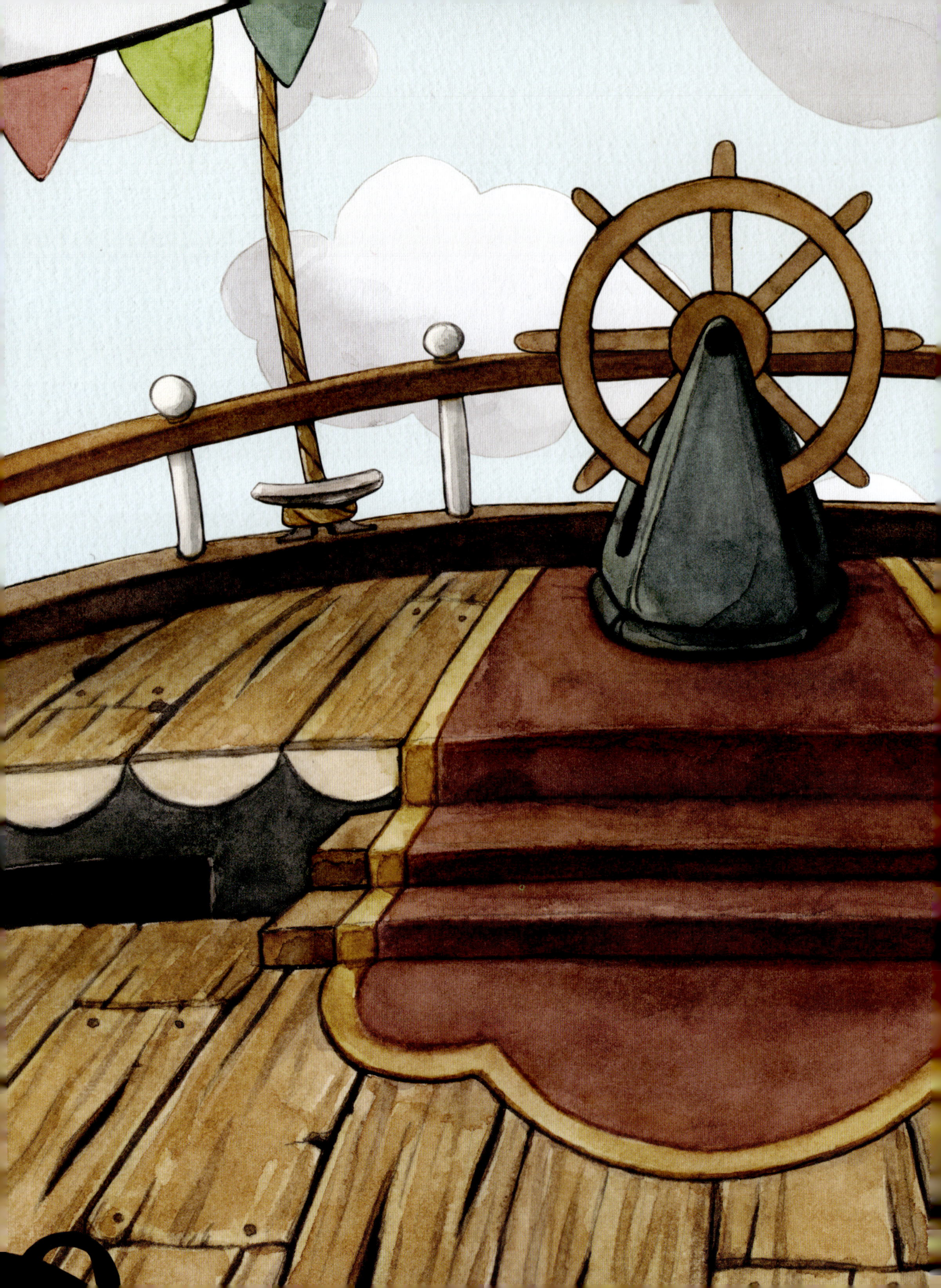

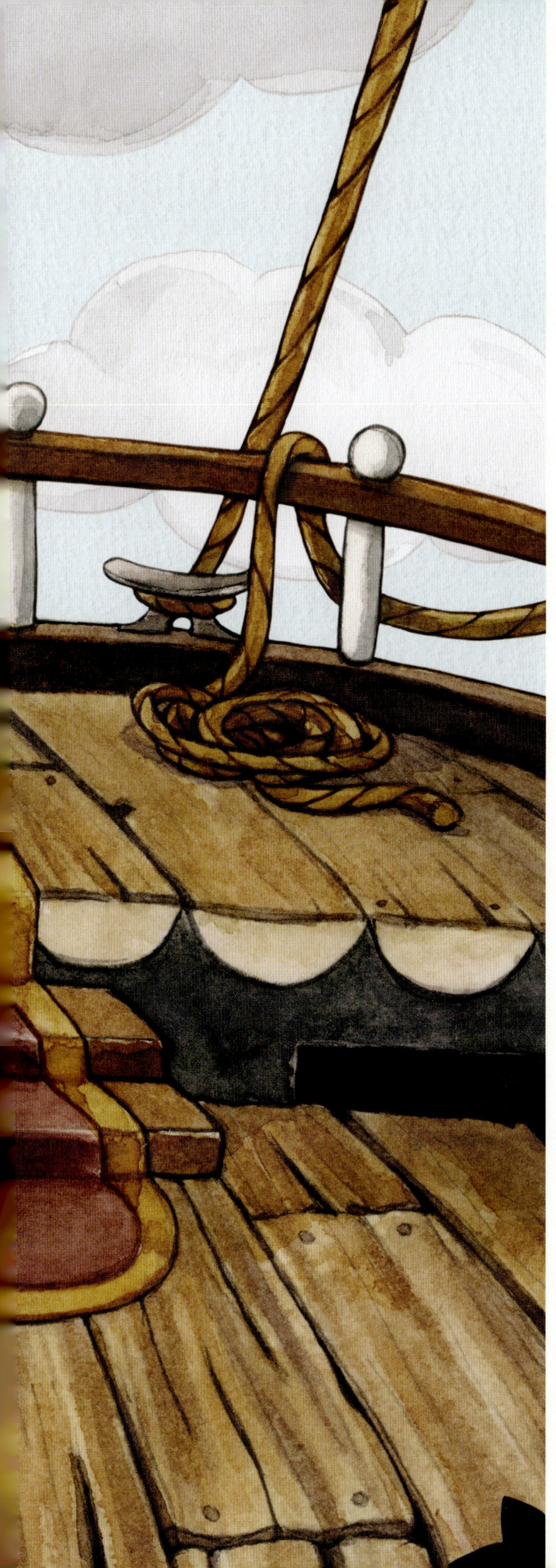

Chapter XV:
Lost Levels

GAME DEVELOPMENT IS RARELY a straightforward or simple journey, and the path toward the best possible game is often strewn with levels, characters, and designs lost along the way to release. This was perhaps doubly true for *Cuphead*, whose trademark rubber hose animation style required an exorbitant amount of effort to bring to life. Oftentimes, this meant being decisive very early in the creative process about which concepts to move forward with and which ones to abandon. With that said, the shifting priorities and changing scope that came with making our very first game meant that some unused ideas ventured further along the path to completion than others. Without further ado, let's open the doors to the vault and take a look at *Cuphead*'s very own lost levels–the bosses, characters, and stages that could have been, and the concepts that never quite made it off the page and into the Inkwell Isles.

Airship

SAILING THE SKIES OF the Inkwell Isles and granting opportunities for Cuphead to best beasts for boffo bucks, the flying Airship was an early concept from the base *Cuphead* game. Director Jared Moldenhauer wanted a mobile structure that could touch down anywhere on the map, only appearing when the player met secret criteria. These spontaneous encounters would challenge players to beat skill-testing mini battles that relied only on your character's parry move, before flying away into the clouds. Ultimately cut for scoping purposes, this concept was revisited in *The Delicious Last Course* under a new name: The King's Leap.

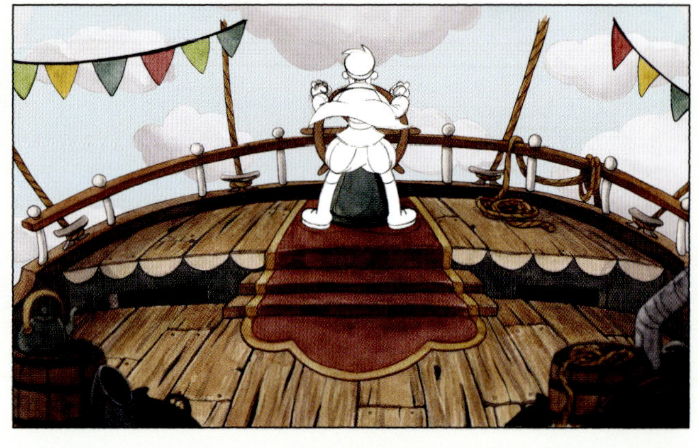

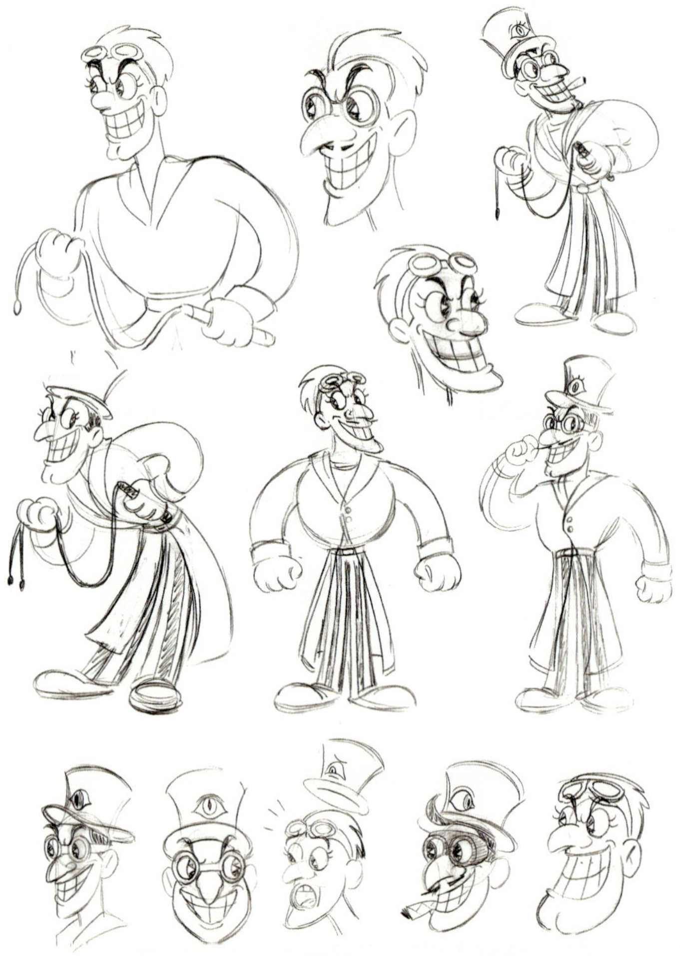

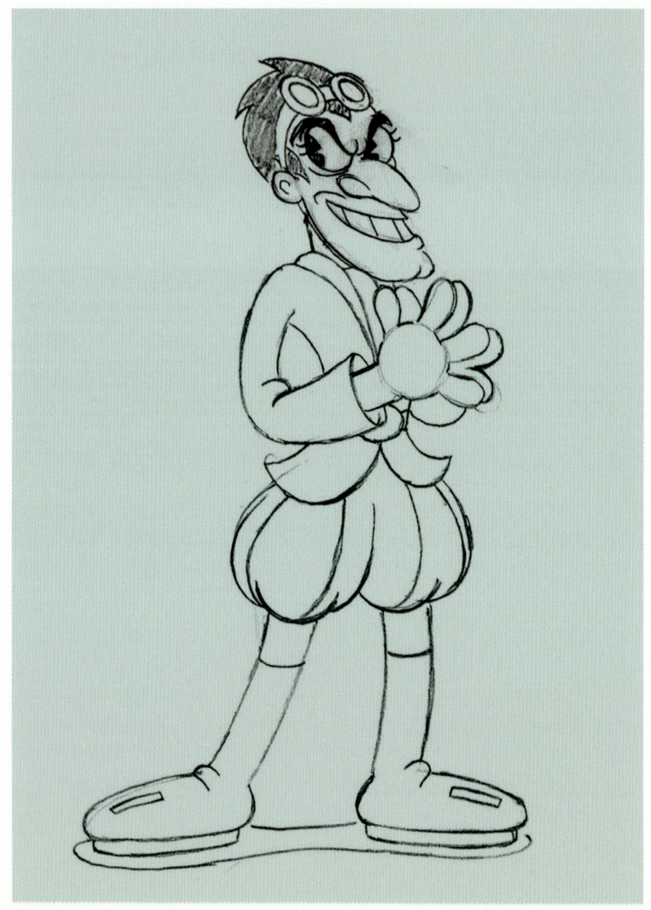

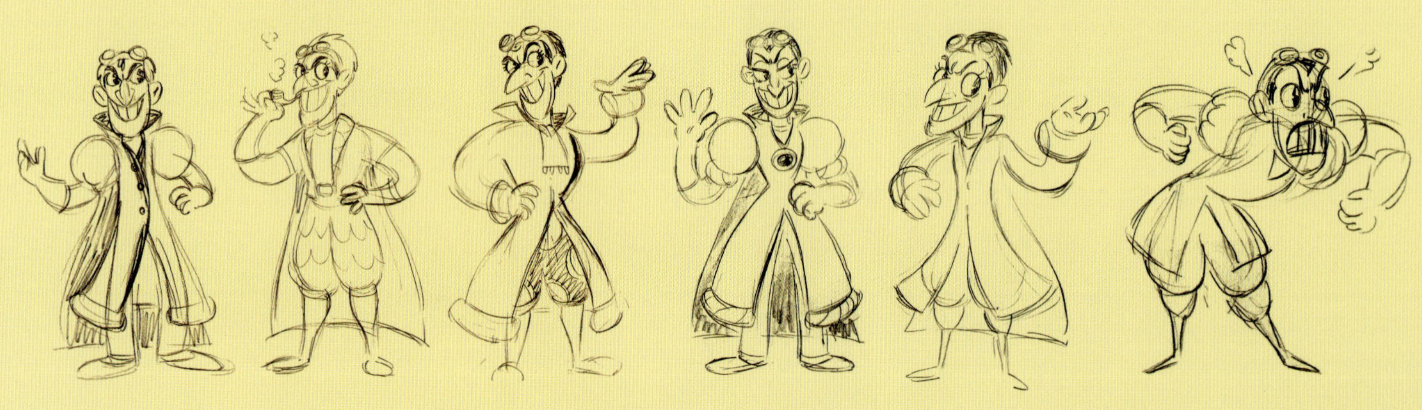

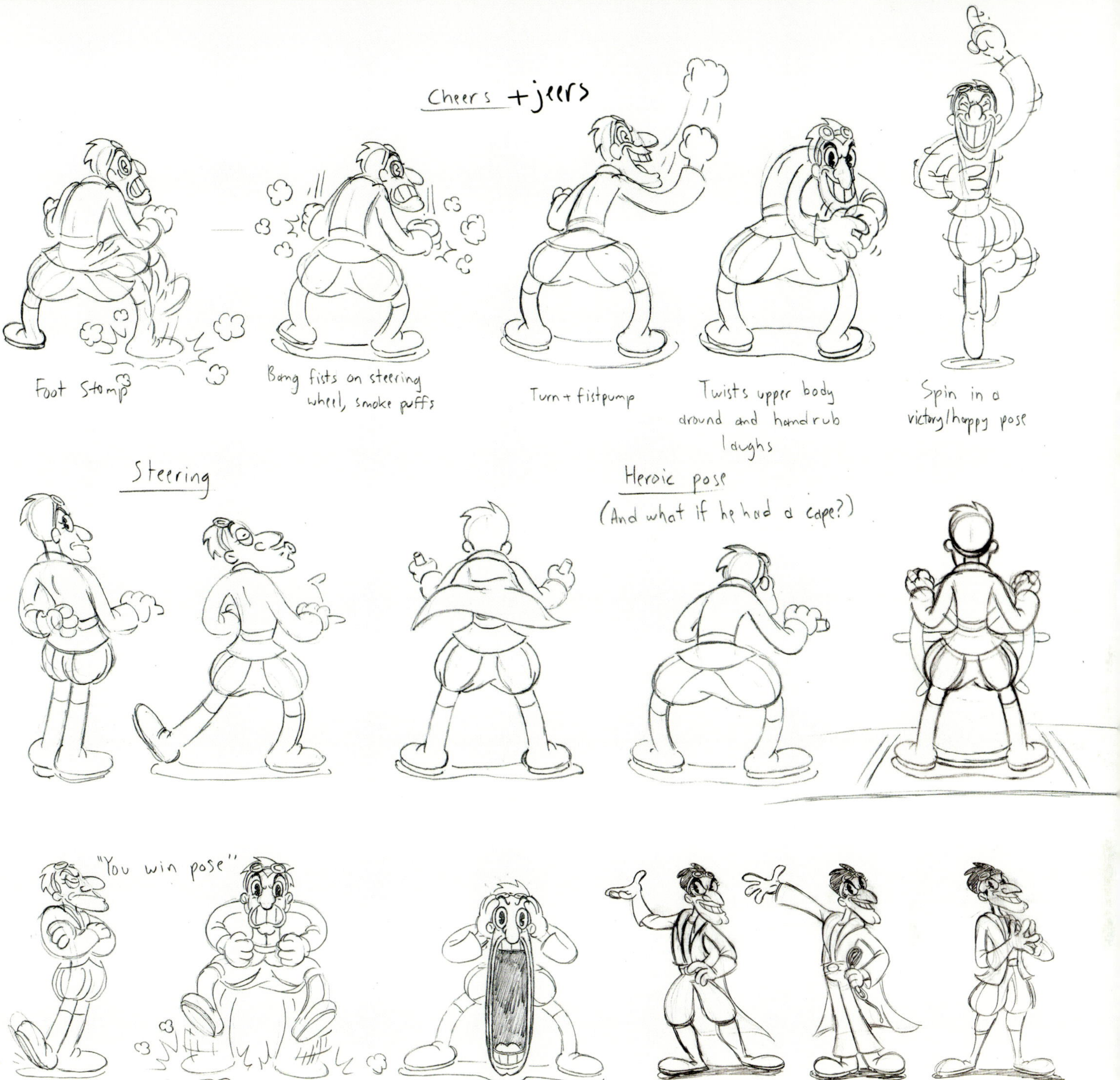

Cheers + jeers

Foot Stomp

Bang fists on steering wheel, smoke puffs

Turn + fistpump

Twists upper body around and hand rub laughs

Spin in a victory/happy pose

Steering

Heroic pose
(And what if he had a cape?)

"You win pose"

TAP
TAP
TAP

"Pff... whatever... hmph..."

Angry stomp jump

Jaw Drop

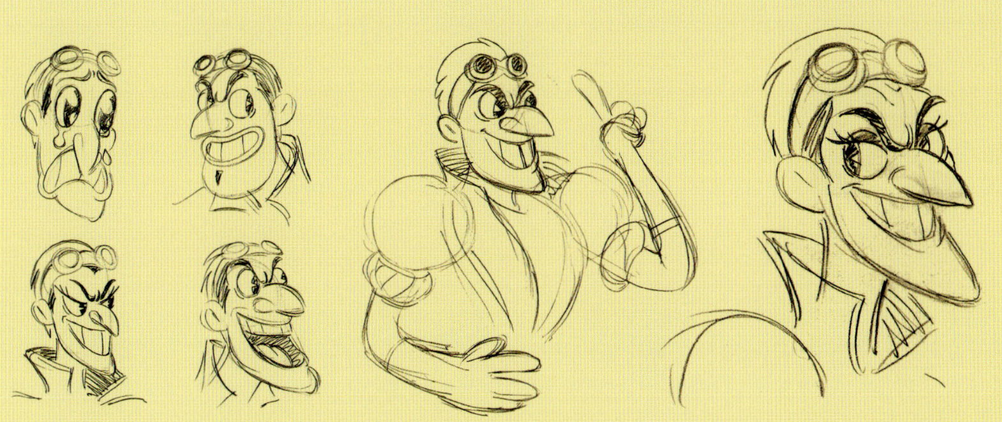

Paying homage to the preeminent airship pilots of gaming history, we added notes of Cid from Final Fantasy 7 *(1997) to the captain's visual design. Above and left, Animator Jake Clark explores the captain's mercurial personality.*

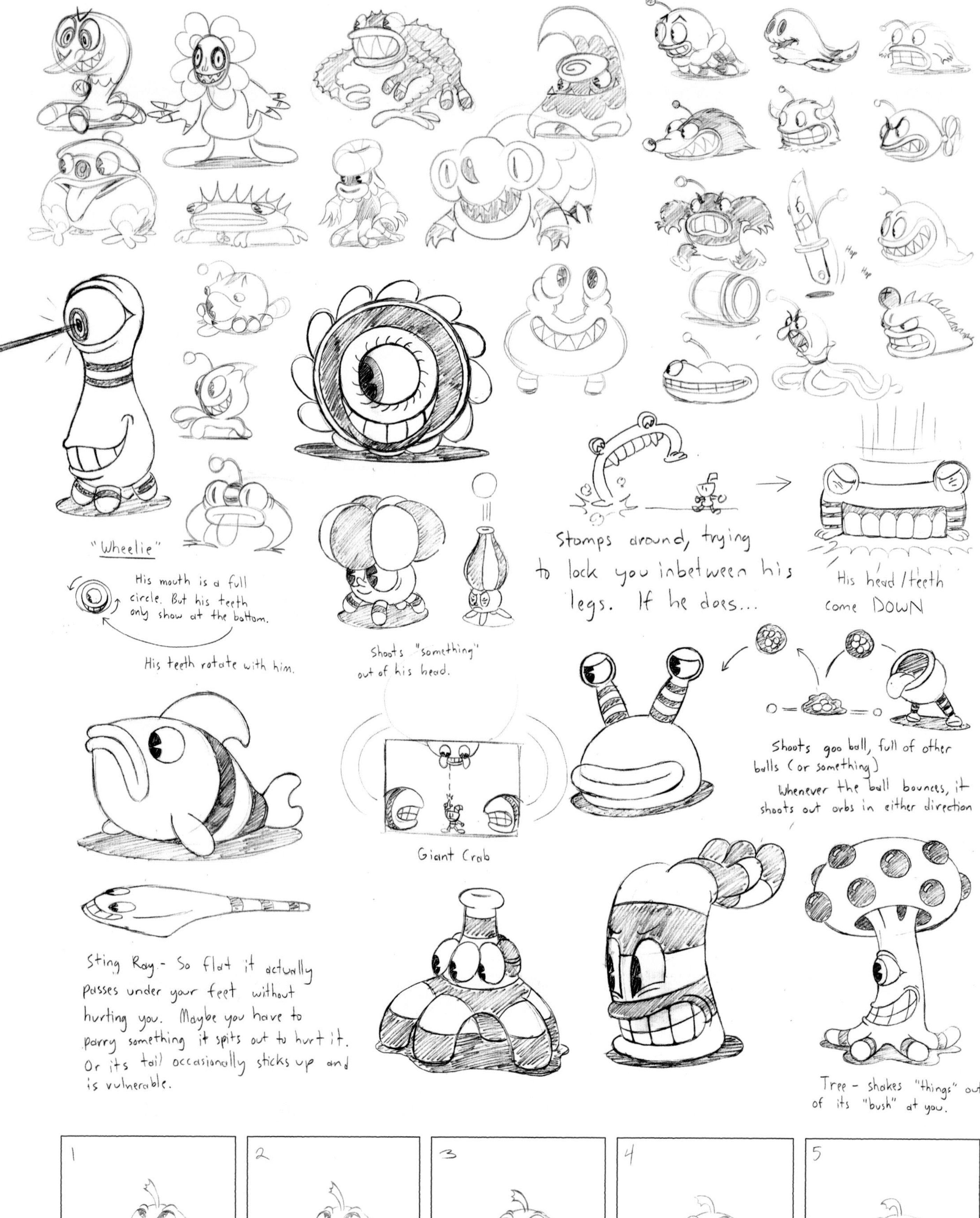
Hop
Hop
"Wheelie"
His mouth is a full circle. But his teeth only show at the bottom.
His teeth rotate with him.
Shoots "something" out of his head.
Stomps around, trying to lock you inbetween his legs. If he does...
His head / teeth come DOWN
Shoots goo ball, full of other balls (or something)
Whenever the ball bounces, it shoots out orbs in either direction
Giant Crab
Sting Ray.- So flat it actually passes under your feet without hurting you. Maybe you have to parry something it spits out to hurt it. Or its tail occasionally sticks up and is vulnerable.
Tree - shakes "things" out of its "bush" at you.
1
2
3
4
5

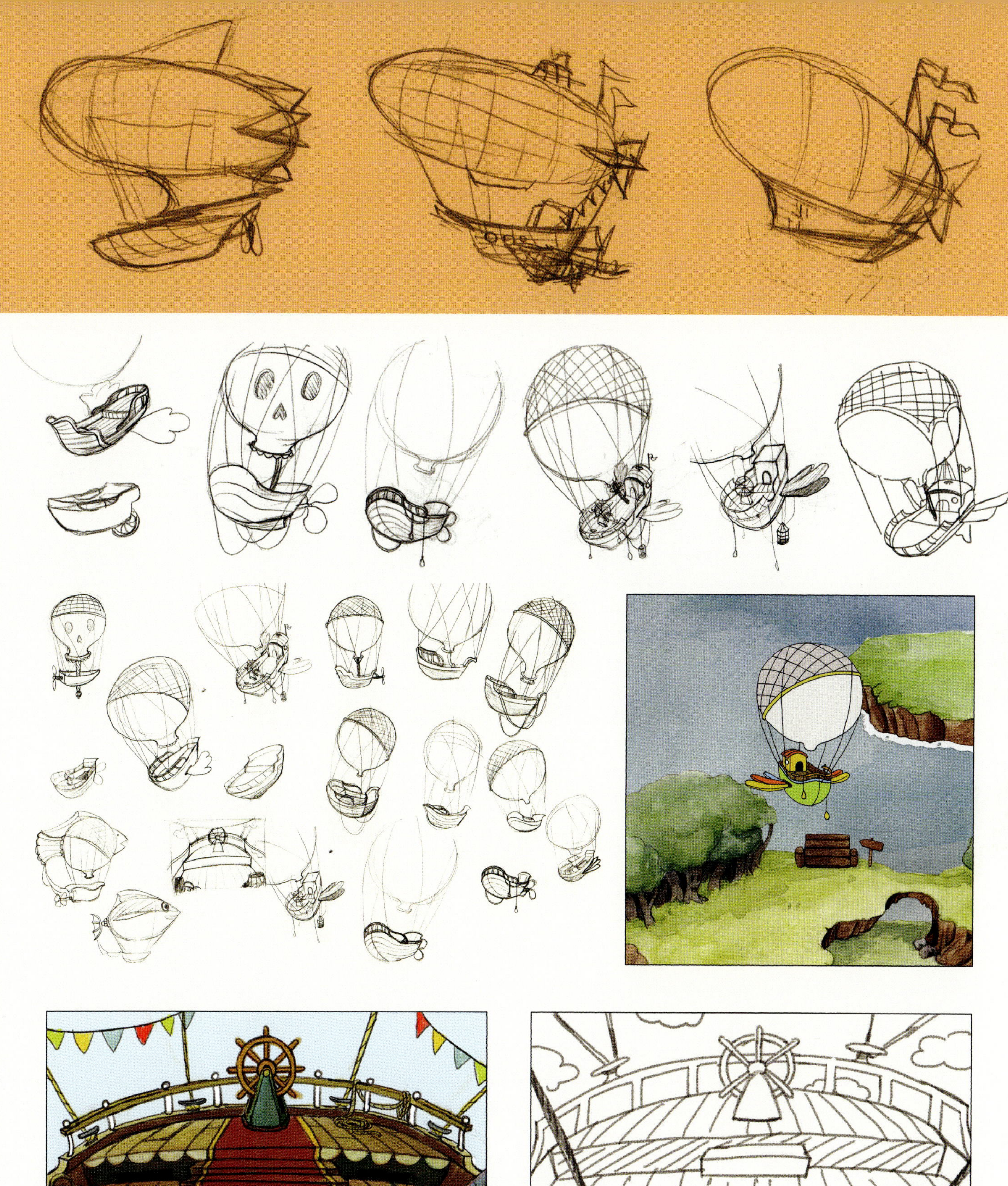

When designing the boss concepts for the Airship battles, we wanted to emphasize surreal form and color–selling the idea that the Captain had collected these rare animals from the most remote and foreign places in the world. The neon-colored octopus by Animator Jake Clark, shown in pencil form at left, even made it far enough along in prototyping that it was shown publicly in one of our trade show demonstration builds of *Cuphead*.

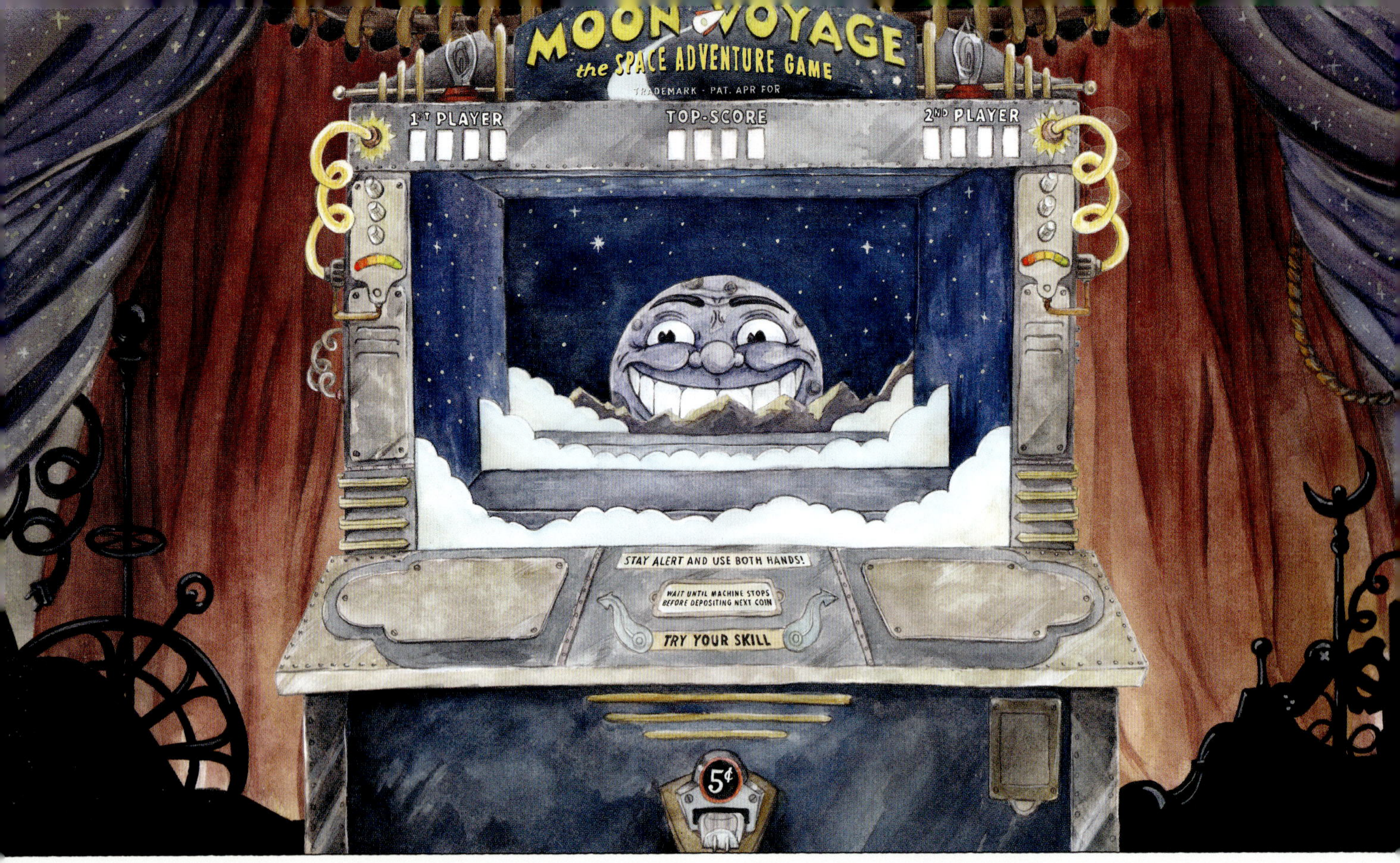

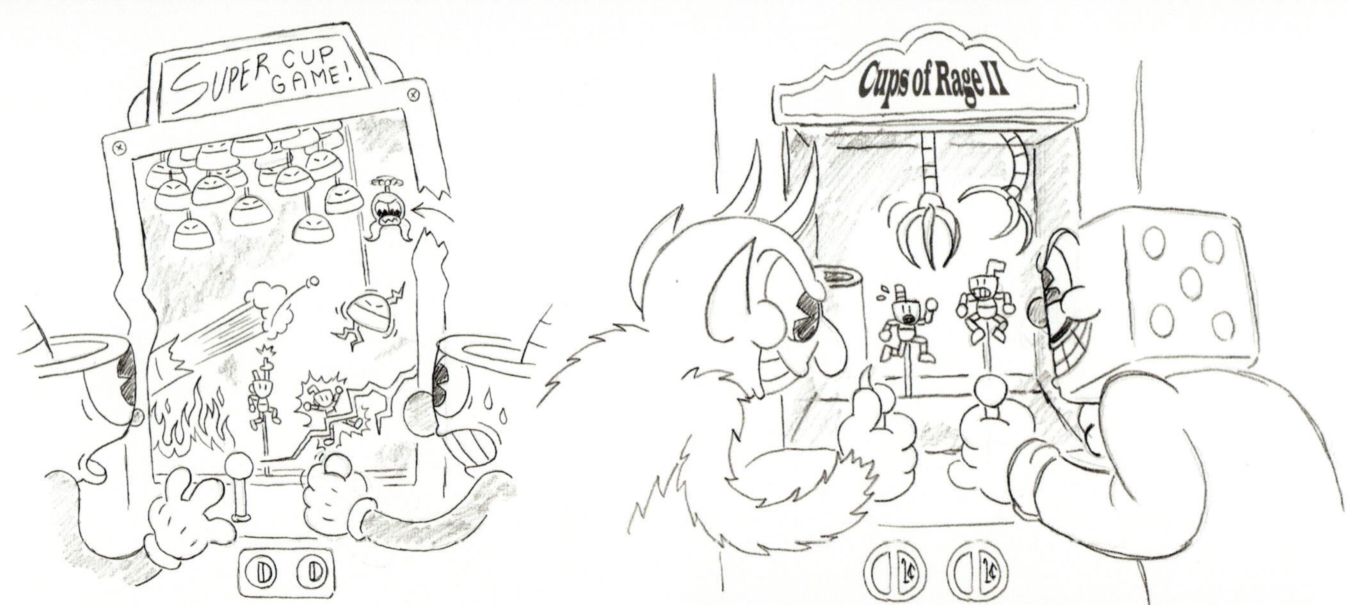

Coin-Op Bop

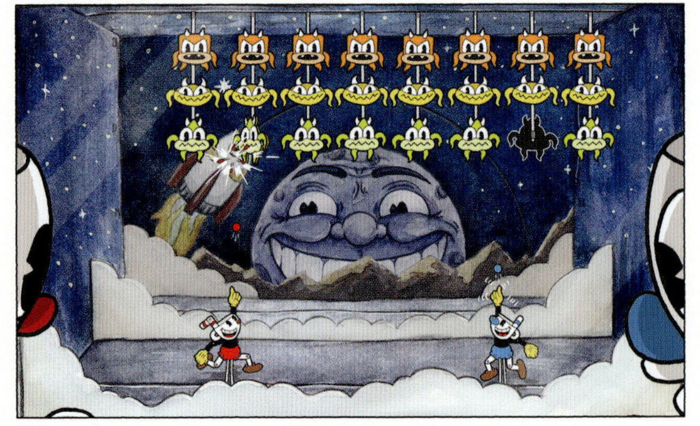

FOR VARIETY, WE ORIGINALLY PLANNED on having unique "bonus round" stages on each Inkwell Isle that would reward players with more of the game's coin currency. The most elaborate of these concepts was a visual homage to early mechanical arcades, with mini-games inspired by video game industry pioneer Atari. It was even set to have animated Cuphead and Mugman characters playing the games-within-a-game, pressing buttons in time with the players' inputs. The sequence went through a number of iterations, eventually being cut due to overall scope.

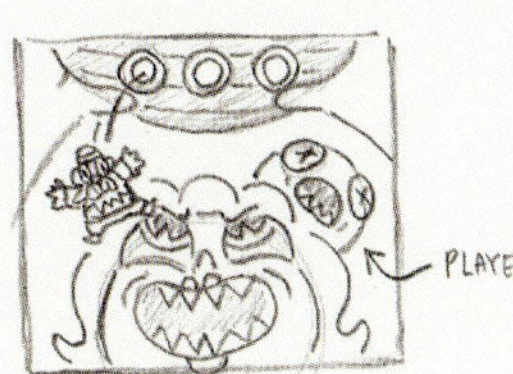

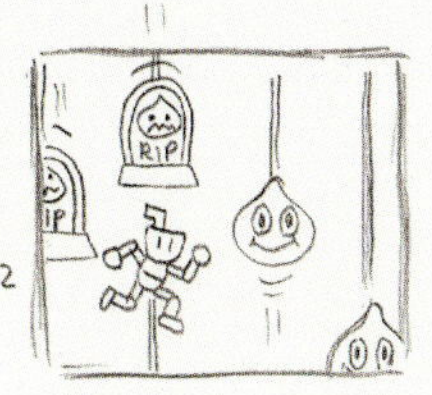

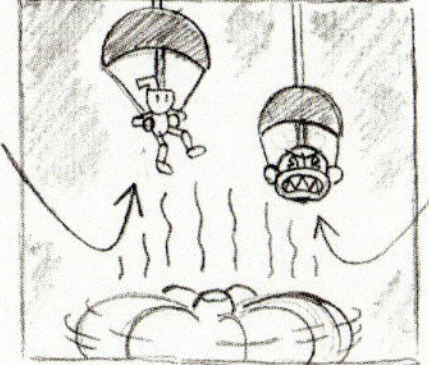

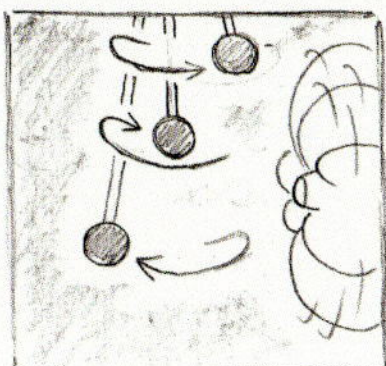

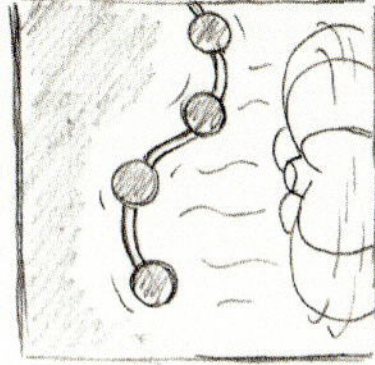

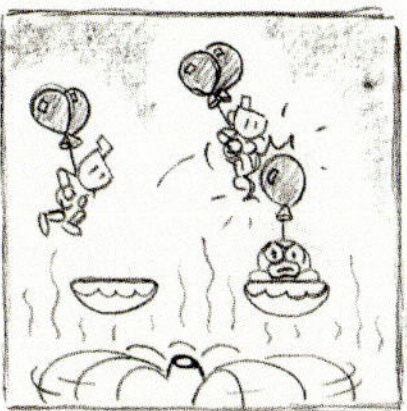

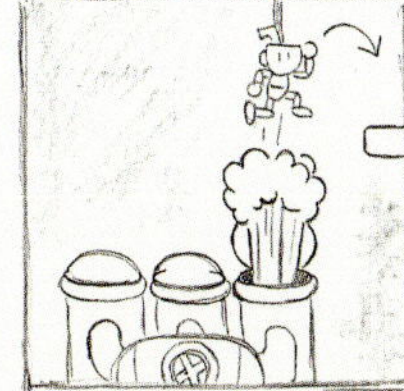

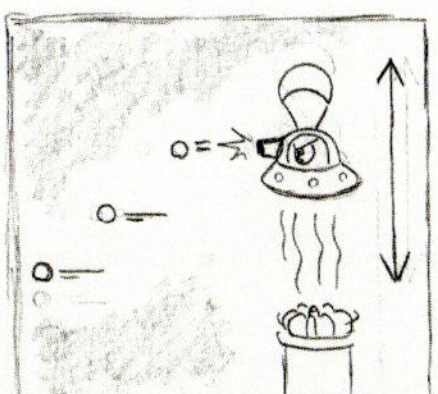

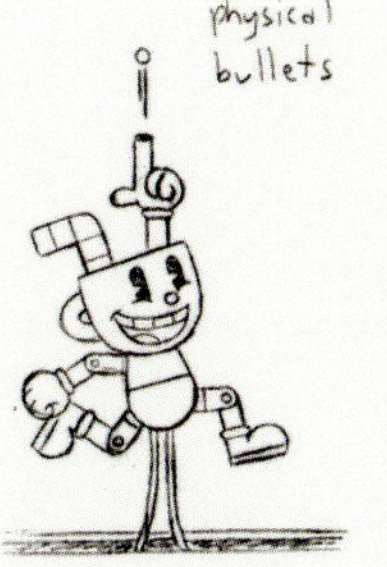
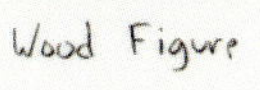
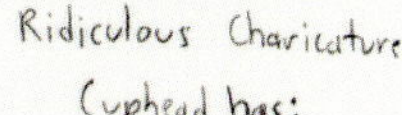

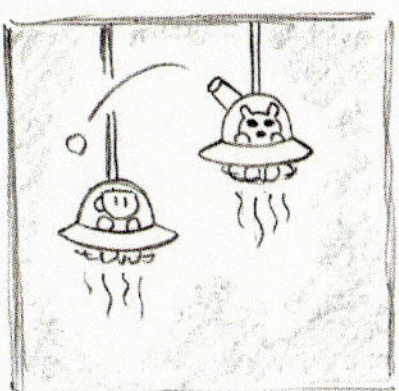

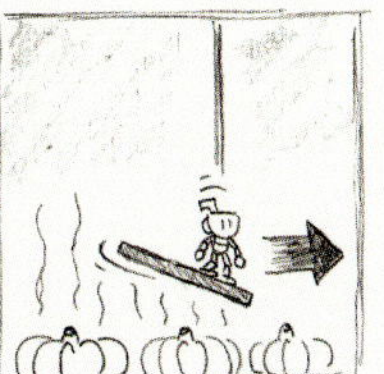

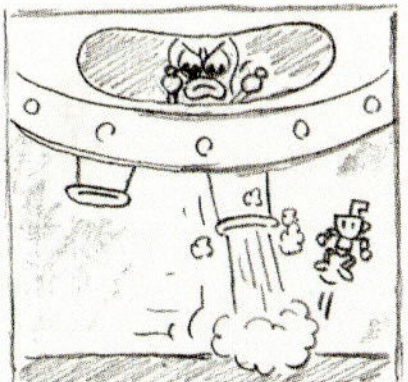
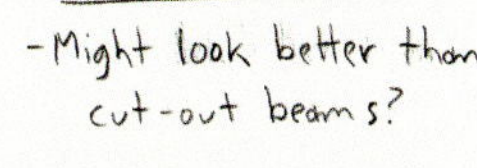

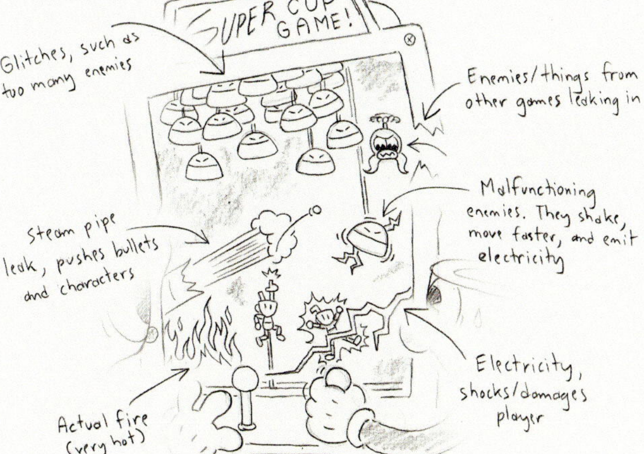

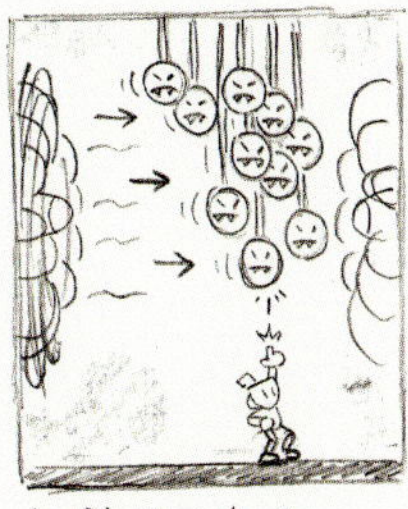

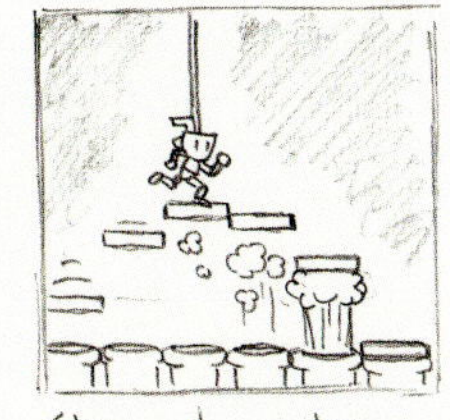

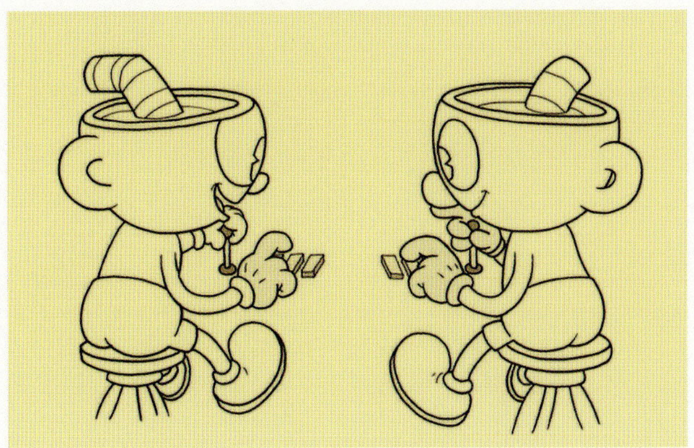

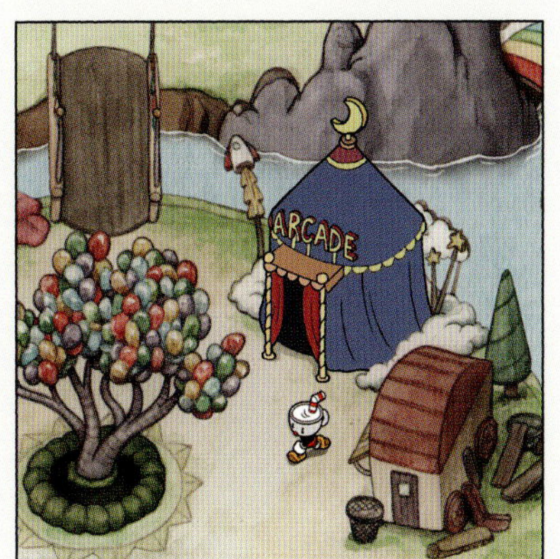

Above, Animator Jake Clark tested out different concepts in order to make the setup adhere to a mechanical board structure. Left: a sign that the concept remained in development long enough to receive a world map icon.

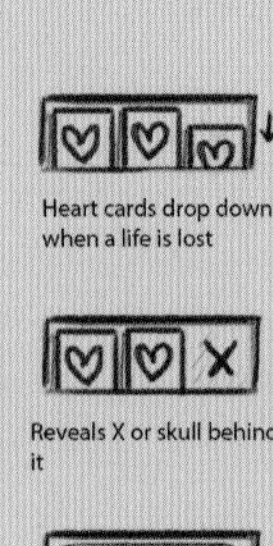

Heart cards drop down when a life is lost

Reveals X or skull behind it

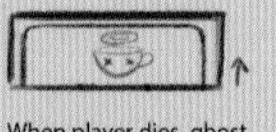

When player dies, ghost card pops up

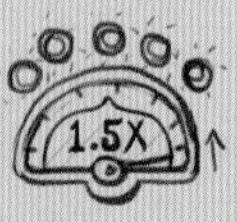

Lights match dial progression

When gauge is full multiplier card pops up

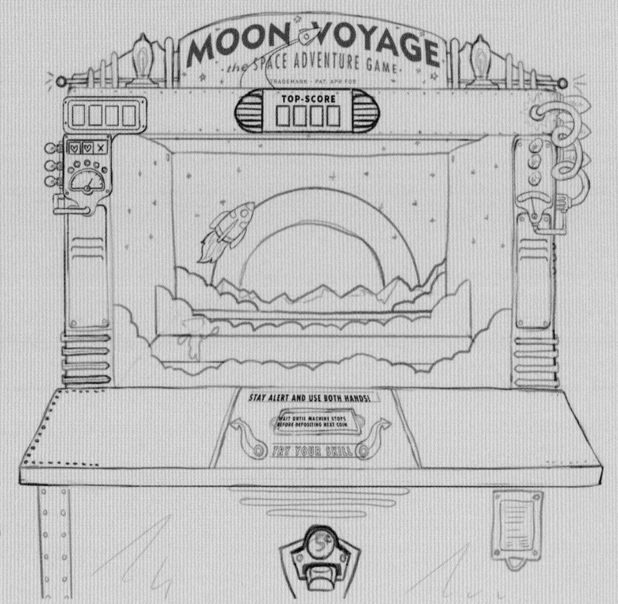

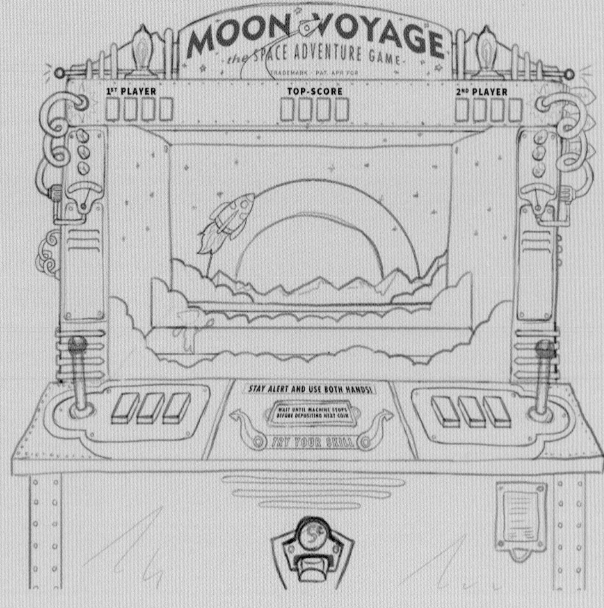

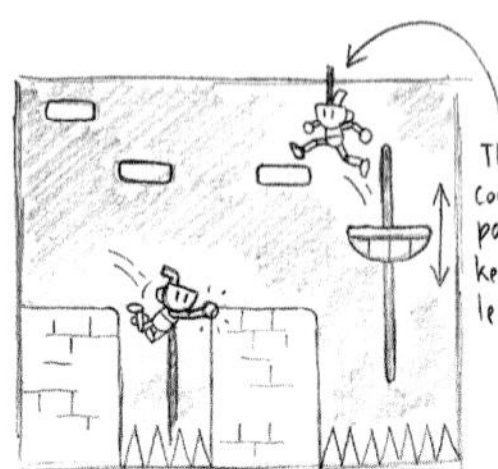

The pole could change position to keep the screen less cluttered

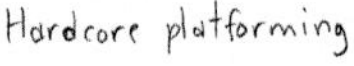

Hardcore platforming

- You're in a vehicle, shooting sideways or up (or maybe diagonal)
- BG always scrolling left

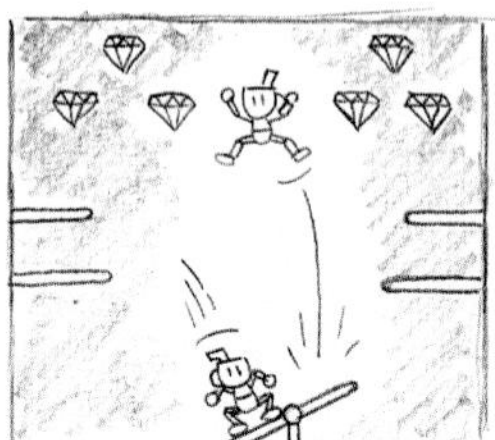

Play as Ribby & Croaks?

Sidescrollin' Beat-em-Up

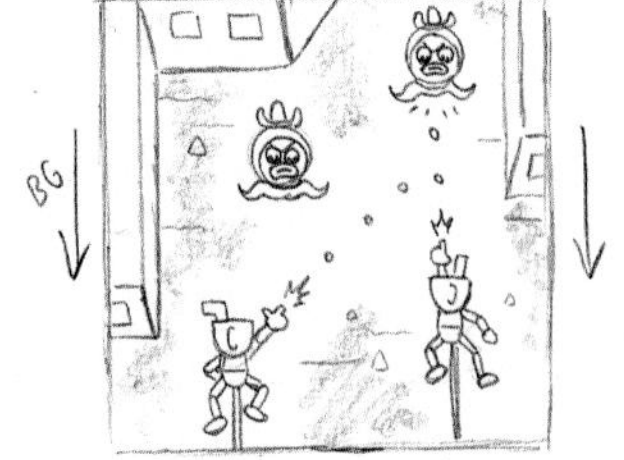

- Back view sprites
- Free movement
- BG always scrolling down

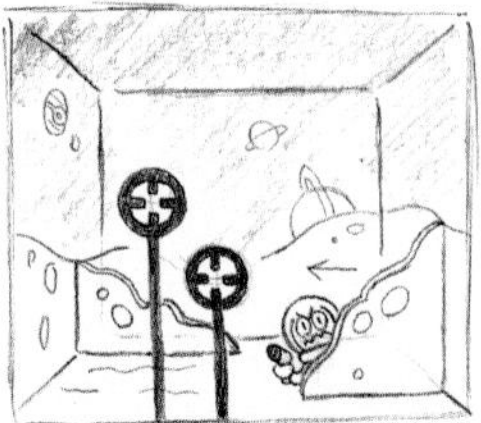

Crosshair Shooter

You control crosshairs on sticks. Enemies pop out and you shoot em - or many other possible scenarios

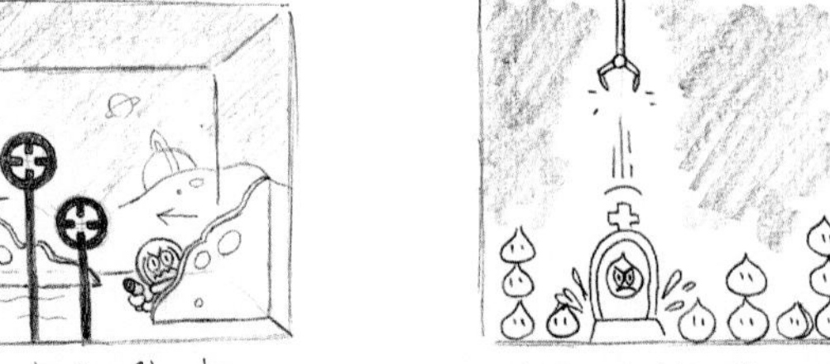

Smash the Slimes

- Some kind of classic puzzle game

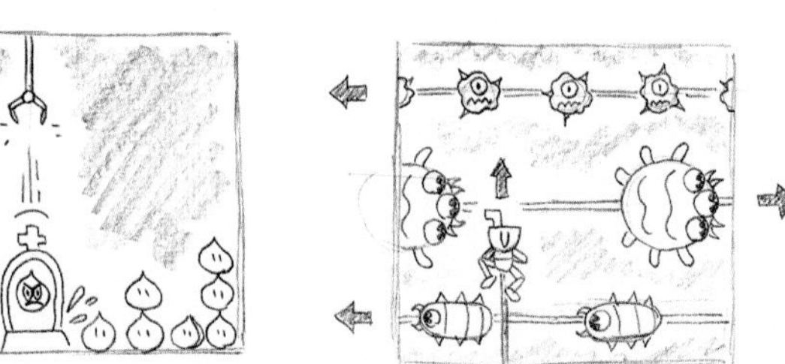

Get to top of screen, avoiding alien bugs, alien space vehicles, or w/e

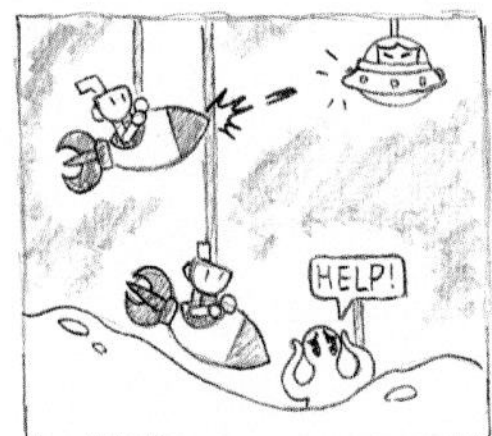

Rocket Riders

- Press up/down = tilt up/down
- Gradual tilting within a range:
- Shoot enemies, save friendly aliens

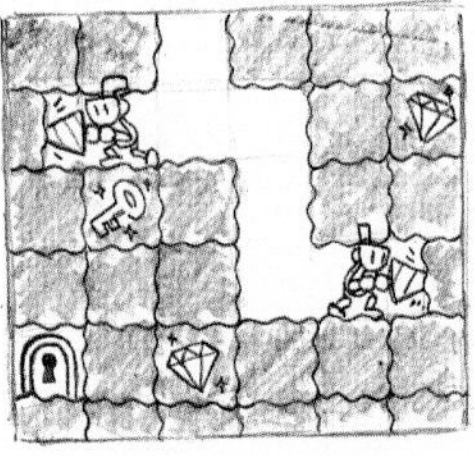

- Grid based "destroy"able terrain
- If you "destroy" a piece, it just moves behind the piece next to it

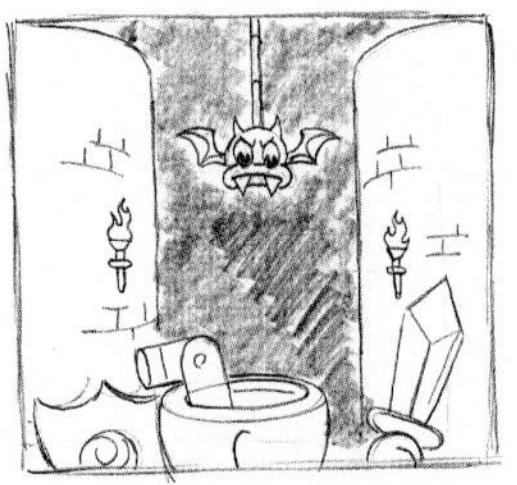

Dungeon Crawler

- Stab enemies with sword
- Block/dodge their attacks

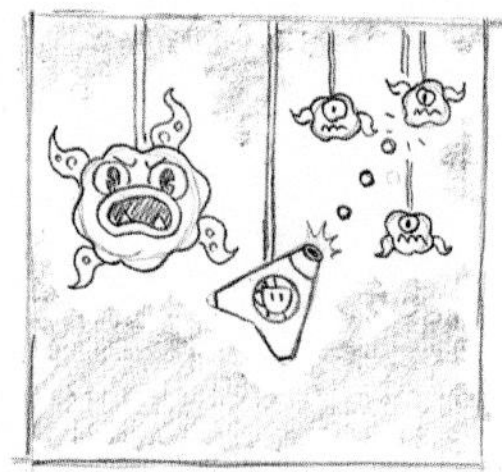

Plays like classic Asteroids (move around, rotate and shoot in any direction)

- Big aliens break into multiple smaller aliens when destroyed.

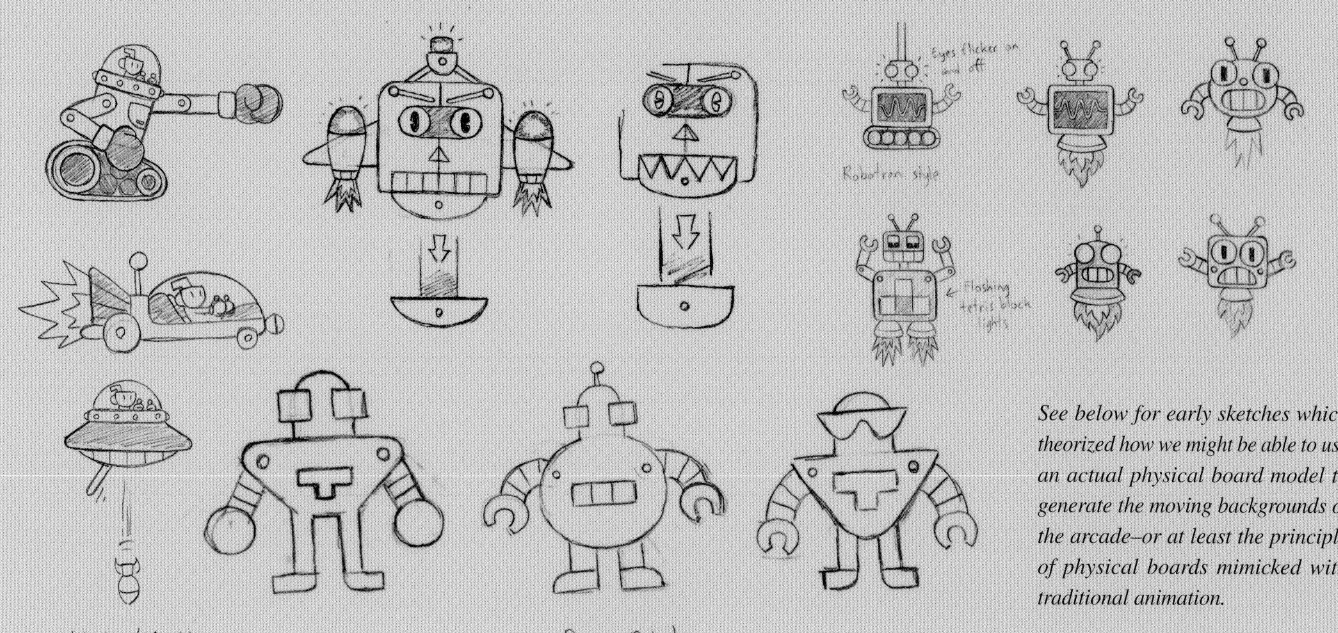

See below for early sketches which theorized how we might be able to use an actual physical board model to generate the moving backgrounds of the arcade–or at least the principle of physical boards mimicked with traditional animation.

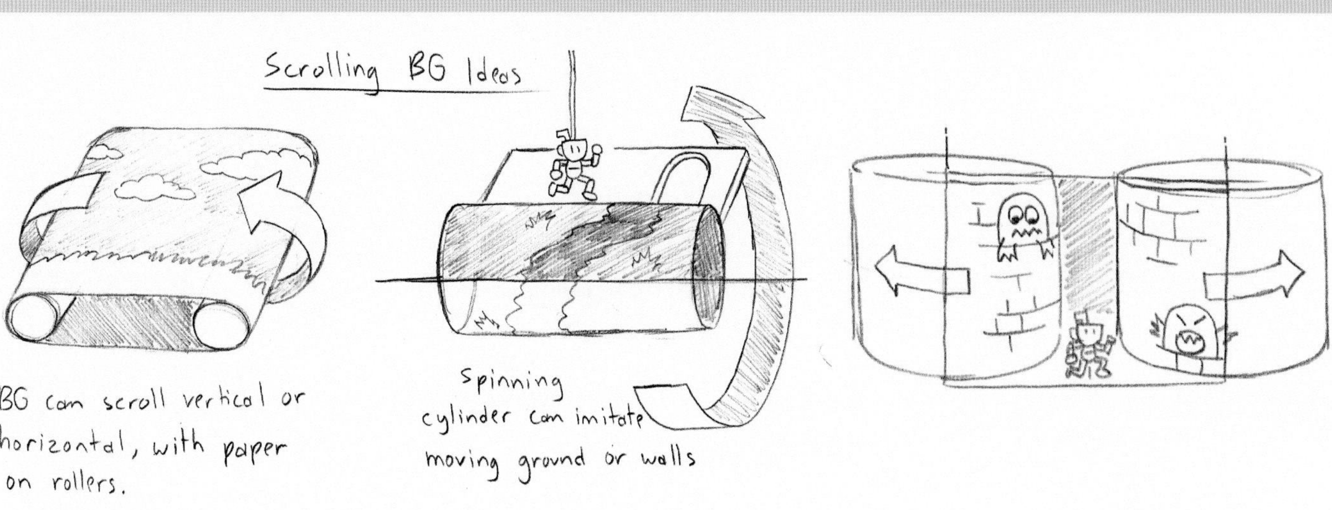

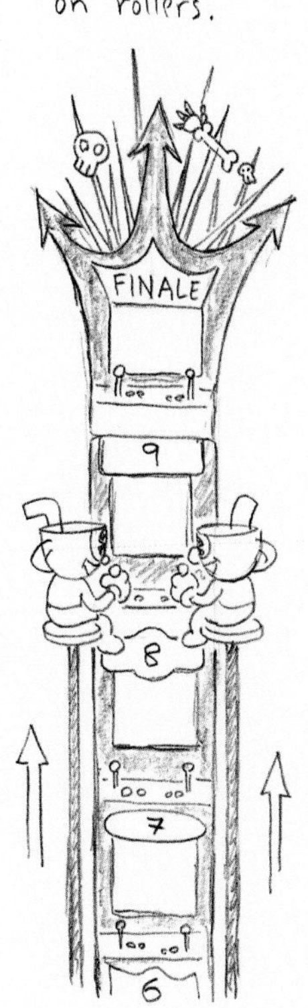

Arcade Tower

- Cup+Mug scale a tower of arcade cabinets, game after game.
- Game order could be randomized
- Cup+Mug have extendable chairs

Alternatively they destroy the tower one game at a time

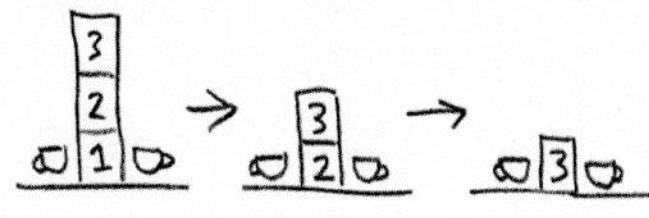

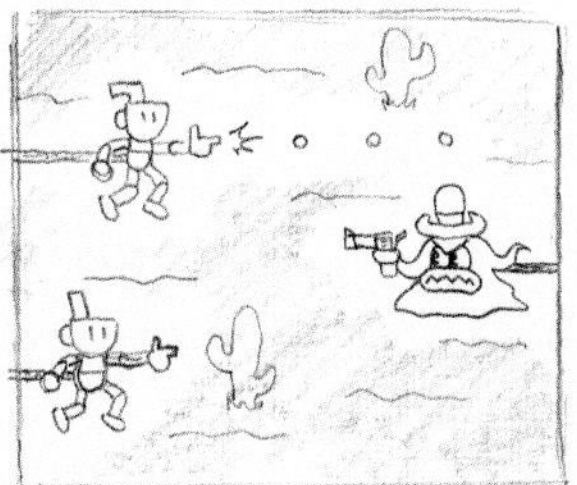

- Move around freely, shoot sideways only.

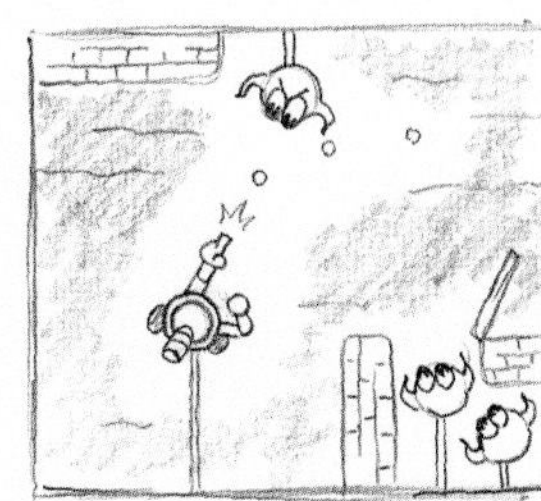

- Top-down "sprites"
- You can rotate/move/shoot all around, as can enemies

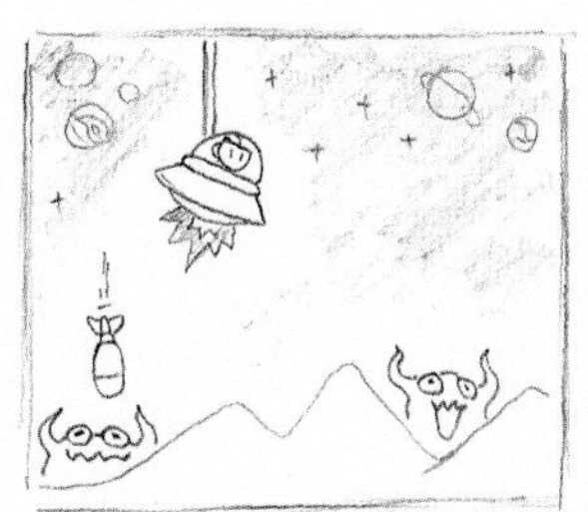

Fire piece hidden when not thrusting

- You can rotate left/right, and thrust upward only
- Drop bombs?

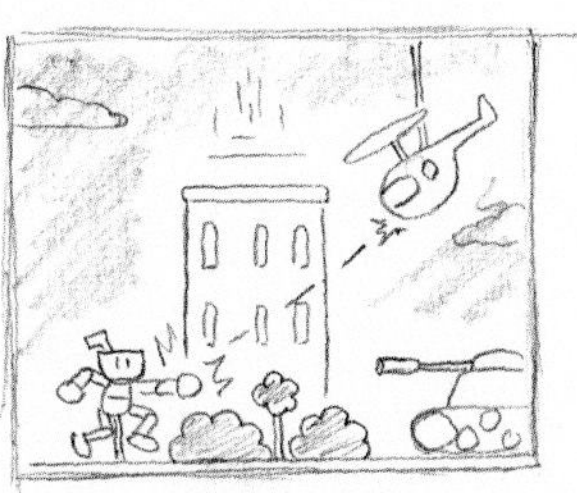

- Smash buildings, and the enemies trying to stop you

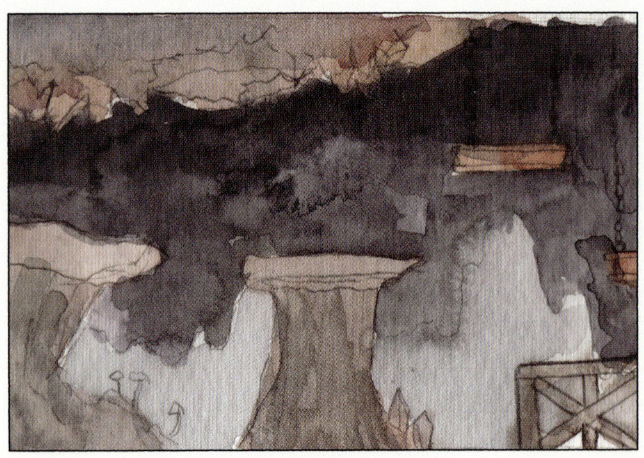

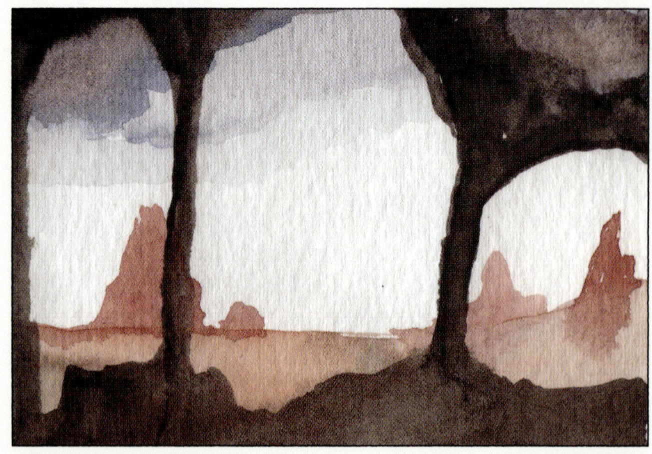

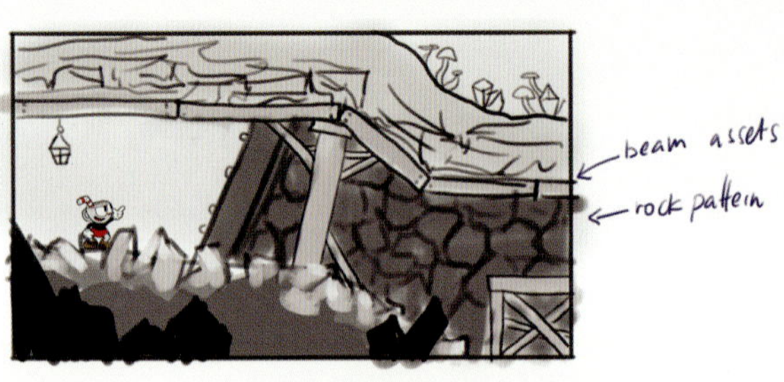

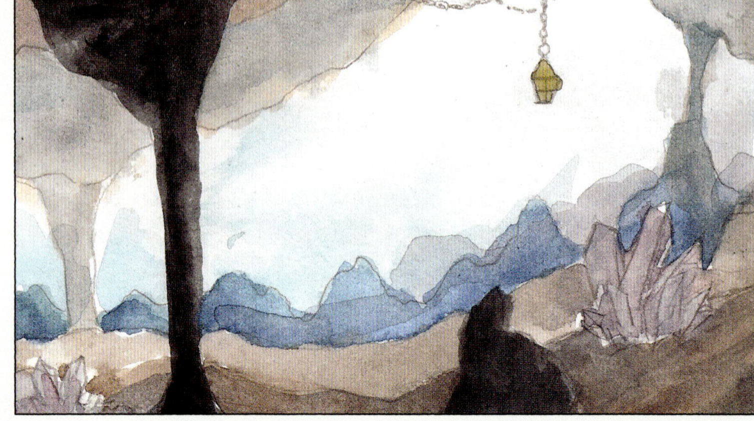

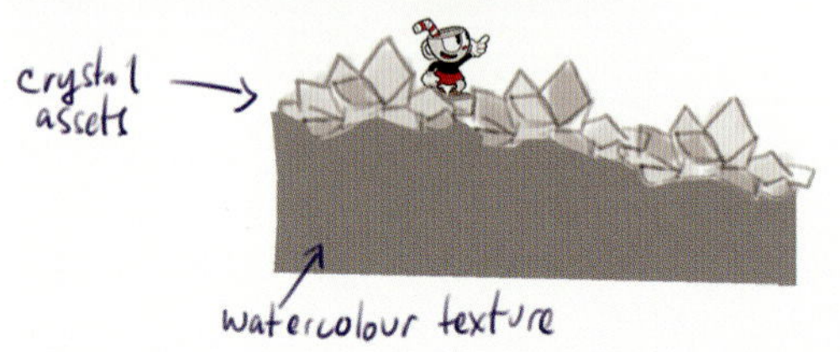

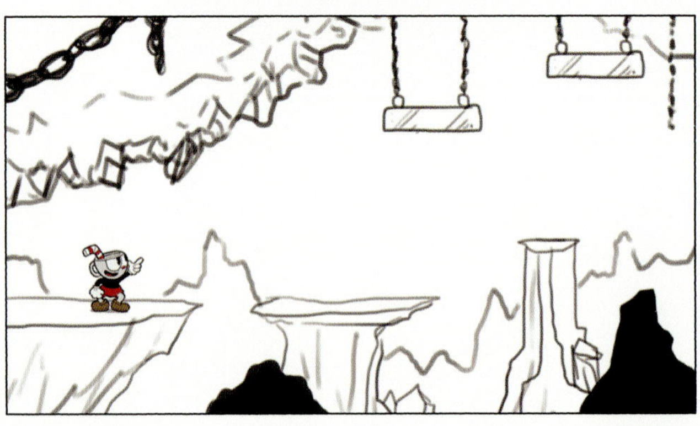

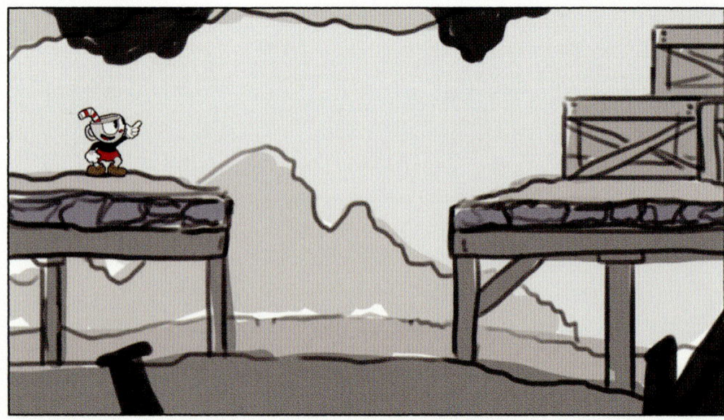

Crystal Caves

VERY EARLY IN THE INITIAL PROTOTYPING of *Cuphead*'s run and gun levels, we planned for two additional stages that would have been used either as platforming levels for the final "Inkwell Hell" zone, or additional stages located on the preceding Inkwell Isles. Game flow and production realities ended up reducing the overall number of platforming levels in the game, however; therefore the mining-themed Crystal Caves never made it out of initial art testing by Background Painter Caitlin Russell.

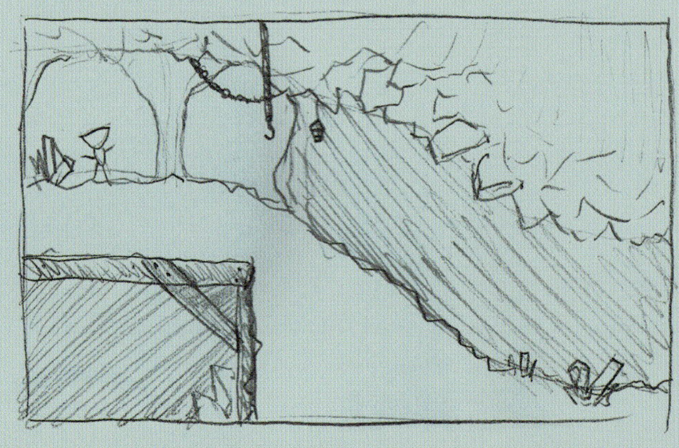

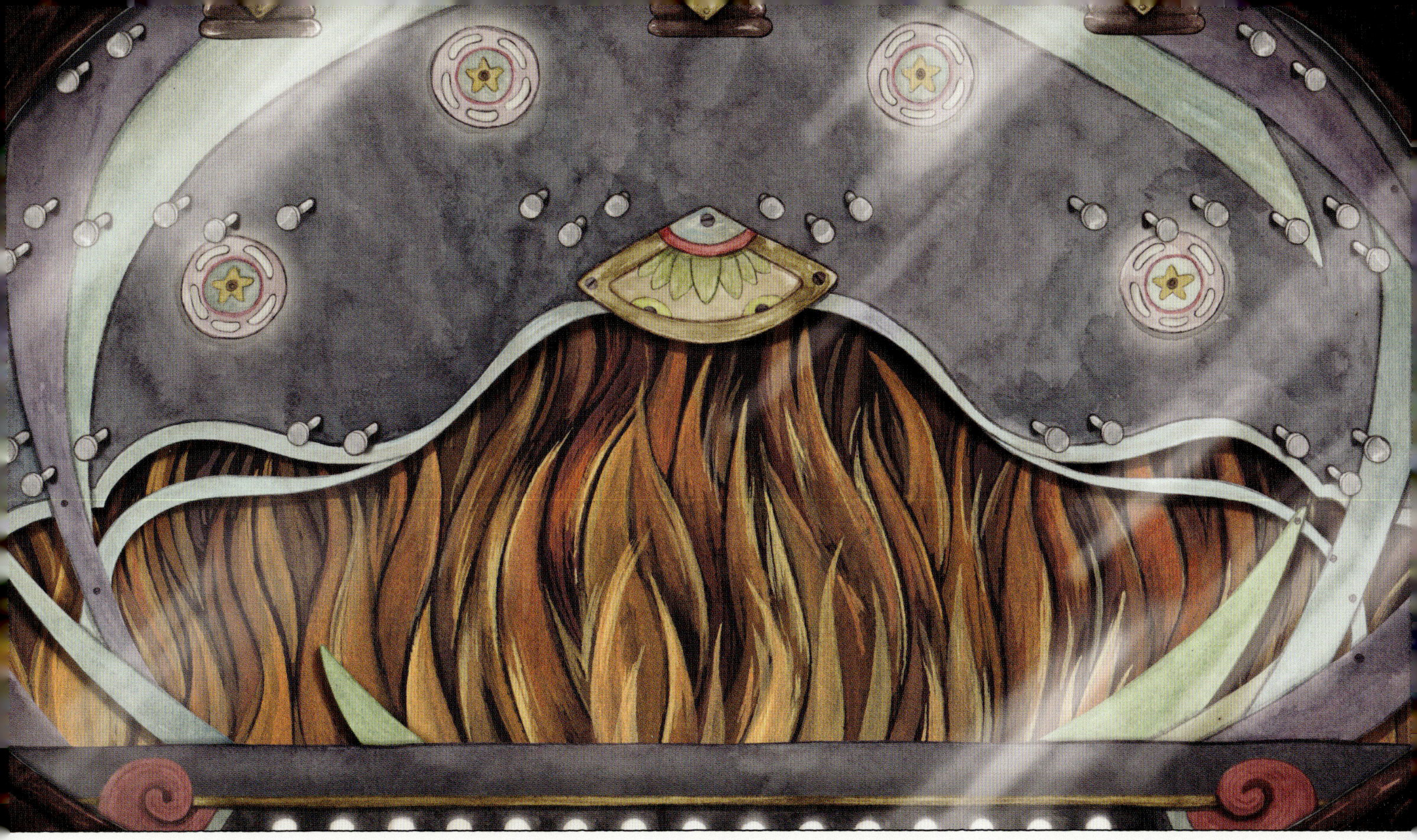

Pachi Pachi

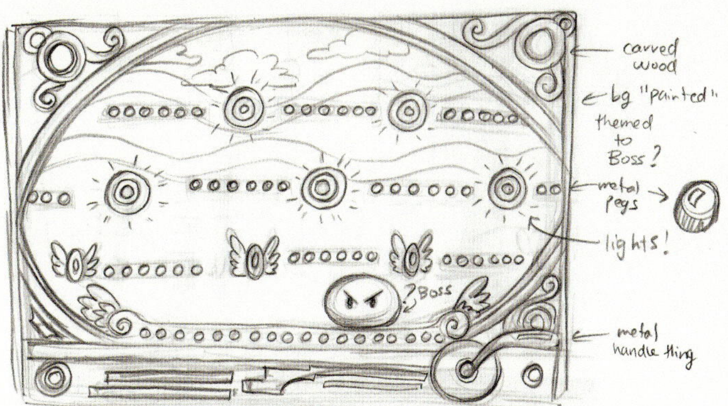

THE PACHINKO THEMED FIGHT, internally named "Pachi Pachi," was to be a secret battle accessed during the mini-boss gauntlet found in the King Dice stage. By completing every individual space on the board before facing the big man himself, the "Start Over" square would have flipped around to reveal the number "10," imparting access to the hidden clash. Ultimately, the encounter was cut because it was mechanically less interesting than the other minions, and did not feel like an adequate reward for besting the whole gauntlet.

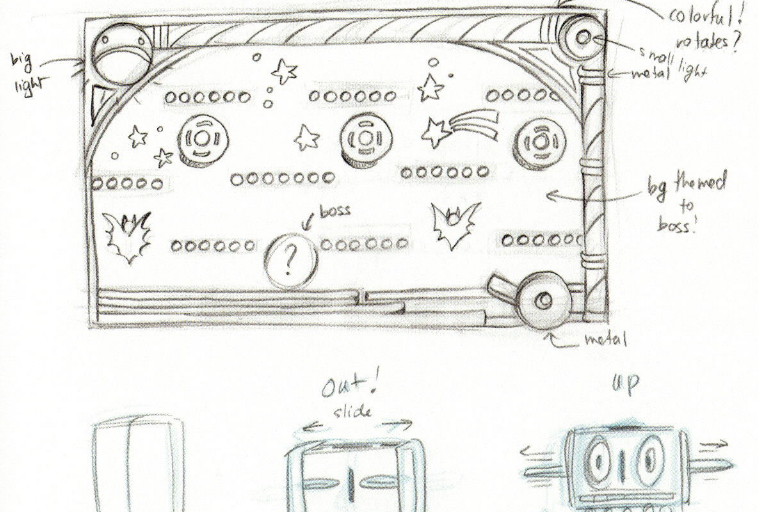

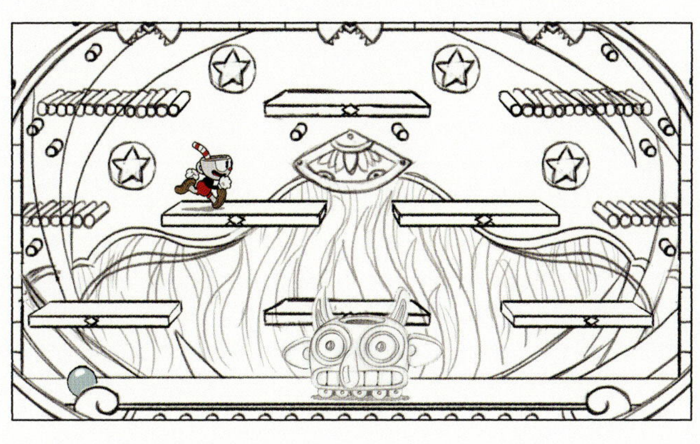

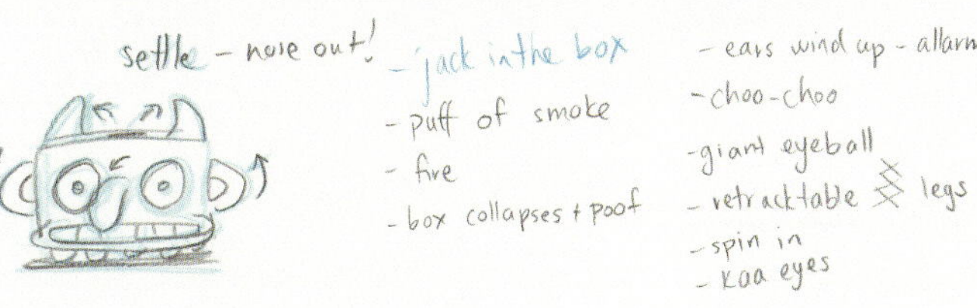

Early concepts for Pachi Pachi by Animator Tina Nawrocki had him made up of pachinko balls.

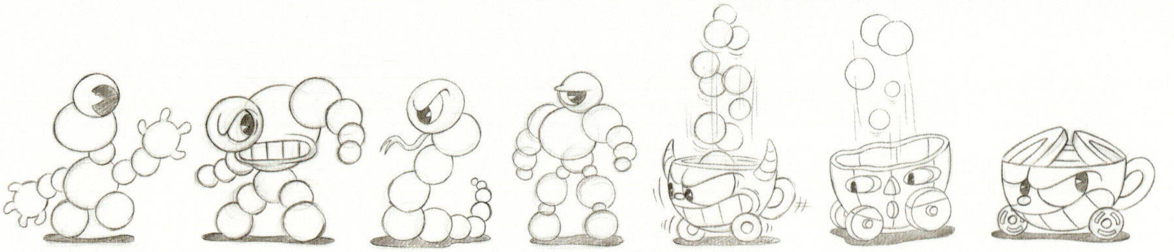

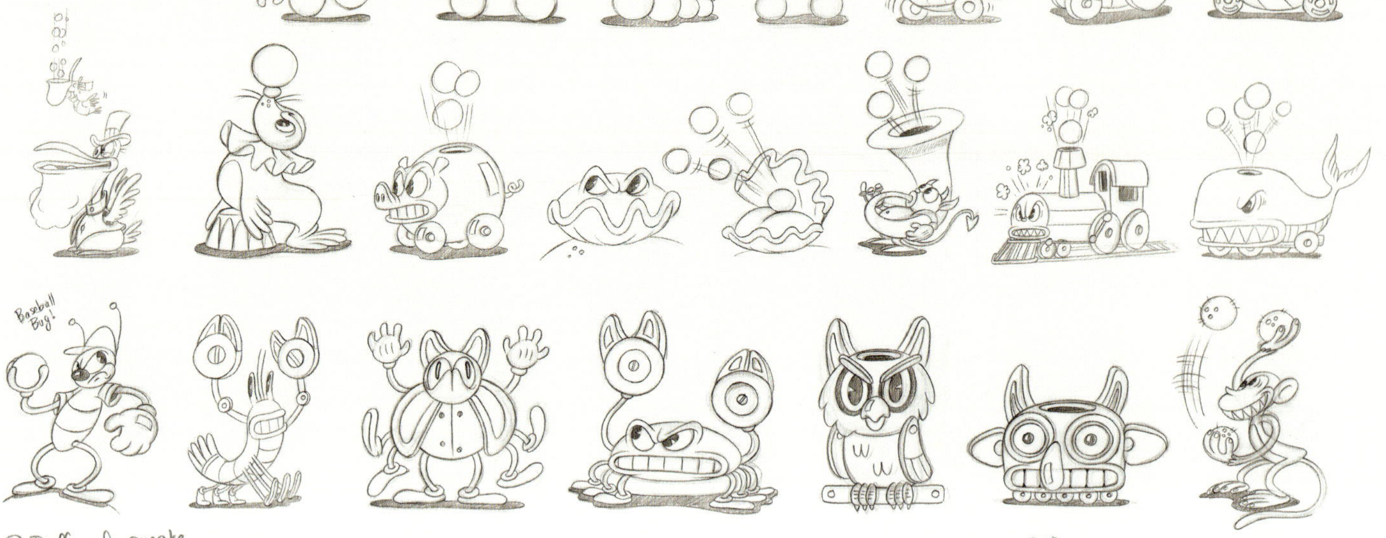

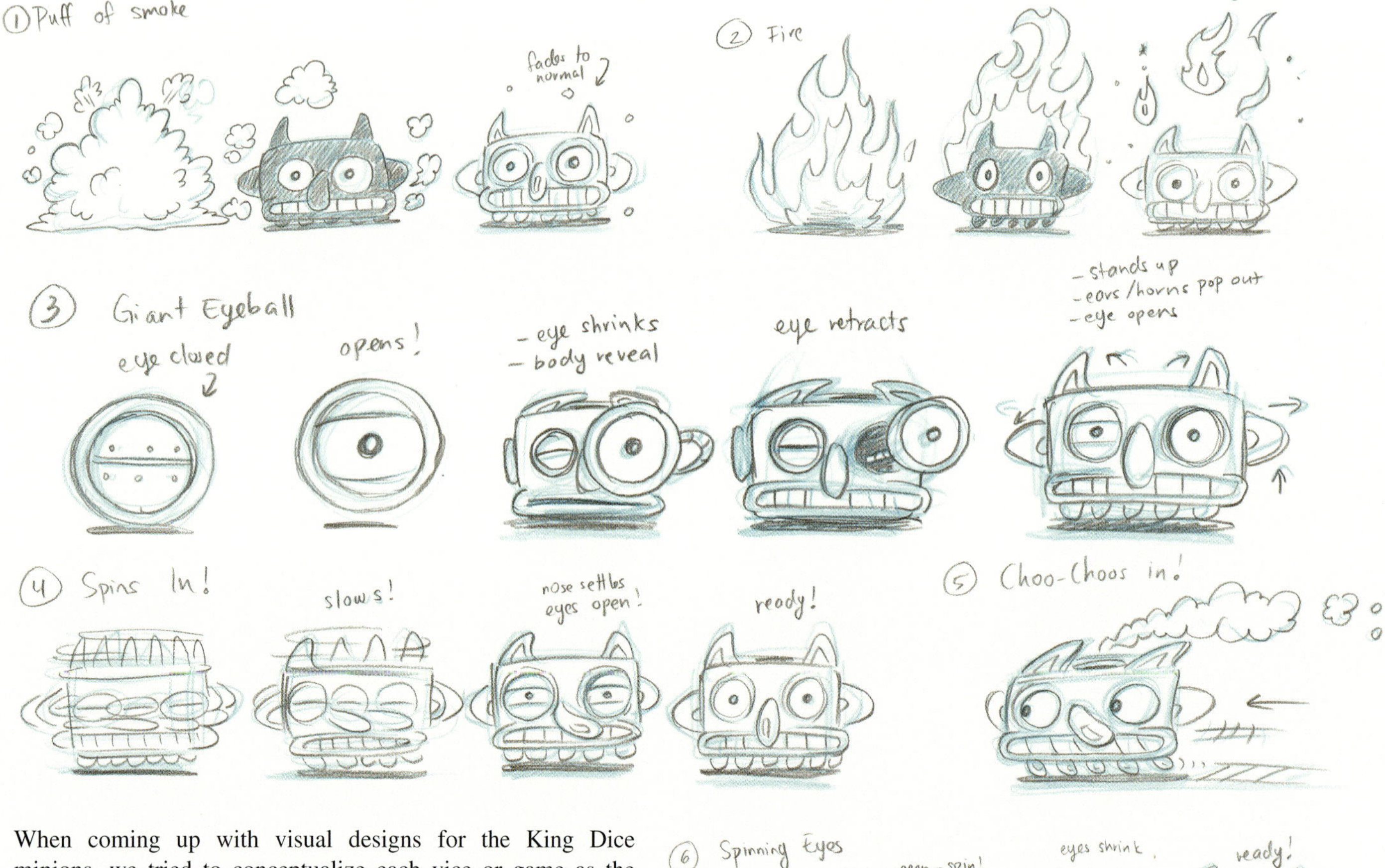

When coming up with visual designs for the King Dice minions, we tried to conceptualize each vice or game as the player's primary obstacle to victory–for example, a dancing roulette spinner, or a living set of booze bottles. Pachinko offered a unique challenge, however, as it's the classic game's vertical board itself impeding your success. Through iteration, we settled on an anthropomorphic win pocket, with the animatronic receiver gates acting as ears. For the stage, we added art deco flourishes that–while somewhat inconsistent with the drab pachinko machines of the era–felt perfectly in line with the other King Dice backgrounds.

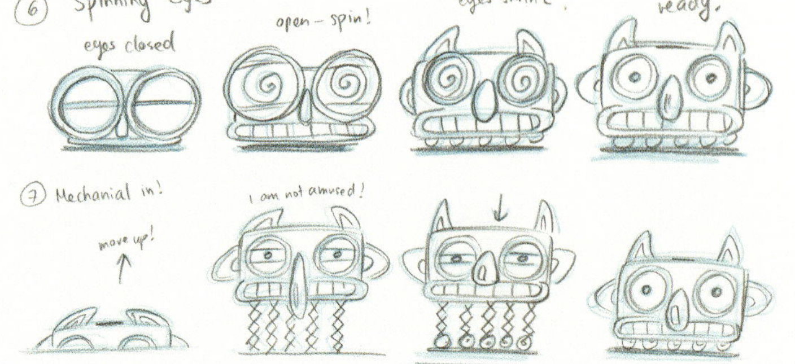

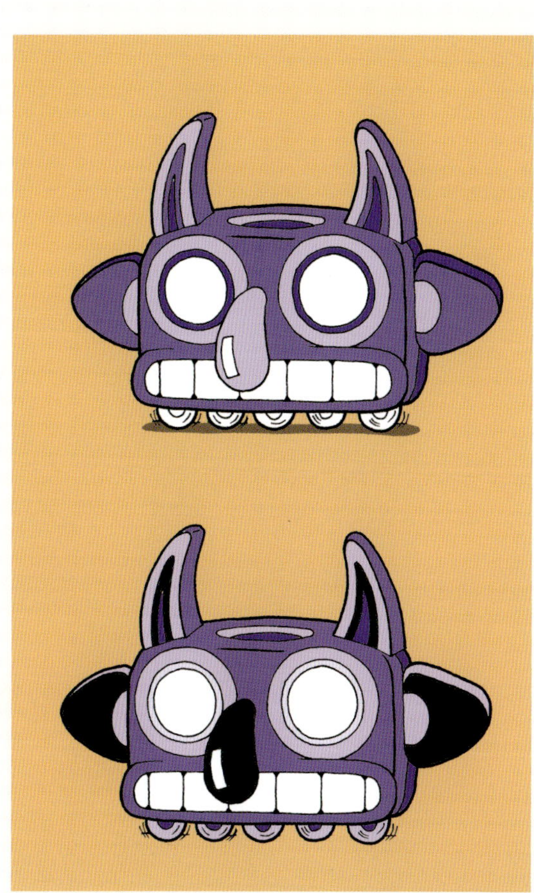

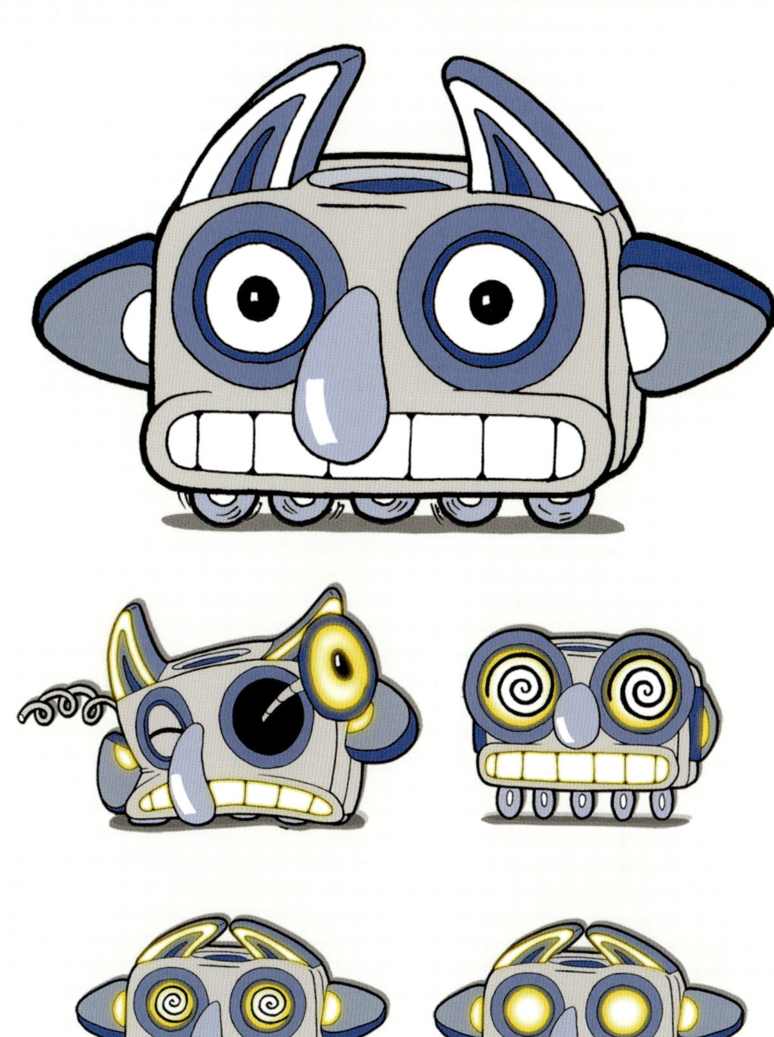

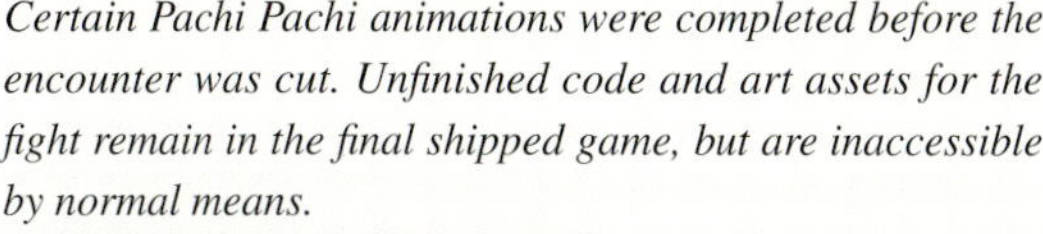

Certain Pachi Pachi animations were completed before the encounter was cut. Unfinished code and art assets for the fight remain in the final shipped game, but are inaccessible by normal means.

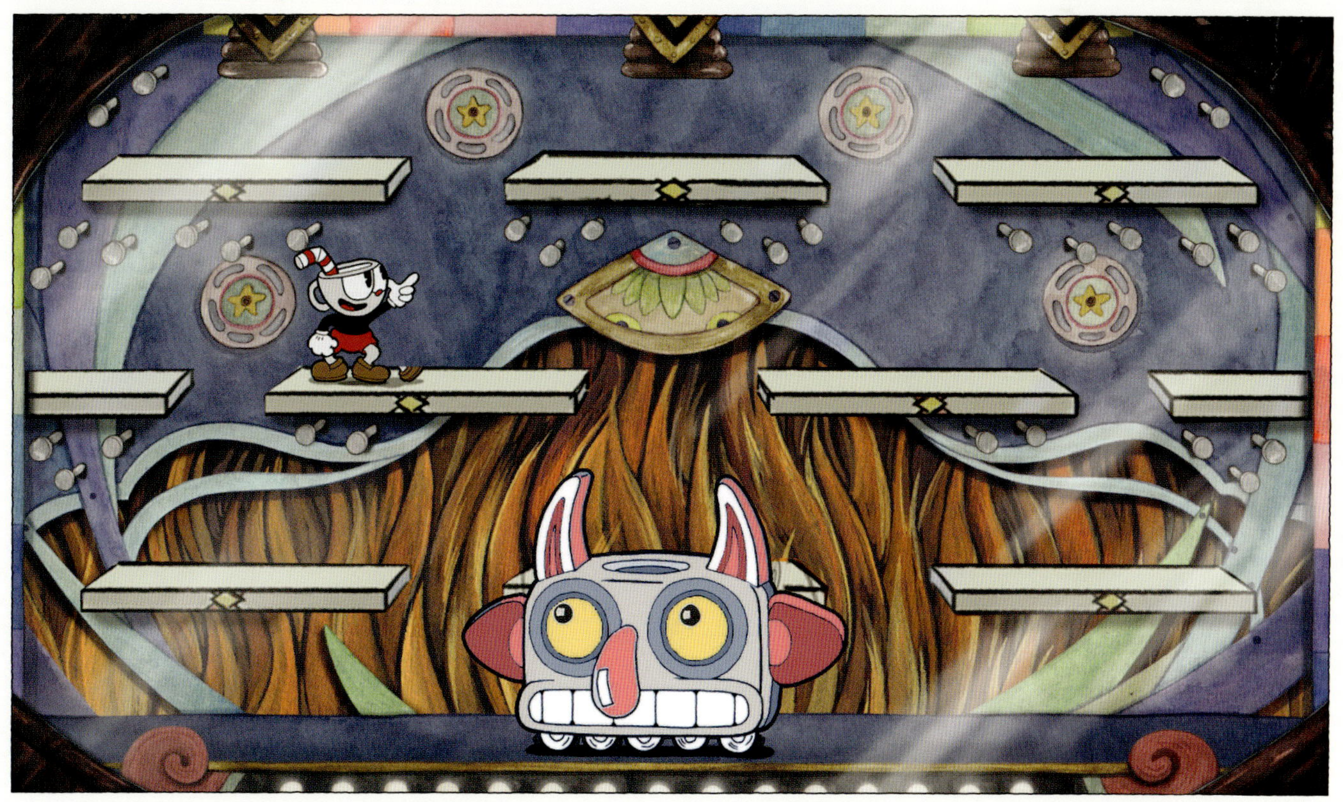

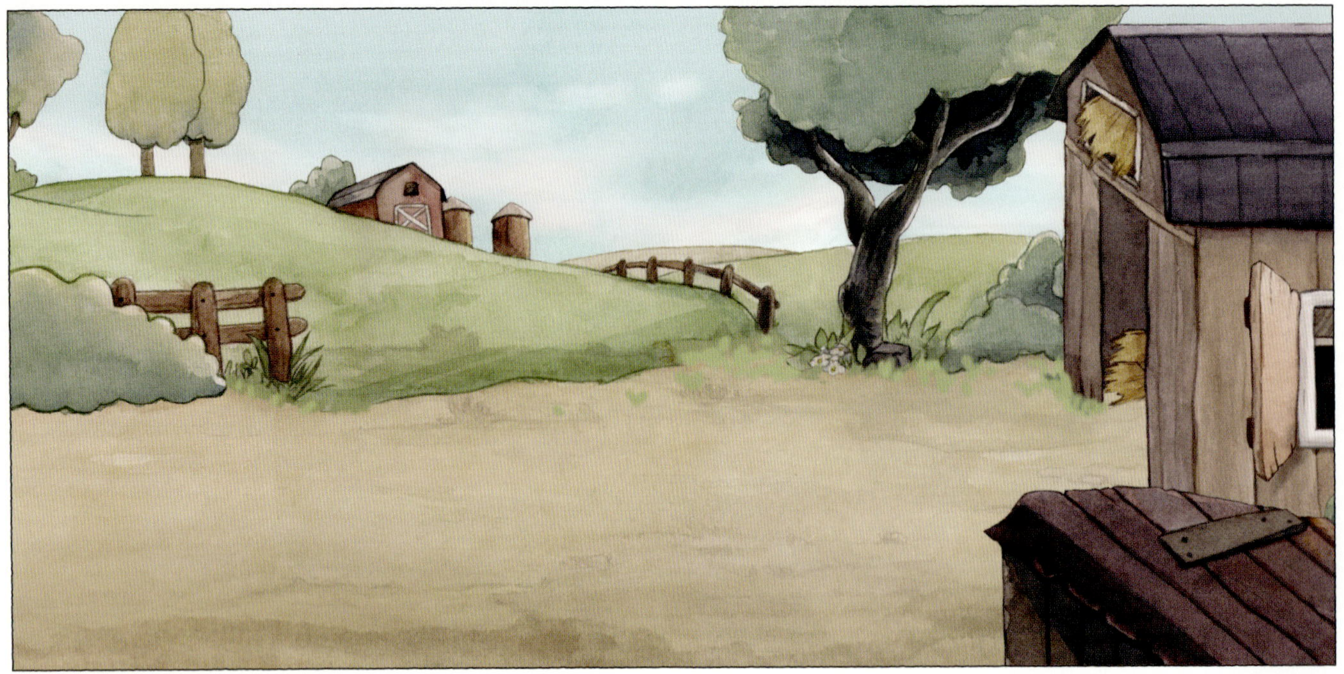

Pig Jump

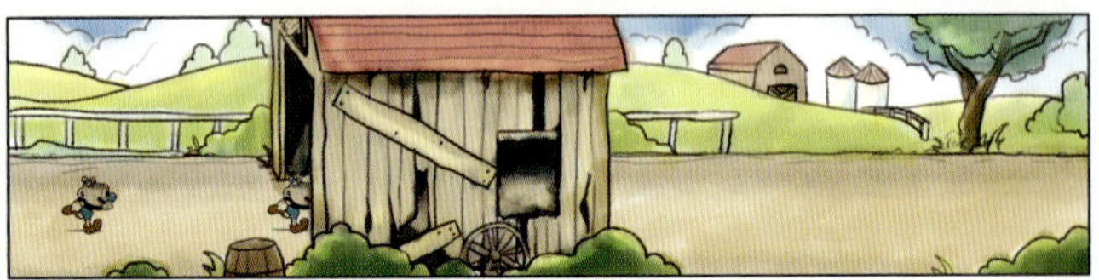

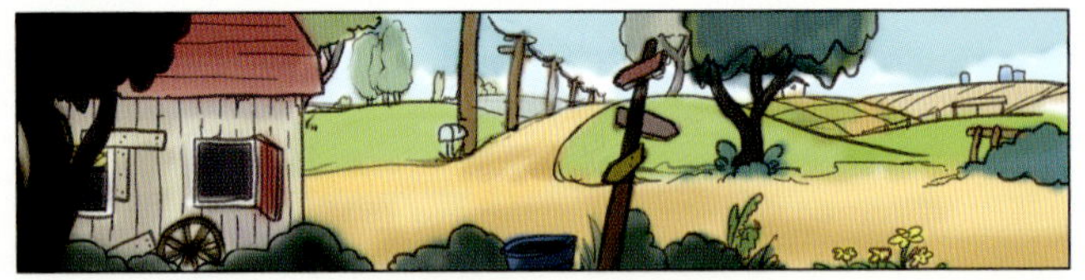

THE DEVELOPMENT OF THIS "Pig Jump" stage inadvertently became origin of the run and gun levels in *Cuphead*. Like the cut arcade game on Isle 2, Pig Jump was to be the bonus stage for Isle 1, acting as a unique encounter that would reward players with additional coins. This autoscrolling level was designed as a platforming challenge against parryable pigs. Through the initial art tests, we ultimately realized the magnitude of work involved in scrolling stages, and decided to redirect our energies toward fully realizing run and gun levels in the game.

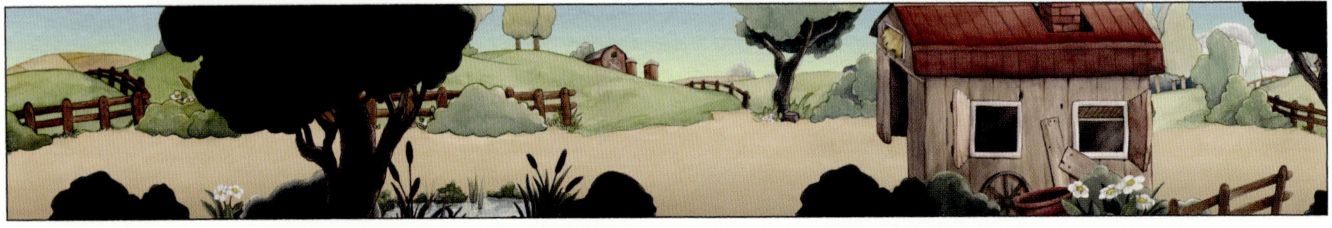

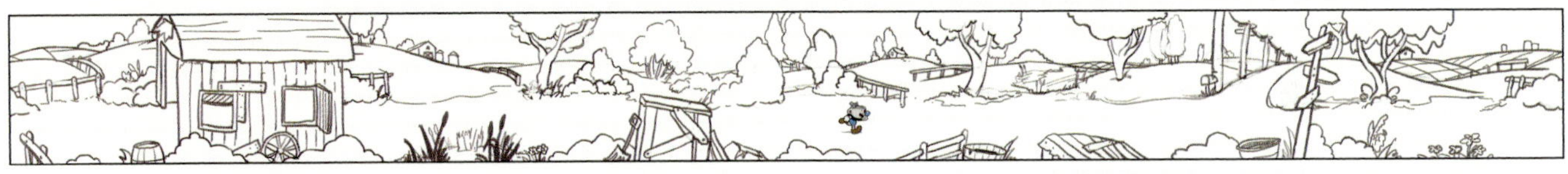

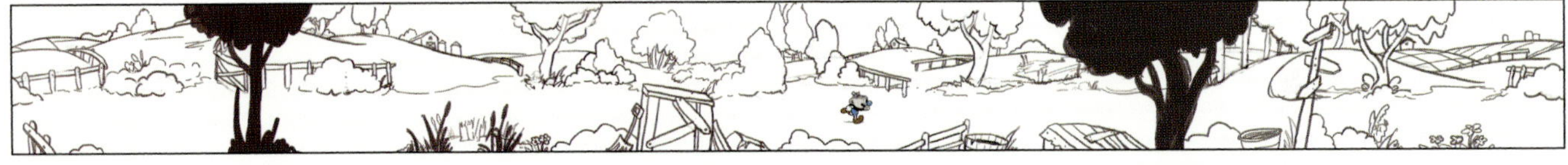

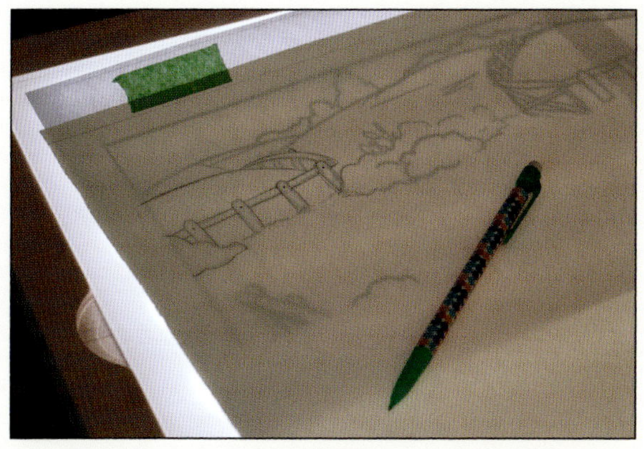

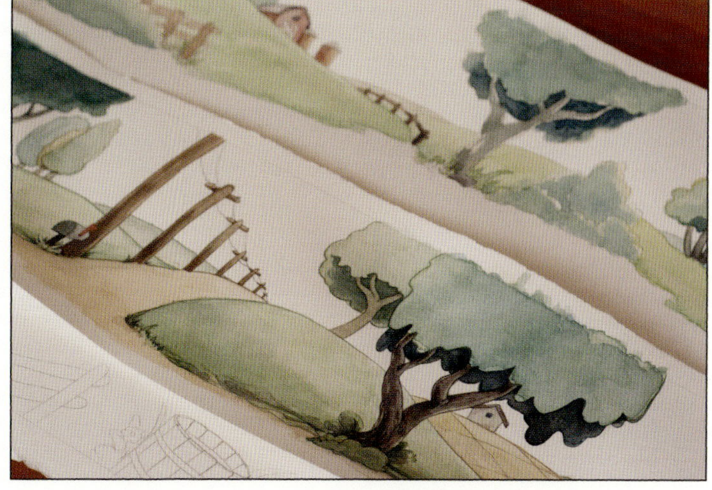

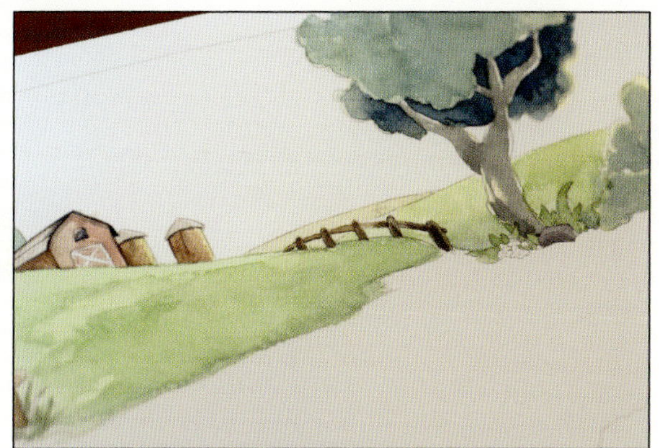

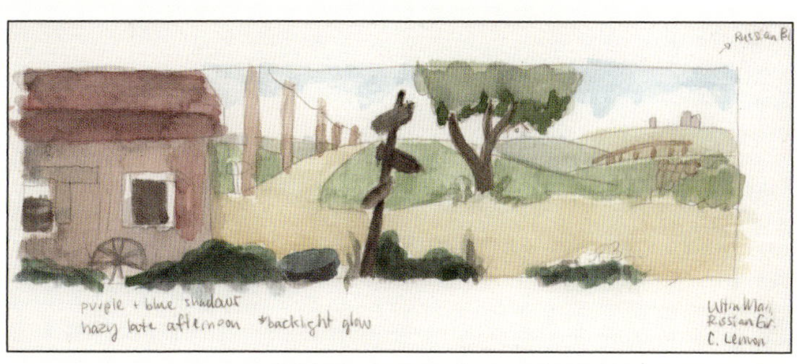

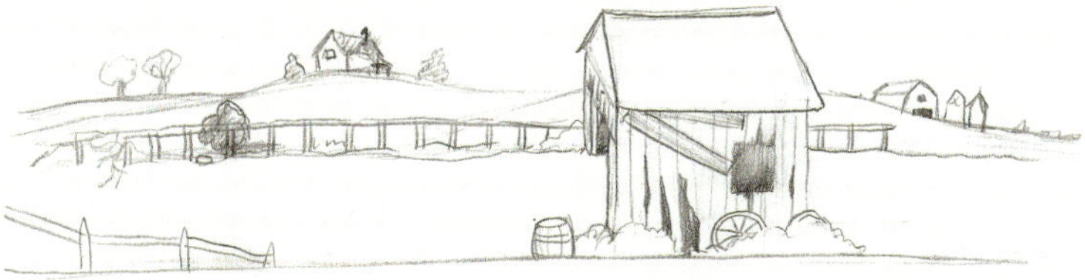

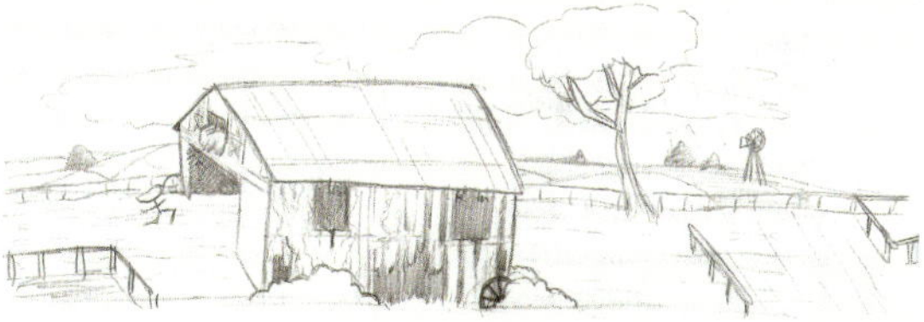

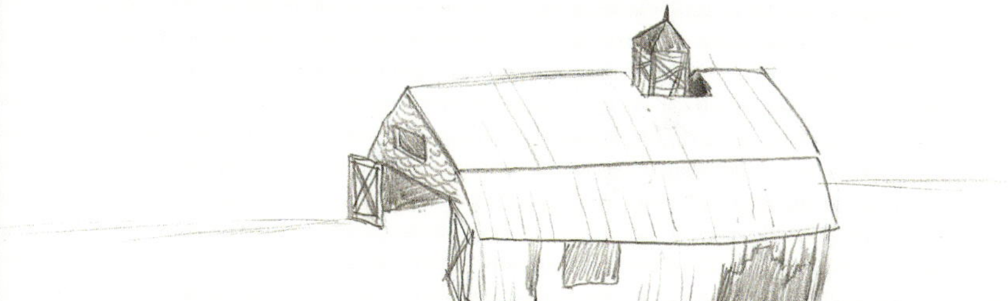

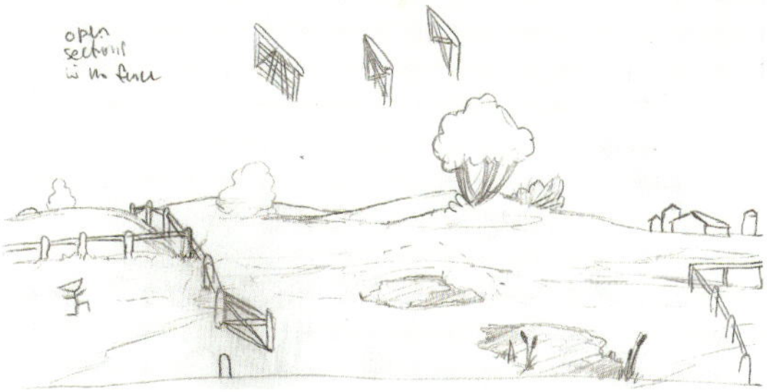

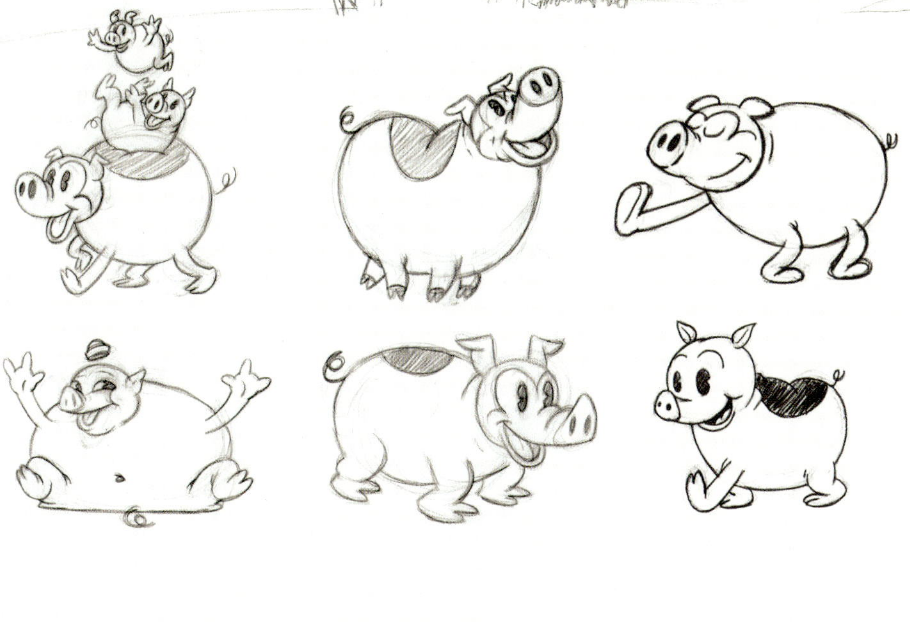

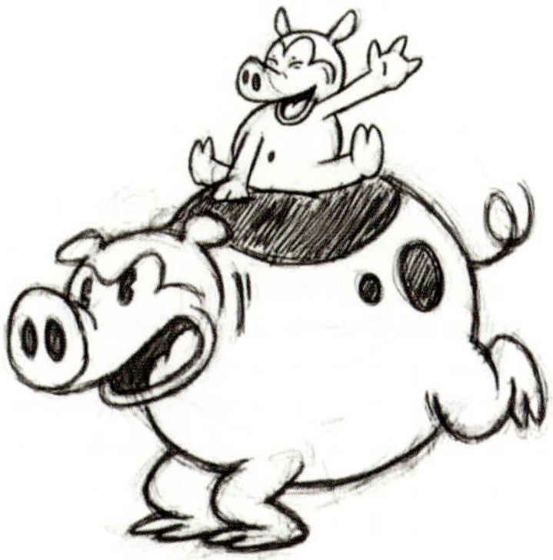

With particular inspiration from the Warner Brothers' 1930 Bosko short *The Booze Hangs High*, Animator Joseph Coleman imbued our pigs with a sense of playfulness.

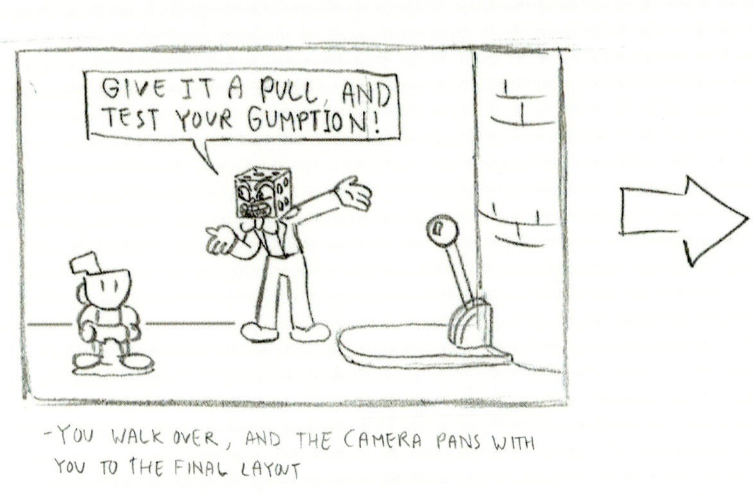

-YOU WALK OVER, AND THE CAMERA PANS WITH YOU TO THE FINAL LAYOUT

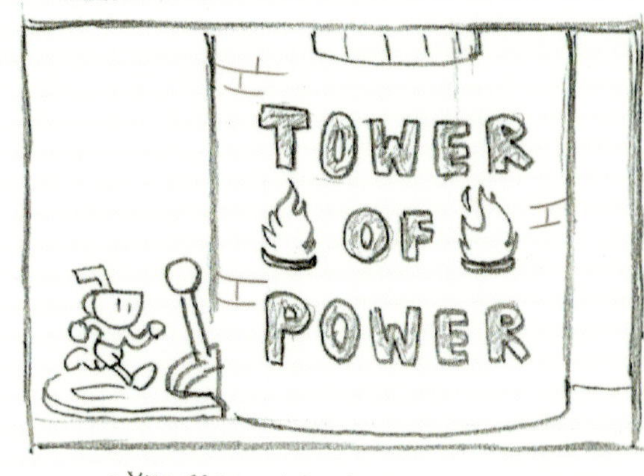

-YOU PARRY THE LEVER AND IT STARTS

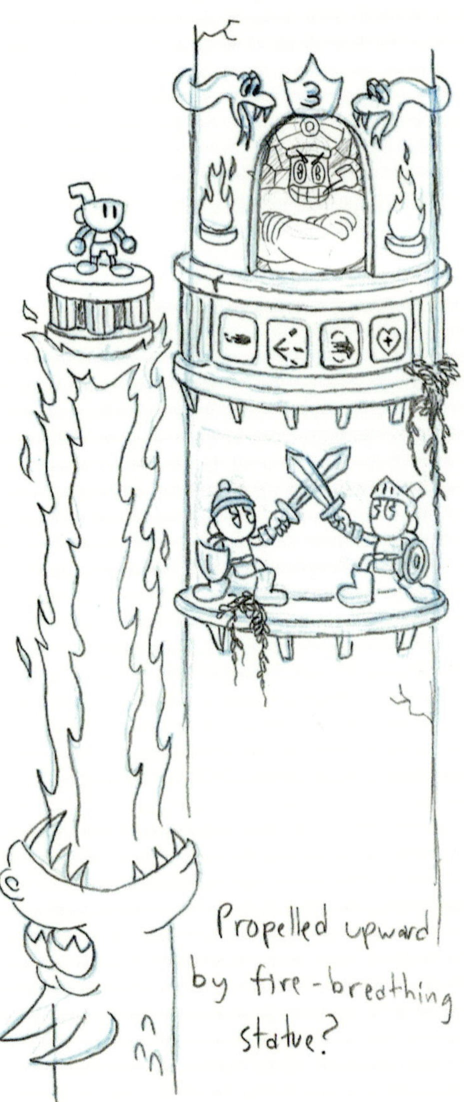

Grappling Hook

Elevator

Bucket w/ Rope

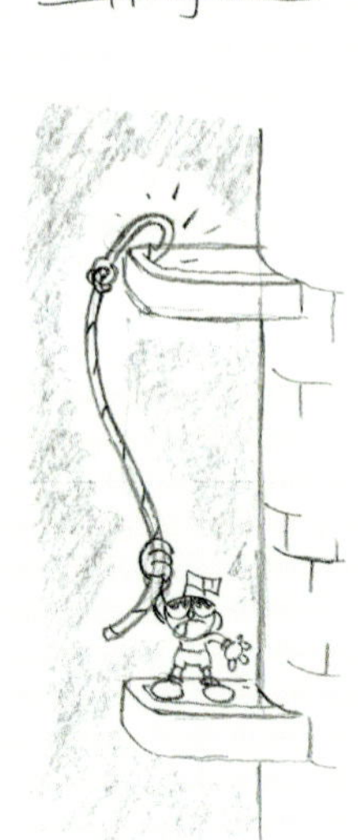

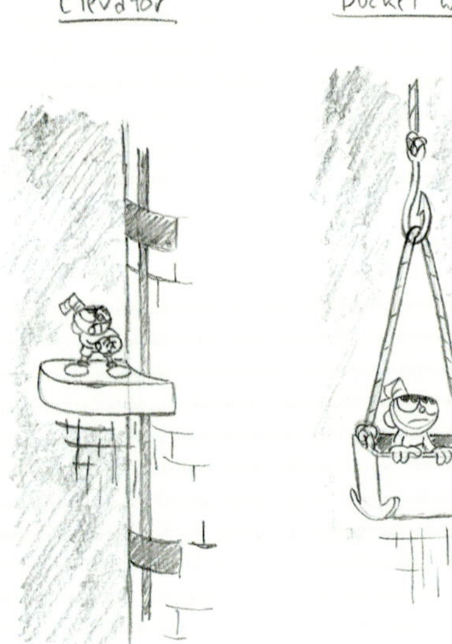

CASINO STYLE

HELL SPIRE

TREE

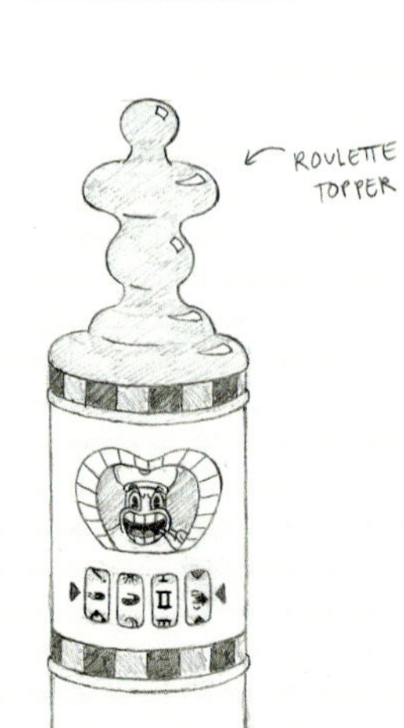

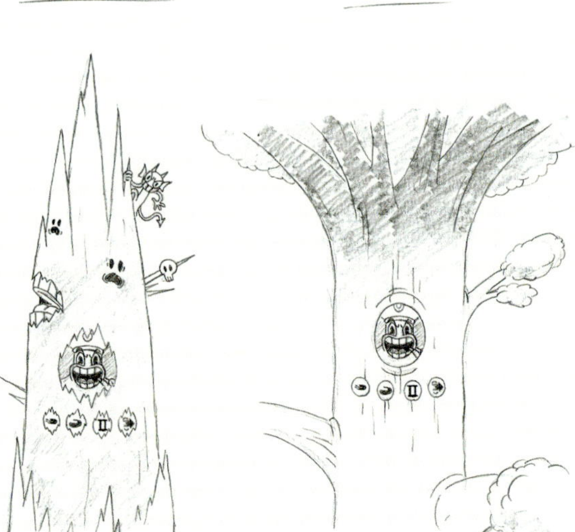

Tower of Power

EARLY ON IN THE DEVELOPMENT of *The Delicious Last Course*, we tried thinking of ways we could leverage existing *Cuphead* boss fights in new and exciting ways. This thought experiment led to the concept for the roguelike-inspired "Tower of Power." Conceptualized as a repeatable endurance challenge, players would fight increasingly difficult bosses in succession, with weapons and charms randomly rewarded after each fight and retry and remix tokens granted for getting high-grade wins. While early prototypes were certainly fun, our assessment of art demands for this feature pushed us to focus instead on more entirely new bosses for the *DLC* expansion.

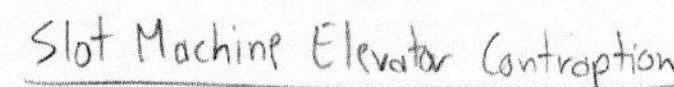

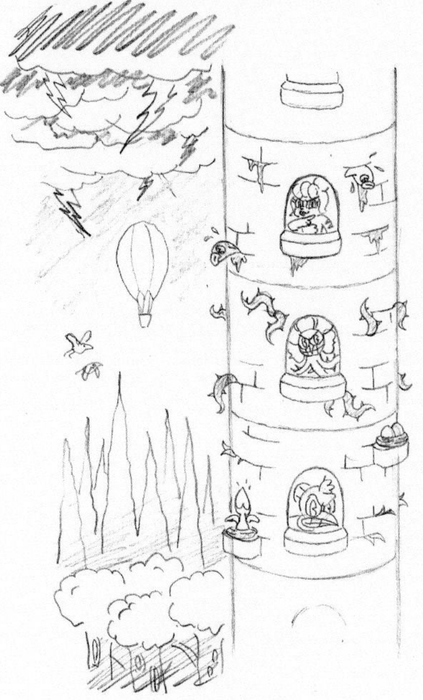

Themed

Tower

- Each boss has a unique tower section:

Cala Maria: Water/Fish

Cagney: Thorns

Wally: Nests/Birds/Feathers

etc.

- They would be drawn/painted to be interchangeable

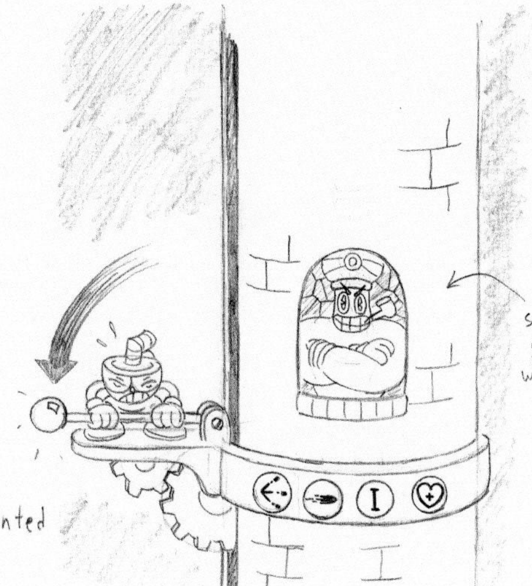

① He pulls the lever

② Elevator moves up **AND**

The 4 equip slots start cycling

③ He arrives at next boss, and the equip slots stop on what you get.

IS THERE SOMETHING AT THE TOP?

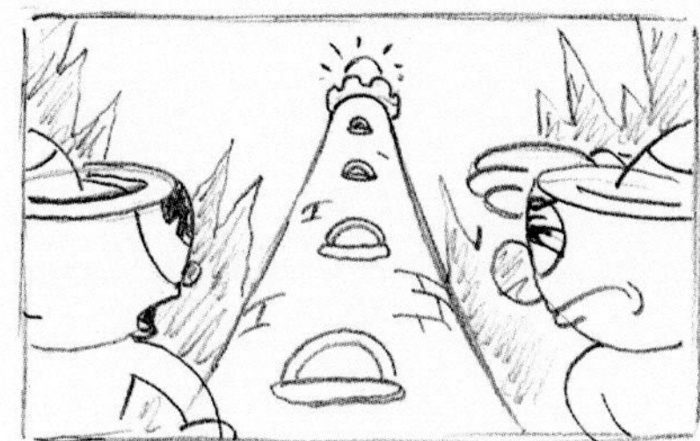

"You see that, Mug? What could it be?"

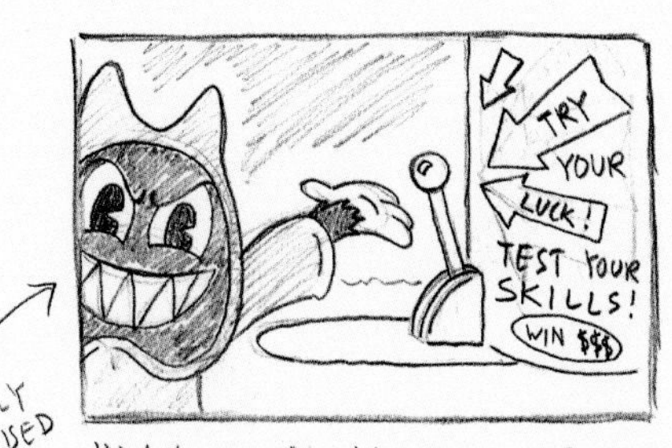

"Welcome to the Tower of Power! Go ahead, give it a pull!"

Early concepts by Animator Jake Clark showed off various framing device for the Tower of Power, from a challenge by King Dice to the notion that the tower itself was a character who needed your help.

Sick Tower

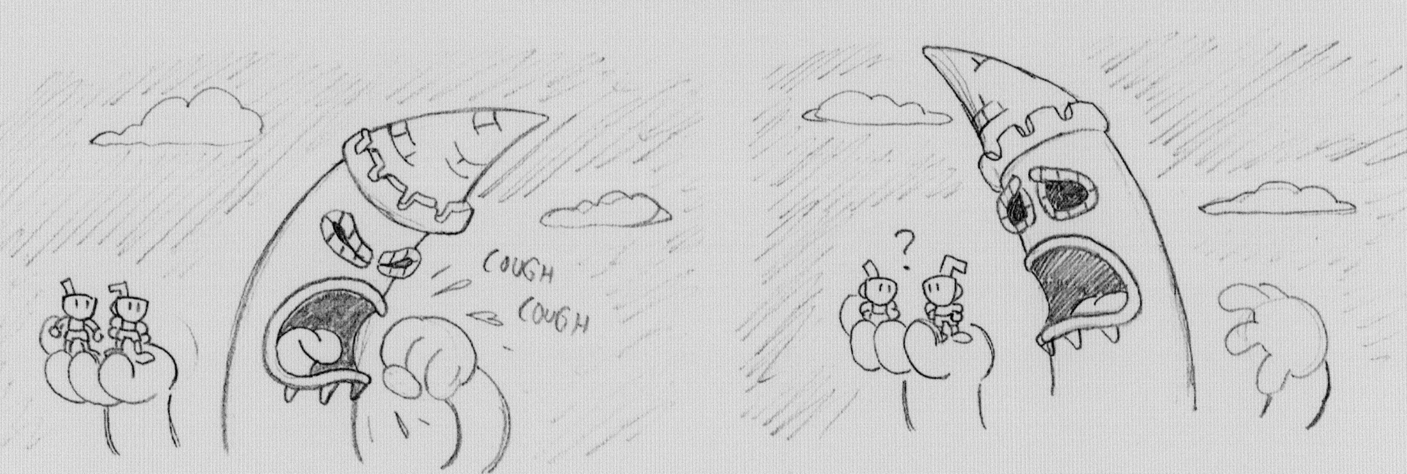

"Some ragamuffins moved in, and they've been constantly roughhousing and making a racket! The stress is making me SICK!!! Could you evict them for me? They don't even pay their rent! I promise I'll make it worth your while..."

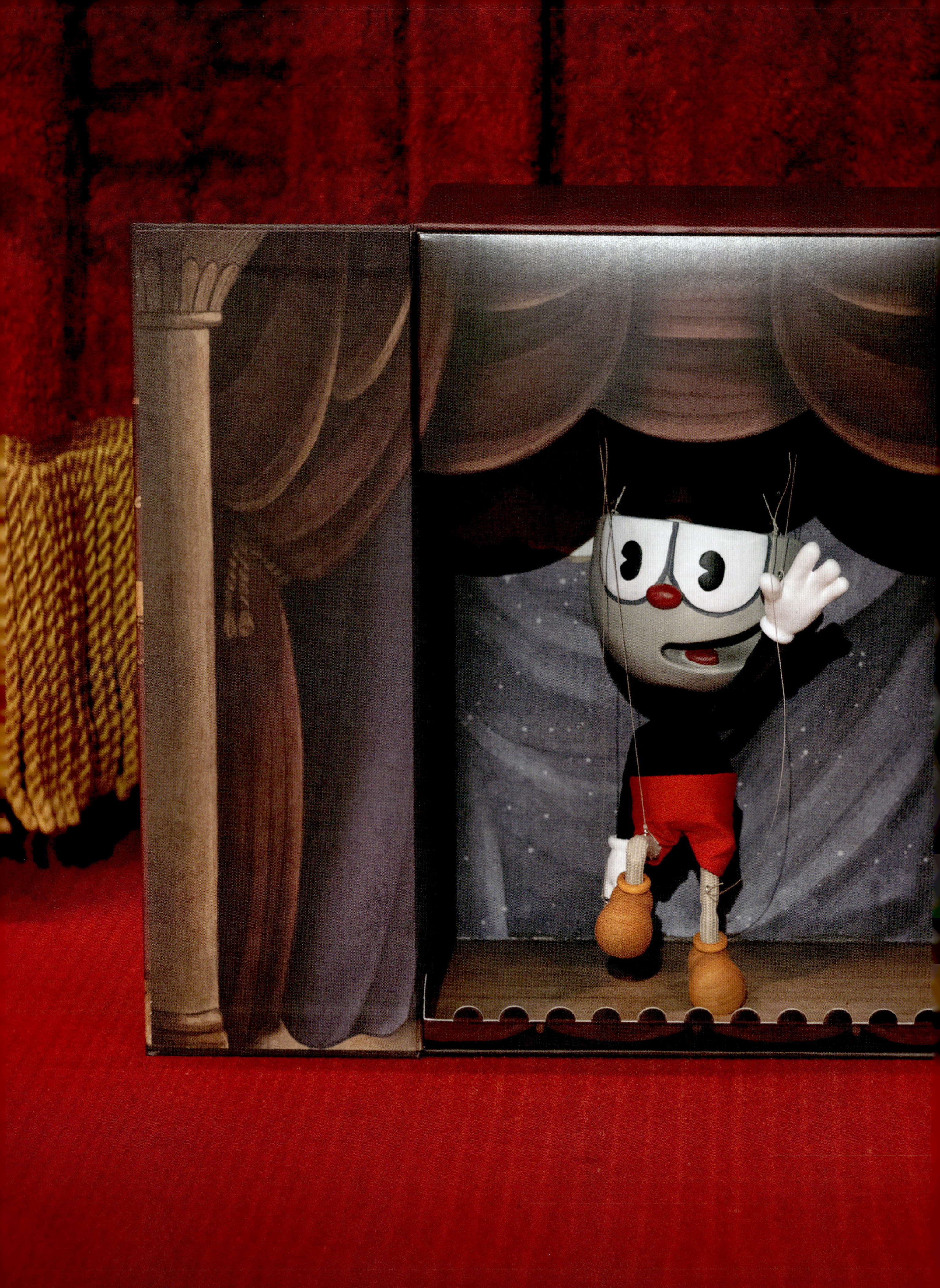

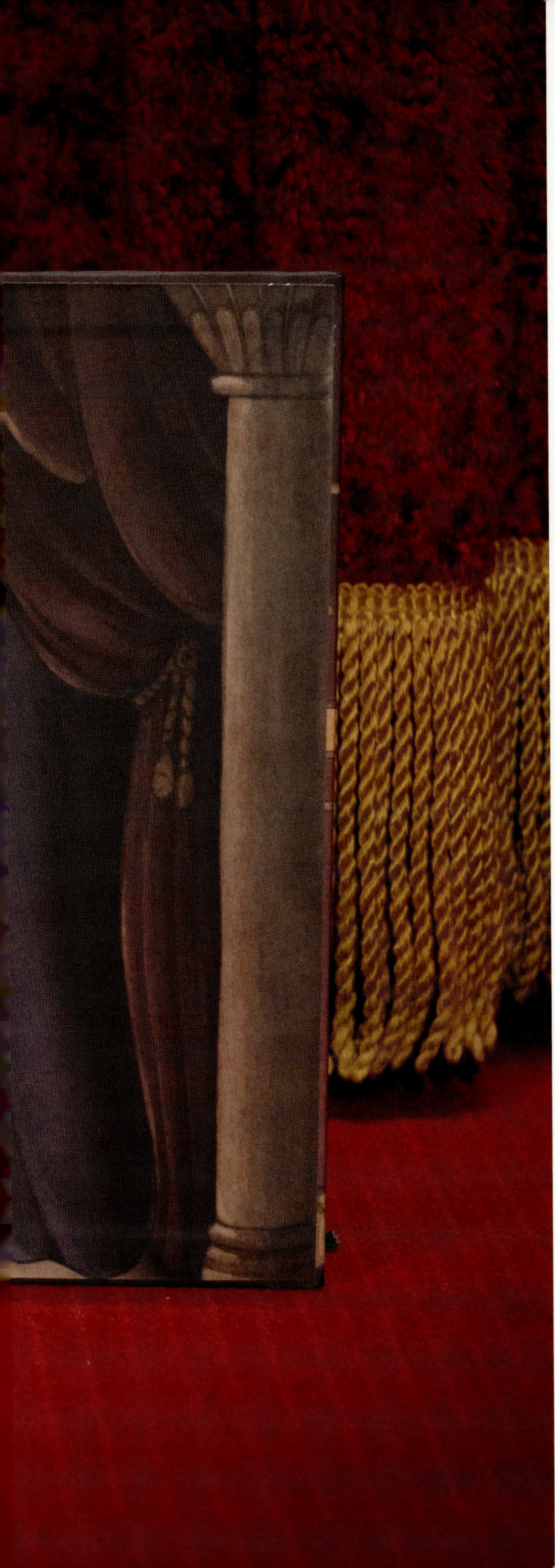

Chapter XVI: Books, Toys, and More!

ASK ALMOST ANY first-time developer what their goal is with the release of their game and you'll inevitably get some variation of the same answer: to do well enough to keep making more games. The same rang true for us on the cusp of *Cuphead*'s release–we didn't dare imagine reaching a wide enough audience to justify the creation of books, toys, or vinyl records. It should come as no surprise then that one of our greatest honors in the years since the game launched has been the ability to collaborate with wonderful partners to bring the Inkwell Isles to life outside of games.

For us, the idea of quick-fix "merch" has always been at odds with the meticulous (perhaps *overly* meticulous!) way we do things at Studio MDHR. So rather than let someone else take our characters and put them on products to sell, we've taken an in-house approach instead. The very same artists, designers and creatives who help to create the *Cuphead* you see on the screen are the people who work with our partners to transport a little bit of the Inkwell Isles directly to you. Our sincerest hope is that as you read, listen to, look at, or play with anything *Cuphead*-related, the real world melts away for just a moment, and with it so do your troubles and worries.

Physical Editions

AFTER THE RELEASE OF *The Delicious Last Course*, we knew it was time to bring a long-held dream to life and create physical editions of the complete *Cuphead* experience. Our partners at iam8bit helped us to capture that nostalgia and joy of owning a physical disc or cartridge. Every package includes reversible cover by Studio Artist Lance Inkwell featuring iconic bosses from across both games, a series of Cuphead Funnies comic strips, and an individually serialized "Cuphead Club" card–modelled after the early aesthetic of Disney's Mickey Mouse Club membership cards.

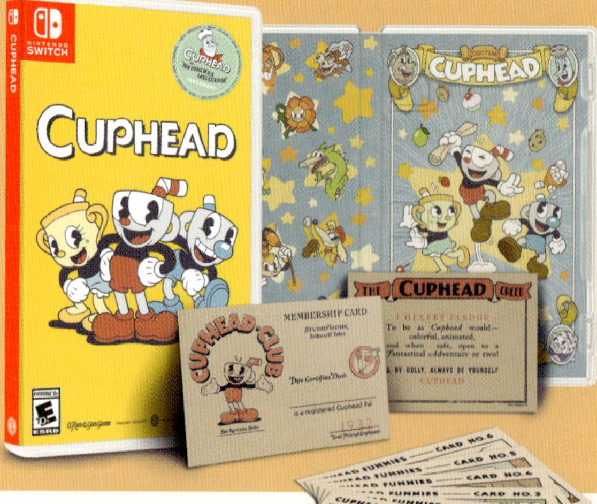

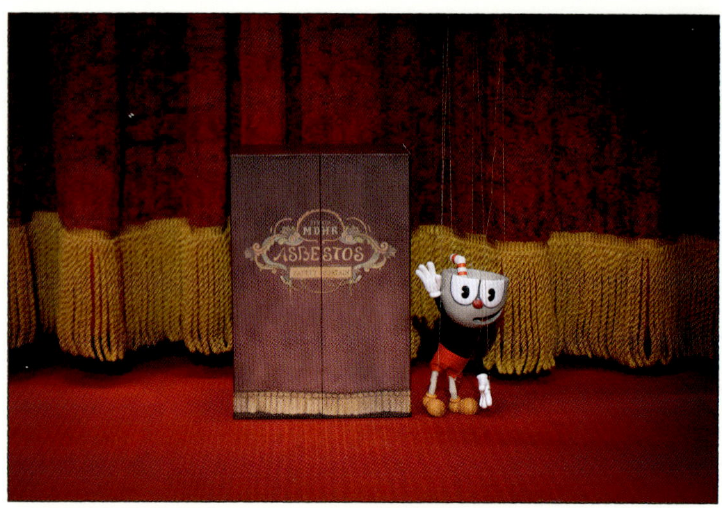

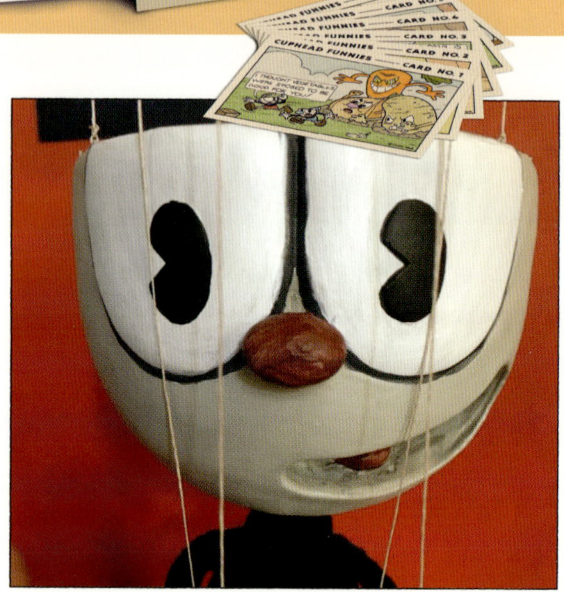

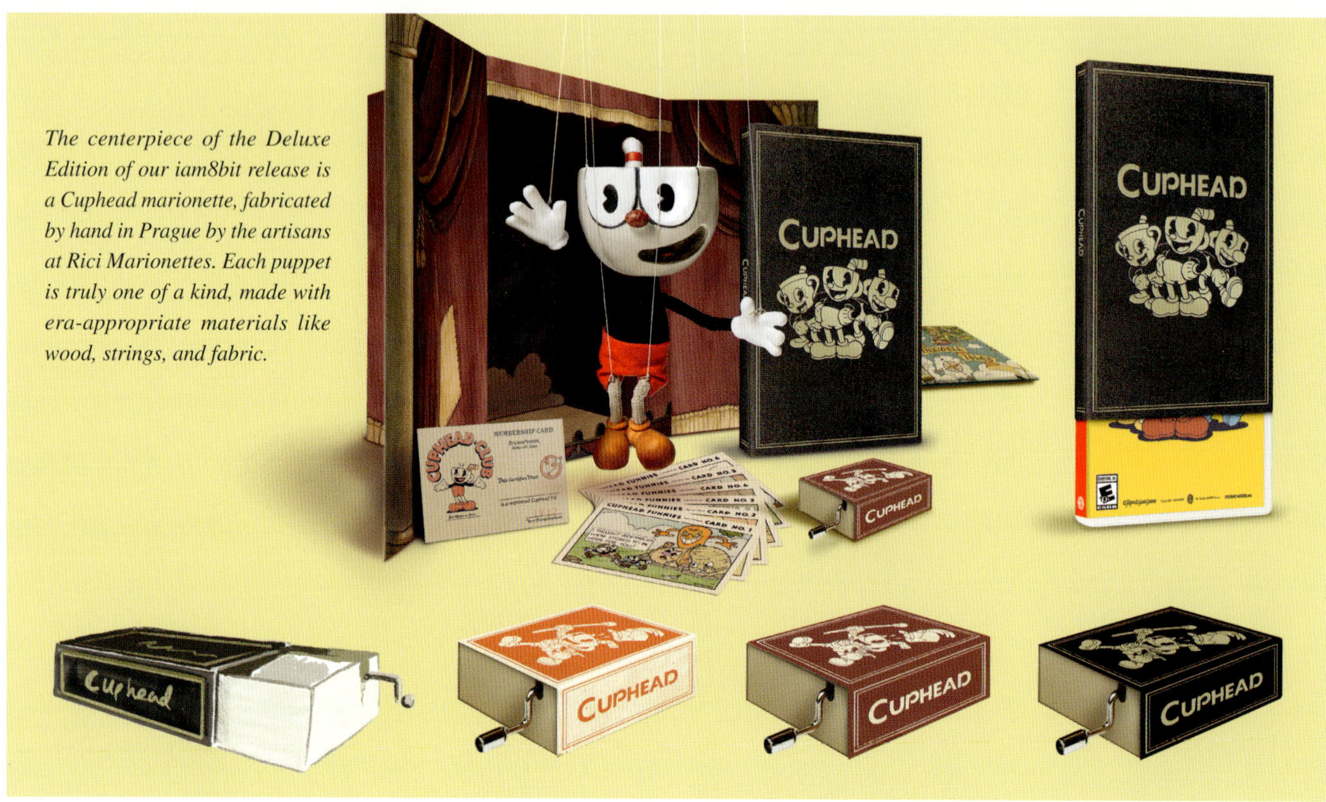

The centerpiece of the Deluxe Edition of our iam8bit release is a Cuphead marionette, fabricated by hand in Prague by the artisans at Rici Marionettes. Each puppet is truly one of a kind, made with era-appropriate materials like wood, strings, and fabric.

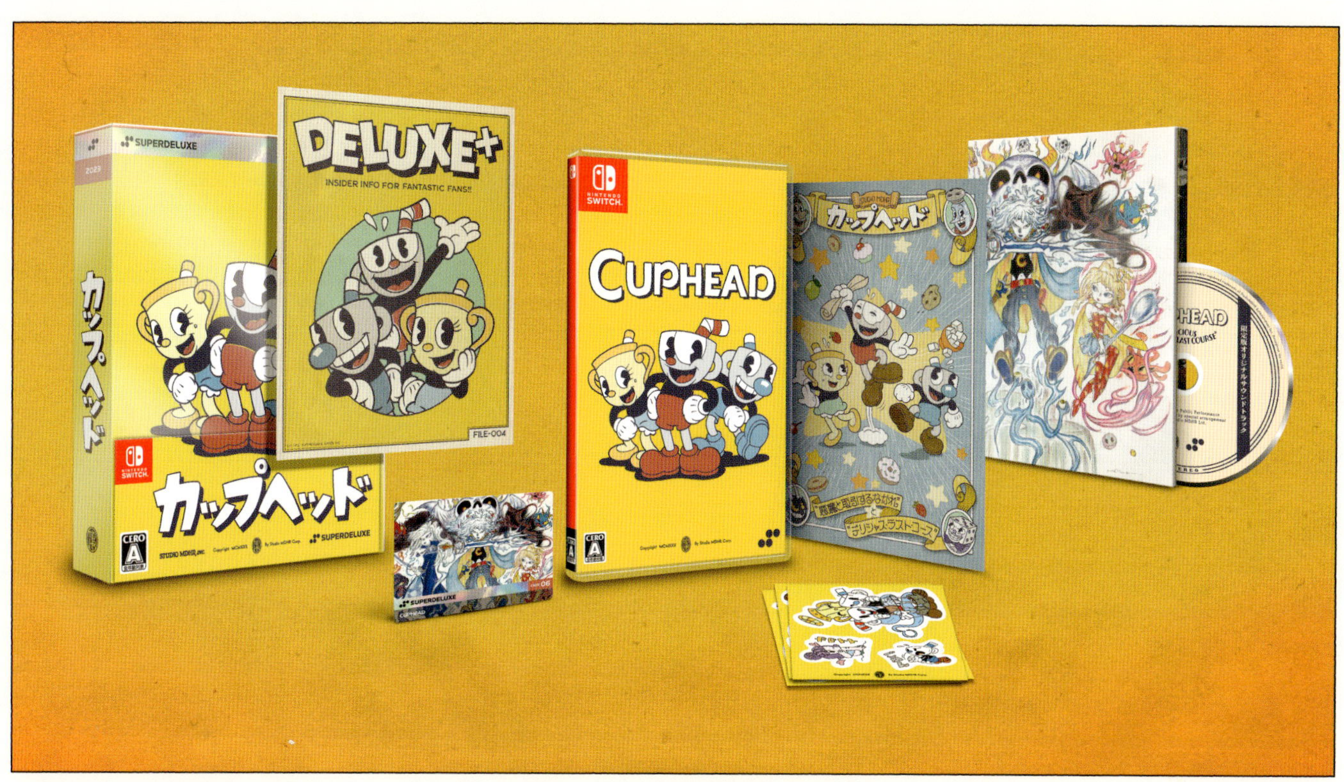

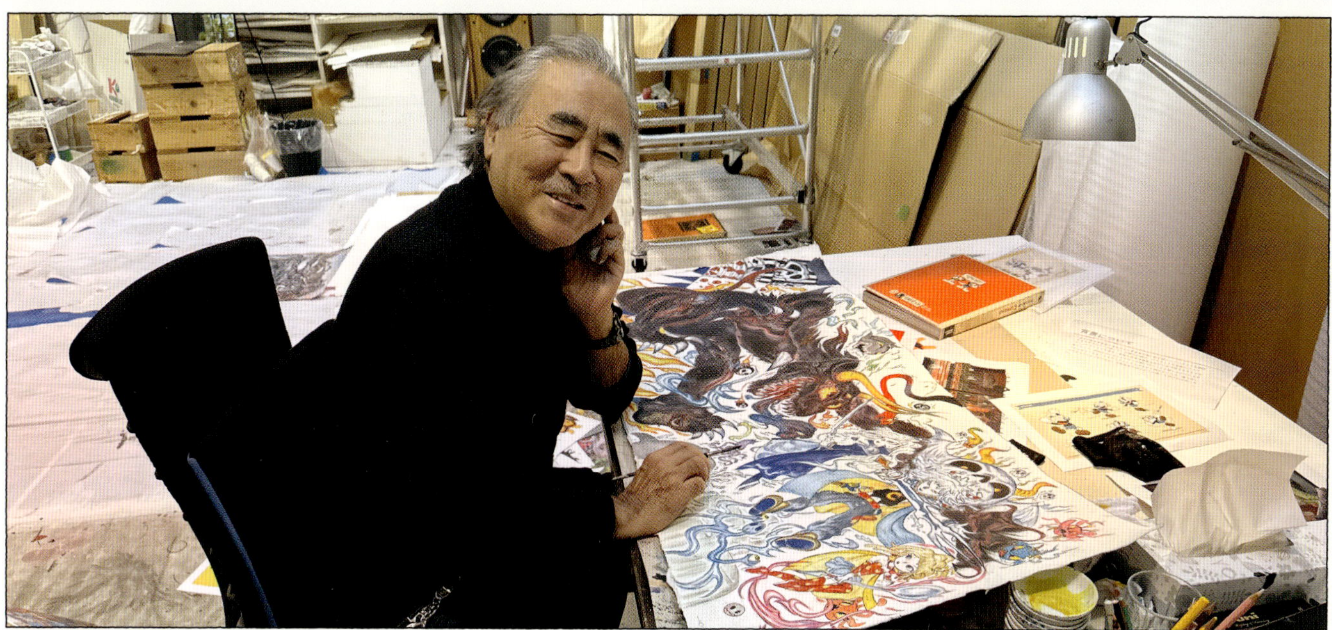

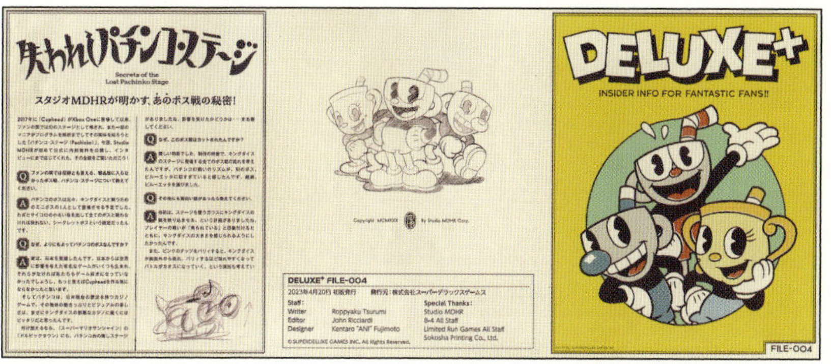

For our amazing Cuphead community in Japan, we worked with the team at SuperDeluxe Games to create a completely unique edition of the game, including an insert CD with cover art painted by legendary artisan Yoshitaka Amano. SuperDeluxe also painstakingly researched and executed a moonshot idea of ours: a box cover containing color blocks of our characters with a clear slip that slides on to mimic the 1930s marriage between paint and celluloid!

Physical Release Trailer

FOR AS LONG AS the *Cuphead* community had been waiting for a physical release of the game on disc and cartridge, we wanted to make the announcement feel like a truly special moment worthy of excitement. In tandem with our partners at iam8bit and Skybound, we called on trusted collaborators Screen Novelties to create a trailer full of physical sets and practical effects. Dubbed "Sunken Treasures," the short vignette sees pals Cuphead, Mugman, and Ms. Chalice diving to the bottom of the ocean in search of jewels, baubles, and the ultimate self-referential treasure…pack-in items from our *Cuphead* physical edition!

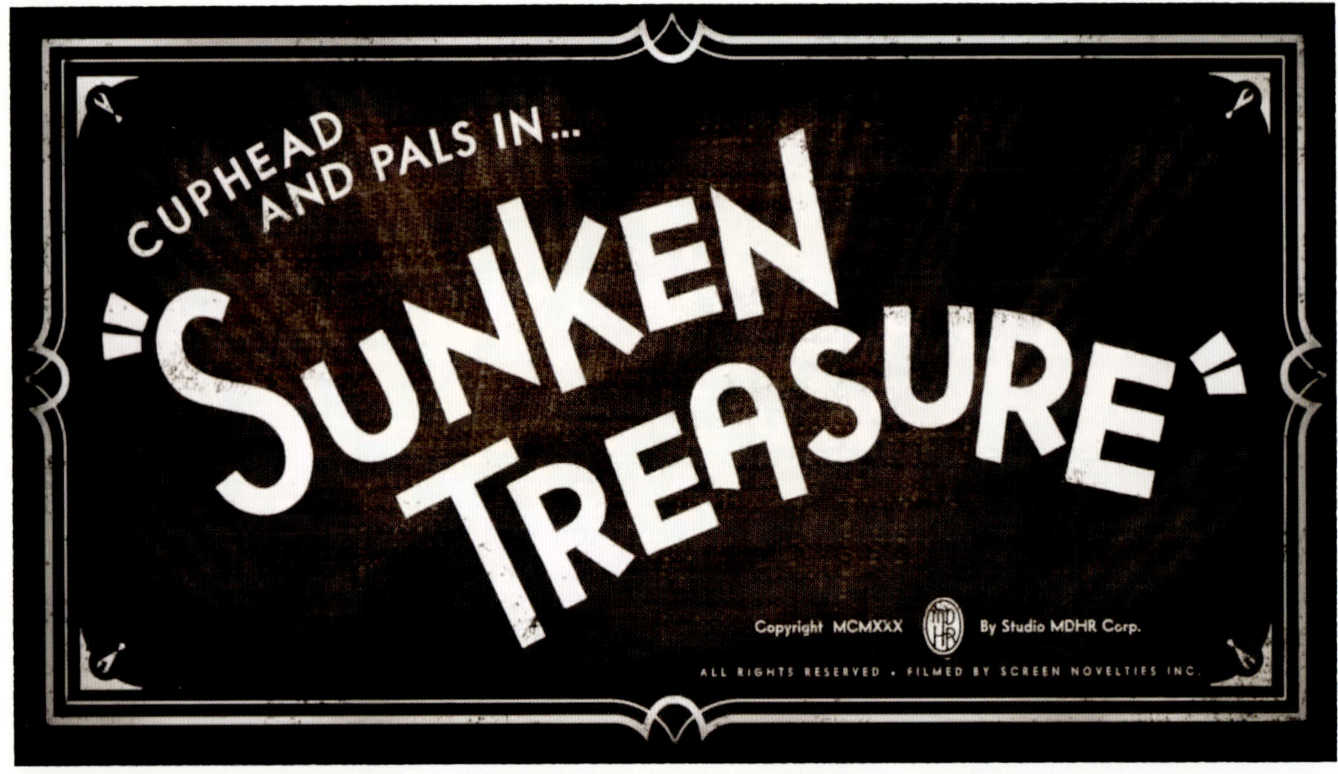

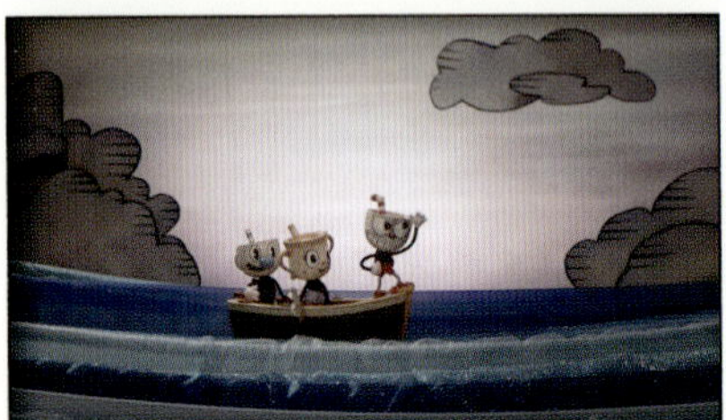

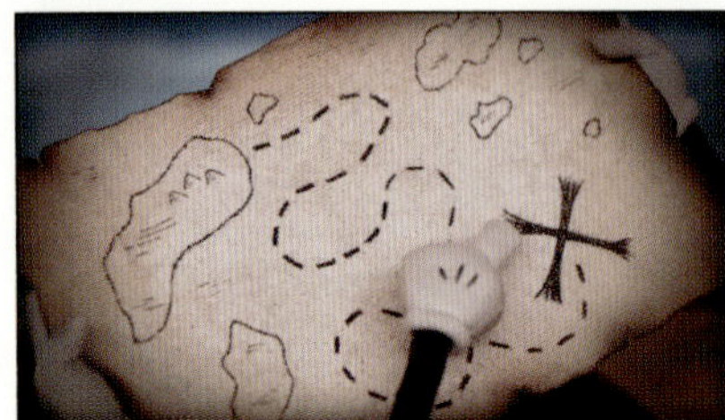

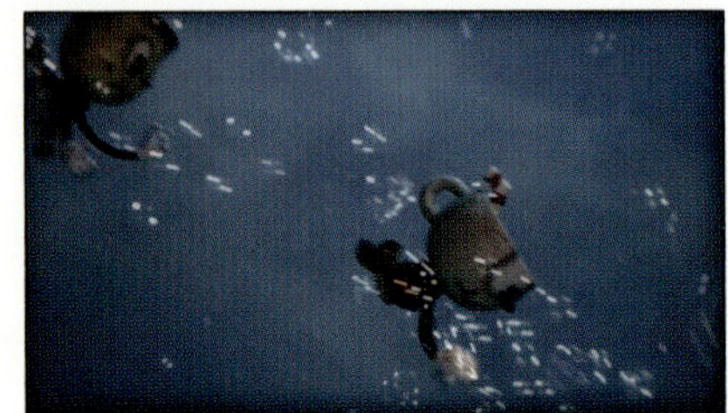

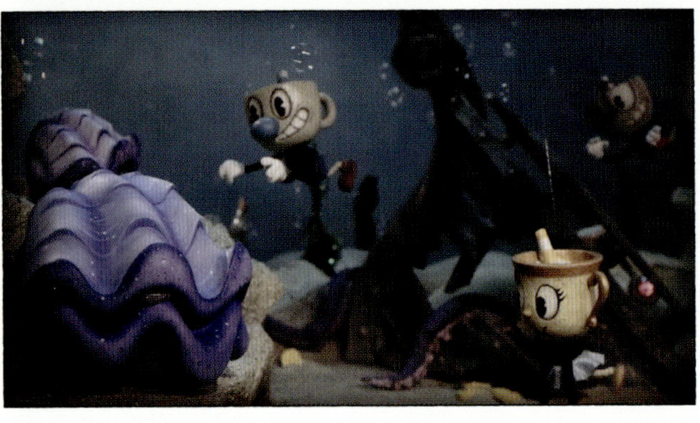

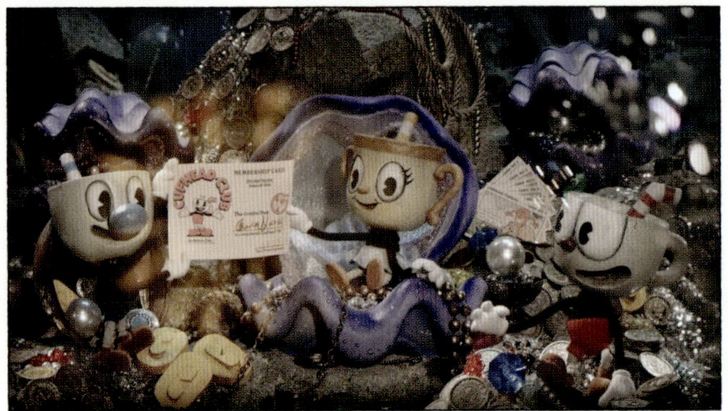

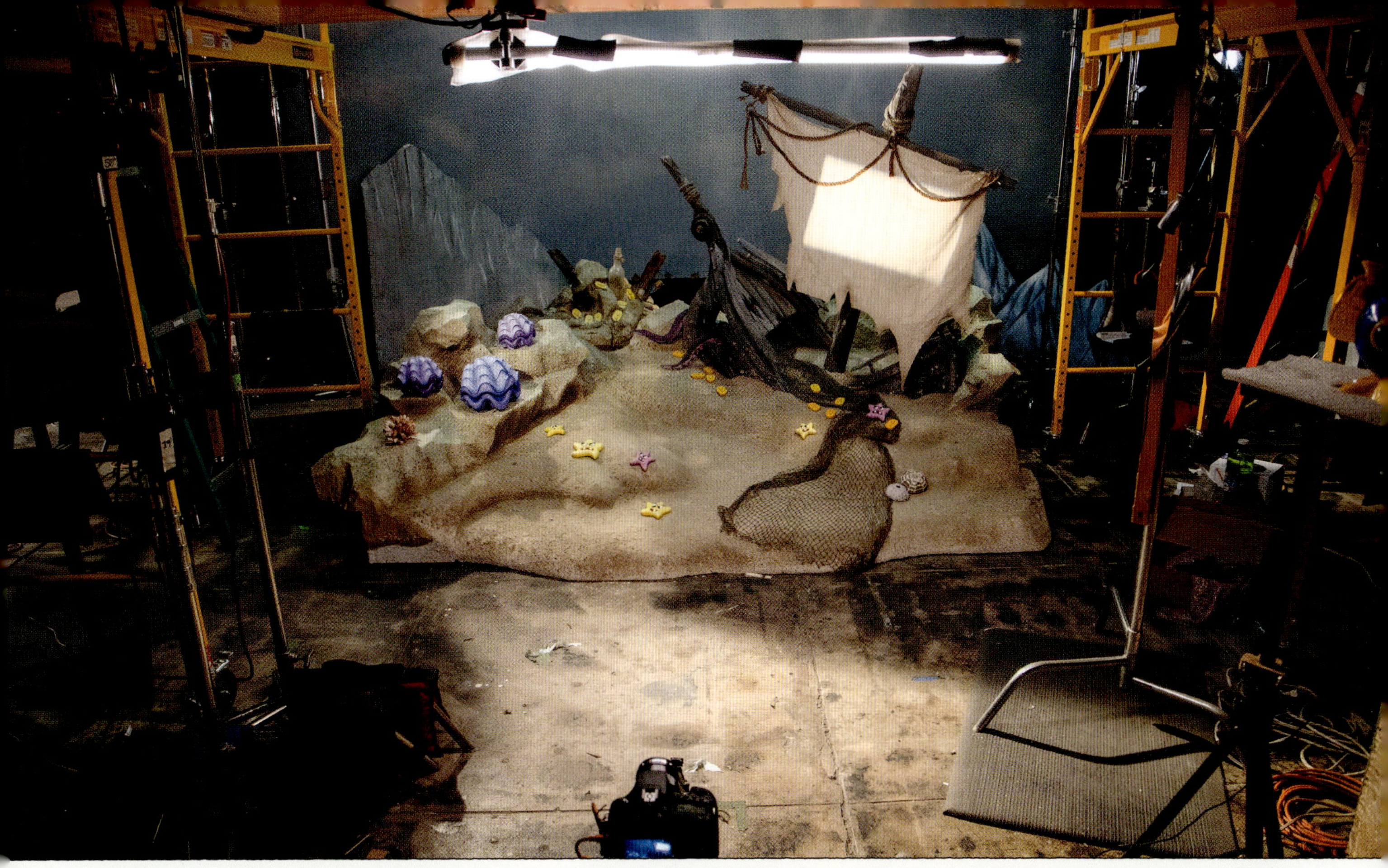

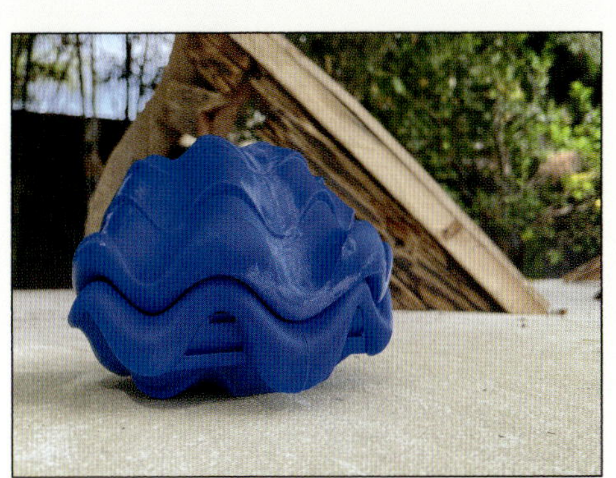

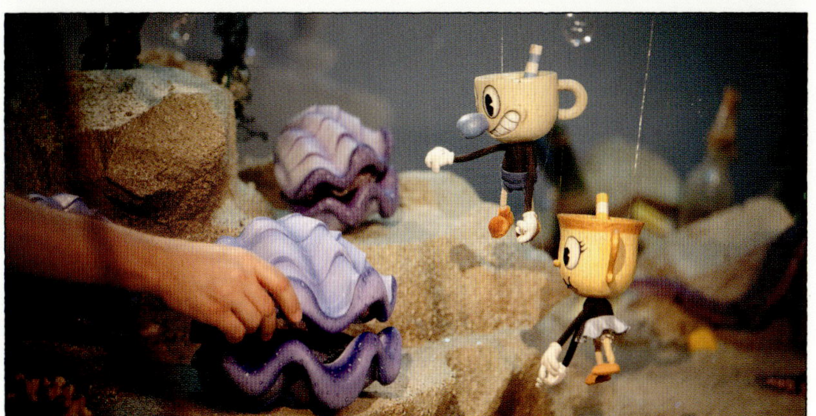

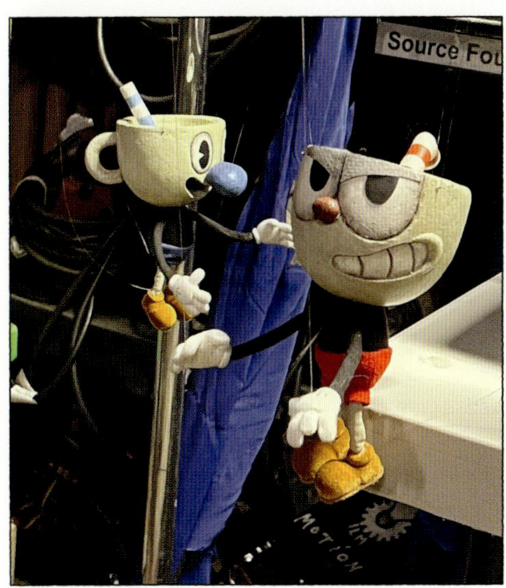

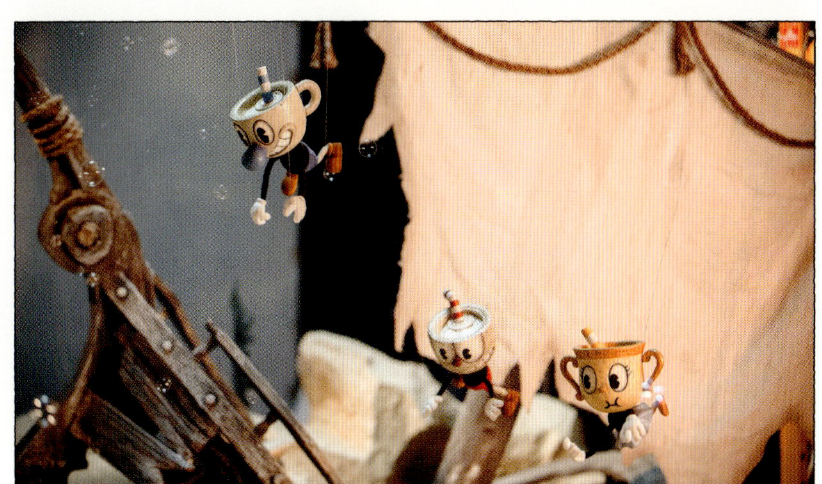

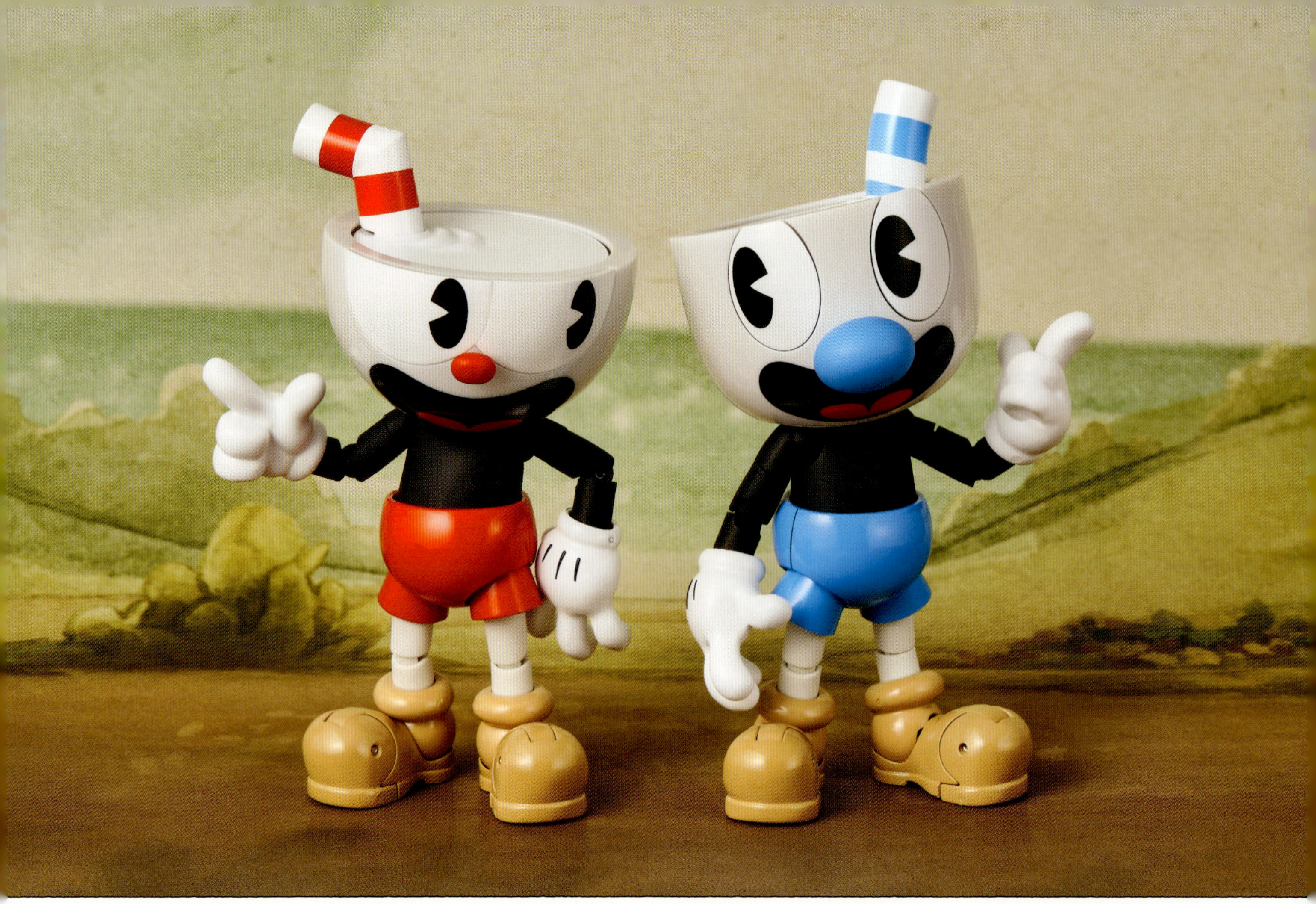

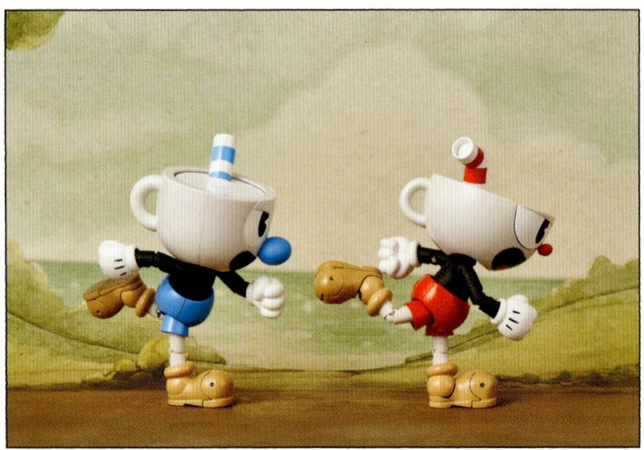

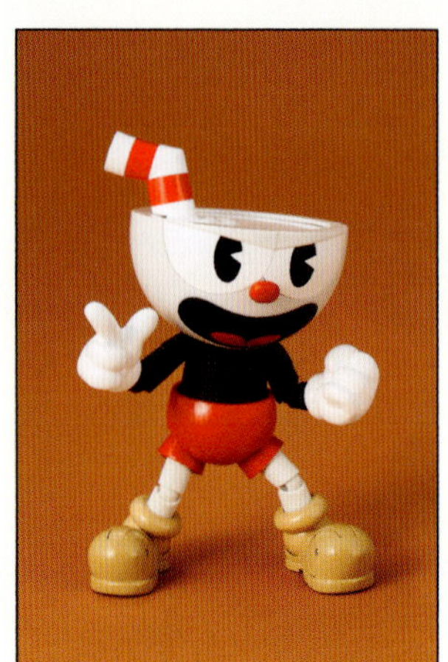

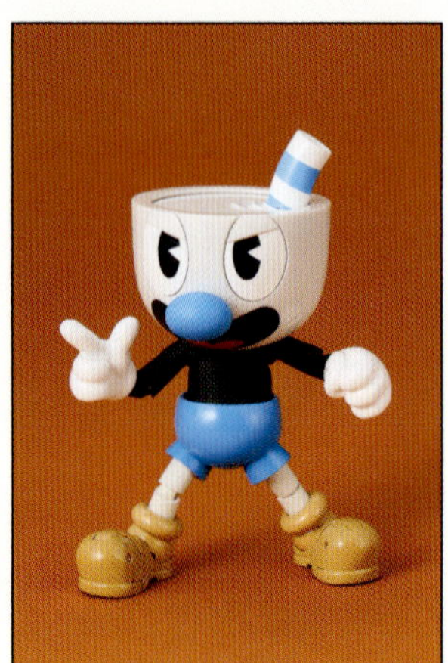

Vinyl Toys and Figures

WHETHER IT'S DELIGHTFUL DESK DOODADS or pristine posable pals, we have had the immense pleasure of working with a range of partners over the years to realize our characters in figurine form. From Funko to YouTooz to 1000Toys and many more, partners always pair up with a Studio MDHR artist to receive "draw overs" that help refine their initial concepts into silhouettes and faces that best capture the essence of characters they're working on. It can be tricky at a smaller scale, but maintaining things like the 1930s "pie eye" and honing in on recognizable poses goes a long way. Pictured above, the team at 1000Toys went all out in crafting their fully articulated Cuphead and Mugman figurines, which feel less like purely playable toys and more like a photography centerpiece.

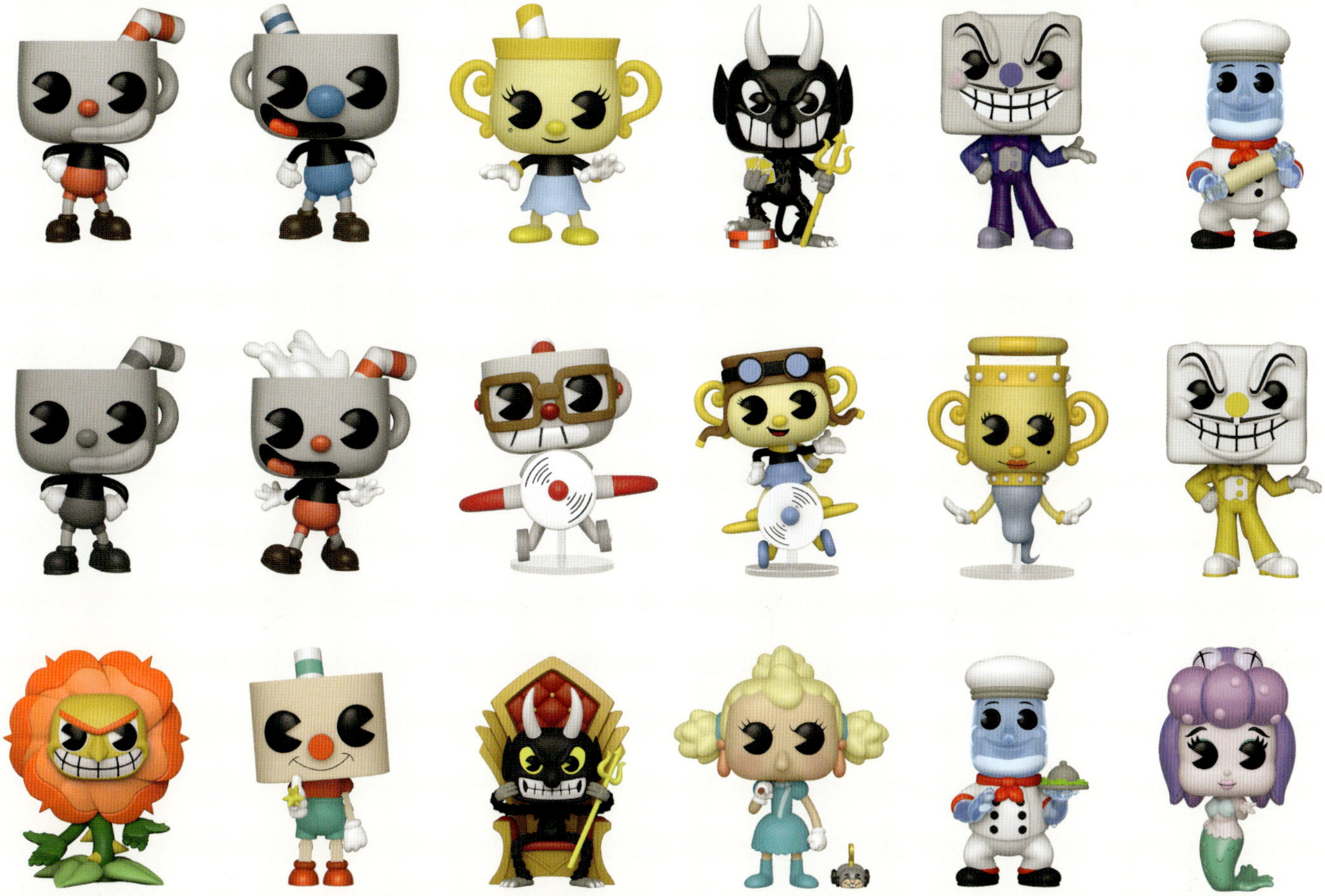

Renowned Japanese toymaker Good Smile collaborated with us to bring Cuphead and Mugman to their "Nendoroid" toy line (seen right, and bottom). Fun fact: the Nendoroid figure of Cuphead is the first time his iconic "pea shooter" has ever been physically modelled!

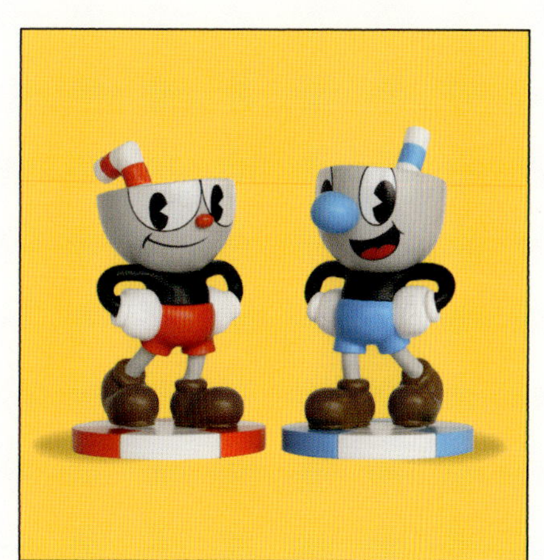

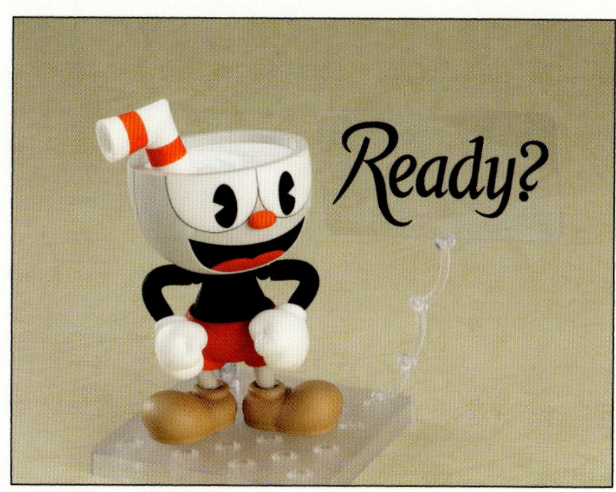

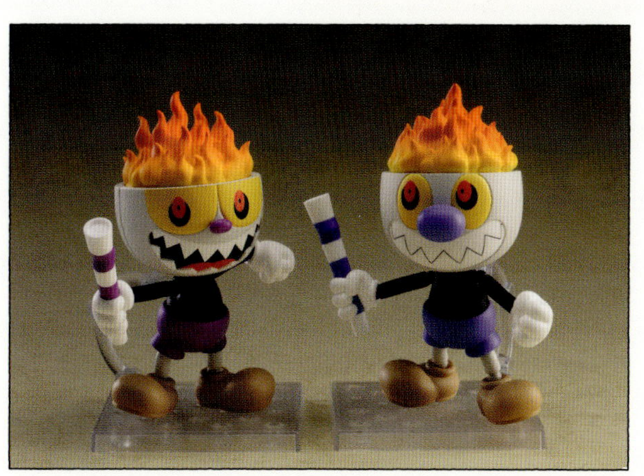

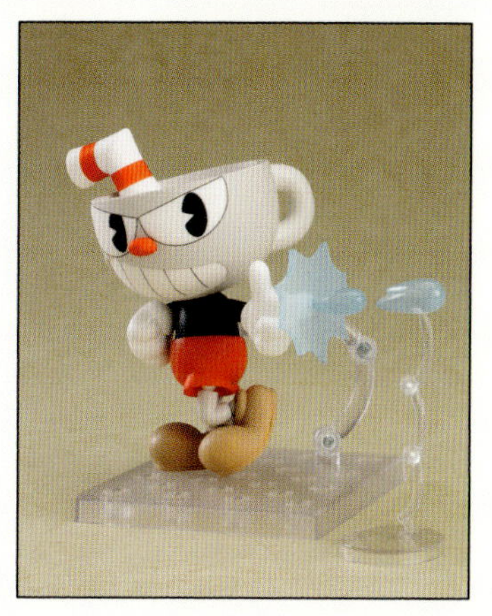

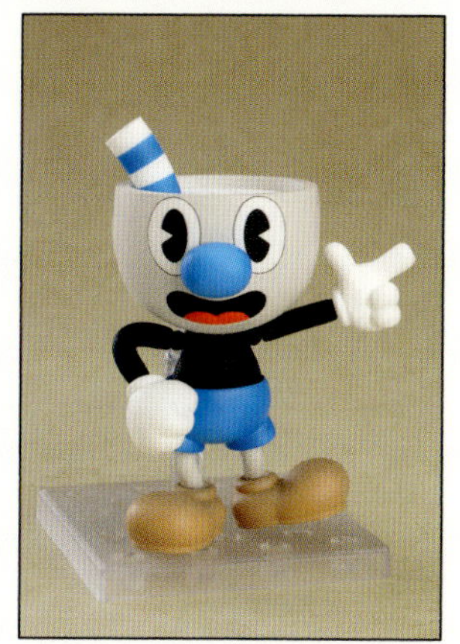

We like to lean into the playful nature of figures to stretch the rules of depicting our core characters in ways we otherwise wouldn't in the world of our games. Led by Austin Long, the team at YouTooz are always looking to find ways to push the boundary between art and collectible, like with their "Cuphead Revealed" figurine pictured right. Standing twelve inches tall, it depicts Cuphead as being quite literally made up of iconic moments from his journey through the Inkwell Isles.

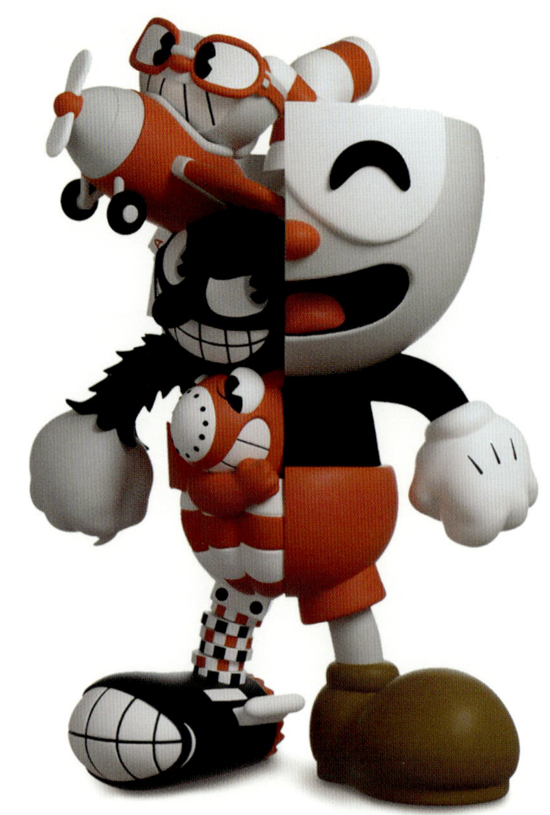

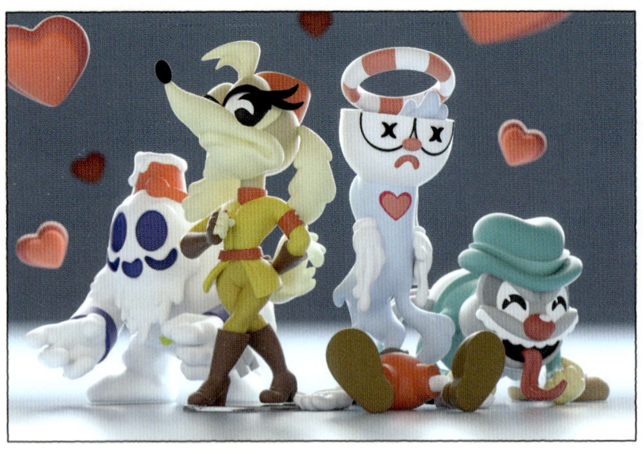

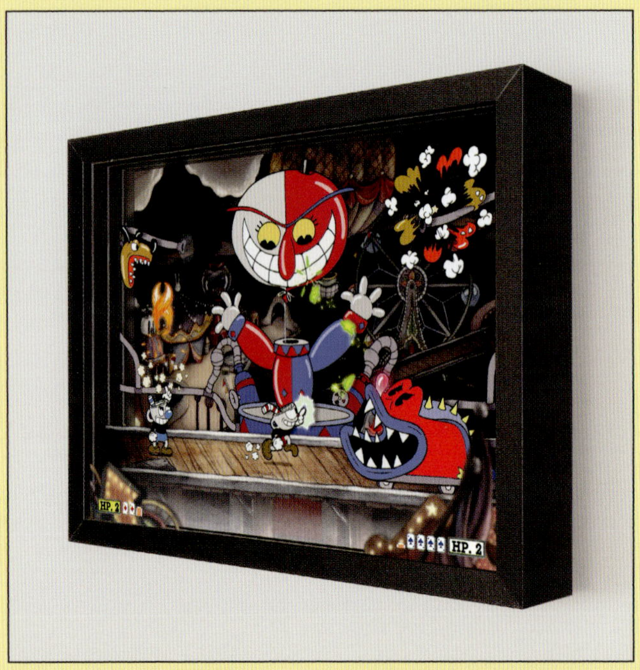

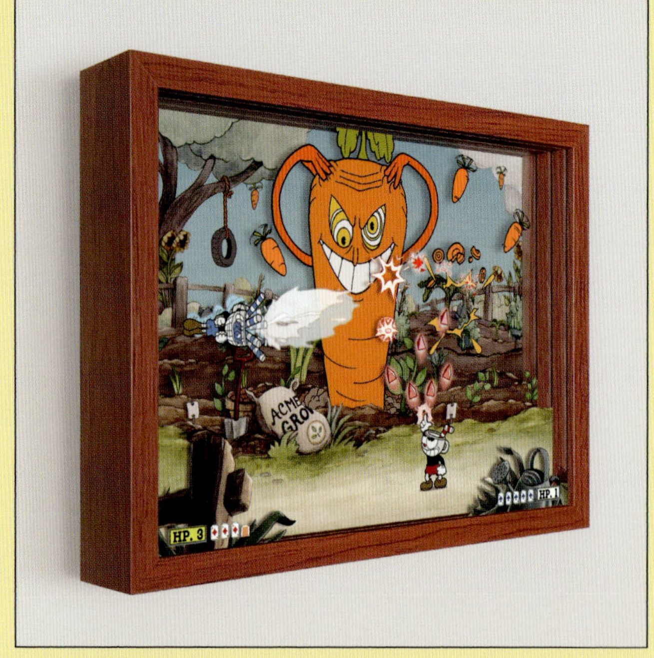

Shadowboxes

WE ARE ALWAYS KEEN to represent the world of the Inkwell Isles in artistic ways, and these shadowboxes from the fine folks at Artovision are a perfect example of the craftsmanship we're drawn to. Led by founder Stuart Sandler, the team at Artovision creates desktop art pieces that pull you into the worlds they're depicting by separating a scene out into multiple layers. The process starts with Stuart selecting moments from *Cuphead* boss battles that best suit the medium. From there, Studio MDHR Brand Design Director Ian Clarke meticulously rebuilds those moments using higher resolution assets. Every character and projectile and smoke puff is an individual image posed to feel as if it came from the middle of a tense boss play-through!

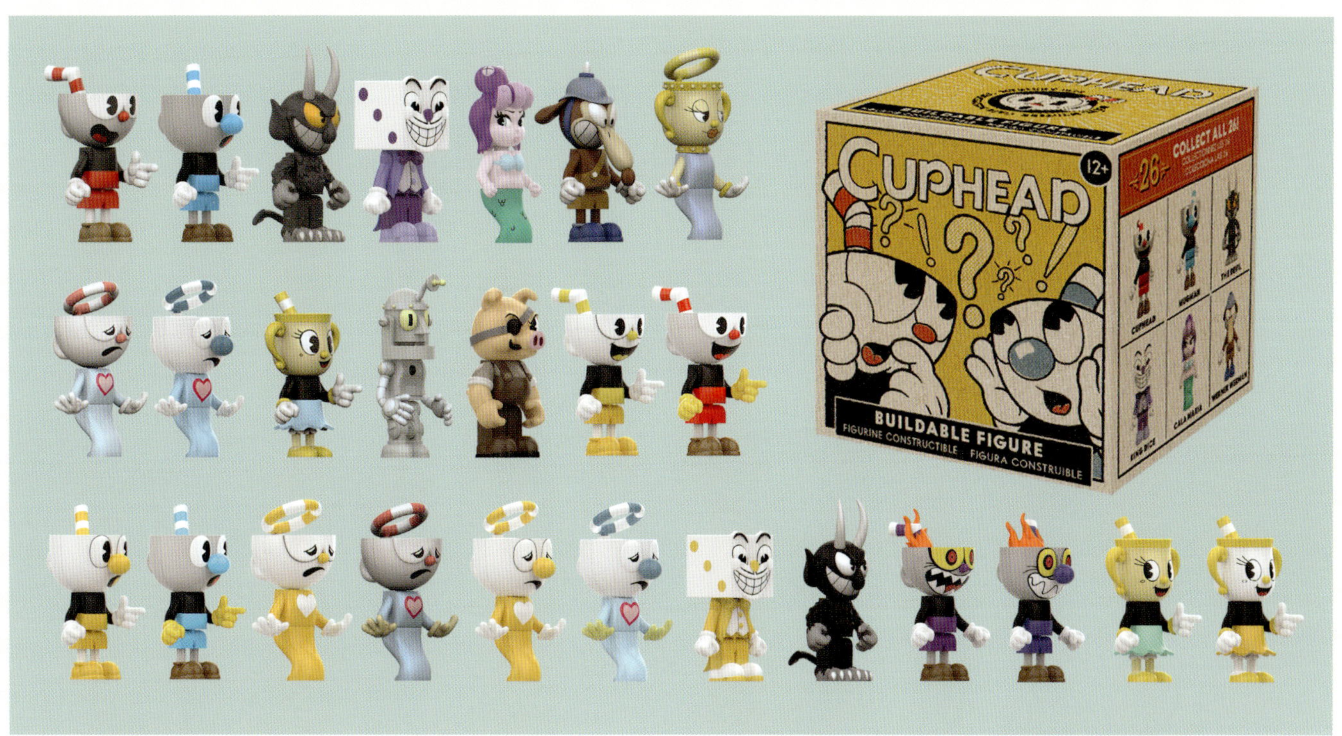

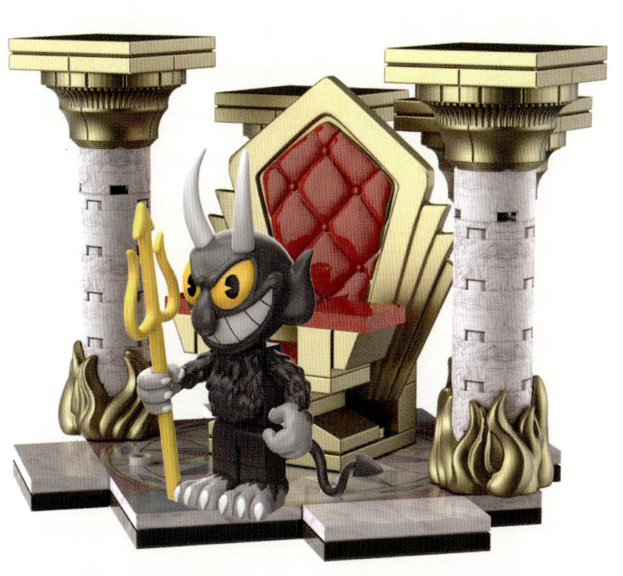

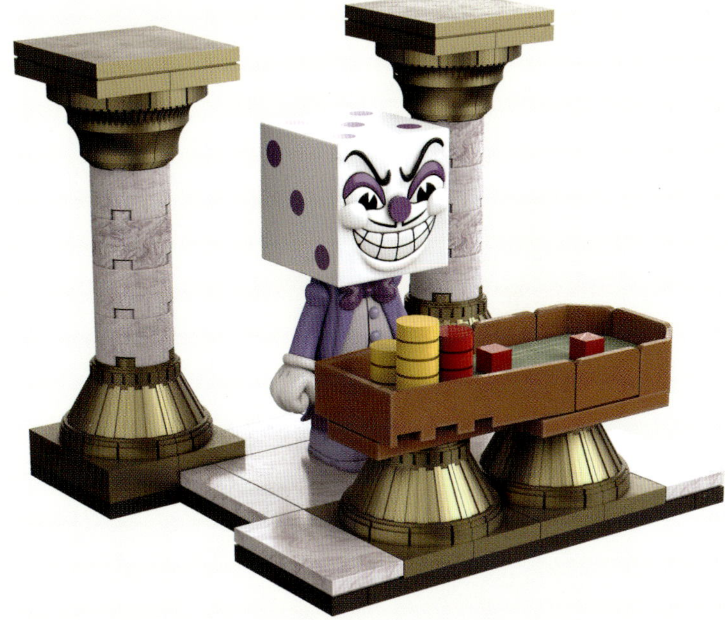

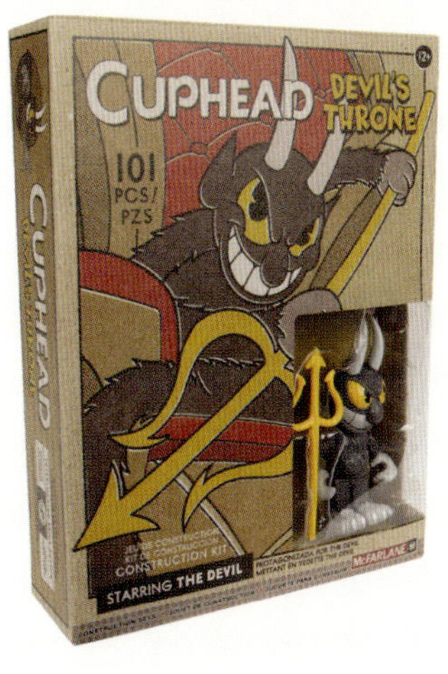

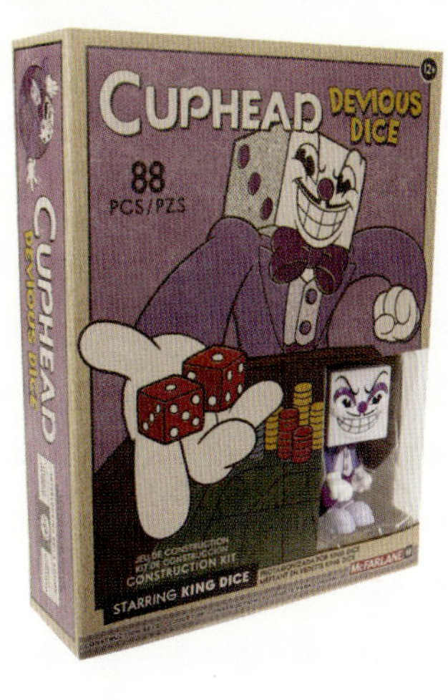

Construction Toys and Figures

A DEFINITE "BUCKET LIST" MOMENT for us was the chance to collaborate with the legendary toymakers at McFarlane on a range of construction kits and buildable miniatures. In both the larger sets and individual figurines, McFarlane supported our push for immersive detail, whether it was the desire to capture the flames in Evil Cuphead's cup or mold individual casino chips on King Dice's craps table. In true Studio MDHR fashion, Brand Director Ian Clarke worked tirelessly on exterior packaging which reflects the texture, stylization, and aesthetic of the era—including brand-new character illustrations done in-house by Animator Joseph Coleman.

Posters

MORE THAN JUST SOMETHING to put on the wall, we've always seen posters as canvases on which other talented artists can interpret the Cuphead characters. Our strong preference is toward small-batch, limited runs that emphasize high quality materials and unique treatments. Soon after *Cuphead*'s release, we were lucky to find a like mind in Joseph Bouganim of New York-based gallery Bottleneck, whose eye for quality and push to experiment always elevates the artwork. For example, the trio of posters pictured below from Japanese artist Yuki Hayashi were produced to celebrate *Cuphead*'s launch on Nintendo Switch, and had a small number of prints available in shiny Metallic Giclee. Meanwhile, the "Fateful End" print from Designer Justin Erickson was custom-commissioned as a spooky celebration of Halloween!

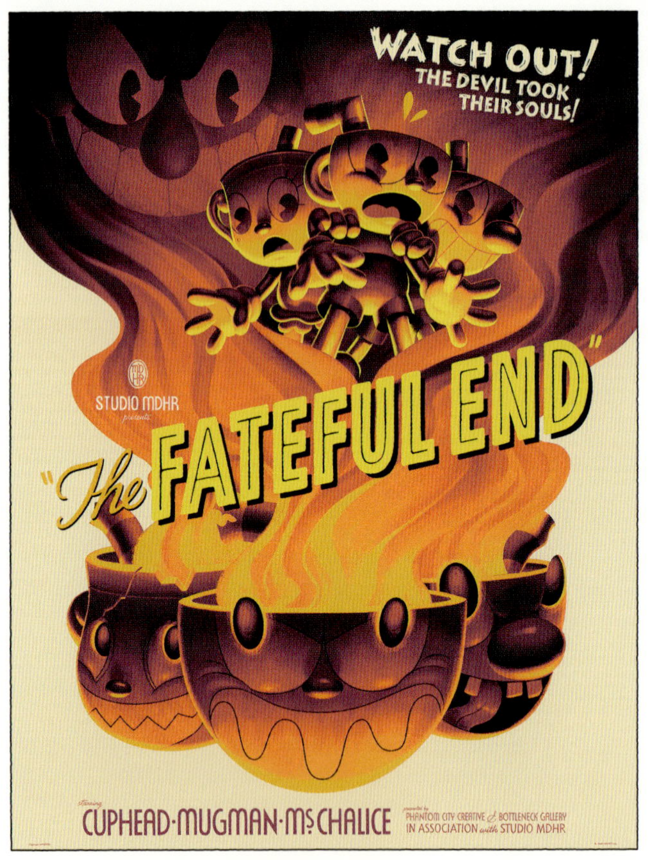

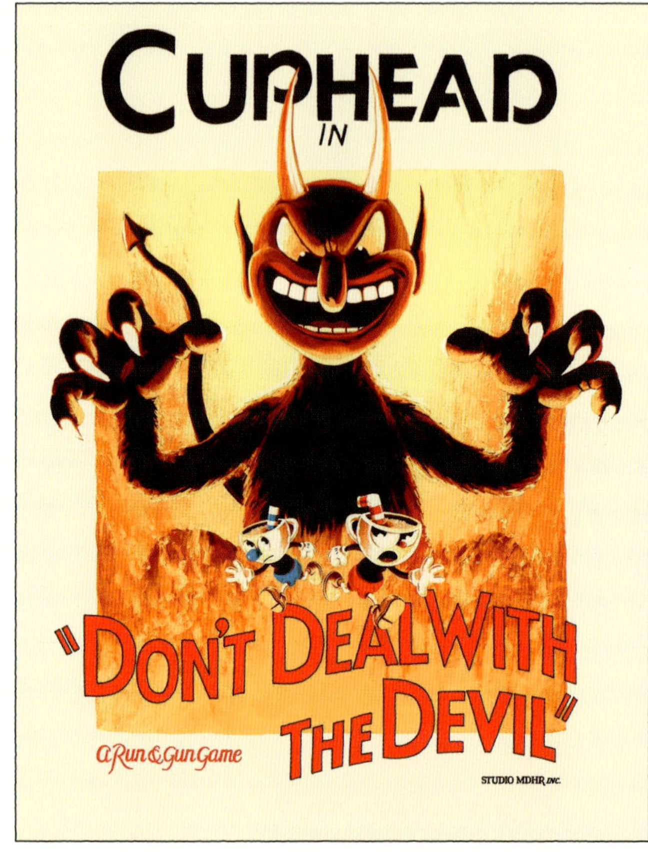

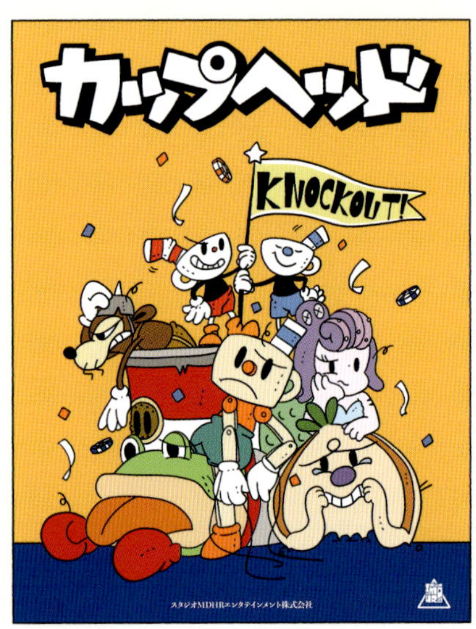

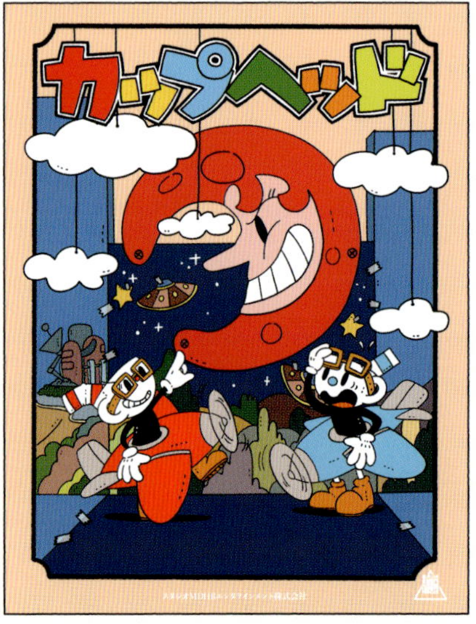

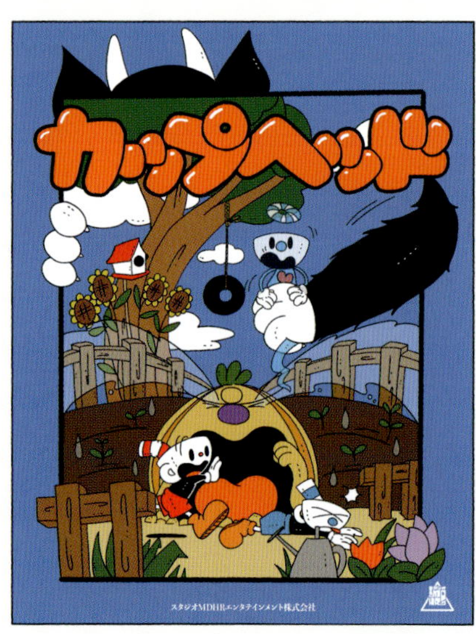

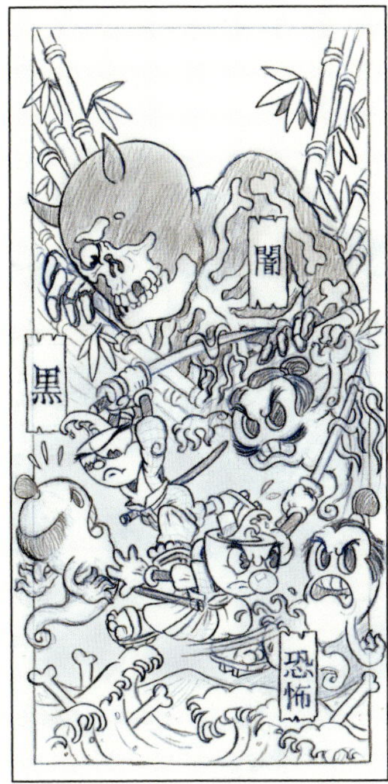

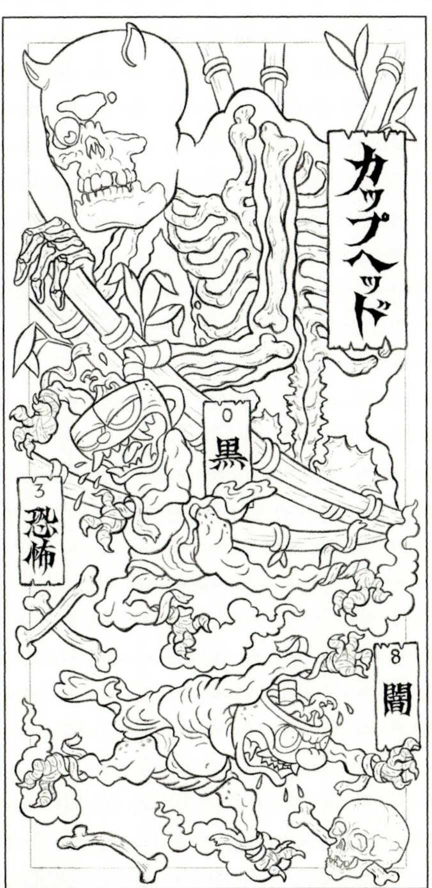

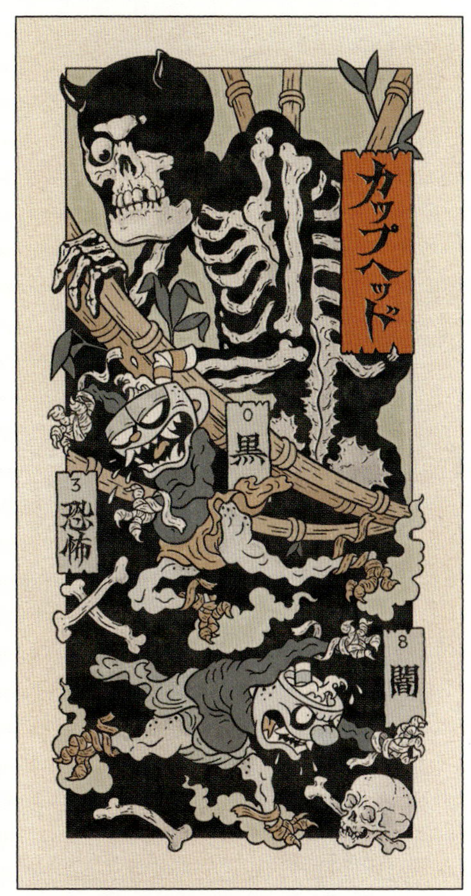

Pictured above, an unused samurai-inspired design for our limited edition Cuphead *woodblock print from Illustrator Lance Inkwell. The final form, seen right, is significantly spookier!*

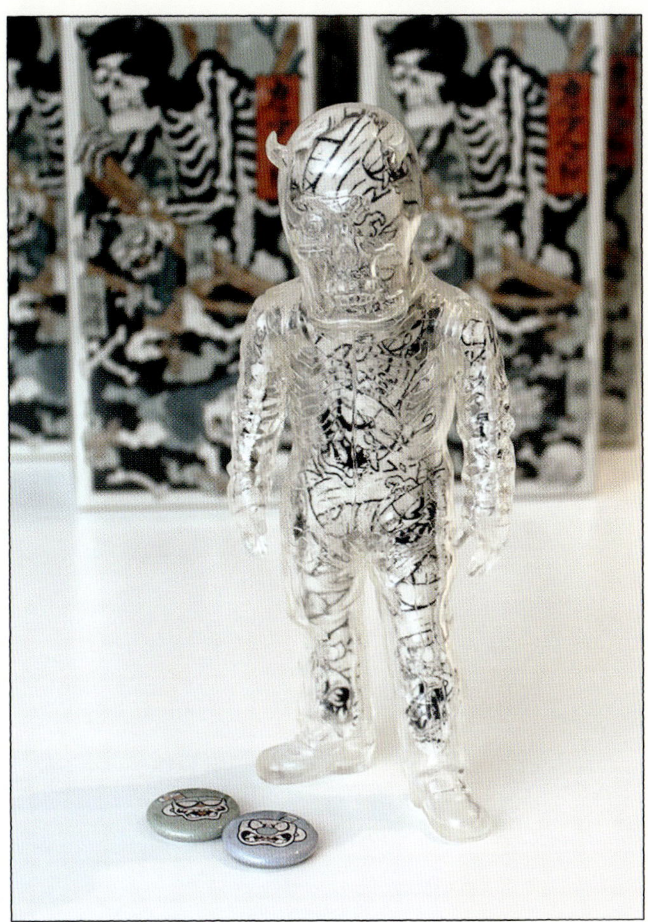

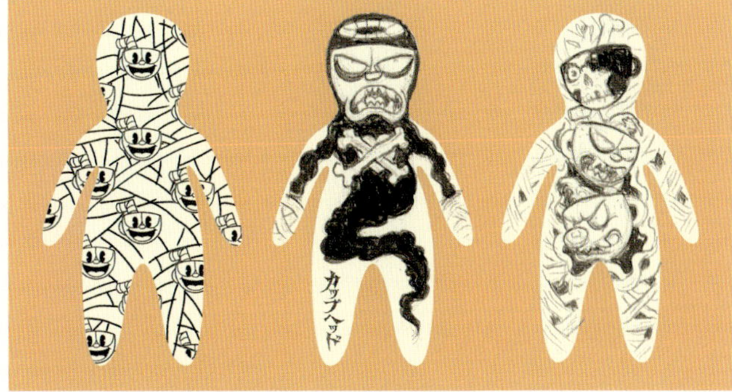

Balzac Collaboration

SOMETIMES, YOUR PERSONAL AND professional lives can collide in serendipitous ways. This much was true for Studio MDHR Art Director Ryan Moldenhauer as we neared *Cuphead*'s launch on the Nintendo Switch system. During his years living in Japan, Ryan cultivated a friendship with members of Japanese indie punk-rock band Balzac, even spending some of his time as a tour and social media manager for the group. As we contemplated ways to artfully celebrate Japanese iconography in tandem with the Nintendo Switch launch, Ryan suggested a partnership with Balzac, whose "Skullman" character is iconic to fans of the band. The result? A limited run of Japan-exclusive Skullman figurines bearing a custom illustration drawn in-house, which was later featured on an authentic *Mokuhanga* woodblock print by Stephen Winiecki and produced by our pals at iam8bit!

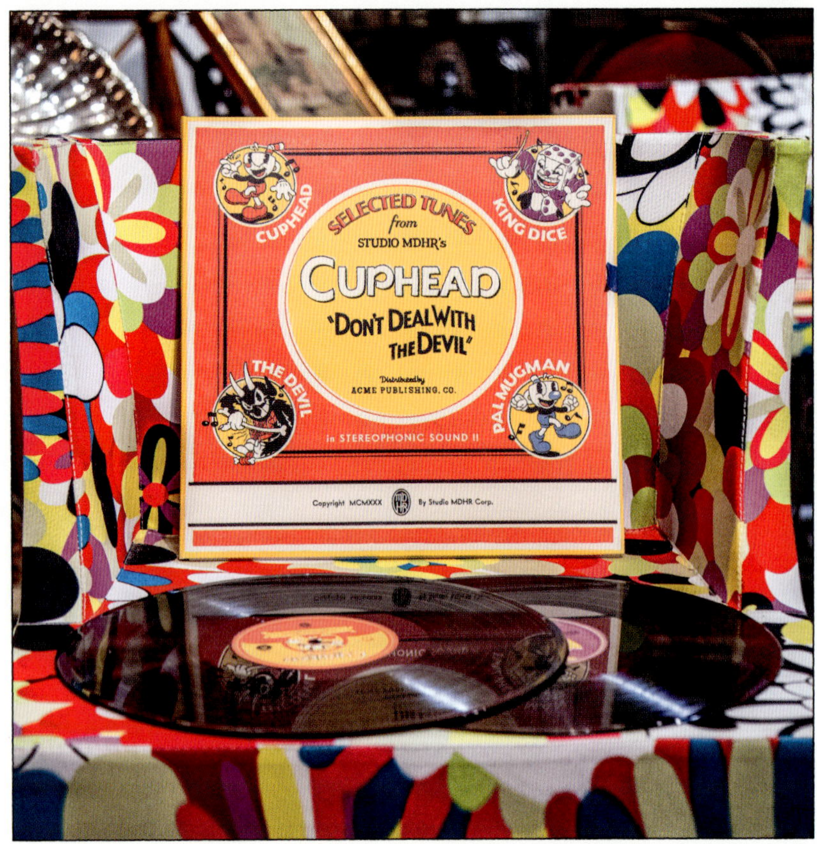

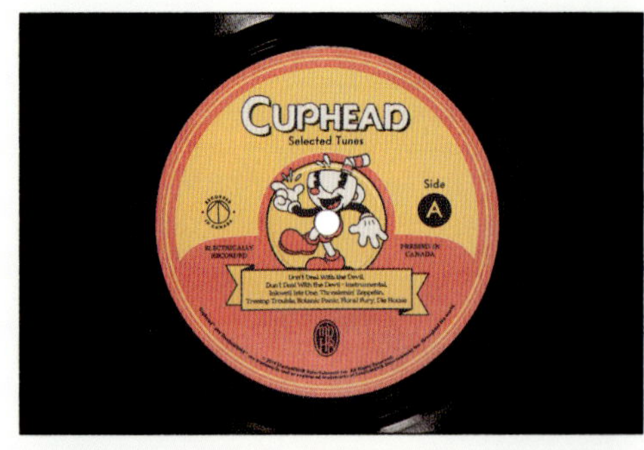

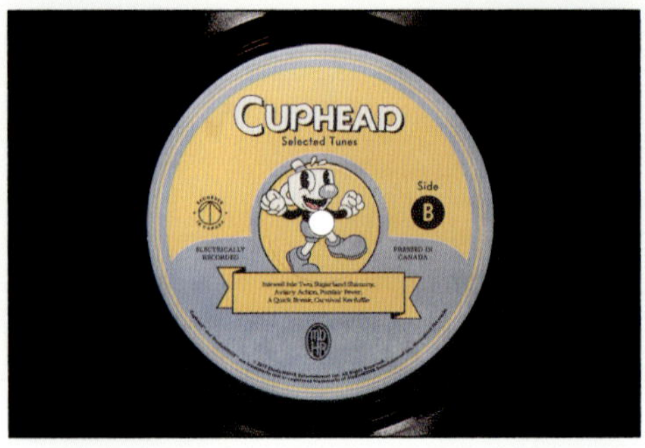

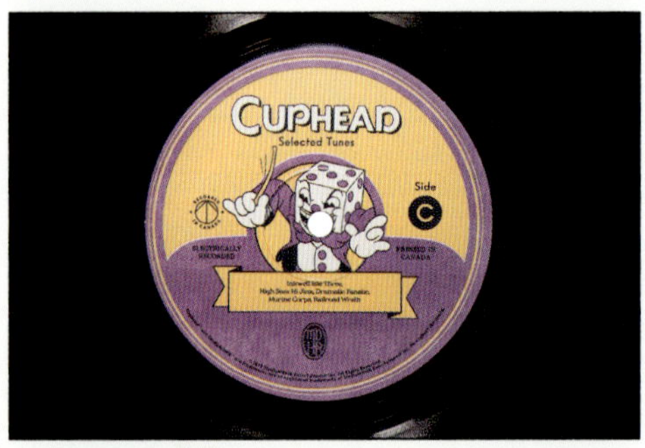

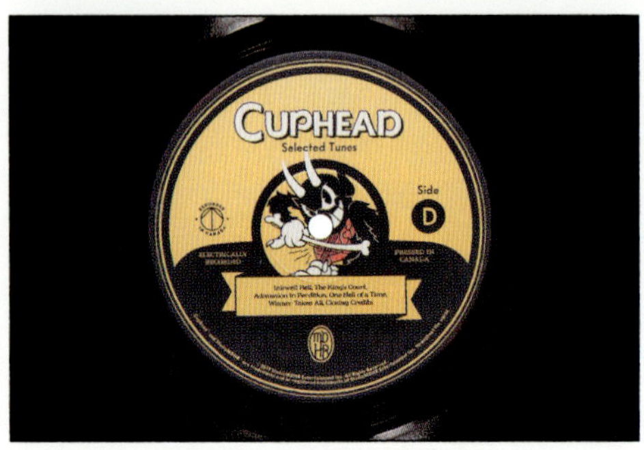

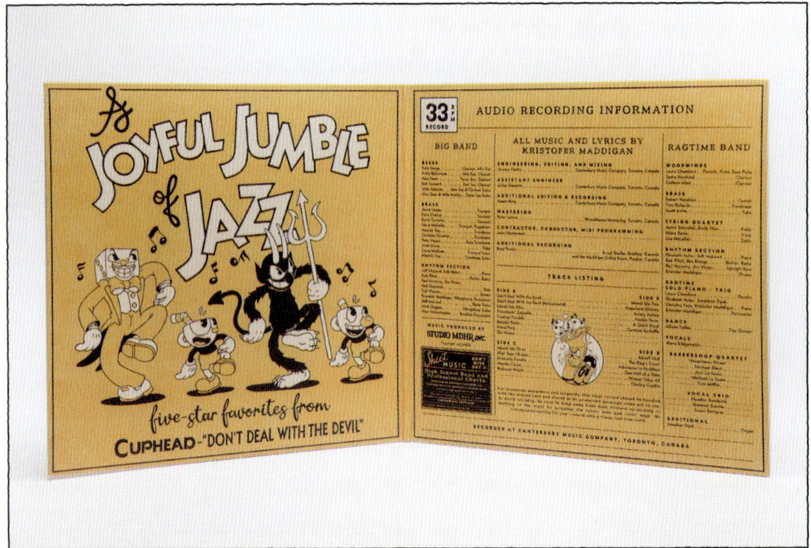

Records

WITH MUSIC SO WOVEN into the DNA of what makes *Cuphead* Cuphead, it has always been important for us to bring our game soundtracks to life on vinyl. A tight collaboration between the studio, Composer Kristofer Maddigan, and the team at iam8bit, each record set is crafted with rigorous audio and artistic standards in mind. We also have a habit of packing the gatefold jackets with hidden references–like mock advertisements on the *Delicious Last Course* LP which promote the same ingredients you collect in-game for Chef Saltbaker!

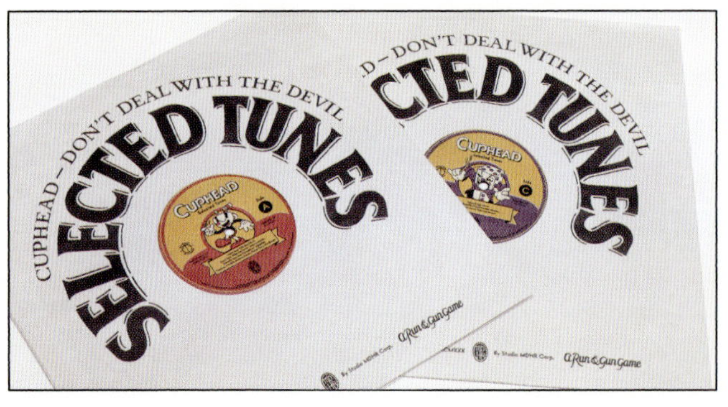

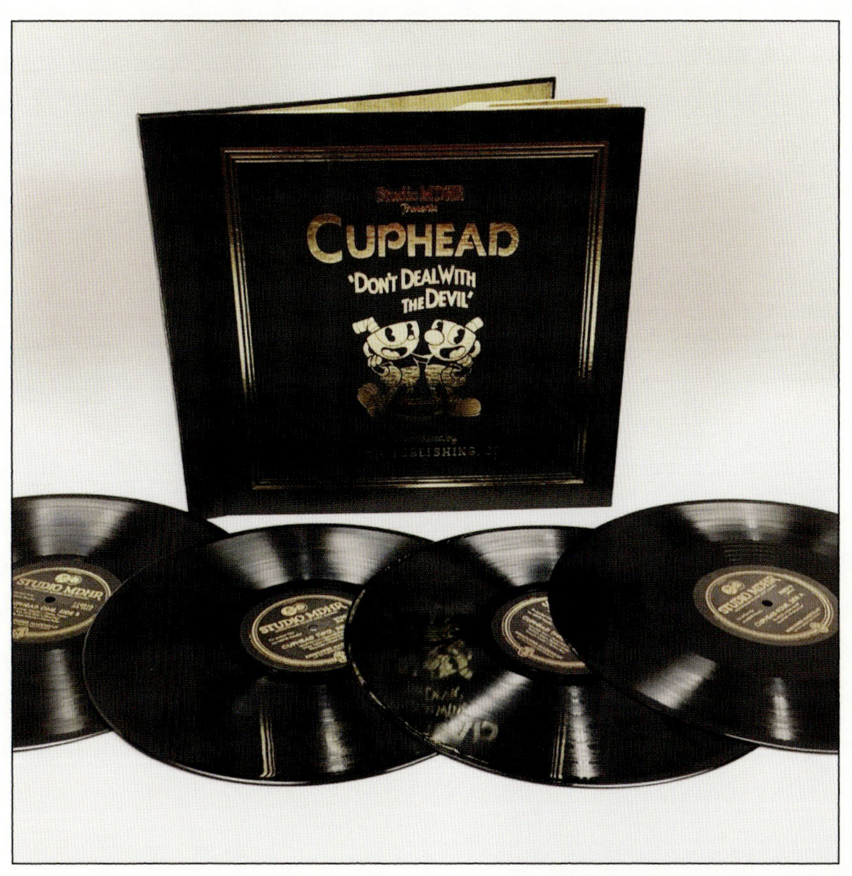
Studio MDHR
Presents
CUPHEAD
'DON'T DEAL WITH THE DEVIL'

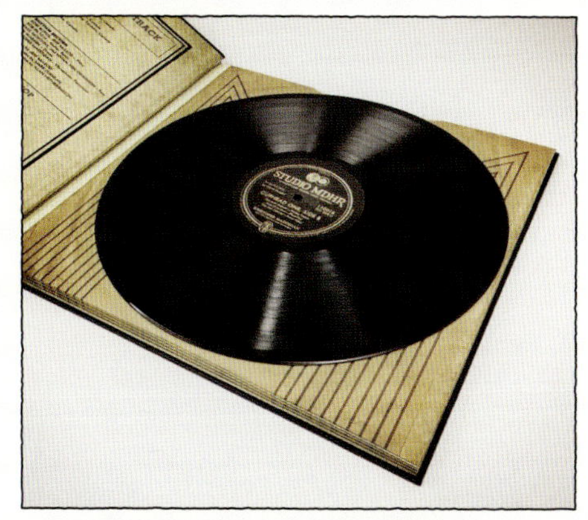

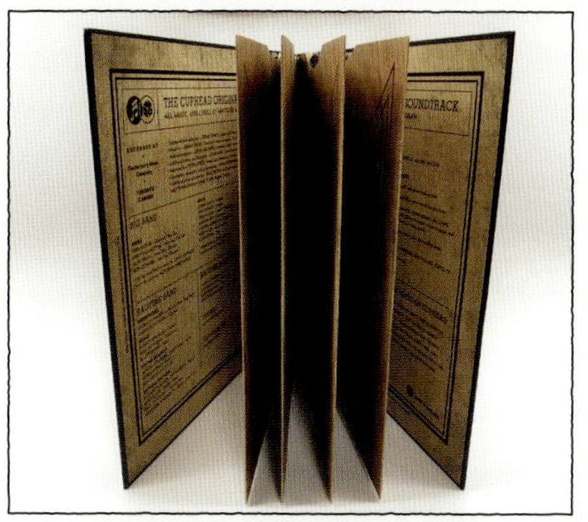

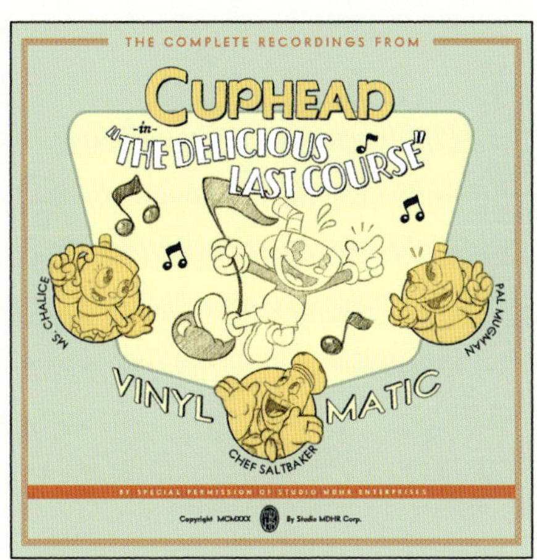
THE COMPLETE RECORDINGS FROM
CUPHEAD
-in-
"THE DELICIOUS LAST COURSE"
MS. CHALICE
PAL MUGMAN
VINYL
MATIC
CHEF SALTBAKER
BY SPECIAL PERMISSION OF STUDIO MDHR ENTERPRISES
Copyright MCMXXX
By Studio MDHR Corp.

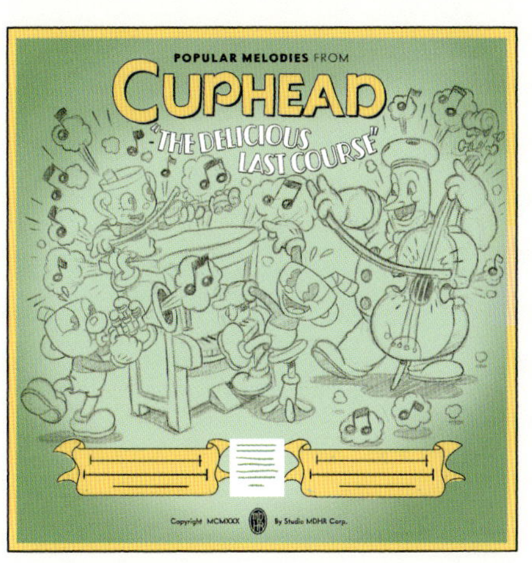
POPULAR MELODIES FROM
CUPHEAD
"THE DELICIOUS LAST COURSE"
Copyright MCMXXX
By Studio MDHR Corp.

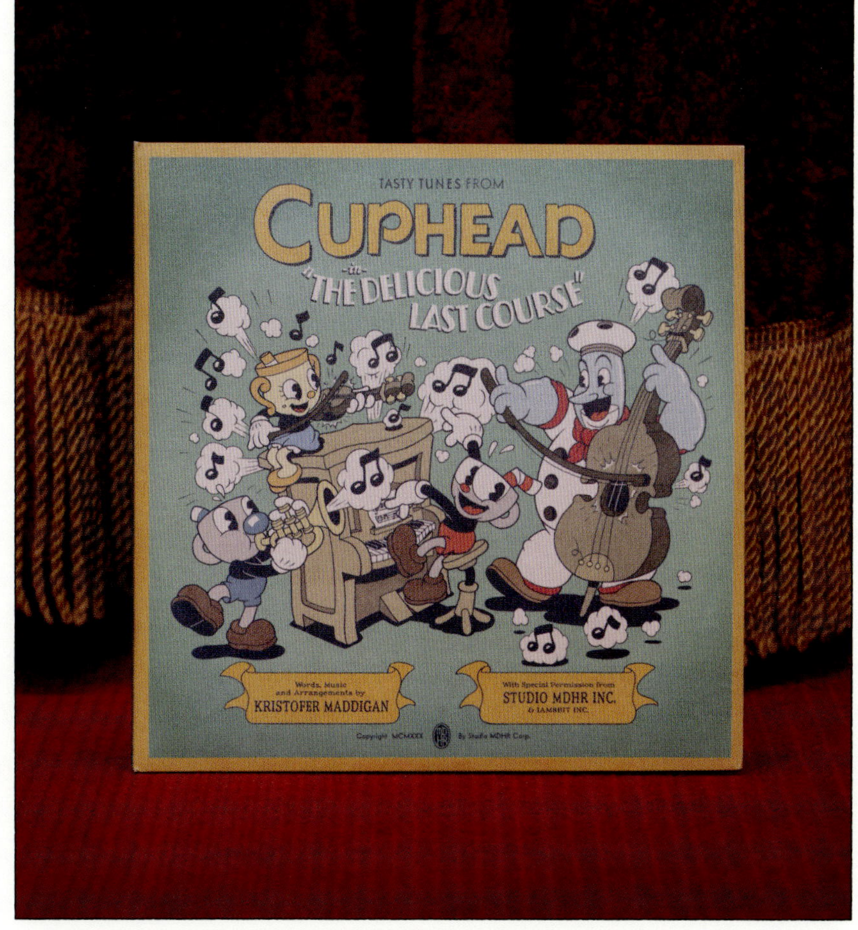
TASTY TUNES FROM
CUPHEAD
-in-
"THE DELICIOUS LAST COURSE"
Words, Music and Arrangements by
KRISTOFER MADDIGAN
With Special Permission from
STUDIO MDHR INC.
Copyright MCMXXX
By Studio MDHR Corp.

Dark Horse Books

IT ISN'T BLOWING SMOKE to say that one of our favorite collaborations is with our partners at Dark Horse (although there is something existentially eerie about discussing the book within the book itself). We often say that it would be a dream of ours for *Cuphead* to be remembered and discussed decades from now, like the cartoon works it was inspired by, and Dark Horse's fastidious dedication to helping us document our process and inspirations within Art Books makes that dream feel closer to reality.

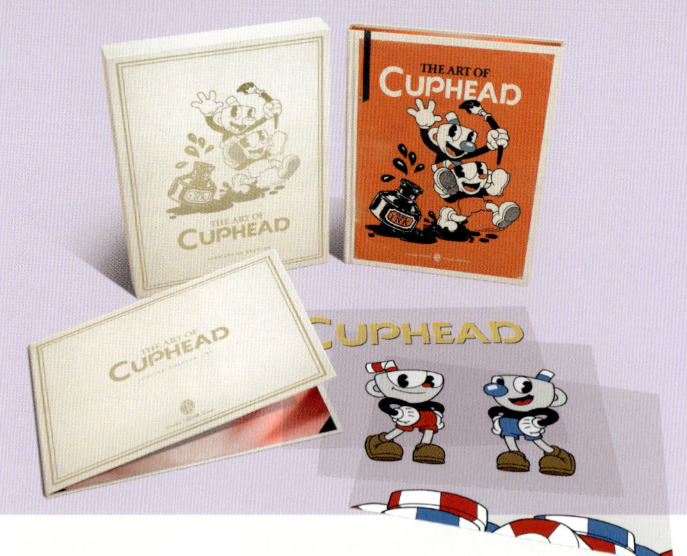

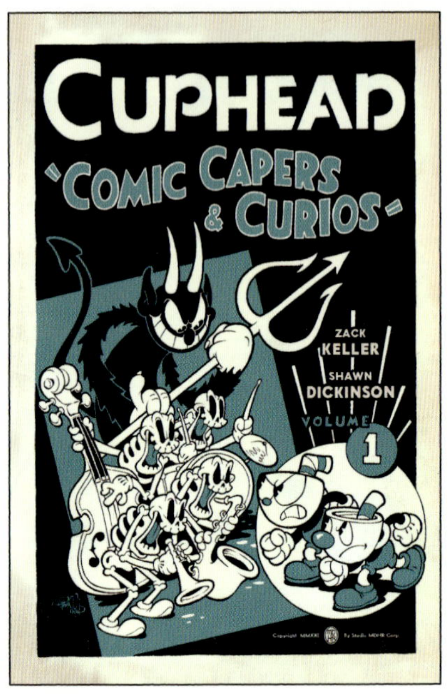

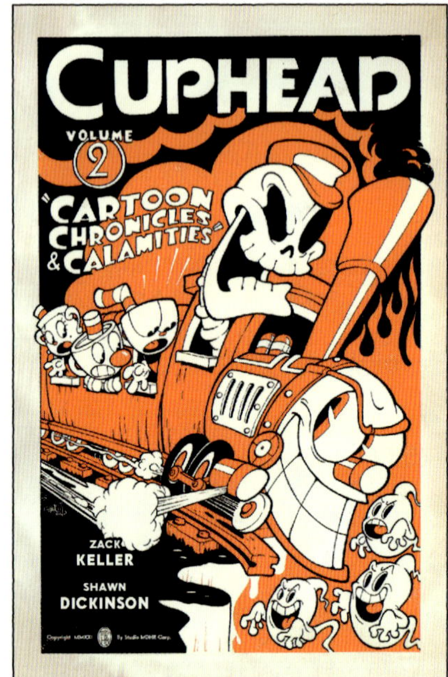

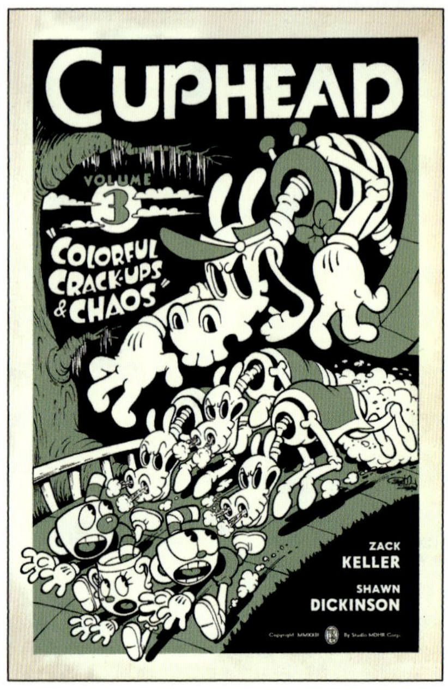

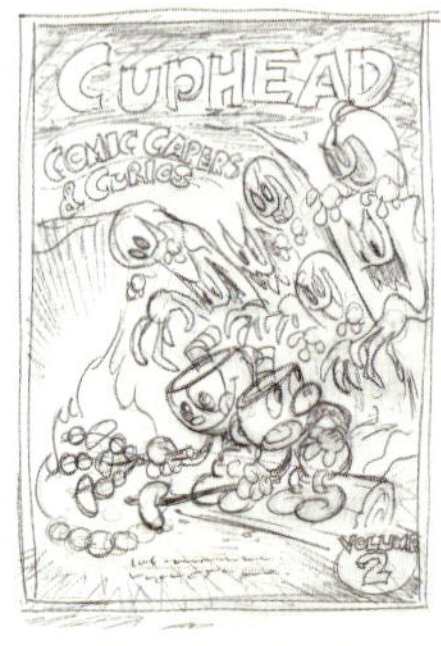

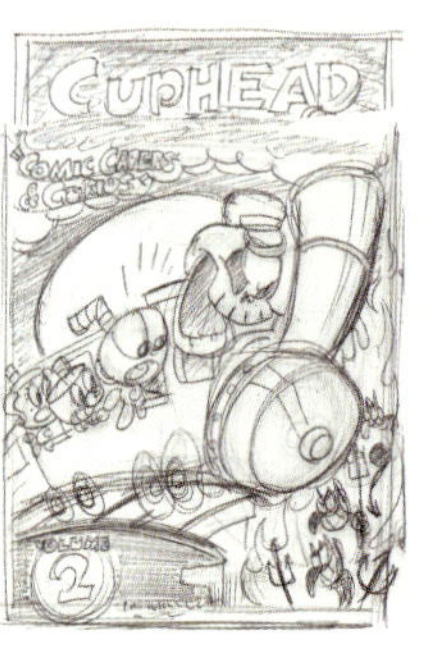

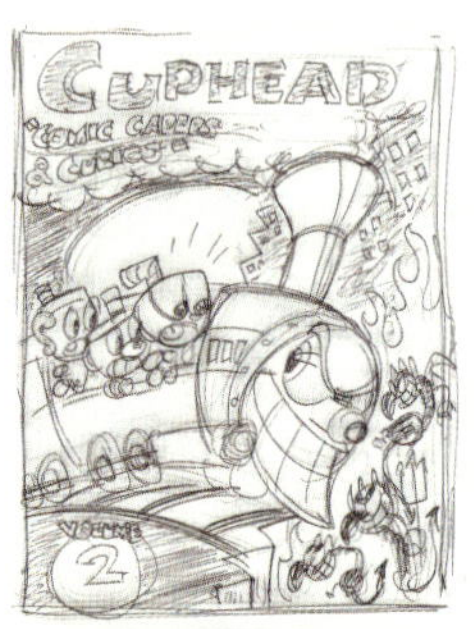

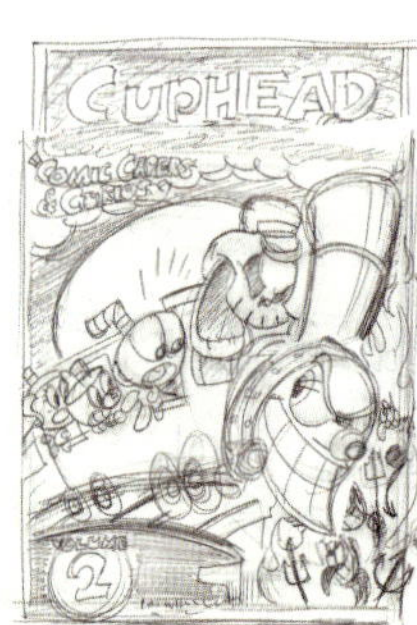

Written by Zack Keller, with wonderfully whimsical art by Shawn Dickinson, the trio of Cuphead graphic novels contain collections of zany side stories in comic form.

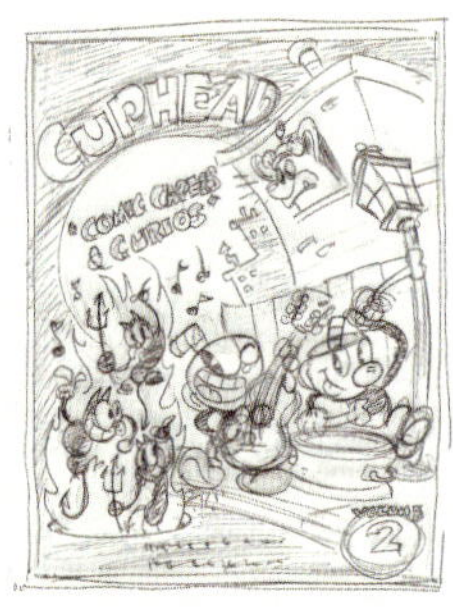

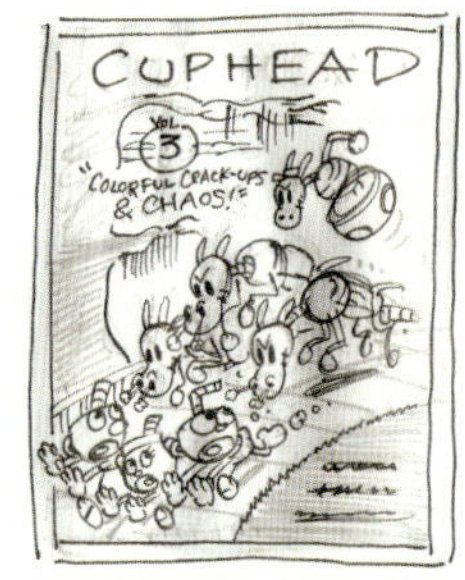

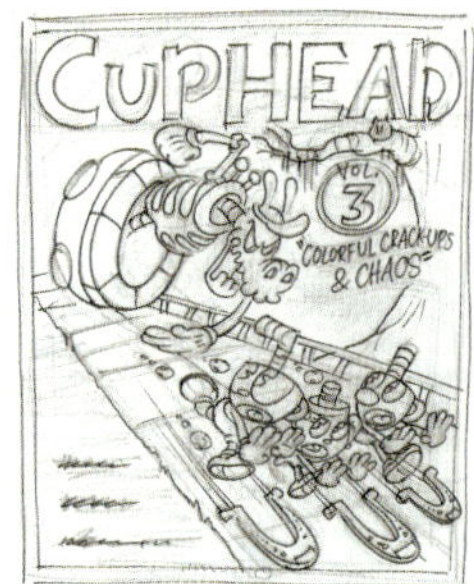

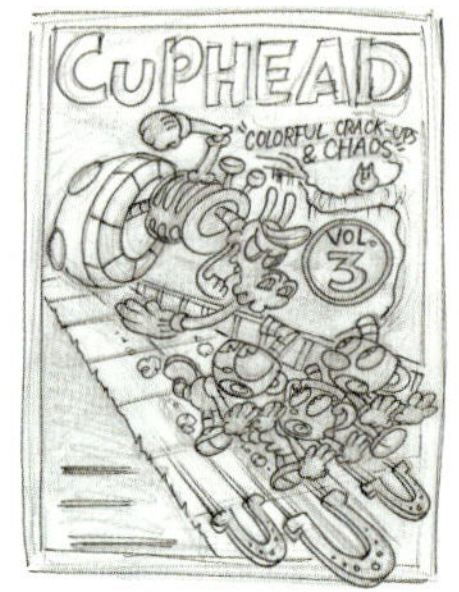

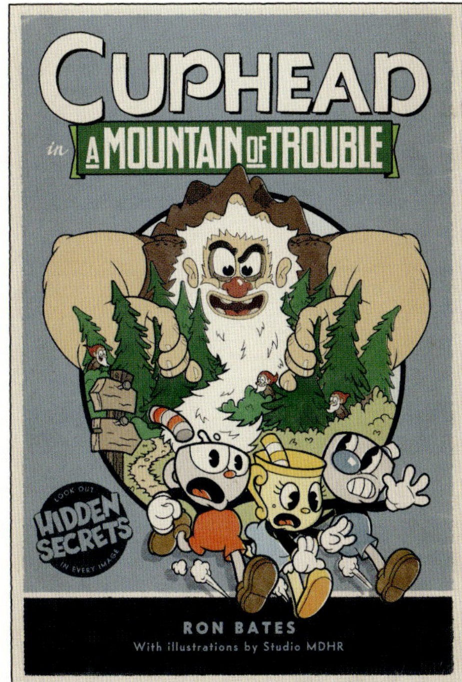

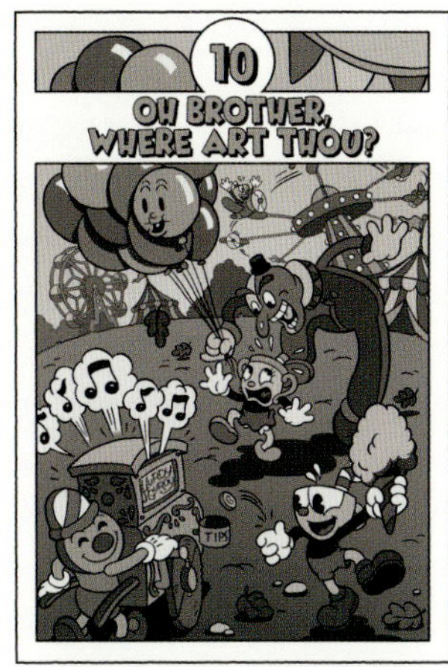

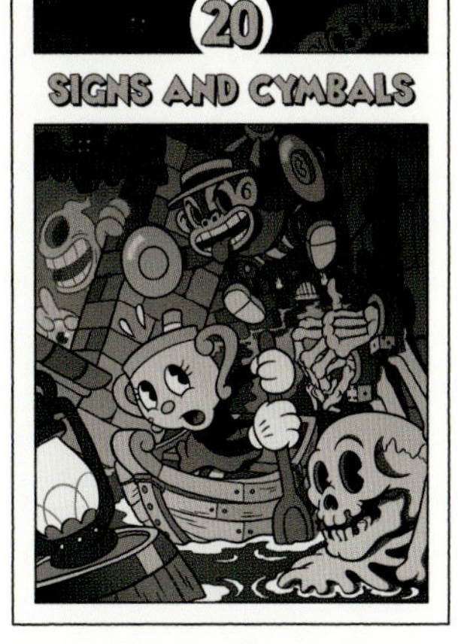

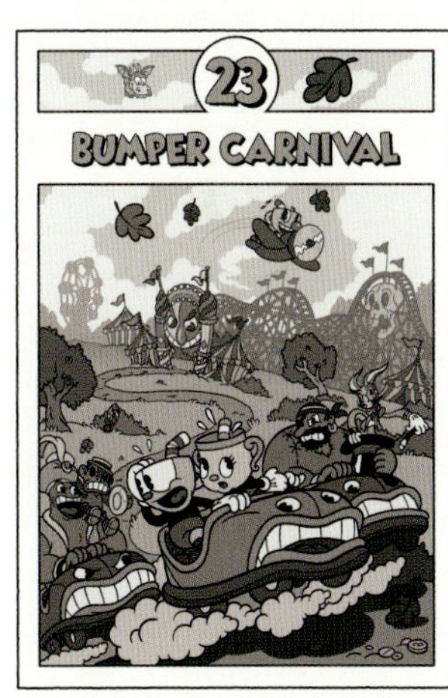

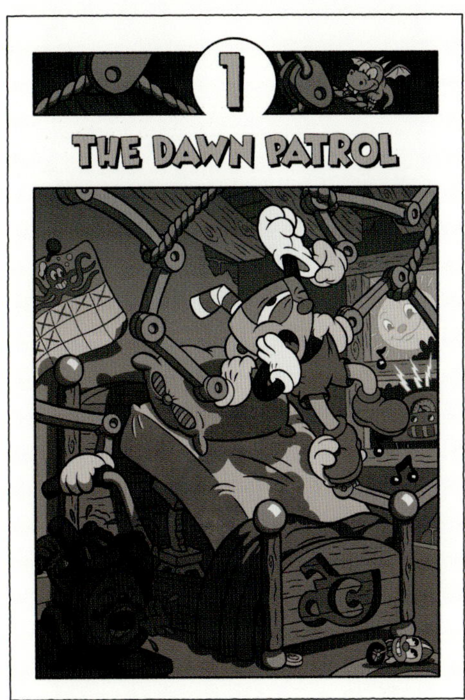

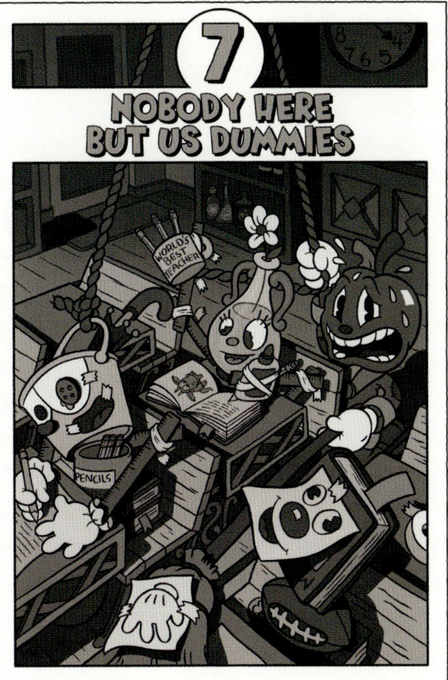

Little Brown Books

ONE OF THE MOST HEARTWARMING partnerships we've been able to forge over the years is with publisher Little Brown, who helped us reimagine the sometimes-creepy world of the Inkwell Isles through the lens of children's stories. Penned by Author Ron Bates, these middle grade books contain heart and humor in equal measure, and were written in close consultation with the writing and lore teams here at the studio. Each book features interior illustrations by Studio MDHR artists and contain hidden secrets for young readers to find as they make their way through the stories!

Zoetrope

ACMI–THE AUSTRALIAN CENTRE for the Moving Image–is Australia's national museum celebrating screen culture. We were flabbergasted when they asked us to collaborate on a Zoetrope installation that would live in the museum for a whopping *ten years*! Together with ACMI and fabricator MegaFun, we pulled out all the stops to help conceptualize a single exhibit that could capture our love of the moving image, from animation to video games, through the lens of Cuphead. The result is "Cuphead: Inspiration from the Inkwell," a massive spinning model that appears to come to life as lights in the room strobe…it truly has to be seen to be believed!

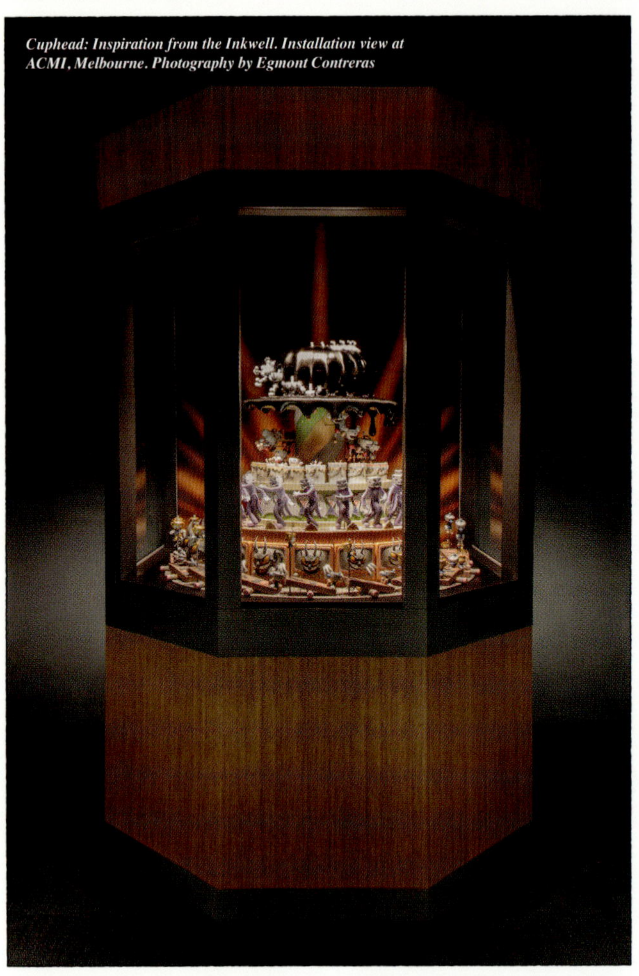

Cuphead: Inspiration from the Inkwell. Installation view at ACMI, Melbourne. Photography by Egmont Contreras

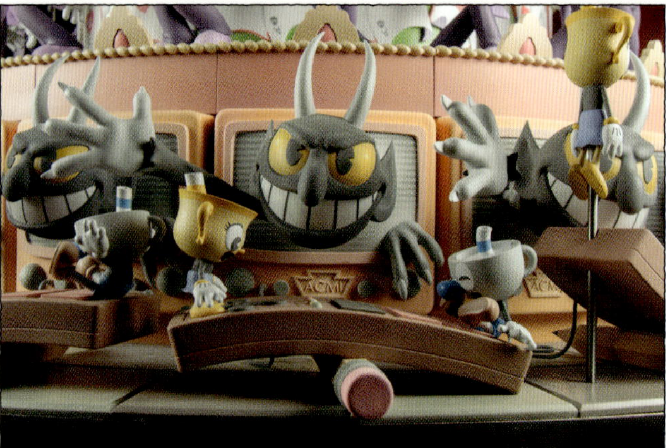

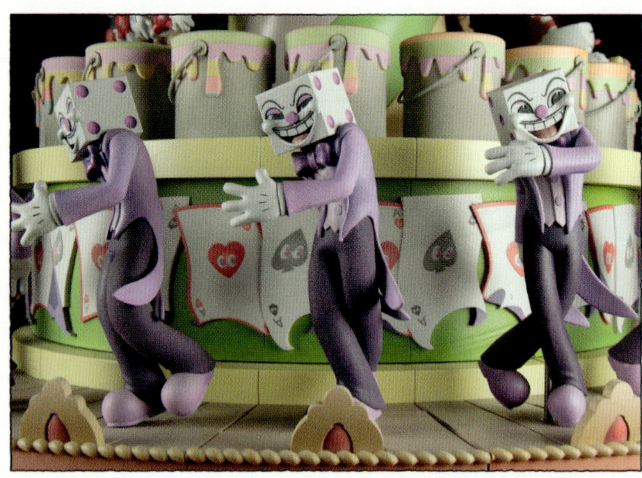

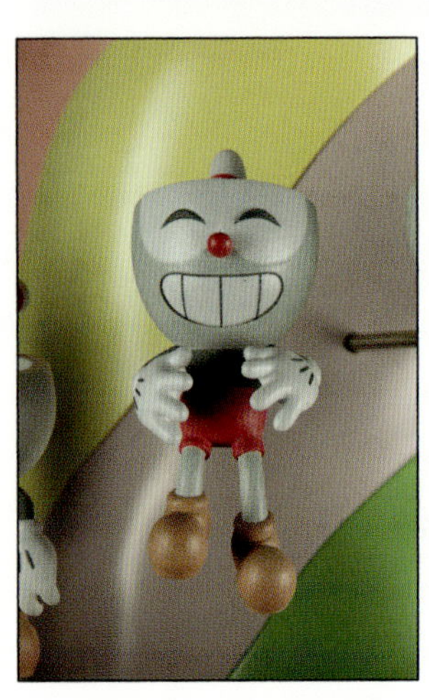

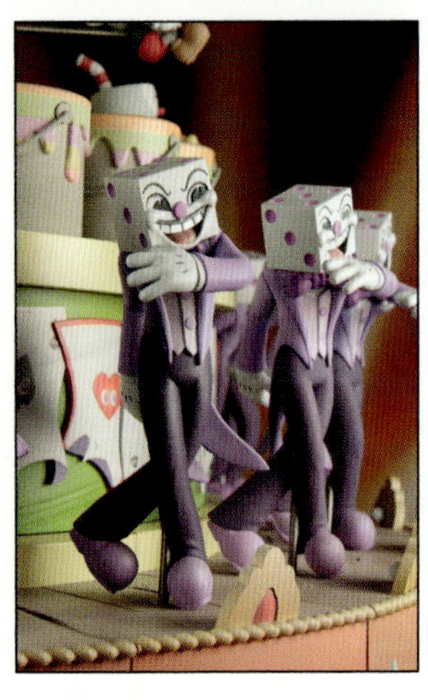

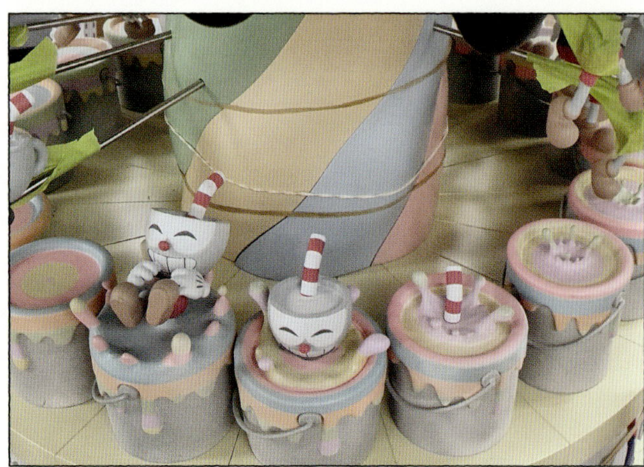

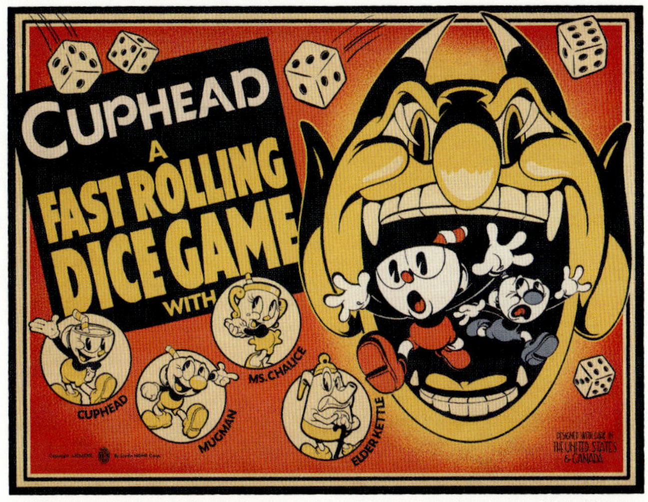

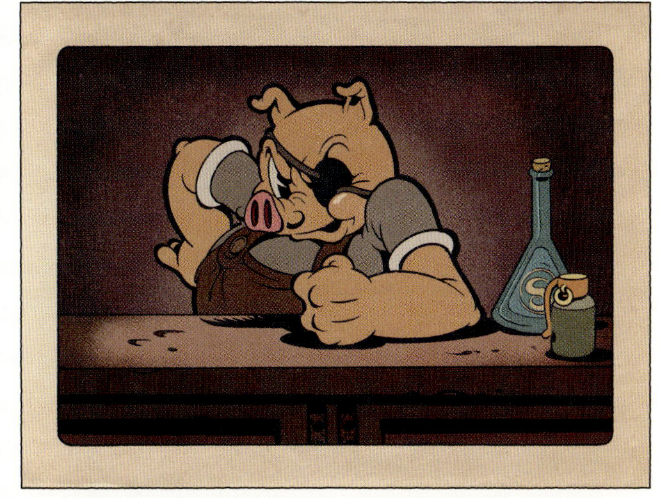

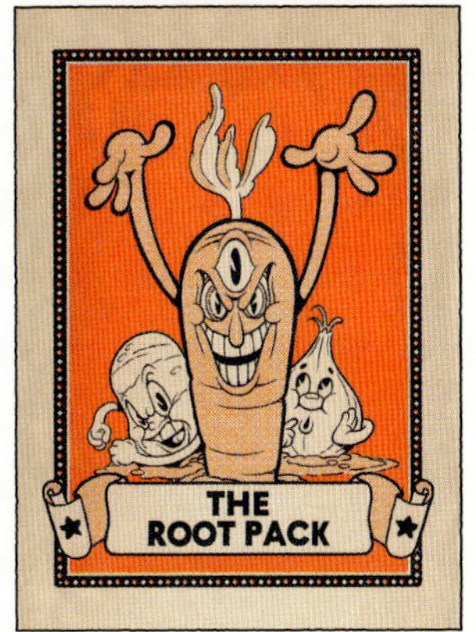

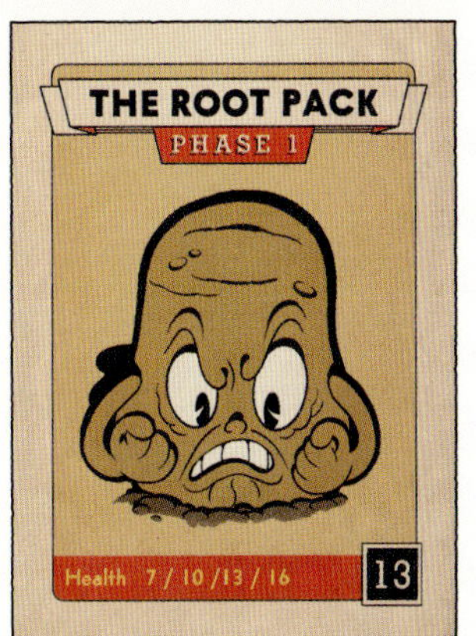

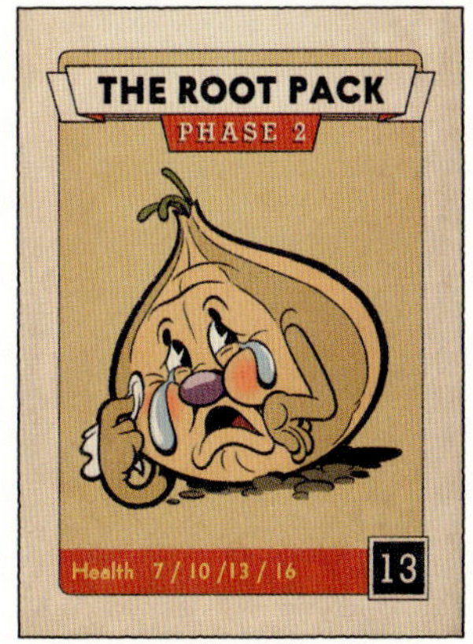

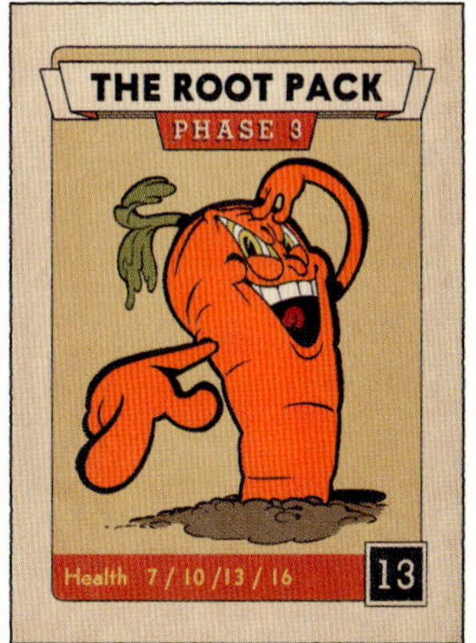

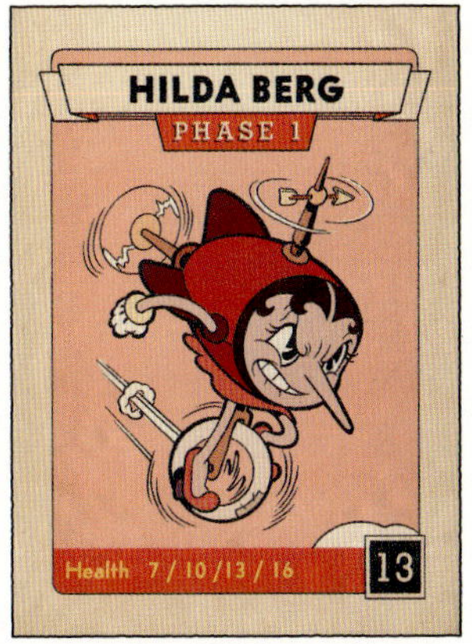

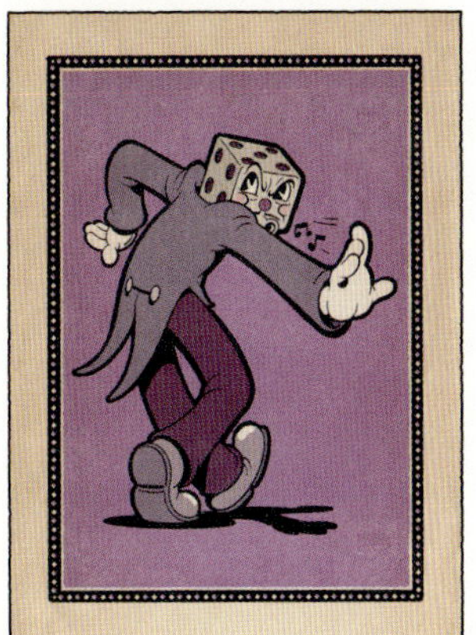

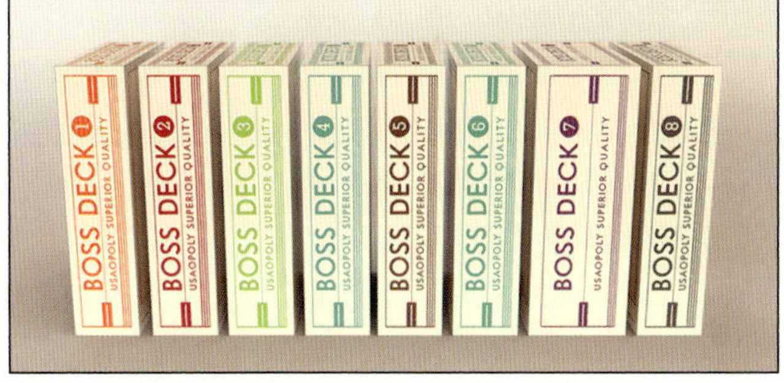

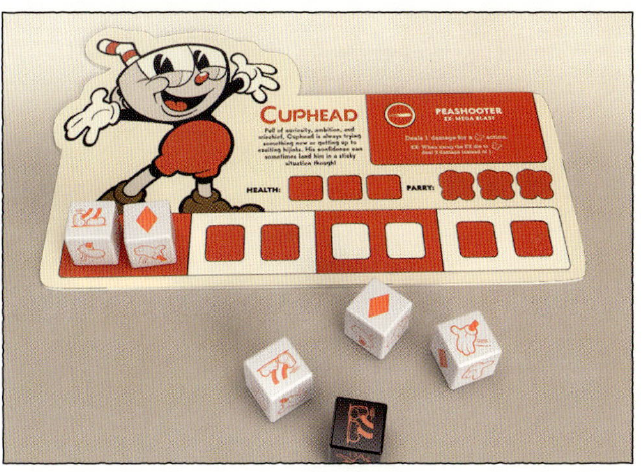

Cuphead Dice Game

MANUFACTURED BY THE TEAM at The Op Games, the *Cuphead Fast Rolling Dice Game* has the distinction of being the *only* official board game based on our characters! Working with talented Illustrator Stephen DeStefano, we honed in on an aesthetic for the game and packaging that was rooted in the look and feel of classic collectible baseball cards. In true Studio MDHR fashion, the game contains over fifty completely unique art pieces!

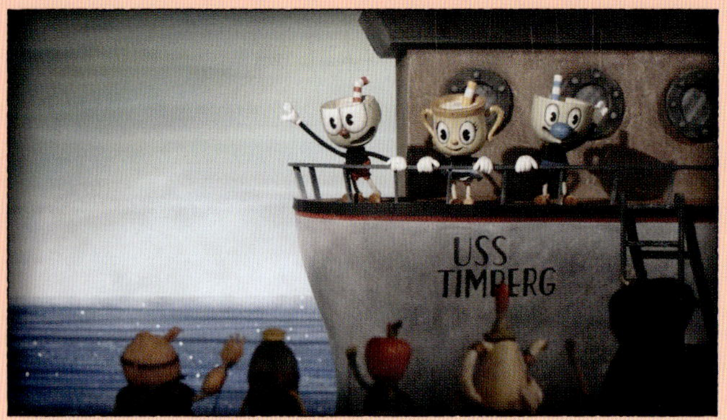

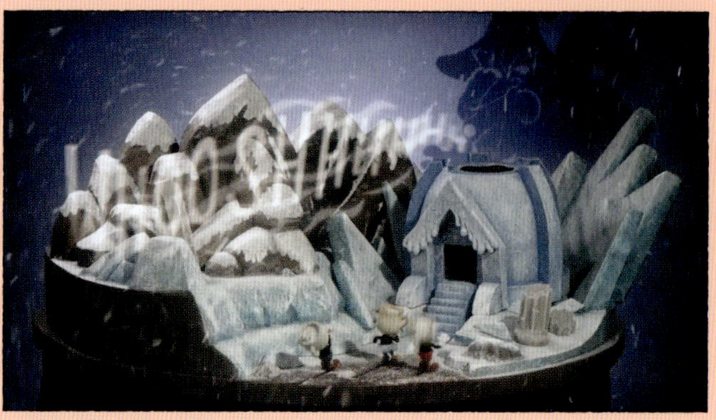

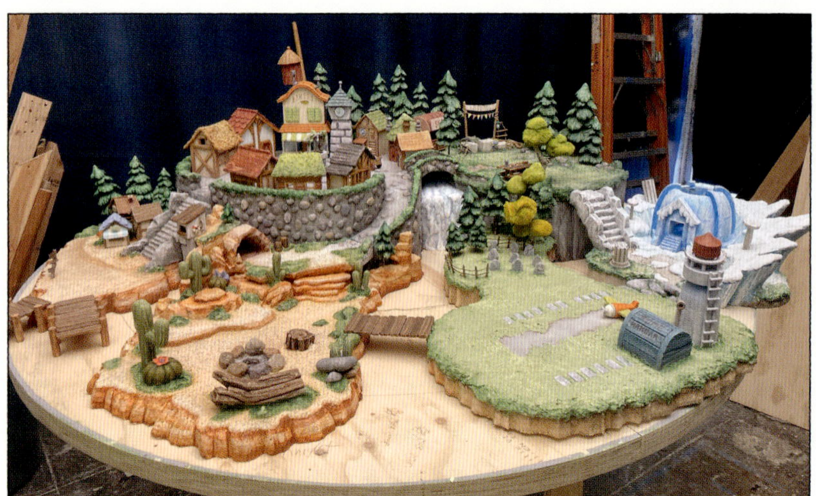

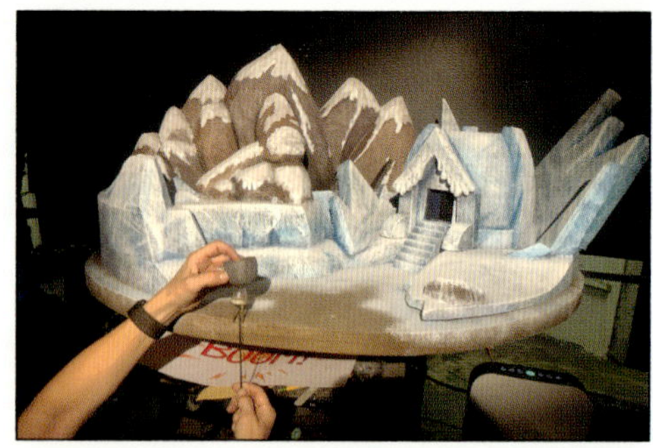

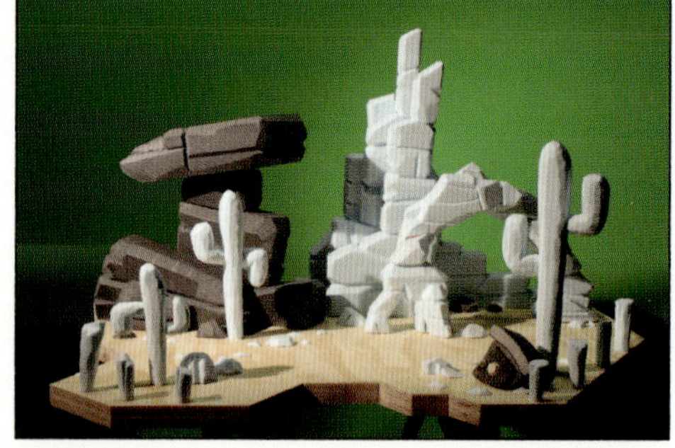

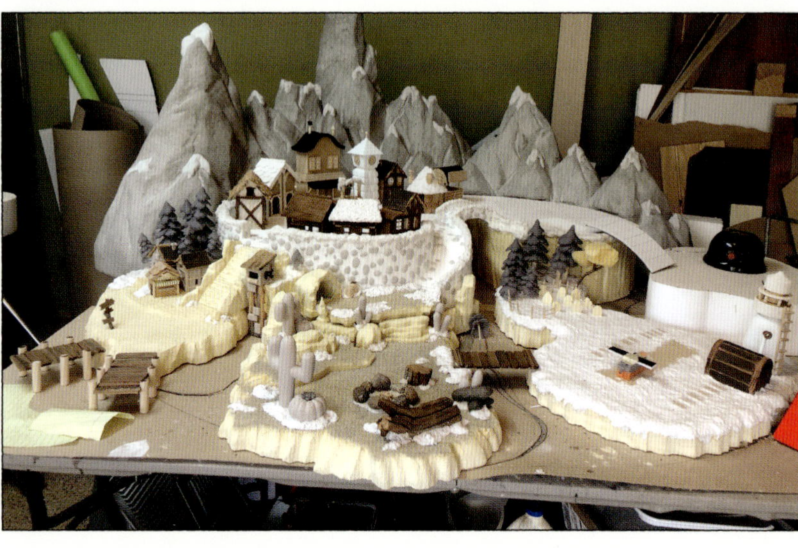

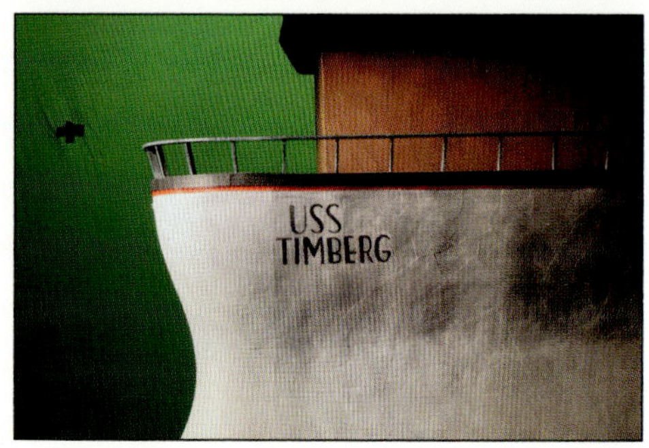

DLC Release Trailer

AS OUR RELEASE DATE FOR *The Delicious Last Course* came into focus, we knew we wanted to do something that felt special and thrilling to share the news with our community. So, we reached out to our pals at LA-based stop motion master Screen Novelties to create a bespoke trailer inspired by classic travelogues and vintage tourism videos. The result was a dizzyingly complex mixture of stop motion, maquette work, rear projection animation, and puppeteering. Fun fact: the cruise ship featured in the beginning of the trailer bears the name of storied Fleischer-era composer Sammy Timberg!

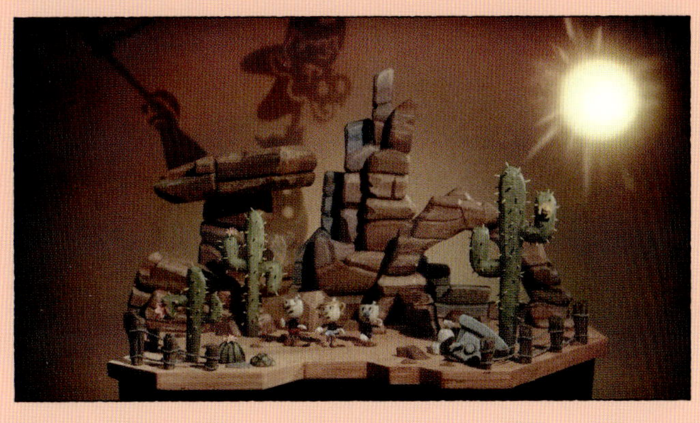

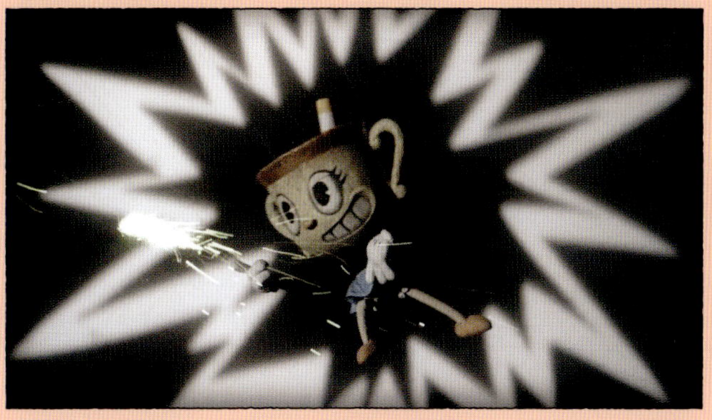

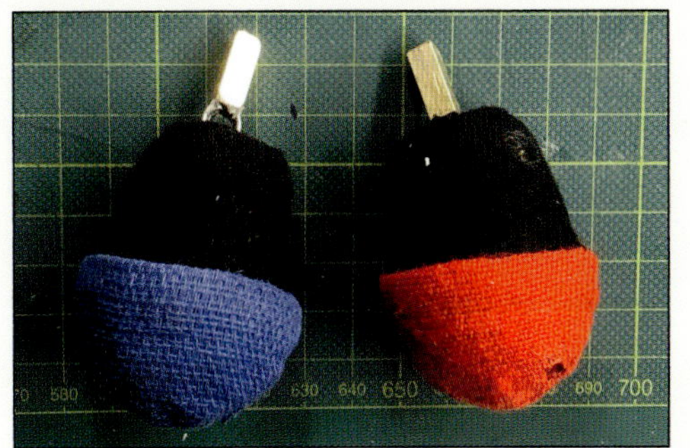

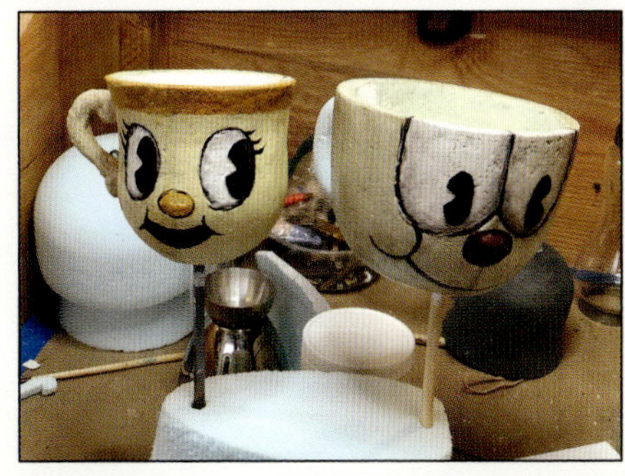

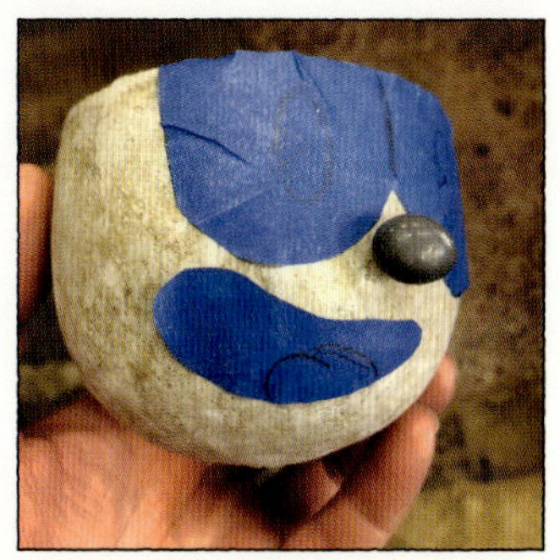

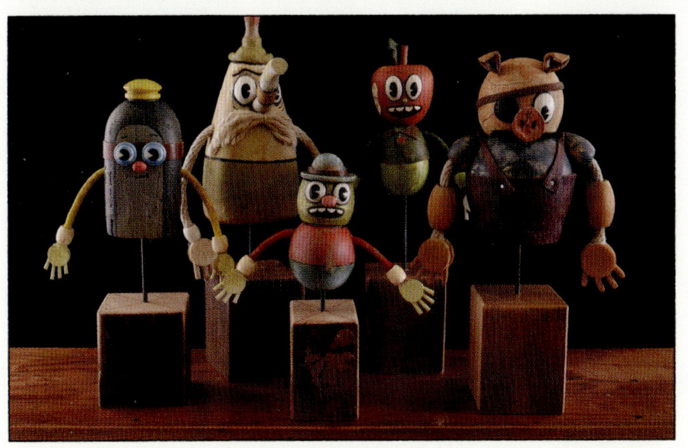

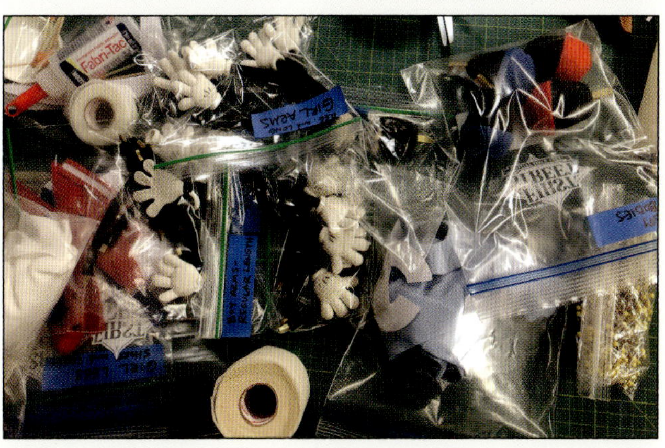
Fabri-Tac

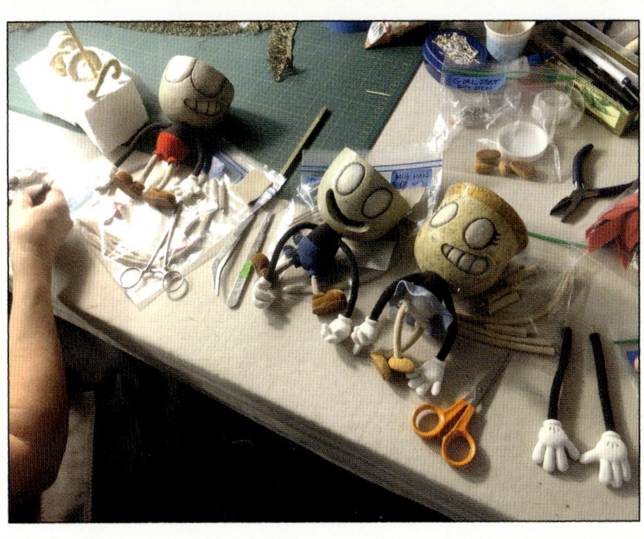

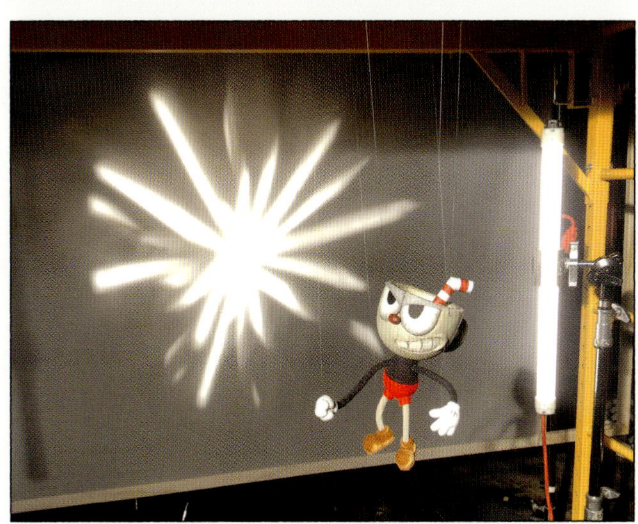

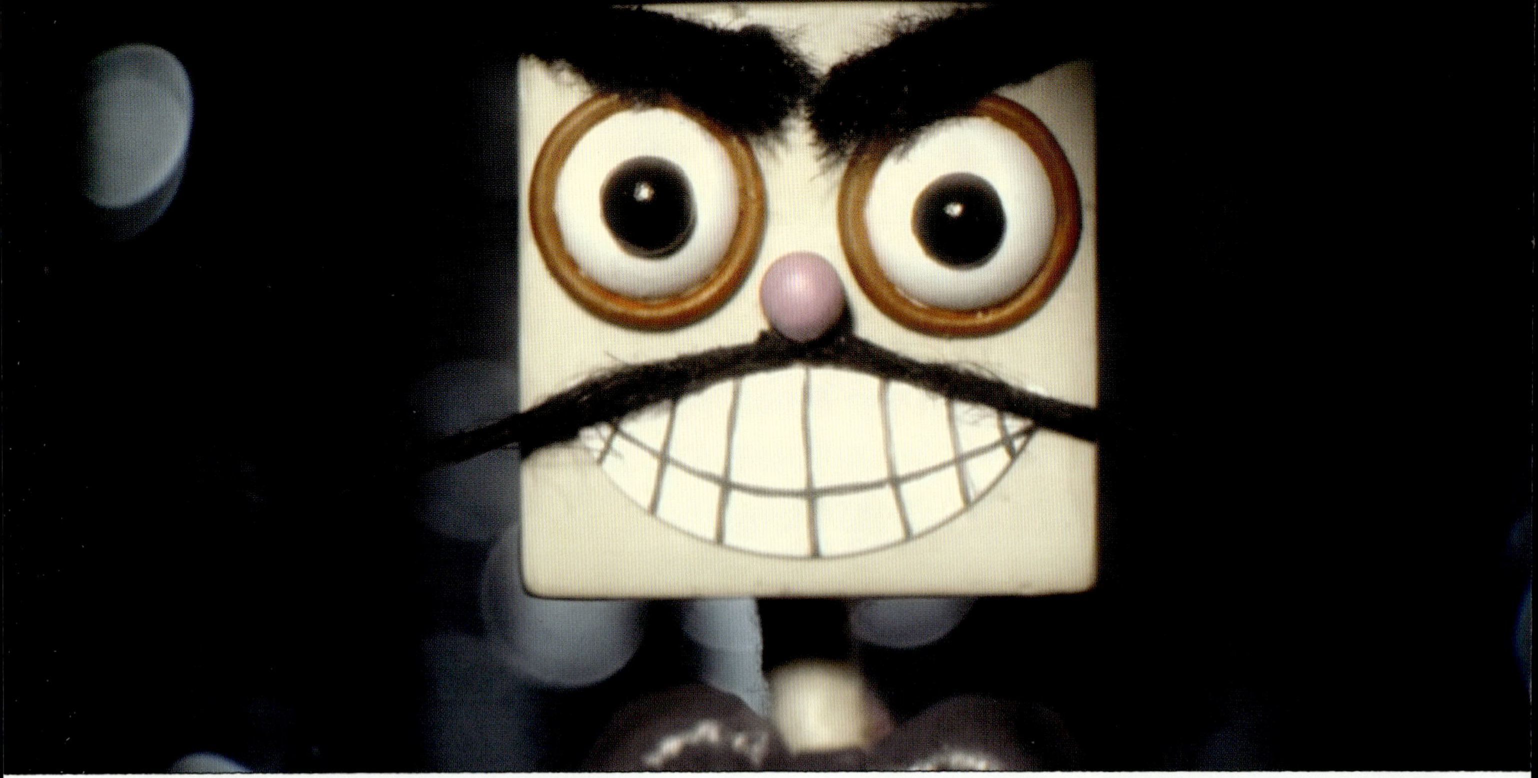

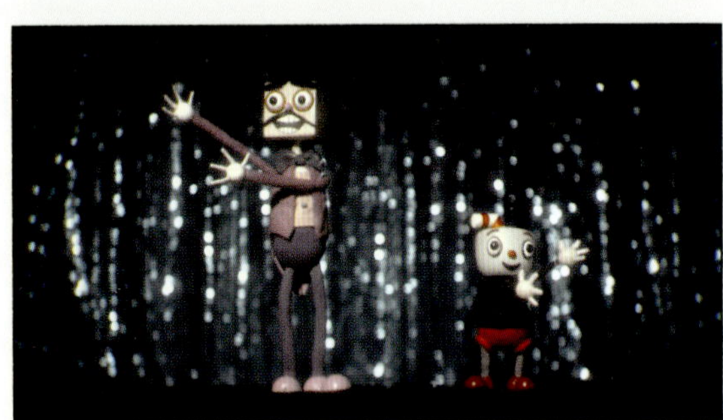

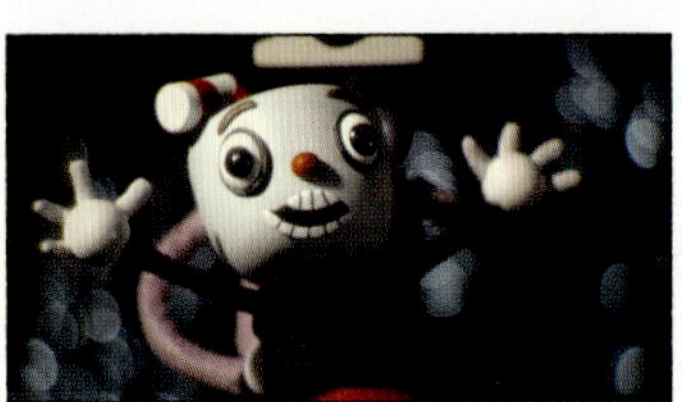

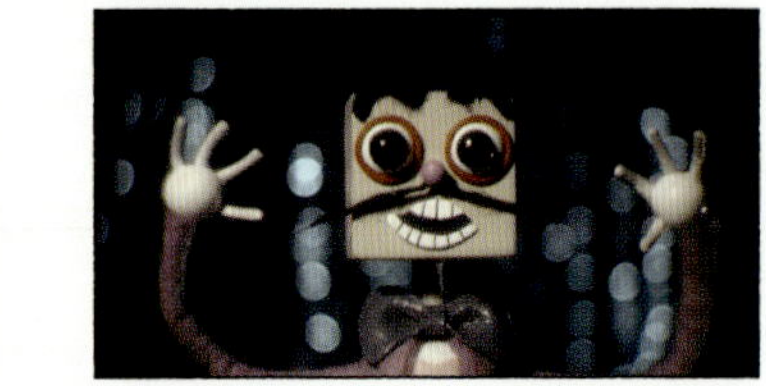

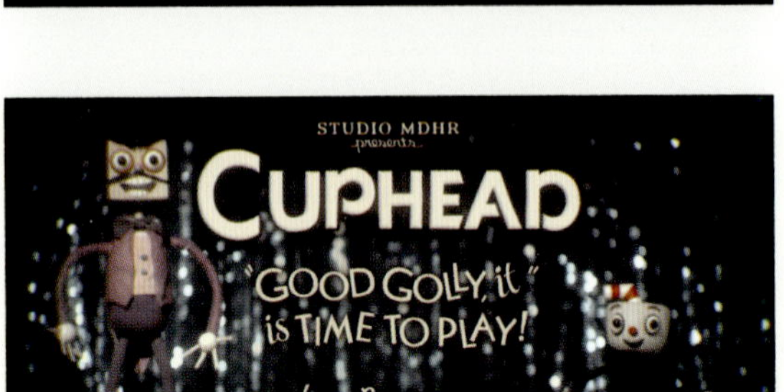

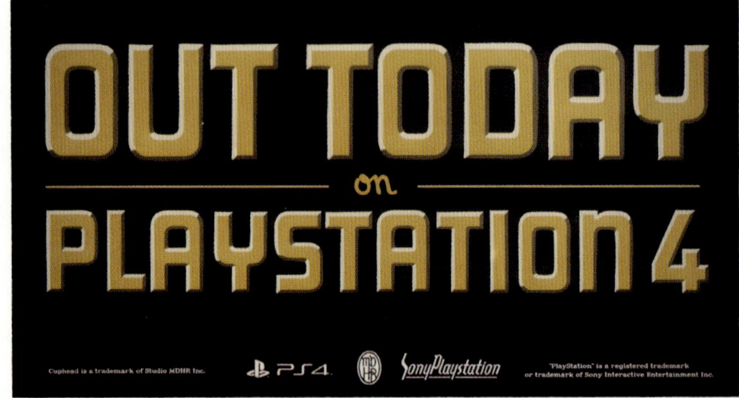

PlayStation Release Trailer

CUPHEAD'S RELEASE ON PLAYSTATION 4 was a surprise "stealth launch," in which a game becomes available on the same day it is announced. To commemorate the moment, we partnered with Toronto studio Stop Motion Department to create an off-kilter video modeled after one of the first-ever stop motion shorts–Dave Fleischer and Seymour Kneitel's *The Peanut Vendor* (1933). Puppet Fabricators Karen Valleau and Lauren Craig built the King Dice and Cuphead puppets with wooden heads, leather hands, and lots of primary shapes to reflect the children's toys of the 1930s, which were made with simple manufacturing like drill presses and saws. We also couldn't resist whipping up a faux vintage Sony PlayStation Logo, seen above, inspired by the classic Sony logos of yesteryear!

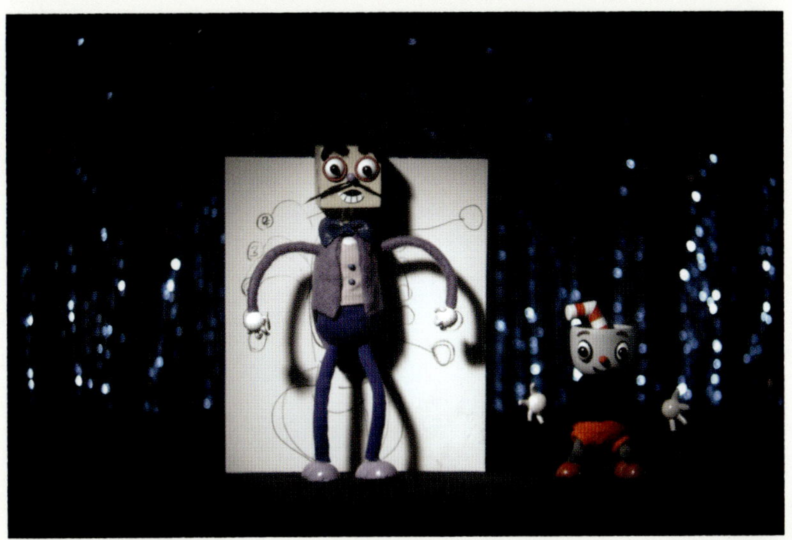

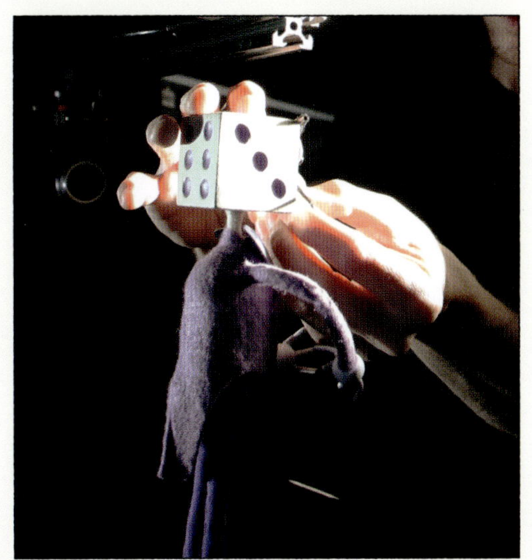

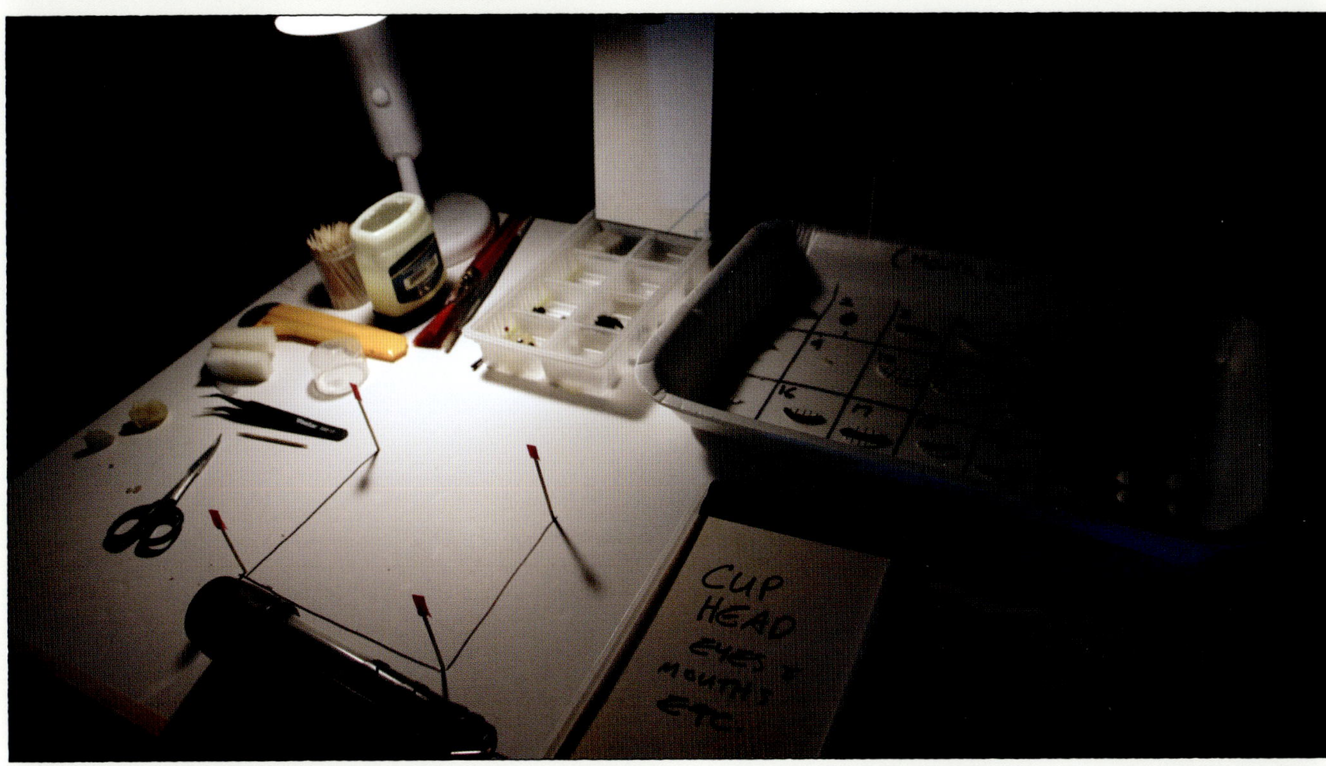
CUP
HEAD
EYES &
MOUTHS
ETC.

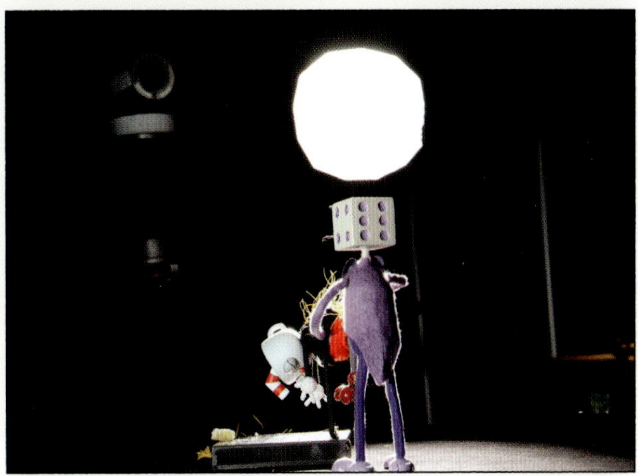

Social Media Art & Holiday Cards

IT MEANS A GREAT DEAL to all of us here at Studio MDHR that wherever you encounter our characters–in our games, on a figurine, or in a holiday greeting on social media–it feels like you're being transported to the world of the Inkwell Isles. We cannot properly express how thankful we are that people have embraced our little animated adventure the way that they have, but we can promise that we will always put into the things we do all the love and craftsmanship we can muster.

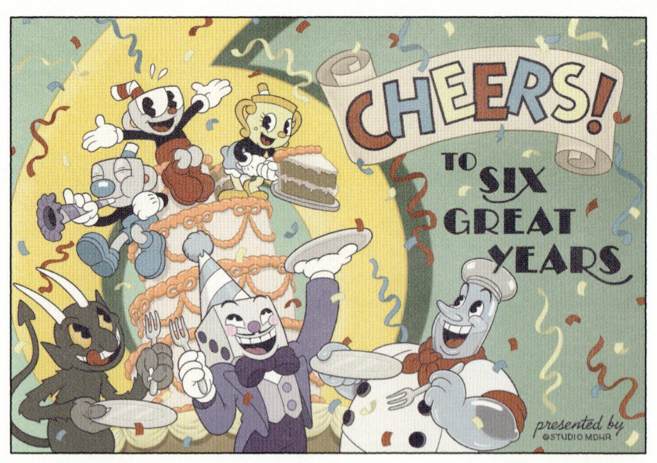

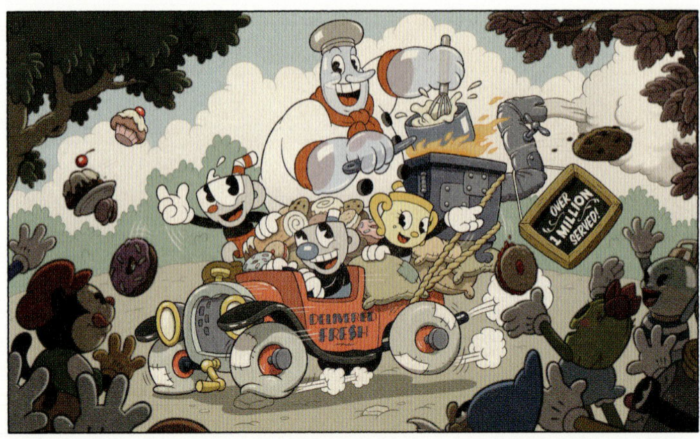

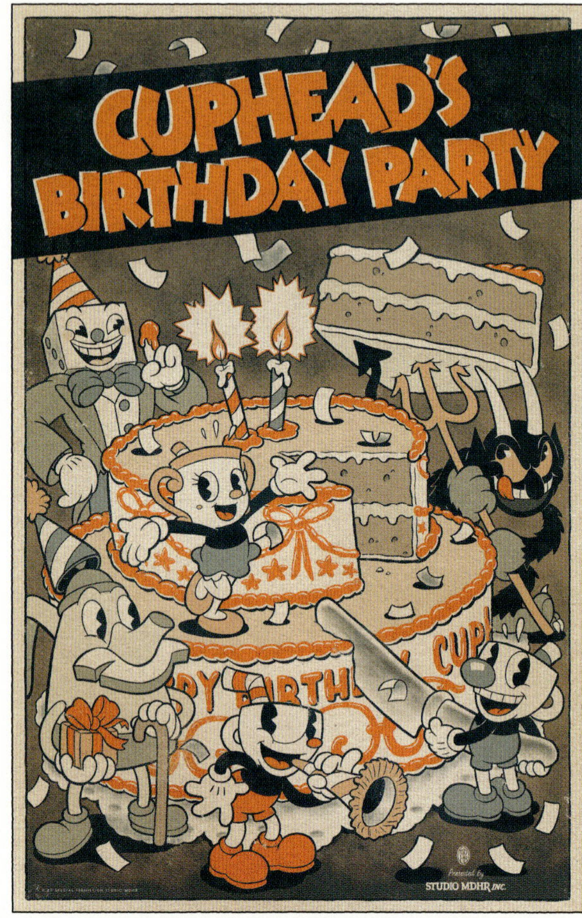

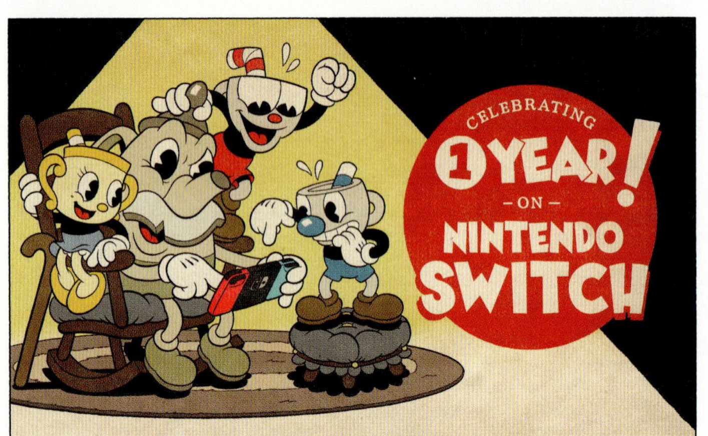

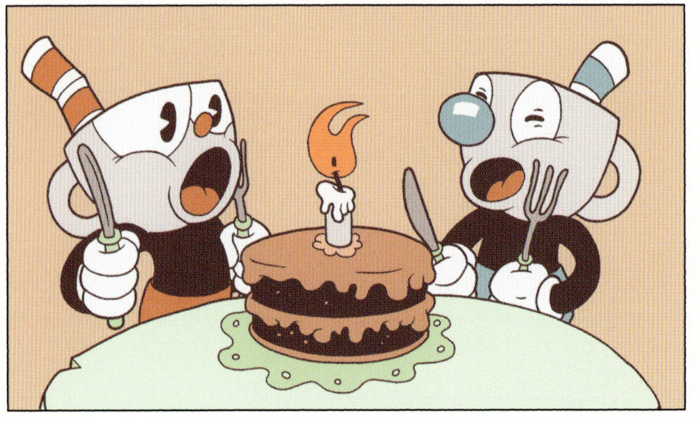

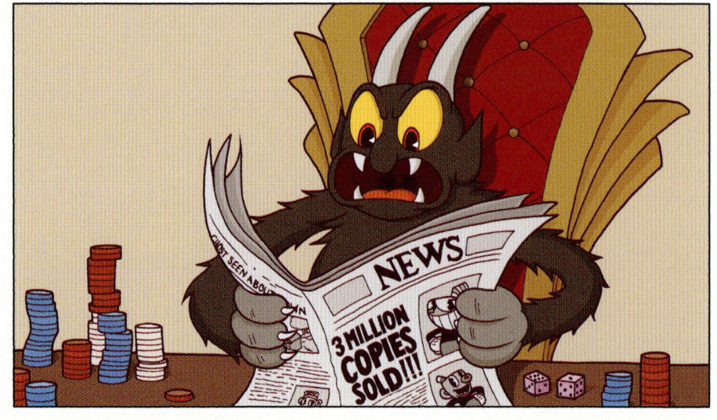

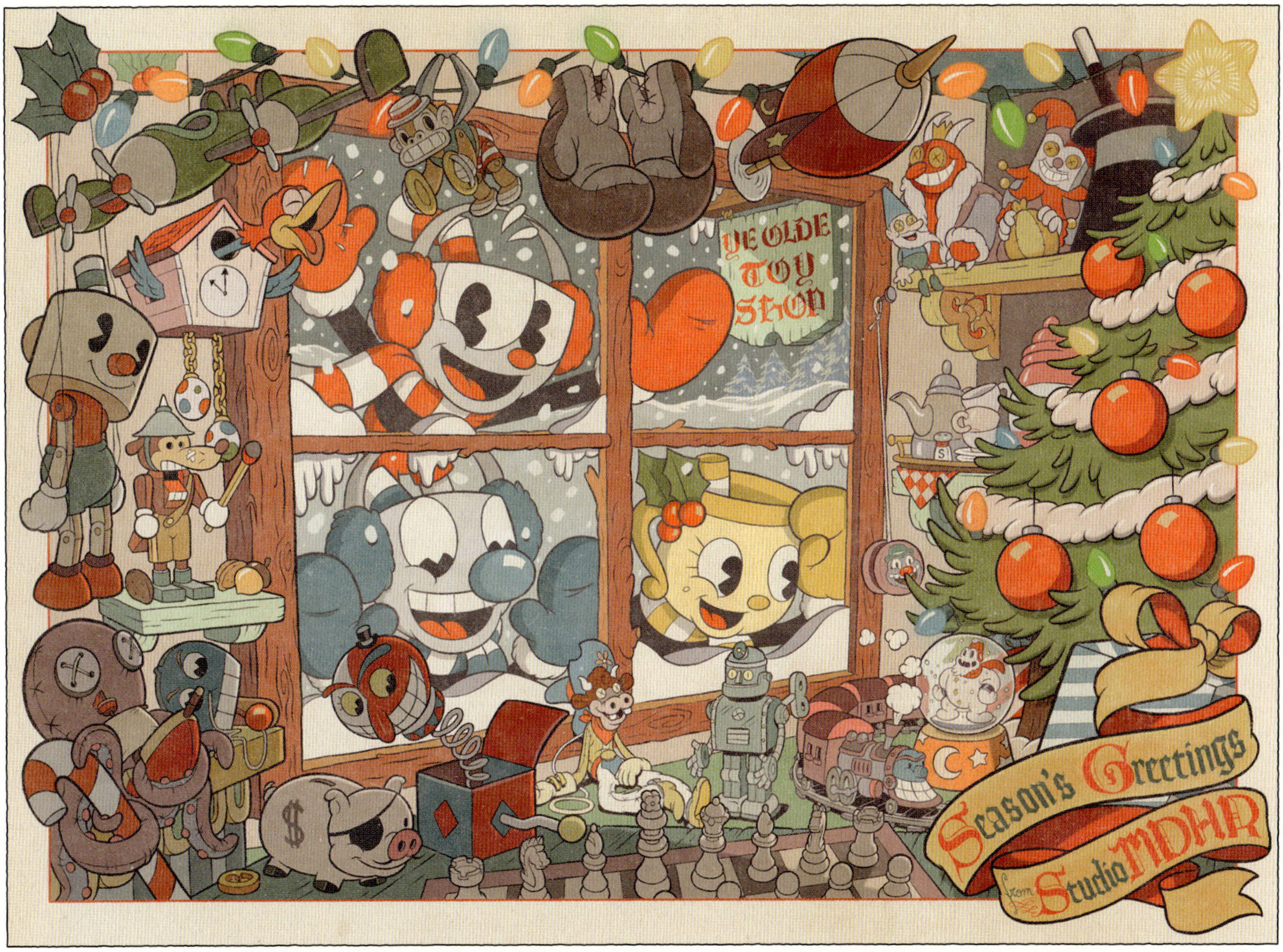

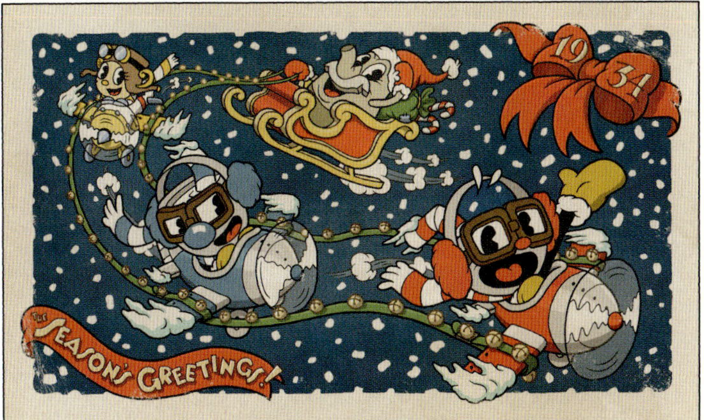

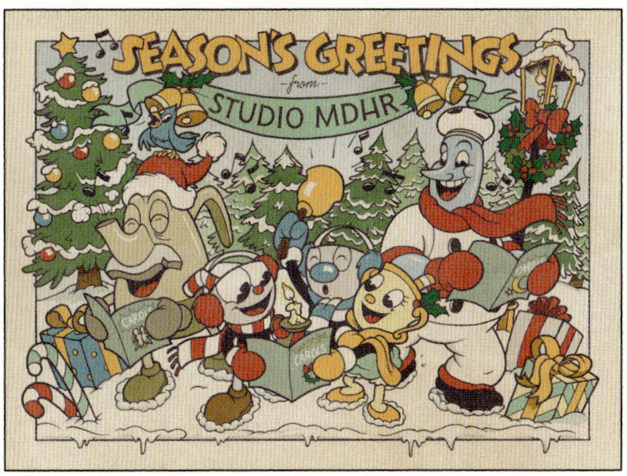

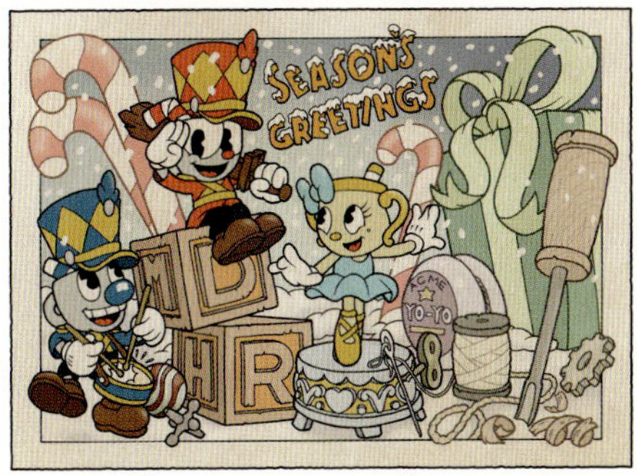

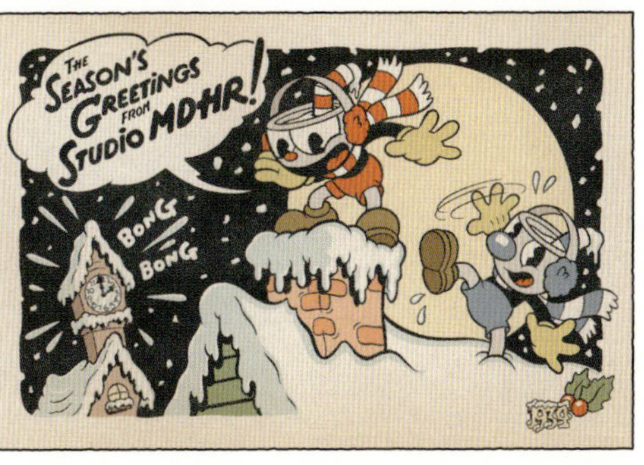

Illustrated by Lance Inkwell, our yearly holiday cards have become a tradition here at the studio. Inspired by the employee holiday cards distributed at Disney in the thirties and forties, each one is packed to the gills with details and references.

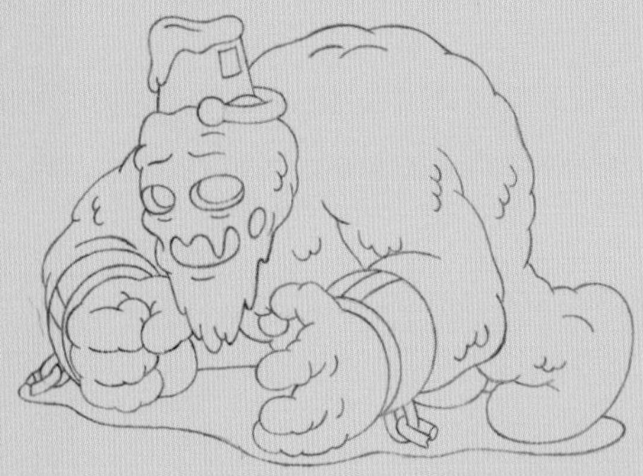
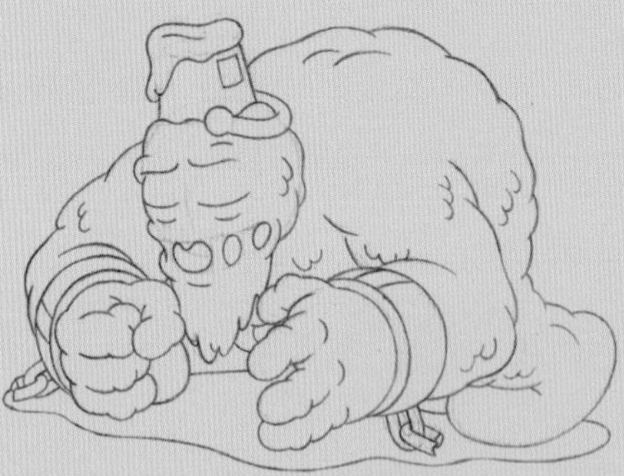
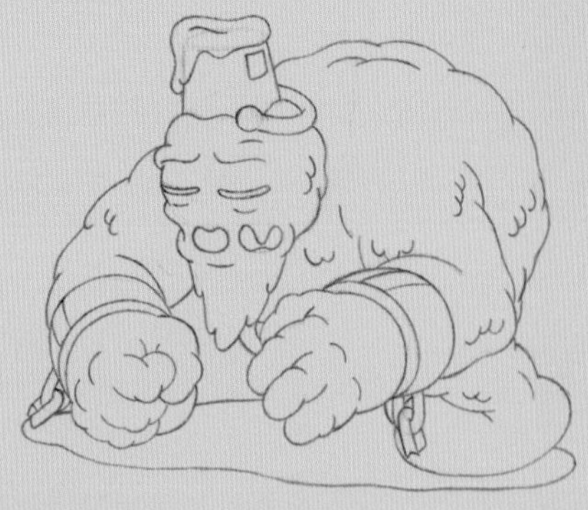

The Delicious Last Course would not have happened without the unbelievable efforts of a talented team. While many of those individuals were mentioned throughout the book, we were not able to call out the contributions of each and every team member, contractor, and contributor. To that end, the credits below represent a fuller picture of those who helped us bring the game to life. We also extend our immense gratitude to our translators, musicians, PR team, release managers, and so many more without whom this endeavor would not be possible.

Directors
Chad Moldenhauer
Jared Moldenhauer

Studio Director, Executive Producer & Supervising Inker
Marija "Maja" Moldenhauer

Producer & Co-Writer
Eli Cymet

Deputy Game Designer, Senior Production Artist, Light & Shadow Painter & Co-Writer
Tyler Moldenhauer

Programmers
Adam Winkels
Peter Malamud Smith
Kezia Adamo

Assistant Art Director & Senior Production Artist
Ryan Moldenhauer

Assistant Art Director, Supervising Animator, Light & Shadow Painter
Hanna Abi-Hanna

Concept Art Lead, Visual Supervisor & Inking Artist
Lance "Inkwell" Miller

Animators
Jared Beckstrand
Jake Clark
Simone Cirillo
Joseph Coleman
Rapeepat "Patt" Jewanarom
Danielle Johnson
Tina Nawrocki
Jamie Oliff

Additional Animators
Stephanie Alexander
Jefferson Bastida
William Bradford
Piti Yindee

Light & Shadow Animators
Stephanie Alexander
Rapeepat "Patt" Jewanarom
Joey Mildenberger
Loris Pernaut
Piti Yindee

Background Artist & Painter
Caitlin Russell

Inking Artists
Danielle Johnson
Lance Miller
Molly Miller

Digital Painters
Lauren Affe
Ian Clarke
Ryan Moldenhauer
Tyler Moldenhauer
Ali Morbi
Caitlin Russell

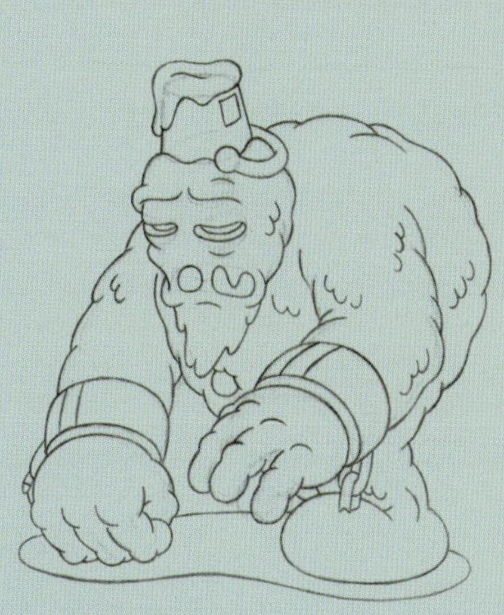
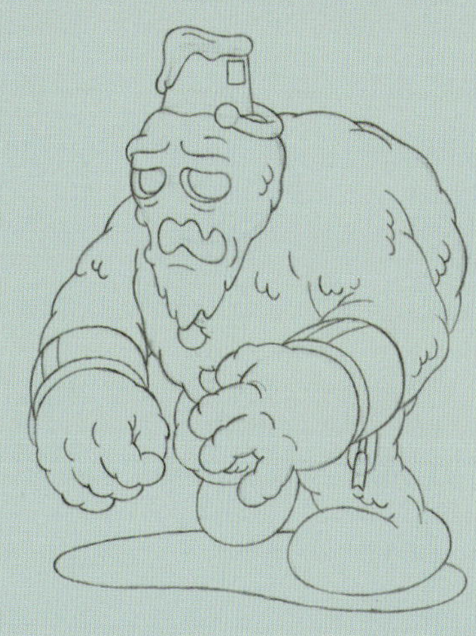
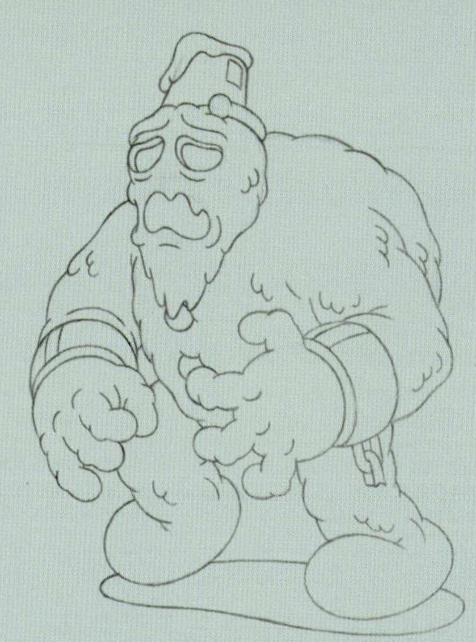

Additional Visual Design
Ian Clarke

Hand-Lettering
Warren Clark
Chiba Keisuke

Soundtrack Composed By
Kristofer Maddigan

Sound Fx
Sweet Justice

Ms. Chalice Tutorial Cart & Devil Skeleton Models
Ali Morbi
With Assistance by
Sarah Ball

King Of Games Castle
Screen Novelties Team
Kelly Mazurowski – *Stop Motion Director*
Casey Follen – *Production Manager*

Producers
Mark Caballero
Chris Finnegan
Seamus Walsh

Director Of Photography
Aaron Wise

Model Makers
Willy Fair
Rachel Ferris
Barney Marquez
Sadie Nash
Greg Pinsoneault

Production Designer
Kelly Mazurowski

Lead Scenic Painter
Alicia Ellsworth

VFX Supervisor
Andrew Babick

Lighting Technician
Riguel Yaluk Mosquera

Animation Assistant
Willy Fair

Additional Tutorial Model Fabrication
Sarah Ball

Type, Lettering & Fonts
Mark Simonson

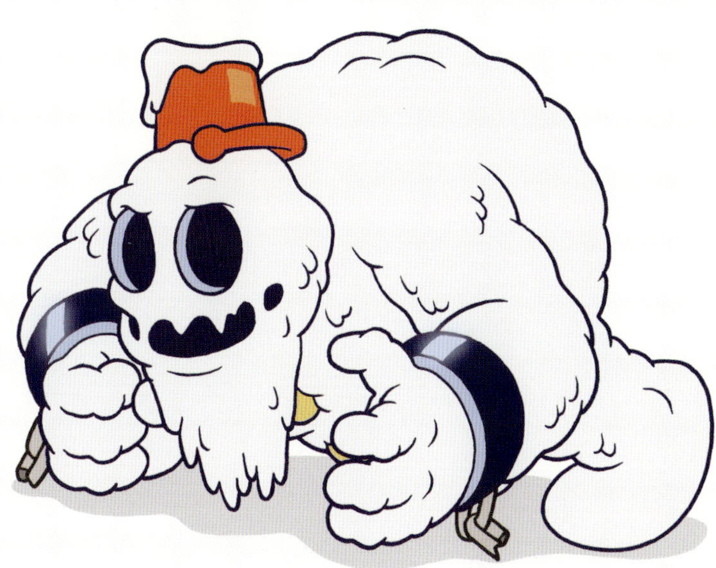

Fin

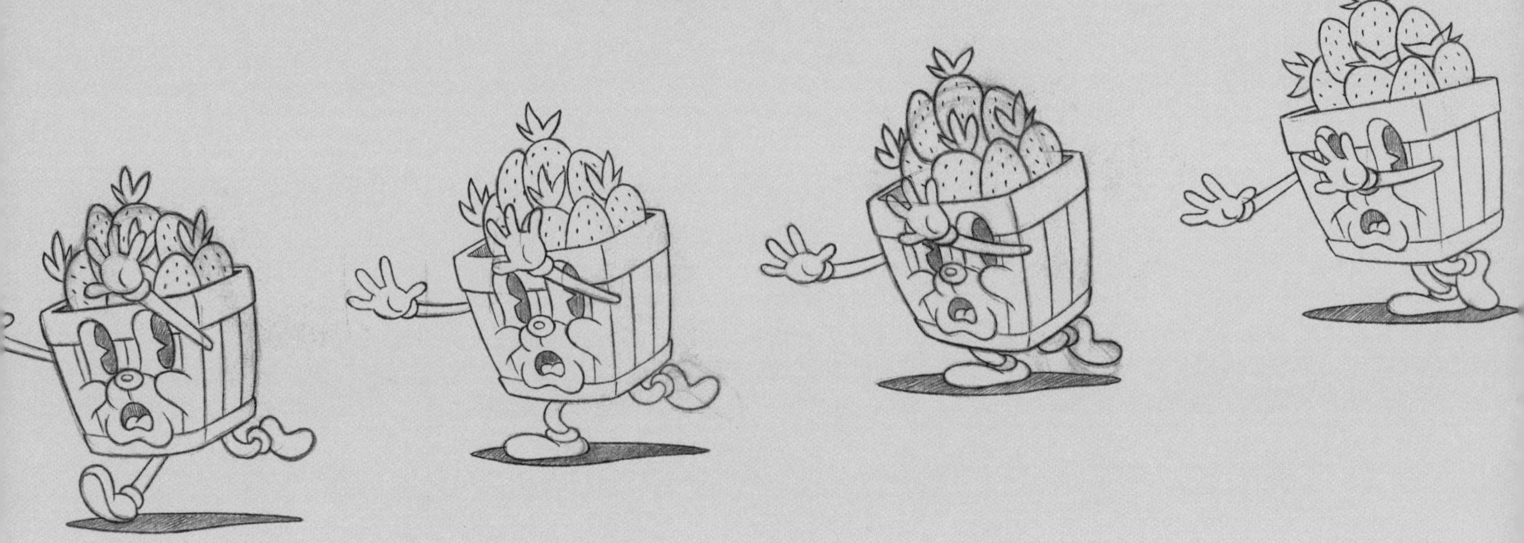